International Directory of
COMPANY
HISTORIES

International Directory of
COMPANY
HISTORIES

VOLUME 133

Editor

Jay P. Pederson

ST. JAMES PRESS
A part of Gale, Cengage Learning

Detroit • New York • San Francisco • New Haven, Conn • Waterville, Maine • London

GALE
CENGAGE Learning

International Directory of Company Histories, Volume 133

Jay P. Pederson, Editor

Project Editor: Miranda H. Ferrara

Editorial: Virgil Burton, Donna Craft, Peggy Geeseman, Hillary Hentschel, Sonya Hill, Keith Jones, Matthew Miskelly, Paul Schummer, Holly Selden

Production Technology Specialist: Mike Weaver

Imaging and Multimedia: John Watkins

Composition and Electronic Prepress: Gary Leach, Evi Seoud

Manufacturing: Rhonda Dover

Product Manager: Jenai Drouillard

For product information and technology assistance, contact us at **Gale Customer Support, 1-800-877-4253.**
For permission to use material from this text or product, submit all requests online at **www.cengage.com/permissions.**
Further permissions questions can be emailed to **permissionrequest@cengage.com**

Gale
27500 Drake Rd.
Farmington Hills, MI, 48331-3535

LIBRARY OF CONGRESS CATALOG NUMBER 89-190943
ISBN-13: 978-1-4144-6883-9
ISBN-10: 1-4144-6883-0

This title is also available as an e-book
ISBN-13: 978-1-4144-8211-8   ISBN-10: 1-4144-8211-6
Contact your Gale, a part of Cengage Learning sales representative for ordering information.

BRITISH LIBRARY CATALOGUING IN PUBLICATION DATA
International directory of company histories, Vol. 133
Jay P. Pederson
33.87409

Printed in Mexico
1 2 3 4 5 6 7 16 15 14 13 12

Contents

Preface

The St. James Press series *The International Directory of Company Histories* (*IDCH*) is intended for reference use by students, business people, librarians, historians, economists, investors, job candidates, and others who seek to learn more about the historical development of the world's most important companies. To date, *IDCH* has profiled more than 12,185 companies in 133 volumes.

INCLUSION CRITERIA

Most companies chosen for inclusion in *IDCH* have achieved a minimum of US$25 million in annual sales and are leading influences in their industries or geographical locations. Companies may be publicly held, private, or nonprofit. State-owned companies that are important in their industries and that may operate much like public or private companies also are included. Wholly owned subsidiaries and divisions are profiled if they meet the requirements for inclusion. Entries on companies that have had major changes since they were last profiled may be selected for updating.

The *IDCH* series highlights 25% private and nonprofit companies, and features updated entries on approximately 35 companies per volume.

ENTRY FORMAT

Each entry begins with the company's legal name; the address of its headquarters; its telephone, toll-free, and fax numbers; and its web site. A statement of public, private, state, or parent ownership follows. A company with a legal name in both English and the language of its headquarters country is listed by the English name, with the native-language name in parentheses.

The company's founding or earliest incorporation date, the number of employees, and the most recent available sales figures follow. Sales figures are given in local currencies with equivalents in U.S. dollars. For some private companies, sales figures are estimates and indicated by the abbreviation *est.* The entry lists the exchanges on which the company's stock is traded and its ticker symbol, as well as the company's NAICS codes.

Entries generally contain a *Company Perspectives* box which provides a short summary of the company's mission, goals, and ideals; a *Key Dates* box highlighting milestones in the company's history; lists of *Principal Subsidiaries*, *Principal Divisions*, *Principal Operating Units*, *Principal Competitors*; and articles for *Further Reading*.

American spelling is used throughout *IDCH*, and the word "billion" is used in its U.S. sense of one thousand million.

SOURCES

Entries have been compiled from publicly accessible sources both in print and on the Internet such as general and academic periodicals, books, and annual reports, as well as material supplied by the companies themselves.

CUMULATIVE INDEXES

IDCH contains three indexes: the **Cumulative Index to Companies**, which provides an alphabetical index to companies profiled in the *IDCH* series, the **Index to Industries**, which allows researchers to locate companies by their principal industry, and the **Geographic Index**, which lists companies alphabetically by the country of their headquarters. The indexes are cumulative and specific instructions for using them are found immediately preceding each index.

SPECIAL TO THIS VOLUME

This volume of *IDCH* profiles Consorzio del Formaggio Parmigiano-Reggiano, responsible for the production of one of the world's most famous cheeses; the long-running nonprofit Muscular Dystrophy Association, which pioneered the telethon format of fundraising; and the flag carrier for Jordan, Royal Jordanian Airlines Company PLC.

SUGGESTIONS WELCOME

Comments and suggestions from users of *IDCH* on any aspect of the product as well as suggestions for companies to be included or updated are cordially invited. Please write:

The Editor
International Directory of Company Histories
St. James Press
Gale, Cengage Learning
27500 Drake Rd.
Farmington Hills, Michigan 48331-3535

St. James Press does not endorse any of the companies or products mentioned in this series. Companies appearing in the *International Directory of Company Histories* were selected without reference to their wishes and have in no way endorsed their entries.

Notes on Contributors

M. L. Cohen
Novelist, business writer, and researcher living in Paris.

Jeffrey L. Covell
Seattle-based writer.

Ed Dinger
Writer and editor based in Bronx, New York.

Arianna Dogil
Writer, editor, and content strategist living in San Francisco.

Paul R. Greenland
Illinois-based writer and researcher; author of two books and former senior editor of a national business magazine; contributor to *The Encyclopedia of Chicago History, The Encyclopedia of Religion,* and the *Encyclopedia of Emerging Industries.*

Robert Halasz
Former editor in chief of *World Progress* and *Funk & Wagnalls New Encyclopedia Yearbook*; author, *The U.S. Marines* (Millbrook Press, 1993).

Frederick C. Ingram
Writer based in South Carolina.

Nelson Rhodes
Editor, writer, and consultant in the Chicago area.

Carrie Rothburd
Writer and editor specializing in corporate profiles, academic texts, and academic journal articles.

Roger Rouland
Writer and scholar specializing in company histories, literary criticism, literary essays, and poetry; freelance photographer specializing in nature photography.

David E. Salamie
Part-owner of InfoWorks Development Group, a reference publication development and editorial services company.

Mary Tradii
Colorado-based writer.

Frank Uhle
Ann Arbor-based writer; movie projectionist, disc jockey, and staff member of *Psychotronic Video* magazine.

A. Woodward
Wisconsin-based writer.

List of Abbreviations

€ European euro
¥ Japanese yen
£ United Kingdom pound
$ United States dollar

A

AB Aktiebolag (Finland, Sweden)
AB Oy Aktiebolag Osakeyhtiot (Finland)
A.E. Anonimos Eteria (Greece)
AED Emirati dirham
AG Aktiengesellschaft (Austria, Germany, Switzerland, Liechtenstein)
aG auf Gegenseitigkeit (Austria, Germany)
A.m.b.a. Andelsselskab med begraenset ansvar (Denmark)
A.O. Anonim Ortaklari/Ortakligi (Turkey)
ApS Amparteselskab (Denmark)
ARS Argentine peso
A.S. Anonim Sirketi (Turkey)
A/S Aksjeselskap (Norway)
A/S Aktieselskab (Denmark, Sweden)
Ay Avoinyhtio (Finland)
ATS Austrian shilling
AUD Australian dollar
Ay Avoinyhtio (Finland)

B

B.A. Buttengewone Aansprakeiijkheid (Netherlands)
BDT Bangladeshi taka

BEF Belgian franc
BHD Bahraini dinar
Bhd. Berhad (Malaysia, Brunei)
BND Brunei dollar
BRL Brazilian real
B.V. Besloten Vennootschap (Belgium, Netherlands)
BWP Botswana pula

C

C. de R.L. Compania de Responsabilidad Limitada (Spain)
C. por A. Compania por Acciones (Dominican Republic)
C.A. Compania Anonima (Ecuador, Venezuela)
C.V. Commanditaire Vennootschap (Netherlands, Belgium)
CAD Canadian dollar
CEO Chief Executive Officer
CFO Chief Financial Officer
CHF Swiss franc
Cia. Compagnia (Italy)
Cia. Companhia (Brazil, Portugal)
Cia. Compania (Latin America [except Brazil], Spain)
Cie. Compagnie (Belgium, France, Luxembourg, Netherlands)
CIO Chief Information Officer
CLP Chilean peso
CNY Chinese yuan
Co. Company
COO Chief Operating Officer

Coop. Cooperative
COP Colombian peso
Corp. Corporation
CPT Cuideachta Phoibi Theoranta (Republic of Ireland)
CRL Companhia a Responsabilidao Limitida (Portugal, Spain)
CZK Czech koruna

D

D&B Dunn & Bradstreet
d.d. Deiniška družba (public limited company/joint-stock company) (Slovenia, Croatia)
d.o.o. Družba z omejeno odgovornostjo (limited liability company/ private limited company) (Slovenia, Croatia)
DEM German deutsche mark (W. Germany to 1990; unified Germany to 2002)
Div. Division (United States)
DKK Danish krone
DZD Algerian dinar

E

E.P.E. Etema Pemorismenis Evthynis (Greece)
EBITDA Earnings before interest, taxes, depreciation, and amortization
EC Exempt Company (Arab countries)

Edms. Bpk. Eiendoms Beperk (South Africa)
EEK Estonian Kroon
eG eingetragene Genossenschaft (Germany)
EGMBH Eingetragene Genossenschaft mit beschraenkter Haftung (Austria, Germany)
EGP Egyptian pound
Ek For Ekonomisk Forening (Sweden)
EP Empresa Portuguesa (Portugal)
ESOP Employee Stock Options and Ownership
ESP Spanish peseta
Et(s). Etablissement(s) (Belgium, France, Luxembourg)
eV eingetragener Verein (Germany)
EUR European euro

F
FIM Finnish markka
FRF French franc

G
G.I.E. Groupement d'Interet Economique (France)
gGmbH gemeinnutzige Gesellschaft mit beschraenkter Haftung (Austria, Germany, Switzerland)
GmbH Gesellschaft mit beschraenkter Haftung (Austria, Germany, Switzerland)
GRD Greek drachma
GWA Gewerbte Amt (Austria, Germany)

H
HB Handelsbolag (Sweden)
HF Hlutafelag (Iceland)
HKD Hong Kong dollar
HUF Hungarian forint

I
IDR Indonesian rupiah
IEP Irish pound
ILS Israeli shekel (new)
Inc. Incorporated (United States, Canada)
INR Indian rupee
IPO Initial Public Offering
I/S Interesentselskap (Norway)
I/S Interessentselskab (Denmark)
ISK Icelandic krona

ITL Italian lira

J
JMD Jamaican dollar
JOD Jordanian dinar

K
KB Kommanditbolag (Sweden)
KES Kenyan schilling
Kft Korlatolt Felelossegu Tarsasag (Hungary)
KG Kommanditgesellschaft (Austria, Germany, Switzerland)
KGaA Kommanditgesellschaft auf Aktien (Austria, Germany, Switzerland)
KK Kabushiki Kaisha (Japan)
KPW North Korean won
KRW South Korean won
K/S Kommanditselskab (Denmark)
K/S Kommandittselskap (Norway)
KWD Kuwaiti dinar
Ky Kommandiitiyhtio (Finland)

L
L.L.C. Limited Liability Company (Arab countries, Egypt, Greece, United States)
L.L.P. Limited Liability Partnership (United States)
L.P. Limited Partnership (Canada, South Africa, United Kingdom, United States)
LBO Leveraged Buyout
Lda. Limitada (Spain)
Ltd. Limited
Ltda. Limitada (Brazil, Portugal)
Ltee. Limitee (Canada, France)
LUF Luxembourg franc
LYD Libyan dinar

M
MAD Moroccan dirham
mbH mit beschraenkter Haftung (Austria, Germany)
Mij. Maatschappij (Netherlands)
MUR Mauritian rupee
MXN Mexican peso
MYR Malaysian ringgit

N
N.A. National Association (United States)
N.V. Naamloze Vennootschap (Bel-

gium, Netherlands)
NGN Nigerian naira
NLG Netherlands guilder
NOK Norwegian krone
NZD New Zealand dollar

O
OAO Otkrytoe Aktsionernoe Obshchestve (Russia)
OHG Offene Handelsgesellschaft (Austria, Germany, Switzerland)
OMR Omani rial
OOO Obschestvo s Ogranichennoi Otvetstvennostiu (Russia)
OOUR Osnova Organizacija Udruzenog Rada (Yugoslavia)
Oy Osakeyhtiö (Finland)

P
P.C. Private Corp. (United States)
P.L.L.C. Professional Limited Liability Corporation (United States)
P.T. Perusahaan/Perseroan Terbatas (Indonesia)
PEN Peruvian Nuevo Sol
PHP Philippine peso
PKR Pakistani rupee
P/L Part Lag (Norway)
PLC Public Limited Co. (United Kingdom, Ireland)
PLN Polish zloty
PTE Portuguese escudo
Pte. Private (Singapore)
Pty. Proprietary (Australia, South Africa, United Kingdom)
Pvt. Private (India, Zimbabwe)
PVBA Personen Vennootschap met Beperkte Aansprakelijkheid (Belgium)
PYG Paraguay guarani

Q
QAR Qatar riyal

R
REIT Real Estate Investment Trust
RMB Chinese renminbi
Rt Reszvenytarsasag (Hungary)
RUB Russian ruble

S
S.A. Sociedad Anónima (Latin America [except Brazil], Spain, Mexico)

S.A. Sociedades Anônimas (Brazil, Portugal)

S.A. Société Anonyme (Arab countries, Belgium, France, Jordan, Luxembourg, Switzerland)

S.A. de C.V. Sociedad Anonima de Capital Variable (Mexico)

S.A.B. de C.V. Sociedad Anónima Bursátil de Capital Variable (Mexico)

S.A.C. Sociedad Anonima Comercial (Latin America [except Brazil])

S.A.C.I. Sociedad Anonima Comercial e Industrial (Latin America [except Brazil])

S.A.C.I.y.F. Sociedad Anonima Comercial e Industrial y Financiera (Latin America [except Brazil])

S.A.R.L. Sociedade Anonima de Responsabilidade Limitada (Brazil, Portugal)

S.A.R.L. Société à Responsabilité Limitée (France, Belgium, Luxembourg)

S.A.S. Societe Anonyme Syrienne (Arab countries)

S.A.S. Societá in Accomandita Semplice (Italy)

S.C. Societe en Commandite (Belgium, France, Luxembourg)

S.C.A. Societe Cooperativa Agricole (France, Italy, Luxembourg)

S.C.I. Sociedad Cooperativa Ilimitada (Spain)

S.C.L. Sociedad Cooperativa Limitada (Spain)

S.C.R.L. Societe Cooperative a Responsabilite Limitee (Belgium)

S.E. Societas Europaea (European Union Member states)

S.L. Sociedad Limitada (Latin America [except Brazil], Portugal, Spain)

S.N.C. Société en Nom Collectif (France)

S.p.A. Società per Azioni (Italy)

S.R.L. Sociedad de Responsabilidad Limitada (Spain, Mexico, Latin America [except Brazil])

S.R.L. Società a Responsabilità Limitata (Italy)

S.R.O. Spolecnost s Rucenim Omezenym (Czechoslovakia)

S.S.K. Sherkate Sahami Khass (Iran)

S.V. Samemwerkende Vennootschap (Belgium)

S.Z.R.L. Societe Zairoise a Responsabilite Limitee (Zaire)

SAA Societe Anonyme Arabienne (Arab countries)

SAK Societe Anonyme Kuweitienne (Arab countries)

SAL Societe Anonyme Libanaise (Arab countries)

SAO Societe Anonyme Omanienne (Arab countries)

SAQ Societe Anonyme Qatarienne (Arab countries)

SAR Saudi riyal

Sdn. Bhd. Sendirian Berhad (Malaysia)

SEK Swedish krona

SGD Singapore dollar

SIT Slovenian tolar

S/L Salgslag (Norway)

Soc. Sociedad (Latin America [except Brazil], Spain)

Soc. Sociedade (Brazil, Portugal)

Soc. Societa (Italy)

Sp. z.o.o. Spólka z ograniczona odpowiedzialnoscia (Poland)

Ste. Societe (France, Belgium, Luxembourg, Switzerland)

Ste. Cve. Societe Cooperative (Belgium)

T

THB Thai baht

TND Tunisian dinar

TRL Turkish lira

TTD Trinidad and Tobago dollar

TWD Taiwan dollar (new)

TZS Tanzanian shilling

U

U.A. Uitgesloten Aansporakeiijkheid (Netherlands)

u.p.a. utan personligt ansvar (Sweden)

UGX Ugandan shilling

V

V.O.f. Vennootschap onder firma (Netherlands)

VAG Verein der Arbeitgeber (Austria, Germany)

VEB Venezuelan bolivar

VERTR Vertriebs (Austria, Germany)

VND Vietnamese dong

VVAG Versicherungsverein auf Gegenseitigkeit (Austria, Germany)

W – Z

WA Wettelika Aansprakalikhaed (Netherlands)

WLL With Limited Liability (Bahrain, Kuwait, Qatar, Saudi Arabia)

YK Yugen Kaisha (Japan)

ZAO Zakrytoe Aktsionernoe Obshchestve (Russia)

ZAR South African rand

ZMK Zambian kwacha

ZWD Zimbabwean dollar

A2A S.p.A.

Via Lamarmora 230
Brescia, 25124
Italy
Telephone: (+39 030) 35531
Fax: (+39 030) 3553204
Web site: http://www.a2a.eu

Public Company
Incorporated: 2008
Employees: 2,210
Sales: EUR 6.04 billion ($8.68 billion) 2010
Stock Exchanges: Milan
Ticker Symbol: ASM
NAICS: 221122 Electric Power Distribution; 221210 Natural Gas Distribution; 221310 Water Supply and Irrigation Systems; 562111 Solid Waste Collection

■ ■ ■

A2A S.p.A. is one of Italy's leading utility companies. Through its Energy division, A2A is Italy's leading power generation company, with a total installed capacity of 6.5 gigawatts (GW) in 2011. The company's power generation portfolio includes both hydroelectric and thermal power plants. The Energy division also includes A2A's natural gas distribution business, which had a total sold volume of nearly two billion cubic meters in 2010. The company's Heat & Services division focuses on the operation of cogeneration plants and district heating facilities, primarily to the cities of Bergamo, Brescia, and Milan and their surrounding regions.

This division also produces and sells electricity to these markets. The company's Environment division focuses on waste collection, street cleaning, and waste management and disposal, as well as waste energy recovery in the form of electricity and heat. The Networks division is the company's transmission and distribution wing, both for electricity and gas, as well as for the integrated water cycle management for the Brescia and Bergamo provinces.

A2A was formed in 2008 through the merger of ASM, AEM, and AMSA, the municipal utility operators in Milan and Brescia. The company is listed on the Borsa Italiana, with both the Milan and Brescia municipalities serving as major shareholders, with 27.5 percent each. Giuliano Zuccoli is the group's chairman. Renato Ravanelli is CEO of A2A's corporate and market area, while Paolo Rossetti serves as CEO of its technical operations.

ORIGINS IN THE EARLY 20TH CENTURY

A2A was created from the merger of three municipal utility and services companies, AEM, ASM, and AMSA, in January 2008. All three companies traced their origins to the development of municipal services in Italy's Lombardy region in general, and the Milan and Brescia markets in particular.

AEM, which stood for Azienda Energetica Municipale, was formally founded in 1910. Movement toward the creation of a city-owned utility company had already been in place for more than a decade prior to the company's founding. At the end of the 19th century, the electrical power industry had become a source of some political contention.

An early contract made by the Milan city government had given a private company, Società generale italiana di elettricità, sistema Edison, the contract to supply electricity to the city. By 1898, however, this contract had turned into a virtual monopoly. This prompted a bitter debate, which ultimately reached a national level. On one side, conservative forces favored maintaining a privately owned utility market. On the other, so-called innovators called for the Milan municipality to take control of its power supply.

The innovators won the day, and in 1903 the Milan government passed a "municipalization" law, enabling the city to produce its own electricity. Construction began on a series of urban power plants, the first of which, located at the Piazzo Trento, began generating electricity in 1905.

In 1909, following a referendum, the Milan government created a new company in order to regroup the city's power generation facilities. Azienda Elettrica Municipale di Milano (Milan Municipal Electricity Company), or AEM, became operational in 1910. Among the company's mandates was the provision of electricity at rates affordable to the private community. The company also developed reduced rates for public housing lighting. At the same time, AEM played a significant role in stimulating the region's economy, introducing special rates for small businesses.

REBUILDING AFTER WORLD WAR II

While AEM's Milan-based power plants were thermal fuel-based, the company also recognized the potential for harnessing the Lombardy region's rivers particularly in the Valtellina region, for its electricity generation. The company built its first hydroelectric plant in Grosotto, on the Adda river, in 1910. Over the next two decades, the company built several more small-scale hydroelectric plants, as well as three storage reservoirs.

AEM came into its own in the period between the two world wars particularly under Benito Mussolini's rule. Through the 1920s and 1930s, the company expanded its network of power plants, including building a major hydroelectric plant at Valtellina. Among the company's projects during the period was a new power plant at Roasco, construction of which began in 1918. This plant was fed by the Fusino dam, built in 1922. By the end of the 1930s, AEM had become the dominant provider of electrical power in the Milan area.

With much of its infrastructure damaged during World War II, AEM was forced to rebuild. Through the 1950s, the company invested heavily in order to restore and modernize the region's power supply. Hydroelectric power now became a primary focus of the company's expanding generation capacity. In 1956, the company launched construction of a new series of large-scale hydroelectric plants in the Valtellina region. The inauguration of the first two power plants in 1960 permitted the company to double its power generation capacity. A third unit was commissioned in 1964, bringing the AEM's total number of hydroelectric plants to six.

ADDING SERVICES IN THE EIGHTIES

The ready availability of relatively inexpensive, sustainable electricity helped fuel Milan's economic growth through the boom years of the 1960s and beyond, helping to transform the city into one of Italy's major financial and industrial centers. At the same time, AEM had also continued to extend its thermal power generation capacity as well, notably with the construction, in partnership with Brescia counterpart ASM, of a plant in Cassano d'Adda, in 1959.

During the 1970s, AEM had put the construction of a fourth large-scale hydroelectric plant in Valtellina on hold. At the end of the decade, however, the company moved ahead with the construction of what was to become its seventh hydroelectric plant in Valtellina, in the Braulio Valley in the protected region of Stelvio National Park. In order to address concerns over the alteration of the natural beauty of the landscape, the company built the power plant inside a cavern located at 2,000 meters above sea level. This plant was commissioned in 1986. By then, the company had also completed a major expansion of capacity at the Cassano d'Adda thermal power plant.

Throughout its history, AEM had focused exclusively on the electricity market. In the beginning of

KEY DATES

1908: Azienda dei Servizi Municipalizzati (ASM) is founded in Brescia.
1910: Azienda Elettrica Municipale di Milano (AEM) is founded in Milan.
1929: AMSA is founded in Milan.
1956: AEM launches construction of a large-scale hydroelectric plant in Valtellina region.
1980: AEM expands into gas distribution and district heating and changes its name to Azienda Energetica Municipale.
2008: ASM, AEM, and AMSA merge, becoming A2A S.p.A.
2009: A2A acquires a stake in Montenegro's EPCG.
2011: A2A wins a contract to build a waste treatment plant in the United Kingdom.

the 1980s, however, the company decided to diversify by adding gas distribution and district heating services to the Milan region. As a result, the company changed its name, to Azienda Energetica Municipale, in 1980. The company soon consolidated its entry into these new segments with the takeover of the operation of Montedison's Milan gas network in 1981.

PRIVATIZATION PROCESS IN 1996

The impending liberalization of the European energy markets led the municipality of Milan to launch the privatization of AEM in the 1990s. As a first step, the company reincorporated as a joint stock company, AEM S.p.A., in 1996. Two years later, AEM's privatization got underway, with the listing of 49 percent of its shares on the Borsa Italiana. The Milan city government maintained majority control of AEM until 2004, when it sold another 17.6 percent, dropping its stake to 33.4 percent. The following year, as the Italian government liberalized the country's energy markets under the Bersani Decree, AEM restructured, placing its various operations into separate subsidiaries. AEM then became the holding company for the group.

The newly public company soon began its expansion drive. In 2000, the company entered the telecommunications sector, building a fiber-optics network for the city of Milan. The following year, the company launched its energy trading operations, at a national and then international level. This business later became known as A2A Trading.

In 2002, AEM acquired rival ENEL's Milan electricity business. This purchase gave AEM the monopoly over electricity distribution in Milan. Also in 2002, the company acquired a stake in GENCO Eurogen, through its 20 percent share of the Edipower consortium. This was followed by the acquisition of Edison S.p.A., in partnership with France's EDF, in 2005.

MERGER TALKS WITH ASM IN 2006

The increasing competitiveness of the Italian and European energy and utilities sectors led AEM to the next phase in its growth. In 2006, the company began merger discussions with its longtime partner ASM. That company had been founded in 1908, initially to operate the city of Brescia's tram service, as well as its ice production factory. The new company's name, Azienda dei Servizi Municipalizzati (Municipal Services Company), reflected its mandate to provide public utility services to the city. In 1909, ASM expanded its operations to include electrical power distribution. The company later added gas distribution in 1924, and management of the city's aqueduct system in 1933.

ASM diversification continued particularly from the late 1960s. In 1968, the company added street cleaning services, followed by the addition of district heating services in 1972, with the construction of the South Lamamora plant. The company later expanded its district heating operations with the Central South cogeneration plant, completed in 1981. The company began providing thermal plant and heating systems services to the city's public buildings from 1989, and also took over operations of its car parks and parking meters in 1990. Starting in 1995, ASM extended into waste handling and wastewater treatment.

Like AEM, ASM converted to a joint stock company in 1998. The company began natural gas imports during this time, and in 2001 formed Plurigas. This company then won a bid to import three billion cubic meters of natural gas per year, for a 10-year period. Also in that year, ASM expanded its electrical generation capacity, joining with Spain's Endesa and Banco Santander Central Hispano to acquire Elettrogen. This company, which became known as Endesa Italia, was the country's third-largest power generator with an installed capacity of 6,590 megawatts (MW).

ASM became the first to lead the consolidation of the region's utilities operations, merging with Bergamo Ambiente e Servizi in 2005. In this way, the expanded ASM took over a variety of public services for the Bergamo municipality, including water, gas, public lighting, street cleaning, and electrical power generation services.

CREATING A2A IN 2008

As talks between AEM and ASM progressed into 2007, the companies added a third partner to the merger, ASM's Milan counterpart, AMSA. This company originated with the creation of Servizi Pubblici Anonima Italiana in 1929, succeeding the city's waste collection and disposal service originated in 1907. The company remained focused on waste collection, changing its name to Azienda Municipale Nettezza Urbana in 1970, and then to Azienda Municipalizzata Servizi Ambientali (AMSA) in 1985. The company later went public as Azienda Milanese Servizi Ambientali in 2001.

AEM played the role of leading partner in the merger, signing separate agreements with ASM and AMSA in December 2007. Under terms of the merger agreement, the municipalities of Milan and Brescia became equal partners, holding stakes of 27.5 percent. A2A S.p.A. officially started business on January 1, 2008. The new company started out as one of Italy's leading power generation companies, with an installed capacity of more than 5,000 MW.

A2A quickly got its expansion strategy underway, buying up 90 percent of Aspem S.p.A., the local utility operator owned by the city of Varese in September 2008. The company followed this purchase up by expanding its power generation capacity. In July 2009, the company acquired the Monfalcone thermoelectric power plant, adding its 976 MW of capacity. At the same time, the company made its first acquisition outside of Italy's northern region, buying a 484 MW hydroelectric plant in Calabria.

The company also eyed expansion beyond the Italian utilities market. This brought the company into Macedonia, where it bought 18.3 percent of Montenegro's Elektroprivreda Crne Gore AD Niksic (EPCG). The company continued building its stake in EPCG, raising its share in the company to 43.7 percent by 2011. By then, the company had initiated a number of other international projects, notably the construction of waste management facilities in Spain, Greece, and the United Kingdom. These included the contract to build a EUR 26 million waste treatment plant, in partnership with Shanks Waste Management and Scottish and Southern Energy.

By the beginning of 2011, A2A had emerged as one of Italy's leading diversified utilities companies, with annual revenues of more than EUR 6 billion. The company's total installed power generation capacity topped 6.5 GW, enabling the company to sell more than 35,500 gigawatt hours in 2010. The company also remained the major partner with France's EDF in controlling the Edison electricity group.

M. L. Cohen

PRINCIPAL SUBSIDIARIES

A2A Coriance S.A.S. (France); A2A Energia S.p.A.; A2A Montenegro d.o.o.; A2A Reti Elettriche S.p.A.; A2A Reti Gas S.p.A.; A2A Servizi alla Distribuzione S.p.A.; A2A Trading S.r.l.; AMSA S.p.A.; Aprica S.p.A.; AS-MEA S.r.l.; Aspem S.p.A.; Ecodeco S.r.l.; Elektroprivreda Cnre Gore AD Niksic (EPCG) (Montenegro; 43.7%); EPCG d.o.o. (Serbia); Retragas S.r.l.; Selene S.p.A.

PRINCIPAL DIVISIONS

Energy; Heat & Services; Environment; Networks.

PRINCIPAL OPERATING UNITS

A2A Reti Elettriche; A2A Reti Gas; A2A Trading; Coriance; Selene; EPCG.

PRINCIPAL COMPETITORS

Enel S.p.A.; Energia & Servizi S.r.l.; Eni S.p.A.; Fedi Impianti s.r.l.; Hera S.p.A.; SolarMarkt AG.

FURTHER READING

"A2A Agrees to Buy 90 Pct of Local Utility Aspem as Part of Expansion Strategy." *AFX Europe (Focus)*, September 30, 2008.

"A2A Energia SpA Bags Tender for Electricity Supply." *TendersInfo News*, June 22, 2011.

"A2A Energia SpA Wins Tender for Electricity Distribution Services." *TendersInfo News*, April 19, 2011.

"A2A Servizi Alla Distribuzione SpA Declared the Winner of Construction Work for Water and Sewage Pipeline." *TendersInfo News*, June 28, 2011.

"A2A Signs Deal with Renault-Nissan to Develop, Market Electric Car in Italy." *ADP News Italy*, July 2, 2009.

"A2A SpA Allocated Contract for Construction Works of Power Plants and Heating Plants." *TendersInfo News*, October 18, 2011.

"A2A to Pick up Talks with EDF over Edison." *M&A Navigator*, September 29, 2011.

"A2A Unit Ecodeco Wins EUR 26m Waste Treatment Plant Contract in UK." *ADP News Italy*, June 15, 2011.

"Italian A2A to Buy 18% in Montenegro EPCG." *ADP News Italy*, September 4, 2009.

"Italian A2A to Divest Stake in Metroweb." *M&A Navigator*, August 24, 2011.

"Italy's A2A Net Profit Rises to EUR 308m in 2010." *ADP News Italy*, March 30, 2011.

"Mergers Commission Approves Italian Retail Gas Joint Venture between A2A and Gazprom." *Right Vision News*, June 28, 2010.

A. Schulman, Inc.

3550 West Market Street
Akron, Ohio 44333-2658
U.S.A.
Telephone: (330) 666-3751
Toll Free: (800) 547-3746
Fax: (330) 668-7204
Web site: http://www.aschulman.com

Public Company
Incorporated: 1928
Employees: 3,000
Sales: $2.19 billion (2011)
Stock Exchanges: NASDAQ
Ticker Symbol: SHLM
NAICS: 325211 Plastics Material and Resin Manufacturing; 325991 Custom Compounding of Purchased Resins; 424690 Other Chemical and Allied Products Merchant Wholesalers

■ ■ ■

A. Schulman, Inc., is a leading global producer and supplier of plastic compounds and resins, which are used by manufacturers as raw materials for packaging products and film, durable goods, household items, automobile parts, and other plastic items. The company specializes in masterbatches, which are highly concentrated plastic compounds enhanced, at customer request, by any number of additives. Although it has been based in Akron, Ohio, since its founding, A. Schulman has extensive operations in Europe and derives 70 percent of its revenues from Europe, the Middle East, and Africa.

About 24 percent of sales are generated in the Americas, with the remaining 6 percent originating in the Asia-Pacific region. The company operates more than 30 manufacturing facilities around the world. In addition to its core manufacturing operations, A. Schulman also leverages its global distribution and supply capabilities by serving as a distributor for other polymer producers.

ROOTS IN RUBBER

Alex Schulman established a rubber brokerage in Akron, Ohio, in 1928 that he incorporated as A. Schulman, Inc. Working out of a small shop, Schulman purchased and resold wholesale and scrap rubber, which his customers would refashion into a variety of rubber products. While Schulman cultivated a clientele, the business remained small. The largest consumers of rubber were tire makers, automobile companies, and hose manufacturers. These companies purchased raw virgin rubber on a huge scale, providing few large sales opportunities for Schulman's enterprise.

In 1930, just as Schulman's business became stable, the nation was plunged into the Great Depression. Demand for most products, including rubber, fell precipitously. Before rubber stocks were depleted, prices nosedived, eliminating demand for used rubber. A few years later, when rubber became scarce, this demand recovered, providing some support to Schulman's business and enabling him to realize a small margin on his sales. A. Schulman, Inc. recovered from the Great Depression slowly, as the company's business depended almost entirely on the successes and resources of his customers. Fortunately, A. Schulman was not crushed by fluctuations in the broader rubber market or larger final markets, as were many tire, automobile, and hose manufacturers.

By the late 1930s and early 1940s, the onset of war in Europe and then in the Pacific caused industrial demand for rubber to increase. Rubber was an important war commodity, and sources of rubber were limited. As a result, a premium was placed on companies that could recycle scrap rubber, producing a useful product from waste. A. Schulman and several other companies in the scrap rubber business were placed under the authority of a war production board that had responsibility for coordinating efficient production of essential commodities and setting prices. Often Schulman did not know who his customers ultimately were. While it took a few months to gain footing, Schulman's company went into full production, supplying mulched rubber for recasting into tires, window seals, and numerous other products.

EXPANDING INTO SCRAP PLASTIC AND THEN PLASTICS MANUFACTURING

The scarcity of rubber during the war helped to accelerate the development of substitute and synthetic rubber products. The most important of these was plastic, which was extremely useful in small castings, exhibiting many of the same resilient and durable qualities as rubber. Although the primary ingredient in plastic was petroleum, also a crucial and limited war commodity, plastic (like rubber) could be recycled. As the war progressed, A. Schulman began to accept scrap plastic for chipping and shipment to casting mills. By the end of the war, A. Schulman had doubled its product line to include scrap rubber and scrap plastic. In 1950, having heard some persuasive arguments from a young salesman named William Zekan, Schulman realized he stood on the threshold of a new industry.

Schulman hired Zekan in 1937 after meeting him on the golf course of the Rosemont Country Club, where the 18-year-old Zekan worked as a caddie. Although Zekan started at A. Schulman as an office boy, earning less than he could as a caddie, he stayed with the business and was promoted to salesman just before he enlisted in the army at the outbreak of the war. Zekan returned to the company after his tour, and in 1947 he was tapped by Schulman to head his New York sales office. Here the shy and reserved Zekan learned the art of sales, eventually honing his skills of persuasion. Zekan performed exceptionally well in New York, and when he was called back to Akron in 1953, it was to take the number two position under Alex Schulman.

Schulman and Zekan developed a new strategy during this period to abandon the scrap markets and move the company into the plastics manufacturing business. Rather than molding its own products, A. Schulman would draw on its substantial reputation as a raw product supplier and concentrate on making plastic compounds, which were manufactured in the form of pellets, smaller than peanuts. By applying heat, these pellets could be extruded or molded into many types of finished products.

The company grew considerably during the 1950s, mostly on the strength of inexpensive oil as well as the increasing number of applications for plastic. For the first time, automobile manufacturers began molding plastic parts for cars, including dashboards, interior side panel trim, and window insulation.

Searching for new growth markets, Schulman established a network of small plants in Britain, France, and Germany. There he hoped to get in on the ground floor of emerging industries in postwar Europe. The company later established a plant in Canada that served various plastics consumers in that country, including the automotive industry.

Alex Schulman died in 1962, and his will specified that Zekan should succeed him as president of the company. For his part, Zekan had become so deeply involved with executive decisions under Schulman that, despite the founder's sudden death, the transition to new leadership was smooth.

The 1960s were a period of strong growth for A. Schulman. It was during the decade after Schulman's death that the company began to really define its place in the industry. The company began to produce plastics, albeit in smaller quantities than competitors, with

KEY DATES

1928: Alex Schulman incorporates A. Schulman, Inc. as a rubber brokerage in Akron, Ohio.

Mid-1940s: A. Schulman expands into scrap plastic.

1950s: Company begins manufacturing plastic compounds.

1962: Alex Schulman dies; William Zekan assumes company leadership.

1972: Company goes public.

1991: Zekan dies; Terry Haines takes over as CEO.

2000: Company ends production at its Akron plant.

2008: Joseph M. Gingo comes onboard as A. Schulman's new CEO.

2009: Production begins at a new masterbatch plant in Akron.

2010: A. Schulman acquires Houston-based ICO, Inc.

special characteristics. Often the customer specified the tolerances of these products in advance of manufacture. The company then instructed its laboratories to design a plastic to meet those specifications. Thus, with the employment of technology, A. Schulman was able to offer a limited quantity of plastics that could outperform other plastics.

DEALING WITH THE CHALLENGES OF THE SEVENTIES AS A PUBLIC COMPANY

As a major player in this vital niche market, A. Schulman was somewhat insulated from the competition elsewhere in the industry. Because A. Schulman dealt in a unique family of products, it was able to sell on quality and not price. This produced a new sales philosophy, described by Zekan as: "We don't talk price, we talk quality."

The company's ability to build such a strong position in the market led Zekan to consider expansion. Rather than just the addition of production facilities, Zekan was concerned with innovations in his product line. Unable to adequately fund technological research internally, he went forward with plans to take the company public in 1972.

In 1973 an Arab-Israeli war triggered an oil embargo against the United States that caused the price of petroleum to skyrocket. For plastics producers such as A. Schulman, this meant temporary shortages of raw

materials and necessary price increases. While these price increases were ultimately passed along to the consumer, the net effect was a serious recession that forced many companies in the plastics industry to go out of business. A. Schulman remained insulated from much of this activity because it produced a product defined by quality and technology rather than simply by price. Nonetheless, the company did suffer some reverses because of the onset of recession.

By 1977 inflationary pressure had stabilized, but a second oil crisis two years later caused additional price shocks that continued to cut into demand. By 1982, automobile manufacturers had entered a prolonged period of serious financial trouble. Because they were large consumers of specialty plastics, A. Schulman's growth continued to lag.

CULTIVATING NEW CUSTOMERS AND EXPANDING PRODUCTION FACILITIES

Hoping to tie its products to growing companies in the automotive industry, A. Schulman began cultivating relationships with Japanese plastics manufacturers, with the intention of gaining supply contracts with Japanese carmakers. The timing was perfect. Several companies, including Honda and Toyota, began building large production facilities in the United States during this time. In 1988 A. Schulman established a joint venture with Japan's largest chemical company, Mitsubishi Kasei Corporation, and the venture, called The Sunprene Company, set up a new plastics plant in Bellevue, Ohio. With the help of Mitsubishi Kasei (later Mitsubishi Chemical Corporation), A. Schulman concluded numerous supply contracts with Honda, Nissan, and Toyota.

The addition of new customers forced A. Schulman to modernize and expand its production facilities. The company spent $33 million to increase worldwide capacity by 25 percent. Nonetheless, the company avoided becoming overly reliant on only a few customers in a single industry. The company's five largest accounts constituted less than 10 percent of sales.

Zekan had a hands-on leadership style and a genuine love of selling. He kept the reins of the company tightly in his hands, prompting some critics to fear that this concentration of power could leave a void in management. However, A. Schulman had a highly capable second tier of management that would be put to the test and would ultimately rise to the challenge in 1989, when Zekan, aged 69, underwent surgery for treatment of cancer. It was at this juncture that Zekan promoted three senior managers in preparation for his retirement. One of these was Terry Haines, who was named president, while Zekan remained chairman and CEO.

Retirement, however, never came. Zekan remained in charge of the company until his death in January 1991. Haines remained president and took on the duties of CEO as well. Robert Stefanko, who ran the finance department, was elected chairman. With the death of Zekan, A. Schulman, Inc. lost the last link to its founder. This also marked the beginning of a new era.

While the company had shunned growth by acquisition for nearly its entire existence, A. Schulman took over the French plastics company Diffusion Plastique in August 1991. Initial integration of the business was difficult but ultimately successful. In addition, the Sunprene joint venture recorded its first profit in 1992. That year, A. Schulman posted its 10th consecutive record for annual net income and was ranked 12th on the *Fortune* 500 list of companies with highest total return over 10 years, averaging 37.2 percent.

The run of earnings increases ended in 1993, however, as economic weakness in Europe and unfavorable exchange rates led to declines in both sales and earnings, the latter falling by 12 percent. Seeking new markets for growth, A. Schulman had earlier in the decade earmarked Mexico as a key market, opening an office in Mexico City in 1990. Around the same time as the passage of the North American Free Trade Agreement (NAFTA) in late 1993, A. Schulman announced plans to build a $15 million plant in Mexico. In September 1995 the compounding plant, located in San Luis Potosí, began operation, with a focus on serving the automotive and packaging sectors in Mexico. This was A. Schulman's 11th plant worldwide and its first in Latin America.

FUELING GROWTH VIA ACQUISITIONS

Domestically, A. Schulman turned to acquisitions to fuel growth in the mid-1990s. In 1994 the company acquired Nashville, Tennessee-based ComAlloy International Corporation, an affiliate of Exxon Corporation's Exxon Chemical Company. Generating about $30 million in annual revenue, ComAlloy specialized in thermoplastics used in high-strength applications for the electrical, appliance, and automotive sectors. During 1995 Eastman Chemical Company sold its compound polypropylene business to A. Schulman. This unit produced colored and filled polypropylene and foam products that were used primarily in the manufacturing of injection-molded plastic automotive parts. A second acquisition in 1995 was that of Texas Polymer Services, Inc., a division of J.M. Huber

Corporation with annual revenues of $15 million. Based in Orange, Texas, the division supplied custom compounding, tolling services, and engineered plastics compounding. In November 1996 A. Schulman acquired the Specialty Compounding Division of Laurel Industries, Inc., which included a manufacturing plant in Sharon Center, Ohio.

Both revenues and profits fell during fiscal 1996. The latter tumbled by 21 percent, because of a steep drop in plastic resin prices, which led customers to reduce inventories, and also because of high start-up costs associated with the company's new initiatives in Mexico and elsewhere. Despite major auto strikes, the company recovered during fiscal 1997 thanks to improving market conditions, as profits increased from $42.2 million to $50.7 million.

Continuing its overseas expansion in the last years of the century, A. Schulman acquired the assets of a distributor and merchant in Warsaw, Poland, in August 1997. This business became the basis for a new Polish subsidiary. Later that year, the company acquired Isopolymer, Inc., which had been the distributor of A. Schulman products in Italy and which had annual sales of about $30 million. In January 1998, production began at a new plastics compounding plant in Surabaya, Indonesia, that had been built through a joint venture to serve the Asia-Pacific region. This was the firm's seventh plant located outside the United States. Also during 1998, the company opened an office in Hungary.

Back home, the firm opened its Product Technology Center in Akron and its Color Technology Center in Sharon Center that same year. At the Product Technology Center, A. Schulman employees could work with customers to formulate custom compounds and, at the center's laboratories, create trial runs of customized products both to test the manufacturing process and to evaluate the end product. Similarly, the Color Technology Center was designed to provide customers with a full range of color services, aided by the staff and by a variety of equipment for analysis, color formulation, and testing. Similar technology centers were opened in Europe as well.

Partly in reaction to the company's difficulties during 1996, a powerful activist pension fund, the California Public Employees' Retirement System (CALPERS), identified A. Schulman as one of several "underperforming" public companies in a report issued in early 1998. CALPERS accused the company of speculating on resin prices, a criticism firmly denied by the company, and of failing to articulate a strategic plan for the company. The pension fund also called on the company to add more independent directors to the company board and to change the way the board was elected so that the entire board had to stand for election each year, with the latter demand being one way to make a company takeover easier. Although A. Schulman refused to change the election rules, the firm did reduce the size of the board from 13 to 10, with the three departing members being company insiders. This gave a larger percentage of seats to outsiders. The company also announced that it was working on a strategic plan and said that neither of the moves was in response to the pressure from CALPERS.

Later in 1998, during the firm's annual meeting, shareholders approved a nonbinding resolution asking the board to consider adopting the annual election of all board members, but shareholders rejected a resolution that urged the board to "arrange for the prompt sale of A. Schulman, Inc. to the highest bidder." Such pressure from shareholders was inevitable given the poor performance of the company's stock over most of the bullish 1990s. One response of the company's board was to initiate an aggressive stock repurchasing plan to improve per-share earnings.

A. Schulman continued an ongoing program of renovating and upgrading its manufacturing facilities, spending $35 million on capital expenditures in 1999, $32 million in 2000, and $33.4 million in 2001. During this period new manufacturing lines were added to the firm's plants in Givet, France; Nashville, Tennessee; and San Luis Potosí, Mexico. Additional capacity was gained through the purchase of a plant in Gorla Maggiore, Italy, in July 2000.

EARLY 21ST-CENTURY STRUGGLES

After achieving record earnings per share of $1.51 in 1999, A. Schulman began faltering. The company recorded earnings per share of $1.25 and $0.43 in 2000 and 2001, respectively. Demand was down because of slowdowns in the world's economies, particularly the U.S. economy; profit margins were affected by the higher cost of plastic feedstocks; and A. Schulman, with its extensive European operations, was also being hit hard by the weakness of the euro. The company responded with an effort to save $15 million a year by cutting jobs, manufacturing lines (at least temporarily), and other operations.

In December 2000 production was ended at the plant in Akron although the facility continued to be used for other functions, including warehousing, logistics, and the Product Technology Center. This was the biggest cost-cutting move, and it involved the elimination of 129 jobs. The company also closed six district sales offices, centralizing such operations at the

company headquarters. Also during 2001, product innovation continued at A. Schulman with the introduction of Invision, which the company called "a lightweight, soft-to-the-touch, environmentally friendly alternative to polyvinyl chloride."

Although sales increased past the $1 billion mark by the fiscal year ending in August 2003 and then increased to $1.24 billion a year later, achieving similar improvements in the bottom line proved more elusive. Despite aggressive cost-cutting measures that were undertaken between 2000 and 2003, including a one-third reduction in the U.S. workforce and a 35 percent reduction in U.S. manufacturing capacity, profits for fiscal 2004 ($27.9 million) were actually lower than that of fiscal 2000 ($32.5 million). In a further cost-saving effort, and to meet increased demand overseas, A. Schulman opened new manufacturing plants in two lower-wage markets, Poland and China, in 2004.

A. Schulman's stock was a consistent laggard during this period and underperformed in comparison with the company's peers. By 2005, with earnings under continued pressure because of rising resin costs and weakness in the automotive sector, a new challenge arose. Barington Capital Group, a New York City-based activist hedge fund, began scooping up company shares that year, amassing a nearly 9 percent stake by October. Barington pressured A. Schulman to make significant changes, including considering a sale of the company, and eventually launched a proxy fight to gain control of A. Schulman's board. Late in October, however, the company reached a deal to derail the proxy battle by agreeing to buy back at least $175 million of its own stock and to appoint a Barington official to the board.

The company remained the focus of shareholder unrest as profits grew only slightly in fiscal 2006 before plummeting 30.9 percent the following year. Facing a dual proxy fight from both Barington and another New York City-based activist investment firm, Ramius Capital Group LLC, which owned a stake of about 7.5 percent, A. Schulman reached an agreement with the dissident shareholders late in 2007 that included the retirement of Haines. At the beginning of 2008, Joseph M. Gingo came onboard as the new CEO. Gingo was a longtime executive at The Goodyear Tire & Rubber Company.

REVAMPING OPERATIONS UNDER NEW LEADER

Gingo moved quickly on a number of fronts. He shook up the company's management team by replacing several top executives. To turn around A. Schulman's long-troubled North American operations, another round of cost-cutting was launched that included the closure of two more plants located in Ontario and Texas. In addition, the company's operations on the continent shifted focus away from the struggling automotive industry and toward producing plastic compounds and resins for manufacturers of packaging for food items and household goods. To support the latter initiative, A. Schulman began construction on a new masterbatch manufacturing facility in Akron where production of high-performance additives for the North American packaging and film markets began in 2009. The company also elected to shut down its Invision business, which had failed to get off the ground.

This overhaul was far from complete when the global economic downturn hit and severely undermined demand for the company's products. As a result, sales for fiscal 2009 plunged more than 35 percent to $1.28 billion. Net income before one-time items amounted to less than half the fiscal 2008 total, while various restructuring and goodwill impairment charges sent A. Schulman into a net loss for the year of $2.8 million.

These results were disappointing but not unexpected given the poor economic environment. The results for fiscal 2010, as a tentative economic recovery took hold, were more indicative of the long-term impact of the strategic moves that Gingo had implemented. That year, A. Schulman had its most profitable year overall since the late 1990s, earning $43.9 million on sales of $1.59 billion. More importantly, the company's North American operations posted profits in all four quarters of the year thanks largely to the shift in focus to higher-growth, higher-margin product lines.

RENEWED PURSUIT OF TARGETED ACQUISITIONS

A renewed confidence at A. Schulman was reflected in a series of targeted acquisitions that strengthened and expanded its core operations. In April 2010 the company acquired Houston-based ICO, Inc. for $237.7 million. ICO was a major global producer of specialty resins and concentrates used in the manufacture of a variety of products, including plastic bags and films, toys, and water tanks. The company had generated sales of about $300 million in its fiscal year ending in September 2009. By purchasing ICO, A. Schulman increased its presence in the U.S. masterbatch market; gained plants in the high-growth Brazilian market; expanded further in the Asia-Pacific region by securing production facilities in Australia, New Zealand, and Malaysia; and solidified its operations in its largest market, Europe, while gaining ground in particular in three countries where its presence had been limited: France, Italy, and the Netherlands. The deal also

expanded A. Schulman's capabilities in rotational molding (commonly called rotomolding), a process used to create hollow items, such as water tanks and kayaks.

Also acquired in the early months of 2010 was McCann Color, Inc., a North Canton, Ohio-based producer of high-quality color concentrates. This $8.8 million deal enabled A. Schulman to shut down its Sharon Center plant, replacing it with a state-of-the-art facility built in 1998. In November 2010 A. Schulman spent $15.2 million to purchase Mash Indústria e Comércio de Compostos Plásticos LTDA, an engineered plastics compounder and producer of masterbatch additives headquartered in São Paulo, Brazil. In other developments overseas, the company in early 2011 announced plant consolidations in both Italy and Australia that entailed the closure of a single plant in each country. Later that year, A. Schulman enhanced its position in the rotational molding market by acquiring a majority stake in the Argentine firm Surplast S.A., based in Buenos Aires, Argentina. Surplast thus became a joint venture between A. Schulman and Alta Plastica S.A., a major Argentine resin distributor. At this same time, A. Schulman was working to make further inroads into Asia-Pacific markets by building a plant in India to produce additive masterbatches for polypropylene film and other products.

As part of its continued pursuit of improved profitability, A. Schulman in August 2011 announced the closure of its engineered plastics plant in Nashville, Tennessee. Production shifted to the company's Akron plant, where compounding capacity was increased through $7 million in upgrades. Later in 2011, the Sunprene thermoplastic elastomer joint venture with Mitsubishi Chemical was dissolved, with Mitsubishi taking over full control of the business. For fiscal 2011, A. Schulman's sales surged nearly 38 percent to $2.19 billion, marking the firm's first $2 billion-plus year. Although net income was down slightly from 2010, profits actually grew more than 20 percent when certain exceptional items were excluded. The overhaul and expansion Gingo had overseen since coming onboard at the beginning of 2008 thus seemed to be showing dividends, especially considering that the global economic climate remained a challenging one.

John Simley
Updated, David E. Salamie

PRINCIPAL SUBSIDIARIES

A. Schulman Plastics, BVBA (Belgium); A. Schulman, S.A.S. (France); A. Schulman Plastics, S.A.S. (France); A. Schulman GmbH (Germany); A. Schulman, Inc.,

Limited (UK); A. Schulman Canada Ltd.; A. Schulman AG (Switzerland); ASI Investments Holding Co.; ASI Akron Land Co.; A. Schulman International, Inc.; A. Schulman de Mexico, S.A. de C.V.; ASI Employment, S.A. de C.V. (Mexico); AS Mex Holding, S.A. de C.V. (Mexico); A. Schulman Polska Sp. z.o.o. (Poland); A. Schulman Plastics SpA (Italy); A. Schulman International Services BVBA (Belgium); A. Schulman Hungary Kft.; PT A. Schulman Plastics, Indonesia (65%); A. Schulman Plastics S.L. (Spain); A. Schulman Europe & Co. KG (Germany); A. Schulman Plastics (Dongguan) Ltd. (China); A. Schulman Italia S.p.A. (Italy); A. Schulman S.á.r.l. et Cie SCS (Luxembourg); A. Schulman S.á.r.l. (Luxembourg); A. Schulman Holdings S.á.r.l. (Luxembourg); A. Schulman Invision, Inc.; DeltaPlast AB (Sweden); DeltaPlast BVBA (Belgium); A. Schulman Plastik Sanayi Ve Tic A.S. (Turkey); A. Schulman Holdings S.A.S. (France); A. Schulman Europe Verwaltungs GmbH (Germany); A. Schulman s.r.o. (Slovakia); Surplast S.A. (Argentina; 51%); Bayshore Industrial, L.P. (Texas); Courtenay Polymers Pty Ltd. (Australia); ICO (UK) Limited; ICO Europe B.V. (Netherlands); ICO Global Services, Inc.; ICO Holdings Australia Pty Limited; ICO Holdings New Zealand Limited; ICO Holland B.V. (Netherlands); ICO P&O, Inc.; ICO Polymers do Brasil Ltda. (Brazil); ICO Polymers France S.A.S.; ICO Polymers Italy S.r.l.; ICO Polymers North America, Inc.; ICO-Schulman, LLC; ICO Technology, Inc.; J.R. Courtenay (N.Z.) Limited (New Zealand); ICO Polymers (Malaysia) Sdn. Bhd.; Soreco S.A.S. (France); Wedco Technology, Inc.; A. Schulman Plastics India Private Limited; The Innovation Company, S.A. de C.V. (Mexico); Worldwide GP LLC; Worldwide LP LLC; Bayshore Industrial GP LLC; Bayshore Industrial LP LLC; ICO Polymers, Inc.; ICO Europe C.V. (Netherlands); ICO Petrochemical Cayman Islands; ICO Holdings LLC; ICO Polymers Hellas Ltd. (Greece); ICO Polymers Cayman Islands; ICO Australia RE Holdings Pty. Ltd.; MASH Industria e Comercio de Compostos Plasticos Ltda. (Brazil).

PRINCIPAL COMPETITORS

Ampacet Corporation; Asahi Kasei Corporation; Clariant AG; Cytec Industries Inc.; E. I. du Pont de Nemours and Company; Ferro Corporation; PolyOne Corporation; Saudi Basic Industries Corporation; Spartech Corporation; Techmer PM, LLC; Washington Penn Plastic Co., Inc.

FURTHER READING

Bewley, Lindsey. "Schulman Consolidates U.S. Engineering Plastics Business, Revises Guidance." *Chemical Week*, August 29, 2011, 11.

Brockinton, Langdon. "Zekan's Rise from Office Boy to Chief Executive." *Chemical Week*, July 13, 1988, 29+.

Chang, Joseph. "Schulman under Siege." *ICIS Chemical Business Americas*, October 10–16, 2005, 11.

Esposito, Frank. "Schulman Buys Color Concentrates Maker." *Plastics News*, March 8, 2010, 8.

———. "Schulman Makes Deal to Pacify Barington." *Plastics News*, October 30, 2006, 28.

Hollander, Sarah. "A. Schulman Shifts Focus to Packaging." *Cleveland Plain Dealer*, November 12, 2008, C1.

Krouse, Peter. "A. Schulman Inc. CEO Resigns." *Cleveland Plain Dealer*, November 17, 2007, C1.

Mackinnon, Jim. "A. Schulman Picks Chief Executive." *Akron (OH) Beacon Journal*, December 18, 2007, C6.

———. "Ramius Wins Schulman Proxy Fight." *Akron (OH) Beacon Journal*, January 11, 2008, C6.

———. "Schulman Reports Higher Sales but Lower Income for the Year." *Akron (OH) Beacon Journal*, October 27, 2011.

Russell, John. "Future Looks Bright: Schulman to Add Plants." *Akron (OH) Beacon Journal*, March 21, 2004, D1.

Seewald, Nancy. "RPM and Schulman Return to Profit as Demand Improves." *Chemical Week*, April 11–18, 2011, 12.

Slakter, Ann, and Homer Starr. "Schulman: A Timely Switch to Plastics." *Chemical Week*, July 9, 1986, 34+.

Walsh, Kerri. "Schulman to Expand Geographic Reach with ICO Purchase." *Chemical Week*, December 7–14, 2009, 28.

Abu Dhabi Islamic Bank PJSC

—■—

PO Box 313, Najda St.
Abu Dhabi,
United Arab Emirates
Telephone: (+971 02) 6100600
Fax: (+971 02) 6654340
Web site: http://www.adib.ae

■ ■ ■

Public Company
Founded: 1997
Incorporated: 1998
Employees: 1,654
Total Assets: AED 75.3 billion ($20.49 billion) (2010)
Stock Exchanges: Abu Dhabi
Ticker Symbol: ADIB
NAICS: 522110 Commercial Banking

Abu Dhabi Islamic Bank PJSC (ADIB) is a leading Islamic bank based in the United Arab Emirates (UAE). One of the fastest-growing Islamic banks in the Middle East and North African region, ADIB operates 66 branches throughout the UAE, backed by a network of more than 250 automated teller machines (ATMs). The company has begun an expansion beyond the UAE, opening branches in London and Baghdad, has developed plans to open branches in Sudan and Qatar, and has applied for banking licenses in a number of other countries. The company owns 51.3 percent of National Bank for Development, based in Egypt, which operates 69 branch offices there, and was a sponsor and shareholder in Bosnia International Bank. ADIB is listed on the Abu Dhabi Stock Exchange and boasted total assets of AED 75.3 billion ($20.49 billion) in 2010. The company is led by CEO Tirad Mahmoud.

RISE OF MODERN ISLAMIC BANKING IN THE 20TH CENTURY

Modern Islamic banking developed in the second half of the 20th century, especially following the creation of the Islamic Development Bank in 1975. The new type of banking was created in order to address conflicts between traditional commercial banking and Islamic law, or Sharia. In particular, Sharia forbid the charging of interest on loans, considering the practice as a form of usury. In addition, Islamic banking addressed other conflicts, such as barring investments contrary to other aspects of Sharia principles.

Islamic banking developed based on the practical application of a number of concepts. Among these were *Wadiah*, or Safekeeping, in which a bank accepts deposits on an interest-free basis while guaranteeing the safety of the deposited funds. Banks retained the right to charge fees for its services. Although barred from paying a fixed interest on deposited funds, banks were enabled to provide payouts in the form of *hibah*, or gifts, to their customers.

Islamic banking rules also established profit-sharing agreements, called *Mudharabah*, to govern commercial relationships, such as the funding of business ventures. The two parties agreed on terms or a ratio of the sharing of profits, if any, resulting from the venture. In the event of a loss, the provider of capital (usually the

COMPANY PERSPECTIVES

Our Mission: To provide Islamic financial solutions for the global community. Our Vision: To be a top tier Islamic financial services group. Our Values: We keep it Simple and Sensible. We are Transparent. We work for Mutual Benefit. We nurture Hospitality & Tolerance. We are Shari'a inspired.

entrepreneur), bore the cost through a reduction of assets or investments placed with the bank as collateral.

Real estate transactions were covered under *Bai' Bithaman Ajil* (or BBA), which referred to a system whereby the bank agreed to purchase a property and then resell it to the property buyer at a fixed profit margin. Buyers were allowed to pay the bank with a lump sum payment or through installments. *Murabahah*, or Cost Plus, provided similar terms for transactions involving other goods, while *Ijarah Thumma Bai'*, or Hire Purchase, was developed as a form of leasing service to cover consumer goods, particularly motor vehicles. Lastly, Islamic banking also developed Sharia-compliant bonds, known as *sukuk*, and insurance products, called *takaful*. *Takaful* products enabled banks to comply with Sharia prohibitions over the taking of financial risks by extrapolating personal risk (such as health, theft, and fire loss) over a larger population.

NEW ISLAMIC BANK IN 1997

Islamic banking took off at the beginning of the 1990s, spreading throughout the Muslim world, although there remained a great deal of variation in individual markets. The more highly developed Persian Gulf region soon emerged as the center of the Islamic banking sector. The growth of the United Arab Emirates as a major shipping and financial center made these states particularly promising markets for building an Islamic banking industry. Dubai had long been the home of the region's first commercially operating Islamic bank, Dubai Islamic Bank.

During the mid-1990s, movement began toward the development of a second Islamic bank in the UAE. In 1996, the Abu Dhabi Investment Authority (ADIA) carried out a feasibility study, determining that the market had expanded sufficiently to support a new Islamic bank. This led to a royal decree in 1997 calling for the creation of Abu Dhabi Islamic Bank. Khalil Mohammed Foulathi, who had previously worked with

ADIA in London, and at the National Bank of Abu Dhabi, as well as directly under UAE president Shaikh Zayed bin Sultan al-Nahyan, was named the bank's first managing director. The shaikh also became a major shareholder in the new bank, with nearly 13 percent, alongside the Abu Dhabi government, which held 26 percent.

Abu Dhabi Islamic Bank began commercial operations in November 1998, with a capital of AED 1 billion, and was formally inaugurated in April of the following year. The bank operated from a single office and initially took a cautious approach to attracting customers, establishing relatively high minimum deposit requirements for customer accounts. By the end of the year, ADIB had already begun planning its expansion, announcing its intention to establish branch offices in Al Ain and Dubai before the end of 1999. The company also eyed a future extension into the northern emirates, including Sharjah.

At the same time, ADIB participated in a number of high-profile bank deals. These included an 8.33 percent stake in a $60 million leasing arrangement for Telekom Malaysia. The bank also made its first investments, acquiring a share of Perception Group, a manufacturer of kayaks and other sports boats based in Delaware, and in Davis IIBU Realty Securities Trust, also based in the United States. Nonetheless, the company took a cautious approach to its own growth. As Foulathi told *MEED* in December 1998: "We have to judge the pace of business before expanding. All expansions have to be justified by the market."

PUBLIC OFFERING IN 2000

By the end of 1999, ADIB had become the third-largest Islamic bank in the Gulf region. By then, the company had already opened its Al Ain and Dubai branches, and had laid out plans for the opening of a Sharjah branch as well. ADIB had also reached an agreement to develop two joint ventures with Dubai Islamic Bank, in order to add insurance and financing services. The company also began preparing its first real estate and vehicle financing products.

By the end of its first full year in operation, ADIB had exceeded its initial expectations, posting a profit of AED 49.9 million. The company had also pioneered the development of Islamic asset allocation funds, setting up the Al Hilal Fund, and had provided $100 million in financing for the Thuraya telecommunications satellite project (the first to be financed in the Middle East region), begun in 2001. By the end of 2000, ADIB had expanded its branch network to nine locations and had launched telephone-based banking services as well.

KEY DATES

1997: Abu Dhabi Islamic Bank (ADIB) is established in Abu Dhabi.
2000: ADIB goes public on the Abu Dhabi Stock Exchange.
2007: ADIB acquires 51.3 percent of National Bank for Development in Egypt.
2010: ADIB is named the Best Islamic Bank for 2010.
2011: ADIB enters Qatar and the United Kingdom.

ADIB went public in November 2000, becoming one of the pioneering stocks on the newly opened Abu Dhabi Stock Exchange. The offering attracted more than 100,000 investors, who combined for a total of 61 percent of the bank's shares. As it developed its operations in the UAE, ADIB also contributed to spreading the Islamic banking movement to other areas of the world. In 2001, for example, the company became one of three sponsors behind the creation of Bosnia International Bank, the first Islamic bank in that country.

Back at home, ADIB emerged as a driving force in regional development projects as well. In 2002, for example, the bank oversaw the Islamic financing tranche for the Shuweihat Independent Water & Power Project, a power generation and water desalination project, the largest-ever carried out in the Middle East. ADIB's portion of the financing stood at $250 million, the largest Islamic financing deal ever arranged in the UAE. The bank also completed its first major *sukuk* deal during this time, worth $800 million. In 2007, ADIB completed a second *sukuk*, a five-year deal worth $750 million.

ENTERING EGYPT IN 2007

While participating in such high-profile projects, ADIB also expanded its retail operations through the first half of the decade. The bank expanded its branch office network to 14 by 2004, and again to 24 branches by the end of 2005. The bank also added a real estate finance subsidiary, Burooj Real Estate Company. The bank had, in addition, launched an intensive training program in order to "Emiratize" its branches, that is, shift its employee balance increasingly toward Emirate nationals. In June 2006, for example, the bank opened its fifth branch office in Al Ain, which was staffed entirely with citizens of the UAE. During that same

month, ADIB introduced a new online banking service, e-ADIB, with an expanded range of transaction services as well as enhanced security features.

In the second half of the decade, ADIB began eyeing international expansion as well. The company tested the waters in Sudan, joining with Dubai Islamic Bank and National Bank of Sharjah to establish Emirates and Sudan Bank in Khartoum. The company entered Egypt in 2007, joining with Emirates International Investment Company to acquire 51.3 percent of National Bank for Development, which operated a branch network of 69 offices. In 2008, the bank filed an application for a banking license in Algeria, while also announcing its interest in expanding into the Libyan, Qatar, and Saudi Arabian markets.

In the meantime, ADIB had doubled its UAE branch network, reaching 50 offices by the end of 2008. The company stepped up expansion of its ATM network as well, nearly doubling the number of machines in operation to 204 by the beginning of 2010. By the end of 2011, ADIB's UAE presence neared 70 branch offices and topped 250 ATMs.

NEW SERVICES FROM 2009

ADIB brought in a new general manager, Tirad Mahmoud, in 2008. Mahmoud, who had previously worked as CEO of Citibank's Central Europe division at Citigroup, as well as holding high-level posts at Saudi American Bank, led ADIB through a major rebranding exercise in part in order to reinforce the bank's customer services. The company launched a wealth management division in 2009, and began extending its hours at many of its locations, which now remained open from 10 a.m. to 10 p.m.

In December 2009, the bank added a branch at the Abu Dhabi International Airport, providing 24-hour service. Also in 2009, ADIB unveiled a new VISA-backed "covered" card, the Sharia-compliant equivalent of a credit card, targeting the small and medium (SME) enterprise market. In 2010, the company became the first in the UAE to offer mobile banking services, in a partnership with mobile telephone services provider Etisalat. The company launched a children's savings account in May 2011, and expanded its range of products and services for women. These included a *takaful*, introduced in October 2011, providing insurance coverage for breast cancer.

These efforts earned ADIB the title of Best Islamic Bank in the Middle East for 2010. Mahmoud himself received honors, including Islamic Banker of the Year at the 2010 Islamic Business & Finance Awards, and, in 2011, Best Emiratisation CEO from the Emirates Institute for Banking and Financial Studies.

ADIB's internationalization effort gained traction as well. The bank received a license to operate in Qatar in August 2011. ADIB then entered the United Kingdom, opening a branch at One Hyde Park in London in November of that year. At the same time, the company announced preparations to launch a new *sukuk*, now through ADIB Sukuk Company Ltd., listed on the London Stock Exchange.

With total assets of AED 75.3 billion ($20.49 billion), ADIB had become one of the leading Islamic banks in the Middle East region. While Islamic banking remained a work-in-progress, and faced criticism for being available only to the wealthier members of the population, ADIB had become a prominent example of the capacity of the banking industry to operate within the requirements of Sharia law.

M. L. Cohen

PRINCIPAL SUBSIDIARIES

Abu Dhabi Islamic Securities Company LLC (95%); ADIB Sukuk Company Ltd. (Cayman Islands); Bosna Bank International D.D. (Bosnia and Herzegovina; 27%); Burooj Properties LLC Real Estate Investments; Kawader Services Company LLC; National Bank for Development (Egypt; 49%).

PRINCIPAL DIVISIONS

Wholesale Banking; Retail Banking; Private Banking and Wealth Management; Treasury; Real Estate.

PRINCIPAL OPERATING UNITS

Abu Dhabi Islamic Bank; ADIB Securities; Burooj Properties.

PRINCIPAL COMPETITORS

Abu Dhabi Commercial Bank PJSC; Commercial Bank of Dubai PSC; Dubai Islamic Bank PJSC; Emirates NBD Bank PJSC; First Gulf Bank PJSC; National Bank of Abu Dhabi PJSC; Standard Chartered Bank.

FURTHER READING

"Abu Dhabi Bank Plans November Launch into UK." *Mortgage Strategy*, October 10, 2011, 4.

"Abu Dhabi Islamic Bank Continues Its Expansion Plan by Extending Opening Hours." *CPI Financial*, June 15, 2009.

"Abu Dhabi Islamic Bank Plans Roadshow." *CPI Financial*, November 10, 2011.

"Abu Dhabi's ADIB Launches Gold Priority Banking." *Global Banking News*, June 14, 2011.

"ADIB Offering Health Takaful for Its Women Customers." *Global Banking News*, October 19, 2011.

"ADIB Plans Expansion in the UAE and Gulf Countries." *Global Banking News*, December 16, 2008.

Dudley, Nigel. "Islamic Banks Tap a Rich New Business." *Euromoney*, December 2001, 92.

"A Master of Reinvention." *Banker Middle East*, August 17, 2011.

Mian, Yawar. "New Islamic Bank Makes Its Mark." *MEED Middle East Economic Digest*, December 18, 1998, 18.

"NBD Partners with ADIB to Launch Ijara Services." *Global Banking News*, August 1, 2011.

"QFCRA Grants Licence to Abu Dhabi Islamic Bank." *CPI Financial*, August 4, 2011.

PT Adaro Energy Tbk

———————————— ■ ————————————

23/F Menara Karya, Jl H R Rasuna Said block x-5
Kav 1-2
Jakarta, 12950
Indonesia
Telephone: (+62 021) 2553-3040
Fax: (+62 021) 5794-4687
Web site: http://www.adaro.com

■ ■ ■

Public Company
Incorporated: 2004
Employees: 6,276
Sales: IDR 24.69 billion ($2.90 billion) (2010)
Stock Exchanges: Jakarta
Ticker Symbol: ADRO
NAICS: 212112 Bituminous Coal Underground Mining

■ ■ ■

PT Adaro Energy Tbk is Indonesia's second-largest coal-mining company and operates the largest single-site coal mine in the Southern Hemisphere. The company markets its coal under the Envirocoal brand, underscoring the low-sulfur and low-ash content of the coal it produces. In 2011, Adaro's production reached 48 million metric tons of coal. In that year, the company announced plans to raise its total coal production to 80 million metric tons per year. Adaro Energy is led by CEO Sonny Sidjaja. Adaro recorded revenues of IDR 24.69 billion ($2.9 billion) in 2010.

BEGINNINGS IN 1982

The surge in oil prices during the 1970s prompted the Indonesian government to step up efforts to exploit the country's vast coal deposits. Indonesia had previously relied on petroleum and natural gas as its primary fuel sources. The rising prices of these fuels had made the mining of Indonesian coal cost-competitive. Indonesian coal had an added advantage, in that it contained low amounts of sulfur and ash. With a sulfur content of less than 0.1 percent, Indonesian coal helped meet the growing demand for less environmentally destructive fuels.

The Indonesian government, then under President Suharto, adopted policies designed to stimulate the domestic coal market. In particular, the government passed decrees requiring Indonesian industries to make use of coal as their fuel source. The government then set out to attract investors willing to develop the country's mining industry. In 1976, the government put up eight blocks of land in coal-rich East and South Kalimantan for tender. Enadimsa, owned by the Spanish government, bid for Block 8, representing 34,400 hectares, located in the Tanjung district of South Kalimantan.

Enadimsa won its bid, largely because it was the only bidder for this block. Located farther inland than the other coal blocks, the parcel was considered to be too difficult to exploit, with too far a distance to transport its coal. The coal was also considered to be of inferior quality. Nonetheless, Enadimsa pressed on with its tender, signing its Coal Cooperation Agreement in 1982. Under this agreement, Enadimsa acquired exploitation rights to the area through 2022, in exchange for a 13.5 percent royalty payment on its sales.

Enadimsa established a new company to launch the mining business, Adaro Indonesia. The Adaro family had been central figures in the history of Spain's own coal industry. The company launched exploration operations in 1983 and by 1989 had largely completed the initial mapping and drilling of the area, as well as put in place preliminary engineering studies. These included means for surmounting the major obstacle of transporting the coal to Indonesia's seaports for shipping to export markets in the exploitation of the South Kalimantan region.

FIRST SHIPMENT IN 1991

For this phase of the operation, the company found itself under new ownership, when Enadimsa sold 80 percent of Adaro to an Australian-Singaporean consortium. Adaro was given new management, led by David Palmer as construction manager and Alastair Grant as general manager. The new team set out to tackle the logistics of the new business, planning out a 70-kilometer roadway to the Barito river.

The project cost of building the mine and the roadway were $28 million. The company sought financing from the banking sector, but failed, in part because the type of coal found in Kalimantan had not yet been traded internationally, and therefore could not be properly valued. Instead, Adaro's investors agreed to back the company with $20 million in development funding. The company was responsible for funding the remainder through its own cash flow.

This meant that Adaro needed to bring its coal to market as quickly as possible. Construction of the roadway began in September 1990, followed by the construction of a crushing plant, complete with stockpiling and barging facilities, in March 1991. The total capacity of the crushing plant was two million metric tons per year. At the same time, the company

opened its first pit, at Paringin, starting with a 30-meter-thick seam in March 1991. Throughout this period, Adaro was forced to overcome a number of difficulties. This included building the mine during Indonesia's rainy season and extending a roadway across nearly 30 kilometers of swampland.

Adaro also began developing the marketing effort to promote its low-sulfur, low-ash coal on the international market. The company developed its own brand, Envirocoal, in order to highlight the reduced environmental impact from burning its coal. The company took its story on the road, exhibiting at major conferences around the world, including at the World Coal Institute exhibition in London in 1990. This effort enabled the company to make its first sale, of a shipment of test coal to Germany's Krupp Industries. In order to meet that contract, the company set up a temporary coal crushing plant and succeeded in loading its first shipment of nearly 69,000 metric tons of coal in October 1991.

BUILDING CAPACITY THROUGH THE NINETIES

By the end of that year, Adaro had also sent test coal shipments to Spain, Japan, and the United States, as well as to its first customers in Indonesia. By March 1992, the company had already received commitments from the United States alone for one million tons per year. Through 1992, the company continued to expand its range of potential customers, targeting especially the North American and European markets. Eastern Europe, then just emerging from decades of environmental pollution during the Soviet era, represented another potentially large market for Adaro's more environmentally friendly coal.

Adaro officially launched its commercial operations in October 1992. The company at first focused its coal production on the Paringin mine, raising its total output to 2.5 million metric tons by 1994, and again to 8.3 million metric tons by 1996. This represented a peak for the Paringin site, which dropped back to below one million metric tons in 1999, before being decommissioned.

Instead, Adaro had switched its mining focus to its new Tutupan deposit. This mine started production in 1997, and expanded rapidly to 15.5 million metric tons in 2000. Tutupan quickly became the largest single-site coal mining operation not only in Indonesia, but in the entire Southern Hemisphere.

This rise in capacity was spurred in part by the Indonesian government's continued effort to shift the balance of its fuel consumption. Into 1995, coal represented just 8.8 percent of the country's total energy consumption, compared to oil's 58 percent. Part of the

1982: Adaro Indonesia is established to exploit a 34,400 hectare coal concession in South Kalimantan, Indonesia.

1992: Adaro launches commercial coal production.

1997: Adaro acquires a new concession in Tanjung, Kalimantan.

2008: Adaro completes Indonesia's largest-ever initial public offering.

2011: Adaro acquires control of PT Mustika Indah Permai and Pt Bukit Enim, in South Sumatra.

effort involved the construction of a new generation of coal-firing power plants. In 1995, for example, Adaro won the contract to supply coal to a new $2.5 billion, 4,000 megawatt (MW) power plant complex at Paiton, in eastern Java. The government also established new targets for the country's coal production, calling for a rise in capacity from 38.5 million metric tons in 1995 to 80 million tons by 2000, and to 95 million by 2005.

STALLED IPO IN 2004

Adaro expanded its own coal concession during the 1990s when it was awarded the contract to operate a coal mine in Tanjung, also in South Kalimantan. Under terms of the contract, acquired in 1997, Adaro held the rights to the concession for 25 years. By then Adaro's shareholder structure had changed again, as a group of Indonesian tycoons, led by Suharto's son Prabowo Soebianto, gained 49 percent of the company through Singapore-listed Beckett Pte. Australia's New Hope was Adaro's other major shareholder, with a 41 percent stake.

Adaro's shareholding structure remained somewhat volatile, however, as Indonesia's Swabara Group became a major shareholder into 1999. By the end of that year, New Hope had raised its share in the company to 50 percent, followed by PT Asmindo Bara Utama's 40 percent.

Adaro's changing shareholding structure nonetheless had an effect on the company's growth, as it continued to expand its total output. In 2001, the company announced plans to raise its output to 19 million metric tons. By then, the company had also received recognition as the World's Best Coal Miner, part of the *Financial Times* Energy Awards in 1999. By 2004, the

company's total output had grown again, to 24.3 million metric tons.

Adaro announced plans for an initial public offering (IPO) in 2004. This announcement came from PT Dianlia Setiamukti, owned by Edwin Soeryadjaja and Benny Soebianto, which had acquired a 51 percent stake in Adaro by then. The company was forced to put its IPO on hold, however, when a dispute arose over its shares. Deutsche Bank, which had been the creditor bank behind Beckett's purchase of its stake in Adaro in the 1990s, had gained control of Beckett's shares in the company after Beckett defaulted on its $100 million in debt to Deutsche Bank. Deutsche Bank had subsequently sold these shares to Dianlia Setiamukti. Beckett sued Deutsche Bank, stalling Adaro's IPO. As a further complication, New Hope sold its 41 percent stake in Adaro in 2005 to a consortium led by Soeryadjaja and Soebianto, and including T. P. Rachmat and Garibaldi Boy Thohir.

PUBLIC LISTING IN 2008

Adaro's investors announced a new plan to take the company public in July 2007. At the time, the company sought to raise about $600 million in the IPO, which would have set a new record on the Indonesian Stock Exchange. Adaro came to the market only a year later. With oil prices soaring and helping to drive up demand for coal, Adaro's offering outpaced its original projections. Instead, the company sold 34.8 percent of its shares raising $1.32 billion, setting a new record for an IPO by an Indonesian company.

The offering helped fuel Adaro's expansion plans through the end of the decade and beyond. The company announced its intention to spend $500 million through 2011 in order to build a new 68-kilometer conveyor to transport its coal to a Central Kalimantan river port. The new conveyor system was expected to cost more than $400 million. The company also planned to build a 60 MW coal-fired power plant.

These investments came as part of the group's "pit to port" vertical integration strategy. Other parts of this strategy came into place through the end of the decade, including the acquisition of a barging and shiploading company in 2009. The company also bought 35 percent of logistics company Servo Meda Sejahtera in October 2011.

Adaro also targeted a major increase in its coal output, to as much as 80 million metric tons by 2014. The company had already made significant advances in expanding the Tutupan mine's output, which reached 26.7 million metric tons in 2005 and climbed to 40.6 million metric tons by 2009. In order to reach its goal, however, the company needed to expand its range of concessions. Toward this end, Adaro began production at a new mining site at Wara, with an initial capacity of five million metric tons per year in 2009.

NEW REGIONS IN 2011

Adaro also announced plans to spend nearly $600 million on new mining concessions in order to reach its goal of 80 million metric tons per year. In September 2010 the company bought PT Bhakti Energi Persada, which held concessions to four coal mines in Kutai, in East Kalimantan. These mines held total reserves of 5.6 billion tons.

This purchase was followed by an agreement to acquire 25 percent of Indomet Coal, held by Australia's BHP Billiton, for nearly $358 million in May 2011. By August of that year, Adaro had acquired 75 percent of PT Mustika Indah Permai, marking the company's move into the South Sumatra region. Mustika held the rights to a 2,000-hectare concession in that region.

Adaro's expansion drive remained focused on the

SouthSumatra region through the end of 2011. The company began acquiring a stake in PT Bukit Enim Energi, a company in the process of developing a greenfield mine site at Muara Enim. Adaro acquired another 46 percent of Bukit in October of that year, raising its total stake in the company past 61 percent.

By then, Adaro was on track to reach a total output of 48 million metric tons for the year. The strong price of coal helped the company achieve equally strong profit growth as it nearly doubled its profits over the previous year. With demand rising from China and India, the company also announced plans to raise its total output to 53 million metric tons by the end of 2012. Adaro had grown to become Indonesia's second-largest coal producer, fueling the international export market into the future.

M. L. Cohen

PRINCIPAL SUBSIDIARIES

PT Adaro Indonesia; PT Alam Tri Abadi; PT Dianka Setyamukti; PT Jasapower Indonesia; PT Makmur Sejahtera Wisesa; PT Saptaindra Sejati.

PRINCIPAL DIVISIONS

Mining; Contract Mining; Barging; Hauling Road; Sea Channel Operations; Shiploading; Coal Terminal Services.

PRINCIPAL OPERATING UNITS

PT Adaro Indonesia; PT Saptaindra Sejati; Hauling Road; Kelanis; PT Maritim Barito Perkasa; PT Sarana Daya Mandiri; PT Indonesia Bulk Terminal.

PRINCIPAL COMPETITORS

Glencore International AG; Noble Group Ltd.; RAG AG; Rio Tinto PLC; Shandong Energy Zibo Mining Group Company Ltd.; Tiefa Coal Industry Group Corporation Ltd.; Utahamerican Energy Inc.; Venezuelan National Petroleum Co.; Wesfarmers Ltd.; Xstrata PLC; Yuzhkuzbassugol Joint Stock Co.

FURTHER READING

"Adaro Acquires S. Sumatra Coal Miner." *Jakarta Post*, August 25, 2011.

"Adaro Group." *Indonesian Commercial Newsletter*, October 2010, 27.

"Adaro Third Fastest Growing Asian Energy Company." *Jakarta Post*, November 4, 2010.

"Adaro's Aggression Pays off as Four Banks Agree 10 yr Deal." *Euroweek Asia*, June 3, 2011.

"Indonesian Coal Miner Adaro Energy Reports 96.5% Surge in Profit." *AsiaPulse News*, November 2, 2011.

"Indonesia's Adaro Acquires New Coal Concession for US$222 Million." *AsiaPulse News*, August 24, 2011.

"Indonesia's Adaro Energy Buys Logistics Company." *AsiaPulse News*, October 14, 2011.

"Indonesia's Adaro Energy Pays US$358 M for Stake in Indomet Coal." *AsiaPulse News*, May 11, 2011.

"Indonesia's Adaro Energy to Acquire Bhakti Energi." *AsiaPulse News*, September 3, 2010.

"Indonesia's Adaro Energy to Invest $470 Mln in 2010." *AsiaPulse News*, December 10, 2009.

"Indonesia's Adaro Energy to Set Aside US4464MLN for Pjts." *AsiaPulse News*, November 11, 2010.

"Indonesia's Adaro Takes Further 46% Stake in Miner Bukit Enim." *AsiaPulse News*, October 19, 2011.

"Indonesia's Adaro to Provide US$230 mln for Pemalang Power PJT." *AsiaPulse News*, September 23, 2011.

"PT Adaro Energy Reports Increase 2010 Coal Sales." *International Resource News*, February 1, 2011.

The AES Corporation

4300 Wilson Boulevard, 11th Floor
Arlington, Virginia 22203
U.S.A.
Telephone: (703) 522-1315
Fax: (703) 528-4510
Web site: http://www.aes.com

Public Company
Incorporated: 1981 as Applied Energy Sources
Employees: 29,000
Operating Revenues: $16.64 billion (2010)
Stock Exchanges: New York
Ticker Symbol: AES
NAICS: 221122 Electric Power Distribution; 221121 Electric Bulk Power Transmission and Control; 221112 Fossil Fuel Electric Power Generation; 221119 Other Electric Power Generation

■ ■ ■

The AES Corporation is one of the world's leading power generation and distribution companies, with operations in approximately 29 countries. With a workforce of about 29,000 people, AES operates 14 different utilities. The bulk of the company's power generation capacity is in North America (36%), followed by Latin America (30%), Europe (20%), Asia (10%), Africa (3%), and the Middle East (1%).

DEVELOPMENT OF PURPA

AES was the invention of Roger W. Sant and Dennis W. Bakke, who had served together in the U.S. Federal Energy Administration (FEA) during the Nixon and Ford administrations in the early to mid-1970s. Sant had been a lecturer at the Stanford School of Business. Bakke, a Harvard M.B.A. and career government employee, was his assistant. As part of their work at the FEA, the two had been instrumental in drafting preliminary versions of the Public Utility Regulatory Policies Act (PURPA).

The law was part of the federal government's attempt to deal with the nation's energy crisis, which, according to prevailing opinion at the time, was caused largely by U.S. dependence on foreign oil. Seeking to reduce this dependence, PURPA mandated that electrical utilities fulfill any need they might have for new power by seeking qualified cogenerators and independent, small-scale, private-sector power producers. The law further stipulated that the cost of power provided by these facilities be less than a utility's "avoided cost," that is, the cost incurred by the utility if it generated the power itself.

PURPA was enacted into law in 1978, four years after Sant and Bakke had left the government to found an energy research institute, or "think tank," at Carnegie Mellon University. That was also the year in which President Jimmy Carter declared the nation's energy crisis to be the "moral equivalent of war," as citizens experienced oil and gas shortages, long lines at the gas pumps, and fear of what the crisis portended for its future. Because of their formative work experience in government at the height of this crisis and their subsequent related work experience in academe, Sant and Bakke were well familiar with the contours of this

COMPANY PERSPECTIVES

Every day, all around the world, our people generate and distribute the electricity that accelerates businesses, energizes hospitals and schools, and elevates the quality of life.

problem, and familiar as well with the rapidly emerging business opportunities spawned by the new law.

What Sant and Bakke were quick to realize was that PURPA had paved the way for a burgeoning market in independent, private-sector power production. In part this was because of the new law's mandate that outside purchases of power be made from cogenerators and independent, small-scale, private-sector power producers. It also stemmed, however, from the fact that PURPA shielded new producers from costly state government regulation and subjected them instead to less onerous federal rules and strictures. In practice, this meant that new producers typically could undercut a utility's avoided cost.

APPLIED ENERGY SOURCES IS ESTABLISHED

AES was founded in 1981 as Applied Energy Sources, and it took several years for Sant and Bakke to taste real success. The novelty of their idea and the untested nature of the market in which they sought to do business made it difficult to attract capital financing. Investors were understandably wary and skeptical of the firm's chances for success. One year's worth of effort netted the firm only $1.1 million in venture capital, an inadequate sum on which to build an electric power company. "From 1981 to 1985," reported the *Washington Post* in May 1995, "one potential project participant after another—including ARCO, IBM, Bechtel Corp. and other large companies—marched in and then backed out of agreements with tiny AES."

The firm's luck took a turn for the better in 1985, when Sant and Bakke invested all of AES's assets in a single deal: a Beaver Valley, Pennsylvania, coal-burning plant. The deal was closed in September 1985 and the plant commenced production in 1987, marking a turning point for the company, which would never again have to depend upon the success of a single project for its very survival.

By then, in fact, AES had two plants up and running: its Beaver Valley facility supplied 125 megawatts

(MW) of electricity to residents and commercial outfits in the Pittsburgh area. Its Deepwater, Texas, power plant, which, fueled by petroleum coke, went online in June 1986, supplied 143 MW of electricity to homeowners and businesses in the Houston area. Financial arrangements for Deepwater had been completed on December 30, 1983, and, in addition to AES, involved 12 other companies: ARCO, Bechtel, J.P. Morgan, eight supporting banks, and General Electric Credit Corporation.

It was an auspicious start for the struggling company, which, over the course of the next 11 years (1984–94), proceeded to build or acquire 10 new power plants. AES sales, consequently, more than tripled in two years, rising from $55.4 million in 1988 to $190.2 million in 1990. Sales grew an additional 75 percent the following year, while net company income witnessed similarly spectacular growth, soaring from $1.6 million in 1988 to $42.6 million in 1991.

AES GOES PUBLIC

Buoyed by its success, the company changed its name from Applied Energy Sources to The AES Corporation and became a publicly traded company on the NASDAQ in 1991. The company listed on the New York Stock Exchange in 1996. Sant assumed the position of company chairman, while Bakke became the firm's president and CEO. Together, they owned approximately 27 percent of all AES stock.

In these early growth years, AES's primary source of profits and revenue was the domestic U.S. power market. Bakke, for instance, estimated that up until mid-1992, 70 percent of the money that AES spent on new business activity was spent in the United States. The remaining 30 percent, he noted, was spent in the United Kingdom. These investments yielded very good results. A November 1993 report by the investment banking firm of Kidder Peabody, for example, found that from 1988 to 1992 AES revenues grew at an annual compounded rate of 64 percent. Company earnings during that same period, the report noted, likewise soared at an annual rate of 136 percent. In 1991, AES was recognized by *Forbes* magazine as one of "America's fastest growing companies," an honor it again earned in 1992 and 1993.

DECENTRALIZED CORPORATE CULTURE

Organizationally, AES established a decentralized corporate culture that gave company employees responsibility for nearly all aspects of business

KEY DATES

1978: Public Utility Regulatory Policies Act (PURPA) is enacted into law.

1981: Roger W. Sant and Dennis W. Bakke establish Applied Energy Sources.

1991: Firm changes its name to The AES Corporation and goes public.

1995: AES begins to pursue ventures in developing countries.

1999: Company enters the retail electricity market.

2002: AES launches a major restructuring effort and announces the sale of several assets and plants.

2004: Company begins focusing on the renewable energy market.

2011: AES agrees to acquire DPL Inc. in a deal worth $3.5 billion.

management. "Frequent and intensive cross-training, role rotation, and finance education for everyone are the rule," reported *CFO* magazine in March 1995. At AES, no more than three layers of management separated an AES entry-level employee from the firm's plant supervisor, each power-generating facility was responsible for its own affairs, and there were no company-wide departments for finance, human resources, operations, purchasing, or public relations.

Consequently, the few company officers assigned to these areas acted typically as distant in-house advisers to the plant project management team responsible for a given project rather than as more conventional hands-on corporate facilitators. For plant financing, for example, CFO Barry Sharp raised less than 10 percent of the estimated $3.5 billion needed for AES's first 10 power plants. Most of the necessary financing was raised by each plant's own multidisciplinary project team, composed of a broad cross-section of AES employees. By all accounts, this management system worked spectacularly well for AES. By giving workers a greater sense of involvement in, and responsibility for, their own professional destiny, employee morale was boosted. In 1995, annual employee turnover was averaging less than 1 percent, according to company executives.

Like all management systems, however, the AES program faced challenges. One of the earliest and most significant breakdowns occurred in 1992 when the company disclosed that employees at its plant in Oklahoma had falsified the results of wastewater test samples in order to retain pollution permits from the Environmental Protection Agency (EPA). The workers responsible for the infraction said they feared losing their jobs if their violation of EPA pollution standards became known.

ENVIRONMENTAL CHALLENGES

In fact, the infraction actually had little substantive impact on AES since the pollution effect being covered up proved negligible and the company itself disclosed to the government that it had broken the law. The workers responsible were fined, demoted, and placed on probation, but not fired. Sant and Bakke voluntarily cut their own bonus pay for that year by 65 percent and 85 percent, respectively. The company publicly apologized for the incident and paid a $125,000 EPA fine. In addition, employees at the Oklahoma plant imposed upon themselves another layer of management supervision and environmental monitoring before eventually readopting AES's standard management system.

Also in 1992, the state of Florida charged AES with misleading state officials about the environmental impact of a coal-fired power plant then under construction in Jacksonville. A subsequent state investigation cleared AES of any wrongdoing. By the time the state eventually concluded its investigation, however, the banks providing financing for the facility had cut off funding for the power plant, thus forcing AES to sell off its financial interest in the facility, cut its losses, and abandon the project, despite the fact that construction was nearly complete.

In spite of these difficulties, AES appeared to have a bright and promising future. In the early 1990s, independent, small-scale, private-sector power producers generated only 9 percent of electricity in the United States. The U.S. Department of Energy estimated, however, that they would account for nearly 40 percent of all new electrical generating capacity added in the United States by 2000. Certainly, AES's growth record bore this out, as company profits grew by some 650 percent from 1990 to 1994, and earnings per share during that same period also grew dramatically, by approximately 500 percent.

INTERNATIONAL EXPANSION

Despite the opportunities for continued growth in the U.S. power market, however, AES began to look abroad for most of its new business ventures in the early 1990s. In fact, by 1995 the firm was spending an estimated 85 percent of its venture capital abroad. Six AES divisions worldwide emerged: AES Electric, which serviced

Europe, the Middle East, and Africa; AES Enterprise; AES Chigen, which serviced China; AES Transpower (Asia, Hawaii, and the American West Coast); AES Shady Point; and AES Americas (Latin America).

The company's shift to the developing world was in part a natural reaction to its experience with its defunct Jacksonville power plant. The plant's failure underscored the relative difficulty independent power producers had doing business in the United States as opposed to overseas, where environmental restrictions were more flexible in part because the cost of pollution there was more easily offset by the benefits of electrical power. As AES company executive Sheryl Sturges told the *Washington Post* in May 1995: "In the developing world, electricity produced from coal and other sources can make the difference between life and death. It can mean refrigeration for medicines and light for schoolchildren to study by."

AES's U.S. government tax levy rose sharply in the mid-1990s, from an effective rate of taxation of 23 percent in 1993 to 40 percent in 1996. In the developing world, by contrast, which was hungry for electrical energy, governments were eliminating tax and regulatory barriers that stymied the efforts of independent power producers.

In fact, the developing world's heightened need for electrical power was the chief reason AES shifted most of its new business ventures abroad. Electricity consumption in the United States, for instance, was expected to grow at an average annual rate of 1.9 percent until 2010, according to the Edison Electric Institute. The demand for electricity in the rest of the world, however, was projected to grow at nearly twice that rate, at an estimated annual rate of 4 percent, according to the International Energy Agency.

GLOBAL FOCUS CONTINUES

According to Sant, the world needed $30 billion worth of new power plants a year through 2000. China and India alone, he suggested, would need three times more generating power over the next 10 years than all of North America combined, and thus would require some $500 billion in power plant financing. As such, AES began an international expansion effort that would position it as the world's largest independent power company. As overseas governments began privatizing their utilities sectors, AES stepped in by making acquisitions and constructing new plants.

By 1999, the Virginia-based company operated in 24 countries and over half of its profits stemmed from its operations outside the United States and Europe. That year, AES paid National Power Plc $3 billion for

the Drax power station, which supplies power to England and Wales. The company also began diversifying into telecommunications and investing in fiber-optic networks in Brazil and Bolivia.

While the company completed a series of acquisitions during the late 1990s and 2000 as part of its global strategy, it made several key moves on the home front as well. In 1998, it announced its $885 million purchase of U.S.-based Cilcorp Inc., which was completed the following year. The firm also acquired California-based NewEnergy Inc. in July 1999. AES then took advantage of deregulation in the U.S. energy sector by creating Power Direct, a retail subsidiary that served U.S. consumers in deregulated markets. Then, in 2000, the firm acquired Indiana-based IPALCO Enterprises Inc. for $3 billion.

Success for AES continued into the new century. The company acquired Venezuelan utility C.A. La Electricidad de Caracas in a $1.7 billion hostile takeover. The firm also set plans in motion to acquire a stake in Chilean utility Gener S.A., and expanded into Bolivia, Nigeria, and Oman. In 2000, revenues climbed to $7.5 billion, up from $2.2 billion in 1997. In early 2001, AES's growth and expansion appeared to be unflappable.

OVERCOMING HARDSHIPS

By this time, the majority of the firm's revenues stemmed from its South American operations. The firm's reliance on global economies, however, eventually caught up with it. An economic slowdown, which worsened after the terrorist attacks on the United States of September 11, 2001, threatened future growth at AES. Falling power prices in Britain, a political and social crisis in Argentina, and faltering currency exchange rates in Brazil also caused earnings to plummet. Overall, earnings fell to $273 million in 2001, down from $795 million in 2000.

In order to combat falling electricity prices, tumultuous emerging markets, and a slowdown in capital, AES announced a major restructuring and cost-cutting effort in early 2002, which included a possible sale of various Latin American holdings. Select construction projects were put on hold and capital spending was reduced by $490 million. The company announced plans to sell Cilcorp, an interest in IPALCO, a portion of Dominican Republic-based Itabo, and certain AES facilities. The firm also began to divest its merchant generation businesses and in June 2002 announced the sale of its NewEnergy arm to Constellation Energy Group. That month, Paul Hanrahan took over as president and CEO after Bakke announced his retirement.

DIVESTING OPERATIONS

In mid-2002 AES prepared to bring a coal-fired power plant online in Guayama, Puerto Rico. The company also lost Drax, the largest power station in the United Kingdom, to creditors. Additionally, in Brazil AES was exploring the sale of its Brazilian Uruguaiana utility, as well as its AES Sul Distribuidora Gaucha de Energia distribution business. After selling three Australian power plants for $165 million, AES began 2003 by exiting sub-Saharan Africa, where CDC Group acquired the company's stakes in two different energy projects. Around the same time AES finalized its sale of Cilcorp to St. Louis-based Ameren Corporation for $1.4 billion. In addition, in the Middle East, the company sold its 32 percent ownership interest in AES Oasis in a $150 million deal with Emerging Markets Partnership.

Net losses totaled $35 million during the first half of 2003, which was a marked improvement over losses of $428 million during the first half of 2002. In order to lower its interest expenses, AES secured $1 billion in loans to refinance its debt in mid-2003. Overseas divestitures continued when Russia-based Unified Energy System acquired the company's majority stake in the electric utility serving Georgia's capital.

RENEWABLE ENERGY FOCUS

In early 2004 AES put power plants in New Hampshire and Texas on the market, with hopes of selling them before they were seized by bank creditors. Midway through the year the company acquired $97.8 million worth of stock in its Santiago, Chile-based AES Gener affiliate. In September of that year, AES began putting an emphasis on the renewable energy market. In keeping with this strategy, a partnership was made with US Wind Force, with which the company planned to pursue wind farm projects.

In mid-2005, AES received $45 million worth of loans from International Finance Corporation. The funds were to be used by the company's distribution operations in Ukraine to improve infrastructure and electricity services there. AES saw its revenues reach $12.3 billion in 2006.

Progress continued as the company headed into the end of the decade. In 2007 the Edison Electric Institute presented AES's Latin American operations with the prestigious Edison Award. The award was given in recognition of the company's advancement of and outstanding contributions to the power industry. It also was in 2007 that AES established a joint venture in China with Guohua Energy Investment Co. Ltd., for the purpose of constructing a wind farm in Hebei Province, near Beijing.

More renewable energy-related developments unfolded in 2007. AES commenced operations of its Buffalo Gap wind farm expansion near Abilene, Texas, which was the state's third largest. By this time the company's domestic wind projects exceeded 1,000 MW, and it had roughly 3,000 MW of global wind power projects under development.

SOLID FOOTING

In mid-2008 AES acquired the Nejapa Landfill Project in El Salvador, which included a system used to convert landfill gas to renewable energy. The acquisition was in keeping with the strategy of AES's Climate Solutions business, which had set a goal of reducing greenhouse gas emissions by more than 34 million tons annually before 2012. Another international development took place in late 2009 when the company agreed to sell $1.58 billion worth of stock to China Investment Corp., a Chinese sovereign wealth fund.

AES ended 2010 on a high note, having repurchased approximately $99 million worth of its stock and eliminated almost $1 billion worth of debt. On the heels of strong growth in areas such as Vietnam, Turkey, and Chile, the company devoted roughly $1 billion to new projects that year. Hanrahan remained at the helm of AES in 2011. Early that year, subsidiary AES California Management Co. agreed to sell the company's gas-fired power plant in Newhall, California, to Clean Energy Systems.

Progress continued in early 2011 when AES agreed to acquire the Dayton, Ohio-based regional energy company DPL Inc. in a $3.5 billion deal. The two companies anticipated concluding the deal toward the end of the year, or in early 2012, after securing the appropriate regulatory approvals. After weathering some difficult times, AES appeared to be on solid footing as the company headed into the 21st century's second decade.

John R. Guardiano
Updated, Christina M. Stansell; Paul R. Greenland

PRINCIPAL SUBSIDIARIES

IPALCO Enterprises Inc.; AES Cameroon Holdings S.A.; AES El Salvador, S.A. de C.V.; Indianapolis Power & Light Company; Eletropaulo Metropolitana Eletricidade de São Paulo S.A. (Brazil); AES Energy Storage; AES Wind Generation, LLC; AES Solar Energy, LLC; AES Solar Power, LLC; AES Southland, L.L.C.; Companhia Energetica de Minas Gerais (CEMIG) (Brazil); AES AgriVerde Services (Ukraine) Limited Liability Company.

PRINCIPAL COMPETITORS

Alliant Energy Corporation; Calpine Corporation; CenterPoint Energy, Inc.

FURTHER READING

"AES: Back to Basics." *Project Finance*, March 2002, 6.

"AES Makes Push into Renewable Energy." *Power, Finance and Risk*, September 13, 2004, 3.

"AES Reports Full Year Results." *Wireless News*, March 3, 2011.

"AES Strengthens Asian Ties." *Power, Finance and Risk*, November 9, 2009.

Birchard, Bill. "Power to the People." *CFO: The Magazine for Senior Financial Executives*, March 1995, 38–43.

"DPL to Merge with AES." *Wireless News*, September 29, 2011.

Egan, John. "Power Plays." *Financial World*, February 4, 1992, 28–29.

Southerland, Daniel. "The International Power Generators: Arlington's AES Corporation Leads a Battery of U.S. Energy Companies Expanding Overseas." *Washington Post*, May 22, 1995, Bus. Sec., 1, 12–13.

"US Power Giant AES Expands Wind Generation Business into China." *AsiaPulse News*, August 10, 2007.

Aetna Inc.

---

151 Farmington Avenue
Hartford, Connecticut 06156
U.S.A.
Telephone: (860) 273-0123
Toll Free: (800) 872-3862
Fax: (860) 975-3110
Web site: http://www.aetna.com

Public Company
Incorporated: 1853 as Aetna Life Insurance Company
Employees: 34,000
Total Assets: $37.73 billion (2010)
Stock Exchanges: New York
Ticker Symbol: AET
NAICS: 524114 Direct Health and Medical Insurance
    Carriers; 524113 Direct Life Insurance Carriers;
    524210 Insurance Agencies and Brokerages

■ ■ ■

Aetna Inc. is one of the largest health care insurers in the United States, serving approximately 35.3 million individuals. Based on enrollment, Aetna ranks as the nation's third-largest health care insurer. Aetna offers medical, pharmacy, dental, behavioral health, group life, and disability plans, as well as medical management capabilities and Medicaid health care management services. The company provides benefits through employers in all 50 states and its network encompasses over one million health care professionals.

PROMINENT NEW ENGLAND LAWYER ESTABLISHES AETNA: 1853

Aetna was founded in Connecticut in 1853 as Aetna Life Insurance Company. Aetna Life was originally formed as an affiliate of the older Aetna Insurance Company, which specialized in fire insurance (and was named after Mt. Etna, the Sicilian volcano), and it profited from its association with Aetna's reputation for reliability and speed in paying claims. However, a new state insurance regulation passed in nearby New York State in 1849, and strengthened in 1853, prohibited the same company from providing both fire and life insurance. In 1853 the Connecticut legislature granted a petition for the separate incorporation of Aetna Life Insurance Company.

Aetna Life's founding president, Eliphalet Bulkeley, originally divided his time between practicing law and developing the fledgling life insurance firm. He was also active in the formation of the Republican Party in Connecticut, starting a long tradition of political activism by Aetna leaders. Bulkeley guided Aetna through its difficult first years, when new insurance laws in some states required capital deposits beyond the stockholders' resources, hindering Aetna from doing business in those states. The depression of 1857 further threatened the firm's financial stability, but Aetna survived in the face of multiple bank closings. During this period the company regained its financial footing in part by hiring its first midwestern agent, a Connecticut man, who opened an office in Wisconsin to serve the burgeoning market in those states.

COMPANY PERSPECTIVES

We help people achieve health and financial security by providing easy access to cost-effective, high-quality health care. And we continue to be a leader in building a stronger, more effective health care system by working with doctors, hospitals, employers, patients, public officials and others.

In 1861 the Civil War began and Aetna modified its form of ownership. Both events profitably affected the company's growth. Seeking security during the uncertain war years, many people bought life insurance policies for the first time. In addition, Aetna modified its form of investor ownership to permit policyholders to control their own funds in a separate mutual department that operated within the overall management structure. Originally, Bulkeley had resisted the mutual plan that placed ownership in the hands of policyholders. He disliked the speculative nature of dividend payment and could not countenance an approach to management that divided responsibility among all policyholders.

Pressure from the public and from competing insurance companies helped change Bulkeley's mind. The result was the creation of a mutual department whose accounting system was separate from that of management. Within this department, policyholders controlled their own funds and received dividends, but did not vote for the management of the company. The firm as a whole continued as an investor-owned company with all the efficiency of management Bulkeley believed was inherent in that arrangement. Partly because of this revision of the ownership structure, in just five years, from 1861 to 1866, Aetna jumped from 15th among 40 life insurance companies nationwide to fifth among 80.

MORGAN G. BULKELEY ERA BEGINS: 1879

Bulkeley died in 1872 and was succeeded by Thomas O. Enders, who had served as both a clerk and secretary for the firm. Bulkeley had presided over Aetna during the speculative postwar years, and had maintained careful control of the risks the company assumed. The 1870s was a period of nationwide economic crisis, and Enders was hard-pressed to keep the firm alive, despite its earlier successes. Not only did he have to contend with a nationwide depression that began in 1873, but he also was burdened with the disastrous results of a major change in the method of premium payment made toward the end of Bulkeley's presidency.

Until then, Aetna and most other insurance companies had accepted interest-bearing notes as half payment for premiums. In the wake of questions from the state insurance commissioner about the booking of these notes as assets, and the negative press elicited by the commissioner's report, Aetna management decided to start requiring full cash payment for premiums. Although Aetna was innovative in this change and most other insurance companies soon began to follow the new practice, the firm's policyholders were outraged. Many canceled their policies, and new policyholders were not forthcoming. In desperate straits following the policy change and weakened by the financial crisis of the 1870s, Aetna steadily declined. Enders resigned in 1879.

Aetna passed back into family hands when Morgan G. Bulkeley, Eliphalet Bulkeley's son, took over leadership of the firm, a position he was to retain for the next 43 years. Although Morgan Bulkeley had been a director on the Aetna board since his father's death, he had chosen to apprentice as a dry goods merchant rather than rise through his father's firm. His primary interest was in politics. He was active in the state Republican Party his father had helped to form. By 1879 he had been a councilman and alderman and was successfully running for mayor of Hartford. He subsequently became governor of Connecticut and then a U.S. senator. Bulkeley maintained firm control over both his government office and his corporate office. While governor, Bulkeley lent the state of Connecticut $300,000 from Aetna's funds during a period of financial need. In 1911 Bulkeley lost his senate seat and returned full-time to his position with Aetna.

DIVERSIFICATION AND INNOVATION: 1879–1919

Aetna did very well under Morgan Bulkeley. Its total assets increased from $25.6 million in 1879 to $207 million in 1922, while premium income increased more than 20-fold during the same period. The number of employees grew from 29 to 2,000. Aetna's success was in large part due to innovations in forms of insurance. The first years of Bulkeley's presidency were spent getting the ailing company back on its feet, but in the 1890s Aetna made its first move to diversify, initiating a period of rapid expansion.

In 1891, under its existing charter, Aetna began to write accident insurance, and in 1899 added health insurance. In 1893 its charter was expanded, allowing the company to become a pioneer in the development

KEY DATES

1853: Aetna Life Insurance Company is incorporated in Connecticut.
1891: Company diversifies into accident insurance.
1899: Aetna enters the field of health insurance.
1960: Aetna enters the international market by purchasing Toronto-based Excelsior Life Insurance Company.
1968: Company's stock is listed on the New York Stock Exchange.
1992: American Re-Insurance is divested for $1.31 billion.
1996: Aetna sells its property-casualty operations to Travelers Group for $4.1 billion and pays $8.9 billion for U.S. Healthcare, Inc.
1998: U.S. individual life insurance business is sold to Lincoln National Corporation.
1999: Aetna acquires the health care business of Prudential Insurance Company of America.
2000: Aetna Inc. spins Aetna U.S. Healthcare off to its shareholders.
2011: Mark T. Bertolini is named chairman five months after being appointed CEO.

of liability insurance. In 1902 Aetna opened a separate accident and liability department to handle employers' liability and workmen's collective insurance. Eager to profit from the rapidly growing market for automobile insurance, in 1907 Aetna management transformed the liability department into Aetna Life's first affiliate, Aetna Accident and Liability Company.

For a few years, this new company issued all the new forms of insurance Aetna offered, but soon further diversification was necessary. In 1912 Aetna offered the first comprehensive auto policy, providing all kinds of auto insurance in one contract. In 1913 a second Aetna affiliate was formed, Automobile Insurance Company. The charter of this second affiliate also allowed it to handle other insurance lines including loss of use, explosion, tornado and windstorm, leasehold, and rent. In 1916 Aetna Auto began to offer marine insurance, a line that was greatly broadened during World War I. Meanwhile, Aetna Accident and Liability Company was expanding its business in fidelity and surety bonds, and in 1917 changed its name to Aetna Casualty and Surety Company. In 1913 Aetna formed a group department to sell group life insurance. Group disability policies were offered for the first time in 1919.

STREAMLINING PROCEDURES: 1922–29

When Morgan Bulkeley died in 1922, Morgan Bulkeley Brainard, grandson of Eliphalet Bulkeley, succeeded his uncle as president. Unlike his uncle, Brainard was a company man. Following college, law school, and two years in a law firm, he joined Aetna as assistant treasurer, later becoming treasurer and then vice president. According to Richard Hooker's *Aetna Life Insurance Company: Its First Hundred Years, a History*, Brainard described his uncle as having "built up an unusually strong organization by the sheer force of his personality." Brainard, by contrast, intended to initiate a new style of leadership. "Where Governor Bulkeley could bring men around him and have them work for him by the inspiration of his presence, I cannot. I have got to surround myself with as able a group of men as I possibly can." Accordingly, Brainard focused on efficiency of administration, concentrating particularly on relations and communications with agents in the field. He streamlined procedures, regularized paperwork, and reduced the costs of doing business. The new approach worked. In 1922 life insurance in force was $1.3 billion. By 1929 assets amounted to $411 million and life insurance in force to $3.79 billion. In 1924, Aetna also had acquired a third affiliate, Standard Fire Insurance Company, which further strengthened its position.

Such expansion, however, did not come without costs. Automobile Insurance Company, one of Aetna Life's affiliated companies, had contributed to the spectacular increases of the 1920s. In 1922 the affiliate's premium income reached $11 million, climbed to $19 million in 1923, and reached $30 million the following year. The affiliate's success, however, was not grounded in a solid financial base. In March 1926, Brainard discovered that Automobile Insurance Company had understated its liabilities and taken on more business than it could handle. The marine division of the affiliate had expanded swiftly during the war years, but had exercised poor judgment in the selection of risks, especially following World War I, when solicitation of marine business should have been curtailed. Automobile Insurance Company also had gained new business by assuming risks from other companies. Brainard rapidly retrenched. He cut business drastically, resulting in premium income of just $7.9 million in 1927 for the auto affiliate. Reserves were increased to cover liabilities and future underwriting losses.

This crisis during the mid-1920s helped prepare Aetna for the economic shock of the Great Depression. Brainard had, in effect, stemmed the tide of financial speculation within Aetna while the rest of the business community continued to speculate until the stock market crash of 1929. As a result, during the worst years of the Depression, Aetna's income dropped by only a little more than 10 percent. Cautious management kept the company solvent. Dividends were not paid between 1932 and 1934, but no Aetna employees were dismissed. In 1929 only 11.7 percent of Aetna's assets were in common stock, and almost half of that in the stock of Aetna affiliates, another condition that helped Aetna survive during the 1930s.

Although the company did suffer because it had assumed growing numbers of farm mortgages that defaulted during the Depression, Brainard's careful business practices kept the losses to a minimum. Aetna also opened up two new lines of business during these difficult years: pensions in 1930 and group hospitalization policies in 1936.

EXPANSION RESUMES: 1941

World War II finally helped pull Aetna and the nation out of the Depression. The war gave Aetna several opportunities to develop new types of insurance coverage. In cooperation with other insurers, Aetna issued a bonding contract for $312 million that insured the construction of seven aircraft carriers. Aetna also was involved in insuring the production of the atom bomb under the Manhattan Project, a uniquely challenging actuarial task because much of the information was classified. In addition, Aetna was centrally occupied with developing its lines of employee group insurance during these years. Ordinary life insurance premiums remained almost steady during World War II, but group insurance rose dramatically, increasing overall premium income by almost 65 percent. Group insurance premiums declined quickly after the war with the switch to a peacetime economy, but Aetna's prewar experience with group insurance helped the company rally with relative ease.

In the postwar years, Aetna continued to diversify cautiously. The company explored the possibilities of insurance coverage for air travel, became involved in several large bonding issues, and became a pioneer in the area of driver's education. In 1955, two years after Aetna's centennial, Brainard resigned the position of president to become Aetna's first chairman. Vice President Henry Beers succeeded him as Aetna's fifth president.

With Beers's inauguration, the long history of family control ended and a new era of shorter presidencies began. In 1962 Beers became chairman and J. A. Hill took over as president. One year later Olcott D. Smith succeeded Beers as chairman. In 1972 John H. Filer succeeded Smith as chairman, and Donald M. Johnson was named president in 1970. In 1976 William O. Bailey

succeeded Johnson. Through these years of fairly rapid changes in management, the position of chairman and chief executive officer gained ascendancy over that of president and chief operating officer.

ENTERING THE INTERNATIONAL MARKET: 1960

In 1960 Aetna entered the international market with the purchase of Excelsior Life Insurance Company of Toronto. Six years later Aetna entered into an international cooperation agreement with Italy's Assicurazioni Generali S.p.A. through which each company provided reciprocal services to the other's clients while abroad. To facilitate flexible management of these expanding operations and allow diversification into noninsurance fields, Aetna Life & Casualty Company, a holding company, was created in 1967 with subsidiaries Aetna Life Insurance Company, Aetna Casualty and Surety, Standard Fire Insurance, and Automobile Insurance Company. Later that same year Aetna purchased Participating Annuity Life Insurance Company, becoming the first major insurance firm to enter the variable annuity market. In 1968 Aetna was first listed on the New York Stock Exchange.

In the late 1960s Aetna experienced a sharp drop in earnings, a trend that reflected an industry-wide increase in claims. The decline was reversed in the early 1970s, in part because of nationwide decreases in losses and increases in premiums and in part because of Aetna's move to control costs and concentrate on the most profitable lines of insurance. Nevertheless, rapid diversification into noninsurance fields later in the same decade undermined earlier gains. Particularly ill-fated acquisitions were Geosource Inc., an oil field services concern, and Satellite Business Systems, a communications firm.

DIVERSIFICATION AND REORGANIZATION: 1972–81

In 1972 Chairman Smith initiated a management change that resembled Brainard's initiation of his new leadership style 50 years before. In place of administration by one man, Smith introduced the "corporate office" approach, a consensual relationship of the four top executives with the chairman still slightly dominant. Corporate structure also was reorganized. In addition, in a move that would become much more important in subsequent decades, Aetna created a health maintenance organization (HMO) subsidiary in 1973.

In 1981 the company reorganized its operations into five insurance divisions. The employees benefits division offered group insurance, health care services, and pension and related financial products to business, government units, associations, and welfare trusts. The personal/financial/security division provided automobile and homeowner insurance, life and health insurance, and retirement funding and annuity products to individuals, small businesses, and employer-sponsored groups. The commercial insurance division marketed property-casualty insurance and bonds for businesses, government units, and associations, including workers' compensation. The American Re-Insurance Company reinsured commercial property and liability risks in domestic and international markets. The international insurance division handled insurance and investment products in non-U.S. markets. The activities of these five insurance sectors were supported by the operations of a financial division that managed all of the firm's investment portfolios.

BACK TO THE INSURANCE
BASICS: 1981–89

Income declined in the early 1980s. In 1981, hoping to lead industry-wide price increases, Aetna raised commercial insurance prices, a mistimed move that cost the company as much as 10 percent of its business. In addition, Aetna was forced to lower its 1982 statement of earnings by 39 percent, in response to a ruling by the Securities and Exchange Commission that disallowed Aetna's practice of booking future tax credits as current earnings.

In 1984 James T. Lynn became chairman and CEO. Like his predecessors in the Bulkeley family, Lynn was active in Republican politics when he accepted the post with Aetna. Trained as a lawyer, he served as secretary of the U.S. Department of Housing and Urban Development from 1973 to 1975, and as director of the Office of Management and Budget from 1975 to 1977. Lynn implemented a policy of prudent retrenchment, selling subsidiaries that were not performing well and emphasizing Aetna's long-standing priority on insurance. This policy proved profitable for Aetna once again as earnings more than doubled from 1984 to 1985, with record increases in 1986 and 1987.

Ronald E. Compton became president of Aetna in 1988. Earnings declined by 23 percent from the previous year, a downturn reflecting increased competition in the commercial property-casualty business, rising loss costs in auto and homeowners insurance lines, and losses in its highly competitive multinational corporations operations. In 1989 the decline continued at the rate of 5 percent from the previous year, with commercial property-casualty insurance lines affected by two natural disasters, Hurricane Hugo, which came struck

the Carolinas and Mid-Atlantic reagion, and the San Francisco Bay area earthquake.

NEW CHALLENGES FROM
CHANGING ECONOMY: 1991–92

In the fluctuating economic climate of the 1990s, Aetna began to redraw its traditional market sector, as well as to reorganize its three domestic insurance divisions into 15 strategic business units. In response to several state legislatures' efforts to roll back or otherwise restrict the rise in auto insurance rates, the company attempted to pull out of both Pennsylvania's and Massachusetts' auto insurance markets, although such efforts drew resistance from both state regulators and consumers. The company would withdraw from the auto insurance business in 13 other states over the next few years. The company also began to curtail its expansion of personal property and casualty insurance markets in several states, and cut back personal mortgage insurance early in the decade.

While pulling out of the auto insurance market, the company was investing heavily in the growing field of managed health care insurance. By 1990 Aetna Life & Casualty had spent more than $400 million to establish its own HMO, a profitable venture that helped buoy net income for that year to $614 million, against a slight drop in overall earnings. Losses taken against plummeting real estate prices in the Northeast further eroded earnings in 1991 because of the company's extensive property holdings. Net income for 1991 was reported at only $505 million, the downturn aggravated by property claims resulting from Hurricane Bob, which hit the Atlantic coast.

A further sign that Aetna was serious in its efforts to reposition itself by narrowing its focus to health and life insurance and financial services came in November 1991, when the company announced that Compton would be appointed chairman upon the retirement of Lynn in early 1992. The company also divested its American Re-Insurance subsidiary in September 1992, selling it to American Re Corporation for $1.31 billion and raising much needed cash. In an effort to retain customers lured away from insurance by mutual fund offerings, Aetna Life & Casualty began offering five mutual funds on the retail marketplace in September 1992.

Despite a slowly improving national economy, the continuing deterioration of the company's mortgage loan portfolio would force Aetna to engage in further streamlining efforts, and in June 1992 the company laid off 10 percent of its workforce. Plagued by natural disasters and bad weather for the remainder of the year, as well as a $55 million charge for withdrawing its automobile insurance services from Massachusetts, the company saw its 1992 net income eroded to $56 million.

RETRENCHMENT AND CUTBACKS: 1993–94

Continuing its slide, Aetna posted a net loss of $365 million in 1993, although much of that loss was attributable to charges related to downsizing. By April 1994 the company announced further layoffs, cutting staff by 4,000 jobs. Despite the layoffs, the efforts to shrink the company's unprofitable pension business, and the implementation of other cost-containment measures, industry analysts were skeptical that the sprawling insurance giant could stem continued losses. In mid-1994 Aetna took another hit: $1.75 billion charged toward loss reserves for the purpose of paying out pollution- and asbestos-related claims against policies written for large industrial businesses as long ago as the 1950s. This action, which shadowed a similar charge against reserves made in 1992, made it the first among the nation's insurance giants to recognize corporate environmental liability.

Efforts to enter the Mexican market after the passage of the North American Free Trade Agreement were among the company's attempts to forestall further decreases in net earnings in 1994 and 1995. Aetna also moved into the Philippines, where it was granted a license in 1995, to Latin America, where it invested $390 million in Brazil's Sul América Seguros in 1997, and to China, where it established two offices with the expectation that the country would soon be open to foreign insurance offices. Year-end 1994 saw net income rise to $467.5 million.

Against this long-awaited rise in net income, the company announced that it intended to sell its property-casualty subsidiary, which had contributed mounting losses to the corporate balance sheet over the past several decades through its policies for individuals and businesses. Travelers Group agreed to a merger with the Aetna division in November, paying Aetna $4.1 billion for a 72 percent interest in the company and making the newly formed Travelers/Aetna Property Casualty Corp. one of the fifth-largest carriers of such insurance in the nation. The deal closed in April 1996.

HEALTH INSURANCE ACQUISITIONS: 1996–99

In 1996, under Compton and newly appointed Chairman of Strategy and Finance Richard L. Huber, Aetna began to shed both its corporate malaise and its

tradition-bound methods of operation. Continuing to divest losing real estate investments after the sale of its property and casualty division, Aetna now focused on aggressively growing its interests in managed health care and retirement services, a potentially risky mix according to some industry analysts. In April 1996 the company paid $8.9 billion for HMO provider U.S. Healthcare, Inc., transforming Aetna into the nation's largest managed health care provider. The parent company Aetna Life & Casualty was renamed Aetna Inc., with the company realigning itself around the new name and new identity. Aetna's existing health insurance operations were merged into U.S. Healthcare, which became an Aetna subsidiary and was renamed Aetna U.S. Healthcare Inc.

A change of leadership in mid-1997 saw former banking executive Huber named president and CEO. In February 1998 Huber was named chairman as well, succeeding the retiring Compton. Huber oversaw several deals in the late 1990s that further bolstered Aetna's position as a major health insurer. In July 1998 the company spent more than $1 billion to acquire New York Life Insurance Company's health insurance operations, which were known as NYLCare Health Plans. The deal added 2.5 million members to the 13.7 million people already enrolled in Aetna plans. NYLCare HMOs operated in several large metropolitan areas, including Washington, D.C., Houston, and Dallas, as well as a number of cities in the states of Illinois, Maine, New Jersey, New York, and Washington.

Continuing to shed noncore operations, Aetna sold its U.S. individual life insurance business to Lincoln National Corporation for $1 billion in cash in October 1998. Then in August 1999 Aetna completed its third major acquisition in as many years, spending about $1 billion for the money-losing health care business of Prudential Insurance Company of America. The deal increased the number of Americans covered by Aetna health plans from 16 million to 22 million, and it also more than doubled Aetna's dental insurance business to 15 million members. To gain antitrust approval from the U.S. Department of Justice, Aetna had to divest its NYLCare HMO businesses in Dallas and Houston. The Texas Medical Association had opposed the deal, concerned that it would give Aetna too large a share of the market in those two cities. The American Medical Association was also against the deal, arguing that it would give Aetna too much power over physicians and be bad for consumers as well.

In fact, by this time many doctors and health care consumers were in open rebellion against the policies that had prevailed at Aetna since its purchase of U.S. Healthcare. It turned out that Aetna had made this acquisition at a peak point and, therefore, had paid a premium price. The company began squeezing both doctors and patients to improve profits. Physicians did not like the restrictions that Aetna contracts placed upon them, and the company began facing a rash of class-action lawsuits not only from doctors but also from patients claiming they had been denied care. Aetna's travails were compounded by the difficulty it had integrating its operations with those of U.S. Healthcare and also by the discovery that the newly acquired Prudential health unit was losing more money than anticipated. Despite steadily increasing revenues, profits were falling, dropping from $901 million in 1997 to $848.1 million in 1998 to $716.9 million in 1999.

GLOBAL HEALTH AND GLOBAL FINANCIAL SERVICES ARE SOLD: 2000

By February 2000 Aetna's stock had fallen to $39, having lost two-thirds of its value since August 1997. Mounting pressure from shareholders led to Huber's sudden resignation that month. William H. Donaldson, cofounder of the investment banking firm Donaldson, Lufkin & Jenrette, Inc., was named chairman and CEO. In late February managed-care firm WellPoint Health Networks Inc. and the U.S. arm of the Dutch financial services giant ING Groep N.V. jointly approached Aetna about a $10.5 billion takeover. The company's board rebuffed this unsolicited bid and instead announced in March that the company would split, creating two separate businesses focusing on health care and financial services.

ING remained interested in a deal, however, and in July the two parties reached an agreement. The complicated transaction was completed in December 2000. Aetna Inc. spun off to its shareholders the Aetna U.S. Healthcare Inc. subsidiary. What remained of Aetna (the company's international and financial services units) was acquired by ING for about $7.75 billion. Aetna U.S. Healthcare was then renamed Aetna Inc. (meaning that the "new" Aetna would trace its incorporation back to that of United States Health Care Systems, Inc. in 1982). As a result, the new Aetna was focused almost solely on U.S. medical and dental insurance and related products. It did retain much smaller operations in group life, disability, and long-term-care insurance and in large-care pensions.

To turn around the troubled company, Donaldson brought John W. Rowe onboard as president and CEO in September 2000. A noted gerontologist, Rowe had most recently served as head of Mount Sinai NYU Health, a group of nonprofit New York City hospitals. Rowe was appointed chairman of Aetna as well in April 2001. Another key appointment was that of Ronald A. Williams, who was named executive vice president and chief of health operations in March 2001. Hired away from Aetna rival WellPoint Health Networks, Williams was promoted to president of Aetna in May 2002.

AETNA BOUNCES BACK: 2002–04

One of the key steps taken by the new leadership team was to mend fences with both doctors and patients. Aetna changed many of the restrictive policies that it had implemented in an attempt to contain costs. It began providing clearer information on coverage to doctors and patients, speeded up payments, and reduced red tape. In May 2003 the company broke ranks with its industry rivals and agreed to settle a massive class-action lawsuit that had been brought against the nation's major managed-care insurers. The suit, whose class included nearly all U.S. physicians, had listed a number of complaints, including unfair billing practices and interference with treatment recommendations. The value of the settlement was estimated at about $470 million. Aetna also introduced new health plans, such as Aetna HealthFund (launched in 2001), that gave plan members more direct control over their health care decisions.

To repair the company's finances, Rowe cut about 15,000 jobs and raised insurance premiums by about 16 percent per year to keep ahead of medical inflation. He also reduced Aetna's customer base from 19.3 million members to 13 million by abandoning unprofitable markets, including almost half of the counties nationwide in which it offered Medicare products. Aetna also dropped members who were generating high medical costs and paying low premiums. Because of the drop in membership, Aetna was no longer the nation's largest managed-care insurer, but it returned to profitability, posting $933 million in net income in 2003.

LEADERSHIP CHANGES: 2006–11

After slimming down, Aetna began to bulk up, adding steadily to its ranks of medical care members. By 2005 membership had climbed to 14.7 million, an increase that occurred alongside rising financial results. The company's turnaround considered complete, Rowe announced his decision to step down as CEO, paving the way for Williams to take the helm. A former senior executive at WellPoint Health Networks Inc., Williams joined Aetna in 2001 and was named president a year later. Working in tandem with Rowe, he distinguished himself during Aetna's revival. "The two executives," *Hartford Courant*'s Diane Levick wrote in the newspaper's February 10, 2006 edition, referring to

Rowe and Williams, "are credited with leading a stunning reversal of Aetna's financial losses and rehabilitating its much-maligned reputation among physicians, employers, benefits brokers, and consultants."

Williams formed his own cadre of executives to lead Aetna forward. The last member to join the team was Mark T. Bertolini, who was named president in July 2007, two months after he was promoted from executive vice president of regional businesses to lead all of Aetna's business operations. Williams and Bertolini faced a period of uncertainty as a leadership team, a period that included a global financial crisis and the promise of health care reform at the federal level. Bertolini canvassed governors and legislators, articulating Aetna's stance on the subject of health care reform. Although opposed to the public insurance option supported by President Barack Obama, the company favored requiring everyone in the United States to have at least basic health insurance and basing doctor salaries on the quality of care they provided to patients.

The ultimate effect of health care reform had yet to be determined by the time leadership of the company passed to a new CEO and chairman. Bertolini was named CEO in late 2010 and chairman in the spring of 2011. Under his leadership, Aetna faced the challenges ahead, confident its legacy of overcoming adversity and adapting to changes in its industry would hold it in good stead in the years to come.

Lynn M. Voskuil
Updated, Pamela L. Shelton; David E. Salamie;
Jeffrey L. Covell

PRINCIPAL SUBSIDIARIES

Aetna Health Holdings, LLC; Chickering Claims Administrators, Inc.; Schaller Anderson Medical Administrators, Incorporated; Aetna Life Insurance Company; Aetna Financial Holdings, LLC; Aetna Behavioral Health of Delaware, LLC; Aetna Partners Diversified Fund (Cayman), Limited (Cayman Islands); Aetna Health and Life Insurance Company; Aetna Health Insurance Company; Aetna Health Insurance Company of New York; Aetna Risk Indemnity Company Limited (Bermuda); Aetna Global Benefits (UK) Limited; Aetna Health Services (UK) Limited; Aetna Health Insurance Company of Europe Limited (Ireland); Aetna Global Benefits (Singapore) Pte. Ltd. (China).

PRINCIPAL COMPETITORS

Blue Cross and Blue Shield; CIGNA Corporation; UnitedHealth Group Incorporated; WellPoint, Inc.

FURTHER READING

"Aetna: A Long Way to the Recovery Room." *Business Week*, July 16, 2001.
"Aetna Explodes." *Economist*, March 18, 2000.
Benko, Laura B. "Makeover at Aetna Lags." *Modern Healthcare*, March 18, 2002.
Gorham, John. "Train Wreck in Hartford." *Forbes*, March 6, 2000.
Gosselin, Kenneth R. "Aetna President Decries Health Debate Noise; Claims 'High Road.'" *Hartford Courant*, August 19, 2009.
Hooker, Richard. *Aetna Life Insurance Company: Its First Hundred Years, a History*. Hartford, CT: Aetna Life Insurance Company, 1956.
Jackson, Susan. "Aetna's Brave Old World." *Business Week*, March 30, 1998.
Lagnado, Lucette, and Joann Lublin. "Hospital Chief Picked to Revive Distressed Aetna." *Wall Street Journal*, September 6, 2000.
Levick, Diane. "Aetna's Stock Reaches Record High." *Hartford Courant*, February 10, 2006.
Lohse, Deborah. "Aetna to Sell Some Assets to Lincoln." *Wall Street Journal*, May 22, 1998.
Rublin, Lauren R. "Temperature Rising." *Barron's*, March 27, 2000.
Treaster, Joseph B. "Aetna Agreement with Doctors Envisions Altered Managed Care." *New York Times*, May 23, 2003.
Wojcik, Joanne. "Aetna's Shift to Health Focus Brings Struggles." *Business Insurance*, August 13, 2001.

Aggreko Plc

120 Bothwell Street, 8th Floor
Glasgow, G2 7JS
United Kingdom
Telephone: (+44 141) 225-5900
Fax: (+44 141) 225-5949
Web site: http://www.aggreko.com

Public Company
Incorporated: 1962
Employees: 3,714
Sales: £1.23 billion ($1.94 billion) (2010)
Stock Exchanges: London
Ticker Symbol: AGK
NAICS: 532490 Other Commercial and Industrial
Machinery and Equipment Rental and Leasing

■ ■ ■

Aggreko Plc is a leading "temporary utility" company. The Glasgow, Scotland-based company specializes in the rental of power generators and other equipment, including air compressors, mobile air conditioning units, and other temperature control equipment, chiefly to industry. The company's prestigious clients hail from a wide range of industries, and have included the Super Bowl, the Olympic Games, and the movie industry. The company's operations include more than 148 locations serving customers in approximately 100 countries.

DUTCH BEGINNINGS, SCOTTISH GROWTH

Aggreko began as a small mobile generator rental business in the Netherlands in 1962 (*Aggreko* comes from the Dutch word for "generator"). Over the next decade, the company expanded its operations into other European market countries in continental Europe. At the beginning of the 1970s, Aggreko turned to the United Kingdom. In 1973 Aggreko opened an office in Glasgow, Scotland, headed by David Yorke and Gordon Tourlamain. The Scottish office quickly outpaced its parent company, and Aggreko's headquarters, and market focus, eventually moved to the United Kingdom. Aggreko grew rapidly over the next decade, expanding notably into Norway to support the booming North Sea oil industry. Lacking the funds for further expansion, Aggreko began to look for a larger partner.

In the early 1980s British conglomerate (and former leader of the worldwide whaling industry) Christian Salvesen had been looking for new business opportunities in order to shore up its operations damaged by the economic recession of the period. Already strongly present in Norway (the company's roots were historically Norwegian) Salvesen acquired Aggreko in 1984. The following year, Salvesen went public, and Aggreko became one of the company's key divisions.

RAPID EXPANSION

Under Salvesen, Aggreko, which continued to be led by Tourlamain and Yorke, started to expand rapidly. By 1986 the subsidiary had increased its number of U.K. depots, while also boosting its presence on the European continent, adding depots in Paris and Marseille to build on its existing French presence. In 1987 Aggreko added a new depot in Germany, two more in England, and then acquired rival Dutch company Van Rijn to

COMPANY PERSPECTIVES

Aggreko prides itself in inspiring confidence in its customers worldwide: Confidence in the equipment and services we provide. Confidence in the promises we make. Confidence in the relationships we build. Confidence in the knowledge that we always get the job done.

reestablish itself as a major generator rental company to the Netherlands' market.

The year 1986 marked another turning point for Aggreko. In that year, the company made its first acquisition in the United States, of Electric Rental Systems in Louisiana, marking Aggreko's entry into the North American markets. The company's new U.S. component, led by Tourlamain, began a rapid expansion drive. By the beginning of 1987, Aggreko had doubled its U.S. operations, with new facilities in Texas, Alabama, Florida, Los Angeles, and San Francisco.

Aggreko's North American presence took on still greater importance in 1988. In that year the company paid $4 million to acquire Mobil Air and Pierce Industrial Air. The purchase not only gave Aggreko the new business area of mobile air conditioning and other temperature control rental equipment, but also a position as leader of that market in the United States.

Part of Aggreko's success, both in the United States and in Europe, was its commitment to developing its own generator and equipment designs, allowing the company to adapt quickly to customers' needs. In 1986 the company introduced the first in a range of super-quiet generators. The following year Aggreko began offering customized rental equipment.

At the end of the 1980s, Aggreko continued to explore new markets. In 1989 the company made its first move into the Asian Pacific markets with the acquisition of Singapore's Yeok Kong Electrical Company. The following year, the company expanded its position in that part of the world with the purchase of Generator Rentals Pty, based in Australia.

INTERNATIONAL LEADER

Changes at Salvesen had led that company to shed a large number of its operations to focus on a smaller core of logistics, food processing, and Aggreko. Aggreko itself represented the fastest-growing component of its parent company. While many other companies suffered through the economic recession at the end of the decade, Aggreko's business benefited from industry's increased interest in outsourcing for their generator and other climate control needs. After building up its temperature control wing in the United States, Aggreko introduced those operations to its European base in 1991. The company added temperature control rentals through an Antwerp, Belgium, depot, and then introduced that operation to the United Kingdom, where it quickly became a segment leader.

It also was in 1991 that Aggreko acquired BDD, giving it another business component, industrial drying equipment rentals. Based in the United Kingdom, the new component also gave the company an entry into the Middle East markets. The company expanded elsewhere in that region, opening depots in Sharjah and Abu Dhabi in the United Arab Emirates. Meanwhile, in Asia, Aggreko set up facilities in Malaysia and Indonesia. Its Australian component was also growing, extending its network to six depots and 14 sales agencies. Aggreko then brought its new desiccant drying expertise to the United States, starting in 1992.

Back in Europe, Aggreko was eyeing a number of prestigious contracts. In 1992 the company won the contract to supply power to the 1992 Olympic Games in Barcelona, as well as the Winter Games in Albertville, France. Backing this effort was the opening of three new depots, in Barcelona, Seville, and Bilbao. In 1994 the company received the power generation contract for the Winter Olympics in Lillehammer, Norway, as well. The company's Spanish success proved short-lived and the company was forced to close its new Spanish depots by mid-decade.

Around the same time, the company was exiting from another unsuccessful expansion move. In 1992 Aggreko had attempted to enter the lighting systems rental market in the United Kingdom, purchasing Light & Sound Design. Unable to find its place in that market, however, Aggreko sold off that operation in 1995.

RESTRUCTURING AND SPIN-OFF

Aggreko was restructured as part of an overall retooling of the Salvesen group, which decentralized its operations and placed responsibility more firmly in the hands of the management of the individual businesses. David Yorke had by then taken over day-to-day leadership of Aggreko, while Dr. Chris Masters had been named chief executive of Salvesen. Aggreko's operations were now organized along regional lines, rather than product segments, with divisions for North America, Europe, the United Kingdom, and the Pacific Rim. In the United

KEY DATES

1962: Aggreko is founded in the Netherlands as a power generator rental business.

1973: David Yorke and Gordon Tourlamain open Aggreko's U.K. subsidiary in Glasgow, Scotland.

1984: Christian Salvesen acquires Aggreko as part of a diversification program.

1986: Aggreko enters United States with acquisition of Electric Rental Systems Inc.

1997: Aggreko is spun off from Salvesen and becomes a separate publicly listed company.

2006: Company acquires GE Energy Rentals from General Electric Company.

States, the company set up its first national accounts program, appealing to the growing number of large corporate clients. That market had also grown to become the company's largest single market, building up to some 50 percent of Aggreko's total sales.

In 1995 Aggreko launched its own series of oil-free air compressors, particularly prized by the food processing and electronics industries, as these air compressors did not disperse the fine particles of oil thrown off by standard air compressors. The following year Aggreko introduced its GreenPower series of environmentally friendly power generators. This new generation of generators was first used for the Olympic Games held that year in Atlanta.

A takeover attempt launched by rival logistics group Hays Plc for Christian Salvesen set in motion a chain of events that saw Aggreko become a separate company in 1997. While Salvesen had rejected the takeover offer, shareholder discontent forced Salvesen's board to restructure the company again, now tightening its focus to become a pure logistics player. Aggreko was spun off as a separate, publicly listed company headed by Masters as chairman and Yorke as managing director. The spin-off helped Salvesen raise funds to begin an aggressive acquisition program, while Aggreko became a more visible company in its own right.

The move was greeted warmly by the financial community and Aggreko Plc's initial public offering on the London Stock Exchange was a success. The company continued to strengthen its position as worldwide leader of the equipment rental market. While power generation remained the company's primary operation, its temperature control and other equipment

rentals were also becoming significant revenue generators.

INTRODUCTION OF OIL-FREE COMPRESSORS

In 1998 Aggreko brought its oil-free compressor equipment to the United Kingdom and other countries in Europe. In the United States, the company bought Tower Tech, a provider of modular cooling towers and equipment for the chemicals, nuclear power, pharmaceutical, and other industries. That purchase cost the company $8.4 million.

Aggreko's power generation business had not only developed itself as a leading supplier of mobile power generation equipment and solutions, but also as a leading "temporary utility" company. Already by 1993, the company was completing projects developing as much as 100 megawatts of generating capacity. In 1999 the importance of this branch of operations was highlighted by the creation of a new division, Aggreko International Power Projects. The new entity was formed in order to be able to provide multi-megawatt temporary power facilities around the world.

The company quickly developed clients among many local and national governments. Its generator fleet found service in such far-flung locations as the war-torn Balkans, drought-crippled Africa, and in the United States, providing crucial supplementary power to such cities as New York. The state of California became another primary U.S. customer, as deregulation of the state's utility market had caused major power shortages in 2001. Many private companies turned to Aggreko at the same time. The growing reliance on electronics and computers made continuous, stable power sources an absolute necessity.

ACQUISITION OF L&S

Aggreko's focus in the United States had been primarily on generator rentals. However, in 1999 the company acquired L&S Industries Inc., based in Baltimore, Maryland. That company had been Aggreko's first sales agent in the United States in the late 1980s. Founded in 1983, L&S had initially targeted the engine repair and maintenance market, before changing its own focus to equipment rentals. The addition of L&S's strong service component helped expand Aggreko's service operations. It also marked the first time the company had acquired one of its sales agents.

In 2000 Aggreko, which was able to boast about its contribution to the blockbuster movie *Titanic*, added another worldwide operation, the air compressor rental fleet of Ingersoll-Rand. The two companies also announced a strategic alliance agreement as part of the acquisition. The company also secured a number of other prestige contracts that year, including power generation for Euro 2000 and the PGA Championships.

The announcement by General Electric (GE) that it was entering the power supply market at the beginning of the century, with the business expected to be online by 2002, sparked speculation that Aggreko might become GE's takeover target. Aggreko affirmed its intention to remain independent, while at the same time playing down the coming competition from the global giant. Some observers, however, cautioned that Aggreko's fleet of primarily diesel-based generators placed it at a disadvantage, as GE, capable of building its fleet from scratch, was able to choose among a number of new generator fuel technologies.

Nonetheless, Aggreko remained buoyant entering the new century. The company secured the contract to supply power to the 2002 Olympic Games to be held in Salt Lake City. Aggreko also received a new managing director, when David Yorke retired in April 2001, turning over the company's operational leadership to Philip J. Harrower. Aggreko meanwhile was riding high on a wave of power blackouts affecting California, which were expected to continue for some time as that market adjusted to the realities of deregulated utilities.

By early 2002 a team of 107 staff members had been working for 18 months to install the necessary equipment for the 2002 Winter Games. In all, Aggreko installed 250 transformers, 350 generator sets, and 3,000 electrical distribution panels to provide 100 megawatts of power. After the Olympics, Aggreko relocated all of the equipment to Japan, where it was needed for the 2002 World Cup. It also was in 2002 that Aggreko introduced a portable line of electrical distribution equipment, which was the first to be listed by Underwriters Laboratories.

RESTRUCTURING

Midway through 2003 Aggreko established a new full-service depot in McAllen, Texas. The new facility was constructed in response to strong customer demand, and it enabled the company to provide better service to the Rio Grande Valley, as well as Mexico's Maquila territory. Early the following year, however, Aggreko announced a restructuring of its depots in both Europe and North America. The net effect was the closure of approximately 30 European locations, as well as 40 in North America. By this time the company was led by CEO Rupert Soames.

Aggreko's restructuring program meant more than simply closing a few depots. The company began mov-

ing away from autonomous stores and toward a more centralized structure in which rental centers were given responsibility for functions such as telemarketing, pricing, and taking sales calls. For example, the company divided its operations in the United Kingdom into four different zones, served by main hubs in London, Bristol, Doncaster, and Dumbarton.

A major deal took place in September 2006 when Aggreko agreed to acquire GE Energy Rentals from General Electric Company for $212 million. The transaction, which was finalized in December, had a number of advantages. In North America, Aggreko's operations expanded to include more than 50 locations. In addition, the deal allowed Aggreko to grow in Asia, Australia, the Middle East, and both South America and Central America.

INTERNATIONAL GROWTH

Aggreko began operations in China in November 2006, when it established a new operation named Aggreko (Shanghai) Energy Equipment Rental Co. That business commenced operations in February 2007. Developments continued in early 2009 when Sweden-based Atlas Copco acquired Aggreko's oil-free compressor rental business in Europe.

The company began 2010 on a positive note, having opened a new 30,000-square-foot service center in Plainview, New York, in 2009. In addition, Aggreko stood to benefit from large events including the Winter Olympics in Vancouver, Canada, for which it was named the official power and temperature control supplier. The company also was prepared to provide energy services for the World Cup in South Africa. Aggreko ended 2010 by acquiring Gillette, Wyoming-based Northland Power Services, a power solutions company serving the oil and gas exploration industry, in a deal worth approximately $26 million.

International growth continued in early 2011 when Aggreko parted with $20.3 million to acquire Auckland, New Zealand-based temporary power rental company N.Z. Generator Hire Ltd. Midway through the year the company established a new 7,000-square-foot service center in Fort McMurray, Alberta, Canada. Around the same time the company began doing business in Xinjiang, China.

By 2011 Aggreko served a global customer base from approximately 148 different sites worldwide. Each year, the company fulfilled roughly 40,000 assignments for its customers, which were dispersed across 100 countries. The company had become the service provider of choice for many of the world's largest events. Moving forward, Aggreko appeared to have excellent prospects for continued success.

M. L. Cohen
Updated, Paul R. Greenland

PRINCIPAL SUBSIDIARIES

Aggreko Generator Rentals (PNG) Limited (Papua New Guinea); Aggreko Peru S.A.C.; Aggreko Trinidad Limited; OOO Aggreko Eurasia (Russia); Aggreko (Singapore) PTE Limited; Aggreko Energy Rental South Africa (Proprietary) Limited; Aggreko Iberia SA (Spain); Aggreko Americas Holdings B.V. (Netherlands); Aggreko Euro Holdings B.V. (Netherlands); Aggreko Rest of the World Holdings B.V. (Netherlands); Aggreko (Investments) B.V. (Netherlands); Aggreko Nederland B.V. (Netherlands); Generatoren Koopmans B.V. (Netherlands); Aggreko Finance Limited; Aggreko Holdings Limited; Aggreko European Finance; Aggreko International Projects Limited; Aggreko Pension Scheme Trustee Limited; Aggreko UK Limited; Aggreko US Limited; Aggreko Generators Limited; Aggreko Luxembourg Holdings; Aggreko Quest Trustee Limited; CS1 Limited; Dunwilco (680) Limited; Rotor Wheel UK Limited; Aggreko Uruguay S.A.; Aggreko Holdings Inc. (USA); Aggreko USA LLC (USA); Aggreko LLC (USA); Aggreko de Venezuela C.A.; Aggreko Argentina S.R.L; Aggreko Generator Rentals Pty Limited (Australia); Aggreko Barbados Limited; Aggreko Belgium NV; Aggreko Energia Locacao de Geradores Ltda (Brazil); Aggreko Canada Inc.; Aggreko Financial Holdings Limited (Cayman Islands); Aggreko Chile Limitada; Aggreko (Shanghai) Energy Equipment Rental Company Limited (China); Aggreko Colombia SAS; Aggreko Cote d'Ivoire S.A.R.L.; Aggreko (Middle East) Limited (Cyprus); Aggreko DRC S.P.R.L. (Congo); Aggreko Energy Ecuador CIA; Aggreko Finland Oy; Aggreko France SARL; Aggreko Deutschland GmbH (Germany); Aggreko Hong Kong Limited; Aggreko Energy Rental India Private Limited; Aggreko Ireland Limited; Aggreko Italia S.R.L (Italy); Aggreko Malaysia SDN BHD; Aggreko Energy Mexico SA de CV; Aggreko Services Mexico SA de CV; Aggreko SA de CV (Mexico); Aggreko (NZ) Limited (New Zealand); Aggreko Projects Limited (Nigeria); Aggreko Gas Power Generation Limited (Nigeria); Aggreko Norway AS.

PRINCIPAL COMPETITORS

Cummins Inc.; Neff Rental LLC; RSC Holdings Inc.

FURTHER READING

"Aggreko Again Expands in Western Canada." *Business Wire*, June 8, 2011.

"Aggreko Buys Northland Power Services." *Manufacturing Close-Up*, December 8, 2010.

"Aggreko Completes GE Energy Rentals Acquisition." *Rental Equipment Register*, December 8, 2006.

"Aggreko Opens Shanghai Service Center." *Rental Equipment Register*, May 4, 2007.

"Aggreko to Enter Xinjiang." *SinoCast Daily Business Beat*, June 13, 2011.

"Swedish Atlas Completes Acquisition of Aggreko Unit." *Nordic Business Report*, March 10, 2009.

Arab National Bank

PO Box 56921
Riyadh, 11564
Saudi Arabia
Telephone: (+966 01) 402 9000
Fax: (+966 01) 402 7747
Web site: http://www.anb.com.sa

Public Company
Incorporated: 1979
Employees: 3,600
Total Assets: SAR 116 billion ($30.94 billion) (2010)
Stock Exchanges: Saudi
Ticker Symbol: ANB
NAICS: 522110 Commercial Banking

■ ■ ■

Arab National Bank (ANB) is one of the 10 largest commercial banks in the Middle East. The bank also ranks as the seventh-largest bank in Saudi Arabia in terms of total assets. In 2010, ANB reported total assets of SAR 116 billion ($30.94 billion). The bank is the second-largest provider of remittance services in Saudi Arabia, backed by a network of 78 "Tele-money" centers. ANB operates through five primary divisions, Retail Banking, Corporate Banking, Commercial Banking, Islamic Banking, and Treasury. The company also has a branch office in London, its only operations outside of Saudi Arabia. ANB's branch office network in Saudi Arabia spans nearly 250 locations, including 37 branches or sections reserved exclusively for women. The bank has also entered the Islamic banking market, and

provides these services from 101 of its branch offices. ANB is listed on the Saudi Stock Exchange and operates as an affiliate of Jordan's Arab Bank, which controls 40 percent of its shares. The remaining 60 percent is controlled by Saudi investors, including General Organization for Social Insurance (10.81%), Al-Jabr Trading Company (5.65%), and Abudi Rahman Al-Rashed and Sons (9.97%). Bank Chairman Abdullatif Hamad Al-Jabr also holds a 6 percent stake. ANB generated net income of SAR 1.91 billion ($510 million) in 2010.

ROOTED IN ARAB BANK

Arab National Bank had its roots in Arab Bank, itself formerly known as Arab National Bank. Arab Bank was founded by Abdel Hameed Shoman (also written as Schuman), born in 1890 in Beit Hanina, near Jerusalem. By the time he was seven, Shoman had already begun working as a stone mason. Shoman left the region in 1910 to immigrate to the United States, arriving with just $32. Shoman went to work as a door-to-door salesman. Ultimately, he went into business for himself, founding a clothing factory in Manhattan. Shoman's son, Abdul Majeed Shoman, joined him in the United States at the age of 14 and went on to complete a master's degree in economics and banking at the New York University.

The younger Shoman's choice of study was no accident. During the 1920s, his father had returned to the Middle East with plans to establish an Arab-owned bank in British-occupied Palestine. To this end, Shoman met with the chairman of the Bank of Egypt, proposing to create a jointly owned bank, with a capital of £100,000.

This plan fell through, however. Instead, Shoman went in search of other financial backing. By 1930 he had succeeded in gathering seven investors who agreed to put up £15,000 to found the new bank. Arab National Bank officially registered for business on May 21, 1930, and commenced commercial operations at its first office in Jerusalem less than two months later. Shoman's son joined the bank in 1931 after completing his studies, and became an important part of the young bank's success. The bank expanded beyond Jerusalem, opening a number of branch offices, including in Jaffa and Haifa.

Arab Bank initially focused on the Palestinian region. The British withdrawal from the region and the subsequent creation of the state of Israel threw much of the bank's operations in turmoil into 1948. The bank moved its headquarters to a new location within Jerusalem's old city, which under the partition had been placed under control of the Arab population. Arab Bank also shut down its branches in Haifa and Jaffa, opening instead new branches in Beirut, Amman, Nablus, and Ramallah. By the end of 1948, the bank had transferred its headquarters to Amman as well.

REGIONAL EXPANSION IN THE FIFTIES

Through the difficulties of the period, Arab Bank established its reputation among the Palestinian community and the Arab world in general. As large numbers of Palestinians fled their homes, Arab Bank made it a point of honoring their claims to their deposits with the bank. This policy helped build a strong degree of loyalty from its customers, which in turn played a significant role in the bank's expansion.

With further growth in the region hampered by the political situation, Arab Bank set out a strategy of regional expansion during the 1950s. For this, the bank followed the Palestinian diaspora, opening branches throughout Jordan, in Egypt, Syria, Iraq, Aden, Sudan, Libya, and other markets. One of the most important of

these was Saudi Arabia, where the bank established its first presence in 1950.

Arab Bank's Saudi operations focused particularly on the kingdom's northern Arab populations, especially the growing community of Jordanian-Palestinians. This population developed a major presence in Saudi Arabia's trading and contracting sectors. Arab Bank's development in Saudi Arabia thus became firmly linked with the country's private sector, even as the Saudi government began putting into place the country's banking system.

By the end of the 1970s, Arab Bank's operations in Saudi Arabia spanned six branches and included nearly 400 employees. By then, Arab Bank had been caught up in the wave of nationalism that had been sweeping through the region since the 1960s. As a result, many of the bank's foreign branches were nationalized.

SAUDI ARABIA BANK IN 1979

Rather than nationalize the banks operating within its borders, the Saudi Arabia government instead instituted a policy of requiring that foreign banks operating in the country bring in Saudi nationals as majority partners in the bank. This policy, introduced in 1975, led Arab Bank to convert its Saudi operations into a separate but affiliated company, Arab National Bank (ANB), in 1979. Saudi nationals then acquired 60 percent of the bank's capital, while Arab Bank retained the largest single stake, at 40 percent. ANB began operations in 1980.

ANB grew strongly through the first half of the 1980s, as the Saudi economy, flush with a massive increase in oil revenues, immersed itself in intensive spending programs. ANB's strong connection with the prominent Jordanian-Palestinian traders in the country allowed the bank to play an important role in the growth of the country's private sector as well. At the same time, ANB received a major contract with the Saudi government, as it gained the Saudi Pension Fund Authority as an exclusive client. As a result, ANB became the administrator for pension funds for government employees.

By 1985, ANB had expanded to 79 branches throughout Saudi Arabia, while its employee base neared 2,500. By then, the bank had built up total assets of SAR 10.4 billion (approximately $2.8 billion). The company, which touted its business strategy as "very conservative," enjoyed strong profits during this period, and claimed to be the most profitable private sector bank in Saudi Arabia.

ANB opened a representative office in London, near the Saudi embassy, in order to provide services to the

KEY DATES

1930: Arab Bank is founded by Abdel Hameed Shoman.
1950: Arab Bank establishes its first branch in Saudi Arabia.
1979: Arab National Bank (ANB) is founded to acquire the Saudi assets of Arab Bank.
1991: ANB converts its London office to full branch status.
2000: ANB becomes the first Saudi bank to offer online banking services.
2010: ANB's total assets reach SAR 116 billion ($30.94 billion).

Arab community in that financial capital. This office was expanded to full branch status in 1991. The bank also completed a capital increase, which doubled in size to SAR 300 million ($80 million) in 1988. By 1990, the bank's Saudi branch office network had grown to 100 locations.

COST-CUTTING IN THE NINETIES

The bank's growth, like the rest of the Saudi Arabian economy, came to a sudden halt leading into the 1990s. Amid a new economic crisis, exacerbated by the Iraqi occupation of Kuwait and the subsequent Persian Gulf War, the Saudi government froze spending. This sent the bank sector into a downward spiral.

While ANB's conservative strategy helped protect it from the worst of the crisis, it nonetheless remained heavily exposed to the difficulties in the private sector. In addition, the bank's strong ties to the Palestinian diaspora hurt the bank as well, given this community's political positioning during the Persian Gulf War.

In order to meet its difficulties, ANB restructured and cut costs. The bank reduced its staff, and instead initiated a new technology-driven strategy. In particular, the bank rolled out its own network of ATMs, acquiring nearly 240 machines by the end of the decade. While this emphasis on technology later helped position the bank among the leaders in Saudi Arabia, the company's cost-cutting efforts were less than successful elsewhere. As one credit rating agency told the *Financial Times* in November 2002, the restructuring "backfired, as costs were cut in many of the wrong areas."

NEW MANAGEMENT IN 1998

ANB continued to struggle to regain its momentum during the 1990s, even as its total assets neared SAR 35 billion. In 1998, the bank brought in a new managing director to revitalize its operations. Nemeh Sabbagh had more than 15 years experience as the second-in-command of National Bank of Kuwait. Under Sabbagh, ANB instituted tighter credit controls, and also a more conservative policy for its bad debt provisioning. The company also focused its efforts on improving its customer services, rather than seeking solely to expand its customer base.

Among the bank's new services was its online banking platform, begun in 2000. As a result, ANB became the first Saudi bank to provide online banking services. The new service, introduced in February of that year, quickly attracted more than 120,000 users, and was expected to near 250,000 by the end of the year, or approximately half of its total customer base. In 2002, the company marketed a new VISA credit card, in conjunction with B.A. Airline Company. At the same time, ANB had also been broadening its range of Islamic banking services and products, including expanding its women-only branch banking network. In 2002, the company introduced its Hesab Al Mubarak banking packaging, featuring a portfolio of Sharia-compliant products. This package was launched alongside a conventional banking package, Manafa Al Arabi, also introduced that year. ANB also introduced a banking package specifically for its pension fund customers, in 2001.

Sabbagh's leadership helped turn the bank around as it recorded strong growth both in its total assets and in its net income. By 2004, the former topped SAR 63 billion, while net profits had soared to SAR 1.17 billion, nearly triple its profits at the beginning of the decade.

ISLAMIC BANKING EXTENSION INTO 2010

ANB launched a refurbishing program for its branch office network in 2005. This program, which also involved a number of branch relocations, included the conversion of a number of branches into exclusively Sharia-compliant branches. In addition, the company introduced a cover card, the Sharia-compliant version of a credit card, and a Sharia-compliant financing wing as well. This led to the creation of a housing finance joint venture with Kingdom Settlement Company, Dar al-Arkan, and the International Finance Corporation in 2006. The new company became the largest Islamic housing finance operation in the Middle East. ANB held a 40 percent stake in the new company, which started with a capital base of $534 million.

The bank continued to add to its Islamic banking operations through the decade. In 2007, the bank announced plans to enter the *takaful* (the Sharia-compliant equivalent of insurance products) sector. ANB also prepared to introduce equipment leasing and mortgage operations for the Islamic market. ANB's extension into the Islamic banking sector played a part in the rapid growth of the bank's branch office network during the decade. By 2011, the company had expanded its total number of locations to 250 offices. This number included 37 women-only branches. At the same time, the bank offered Islamic banking services at more than 100 branches.

ANB briefly flirted with expanding its operations beyond the Saudi market in the second half of the decade, following the appointment of Robert Eid as managing director in 2006. In that year, the company launched a failed bid to acquire Egypt's Bank of Alexandria in 2006. ANB did not rule out further attempts to establish a regional presence. Nonetheless, in June 2007 Eid told *MEED*: "In the broader scheme of things ... our key focus is on Saudi Arabia, which presents bountiful prospects."

ANB maintained its focus on the Saudi market leading into the next decade, targeting growth in the retail sector, which at the beginning of 2011 represented 39 percent of the group's income. Treasury services added 22 percent, while the bank's Corporate division represented 17 percent. The bank continued to post strong profit growth through that year. By the third quarter of 2011, ANB had increased its net income 50 percent over the previous year. With deposits of nearly SAR 86 billion and total assets of SAR 116 billion ($30.94 billion), ANB had succeeded in becoming not only one of Saudi Arabia's top 10 banks, but also one of the 10 largest banks in the Middle East region.

M. L. Cohen

PRINCIPAL SUBSIDIARIES

ANB Invest; Arabian Heavy Equipment Leasing Company (62.5%); Saudi Home Loan (40%).

PRINCIPAL DIVISIONS

Retail Banking; Corporate Banking; Commercial Banking; Islamic Banking; Treasury; London Branch.

PRINCIPAL COMPETITORS

Al Rajhi Bank; Banque Saudi Fransi; Islamic Development Bank; The National Commercial Bank; Riyad Bank; Samba Financial Group; The Saudi British Bank; Saudi Hollandi Bank.

FURTHER READING

"Arab Bank Looks for Buys." *MEED Middle East Economic Digest*, June 15, 2007, 29.

"Blood Links of Family and Tribe." *Financial Times*, November 20, 2002.

"Lending by Proxy." *MEED Middle East Economic Digest*, May 19, 2006, 59.

Martin, Matthew. "Arab National Bank: While the Riyadh-Based Lender Can Look Forward to Growth in the Year Ahead, Competition Will Be Tough." *MEED Middle East Economic Digest*, January 21, 2011, 22.

———. "Focus Turns to Retail Business." *MEED Middle East Economic Digest*, May 18, 2007, 47.

"NB Launches e-Banking." *MEED Middle East Economic Digest*, February 18, 2000, 25.

"New Strategy Bears Fruit." *Banker*, August 2002, S22.

"Region's Biggest Home Finance Company Formed." *MEED Middle East Economic Digest*, August 18, 2006, 30.

"Saudi's Arab National Bank Reports Results." *Global Banking News*, October 13, 2011.

Asiana Airlines, Inc.

Asiana Town
Kangseo P.O. Box 98
#47, Osae-Dong, Kangseo-Ku
Seoul,
South Korea
Telephone: (+82 2) 669-3183
Toll Free: (800) 227-4262
Fax: (+82 2) 669-3170
Web site: http://flyasiana.com

Public Company
Incorporated: 1988
Employees: 7,500
Sales: KRW 5.07 trillion ($5.37 billion) (2010)
Stock Exchanges: KOSDAQ
Ticker Symbol: 020560
NAICS: 481111 Scheduled Passenger Air Transportation; 481112 Scheduled Freight Air Transportation; 481211 Nonscheduled Chartered Passenger Air Transportation; 481212 Nonscheduled Chartered Freight Air Transportation; 488190 Other Support Activities for Air Transportation

■ ■ ■

Asiana Airlines, Inc., Korea's second national airline, has carved out an impressive place for itself during its relatively brief time in the skies. Founded by the Kumho Group as a chiefly domestic carrier, Asiana has invested in new planes from the start and has sought to compete on quality rather than price. Asiana flies a fleet of 72 planes to 68 destinations in 22 countries and has extensive cargo and catering operations in addition to its passenger business.

ORIGINS

Asiana Airlines was formed in February 1988. Korea's newfound prosperity was creating rising consumer demand for airline tickets, according to aviation historian R. E. G. Davies, and the transitioning of the country from Third World to industrial made having a single national airline (Korean Airlines Co. Ltd., or KAL) seem an obsolescent idea. With KAL unable to maintain market share in the face of unprecedented demand, Korean president Chun Doo Hwan granted a license for a second national airline to the Kumho Group. This was to be headquartered in the southern city of Kwangju in the Chollanam-do Province, an area somewhat removed economically and politically from the Korean mainstream.

The Kumho Group worked its way into aviation literally from the ground up, starting in taxis in 1946 before moving on to buses and, finally, planes. It was also the country's largest tire producer. Kumho founder Park In-Chon, a former police officer, dreamed of forming an air empire. However, he died in 1984 before this could be realized.

His son, Dr. Park Seong-Hwang, Kumho Group chairman and former transport minister, saw the dream through as Asiana's first chairman. A former economics professor trained at Yale, he helped secure $36.5 million in start-up capital for the new venture. Thirty-five percent of it came from the Korean Development Bank.

COMPANY PERSPECTIVES

Asiana Airlines—the company that comes closest to its customers with a smile as beautiful as a wing with stripes of many colors, puts safety first with advanced equipment and a new fleet. Asiana Airlines is the company that realizes customer satisfaction and a service that is based on the customer's expectations. Asiana Airlines is always evolving to ensure enjoyable and comfortable travel.

Asiana began scheduled services the week before the government lifted restrictions on foreign travel on January 1, 1989. The pent-up demand was immense. Asiana began with domestic routes based on hubs in Seoul and Cheju. Within a year and a half, it was also flying to four Japanese destinations.

With domestic fares already low in Korea, Asiana competed on service quality. It operated relatively new planes from the beginning, starting with Boeing 737s leased from Ireland's GPA Group. Asiana ordered more planes in April 1989. This show of confidence continued in September 1990, when the very young airline ordered or optioned $6 billion worth of planes from Boeing.

Asiana's revenues were less than $100 million in 1989, and the carrier lost $46 million. Losses of about $90 million were posted the next two years, although revenues reached $150 million in 1990 and doubled in 1991. The company had about 3,000 employees at the time.

SPREADING ITS WINGS IN 1991

In early 1991, Asiana's international network spread to Taipei, Hong Kong, Bangkok, and Singapore, all important commercial centers. That November, the carrier launched an ambitious passenger/freight service to Los Angeles via Boeing 747. By the end of 1992, Asiana had also added separate routes to San Francisco and New York. The carrier would have preferred Chicago over San Francisco, but it was already served by KAL and the U.S. government would not allow Asiana to fly there as well. International flights accounted for 65 percent of Asiana's revenues of $404 million in 1992.

Asiana's international expansion outpaced the Korean government's ability to hammer out air traffic agreements with other countries. Korea and China were working on a bilateral agreement covering the Beijing–

Seoul route in early 1993. China wanted to allow only one of Korea's airlines to operate between the two cities. Guidelines established in 1990 had permitted only Asiana to fly to Japan, Southeast Asia, and the United States, but these rules were soon bent.

Routes to two very different destinations were launched in July 1993: Ho Chi Minh City and Honolulu. Unfortunately, Asiana also experienced its first crash that month when one of its Boeing 737s hit a mountain on the Korean coast. By this time, Asiana had a fleet of 29 new Boeing aircraft flying six million passengers a year to 16 domestic and 19 international destinations. It had 6,000 employees and planned to double in size within seven years.

PROFITABLE IN 1994

Asiana's president since 1991, Park Sam-Koo, was the younger brother of company founder Park Seong-Hwang. Park Sam-Koo banned smoking from all planes upon learning the majority of passengers preferred nonsmoking seats. The carrier carved out its place in a competitive market and posted its first profit in 1994, KRW 14.2 billion ($18 million) on sales of KRW 792.5 billion ($993 million). The airline had lost $200 million during the previous five years. Kumho periodically infused capital into the airline to keep it running. The group did dilute its holdings. It owned 75 percent of Asiana in 1993.

Asiana signed a code-share agreement with Northwest Airlines Corp. in August 1994, operating transpacific routes in tandem with Northwest and giving it access to passengers transferring from the U.S. carrier's extensive network. In 1995, Asiana began operating a Shanghai–Seoul service in collaboration with China Eastern Airlines, which had previously partnered with KAL on that route. However, in November 1996, the South Korean government halted a space-sharing arrangement with Virginia-based Gemini Air Cargo on the New York–Seoul route, contending that this represented a wet lease, which was illegal in South Korea. In a wet lease, one company provided planes, fuel, and crew for another.

By the end of 1996, Asiana was flying cargo flights to three countries, including service to Delhi and Macau, where Asiana shipped cargo on barges from nearby Hong Kong. Cargo accounted for a quarter of Asiana's revenues in 1996.

In the fall of 1997, Asiana became one of several Pacific Rim airlines to sign a code-share agreement with American Airlines, which was attempting to expand its presence in the East. Sabena, Austria Airlines, and Air China were other code-share partners.

WEATHERING THE ASIAN FINANCIAL CRISIS

Asiana and Korean Air both suffered during the Asian financial crisis as both the Korean won and passenger counts fell. Asiana logged a loss of KRW 53.6 billion on revenues of KRW 684 billion for 1997. Both airlines began selling off planes to reduce their debt. Asiana had borrowed $3 billion to expand its fleet. Both Asiana and Korean Air also petitioned the government to allow a greater percentage of ownership from foreign investors. Since Korean Air was publicly traded, the government allowed it to be half-owned by foreigners, although it was only 21 percent foreign-owned at the time. Asiana was limited to 20 percent foreign ownership and was in fact 19 percent owned by foreign interests since Swiss-based Pacific Investment Capital had invested in parent company Korean Air Transportation Co. in 1996.

A new bilateral agreement between the United States and Korea in 1998 opened the U.S. market to Korean carriers. Asiana soon was posting profits again, thanks in part to a focus on high-yield routes to China and Japan and the recovery of the national economy. A string of accidents at rival Korean Air boosted Asiana's passenger loads. In 1999, Asiana recorded a net profit of KRW 109.6 billion on sales of KRW 1.78 trillion, after losing KRW 141.5 billion on sales of KRW 1.54 trillion the year before.

Asiana launched an initial public offering (IPO) on the local KOSDAQ exchange on December 24, 1999. The carrier earmarked the capital to restructure its debt. The airline, along with the rest of the Kumho Group, was helping to pay for the development of Inchon International Airport. After the IPO, Kumho Group's

ownership in Asiana fell from 66.7 percent to 47 percent.

CHALLENGES LEADING TO GOVERNMENT BAILOUT

Unfortunately, the carrier could not maintain its good results. It posted a net loss of KRW 156 billion for 2000, thanks largely to higher fuel prices and a weaker currency. Another cause for concern was the reentry of more foreign carriers, such as All Nippon Airways (ANA), into the Korean market. The airline nevertheless joined ANA in a code-sharing agreement on the Seoul–Tokyo route, Asiana's busiest.

Asiana started a high-speed delivery service in the spring of 2000 that paired its planes with motorcycle couriers. In June of that year, Asiana was tasked with carrying a South Korean delegation to Pyongyang in a historic first flight to North Korea since the country was divided in 1945.

As part of its effort to attract lucrative business travelers, Asiana installed sleeper beds in its first-class cabins, which were limited to only a dozen seats. In-flight entertainment systems were also top rate, and Asiana compared its business-class cabin to other airlines' first class. A generous mileage program and excellent on-time performance were two other key selling points for the business client.

Flight attendants and ground staff staged a strike at Asiana in June 2001. That summer, Asiana was protesting a ruling by the U.S. Federal Aviation Administration that lowered Korea's air safety rating, preventing any of its carriers from expanding or changing operations to the United States. Asiana felt it was being unfairly penalized, as its own safety record was above average.

Asiana continued to vie aggressively for transpacific cargo business. In June 2001, it launched a service to carry fresh fruit and seafood from Seattle to Asia. In late September, the carrier announced cutbacks to its Los Angeles service at the same time as it was trimming 360 jobs from its 8,600-strong workforce. Asiana also cut routes in Asia and Europe.

The Korean government announced a KRW 250 billion ($192 million) bailout package for both Asiana and Korean Air in November 2001. Asiana was to receive a low-interest loan for KRW 110 billion ($85 million).

NEW AIRPORT IN 2001

A new international airport opened near Seoul in 2001, giving Korea's international carriers an impressive and efficient launching pad. With such large markets as Japan and China nearby, Asiana did not need to invest in long-haul airliners to the same extent as airlines with more global reach, noted *Air Transport World* in its August 2003 issue. Chairman and CEO Park Sam-Koo, also head of the parent Kumho Group, told the journal the monetary crisis of the late 1990s had left it less interested in growth. However, it did open service to London's Heathrow Airport in May 2002. It controlled a little less than one-quarter of Korea's international traffic.

In 2002 the airline posted a pretax profit of KRW 150.1 billion ($125 million), its first in three years, on revenues of KRW 2.60 trillion. There were about 7,000 employees, including 800 flight crew members. Airfreight accounted for nearly one-third of revenues. Scheduled cargo destinations in North America included Anchorage, Los Angeles, San Francisco, and New York. Service to Calgary was added in 2004.

ALLIED IN 2003

Asiana was buffeted by yet another crisis, SARS, in 2003. This resulted in cancellations of some international routes and shifting of capacity to the domestic market. There was one rather auspicious development in the otherwise troubling year. In March 2003 Asiana officially joined the Star Alliance global airline group. This provided seamless connections for its passengers to thousands of destinations around the world, while providing a sure source of feeder traffic. (Rival KAL had joined the Delta-led SkyTeam three years earlier.)

In 2003 Asiana also sold an 80 percent stake in its catering business to Lufthansa's global LSG Sky Chefs operation. The deal was valued at KRW 65 billion ($52 million) plus performance bonuses of up to 50 percent more. By 2005, Asiana made an operating profit of KRW 57.56 billion on revenues of KRW 3.07 trillion. It had 7,800 employees and a fleet of 59 aircraft.

The airline served 15 domestic destinations and 58 international ones extending to the Pacific Rim and Europe. It was still competing on the basis of superior customer service, although rival KAL was trying to woo well-heeled international passengers with improved in-flight amenities. There was intense competition on flights to China.

The cooperation between Asiana and ANA was strengthened when each took $12 million stakes in the other in 2007. Their code-sharing was extended to more strategic Pacific Rim destinations as far as Honolulu and Shanghai. Asiana posted a net gain of $113.5 million, down 20 percent, on revenues up 5 percent to $3.89

billion in 2007. Cargo was very important, accounting for 34 percent of revenues.

It carried 13.1 million passengers in 2008 on a network of 65 international and 12 domestic destinations. In addition, it ran freighters between 25 cities in 16 countries. Asiana ended the year with a very young fleet of 69 aircraft and had just extensively refurbished the cabins on its international routes. *Air Transport World* pronounced Asiana its airline of the year for 2009.

China was the fastest-growing market, showing traffic gains of more than 20 percent a year. Asiana continued to open new routes there, blessed by the Korean government because of its superior safety record.

STILL EVOLVING

Asiana faced increasing competition from budget airlines in the domestic market. It paid KRW 23 billion ($24 million) for a 46 percent stake in low-cost start-up Air Busan Co., which began service in October 2008. Asiana reported revenues of KRW 5.07 trillion ($5.37 billion) for 2010, a 30 percent rise from the previous year. It made a net profit of KRW 236 billion ($211.3 million) after losing KRW 266.3 billion in 2009.

Asiana had nearly 7,500 employees at the end of 2010. It was operating a fleet of 72 aircraft to 12 cities within Korea and 67 destinations in 22 other countries. The company lost a Boeing 747 freighter when it crashed in the sea en route to Shanghai in July 2011.

Known for excellence in operational safety as well as customer service, Korea's second-largest airline had secured a loyal customer base. A secure foothold in Japan and preferential access to the vast Chinese market supplied it ample room to grow, while membership in the Star Alliance connected it to airline passengers around the world. Although perilously exposed to calamities such as the Asian financial crisis, Asiana had consistently demonstrated resourcefulness combined with an unrelenting commitment to its customers.

Frederick C. Ingram

PRINCIPAL COMPETITORS

Korean Airlines Co. Ltd.

FURTHER READING

"Asiana Lists on Kosdaq as Profits Rise." *Airfinance Journal*, November 1999, 12.

"Asiana on Brink of Corporate Overhaul by Selling Fleet." *Airfinance Journal*, February 1998, 6.

"Asiana President Summoned; KAL Gets New Safety Head." *Airfinance Journal*, February 2000, 5.

Bangsberg, P. T. "Korean Airlines Shedding Planes to Pare Their Debt." *Journal of Commerce*, April 29, 1998, 13A.

———. "South Korean Air Carriers Spread Their Wings, Put Focus on Cargo." *Journal of Commerce*, November 1, 1996, 8B.

Barnett, Chris. "Korean Competitor; Asiana Airlines Fights for Market Share as It Seeks Waiver from FAA Ruling." *Journal of Commerce*, September 10, 2001, 39.

Cameron, Doug. "Asiana Stays for the Long Haul." *Airfinance Journal*, March 1995, 30.

Cheesman, Bruce. "Asiana Airlines: Korean Upstart Comes of Age." *Asian Business*, September 1993, 17.

Clifford, Mark. "Upstart Still Rising: Airline Is Group's Loss Leader." *Far Eastern Economic Review*, April 18, 1991, 64.

Darlin, Damon. "Two Sons Rise in the East." *Forbes*, September 26, 1994, 58.

Davies, R. E. G. "Airlines of South Korea." *Airlines of Asia since 1920.* London: Putnam Aeronautical Books; McLean, VA: Paladwr Press, 1997, 515–32.

Donaghue, J. A. "Asiana's Competitive Code." *Air Transport World*, July 1996, 30.

Flint, Perry. "All Dressed Up and No Place to Go." *Air Transport World*, May 1991, 22.

———. "The Treasure Chest in the Backyard: With China and Japan as Neighbors, Asiana Airlines Doesn't Have to Look for Gold in Long-Haul Markets." *Air Transport World*, August 2003, 26+.

Jones, Dominic. "On the Rebound?" *Airfinance Journal*, December 1999, 34–36.

Kayal, Michele. "Open Skies Could Put Korea in the Cockpit; Drop in Cargo Rates to US Feared as Lines Aggressively Add Capacity." *Journal of Commerce*, April 29, 1998, 1A.

———. "South Korea Halts US Airline." *Journal of Commerce*, November 27, 1996, 1B.

"Market Development Award: Asiana." *Air Transport World*, February 1997, 47–48.

Moorman, Robert W. "The Other Korean Airline." *Air Transport World*, June 2000, 57–59.

Proctor, Paul. "Asiana Nears Profitability after Bankruptcy Scare." *Aviation Week & Space Technology*, May 31, 1999, 36.

Rainat, Joyce. "A Cabbie's Legacy." *Asian Finance*, March 15, 1991, 12.

Thomas, Geoffrey. "Asiana's Magic." *ATWOnline*, May 31, 2008.

Westlake, Michael. "Fly in the Ointment: South Korean Carriers Vie for Passengers." *Far Eastern Economic Review*, September 3, 1992, 55.

Bangkok Bank Public Company Ltd.

---

333 Silom Rd.
Bangkok, 10500
Thailand
Telephone: (+66 02) 231-4333
Fax: (+66 02) 231-4742
Web site: http://www.bangkokbank.com

Public Company
Founded: 1944
Incorporated: 1994
Employees: 19,833
Total Assets: THB 1.72 trillion ($64.83 billion) (2010)
Stock Exchanges: Bangkok
Ticker Symbol: BBL
NAICS: 522110 Commercial Banking

∎∎∎

Bangkok Bank Public Company Ltd. is the largest commercial bank in Thailand. With total assets of 1.73 trillion baht ($64.83 billion), it is also one of the leading banks in Southeast Asia. Bangkok Bank provides a full range of corporate and retail banking services to a customer base of more than 17 million accounts. The company is the leading corporate banker in Thailand, and also leads the country in banking services to the small and medium-sized enterprise (SME) sector. Bangkok Bank operates an extensive network of 1,000 branch offices, as well as 230 business-focused offices. The company also operates Thailand's largest network of automated teller machines (ATMs) and cash deposit machines, which numbered 7,600 in 2011. Bangkok

Bank is listed on the Bangkok Stock Exchange and is led by Chairman Chatri Sophonpanich and CEO Chartsiri Sophonpanich, the son and grandson of the bank's founder, Chin Sophonpanich.

FINANCIAL GENIUS IN THE FORTIES

Prior to World War II, the Thai banking sector was dominated by foreign banks, especially from the United States and Europe. The Japanese occupation of Thailand during the war forced these banks to withdraw from the country. The departure of these banks opened the opportunity for the creation of a new, Thai-owned banking industry. In 1944, a group of Thai government officials, military figures, and other notables, led by Field Marshal Phin Choonhaven and including General Phao, joined together to create Bangkok Bank. The new bank, created as an umbrella body for its owner's financial deals, was long suspected of financing the Thai heroin trade, itself dominated by the country's military rulers. Among the directors of the bank was Chin Sophonpanich.

Born in 1910 to a Chinese father and a Thai mother, Chin was sent to school in Swatow, Chao-yang Hsien, the center of the ethnic Teochew (also transliterated as Teochiu) population, at the age of five. The move served to reinforce Chin's ties to the Teochew and the Teochew diaspora, which had spread throughout Southeast Asia and elsewhere, becoming a dominant force in the Asian financial and industrial sectors, including in Thailand.

Chin remained in China until the age of 17, when his father lost his job as a sawmill clerk. Chin dropped

COMPANY PERSPECTIVES

With a complete range of financial services, modern technology and friendly staff, Bangkok Bank can help customers with their personal and business banking needs as they journey through life. For more than half a century, Bangkok Bank has been Thailand's leading bank.

out of school and went to work for a time as a coolie for a construction company, where he rose to the position of assistant manager. During this time, Chin attended night school and learned to speak Thai.

After the construction company was destroyed by fire in 1930, Chin went to work on a Teochew-owned junk smuggling rice from Bangkok to Swatow. After several voyages, Chin gave up a life at sea and instead turned to his friend, Udane, the adopted son of Phin Choonhaven who, like Chin, had his roots in Chaoyang Hsien. Udane helped Chin find work as a bookkeeping clerk at one of Phin's businesses, a building supply firm. Despite a lack of formal education, Chin displayed a natural gift for figures.

This led Phin to agree to provide the financial backing to allow Chin to go into business for himself. In 1935, Chin set up Asia Trading, a company involved in the trade of lumber, construction materials, hardware, and other products. Chin's financial talents enabled him to parlay his earnings from Asia Trading into the Teochew-controlled gold trade in the early 1940s. By 1945, Chin had already earned his first fortune.

CONTROLLING BANGKOK BANK FROM 1951

Chin continued to expand his own business interests, with the support of General Phin. Chin's primary focus remained on the gold trade, and following the military coup (led in part by Phin and his son-in-law General Phao Siyanon) of the Thai government in 1947, Chin received the monopoly over all gold trading in Thailand. At the same time, Chin gained, through his other businesses, including Asia Trust, the monopolies over remittances and foreign exchange transactions in Thailand. Chin also established operations overseas, acquiring Hong Kong and Swatow Bank in Kowloon. This bank became the basis of Commercial Bank of Hong Kong, one of the major financial institutions in Hong Kong and a second pole for the family's financial empire.

At the same time, Chin also gained control at Bangkok Bank. From the beginning, Bangkok Bank had been afflicted by a chronic lack of liquidity, the result of profit-taking by its owners. By 1951, with the bank on the verge of collapse, Chin was given the mandate to take charge of the bank and restructure its operations. Chin promptly fired the bank's management and brought in a new team of professional managers from Asia Trust and reoriented the bank as a Western-styled bank. Chin set out to attract savings, particularly from Thailand's farmers and small-store owners, by offering higher monthly interest rates than Thailand's other banks. For its largest clients, Bangkok Bank also introduced personal banking services. As a result, Thais flocked to the bank. The bank also persuaded large numbers of Chinese-owned foreign businesses operating in Thailand to transfer their business to the bank. At the same time, the influence of General Phin and his son-in-law General Phao Choonhaven brought the bank large deposits from the Ministry of Commerce as well.

Chin gained full control of Bangkok Bank during a boardroom coup in 1952. With Phao and Phin's backing, he began developing Bangkok Bank into one of Thailand's largest and most international banks, opening its first overseas branch office in Hong Kong in 1954. The bank next added an office in Tokyo in 1955, followed by offices in London and Singapore in 1957.

RETURNING FROM EXILE IN THE SIXTIES

The Sarit-led coup of 1957 forced both Phao and Phin to flee Thailand. Chin now faced losing control of Bangkok Bank. Instead, Chin brought in General Praphat, who had taken over as interior minister of the Sarit government and who remained a powerful figure in his own right, as the bank's chairman. In this way, Chin had succeeded in shielding the bank from Sarit. The move, however, forced Chin into exile to escape from Sarit's anger. Chin moved to Hong Kong, where he began grooming his sons, Robin Chan and Chatri Sophonpanich, to take over his banking empire.

Chin's exile enabled him to consolidate the Teochew financial circuit around Commercial Bank and Bangkok Bank. Chin himself became one of the wealthiest of the Chinese diaspora, and one of the most powerful members of the Teochew community. Chin's time in exile also gave him the opportunity to study Western banking in depth, later applying what he learned to transform Bangkok Bank into Thailand's largest commercial bank.

Following Sarit's death in 1963, Chin returned to Thailand, taking up his position as Bangkok Bank's

KEY DATES

1944: Bangkok Bank is established, with Chin Sophonpanich as a director.
1951: Chin gains management control of the bank.
1954: Bangkok Bank opens its first overseas office, in Hong Kong.
1980: Chin's son, Chatri Sophonpanich, becomes bank president.
1996: Bangkok Bank opens its first branch in China.
2009: Bank's Chinese operations receive full bank status.
2011: Bangkok Bank establishes THB 5 billion relief fund for Thai flooding victims.

president once again. Praphat remained the bank's chairman, and Chin's business partner. In this way, Bangkok Bank benefited from Chin's financial genius and Praphat's political connections through the 1970s.

NEXT GENERATION IN 1980

Chin turned over the presidency to Boonchu Rojanasatien in 1977. Rojanasatien set out a modernization program for the bank, but left the bank to become Thailand's deputy prime minister in 1980. Chatri Sophonpanich took over as bank president, and gained full control over the bank after his father's death in 1988. Chatri, born in 1934, remained as president of the bank until 1992, leading the bank through what became known as its "golden years." Under Chatri, Bangkok Bank grew to become not only Thailand's largest bank, but the country's largest corporation. Bangkok Bank also claimed a spot among the world's top 200 banks during this time. More importantly, as the bank's net profits topped THB 10 billion, the bank was named one of the world's five most profitable banks in 1993.

Chatri Sophonpanich stepped down as president in 1992, and the bank once again brought in a nonfamily member as its president. In 1994, however, Chatri's oldest son, Chartsiri Sophonpanich, took over as bank president. Under Chatri as chairman and Chartsiri as president, Bangkok Bank continued to grow, building its total assets from $20.6 billion in the early 1990s to $41.4 billion (twice those of its next-largest competitor, Thai Farmers Bank) in 1996. Bangkok Bank alone represented approximately 25 percent of the entire Thai commercial banking sector, and was its most profitable, posting net profits of nearly $789 million in 2006.

Nonetheless, Bangkok Bank faced new pressures in the decade. For one, the liberalization of the Thai banking sector in 1992 saw a wave of new competitors. As a result, Bangkok Bank's market share slipped from 30 percent at the end of the 1980s to just 21 percent during the second half of the 1990s. The company also faced increased competition from Thai Farmers, which launched an ambitious expansion program during the decade. In response, Bangkok Bank launched its own $150 million investment program, designed to upgrade its branch offices and equipment, as well as expand its network of ATMs.

SURVIVING THE BAHT CRISIS IN 1997

Bangkok Bank also expanded its foreign operations, building out its international branch network to 22 offices, including in New York, while creating a full-fledged banking subsidiary for its Malaysian operations. In March 1996, the company also entered China for the first time, opening an office in Swatow, as a symbolic nod to the bank's Teochew roots.

This foreign expansion played a role in enabling Bangkok Bank to survive the economic crisis that swept through Thailand and much of the Asian region in 1997. While much of the Thai banking sector collapsed amid the devaluation of the baht, Bangkok Bank's traditionally conservative lending portfolio helped to shield the bank from the worst of the crisis. Nonetheless, Bangkok Bank struggled through the end of the decade, turning to the foreign investment community to shore up its capital base. This meant that the share of foreign ownership in the bank rose from 25 percent before the crisis to nearly 49 percent by the end of 1999. During this time, Singapore Investment Corporation became a major shareholder.

Despite the change in shareholding, the Sophonpanich family maintained management control of the bank. The bank instituted a number of changes designed to strengthen the group's financial foundation. The company worked at reducing its nonperforming loan portfolio. At the same time, the bank carried out a streamlining of its employee base, which dropped from a high of 26,500 in 1997 to just 18,000 by the end of 2002.

The bank also set out to broaden its customer base. Bangkok Bank had traditionally focused on the corporate and SME banking sector. With the start of the new century, the company began an effort to attract private retail customers as well, launching a number of new customer service initiatives. Among these was the group's online banking site in 2002. The company also continued expanding its branch network, which reached 600 offices in 2005, and climbed to 1,000 into the next decade. At the same time, Bangkok Bank invested heavily in building its ATM network, reaching a total of 7,600 ATMs and cash-deposit machines by 2011.

FULL BANK STATUS IN CHINA IN 2011

These efforts helped boost the bank's total accounts from 10 million at the beginning of the decade to 17 million into 2011. The company's total assets also grew strongly, topping THB 1.72 trillion ($64.83 billion). During the decade, Bangkok Bank rolled out a number of new services, including securities broking and private banking and bancassurance products.

Bangkok Bank also refocused its foreign operations during the decade, exiting a number of markets, including Cambodia, and reducing its international branch office network to just 13 offices. Instead, the bank fixed its attention on building up its operations in mainland China. In 2009, the bank received a license from the Chinese government enabling its Thai operations to act as a yuan clearinghouse. The company also received a license to convert its four Chinese branch offices to full bank status, grouped under a new, China-incorporated subsidiary, Bangkok Bank (China) Company. This bank, which started with a capital of $585.5 million, opened its first office in Shanghai in December 2009. Soon after, Bangkok Bank launched its own credit card in China, in partnership with that country's leading credit card group, China UnionPay.

Through 2011, Bangkok Bank renewed its focus on the Thai retail banking sector, particularly its credit card and home loan business. The company hoped to add as many as 450,000 new customers in 2011 to its existing credit card base of 1.6 million. At the same time, the bank sought to expand its home loan portfolio by 50 percent per year. The company expected to raise the share of retail banking in its overall operations from 17 percent.

Throughout its history, Bangkok Bank had played a central role in underpinning Thailand's industrial and economic growth. This position was underscored when, after the country was struck by unprecedented floods in late 2011, the company joined in the relief effort, setting aside THB 5 billion in loans to the companies in the flooded areas in November 2011. After nearly 70 years, the bank remained a centerpiece of the Thai commercial banking industry.

M. L. Cohen

PRINCIPAL SUBSIDIARIES

Bangkok Bank (China) Company Limited; Bangkok Bank Berhad (Malaysia); BBL Asset Management Co., Ltd.; Bualuang Securities Public Company Limited; Sinsuptawee Asset Management Co., Ltd.

PRINCIPAL DIVISIONS

Commercial; Small Business; Consumer; International Banking; Treasury; SAM/Recovery; Investment Banking.

PRINCIPAL COMPETITORS

Bank of Ayudhya PCL; Kasikornbank PCL; Krung Thai Bank PCL; Siam City Bank Public Company Ltd.; Siam Commercial Bank PCL; Thanachart Bank PCL; TMB Bank PCL.

FURTHER READING

"Bangkok Bank Contributes Baht 5 Million to Establishment of Flood Relief Fund by Thai Listed Companies Association." *ENP Newswire*, November 4, 2011.

"Bangkok Bank Given a Jolt." *Nation*, October 14, 2011.

"Bangkok Bank Joins Another Japan Partner." *Nation*, September 14, 2011.

"Bangkok Bank Reports Fiscal Results." *Global Banking News*, October 20, 2011.

"Bangkok Bank Targets Retail Clients." *Nation*, May 18, 2011.

"Bangkok Bank's Chinese Branches Upgraded to Local Banks Status." *Global Banking News*, December 29, 2009.

"BBL Poised for Strong Lending Growth." *Nation*, July 4, 2011.

Chua, Jean, and Steven Gwynn-Jones. "Growth Expected to Stall at Thai Bank." *International Herald Tribune*, June 29, 2007, 12.

Gearing, Julian. "Autumn of the Patriarch." *Asiaweek*, June 7, 1996.

Montlake, Simon. "Thai Banks Shine Bright." *Banker*, February 1, 2011.

Robinson, Karina. "Revving the Profit Engines." *Banker*, December 2002.

Seagrave, Sterling. *Lords of the Rim: The Invisible Empire of the Oversea Chinese.* New York: G.P. Putnam's Son, 1995.

BCE Inc.

—————————————————■—————————————————

1, Carrefour Alexander Graham Bell, Building A
Verdun, Quebec H3E 3B3
Canada
Telephone: (514) 786-8424
Toll Free: (888) 932-6666
Fax: (514) 766-5735
Web site: http://www.bce.ca

Public Company
Incorporated: 1880 as Bell Telephone Company of
   Canada
Employees: 50,200
Sales: CAD 18.07 billion (2010)
Stock Exchanges: Toronto New York
Ticker Symbol: BCE
NAICS: 517210 Wireless Telecommunications Carriers
   (Except Satellite); 517110 Wired Telecommunica-
   tions Carriers; 517919 All Other Telecommunica-
   tions; 515120 Television Broadcasting

■ ■ ■

BCE Inc. is the largest communications company in
Canada. The company, operating under the Bell and
Bell Aliant brand names, provides a range of communications services to Canadian residential and business customers. BCE offers local and long-distance communications and data services, wireless digital voice and
Internet services, and mobile-TV service with access to
live and on-demand content. The company's Bell Media
unit is Canada's leading multimedia company and has
assets that include the country's number one television

network CTV, radio, digital media, and the country's
most popular specialty TV channels.

EARLY HISTORY

The history of BCE Inc. can be traced to Canada native
Alexander Graham Bell and his early communications
experiments, which eventually led to the formation of
Bell Telephone Company of Canada. Chartered by the
Canadian Parliament on April 29, 1880, the company,
known informally as Bell Canada, spent the next 100-
plus years growing and diversifying into one of Canada's
largest and most successful organizations. In fact, by
1983, Bell Canada could be described as both a
telecommunications company and a holding company,
with controlling interests in more than 80 other
organizations. In 1983 a new parent company, Bell
Canada Enterprises Inc. (BCE), was created.

The Canadian phone company's history began in
the late 1870s, when Canada's first telephone exchange
opened in 1878 in Hamilton, Ontario. Next came a
Toronto exchange in 1879. By 1881 the company had
exchanges in 40 cities. By 1890 the firm was offering
long-distance service over 3,670 miles. From early on,
the firm used the slogan, "A telephone business run by
Canadians for Canadians."

Initially, telephone service was offered only during
business hours to about 2,100 telephones. Business
owners could use the service by buying pairs of instruments to communicate from home to office, from office
to factory, or between other pairs of locations. To
expand service, the company in 1890 began offering
evening and Sunday service. Although U.S.-based

American Telephone and Telegraph Company (AT&T) owned 48 percent of Bell Canada's stock in 1890, Canadians began buying more of that stock as the company grew. Bell Canada in 1895 incorporated its manufacturing arm, Northern Electric & Manufacturing Company Limited, which was partially owned by AT&T's Western Electric.

By 1925 the company was well on its way to living up to its motto, as Canadians owned 94.5 percent of its stock. The late 1920s saw several advances, including a phone service that linked Canada to Britain via the United States; a carrier system; and, in 1931, the formation of the TransCanada Telephone System. The following year the system made possible the first long-distance call from Montreal to Vancouver via an all-Canadian route. In 1933 the U.S. federal securities act ended AT&T's right to purchase new shares.

EXPANSION: FIFTIES THROUGH SEVENTIES

During the Great Depression, the need for telephone service dropped substantially. Operators worked about half the hours they had put in previously, only three days per week. When World War II began, all operators were summoned back to long weeks of work. Following the war, in 1945, Bell Canada installed its one millionth phone. Bell Canada in 1954 merged two subsidiaries, Eastern Townships Telephone Company and Chapleau Telephone System. In 1956, the company merged with Kamouraska Telephone Company and expanded again in 1957 when it acquired Mount Albert Telephone Company Ltd. That same year Bell Canada acquired most of Western Electric's share of Northern Electric, which Western held through a subsidiary, Weco Corporation. In 1964 it bought the remainder. By 1958 customers in Canada and the United States could dial other telephone users directly without going through an operator.

Bell Canada acquired Madawaska Telephone Company in 1960. It gained control in 1962 of Avalon Telephone Company Ltd., which would later be known as Newfoundland Telephone Company Ltd. The follow-

ing year, Bell Canada bought Monk Rural Telephone Company, changing its name to Capital Telephone Company Ltd. in 1966. That same year Bell Canada gained a new general counsel, A. Jean de Grandpre, a lawyer with two decades of private-practice experience who would soon become a major leader in the company's growth and diversification. Under his leadership, the firm grew rapidly through capital expansion and acquisition. In 1970, for example, the firm acquired control of Oxford Telephone Company Ltd. and Caradoc Ekfrid Telephone Company Ltd., as well as an interest in Telesat Canada, a communications satellite operation that in 1972 launched Canada's first commercial communications satellite. During the early 1970s, Bell-Northern Research Ltd. was established to consolidate the research and development efforts of Northern Electric and Bell Canada. By 1973 de Grandpre had risen to the post of president of Bell Canada before being named chairman and chief executive officer three years later.

Bell Canada in 1973 sold a portion of Northern Electric to the public. In 1976 Northern Electric changed its name to Northern Telecom Limited. Bell Canada in 1976 created Bell Canada International Management, Research and Consulting Ltd. (BCI). The firm, which succeeded Bell's Consulting Services Group founded in the mid-1960s, was designed to offer expertise in telecommunications management and technical planning. The Ottawa-based BCI's clients included common carriers, private corporations, defense companies, contractors, manufacturers, other consultants, and Northern Telecom. In addition, the firm had business dealings across the globe, in Africa, the Middle East, Europe, the Caribbean, South America, and the United States, transferring technology to other nations in the process.

In addition, Northern Telecom and Bell Canada formed B-N Software Research Inc. for the research and development of new software. Late in 1978 Bell Canada introduced a fiber-optic system developed by Northern Telecom Ltd. Designed to simultaneously transmit telephony, data, and video, the company introduced the revolutionary new system during a video telephone conference call between Toronto and London. In 1981 the software firm was merged into Bell-Northern Research.

FORMATION OF BELL CANADA ENTERPRISES INC.

By 1982 Bell Canada controlled nearly 80 other companies. Switching control of the organizations, including that of Bell Canada, to a new parent company would simplify the business, de Grandpre believed.

KEY DATES

1880: Bell Telephone Company of Canada (Bell Canada) is established.

1983: Bell Canada Enterprises Inc. (BCE) is created to act as a holding company for Bell Canada and its subsidiaries.

1997: Jean C. Monty is named chief operating officer and president of BCE.

2000: BCE purchases the *Globe and Mail* newspaper and joins its recently acquired print and TV assets with its Sympatico-Lycos portal.

2001: BCE combines its media assets to form Bell Globemedia.

2004–06: BCE sells Emergis, a majority stake in Globemedia, CGI Group, and Telesat.

2011: BCE reacquires all of what was formerly Globemedia, including CTV.

Consequently, in 1983 Bell Canada Enterprises Inc. (BCE Inc.) was created to act as a holding company for a corporate family whose assets amounted to $15 billion and included Bell Canada itself. By designating most of the company's businesses as separate BCE subsidiaries, Bell Canada was the only company that remained under the regulatory control of the Canadian Radio-Television and Telecommunications Commission (CRTC).

In addition to leadership and coordination, BCE provided equity investments to further the development of its various businesses and to finance their growth via new products, markets, internal growth, or acquisitions. BCE in 1983 acquired a sizable percentage of TransCanada PipeLines Ltd. (TCPL), a move described in BCE's 1983 annual report as "a significant commitment by BCE to western Canada and to the resource sector of the Canadian economy." Although Radcliffe Latimer, president of TCPL and a personal friend of de Grandpre, cautioned shareholders to ignore BCE's offer of $31.50 per share, BCE still managed to swiftly take over 42 percent of the company.

BCE's operations by 1984 included Bell Canada and several other locally regulated telecommunications operations: Northern Telecom Limited, a telecommunications manufacturer; Bell-Northern Research Ltd., owned by Bell Canada and Northern Telecom Ltd.; Bell Canada International Inc., a consulting firm; Bell Communications Systems Inc.; TCPL; Tele-Direct (Publications) Inc., owned by Bell Canada; and Tele-Direct (Canada) Inc.

AGGRESSIVE EXPANSION LEADS TO DIVESTITURE

BCE's growth spurt continued throughout the 1980s. In fact, corporate assets jumped from CAD 14.8 billion in 1983 to CAD 39.3 billion in 1989. There were investments in energy, real estate, printing and packaging, mobile and cellular communications, and financial services. BCE became the first Canadian corporation to earn a net income of more than CAD 1 billion. Despite that success, however, other aspects of BCE's business did not fare as well. One such failure was the firm's venture into real estate in 1985 through BCE Development Corporation, a new subsidiary. The company's experiments with printing and with oil and gas investments also brought poor reviews from shareholders.

During the second half of the 1980s, BCE had several conflicts with the CRTC. The company, for example, was the subject of a six-week, 1986 CRTC hearing held to examine Bell Canada's profits from 1985 through 1987. As a result, the CRTC ordered Bell Canada to refund to consumers CAD 206 million worth of excess payments. In addition, the commission forced the company to decrease its projected profits for 1987 in the amount of CAD 234 million by lowering long-distance rates in Ontario and Quebec by nearly 20 percent.

In 1989 de Grandpre retired as chairman but remained on the board of directors as founding director and chairman emeritus. J. V. Raymond Cyr, who had been chief executive officer of BCE since May 1988, assumed the additional post of chairman. Jean C. Monty was named the new Bell Canada president.

To restore stockholder faith, company leaders decided to review BCE's portfolio of businesses. They determined that telecommunications would naturally remain BCE's core business, but the firm's involvement in real estate was dissolved. Six years after taking control of TCPL, which BCE viewed as a solid, long-term investment, the company sold its stake in the energy business, which was not consistent with BCE's core businesses. BCE chose to concentrate on telecommunications and financial services and acquired the well-established Montreal Trustco Inc. It was, however, Bell Canada that brought the most revenue to the parent company. With a record year in 1989, Bell Canada contributed CAD 2.75 per share to BCE's 1989 earnings. In addition, BCE stock continued to be the most widely held stock in Canada, consistently viewed as a good investment, a stock for "widows and orphans."

REDUCED SCOPE OF BUSINESS: 1990–95

By the early 1990s, BCE owned subsidiaries operating in three primary areas: telecommunications services, telecommunications equipment manufacturing, and financial services. Although these subsidiaries made crucial contributions to the success of BCE, many were successful enough to develop recognized reputations of their own. Bell Canada, the country's largest telecommunications company, provided most of the firm's services in that area; Northern Telecom Limited was responsible for the manufacturing end of the business and was the second-largest such company in North America. BellNorthern Research, the largest private industrial research and development organization in the country, also played a vital role in BCE's research and development activities, while financial services were provided by Montreal Trust.

Following BCE's 1983 restructuring, the company began to face increasing competition, especially in the 1990s when the telecommunications industry gained several new entrants. In fact, BCE's earnings in the early 1990s were less than spectacular. They fell dramatically from CAD 1.2 billion in 1994 to CAD 782 million in 1995. Bell Canada, responsible for nearly 50 percent of the company's earnings at the time, faced increased competition due to deregulation in the long-distance phone industry. Its market share fell by nearly 22 percent in 1994, as companies, including Sprint Canada Inc. and Unitel Communications Inc., entered the fray, vying for a piece of the Canadian long-distance market.

At the same time, Northern Telecom (renamed Nortel in 1995) also faced expanding competition. This was especially true in foreign markets where Nortel hoped to boost sales related to wireless operations. The firm was known, however, for its central switches, a market that reached maturity in the late 1980s. As Nortel faced an uphill battle in trying to break into the foreign wireless technologies sector, most of BCE's other businesses likewise battled for market share in their fields.

CHANGES IN FOCUS, MANAGEMENT, AND COMPETITION: LATE NINETIES

In 1996 Rob Osborne, an executive from Maclean Hunter who had joined BCE in 1994, was named BCE president. Under his leadership and that of CEO and new Chairman Lynton Wilson, BCE began a turnaround, recording CAD 1.15 billion in profits in 1996, a substantial increase over 1995. In fact, a 1997

Canadian Business article claimed that BCE had been "overweight, unfocused, and slow to budge" during the late 1980s and early 1990s, but that, "spurred by new competition, the obese giant has pulled off an amazing transformation."

While it cleaned up its image and shed businesses unrelated to its telecommunications focus, BCE also underwent a series of management changes. In 1997 Monty, CEO of Nortel credited for its rebirth in the 1990s, was named chief operating officer and president of BCE. A proponent of a convergence strategy, combining multiple content services from disparate mediums delivered through telecommunications lines, Monty assumed the CEO title the next year. Osborne moved over to head Bell Canada. In February 1998 Osborne resigned unexpectedly from Bell to take over operations at Ontario Hydro and was replaced by John A. MacDonald, a former BCE chief technology officer.

Amid the management reshuffling, the CRTC decided in 1997 to allow phone companies to enter the cable-TV market, opening up a potentially lucrative market for BCE. In turn, cable firms could enter the local-calling markets. During this period, the landscape of the telecommunications industry as a whole began to change dramatically due to consolidation and merger activity. Deals including Worldcom Inc.'s purchase of MCI Communications Corp. and Teleport Communications Group Inc.'s acquisition of ACC Corp. threatened Bell Canada's hold on the local-calling market in Canada.

BCE deployed plans during the late 1980s to develop Internet and e-commerce businesses. In 1998 the company created Bell Nexxia, a national broadband company, and BCE Emergis, an e-commerce business focused on the insurance, health care, and financial fields. Meanwhile, Nortel acquired Broadband Networks Inc., a leading manufacturer of fixed broadband wireless communications networks. It also purchased a leading Internet service provider (ISP) networking firm, Bay Networks, in 1998, changing its name to Nortel Networks after the purchase. In line with a convergence strategy, BCE then created the ISP and portal Sympatico.ca.

In order to gain a stronger foothold in North American markets, BCE sold a 20 percent stake in Bell Canada to Ameritech in 1999, and Bell Mobile Communications Inc. was renamed Bell Mobility and became a wholly owned Bell Canada subsidiary. That same year BCE organized a merger of four Atlantic incumbent local-exchange carriers (ILECs) to create AtlanticCo, in which BCE owned 41.6 percent.

DEPLOYMENT OF CONVERGENCE
STRATEGY: 2000–03

In 2000 Monty assumed the additional title of chairman, and Michael J. Sabia became president. Following the much heralded merger between the publisher Time Warner and AOL, BCE attempted its own version of convergence of mass media, bringing together Internet hosting, telecommunications connectivity, and content distribution. In 2000 BCE purchased 77 percent of the U.S.-based global Internet and data-services provider Teleglobe that it did not already own.

That same year the company acquired Canada's largest privately controlled television network, CTV, and formed a joint-venture Internet company with Lycos, Inc. The new business, Sympatico-Lycos, joined the Internet portals of the two companies and provided Canadians a major portal from which to access e-mail and conduct Web searches. As part of the BCE-Lycos deal, Bell Canada invested CAD 37 million ($25 million) in the venture, in which BCE took a majority stake. Further expanding its media empire, BCE purchased the nationally distributed Toronto-based *Globe and Mail* newspaper and joined its recently acquired print and TV assets with its Sympatico-Lycos portal.

To advance its convergence strategy, the company in 2000 began a three-year, $1.5 billion investment in expanding high-speed Internet access. Bell Mobility that year launched a $100 million expansion of its digital network in Quebec and Ontario and began serving western Canada. In addition, BCE in 2000 spun off its 94 percent stake in Nortel through a share distribution to its stockholders. In January 2001 BCE combined its media assets and garnered an investment from The Thomson Corporation to form Bell Globemedia, owning CTV, the *Globe and Mail*, the sports network TSN, and other assets, and representing the largest media company in Canada with annual sales of about CAD 1.25 billion ($827 million).

In 2001 Bell Mobility forged a pact with Nortel to expand digital cellular services into the provinces of Alberta and British Columbia. Bell Mobility also joined with other Canadian mobile operators to begin offering texting services. BCE announced plans to roll out a ComboBox, or set-top box, that would allow users to interact with their TVs like a computer. The company's Bell ExpressVu division also debuted Canada's first interactive game channel. Bell ExpressVu teamed with European firm Visiware to launch the channel Ludi TV, available to direct-broadcast subscribers using the company's set-top boxes.

In May 2002 Monty resigned after continuing declines in earnings and signs his convergence strategy was not working. Sabia, president of BCE, was named to the additional post of CEO. Sabia reoriented BCE to focus on traditional telecommunications operations. The company that year staged a stock offering, raising CAD 1.53 billion ($99.3 million) in order to reacquire the 20 percent stake in Bell Canada it earlier sold to SBC Communications. BCE also sold Teleglobe and its phone directory business and sold back the Sympatico-Lycos portal to Bell Globemedia. In 2002 BCE launched Canada's first wireless network for data in Toronto and later expanded the service to other major Canadian cities. The launch was part of BCE's first-phase rollout of a 3G wireless network. Bell Canada meanwhile teamed with Manitoba Telecom Services Inc. to jointly provide Alberta and British Columbia businesses with wire-line phone and data services as part of its expansion in western Canada.

In 2003 Bell Canada began expanding DSL services in Quebec and Ontario. BCE formally ended its convergence strategy in February 2003. The company reacquired complete control of its internal Internet portal Sympatico.ca and transferred the business from Globemedia to Bell Canada and reduced its ownership in Globemedia. BCE then reintegrated Globemedia's Web-based products into different BCE-owned companies.

By the close of 2003, BCE had four primary business units: Bell Canada, generating more than 85 percent of company revenues; its stake in Globemedia, responsible for 7 percent of sales; BCE Ventures, which included the information technology services business CGI and the satellite systems company Telesat that generated about 6 percent of revenues; and BCE Emergis, the electronic business services provider, which accounted for 2 percent of sales.

DIVESTITURES AND WESTERN
CANADA EXPANSION: 2004–08

In 2004 Bell Mobility expanded into northern British Columbia and Yukon, in the process providing northern Canadian customers with texting services for the first time. That same year, BCE acquired the 40 percent of Bell West that it did not own as part of its strategy to continue growing its services in western Canada. BCE also sold Emergis. In 2005, the company began delivering high-speed Internet to more than 400 rural Alberta towns. BCE also launched 3G service there.

In December 2005 BCE sold a 48.5 percent interest in Bell Globemedia, reducing the company's stake to 20 percent, and sold its 29.9 percent share of CGI Group. The two divestitures netted the firm more than CAD 2.3 billion. BCE in 2006 sold its entire satellite business, Telesat Canada, for CAD 3.42 billion ($2.96 billion). The sales were part of Sabia's strategy of reducing BCE's holdings to what were considered core assets and placed the company in a position to be debt free. In 2006 BCE announced it would reorganize the company, eliminating its holding company structure, and convert its assets to an income trust, named Bell Canada Income Fund. The Canadian crown, however, passed new taxation laws in late 2006, and the company backed away from its plans to become a trust in December. Bell Canada joined with Aliant to create a business that combined Aliant's wireless and information technologies on Canada's Atlantic Coast with BCE's wire-line operations in Ontario and Quebec, establishing Bell Aliant Regional Telecommunications Income Fund.

In 2007 BCE became a prime acquisition target. In June its board approved a bid from a group led by the Ontario Teachers' Pension Plan, in what would have been the largest Canadian acquisition ever. A lengthy court process followed, during which time the Quebec Superior Court blocked the acquisition and the Superior Court of Canada overturned the provincial ruling. With the deal appearing certain, Sabia announced he was leaving the company and was replaced in mid-2008 as CEO by George Cope, who had become BCE president two years earlier after serving as Bell Canada president. In late November 2008, however, the solvency of BCE was called into question, and the acquisition was nixed. That same year, the company moved its corporate headquarters from its 80-year-old home in Montreal to Quebec.

CONVERGENCE 2.0

Bell Mobility in 2009 launched what it billed as the world's most advanced broadband network. In 2010 the company also began testing an LTE network, a next-generation 4G wireless network. For consumers to take advantage of the company's network enhancements, BCE offered consumers a variety of new smartphones and gaming turbo sticks. In September 2010 BCE announced it would again remake itself as a vertically integrated media company by reacquiring 100 percent of Canada's largest television broadcast operation, the CTV Television Network, for CAD 1.3 billion, as well as all of what had been Globemedia. The acquisition included full ownership of CTV and 33 affiliates; 33 radio stations; and several Web sites, including Sympatico.ca; as well as a stake in 30 specialty channels, including the Comedy Network and Discovery Channel; and 15 percent of the *Globe and Mail*, with Thomson owning 85 percent of the newspaper.

The purchase was designed to place BCE in a position to take advantage of new and evolving methods of

distributing content through Internet and wireless networks. It also prevented BCE's major cable competitors Quebecor and Rogers from dominating Canadian cable ownership.

In line with its re-embracing of convergence, BCE was selected as exclusive telecommunications provider for the 2010 Vancouver Olympics. The company became the first telecommunications partner of the Olympics to develop both wire-line and wireless connectivity to the games, constructing more than 620 miles of cable linking games sites and technical support centers. This included more than 185 miles of high-speed broadband fiber that connected Vancouver to the mountain resort of Whistler. That same year BCE launched a three-year program to develop fiber-to-the-home in Quebec and Ontario. The expensive type of fiber-optic cable replaced standard copper wire and provided broadband integration of voice data, video, and other services.

In March 2011 the CRTC approved BCE's mega-acquisition featuring CTV and other assets, and BCE formed the new company Bell Media, which became a wholly owned BCE subsidiary and owner of the media properties acquired. In looking beyond 2011, BCE planned to increase TV program availability on tablet computers and smartphones in order to connect to and draw in more viewers. The company planned to further invest in its high-speed broadband network to make digital video and additional content available through television, Web, tablet computer, and smartphone mediums. BCE anticipated having 15 million customers by 2015 using at least one of these mediums to view its programs.

Kim M. Magon
Updated, Christina M. Stansell; Roger Rouland

PRINCIPAL SUBSIDIARIES

Bell Aliant (44%); Bell Canada; Bell Canada Holdings Inc.; Bell Media Inc.; Bell Mobility; Virgin Mobile Canada.

PRINCIPAL COMPETITORS

Cogeco Cable Inc.; Quebecor Inc.; Rogers Cable Communications Inc.; Shaw Communications Inc.; TELUS Corporation.

FURTHER READING

"BCE Replaces CEO, Limits Teleglobe Support." *Communications Today*, April 25, 2002.

"BCE Selling Stake in CGI Group." *CBC News*, December 16, 2005. Accessed November 29, 2011. http://www.cbc.ca/news/business/story/2005/12/16/cgi-051216.html.

"BCE Sells Major Stake in Bell Globemedia to Torstar, Teachers'." *CBC News*, December 2, 2005. Accessed November 29, 2011. http://www.cbc.ca/news/business/story/2005/12/02/bellglobe-051202.html.

Chipello, Christopher J. "Of Its Stake in Bell Globemedia." *Wall Street Journal Online*, December 3, 2005. Accessed November 29, 2011. http://www.marketwatch.com/story/bce-sells-stake-in-media-unit-2005-12-03.

DeCloet, Derek. "The New Convergence: A Lot Like the Old Version but Much, Much Cheaper." *Globe and Mail*, September 10, 2010.

"Hollowing Out? The Bell Canada Takeover; The World's Biggest Private-Equity Deal." *Global Agenda*, July 2, 2007.

Kelly, Brendan. "Canuck Conglom BCE Retools Web Strategy." *Daily Variety*, February 10, 2003, 9.

Kilgore, Tomi. "BCE Sells Telesat Canada Sub for C$3.42 Billion." *Wall Street Journal Online*, December 18, 2006. Accessed November 30, 2011. http://www.marketwatch.com/story/bce-sells-telesat-canada-sub-for-c342-billion.

Kirby, Jason. "How to Squander a $52-Billion Empire: The Michael Sabia Story." *Maclean's*, July 23, 2007, 40+.

LaSalle, LuAnn. "BCE Creates Bell Media after Completing $3.2B Acquisition of CTV." *Canadian Press*, April 1, 2011. Accessed November 30, 2011. http://www.therecord.com/news/business/article/510550—bce-creates-bell-media-after-completing-3-2b-acquisition-of-ctv.

McNish, Jacquie, and Paul Waldie. "Olympic Moment Turned Bell CEO into Champion for Mobile Media." *Globe and Mail*, September 11, 2010.

"Media Convergence, Acquisitions and Sales in Canada." *CBC News*, April 30, 2010. Accessed November 29, 2011. http://www.cbc.ca/news/business/story/2010/04/29/f-media-ownership-canada.html.

Onstad, Katrina. "Chomp!" *Canadian Business*, May 1997, 56.

Belle International Holdings Limited

PO Box 2804
George Town,
Cayman Islands
Telephone: (+86 755) 8287-7388
Web site: http://www.belleintl.com

Public Company
Founded: 1981 as Lai Wah Footwear Trading Limited
Employees: 87,619
Sales: RMB 23.71 billion ($3.66 billion) (2010)
Stock Exchanges: Hong Kong
Ticker Symbol: 1880
NAICS: 316214 Women's Footwear (Except Athletic)
  Manufacturing

■■■

Belle International Holdings Limited is China's leading retail footwear group, overseeing a network of nearly 13,200 stores in mainland China, and 164 stores in Hong Kong and Macau. Belle International is the leading women's footwear retailer in China. With six of the top 10 women's footwear brands, including leading brand Belle, as well as Teenmix, Tata, Staccato, Senda, and Basto, Belle International commands nearly one-fourth of the total market. Other company brands include Joy & Peace, Mirabell, Millie's, and Jipi Japa. Belle International also holds the Chinese license for a number of international brands, including Bata, Geox, Mephisto, and Caterpillar. In addition, the company also holds the retail license for such international sports footwear and sportswear brands as adidas, Nike, Converse, Puma, and Reebok, and is also a licensed retailer for leading Chinese sports brand Li-ning.

Belle International is also a vertically integrated footwear manufacturer, providing the product design and development, procurement, manufacturing, and distribution support for its own brands. The company operates from five factories in the provinces of Shenzhen, Dongguan, Jiangsu, Hubei, and Anhui, with a total annual production capacity topping 25 million pairs of shoes in 2011. Belle International is listed on the Hong Kong Stock Exchange and was admitted to the exchange's Hang Seng Index in September 2010. The founding Tang family, led by group Chairman Tang Yiu, holds more than 31 percent of the company. After Tang suffered a stroke in 2011, CEO and cofounder Sheng Bai Jiao took over as acting chairman.

HONG KONG TRADER IN 1981

Belle International originated as a small trading company focused on footwear founded in 1981 as Lai Wah Footwear Trading Limited. The driving force behind this business was Tang Yiu, who was then 46 years old. Despite his relatively late start in footwear, Tang soon became a major figure in the Hong Kong market. Tang's early success earned him a position as chairman of Federation of Hong Kong Footwear Ltd.

Hong Kong's relatively small size, and the impending handover of control of the island to the Chinese mainland government, led Tang to broaden his company's horizons. Tang targeted two complementary directions. The first of these was an entry into manufacturing, starting from a production base in Shen-

COMPANY PERSPECTIVES

"A new year is a new beginning, always with risks and uncertainties, yet full of excitement and opportunities. In the past 20 years we experienced great difficulties but also achieved great success, creating a solid foundation for the future. All of us at Belle are determined to stay true to our core values: perseverance, confidence, discipline and devotion. I am confident that the Group will sail steadily and far against all headwinds ahead."—Tang Yiu, chairman

zhen, on the Chinese mainland, with an eye toward developing the company's own footwear brands and retail operations in Hong Kong. At the same time, the company also began preparing to extend its business into the Chinese wholesale footwear market.

In 1991, Tang founded a new company, Shenzhen Belle Footwear Co. Ltd. Tang was joined by Sheng Bai Jiao, then 40 years old, who had already gained significant experience in the Chinese footwear and apparel industries. Sheng's experience also included a stint at the China Merchants Shekou Industrial Zone Light & Textile Industries Development Company. Tang and Sheng made preparations for opening the company's first manufacturing facility. This was placed under a separate company, Lai Kong Footwear (Shenzhen) Co., Ltd., established in 1994.

RETAIL BRANDS IN 1998

Belle Footwear's production included custom-made footwear but focused especially on developing its own branded lines of footwear for the Chinese and Hong Kong wholesale markets. The company's Belle brand quickly became popular on the mainland, and continued to play the role of company flagship. By 1997, the Belle brand claimed the leading spot among the top women's footwear brands in China. The success of the brand encouraged Belle to begin planning an entry into the retail sector, as early as 1997.

Chinese legislation at the time, however, barred foreign corporations from operating in the country's retail sector. Instead, Belle began developing a network of third-party distributors to reach the mainland market. This network included 10 distribution groups, which in turn represented 16 individual distribution companies, each operating in a different region of China. These distributors appeared to have been controlled by relatives of both Sheng and Tang.

The company's distributors were granted exclusive distribution rights to Belle products in their regions. The distributors became responsible for building a retail network for Belle's products. By the early 2000s, the distributors had already opened more than 600 stores.

In the meantime, Belle also built up its own directly controlled retail operations. For this, the company initially targeted the Hong Kong market, establishing a new retail brand, Staccato Footwear Company Ltd., in 1998. This business later extended into the Macau market in 2003, then opened its first stores in the United States in 2004.

MAINLAND RETAILER IN 2002

Belle continued developing its brand lineup. The company launched a new women's footwear brand for the Chinese market, Teenmix, in 1999. This brand quickly grew into another favorite, and into the next decade became the second-highest-selling women's footwear brand in China, behind the Belle brand. In 2002, Belle's brand effort found new success, with the introduction of its Tata brand. This brand soon caught up to Teenmix, sharing the number two position among top-selling women's shoe brands in China.

China's entry into the World Trade Organization during the decade led to changes in the country's foreign investment rules, particularly in the relaxation of the rules barring foreign corporations from establishing retail operations. Belle now became eligible to build its own directly controlled retail business in China. In preparation for these changes, the company's individual distributors were brought together under a single entity, Shenzhen Belle Investment Company Ltd., in 2002. When the new rules came into effect in April 2004, Belle began the process of absorbing Belle Investment's operations. This involved the establishment of a company registered in the British Virgin Islands, which acquired 90 percent of Belle Investment. In August 2005, Belle terminated its distribution agreement with Belle Investment, taking direct control of its retail operations, which then counted more than 1,900 stores. The following year, the company also took over Belle Investment's retail sportswear operations.

These were shortly to commence a major expansion. Starting in September 2005, the company opened nearly 1,100 new footwear stores in mainland China through the end of 2006. The company also boosted its position in the retail sportswear market, opening nearly 325 sportswear stores during the period as well. By December 2006, the company had doubled its total retail base, to more than 3,800 stores, including nearly 730 sportswear outlets.

KEY DATES

1981: Tang Yiu founds Lai Wah Footwear Trading Limited in Hong Kong.

1991: Tang founds Shenzhen Belle Footwear in mainland China.

1998: Company forms the Staccato retail chain in Hong Kong.

2004: Belle begins direct retail operations in mainland China.

2007: Company goes public on the Hong Kong Stock Exchange as Belle International Holdings.

2011: Belle invests in the e-commerce sector; Tang suffers a stroke.

IPO SUCCESS IN 2007

Belle's sportswear division made a major leap forward in 2006 when the company acquired the distribution rights to both the Nike and adidas brands on the Chinese mainland. The company quickly became the leading retailer of both brands in China. This extension of the group's sportswear operations also provided Belle with a platform for developing a wider portfolio of licensed brands. In this way, the company positioned itself to take advantage of the fast-growing consumer market in China, both for Chinese brands as well as for the booming demand for international brands.

By the beginning of 2007, Belle had become China's leading footwear retailer. The Belle brand retained its place atop the women's footwear market. The company's other brands had also performed well, with Teenmix rising to fourth place, Staccato at eighth, and Tat at 10th. The company had also added a number of other brands, including Fato and JipiJapa, as well as the licenses to the Bata and Joy & Peace brands. Belle had also added sales of bags and accessories, as well as men's footwear, to its operations. Belle had also recorded strong revenue growth, with its total sales rising from RMB 870.5 million in 2004 to more than RMB 6.2 billion at the end of 2006.

This growth helped set the stage for the company's initial public offering (IPO). In May 2007, the company listed its shares on the Hong Kong Stock Exchange under the name of Belle International Holdings. The IPO, oversubscribed by some 500 times, became the largest-ever on the Hong Kong exchange, raising $1.1 billion and giving the company a market capitalization of $8.6 billion. Founder Tang's ap-

proximately 34 percent share was then worth nearly $3 billion. Other members of the Tang family had also joined the business, including Tang's daughter Tang Wing Mai, who held a degree in business administration from the University of Texas at Austin, and who had been instrumental in preparing the group's IPO.

MIRABELL ACQUISITION IN 2008

Belle International quickly put its new funds to work. In August 2007, the company reached an agreement to acquire the license to the Fila sportswear brand for markets in China, Hong Kong, and Macau for $48 million. As part of that agreement, the company acquired HK Retail Co., holder of the Fila trademark in Hong Kong. The company then formed a joint venture with Fila Luxembourg, called Full Prospect and held at 85 percent by Belle. The partnership proved short-lived, however, as Belle sold off its stake in Full Prospect in August 2009.

In the meantime, Belle International had made several new acquisitions in order to boost its share of both the mainland Chinese and Hong Kong footwear and sportswear markets. In November 2007, the company bought Ossia International, owner of the Millie's retail footwear brand, for approximately $76 million. Ossia operated 150 stores in Hong Kong, Macau, and mainland China.

Soon after, Belle reached an agreement to acquire five subsidiaries of Jiangsu Senda Group, including the Senda footwear brand. Belle paid more than $215 million for the five companies, which included Jiangsu Senda Footwear Co., Zigui Yongxu Footwear Co., Jiangsu Senda Group Sanxia Footwear Co., Shanghai Basto Footwear Co., and Shanghai Xiweideng International Trading Co. The company completed a second transaction with Jiangsu Senda soon after, paying $75 million for the Shanghai Aurora Footwear Co. and its manufacturing and warehousing capacity.

In 2008, Belle set its sights on acquiring another major rival. In February of that year, the company agreed to pay $215 million for Mirabell International, operator of nearly 350 retail stores. These stores operated under such brand names as Mirabell, Joy & Peace, Inshoesnet, and international brands including Fiorucci and Geox. Mirabell's operations included 207 company-owned stores in mainland China, as well as 133 Joy & Peace franchises, with 105 stores in Hong Kong and 17 stores in Taiwan.

MOVING ONLINE IN 2011

These acquisitions added another 950 stores to the company's retail operations. Belle also continued its own new store opening program, adding more than 1,000 new stores through 2008 alone. By the end of that year, Belle's total retail portfolio numbered more than 6,000 footwear locations and more than 3,100 sportswear stores. In order to fuel this expansion, Belle completed two secondary offerings in 2007 and 2008, raising an additional $775 million. The company also added a new licensed brand, Geox, in 2008, announcing plans to open more than 200 Geox stores in China by the end of the decade.

Belle remained upbeat into 2009, despite the prevailing economic gloom amid the gathering global crisis. The company announced plans to invest RMB 500 million in further expansion and refurbishing of its existing retail network. The group's U.S. operations, however, proved less resilient, leading to the group's exit from that market. Nonetheless, the robust growth of the Chinese market provided the foundation for the company's own expansion. By 2010, Belle had opened its 10,000th store. In that year, the company, which posted revenues of RMB 23.71 billion ($3.66 billion), was admitted to the Hong Kong Stock Exchange's Hang Seng Index.

Belle continued opening new stores, topping 12,000 outlets at the beginning of 2011, then rising again to more than 13,000 by the middle of the year. By then, the company had expanded its retail operations to include all of China's provinces. Belle remained the group's largest brand, with more than 1,500 Belle Stores in 200 cities.

Belle also began seeking out new business horizons. The company dipped its toes into the e-commerce sector in late 2009, launching Topshoes.cn. In April 2011, the company announced plans to team up with online service provider Baidu Inc. to develop an online footwear and apparel shop. Then, in July 2011, the company acquired control of Yougou.com, which was then merged with Topshoes.cn. The company backed these extensions with the construction of a new e-commerce-only warehouse, in Shenzhen. In September 2011, the company announced its intention to invest $200 million in 17ugo.com, a business-to-consumer Web site, into 2014.

Belle International faced a setback when Tang Yiu suffered a stroke in April 2011. While the 75-year-old Tang was expected to recover, cofounder and company CEO Sheng took over as the company's acting chairman. Under Tang and Sheng's leadership, Belle International had grown from a small footwear wholesaler to become China's leading integrated footwear and sportswear company. Belle International hoped to continue this successful record as it moved ahead.

M. L. Cohen

PRINCIPAL SUBSIDIARIES

Artigiano Footwear Limited; Belle Footwear (Hong Kong) Company Limited; Belle Group Limited; Belle International (China) Limited; Belle Worldwide Limited; Bestfull International Limited; Famestep Management Limited; Full Sport Holdings Limited; Full State Corporation Limited; Fullbest Investments Limited; Lai Wah Footwear Trading Limited; Millie's Company Limited; Mirabell International Holdings Limited; Shoesnet Co. Limited.

PRINCIPAL DIVISIONS

Footwear; Sportswear.

PRINCIPAL COMPETITORS

Far East Industrial Stock Company Ltd.; Hongguo International Holdings Ltd.; Jihua Group Corporation Ltd.; Qingdao Doublestar Company Ltd.; Stella International Holdings Ltd.; Zhongshan Xinbao Shoes Company Ltd.

FURTHER READING

Balfour, Frederik. "Shoe Seller Belle Conquers China." *Business Week*, September 5, 2008.

Bei Hu. "Bell's IPO Said to Set Consumer Firm Record." *International Herald Tribune*, May 17, 2007.

"Belle Earnings Up on Spending." *Business Daily Update*, March 25, 2010.

"Belle Eyeing Ecommerce." *SinoCast Daily Business Beat*, September 1, 2011.

"Belle Footwear Billionaire Tang Yiu Hospitalized after Stroke." *Forbes*, April 25, 2011.

"Belle International Offers HK$1.67bn for Mirabell." *just-style. com*, February 29, 2008.

"Belle Int'l to Invest US$200 mln in B2C Website 17ugo. com." *China Knowledge Newswires*, September 6, 2011.

"Belle Set to Expand Footprint." *Standard*, March 25, 2009.

Flannery, Russell. "Belle IPO Makes Tangs Billionaires." *Forbes*, May 23, 2007.

"New Belle to Purchase 5 Companies with CNY1.6bn." *Al-estron*, November 15, 2007.

BlueScope Steel Ltd.

Level 11, 120 Collins Street
Melbourne, VIC 3000
Australia
PO Box 18207, Collins Street E
Melbourne, VIC 8003
Australia
Telephone: (+61 3) 9666-4000
Fax: (+61 3) 9666-4111
Web site: http://www.bluescopesteel.com

Public Company
Founded: 1968
Employees: 18,000
Sales: AUD 10.34 billion ($9.8 billion) (2011)
Stock Exchanges: Australian London New York
Ticker Symbol: BSL
NAICS: 331111 Iron and Steel Mills

∎ ∎ ∎

BlueScope Steel Ltd. is Australia and New Zealand's largest steel company. The Melbourne-based company focuses its steel production on flat steel products, including slab, plate, cold-rolled coil, and hot-rolled coil products. BlueScope is a leading producer of value-added metallic-coated and painted steel products in Australia and New Zealand and throughout the Asian region. The company also produces and distributes steel products in North America through its 50 percent stake in the North Star BlueScope Steel joint venture. The company's brands include Lysaght, Xlerplate, Color-bond, Zinclume, Waterpoint, Butler, Colorbond, Smart-russ, and PED.

BlueScope was spun off from BHP following that company's merger with Billiton in 2001. BlueScope is listed on the Australian, London, and New York stock exchanges. Graham Kraehe is the group's chairman and Paul O'Malley is its managing director and CEO.

STEEL BEGINNINGS IN 1915

BlueScope Steel had its origins in the early years of the 20th century, as Australia's Broken Hill Proprietary (BHP) faced an impending decline in its mining activities. With ready access to coal and to iron ore, BHP decided to extend its operations into steel production. The company opened its first foundry at Newcastle on the New South Wales coast in 1915.

The country's entry into World War I meant that the steelworks operated at full capacity from the start. BHP also supported the growth of homegrown industry, creating a strong domestic customer base for its steel products.

Among these customers was John Lysaght (Australia) Pty., founded in 1918 as a producer of sheet rolling and galvanized steel. Lysaght traced its own origins to an ironworks founded in Bristol, England, by John Lysaght in 1857. Lysaght entered the Australian market in 1880, opening a sales office in Melbourne. By then, Lysaght had already become a major producer of corrugated iron worldwide. Lysaght, acquired by Guest Keen and Nettlefolds (GKN) in 1920, added a second works, called Springhill, in Port Kembla, in 1936, which launched production in 1939.

Lysaght's Port Kembla works came in support of BHP's acquisition of Australian Iron & Steel Company (AIS), its sole competitor in the domestic market, in 1935. BHP continued to expand its steel production through the decade, adding a new steel works and port at Whylla in 1937. By then, BHP's total steel production had topped 500,000 tons. The company was also one of Australia's largest private-sector employers, with a workforce of 10,000.

In support of the run-up to World War II, BHP carried out a major expansion of its Port Kembla works, supporting Lysaght's own expansion as that company diverted parts of its operation to the production of the Owen submachine gun and other products. After opening its Port Kembla works, Lysaght joined with American Rolling Mills Company to create a joint venture, Commonwealth Rolling Mills, also at Port Kembla. This factory initiated production of specialty steels, such as bulletproof plate, and steel for helmets, aircraft, and other military applications. Commonwealth also produced steel products for Australia's automotive and home appliance industries. Lysaght became full owner of the joint venture following World War II.

FLAT PRODUCTS IN 1946

Through AIS, BHP extended its steel operations into the production of flat products, setting up a new division in 1946. The company then launched construction of a new hot strip mill, which began production in 1955, at a cost of £40 million. The new mill boasted a total production capacity of one million tons per year. Lysaght once again joined BHP in this extension, upgrading its own machinery to the new continuous cold reduction process.

The postwar economic boom led BHP to expand AIS again with the addition of a second steel works, featuring an open hearth furnace, starting in 1956. Through the decade, BHP added a sinter plant and a

fourth blast furnace. In 1961 it opened a ferro-alloy factory, based in Bell Bay in Tasmania. At the original Newcastle site, BHP carried out a major upgrade, replacing its open hearth furnace with the more modern Basic Oxygen System (BOS) furnace, in 1962. The company outfitted its Whylla works with a BOS furnace as well, in 1965. This site was also expanded during the decade to include a second blast furnace, as well as a rolling mill.

Lysaght in the meantime had also expanded considerably, adding continuous galvanizing line in Port Kembal in 1961 and opening a number of steel service centers throughout Australia. The company also launched production of special sheet steels, including coated steels for use in the production of fuel tanks and other applications. The Colorbond brand of prepainted steel was introduced in 1966, followed by a line of vinyl coated steel. In 1967, Lysaght began construction of a new, larger sheet steel plant in Western Port, replacing its Newcastle operation. The company also carried out the expansion of its Springhill site.

The relationship between BHP and Lysaght had long been close. In 1969, BHP acquired 50 percent of Lysaght from GKN. Ten years later, BHP acquired full control of Lysaght. The acquisition included a number of new operations, including a hot strip mill built at Lysaght's Western Port plant in 1978. Also during the decade, the company debuted its Zincalume steel brand, a zinc-aluminum alloy with enhanced protection from corrosion, developed in partnership with the United States' Bethlehem Steel.

RESTRUCTURING IN THE EIGHTIES

Despite this growth, BHP's steel division struggled in the early 1980s, even as BHP itself faced a hostile takeover attempt from Australian tycoon Robert Holmes à Court. The steel industry had become increasingly international, and even global, forcing BHP to compete against more modern and more efficient steel producers in Japan and elsewhere. The economic crises of the 1970s and early 1980s also had a toll on the group. By 1983, the company had been forced to lay off nearly one-third of its workforce.

The group's battle with Holmes à Court had the paradoxical effect of forcing through a major restructuring of BHP steel operations. In 1985, BHP restructured into its three main components: Steel, Minerals, and Oil. The group's steel operations were reorganized under a new company, BHP Steel International. Under the leadership of John Prescott, and BHP CEO Brian Loton, BHP Steel undertook a major modernization effort,

KEY DATES

1915: Broken Hill Proprietary (BHP) enters the steel industry.
1935: BHP acquires Australian Iron & Steel Company.
1969: BHP acquires 50 percent of John Lysaght (Australia).
1979: BHP acquires full control of Lysaght.
1989: BHP acquires New Zealand Steel.
1995: Company opens its first factory in Shanghai, China.
2002: BHP Steel is spun off as a public company and becomes BlueScope Steel.
2008: BlueScope acquires IMSA Steel in the United States.

spending some AUD 22 billion over the next decade. BHP Steel's efforts were supported by Australia's Labour government, which instituted a five-year Steel Industry Plan that helped prevent worker unrest by guaranteeing employment to union members. The plan enabled BHP to achieve significant gains in productivity, transforming BHP Steel into one of the world's most efficient steelmakers, and one of the few to achieve profits in the early 1990s. By then, BHP Steel's total output topped six million tons per year.

BHP Steel had taken on an increasingly international dimension in the 1990s. The company added operations in New Zealand, acquiring New Zealand Steel in 1989. The company also entered the United States, setting up a steel trading arm there in 1987. From that base, BHP Steel established a large steel trading hub, BHP Trading Inc.

At the same time, BHP Steel increasingly shifted its steel production focus from semifinished steel products to its higher valued-added coated steel lines. To this end, the company spent $110 million building a new coating line at Western Port, which opened in 1991, more than tripling the group's coated steel capacity. In 1994, the company added a coated sheet steel line at its New Zealand subsidiary, launching production of the Zincalume brand there.

ASIAN EXPANSION IN THE NINETIES

BHP Steel's focus turned to the Asian markets during the decade. The company built an $82 million zinc-

aluminum coil coating line in Malaysia, beginning production in 1996. This facility was slated to reach 150,000 metric tons capacity. By then, BHP Steel had also gained permission to enter China, opening a roll forming plant in Shanghai in 1995. The push into the Asian region was accompanied by a reorganization of BHP Steel's operations along geographic lines in the middle of the decade.

In the United States, BHP Steel became a steel producer, forming a 50-50 joint venture with North Star Steel Co. and building a $400 million slab minimill with a capacity of 1.5 million metric tons of coated coils per year. That company became operational in 1996. BHP Steel also spent nearly $300 million expanding its coated coil production in Australia, while at the same time adding a coated steel factory in Thailand.

At the end of the decade, BHP Steel's Newcastle Steelworks had sunk into losses, in part because of the oversupply of steel capacity on the global market. BHP Steel decided to shut down the works in 1999. At the same time, the company announced plans to pursue a wider divestment program. This led the company to sell off its long steel production in 2000, spinning off the Whylla Steelworks, together with a number of mills attached to the Newcastle operation, as publicly listed OneSteel Limited. The company also announced its intention to exit the North Star BHP Steel joint venture.

BECOMING BLUESCOPE IN 2003

In 2001, however, BHP announced it had reached an agreement to merge with The Anglo-South African mining giant Billiton, creating BHP Billiton. Following on that agreement, BHP Billiton announced its intention to spin off its steel arm. This was completed in July 2002, when BHP Steel listed on the Australian Stock Exchange. The company initially sought to keep the BHP Steel name but when BHP Billiton refused to allow this, the company changed its name, to BlueScope Steel, in 2003.

BlueScope now pinned its growth on further expansion in the Asian region, primarily through investments in producing downstream, value-added steel products. The company expanded its production in China and Thailand, and added operations in Indonesia and Vietnam as well. Investments included an AUD 160 million metallic coating and painting plant in Vietnam, and an AUD 280 million metallic coating and painting facility in Jiangsu, China.

The company also expanded its U.S. presence, paying $250 million for Butler Manufacturing, a manufacturer of preengineered buildings. The company further expanded its U.S. footprint in 2008, paying $730 million for IMSA Steel Corp., adding its operations in preengineered buildings, coil-coating, insulated steel panel production, and building components, including architectural roof and wall systems.

BILLION-DOLLAR LOSS IN 2011

Other acquisitions in the decade included the purchase of Smorgon Steel Distribution, a move designed to increase BlueScope's access to the Australian steel distribution market. Through Bluescope Lysaght, the company acquired Ranbuild, a producer of sheds, in 2004. The company also entered the retail market, opening a chain of Lysaght Home Improvement Centers.

The global economic crisis cut short BlueScope's growth at the end of the decade. As demand for steel plummeted, the company took steps to protect its balance sheet, an effort that enabled the company to recover from a loss of AUD 66 million in 2009 with a net profit of AUD 126 million on AUD 8.3 billion in revenues in 2010. This profit came despite a drop in revenues of more than AUD 1.5 billion.

BlueScope managed to restore its revenues to AUD 10.34 billion ($9.8 billion) in 2011. At the same time, however, BlueScope reported its largest-ever loss, of AUD 1.05 billion. In response, BlueScope announced plans to carry out a major restructuring of its operations in August 2011. Under the restructuring plan, the company announced its intention to close its Western Port mill, and shut down the number six blast furnace at Port Kembla. The closure of the latter plant also meant that BlueScope was exiting the steel exports market.

Reflecting on the difficulties of the steel market in the new decade, BlueScope Chairman Graham Kraehe told the *Courier-Mail* in August 2011: "I've been in manufacturing all my life and I've seen a lot, but nothing like what we've got at the moment." As the flagship of Australia's steel industry, BlueScope Steel hoped its restructuring would prepare it for a stronger future.

M. L. Cohen

PRINCIPAL SUBSIDIARIES

North Star BlueScope Steel Inc. (USA; 50%); Butler Manufacturing Inc. (USA); Castrip LLC (USA; 47.5%); Port Kembla Steelworks Pty. Ltd.; BlueScope Steel China Co.; BlueScope Steel (Thailand) Limited; BlueScope Steel Indonesia; BlueScope Lysaght Vietnam.

PRINCIPAL DIVISIONS

Coated & Industrial Products Australia; Australia Distribution & Solutions; New Zealand & Pacific Steel Products; Coated & Building Products Asia; Hot Rolled Products North America; Coated & Building Products North America; Metl-Span Inc. (USA).

PRINCIPAL COMPETITORS

ArcelorMittal S.A.; Baosteel Group Corp.; Cargill Inc.; Daido Steel Company Ltd.; Libyan Iron and Steel Co.; Nippon Steel Corporation; Tata Sons Ltd.; Xingtai Iron and Steel Corporation Ltd.

FURTHER READING

"Aussie Steel Maker Builds New Plant." *Vietnam Investment Review*, December 22, 2003, 5.

"BHP Billiton Steel Sub-listing Could Be Largest IPO of 2002." *Euroweek*, May 17, 2002, 21.

"BHP to Expand in Asia." *Asia Today International*, June–July 2003, 16.

"BHP Will Spin Off BHP Steel." *New Steel*, May 2001, 7.

"BlueScope Buying IMSA's N. American Plants." *Metal Producing & Processing*, January–February 2008, 7.

Chong, Florence. "Opportunity and Growth—Two Words Driving the BlueScope Strategy." *Asia Today International*, April–May 2004, 19.

Clarke, Jo. "Color Us Bluescope." *American Metal Market*, September 3, 2002, 4.

Roberts, Greg, and Soraya Permatasari. "Revamp for Steel Giant as $1b Lost." *Courier-Mail*, August 23, 2011.

Boston Properties, Inc.

———————————— ■ ————————————

The Prudential Center
800 Boylston Street
Boston, Massachusetts 02199-8103
U.S.A.
Telephone: (617) 236-3300
Fax: (617) 536-5087
Web site: http://www.bostonproperties.com

Public Company
Incorporated: 1970
Employees: 680
Sales: $1.55 billion (2010)
Stock Exchanges: New York
Ticker Symbol: BXP
NAICS: 531320 Offices of Real Estate Appraisers;
    531120 Lessors of Nonresidential Buildings (Except
    Miniwarehouses); 531110 Lessors of Residential
    Buildings and Dwellings

■ ■ ■

Boston Properties, Inc., acquires, develops, and manages
property and Class A office buildings, primarily in
Boston, New York, San Francisco, Washington, D.C.,
and Princeton, New Jersey. The company is one of the
country's largest real estate investment trusts (REITs).
Boston Properties primarily owns and develops office
buildings but also owns and rents hotel, residential, and
retail properties. The company is run by Mort Zuckerman, who also owns New York's *Daily News* and *U.S.
News & World Report*. As of 2010 Boston Properties was
listed on the S&P 500.

ORIGINS AND INITIAL BUSINESS

Born and raised in Montreal, Mortimer B. Zuckerman
earned an M.B.A. and two law degrees (one from Harvard Law School) before going to work for the Boston
developer Cabot, Cabot & Forbes in 1962 at a starting
salary of $8,750. Within three years he was chief
financial officer and a partner in the firm. By the time
he was 30, Zuckerman was worth $5 million. When
Zuckerman left to open his own company at the beginning of 1970, he had a stake in Cabot, Cabot & Forbes
as well as 18 properties, including 12 California
industrial and business parks. He and Edward H. Linde,
a colleague at the firm, also claimed a $4 million share
in a Boston building. When the company offered only
$2.2 million, they took the matter to court and eventu-
ally won their claim, plus $400,000 in interest.

Shortly after founding Boston Properties in 1970,
Zuckerman took on Linde as a quarter-share partner.
Linde had the job of constructing buildings and managing properties, while Zuckerman made deals and arranged financing. At first Boston Properties was most
active on the West Coast. The firm, as the controlling
general partner, constructed the nine-building Hilltop
Business Center in South San Francisco during the early
1970s and also built two industrial properties there.

During its initial years, Boston Properties was
chosen by Boston Mayor Kevin White to build Park
Plaza, a 10-acre, five-tower residential-retail-office
complex overlooking the Public Gardens next to Boston
Common, the city's downtown park. Opposition
quickly arose from neighborhood groups objecting to

COMPANY PERSPECTIVES

The company acquires, develops, and manages its properties through full-service regional offices in Boston, New York City, Washington, D.C., San Francisco, and Princeton, New Jersey. Its property portfolio is comprised primarily of first-class office space and also includes one hotel. Boston Properties is well-known for its in-house building management expertise and responsiveness to tenants' needs. The company has a superior track record in developing Class A, central business district office buildings, suburban office centers, and build-to-suit projects for the U.S. government and a diverse array of high-credit tenants.

the size and height of the development, especially because it would cast a shadow over the park. After seven years a scaled-down version was approved, but Boston Properties walked away from the project, "exhausted by the process," according to Zuckerman.

Boston Properties lost the Park Plaza battle but essentially won the war because Zuckerman and Linde were so busy pushing the plaza that they had no time for other ventures that might have collapsed in the 1974–75 crash of the Boston real estate market. With cash on hand, the company bought sites at very low prices from financially troubled developers. Mayor White approved Boston Properties' plan to build a Marriott hotel (completed in 1982) on public waterfront land even though a committee he had appointed ranked it dead last among eight proposals. The company also won a competition to develop a Cambridge 24-acre urban-renewal site adjacent to the Massachusetts Institute of Technology, on which it constructed 10 buildings, including another Marriott hotel.

In the early 1970s, Zuckerman and Linde identified the area of suburban Boston along Route 128 as ready for the development of modern office buildings. They selected the quadrant west/northwest of Boston between the Massachusetts Turnpike and U.S. 93 as the most desirable area in which to concentrate their efforts. Between 1978 and 1988, Boston Properties acquired 13 key sites in the area where it completed development of 17 office buildings, containing more than two million rentable square feet.

ENTRANCE INTO WASHINGTON, D.C., AND NEW YORK

In 1979 Boston Properties opened a Washington, D.C., office. Two years later it completed Capital Gallery, an office building south of the Mall and southwest of the U.S. Capitol. In 1981 Boston Properties formed a joint venture with *U.S. News & World Report* to construct a new headquarters for the magazine, a luxury hotel, an office building, and two condominium buildings in Washington, D.C. When Zuckerman purchased *U.S. News* in 1984, he acquired the real estate for the publication's headquarters (although his publishing ventures were not integrated into Boston Properties). The magazine's headquarters building was sold in 1987 to Shuwa Corp., a Japanese firm, for about $80 million, reportedly a record price for D.C. office space.

Boston Properties completed a one million-square-foot complex in the nation's capital near Rock Creek Park in 1986 that consisted of 101 condominiums and the mixed-use Whitman Place, where the Association of American Medical Colleges rented five floors. The company also developed a one million-square-foot Federal Judiciary Building near Union Station but did not assume ownership of the structure.

Boston Properties entered New York City in 1983 when it bought for $84 million the land and architectural design for 599 Lexington Avenue, a 47-story office building planned to rise at 52nd Street and Lexington Avenue in midtown Manhattan. Built without any rental commitments, the $300 million speculative venture was completed in 1986. The gamble paid off when more than half of the one million square feet of office space was leased before the end of 1986 without offering discounts. The Lexington Avenue building was Boston Properties' largest development to date and through the late 1990s commanded higher rent per leased square foot than any other company property.

In 1985 Boston Properties made a winning bid of $455.1 million for one of the most valuable remaining parcels of prime Manhattan land, the New York Coliseum site at Columbus Circle on the southwestern periphery of Central Park. The company's bid was a per-acre record and the largest sum of money ever offered for a piece of public land in New York. The company planned giant 58- and 68-story towers of office, hotel, retail, and condominium space flanking an enormous atrium, and it lined up the investment-banking firm of Salomon Brothers as both co-owner and major tenant.

In a controversy similar to that of Park Plaza, however, the proposal drew fierce opposition from community groups and such celebrities as Jacqueline

KEY DATES

1970: Boston Properties is formed.
1997: Boston Properties goes public.
1998: Company opens a San Francisco office and acquires the Embarcadero Center.
2001: Boston Properties acquires Citigroup Center at 153 East Third Street in Manhattan.
2005: Company sells Embarcadero Center West Tower in San Francisco and Riverfront Plaza in Richmond, Virginia.
2006: Boston Properties sells 280 Park Avenue in Manhattan for $1.2 billion and 5 Times Square for $1.3 billion.
2008: Company buys the General Motors Building in New York for a record $2.8 billion.
2010: Firm acquires Boston's tallest building, the 62-story John Hancock Tower.

Kennedy Onassis, Walter Cronkite, Henry Kissinger, and Bill Moyers. A prime objection was that the towers would throw long shadows over the southern part of the park in the afternoon. The opponents lost their case in federal court, but by then Salomon Brothers had backed out of the deal because of the 1987 Wall Street crash. The proposal was subsequently scaled down and did not officially die until 1994, when negotiations between Boston Properties and the site owner, the Metropolitan Transportation Authority, ended in acrimony.

During the 1980s Boston Properties was active in Montgomery and Prince Georges Counties in Maryland and Fairfax County in Virginia. Between 1982 and the end of 1990, the company completed 14 office buildings on a 127-acre Springfield, Virginia, site and retained ownership of 11 of them. Democracy Center, a three-building office complex in Bethesda, Maryland, was completed in 1988. By that time seven of nine planned buildings had been completed for the 66-acre Maryland 50 Industrial Park in Landover, of which the company retained three.

In 1987 the company completed development of the U.S. International Trade Commission Building in Washington, D.C. During the late 1980s, Boston Properties also bought two full blocks in Washington, D.C., for its Independence Square development. A 360,000-square-foot building for the Office of the Comptroller of the Currency in Washington, D.C., was completed on this site in 1991. The following year a Boston Properties-led partnership completed a new

National Aeronautics and Space Administration (NASA) headquarters located just east of Independence Square. The partnership garnered a 20-year, $383 million lease from NASA.

ACQUISITIONS AND PROJECTS IN THE NINETIES

During the mid-1980s, Zuckerman and Linde acquired land and formed a partnership to develop an office park on an 18-acre Concord, Massachusetts, site. Development of the site, located only 700 yards from 19th-century essayist Henry David Thoreau's Walden Pond, was approved by zoning authorities. The project, however, sparked considerable controversy and objections from a group led by musician Don Henley to preserve 2,680-acre Walden Woods. By 1993 Linde and Zuckerman had formally nixed the project and sold the land to the Walden Woods Project.

In 1995 Boston Properties, in order to focus on commercial real estate, made one of its rare sales. The company sold the Park Hyatt Hotel in Washington, D.C., for $43.5 million to Hyatt Corp. In 1996 Boston Properties began construction on its first speculative office project in seven years, starting work on a three-story, 102,000-square-foot building in Lexington, Massachusetts, a suburb of Boston. Boston Properties weathered the real estate recession of 1989–93 and claimed an average annual return of about 14.2 percent between 1992 and 1996. Between 1989 and 1996, it completed eight third-party development projects on a fee basis in the Baltimore, Boston, New York, and Washington, D.C., metropolitan areas.

Boston Properties announced in August 1997 that it had agreed to buy 280 Park Avenue, a complex of two large office towers in midtown Manhattan between East 48th and 49th Streets, from Bankers Trust Co., for $321 million. Bankers Trust and other existing corporate tenants remained in the tower through the acquisition. The company's projects during the late 1990s also included two Springfield, Massachusetts, office buildings, to be leased to the U.S. Customs Service and Autometric, Inc., respectively. Boston Properties also developed two office buildings in Reston, Virginia, one of which became headquarters for BDM International and two office buildings in Herndon, Virginia.

IPO AND MAJOR ACQUISITIONS: LATE NINETIES

By February 1997 Boston Properties owned more than 90 properties and 12 million square feet of office buildings in the Boston area, Manhattan, and Washington,

D.C. The majority of those were managed by the company, and 10 percent of its space was leased to federal agencies. Boston Properties had a $300 million credit line, considered modest by the standards of the late 1990s. Its federal government tenants, although creditworthy, were not paying top dollar. With several REITs considering a public offering, and with high investor interest, Boston Properties in 1997 went public on the New York Stock Exchange with a $903 million offering, the second-largest REIT initial public offering (IPO) ever. Merrill Lynch and Goldman Sachs co-led the IPO with shares sold at $25. The offering helped fund the acquisition that year of 280 Park Avenue and 875 Third Avenue in New York. That same year Boston Properties purchased 100 East Pratt Street in Baltimore, Maryland.

In 1998 Boston Properties completed the second-largest equity offering ever for a REIT: $808 million. The company quickly put its new funding to use and grew that year through major acquisitions, including the purchase of the 2.3 million-square-foot Prudential Center, a Boston office and mixed-use building with rights to develop another 1.7 million square feet for $546 million (Prudential received $100 million worth of Boston Properties' preferred shares in the deal). Boston Properties also acquired the 531,000-square-foot office complex Reservoir Place in Waltham, Massachusetts. The company additionally joined with Gould Property Co. to begin development of D.C.'s Market Square North, a mixed-used high-end property between the U.S. Capitol and White House. That same year the firm opened a San Francisco office and acquired for $1.23 billion the six-building, four million-square-foot iconic Embarcadero Center, a downtown office development.

In 1999 Boston Properties acquired the Gateway complex in South San Francisco, including two office towers 98 percent occupied on Gateway Commons, a master-planned business district, for $118 million. The company also invested in One South Market in San Jose, California. During the next three years, 611 Gateway Commons was completed. Boston Properties in 1999 also partnered with the developer George Klein and the Blackstone Group and obtained rights to develop 2.3 million square feet in Times Square, Manhattan, including Times Square Tower and 5 Times Square, two prime locations with more than one million square feet of office space. That same year Boston Properties landed a major tenant for 5 Times Square as Ernst & Young signed a 20-year lease for a 37-floor headquarters worth $1.2 billion, one of the biggest real estate deals in New York history. During the late 1990s, Boston Properties also developed more than two million square feet of northern Virginia office space in Reston

Town Center. By the end of the decade, Boston Properties ran the country's second-largest REIT.

DEVELOPMENT OF "TROPHY" PROPERTIES

With a robust economy and Internet boom, and with vacancy rates at a two-decade low, the Manhattan real estate market in 2000 was the strongest it had been in decades. To fund future development, Boston Properties in 2000 completed a $607 million equity offering. That same year the company began development of a "mini-Embarcadero" in San Jose. Boston Properties also added to its so-called trophy properties in its home city, acquiring the 21-floor office tower at 265 Franklin Street. In late 2000 Boston Properties acquired a parking lot at 901 New York Avenue Northwest in Washington, D.C., to develop an 11-story office building. Late in the year the company broke ground on a joint development with Terrabrook, the new 16-story, Class A office building, Reston Town Center at Two Freedom Square in Virginia.

Despite the initial signs of a dot-com bust, the company continued acquiring properties. In 2001 Boston Properties and Allied Partners acquired the Citigroup Center at 153 East Third Street in Manhattan, a 1.6 million-square-foot, 59-story building, recognized for its unique structure with an angled roof. Boston Properties also purchased 601 Lexington Avenue in New York and completed a Boston Back Bay tower at 111 Huntington Avenue.

In 2002 the company completed 5 Times Square and secured Ernst & Young as an anchor tenant to a 20-year lease. That same year Boston Properties acquired 399 Park Avenue, a 1.7 million-square-foot Manhattan building, for $1.1 billion and purchased the 39-story tower at 399 Park Avenue. In 2003 Boston Properties completed a $1.5 billion offering of senior unsecured notes and a $294 million equity offer. Also in 2003, the firm acquired interests in One and Two Freedom Square in Virginia and a 507,000-square-foot parcel near Reston Town Center.

In 2004 the 1.2 million-square-foot Times Square tower was completed. That year Boston Properties was part of a three-firm consortium that acquired a 21-acre property on Boston Harbor's waterfront in the midst of the city's financial district. The consortium planned to develop three million square feet of office, residential, retail, and hotel space. In 2005 Boston Properties sold two of its trophy properties, Embarcadero Center West Tower in San Francisco for $206 million and Riverfront Plaza in Richmond, Virginia, for $247 million. For the second straight year, *Fortune* named Boston Properties the number one real estate company in its list of the most admired companies in the United States.

In 2006 Boston Properties acquired Allied Partners' minority stake in Citigroup Center and also purchased the rights to rename the structure. With New York prices at unprecedented levels, the firm sold 280 Park Avenue in Manhattan for $1.2 billion and sold 5 Times Square for $1.3 billion. In late 2006 the company joined with Related Companies to develop an 800,000-square-foot Manhattan office tower. In May 2007 Douglas Linde, treasurer and CFO, became Boston Properties president, succeeding Edward Linde who remained CEO. By July 2007 the company's stock was trading at more than $100 a share, up from $25 at its 1998 IPO and about $43 in 2000 during the pre-dot-com bust. During that time, the company's rentable space had grown to two million square feet.

RECESSION AND REAL ESTATE REBOUND

In May 2008 Boston Properties purchased the General Motors Building in New York for $2.8 billion (a historic high for an office building price) as part of a four-property $3.95 billion deal. Boston Properties gained a 60 percent stake in the GM Building, another Manhattan trophy building for the company, located at the convergence of midtown Manhattan and Central Park. The building generated some of New York's highest rents and attracted A-list clients. The GM Building acquisition was financed in part by two parties, one being a Goldman Sachs-led consortium of investors from Qatar and Kuwait and the other being Dubai's ruling family. That same year Boston Properties renamed the Citigroup Center as 601 Lexington Avenue.

In 2008 Boston Properties was involved in one-third of the 12 largest acquisitions in Manhattan, which generated more than 40 percent of the firm's net income. By 2009 Boston Properties was the nation's leading leaser of office rental space. With the property market suffering due to a recession, the company reduced its financial commitments, putting some development projects on hold through 2011. Many of the company's major corporate clients were in the financial sector, which was heavily impacted by the recession. By the end of 2009, Boston Properties had absorbed about half the losses it suffered from declining rentals. The company refinanced some assets and reduced the amount it had leveraged, cut rents, and sold $842 million in stock, or 6 percent of the firm.

In January 2010 company cofounder and CEO Edward Linde died. Zuckerman, then chairman, assumed the additional title of CEO. The company that year sold $700 million in unsecured senior notes, netting about $693 million. Boston Properties and New York's three other leading public REITs, by 2010, had largely recovered from the real estate collapse that had begun a few years earlier. In 2010 Boston Properties acquired Boston's tallest building, the 62-story John Hancock Tower, for $930 million. The blue-glass skyscraper, with a 360-degree view of the Back Bay of Charles River, was one of the city's most identifiable structures. The company also acquired for $280.5 million New York's 510 Madison Avenue, a brand-new office complex requiring additional capital to prepare it for office occupants. In 2010 the company also opened the newly developed Weston Corporate Center in Weston, Massachusetts.

In early 2011 Boston Properties acquired Bay Colony Corporate Center, located in a 58-acre Waltham, Massachusetts, Class A office park. As of 2011, Boston Properties expected Manhattan rents to once again rise during the forthcoming two years. Boston Properties was also expected to resume construction on one project that had been two years on hold, the 39-story office complex at 250 West 55th Street. The company also planned a $600 million common stock offering. Midyear financial results showed double-digit revenue growth, and financial analysts proclaimed the industry had bottomed out.

In late 2011 Boston Properties and its partners sold Two Grand Central Tower, one of the properties acquired in the 2008 acquisition of the GM Building. The company's strategy moving forward was to focus on a few major markets, including Boston, Washington, D.C., midtown Manhattan, San Francisco, and Princeton, New Jersey. In those markets, Boston Properties planned to continue to be one of the leading owners and developers. The company believed its reputation, relationships with developers and brokers, and Class A properties would serve it well and help fuel continued growth.

Robert Halasz
Updated, Roger Rouland

PRINCIPAL SUBSIDIARIES

Boston Properties Limited Partnership; Boston Properties LLC; Boston Properties Management LLC; BP 125 West 55th Street LLC; BP Gateway Center LLC; BP Hancock LLC; BP Market Square North GP LLC; BP Russia Wharf LLC; BP Times Square Tower Mezzanine LLC; Embarcadero Center Associates; Embarcadero Center, Inc.; Market Square North Associates Limited Partnership; No. 1 Times Square Development LLC;

No. 5 Times Square Development LLC; Reston Corporate Center Limited Partnership; Times Square Tower Associates LLC.

PRINCIPAL COMPETITORS

Beacon Capital Partners, LLC; CommonWealth REIT; LeFrak Organization Inc.

FURTHER READING

"Boston Properties to Acquire the John Hancock Tower in Boston." *Manufacturing Close-Up*, October 7, 2010.

Feldman, Amy. "Zuckerman Leads Flood of REITs Cashing In on NY." *Crain's New York Business*, February 10, 1997, 3+.

Fung, Amanda. "Mort's Triumphs Turning Sour; Stalled Building Projects, Falling Values Hit Hard." *Crain's New York Business*, February 16, 2009, 1.

Geiger, Daniel. "Macklowe Sells 510 Madison: $280m Deal Puts Boston Properties in Driving Seat." *Real Estate Weekly*, August 25, 2010, B1.

———. "Zuckerman Expecting Big Things from GM Building." *Real Estate Weekly*, June 18, 2008, 1+.

"Macklowe Portfolio Fetches Almost $4 Billion." *National Real Estate Investor*, May 27, 2008.

Marks, Andrew. "Big 4 Make Comeback; After Raising Funds, Refinancing Debts, REITs Ready to Pounce." *Crain's New York Business*, February 15, 2010, 13.

Piore, Adam. "Mort Zuckerman Gets Last Laugh." *Real Deal*, September 1, 2008.

Vinocur, Barry. "Boston Properties Wins Raves for Its Portfolio." *Barron's*, June 9, 1997, 41–42.

"Zuckerman Unbound." *Institutional Investor*, January 1998, 106.

Canadian Oil Sands Limited

—————— ■ ——————

2500 First Canadian Centre
350-7th Avenue Southwest
Calgary, Alberta T2P 3N9
Canada
Telephone: (403) 218-6200
Fax: (403) 218-6201
Web site: http://www.cdnoilsands.com

Public Company
Incorporated: 1995 as Athabasca Oil Sands Trust
Employees: 22
Sales: CAD 3.18 billion (2010)
Stock Exchanges: Toronto
Ticker Symbol: COS
NAICS: 211111 Crude Petroleum and Natural Gas
Extraction

■ ■ ■

Canadian Oil Sands Limited is the largest owner of Syn-crude Canada Ltd., the largest oil sands mining opera-tion in the world. Canadian Oil Sands owns a 36.74 percent stake in Syncrude, which operates in the Atha-basca Oil Sands in northeastern Alberta, Canada. The Athabasca Oil Sands is an oil sands deposit containing an estimated 1.7 trillion barrels of oil, according to the Alberta Energy Resources and Conservation Board. Canadian Oil Sands shares ownership of Syncrude with six other companies. The company's president and CEO, Marcel R. Coutu, also serves as chairman of Syn-crude Canada Ltd.

THE SEARCH FOR OIL IN ATHABASCA VALLEY: 1906–64

Throughout the 20th century attempts were made to commercially develop the Athabasca Oil Sands, begin-ning in 1906, when Alfred von Hammerstein drilled his first well. Hammerstein believed the bitumen-laced sand in the region indicated pools of oil deep beneath the surface. He was wrong. His drilling efforts, conducted over the next decade, unearthed only salt.

Entrepreneurs, engineers, and scientists who made subsequent forays in the oil sands realized it was the bitumen they were after and not what lay beneath the bitumen. According to geologists, a large volume of oil was pushed into northeastern Alberta tens of millions of years ago, traveling upward through sloping layers of sediment as it moved. Eventually the oil reached depths cool and shallow enough to bring it into contact with bacteria, which gradually degraded the light crude to bitumen, a hard, tar-like substance.

Although Hammerstein's successors realized bitu-men was a grade of crude oil, the chore of converting it to its former state confounded generations of would-be oil producers. Once some of the technological challenges were resolved, one glaring problem remained. Put simply, the cost of extracting a barrel of oil from the oil sands cost more than the price of a barrel of oil, present-ing an insurmountable obstacle blocking commercial development. As time passed, however, the prospect of commercially developing the oil sands improved. Advances in technology, improved extraction techniques, and the escalating price of oil began to make com-mercial operations possible. Attention naturally turned to the Athabasca deposit, the largest of Alberta's three main oil sands deposits, where Canadian Oil Sands would become the largest owner of the world's largest oil sands mine, Syncrude.

SYNCRUDE TAKES SHAPE AND TWO TRUSTS EMERGE: 1964–96

Syncrude's roots stretched to 1964, two years after the government of Alberta announced an oil sands policy that allowed for the development of oil sands. Upon formation, Syncrude was a consortium of interests dedicated to researching the economic and technical feasibility of mining oil from the Athabasca deposit. The consortium offered a proposal for the construction of a production facility, which was approved in 1969. The site of the proposed mining operation was 40 kilometers north of Fort McMurray, a site not far from where Hammerstein drilled his first well, near Mildred Lake. Construction at the site commenced in 1973 and in 1978 the first barrel of Syncrude Sweet Blend was shipped from the Syncrude operation, the first of one billion barrels of synthetic crude oil that would travel through pipelines to refineries in Alberta, Ontario, and the United States in the next 20 years.

The roots of Canadian Oil Sands stretched indirectly to the commencement of production at Syncrude and directly to Athabasca Oil Sands Trust. Athabasca Oil Sands Trust was formed in 1995, an income trust managed by Gulf Canada Resources Limited, one of the original participants in the Syncrude project. Athabasca Oil Sands Trust, upon formation, owned an 11.74 percent stake in the Syncrude project, operated and managed by Syncrude Canada Ltd. Another income trust (an entity that pays out most of its earnings in the form of cash distributions) was formed by another Syncrude participant, PanCanadian Petroleum Limited, which sold a 10 percent stake in the project to Canadian Oil Sands Trust, formed in 1996.

The importance of the two trusts to the operations of Syncrude increased substantially when they merged in 2001. Athabasca Oil Sands Trust and Canadian Oil Sands Trust joined forces in July, emerging as Canadian Oil Sands Trust, a firm with a market capitalization of CAD 2 billion that ranked as the largest oil and gas royalty in Canada. Significantly, the combined trusts ranked as the second-largest owner of the Syncrude project, controlling a 21.74 percent stake, trailing only the 25 percent owned by the Exxon Mobil's subsidiary Imperial Oil Ltd.

At the time of the merger, production at Syncrude averaged roughly 250,000 barrels per day, an increase from the 49,000 barrels per day produced at the project during its first full year in 1979. Canadian Oil Sands and its nine other partners in the project envisioned a far greater daily production total, inking agreement for a $5.7 billion expansion project, dubbed "Syncrude 21," that would lift the project's daily output to more than 465,000 barrels per day by 2008. It was the capital requirements of Syncrude 21 that brought Athabasca Oil Sands Trust and Canadian Oil Sands Trust together. The merged trust, according to the thinking of the executives in charge, would be more easily able to fund the expansion project than as separate trusts.

THE SCALE AND POTENTIAL OF SYNCRUDE: 2001–06

The $5.7 billion expansion was just one of the projects planned in the Athabasca region. Approximately CAD 20 billion worth of expansion projects were scheduled at the time of the merger, reflecting the rising level of excitement in mining for oil. New technologies had cut extraction costs in half since the mid-1980s, reducing production costs from $30 per barrel to $18 per barrel. Meanwhile, the price of a barrel of oil had increased, making an oil sands operation, in turn, increasingly profitable. Although producing a barrel of oil from the oil sands cost far more than the $4 per barrel to produce conventional oil, the difference between extraction costs and the price of a barrel of oil translated to profits. The average price of a barrel of oil in 2001 was $23 and it was projected to climb vigorously (the price would skyrocket above $90 in 2008), fanning excitement within the industry. The profits were there and the supply was massive. The Athabasca Oil Sands were believed to contain 175 billion barrels of recoverable oil, enough to meet North American oil needs for the next four decades. The Alberta oil sands, a 54,000-square-mile region, were believed to hold enough oil to meet the world's needs for the next 10 years.

Mining for oil was big business, in terms of both the financial worth and the scale of operations. At the

KEY DATES

1978: Syncrude mine in Alberta, Canada, produces its first barrel of oil.
1995: Athabasca Oil Sands Trust, an 11.74 percent owner of Syncrude, is formed.
1996: Canadian Oil Sands Trust, a 10 percent owner of Syncrude, is formed.
2001: Athabasca Oil Sands Trust and Canadian Oil Sands Trust merge.
2003: Canadian Oil Sands purchases a 13.75 percent stake in Syncrude in two transactions valued at CAD 1.48 billion.
2007: Canadian Oil Sands purchases a 1.25 percent stake in Syncrude for CAD 475 million.
2010: Canadian Oil Sands converts from a trust to a corporation, becoming Canadian Oil Sands Limited.

nearly 14-square-mile Syncrude site near Mildred Lake, five-story-high electric shovels clawed into an enormous open-pit mine, 24 hours per day, seven days a week. Each pass of the shovel was capable of excavating more than 100 tons and the trucks used to haul the material excavated were capable of carrying nearly 450 tons per load. To extract one barrel of oil, the shovels removed an average of two tons of peat and dirt that covered the oil sands, then two tons of the oil sand itself. Next, several barrels of water were heated to strip the bitumen from the sand and upgrade it. At the upgraders, the bitumen was heated to 900 degrees Fahrenheit and compressed to more than 100 atmospheres, a process, called "cracking," that either subtracted carbon or added back the hydrogen removed by bacteria millennia ago. Afterward, the contaminated water was discharged into tailing ponds, or toxic pools of oily water. One such pond near Mildred Lake, the Mildred Lake Settling Basin, measured four square miles, contained by a sand dike that by volume ranked as one of the largest dams in the world.

The laborious and costly process of extracting oil from the oil sands also took a heavy toll on the environment, making the business of mining for oil a controversial one. The Syncrude operation occupied what had been part of Canada's boreal forest, an area denuded to make way for the massive shovels and trucks that clawed downward, creating a sprawling pit 80 meters deep. The process of digging and cooking a barrel of crude oil from the oil sands emitted as much as

three times more carbon dioxide than obtaining a barrel of oil from a conventional drilling operation. Further, the tailings ponds, which covered 50 square miles in Alberta's oil sands, littered the region.

In 2008, 1,606 ducks landed on the oily surface of one of Syncrude's tailing ponds and died, sparking outrage from groups opposed to mining the oil sands. "Oil sands represent a decision point for North America and the world," Simon Dyer, a spokesperson for the Pembina Institute, a Canadian environmental group, said in the March 2009 issue of *National Geographic*. "Are we going to get serious about alternative energy, or are we going to go down the unconventional oil track? The fact that we're willing to move four tons of earth for a single barrel really shows that the world is running out of easy oil."

CANADIAN OIL SANDS TAKES A BIGGER SHARE OF SYNCRUDE: 2003–07

Despite opposition from some fronts, the demand for oil and the massive amount of it contained in Alberta's oil sands kept Syncrude and other operations pressing forward. When *Oil & Gas Journal* included Alberta's oil sands in its list of proven reserves in 2003, Canada, which derived 97 percent of its reserves from oil sands, leapt to second place among the world's oil-producing nations, trailing only Saudi Arabia. Canadian Oil Sands, operating as the second-largest owner in the world's largest oil sands mine, was not content with its share of what had become the world's oil jewel.

In March 2003, the trust purchased the 10 percent stake owned by Calgary-based EnCana Corporation, paying CAD 1.07 billion to become Syncrude's largest owner with a 31.74 percent interest in the project. The deal also included an option for Canadian Oil Sands to acquire EnCana's remaining 3.75 percent share, which the trust did three months later, paying CAD 417 million. After purchasing the optional 3.75 percent stake, Canadian Oil Sands owned 35.49 percent of the project, heading an ownership group that comprised Imperial Oil (25 percent), Petro-Canada (12 percent), ConocoPhillips (9.03 percent), Nexen Inc. (7.23 percent), Murphy Oil (5 percent), Mocal Energy (5 percent), and Talisman Energy (1.25 percent).

Together the ownership partners invested heavily in the expansion of the Syncrude project. The projected $5.7 billion expansion begun in 2001 cost $8.4 billion by the time it was completed in 2006 adding 100,000 barrels of oil per day to Syncrude's production total. Further expansion projects were being considered to increase Syncrude's production to more than 500,000 barrels per day. Before any plans were formalized, however, Canadian Oil Sands again increased its owner-ship of Syncrude. In late 2006, the trust announced it had agreed to purchase Talisman Energy's 1.25 percent interest for CAD 475 million. The transaction, completed in early 2007, gave Canadian Oil Sands a 36.74 percent stake in Syncrude.

THE TRUST BECOMES A CORPORATION: 2010

Canadian Oil Sands' ownership interest in Syncrude remained at 36.74 percent at the end of the decade, when the project had a capacity of 350,000 barrels per day. There were ambitious plans for future expansion, plans made more attractive by an International Energy Report in late 2009 that forecast $120-a-barrel oil in 2030. By 2020, Canadian Oil Sands and its partners planned to increase daily production to 600,000 barrels, a production level that the ownership partners believed they could sustain for the ensuing 60 years. As Canadian Oil Sands prepared for its promising future, it converted from a trust to a corporation, completing the process in December 2010, when it began operating under the name Canadian Oil Sands Limited.

Jeffrey L. Covell

PRINCIPAL SUBSIDIARIES

Canadian Arctic Gas Ltd.; Canadian Oil Sands Market-ing Inc.; 1506627 Alberta Ltd.; Canadian Oil Sands Partnership (99.99%).

PRINCIPAL COMPETITORS

Canadian Natural Resources Limited; EnCana Corpora-tion; Imperial Oil Limited.

FURTHER READING

"Canadian Oil Sands Completes Corporate Conversion." *Mar-ketwire Canada*, December 31, 2010.

"Canadian Oil Sands Duck Kill Tripled." *UPI NewsTrack*, March 31, 2009.

"Canadian Oil Sands to Acquire 1.25 Per Cent Interest in Syn-crude Joint Venture." *CNW Group*, November 29, 2006.

"EnCana Opts Out of Syncrude; Canadian Oil Sands Trust Adds Stake." *Oil Daily*, February 4, 2003.

Kunzig, Robert. "The Canadian Oil Boom." *National Geographic*, March 2009.

"2 Canadian Trusts Plan Merger." *Oil Daily*, March 12, 2001.

Catlin Group Limited

---

16 Church Street, 5th Floor, Washington House
Hamilton, HM11
Bermuda
Telephone: (+441) 296-0060
Fax: (+441) 296-6016
Web site: http://www.catlin.com

Public Company
Founded: 1984 as Catlin Underwriting Agencies Limited
Incorporated: 1999 as Catlin Group
Employees: 1,600
Total Assets: $12.08 billion (2010)
Stock Exchanges: London
Ticker Symbol: GCL.L
NAICS: 524126 Direct Property and Casualty Insurance
   Carriers

■ ■ ■

Catlin Group Limited is a world-leading insurance and reinsurance underwriter, with 50 offices in 20 countries, and a staff of nearly 700 underwriting employees. Catlin operates from six underwriting hubs, in London, Bermuda, the United States, Canada, Asia-Pacific, and Europe. Each hub specializes both on its core market as well as on a specific range of insurance and underwriting products. The London hub represents the company's original operation as a Lloyd's of London member and remains the group's largest, posting more than half of Catlin's $4.07 billion in gross premiums written (GPW) in 2010. The U.S. hub is the group's second-largest, and focuses on the specialty insurance and reinsurance

products. This division contributed more than 17 percent to the group's GPW in 2010. In Bermuda, where the company is registered, Catlin focuses primarily on reinsurance products for international markets, while the European hub is an insurance and reinsurance underwriter.

In 2011, the company entered the European reinsurance market, founding Catlin Re Switzerland in Zurich. Catlin has also been building its presence in the fast-growing Asia-Pacific markets, including Australia. The Asia-Pacific hub represented more than 5 percent of group sales in 2010. Catlin's smallest hub is its Canada hub, which focuses on providing underwriting products to that market. Catlin is listed on the London Stock Exchange. The company is led by CEO and founder Stephen Catlin.

TEABOY IN 1973

While Stephen Catlin's family had hoped he would pursue a career in medicine, Catlin himself had other ideas. As a compromise, Catlin agreed to attend dental school but failed to make the grade. As Catlin explained to the *Daily Telegraph* in February 2005: "I perhaps didn't work as hard as I could at school. I didn't really want to be a dentist. … I am a stick and carrot merchant. I like to do something where I can see benefit."

Instead, Catlin at the age of 18, in 1973, took up an offer to work as a teaboy at the box (trading desk) of Lloyd's of London underwriter Anton Underwriting Agency. Catlin, who cut off his long hair before taking the job, quickly discovered a vocation in underwriting.

Over the next decade, Catlin climbed the ranks at Anton, becoming a deputy underwriter in 1982. Catlin soon began to specialize in excess of loss and energy accounts. In 1984, however, Anton agreed to be sold to another Lloyd's underwriter, Merritt. Despite his success at the company, Catlin's position was not high enough for him to profit from the sale. As Catlin told the *Daily Telegraph*: "It became very apparent to me that a lot of people were making money out of this transaction and I wasn't one of them."

This realization encouraged Catlin to form his own underwriter. For this, Catlin teamed up with his own deputy underwriter, Rupert Atkin, taking a two-seater box at Lloyd's and founding Catlin Underwriting Agencies Limited. The partners started out with a capital of just £25,000. Catlin's share of that capital, borrowed from a bank, stood at £15,000.

With little more than an underwriting stamp, and a copy machine borrowed from a neighboring box, the new company set out developing its insurance business. Catlin based the company's underwriting business on long-term, sustainable development, rather than on high-volume, short-term profits. By committing to long-term growth, the company hoped to maintain its earnings across the dips in the highly cyclical underwriting market. As such, Catlin started small, writing just £2.5 million worth of insurance over the firm's first 16 months. These operations proved profitable nonetheless, as the company's fixed costs during the period reached just £180,000.

SYNDICATE 1003 IN 1985

By 1985, Catlin had grown sufficiently to launch its own syndicate (which provided underwriting services on behalf of the Lloyd's private investors known as Names). Syndicate 1003 was established that year under Catlin's management with a premium capacity of £6 million. Syndicate 1003 initially focused on providing marine insurance products.

Under Catlin's management, Syndicate 1003 grew to a premium capacity of £170 million by 1995. This

success was all the more remarkable given the extreme volatility of the Lloyd's markets during this period, which amid the economic upheavals and massive losses resulting from asbestosis claims, saw the bankruptcy of many of Lloyd's underwriting firms.

The Catlin agency's youth, and therefore lack of exposure, provided some insulation from a stormy climate during this period. At the same time, the company's more cautious, long-term focus gave it a degree of stability among other Lloyd's underwriters. As a result, Catlin managed to post profits throughout the period, during which the rest of the Lloyd's markets lost more than £8 billion. The difficulties in the market also brought growth opportunities for Catlin. In 1993, for example, the company acquired the business of another Lloyd's syndicate, Syndicate 179, which was folded into Syndicate 1003.

Catlin's success caught the attention of the larger, international insurance market. At the same time, Lloyd's of London had adopted new rules allowing corporations to become Lloyd's investors for the first time. This development made Catlin particularly attractive, and in 1995 the company brought in Bermuda-based Western General Insurance as a major shareholder. With this increase in equity, Catlin established a new syndicate, Syndicate 2003, entirely funded from the company's own capital. Syndicate 2003 initially operated in parallel to Syndicate 1003, which remained funded by Lloyd's Names and other investors.

OVERSEAS MOVES FROM 1999

The investment by Western General became the impetus for a change in direction for Catlin. Whereas previously the company had focused entirely on the U.K.-based Lloyd's markets, Catlin now began to eye expansion as an internationally operating insurance and underwriting group.

In preparation for this expansion, the company transferred its registration to Bermuda, where it incorporated a new holding company, Catlin Group Limited. The company then began opening its first international offices. For this the company targeted both the Asia-Pacific region and the United States, opening offices in Kuala Lumpur and Singapore, and in New Orleans and Houston. In the United Kingdom, the company also moved beyond the London market, adding an office in Glasgow in 2001, and in Leeds and Derby in 2003. The company also added its first continental European operations that year, with an office in Cologne, Germany.

If Catlin had successfully skirted the worst of the turmoil surrounding Lloyd's Reconstruction and

KEY DATES

1984: Stephen Catlin and Rupert Atkin found Catlin Underwriting Agencies Limited at Lloyd's of London.

1995: Company brings in Western General Insurance as an equity investor.

1999: Company forms Catlin Group as a Bermuda-based holding company and launches its international expansion.

2004: Catlin Group goes public on the London Stock Exchange.

2006: Company acquires Wellington Underwriting Plc and nearly doubles in size.

2011: Catlin enters the European reinsurance market with Catlin Re Switzerland.

Renewal program during the 1990s, the company nonetheless stumbled entering 2000. Hit by indemnity claims from the United States, Catlin took its first-ever underwriting loss that year. The following year, the company, which had underwritten game insurance for the National Football League, faced a loss of $10 million when the league canceled all of its games on the Sunday following the September 11, 2001, terrorist attacks on the United States (9/11). Overall, the company's losses from 9/11 reached just $32 million. These were compounded, however, by still greater losses following the bankruptcy of accident claims company The Accident Group that year.

PUBLIC OFFERING IN 2004

These difficulties forced the company to seek new financing, and in 2002 Catlin completed a private equity placement, raising $482 million. The increased capital permitted the company to complete two significant expansion moves. The first of these involved the creation of a dedicated subsidiary providing underwriting products for the Bermuda market. The second was the acquisition of the entire capacity of Syndicate 1003. This syndicate was then merged into Syndicate 2003.

Catlin renewed its growth into the middle of the decade, in part as a result of the increasing number of large-scale natural disasters, such as the tsunami that swept through much of the Asian region, or the string of hurricanes that hit the Florida coast in 2004. As one result, the increasing frequency and scope of these disasters produced a surge in business for Catlin's underwriting operations. The new demand also enabled Catlin and other companies to raise premiums accordingly.

With the underwriting industry once again entering a growth cycle, Catlin went public, listing its shares on the London Stock Exchange in April 2004. The offering enabled the company to generate nearly $200 million in fresh capital. Success of the offering placed Catlin's market capitalization at more than $500 million.

The public offering helped to fuel Catlin Group's further expansion. The company extended its operations beyond the Lloyd's market and launched a new insurance underwriting subsidiary, Catlin U.K. The company also opened several new offices, entering the Australian market with an office in Sydney, and opening offices in Antwerp, Toronto, and Guernsey, as well as in Watford and Birmingham. Into 2006, the company also added offices in Calgary and Hong Kong.

LLOYD'S LARGEST IN 2006

Catlin increasingly moved toward a hub-based operational structure in the second half of the decade. This included the creation of Catlin U.S. as the central underwriting platform for the group's U.S. underwriting business. Catlin U.S. quickly expanded, adding offices in New York and Atlanta.

Back in London, Catlin prepared to join the major leagues at Lloyd's of London. In November 2006, the company reached an agreement to acquire Wellington Underwriting Plc for £532 million ($1.01 billion). The purchase nearly doubled Catlin's size, with a capital of £1.2 billion ($2.28 billion), and GPW of £2.4 billion ($4.56 billion). Following the purchase, Catlin closed down Wellington's Syndicate 2020, transferring its capital to Syndicate 2003. Completed in 2007, this transfer established Syndicate 2003 as the largest at Lloyd's. Catlin Underwriting Agencies Limited also became the largest underwriting agency in the Lloyd's market.

Catlin had also formulated plans to expand its international operations in its continuing effort to diversify from its core Lloyd's business. This led the company to open four new European offices, in Barcelona, Paris, Zurich, and Innsbruck, Austria. The company also stepped up its U.S. expansion, adding new offices in Cleveland, Philadelphia, and Lexington, Kentucky, in 2007. The company then added offices in Boston and in Woodland Hills, California, as well as in Tokyo and Munich in 2008.

In order to fund this expansion, the company completed a new preferred shares issue, netting $600 million in 2007. This was followed by a $289 million rights issue in 2009. The new capital allowed the company to add offices in Genoa and Rome in Italy, Mumbai (Bombay), Bergen, Bogota, and Hitchin, England, in 2009. Through 2010, Catlin's network extended to include offices in Oslo, Melbourne, Miami, Montreal, and Vancouver as well.

EUROPEAN REINSURANCE IN 2011

Catlin continued to seek out a limited number of acquisitions in the new decade. In April 2010, the company's Catlin U.K. subsidiary agreed to acquire the underwriting assets of Angel Underwriting, based in Colchester, England. In the United States, Catlin bought Blue Ridge Insurance Company, a subsidiary of General Casualty Company of Wisconsin owned by QBE Insurance Group. Under terms of the acquisition, QBE retained all of Blue Ridge's previously written business, leaving Catlin with a shell company from which to expand its U.S. operations. Following the purchase, completed in January 2011, Catlin changed Blue Ridge's name to Catlin Indemnity Company.

By then, Catlin had added a new line of business. In July 2010, the group announced plans to enter the European reinsurance market, traditionally centered in Switzerland. Catlin's plans included founding a new subsidiary, Catlin Re Switzerland, backed by a capitalization of $1.1 billion. The company received approval from the Swiss Financial Market Supervisory Authority in December 2010, and Catlin Re Switzerland formally commenced operations in January 2011.

By then, Catlin had emerged as a leading international specialist insurance underwriter, with GPW of more than $4.07 billion in 2010. The company had successfully expanded to more than 50 offices in 20 countries, covering nearly all of the major underwriting markets through its six underwriting and insurance hubs. The company's strong growth earned founder Stephen Catlin the title of U.K. Entrepreneur of the Year from Ernst & Young in September 2011. Catlin remained firmly at the company's helm, targeting an increasing presence in Asia, as well as in continental Europe.

M. L. Cohen

PRINCIPAL SUBSIDIARIES

Catlin Asia Pte. Ltd. (Singapore); Catlin Australia Pty Limited; Catlin Ecosse Insurance Ltd. (UK); Catlin GmbH (Germany); Catlin Holdings (UK) Ltd.; Catlin Holdings Ltd. (UK); Catlin Indemnity Company; Catlin Labuan Ltd. (Malaysia); Catlin Syndicate Ltd. (UK); Catlin Underwriting Agency U.S., Inc.; Catlin, Inc. (USA); Southern Risk Operations, L.L.C. (USA).

PRINCIPAL DIVISIONS

Underwriting; Reinsurance.

PRINCIPAL OPERATING UNITS

London/U.K.; Bermuda; U.S.; Asia-Pacific; Europe; Canada.

PRINCIPAL COMPETITORS

Ageas N.V.; Allianz Belgium S.A./N.V.; Allianz SE; American International Group Inc.; AXA Group; BNP Paribas S.A.; BPCE S.A.; Caisses d'Epargne Participations S.A.; Citigroup Inc.; Confederation Nationale du Credit Mutuel; Credit Suisse Group AG; Dexia S.A./N.V.; Life Insurance Corporation of India.

FURTHER READING

"Catlin CEO Named Entrepreneur of the Year." *Reactions* (UK), September 2011.

"Catlin GPW Growth." *Post Magazine*, May 19, 2011.

"Catlin Heading Back out in the Cold." *Business Insurance*, March 1, 2010, 27.

"Catlin to Launch $1bn European Reinsurer." *Reactions* (UK), June 1, 2010.

"Catlin UK Unveils Disaster Recovery Solution." *Reactions* (UK), May 2011.

Cave, Andrew. "Underwriter Whose Big Risk Paid off Handsomely." *Daily Telegraph*, February 19, 2005, 32.

"East Beats West, Says Stephen Catlin." *Reactions* (UK), September 2011.

"Insurer Catlin of Bermuda Launches IPO." *Reactions* (UK), January 2011.

Chipotle Mexican Grill, Inc.

1401 Wynkoop Street, Suite 500
Denver, Colorado 80202-1729
U.S.A.
Telephone: (303) 595-4000
Fax: (303) 595-4014
Web site: http://www.chipotle.com

Public Company
Incorporated: 1993
Employees: 26,500
Sales: $1.84 billion (2010)
Stock Exchanges: New York
Ticker Symbol: CMG
NAICS: 722211 Limited-Service Restaurants

■ ■ ■

Chipotle Mexican Grill, Inc., is one of the leading fast-casual Mexican restaurant chains in the United States, with more than 1,200 company-owned outlets in about 38 states. Known for its fresh, high-quality ingredients, including meats from "naturally raised" animals, Chipotle (pronounced chi-POAT-lay) offers a simple menu of burritos, tacos, salads, and burrito bowls, with each item filled or topped with the customer's choice of pork, shredded beef, chicken, steak, or beans, as well as additional customer-selected fillings or toppings. In 2011 the company launched a new dining concept with the opening of a fast-casual pan-Asian restaurant in Washington, D.C., called ShopHouse Southeast Asian Kitchen.

EARLY NINETIES BRAINCHILD OF STEVE ELLS

Born on September 12, 1965, in Indianapolis, Steve Ells, the founder of Chipotle, developed a deep interest in cuisine, cooking, and restaurant eating at an early age. He told *Nation's Restaurant News*, for a January 25, 1999, article, that in family travels across the United States and Europe he had an opportunity to taste many different foods and to develop an appreciation for fine cuisine at an unusually young age. Instead of cartoons, he was interested in watching Julia Child cooking shows. "When I was in fourth grade, I used to make eggs Benedict before I had to catch the school bus."

Ells attended the University of Colorado at Boulder, where he received an art history degree in 1988. He then decided to pursue his lifelong interest in fine food by attending the Culinary Institute of America in Hyde Park, New York. After graduating in 1990, he worked for two years at the high-end Stars restaurant in San Francisco under famed chef Jeremiah Tower. His inspiration for creating Chipotle, however, came from his frequent off-hour visits to little *taquerias* in San Francisco's Mission District. There he was struck by the fat burritos prepared to order, everything bundled in a giant flour tortilla wrapped in foil. Ells's idea was to put a twist on this traditional Mexican peasant food by stuffing the tortillas with gourmet ingredients, leveraging his culinary knowledge.

After a year of planning, during which he arranged an $80,000 loan and persuaded his father, a former president of the pharmaceuticals firm Syntex Corporation, to invest an additional $85,000, the then 27-year-old Ells returned to the Denver area, where he had lived during his junior/senior high years, to open the first Chipotle Mexican Grill. It was named after a smoked and dried jalapeño pepper that figured prominently among the ingredients, particularly the marinades used to flavor the meats. Located on Evans Avenue in Denver near the campus of the University of Denver, the restaurant opened in July 1993. The configuration of the restaurant made for a somewhat rough beginning. The kitchen was in the back, and customers and employees had to yell back and forth during ordering. Ells soon developed an open-kitchen design in which the food prep was brought out front, and the customers could interact directly with the staff and have more control over the food they were ordering.

The simple menu enabled customers to choose among burrito, taco, and fajita items; select a filling of steak, chicken, pork carnitas, or vegetarian; and then add various other fillings or toppings, all as they moved along a serving line. The huge burritos, weighing a pound and a quarter and wrapped in enormous 14-inch flour tortillas, held rice and beans in addition to the aforementioned fillings. Ells put special gourmet touches on nearly everything: cilantro and lime juice in the rice; chopped serranos, more cilantro, and marinated red onions in the guacamole; romaine lettuce rather than the typical iceberg in the tacos. In an early, rave review, Bill St. John, writing in the October 22, 1993, issue of

the *Rocky Mountain News*, enthused: "Nothing is plain here; everything has depth, character, nuance, layers of flavor." The main items on the menu were quite reasonably priced, initially ranging from $3.95 to $4.55. Among the drink offerings were margaritas and beer.

After working out the initial kinks, the first Chipotle became a huge hit. Ells's father got his investment back within a month or so. Over the next few years, more outlets were opened in the Denver metro area, funded by an additional $1.5 million investment by Ells's father and a $1.5 million private stock offering. The second store opened in February 1995, and then six more debuted during 1996. Ells concentrated first on siting restaurants in Denver's trendier neighborhoods before moving into the suburbs. Backing this growth initiative and adding efficiency to the overall operations was the addition of a central commissary where some of the ingredients were prepared.

By this time, Chipotle was considered a pioneer in two national restaurant trends: so-called wraps and the fast-casual sector. The latter category encompassed chains that were fancier than typical fast-food restaurants such as Taco Bell and faster than casual-dining chains such as Chevys. Each Chipotle was estimated to be generating just over $1 million in annual sales at this time. Sales were divided about 50–50 between eat-in and carry-out customers. Chipotle's clientele was mainly composed of adults between the ages of 18 and 49, a contrast to most fast-food restaurants, which catered to teenagers and families.

Whereas the first Chipotle was a cramped 800 square feet in size, the subsequent units covered 1,600 to 2,800 square feet, and they employed about 17 workers each. Although the design differed from unit to unit, the architecture aimed for a hip, urban feel. The decor was spare and industrial: halogen lighting, metal tabletops, wooden benches and seats, concrete floors, and arched metal ceilings. At this time, design and construction costs totaled about $249,000 per unit. Also noteworthy during this initial period of growth was that Chipotle did little in the way of advertising or promotion, relying instead on word-of-mouth testimonials.

RAPID EXPANSION FUNDED BY LATE-NINETIES MCDONALD'S BUYOUT

As six more Chipotle Mexican Grills opened in the Denver area during 1997, bringing the total to 14, Ells and other company leaders were seeking more funding to accelerate the growth rate. Venture capital firms were more interested in the high-flying tech world at the time, so a member of the Chipotle board of directors

KEY DATES

1993: Steve Ells opens the first Chipotle Mexican Grill in Denver, Colorado.

1995: Second Chipotle restaurant opens.

1997: Six more Chipotle Mexican Grills open, bringing the total to 14.

1998: McDonald's Corporation purchases a minority stake in Chipotle; first units outside Colorado open.

1999: McDonald's purchases majority control of Chipotle.

2001: Menu begins featuring free-range pork in the first move into "naturally raised" ingredients.

2006: Chipotle is taken public; McDonald's later disposes of its remaining shares, making Chipotle completely independent.

2010: The 1,000th Chipotle restaurant opens.

2011: Company opens its first ShopHouse Southeast Asian Kitchen.

sent an unsolicited business plan to fast-food leader McDonald's Corporation.

The timing was perfect. Domestic sales were flattening at the burger giant, and executives were seeking a way to jump-start growth. In February 1998, after a year of negotiations and due diligence, McDonald's made its first-ever investment in a restaurant chain it did not itself develop, buying a minority stake in Chipotle. (Later, it bought the Boston Market chain and owned the Donatos Pizza chain for a few years.) Chipotle continued to be run independently, headed by Ells as CEO, and neither its management structure nor its menu changed. Growth would continue to be generated through company-owned outlets, but now with the backing of much deeper pockets.

Following the McDonald's infusion, Chipotle began expanding outside of Colorado, sometimes aided by McDonald's expertise in site selection. Two units were opened in Kansas City (one in Kansas and one in Missouri) in 1998, and several new markets were entered in 1999: Chicago; Cleveland, Columbus, and Dayton, Ohio; Minneapolis-St. Paul; Phoenix; Dallas; and Washington, D.C. The restaurant count more than doubled in 1999, ending at 37. Revenues for the year totaled approximately $31 million, compared to $13 million for 1997. McDonald's increased its stake in Chipotle to more than 50 percent in 1999 and would later bump its ownership interest to 90 percent.

Another early benefit of the McDonald's relationship was that Chipotle could leverage McDonald's industry clout in, for example, getting a better supplier of avocados. Chipotle was also able to have supplies such as avocados shipped immediately through McDonald's massive distribution system. Such access was indispensable as Chipotle's operations spread out geographically.

ACCELERATING GROWTH, SHIFTING TO ORGANIC INGREDIENTS

Expansion accelerated in the first years of the 21st century, with the store count reaching 100 by the end of 2000 and then 175 at year-end 2001. Among the new markets were Baltimore, Houston, Los Angeles, and San Francisco. Around this same time, the company made the first significant changes to the menu since the first store opened. In addition to fine-tuning the recipe for its homemade guacamole, Chipotle switched to free-range pork for its carnitas. The supplier, Oakland, California-based Niman Ranch, raised its pigs "naturally." Niman allowed them to roam free, fed them a pure vegetarian diet, and did not give them any antibiotics or hormones. The result, according to Ells, was better-tasting pork. To use the higher-end and higher-priced product, Chipotle had to raise the price of its pork burritos by more than $1, to $5.50, but sales hardly suffered. Ells told *Nation's Restaurant News* for a July 30, 2001, article that "our customers can't get enough of the new recipe. ... In fact, we are selling two-and-a-half times more carnitas than before, and sales continue to rise." Overall revenues at Chipotle nearly doubled in 2001, reaching $131.6 million.

About 55 more Chipotles opened in 2002 and another 70 the following year, bringing the total to 300. As it celebrated its 10th anniversary, Chipotle ranked as one of the fastest-growing restaurant chains in the country. The chain entered the Las Vegas, Atlanta, and New York markets, among others, in 2003, by which time revenues had grown to $315.5 million. Same-unit sales were growing at an impressive rate of 20 percent per year. Late in 2003 McDonald's announced, contrary to earlier rumors, that it would sell neither Chipotle nor Boston Market, both of which were operating in the black (it soon sold Donatos Pizza, however). Chipotle remained a major growth avenue for McDonald's.

"FOOD WITH INTEGRITY"

Continuing to upgrade his food ingredients, Ells switched from yellow corn, which could contain genetically modified stock, to organic white corn, which did not have any genetically modified stock. He also began switching to organic beans, but a shortage of suppliers meant that Chipotle could get only 10 percent of the beans it needed from organic sources. In addition, he was running into similar problems finding suppliers of organic chicken. By mid-2004 Chipotle was offering naturally raised, antibiotic-free chicken from Bell & Evans in 50 restaurants in Washington, D.C., New York, and Ohio. Eight restaurants in Chicago and New York were using naturally raised beef. Overall, in making these and other changes to its food supplies, Chipotle showed that it was concerned with much more than us- ing simply fresh ingredients. The company also wanted to know where ingredients came from and how animals were raised. Ells encapsulated this increasing concern for the environmental and societal impact of his company by making "food with integrity" a guiding philosophy for how Chipotle operated as a business.

Starting with 2004, Chipotle increased its growth rate to 100 new units per year, which enabled the firm to approach the 500 restaurant mark by the end of 2005. The chain expanded into the Pacific Northwest by entering the Seattle and Portland, Oregon, markets and also moved into Florida, specifically Orlando and Tampa. Chipotle also beefed up its marketing efforts by hiring its first outside advertising agency, the New York office of an irreverent British agency, Mother. Chipotle had been producing its own humorous radio, print, and billboard ads featuring a photo of a burrito wrapped in foil accompanied by brief, witty copy, such as "A complete, four-course meal in a handy tortilla carrying pouch" or "Burrito? Or body pillow?" Chipotle's marketing budget was estimated to be $10 million per year.

Another development was an addition to the menu in response to the low-carb diet craze: Chipotle began offering its burritos in a bowl, sans tortilla, and with ro- maine lettuce standing in for rice. Within a year of its introduction, Chipotle restaurants had sold about seven million of these so-called burrito bowls. In 2004, in a change made well ahead of many others, Chipotle began using frying oil that was free of artery-clogging trans fats. The following summer, the company's restaurants added another new item to the menu: entrée salads. These romaine lettuce-based salads could be customized with the same assortment of ingredients customers could select for the chain's burritos or tacos, and they were topped with a chipotle-honey vinaigrette dressing that was made fresh daily in each restaurant. Chipotle reported revenues for 2005 of $627.7 million, nearly double the total for 2003, while net income for 2005 amounted to $37.7 million, a sixfold increase over that of the previous year.

RETURNING TO INDEPENDENCE AS PUBLIC COMPANY: 2006

During 2005 McDonald's reversed course and decided to spin off Chipotle, in part because the burger giant wanted to concentrate on its core business. In January 2006 Chipotle Mexican Grill, Inc. was taken public on the New York Stock Exchange through an initial public offering (IPO) of 7.88 million shares. By the end of the first day of trading, the shares had doubled in value, from the offering price of $22 per share to $44. The proceeds of more than $173 million were used to open up additional restaurants and to repay the chain's credit line with McDonald's. In May 2006 McDonald's sold a portion of its remaining majority stake in Chipotle through a secondary offering, and then in October of that same year McDonald's disposed of its remaining interest via a tax-free exchange that enabled shareholders to trade their McDonald's shares for shares in Chipotle.

During 2007, its first full year of post-McDonald's independence, Chipotle opened an additional 125 restaurants across the United States to bring the chain total to more than 700. Revenues that year increased 31.9 percent, surpassing the $1 billion mark for the first time, while the company also recorded its 10th consecu- tive year of double-digit same-unit sales growth. Chipot- le's growing popularity led to a major challenge at certain locations: lines at peak eating times that grew so long that some customers left, unwilling to wait. The chain worked to speed up the lines by adding automatic change machines to cash registers and employing hand- held credit-card devices to take orders from customers waiting in line.

Chipotle also continued to augment its "food with integrity" initiatives. In 2007 the company completed a transition to serving cheese and sour cream made only with milk from cows not treated with synthetic growth hormones. By the end of 2007, all of Chipotle's restaurants were serving naturally raised pork, while 55 percent offered naturally raised beef. In addition, 25 percent of the black and pinto beans served by the chain came from organic farms, and Chipotle restaurants began using locally sourced produce when seasonally available. By the spring of 2008, the company completed the rollout of naturally raised chicken to the entire Chipotle chain.

Among the 136 new restaurants opened in 2008 was a Toronto, Canada, unit, the first located outside the United States. Higher costs for almost all of the chain's raw ingredients led to the implementation dur- ing the fourth quarter of 2008 of across-the-board increases in menu prices at most of the chain's restaurants. Continued upward pricing pressures led Chipotle to institute a series of price increases on a regional basis over the next few years. Although higher prices and the sharp economic downturn were factors in same-unit sales growth of just 2.2 percent during 2009, the opening of 121 more restaurants that year helped push overall sales up 14 percent to $1.52 billion. Chipotle also posted the highest profit margin in its history that year as the company's relentless focus on efficiency, including a major effort to reduce the costs associated with opening a new restaurant, continued to pay dividends. The 2009 net income total of $126.8 million was 62 percent higher than that of the previous year.

PAST THE 1,000-RESTAURANT MARK

In the meantime, at the beginning of 2009, Monty Moran was promoted from president and COO to co-CEO of Chipotle, with Ells's CEO title changing to co-CEO. Moran had served as president and COO since March 2005 and before that had for a number of years acted as Chipotle's general counsel. Moran was charged mainly with handling the company's day-to-day activities, which enabled Ells to focus more of his time on ingredient sourcing, overseeing the chain's menu, restaurant design, marketing, and consumer outreach. Overall, Chipotle remained on the same path through 2010. The company opened 129 new restaurants that year, pushing the total over the 1,000-unit mark. Among the openings was a London, England, Chipotle, the first located outside North America.

Late in 2010 Chipotle ran afoul of a government crackdown on illegal immigrants when an audit conducted by the Immigration and Customs Enforcement arm of the U.S. Department of Homeland Security found more than 500 undocumented workers employed at Chipotle restaurants, mostly in Minnesota. The company was forced to let these workers go, which disrupted the operations of a number of restaurants. In 2011 the U.S. attorney's office in Washington, D.C., began a criminal probe into Chipotle's hiring practices, although the company denied breaking any laws, saying that some illegal immigrants had been hired "unintentionally." As this investigation unfolded, Moran began lobbying members of the U.S. Congress to overhaul the country's immigration laws. Documented immigrant workers were considered a key to Chipotle's success. About half of the workers at the company, which offered starting salaries well above the national minimum wage, were Hispanic.

Chipotle continued to accelerate its expansion, as the restaurant count exceeded 1,200 by the end of 2011 with plans for 155 to 165 openings in 2012, including the first unit located in Paris, France. In addition, the company launched a possible new avenue for growth: a fast-casual pan-Asian restaurant called ShopHouse Southeast Asian Kitchen, the first of which opened in Washington, D.C., in September 2011.

The inspiration for this new restaurant concept came from the traditional shophouses commonly found in Thailand, Malaysia, and Vietnam. In these two- or three-story buildings, families lived upstairs and ran restaurants on the ground floor. Ells's ShopHouse was essentially the Chipotle format in terms of food ordering and preparation, as well as the emphasis on fresh, "sustainably raised" ingredients, but featuring ingredients inspired by Southeast Asian cuisine, including grilled and braised meats, fresh vegetables, herbs, spicy sauces, and a variety of garnishes. The ShopHouse entrée selections included rice bowls and *bahn mi* sandwiches, a traditional baguette sandwich.

The Chipotle chain had proven to be a huge success for Ells. Revenues continued to mount and in 2011 the company was added to the prestigious S&P 500 stock index. It seemed unlikely that Ells could duplicate the success of his original concept with ShopHouse, but even a more modestly successful new chain would provide an important growth vehicle for Chipotle Mexican Grill and perhaps pave the way for other concepts using Chipotle's successful formula.

David E. Salamie

PRINCIPAL SUBSIDIARIES

Chipotle Mexican Grill of Colorado, LLC; Chipotle Mexican Grill of Maryland, LLC; Chipotle Mexican Grill of Kansas, LLC; Chipotle Mexican Grill Service Co., LLC; Chipotle Mexican Grill U.S. Finance Co., LLC; CMGGC, LLC; Chipotle Mexican Grill Texas Holdings, LLC; Chipotle Texas, LLC; Chipotle Mexican Grill Canada Corp.; Chipotle Mexican Grill Holdings GmbH (Switzerland); Chipotle Mexican Grill Management GmbH (Switzerland); Chipotle Mexican Grill UK Limited; Chipotle Mexican Grill France SAS.

PRINCIPAL COMPETITORS

El Pollo Loco Holdings, Inc.; Fresh Enterprises, LLC; MSWG, LLC; Panchero's Franchise Corporation; Qdoba Restaurant Corporation; Rubio's Restaurants, Inc.

FURTHER READING

Adamy, Janet. "Burrito Chain Assembles a Winning Combo: Ignoring Fast-Food Formula, Chipotle Promotes Service, Costly Natural Ingredients." *Wall Street Journal*, November

23, 2007, B1, B2.

Alsever, Jennifer. "Quest for a New Burrito: CEO Brings Natural Foods to Fold." *Denver Post*, May 9, 2004, K1.

Bernstein, Charles. "The Right Combination: Chipotle Grows with Steve Ells' Youth and Food Fanaticism Plus McDonald's Experience and Deep Pockets." *Chain Leader*, May 2001, 54–56, 58, 60.

Brand, Rachel. "Chipotle Founder Had Big Dreams." *Rocky Mountain News*, December 23, 2006, 1C.

Cavanaugh, Bonnie Brewer. "Steve Ells." *Nation's Restaurant News*, October 4, 2004, 114, 116.

Forgrieve, Janet. "Feeding Frenzy: Investors Snap Up Chipotle Shares, Doubling IPO Price." *Rocky Mountain News*, January 27, 2006, 1B.

Frumkin, Paul. "McD Divesting 88-Percent Chipotle Stake through Stock Swap." *Nation's Restaurant News*, September 18, 2006, 9.

Garber, Amy. "McD to Spin Off Stake in Chipotle Burrito Brand Early Next Year." *Nation's Restaurant News*, October 3, 2005, 1, 89.

Jordan, Miriam. "A CEO's Demand: Fix Immigration." *Wall Street Journal*, December 19, 2011, B1, B8.

———. "Chipotle Workers Draw Scrutiny." *Wall Street Journal*, February 8, 2011, B1.

Kaplan, David A. "Chipotle's Growth Machine." *Fortune*, September 26, 2011, 34+.

Markels, Alex. "Chipotle's Secret Salsa." *U.S. News and World Report*, January 21, 2008, 41.

Raabe, Steve. "Probe Weighs on Chipotle: Chain a High-Profile Target as Immigration Investigations Increasingly Focus on Employers." *Denver Post*, May 8, 2011, K1.

Ruggless, Ron. "Steve Ells: Taking Quick Service to New Levels of Sophistication at Chipotle Mexican Grill." *Nation's Restaurant News*, January 25, 1999, 68, 77.

St. John, Bill. "Chipotle Mexican Grill: Just Like the Pepper, It's All Jazzed Up." *Rocky Mountain News*, October 22, 1993, 20D.

Zuber, Amy. "Chipotle Upgrades Menu Items, Will Drop 'Mexican Grill' Name." *Nation's Restaurant News*, July 30, 2001, 4, 69.

Colony Capital, LLC

2450 Broadway, 6th Floor
Santa Monica, California 90404
U.S.A.
Telephone: (310) 282-8820
Fax: (310) 282-8808
Web site: http://www.colonyinc.com

Private Company
Incorporated: 1991
Employees: 200
Sales: $200 million (2010 est.)
NAICS: 525930 Real Estate Investment Trusts; 525990 Other Financial Vehicles

■ ■ ■

Colony Capital, LLC, is the third-largest private equity real estate company in the world, controlling $36 billion in private equity and real estate investments. Colony Capital also invests in nonperforming loans and distressed assets. The company maintains offices in Los Angeles, New York, Boston, London, Madrid, Paris, Rome, Beirut, Hong Kong, Beijing, Tokyo, Seoul, and Taipei.

FOUNDER'S BACKGROUND: 1976–91

At the helm of one of the most prolific investment firms in the United States was its founder, Thomas J. Barrack. The son of a grocer, Barrack grew up in Culver City, California, during the 1950s, attended law school at the University of San Diego, and worked as a lawyer until embarking on his real estate career in 1976. Barrack's switch in professions introduced him to Texas financier Robert M. Bass, one of the four Bass brothers who parlayed an estate left to them by their father (Perry R. Bass) and uncle (the Texas wildcatter Sid Richardson) into a much bigger fortune. Each of the Bass brothers became billionaires during their careers. Robert Bass built part of his empire by launching his own investment firm, the Robert M. Bass Group, in 1986, through which he invested more than $1.2 billion in two dozen transactions. Barrack aided Bass during the period, serving as managing director of RMB Realty Inc., Bass's real estate investment and management vehicle. During the second half of the 1980s, Barrack oversaw several large deals, including the purchase of Westin Hotels & Resorts and California-based American Savings Bank. In 1991 Barrack left Bass and struck out on his own, forming Colony Capital.

Barrack, through Colony Capital, managed an opportunity fund, sometimes referred to as a vulture fund. Opportunity funds arose during the savings and loan banking crisis of the late 1980s and early 1990s, when 747 out of the 3,234 savings and loans associations in the United States collapsed. To resolve the crisis, a government-owned asset management company was formed, the Resolution Trust Corporation (RTC), which was tasked with liquidating the assets that had been controlled by the failed savings and loan associations. The assets were primarily real estate-related assets such as mortgage loans, assets that drew the attention of Barrack and a small group of other shrewd investors. They saw opportunity in the financial mess, while the major-

COMPANY PERSPECTIVES

Through the identification of supply-demand source imbalances in capital, product types and information availability, Colony achieves attractive risk-adjusted returns by investing in real estate, non-performing loans, distressed assets, real estate-dependent operating companies, and select commercial and residential development opportunities throughout the world.

ity of the investment community looked askance at the sour mortgages seized by the RTC.

In 1991, in a deal that coincided with the formation of Colony Capital, Barrack purchased part of the first pooled RTC portfolio of assets. Colony Capital, along with General Electric Capital Corp. and Barrack's former employer, the Robert M. Bass Group Inc., acquired a group of apartment buildings, properties with a face value of $1.1 billion that the joint venture purchased for $527 million.

ENTICING RETURNS: 1991–95

The savings and loan crisis presented an opportunity to buy real estate for between 20 cents and 50 cents on the dollar. Colony Capital, Goldman Sachs, Morgan Stanley, Apollo Real Estate Advisors, and perhaps six or seven other firms seized the opportunity, forming the first wave of investors that would purchase $400 billion in real estate assets from the RTC during the next four years. The premise of the investment strategy was simple. "It was a basic idea," Barrack said in the October 2001 issue of *National Real Estate Investor*. "Buy when everything is down and sell when it goes back up." The investment firms typically sold the real estate back to the original owners or developers for roughly 60 cents on the dollar. "We also loaned about 70 percent of the purchase price to the developers," Barrack told *National Real Estate Investor*. "In that period, we were making incredible returns, north of 70 percent," he added.

Barrack made his name and cemented Colony Capital's reputation in the RTC era. He orchestrated massive deals, made jaw-dropping profits, and established Colony Capital as a known name in the investment community. The period of RTC-led liquidation lasted for only a handful of years, however. The RTC, formed in 1989, was shut down in 1995, its task of dealing with the assets held by failed savings and loan

associations completed. Market conditions had stabilized in the United States, but instability and market inefficiencies existed elsewhere. Barrack's objective was to find those opportunities, and he found them in Europe, where he directed Colony Capital's investment activities in 1995.

BARRACK HEADS TO EUROPE: 1995

Midway through the decade, property markets in Western Europe and the United Kingdom resembled conditions that existed during the RTC era in the United States. Barrack swooped in, purchasing distressed real estate property. After a change in German tax law, incentives were created that encouraged German investment funds to purchase real estate in neighboring countries, which they did, demonstrating a willingness to pay large sums for their purchases. In Europe, during the second half of the 1990s, Colony Capital averaged an approximately 25 percent return on investment.

The common theme and distinguishing trait of Barrack's first decade of leading Colony Capital was his preference for buying companies whose business was dependent on real estate. Barrack did not buy real estate to function as a landlord. "We find operating companies that use real estate, where there's complexity or they're out of current appeal," he said in the June 2000 issue of *Continental Magazine*. Tellingly, when he decided to take part in the explosive growth of the dot-com sector in the late 1990s, he purchased a stake in a company that owned buildings housing computer servers.

By the end of the decade, Barrack had invested $6 billion through four Colony Capital funds. The firm's funds, open to only the largest of institutional investors, yielded impressive returns, ensuring that Barrack's investment activities in the next decade would intensify. Colony Capital invested $6 billion during its first nine years of existence. During the succeeding years, the firm would come close to equaling the total in a single transaction.

A FOCUS ON CASINOS AND HOTELS: 2001–05

One area of particular interest to Barrack in the decade ahead was the gaming industry, where stocks were trading at historic lows. He obtained a gaming license in the late 1990s and became one of the few investors licensed to own gaming companies. His first major deal was the purchase of Harvey's Casino Resorts, which owned properties in Iowa, Colorado, and Lake Tahoe, Nevada. Colony Capital paid $405 million for the company in 1998 and sold it for $675 million in 2001.

During the first decade of the 21st century, Colony Capital became one of the largest private equity real estate investors in the world. The firm's largest deals involved acquiring gaming properties, hotels, and resorts, deals that were completed through four funds, Colony Investors V through Colony Investors VIII. Through Colony Investors V, the firm invested $340 million in 2003 to acquire four hotels and a 51 percent interest in 6,000 acres of undeveloped oceanfront land at Costa Smeralda, in Sardinia, Italy. Several months later, the firm paid $722 million to purchase the Fukuoka Dome baseball park, a shopping mall, and hotel located in Fukuoka, Japan. Acquiring the properties, owned by Daiei Inc., a financially ailing supermarket operator, primarily involved the transfer of interest-bearing debt and other liabilities.

High-profile acquisitions followed in 2004, as Colony Capital increased its involvement in the gaming industry. In June the firm purchased the Las Vegas Hilton Hotel and Casino from Park Place Entertainment Corp. for $280 million. Colony Capital announced it would invest up to $67 million over a four-year period to renovate the property. In September Barrack brokered a massive deal with Harrah's Entertainment and Caesars Entertainment, the new name for Park Place Entertainment. Harrah's Entertainment and Caesars Entertainment were preparing to merge in a $9.4 billion deal that required the two parties to divest certain assets. Colony Capital benefited from the merger, agreeing to pay $1.24 billion for two casinos in Tunica, Mississippi; the Atlantic City Hilton in New Jersey; and Harrah's East Chicago. The acquisition was completed in 2005.

The scale of Barrack's investments increased during the second half of the decade, elevating Colony Capital's

stature. The firm became of the three largest private equity real estate firms in the world during the period, trailing only Blackstone Group and Morgan Stanley Real Estate. In 2005 the firm paid roughly $1 billion to acquire Singapore-based Raffles International Ltd., which operated 41 hotels and resorts under the Raffles Hotel and Swissotel banners. The following year Colony Capital joined forces with Kingdom Hotels International, owned by Saudi Prince Alwaleed bin Talal, to buy Fairmont Hotels & Resorts Inc. for $3.9 billion. Based in Toronto, Canada, Fairmont owned 87 properties with an aggregate of 34,000 rooms. Following the acquisition, Colony Capital revealed plans to combine Fairmont and Raffles to create a single hotel brand for 120 hotels in 24 countries.

ACQUISITIONS AND DISTRESSED DEBT: 2007–11

One of the largest deals in Colony Capital's first 20 years of existence took place one year after the investment in Fairmont. In 2007 the firm led a group that made a bid for Las Vegas-based Station Casinos Inc., which owned 18 hotels and casinos. Colony Capital invested $2.6 billion for a 75 percent interest in the company, taking the biggest share of a deal valued at $8.9 billion when the assumption of Station's $3.4 billion in debt was included. The investment proved to be one of Barrack's mistakes, however, after Station filed for bankruptcy in 2009.

Barrack hoped to improve his position with the Station properties after reorganizing under the protection of Chapter 11, but the sting of the miscue did little to temper his desire for risky investments. The end of the decade brought economic conditions that presented numerous opportunities to Barrack. The global financial crisis of the period was a clear example of market instability, prompting Barrack to plunge headlong into the economic morass. In 2009 Colony Capital concluded a deal with the Federal Deposit Insurance Corporation (FDIC), a U.S. government-run corporation, to acquire approximately 1,200 loans with an aggregate, unpaid principal balance of $1.02 billion, substantially all of which was commercial real estate loans. The deal to acquire distressed debt was completed in January 2010. Several months later, Colony Capital was part of a group that paid more than an estimated $1 billion to buy San Francisco's First Republic Bank, which operated in six U.S. states.

Barrack and Colony Capital showed no signs of lessening their investment activities as the firm celebrated its 20th anniversary in 2011. In January, Colony Capital and another private equity firm, Cogsville Group, purchased two real estate portfolios filled with the distressed assets of 14 failed financial institutions from the FDIC. The following month, Colony Capital struck another deal with the FDIC, acquiring distressed real estate loans with an unpaid principal of $817 million for $193 million. The deal making, as it had throughout Colony Capital's history, continued, promising the firm would remain a prolific real estate investor in the years ahead.

Jeffrey L. Covell

PRINCIPAL SUBSIDIARIES

Colony Resorts LVH Acquisitions, LLC; Colony Capital Inc.; Colony Financial, Inc.

PRINCIPAL COMPETITORS

Apollo Global Management, LLC; Equity Group Investments, L.L.C.; Four Seasons Holdings Inc.

FURTHER READING

Berke, Jonathan. "Colony to Make $1.24B Casinos Deal." *Daily Deal*, September 27, 2004.

Clifford, Hal. "Ahead of the Curve." *Continental Magazine*, June 2000.

"Colony Capital, LLC and Investor Consortium Announce Two Transactions with FDIC." *Bezinga.com*, December 20, 2010.

Fickes, Mike. "Feasting on Market Inefficiency Worldwide: Successful 'Vulture' or Opportunity Funds Capitalize on High-Risk Properties with Unrecognized Value." *National Real Estate Investor*, October 2001.

Holtmann, Andy. "Private Acceptance: Revised Buyout Bid of $90 Per Share Accepted by Station Casinos' Board." *Casino Journal*, April 2007.

"Park Place Announces Agreement to Sell Las Vegas Hilton to Colony Capital." *Business Wire*, December 24, 2003.

Smith, Charles. "Daiei Assets Go to Colony." *Daily Deal*, December 3, 2003.

Consorzio del Formaggio Parmigiano-Reggiano

—■—

Via Kennedy, 18
Reggio Emilia, 42124
Italy
Telephone: (+39 0522) 307741
Fax: (+39 0522) 307748
Web site: http://www.parmigiano-reggiano.it

Private Organization
Founded: 1934
Incorporated: 1954
NAICS: 311513 Cheese Manufacturing

■ ■ ■

Consorzio del Formaggio Parmigiano-Reggiano is the consortium supporting the interests of the more than 460 dairies and nearly 3,700 farmers involved in the production of world-famous Parmigiano-Reggiano, or Parmesan, cheese. Each year, members pay an annual fee representing approximately 1 percent of the wholesale value of the total number of their cheeses that have been stamped (approved) by the consortium. In 2011, the total production of Parmigiano-Reggiano cheese reached 114,000 metric tons, 82 percent of which is sold in Italy.

ORIGINS OF PARMIGIANO-REGGIANO CHEESE

While Parmigiano-Reggiano was granted its status as an Appellation of Origin (AO) in 1951, the cheese's history dates back at least 1,000 years. At the collapse of the Roman Empire, the mountainous region of northern Italy, particularly the future provinces of Parma and Reggio Emilia, as well as parts of Modena and Bologna, were considered too marshy to be of value for agricultural purposes. In the late Middle Ages, however, groups of Benedictine monks moved into the region around the River Po, where they had been granted extensive landholdings, both from the civil and religious authorities of the time, as well as from the general population. The monks began land reclamation activities, converting large areas of land to fertile agricultural fields, where they planted grains and other cereals, and made use of the small number of cattle in the area to help them work the fields. The plains to the south of the river were in general reserved as pastureland for cattle. This in turn brought about major increases in the region's cattle herds.

The presence of larger herds of cattle meant that production of cow milk-based cheese became viable for the first time. Previously, the region's cheese production, which itself dated back to the Roman era, had been exclusively confined to sheep's milk cheese. The Benedictine monks proved instrumental in the development of the region's classic cheese varieties, which included a similar cheese to Parmigiano-Reggiano, called Grana. Both cheeses were produced using a double-heating method developed by the Benedictines. The Benedictine order proved central to the creation of many of Europe's iconic cheeses, such as French Munster, Cluny, and Saint-Maur, named for the monasteries that first produced them.

Parmigiano cheese had its center in Parma but was also produced in surrounding areas, including Reggio

COMPANY PERSPECTIVES

Parmigiano-Reggiano is a cheese with a long history and famous today throughout the world. Parmigiano-Reggiano is a true product of the land and of the traditions of the people who produce it. Those who like good food and fine flavor, those who appreciate the importance of heritage and those who have a true respect for nature and origin will really enjoy this cheese.

Emilia, named for its position along the Roman road Via Emilia. Parmigiano's fame spread far beyond its home region, however, becoming one of the favorite cheeses not only in Italy, but elsewhere in Europe. A first official mention of the Parmigiano name appeared in 1344 in the ledgers of the Prior's Refectory in Florence. Evidence of the cheese's widespread popularity was underscored in its appearance in Boccaccio's *Decameron* just four years later.

REACHING THE UNITED STATES IN THE 18TH CENTURY

Over the next centuries the process for producing the cheese saw continued refinements. Among the notable innovations was the practice of "salting" the cheese, that is, leaving a wheel of cheese in a vat of brine so that the cheese absorbed the salt. Cheese makers also began ripening the cheeses, leaving them to mature for increasingly longer periods, a process essential to the flavor and texture of parmesan cheese. From the 16th century, as the influence of the Benedictines in the region waned, cheese making became the province of an increasing number of small dairies, largely controlled by the nobility and other wealthier members of society.

Farming in the region also improved considerably and became responsible for another important part of the future Parmigiano-Reggiano specification. Through the 18th century, farmers adopted crop rotation techniques, planting fields with clover and alfalfa, both of which played a part in Parmigiano's distinctive flavor. This period also saw early cooperative efforts, such as the institution of "turning" or mutual cheese dairies, in which each member of a group was given a turn at producing cheese. In this way, even smaller farmers were able to produce and sell cheese.

The political and economic turmoil and corresponding drop in production in the Parma region, during the 18th century and into the 19th century, provided an early signal of the need to protect the Parmigiano cheese variety. A group of merchants in Parma took advantage of the situation, bringing in cheese from Lodi, in Reggio Emilia, and marketing it as Parmigiano. This cheese was also known as Lodigniano. In the late 19th century, the Lodi cheese adopted the new name of Reggiano.

During the 19th century, the turning cheese dairy system began to break down, in part because of the distrust between farmers and cheese makers. Instead, the market became dominated by commercial dairies, which not only produced cheese but also marketed and distributed it. By the end of the 19th century, the region counted a growing number of commercial dairies.

By then, Parmigiano's fame had spread well beyond Italy. France had long been an important export market, and by the 18th century, Parmigiano had become, alongside Gruyère, one of the staple cheeses of fine French cuisine. France's gastronomic influence helped establish Parmigiano's reputation worldwide, including in the United States. In the second half of the 18th century, parmesan cheese had already begun to appear as an ingredient in cookbooks. As president, Thomas Jefferson played a role in boosting imports of the cheese, which grew to become one of the best-selling cheeses in the country.

DISPUTES IN THE EARLY 20TH CENTURY

The number of commercial cheese dairies in the Parmigiano-Reggiano region grew strongly through the end of the 19th century and into the 20th century. From around 50 dairies in Parma in the 1850s, the sector jumped to nearly 1,000 dairies at the end of the century. These included dairies in Reggio Emilia and Modena, starting in the 1870s. By the 1920s, the Parma region alone counted nearly 1,000 dairies, while Reggio Emilia numbered 500, and Modena more than 700.

The rise in dairies was accompanied by a new dispute in the Parmigiano-Reggiano appellation. In 1895, the province of Milan, which included the town of Lodi, declared that only cheese produced in its region could claim the Parmigiano-Reggiano name. The dairy industry in Parma responded by challenging this decision in court. As a result, the Milan cheese makers were denied the right to call their cheese Parmigiano-Reggiano in 1899.

A dispute soon broke out between Parma and Reggio Emilia, however. In 1901, Reggio proposed the creation of a trade union, linking cheese makers and distributors, which would also establish specifications for

KEY DATES

1934: Consorzio Volontario Interprovinciale del Grana Tipico is created to oversee the production and marketing of Parmigiano-Reggiano cheese.

1954: Consortium changes its name to Consorzio del Formaggio Parmigiano-Reggiano.

1995: Consortium allows corporations into its membership.

1999: Consortium wins a landmark case against Nuova Castelli.

2007: European Union rules that "Parmesan" is not a generic term.

2011: Cheeses from two U.S. companies are seized as imitation Parmigiano-Reggiano.

the Parmigiano-Reggiano variety. Parma's response came in 1904, with an attempt to shorten the cheese's name, to simply "Parmigiano." This resulted in a feud of sorts between the two towns, with Parma calling its cheese Grana Parmigiano and Reggio calling its cheese Reggiano.

The dispute continued on and off for the next three decades. An attempt was made to codify and name the cheese produced in Parma and Reggio Emilia, as well as in parts of Modena and Mantua in 1909, when the chambers of commerce of the four towns met to discuss creating a common mark for the cheese. The parties could not reach an agreement, however. Instead, Parma and Reggio Emilia each began developing their own marks, to be imprinted into the cheese itself, with the initials F.P. (Formaggio Parmigiano) and G.R.R.E. (Grana reggiano di Reggio Emilia, i.e., Reggiano Hard Cheese from Reggio Emilia), respectively.

CREATING A CONSORTIUM IN 1934

Neither town made much progress in implementing their new appellations, in part due to the outbreak of World War I. In the beginning of the 1920s, however, the two regions faced a new, common threat. Italian immigrants to Argentina had brought with them the technique for making their own variant of Parmigiano-Reggiano cheese. Because they produced smaller wheels (less than seven kilograms, as compared to the average weight of 39 kilograms per wheel of Parmigiano Reggiano), they called their cheese Reggianito. This cheese, saltier than its Italian parent, was also aged for far less

time, under six months as opposed to the minimum of 12 months for Parmigiano-Reggiano.

The far less expensive Reggianito found a strong market in the United States, where a number of major food brands began marketing the cheese as "Parmesan." Faced with this pressure, which only exacerbated the effects of the Great Depression on the region's cheese industry, the Parma and Reggio Emilia sides at last recognized the need to join together and create a single organization to defend their interests. Another motivation came from the province of Milan, which attempted to establish a single overriding brand name for Italy's "Grana" type cheeses.

In 1934, the parties agreed to the creation of the Parmigiano-Reggiano brand. A new organization was established, initially called the Consorzio Volontario Interprovinciale del Grana Tipico (Voluntary Interprovincial Consortium of Typical Grana). This consortium became the first in Italy established in order to protect a regional specialty. The charter for the new organization defined the Parmigiano-Reggiano region as including Parma, Reggio, and Modena provinces, as well as the region south of the River Po in Mantua. Three years later, under the guidance of the Ministry of Agriculture, a small strip of the province of Bologna was added to the definition.

APPELLATION OF ORIGIN IN THE FIFTIES

The consortium struggled through the years of World War II, and had all but collapsed by 1945. Into the early 1950s, the consortium remained at a virtual standstill. During this decade, however, the movement toward the recognition of, and protection of, regional foods and their specificity was soon to result in the creation of the World Intellectual Property Organization (WIPO) and the official creation of the Appellation of Origin (AO) system. This effort had begun in the 1920s, when the Dairy International Congress had begun including place of origin in the definition of certain types of cheese. The AO system was formally established in 1951, and included Gorgonzola, Pecorino, Romano, Roquefort, and Parmigiano-Reggiano as the first to receive protected status.

The Parmigiano-Reggiano consortium was reformed in 1954 under the name Consorzio del Formaggio Parmigiano-Reggiano. The following year, the Italian government passed legislation providing Parmigiano-Reggiano with legal status as a trademark, with the stipulation that this cheese come only from the Parmigiano-Reggiano region and also comply with certain restrictions and characteristics. Among these, only raw milk was to be used, and only milk from grass-fed cattle. In addition, no additives, colorings, or other artificial ingredients were allowed to be used. The consortium also put into place a grading system, based on length of aging.

Further enforcement of the AO system came in 1958, with the signing of the Lisbon Agreement for the Protection of Appellations of Origin and their International Registration. Parmigiano-Reggiano's formal registration as an AO came in 1969. By then, the consortium had developed its own mark, featuring a dotted inscription circling the cheese wheels, introduced in 1964.

ADVERTISING EFFORT IN THE SEVENTIES

The devaluation of the Italian lira during the 1970s threw the region's cheese industry into crisis, as Parmigiano-Reggiano cheeses experienced a dramatic price increase. With sales dropping sharply, the consortium launched its first-ever national advertising campaign. This effort sought to underscore the nutritional value of the cheese, as well as justify its price, by publicizing the fact that more than 16 liters of milk were required to produce just one kilo of cheese.

The consortium steadily increased its advertising budget in the 1980s, launching a series of promotions in supermarkets and in schools starting in 1984. Part of this effort was directed toward introducing new ways of eating the cheese. While Parmigiano-Reggiano was traditionally grated as a topping for pasta and other recipes, the consortium promoted its use as a simple snack as well. One of the companies joining in this effort was Parmareggio, founded in 1984 by William Iori, which became a pioneer in new packaging for the cheese. Among this company's innovations was its "Mito" branded snack food. Destined for vending machines, the package featured a 20-gram piece of Parmigiano-Reggiano, along with a cracker. Parmareggio received special permission to market the product from the consortium.

The consortium's advertising budget grew even larger at the end of the 1980s and into the 1990s, in part in order to compensate for the overproduction of cheese, as new farmer technologies enabled dairy farmers to achieve higher milk yields. The consortium began sponsoring sports and other events during this time, as well as participating in trade fairs around the world. The consortium also adopted a quota system in order to control the production volume of its members. This system was abandoned, however, after it was challenged by the Italian antitrust authority in 1996.

LANDMARK CASE IN 2002

The consortium faced other challenges leading into the new century. In 1995, the organization yielded to pressures from its external network of maturing firms, wholesalers, and distributors and modified its constitution to allow commercial organizations to become members of the consortium for the first time. This decision, however, placed the group's dairy farmers and cheese makers at risk of becoming dominated by the more economically powerful commercial enterprises. In addition, unlike the farmers and cheese makers, these companies did not necessarily share an exclusive focus on a single product, and might also have interests in competitive products, including Grana Padano.

A more significant threat came from outside of the consortium's core region. One of the consortium's primary objectives was the defense of the Parmigiano-Reggiano brand. To this end, the consortium stepped up its efforts to shut down imitation cheeses and head off what the Italian government labeled as "agro-piracy." Among the consortium's actions was to include, in 1991, specifications stipulating the cheese must be packaged in the region defined by the Parmigiano-Reggiano AO.

The consortium also defended the integrity of its trademark, and in particular targeted manufacturers marketing cheese as "Parmesan." In 1996, the consortium officially registered the Parmigiano-Reggiano trademark with the European Union. This set the stage for the company's assertion that the label "Parmesan" represented a variation of the term *Parmigiano-Reggiano* and therefore was protected under the same trademark and appellation of origin.

In 1999, the consortium won a landmark case against Nuova Castelli SpA, a company located in Reggio Emilia that had been marketing a product in Europe labeled "Parmesan," even though the product contained no Parmigiano-Reggiano at all. Despite protests from the German and Austrian governments, the European court ruled in the consortium's favor, extending the cheese's AO protection to include the term *Parmesan* as well as other similar variants.

THWARTING IMITATIONS IN 2011

The consortium continued to score victories over imitators through the decade. In 2004, for example, Spanish foods giant Campofrio agreed to honor the Parmigiano-Reggiano and Parmesan trademarks. The company scored a new victory in the United States the following year, successfully blocking Wisconsin-based Blaser's USA from using its trademarks. The consortium also locked horns with foods giant Kraft Foods, which attempted to market a so-called "fast-cured" parmesan cheese, aged for only six months.

In 2007, the European Union reaffirmed that the word *Parmesan* could not be used as a generic term, against a challenge launched by Germany. This decision was reaffirmed in 2008, by a ruling from the European Court of Justice. The first successful application of this ruling came in 2010, when the Court of Cologne banned Fuchs Gewürze GmbH from marketing a cheese called Parmetta.

The consortium's efforts continued into 2011, leading to seizures of imitation parmesan cheeses produced by two companies in the United States. The company also successfully defended itself against the marketing of "parmesano" and "reggianito" cheeses in South America.

At the same time, the consortium took other steps to promote its cheese and ensure its quality. In 2006, the consortium joined with the provinces of Bologna, Modena, Parma, and Reggio Emilia to found a Cheese Maker's School, in order to ensure the supply of future cheese masters. The company scored a marketing coup when Parmigiano-Reggiano was named part of the official diet of the International Space Station. The Consorzio del Formaggio Parmigiano-Reggiano remained committed, presumably for decades to come, to protecting and promoting one of the world's most famous cheeses.

M. L. Cohen

PRINCIPAL COMPETITORS

Consorzio di Grana Padano.

FURTHER READING

"Annual Parmigiano Reggiano 'Crack Off' at Whole Foods Market Celebrates Italian King of Cheese." *Food Business Week*, April 21, 2011, 11.

Bentz Crowley, Marilyn. "King of Cheese." *Chatelaine*, June 1999, 160H.

Croft, Martin. "European Court Blocks Sales of 'Fake' Parmesan." *Marketing Week*, June 27, 2002, 10.

De Roest, Kees. *The Production of Parmigiano-Reggiano Cheese: The Force of an Artisanal System in an Industrialised World.* Amsterdam: Uitgeverij Van Gorcum, 2000.

Fletcher, Janet. "A Visit to Italy Rekindles a Love Affair." *San Francisco Chronicle*, January 22, 2004, D4.

"Government Bails out Parmesan Producers." *Dairy Industries International*, January 2009, 11.

"Parmesan—The King of Cheeses." *WIPO*, February 2011.

"Parmigiano Reggiano." *Dairy Industries International*, January 2011, 7.

"Parmigiano Reggiano Cheese Output Down, Exports Up." *Dairy Markets Weekly*, March 1, 2001, 9.

"Parmigiano-Reggiano Consorzio and Rienzi & Sons Settle Lawsuit." *Gourmet Retailer*, September 2002, 10.

"Playing with Packs." *Dairy Industries International*, March 2005, 19.

"Shortages May Push up Parmesan Price." *Grocer*, December 5, 2009, 64.

"Six-Month Parmesan? No, Say Producers." *Dairy Industries International*, March 2006, 10.

Cooper Industries plc

5 Fitzwilliam Square
Dublin, 2
Ireland
600 Travis Street, Suite 5600
Houston, Texas 77002
U.S.A.
Telephone: (713) 209-8400
Fax: (713) 209-8996
Web site: http://www.cooperindustries.com

Public Company
Incorporated: 1895 as the C. & G. Cooper Company
Employees: 24,795
Sales: $5.06 billion (2010)
Stock Exchanges: New York
Ticker Symbol: CBE
NAICS: 332212 Hand and Edge Tool Manufacturing; 332510 Hardware Manufacturing; 335122 Commercial, Industrial, and Institutional Electric Lighting Fixture Manufacturing; 335311 Power, Distribution, and Specialty Transformer Manufacturing; 335999 All Other Miscellaneous Electrical Equipment and Component Manufacturing

■ ■ ■

Cooper Industries plc is a global electrical products manufacturer that serves the residential, commercial, and industrial construction markets. Products include wiring devices, power management and distribution equipment, and circuit protection equipment. Notable brands include Bussmann electrical and electronic fuses, Halo and Metalux lighting fixtures, Kyle and McGraw-Edison power systems, and Crouse-Hinds electrical equipment. Cooper maintains approximately 130 manufacturing plants in 21 countries, deriving 39 percent of its annual revenue from outside the United States. Cooper's corporate headquarters are based in Dublin, Ireland, and its administrative headquarters are based in Houston, Texas.

EARLY HISTORY: 1833–95

Brothers Charles and Elias Cooper built a foundry in 1833 in their hometown of Mount Vernon, Ohio, and called it Mt. Vernon Iron Works. Soon better known as C. & E. Cooper Company, the firm's first products were plows, maple syrup kettles, hog troughs, sorghum grinders, and wagon boxes. Charles Cooper was the stronger leader. Aggressively antislavery and a dedicated prohibitionist, he became a respected community leader, even though many of his views differed greatly from those of his neighbors. When Elias Cooper died in 1848, Charles Cooper took a succession of partners, and with each the company name changed accordingly.

Mount Vernon was linked to the rest of the nation by the railroad in 1851, and the following year Cooper was able to ship its first steam-powered compressors for blast furnaces. Cooper's relationship with the railroad had its difficulties, however. When the Sandusky, Mansfield, and Newark Railway was delinquent in paying for wood-burning locomotives from the company, Charles Cooper was driven to chain the wheels of a locomotive to the track, padlock it, and stand sentry until he was paid in full.

COMPANY PERSPECTIVES

Cooper's portfolio is well-positioned to the most critical, fastest growing global end markets. Additionally, the majority of our portfolio now participates in one or more of four key global trends: increasing worldwide electricity consumption and the need to upgrade the electrical grid; growing demand for alternative, sustainable and energy-efficient technologies; the continuing global infrastructure build-out; and the increasing need for ensuring the safety and protection of people, equipment and facilities.

By the time of the Civil War, Cooper products included wood-burning steam locomotives and steam-powered blowing machines for charcoal blast furnaces. After Charles Gray Cooper, son of Elias, served in the Union army and attended Rensselaer Institute, he became a partner with his uncle.

In 1869 Cooper became the first company in what was then the West to produce the new, highly efficient Corliss engine. Six years later, it offered the Cooper traction engine, the first farm tractor in the United States. Throughout the rest of the century, the Corliss engine was Cooper's principal product.

FROM STEAM TO NATURAL GAS: 1895–1929

The company was incorporated as C. & G. Cooper Company in 1895. Frank L. Fairchild, a respected salesman of the Cooper-Corliss engine, was named its first president. Fairchild so enjoyed selling that throughout his 17-year presidency he continued to serve as sales manager. By 1900 gas was being discovered in new fields and shipped more than 100 miles through primitive pipelines. At the same time, the oil industry was also beginning to develop. Not long after Charles Cooper's death in 1901, it became clear that steam turbine engines were destined to replace the Corliss engine. Cooper management recognized the necessity of focusing on a small segment of the market, and in 1908 it wisely chose to make a gradual change to natural-gas internal-combustion engines, which were being used successfully at the compression stage of pipeline transmission.

During World War I, Cooper built high-speed steam-hydraulic forging presses for government arsenals, munitions plants, and shipyards, as well as giant gas engines and compressors and triple-expansion marine engines. The company's wartime production demands slowed its transformation from a producer of steam to gas engines, since steam engines were needed for the war effort. After the war, it became clear that the company had chosen its direction wisely when it set its sights on developing gas internal-combustion engines. The old Corliss was quickly becoming outmoded by competition from steam turbines and gas-powered engines.

Fairchild died suddenly in 1912 and Charles Gray (C. G.) Cooper, took his place. In 1919 C. G. Cooper became chairman and Desault B. Kirk, the company's treasurer, became president. Just a year later, Cooper began a long-range program for growth, and the directors elected Beatty B. Williams president. Although he had married the boss's daughter, few credited Williams's rise to simply marrying into the family. Serving as vice president and general manager during the war years, Williams was single-minded in his dedication to the company's success and directed Cooper (and subsequently Cooper-Bessemer) with great energy and foresight for 22 years. Always mindful of the distance that could develop between office and factory workers, Williams held conferences in which factory workers were invited to air their views and offered evening courses in production and management in which any employee could enroll.

Natural gas was gaining growing importance in the manufacture of steel and glass and in the emerging petrochemical industry. Cooper field service engineers were often on hand for months at a time to oversee the installation of huge four-cycle Cooper engines and compressors in compressor stations as new pipelines were routed through West Virginia, Louisiana, Arkansas, Oklahoma, and Texas.

MERGER WITH BESSEMER: 1929

Within just a few years, Cooper became the country's leading producer of pipeline compression engines. Although Cooper also produced smaller two-cylinder engines used in natural-gas fields to extract gas as it came from the well, the Bessemer Gas Engine Company of Grove City, Pennsylvania, dominated that field.

Founded in 1897, Bessemer had produced oil-pumping engines for most of its existence and had invested heavily in diesel engine development during the 1920s. While Cooper and Bessemer had some product overlap, their major strengths were in different areas.

By 1929 Cooper needed additional production facilities to meet the mounting orders for large natural-gas engine compressor units. Bessemer, after its lengthy period of diesel development, badly needed new capital.

KEY DATES

1833: Brothers Charles and Elias Cooper build a foundry in Mount Vernon, Ohio.
1929: Company merges with Bessemer Gas Engine Company, forming Cooper-Bessemer Corporation.
1960: Company introduces the world's first industrial jet-powered gas turbine.
1965: Company changes its name to Cooper Industries.
1985: Cooper merges with McGraw-Edison Co. in a deal that nearly doubles its size and makes it one of the world's largest lighting manufacturers.
1995: Company spins off its petroleum and industrial equipment business.
1998: Company sells its automotive business to Federal-Mogul Corporation for $1.9 billion.
2000: Cooper acquires Eagle Electric Manufacturing and B-Line Systems.
2006: Cooper acquires Cannon Technologies, its first purchase of a software company.
2010: Cooper's hand and power tools business is spun off in a joint-venture company, Apex Tools Group, LLC.

entering new markets. The company was convinced that the diesel would replace steam-powered railroad engines and it developed one for the new market.

THE WAR YEARS: 1941–45

Charles B. Jahnke was elected president in 1940 and Williams moved to chairman of the board, but Jahnke died a year later and Williams returned to the presidency for two more years. Only when Cooper-Bessemer embarked on a wartime production schedule in 1941 did its sales figures surpass their pre-Depression level. The company had sold engines to several branches of the military before the war and was thus in a favored position to receive large orders during World War II. It became a major producer of diesel engines for military vessels of all kinds and also increased production of locomotive engines. At the peak of its wartime production, Cooper-Bessemer had 4,337 employees working in round-the-clock shifts.

In 1941 Cooper-Bessemer's net sales jumped to an all-time high, and just two years later they had more than tripled. The company was listed for the first time on the New York Stock Exchange in 1944. Gordon Lefebvre was elected company president in 1943. He had previously served as vice president and general manager. Formerly the head of General Motors's Pontiac division, he had a background in engineering and was energetic, likable, and a tough negotiator.

INTERNATIONAL EXPANSION AND PRODUCT DEVELOPMENT: 1945–57

After World War II, Cooper-Bessemer became increasingly interested in selling its products worldwide. It formed an international sales office and announced its first sales-service branch outside the United States, in Caracas, Venezuela, in 1945. Later in the decade, it expanded warehouse facilities in Canada and established a subsidiary sales unit, Cooper-Bessemer of Canada, with three offices, and received its first postwar orders from the Soviet Union.

Cooper-Bessemer had developed its innovative "turbo flow" high-compression gas-diesel engine in 1945, and two years later it introduced the GMW engine, which delivered 2,500 horsepower and could be shipped in one assembled unit. In these postwar years Cooper officials began to discuss diversification, resolving to find new markets for old products and new products for old markets, rather than moving into fields with which the company was not familiar.

In 1951 Cooper-Bessemer's sales of $52 million surpassed its wartime high by nearly $10 million. Busi-

Both companies had posted nearly identical average earnings for the previous three years. The companies negotiated a merger for several months, and the Cooper-Bessemer Corporation came into being in April 1929. The merger made the company the largest builder of gas engines and compressors in the United States. Soon afterward it was listed on the American Stock Exchange.

Cooper-Bessemer's business boom was brief. The company continued the Bessemer line of diesel marine engines, and since most ships were built or converted on the East Coast, Cooper-Bessemer soon decided to open a sales office in New York. The office was opened on October 23, 1929, however, at the very beginning of the Great Depression. Two years later, annual sales had dropped more than 90 percent, reflecting the almost total halt of construction on long-distance pipelines and in U.S. shipyards. Half of all sales that year were for repair parts. Along with thousands of other U.S. companies, Cooper-Bessemer was forced to lay off workers.

Cooper-Bessemer slowly revived in the middle and late 1930s by continuing to improve products and by

ness that year was boosted by the Korean War because company shipments were almost solely to markets supported by the war effort, such as the petroleum, aluminum, chemical, and railroad industries.

In 1954 a combination of internal and external circumstances led to a startling 38 percent decrease in net sales and Cooper-Bessemer's first net loss since 1938. The company's problems included a seven-week strike at the Grove City plant and a nationwide recession, but the main difficulty was the U.S. Supreme Court's decision in the Phillips Petroleum case, which ruled that producers selling gas to interstate pipelines had to submit to the Federal Power Commission's jurisdiction. This decision produced upheaval and uncertainty among pipeline operators, and therefore for Cooper-Bessemer.

While the company was rebuffing a 1955 takeover attempt by a private investor named Robert New, Lefebvre resigned unexpectedly, and Lawrence Williams, Beatty Williams's son, became president. He served beside his father, who was chairman of the board. Lawrence Williams had already served the company in many capacities and had taken early retirement to pursue other interests. He considered his return a temporary one. The takeover attempt had shaken management. In an attempt to bring an infusion of young talent to the company, Williams made a number of top management changes, including elevating Eugene L. Miller to COO. Due to revitalized demand, sales bounced back in 1956 to a record high of $61.2 million, but it was becoming increasingly clear that Cooper-Bessemer needed to diversify in order to avoid the cyclical pitfalls of energy-related manufacturing.

CHANGES IN GOVERNANCE: 1957–60

In 1957 Gene Miller was elected president. At 38, he was the youngest man to hold the position since the company's original founder. Miller had begun at Cooper-Bessemer in 1946. A year after he became president, the company acquired Rotor Tool Company of Cleveland, the makers of pneumatic and high-cycle electric portable tools.

Over the next few years Cooper-Bessemer struggled to develop an engine to meet the challenge of General Electric's new combustion gas turbine engine, which threatened to supplant several of Cooper's engines in the pipeline transmission market. Its efforts resulted in the world's first industrial jet-powered gas turbine, introduced in 1960.

Under Miller's leadership, the distinction between Cooper-Bessemer administrative and operational

management grew more pronounced, as was happening in companies throughout the country. Innovations such as computerization, fluctuations in worldwide monetary exchanges, increased government controls, and changing tax structures had made operating a large business increasingly complicated. In recognition of this, Miller moved the corporate offices from the Mount Vernon plant to offices on the city square to establish a corporate group capable of administering many relatively independent divisions. Meanwhile, Cooper-Bessemer's international division was also growing. By the end of the 1950s, Cooper had sales agents in 10 countries, licensees in three, and franchises in two. In 1964 it opened an office in Beirut and also formed a wholly owned British subsidiary, Cooper-Bessemer (U. K.), Ltd.

DIVERSIFICATION THROUGH ACQUISITION: 1960–81

Cooper-Bessemer was no exception to the trend toward large conglomerates during the 1960s, but it did try to limit its acquisitions to those that could be mutually beneficial. In the early 1960s, it acquired Kline Manufacturing, a producer of high-pressure hydraulic pumps, Ajax Iron Works, which built gas engine compressors and a water flood vertical pump for oil and gas production, and the Pennsylvania Pump and Compressor Company. Between 1960 and 1965, the company's sales grew from $68 million to $117 million.

Cooper had grown into a large, diverse company. To better reflect its nature, it changed its name to Cooper Industries, Inc., in December 1965. Two years later it moved its corporate headquarters to Houston in order to be more in the geographic mainstream of U.S. business. Cooper acquired Lufkin Rule Company of Saginaw, Michigan, in 1967. It was the first of many acquisitions for what the company called a "tool basket," a high-quality hand tools manufacturing group. Subsequent hand tool-related acquisitions included Crescent Niagara Corporation (wrenches) in 1968, Weller Electric Corporation (soldering tools) in 1970, Nicholson File Company (rasps and files) in 1972, Xcelite (small tools for the electronics industry) in 1973, J. Wiss & Sons Company (scissors) in 1976, McDonough Company's Plumb Tool subsidiary (striking tools) in 1980, and Kirsch Company (drapery hardware) in 1981.

The company branched out into aircraft services in 1970 by acquiring Dallas Airmotive, and later acquired Southwest Airmotive Company in 1973 and Standard Aircraft Equipment in 1975. Although these acquisitions performed satisfactorily, the company sold its airmotive segment to Aviation Power Supply in 1981 because it did not see much potential for further growth. The 1973 oil embargo threw many industrialized nations into an uproar. Cooper's Ajax division struggled to keep up with orders from domestic crude-oil producers and Cooper received a large order for its Coberra gas turbines for the Alaskan pipeline.

After having served as president and chief operating officer since 1973, Robert Cizik was named CEO in 1975. Lured to the company from Standard Oil New Jersey in 1961, Cizik started his career at Cooper as executive assistant for corporate development.

GARDNER-DENVER ACQUISITION: 1979

Cizik stepped up the company's acquisition program. After satisfying a Justice Department challenge, Cooper acquired the White Superior engine division, a heavy-duty engine maker, from the White Motor Company in 1976. In 1979 Cooper realized a dream of acquiring the Dallas-based Gardner-Denver Company, a company roughly the same size as Cooper. Cooper was confident the company's three energy-related business segments could be successfully merged into its own energy-related manufacturing operations. That year the company passed the $1 billion sales milestone, only three years after it had reached the $500 million mark. At the time, Cooper was criticized for handling acquisitions coldheartedly. After acquiring Gardner-Denver, it closed the company's corporate headquarters, decentralized it, reduced employment, and cut benefits.

Cooper was also known for its manufacturing efficiency and willingness to make capital investments to improve production or market position. For instance, when the last domestic producer of the very hard steel needed to manufacture files stopped making it, Cooper developed a process for making its own steel that was different from the traditional method but still suitable for making files, at half the cost.

ACQUISITION CAMPAIGN CONTINUES: 1981–89

In 1981 Cooper acquired the highly respected Crouse-Hinds Company of Syracuse, New York, makers of electrical products, after a long battle in which Cooper played white knight, rescuing Crouse-Hinds from Inter-North Corporation. Cooper also acquired the Belden Corporation, a wire and cable manufacturer that Crouse-Hinds had been in the process of purchasing. This acquisition expanded Cooper's size by 50 percent. When demand for gas and oil began to slump in 1981, Cooper's diversification paid off. Sales of the company's

energy-related products dropped by 60 percent but its other two divisions were hurt far less.

Cizik continued to look for new acquisitions. Cooper's next bold move was a 1985 merger with McGraw-Edison Company, a manufacturer of electrical energy-related products for industrial, commercial, and utility use. The merger nearly doubled Cooper's size and made the company one of the largest lighting manufacturers in the world. Cooper's 1985 sales passed $3 billion.

After the McGraw-Edison acquisition, most Cooper acquisitions were on a somewhat smaller scale in the 1980s. In 1987 they included the molded rubber products division and the petroleum equipment and products group from Joy Technologies. In 1988 Cooper acquired RTE Corporation, a Wisconsin-based manufacturer of electrical distribution equipment, and Beswick, a manufacturer of fuses and related products in the United Kingdom. In 1989 Cooper made another major acquisition, purchasing Champion Spark Plug Company, the world's leading manufacturer of spark plugs for combustion engines. Champion, based in Toledo, Ohio, was also a major producer of windshield-wiper blades. Later in the year, Cooper also acquired Cameron Iron Works, a Houston-based company with annual sales of $611 million. Cameron was a maker of oil tools, ball valves, and forged products.

By the early 1990s, Cooper manufactured more than a million products in 145 plants, 41 of them in foreign countries, and its annual revenues exceeded $4 billion. International expansion continued during this period. In 1991 three Canadian-based businesses were acquired. The following year, Cooper purchased Ferramentas Belzer do Brasil, a Brazilian-based hand tool manufacturer.

A NEW STRATEGY: 1995–99

Management began to take a different approach to expansion in the mid-1990s as competition became fierce in many of its markets. In 1995 the firm spun off its petroleum and industrial equipment business, signaling the start of its new strategy. H. John Riley Jr. was named CEO that year, and under his direction, Cooper began strictly focusing on its Electrical Products, Tools and Hardware, and Automotive Products business segments.

Cooper made eight acquisitions in 1997, the largest being that of the Menvier-Swain Group, an emergency lights and alarm manufacturer. It also divested Kirsch, its window treatment business, along with other units considered to be low margin and unrelated to the firm's new direction.

The company continued with its transformation in 1998, significantly changing its holdings with the sale of its automotive businesses. While this segment secured nearly 35 percent of Cooper's revenues, it was responsible for just 25 percent of earnings. The segment was also in dire need of capital investment to improve performance, an investment that did not fit in with Cooper's strategy. In October of that year, Federal-Mogul Corporation bought the division for $1.9 billion.

The firm also made 11 acquisitions that year, expanding its power tool business by 50 percent. U.S. power tool manufacturer Intool Inc. was purchased, along with three European-based companies. Cooper's reach in the electrical products market also increased in size that year through several key mergers in Latin America.

While market conditions weakened throughout the manufacturing industry, Cooper continued to bolster its two key business segments. During 1999 the company acquired 10 businesses and significantly expanded its reach in European markets. International revenues increased by 17 percent to $1.1 billion during the year.

STRONG MARKET POSITION: 2000–03

After nearly a decade of restructuring and divestiture, Cooper entered the new millennium a leaner, more focused company. The firm made several key acquisitions in 2000, including the B-Line Systems business of Aldrich Corp. and Eagle Electric Manufacturing, which was incorporated into the company's Wiring and Devices division. By the start of the century, Cooper's main two business segments, Electrical Products and Tools & Hardware, were securing nearly $4.5 billion in sales, up from $2.8 billion in 1995. In fact, Cooper held leading positions in many of its markets, which, coupled with its positive revenue and earnings results and its track record of success, made it a takeover target. In 2001 a bid from a suitor, Danaher Corporation, arrived. Cooper turned down the unsolicited offer from its rival, claiming that the proposal undervalued the firm.

After the parried approach by Danaher, Cooper continued to work on redefining its role. The Cooper of the 21st century bore little resemblance to the company that made its living by making hog troughs and plows nearly two centuries earlier. Cooper's ability to evolve as conditions around it changed was on display during the decade ahead, a decade that would include the celebration of its 175th anniversary. The company successfully incorporated high technology into its product lines, executing a strategy embraced by Kirk S. Hachigian.

Hachigian joined Cooper in 2001 as executive vice president of operations and quickly earned a promotion to the post of COO. In 2005 he was named CEO, succeeding Riley, and furthered his efforts in the technology sector begun while he was COO. In 2006 Cooper acquired Cannon Technologies for $190 million, the company's first acquisition of a software company. "The future is going to be communications, system automations, integration, and safety," Hachigian said in an interview published in the September 14, 2008, edition of the *Houston Chronicle*. "Your kids won't know what an incandescent bulb is," he added.

Cooper had moved away from making incandescent lightbulbs to producing more energy-efficient LED lighting, just one of the examples of its ability to change with the times. Cooper, in the 21st century, installed radio frequency technology into its power drills, enabling the drill's user to determine which bolt or rivet had been over-tightened or missed altogether. Similar technology was used with electrical fuses, which were connected to a wireless network, enabling the pinpoint location of a blown fuse without having to scan hundreds of fuses. As Hachigian stepped up Cooper's high-technology efforts, he also focused more on providing equipment used in energy infrastructure to compensate for the cyclical residential construction market. Copper's revenues from the industrial sector increased from $600 million the year Hachigian joined the company to $1.4 billion by 2008.

ECONOMIC CRISIS AND A MOVE TO IRELAND: 2008–10

Cooper's 175th anniversary in 2008 coincided with a severe economic downturn. To weather the storm, Hachigian borrowed a page from the company's response to a sour economic climate in the early 1990s. He increased Cooper's involvement in international markets, which accounted for 34 percent of the company revenues in 2007. By 2012, Hachigian wanted the company's revenue to be evenly split between domestic and international business. The company did not escape the global economic crises unscathed, however. Cooper laid off 2,200 employees in 2009, representing 8 percent of the company's salaried workers and 7 percent of its hourly workers. Revenues slipped during the period, dropping from $6.5 billion in 2008 to $5 billion in 2010. Net income fell as well, decreasing from $632.2 million in 2008 to $443.8 million in 2010.

In the midst of the economic turmoil, Cooper made a significant alteration to its place of incorporation. In 2009 the company switched its registration from Bermuda to Ireland, a move intended to strengthen its efforts to expand the international portion of its business. The move resulted in the establishment of corporate headquarters in Dublin (administrative headquarters remained in Houston) and in a new name for the parent company of the Cooper divisions, as Cooper Industries plc became the company's official corporate title, replacing Cooper Industries, Ltd.

Cooper ended the decade by striking a deal with its former suitor, Danaher. In 2010 Apex Tools Group, LLC, was formed as a joint-venture company by Cooper and Danaher. The new company took control of Cooper's power and hand tool businesses and assets from Danaher's tools and components segment. Cooper and Danaher each owned a 50 percent interest in Apex.

Updated, Christina M. Stansell; Jeffrey L. Covell

PRINCIPAL SUBSIDIARIES

Cooper B-Line, Inc.; Cooper Bussmann, LLC; Cooper Crouse-Hinds, LLC; Cooper Hungary Group Financing Limited Liability Company; Cooper Lighting, LLC; Cooper Power Systems, LLC; Apex Tools Group, LLC (50%).

PRINCIPAL DIVISIONS

Cooper B-Line; Cooper Bussmann; Cooper Crouse-Hinds; Cooper Lighting; Cooper Power Systems; Cooper Safety; Cooper Wiring Devices.

PRINCIPAL COMPETITORS

ABB Ltd.; General Electric Company; Hubbell Incorporated.

FURTHER READING

Chappell, Lindsay. "Cooper Moves Forward Despite Setbacks." *Automotive News*, June 29, 1998.

"Cooper Acquires Crompton Lighting." *Appliance Manufacturer*, December 1999.

"Cooper Planning to Slash Jobs." *American Metal Market*, January 4, 1999.

"Cooper Rejects Danaher Bid; Looks to Alternatives." *Industrial Distribution*, September 2001.

Couretas, John. "Federal-Mogul Completes Buy." *Automotive News*, October 12, 1998.

Greer, Jim. "Cooper Shuns Suitor as Details of Failed 1999 Deal Surface." *Houston Business Journal*, August 10, 2001.

Hem, Brad. "Manufacturing: Despite the Economic Downturn, Cooper Industries Has Been Able to Branch Out, Both Technologically and Geographically." *Houston Chronicle*, September 14, 2008.

Keller, David N. *Cooper Industries: 1833–1983*. Athens: Ohio University Press, 1983.

Papanikolaw, Jim. "Sigma-Aldrich Sells Its B-Line Systems to Cooper Industries." *Chemical Market Reporter*, April 3, 2000.

Deutsche Lufthansa AG

Von Gablenz St. 2-6
Cologne, 50679
Germany
Telephone: (+49 221) 826-3992
Fax: (+49 221) 826-3646
Web site: http://www.lufthansa.com

Public Company
Incorporated: 1926 as Deutsche Luft Hansa AG
Employees: 117,066
Sales: EUR 27.32 billion ($39.89 billion) (2010)
Stock Exchanges: Frankfurt Stuttgart Munich Hanover
 Dusseldorf Berlin Bremen Hamburg Xetra
Ticker Symbols: DLAKY LHA
NAICS: 481111 Scheduled Passenger Air Transportation; 481112 Scheduled Freight Air Transportation; 488119 Other Airport Operations; 488190 Other Support Activities for Air Transportation; 722320 Caterers

■ ■ ■

Deutsche Lufthansa AG (commonly referred to as Lufthansa) is the largest airline in Germany and one of the largest airlines in the world. More than 91 million passengers take Lufthansa flights each year. Lufthansa Group operates a fleet of more than 700 aircraft and is a founding member of the Star Alliance.

The Lufthansa Group also includes Swiss, Austrian Airlines, bmi, and the Eurowings Group. Other units, such as data processing specialist Lufthansa Systems and Lufthansa Flight Training, are world-leading businesses in their own right. Lufthansa Cargo AG is one of the world's largest carriers of international airfreight, while LSG Sky Chefs heads the world's largest alliance of inflight caterers. Lufthansa also holds a 50 percent interest in leading European travel group Thomas Cook AG.

ORIGINS

The history of Lufthansa parallels the development of aviation in Germany, dating back to a time when the first aviators were just beginning to fly. However, Lufthansa was not established as a commercial airline in Germany until the 1920s.

After World War I, the German government favored the development of a national airline system made up of a number of associated regional airlines. One of the largest airline companies, Deutscher Aero Lloyd, was incorporated in 1923 and centered its operations on Berlin's Temple Field. The following year, Junkers Luftverkehr was founded. Junkers built airplanes in addition to operating an airline. Together the two companies dominated German aviation.

The two companies merged with all the other German aeronautic concerns in 1926 to form Deutsche Luft Hansa Aktiengesellschaft (the name "Hansa" was taken from the north-German Hanseatic trading league, which had contributed most of the airline's private capital). Luft Hansa was a government-run private monopoly, the chosen instrument for all German air services. The company's logo was taken from Aero Lloyd and its blue and yellow colors were taken from Junkers. By May 1926, Luft Hansa served 57 domestic and 15 international airports.

In 1934, under the new name "Lufthansa," the company opened an airmail service between Stuttgart and Buenos Aires. As an instrument of state commerce and diplomacy, Lufthansa flew to numerous destinations around the world, including Beijing, New York, Cairo, Bangkok, and Tokyo. Regarded as an instrument of the state, Lufthansa increasingly came under the control of the ruling Nazi Party. Lufthansa began service to destinations in the Soviet Union during 1940. These routes provided the German Luftwaffe (air force) with valuable strategic information used in Adolf Hitler's surprise invasion of the Soviet Union two years later. In 1941, the Luftwaffe assumed control of Lufthansa's airplanes and converted many of them for military use. As World War II continued, many Lufthansa employees were drafted into military service in support of the Luftwaffe, and many lost their lives.

REBORN AFTER THE WAR

After the war, Germany was occupied by the Soviet Union, the United States, France, and Britain. The Soviet-occupied zone later became the German Democratic Republic (East Germany), and the U.S., French, and British zones became the Federal Republic of Germany (West Germany). A general state of belligerency between the Soviet Union and the Western Allies further divided East and West Germany. Under the conditions of the occupation, both East and West Germany were forbidden in 1945 to establish their own airline companies. British, French, and U.S. airlines had a monopoly on air service in West Germany, while the Soviet airline Aeroflot assumed all air services in East Germany.

By 1951, the reestablishment of a national airline for West Germany was proposed. The following year, the West German government in Bonn set up a preparatory airline corporation, and on January 6, 1953, Luftag (Aktiengesellschaft für Luftverkehrsbedarf) was created in Cologne. Hans Bongers, who joined Lufthansa in 1926, was reinstated as director of the national airline. Luftag began service with four Convair 340s, later joined by three DC-3s and four Lockheed Constellations.

Luftag's airplanes were piloted by foreign airline personnel while former Lufthansa pilots were retrained in the United States. The Germans later flew as copilots until 1956, when all-German crews were assigned. In 1954, Luftag instituted its old name, Lufthansa (Deutsche Lufthansa Aktiengesellschaft), and in the following years reestablished its services to North and South America and the Middle East.

JET-POWERED EXPANSION

Lufthansa began flying Boeing 707 passenger jets on its international routes in 1961. The introduction of jets marked the beginning of an equipment rotation at Lufthansa. The older propeller-driven airplanes were slowly phased out and replaced by jets. With this new equipment, Lufthansa firmly reestablished itself as one of the world's premier air carriers.

The expansion of Lufthansa continued with the reintroduction of services to Africa. The airline established service to Nigeria in 1962 and later that year began service to Johannesburg, South Africa. Despite the heavy investment required for the airline's expansion, Lufthansa was able to declare its first profitable year in 1964. Previously the airline had charged its losses to the federal government.

Lufthansa joined a maintenance pool called ATLAS in 1969. As a member of ATLAS, Lufthansa cooperated with Air France, Alitalia, Sabena, and Iberia in the repair and maintenance of aircraft and other equipment. Lufthansa's Hamburg facility was designated to perform repairs for the pool's B747s, DC-10s, and A300s.

The updating of equipment at Lufthansa continued over the next few years as the airline introduced Boeing's 737 for short distance shuttle routes, and a 747 jumbo jet for heavily traveled long-distance services. In addition to the 747, Lufthansa purchased several McDonnell Douglas DC-10s. The new aircraft replaced the older turboprops, the last of which was removed from the fleet in 1971. During this period, Lufthansa developed its airfreight services with a fleet of 747s specially designated to haul cargo. The airline constructed automated freight handling facilities in a number of destinations across the world. Lufthansa recognized the importance of cargo services before most of its competition. The company established one of the most modern freight handling systems in the world, and cargo services became a major source of revenue.

KEY DATES

1926: Deutsche Luft Hansa is formed from consolidation of German aviation interests.
1941: Luftwaffe assumes control of Lufthansa aircraft.
1945: Germany is banned from operating its own airlines after World War II.
1953: New airline is launched in West Germany as Luftag.
1954: Luftag, renamed Lufthansa, reestablishes intercontinental routes.
1976: First Airbus A300, a mostly German-made airliner, enters the company's fleet.
1997: Star Alliance is formed with Lufthansa as a founding member.
2005: Swiss International Airlines and Eurowings Group are acquired.
2009: Austrian Airlines and British Midland (bmi) are acquired; AeroLogic cargo partnership is launched with DHL.

CHALLENGES

Being a European airline, Lufthansa was exposed to terrorist activities during the 1970s. Security was inadequate at many airports served by the company, which made it easy for terrorists to board and commandeer an airplane. However, not one Lufthansa passenger lost his life despite numerous hijackings on the airline. The chairman of the company during the 1970s, Rolf Bebber, established a crisis management procedure that enlisted the diplomatic influence of the West German government. Through this procedure, the company could respond quickly to terrorist demands in order to resolve a crisis. In addition, security at all Lufthansa airports was significantly upgraded.

The airline experienced considerable problems with German air traffic controllers who staged a "go-slow" from May to November 1973. Lufthansa estimated that it lost $71 million due to flight cancellations during that period. The controllers, who were civil servants, had been demonstrating their displeasure with working conditions in this manner since 1962. Lufthansa tried to persuade the federal government to change the status of the controllers in an effort to avoid future slowdowns but was unsuccessful.

Lufthansa received its first A300 jetliner in 1976 from Airbus, the French-German-British-Spanish aircraft consortium. The A300 was the first commercial aircraft to be built primarily by Germans in more than 30 years. The German member of the Airbus group, Messerschmitt-Bölkow-Blohm (MBB), continued to contribute to the development of more advanced Airbus jetliners which Lufthansa added to its fleet. In 1983, the airline commissioned its first A310 and later purchased the consortium's A319, A320, A321, and A340 jets.

MBB was particularly willing to involve Lufthansa in the Airbus projects. Since both companies were German, they were encouraged by the federal government to coordinate and serve each other's economic interests. As a result, Airbus was especially sensitive to Lufthansa's design requirements. Moreover, because Lufthansa was highly respected as a modern air carrier, the jetliners built to its specifications were more marketable to other airline companies.

A WORLD LEADER

In 1982, 80 percent of Lufthansa's stock was owned by the West German government. The board of directors, however, was appointed by Lufthansa's private investors. On June 22 of that year, the board of directors narrowly elected a new chairman to succeed Herbert Culmann. Culmann was a popular chairman, but he retired two years early to save his company embarrassment over allegations of kickbacks to travel agents.

The new chairman was Heinz Ruhnau, a career bureaucrat with strong affiliations with the West German Social Democratic Party. His appointment generated an unusual amount of concern because many feared the ruling Social Democrats were attempting to politicize the airline. Ruhnau was an undersecretary in the Transport Ministry and a former chief assistant to the head of West Germany's largest trade union, IG Metall. He did not, however, have experience in private enterprise, and Lufthansa was being prepared for a further privatization of its stock. In 1985, the federal government held 74.31 percent of Lufthansa; 7.85 percent was held by government agencies; and the remaining 17.84 percent was held by private interests.

Ruhnau assumed his post on July 1, 1982, in a smooth transition of leadership. Ruhnau's immediate tasks were to improve Lufthansa's thin profit margin and win the support of the company's 30,000 skeptical employees. The company's performance in 1982 was impressive and resulted in its selection as airline of the year by the editors of *Air Transport World*.

WEATHERING CHANGE

The early to mid-1990s was a period of enormous change in Europe, change that proved extremely challenging for Lufthansa. Most obvious was the 1990 reunification of Germany, a difficult process that nonetheless afforded Lufthansa the opportunity to fly to Berlin under its own colors for the first time since the Allied occupation. The period also featured steadily increasing competition which forced down ticket prices worldwide and cut into Lufthansa's market share. The company was particularly vulnerable because of its cumbersome bureaucracy and its relatively high-wage workforce, with the workers traditionally protected by the company's state-run status. Other forces reshaping the operating environment for Lufthansa included the gradual deregulation of the airline industry in Europe, the trend toward privatization sweeping the continent, and the planned economic integration of Europe during the 1990s. By the start of the 21st century, Lufthansa had made numerous changes in response to these challenges, emerging as a very different company.

Leading Lufthansa through most of the 1990s was Jürgen Weber, who became chairman in September 1991. The company was hemorrhaging at the time amid fierce competition and a sharp decline in European air travel in 1991, with the Gulf War a major catalyst for the drop. For the first time since 1973, Lufthansa lost money, posting a net loss of DEM 425.8 million in 1991, followed by another loss of DEM 391.1 million in 1992. Starting in mid-1992, Weber began working feverishly to bring the company's costs in line. By 1994, job cuts totaling 8,400 had been made, and Weber got workers to agree to an unprecedented one-year wage freeze in 1993. He also dumped unprofitable routes and cut some services, such as first class within Europe. Through these measures, $1 billion in annual cost savings was realized, leading Lufthansa back into the black by 1994, when it made DEM 302 million.

Not everything went smoothly, however. A new low-cost domestic shuttle service, Lufthansa Express, was launched in 1992 but caused confusion among customers and was eventually scrapped. Meantime, Lufthansa faced a new and potentially formidable competitor in its home market when in 1992 British Airways plc acquired a 49 percent interest in a Berlin-based carrier, newly dubbed Deutsche BA. The regional airline offered high-quality service to business travelers and competed directly with Lufthansa's regional airline, known as Lufthansa CityLine, which also catered to business travelers and which Lufthansa gained 100 percent control over in 1993. By the mid-1990s, Deutsche BA had firmly established itself as Germany's number two scheduled airline, with a market share of 14 percent.

In 1993, the German government still held 51.6 percent of Lufthansa. A rights issue soon reduced the stake to 35 percent, giving company workers less

government protection. In July 1993, Weber began restructuring Lufthansa. With a vision of Lufthansa as a holding company for several separately operated units, he spun off Lufthansa Cargo as a stand-alone, but wholly owned, business, the largest specialized air cargo carrier in the world. In succeeding years, several additional operations were similarly spun off, creating Lufthansa Technik in the maintenance area, Lufthansa Systems in data processing, LSG Lufthansa Service in catering, and Lufthansa Flight Training. Lufthansa City-Line and air charter specialist Condor Flugdienst also operated autonomously. The culmination of this process came in April 1997 when Lufthansa's flagship scheduled passenger business was made independent as well, under the name Lufthansa German Airlines. Deutsche Lufthansa had thereby evolved into a holding company for what was referred to as the Lufthansa Group.

STAR ALLIANCE: 1997

Another key goal of Weber's was to seek international partnerships, as alliances became increasingly common and vital for survival in the 1990s. In October 1993, Lufthansa and United Airlines, the leading U.S. airline, began a code-sharing arrangement whereby a single flight number in a reservation system could involve a journey consisting of a Lufthansa leg and a United leg. This partnership eventually led to the May 1997 formation of the Star Alliance, which initially involved Lufthansa, United, Air Canada, Scandinavian Airlines System (SAS), and Thai Airways International. The Star Alliance included not only code-sharing but also reciprocal frequent flyer programs, reciprocal lounge access agreements, and scheduling and pricing coordination efforts. In October 1997, the Brazilian airline Varig joined the alliance, followed within two years by Air New Zealand and Ansett Australia. In 1997 and 1998, Lufthansa also entered into separate bilateral partnerships with Singapore Airlines and All Nippon Airways of Japan.

In October 1997, Lufthansa was fully privatized with the sale of the government's remaining 37.5 percent stake in the airline, raising about DEM 4.7 billion ($2.8 billion). The company was now free of its government ties, operating within a new group structure, and was considered one of the most profitable airlines in the world (net profits for 1997 were DEM 834.7 million), an amazing turn of events from the depths of the early 1990s. With the airline industry fully open to competition throughout the European Union, Lufthansa was presented with new challenges (even greater competition) as well as additional opportunities. In the globally competitive industry environment, it seemed likely that the company's future depended heavily upon that of the Star Alliance.

In 1999, Lufthansa subsidiary GlobeGround GmbH acquired Hudson General Corp., the world's largest publicly traded airport services company. The deal was worth $132.6 million. GlobeGround had been formed in 1990 as Lufthansa Airport and Ground Services. A subsidiary of Lufthansa Commercial Holding, it was renamed in January 1999 and was acquired by Penauille PolyServices of France in 2001.

Lufthansa Cargo AG was considered the world's largest carrier of international airfreight, carrying more than 1.6 million tons of cargo a year among 450 destinations. The unit operated a fleet of 22 dedicated freighters and used cargo capacity on the passenger flights of Lufthansa and partner Spanair. Its revenues were $2.64 billion in 2000, when it had 5,000 employees.

Group net profit rose 9 percent to $620 million (EUR 689 million) in 2000, even in the face of rising fuel costs. Revenues were about $14 billion (EUR 15.2 billion). Nearly 47 million people flew the airline during the year. Lufthansa had about 250 planes, plus another 60 operated by CityLine. Operationally, Lufthansa was developing a second hub at Munich as its Frankfurt base became crowded.

A "D-CHECK" IN 2001

In April 2001, Weber, a former maintenance head, announced a "D-Check" for the entire company (the name refers to an aircraft's most comprehensive inspection), hoping to generate an additional $1 billion a year in cash flow by 2004. The month after the announcement, however, a pilot's strike cost the airline more than $50 million.

In the Future European Operations initiative, Lufthansa reorganized its regional services. A new commuter subsidiary, Lufthansa CityLine, was formed, while PrivatAir of Switzerland was contracted to handle certain business routes. These were both low-cost operations, unfettered by traditional collectively bargained wage agreements. Lufthansa also acquired a 25 percent stake in budget start-up Eurowings.

The airline also upgraded its business class service and made plans to provide a broadband Internet connection on flights. The Star Alliance continued to attract new members among the world's airlines, bringing Lufthansa additional feeder traffic sources from abroad.

Following the September 11, 2001, terrorist attacks on the United States, Lufthansa coped with the general downturn in aviation by reducing capacity while retaining employees. The company's Sky Chefs catering business was particularly hard hit, leading to layoffs of 30 percent of staff. As the world's aviation industry reeled, *Forbes Global* remarked in February 2003 at how well Lufthansa was able to fare, given Germany's reputation for high social costs. By November 2002, the airline was planning to add 2,000 jobs while some of the biggest airlines in the United States were trying to stave off bankruptcy. Analysts credited Lufthansa's survival to its quick and flexible responses to the crises of the previous decade, as well as its ability to forecast future business conditions. Net profit was EUR 717 million for 2002. Lufthansa made several key divestments in 2002, selling its 25 percent holding in DHL World Wide Express for $514 million to Deutsche Post World Net, and disposing of its Start Amadeus GmbH travel package company for $95 million.

DIFFICULT YEAR IN 2003

In 2003, a very difficult year, Lufthansa posted a net loss of EUR 984 million ($1.2 billion) on sales of EUR 15.96 billion ($20.03 billion). Like other airlines, Lufthansa struggled with the severe acute respiratory syndrome (SARS) crisis in Asia and the war in Iraq. The economy was also slow, particularly in Germany. The year also saw some significant changes. Wolfgang Mayrhuber, formerly head of Lufthansa Technik, then the passenger business division, replaced Weber as Lufthansa Group's new chairman and CEO. The airline had a fleet of about 370 planes and more than 93,000 employees. Lufthansa was again tweaking its regional operations and searching for cost-cutting opportunities. It finally hammered out a new pay agreement with the pilots' union Vereiningung Cockpit in December 2004. The pilots agreed to a pay freeze and extra work hours.

Lufthansa was also looking for places to grow, as with a new nonstop route from Frankfurt to Portland, Oregon. The airline was aiming to grow its capacity to China by 50 percent after a new 2004 bilateral agreement increased access to the country's skies.

Lufthansa acquired Swiss International Airlines in January 2005 for a reported EUR 310 million ($406 million). The Swiss national carrier had been relaunched just three years earlier but soon accrued losses of $1.6 billion. At the end of 2005 Lufthansa acquired the Eurowings Group, including germanwings, a budget operator. Lufthansa also explored a new sales channel, rolling out an executive jet program at Frankfurt and Munich in March 2005 in collaboration with NetJets.

Lufthansa was profitable as 2005 sales rose 7 percent to EUR 18.1 billion. Passenger revenues accounted for 64 percent of revenues. Cargo contributed sales of about EUR 2.8 billion ($3.8 billion). LSG Sky

Chefs was still the largest airline catering company in the world with revenues of about EUR 3 billion. Both it and the Thomas Cook travel agency recovered their profitability during the year.

In 2006 Air France–KLM eclipsed Lufthansa as the world's largest airline group by revenue. Nevertheless, Lufthansa's revenues were steadily increasing, from EUR 19.9 billion in 2006 to EUR 22.4 billion in 2007, as operating income climbed from EUR 845 million to EUR 1.4 billion.

INVESTING THROUGH THE DOWNTURN

Lufthansa committed to significant capital outlays at its subsidiaries before the world economy entered a slump due to the credit crisis of late 2008. Lufthansa Cargo upgraded the security at key hubs at Frankfurt, Munich, New York, Shanghai, Chicago, and Los Angeles. The maintenance organization had a new maintenance, repair, and operations (MRO) base in India (complementing existing operations in China and the Philippines), and in early 2008 opened a 270,000-square-foot hangar at Frankfurt capable of storing two of the massive new Airbus A380 superjumbos.

The business travel market, traditionally the most lucrative part of the business, contracted sharply in the global economic slowdown that began in late 2008. Lufthansa lost EUR 112 million ($152 million) in 2009 after posting a EUR 542 million profit (restated) the previous year. In spite of efforts to reduce capacity, the cargo unit was particularly hard hit, losing EUR 152 million in 2009 after earning EUR 201 million on revenues of $3.8 billion in 2008.

Lufthansa used the weakened economy as an opportunity to take over more smaller carriers. It bought Air Dolomiti, which it operated under the Lufthansa Italia brand for three years before reverting it to the original name. In 2009 Lufthansa acquired Austrian Airlines AG, paying more than $230 million. It also acquired struggling British Midland (bmi). It laid off several hundred employees and trimmed the timetable and fleet in a turnaround bid, while some of bmi's valuable landing slots at Heathrow went to other Lufthansa Group airlines. During the year Lufthansa bought a 45 percent interest in Brussels Airlines as well.

The acquired airlines typically retained their identities while benefiting from Lufthansa's connecting traffic as well as economies of scale in aircraft purchases. The group ordered 40 Airbus aircraft worth $4.3 billion in September 2010. For shorter routes operated by Eurow-ings, Lufthansa was phasing out its BAe 146 and Avro RJs in favor of Bombardier Canadair aircraft.

LEADING ITS PEERS

Lufthansa extended its collaborations into the airfreight business. It formed a charter joint venture with its new Chinese affiliate Jade Air Cargo in 2008. A partnership with DHL called AeroLogic began operating in June 2009 at Leipzig. DHL had just opened a $475 million hub at the old East German military airbase there. Lufthansa had been flying cargo out of Leipzig for two years, avoiding the higher costs and night-flight restrictions at Cologne.

In spite of a one-day pilots' strike that saw more than 800 flights canceled and severe winter weather, Lufthansa Group led its European peers with a net profit of EUR 1.1 billion on revenues of EUR 27.3 billion ($39.9 billion) in 2010. Passenger traffic rose 10 percent as the market recovered from the worst of the global downturn.

Christoph Franz succeeded Mayrhuber as group chairman and CEO in January 2011. Franz had previously been deputy chairman. Lufthansa Group was soon planning to add 4,000 new employees in Germany alone. It was upgrading its cabins and expanding its network. Swiss was also growing and hiring new employees.

Lufthansa ordered 30 A320 neo-series aircraft valued at $2.8 billion in March 2011. This gave it a total of 78 Airbus aircraft on order, including 10 A380s. A total of 150 new aircraft were due for delivery in the next five years. Lufthansa Cargo, which operated a fleet of 18 MD-11 freighters, was shopping around for a more efficient replacement aircraft. Lufthansa began testing a mix of regular jet fuel and biosynthetic kerosene on a regular scheduled service in July 2011, a first. The 51 percent owned information technology (IT) subsidiary, Lufthansa Systems, posted revenues of EUR 595 million ($856 million) for the year. It was offered for sale as its profitability dwindled.

Much of Lufthansa's sustained success came from anticipating changes in the industry. As the global aviation field continued to consolidate, with British Airways joining Iberia and United taking over Continental, Lufthansa remained among the most admired and most emulated corporations in passenger and cargo operations. It was willing, however, to shed a once promising high-tech segment, its IT operations. An influential carrier throughout the history of commercial aviation, Lufthansa was assured a prominent place in the future of the industry as well.

Updated, David E. Salamie; Frederick C. Ingram

PRINCIPAL SUBSIDIARIES

Lufthansa Passenger Airlines; SWISS; Austrian Airlines; bmi; Brussels Airlines; Germanwings; Sun-Express; Lufthansa Cargo; Lufthansa Technik; Lufthansa Systems; LSG Sky Chefs.

PRINCIPAL DIVISIONS

Passenger Airline Group; Logistics; MRO; IT Services; Catering.

PRINCIPAL COMPETITORS

Air Berlin PLC & Co. Luftverkehrs KG; Air France–KLM; AMR Corporation; British Airways plc; FedEx Corporation.

FURTHER READING

Bruch, Heike, and Thomas Sattelberger. "Lufthansa's Transformation Marathon: Process of Liberating and Focusing Change Energy." *Human Resource Management*, Fall 2001, 249+.

Davies, R. E. G. *Lufthansa: An Airline and Its Aircraft*. New York: Orion Books, 1989.

Flint, Perry. "Friends Again (Lufthansa Technik as a Standalone Subsidiary of Lufthansa)." *Air Transport World*, August 2001, 24.

Flottau, Jens. "German Makeover: Lufthansa Plans to Slash Costs, Restructure European Operations in Ongoing Effort to Restore Profitability." *Aviation Week & Space Technology*, October 27, 2003, 39.

Hill, Leonard. "'Same Mountain, Different Angle.'" *Air Transport World*, June 2001, 42.

———. "Training (R)Evolution." *Air Transport World*, April 2002, 64.

Josselson, Steven. "Reality Check from Germany." *Airfinance Journal*, May 2002, 34+.

Moores, Victoria. "Rescue Mission." *Airline Business*, October 29, 2010.

Morrison, Murdo. "Agile Lufthansa Looks Near and Far." *Airline Business*, January 1, 2002, 18.

Steinborn, Deborah. "The Crane Keeps Aloft." *Forbes Global*, February 17, 2003, 37.

Wachtel, Joachim. *The Lufthansa Story*. Cologne: Lufthansa German Airlines, 1980, 135.

Dollar Tree, Inc.

500 Volvo Parkway
Chesapeake, Virginia 23320
U.S.A.
Telephone: (757) 321-5000
Fax: (757) 321-5111
Web site: http://www.dollartree.com

Public Company
Incorporated: 1986 as Only One Dollar, Inc.
Employees: 64,000
Sales: $5.89 billion (2010)
Stock Exchanges: NASDAQ
Ticker Symbol: DLTR
NAICS: 424410 General Line Grocery Merchant
    Wholesalers; 424490 Other Grocery and Related
    Products Merchant Wholesalers; 445110
    Supermarkets and Other Grocery (Except
    Convenience) Stores; 445120 Convenience Stores;
    452990 All Other General Merchandise Stores

■ ■ ■

Dollar Tree, Inc., is a leading discount retailer with merchandise priced at $1 or less at most of its locations. The company's more than 4,200 stores include several incarnations of extreme discounters including the original Dollar Tree outlets as well as Dollar Bills, Dollar Giant, and Deal$. Each location offers a wide assortment of goods including food, toys, housewares, cleaning supplies, health and beauty aids, hardware, books, stationery, and other consumer and seasonal items, the majority of which are imported from Asia. Selling merchandise (including many well-known brands) at exceptionally low prices has made Dollar Tree the third-largest value discounter in North America, nipping at the heels of Canada's Dollar General and U.S.-based Family Dollar, Inc.

FROM TOY STORE TO DOLLAR STORE: 1986–90

The founders of Dollar Tree, Inc., first worked together managing K&K Toys, Inc., building from one store to a 136-store retail success story. In 1986 the three partners (J. Douglas Perry, Macon F. Brock Jr., and H. Ray Compton) decided to diversify by establishing a new company, Only One Dollar, incorporated in Virginia.

"We had all started out in the variety store business, so it seemed a natural transition," Brock told *Chain Store Executive* in November 1997. The company opened with five stores in Virginia, Georgia, and Tennessee, and, typical of the dollar format, offered primarily closeout merchandise. Perry became chairman of the new company, Brock served as president, and Compton was executive vice president and chief financial officer.

While the three men continued to manage K&K Toys, the new venture grew to 171 stores over the next five years. In October 1991 they sold the toy chain, one of the largest mall-based toy retailers in the country, to a subsidiary of Melville Corporation and turned their full attention to the Dollar discount operation.

COMPANY PERSPECTIVES

Dollar Tree, Inc. is a customer-oriented, value-driven variety store operating at a one dollar price point. We will operate profitably, empower our associates to share in its opportunities, rewards and successes; and deal with others in an honest and considerate way. The company's mission will be consistent with measured and profitable growth.

CHANGING INVENTORY AND LOCATIONS: 1991–93

The discount chain implemented two major strategic shifts in the early 1990s. First, rather than continue as a purveyor of closeout merchandise, the partners wanted to become the modern equivalent of traditional variety stores with a wider assortment of basic goods, priced at no more than a dollar. To do this, they had to change purchasing strategies that had emphasized deals and novelties. Consequently, they started buying directly from foreign manufacturers and worked with U.S. suppliers to offer customized packaging, a broader selection, and larger products.

Management's aim was to not only meet customer expectations with the range of products available but to offer items usually priced well beyond a dollar at competitors. In support of these new endeavors, location became key with new stores opening not in enclosed malls but instead in strip centers anchored by large grocery stores or such mass merchandisers as Kmart, Target, or Wal-Mart that it could undersell. The strategy not only helped customers compare prices, but saved the company rent money as strip malls were generally more economical than enclosed, higher-end mall locations. By the end of 1992 the company had 256 stores with net sales of $120.5 million and net income of $10.8 million.

During 1993 Brock was named CEO and the company changed its name to Dollar Tree Stores, Inc. The newly christened firm also continued its expansion, gaining 72 new stores, all of which were located in strip shopping centers. Because management believed stores had a relatively small shopping radius, several locations within a single market were often opened without fear of market cannibalization. Most were located in mid-sized cities and small towns. The rest operated in major metropolitan areas. New stores were usually profitable within their first year of operation and reinforced growth expectations without acquisitions or mergers.

The typical Dollar store was approximately 3,200 square feet with 85 to 90 percent of this area as selling space. Unlike many of its competitors, Dollar Tree paid a great deal of attention to the design of its stores and the physical presentation of its merchandise. The chain used the same layout plan in each of its stores, with merchandise organized by category and displayed in densely stocked bins and shelves. Carpeting, bright lighting, background music, and the use of vibrant colors such as red checkout stands made the stores attractive and comfortable.

With an average purchase of $6.50 per customer, the chain did not accept credit cards, nor did it scan purchases at checkout. "We locate our stores where people are already shopping, hoping they will be curious enough to check us out," Brock had commented to *Chain Store Executive*. "And then we try and make the outlets as easy as possible for customers to get in and out of."

By the end of 1993, the chain had 328 locations, sales of $167.8 million, and net income of $9.5 million. The slight drop in income from the previous year was due to $4 million in recapitalization costs. As part of the recapitalization, the founders and their spouses sold 50 percent of the outstanding stock to the SK Equity Fund, L.P., and four associates for a total of $23.6 million.

MAJOR GROWTH: 1994–96

The company continued its successful formula in 1994, expanding to 409 stores with sales topping the $200 million mark for the first time, reaching $231.6 million. A key factor of the chain's ongoing success was its distribution system. Sharing space (186,000 square feet) at the Norfolk headquarters was one of the company's two distribution centers. The other, with 244,000 square feet, was located in Memphis, Tennessee.

This capacity allowed the company to buy large quantities at good prices and receive early shipment discounts, thus keeping prices within its one dollar range. Given the relatively small size of most units, backup inventory was kept at the distribution centers with stores receiving weekly shipments. During busy holiday seasons, the company often doubled weekly deliveries to high-volume stores.

In 1995 the company began the year by creating two subsidiaries, Dollar Tree Management, Inc. and Dollar Tree Distribution, Inc. In March, management took Dollar Tree public on the NASDAQ and opened its 500th store. Sales for the year topped $300 million, with per share earnings of 76 cents.

The dawn of the following year, 1996, brought major expansion with the acquisition of Dollar Bills,

KEY DATES

1986: J. Douglas Perry, Macon F. Brock Jr., and H. Ray Compton establish Only One Dollar Inc.

1993: Company changes its name to Dollar Tree Stores, Inc. with Brock as chief executive.

1995: Dollar Tree goes public on the NASDAQ.

1996: Dollar Bills Inc. is acquired.

1998: Company adds California-based 98 Cents Clearance Centers to its arsenal; Bob Sasser joins the company as chief operating officer.

2000: Expansion continues with the purchase of Dollar Express Inc.

2001: Sasser is named president of the company.

2003: Greenbacks Inc. is acquired, adding stores in several western states.

2004: Sasser becomes chief executive officer.

2006: Deal$ discount chain is acquired from Supervalu.

2008: Company changes its name to Dollar Tree, Inc. to reflect the diversity of its holdings.

2011: Dollar Tree expands into Canada with stores in Alberta, British Columbia, Ontario, and Saskatchewan.

Inc. for approximately $52.6 million in cash and $2 million in inventory. The purchase moved the company into three new states (Iowa, Minnesota, and Wisconsin) and added 136 stores, increasing Dollar Tree's store base by 27 percent. A modern 250,000-square-foot distribution center and a wholesale division in the Chicago area completed the acquisition.

Most of the Dollar Bills stores were concentrated in urban areas, a different retail market than existing Dollar Tree stores. The new additions were typically larger, had higher average sales, and carried less inventory per square foot. They also had a higher proportion of low-margin items such as food, health and beauty aids, and household supplies. By the end of the year, the new acquisitions were successfully integrated into the company. To help make sure all locations followed the same operational procedures, Dollar Tree instituted a new training program ("Dollar Tree University") at its Virginia headquarters.

In mid-1996 the company made a second public stock offering and expanded its international reach beyond Asia with new suppliers from Italy, Brazil, Argentina, and Mexico. Imports made up over a third of Dollar Tree's merchandise and around 40 percent of its sales. Closeout merchandise, which had been the company's initial concept, now made up less than 15 percent of its offerings.

In evaluating the overall merchandise mix, the company added more higher-margin inventory such as toys and gifts to the items available at the Dollar Bills locations and more consumable products on the shelves of the Dollar Tree stores. The integration was accomplished with little disruption, while an additional 104 new stores were opened throughout the country. The company ended 1996 with 737 stores at a time when competitors struggled with the dollar format and several closed their doors. Dollar Tree, however, finished the year with sales up more than 64 percent to $493 million, with about half this revenue attributable to Dollar Bills stores.

NEW HQ AND MORE: 1997–99

Construction on a new $34 million headquarters and support center began in 1997, just 10 miles from the company's current offices. A few months later, the founders, SK Equity Fund, and other shareholders offered four million shares of Dollar Tree stock for sale. While the company itself did not receive any of the proceeds of that sale, in July it issued a three-for-two stock split.

During the year, 150 new stores were opened, bringing total locations to 887. Many of the new stores were an experimental, larger prototype increasing space by an additional 3,500 to 4,000 square feet. Management hoped larger aisles and shopping carts would spur purchases. They were right as net sales rose nearly 29 percent to $635.5 million for 1997, with same store sales up more than 7 percent. Net earnings increased to $48.6 million from the previous year's $33.8 million, as one of the company's longtime variety store competitors, Woolworth's, closed all stores in the United States.

Although staff moved into the new HQ before the year ended, the state-of-the-art distribution center began operating in January 1998. With an automated conveyor and sorting system, the new facility had the capacity to support up to 800 stores. This was a bit short, however, since the company had not only bought the California-based 98 Cents Clearance Center chain, but also expanded into Oklahoma, Connecticut, and Massachusetts, while opening its 1,000th store in the fall.

Dollar Tree President and CEO Brock also announced the company was in the process of buying land in Olive Branch, Mississippi, for a distribution center to replace the nearby Memphis facility. The new $20 million Olive Branch facility, some 425,000 square feet in size, began operation in early 1999, the same year the company surpassed $1 billion in sales and hired Bob Sasser, formerly of Rose Stores, Inc. as its chief operating officer.

A NEW ERA: 2000–04

In the new millennium, Dollar Tree bought the similarly named Dollar Express Inc. for $306.8 million and added over 100 stores in six mid-Atlantic states, for a total store count of 1,729 units. Sasser continued to climb within the company's ranks, taking over as president in 2001. To support its ever extending supply chain, the company also opened new warehouse/distribution centers in California, Georgia, Pennsylvania, and Oklahoma. Its next acquisition came in 2003 with the purchase of Greenbacks Inc., giving Dollar Tree a presence in Colorado, Arizona, Montana, New Mexico, Utah, and Wyoming, effectively positioning it as the first dollar store chain with a national reach.

Dollar Tree broke the $2 billion mark in 2002 as sales and net income continued their upward trend. While the company focused on growing both organically and through acquisitions, it also made technology a cornerstone in its expansion platform. In addition to its high-tech distribution center in Virginia, the company had begun implementing a point-of-sale (POS) scanning system in 2001 to simplify sales and provide better inventory control. By 2003 nearly 1,500 of the company's stores were using POS systems.

Sasser, who had served as president since 2001, took over as CEO in January 2004 while Brock continued on as chairman. The company continued its growth in both store locations and revenue, finishing the year with sales of just under $2.8 billion and net income of $177.6 million. Locations numbered 2,318 in 41 states, with a workforce of 28,700, placing the chain third in the North American discount segment behind Canada's Dollar General ($6.9 billion, 6,700 stores) and North Carolina-based Family Dollar ($4.6 billion, 5,208 stores).

Despite being bested in size and sales by its top two rivals, Dollar Tree was ranked higher in a July 2004 survey by *Women's Wear Daily*, which polled consumer loyalty to the top 20 most-visited retailers. While Walmart, Target, and Kmart occupied the top three slots, Dollar Tree ranked fifth, besting Dollar General (sixth) and Family Dollar (11th).

EXPONENTIAL GROWTH: 2005–09

As Dollar Tree hit the midpoint of the decade, its competitors in both dollar and big box formats were stocking more value-added and convenience food items, hoping to lure additional shoppers to their stores. In this instance, Dollar Tree was ahead of the curve as stores in Pennsylvania and New Jersey (from the Dollar Express acquisition) had always carried frozen and packaged entrees, capturing market share from nearby convenience stores. Management considered a full scale rollout of frozen and refrigerated foods, as consumables accounted for more than 40 percent of its sales.

As Dollar Tree continued its aggressive expansion, opening more than 200 stores each year and either enlarging or relocating smaller versions, an ACNielsen poll found over two-thirds of consumers shopped at dollar stores, supporting more than 17,000 nationwide outlets. Sasser was quoted in a July 2005 *Convenience Store News* article as stating, "We believe there is plenty of room to grow and we still believe we could double store count in the country."

True to Sasser's words, the company added units and sales, finishing 2005 with $3.4 billion in revenue and net income of $173.9 million. The following year, 2006, was particularly successful as sales leapt to nearly $4 billion and net income rose to $192 million, due in part to the acquisition of the Deal$ discount chain from Supervalu and the continued addition of freezers and coolers to existing stores and all new locations. Correspondingly, Dollar Tree's workforce mushroomed from 30,155 in 2004 to 42,200 in 2006.

As the economy slid into a recession in 2008, Dollar Tree repositioned itself, changing its name to Dollar Tree, Inc. to reflect the growing diversity of its holdings. As other companies failed and unemployment skyrocketed, Americans turned away from higher-priced retailers to discounters, with dollar stores reaping the rewards: Dollar Tree's stock soared from a high of $21.85 in 2007 to $30.65 in 2008, with sales rising from $4.2 billion to $4.6 billion for the same period. The retailer had added 313 new locations during the year, bringing its total to more than 3,400 stores in 48 states.

The next year, however, Dollar Tree stumbled a bit after trying to mimic other discounters and its Deal$ stores, pricing some merchandise higher than a dollar. While the departure from its namesake price policy worked in the Deal$ units, increasing both traffic and sales, it confused Dollar Tree shoppers and sent others scurrying out the door. Share prices for 2009 fell to a low of $16.25 before rebounding to finish the fiscal year at $28.47. Sasser characterized the experiment, in a March 2009 *Supermarket News* article, as a definite "oops." Despite the mistake, the company still managed to increase sales to $5.2 billion and net income to a robust $320.5 million.

ONWARD AND UPWARD: 2010 AND BEYOND

As the first decade of the new century came to a close, Dollar Tree's growth seemed to know no bounds as sales and profits exceeded both management's and analysts' expectations. Shoppers squeezed by higher gas prices opted not to drive across town to big box or primary grocery chains, instead choosing dollar stores closer to home. To keep customers coming, extreme discounters not only broadened product lines but gave shoppers more familiar brands such as Campbell's, Nestlé, and Smucker's.

For its part, Dollar Tree was able to continue its expansion plans, taking advantage of the slumping real estate market to open more stores for less cost. The discounter planned to open more than 200 stores in 2010 and succeeded in adding 235 new units, ending the fiscal year with a total of 4,101 North American locations. In addition, coolers and freezers were added to more outlets, bringing the total to just over 40 percent of stores. "We continue to expand this category because it serves the current needs of our customers and drives traffic into our stores," Sasser commented to *Supermarket News* in August 2010. "While adding more stores, we also continue to learn more precisely what our customers need, and we are refining our frozen and refrigerated assortments to provide more value and excitement in our stores."

While Dollar General continued to lead the super-value retail segment, Dollar Tree began to invade its turf with the acquisition of 86 stores in four provinces: Ontario in the East, and British Columbia, Alberta, and Saskatchewan in the Northwest. Year-end 2010 figures suggested Dollar Tree was gaining ground, literally and figuratively, with revenues reaching $5.8 billion and yielding net income of $397.3 million.

In its 35th year in 2011, Dollar Tree had succeeded far beyond its founders' expectations, finding its niche and not only carving a healthy slice of the extreme discounter's pie, but also creating a legion of loyal shoppers from coast to coast and even in Canada. As tough economic times persisted in the 2010s, shoppers increasingly turned away from grocery chains and big box discounters to dollar stores, with Dollar Tree and its competitors reaping the rewards.

Ellen D. Wernick
Updated, Christina M. Stansell; Nelson Rhodes

PRINCIPAL SUBSIDIARIES

Dollar Tree Distribution Inc.; Dollar Tree Management, Inc.; Dollar Tree Stores Inc.

PRINCIPAL COMPETITORS

99 Cents Only Stores; Dollar General Corporation; Family Dollar Stores, Inc.; Target Corporation; Walmart Stores, Inc.

FURTHER READING

Berner, Robert, and Brian Grow. "Out-Discounting the Discounter." *BusinessWeek*, May 10, 2004, 78.

Burritt, Chris. "Came for the Bargains, Stayed for the Brands." *BusinessWeek*, August 2, 2010, 23.

"Customer Loyalty." *Women's Wear Daily*, July 15, 2004, 10.

Francella, Barbara G. "Dollar Tree Bears Loot." *Convenience Store News*, July 18, 2005, 57.

Gentry, Connie, et al. "Big Builders." *Chain Store Age*, December 2009, 61.

Gregory, Sean. "The Buck Stops Here." *Time*, December 20, 2010, 54.

Hitt, Jack. "The Buck Stops Here." *New York Times Magazine*, August 21, 2011, 18.

Hoover, Ken. "Customers Find Value in Dollar Tree Offerings." *Investor's Business Daily*, July 27, 2009.

Hudson, Kris. "Making Sense of 'Dollar Stores.'" *Wall Street Journal* (Eastern Edition), September 21, 2005, C1.

Jonnarone, John. "Dollar Tree Profits Come in Small Sizes." *Wall Street Journal*, January 22, 2011, B18.

McGrath, Courtney. "Best of the Best: King of Dollar Stores." *Kiplinger's Personal Finance*, September 2003, 36.

Much, Marilyn. "Bargain-Hunting Consumers Find Value and Quality in a Dollar." *Investor's Business Daily*, July 23, 2009.

———. "Discounters Dollar Tree, TJX Top Views as Shoppers Continue to Spend Carefully." *Investor's Business Daily*, February 25, 2010, A1.

"Racking Up Profit at Dollar Tree Stores." *Chain Store Age Executive*, November 1997, 54.

Springer, Jon. "Dollar Tree Ends Multi-price Test." *Supermarket News*, March 2, 2009, 10.

Wellman, David. "Dollars on Ice." *Frozen Food Age*, March 2004, 55.

Zwiebach, Elliot. "Dollar Tree Expands Coolers." *Supermarket News*, August 30, 2010, 26.

AB Electrolux

St. Göransgatan 143
Stockholm, SE-105 45
Sweden
Telephone: (+46 8) 738 60 00
Fax: (+46 8) 738 74 61
Web site: http://www.electrolux.com

Public Company
Founded: 1919 as Aktiebolaget Elektrolux
Incorporated: 1910 as Elektromekaniska AB
Employees: 52,693
Sales: SEK 106.33 billion ($14.76 billion) (2010)
Stock Exchanges: NASDAQ OMX Stockholm Over the Counter (OTC)
Ticker Symbols: ELUXB (Stockholm); ELUXY (OTC)
NAICS: 333411 Air Purification Equipment Manufacturing; 335211 Electric Housewares and Household Fan Manufacturing; 335212 Household Vacuum Cleaner Manufacturing; 335221 Household Cooking Appliance Manufacturing; 335222 Household Refrigerator and Home Freezer Manufacturing; 335224 Household Laundry Equipment Manufacturing; 335228 Other Major Household Appliance Manufacturing

■ ■ ■

AB Electrolux is the second-largest appliance manufacturer in the world, trailing only Whirlpool Corporation. Electrolux manufactures a variety of household appliances, including refrigerators, washing machines and dryers, stoves, dishwashers, vacuum cleaners, and air purifiers. The firm also manufactures professional foodservice and laundry equipment used by hotels, restaurants, and laundromats. Overall, Electrolux sells more than 40 million products each year to customers located in more than 150 countries around the world. In addition to its flagship Electrolux brand, the company also sells these products under such well-known names as AEG, Eureka, Frigidaire, and Zanussi. The Wallenberg family dynasty of Sweden, through Investor AB, owns about 30 percent of the shareholder voting rights in Electrolux, a holding dating back to 1956.

BEGINNINGS IN VACUUM CLEANERS

The Electrolux empire originated with the perspicacity and marketing flair of Axel Wenner-Gren, who spotted the potential of the mobile vacuum cleaner only a few years after its invention by Englishman H. C. Booth in 1901. In 1910 the young Wenner-Gren bought a part share in the European agent of a U.S. company producing one of the early vacuum cleaners, the clumsy Santo Staubsauger. After several years as a Santo salesman for the German-based agent, Wenner-Gren sold his share of the company and returned to Sweden, where the building blocks for the future Electrolux, AB Lux and Elektromekaniska AB, were already in place.

Sven Carlstedt had formed Elektromekaniska in 1910 to manufacture motors for a vacuum cleaner based on the Santo, which was produced by Swedish engineer Eberhardt Seger. Since its founding in 1901, Lux had manufactured kerosene lamps. Confronted with a shrinking market owing to the introduction of electric lighting, the head of Lux, C. G. Lindblom, proposed to Carlstedt that the two companies form a joint venture

COMPANY PERSPECTIVES

"Thinking of you" expresses the Electrolux offering: To maintain continuous focus on the consumer, whether it's a question of product development, design, production, marketing, logistics or service.

for the production and marketing of a new vacuum cleaner.

In 1912 Wenner-Gren became the agent for the Lux 1 vacuum cleaner in Germany, subsequently taking on the United Kingdom and France as well. Over the next few years Wenner-Gren's role in the company grew, and the machine gradually became lighter and more ergonomic. Wenner-Gren foresaw a potential sales bonanza in Europe after the end of World War I. Initially unable to persuade his colleagues to step up production capacity, he overcame their reluctance by guaranteeing a minimum sales figure through his own sales company, Svenska Elektron (later known as Finans AB Svetro).

Lux and Elektromekaniska merged in 1919 as Aktiebolaget Elektrolux (the spelling was changed to Electrolux in 1957). Wenner-Gren became president and a major shareholder of the new company. In 1921 the Lux V was introduced. This new model resembled a modern cylindrical vacuum cleaner, but it glided along the floor on ski-like runners instead of wheels. The Lux V was to present serious competition to the upright Hoover machines in the 1920s.

REVOLUTIONARY SALES TACTICS

The convenience and attractive styling of its product helped to get the new company off to a promising start, but the salesmanship of Electrolux's president probably played an even bigger part. Wenner-Gren was a great believer in the door-to-door sales techniques already espoused by competitors such as Hoover in the United States. Vacuum cleaners were demonstrated to potential customers in their own homes, and buyers were allowed to pay for their machines in installments. Wenner-Gren knew how to get the best out of his sales force.

Sales training, competitions, and such slogans as "Every home an Electrolux home" later became familiar methods of boosting sales, but when Wenner-Gren introduced them they were revolutionary. He also believed in leading from the front. The story of how he sold a vacuum cleaner to the Vatican is part of company mythology. Four competitors demonstrated their

machines first, each vacuuming their allocated area of carpet. When Wenner-Gren's turn came, instead of vacuuming the fifth area, he went over the first four again. The resultant bagful of dust persuaded the pope to add his palace to the growing number of Electrolux homes. Advertising, too, was imaginative. Not only did Electrolux make extensive use of the press, but in the late 1920s citizens of Stockholm, Berlin, and London were liable to encounter bizarre vacuum cleaner-shaped cars in the streets.

Bizarre or not, the sales methods worked, and the company grew. Throughout the 1920s, new sales companies sprang up, not only all over Europe but also in the United States in 1924, Australia in 1925, and South America. Many of these were financed by Wenner-Gren himself rather than by Electrolux in Sweden. Vacuum cleaner manufacturing plants also started to open overseas, first in Berlin in 1926 and a year later in Luton, England, and Courbevoie, France.

By 1928 Electrolux had sales of SEK 70 million. It had five manufacturing plants, 350 worldwide offices, and 20 subsidiaries. In spite of this geographic expansion, the company was often short of funds, in part because of the system of payment by installments. It became clear that further growth would require increased capital, and it was decided to float the company on the London Stock Exchange and to issue more shares. Prior to flotation in 1928, Electrolux bought out many of the related companies owned by Wenner-Gren, although he retained his minority shareholding in the American Electrolux Corporation until 1949.

Flotation on the Stockholm stock exchange was postponed until 1930 owing to the stock market crash of 1929. When the shares did appear they were greeted with some mistrust, as it was thought that the company was overvalued and that sales would suffer during the anticipated recession. These doubts, however, were to prove unfounded.

DIVERSIFYING INTO REFRIGERATORS

During the 1920s Electrolux introduced a number of new products, including floor polishers, which were a natural progression from vacuum cleaners and debuted in 1927. The main diversification of the 1920s, however, came through the acquisition in 1925 of AB Arctic, a company manufacturing a novel machine, the absorption refrigerator. This type of refrigerator had no moving parts, although early models required a connection to a source of running water. Power was provided by electricity, gas, or kerosene, in contrast with the compression method of refrigeration, which relied on electric power. Early compressors were noisy and bulky,

KEY DATES

1919: Swedish firms AB Lux and Elektromekaniska AB merge to form Aktiebolaget Elektrolux, with Axel Wenner-Gren serving as president.

1928: Public trading of the company's stock begins on the London Stock Exchange.

1956: Wenner-Gren sells his stake in the firm to the Swedish finance group Wallenberg.

1957: Company changes the spelling of its name to Electrolux.

1974: Electrolux purchases the U.S.-based Eureka-Williams Company.

1986: Through purchase of White Consolidated Industries Inc., Electrolux adds the Frigidaire brand.

2000: Company reacquires the rights to the Electrolux brand in North America, which it had sold in 1968.

2011: Electrolux acquires leading appliance makers based in Egypt and Chile.

so the new Electrolux system had several advantages over its competitors' compression refrigerators.

A new air-cooled version of Electrolux's absorption refrigerators was introduced in 1931, and by 1936 more than one million had been sold. Demand for the machines grew as various countries placed restrictions on the use of food preservatives. In the United States, Servel, Inc. had acquired a license to manufacture Electrolux's refrigerators.

Electrolux's original vacuum cleaner factory on Lilla Essingen was devastated by fire in 1936. When it was rebuilt the following year, the opportunity was taken to fit it with the latest equipment and to install a central research laboratory.

In 1926 Wenner-Gren became chairman of the board, with Ernst Aurell taking over as president. During the 1930s Wenner-Gren remained chairman but reduced his involvement in the running of the company, prior to resigning from his post in 1939. Harry G. Faulkner, a British accountant who had been instrumental in the company's consolidation prior to the 1928 flotation, succeeded Aurell in 1930 and remained president throughout the 1930s.

With intensive marketing and continued investment in research and development, Electrolux rode out the Great Depression. By 1939 annual sales stood at SEK

80 million. That year, Gustaf Sahlin, former president of the United States Electrolux Corporation, took over the presidency of the parent company from Faulkner. Throughout World War II, despite the loss of some manufacturing plants, Electrolux managed to maintain many of its usual activities, opening operations in Australia, Venezuela, and Colombia. At home in Sweden, it acquired companies in the fields of commercial laundry equipment and outboard motors. Much energy, however, was diverted into the war effort, including the manufacture of munitions and of air cleaners for the Swedish forces.

After the war Electrolux resumed its normal operations, initially under Elon V. Ekman, who became president in 1951, and from 1963 to 1967 under his successor, Harry Wennberg. The period was not without setbacks, however. Many subsidiaries that had been opened in Eastern European countries before the war disappeared from view behind the Iron Curtain. In addition, despite a British government contract to supply 50,000 built-in absorption refrigerators for prefabricated temporary houses, the company began to face problems in the refrigerator market. Compression technology had advanced and was proving more effective for the larger refrigerators that consumers began demanding. Although at first the company concentrated on improving the design of the absorption refrigerator, Electrolux eventually was obliged to adopt compression technology.

FURTHER DIVERSIFICATION IN POSTWAR PERIOD

Meanwhile, diversification continued. During the 1950s Electrolux started making household washing machines and dishwashers, and the company extended floor-cleaning equipment production to an increasing number of countries, including Brazil and Norway. When, in 1956, Wenner-Gren sold his remaining shares in Electrolux to the Swedish finance group Wallenberg, revenue had reached more than SEK 500 million. Over the succeeding decades, the association with Wallenberg often stood Electrolux in good stead, helping, for example, to arrange overseas funding and to insulate the group from any hostile takeover bids.

In 1962, in an attempt to solve its refrigerator problems, Electrolux bought the Swedish firm of ElektroHelios for SEK 36 million. This firm, founded in 1919, had a major share of the Scandinavian market in compressor refrigerators and freezers, and it also produced stoves. In the year following the acquisition, Electrolux launched a wide range of food-storage equipment, putting it in a strong position to benefit from the demands generated by the flourishing frozen food industry.

PURSUING MAJOR ACQUISITIONS

Until the 1960s Electrolux had continued to operate along the lines conceived by Wenner-Gren in the early years. A new phase began in 1967, when Hans Werthén was recruited from Ericsson, another member of the Wallenberg group of companies. Werthén remained with Electrolux for more than 25 years, first as president, and from 1975 to 1991 as chairman, with Gösta Bystedt and then Anders Scharp succeeding him as president. Under this regime, a series of momentous acquisitions was to allow Electrolux to multiply its sales by a factor of 60 in 20 years.

When Werthén took over management of the Electrolux group the company was in the doldrums. It had run into internal and external problems, and its technology was outmoded. Electrolux, an international company, had not been effectively integrated with its acquisition ElektroHelios, which still focused on the Scandinavian market. In many ways the merged companies had continued to behave as if they were still competitors, resulting in a net loss of market share in the refrigerator market. Only the vacuum cleaners were profitable: To use Werthén's own words, "they represented 125 percent of the profits."

Approaching the problem from a new perspective, Werthén managed to resolve the Electrolux-Elektro-Helios conflict and get rid of the organizational overlap. Scharp, his new head of production, set about updating production technology to challenge the much more advanced techniques he had seen in U.S. appliance factories. Werthén believed that Electrolux's problems could not be overcome simply through operational improvements. The company had a more fundamental problem: size.

As Werthén saw it, Electrolux was neither small enough to be a niche player, nor large enough to gain the economies of scale it needed to compete with such giants as Philips and AEG. Growth was the only way forward, and in the overcrowded market place for household goods, growth meant acquisitions.

The initial focus was on Scandinavia. One small competitor after another, many of them struggling for survival, was bought up by the growing company. The Norwegian stove manufacturer Elektra, the Danish white goods company Atlas, and the Finnish stove maker Slev were among the first acquisitions of the late 1960s. Soon Electrolux was shopping for competitors outside Scandinavia. The 1974 acquisition of Eureka-Williams Company (later renamed The Eureka Company), one of the longest-established vacuum cleaner companies in the United States, gave Electrolux a large slice of a valuable market overnight.

At around this time there were glimmerings of hope for the reemergence of the absorption refrigerator. The quiet-running units were ideally suited to installation in smaller living spaces, such as mobile homes and hotel rooms. Electrolux managers soon sensed these new opportunities. After taking over competitors Kreft (of Luxembourg) and Siegas (of Germany) in 1972, the group became the world leader in this sector.

In addition to expanding its share of the company's existing markets, Electrolux soon started to see acquisitions as a way of entering new areas, particularly those related to existing product lines. Electrolux acquired the British lawnmower manufacturer Flymo in 1968 because Werthén saw lawn mowing as an activity allied to floor cleaning. The provision of cleaning services seemed a logical extension to the production of cleaning equipment, prompting the purchase of a half share in the Swedish cleaning company ASAB.

Buying the venerable Swedish firm Husqvarna AB in 1978 gave Electrolux not only a new pool of expertise in commercial refrigeration but also a flourishing chainsaw-manufacturing concern, which complemented its interests in outdoor equipment. Taking over a clutch of other chainsaw manufacturers over the following decade, including the U.S. firm Poulan/Weed Eater in 1986, enabled Electrolux to claim leadership of the worldwide chainsaw market. The outdoor products sector was further strengthened and broadened through the acquisitions of Roper Corporation's garden products business (subsequently renamed American Yard Products) in 1988 and of Allegretti & Co., a U.S. maker of battery-driven garden tools, in 1990.

This program of acquisitions brought some more radical departures from existing product lines. In 1973 Electrolux bought Facit, a Swedish office equipment company. The deal also brought to Electrolux the production of Ballingslöv kitchen and bathroom cabinets. Initial doubts about whether Electrolux had the knowhow to manage a high-tech company proved unfounded. The purchase of Swedish metal producer Gränges was greeted with equal skepticism, because again the connection between the new and existing businesses appeared to be rather tenuous. Gränges was seen as a troubled company, but when Electrolux bought it in 1980 for SEK 725 million, Werthén had already been chairman of its board for three years and had overseen a marked upturn in its fortunes. By the late 1980s Gränges's aluminum products and car seat belts represented a major aspect of Electrolux's business, although other parts of Gränges were sold off.

REACHING FOR WORLD APPLIANCE LEADERSHIP

Under the presidency of Scharp, which began in 1981, Electrolux's program of acquisitions began to focus on the consolidation and expansion of existing lines.

Takeovers became increasingly ambitious as Electrolux saw within its reach the chance to become one of the world leaders in household appliances. Major steps toward this goal were the acquisitions of Zanussi S.p.A. in Italy, White Consolidated Industries Inc. in the United States (the third-largest white goods company in that country whose brands included Frigidaire), and the white goods and catering equipment divisions of the United Kingdom's Thorn EMI, in 1984, 1986, and 1987, respectively. Through the years, Electrolux gained a reputation for buying only when the price was right and for turning around sick companies, even at the cost of heavy staff cuts and management shakeups.

Electrolux made divestments as well as acquisitions. One of Werthén's earliest acts as president had been the 1968 sale of AB Electrolux's minority shareholding in the U.S. firm Electrolux Corporation to Consolidated Foods, which raised SEK 300 million, although the subsequent Eureka purchase had placed the company in the curious position of competing against its own brand name. Management continued this policy of judicious divestment following acquisitions, when it was concluded that all or part of the new member did not fit in with the group's strategy, however, the sell-offs also served to improve the balance sheet in the wake of an acquisition. Facit, for instance, was sold to Ericsson in 1983, and shortly after the purchase of White Consolidated, its machine-tool division, White Machine Tools, was also sold.

Another method of raising cash following an acquisition was through the sale of assets, although Electrolux acquisitions were not primarily motivated by a desire to strip assets. In the case of Husqvarna, the purchase price of SEK 120 million was more than covered within six months by the sale of its land and other property. A third way of recovering the costs of acquisition was the use of a troubled company's accumulated losses wherever possible to reduce the group's tax liability. This was a major incentive in the acquisition of Gränges.

Not every company was delighted to hear Electrolux knocking on its door. Many a takeover was resisted by the target company, even though Electrolux was also sometimes called in to rescue a troubled company (as happened with Zanussi) or asked to act as a white knight (notably for the U.S. household appliance company Tappan in 1979).

GEOGRAPHIC EXPANSION AND RESTRUCTURINGS IN THE NINETIES

The 1990s brought major changes to Electrolux, spearheaded by a new management team. Werthén resigned as chairman in early 1991, Scharp became chairman and CEO, and Leif Johansson was named president of the firm, taking over as CEO himself in 1994. During Werthén's long reign, Electrolux had grown tremendously through acquisitions but had failed to effectively consolidate the acquired operations into existing ones. The result was an unwieldy array of brands, each of which needed the support of separate production and marketing operations. Electrolux was further hurt in the early 1990s by an economic downturn in its core European and North American areas of operation and by the maturing of the white goods sectors in those same markets, which intensified competition. All told, profits for Electrolux from 1990 through 1994 were much lower than the heights reached during the late 1980s. The new management team responded by seeking out new markets for its core products, by gradually divesting its noncore industrial products operations, and by streamlining its remaining business units.

Electrolux targeted Eastern Europe, Asia, South America, the Middle East, and southern Africa in its 1990s push for global growth. The company had already, in 1989, arranged for Sharp Corporation to distribute some of Electrolux's products in Japan. Subsequent moves in Asia included the setting up of joint ventures in China for the manufacture of compressors, vacuum cleaners, and water purifiers, and the acquisition of majority stakes in refrigerator and washing machine factories in India. In January 1996 another Chinese joint venture was established for the production of refrigerators and freezers for commercial users.

The newly opened markets of Eastern Europe were first targeted with the 1991 purchase of the Hungarian white goods company Lehel. A 1995 joint venture with Poland's Myszkow FNE Swiatowit began making washing machines under the Zanussi brand. In Latin America, where Whirlpool was dominant, Electrolux acquired 99 percent of Refrigeração Paraná S.A. (Refripar) in 1996. Refripar (soon renamed Electrolux do Brasil) held the number two position among Brazilian white goods companies. Also in 1996, Electrolux purchased a 20 percent stake in Atlas Eléctrica S.A. of Costa Rica, the leading producer of refrigerators and stoves in Central America. By 1994, about 10 percent of Electrolux's sales came from outside the European Union (EU) and North America. This figure more than doubled by 1996 to 20.4 percent, with non-EU Europe accounting for 7 percent; Latin America, 6.4 percent; Asia, 5.1 percent; Oceania, 1 percent; and Africa, 0.9 percent.

While undergoing this global expansion, Electrolux also moved gradually to concentrate solely on three core sectors: household appliances, commercial appliances, and outdoor products. Profits in the company's industrial products sector were falling, and Scharp and Johansson determined that these noncore operations should be jettisoned. The culmination of this process came in 1996 and 1997, with the divestment of the Constructor group (producers of materials-handling equipment), the Swedish electronics operations of Electrolux Electronics, and a sewing machines unit; and with the spin-off of Gränges to the public. The final divestment came in August 1997 when Electrolux's goods protection operation, which sold tarpaulins and storage halls, was sold to MVI, a privately owned investment fund.

Electrolux greatly reduced its acquisitions activity in the EU and North America in the 1990s, although there was one major addition. In 1992 the company bought a 10 percent stake in AEG Hausgeräte, the household appliance division of Germany's Daimler-Benz. This stake was increased to 20 percent in 1993 and the following year Electrolux purchased the remaining 80 percent for about $437 million. The purchase brought the company another strong European brand, which fit well into a renewed brand strategy for Electrolux. The company sought to position the Electrolux brand as a global brand and Electrolux, Zanussi, and AEG as pan-European brands, while continuing to maintain strong local brands such as Faure in France and Tricity Bendix in the United Kingdom.

Along with the new brand strategy, Electrolux began to reduce its fragmented operations and become more efficient. In 1996 a pan-European logistics function was set up for white goods and floor-care products. Late that year, the company's North American white goods operation, Frigidaire Company, was combined with the two North American outdoor products companies, Poulan/Weed Eater and American Yard Products, to form Frigidaire Home Products. Merging these operations made strategic sense because the trend in retailing was toward single retailers selling both indoor and outdoor appliances. Similar consolidations were planned for Electrolux's operations elsewhere in the world.

In April 1997 Johansson left Electrolux to become the chief executive at AB Volvo. Replacing him as Electrolux president and CEO was Michael Treschow, who had been president and CEO at Atlas Copco AB, a maker of industrial equipment and, like Electrolux, part of the Wallenberg dynasty. It was thus left to Treschow to announce, in June 1997, a major restructuring plan, which had already been agreed on before he took over. Over a two-year period, Electrolux would lay off more than 11,000 of its workers (constituting 11 percent of its workforce) and close 23 plants and 50 warehouses (half of its global total), with the reductions coming

mainly in Europe and North America. In addition, a restructuring charge of SEK 2.5 billion ($323 million) was incurred in the second quarter of 1997.

Under the leadership of Treschow, Electrolux further streamlined its operations in 1998, divesting its recycling business, its kitchen and bathroom cabinets interests, and various professional cleaning and heavy-duty laundry equipment units. The following year, the firm sold its food and beverage vending machine businesses and its professional refrigeration equipment business. That year, Electrolux laid off a large portion of its direct sales force. The company completed these restructuring efforts in 1999 and began to focus on maintaining its leadership position.

Toward this end, the company began to develop new products that incorporated cutting-edge technology. In 1999 it teamed up with Ericsson to develop and market products for the "networked home." Managed under a joint venture called e2Home, these products would be connected via the Web to a variety of information and service providers. Another product line, the Live-In Kitchen, connected appliances to mobile phones, which among other features, allowed owners to preheat their oven from their cell phone. As part of its foray into new technology, Electrolux also developed the Trilobite vacuum cleaner, a robotic product that used sensors to vacuum a room, and a Smart Fridge, a top-of-the-line refrigerator complete with a built-in computer screen and Internet access.

BOOSTING PROMINENCE OF ELECTROLUX BRAND

By 2000, both sales and net income had increased steadily over the previous three years. During that year, the company repurchased the rights to the Electrolux brand in North America, which it had sold in 1968 upon divesting its U.S. floor-care company. The purchase was part of its plan to align its brand names, especially in North America.

The company's operating environment became turbulent in 2001. Weakening demand and high costs related to upgrades at its refrigerator factories in North America led to a 23 percent drop in operating income compared to the previous year. Despite these challenges, the company made two significant acquisitions: the major appliance division of Email Limited, Australia's largest household appliance manufacturer, and Marazzini Ernesto S.p.A., a lawnmower manufacturer based in Italy.

In April 2002 Hans Stråberg took over as president and CEO as Treschow left the firm to head Ericsson. Under Stråberg, Electrolux continued to keep a keen eye on costs. In December 2002 another restructuring was launched that involved a further 6 percent workforce reduction, representing the elimination of more than 5,000 jobs. Focusing on several underperforming operations, this overhaul included the closure of a room air-conditioning plant in Edison, New Jersey, and revampings of refrigerator production in China and compressor operations in India.

Electrolux also accelerated the brand realignment that had begun under Stråberg's predecessor. The main goal was to build Electrolux into a leading global brand. This was accomplished in part through double-branding, an initiative launched in 2003 in which a strong local or regional brand was paired with the flagship brand. For example, the Juno brand in Germany was renamed Juno-Electrolux. By 2004, in part thanks to the double-branding, sales of Electrolux-branded products accounted for 40 percent of overall sales, compared to the 10 percent figure for 2000. In 2005 the pan-European AEG brand was likewise double-branded AEG-Electrolux.

In the meantime, an equally important branding event occurred across the Atlantic when the company introduced its first products bearing the Electrolux name in North America since regaining control of the brand on that continent three years earlier. After this 2003 launch of floor-care products, Electrolux major appliances followed a year later, starting with the high-end Electrolux ICON range. Concurrent with these brand realignment initiatives, Electrolux concentrated on shifting the corporate culture away from a manufacturing focus toward the creation of products based on identified consumer needs and demands.

SHIFTING PRODUCTION TO LOW-COST COUNTRIES

Stråberg also launched a major, multiyear reorganization of the firm's global manufacturing operations to drive down costs and hold the line against rapidly growing Asian competitors such as the Chinese firm Haier Group Company and Korea's LG Corp. and Samsung Group. By the end of the decade, more than 30 factories, most located in high-wage North American and European countries, were shut down as production was shifted to facilities in Mexico and other low-cost countries in Eastern Europe and Southeast Asia. Nearly 60 percent of Electrolux's production was taking place in low-cost countries by 2010, a huge increase compared to the 15 percent figure for 2002. Among the facilities closed as part of this globalization of production were a refrigerator plant in Greenville, Michigan; vacuum cleaner plants in Västervik, Sweden, and El Paso, Texas; a stove factory in Reims, France; a tumble dryer factory in Tommerup, Denmark; a major appliances plant in

Nuremberg, Germany; and a small appliances factory in Torsvik, Sweden.

In a move that enabled the company to concentrate all its efforts on its core business of producing and selling indoor appliances for the household and professional markets, Electrolux in June 2006 spun off its outdoor products operations to its shareholders as the independent, publicly traded Husqvarna AB. Over the next couple of years, as part of a revitalized product development effort, Electrolux introduced comprehensive lines of new products under its flagship brand in both Europe and North America for the premium segment of the market. Additionally, in North America the company relaunched the Frigidaire brand for the mass-market segment in 2009.

With about a third of its sales originating in the United States, the bursting of the housing bubble in that country seriously affected Electrolux's results as demand for major appliances fell off. As the global economy sank into a deep recession in 2008, Electrolux's overall sales were flat that year in comparison to the previous one, while profits plunged 87 percent to just SEK 366 million ($56 million). The bottom line was reduced by more than SEK 1 billion ($153 million) in restructuring costs that were incurred as part of an overhaul that entailed further job cuts of about 3,100, or 5 percent of the workforce.

By 2010 the North American and European economies had made only halting recoveries from the deep slump, leaving consumers cautious about making large-ticket purchases of durable goods. At the same time, Electrolux and its U.S.-based rival Whirlpool were being squeezed by rising costs for such raw materials as steel, copper, and plastics and fierce price competition from Korean rivals LG and Samsung. The competitive environment made it difficult for Electrolux to pass the increased costs onto consumers through price increases. Late in 2010, the company announced another restructuring involving 2,100 more job cuts in Europe and North America. In addition, Electrolux planned to consolidate its North American cooking appliance manufacturing at a newly built factory in Memphis, Tennessee, leading to the closure of a large facility in L'Assomption, Quebec, Canada.

At the beginning of 2011, Stråberg left Electrolux to pursue other business endeavors. He was succeeded by Keith McLoughlin, who had most recently headed the company's global major-appliance manufacturing operations and had earlier led the turnaround of the North American major appliances unit, including overseeing the revitalization of the Frigidaire brand. Born in the United States, McLoughlin became Electrolux's first non-Swedish CEO.

While contending with the challenges of the highly competitive markets of North America and Europe, McLoughlin accelerated Electrolux's pursuit of growth in faster-growing emerging markets. During the third quarter of 2011, Electrolux completed an acquisition that had been announced the previous year, purchasing Cairo-based Olympic Group, the largest home appliance maker in the Middle East and North Africa, for SEK 2.56 billion ($401 million). In October 2011 Electrolux acquired the Chilean firm Compañia Tecno Industrial S.A. (CTI), which had been a publicly traded company majority owned by Sigdo Koppers S.A. CTI was the leading producer of appliances in Chile and Argentina, and purchasing it enhanced Electrolux's already strong presence in Latin America. These deals increased the portion of sales that Electrolux derived from emerging markets to 35 percent, a figure that the company aimed to increase to 50 percent by 2016. Electrolux planned to rely on emerging markets for growth as it contended with the prolonged slowdown in the more mature markets of Europe and North America.

Alison Classe
Updated, Christina M. Stansell; David E. Salamie

PRINCIPAL SUBSIDIARIES

Electrolux Laundry Systems Sweden AB; Electrolux HemProdukter AB; Electrolux Professional AB; Electrolux Floor Care and Small Appliances AB; Electrolux Home Products Pty. Ltd (Australia); Electrolux Hausgeräte G.m.b.H. (Austria); Electrolux CEE G.m.b.H. (Austria); Electrolux Home Products Corporation N.V. (Belgium); Electrolux Belgium N.V.; Electrolux do Brasil S.A. (Brazil); Electrolux Canada Corp.; Electrolux (Hangzhou) Domestic Appliances Co. Ltd (China); Electrolux (China) Home Appliance Co. Ltd; Electrolux Home Products Denmark A/S; Oy Electrolux Ab (Finland); Electrolux France SAS; Electrolux Home Products France SAS; Electrolux Professionnel SAS (France); Electrolux Deutschland GmbH (Germany); Electrolux Rothenburg GmbH Factory and Development Germany; Electrolux Lehel Hütögépgyár Kft (Hungary); Electrolux Appliances S.p.A. (Italy); Electrolux Professional S.p.A. (Italy); Electrolux Italia S.p.A. (Italy); Electrolux Luxembourg S.à r.l.; Electrolux de Mexico, S.A. de CV; Electrolux Associated Company B.V. (Netherlands); Electrolux Home Products (Nederland) B.V. (Netherlands); Electrolux Home Products Norway AS; Electrolux Poland Spolka Z.o.o.; Electrolux Home Products España S.A. (Spain); Electrolux Home Products Operations España S.L. (Spain); Electrolux AG (Switzerland); Electrolux Plc (UK); Electrolux Professional Ltd (UK); Electrolux Home Products Inc. (USA); Electrolux North America, Inc. (USA); Electrolux Professional Inc. (USA).

PRINCIPAL OPERATING UNITS

Floor Care and Small Appliances; Major Appliances Asia/Pacific; Major Appliances Europe, Middle East, and Africa; Major Appliances Latin America; Major Appliances North America; Professional Products.

PRINCIPAL COMPETITORS

Ali SpA; Alliance Laundry Holdings LLC; BISSELL Homecare, Inc.; BSH Bosch und Siemens Hausgeräte GmbH; Candy Hoover Group Srl; Controladora Mabe S.A. de C.V.; Dyson Ltd.; Fisher & Paykel Appliances Holdings Limited; General Electric Company; Girbau, SA; Haier Group Company; Indesit Company S.p.A.; LG Corp.; Manitowoc Foodservice Companies, Inc.; The Middleby Corporation; Miele & Cie. KG; Primus BVBA; Rational AG; Royal Philips Electronics N.V.; Samsung Group; SEB SA; Stanley Black & Decker, Inc.; Techtronic Industries Company Limited; Whirlpool Corporation.

FURTHER READING

Brown-Humes, Christopher. "Electrolux Moves Out of Its Markets." *Financial Times*, July 28, 2005, 30.

Burt, Tim. "Electrolux Set to Pull Out of Industrial Goods." *Financial Times*, October 30, 1996, 28.

Canedy, Dana. "Electrolux to Cut 12,000 Workers and Shut Plants." *New York Times*, June 13, 1997, D2.

Electrolux: Two Epochs That Shaped a Worldwide Group. Stockholm: Electrolux, 1989.

Hagerty, James R., and Bob Tita. "Appliance Sales Tumble: Whirlpool, Electrolux Set Production Cuts; Frugal Customers Become Handymen." *Wall Street Journal*, October 29, 2011, B1, B2.

Hagerty, James R., and Sven Grundberg. "Rising Costs Squeeze Appliance Makers." *Wall Street Journal*, February 3, 2011, B6.

Marsh, Peter. "Electrolux Awaits Results of Clean-Up." *Financial Times*, February 13, 2007, 25.

Marsh, Peter, and Robert Anderson. "Electrolux Axes 3,000 Jobs as Sales Decline." *Financial Times*, December 16, 2008, 16.

McIvor, Greg. "Electrolux Comes under the Scalpel." *Financial Times*, October 29, 1997, 19.

Quinn, Matthew. "Electrolux: No Plans to Withdraw from U.S." *Wall Street Journal*, August 27–28, 2011, B3.

Reed, Stanley. "The Wallenbergs' New Blood." *Business Week*, October 20, 1997, 98, 102.

Stone, Rod. "Electrolux to Cut Jobs to Bolster Productivity." *Wall Street Journal Europe*, December 18, 2002, A6.

Ward, Andrew. "Electrolux Appoints Its First Non-Swedish Chief." *Financial Times*, September 24, 2010, 15.

Embraer S.A.

—————————■—————————

Avenida Brigadeiro Faria Lima, 2170
São José dos Campos, SP 12227-901
Brazil
Telephone: (+55 12) 3927-4404
Fax: (+55 12) 3927-6070
Web site: http://www.embraer.com.br

Public Company
Incorporated: 1969 as Empresa Brasileira de Aeronáutica
S.A.
Employees: 18,884
Sales: $5.36 billion (2010)
Stock Exchanges: São Paulo New York
Ticker Symbols: EMBR3; ERJ
NAICS: 336411 Aircraft Manufacturing; 336413 Other
Aircraft Part and Auxiliary Equipment Manufacturing;
488190 Other Support Activities for Air
Transportation

■ ■ ■

Embraer S.A. is a leading manufacturer of civil and
military aircraft. It is one of Brazil's most successful
exporters. The company was formed to supply the
military, but defense and security sales accounted for
just 12.5 percent of revenues in 2010. In the previous
two decades, Embraer had become one of the world's
largest civil aircraft manufacturers by riding the regional
jet trend. Commercial aviation accounted for 53.9
percent of 2010 revenues and aviation services, 10.5
percent. The group's other interests include defense
electronics.

When the market for regional airliners became
saturated, Embraer developed a line of executive jets. It
continued to produce increasingly advanced military
aircraft in partnership with foreign companies such as
Dassault, which allowed it to offer its first supersonic
fighter, a variant of the Mirage 2000. It also brought out
unmanned aerial vehicles (UAVs) developed with Elbit
and others.

MILITARY ORIGINS

Three military cabinet leaders (army, navy, and air force)
took over Brazil in 1968 after elected president General
Artur Costa e Silva was incapacitated by strokes.
General Emilio Medici was installed as the new head of
state. The military wanted Brazil to have its own
aircraft-manufacturing capacity and created Empresa
Brasileira de Aeronáutica S.A. (Embraer) the next year.

The Brazilian government held 51 percent of the
voting shares while private investors held the rest. Embraer
was based in the provincial town of São José dos
Campos in São Paulo State. Operations started in 1970
and the company broke even the next year.

Embraer's first design, the EMB-110 Bandeirante
("Pioneer"), was the first aircraft produced in Brazil.
Powered by two turboprop engines, the plane could
carry up to 21 passengers and was quite popular with
U.S. commuter airlines. Embraer also developed military
versions of this versatile plane. Another early design was
the Xingu, which carried six to nine passengers. Embraer's
Neiva subsidiary built the Ipanema crop duster
and various Piper light planes under license.

COMPANY PERSPECTIVES

Human flight is a wondrous thing. Flight makes the world smaller, bends time in our favor, and keeps danger a little farther from our doorsteps. We are Embraer, a global company creating innovative aircraft and technologies, because we believe that, while the destination is important, the journey is everything.

Embraer built a version of the Italian Aermacchi MB-326BG military jet trainer under license for the Brazilian air force. The company then teamed with Aermacchi and Aeritalia in developing the AMX subsonic fighter aircraft to replace Fiat G-91 and Lockheed F-104 fighters in the Italian air force. The program was valued at $600 million. Embraer also developed its own basic trainer, the EMB-312 Tucano. The Brazilian air force ordered 168 of them in the early 1980s.

A VARIETY OF PROJECTS

Embraer had been profitable from its second year in operation, but posted an annual loss in 1981. By 1982, Embraer had 6,000 workers and had produced 2,500 aircraft. The company was developing a maritime surveillance version of the Bandeirante in the early 1980s. Work had also begun on the EMB-120 Brasilia, a 30-seat turboprop with similar applications to its smaller predecessor. Embraer held more than 130 orders and options for the Brasilia before it entered production in 1985. However, airlines were slow to convert options into firm orders. Sales were between $170 million and $180 million in 1984. The company garnered 40 percent of its revenues abroad. Although Brazil was suffering an economic depression, trade barriers protected the company's home market.

The first prototype AMX crashed in May 1983, but the program continued. Embraer began filling a large order from Egypt for the Tucano trainer in 1985. Meanwhile, Short Brothers of Belfast, Northern Ireland, was bidding to produce the Tucano under license for the Royal Air Force. Production continued on military variants of the Bandeirante. Embraer also developed missiles, and was part of a consortium that in 1988 agreed to help Iraq develop satellite and missile technology.

Embraer remained dependent on imported avionics and communications equipment. When it tried to buy a Model 3090 computer from IBM in 1990, the sale was blocked after Brazil would not guarantee that the computer would not be used for military purposes or transferred to other countries.

PRIVATIZATION IN 1994

The recession that followed the Gulf War affected the whole aviation industry, and Embraer suffered with everyone else. By 1994, the company was bankrupt, on its way to losing $337 million for the year. The Brazilian government sought a world-class aerospace company to help rescue it during its privatization in May 1994. However, other makers of regional aircraft were blocked from participating.

Ultimately, a group led by Banco Bozano, Simonsen S.A. acquired 60 percent of the company's voting shares. Two large pension funds joined the Rio de Janeiro-based holding company: Caixa de Previdência dos Funcionários do Banco do Brasil S.A. (PREVI) and Fundaçao SISTEL de Seguridade Social (SISTEL). Seeking to create a leaner, more efficient manufacturer, after a six-month ban on layoffs, the new owners cut a third of the company's 5,500 jobs. Mauricio Botelho, an engineer and executive at Bozano Simonsen, became company president in September 1995.

By the mid-1990s, the Brasilia had reportedly become the most widely used turboprop in the United States. However, since the introduction of Bombardier Aerospace's Canadair Regional Jet (RJ) in 1993, the whole category was being displaced by regional jets: small airliners that were less noisy, more spacious, and faster, yet still economical to operate on short routes.

EMBRAER REGIONAL JETS

Embraer's entrant, the ERJ-145 (also called the EMB-145), took its first test flight in August 1995. The planes sold for $14.5 million each, somewhat less than its only direct competitor the Canadair but twice as much as the Brasilia. Embraer's own regional jet had originally been conceived in 1989, but was slower to market due to organizational sluggishness. (Fairchild Aerospace, formed when U.S.-based Fairchild Aircraft took over the German Dornier Luftfahrt in 1996, also made airliners with fewer than 100 seats.)

Continental Express ordered 25 of the 50-seat ERJ-145s for $375 million in the fall of 1996, and reserved options for 175 more. Within a year, American Eagle had ordered 42. (A number of smaller foreign operators had been the first to sign up for the jet.) Plans for a shorter, 35-seat derivative called the ERJ-135 were soon in the works. Embraer also began designing a larger series of aircraft, the ERJ-170/190, for the 70- to 110-seat market.

KEY DATES

1969: Embraer is founded by Brazil's military dictatorship.
1981: Embraer posts only the second annual loss in its history.
1985: High-performance EMB-120 Brasília turboprop is certified.
1994: Nearly bankrupt, Embraer is privatized.
1996: Embraer certifies the first of its highly successful regional jets, the ERJ-145.
1999: French aerospace consortium buys 20 percent of company's voting shares.
2000: Embraer attains listing on the New York Stock Exchange.
2002: Legacy executive jet enters service; Embraer opens first foreign plant, in China.
2005: U.S. manufacturing facility opens near Jacksonville, Florida.
2011: Embraer pursues UAV and supersonic fighter markets through joint ventures.

The regional jet would help save the company, but it would take time. Embraer, which still carried $600 million in debt, posted a loss of $40 million (BRL 42 million) in 1996 and a loss of $30 million (BRL 33 million) in 1997.

Competition between Embraer and Bombardier, and between Brazil and Canada, was intense. Bombardier ran want ads for engineers in Brazil, luring them to Canada with superior pay and quality-of-life benefits. Embraer alleged that in 1997 Bombardier dropped the company from a $100 million NATO contract to supply Tucano trainers due to the success of Embraer's EMB-145.

Embraer and Bombardier each accused the other of thriving because of government subsidies. Bombardier criticized the special financing the Brazilian government offered through its Proex export promotion program. However, Brazil countered that as a developing country it was not required to follow World Trade Organization (WTO) rules until 2002. The country did agree to modify its Proex program to comply with a WTO ruling in 1999. The WTO ruled that Proex still kept financing rates below international levels, and ordered Brazil to stop this subsidy. Embraer had become Brazil's second-largest exporter, with foreign sales of $1.2 billion in 1998. It was the fourth-largest aircraft manufacturer in the world.

The Brazilian real lost 40 percent of its value in the first few weeks of 1999. Although most of Embraer's revenues came in hard currency, rising interest rates accompanied the real's devaluation, making money to finance sales and develop new designs harder to find. Ultimately Embraer benefited from lowered manufacturing costs.

Embraer pressed on with plans to develop larger versions of the EMB-145, dubbed the EMB-170 and EMB-190. The project was expected to cost $750 million. Embraer expected to contribute $250 million itself, and to raise another third each from a strategic partner and the international financial markets.

In June 1999, Embraer announced a record $4.9 billion order from Crossair, a Swiss regional airline. Crossair placed firm orders for 15 ERJ-145s, 30 ERJ-170s, and 30 ERJ-190s. The latter two had delivery dates of 2002 and 2004. Crossair also placed options on another 125 aircraft.

NEW CAPITAL FOR THE NEW MILLENNIUM

A consortium of four French aerospace companies (Aerospatiale-Matra, Dassault Aviation, Snecma, and ThomsonCSF) acquired 20 percent of Embraer's voting shares in 1999. The Brazilian government retained 20 percent under a "golden share" provision. Brazilian air force officials were wary of letting foreign aerospace companies own part of Embraer. However, Embraer seemed likely to benefit from applying French technology in its military jets. At the time, the company was only devoting 10 percent of its production to jet fighters. In the same year, Embraer created a landing gear and hydraulics joint venture with a German company, Liebherr International.

Embraer realized record earnings of BRL 412 million ($240 million) in 1999 due to strong sales in Europe as well as the United States. The company sold 100 jets during the year, and sales were expected to rise by 50 percent in 2000. Revenues and profits doubled for the first half of 2000. Embraer was listed on the New York Stock Exchange in July 2000. The company had a $20 billion backlog and was developing its Legacy business jet.

As the market for regional jet airliners became saturated, Embraer prepared a line of smaller aircraft to compete for executive jet buyers. The Legacy 600, based on the ERJ-135, was priced relatively low at just under $20 million and entered service in 2002. Larger derivatives followed.

Economic difficulties early in the decade stalled sales of the company's upgraded Super Tucano in South

America. Its partnership with Dassault allowed it to prepare to offer its first supersonic aircraft, a version of the Mirage 2000, for consideration as Brazil's next fighter.

Orders fell after the September 11, 2001, terrorist attacks on the United States that dampened the aviation industry worldwide. However, Embraer's large customer base in South America was less affected than others. Net earnings increased 70 percent in 2001 to $468 million. The company then employed nearly 11,000 people and had established its own aeronautical engineering and M.B.A. programs.

NEW FACILITIES AT HOME AND ABROAD

The company was in the midst of a building spree. In 2000 it had broken ground on a $25 million, 48,500-square-foot plant to assemble its new ERJ-170 and ERJ-190 jets. Partners such as Kawasaki Heavy Industries, its wing supplier, were constructing their own facilities in Brazil to support the projects.

In December 2002, Embraer announced an agreement to build its first foreign plant, in China, as 51 percent partner in a joint venture with a state-owned company. Its first ERJ-145 here was completed within 12 months. In October 2007 Embraer celebrated delivery of its 1,000th ERJ-145, which had been produced at its China joint venture.

Embraer had established several international subsidiaries dedicated to sales and service. By 2008, there were 38 in all, including two dozen in the United States. In 2005 Embraer opened a 71,000-square-foot manufacturing facility near Jacksonville, Florida, where a cluster of aerospace companies was forming around the old Cecil Field Naval Air Station. Embraer was joining Lockheed Martin to field a bid for the U.S. Army's Aerial Common Sensor program based on the ERJ-145. In 2008 Embraer began building plants in Melbourne, Florida, and Evora, Portugal.

SMALLER AND LARGER JETS AND UAVS

In 2005 Embraer began developing its Phenom 100 and 300, its first entrants in the emerging very light jet and light jet categories of executive aircraft. The next year the company launched an ultra-large business jet called the Lineage 1000, which was based on the EMB-190 regional jet airliner. The company in 2009 began development of a new transport for the Brazilian Air Force called the KC-390. It was expected to begin flight testing in five years.

The next frontier for Embraer was UAVs, spurred by interest from the Brazilian military. In April 2011 the company entered a joint venture with the Aeroelectronica (AEL) unit of Israeli company Elbit Systems, known for its Hermes 450 UAV. It had recently acquired a majority holding in UAV manufacturer Orbi-Sat da Amazônia S.A. and was backing the local start-up Santos LAB.

REORGANIZATION IN 2006

A holding company, Embraer–Empresa Brasileira de Aeronáutica S.A., took over the old Embraer in a 2006 corporate reorganization. In 2010 it was renamed Embraer S.A. In 2010 pretax profit rose 25 percent to $408.1 million on revenues down slightly to $5.36 billion. Net profits fell from $478.9 million to $345.4 million.

The business continued to evolve and expand. It acquired a 50 percent stake in Atech Negócios em Tecnologias S.A. for BRL 36 million in April 2011, an investment in the booming C4I (command, control, communications, computer, and intelligence) sector. It was also making plans to set up a Legacy 600/650 production line in China with its joint venture Harbin Embraer Aircraft Industry Company Ltd. (HEAI).

INCREASING GLOBAL INFLUENCE

Millions of airline passengers flew on Embraer's regional jets every year. Brazil's hosting of the Soccer World Cup in 2014 and the Summer Olympic Games two years after that was sure to bring more visibility to a company whose reach far exceeded its name recognition.

The company rose to the top of its industry in an era that saw the launch of very few successful aircraft manufacturers. By transferring expertise learned in its original military mission to civil aviation and back again, it secured a place as a cost-effective alternative in many market segments. Government aid played a role in the company's development, as did Embraer's flexibility in adapting and developing new products. The contractor formed to give Brazil a toehold in the aviation industry had become a giant publicly traded, globally sourced corporation, positioned in some of the fastest-growing segments of the aerospace market.

Frederick C. Ingram

PRINCIPAL SUBSIDIARIES

Embraer Aircraft Holding, Inc. – EAH (USA); Embraer Aircraft Customer Services, Inc. – EACS (USA); Embraer Aircraft Maintenance Services, Inc. – EAMS (USA); Embraer Services, Inc. – ESI (USA); Embraer Executive Jet Service, LLC – EEJS (USA); Embraer Executive Aircraft, LLC – EEA (USA); Embraer Training Services – ETS (USA); Embraer CAE Training Services – ECTS (USA); Embraer Credit Ltd. – ECL (USA); Embraer Representations, LLC – ERL (USA); Indústria Aeronáutica Neiva Ltda.; ELEB Equipamentos Ltda.; Embraer GPX Ltda.; ECC do Brasil Cia de Seguros; Embraer Merco S/A – EMS (Uruguay); Embraer Aviation Europe SAS – EAE (France); Embraer Aviation International SAS – EAI (France); Embraer Europe SARL – EES (France); Embraer Australia Pty Ltd. – EAL; Harbin Embraer Aircraft Industry Company, Ltd. – HEAI (China; 51%); Embraer (China) Aircraft Technical Services Co., Ltd; Embraer Spain Holding Co., SL – ESH; ECC Investment Switzerland AG; ECC Insurance & Financial Company Ltd. (Cayman Islands); Embraer Finance Ltd. – EFL (Cayman Islands); Embraer Overseas Limited (Cayman Islands); Listral Estruturas Aeronáuticas S.A. (Portugal); Embraer Portugal – SGPS, S.A.; Embraer Portugal Estruturas Metálicas S.A.; Embraer Portugal Estruturas em Compósito S.A.; Air Holding SGPS, S.A. (Portugal); OGMA – Ind. Aeronáutica de Portugal S.A.; ECC Leasing Company Ltd. (Ireland); Embraer Asia Pacific Pte-Limited – EAP (Singapore); Embraer CAE Training Services (UK) Ltd.

PRINCIPAL COMPETITORS

Bombardier Inc.; Cessna Aircraft Company; Finmeccanica S.p.A.; Gulfstream Aerospace Corporation; Hawker Beechcraft Corporation.

FURTHER READING
"Building a Legacy." *Flight International*, April 25, 2006.

Cassiolato, José, Roberto Bernardes, and Helena Lastres. *Transfer of Technology for Successful Integration into the Global Economy: A Case Study of Embraer in Brazil.* New York: United Nations, 2002.

Godeiro, Nazareno, Cristiano Monteiro da Silva, and Edmir Marcolino da Silva. *A Embraer é nossa! desnacionalização e reestatização da Empresa Brasileira de Aeronáutica.* São Paulo: Editora Instituto Jose Luís e Rosa Sundermann, 2009.

Lima, Edvaldo Pereira. "Flying High: Embraer's Mauricio Botelho Has Taken a Flagging, State-Owned Company and Turned It into the Fourth-Largest Aircraft Maker in the World." *Chief Executive* (U.S.), January–February 2003, 48+.

Norris, Guy. "Brazil's Big Shot." *Flight International*, July 20, 2004, 50+.

Rodengen, Jeffrey L., Elizabeth Fernandez, and Sandy Cruz. *The History of Embraer.* Fort Lauderdale, FL: Write Stuff Enterprises, Inc., 2009.

Trimble, Stephen. "Breaking Through." *Flight International*, March 23, 2004, 41+.

Warwick, Graham. "Targeted Growth." *Aviation Week & Space Technology,* March 28, 2011, 46+.

Envoy Medical
Corporation

5000 Township Parkway
St. Paul, Minnesota 55110-5852
U.S.A.
Telephone: (651) 361-8000
Web site: http://www.envoymedical.com

Private Company
Incorporated: 1995 as St. Croix Medical, Inc.
Sales: $50 million (2011 est.)
NAICS: 339112 Surgical and Medical Instrument
    Manufacturing

■ ■ ■

Envoy Medical Corporation is a St. Paul, Minnesota-based medical device company. Privately owned, Envoy has one product on the market, the Esteem middle-ear implant that overcomes moderate to severe sensorineural hearing loss in the range of 55 to 85 decibels. An implanted sensor sound processor, and long-life battery, invisible to the eye, converts vibrations picked up from the eardrum, malleus, and incus bones into electrical signals. After being filtered and magnified, they are sent to a driver attached to the stapes bone of the middle ear. Mechanical vibrations are then created and sent to the stapes and cochlea, allowing users to hear sounds that are far clearer and more distinct than what traditional hearing aids produce. Moreover, traditional hearing aids are removed for sleep, must avoid moisture, and often cause ear infections. Esteem recipients use a remote control to turn off the system, adjust the volume, and select among three different program settings. In addi-

tion to its U.S. headquarters, Envoy maintains sales offices in Germany, France, Italy, Brazil, and the United Arab Emirates.

FORMATION STEMMING FROM EXPERIENCE AND NEED: 1995

Envoy traces its history to the work of Wisconsin entrepreneur and audiologist Donald Schaefer, who in 1988 patented a hearing aid device called the Incus Plus. Schaefer died in 1990. The patent was acquired by Minneapolis, Minnesota-based St. Croix Medical Inc., founded in November 1995 by Ted P. Adams, the company's chief executive officer and chairman, and partner Bruce A. Brillhart. Adams was especially qualified to develop the device into a commercial project. He suffered from hearing loss and wore binaural hearing aids, making him particularly sympathetic to the hearing-impaired. He was also very familiar with implantable products. He had 25 years of experience in the field and held some 40 patents covering pacemakers. The procedure for implanting the hearing device, now recast as the Deafiance Soundbridge, was virtually the same as with pacemakers. "In a lot of ways," Adams told *Advance* in October 1996, "the design technology is very similar to a pacemaker; it's like it in almost every respect." The device relied on a pair of implanted piezoelectric transducers, the same technology used in pacemakers. They would remain untouched even after the battery and electronics were replaced every few years, a gain similar to pacemakers.

Brillhart played a key role in raising start-up funds, but much of the money was the result of good fortune

COMPANY PERSPECTIVES

Envoy Medical provides superior value to the field of otology through innovative technology, quality products, continuous improvement, and customer service.

and word of mouth. Roger Lucas, a biotechnology entrepreneur, learned about St. Croix from a broker who had just shown office space to Adams and Brillhart. Lucas, whose father and grandfather suffered from hearing problems and was concerned that both he and his children might one day suffer the same fate, contacted Adams and Brillhart. "They had this device, and they drew it out on the back of the proverbial napkin," Lucas told *Twin Cities Business* in an August 2010 article. "I immediately wrote them a check for $150,000." Over the years, he would continue to write checks to a company that he admitted he "kept falling more and more in love with."

ANIMAL TRIALS BEGIN: 1997

St. Croix Medical became operational in March 1996 and began turning Schaefer's concept into a marketable product. Animal trials were begun at the University of Minnesota's Auditory and Physiology Laboratory in the fall of 1997. At this stage, the company was only trying to demonstrate the electrical and mechanical performance of the implants, determine the proper placement of the transducers, test the biocompatibility of the materials, and evaluate the overall system performance. Only human trials would allow researchers to fully understand the true efficacy of the system, however. St. Croix Medical also laid the foundation for eventually marketing a device in Europe, where the market potential was estimated at 10 million people. In late 1997, the company forged a partnership called Hannover Medical GmbH with the German state of Niedersache to manufacture and distribute the hearing restoration system when it became available.

St. Croix had hoped to perform the first complete implant of a system in three years, begin sales in Europe, and be close to completing the regulatory review and approval process in the United States by the end of the 1990s. Although development of the product took more time than expected, the company continued to find willing investors. Entrepreneurial brothers Patrick, Michael, and Daniel Spearman bought a stake in the company. Their brother-in-law, basketball player

Kevin McHale, invested $200,000 in the company in 2000.

FIRST USER: 2000

Testing of the device, recast as the Envoy System, was begun in Germany in 2000. The first recipient of the device was a 59-year-old woman who enjoyed excellent results. In January 2001, the system was approved for study by the U.S. Food and Drug Administration (FDA), and the following year clinical trials were begun at Allegheny General Hospital in Pittsburgh, Pennsylvania, and the Virginia Mason Listen for Life Center in Seattle, Washington. The first person in the United States to receive the Envoy System was 66-year-old Conrad Hart of Pittsburgh. He was one of four initial recipients, two of whom had to undergo second surgeries because the driver was not properly connected to the stapes bone. Hart and another patient, however, reported excellent results.

Some investors grew frustrated with the slow pace of bringing the device to market. In September 2002, a new president and chief executive was found in Hanz Neisz, a trained mechanical and electrical engineer and former executive with Medtronic, Inc. and American Medical Systems, Inc. In 2003, he made plans to engineer a reverse 10-to-1 stock split to improve the share price. Unhappy with that approach, Patrick Spearman asked the board of directors to allow him to seek new investors instead. They agreed, and through Kevin McHale, Spearman secured an investment from the owner of the National Basketball Association's Minnesota Timberwolves, Glen Taylor. Lucas and the Spearmans increased their investments as well. Patrick Spearman would become co-CEO with Neisz, eventually assuming the post by himself.

The initial clinical trials led to improvements in the design of the device. The all-important Phase II clinical trials began in the United States and Germany in 2004 to determine the safety and effectiveness of the system. A larger number of patients were enrolled in the study and additional medical facilities participated.

NAME CHANGE: 2005

The company also underwent a name change at the start of 2005, embracing its signature product to become Envoy Medical Corporation. The name of the product, however, would undergo a change. "Envoy" gave way to "Esteem." Because hearing aids carried a stigma, an invisible, implantable product developed self-confidence, hence the move to the Esteem brand name.

In May 2006, Envoy Medical received CE Mark approval, allowing the company to market the Esteem

KEY DATES

1995: St. Croix Medical, Inc. is founded.
2000: First device is successfully implanted in Germany.
2004: Phase II trials begin in Germany and the United States.
2005: Company is renamed Envoy Medical Corporation.
2009: Unanimous FDA approval is received.

system in the European Union. The company's German subsidiary began manufacturing and marketing the device. Later in the year, the Esteem system was recognized by *Popular Science*. It was listed among the "100 Best Innovations of the Year." In the United States, meanwhile, the final phase of testing was conducted to gain FDA approval. The company also moved its headquarters from Minneapolis to St. Paul, Minnesota.

Securing FDA approval was a lengthy process for Envoy, but the company did not stand still. It continued to attract investors. In 2007, the company raised another $12 million to fund the marketing of the Esteem in Europe and ongoing clinical trials in the United States. Since its founding, the company had now raised $80 million. Envoy also received a major vote of confidence in 2007 when Kenneth H. Dahlberg, founder of Miracle Ear, Inc., a pioneer in the hearing aid industry, became an investor and director of the company.

FDA GIVES ITS APPROVAL: 2010

Envoy submitted its premarket approval application to the FDA in August 2009. A scientific panel unanimously recommended in December of that year that the Esteem be granted approval. In March 2010, Envoy received its formal premarket approval letter allowing the company to begin the commercial distribution of the device in the United States. A nationwide marketing campaign was launched in May featuring television ads in 19 cities, mostly airing on news stations. The company also secured a coveted advertising deal with radio talk show host Rush Limbaugh at a cost of $250,000 a month. Limbaugh was particular about the products he promoted, but he was also sympathetic to people suffering from hearing loss, a condition he experienced. He had resorted to cochlear implants to restore much of his hearing.

Interest in the Esteem spiked, as demonstrated by the surge in hits to the company's Web site. Envoy's profile with investors also increased. In October 2010, the company netted $16.4 million, including $10 million from Starkey, the world's largest manufacturer of hearing aids. Another round of fundraising in the spring of 2011 fetched a further $6.5 million. Plans would also be laid to take the company public in the near future.

Envoy faced a number of challenges in making a commercial success of the Esteem. The surgical procedure was delicate and required surgeons to be willing to undergo the necessary training. Initially, the device was able to be sold in only five medical centers in the United States, however, the number quickly grew. Also of concern was the high price of the device. Unlike traditional hearing aids that cost about $2,000, the Esteem cost $20,000, plus $10,000 for the surgery. Although the company provided patients with an option to make a $15,000 down payment and monthly payments of $450 for five years, it was a hefty price tag.

Despite the high cost, and the lack of health insurance reimbursement, the Esteem possessed one significant attribute: It worked extremely well. The device received an unexpected marketing boost from one of its satisfied patients in the fall of 2011. A 29-year-old wife and mother of two from Burleson, Texas, Sarah Churman, was recorded by her husband when her Esteem system was first turned on in a medical clinic. Because of a genetic deformity in her inner ear, she had experienced difficulty hearing since birth, and the hearing aids that she had first worn at the age of two offered little more than access to vibrations and loud noises. Her emotional response to hearing the world clearly for the first time in her life was a mix of surprise, joy, and tears. The video was posted on YouTube by the couple, and it quickly went viral. Churman became a guest on national television shows and Envoy received a level of promotion it could never afford through regular advertising.

Envoy's future appeared promising. A public offering of stock seemed inevitable. As with most electronic devices, the price would likely decrease in time, spurring greater sales, and allowing the device to become more mainstream. There was an estimated 15.2 million people with moderate to moderately severe hearing loss in the United States, but only about 30 percent of those people owned a hearing aid, and many of them did not use the device they owned. The unwieldy and unattractive nature of traditional hearing aids was a major deterrent. If Envoy was able to tap into even a fraction of this market, it would develop a thriving business for years to come.

Ed Dinger

PRINCIPAL SUBSIDIARIES

Envoy Medical GmbH (Germany); Envoy Medical Eurl (France); Envoy Medical Srl (Italy).

PRINCIPAL COMPETITORS

GN Hearing Care Corporation; Otologics, Inc.; Starkey Laboratories, Inc.

FURTHER READING

Grauer, Yael. "Envoy Medical Corp. Begins Raising $6.5M." *MedCity News*, April 5, 2011.

Grayson, Katharine. "Implantable Hearing-Aid Firm Secures $12M." *St. Paul Business Journal*, March 4, 2007.

Howard, Fran. "Deep Sound." *Twin Cities Business*, August 2010.

"Implantable Device Provides 'Bridge' to Sound." *Advance*, October 21, 1996.

Lee, Thomas. "Envoy Medical Investors Envision Big Returns with Esteem Hearing Device." *MedCity News*, January 1, 2010.

———. "Rush Limbaugh Powers Envoy Medical to New Fame, Investors." *MedCity News*, October 7, 2010.

Parmar, Arundhati. "St. Paul Device Company Envoy Medical Plans IPO." *Finance and Commerce*, May 7, 2010.

Ross, Oakland. "With a Device Called Esteem, Sarah Churman Greets the World of Sound." *Toronto Star*, October 5, 2011.

Snowbeck, Christopher. "FDA OKs Implantable Hearing System." *St. Paul Pioneer Press*, March 18, 2010, C1.

Yoffee, Lynn. "Envoy Medical Poised to Alter Hearing Loss Device Market." *Medical Device Daily*, April 21, 2009.

Experian Information Solutions, Inc.

━━━━━━■━━━━━━

475 Anton Boulevard
Costa Mesa, California 92626
U.S.A.
Telephone: (714) 830-7000
Fax: (714) 830-2449
Web site: http://www.experian.com

Subsidiary of Experian plc
Incorporated: 1996 as Experian Corporation
Employees: 5,553
Sales: $2 billion (2010 est.)
NAICS: 561450 Credit Bureaus

■ ■ ■

Experian Information Solutions, Inc., is the U.S.-based arm of Experian plc, a major global credit reporting agency. One of the Big Three consumer credit bureaus, the company uses a database of more than 215 million consumer and 15 million business files in the United States to provide credit reports to consumers as well as financial services firms, retailers, small businesses, and others. Further services include sales prospecting, direct marketing, skip tracing and collections, and demographic information. The company is best known to the general public for its heavily advertised FreeCredit Report.com. In addition to its Costa Mesa, California, headquarters, Experian maintains offices in eight other cities spread across the United States.

GROWTH OUT OF AUTOMOTIVE ELECTRONICS: SIXTIES

The company that became Experian Information Solutions began as a unit of TRW. TRW was founded in 1901 as Cleveland Cap Screw Co. It began by making cap screws, bolts, and studs, but soon its main product was welded valves for cars made by automotive pioneer Alexander Winton. The company went through several owners and name changes early in the 20th century until in 1926 it took the name Thompson Products Inc. At that time it made a variety of parts for both the automotive and aviation industries. In 1958, Thompson Products merged with Ramo-Wooldridge Corp. and took the name Thompson-Ramo-Wooldridge. Ramo-Wooldridge was a leading company in the defense electronics industry. The merged company became a giant in defense and in automotive parts. It invented many key automotive components such as the permanently lubricated steering linkage and the seat-belt pretensioning device. By the mid-1960s, the company shortened its name to TRW and began a global expansion, acquiring plants in Germany, Brazil, and the United Kingdom.

While TRW was developing rack-and-pinion power steering and seat-belt technology, it also launched a consumer credit information bureau. The company began compiling a consumer database in the mid-1960s. Starting in the mid-1970s, TRW also operated a small-business database. TRW's information division grew by both internal expansion and acquisition. By the mid-1980s, TRW Information Services, as the consumer credit unit was called, had credit histories on file of approximately 90 million Americans. At that time, TRW Information Services was the largest U.S. credit reporting agency.

MAKING A NAME IN THE EIGHTIES

Information services was apparently a profitable business, yet it had little to do with the main products of the rest of TRW. "TRW brass had never been comfortable with the information business," claimed *Direct* in a March 1, 1999, interview with Experian CEO D. Van Skilling. Although TRW hung on to the unit for a long time, there were indications by the 1980s that the information services division was not as well run as it might have been. In 1984, someone stole an account password from the consumer credit division and posted it on an electronic bulletin board. The company moved quickly to change the password and halt any leaks of private credit information, but the event did little for TRW's reputation. TRW also seemed uncertain how to present itself to consumers.

Consumers did not come up against their credit reports in most cases unless there was a problem. In 1986, TRW launched a new consumer-oriented business, TRW Credentials Service, which let subscribers access their credit histories once a year for a $30 fee. Years later, TRW was forced to allow consumers a free annual look at their credit reports. In 1989, the company finished a study of consumer attitudes toward credit reporting. It found a wealth of problems and complaints. Even if consumers had bad experiences with another credit reporting bureau, TRW seemed to take the heat, as it was so large and well known.

That year, Skilling took over as chief executive of TRW's Information Systems and Services division. Skilling's career path was somewhat indicative of TRW's discomfiture with the division. He had a bachelor's degree in chemistry, and worked in naval intelligence during the Korean War. Skilling then worked in various areas, including marketing, of TRW's oil field equipment group, and also in the industrial products group.

Nothing in his background directly prepared him for working in information services, yet he became the head man of the division.

Skilling quickly realized that the company's computer systems were outdated and insufficient. (Perhaps he had help with this. Skilling claimed that he had given Bill Gates the only job he ever held before he went on to found Microsoft.) In addition, the information from the consumer study also showed that much could be improved. The company began investing in upgrades, spending some $30 million between 1989 and 1991. However, Skilling was apparently not able to make changes quickly or thoroughly enough to forestall a public relations disaster.

Two years into Skilling's term, in 1991, a story of egregious credit reporting errors at TRW received wide press. TRW used subcontractors to gather information for the millions of credit reports it had on file. Apparently because of the errors of one part-time worker hired by a subcontractor, thousands of people in New England found themselves with bad credit reports. In the town of Norwich, Vermont, the worker had gone into the town hall and asked for the names of people with liens against their property because of unpaid local taxes. What actually went into the worker's report, however, were the names of the people who had paid their taxes, all 1,400 of them. Some of these people found themselves denied credit, and the problem was revealed. TRW at first claimed the Norwich case was an isolated incident.

As more similar cases cropped up across New England, the company eventually was forced to delete all local tax data from consumer files for people in Vermont, Rhode Island, Maine, and New Hampshire. The *Wall Street Journal* (October 14, 1991) reported on the case of a small-town funeral home director who claimed to have been switched to five different numbers when he called TRW to complain about an erroneous credit report. It took the company a week to respond to him. Months before the New England story broke, more than a dozen states had filed suit against the company. The suits alleged that TRW used sloppy procedures to create credit files on consumers, that the company did not adequately respond to consumer complaints, and that in some instances, after errors were corrected at consumer insistence, the company reinserted the faulty data into the consumers' files. The suits also alleged that TRW illegally sold consumer data to direct marketers.

TRW settled all the cases quickly, signing a consent decree in December 1991 promising to give credit rating information to consumers promptly and clearly. Consumers could order one free copy of their credit report each year. Despite the obvious problems in the

```
┌─────────────────────────────────────────────┐
│                                               │
│              KEY DATES                        │
│                  ▪                            │
│  ─────────────────────────────────────────   │
│                                               │
│  1901:  TRW is founded as Cleveland Cap Screw Co. │
│  1926:  Company's name is changed to Thompson │
│         Products Inc.                         │
│  1984:  TRW Information Services, as the company │
│         was then known, is largest U.S. credit report- │
│         ing agency.                           │
│  1996:  TRW spins off information unit, Experian │
│         Corporation, acquired by Great Universal │
│         Stores.                               │
│  2001:  Experian focuses on four main businesses: risk │
│         management, collections, fraud prevention, │
│         and authentication and marketing.    │
│  2011:  Company introduces a suite of new products. │
│                                               │
└─────────────────────────────────────────────┘
```

information services division, TRW made it plain that it was hanging on to the unit. TRW's overall earnings were slowing, and it had to put several operations on the auction block. Even as it was trimming costs elsewhere, TRW invested more in Information Systems and Services. After spending $30 million between 1989 and 1991, the company budgeted another $26 million for upgrades in the division for 1992.

A SPIN-OFF AND A SALE: MID-NINETIES

There was no doubt that the Information Systems and Services division was valuable to TRW. It did not break out financial figures for the unit except to say that it contributed less than 10 percent of the company's revenues. Even so, the division had about a 35 percent share of the U.S. credit reporting market, and the industry seemed poised for growth. As data management became more sophisticated, the credit reporting industry looked forward to being able to sell precisely targeted lists of consumers to marketers and lenders.

TRW used its database expertise in the mid-1990s to help in its own political lobbying efforts. It created a database called Constituent Relations Information Systems in 1994 which in part kept track of over 8,000 government officials and their stance on issues that might affect TRW. Keeping records of a couple thousand legislators and their aides was small potatoes to a company that now had 180 million individual credit histories on file. It took in some 33 million new pieces of information every single day. Growth potential seemed strong, as long as the company could come up with more ways to organize and market its data.

Nevertheless, information services remained a strange fit with the rest of TRW. Skilling had overseen great changes in the division since taking over in 1989. He believed the division could do more as an independent company. Constrained by top management at TRW, he told them "Play me or trade me," according to the *Direct* article. Skilling and more than 60 other top executives at the unit went in with two leading buyout firms and raised cash to take the Information Systems and Services division private in 1996.

The buyout firms were Bain Capital and Thomas H. Lee Co. Both these firms had been involved in high-profile transactions in the early 1990s. Thomas H. Lee had earned $900 million for itself and its investors when it sold Snapple Beverages to Quaker Oats in 1994, and Bain Capital had managed to acquire the clinical diagnostics unit of chemical giant Du Pont in 1995, just months before the TRW deal. The investment group gave TRW $1.01 billion in cash for the credit reporting unit, along with stock adding up to a 16 percent share in the new company. At the time of the sale, the unit was bringing in about $540 million in annual revenue. TRW was pleased, claiming the cash would allow the company to make investments in its remaining automotive and aerospace businesses.

The newly independent company took the name Experian. It planned to increase its business in target marketing, that is, the tailoring of its databases to suit specific customer needs. It also wanted to expand into overseas markets. Experian made an offer to the British conglomerate Great Universal Stores to buy its credit reporting unit, CCN Group Ltd. Great Universal Stores was perhaps best known for its steadfast outerwear unit, Burberrys. CCN was the largest credit reporting company in the United Kingdom, and it was responsible for some 5 percent of Great Universal Stores' profits. CCN had apparently been interested in buying the information services unit from TRW for years, but talks had gone nowhere.

When Great Universal Stores received the offer from Experian, it responded by asking to buy Experian for $1.7 billion. Experian's spin-off from TRW had not been finalized until September 1996, and the offer from Great Universal Stores came in November. The price was right, as it gave the investment group some $500 million over what they had just paid to TRW. Thomas H. Lee and Bain Capital each tripled the $100 million they had put into the deal, and several millionaires were minted from the group of TRW executives involved in the spin-off.

MUCH MORE THAN A CREDIT REPORTING AGENCY

CCN changed its name to Experian, and the company operated from two headquarters, one in Nottingham, England, and the other in Orange, California. The newly merged company quickly made acquisitions of its own. It bought two direct-marketing firms, Metromail and Direct Marketing Technology. The company touted itself as much more than a credit reporting agency. It had vast files on both consumers and small businesses, and it found more ways to use these resources.

In 1998 Experian debuted a so-called publisher co-op database, called CircBase. This database combined lists of magazine subscribers with catalog ordering information. It covered over 70 million households, and gave magazine publishers more specific data about their customers. Older databases on this model had only been able to generate lists of consumers sorted by more general factors such as age, sex, income, and ZIP code. CircBase was able to identify consumers who had actually bought certain items, such as cookware or fishing gear. This gave subscribers a clearer idea of who might be interested in a cooking or fishing magazine, for example.

By 2000, Experian was strongly interested in building business on the Internet. Moving beyond direct-mail marketing, the company looked into targeted e-mail marketing, forming a joint venture with a volume e-mail company called FloNetwork Inc. FloNetwork used what was called permission-based marketing, where consumers were in a more interactive relationship with the marketer, asking for information. FloNetwork offered Experian its expertise in online communication, and Experian gave the marketer more access to European and U.K. markets. Experian also acquired an e-mail marketing firm, Exactis.com, in 2000, spending $13.5 million for it. Another key piece of online business Experian developed was fraud prevention. It had developed its own consumer identification technology when it began offering credit reports online, so that only the appropriate person could access the report. Experian then offered this technology to other businesses selling merchandise or services online.

In other new businesses, Experian began offering a risk-assessment tool called Cross View Solutions, which helped lenders assess potential customers who had little or no credit history. The company also began pursuing the collections market, selling its database services to companies searching for people who had fallen behind on bills or loan payments. Experian spent millions of dollars in the first decade of the 2000s improving its small business database. It collected information on some 10 million businesses, combing through thousands of phone directories and following up with telephone interviews. In mid-2000 its business database contained files on about 15 million businesses, and the company aimed to add another nine million.

NEW FOCUS: 2001

In 2001, Experian launched a plan to become a one-stop supplier of solutions in four main areas: risk management, collections, fraud prevention, and authentication and marketing. Moreover, it sought to focus more on its business-to-business services, using its National Business Database to become more involved in key growth markets, including financial services, equipment leasing, food services, collections, advertising media, and transportation. Experian also sought in the early 2000s to foster further growth through acquisitions. In 2002, it paid $130 million for Consumer-Info.com, which provided Internet credit reports and scores to consumers. Annual revenues by this stage increased to $1.5 billion.

Experian expanded its geographic footprint in 2003 by acquiring the credit operations and contracts of Credit Bureau of Provo, Utah; Wilkes-Barre, Pennsylvania-based United One Resources; Credit Bureau of El Paso, Texas; and Credit Bureau of Lawton, Oklahoma. In that same year, Experian acquired the identity theft protection company PromiseMark Inc., a Fairfax, Virginia-based provider of products that helped prevent identity theft, viruses, Web hackings, and similar online threats. The PromiseMark product line was then incorporated into the Experian Consumer Direct division.

The Internet opened up new avenues for Experian to use its database of information to serve the business-to-consumer market, allowing individuals to monitor their credit ratings. Experian ran into some trouble, however, through the marketing of "free credit reports" through FreeCreditReport.com and consumerinfo.com. Many users did not realize that by providing their credit card numbers, which the sites maintained were needed in order to provide accurate information, they would be charged a $79.95 annual membership fee if they did not cancel during a 30-day free trial period. Although Experian made changes to the Web sites in September 2003, the company would come under the scrutiny of the Federal Trade Commission (FTC). Two years later the company reached a settlement and agreed to provide refunds to certain customers who had purchased the credit-monitoring product online before changes were made to the Web site.

Experian Information Solutions, Inc.

FREECREDITREPORT: POP CULTURE PHENOMENON

Despite the problems with the FTC, FreeCreditReport.com soon became a rising star among Experian units. The stage was set for the popularity of the product by the development of a new credit risk score that was developed by Experian and its two chief rivals, Equifax and TransUnion. Together, they created VantageScore, LLC, to compile and provide the new VantageScore, which for the first time brought together the credit information housed by the Big Three and created a common scale.

FreeCreditReport made use of the new credit score numbers, but more importantly, it launched a highly successful television and radio advertising campaign in 2007. It featured a young man who sang about the misfortunes of his life that were caused by his failure to check his credit rating. The song, and the ones that followed, soon gained pop culture status. The follow-up campaign was launched the following year, and in 2010, the company conducted a nationwide search to hire a real band to make a new set of commercials. The previous band had been cast by an advertising agency.

Experian grew on a number of other fronts in the new century, completing a bevy of acquisitions. In 2005 a pair of Web sites were acquired: LowerMyBills.com and PriceGrabber.com. Also in 2005, Experian added Baker Hill, a provider of relationship-management, credit-origination, and risk-management solutions to small businesses. The following year, Experian acquired Clarity Blue, a marketing solutions company. That same year, Great Universal (now named GUS plc) demerged into two separate companies: Home Retail Group plc and Experian plc. In 2007 Experian purchased Hitwise, an Internet market intelligence firm. In 2010, Experian acquired RentBureau, a rent payment credit bureau.

In addition to acquisitions, Experian pursued organic growth, developing new services to meet fresh challenges. With credit tightening, the company introduced the Income Insight and Income View tools in 2009 to help lenders estimate a prospective borrower's ability to repay loans. The following year, Experian introduced three peril models to help insurers better understand a household potential for water damage, accidental damage, or malicious damage. New consumer-notification requirements imposed on lenders resulted in Experian introducing a suite of new products to meet that need in 2011. The Federal Reserve Board also created a new rule that allowed lenders to consider only applicants' individual, not household, incomes. Experian, as a result, developed Income Insight W2 to help lenders estimate income based on the individual's credit

report. The future would undoubtedly bring further changes to the world of credit, providing Experian with ample opportunity to grow its business even further.

A. Woodward
Updated, Ed Dinger

PRINCIPAL DIVISIONS

Credit Services; Decision Analytics; Interactive; Marketing Services.

PRINCIPAL COMPETITORS

The Dun & Bradstreet Corporation; Fimalac; Infogroup Inc.

FURTHER READING

"Case of the Missing Password." *Time*, July 2, 1984, 53.

"CCN Group Adopts Experian Name." *American Banker*, June 20, 1997, 12.

Daley, James. "TRW Goes to Washington." *Forbes ASAP*, June 6, 1994, 127–28.

Denari, Tom. "Sing a Song of Bad Credit." *Brandweek*, September 29, 2008, 45.

Freeman, Lisa. "Three National Credit Bureaus Team to Create New Credit Risk Score." *Credit Union Journal*, March 20, 2006, 3.

Hargrave, Sean. "Credit Where It's Due." *New Media Age*, October 28, 2004, 20.

Hirsch, James S. "Buyout Group Hits $500 Million Jackpot." *Wall Street Journal*, November 15, 1996, A5.

"Keeping an Eye on Your Credit Profile." *Business Week*, January 20, 1986, 82.

"Large British Retailer to Buy U.S. Credit-Data Company." *New York Times*, November 15, 1996, D2.

Lee, W. A. "Experian Eyes Payments, Mulls Deals." *American Banker*, May 30, 2003, 1.

Lucas, Peter. "Think Global, Act Local." *Collections and Credit Risk*, July 2001, 26.

Miller, Michael W. "Rash of Errors Blemishes TRW Credit Reports." *Wall Street Journal*, October 14, 1991, B1–B2.

"The Noise Was Great; the Result Was TRW." *Automotive News*, April 29, 1996, S104.

Schultz, Ray. "Skilling's Laws." *Direct*, March 1, 1999, 9.

"TRW Credit Reporting Unit to Be Sold for $1 Billion." *New York Times*, February 10, 1996, 38.

"TRW Promises to Change Its Ways." *Business Week*, December 23, 1991, 38.

"TRW's Credit-Data Unit nears Accord with States." *Wall Street Journal*, December 6, 1991, A7.

First Wind Holdings, Inc.

———— ■ ————

179 Lincoln Street, Suite 500
Boston, Massachusetts 02111-2425
U.S.A.
Telephone: (617) 960-2888
Fax: (617) 960-2889
Web site: http://www.firstwind.com

Private Company
Founded: 2002 as UPC Wind Partners
Incorporated: 2007
Employees: 220
Sales: $56.02 million (2009)
NAICS: 221122 Electric Power Distribution

■ ■ ■

First Wind Holdings, Inc., is an independent power producer specializing in the development and operation of utility-scale wind energy projects in the United States. The company owns and operates 11 wind farms in Maine, Vermont, New York, Utah, and Hawaii, with an aggregate generating capacity of 766 megawatts (MW) of electricity. Other assets include lead generation lines in Maine and Utah, which transfer electricity to the power grids in Maine and California. First Wind sells electricity to power distributors directly and through Renewable Energy Certificates. Wind farms in the Northeast are managed through Northeast Wind, LLC, a joint venture partnership with Algonquin Power and Utilities Corporation and Emera, Inc.

FORMATIVE EXPERIENCE

First Wind Holdings originated as UPC Wind Partners, a subsidiary of UPC Renewables, itself established in Italy by Brian Caffyn and Peter Gish in 1995. Prior to founding UPC Renewables, Caffyn oversaw wind farm operations for Cannon Power, with more than 700 wind turbines near San Diego. During the early 1990s, Caffyn managed the development, construction, operation, and maintenance of wind farms in California and abroad.

Caffyn left Cannon and cofounded UPC International Partnership CV II with Gish, an attorney who specialized in financial and corporate contracts. UPC International developed one of the largest wind farms in the world at that time, in Naples, Italy, with 170 MW of power capacity. With proven success, UPC International turned to the United States in 2000, researching potential opportunities for wind projects.

Caffyn led the effort to establish UPC Wind Partners that year, and then returned to UPC Renewables in 2004. That year, UPC hired Paul Gaynor to lead as chief executive officer at UPC Wind Partners. Caffyn remained chairman of the board for several years.

EARLY ROADBLOCKS

Early on, UPC Wind Partners encountered local resistance to wind farm development. For instance, critics of the Hardscrabble Mountain project, near Sheffield, Vermont, asked, "Will Vermont become the Pinwheel State?" Residents in Lyman, New Hampshire, petitioned the town council to prevent a test turbine

COMPANY PERSPECTIVES

First Wind is proud to play a leading role in helping build energy independence, create jobs, and revitalize the economy—all while protecting our environment for future generations and generating renewable energy for thousands of homes. As an experienced developer, owner, and operator of wind farms, First Wind is committed to the communities where our projects are located, and we are dedicated to helping towns and states gain economic benefits from this clean energy revolution.

from being installed on Mount Washington. UPC retreated from full participation in a wind farm project off of Cape Cod, due to the encumbrances of the local political process.

One exception was Maine, where UPC subsidiary Evergreen Wind Company attempted to develop a wind farm on Mars Hill Mountain. That opportunity came through leases with private landowners, which sidestepped concerns of local residents. Nevertheless, that project took several years to come to fruition.

Another problem weathered by First Wind involved shifting federal tax legislation, which hindered project financing. A federal tax credit law lapsed during most of 2004, from January through October. This delayed project development, as financing was dependent on a subsidy based on per kilowatt hours produced for the first 10 years in operation. Once tax credits were reauthorized in October 2004, wind farm development progressed.

UPC finally established its first wind project, at Kaheawa Pastures, on the southern mountains of Maui, at Maalaea, in 2006. UPC obtained $65 million in financing for construction of the wind farm in April 2005. As a joint venture of Makani Nui Associates and Kaheawa Wind Power, the 30 MW facility began producing power in June 2006. Native plants raised from seed were reintroduced to the project site in early 2007, to restore damage to native habitat incurred during construction.

2006–08: FOCUS OF GROWTH: NORTHEAST

By 2006 UPC had more than 270 MW of wind energy capacity under development. Gish was instrumental in obtaining substantial private-equity funding from two large investment firms. D.E. Shaw purchased a majority

ownership in May 2006. The other sponsor was Madison Dearborn Capital Partners. Investment funds allowed First Wind to implement its wind energy projects.

Construction on the Mars Hill Wind Farm began in early 2006 and commercial operations began in March 2007. With 28 turbines and generating capacity of 42 MW, the wind farm provided enough power for 20,000 homes. Operating income enabled UPC to finally obtain funding for the facility. The company secured $44 million from JPMorgan Capital Corporation and WFC Holdings Corporation, applied to reduce debt.

In September 2006, UPC broke ground on a wind farm in Lackawanna, New York, on land where Bethlehem Steel once operated a mill. A brownfield redevelopment off Lake Erie, the project consisted of eight turbines capable of producing 20 MW of electricity. The Buffalo Niagara region would benefit from enough clean energy to power 6,000 homes annually. Named Steel Winds, the $40 million project became fully operational by the summer of 2007. The project was a joint venture with BQ Energy of Pawling, New York, and Clipper Windpower of Carpinteria, California.

UPC sought wind farm development opportunities on the West Coast and in Hawaii. In March 2007, it initiated the approval process for a 40-turbine, 60 MW facility in Oregon. A joint venture with Makani Nui Associates yielded a letter of intent with the Kauai Island Utility Cooperative for the purpose of building a 15 MW wind farm to power 4,000 homes on the island of Kauai.

PREPARING FOR AN IPO

With several projects in operation or in development, UPC prepared for an initial public offering (IPO) of stock. In May 2007 UPC Wind Partners changed its company name to First Wind Holdings, Inc. The company planned the IPO for the spring of 2008.

In the meantime, First Wind made progress on the Sheffield Wind Project in Vermont. In August 2007, after 18 months of working with local communities and government agencies, First Wind obtained a Certificate of Public Good from the Vermont Public Service Board. Local concerns included minimizing the environmental impact of the project and local job creation. First Wind agreed to hire locally for the 75 positions in design, engineering, and construction. In addition, UPC agreed to establish a 2,700-acre bear habitat for conservation, to be located on forestland already under management.

In late December 2007, First Wind announced that it had signed a long-term power purchase agreement with the Los Angeles Department of Water and Power, to provide electricity from the proposed Milford Wind Corridor project in Utah. The 20-year agreement covered 185 MW, enough to serve 39,000 homes. Once the first phase was completed, the cities of Burbank and Pasadena would receive electricity from the wind farm, as well. Burbank would get 10 MW and Pasadena five MW.

2008–09: FINANCIAL HURDLES OVERCOME

First Wind's plan to hold an IPO in August 2008 was postponed. The company had intended to raise $450 million. In the company prospectus, First Wind stated that it expected annual compound growth to be approximately 26.4 percent through 2013. However, the company did not find support from the investment community, as revenues declined and operating losses increased. In addition, First Wind carried more than $560 million in debt.

Hedging activities that yielded significant gains in 2007, at $9.8 million in revenues for the year, began to bring losses in 2008. For the first quarter of 2008, revenues declined 14 percent. While 88 percent of the first-quarter 2008 revenues came from the sale of electricity, only 38 percent was sold at market price value. Net losses increased to $18.5 million. Only a fraction of the company's wind farms generated electricity. With 5,564 MW of installed wind power, only 92 MW were being generated as of June 30, 2008.

First Wind turned to other financing options. The company raised $165 million in cash and $146.3 million in tax equity financing. First Wind expected a $140 million investment from Lehman Brothers, for a wind farm in Cohocton, New York. However, when Lehman Brothers went into bankruptcy, loss of the investment brought wind energy development to a halt. The

American Recovery and Reinvestment Act of 2009 filled that gap with a convertible tax credit program, allowing projects to move forward.

A $74 million tax benefit allowed the company to complete development of the Cohocton project, located in northeast New York. Cohocton Wind consisted of 50 wind turbines for an aggregate capacity of 125 MW of electricity. The project carried power for 50,000 homes when it was completed in January 2009.

A $40 million tax credit supported development of the Stetson Wind project in Maine. Stetson Wind was completed in two phases. Stetson Wind I, which comprised 38 1.5 MW turbines, for 57 MW capacity, went online in January 2009. Stetson II, with 17 turbines and 26 MW generating capacity, was completed in March 2010.

In Utah, the Milford Wind project completed Phase I in November 2009. Located in Beaver County, the facility comprised 97 wind turbines with 204 MW of power capacity. After much delay, the Sheffield, Vermont, project progressed in 2010. When citizens appealed the project development due to concern over environmental impact, First Wind agreed to meet certain restrictions. The company obtained $76 million in financing for the project in December 2010. First Wind planned 16 turbines with 2.5 MW capacity each, for an aggregate of 40 MW of power, enough to cover 15,000 homes in northeast Vermont.

2011: DEVELOPMENT MOMENTUM BUILDS

First Wind gained momentum in 2011, as the company commissioned several energy projects. With the support of a $117 million loan from the U.S. Department of Energy, construction on Kahuku Wind began in July 2010. Located on the island of Oahu, Kahuku Wind comprised 12 turbines and carried 30 MW of power capacity, enough for 7,000 homes. The project included a large-scale battery storage system, capable of holding 15 megawatt hours of energy, for the purpose of providing consistent energy output to the island's power grid. A product of Xtreme Power, Inc., such a storage system was the first of its kind to be used in a wind energy project in the United States. Construction on Kahuku Wind was completed in March 2011.

The second phase of the Milford, Utah, wind farm progressed in 2011. This part of the project was located in Millard County, primarily. In addition to construction of 68 wind turbines, with 102 MW of capacity, the project involved installation of an 88-mile generator lead to connect the facility to the Intermountain Power Plant in Delta. First Wind contractors used helicopters in construction in order to protect the sensitive desert environment. When completed in May, the generator lead relayed energy to the Southern Transmission System, the power grid for the Los Angeles area.

First Wind formed a joint venture with Algonquin Power and Utilities Corporation (APU) and Emera, Inc., to handle operations at the company's wind farms in the Northeast, with a generating capacity of 370 MW. First Wind owned a 51 percent interest in the new company, Northeast Wind, and continued to hold responsibility as a managing partner. First Wind planned to transfer new projects to Northeast Wind for operation and maintenance, after meeting certain criteria.

APU, Emera, and First Wind planned to develop wind projects as well. APU would provide experience with renewable energy, Emera would bring financial support, and First Wind, development experience. In May 2011 First Wind Capital, LLC, obtained $200 million in bond financing, due in 2018. The funds were allocated to pay existing debt and finance the Hawaii, Washington, Maine, and Vermont wind projects.

First Wind completed power facilities in Maine and Vermont. Rollins Wind consisted of 40 1.5 MW turbines totaling 60 MW in generating capacity. Commissioned in July 2011, the project brought total wind generation capacity in Maine to 185 MW. The project contributed to $125 million in economic benefits to the state of Maine, including job creation and tax revenue, all related to First Wind projects. The Sheffield, Vermont, project came to fruition as well, with operations beginning in October.

2012–14: PROJECTS UNDER DEVELOPMENT

At the end of 2011, First Wind had several projects under development. Expansion at the Lackawanna, New York, wind farm began in 2011. The Steel Winds II project included six additional 3.5 MW Clipper Liberty wind turbines, enough to generate power for 6,000 homes. First Wind expected the project to be completed by early 2012.

In Hawaii plans for wind farm development on Molokai came to a halt due to procedural issues. First Wind continued with development of the Kawailoa, 69 MW project on a former sugarcane farm northeast of Haleiwa, on Oahu's North Shore. First Wind expected that facility to begin operations in 2012.

In the West, development of the Palouse Wind project, in Whitman County, Washington progressed. First Wind obtained a Conditional Use Permit in May 2011, a necessary step in the approval process that al-

lowed the company to begin construction in October. Avista Utilities agreed to purchase power from the facility upon completion, sometime in 2012. First Wind expected to build energy capacity to 70 MW at the site.

Projects in the early stages of development included several in Maine, with approximate generating capacity of 300 MW. First Wind expected the Oakfield wind farm in Aroostook County, Maine, to be completed in 2012. After an earlier Oregon project failed to meet local criteria for environmental protection, First Wind established the Baseline project, to be located on farmland in the Columbia Gorge, south of Arlington, Oregon. The site showed wind power potential up to 500 MW. First Wind set a goal to have installed at least 1,000 MW in total power capacity systemwide by the end of 2012 and 2,000 MW by the end of 2014.

Mary Tradii

PRINCIPAL SUBSIDIARIES

First Wind Capital LLC; First Wind Holdings, LLC; Northeast Wind, Inc. (51%).

PRINCIPAL COMPETITORS

Caithness Corporation; IBERDROLA Renewables, Inc.; Pathfinder Renewable Energy LLC; Pattern Energy Group LP.

FURTHER READING

Alspach, Kyle. "First Wind Aims to Put More Financing in Its Sails: After Passing on IPO, Wind Farm Developer Looks to Raise $300M." *Boston Business Journal*, December 24, 2010. Accessed November 18, 2011. http://www.bizjournals.com/boston/print-edition/2010/12/24/first-wind-aims-to-put-more-financing.html.

Brown, Rodney. "First Wind Issues $200M in Notes for New Wind Projects." *Boston Business Journal*, May 23, 2011. Accessed November 18, 2011. http://www.bizjournals.com/boston/news/2011/05/23/first-wind-issues-200m-in-notes.html.

"First Wind Forms Joint Venture for Northeast." *Maine Sunday Telegram*, May 1, 2011, C5.

"IPO Candidates Bringing Large Losses to the Table." *Boston Business Journal*, August 18, 2008. Accessed November 18, 2011. http://www.bizjournals.com/boston/stories/2008/08/18/story4.html.

"UPC Finds Green Energy Initiatives Face Headwind." *Boston Business Journal*, April 18, 2005. Accessed November 18, 2011. http://www.bizjournals.com/boston/stories/2005/04/18/story8.html.

"UPC Wind to Help Power Los Angeles." *Los Angeles Business Journal*, December 20, 2007. Accessed November 18, 2011. http://www.bizjournals.com/losangeles/stories/2007/12/17/daily28.html.

Gannett Company, Inc.

7950 Jones Branch Drive
McLean, Virginia 22107-0910
U.S.A.
Telephone: (703) 854-6000
Fax: (703) 854-2046
Web site: http://www.gannett.com

Public Company
Incorporated: 1923
Employees: 32,600
Sales: $5.4 billion (2010)
Stock Exchanges: New York
Ticker Symbol: GCI
NAICS: 511110 Newspaper Publishers; 513120 Television Broadcasting; 511120 Periodical Publishers

■ ■ ■

Gannett Company, Inc., calls itself a diversified news and information company because it provides information to consumers through the Internet, newspapers, magazines, and television stations. It publishes more than 80 daily newspapers, including the best-selling *USA Today* (the nation's second-largest newspaper behind the *Wall Street Journal*), about 600 magazines, nearly 1,000 domestic non-daily publications, and operates 23 television stations as well as Internet sites sponsored by its television stations and newspapers. Gannett's subsidiary Newsquest is the United Kingdom's second-largest regional newspaper company. Newsquest publishes more than 300 titles, of which 17 are daily newspapers.

ORIGINS: EARLY 20TH CENTURY

Gannett was the brainchild of Frank Gannett, who paid his way through Cornell University by running a news correspondence syndicate. When he graduated he had $1,000 in savings. Gannett got into the media business in 1906 when he and several associates bought the *Elmira Gazette* in Elmira, New York, with $3,000 in savings, $7,000 in loans, and $10,000 in notes. They bought another local paper and merged them to form the *Star-Gazette*, beginning a pattern of mergers to increase advertising power that the company would follow throughout its history. Six years later, in 1912, Gannett bought the *Ithaca Journal*, beginning his toehold in upstate New York. The company gradually built up a portfolio of 19 New York dailies by 1989.

In 1918 Gannett and his team moved to Rochester, New York, a city whose papers would turn out to be among the company's strongest. Many of Gannett's rising executives were groomed at the Rochester papers. The group purchased two newspapers upon their arrival and merged them into the *Times-Union*. The papers' holdings were consolidated under the name Empire State Group. In 1921 the *Observer-Dispatch* of Utica, New York, was acquired. In 1923 Gannett bought out his partners' interests in the Empire State Group and the six newspapers the group then owned, and formed Gannett Co., Inc. Gannett appointed Frank Tripp general manager. Tripp helped run the everyday business of the papers, and the two were close allies for years. The Northeast was Gannett's focus for the next 25 years, and the company expanded aggressively with acquisitions there. Another key executive, Paul Miller, joined the company in 1947, becoming Gannett's executive

COMPANY PERSPECTIVES

To be the trusted, leading media and marketing solutions company at the forefront of a new era in human engagement.

assistant. By then, the company operated 21 newspapers and radio stations.

The company's role as a leader in technology began in 1929, when Frank Gannett co-invented the teletypesetter. Gannett newsrooms were among the first to use shortwave radios to gather reports from distant sources. In 1938, before color was used much in newspapers, many Gannett presses were adapted for color. Much later, with its *USA Today*, the company would continue to be a leader in color use. Other advantages included a corporate plane that helped reporters get to the site of news quickly.

1957: GROWTH UNDER MILLER

Gannett News Service, as the company became known, was founded in 1942 as Gannett National Service. The wire service subsidiary provided the company's local papers with national stories from Washington, D.C., and 13 bureaus. The stories often featured a local angle or local sources. Gannett grew by buying existing newspaper and radio and TV stations. By the time of its founder's death in 1957, it had accumulated 30 newspapers. Miller, as the new president and chief executive officer, oversaw the company's expansion from a regional to a national chain in the next decade.

In 1966 Gannett founded its first newspaper, *Florida Today*. It was the work of Allen Neuharth, who later was to become the founder of *USA Today*. Neuharth brought the new paper to profitability in 33 months, an incredible feat in the newspaper business, according to analysts. Because the paper was near the National Aeronautics and Space Administration (NASA), it was dubbed "Florida's Space Age Newspaper." The paper was ultimately redesigned to emphasize state and local news and was promoted and sold with *USA Today*, which provided national and international coverage.

Gannett went public in 1967 on the New York Stock Exchange. In 1970 Miller assumed the title of chairman, and Neuharth was promoted to president and chief operating officer from executive vice president, making him the heir apparent to the top position in the

company. Neuharth went on an acquisition spree, leading the company to its current size and status in the media world. He became chief executive officer in 1973 and chairman in 1979.

THE SEVENTIES: GROWTH THROUGH ACQUISITIONS

Two notable mergers were those with Federated Publications in 1971 and with Speidel Newspaper Group in 1977. Two years later, Gannett merged with Combined Communications, the biggest such merger in the industry at that time, for $400 million. The Evening News Association joined the Gannett family later when Gannett bought it for $700 million. One near merger was with Ridder Publications. That company's president, Bernard H. Ridder, Jr., was a golfing partner of Miller. Ridder had concluded that the only way his small, family-held company's stock would ever reach its full potential was for Ridder Publications to merge with a big media company. The two talked, but Ridder proved to be more interested in Knight Newspapers because it had less geographic overlap with Ridder than did Gannett.

In 1989, however, Gannett and Knight-Ridder implemented a joint operating agency to combat the decline in newspaper advertising revenues in Detroit, Michigan. The cooperative venture was the largest ever merging of two competing newspapers' business operations. The arrangement called for the Knight-Ridder's *Free Press* and Gannett's *Detroit News* to divide revenues equally. Since Gannett held more of Detroit's market share before the merger, it took a loss during the venture's first year, 1990.

THE EIGHTIES: NEUHARTH AND THE GANNETT FOUNDATION

In 1986 Neuharth retired as chief executive officer, passing the baton to John J. Curley. Curley had been president and chief operating officer since 1984. He joined Gannett in 1970. Curley took on the title of chairman in 1989. A newsman like most of Gannett's heads, Curley was editor and publisher of several Gannett papers and was founding editor of *USA Today*.

Neuharth continued as chairman of the Gannett Foundation, which was established in 1935 by Frank Gannett to promote free press, freedom of information and better journalism, adult literacy, community problem-solving, and volunteerism. Neuharth spent as freely at the foundation as he had at the company, giving $28 million to various programs in 1989 alone. Despite criticism from some Gannett newspaper execu-

KEY DATES

1923: Frank Gannett buys out his partners in the newspaper business and incorporates Gannett.
1942: Wire service subsidiary Gannett News Service is founded as Gannett National Service.
1967: Company goes public on the New York Stock Exchange.
1982: *USA Today* begins publication.
1999: Gannett acquires Newsquest plc.
2005: Craig Dubow takes over as president and chief executive officer.
2008: Tribune Company, Hearst Corporation, and New York Times Company form quadrantONE with Gannett.
2010: Gracia C. Martore replaces Dubow.

tives, Neuharth also oversaw the foundation's move from Rochester, New York, to Arlington, Virginia, where *USA Today*'s offices were located. Interior design of the charity's new headquarters ran to $15 million.

With expenses rising faster than assets, Neuharth sold the foundation's 10 percent share of Gannett Co. back to the company for $670 million. On July 4, 1991, the philanthropy's name was changed to the Freedom Forum, and its mission was changed to focus on First Amendment and other strictly journalistic issues. Gannett Co. created a $5 million fund to replace money withdrawn from the Gannett Foundation's more community-oriented charities. Other accomplishments of the company in the early 1990s included: increasing the company's use of recycled newsprint to 20 percent of total usage, over 180,000 tons; being named one of the United States' top 20 places for African Americans to work; and becoming the first news service to syndicate a weekly newspaper column dedicated exclusively to gay and lesbian issues.

Neuharth had said in 1982 when he started *USA Today* that it would begin making annual profits in three to five years. By 1990 the paper had had quarterly profits but never a full year of profitability. Between 1982 and 1990, *USA Today* sapped the company of an estimated $500 million. September 1992 marked 10 unprofitable years for *USA Today*. Nonetheless, with 6.6 million readers daily, the United States' most widely read newspaper also celebrated record advertising and circulation revenues. *USA Today* executives claimed that had the U.S. economy not been in recession, the paper would have been in the black by 1990. Fortunately, the

rest of Gannett's business was strong enough to offset *USA Today*'s annual losses. Curley, the paper's president and publisher, hoped that cost-containment measures, lower newsprint prices, and other savings in the production-distribution process would bring *USA Today* into profitability.

THE NINETIES: $5 BILLION IN REVENUES

The year 1991 was Gannett's most difficult since the company had gone public in 1967. The company slipped from second to third in rankings of the top U.S. media concerns as a result of Time Warner's leapfrog to first place. Annual revenues dropped 2 percent and net income was down 20 percent from the year before. Fifty-five of Gannett's 86 local dailies raised circulation prices, and circulation barely rose.

Nonetheless, the national daily newspaper was another demonstration of Gannett's leadership role in the use of technology, as well as journalism. The paper also was an innovator in graphics, especially in the use of color. Media observers credited *USA Today*'s use of color as the spur for industry-wide interest in color graphics. The copy for the paper was composed and edited at *USA Today*'s Arlington, Virginia, headquarters, then transmitted via satellite to 36 printing plants in the United States, Europe, and Asia.

Gannett's most significant activity during the 1990s took place in the divestiture and acquisition arena, an area that some observers believed the company needed to explore more fully. Critics opined that Gannett, renowned for its financially conservative approach, should loosen its purse strings and adopt a more aggressive acquisition strategy. Confronted with suggestions that the company should purchase a movie studio or a television network, Gannett management demurred, preferring to keep its focus set on its core businesses. Despite the company's steadfast adherence to its existing businesses, the 1990s saw Gannett explore new business opportunities and express more than a modicum of acquisitive might.

SERIES OF ACQUISITIONS AND DIVESTITURES

Gannett began the process of adding and paring away businesses in 1995. That year, the company shouldered past rival bidders such as Ellis Broadcasting and NBC in its $1.7 billion acquisition of Greensville, South Carolina-based Multimedia, Inc. The acquisition gave Gannett 11 daily newspapers, 50 other newspaper publications, five network-affiliated television stations, two radio stations, and production and syndication control for television shows hosted by Phil Donahue, Sally Jessy Raphael, Rush Limbaugh, and Jerry Springer. The acquisition of Multimedia also ushered Gannett into the cable business, giving the company 450,000 cable television subscribers.

As the company delved into the previously foreign territory of operating cable television systems and controlling television programming, it withdrew from two other businesses. In 1996 the company sold its outdoor advertising division to Outdoor Systems of Phoenix, divesting the business to free its resources for the development of its newspaper and broadcast properties and to facilitate the incorporation of the Multimedia properties into its fold. Louis Harris & Associates, Gannett's polling subsidiary, also was sold in 1996, a year that saw the company enter into a joint venture with Knight-Ridder and Landmark Communications to form an Internet service provider called InfiNet, created to help publish newspapers online.

Deal making continued to predominate at Gannett headquarters as the company entered the late 1990s. The company had exchanged six of its radio stations for a television station in Tampa, Florida, in 1996. In 1998, it exited the business entirely by selling its remaining five radio stations to Evergreen Media. As the company's radio properties disappeared, the number of its television stations increased with the acquisition of three stations in Maine and South Carolina.

Before the end of the decade, the company completed two more significant deals, which, in keeping with the trend established in the 1990s, included a divestiture and an acquisition. In 1999, the company sold the cable assets obtained in the Multimedia acquisition. According to company officials, the decision to divest the cable properties was not based on a strategic decision, but represented an opportunity to realize a significant profit. Gannett sold the cable business to Cox Communications for $2.7 billion. In a separate announcement, Gannett revealed that it was acquiring 95 percent of Newsquest plc, the largest regional newspaper publisher in England.

The cumulative effect of the acquisitions and divestitures completed during the latter half of the 1990s lifted Gannett's revenues above $5 billion by the end of the decade. Although the company shied away from headlong leaps into other areas of the media industry, unlike many of its competitors, Gannett's consistent record of financial growth suggested that there was no pressing need to develop into a comprehensive, broadly diversified media conglomerate.

THE EARLY 21ST CENTURY

As the 1990s rolled to a close Gannett became embroiled in a $10 million lawsuit with Chiquita Foods International. In May 1998 the *Cincinnati Enquirer*, a Gannett-owned newspaper, ran an 18-page exposé on the banana titan, contending numerous questionable business practices. After it was alleged that *Enquirer* reporter Mike Gallagher had illegally obtained Chiquita voice-mail messages, the *Enquirer* retracted the story on the front page of its Sunday edition, on June 28, 1998. Repercussions from the suit extended into the next century as the reporter and his managing editor filed suits of their own.

Gannett acquired Sacramento's KXTV Channel 10 in February 1999 and sold its Multimedia Cablevision Inc., a 515,000-subscriber operation it had picked up in 1995 through its acquisition of Multimedia. By October 1999, Gannett was back in purchasing mode, picking up eight papers in the New York area from the Tucker Communications group. Additionally, the company expanded its U.K. presence, purchasing 11 British dailies. The trend continued into 2000, when The Thomson Corporation agreed to sell Gannett 21 daily papers for $1.13 billion in June.

Longtime CEO John Curley stepped down from Gannett in June 2000, passing the mantle to his right-hand man, President and Vice Chairman Douglas H. McCorkindale. Curley remained chairman until early 2001, when he retired, leaving McCorkindale chairman, president, and chief executive officer. The orderly changeover caused nary a ripple in Gannett's stock. McCorkindale had been Curley's associate for so long that investors seemed assured that the firm would continue on familiar patterns. Certainly the company strategies remained the same. In that same month, Gannett bid on yet another British company, Newscom, publisher of four daily newspapers, for $702 million. It then cut a check for $2.6 billion for *Arizona Republic* and *Indianapolis Star* publisher Central Newspapers. The acquisitions mounted through the rest of the decade.

In 2003, it purchased several Hawaiian magazines and a related Web site, and Clipper Magazine, a direct-mail ad company. By 2004 Gannett controlled three Scottish papers and 11 related magazines, as well as 34 publications from Brown County Publishing Company, including the *Green Bay News-Chronicle*. Profits for the company remained on the upswing into the middle of 2004, and CEO McCorkindale was voted in by directors to remain chairman until 2006, two years longer than originally scheduled.

Success did not come without some controversy. As late as 2003, the lawsuits related to the Chiquita banana stories in the *Enquirer* were still in the courts.

Ultimately, the courts decided in favor of former editor Larry Beupre and awarded him a $550,000 settlement for his claim that he had been the company's scapegoat. There was likewise trouble in Hawaii, with *Honolulu Star-Bulletin* owner David Black accusing Gannett of various unsavory business practices, including legal manipulations that rendered it cost-prohibitive for his paper, a rival to the Gannett-owned *Honolulu Advertiser*, to purchase newsprint. In late 2004, however, Gannett was secure financially and in its role as an industry leader.

Craig Dubow took over as president and chief executive officer from McCorkindale in 2005. That year Gannett purchased PointRoll, an online media company. The following year, with ad income dropping precipitously, Gannett increased its one-third share of CareerBuilder to 42.5 percent. It also purchased a share of ShopLocal.com, an online shopping site, and Topix.net, a news aggregator site.

ADOPTING NEW APPROACHES TO REMAIN COMPETITIVE

With revenues of $7.6 billion, Gannett launched Gannett Video Enterprises in 2006, providing high-quality, customized programming to other media companies for on-air, online, and wireless distribution. The launch was part of Gannett's attempt to remake itself in the ever-changing online world. Believing that news organizations had driven away readers by becoming too imperious, distant, and slow-to-respond, Gannett also changed the way it gathered and presented the news, involving readers in its reporting and mining online community discussions for stories. It merged its newspaper and on-line operations into a single unit and included non-journalists in a test run at citizen journalism at the *News-Press* in Florida. In another attempt to solicit input from often-ignored perspectives, Gannett developed an internal Web site for sharing best practices. By July 2007, USAtoday.com was reporting a 20 percent year-over-year increase in traffic.

In 2008 Gannett joined with Tribune Company, Hearst Corporation, and The New York Times Company to form quadrantONE, selling national advertising to its members' online publications in 27 of the top 30 newspaper markets. Before long, it had added another 26 newspaper company affiliates. Even with revenues of $4.9 billion that year, however, Gannett's declining ad income and overall sales led to the layoff of 700 employees, 100 of them in management jobs. This was followed by more rounds of layoffs that extended into 2011.

Operating revenues picked up to $5.5 billion in 2009, then dropped again in 2010 to $5.4 billion, the year that Gracia C. Martore replaced Dubow as the company's president and COO. (The company received criticism in 2011 when the *New York Times* reported that Dubow had earned $9.4 million in 2010, almost twice his salary for 2009.) Martore had joined Gannett in 1985 and had worked her way up the financial ladder of the company. She would be faced with the same challenges as the head of any major news and information provider in a rapidly changing industry: how to find new ways to make money. In 2011, the company hired its first chief marketing officer and began to post "A Gannett Company" across all its properties (newspapers, Web sites, television stations). It also hired a vice president of innovation as it looked to its digital properties and its newly created sports media group for growth.

Lisa Collins
Updated, April Dougal; Jeffrey L. Covell;
Howard A. Jones; Carrie Rothburd

PRINCIPAL SUBSIDIARIES

USA Today; USA Weekend; Newsquest plc; Gannett News Service; Gannett Offset; Gannett Retail Advertising Group; Gannett Media Technologies International; Texas-New Mexico Newspapers Partnership; Captivate; Clipper Magazine Inc.; 101 Inc.; Army Times Publishing Company; Gannett UK Ltd.; Central Newspapers; PointRoll, Inc.

PRINCIPAL COMPETITORS

The Associated Press; The E.W. Scripps Company; The Hearst Corporation; Knight-Ridder Inc.; McClatchy Company; The New York Times Company; The News Corporation Ltd.; Tribune Company.

FURTHER READING

Ahrens, Frank. "Gannett to Change Its Papers' Approach." *Washington Post*, November 7, 2006, D1.

"Evolution of Engagement." *Brandweek*, September 10, 2007.

Flamm, Matthew. "Gannett Bets on a New Marketing Push." *Crain's*, August 8, 2011, 2.

"Gannett's Nimbus Delivers the Weather Online." *Presstime*, December 2007, 53.

Gingerich, Jon. "Gannett to Resume Layoffs, Cutting 700 More Newspaper Jobs." *O'Dwyer's*, July 2011, 8.

"Give-and-Take Site Gives Gannett Staffers Great Ideas." *Presstime*, July 2007, 8.

"Off the Page: How Print Players Are Using Mobile to Reach Readers and Advertisers on the Move." *Media Week*, February 25, 2008, 14.

Geberit AG

Schachenstrasse 77
Jona, 8645
Switzerland
Telephone: (+41 55) 221 63 00
Fax: (+41 55) 221 67 47
Web site: http://www.geberit.com

Public Company
Founded: 1874
Employees: 5,820
Sales: CHF 2.15 billion ($2.29 billion) (2010)
Stock Exchanges: Swiss
Ticker Symbol: GEBN
NAICS: 326191 Plastics Plumbing Fixture Manufacturing; 327111 Vitreous China Plumbing Fixture and China and Earthenware Bathroom Accessories Manufacturing; 332913 Plumbing Fixture Fitting and Trim Manufacturing; 332998 Enameled Iron and Metal Sanitary Ware Manufacturing

■ ■ ■

Geberit AG is Europe's leading manufacturer of sanitary technology. The Jona, Switzerland-based company covers every aspect of sanitation systems and components, from water supply to wastewater drainage. The company's products are developed along six primary groups, divided into two major sectors. Under Sanitary Systems, which accounts for about 59 percent of Geberit's sales, the company's products include installation systems; cisterns and mechanisms, including the company's "shower toilets," outfitted with bidet-like spray systems;

faucets and flushing systems, including water- and energy-saving technologies such as electronic dual-volume and flush/stop systems; and waste fittings and traps, for restrooms, bathrooms, and kitchens, as well as for industrial and laboratory units. Installation systems represents the largest single Sanitary Systems market, with about 37 percent of the company's total sales. Under the Piping Systems category, which generates about 41 percent of Geberit's sales, the company includes building drainage systems, with complete piping and fittings assemblies for new construction and building renovations; and supply systems, which include products and systems for household water and gas supply and supply systems for industrial plants.

Geberit maintains offices in more than 40 countries worldwide, with 15 manufacturing plants in Switzerland, Germany, Austria, Liechtenstein, Italy, the United States, and China. Germany represents Geberit's single largest market, at 33.7 percent of sales in 2010. Switzerland, at 13.6 percent, and Italy, at 10.1 percent, are also major markets for the company, while the Benelux countries contributed 8.6 percent of the total; Central and Eastern Europe, 6.7 percent; Austria, 6.3 percent; the Nordic countries, 4.6 percent, France, 4.2 percent; the United Kingdom and Ireland, 2.3 percent; and Spain and Portugal, 1.1 percent. Less than 10 percent of sales were generated outside Europe, including 3.8 percent from the United States, 2.8 percent from the Far East and Asia-Pacific region; and 2.2 percent from the Middle East and Africa. Geberit's decentralized management structure typically places operational responsibility on the managers of its subsidiaries, which enables the company to remain reactive to local markets. Long a family-owned company, Geberit went public in 1999 with a listing on the Swiss Stock Exchange.

SANITARY TECHNOLOGY PIONEER AT THE DAWN OF THE 20TH CENTURY

Caspar Melchior Albert Gebert started out as a plumber in Rapperswil, Switzerland, receiving a trade permit in 1874. Through the end of the century, Gebert built up his plumbing business. At the dawn of the 20th century, however, Gebert decided to enter manufacturing as well, and in 1905 he began producing toilet tanks. Gebert's first tank, called the "Phoenix," was built of wood and lined with lead and also featured a lead flush mechanism. The tank system represented somewhat of a breakthrough in the development of modern sanitary systems, and the company was awarded a patent on the design in 1912. Gebert himself did not live to see that event. Upon his death in 1909, the company was taken over by his sons, Albert and Leo.

By the end of the second decade of the 20th century, Gebert had developed markets for the company's tanks across Switzerland, as well as in neighboring countries. Gebert set up a number of production workshops in order to supply these foreign markets. Production levels began to grow again as World War I drew to a close, prompting the company to begin building a new production plant in Rapperswil in 1917. The new facility included the company's own foundry. The following year, the company added a new range of products, including U-bend pipes and taps and valves, which also were used by the chemicals industry.

In 1921, following completion of construction of the new facility in Rapperswil, the company centralized all of its manufacturing activity there. The company continued to develop its foreign markets, particularly in the German-speaking countries. By the end of the 1920s, however, the Gebert family extended the company's reach into France, with the opening of a sales office in Paris in 1929.

The company continued to develop its product lines, and in the mid-1930s the company once again placed itself at the forefront of sanitary technology. The development of plastic was to take its place among the most significant events of the 20th century, transforming nearly every aspect of people's lives. In 1935 the Gebert family company became one of the first to begin adapting the new plastic material to its toilet tank and piping systems. The noncorroding nature of the new material made it ideally suited for use in producing certain components for toilet systems, particularly in the concealed systems being developed for public facilities.

World War II placed a halt on the company's growth. By the 1950s, however, with much of Europe undergoing a vast reconstruction and a corresponding economic boom, the company returned to its pursuit of innovations in sanitary technology. In 1952, the company debuted its first all-plastic Geberit toilet tank. That product, produced with the newly developed polyethylene plastic, marked a new success for the company.

INTERNATIONAL GROWTH IN THE FIFTIES

The next generation of Geberts, brothers Heinrich and Klaus (sons of Albert Gebert), took over management of the family-owned company in 1953. At that time, the company registered the Geberit trademark and adopted the slightly modified word as the new company name. Geberit then began to expand its European interests, creating a new international distribution subsidiary and opening new foreign offices offering sales and technical services.

Germany represented the market with the largest growth potential, particularly given the vast rebuilding effort needed in the postwar years. In order to position itself in the German market, Geberit created its first foreign subsidiary in 1955 in Pfullendorf, which constructed its own production plant and began developing a dedicated network of sales and technical service offices across Germany.

In addition to pursuing the foreign market, Geberit eyed an expansion of its product line. The flexibility of the new generation of plastics enabled the company to begin developing complementary product ranges, starting with Geberit's first drainage systems products, including U-bends, odor traps, and related components, in 1956.

Geberit launched a new foreign subsidiary in France in 1959, which was followed by the establishment of a subsidiary in Vienna, Austria, in 1965. By then the company had moved to a larger plant in Rapperswil-Jona, constructed in 1962 to meet the growing demand.

KEY DATES

1874: Caspar Gebert opens a plumbing business in Rapperswil, Switzerland.
1953: Company adopts the name and trademark of Geberit.
1956: Company begins producing components for wastewater systems.
1976: Company is reorganized under Geberit Holding SA.
1977: Geberit enters the installation systems market.
1991: First nonfamily member, Günter F. Kelm, is named CEO.
1997: Geberit is acquired by British investment firm Doughty Hanson & Co.
1999: Geberit goes public on the Swiss Stock Exchange.
2002: U.S.-based Chicago Faucet Company is acquired.
2004: Company acquires German firm Mapress Holding GmbH.

In 1964 the company marked a new successful product launch when it introduced its first concealed tank system.

Geberit's growth was particularly strong in Germany, and in 1967 the company built a new manufacturing facility for its Pfullendorf subsidiary. The company expanded its Jona plant and, in particular, added blow-molding production technology, reducing the cost of its toilet tank production. In 1972 Geberit added a third production plant, located in Potterbrunn, a town just west of Vienna. In that year, Geberit moved into a new market with the addition of a subsidiary in Belgium. A subsidiary was formed in the Netherlands in 1973.

During the 1970s, Geberit continued to add new product categories, extending its product range to include full drainage systems and flush-mounted systems and introducing new components for the hygiene sector. The company remained wholly focused on Europe until the mid-1970s. In 1976 Geberit made its first attempt to enter the U.S. market, launching a subsidiary and production plant in Michigan City, Indiana. The United States nonetheless remained a relatively minor market for Geberit. Also in 1976, the company overhauled its corporate structure and was reorganized under Geberit Holding SA.

FURTHER DIVERSIFICATION AND GEOGRAPHIC EXPANSION

A more significant event for the company came with its move into the installation systems market in 1977. That product market became the company's single largest, accounting for more than one-third of its sales by the end of the century. At the same time, Geberit began developing a range of other products, such as the so-called shower toilet, which featured a bidet-like spray attachment for standard and custom-built toilets.

The 1980s saw continued growth for the company. Geberit expanded its Pfullendorf plant again in 1980, while opening a warehouse facility at its Rapperswil-Jona site that same year. In 1984 Geberit moved into the Scandinavian market with the opening of a subsidiary in Denmark. A major step forward in the company's growing installation systems business came with the 1985 acquisition of Sanbloc GmbH, a producer of components for installation systems based in Weilheim, Germany.

The company automated its production process in 1987. In 1989 Geberit moved into new product territories, specifically with an entry into the fresh water supply systems sector, a move accomplished in part by the acquisition of a shareholding in the Swiss firm FAE Fluid Air Energy SA, which gave the company the exclusive license for marketing FAE's products.

Geberit built a new, larger factory in Potterbrunn, which opened in 1990. Another production plant, placed under the company's Pretec subsidiary, was added in Liechtenstein in 1994 in order to take advantage of the newly opening markets in the eastern region of the reunified Germany as well as other Eastern European markets. By then, the company had begun to prepare its transition to a public company. In 1991 the company hired its first CEO from outside the Gebert family. Under Günter F. Kelm, the company altered its management structure, adopting a decentralized structure that gave its subsidiaries greater operation control and responsibility. By 1992, the company's sales had topped CHF 785 million ($535 million), which represented a near-doubling of the company's revenues in just four years.

Geberit continued to invest heavily, at an average rate of some CHF 80 million per year. The company opened a new production plant in its Rapperswil-Jona headquarters and then constructed a plant for its Mepla product range in Givisiez, Switzerland. At the same time, Geberit acquired additional production capacity in Italy and Portugal. In 1994 Geberit launched a new subsidiary, Balena, as the brand for its line of shower toilets. The company successfully developed the brand and its product line, topping 100,000 customers by the end of the decade. Also in 1994, Geberit expanded into China by entering into two production-based joint ventures. The following year, the company acquired Italian PVC-pipe manufacturer Deriplast, S.p.A., and soon thereafter Deriplast bought another Italian company, Società Walking Pipe Italiana.

TRANSITION FROM FAMILY FIRM TO PUBLIC COMPANY

In the meantime, Geberit began investigating its options for the future, and in 1995 the company announced that it was considering an initial public offering (IPO) to enable the founding family to cash out of the business. Instead, Geberit was sold to British investment house Doughty Hanson & Co., manager of the largest private-equity investment fund in Europe, in March 1997 in a transaction valued at CHF 1.8 billion ($1.2 billion). Kelm and the rest of Geberit's management team remained in place, acquiring a minority share in the company, which projected a public offering for later in the decade.

With stronger financial backing, Geberit stepped up its pace of expansion. In 1997 the company acquired Prosan d.o.o., a Slovenian company that produced concealed cisterns and interior fittings for ceramic cisterns. Then, at the beginning of 1999, Geberit moved into the United Kingdom with the purchase of Caradon Terrain Ltd., a maker of drainage systems and other products under the Terrain brand name. Not all of the company's expansion moves came through acquisition, however. Geberit's joint ventures in China eventually turned into company subsidiaries, and the company in 1998 opened a new production plant in China as its drive into the markets of Asia began to gain momentum.

By the end of 1998, with sales topping CHF 1 billion for the first time, Doughty Hanson announced its intention to launch Geberit (by this time named Geberit AG) as a public company in 1999. That listing on Swiss Stock Exchange was accomplished in June 1999. The successful IPO provided Geberit with funds to pursue new acquisitions. In July 1999 the company acquired a further stake in FAE Fluid Air Energy, raising its shareholding position to 70 percent, with an agreement to take full control of FAE by 2001.

Geberit was hit hard in 2001 by a slumping German building sector, which resulted in a slight drop in sales. Geberit hit back the following year with two key acquisitions. The first, made on January 1, 2002, gave the company a controlling stake of Austria's Huter Vorfertigung GmbH, a company established in the 1970s specializing in installation systems. Then, in July 2002,

Geberit strengthened its position in the North American market with the acquisition of The Chicago Faucet Company. The $33.3 million purchase of Chicago Faucet extended Geberit's product range to include commercial faucets and fittings, while also bringing four new production plants in the United States into the company fold. Chicago Faucet reported sales of $70 million for fiscal 2001. Geberit finished 2002 by acquiring WC Technology Corporation (WCTC) from Masco Corporation for $5.5 million. WCTC, which was based in Farmington Hills, Michigan, and was subsequently folded into Chicago Faucet, was the developer and manufacturer of advanced, water-saving pressure-tank technology for toilet flushing for the commercial and public sector.

MAPRESS ACQUISITION AND OTHER GROWTH INITIATIVES

In 2004 Geberit enjoyed a 35.8 percent increase in sales to CHF 1.91 billion ($1.67 billion), with the bulk of the increase stemming from the company's acquisition of Mapress Holding GmbH at the very beginning of the year for EUR 372.5 million ($469 million). Mapress, based in Langenfeld, Germany, was a major European producer of high-quality, metal press fitting pipe and drainage systems made of stainless steel, carbon steel, and copper. These products were used in such applications as residential and commercial construction, building drainage, fire suppression systems, gas distribution, and shipbuilding. During its first year under the Geberit umbrella, Mapress accounted for CHF 369.6 million ($323.9 million) of the parent company's sales.

In other 2004 developments, Geberit purchased full control of Huter Vorfertigung and established a distribution subsidiary in Mexico. At year's end, Kelm stepped down from the CEO position and was succeeded by Albert M. Baehny, who had most recently served as Geberit's head of group division marketing and European sales.

In addition to pursuing growth through acquisition, Geberit continued to churn out innovative new products each year. In 2005, for example, the company debuted its Powerflush technology, which, without relying on electricity, offered a higher-pressure flushing system that used the same amount of water as traditional systems. Chicago Faucets a year later introduced its HyTronic line of electronic faucets, which incorporated a twin-beam infrared system that, when triggered, turned on the water flow. Also during this period, Geberit expanded its line of Balena shower toilets into additional international markets, and it also launched major expansions of several of its European production facilities, including a tripling of the capacity of its plant in Givisiez, Switzerland, where its line of Mepla pipe was manufactured. At the same time, the company jettisoned some noncore operations, including its underground piping systems business, which was divested in 2005, and its PVC piping business in the United Kingdom, which was sold in July 2007 to the U.K. firm Polypipe. The latter divested operation included a production and warehousing facility in Aylesford, a U.K.-based sales team, and the Terrain brand.

Geberit grew steadily through 2007, when revenues reached a record CHF 2.49 billion ($2.2 billion). During 2008, however, the global economic downturn, which hit the construction and building renovation markets particularly hard, began affecting the company's sales. By 2009 revenues had fallen to CHF 2.18 billion ($2.1 billion). A stronger Swiss franc also negatively affected Geberit's results, and the company's net profits for 2009 of CHF 397.5 million ($386 million) represented a drop of nearly 15 percent from the previous year. During 2009, Geberit began phasing out the Balena brand and relaunched its line of shower toilets under the name Geberit AquaClean in the German, Swiss, and Austrian markets. The new brand debuted in the Netherlands and France in 2010.

Although the company reported a 1.6 percent decline in revenues in 2010, in terms of local currencies Geberit's sales actually rose 5 percent that year. Geberit continued to churn out new products, including Geberit Monolith, a toilet system for the renovation market that concealed the cistern behind a glass plate. Also in 2010, the company accelerated its pursuit of growth in a key geographic area by opening a new headquarters for the Asia-Pacific region in Shanghai, China. During 2011 Geberit expressed optimism about what it perceived as a slight recovery in the construction market, although any such recovery seemed precarious at best given the overall economic uncertainty that then prevailed. Through the first nine months of the year, Geberit's sales were down slightly compared to the previous year, while net income fell 4.2 percent despite the company's cost-containment and streamlining efforts.

M. L. Cohen
Updated, David E. Salamie

PRINCIPAL SUBSIDIARIES

Geberit Holding AG; Geberit International AG; Geberit International Sales AG; Geberit Verwaltungs AG; Geberit Vertriebs AG; Geberit Marketing e Distribuzione SA; Geberit Produktions AG; Geberit Apparate AG; Geberit Fabrication SA; Geberit Pty Ltd. (Australia); Geberit Vertriebs GmbH & Co. KG (Austria); Geberit

Produktions GmbH & Co. KG (Austria); Geberit Beteiligungsverwaltung GmbH (Austria); Geberit Huter GmbH (Austria); Geberit N.V. (Belgium); Geberit Finance Ltd. (Channel Islands); Geberit Reinsurance Ltd. (Channel Islands); Geberit Flushing Technology Co. Ltd. (China); Geberit Plumbing Technology Co. Ltd. (China); Geberit Shanghai Trading Co. Ltd. (China); Geberit Shanghai Investment Administration Co. Ltd. (China); Geberit spol. s.r.o. (Czech Republic); Geberit A/S (Denmark); Geberit OY (Finland); Geberit S.a.r.l. (France); Geberit Beteiligungs GmbH & Co. KG (Germany); Geberit Deutschland GmbH (Germany); Geberit Management GmbH (Germany); Geberit Vertriebs GmbH (Germany); Geberit Produktions GmbH (Germany); Geberit Logistik GmbH (Germany); Geberit Mapress GmbH (Germany); Geberit RLS Beteiligungs GmbH (Germany); Geberit Liechtenstein GmbH (Germany); Geberit Weilheim GmbH (Germany); Geberit Kft (Hungary); Geberit Plumbing Technology India Pvt. Ltd.; Geberit India Manufacturing Pvt. Ltd. (India); Geberit Produzione S.p.a. (Italy); Geberit Holding B.V. (Netherlands); Geberit B.V. (Netherlands); Geberit International B.V. (Netherlands); Geberit AS (Norway); Geberit Sp.z.o.o. (Poland); Geberit Tecnologia Sanitaria S.A. (Portugal); Geberit South East Asia Pte. Ltd. (Singapore); Geberit Slovensko s.r.o. (Slovakia); Geberit Sanitarna tehnika d.o.o. (Slovenia); Geberit prodaja d.o.o. (Slovenia); Geberit Southern Africa (Pty.) Ltd. (South Africa); Geberit S.A. (Spain); Geberit AB (Sweden); Geberit Tesisat Sistemleri Ticaret Ltd. (Turkey); Geberit Sales Ltd. (UK); Duffin Manufacturing Co. (USA); The Chicago Faucet Company (USA).

PRINCIPAL COMPETITORS

Elkay Manufacturing Company; Grohe AG; GWA Group Limited; Ideal Standard International BVBA; Kohler Co.; Masco Corporation; Moen Incorporated; Roca Corporación Empresarial, S.A.; Samuel Heath & Sons Plc; Sanitec Corporation; Takara Standard Co. Ltd.; TOTO Ltd.; Uralita, S.A.; Villeroy & Boch AG.

FURTHER READING

"Geberit Acquires W/C Technology." *Contractor*, December 2002, 5.

"Geberit Buys FAE Fluid Air Energy." *Reuters*, July 7, 1999.

Lenius, Pat. "Geberit Acquires Chicago Faucet." *Plumbing and Mechanical*, August 2002, 20, 36.

———. "Geberit Celebrates 25 Years in North America." *Supply House Times*, December 2001, 14.

"Swiss Company Nabs Pipe Extruder Terrain." *Plastics News*, March 15, 1999, 12.

Wicks, John. "Royal Flush: Geberit Makes the Water Flow." *Swiss Business*, January–February 1994, 9.

The Gores Group, LLC

10877 Wilshire Boulevard, 18th Floor
Los Angeles, California 90024
U.S.A.
Telephone: (310) 209-3010
Fax: (310) 209-3310
Web site: http://www.gores.com

Private Company
Founded: 1987 as The Gores Technology Group, LLC
Employees: 19,800
Sales: $1.27 billion (2010)
NAICS: 523999 Miscellaneous Financial Investment Activities

∎ ∎ ∎

The Gores Group, LLC, is a private equity investment and management company that acquires businesses involved in technology, telecommunications, health care, media, retail, and industrial markets. Gores Group purchases businesses with annual revenues ranging between $30 million and more than $1 billion and improves their operating results by managing the businesses. Gores Group employs teams comprising financial and operations experts, who replace an acquired company's senior management and make improvements in the way the company is operated. Frequently, the firm acquires divisions or subsidiaries of large corporate parents. Often, Gores Group's acquisitions are bankrupt or suffering financially. Gores Group maintains offices in North America and Europe. During the first 25 years of its existence, the firm acquired ap-

proximately 80 businesses with combined revenues exceeding $15 billion.

FOUNDER'S BACKGROUND: 1978–87

Alec E. Gores's path to becoming a billionaire began in his parents' basement. The eldest of six children born to a Greek father and a Lebanese mother, Gores spent the first 15 years of his life in Nazareth, Israel, before moving with his family to Flint, Michigan, where his father opened a grocery store in the late 1960s. Gores bagged groceries at his father's store and became the first member of his family to attend college when he enrolled at Western Michigan University. Several years after earning a degree in computer science, Gores started his own business.

When he was 25 years old, Gores borrowed $10,000 from his father and established Executive Business Systems, a company whose main office was located in his parents' basement. Gores used the money to start a distributor business for CADO, a minicomputer maker. He traveled throughout Michigan, selling the computer systems to small businesses, building Executive Business Systems into a thriving enterprise. In 1986 proof of his success could be measured in financial terms. A telecommunications company, Contel Corp., acquired Executive Business Systems, paying Gores $10 million for his entrepreneurial creation.

Within months of selling Executive Business Systems, Gores wanted the company back. Contel's management made a number of missteps when they took control, including reducing commissions to salespeople and ignoring a small but profitable software venture that operated within Executive Business Systems. Gores was angered by the treatment his former company had received and he wanted to purchase it from Contel, but he was outbid by another party. His attempt to restore lost luster to Executive Business Systems was rebuffed, but it sparked a desire to fix ailing businesses suffering from mismanagement. Gores decided to start his own buyout firm.

FORMING AN INVESTMENT FIRM: 1987

For help in starting his second business, Gores turned to Art Pronovost, a former CADO distributor. Their plan was to invest in struggling companies and repair them, using the money Gores had earned from the sale of Executive Business Systems to fund their acquisitions. The pair struggled at first, finding it difficult to broker deals, but gradually their efforts began to pay dividends, putting their firm, The Gores Technology Group, in a distinct niche in the private equity investment community.

With Gores leading the way, an investment strategy emerged. Gores favored acquiring technology companies, preferably candidates with strong cash flow that operated as divisions of large companies. Gores targeted businesses in disrepair or being managed poorly that showed the ability for quick recovery, restricting his investment activities to those businesses with annual sales ranging between $5 million and $50 million. Once Gores Technology Group acquired a business, a team of financial and operations experts quickly took control, taking over senior management positions. The new executives pored through financial records, real estate agreements, and supplier contracts, searching for hidden problems. Meetings were held with managers and employees to discuss payroll reductions and possible

ways to restructure. Once changes were made, Gores Technology Group looked to sell the business or merge it with another business owned by the firm.

Gores established himself during the 1990s, using the profits from one deal to fund the next deal. From the firm's founding in 1987 to the end of the 1990s, Gores Technology Group acquired nearly 40 technology companies, buying companies such as NBI Services, Inc., a division of NBI, Inc., that designed word processing hardware and software. The firm purchased Information Dimensions, a provider of document management software; ONEBOOK Financials, a developer of Web-based business software applications; and bankrupt SSA Global Technologies, a developer of resource planning software for corporate clientele, among dozens more.

Although profitable and growing, Gores Technology Group attracted little attention from industry observers as it progressed through the 1990s. Because the firm focused on small acquisitions, it remained relatively anonymous. Industry observers soon became aware of Gores's firm, however, after a stunning deal that exchanged the firm's anonymity for prominence and made Gores a celebrated figure in the investment community.

ACQUISITION OF THE LEARNING COMPANY: 2000

Gores set his sights on assets that had been a disaster for toy manufacturer Mattel Inc. In May 1999 Mattel paid $3.5 billion for an educational and entertainment software developer named The Learning Company (TLC). The acquisition, spearheaded by Mattel's CEO, Jill Barad, quickly proved costly, losing $1.5 million each day and causing Mattel's stock to plunge from $45 per share to $11 per share. Barad lost her job because of the debacle and her successor announced in April 2000 that Mattel was selling the troubled company less than a year after acquiring it.

Despite being advised against purchasing TLC, Gores leaped at the opportunity to buy the troubled company. In 2000 he forged a remarkable deal with Mattel, paying nothing for a company that had sold for $3.5 billion a year earlier. To gain control of TLC, Gores agreed to pay Mattel 50 percent of any profits produced by TLC and part of any sale of TLC. The transaction, completed in September 2000, put Gores on the investment community's radar, as did his efforts to restore TLC to its previous high status. Gores Technology Group's operations and financial wizards moved in, taking the reins of command at TLC while they looked for what Mattel's management had missed.

KEY DATES

1987: Alec E. Gores starts his own private investment and management firm.
2000: The Learning Company is acquired from Mattel Inc., casting Gores in the spotlight.
2003: Firm launches its first private equity fund.
2007: Gores Capital Partners II closes with $1.3 billion worth of commitments.
2011: Gores Capital Partners III, a $2 billion private equity fund, closes to new investors.

Within weeks, changes were made, including reducing TLC's seven operating divisions to three divisions, establishing controls on spending, and culling TLC's nearly 500 software titles to focus on key brands. A little more than two months later, 75 days after Gores Technology Group completed the acquisition, TLC turned an operating profit, cementing Gores's reputation as a corporate turnaround artist.

Once TLC recovered under the control of Gores Technology Group, the assets were sold. In 2001 the educational unit of TLC was sold to Ireland's Riverdeep Group plc and the entertainment division was sold to France's UbiSoft Entertainment SA. The remainder of TLC was sold to its management in three transactions that were completed by 2002. Meanwhile, Gores had moved on to his next acquisition, demonstrating again his knack for striking a creative deal. In 2001 Micron Electronics Inc., a subsidiary of Boise, Idaho-based Micron Technology, was looking to shed itself of its computer-making business to focus on its Internet business. Gores swooped in and began negotiating with the company's CFO, a discussion that led to Micron paying Gores Technology Group $70 million to take over the business in exchange for a percentage of the sales price if Gores Technology Group sold the business within the ensuing three years.

A TRANSITION TO BIGGER ACQUISITIONS: 2000–06

With the TLC transaction, Gores elevated his and his firm's stature in the investment community. Instead of focusing on businesses that generated between $5 million and $50 million in annual revenue, he began to focus on businesses that generated more than $100 million in annual revenue, sifting through hundreds of prospects each year and typically finding approximately five suitable candidates. He continued to make high-

profile deals during the early part of the decade, purchasing Hewlett-Packard's VeriFone division in 2001 and Elcotel, Inc., a provider of public access terminals, telecommunications networks, and management services, in 2002, but his pursuit of larger companies began to present a problem.

Gores needed to have access to a far larger supply of capital than he had at his disposal during the first 15 years of Gores Technology Group's existence. During those years, he had used his own money and the profits produced by his firm to finance his efforts on the acquisition front, but he began to experience difficulty with larger deals, making unsuccessful bids for Global Crossing Ltd. and Polaroid Corporation. With a larger supply of capital, Gores could move more quickly after larger deals, which prompted him to launch his first private equity fund in 2003. Gores Technology Group invested approximately $100 million in the fund and sought between $400 million and $500 million from outside investors.

With his first fund, Gores made a series of deals. He acquired Wire One Technology, a provider of communications hardware and services, and merged it with a company his firm owned, V-SPAN, to form Wire One Communications (a company sold to BT Conferencing in 2008). In 2005 he purchased Global Tel Link, a developer of network-based call processing and digital recording platforms that served the corrections industry, and merged it with National Public Markets, a provider of inmate telecommunications services, selling the combined entity four years later. He purchased Brand-Rex, a designer and manufacturer of copper and fiber-based cabling systems, from Honeywell International, and Avure Technologies, a designer and manufacturer of high-pressure presses for forming sheet metal, from Flow International. The acquisitions were part of a group of 18 companies acquired by Gores's firm between 2003 and 2006, during which time Gores Technology Group shortened its name to Gores Group.

GORES CAPITAL PARTNERS II AND III: 2007–11

After using the capital from his first fund, Gores started a second fund, Gores Capital Partners II, in 2007. When the fund closed in July, it had secured $1.3 billion worth of commitments, a sum Gores intended to use to acquire mature technology, industrial, and telecommunications services providers. Acquisitions purchased with the funds from Gores Capital Partners II included Lineage Power, a provider of AC-DC and DC-DC power systems; Sagemcom, a provider of broadband communications hardware and software; and Westwood One, Inc., a provider of programming to radio, television, and online businesses. Gores Group also acquired two companies operating under Chapter 11 of the U.S. Bankruptcy Code. In May 2009 the firm took a 51 percent stake in Stock Building Supply, a building supplies provider based in Raleigh, North Carolina, that generated $3.5 billion in sales in 2008. In September 2010 the firm purchased National Envelope Corporation, the largest envelope producer in the United States. The company produced 37 billion envelopes annually, generating more than $600 million in revenue.

The firm continued to compile an impressive record of success in its investment and management activities, earning the confidence of large, institutional investors. After exhausting the funds of Gores Capital Partners II, the firm closed Gores Capital Partners III in February 2011, raising $2 billion, exceeding its target amount by more than 30 percent. With the capital from the fund, Gores Group made several acquisitions on the eve of its 25th anniversary. In June 2011 the firm acquired Scovill Fasteners, Inc., a bankrupt maker of closure products for apparel and industrial uses. In October 2011 Gores Group agreed to acquire the U.S.-based assets of Hypercom Corporation, which included operations that provided electronic payment and transaction devices to retailers. The following month, the firm purchased The Clark Group, Inc., a provider of distribution and transportation services for the print media industry. As it moved ahead, the company could be expected to continue its strong track record of sound and astute investing.

Jeffrey L. Covell

PRINCIPAL COMPETITORS

Bain Capital, LLC; Clayton, Dubilier & Rice, Inc.; Forstmann Little & Co.

FURTHER READING

"Billionaire Raising Capital for First Buyout Fund." *Alternative Investment News*, March 2003.

Canabou, Christine. "Mr. Fix-It." *Fast Company*, June 2003.

"Gores Engineers Rapid Turnaround at Software Maker." *Los Angeles Business Journal*, April 16, 2001.

"The Gores Group Acquires The Clark Group, Inc." *Benzinga.com*, November 4, 2011.

"Gores Group Closes $2 Billion Private Equity Fund." *Wireless News*, February 21, 2011.

Jaffe, Joshua. "Gores Sells The Learning Co. Unit to Riverdeep." *Daily Deal*, September 6, 2001.

Meyer, Cheryl. "Gores to Bid for Global Crossing." *Daily Deal*, July 11, 2002.

Grand Canyon Education, Inc.

3300 West Camelback Road
Phoenix, Arizona 85017
U.S.A.
Telephone: (602) 639-7500
Toll Free: (800) 800-9776
Web site: http://www.gcu.edu

Public Company
Incorporated: 1949 as Grand Canyon College
Employees: 2,600
Sales: $385.63 million (2010)
Stock Exchanges: NASDAQ
Ticker Symbol: LOPE
NAICS: 611310 Colleges, Universities, and Professional
   Schools

■ ■ ■

Grand Canyon Education, Inc., operates Grand Canyon University, a for-profit, nondenominational Christian school that serves about 3,700 students at its Phoenix campus and nearly 40,000 others online. Grand Canyon offers more than 100 bachelor's and master's degrees through its colleges of education, nursing, business, fine arts, and arts and sciences, as well as doctoral degrees in the fields of education, business, and psychology. The school also has nondegree certificate programs in many of the same disciplines. Founded in 1949 by the Arizona Southern Baptist Convention, Grand Canyon became a for-profit institution in 2004 and was later spun off by owner SignificantFederation LLC, which retains a sizable stake.

BEGINNINGS

Grand Canyon College was founded in 1949 by the Arizona Southern Baptist Convention to train ministers and teachers, giving a local option to students who would otherwise have to leave the state to study in such places as Texas and Missouri. It began operations in temporary quarters in Prescott with 93 students and 16 faculty members. In 1951 it moved to a larger site in Phoenix that was donated by the First Southern Baptist Church.

In 1968 the college won regional accreditation from the North Central Association of Colleges and Schools' Commission on Institutions of Higher Education. Approval from the independent body certified that it provided a quality education and made it eligible for federal and state financial aid.

Over the years the number of students and programs offered by Grand Canyon College grew, although its budget was often tight. In the 1980s nursing and master's degree programs in education and business were added. In 1989 the school changed its name to Grand Canyon University (GCU) to reflect its offering of graduate degrees. In 1994 the school overhauled its accounting procedures, and in 1997 it added the option of distance learning.

In 1999 GCU's finances were dealt a severe blow when the Southern Baptist Convention's fundraising unit, the Baptist Foundation of America, was shut down after it was found to be operating a real-estate pyramid scheme that had cost investors $590 million. GCU lost several small endowments, while a number of prospective donors lost sums that the school might later have been given.

SPLIT WITH BAPTIST CONVENTION IN 2000

At this time, GCU's accountants advised its leaders to integrate the school's financial statement into that of the Arizona Southern Baptist Convention, which continued to own the university and appoint its trustees. Some administrators, however, saw this consolidation as threatening the school's all-important accreditation through the North Central Association of Colleges and Schools, which had previously raised concerns about its relationship with the Baptist Convention. Losing accreditation would also impact the acceptance of federal student loans, and cause further financial distress.

Faced with these concerns, in January 2000 GCU's board voted 21 to three (with five abstentions) to split with the Baptist Convention. The school's mission would remain little changed, however, and GCU would continue to focus on offering a Christian-based curriculum, although no longer as an official Baptist institution. Its annual budget now stood at $25 million.

Following the move to independence GCU's financial picture continued to deteriorate, as the number of foreign students dropped following the September 11, 2001, terrorist attacks on the United States and then after GCU raised tuition by 30 percent to help make up losses. Still hoping things would improve, the school built a new student union and 400-bed dormitory, both of which were completed in 2003. It suffered another

setback, however, when two sizable donations that had been promised upon completion fell through, causing the school's debt to balloon to $40 million.

SALE TO SIGNIFICANT EDUCATION IN 2004

In the fall of 2003 rumors began to circulate that GCU would close its doors at the end of the year and leave its 1,600 students in out in the cold. The institution's trustees, who had reportedly been unaware of the depth of its financial problems, approached a Christian-based San Diego firm called Significant Education LLC to help raise emergency funds. After rejecting options such as the sale of the school's distance-learning unit or a merger with another college, the trustees announced in January 2004 that Significant Education would purchase the school. The sale made news as the first time a Christian nonprofit college had been converted into a for-profit operation.

After the sale, Significant Education took over management of the school, while the nonprofit organization that had founded it (now renamed Grand Canyon University Institute for Advanced Studies) would retain ownership of the land and buildings, as well as overseeing the school's endowment and scholarships. In exchange, it would receive a 5 percent royalty on gross earnings. The school's board of trustees would also continue to approve faculty appointments, and two members would join Significant Education's board.

Since its founding in 2002 by a group of five Christian investors, Significant Education had been looking to purchase an existing college, rather than create one out of whole cloth, to avoid the lengthy process of winning accreditation. The firm was headed by Michael K. Clifford, 50, who had dropped out of high school to play in rock bands before becoming a born-again Christian. He then became a fundraiser for conservative Christian organizations including Campus Crusade for Christ and Franciscan University in Steubenville, Ohio. Clifford had lived in Phoenix, where his father owned a radio station, and one of his mentors was John Sperling, the founder of online education giant the University of Phoenix.

Following the purchase Clifford took the title of managing director of the university, with Phoenix megachurch pastor and friend Tommy Barnett named chancellor. Over the next year a number of significant changes were made, including renegotiating or canceling contracts with suppliers and consultants (some of which resulted in lawsuits against the school), creating a technology infrastructure, and implementing a

KEY DATES

1949: Grand Canyon College is founded in Arizona to train Baptist ministers, teachers.

1968: School receives regional accreditation.

1989: Name is changed to Grand Canyon University following addition of graduate degrees.

2000: University becomes financially independent of the Arizona Southern Baptist Convention.

2004: Significant Education buys school, begins to operate it as a for-profit institution.

2008: Grand Canyon Education, Inc. begins trading on the NASDAQ.

pedestrian-friendly makeover of the school's campus. The school's business program was renamed the Ken Blanchard College of Business in a partnership with the *One-Minute Manager* author. GCU's new owners also laid off 22 administrative staff members, added and dropped courses and departments to reflect student needs, boosted faculty pay by as much as 30 percent, and reduced the school's tuition of $14,500. In the first year the number of students on campus grew from 1,600 to 1,750.

ONLINE OFFERINGS BOOSTED, RECRUITMENT RAMPED UP

The school's new owners put their strongest effort into expanding its online education program, which had been launched the year before and was now serving 1,500 students. New Web-based bachelor's and master's degree programs in such popular areas as nursing, pharmacology, and hospitality were added to the existing education and business offerings, while associate degree and nondegree certificate programs were also developed. Some 100 new online support employees and 200 teaching adjuncts were hired, the latter of which could work from a remote location rather than being tied to campus.

While GCU would officially remain a Christian school (although weekly chapel attendance was no longer required), its online programs did not stress this point, and it began to compete directly with the University of Phoenix and other for-profit Web-based schools, using outside recruitment firm Mind Streams LLC to find students. The number of online students doubled within the first year, and continued to grow rapidly.

GCU was now budgeting $6 million on advertising, primarily for the Internet, and Clifford predicted that the figure would double each year. The new owners' eagerness to shed its conservative image, along with Clifford's music-industry background, were apparent in the May 2004 announcement that GCU would grant an honorary doctorate to Phoenix-area rock star Alice Cooper, a born-again Christian who had previously given money to the school.

In May 2005 Grand Canyon University was recertified by the U.S. Department of Education to receive Title IV student loans on a provisional basis, even though concerns were raised about financial and administrative issues. The school would be required to post a letter of credit and accept limitations on growth and greater monitoring of cash intake. GCU's lead investor, Endeavor Capital, subsequently agreed to underwrite the credit requirement and provide money for other working capital. The school's credit and growth restrictions were lifted in October 2006, and the cash monitoring requirements were removed a few months later.

For 2006 revenues topped $72 million, and the firm recorded net income of $600,000. There were now 8,400 online students and 2,250 taking classes on campus. The following year saw GCU's academic accreditation renewed for another 10-year period.

GRAND CANYON EDUCATION GOES PUBLIC: 2008

In May 2008 Significant Education announced it would sell shares in Grand Canyon Education, Inc. on the NASDAQ, hoping to raise $230 million. Following the announcement the company revealed that it was being investigated by the U.S. Department of Education for its commission-based student recruitment practices, and was also being sued by a whistle-blower who claimed student aid funding was being falsely obtained. In June, the firm hired Brian Mueller, the president of University of Phoenix parent Apollo Group, to serve as CEO, and another University of Phoenix administrator, Daniel Bachus, to be chief financial officer. Dozens of other University of Phoenix staffers would subsequently defect to GCU.

In November Grand Canyon Education's initial public offering (IPO) was made as the market was roiling from the mortgage crisis, and the sale of 10.5 million shares of stock raised $126 million, far less than originally projected. Three-fourths of the proceeds were used for a special dividend for existing shareholders, who would keep their stake but see it converted from preferred to common stock. This move would also enable the firm to comply with Department of Education rules about controlling interest in schools. Significant Education (later known as SignificantFederation LLC) also had interests in other schools including Bridgepoint Education.

GCU's enrollment now stood at 22,000, up 63 percent from the year before, with more than 80 percent of students taking online courses. It was ranked as one of the top online schools by the Online Education Database, and had also recently been named one of the top five online colleges for entrepreneurs by *Fortune* magazine.

During 2008 the school added its first doctoral program, the Doctorate of Education in Organizational Leadership. GCU's other degree offerings included Master of Arts in Teaching, Master of Education, Master of Business Administration, Master of Science, Bachelor of Arts, and Bachelor of Science diplomas, and students could choose from 76 majors within these areas. Certificate programs were also offered for those interested in continuing education or the learning of specific skills without a degree.

ENROLLMENT TOPS 40,000 IN 2010

With the U.S. economy in a recession, many people began to go back to school to boost their employability, and the firm's online enrollment continued to expand. By the end of 2010, GCU had over 37,000 online students, as well as 3,750 studying on its Phoenix campus. Nearly half of distance-learning students were pursuing graduate degrees at the master's and doctoral levels.

The school's dramatic online growth was in large part the work of recruitment contractor Mind Streams LLC, which had been founded in 2000 by Gail Richardson, the mother of University Executive Chairman Brent Richardson and GCU General Counsel Christopher Richardson. For its efforts, Mind Streams took a percentage of the total fees paid by students it recruited over their academic career, which amounted to a few thousand dollars each.

Revenues for the year were $385.6 million, more than double the amount of 2008 and five times the figure of four years earlier. Net income grew to $44.4 million. The final totals had been restated, however, due to a too-low calculation of the amount of probable loss due to former students' nonpayment of tuition debts, which were boosted by $15.2 million in the final tally. During the year the firm had also settled the 2008 whistle-blower lawsuit for $5.2 million.

NEW FEDERAL RULES SPARK CHANGES IN 2011

In the summer of 2011 the U.S. Department of Education began to implement new rules that restricted for-profit schools' use of commission-based recruiting, which had become controversial for the high cost involved as well as the relatively large number of such students who went on to default on their federally guaranteed loans. The rules, which had been watered down from the original proposal following one of the most intense lobbying efforts in Washington history, would also restrict loans to students at schools where there were high levels of default, and for programs that did not lead to what was termed "gainful employment."

As a result, GCU ended its contract with commission-based recruiter Mind Streams LLC, paying it more than $8 million to cover all obligations for students recruited to that time, and took over its database of potential recruits. The school's recruiting would now be handled by Mind Streams affiliate Lifetime Learning, which would generate and sell leads for new students to GCU and other institutions. Like Mind Streams, it was headed by Gail Richardson.

In the late summer of 2011, GCU was informed that a Department of Education review of its operations had found several potential problems. These included issues with recruitment policies, the recording of non-passing grades for students with federal loans, and an Interdisciplinary Studies program declared ineligible for loans under the "gainful employment" rule. The institution again was forced to restate its financial results for the first three quarters of 2011 to reflect changes in its estimate of bad student debt.

In September 2011 GCU opened a new 5,000-seat arena that would host basketball games, concerts, and other events. It was the focal point of a $200 million building program that would also add two dormitories, a dining facility, a new classroom building, and a student recreation center. Earlier in the year the school had announced it was freezing on-campus tuition at the 2009 level of $16,500. It was seeking to boost campus enrollment to as much as 12,000 over the next few years, but the costs were significantly higher than public universities, which cost between about $8,500 and $9,700.

In October the university announced the creation of the Colangelo School of Sports Business as part of its Ken Blanchard College of Business. The new unit was named after Jerry Colangelo, who had owned the National Basketball Association's Phoenix Suns and Major League Baseball's Arizona Diamondbacks, among other teams, and was a member of the Basketball Hall of Fame. GCU was hoping to boost sports business majors from 300 to 1,000 students and develop a top-10 program nationally.

More than 60 years after its founding as a small Baptist college, Grand Canyon University had grown into a formidable educational institution with over 40,000 students, most of whom participated via the Internet. The school's offerings ranged from education to nursing to business, and students could receive everything from a learning certificate to a doctorate. Thriving in the economic downturn, the school was nonetheless facing pressure from the increasing scrutiny placed on for-profit schools that had higher rates of student loan defaults, and was adjusting its practices to conform to new, tighter regulations.

Frank Uhle

PRINCIPAL SUBSIDIARIES

Grand Canyon University.

PRINCIPAL COMPETITORS

Arizona State University; Azusa Pacific University; Baylor University; Capella University; Northern Arizona University; Seattle Pacific University; University of Arizona; University of Phoenix; Walden University.

FURTHER READING

Berry, Jahna. "University Addresses Review in SEC Filing." *Arizona Republic*, August 29, 2011. Accessed December 7, 2011. http://www.azcentral.com/business/news/articles/2011/08/29/20110829university-addresses-review-sec-filing.html#ixzz1eS6kxsHz.

Bollag, Burton. "For the Love of God (and Money)." *Chronicle of Higher Education*, September 3, 2004. Accessed December 1, 2011. http://chronicle.com/article/For-the-Love-of-God-and/34996.

"Interview: Michael Clifford." *PBS Frontline*. Accessed December 1, 2011. http://www.pbs.org/wgbh/pages/frontline/collegeinc/interviews/clifford.html#ixzz1f79PQTp7.

Laub, John. "Grand Canyon University Goes Public—Raises $126 Million, Mostly for Investors." *Phoenix CEO-CFO Group*, December 2008. Accessed December 7, 2011. http://www.phoenixceocfo.com/content/articles/2008-12/grand-canyon.bv.

McBride, Laura. "How a Struggling School Got Saved." *Arizona Republic*, October 9, 2011. Accessed November 22, 2011. http://www.azcentral.com/arizonarepublic/viewpoints/articles/2011/10/08/20111008school-saved-mcbride.html#ixzz1eS8MnJTz.

Zepeda, Alyson. "Grand Canyon University Freezes Tuition, Hopes to Attract Students." *Arizona Republic*, April 17, 2011. Accessed December 7, 2011. http://www.azcentral.com/arizonarepublic/local/articles/2011/04/17/20110417grand-canyon-university-tuition-freeze.html#ixzz1eS7FOJyt.

Grupo Los Grobo

Ruta Nacional 5, Km. 308
Carlos Casares, Buenos Aires B6530CFD
Argentina
Telephone: (54 23) 9545-9000
Fax: (54 23) 9545-9100
Web site: http://www.losgrobo.com.ar

Private Company
Founded: 1984 as Los Grobo Agropecuaria S.A.
Employees: 1,000
Sales: $550 million (2010 est.)
NAICS: 111110 Soybean Farming; 111140 Wheat Farming; 115116 Farm Management Services; 311211 Flour Milling; 311923 Pasta Manufacturing; 551112 Offices of Other Holding Companies

■ ■ ■

Grupo Los Grobo consists of a group of companies working and investing in the farmlands of South America. These companies, located in Argentina, Brazil, Paraguay, and Uruguay, are involved in grain production, mostly soybeans and wheat, using technological advances such as transgenic seeds resistant to diseases and insects and the intensive use of fertilizer and agrochemicals. In all, they cultivate some 750,000 acres, of which 90 percent are rented rather than owned, making the group the leading producer of grains in Argentina and the second-largest in Latin America. Los Grobo also produces flour and pasta from grain and sells them as well as fertilizer, agrochemicals, and the crops it grows. The group also offers to other producers a host of agribusiness services, including marketing, warehousing, transport, and financial services such as risk management and hedging.

ESTABLISHING A NEW PARADIGM: 1984–2003

Los Grobo Agropecuaria S.A. was founded in 1984 by Adolfo Grobocopatel, grandson of Jewish immigrants from what is now the Republic of Moldova in Eastern Europe. The enterprise started with 3,500 hectares (8,645 acres) in the province of Buenos Aires, one silo, one truck, and four employees. Although Adolfo and his two brothers ("Los Grobo," as they were known) were successful farmers and grain traders, Adolfo dreamed of becoming a great landowner. This was unlikely, given the high price of farmland in Argentina's fertile pampas.

Adolfo's son, Gustavo, a young agricultural engineer, had a different idea, based on a long tradition in Argentina of subcontracting by rural landowners. Because Los Grobo did not have the capital to grow by land acquisition, he first rented recently flooded land in the province at low cost. By the end of 1989 he had accumulated 10,000 hectares (nearly 25,000 acres).

Gustavo Grobocopatel next developed a network of contractors who became partners in Los Grobo and were paid with a part of the harvested production. They were trained to follow its methodology, which, in 2000, enabled Los Grobo to become the first farming company in the world to be ISO 9001 certified. A software program, based on Global Positioning Systems (GPS) data, was created to allow the enterprise's network members to measure soil characteristics and

COMPANY PERSPECTIVES

Passion for doing. Intelligence to realize. Generosity to share. Energy to take responsibility.

establish the precise density of such inputs as seeds and fertilizers in order to achieve maximum productivity.

Before 2000, Los Grobo's profits, at Adolfo's insistence, were invested in buying land rather than in Gustavo's priorities: employing advanced technology and hiring talented agronomists. By 2003, however, Adolfo had agreed to withdraw the original acreage of the family business for his own use and allow Gustavo and his three sisters, plus their children, to direct the future of the enterprise.

INDUSTRY AND TECHNOLOGY: 2001–03

In 2001 Los Grobo added an industrial division by establishing the first of a network of grain mills. The largest of these was in Guaminí, Buenos Aires. Another, in Puerto Galván, Bahía Blanca, was the only one in Argentina with direct access to the sea. The firm, whose revenues reached about $60 million that year, also founded Los Grobo Agroindustrial do Brasil, a flour producer and distributor.

Los Grobo established an alliance in 2002 with Software Consulting Group to develop a management system that would integrate all its activities: not only production and distribution but also marketing and import-export. The system included a database of suppliers and customers and was to incorporate satellite services to monitor the crops. Los Grobo was buying and selling the cereal crops of other producers as well as marketing its own. It would also soon be establishing, with 60 other producers, a biotechnology company developing genetically modified soybean seeds to resist drought and disease. If it were not for biotechnology, Gustavo maintained, the price of soy would be twice as high and that of chicken three times as high, and meat would be a luxury product.

Los Grobo was also a proponent of no-till planting: punching holes in the ground to which pesticides and fertilizer had been applied and dropping seeds into them. This method of cultivation avoided soil erosion. According to Grobocopatel, no-till agriculture improved soil with use and would allow him to hand over to his children better soil than that which his parents had left him.

EXTENDING ITS SCOPE: 2004–05

The Grobocopatel family established Grupo Los Grobo, during 2002 and 2003, as a holding company for the existing seven firms. Los Grobo gained a presence in Uruguay in 2004, when Marcos Guigou founded Agronegocios del Plata (ADP) with Gustavo's backing. ADP soon became the nation's second-largest soybean producer, and Guigou later became a shareholder in the group. He also was named manager of Tierra Roja, the Los Grobo company founded in Paraguay in 2005.

Grupo Los Grobo was the largest individual operator in the Argentine market of cereals by 2004, when it moved to new corporate headquarters in Carlos Casares, Buenos Aires, about 3½ hours from the city of Buenos Aires. A "smart" building on a 50-acre site, it was said to include the most advanced fiber-optic technology in a totally rural context. It employed materials appropriate to the location, such as bricks and local woods, but also included a curved auditorium clad in corrugated sheets of metal reminiscent of Los Grobo's silos. In addition to this hall, used for staff training and presentations, the complex contained a high-speed Internet connection, still unusual in rural Argentina.

Also in 2004, Los Grobo Agropecuaria established a joint venture with the Argentina candymaker Arcor S.A. I.C. to build a river port in San Pedro, Buenos Aires, for export of goods to other countries. Los Grobo used this port to ship wheat, corn, and soybeans. Commercialization of grains was by this time bringing in about twice as much revenue as the company's own crop production.

Gustavo Grobocopatel was becoming known in some circles as the "king of soy." World demand had doubled in 15 years, and Argentina and Brazil were closing in on the United States as major soybean producers. Argentina more than doubled its acreage in soybeans between 1997 and 2004. Grobocopatel sought to profit from the establishment of Mercosur as an economic bloc encompassing Argentina, Brazil, Paraguay, and Uruguay, foreseeing the possibility of a so-called OPEC of soy. Of 80 million pounds of grains produced for Los Grobo in 2004, 40 percent was soybeans and 40 percent wheat. Los Grobo farmed nearly 200,000 acres that year, but three-quarters was leased rather than owned. Los Grobo Agropecuaria retained between three-quarters and four-fifths of the crops produced on leased land.

By now Gustavo had defined the group as a network business. It included more than 1,000 participants throughout Argentina, including landowners, agronomists, contractors, and branch managers. Landowners checked their accounts on the Los Grobo Web site. They were invited to attend training courses at

KEY DATES

1984: Los Grobo Agropecuaria is founded in the province of Buenos Aires, Argentina.
2003: Grupo Los Grobo has been established as a holding company for seven firms.
2007: Los Grobo takes a Brazilian partner and begins buying farmland in Brazil.
2008: Los Grobo has become the fourth-largest milling group in Argentina.
2010: Group's grain production is well over two million metric tons.

corporate headquarters and encouraged to visit farms that were especially productive.

THE GROUP IN ARGENTINA: 2006–08

Grupo Los Grobo was cultivating 235,000 acres in Argentina, 62,000 acres in Uruguay, and 27,000 acres in Paraguay by 2006, of which about 90 percent was leased rather than owned. By 2008, between its own production and that of others, it was the fourth-largest milling group in Argentina and was marketing 1.5 million metric tons per year of soybeans, wheat, millet, and sunflower seeds and oils.

Los Grobo and other Argentine agricultural groups were expanding into neighboring countries partly because of the high export taxes levied on their products by their government and also because prime farmland was less expensive to acquire outside Argentina's borders. In Paraguay, for example, such land was estimated to cost only one-fifth of what it cost in Argentina.

Agricultural producers had long protested not only export taxes but also restrictions on exporting and price controls intended to keep the cost of food low for urban Argentines. A government decree in March 2008 raised export taxes on agricultural products still higher, touching off a three-month strike by farmers and ranchers that ended only when the Senate rejected the increases, which were based on a sliding scale tied to world commodity prices. In the case of soybeans, the tax rate had been raised from 35 to 44 percent.

BRAZIL AND ELSEWHERE: 2007–08

Los Grobo saw great opportunities in Brazil, which offered more undeveloped or underdeveloped farmland

than any other country in the world. The group's first Brazilian holdings included a 2007 joint venture with the Brazilian enterprise Harinanet that was named Unigral do Brasil. This company bought wheat from Los Grobo in Argentina and imported it to Brazil to convert it to flour in rented mills for distribution by Harinanet. In order to raise money for land acquisition, Los Grobo sold 20 to 25 percent of the holding company in 2007 for $100 million to Pactual Capital Partners (PCP), an investment fund and business developer. PCP, which was soon renamed Vinci Partners, also became a management partner. The two parties also agreed to jointly contribute $400 million to a fund oriented to agricultural investments in the region.

In mid-2008 Los Grobo purchased 35 percent of Ceagro Agrícola Ltda., a Brazilian company that specialized in storing and marketing grains but was now intending to grow soybeans and millet in its home territory of northern Brazil, a region known as Mapito because of its location where three states meet: Maranhão, Piauí, and Tocantins. Ceagro, which was founded in 1994, had a maritime terminal in Porto Franco, Maranhão, from which it exported grains. Also in 2008, Los Grobo purchased Sementes Selecta, a bankrupt soybean producer in the states of Goiás and Minas Gerais. The restructured company opened a soy processing plant the following year.

Los Grobo had less luck in the northern part of South America. Grobocopatel signed a contract in early 2007 with Hugo Chávez, president of Venezuela, to transfer technology to the agricultural offshoot of Petróleos de Venezuela S.A., the nation's state-owned oil producer. He rescinded that contract the following year, leaving behind some 12,500 hectares (31,000 acres) planted with soy and corn seeds and another 50,000 acres ready for the next planting. Grobocopatel complained that progress had been slower than he expected because of bureaucratic problems. By then he had been invited to Colombia by its president, Álvaro Uribe, but a short visit to the western plains of that country yielded no further action.

LOS GROBO'S OPERATIONS IN 2009–10

During the 2009–10 growing season, Los Grobo was operating a production area of 251,000 hectares (620,000 acres) in Argentina, Brazil, Paraguay, and Uruguay, with grain production reaching 2,275,000 metric tons. The group had storage capacity of a million metric tons of grain in 44 owned and rented silos.

Los Grobo provided a one-stop bundle of services to partnering agricultural producers. Some 120 specialists in the field offered technical expertise and other consulting. The group's companies developed and sold technologically enhanced seeds and other inputs. Loans were available to allow local farmers to prepare for planting. Field experts provided constant crop monitoring to maintain quality. Long-term contracts were offered for the sale of grain. The group's logistic network offered transportation and storage solutions. Its trading desk and hedging services leveraged the group's market knowledge.

A typical leasing contract involved between 400 and 4,000 hectares (about 1,000 to 10,000 acres) and was for three years, with annual payments. About 90 percent were renewed after three years. Agricultural production accounted for about 30 percent of the group's revenues. The commercialization of grains to trading companies or the local market accounted for 60 percent of revenues but a lower margin of profit. Inputs such as selling fertilizers, agrochemicals, and seeds accounted for about 10 percent.

According to a case study of Los Grobo published by Harvard Business School, Grupo Los Grobo's revenues were $550 million in fiscal 2010 (the year ended April 30, 2010). A *DNA* story in January 2011 gave $700 million as its revenues in 2010. In a March 2011 article in the Argentine business magazine *Apertura*, Grobocopatel said the group had passed the billion-dollar mark.

In 2010 Los Grobo merged two of its Brazilian companies and acquired another, in Mato Grosso. In 2011 the company opened, in Argentina, its first plant for dry pasta. Los Grobo was now cultivating 60 percent soybeans, 30 percent wheat. Interviewed in 2011 by *Apertura*, Grobocopatel said that Los Grobo was doing 45 percent of its business in Brazil, 40 percent in Argentina, 10 percent in Uruguay, and 5 percent in Paraguay. He predicted that the company would grow much faster in Brazil than the other countries.

FORESEEING A ROSY FUTURE

Los Grobos enjoyed a very good year in 2010 and expected the same in 2011, as a result of the high prices being commanded for food commodities worldwide. During the next three to five years Los Grobo expected to triple its 2010 revenues. Grobocopatel expressed his belief that world demand would continue to increase because of growing population and the fact that demand was outstripping supply. He foresaw consolidation in certain agricultural sectors: in fertilizers, milling, supplies, and logistics, leading to a greater degree of vertical integration. Volatility of commodity prices would be unavoidable, he said, but he maintained that his

company would handle this. "In an enterprise such as ours, the key to competitiveness is the management of risk," he told *Apertura*. "We adopted a management model of risk for agriculture to our agrobusiness enterprise."

Grobocopatel denounced export taxes as being antibusiness, harmful to productivity and to the growth of technology. As long as world prices remained high, he predicted, Argentine politicians would not come under pressure from the producers. The agricultural sector, however, would not be able to attract the investment it needed, and more people would migrate from rural areas to the cities. Earlier, Grobocopatel had maintained that the agriculture and livestock-raising sector was generating more employment than any other industrial sector in Argentina.

Robert Halasz

PRINCIPAL SUBSIDIARIES

Agronegocios del Plata (Uruguay); Ceagro Agrícola Ltda.; (Brazil); Los Grobos Agropecuaria S.A.; Molinos Los Grobo; UPJ.

PRINCIPAL DIVISIONS

Industrial; Raw Materials.

PRINCIPAL COMPETITORS

Adecoagro LLC; Cresud S.A.C.I.F. y A.; El Tejar S.A.; MSU S.A.; SLC Agrícola S.A.

FURTHER READING

Batista, Fabiana. "Ceagro parte para plantio de soja." *Gazeta Mercantil*, July 8, 2008, 8.

Bell, David E., and Cintra Scott. *Los Grobo: Farming's Future?* Harvard Business School Case No. 9-511-088. Boston: Harvard Business School Publishing, rev. ed., 2011.

Crettaz, José. "Concierto en soja mayor." *América Economía*, September 8, 2008, 38–39.

"Expansión agrícola se proyecta en el tiempo con políticas estables." *El País*, August 7, 2004.

Fogaça, Guilherme. "O sem-terra que produz." *Exame*, May 6, 2009, 46–47.

Groba, Alejandra. "Los Grobo entran al negocio del software." *El Cronista*, July 16, 2002.

———. "Los Grobocopatel fusionarán sus siete sociedades en un holding." *El Cronista*, December 31, 2002.

"Gustavo Grobocopatel." *Apertura*, March 2011, 70–72.

McAfee, Andrew, and Alexandra de Royere. *Los Grobo*. Harvard Business School Case No. 9-606-014. Boston: Harvard Business School Publishing, 2005.

Mitchell, Jason, et al. "Argentina Seeks a Crop of Cash." *Euromoney*, April 2008, 56.

"Produtor argentine pede 'Opep da soja.'" *Valor Económico*, December 16, 2003.

Sood, Varun. "World's 'Biggest Farmer' Says Future Is in Outsourcing.'" *DNA - India*, January 5, 2011.

Hammerson plc

10 Grosvenor Street
London, W1K 4BJ
United Kingdom
Telephone: (+44 20) 7887-1000
Fax: (+44 20) 7887-1010
Web site: http://www.hammerson.co.uk

Public Company
Incorporated: 1953 as Hammerson Property and Investment Trust
Employees: 344
Operating Revenues: £353.3 million ($546.5 million) (2010)
Stock Exchanges: London
Ticker Symbol: HMSO
NAICS: 531120 Lessors of Nonresidential Buildings (Except Miniwarehouses); 237210 Land Subdivision; 531190 Lessors of Other Real Estate Property

■ ■ ■

Over the course of more than five decades, London-based Hammerson plc has made its mark as a leading real estate developer and manager. During the early 2010s the company's real estate portfolio in the United Kingdom and France was valued at approximately £5.8 billion. At that time Hammerson had a stake in 18 retail parks and 18 major shopping centers. CEO David Atkins heads the company, which maintained an average 97 percent occupancy rate during 2010.

BUILDING A BUILDING BUSINESS

The Hammerson family, who had been operating a business in the garment industry, entered the real estate market during the years of World War II. Led by Lewis Hammerson, the family sold its garment business in 1942 and used that capital to begin buying London-area properties. The company renovated the properties (often single-family houses), transforming them into apartment buildings and then reselling them. Incorporated as L.W. Hammerson & Co. in 1948, the company had experienced steadily increasing profits, which enabled it to enter the market for retail and commercial properties by the end of the 1940s.

In 1953 the company performed a reverse takeover of an older company named Associated Investment Trust. This not only boosted the company's size but gave it a listing on the London Stock Exchange. Taking on the name of Hammerson Property and Investment Trust, the company slowly began to assert itself on the London market, building up one of the United Kingdom's largest real estate portfolios.

Leading the company's major growth was Sydney Mason, who took over after Lewis Hammerson's death in 1958. Mason turned the company's interest to a relatively new type of building development, the shopping center. As rising numbers of automobiles and better highways enabled more of the population to move outside of the city centers, the shopping center offered an alternative to the typical high street urban shopping district. Hammerson began developing its own shopping centers. Its first center was built at the end of the 1950s in Bradford, in the Yorkshire region.

Hammerson had begun, meanwhile, to develop another interest: international growth. With financial backing from such institutional investors as Standard Life Assurance and Royal London Mutual Insurance, Hammerson started to acquire properties in other parts of the English-speaking world. During the 1960s Hammerson expanded into Australia, New Zealand, and the United States. The company's international growth was spurred on by the passage of legislation in the early 1960s. The so-called Brown Ban of 1964 had placed severe limits on the rate of new developments in the United Kingdom which was Hammerson's core London market. Hammerson's overseas presence helped it to continue its growth.

GLOBAL GROWTH

By the end of that decade the company had extended into Canada, a market that was to become one of the company's most important foreign markets. Back at home, Hammerson also found a new headquarters building at 100 Park Lane in London. Formerly known as Dudley House, the building originally had been built in 1827 by the first Earl of Dudley. Damaged during the air raids of World War II, the building was only partially restored with funds provided by the War Damage Act. A full restoration of the property was not begun until 1969, when Hammerson, then seeking a new headquarters, agreed to carry out the needed repairs.

At the same time, Hammerson looked closer to home, across the North Sea, entering Dutch and Belgian property markets in the late 1970s. Back at home, the effects of the Brown Ban had cut deeply into the company's new development efforts. Instead, Hammerson concentrated on renovating and improving its existing portfolio of properties.

Hammerson's revenues were by then generated by its net rental income rather than by its earlier practice of "flipping" its renovated buildings. If these factors meant that the company's growth in the early 1970s had been more modest than in the decade before, they also helped protect the company during the long slump in the property market that began in 1974. Coupled with a long-lasting recession, itself brought on by the Arab oil embargo of 1973, the bottoming out of the property market spelled the ruin of many of Hammerson's more speculative competitors. Hammerson's own low vacancy levels helped to protect it from the worst of the downturn in the real estate market.

Not all of the company's holdings were performing equally, however. The company's Australian and New Zealand holdings left it particularly vulnerable to the struggling markets in those countries. The return to health of the European and U.K. markets encouraged Hammerson to turn its focus to those markets, which, toward the middle of the decade, had entered into a new boom period.

BOOM TIME

This time, Hammerson joined its competitors in the buoyant market for new property developments that was helping to transform the skylines of many of the world's major cities. Hammerson built up a large portfolio of speculative developments, and its holdings boosted it to the rank of number five in the United Kingdom's real estate investment sector by the end of the decade. The company averted one disaster, a hostile takeover attempt from Dutch property investment giant Rodamco in 1989, to rush headlong into a new building market crash. This time, Hammerson's portfolio left it highly vulnerable to the sudden slump in rents and the soaring vacancy rates that marked the beginning of the 1990s.

Hammerson was hit hard by the crash in the worldwide property market that reached bottom in 1992. The company's angry shareholders, which had seen their investments cut in half, agreed to help the company raise new capital in a rights issue with the condition that Hammerson shed its management, including longtime leader Mason. Taking Mason's place in 1993 was industry veteran Ron Spinney, who previously had held the top position at rival property developer Greycoat.

REFOCUSING FOR THE 21ST CENTURY

Spinney placed Hammerson on an immediate diet, leading a vast sell-off of the company's holdings, including its entire Australian portfolio, AMP Limited, in 1994. Proceeds from that sale and from the sale of other properties in now noncore markets were placed in expanding Hammerson's U.K. portfolio and developing

KEY DATES

1942: Lewis Hammerson sells garment business and begins real estate activity.

1948: L.W. Hammerson & Co. is incorporated.

1953: Reverse takeover of Associated Investment Trust is accomplished; company is listed on the London Stock Exchange; name changes to Hammerson Property and Investment Trust.

1958: Lewis Hammerson dies; Sydney Mason takes over company direction; shopping center development begins.

1993: Ron Spinney takes over as CEO.

2009: Hammerson withdraws from Germany; CEO John Richards is succeeded by David Atkins.

its positions in just two carefully chosen foreign markets, those of Paris and Berlin. The company's choices were to prove the right ones as those two markets began a return to health by the middle of the decade. Meanwhile, the refocus on a smaller number of markets helped the company cut its costs, improving its profit margins. Hammerson coupled its property sales with the acquisition of new properties, enhancing its commercial and office building portfolio. In 1994 the company made a number of purchases. These included 99 Bishopsgate, which had been heavily damaged in an IRA bombing in 1993, and the £140 million cash and share purchase of six buildings from the PosTel post office pension fund.

The following year Hammerson began boosting its French holdings, focusing on Paris, with the acquisition of 54, Boulevard Haussmann, giving the company more than 10,000 square meters on one of the city's busiest shopping streets. Just outside of Paris, Hammerson bought a share in the Espace Saint Quentin shopping center, as well as a holding in the 3 Fontaines shopping center in Cergy-Pontoise. The company added another Parisian site, 40-46, rue de Courcelles, in 1996, paying £67 million.

In 1996 Hammerson boosted its small portfolio of German properties with the acquisition of a controlling interest in Berlin's Markisches Zentrum shopping complex, for the purchase price of £81.5 million. Hammerson extended its new growth strategy not only to the acquisition of existing buildings but to the development of new office and commercial complexes. One such development was the new London landmark building Globe House, a 20-story structure with a view of the Thames River.

The company also joined in with partners for the development of the ambitious Bull Ring development designed to revitalize the Birmingham city center. That development was slated to be completed by 2001. Unlike the company's property developments during the speculative 1980s, most of its new properties were pre-let before completion. Such was the case with Globe House, for example, which had already found BAT as its major tenant.

MERGER ATTEMPT

Hammerson attempted to gain weight in 1997. At that time the company began merger talks with U.K. rival MEPC, which held extensive holdings in the North American market. Although analysts greeted the idea of such a merger warmly, the merger fell through by the end of the year. Hammerson's realignment was more or less completed in 1998 when the company agreed to sell its Canadian assets, which accounted for some 17 percent of its total portfolio, to OMERS Realty Corp. for CAD 600 million. The company turned the proceeds of that sale toward boosting its presence in the Paris market, buying two Parisian shopping centers and their management, including the Italie 2 shopping complex. Back in the United Kingdom, Hammerson reached an agreement with Land Securities, then developing the Martineaux Galleries in Birmingham, to combine that structure with the Bull Ring development, creating a single shopping complex worth some £800 million. Soon after, Hammerson paid £83 million to buy Euston Square, in London, from Japanese company Kajima.

Spinney announced his intention to step down from day-to-day management of the company he had resurrected in May 1999. Taking instead a part-time position as company chairman, Spinney explained to the *Financial Times* in May 1999: "I am 58 years old and the business is just about in the shape that I want it to be. It is the first time I have been able to say to myself that there are no buildings in our portfolio which I wouldn't want to own." Spinney was replaced by John Richards, who had already been serving to coordinate the company's U.K. and European expansion efforts.

A NEW MILLENNIUM

Richards continued to guide Hammerson along the strategy developed by his predecessor. At the beginning of 2000 the company acquired a new Berlin site, the 28,000-square-meter Forum Steglitz shopping center. In

Paris the company acquired the office and retail property of Les Trois Quartiers for £127 million, and then a majority interest in the Bercy 2 shopping complex for £44 million.

The company's West Quay, Southampton shopping complex opened in September 2000. At the end of that year, Hammerson announced the start of construction of the One London Wall complex, a 19,300-square-meter office complex expected to be completed in 2003. Helping to finance these and future developments was the sale, in March 2001, of the company's refurbished rue de Courcelles building, to Munich Re in a deal worth £101 million.

Midway through 2001 Hammerson announced that it was acquiring a 50 percent ownership interest in Paris-based SCI Opera Capucines from the insurance group MAAF. By August 2002 the company's property portfolio was valued at approximately £3.54 billion. Retail properties comprised 63 percent of its portfolio, with offices accounting for 37 percent. The majority of Hammerson's properties (87 percent) were of an investment nature, while 13 percent were developments.

RETAIL FOCUS

Hammerson began 2003 by announcing plans to double its retail park portfolio. By midyear the company was preparing to develop a new town center in Kingston upon Thames in Surrey. After being selected as a preferred development partner by the Kingston Council, the company moved forward with the development of a master plan for the long-term project, which would include at least 500,000 square feet of mixed-use space.

Other developments in 2003 included the sale of the Stockport-based Merseyway Shopping Centre to Buckingham Securities for £128 million. In addition, Hammerson also partnered with Standard Life to acquire a £74 million retail park site in Brent Cross, North London, located across from its Brent Cross shopping center. Development of the site was scheduled to begin in early 2004.

Around the same time, Standard Life sold its 20 percent interest in Hammerson, leaving it with a 1.6 percent stake. Around the same time Hammerson concluded the £47.7 million sale of the former Lazards headquarters building in London. The 150,700-square-foot structure was purchased by the Gertner family.

COMPANY RECONSIDERS SPAIN AND ITALY

Progress continued in early 2004 when Hammerson acquired the site of the London Stock Exchange in a £68 million deal. By the middle of the year plans were underway to pursue a mixed-use, 500,000-square-foot development in Kingston upon Thames, Surrey, via a tie-up with the pension fund CIN. Around the same time the company announced that it was canceling plans to expand into Spain and Italy because the strategy would be cost-prohibitive.

By mid-2005 Hammerson was planning to expand the number of employees at its headquarters on Park Lane, where it had 127 staff members. The company began considering plans to relocate to 10 Grosvenor Street in London, where it eventually moved. That same year Hammerson acquired a two-acre site on the outskirts of London. Known as Northgate, the site was acquired for £4.1 million. The company had plans for a mixed-use development, which would include homes, as well as a hotel and office space.

Hammerson acquired the 72,000-square-foot, eight-story Stockley House office building in London for £71.4 million in mid-2007. By 2008 the company was pursuing plans to build a 51-story, 1.5 million-square-foot tower in the London Borough of Hackney. However, roadblocks emerged after the Hackney Council delayed the company's plans, which involved demolishing a pub called the Light Bar. The council was considering whether or not to include the pub in a conservation area, which would derail Hammerson's development plans.

LEADERSHIP CHANGES

By mid-2009 Hammerson was preparing to withdraw from Germany by selling the Berlin-based shopping center Forum Steglitz to Europa Capital Partners. Another pivotal development took place when, after a 10-year stint at the company's helm, CEO John Richards announced that he would retire at the end of September. Succeeding Richards was 43-year-old David Atkins.

Hammerson partnered with Germany-based Allianz in 2010 in a joint venture formed for the purpose of operating a shopping center named Espace Saint Quentin in France. It also was in 2010 that Hammerson agreed to divest its 51 percent stake in the French shopping center O'Parinor to the National Pension Service of Korea. The deal was valued at $278.5 million. In July 2011 Hammerson announced that the Borough of Hackney had granted its approval for Principal Place, a new proposal to construct a 16-story office building, as well as a residential tower containing 243 apartments. Restaurants and retail sites were to be part of a street-level area, which also included the restoration of the Light Bar, which had complicated Hammerson's initial plans to develop a 51-story tower in Hackney.

It also was in 2011 that Martin Jepson, who led the company's London Group, tendered his resignation. Jepson was temporarily succeeded by Chief Investment Officer Peter Cole. After nearly seven decades of operations, Hammerson appeared to be in a strong position as the company headed into 2012.

M. L. Cohen
Updated, Paul R. Greenland

PRINCIPAL SUBSIDIARIES

Hammerson (99 Bishopsgate) Ltd.; Hammerson (Brent Cross) Ltd.; Hammerson (Bristol Investments) Ltd.; Hammerson Bull Ring Ltd.; Hammerson (Cramlington 1) Ltd.; Hammerson Group Management Ltd.; Hammerson Operations Ltd.; Hammerson (Leicester) Ltd.; Hammerson Oracle Investments Ltd.; Hammerson (Silverburn) Ltd.; Union Square Developments Ltd.; West Quay Shopping Centre Ltd.; Hammerson International Holdings Ltd.; Hammerson UK Properties plc.; Grantchester Holdings Ltd.; Hammerson (125 OBS LP) Ltd.; Hammerson (60 Threadneedle Street) Ltd.; Hammerson SAS (France); Hammerson Holding France SAS; Hammerson Centre Commercial Italie SAS (France); Hammerson Faubourg Saint-Honoré SAS (France); Société Civile de Développement du Centre Commercial de la Place des Halles SDPH (France; 64.5%); Hammerson Europe BV (Netherlands); Hammerson GmbH (Germany).

PRINCIPAL COMPETITORS

Burford Holdings Limited; Great Portland Estates plc; Peel Holdings (Management) Limited.

FURTHER READING

"Deal Snapshot: Hammerson Inks Mall JV with Allianz Real Estate." *M & A Navigator*, June 18, 2010.

"Hammerson Buys Exchange Site." *Property Week*, April 8, 2004, 8.

Heap, Richard. "Portfolio in a Storm: In His First Interview since Taking over Hammerson's London Portfolio, Martin Jepson Talks to Richard Heap about Obstacles and Opportunities Ahead." *Property Week*, September 12, 2008, 74.

Hipwell, Deirdre. "Hammerson Close to Exit from Germany: Last German Asset under Offer to Europa Capital Partners for 70m [Euro]." *Property Week*, May 15, 2009, 13.

"Ron Spinney to Step Down as Hammerson Chief." *Financial Times*, May 14, 1999.

Stevenson, Tom. "Hammerson Gets into Shape." *Independent*, March 19, 1996, 18.

Yates, Andrew, ed. "Hammerson Backs the Boom." *Independent*, March 17, 1998, 24.

HealthSouth Corporation

—■—

3660 Grandview Parkway, Suite 200
Birmingham, Alabama 35243
U.S.A.
Telephone: (205) 967-7116
Toll Free: (800) 765-4772
Fax: (205) 969-3543
Web site: http://www.healthsouth.com

Public Company
Incorporated: 1984 as Amcare, Inc.
Employees: 23,000
Operating Revenues:$1.99 billion (2010)
Stock Exchanges: New York
Ticker Symbol: HLS
NAICS: 621498 All Other Outpatient Care Centers

■ ■ ■

With a presence in 26 states and Puerto Rico, Health-South Corporation ranks as the largest owner and operator of inpatient rehabilitation hospitals nationwide. The company's customers include patients who are recovering from illnesses and injuries in a wide range of categories, including orthopedic, neurological, cardiac, and pulmonary conditions. HealthSouth's operations include inpatient rehabilitation hospitals, outpatient rehabilitation clinics, and home health services.

NEW TWIST ON REHABILITATION SERVICES

HealthSouth was the brainchild of Richard Scrushy. Scrushy grew up in Selma, Alabama, and earned a degree in respiratory therapy from the University of Alabama, Birmingham. By the age of 30 he had advanced to vice president at Lifemark Corp., a Houston-based health care management firm.

At Lifemark, Scrushy witnessed firsthand the changes sweeping the health care industry. The dominant trend was toward a reduction in reimbursement dollars available to traditional medical practitioners. Corporations and insurance companies were trying to cut health care expenditures while, at the same time, costs in the medical field were rising. "I saw the squeezing of reimbursement in the health care system and I wanted to take advantage of that change," Scrushy said in a June 1990 article in *Forbes*. "My idea," he added, "was to provide high-quality hospital-type rehabilitation services in a low-cost setting."

Scrushy got his chance to start his rehabilitation company in 1984, when Lifemark Corp. was purchased by Los Angeles-based American Medical International. Armed with a plan, Scrushy lacked only the money to get started. His break came in a Houston restaurant, when a Citicorp venture capitalist overheard Scrushy outlining his business plan and eventually offered a $1 million grubstake, giving birth to what would become HealthSouth.

PERFECT TIMING

Scrushy persuaded four of his Lifemark associates to break ranks with him and move to Birmingham to build the company's first outpatient facility. Their company was incorporated in January 1984 as Amcare Inc. The organization changed its name to HealthSouth Rehabilitation Corporation in May 1985.

Scrushy got into the rehabilitation industry at a good time. During the early 1980s people began to view rehabilitation as a means of reducing medical expenses. Specifically, rehabilitation could be used to minimize unnecessary, expensive surgeries. It also helped injured workers get back to their jobs more quickly, thus eliminating expensive workers' compensation and disability costs. As health and insurance professionals began to recognize those benefits, the use of rehabilitation services soared. Between 1982 and 1990, in fact, rehabilitation expenditures increased at an average annual rate of about 20 percent and the number of outpatient rehabilitation centers soared. That industry growth contributed to healthy gains for HealthSouth throughout the decade.

A UNIQUE STRATEGY

Perhaps more important than general industry expansion for HealthSouth during the 1980s was Scrushy and his fellow managers' unique operating strategy. When HealthSouth got started in 1984, rehabilitation centers were stereotyped as drab, institution-like facilities with, generally, mediocre staff. Scrushy wanted to change that image.

Borrowing from health clubs, he designed his rehab centers as bright, open-spaced, mirrored rooms with trained physical therapists and sporty equipment. The centers more closely resembled high-priced health clubs than traditional hospital-styled rehab centers, and doctors became increasingly willing to send patients to a HealthSouth facility for treatment. Scrushy added a few more HealthSouth outlets and by 1985 was generating nearly $5 million in annual revenues. HealthSouth added new rehab centers to its chain throughout the middle and late 1980s. Because of the company's unique recipe for success, its centers became known as effective and cost-efficient, and as models for other

companies in the rehab industry. Rather than focusing on a specific rehab niche, such as head or spinal injuries, HealthSouth differed from many of its competitors in that it targeted the larger market for less-expensive, general outpatient rehabilitation services.

HealthSouth's facilities were built around a large gymnasium, in which some patients rode exercise bikes while listening to rock music. Old and young people worked out side by side, often with the help of a therapist, while others received physical, occupational, or speech therapy in private treatment rooms. Some of the machines even were hooked to computers that fed reports to doctors about how patients were responding to treatment.

FOCUSED PROGRAMS

HealthSouth appealed to the medical community by offering a number of rehabilitation programs tailored for different ailments. At the urging of Dr. Scott Burke, a Denver spinal rehabilitation specialist, HealthSouth designed a program to treat back problems. Widely used, the whole package cost only $3,700, which was much less than the patient might otherwise spend on unnecessary surgeries and hospital costs. HealthSouth also began offering special services for the lucrative sports rehabilitation market. To that end, HealthSouth eventually launched an entire sports division with separate facilities and prominent doctors. Dr. Jim Andrews, one of HealthSouth's most renowned surgeons, treated such celebrities as Bo Jackson, Jane Fonda, and Charles Barkley.

While HealthSouth kept the doctors and patients happy with state-of-the-art facilities, it stayed on the good side of the insurance companies by minimizing overhead and treatment costs. It saved money on construction, for example, by using the same basic floor plan and architecture for all of its outpatient centers, including the same carpeting, wallpaper, and furniture. Because the centers processed so many patients (about 15 to 20 per hour, or roughly 200 a day at many HealthSouth facilities), the average cost of a visit was kept at a low $50 to $90. Insurers did not blink at the cost, because it was much less expensive than traditional treatment. A study conducted by Northwestern National Life Insurance Co. estimated that every $1 spent on rehabilitation saved about $30 on disability benefits.

By 1988, two years after going public, HealthSouth was operating a network of 21 outpatient facilities, 11 inpatient facilities, and 7 rehabilitation equipment centers in 15 states, making it a leader in the U.S. rehabilitation industry. Sales had spiraled upward at an average of more than 100 percent annually since 1984,

KEY DATES

1984: Richard Scrushy and four partners form Amcare Inc.

1985: Company changes name to HealthSouth Rehabilitation Corporation.

1986: Company goes public.

1994: HealthSouth surpasses the $1 billion mark in revenues.

2003: Government regulators find the company guilty of overstating earnings by $2.7 billion.

2004: Jay Grinney is named CEO; company finalizes a $325 million settlement with the Justice Department and Department of Health and Human Services over alleged Medicare fraud.

2007: HealthSouth sells its diagnostic, outpatient surgery, and outpatient rehabilitation divisions.

2011: Company's long-term acute care hospital business is sold.

peaking at $75 million in 1988. Revenues shot up to $114 million in 1989 and then to $181 million in 1990, about $13 million of which was netted as income.

In fact, HealthSouth managed to post successive profits every year after 1985. Aside from increasing its customer base at existing centers, the company grew by purchasing other rehab and health care companies and restructuring them to fit into the HealthSouth organization. It was in December 1989, for example, that Scrushy jumped into the sports rehab business when he paid $21 million for a 219-bed general hospital in Birmingham that specialized in orthopedic surgery and sports medicine.

RAPID GROWTH

By the mid-1990s HealthSouth was operating 14 inpatient and 31 freestanding outpatient rehabilitation centers in 21 states. The company continued to add new general rehabilitation centers to its chain in 1991 and 1992. Meanwhile, its specialized sports business flourished and it enjoyed success with its new orthopedic hospitals that featured leading surgeons.

By 1992 HealthSouth had established itself as one of two leaders in the U.S. rehabilitation industry. Its chief nemesis was Continental Medical Systems Inc., of Pennsylvania. Continental, with $20 million in net

earnings in 1991 compared with $22 million for HealthSouth, generated most of its profit from rehabilitation service contracts with hospitals, schools, and nursing homes. Like HealthSouth, it operated inpatient and outpatient rehab centers across the country. Continental and HealthSouth nearly merged in 1992. The resulting company would have been a $2 billion concern had the deal not fallen through. Instead, HealthSouth remained independent and went on to become the largest provider of rehabilitative services in the nation. It attained that status through an aggressive merger and acquisition agenda advanced during the early and mid-1990s.

Chief among its acquisitions was the purchase of National Medical Enterprises Inc. in December 1993. That pivotal buyout added 31 inpatient rehabilitation facilities and 12 outpatient rehabilitation centers to HealthSouth's portfolio, boosting the total number of outpatient centers in its chain from 126 at the end of 1992 to 171 going into 1994. Evidencing the effectiveness of HealthSouth's strategy was a substantial improvement in the performance of National Medical's facilities in the two years following the acquisition.

HealthSouth's revenues for 1993 surged impressively to $575 million and the company assumed the industry lead. HealthSouth achieved its dazzling gains during the early 1990s, in part, by focusing on rehabilitating people who were injured rather than chronically ill. That was the primary growth market, because employers and insurance companies were eager to move those individuals out of the health care system.

HealthSouth's Workstart program was a good example of its core service. The Workstart plan was designed to get most workers back on the job after surgery or an injury within 30 days at an average cost of just $2,700. The program was ideal for employers because HealthSouth, using advanced testing and statistical analysis, was able to determine the extent of the patients' pain and injury. Among other benefits, that kind of analysis discouraged faking or exaggerating the extent of injuries to take advantage of disability payment programs.

ACQUISITIONS INTENSIFY

HealthSouth stepped up its acquisition program in 1994 and 1995 by absorbing a number of new companies. Two major purchases included the September 1994 acquisition of ReLife Inc. and the February 1995 buyout of NovaCare, Inc.'s inpatient rehabilitation hospital division. ReLife brought 31 inpatient rehabilitation facilities and 12 outpatient centers that added roughly $119 million in annual revenues to HealthSouth's income statement.

That and other acquisitions helped to push Health-South's sales past the $1 billion mark to $1.13 billion in 1994. Furthermore, net income vaulted to $53.23 million and the company's stock price raced to a record level. Following the NovaCare acquisition, the company's total network rose to more than 425 facilities located in 33 states.

HealthSouth sustained its aggressive growth drive throughout 1995, snapping up several smaller competitors. Significantly, in October 1995 Health-South announced that it had agreed to purchase the rehabilitation services operations of Caremark International for $127 million in cash. The Caremark operations consisted of 123 outpatient rehabilitation facilities that were generating about $80 million in annual revenues. That gave the company a total of about 440 outpatient facilities and about 40 percent of the total rehabilitation market.

HealthSouth also bought Diagnostic Health Corporation, which offered outpatient imaging services. Perhaps most notable was the early 1995 acquisition of Surgical Health Corporation, which represented Health-South's diversification into an entirely new market: outpatient surgery services. The $1.1 billion acquisition, the company's largest to date, immediately catapulted HealthSouth into the lead as the top operator of outpatient surgery centers in the nation.

CONTINUING DIVERSIFICATION, NEW CHALLENGES

HealthSouth's steady string of acquisitions did not end as the company headed into the second half of the decade. Purchases in 1996 included Surgical Care Affiliates, Inc., which controlled 67 outpatient surgery centers in 24 states, for an estimated $1.4 billion; Advantage Health Corporation, which owned about 136 inpatient and outpatient rehabilitation centers in 11 states, for about $315 million; Professional Sports Care Management, Inc., which included 36 outpatient rehabilitation centers in New York, New Jersey, and Connecticut, for about $59 million; and ReadiCare, Inc., which operated 37 occupational health centers in Washington and California, for about $76 million.

The following year HealthSouth acquired Health Images, Inc., which owned 55 diagnostic imaging centers in the United Kingdom and 13 states in the United States; ASC Network Corporation, which operated 29 surgery centers in eight states; and National Imaging Affiliates, Inc., which ran eight diagnostic imaging centers in six states. The most significant acquisition, however, was the purchase of Horizon/CMS Healthcare, the largest provider of specialty health care

services in the United States. The transaction included 30 inpatient rehabilitation centers and about 275 outpatient rehabilitation centers, in addition to other businesses. After completing the deal, HealthSouth sold Horizon's 139 long-term care facilities, 12 specialty hospitals, 35 institutional pharmacies, and more than 1,000 rehabilitation therapy contracts to Integrated Health Services, Inc.

In 1998 HealthSouth made two major acquisitions. The firm purchased National Surgery Centers, Inc., which operated 40 surgical facilities in 14 states, and also acquired 34 surgery centers from Columbia/HCA Healthcare Corporation. To focus on its core operations, HealthSouth decided in 1998 to sell its nonstrategic businesses, including its home health operations. HealthSouth's numerous acquisitions had significantly strengthened and expanded its dominance and presence in rehabilitative and outpatient surgery services, and by the end of the year HealthSouth had nearly 1,900 centers in 50 states, the United Kingdom, and Australia.

NEW CHALLENGES

Despite HealthSouth's leadership position and long history of steady earnings growth, the company faced new challenges in the late 1990s that cut into its profits. The federal government's Balanced Budget Act of 1997 placed new restrictions on Medicare, which resulted in lower reimbursements for some medical services. A significant portion of HealthSouth's revenues came from Medicare, and the new legislation led to decreasing reimbursements for HealthSouth. In addition, managed care companies and health maintenance organizations (HMOs) were growing in number and power, and their attempts to lower reimbursement costs to health care providers posed a serious threat to HealthSouth, which received 60 percent of its total revenue from managed care.

In October 1998 HealthSouth announced that earnings growth was slowing to 15 to 20 percent from 30 percent a year. As a result, the company's stock tumbled from a high of about $30 per share during the summer to less than $8. HealthSouth's founder and CEO was undaunted, however. Scrushy noted that growth of between 15 and 20 percent a year was quite acceptable and commented that same month on the share price erosion in the *Wall Street Journal*. "It's all paper," Scrushy stated, adding, "I'm very calm."

HealthSouth continued to face difficulties in 1999. In June the company announced plans to divide its inpatient and outpatient operations by spinning off the inpatient services into a new company, to be called HealthSouth Hospital Corporation. The strategy would have allowed HealthSouth to concentrate on its more profitable outpatient operations, but in September the corporation decided to postpone its plans.

HealthSouth also stated that it expected operating profit margins to fall lower than forecast during the third and fourth quarters of 1999. The company said it would take charges of between $250 million and $300 million. As a result, share prices dropped to a low of $4.56 per share. For the third quarter of 1999 Health-South reported revenues of $993.3 million, down from $1.05 billion during the comparable period of 1998. The overall picture was not necessarily bleak, however, and for the nine months ended September 30, 1999, HealthSouth's revenues were $3.07 billion, up from $2.97 billion in the same period of 1998.

Hoping to rise above its recent problems, Health-South endeavored to strengthen and continue building its empire. The company acquired American Rehability Services, which operated outpatient rehabilitation centers in 18 states, from Mariner Post-Acute Network, Inc., in July 1999. HealthSouth also formed a partnership with WebMD, Inc., a provider of health care information on the Internet, and Healtheon Corporation, a provider of electronic commerce services related to the health care industry, to develop and operate a channel dedicated to sports medicine issues on the WebMD Web site.

A NEW MILLENNIUM

HealthSouth's new online channel was launched in early 2000. It offered sports medicine information, links to HealthSouth centers, interactive chat events with physicians and celebrity athletes, and online communities. The venture extended the company's online presence and significantly raised its brand recognition.

In early 2000 HealthSouth operated 125 rehabilitation hospitals, as well as 1,900 outpatient surgery and rehabilitation locations. The company began the new millennium by establishing a new strategic investment division. Chief Financial Officer Michael Martin was promoted to lead the new division, while Controller William Owens was elevated to the CFO position. In August 2001 the company formed a brand marketing partnership with Mandalay Advertising and Mandalay Sports Entertainment.

By late 2002 HealthSouth indicated that, because of reduced Medicare reimbursements, its earnings were suffering. To rectify the situation, plans to spin off the company's outpatient surgery center business were announced. However, when investors and lenders balked, the plan failed to materialize.

SERIOUS TROUBLE

Major problems emerged at HealthSouth in early 2003 when the Securities and Exchange Commission charged both the company and Scrushy with overstating earnings by $1.4 billion. The Justice Department became involved, and by July a dozen former HealthSouth executives had pleaded guilty. Ultimately, regulators found additional evidence of accounting fraud dating back to 1996, indicating that the company overstated its earnings by as much as $2.7 billion. In November Scrushy was indicted on 85 counts of money laundering, conspiracy, and fraud.

The restructuring specialist Alvarez & Marsal was tasked with restoring HealthSouth. Managing Director Guy Sansone carried out the difficult task of negotiating with banks, bondholders, and the government. In May 2004 HealthSouth named Jay Grinney as its new CEO. By late 2004 the company was ready for a fresh start, with a new board of directors, new management, $600 million in cash, additional bank financing, and importantly, financial safeguards to help prevent future accounting irregularities.

In late 2004 HealthSouth took another important step in its recovery. At that time the company finalized a $325 million settlement with the Justice Department and the Department of Health and Human Services' inspector general's office. By doing this HealthSouth settled lawsuits pertaining to alleged Medicare fraud that had occurred on the previous management team's watch.

Although he did not participate in decision-making matters, former Chairman and CEO Scrushy continued to hold a seat on HealthSouth's board of directors in mid-2005, along with a 1 percent ownership stake valued at approximately $20 million. After being found not guilty in his criminal trial, Scrushy announced that he would attempt to reclaim his spot as HealthSouth's CEO. However, the proposed reinstatement was opposed by investors and the company's new leadership, and failed to materialize. Ultimately, Scrushy relinquished his board seat and severed ties with HealthSouth.

DIVESTITURES

In early 2006 HealthSouth revealed plans to reduce its long-term debt via the sale of the company's diagnostic, outpatient surgery, and outpatient rehabilitation divisions. The company announced plans to conduct a one-for-five reverse stock split and regain a listing on the New York Stock Exchange. In early 2007 Select Medical Corp. agreed to acquire HealthSouth's outpatient rehabilitation division in a $245 million deal. In addition, Texas Pacific Group agreed to acquire its outpatient surgery division for $945 million. Finally, The Gores Group agreed to acquire HealthSouth's diagnostic division for approximately $47.5 million.

HealthSouth moved forward with a focus on inpatient rehabilitation services. CEO Jay Grinney acquired $2 million worth of HealthSouth stock, or approximately 115,000 shares, in August 2007. In early 2008 the company announced the sale of its 104-acre, 200,000-square-foot headquarters complex in Birmingham, Alabama, to Daniel Corp. for $43.5 million. As part of the deal, HealthSouth agreed to lease back the facility.

By mid-2009 HealthSouth was seeking opportunities for strategic growth. Plans were made to begin offering hospice services and expand the company's post-acute care business. An important leadership change took place in mid-2010 when Douglas E. Coltharp was named chief financial officer.

RETURN TO GROWTH

HealthSouth entered a growth mode in 2010. In Las Vegas, the company agreed to acquire Desert Canyon Rehabilitation Hospital. This was followed by an announcement to build a new inpatient rehabilitation hospital in Houston, Texas. Finally, HealthSouth ended 2010 by receiving preliminary state approval to construct a new inpatient rehabilitation hospital in Ocala, Florida. In August 2011 HealthSouth sold its long-term acute care hospital business, which included facilities in five states, to LifeCare Holdings Inc., in a $117.5 million deal. In October the company secured state approval to build a comprehensive medical rehabilitation hospital in Martin County, Florida, via a tie-up with Martin Memorial Health System. The company moved forward as the largest inpatient rehabilitation hospital owner/operator in the nation. After withstanding significant challenges, HealthSouth had restored its reputation and was positioned for success in 2012 and beyond.

Dave Mote
Updated, Mariko Fujinaka; Paul R. Greenland

PRINCIPAL SUBSIDIARIES

Advantage Health Harmarville Rehabilitation Corporation; Advantage Health, LLC; AnMed Enterprises, Inc.; HealthSouth, LLC; BJC/HEALTHSOUTH Rehabilitation Center, LLC; Beaumont Rehab Associates Limited Partnership; Central Arkansas Rehabilitation Associates, L.P.; CMS Jonesboro Rehabilitation, Inc.; CMS Rehab

of WF, LP; CMS Topeka Rehabilitation, Inc.; Central Louisiana Rehab Associates LP; Collin County Rehab Associates Limited Partnership; Continental Medical of Arizona, Inc.; Continental Medical Systems, Inc.; Continental Rehabilitation Hospital of Arizona, Inc.; HCA Wesley Rehabilitation Hospital, Inc.; HCS Limited; HealthSouth/GHS, LLC; HealthSouth/Maine Medical Center Limited Liability Company; HealthSouth Aviation, LLC; HealthSouth-Cypress Real Estate, LLC; HEALTHSOUTH LTAC of Sarasota, Inc.; HealthSouth Mesa Rehabilitation Hospital, LLC; HEALTHSOUTH OF HENDERSON, INC.; HealthSouth of Mechanicsburg, Inc.; HealthSouth of Midland, Inc.; HealthSouth of Sarasota Limited Partnership; HEALTHSOUTH OF SEA PINES LIMITED PARTNERSHIP; HEALTHSOUTH OF YORK, LLC; HealthSouth Owned Hospitals Holdings, LLC; HEALTHSOUTH of Yuma, Inc.; HEALTHSOUTH Properties, LLC; HEALTHSOUTH Real Estate, LLC; HEALTHSOUTH Real Property Holding, LLC; HEALTHSOUTH Rehabilitation Center, Inc.; HealthSouth Rehabilitation Hospital of Arlington Limited Partnership; HealthSouth Rehabilitation Hospital of South Jersey, LLC; HEALTHSOUTH Specialty Hospital, Inc.; HEALTHSOUTH Sub-Acute Center of Mechanicsburg, Inc.; HEALTHSOUTH of Altoona, LLC; HEALTHSOUTH of Austin, Inc.; HEALTHSOUTH of Dothan, Inc.; HealthSouth of East Tennessee, LLC; HEALTHSOUTH of Erie, LLC; HEALTHSOUTH of Fort Smith, LLC; HEALTHSOUTH of Houston, Inc.; HEALTHSOUTH of Montgomery, Inc.; HEALTHSOUTH of Pittsburgh, LLC; HEALTHSOUTH of Reading, LLC; HEALTHSOUTH of San Antonio, Inc.; HEALTHSOUTH of Sewickley, Inc.; HEALTHSOUTH of South Carolina, Inc.; HEALTHSOUTH of Spring Hill, Inc.; HEALTHSOUTH of Tallahassee Limited Partnership; HEALTHSOUTH of Texarkana, Inc.; HEALTHSOUTH of Texas, Inc.; HEALTHSOUTH of Toms River, LLC; HEALTHSOUTH of Utah, Inc.; HEALTHSOUTH/Deaconess, LLC; HealthSouth/Maine Medical Center Limited Liability Company; HEALTHSOUTH/Methodist Rehabilitation Hospital Limited Partnership; HealthSouth of Ft. Lauderdale Limited Partnership; HealthSouth of Midland, Inc.; HealthSouth of Nittany Valley, Inc.; HealthSouth of Treasure Coast, Inc.; Healthsouth Bakersfield Rehabilitation Hospital Limited Partnership; Healthsouth Meridian Point Rehabilitation Hospital Limited Partnership; Healthsouth Northern Kentucky Rehabilitation Hospital Limited Partnership; HealthSouth Rehabilitation Center of New Hampshire, Ltd.; HealthSouth Rehabilitation Hospital of Altoona, LLC; Healthsouth Rehabilitation Hospital of Arlington Limited Partnership; HealthSouth Rehabilitation

Hospital of Desert Canyon, LLC; HealthSouth Rehabilitation Hospital of Gadsden, LLC; HealthSouth Rehabilitation Hospital of Manati, LLC; HealthSouth Rehabilitation Hospital of New Mexico, Inc.; Health-South Rehabilitation Hospital of Northern Virginia, Inc.; HealthSouth Rehabilitation Institute of Tucson, LLC; HealthSouth Valley of the Sun Rehabilitation Hospital Limited Partnership; Healthsouth of Largo Limited Partnership; Healthsouth of Sarasota Limited Partnership; K.C. Rehabilitation Hospital, Inc.; Kansas Rehabilitation Hospital, Inc.; Lakeshore System Services of Florida, Inc.; Lakeview Rehabilitation Group Partners; New England Rehabilitation Management Co, LLC; New England Rehabilitation Services of Central Massachusetts, Inc.; HealthSouth Specialty Hospital of North Louisiana, LLC; Piedmont HealthSouth Rehabilitation, LLC; Plano Health Associates LP; Rebound, LLC; Rehab Concepts Corporation; Rehabilitation Hospital Corporation of America, LLC; Rehabilitation Hospital of Colorado Springs, Inc.; Rehabilitation Hospital of Fredericksburg, Inc.; Rehabilitation Hospital of Nevada–Las Vegas, Inc.; Rehabilitation Hospital of Nevada–Las Vegas, LP; Rehabilitation Hospital of Petersburg, Inc.; Rehabilitation Hospital of Phoenix City, LLC; Rehabilitation Hospital of Plano, Inc.; Rehabilitation Institute of Western Massachusetts, Inc.; Rusk Rehabilitation Center, LLC; Sarasota LTAC Properties, LLC; Saint Barnabas/HEALTHSOUTH Rehab Center LLC; SCA-Dalton, Inc.; Sherwood Rehabilitation Hospital, Inc.; Southeast Texas Rehabilitation Hospital, Inc.; Southern Arizona Regional Rehabilitation Hospital, LP; Tarrant County Rehabilitation Hospital, Inc.; Trident Neuro-Sciences Center, LLC; Tyler Rehab Associates LP; University of Virginia/HealthSouth, LLC; Van Matre Rehabilitation Center LLC; Vanderbilt Stallworth Rehabilitation Hospital, LP; West Virginia Rehabilitation Hospital, Inc.; Western Medical Rehab Associates, LP; Western Neuro Care, Inc.; Yuma Rehabilitation Hospital, LLC.

PRINCIPAL COMPETITORS

Kindred Healthcare, Inc.; RehabCare Group, Inc.; Select Medical Holdings Corporation.

FURTHER READING

Barr, Paul. "Scrushy Plots a Comeback; As HealthSouth Works Hard to Put a Fraud Scandal in the Past, Its Acquitted Founder Studies How He Can Regain the Company." *Modern Healthcare*, July 11, 2005, 6.

"HealthSouth Sells Diagnostic Unit to Gores Group for $47.5 Million." *Biomedical Business & Technology*, May 1, 2007.

Iyer, Savita. "Clean Bill of Health for HealthSouth, New Financing Ahead." *Bank Loan Report*, September 27, 2004.

Paris, Ellen. "Straighten That Back! Bend Those Knees!" *Forbes*, June 11, 1990, 92.

Sell, Molly Jackson. "HealthSouth Tumbles on Fraud Allegations." *Loan Market Week*, March 24, 2003, 1.

Sharpe, Anita. "HealthSouth Stock Plunges on Forecast." *Wall Street Journal*, October 1, 1998, A3.

"12th HealthSouth Executive Cooperates." *New York Times*, July 9, 2003, C5.

Zigmond, Jessica. "HealthSouth Ponders IPO for Surgery Centers; After Select Medical Deal, Chains Focus Will Be on Inpatient Rehabilitation." *Modern Healthcare*, February 5, 2007, 12.

HEICO Corporation

3000 Taft Street
Hollywood, Florida 33021-4441
U.S.A.
Telephone: (954) 987-4000
Fax: (954) 987-8228
Web site: http://www.heico.com

Public Company
Incorporated: 1957 as Heinicke Instruments Co.
Employees: 2,500
Sales: $764.89 million (2011)
Stock Exchanges: New York
Ticker Symbols: HEI; HEI.A
NAICS: 334511 Search, Detection, Navigation, Guidance, Aeronautical, and Nautical System and Instrument Manufacturing; 334519 Other Measuring and Controlling Device Manufacturing; 335912 Primary Battery Manufacturing; 336412 Aircraft Engine and Engine Parts Manufacturing; 336413 Other Aircraft Parts and Auxiliary Equipment Manufacturing; 488190 Other Support Activities for Air Transportation; 551112 Offices of Other Holding Companies

■ ■ ■

HEICO Corporation, through its Flight Support Group, is a major supplier of jet engine and aircraft component replacement parts. The company designs these parts, gains Federal Aviation Administration (FAA) approval for their use, and manufactures them for various customers, including Deutsche Lufthansa AG, AMR

Corporation (parent of American Airlines), Delta Air Lines, Inc., Japan Airlines Co., Ltd., and British Airways Plc. The Flight Support Group, which accounts for about 70 percent of HEICO's overall sales and is 20 percent owned by Lufthansa Technik AG (the technical services subsidiary of Deutsche Lufthansa), also repairs, overhauls, and distributes jet engine and aircraft parts for commercial air carriers, aircraft repair companies, and other customers.

The remaining 30 percent of HEICO's revenues is generated by the company's Electronics Technologies Group, which produces various niche electronic, microwave, and electro-optical products for defense contractors and commercial and defense satellite and spacecraft manufacturers. Members of the Mendelson family have managed HEICO since 1990, and the family also owns a substantial minority stake in the publicly traded company.

ORIGINS

HEICO was founded in 1957 as Heinicke Instruments Co., initially focusing on making products for medical laboratories. The company went public in 1960, and its stock was listed on the American Stock Exchange two years later. In 1974 Heinicke entered the aviation business with its purchase of Jet Avion Corporation, a manufacturer of jet engine parts. Five years later the Securities and Exchange Commission sued the company for misrepresenting its engineering expertise. Heinicke settled the suit and agreed to include more outside representation on its board.

In the early 1980s, Heinicke came under the control of Tyco Laboratories, Inc., a New Hampshire-based company that accumulated 46 percent of the company's stock. Tyco, aiming to use Heinicke to expand into the medical supplies market, installed Chester Warner as its CEO. Warner, who replaced the previous president, Rolf Franz, was an experienced laboratory products executive who reorganized the company and revitalized its offerings. Heinicke eventually bought back Tyco's shares.

Increasingly stringent FAA safety regulations, along with deregulated fares, boosted business in the mid-1980s. Earnings were $7.6 million in 1986 on sales of $46 million. Jet Avion accounted for two-thirds of sales. By this time, investors who had held the company's stock for the previous 10 years had seen a return of more than 1,000 percent.

The company changed its name from Heinicke Instruments Co. to HEICO Corporation in 1986. This prompted a 1989 lawsuit from Heico Inc., a manufacturing holding company based in Addison, Illinois, which asserted that the change caused "unnecessary confusion in the trade and financial communities." HEICO succeeded in holding on to its new namesake.

HEICO completed a secondary stock offering on the American Stock Exchange in January 1987. In October of that year, the company announced that plans to buy All Fab Corp. for $11 million fell through. All Fab, based in Everett, Washington, was an aerospace machining operation. At the same time, HEICO stated it was buying Germfree Laboratories Inc. of Miami. It also authorized a stock buyback.

BEGINNING OF MENDELSON ERA IN 1990

In 1988 HEICO was a takeover target for H Acquisition Corp., led by Chicago investor George Fox, who offered $75 million, or $30 a share for the company. An investor group led by Laurans A. Mendelson, a Miami-based real estate developer and stock investor, subsequently raised its shareholding from 9.9 percent to 13.6 percent of the company.

In 1989 the Mendelson group offered $42 million ($21 per share) for the rest of the company. In February the group planned a proxy fight to gain representation on the HEICO board. By December the group controlled four board seats, including one vacated by the resigning chairman and CEO, Robert Surtees. Mendelson was named CEO of HEICO in February 1990 and became chairman as well that year. Also that year, HEICO sold its laboratory business to Naperville, Illinois-based Varlen Corp. for $17 million. Later, in September 1992, a friend of Mendelson, Herbert Wertheim of Coral Gables, Florida, raised his stake in the company to 10.2 percent and requested two board seats.

As the global aviation industry stalled in the early 1990s, HEICO branched out, forming MediTek Health Corporation to enter the medical imaging field. The venture was short-lived. In June 1996 HEICO sold MediTek to U.S. Diagnostic, Inc. of West Palm Beach for $23.8 million.

SOLIDIFYING REPLACEMENT-PARTS NICHE VIA ACQUISITIONS

Sales and profits soared in the mid-1990s, buoyed by a recovering aerospace industry. Analysts praised the company's lean operation, which allowed HEICO to undersell the big engine manufacturers and earn loyalty among its airline clientele. In September 1996 HEICO bought Trilectron Industries, Inc. for $7 million in cash and $2.3 million in assumed debt. The Palmetto, Florida-based company made aircraft ground support equipment such as ground power units and air conditioning units and had annual sales of about $15 million.

In October 1997 Lufthansa Technik AG, the technical services subsidiary of Deutsche Lufthansa AG, invested $26 million in HEICO's Flight Support Group, buying a 20 percent stake in this main HEICO unit. The funds from this alliance enabled HEICO to accelerate the development of additional FAA-approved replacement parts for jet engines, an operation that, following the divestment of MediTek, had become HEICO's core business. Under the continued leadership of Mendelson, HEICO built this business up through acquisitions and organic growth.

On the acquisition front, HEICO in 1998 tried to obtain a controlling interest in Teleflex Lionel-Dupont

S.A. (TLD), a French manufacturer of aircraft and aircraft engine components, for stock worth $63 million (FRF 370 million). The French company had annual sales of about FRF 384 million. In September 1998, however, HEICO announced it would not be able to acquire TLD because of a competing bid.

HEICO acquired McClain International, Inc., a private maker of jet engine parts based in Atlanta, for $41 million in July 1998. Lufthansa provided $9 million to fund the purchase. McClain's annual sales were $11 million. The company was founded in 1962 by a World War II veteran pilot and had 60 employees.

HEICO's revenues rose from $63.7 million in fiscal 1997 to $95.4 million the following year. The company remained on the acquisition trail, seeking to further bolster its core operations. In October 1998 the company bought Associated Composite, Inc. of Miami, which specialized in the repair of exterior aircraft parts. Two months later came the purchase of Rogers-Dierks, Inc., a direct competitor of HEICO in the production of FAA-approved jet engine replacement parts.

During fiscal 1999, Lufthansa invested an additional $5 million in HEICO's Flight Support Group, bringing its total investment to $42 million while maintaining the same 20 percent stake. In January 1999 HEICO's Ground Support Group bought Radiant Power Corp. from Santa Ana, California-based Derlan, Inc., a subsidiary of Toronto-based Derlan Industries

Limited. Radiant Power had revenues of about $4 million in 1998 from the sale of backup power supplies and batteries for a variety of onboard applications. Radiant was known for its propane- or natural gas-based InfraTek aircraft deicing system, which produced specific wavelengths of radiant heat to remove snow and ice.

HITTING THE BIG BOARD IN 1999

After years on the American Stock Exchange, HEICO shares began trading on the New York Stock Exchange in January 1999. A secondary stock offering in February 1999 raised $64 million. The company's revenues had grown more than 50 percent annually over the previous five years.

HEICO continued its growth by acquisition strategy, announcing in May that its Flight Support Group had bought Miami-based Air Radio & Instruments Corp. The purchase cost $3.5 million and complemented HEICO's expertise in repairing and overhauling aircraft components. In June 1999 HEICO bought Turbine Kinetics, Inc. and AeroKinetics, Inc. of Glastonbury, Connecticut. Both manufactured jet engine replacement parts. Their addition to the HEICO fold increased the company's product line to 1,200 jet engine parts.

Several other acquisitions were completed in 1999 as well. Privately held Leader Tech, Inc., based in Tampa, was purchased through HEICO's renamed Electronics and Ground Support Group. Leader Tech was a 20-year-old manufacturer of electromagnetic and radio-frequency shielding for circuit boards. In a deal involving $28.9 million in cash and $4 million in assumed debt, HEICO acquired Corona, California-based Thermal Structures, Inc. and its Quality Honeycomb, Inc. affiliate. The acquired concerns were manufacturers of thermal insulation products and related components for the aerospace and defense industries. HEICO rounded out its 1999 deal-making with the September purchase of Santa Barbara Infrared, Inc., a producer of infrared simulation and test equipment for the defense and aerospace industries.

In September 2000, in a move designed to enable the company to focus more on its aerospace businesses, HEICO sold Trilectron to Hobart Brothers Company, a subsidiary of Illinois Tool Works Inc., in a deal valued at about $64 million. HEICO retained Radiant Power, however, and this subsidiary became part of a newly named Electronic Technologies Group, which also included Leader Tech and Santa Barbara Infrared. Also in 2000, HEICO settled a lawsuit brought against it in 1989 by United Technologies Corporation. The lawsuit claimed that HEICO's Jet Avion subsidiary had infringed on patents for the heat- and corrosion-resistant coatings used in the combustion chambers of Pratt & Whitney gas turbine engines. Through this settlement, HEICO received a permanent license to make and sell the parts that had been the subject of the litigation. The company, through its insurer, made a payment to United Technologies for this license.

The Electronic Technologies Group was expanded again in April 2001 when HEICO acquired Analog Modules, Inc. for $15.6 million. Based in Longwood, Florida, Analog produced certain components used in laser and electro-optical products such as laser rangefinder receivers. Later that year, HEICO acquired Cleveland-based Inertial Airline Services, Inc. for $25 million in cash and stock. Inertial specialized in repairing and overhauling inertial navigation systems for commercial and military aircraft.

FURTHER PARTNERSHIPS WITH AIRLINES

Also in 2001, HEICO entered into a joint venture with AMR Corporation, the parent of American Airlines, that was designed to accelerate HEICO's development and manufacturing of FAA-approved jet engine and aircraft component replacement parts. HEICO followed up on this deal (and its previous one with Lufthansa) by entering into long-term strategic alliances with United Airlines, Inc. (2002), Delta Air Lines, Inc. and Air Canada (2003), and Japan Airlines Co., Ltd. (2004). In each case, the airline agreed to purchase the existing replacement parts sold by HEICO on an exclusive basis. Each airline received a significant discount in return, while also agreeing to work with HEICO on the development of additional replacement parts not yet carried by HEICO. During this financially troubled time for the airline industry, air carriers were eager to partner with HEICO for the substantial savings that could be realized in comparison with the prices that original equipment manufacturers charged for replacement parts. Aided by these partnerships, HEICO by fiscal 2006 was developing about 400 new, FAA-approved parts per year, and it was offering to its customers a total of 5,100 replacement parts.

As these partnerships took shape, HEICO continued to pursue targeted acquisitions, keeping its eye out for modest deals that were strategically important but did not significantly increase the firm's debt load. In November 2005, for instance, HEICO acquired a 51 percent stake in Deer Park, New York-based Seal Dynamics LLC, a leading distributor and designer of FAA-approved hydraulic, pneumatic, mechanical, and electromechanical aircraft components.

Through deals such as this one and ongoing new product development efforts, HEICO was able to maintain a superior level of highly profitable growth. Profits for fiscal 2006, for example, jumped nearly 40 percent to $31.9 million, while revenues surged 45 percent to $392.2 million. With these record results, HEICO's sales and earnings had grown at an annual rate of about 19 percent since 1990, the year Mendelson assumed the company leadership. Also in 2006, HEICO was named one of *Forbes* magazine's "Best Small Companies," the first of six straight appearances on this annual list.

In May 2007 HEICO entered into another long-term strategic alliance centered on aircraft replacement parts with a major airline with British Airways Plc. Among the acquisitions completed that year was EMD Technologies Inc., a firm based near Montreal, Canada, that manufactured high-voltage energy generators for medical, baggage inspection, and industrial imaging systems. HEICO continued on its upward trajectory through fiscal 2008, when earnings were a record $48.5 million on sales of $582.3 million, also an all-time high. The following year, however, HEICO saw orders from airlines and other customers drop off significantly during the depths of the severe economic downturn, resulting in an uncommon occurrence at the company: a fall in sales, one totaling about 7.6 percent. Net income dropped 8 percent as well, totaling $44.6 million for the year.

RESUMING GROWTH UNDER MENDELSON LEADERSHIP

In October 2009 Eric A. Mendelson and Victor H. Mendelson were named copresidents of HEICO, with their father, Laurans Mendelson, retaining his long-standing positions as chairman and CEO. For a number of years, the two brothers had served as heads of the company's two main operating units, with Eric leading the Flight Support Group and Victor the Electronic Technologies Group. They continued to serve in these same capacities after being named copresidents. Also in October 2009, HEICO acquired the Seacom division of privately held Dukane Corporation. The unit, which was subsequently renamed Dukane Seacom, Inc., was the world's largest manufacturer of beacons used to locate aircraft cockpit voice recorders, flight data recorders, and other devices that have been submerged underwater.

In concert with organic growth centering on the addition of hundreds of additional replacement parts to its product offerings, HEICO continued to pursue targeted acquisitions similar to the Seacom deal. These were typically companies with annual revenues of anywhere from

$10 million to $30 million. Deals completed in fiscal 2011 included the December 2010 purchase of an 80.1 percent stake in Blue Aerospace LLC, a firm based in Tamarac, Florida, that supplied military aircraft parts and services, primarily to foreign military organizations allied with the United States.

Results for the fiscal year ending in October 2011 clearly showed that HEICO had resumed its sharply upward trajectory. With its net income of $72.8 million and sales of $764.9 million both representing all-time highs, HEICO could boast of a remarkable record since the beginning of the Mendelson era in 1990, including compound annual growth rates since that year of 17 percent in sales and 19 percent in net income. The company's shareholders reaped the benefits of this well-managed company, as HEICO in January 2012 paid its 67th consecutive semiannual dividend. By the end of fiscal 2011, a $1,000 investment in HEICO stock made in 1990 was worth more than $65,500.

Frederick C. Ingram
Updated, David E. Salamie

PRINCIPAL SUBSIDIARIES

Aero Design, Inc.; Aircraft Technology, Inc.; Analog Modules, Inc.; Connectronics Corp.; dB Control Corp.; DEC Technologies, Inc.; Dielectric Sciences, Inc.; Dukane Seacom, Inc.; EMD Technologies Incorporated (Canada); Engineering Design Team, Inc.; Flight Specialties Corp.; Future Aviation, Inc.; HEICO Aerospace Corporation; HEICO Aerospace Holdings Corp. (80%); HEICO Electronic Technologies Corp.; HVT Group, Inc.; Inertial Aerospace Services, Inc.; Jet Avion Corporation; Jetseal, Inc.; Leader Tech, Inc.; LPI Industries Corporation; Lumina Power, Inc.; McClain

International, Inc.; NIACC-Avitech Technologies Inc.; Prime Air, LLC; Radiant Power Corp.; Santa Barbara Infrared, Inc.; Seal Dynamics LLC; Sierra Microwave Technology, LLC; Sunshine Avionics LLC; Thermal Structures, Inc.; Turbine Kinetics, Inc.; VPT, Inc.; JetAvi Engineering Private Limited (India); Avisource Limited (UK); Prime Air Europe Limited (UK); Essex X-Ray & Medical Equipment Ltd. (UK).

PRINCIPAL OPERATING UNITS

Flight Support Group; Electronic Technologies Group.

PRINCIPAL COMPETITORS

GE Aviation; Hamilton Sundstrand Corporation; Honeywell Aerospace; Pratt & Whitney; Rolls-Royce Group plc.

FURTHER READING

Brannigan, Martha. "No Turbulence for Heico." *Miami Herald*, January 18, 2010, 4G.

Cordle, Ina Paiva. "Heico Teams with AMR." *Miami Herald*, May 24, 2001, 1C.

"Heico Exec Ups Direct, Indirect Ownership." *Miami Daily Business Review*, January 9, 2003.

Hemlock, Doreen. "From Last Resort to First Choice: Hollywood Firm's Generic Parts Have Transformed Industry." *South Florida Sun-Sentinel* (Fort Lauderdale), February 24, 2007, 1D.

Lubove, Seth H. "Heico Stays Cool under Pressure." *Florida Trend*, April 1989, 24+.

Mann, Joseph A., Jr. "Heico's Global Reach." *Miami Herald*, June 19, 2011.

Myers, Anika. "Cruising Along." *Miami Daily Business Review*, January 2, 2002.

Seemuth, Mike. "Family Members Sell Part of Heico Stock." *Miami Daily Business Review*, January 23, 2008, A3.

Henselite (Australia) Pty. Ltd.

320 Darebin Road
Fairfield, Victoria 3078
Australia
Telephone: (61 39) 488-0488
Fax: (61 39) 488-0401
Web site: http://www.henselite.com

Private Company
Founded: 1930
Employees: 45
Sales: $22.14 million (2010)
NAICS: 326199 All Other Plastics Product Manufacturing; 423910 Sporting and Recreational Goods and Supplies Merchant Wholesalers; 454390 Other Direct Selling Establishments

■ ■ ■

Henselite (Australia) Pty. Ltd. is the largest manufacturer and distributor of lawn bowls in the world, controlling 70 percent of the global market. Henselite produces its bowls at a manufacturing facility in Victoria, Australia. The company also sells a range of lawn bowling clothing and accessories. Henselite exports 60 percent of its lawn bowls, serving markets in Asia, Africa, North America, South America, and Europe. Australia accounts for approximately half of the global market for lawn bowls. The company is managed by the fourth generation of the Hensell family, Mark and Bruce Hensell.

ORIGINS

The asymmetric bowls used in the centuries-old sport of lawn bowls underwent profound changes during the evolution of the game to its modern standard. Bowls manufacture changed considerably, both in the material and in the production techniques used, but the object of the game remained the same through the centuries. A bowl is delivered, taking an arcing path because of its bias, toward a smaller object, a "jack." However many bowls are closer to the jack than the opponent's bowls determines the score in that direction of play, an "end." Played on a smooth, manicured rectangle of grass, the sport demands precision and consistency from a bowler, the same qualities demanded of a bowls manufacturer.

During the 18th and 19th centuries, the common material used to make bowls was lignum vitae, a hard, dense wood brought to the birthplace of bowls, the United Kingdom, following the voyages of Christopher Columbus. In England and Scotland, manufacturers such as John Jacques & Son, Thomas Taylor, and William Lindop, established between 1795 and 1850, used lignum vitae to produce bowls. Lignum vitae also was used in Australia, imported by colonists who had learned the game in the United Kingdom. In 1864 Alcock & Co., a Melbourne-based billiard table manufacturer, used its wood-turning expertise to turn several sets of bowls for the Melbourne Bowling Club, becoming the first manufacturer of bowls on the continent. It was there, at Alcock & Co., that the individual who would revolutionize the manufacture of bowls began his career.

WILLIAM DAVID HENSELL BEGINS HIS CAREER: 1898

William David Hensell was born in Richmond, Victoria, in 1882. He was apprenticed to the wood-turning trade at the age of 16 and joined Alcock & Co. when he was 18 years old. At Alcock & Co., he learned to turn wood into billiard balls under the tutelage of M. J. Wood, an avid lawn bowler who became the official bowls tester at Alcock & Co. The company was appointed official tester for the Western Australian Bowling Association two years after Hensell's arrival, which steered Hensell in a new direction. He was sent 1,700 miles west, to Perth, where he spent nearly seven years testing bowls for the Western Australian Bowling Association.

The science of testing the bias consistency of bowls was rudimentary at best when Hensell arrived in Perth. Bowlers and manufacturers desired a consistent bias for each bowl in a set of four bowls, an objective that was difficult to achieve in Hensell's era because of the peculiarities of wooden bowls and because of the methods and equipment used to test bowls. At the time Hensell arrived in Perth, bowls testers used a wooden chute placed atop a 12-foot-long billiard table to conduct their tests. The chute was designed to propel a bowl nine feet along the testing table, a distance approximately one-tenth the length taken by a bowl on a bowling green. The method gave only a crude approximation of the bias of a bowl because of the shorter distance. A bowl that passed the bias test on the testing table often performed erratically on the green and, likewise, a bowl that failed the bias test on the testing table often behaved consistently on the green.

Hensell addressed the flaws in testing methods after he left Perth. In 1908 Alcock & Co. needed to replace its tester for the New South Wales Bowling Association and turned to Hensell to fill the vacancy. Hensell moved from Perth to Sydney and began his pioneering work.

For the New South Wales Bowling Association, Hensell began using a 36-foot testing table, which gave a truer indication of a bowl's bias than the 12-foot table. He also grappled with the testing inconsistencies engendered by the wooden bowls. Climatic changes caused wooden bowls to shrink, causing them to wobble on the green and on the testing table. Hensell realized he needed a way to reshape shrunken bowls, prompting him to design the first Australian machine for reshaping bowls.

FROM WOOD TO RUBBER: 1918–30

With his work in Sydney, Hensell had begun to strive for perfection. He threw himself into the science of manufacturing bowls and of testing bowls, becoming an innovative force in the sport. After developing the first Australian machine to reshape wooden bowls, he began searching for new materials to produce bowls and gravitated toward composite materials. He studied various composites, devoting his nights and weekends to reading up on the subject, and determined that vulcanized, or hardened, rubber possessed the most desirable characteristics for consistency in bowls manufacture. After Hensell returned to Melbourne in 1918, a manager for Dunlop Rubber Co. brought his wooden bowls to Hensell for testing and the meeting led to groundbreaking work.

Hensell turned his research in composites from theoretical to practical and began making rubber bowls. After successfully producing 12, five-inch rubber bowls that tested perfectly, Hensell left Alcock & Co. in 1918 and entered into an arrangement with Dunlop to turn rubber balls into rubber bowls. Hensell established his own business in Melbourne, purchasing a testing table and turning plant, and set to work. Before the end of the year, the first rubber bowls in the world began appearing on bowling greens in Victoria, causing a sensation. Bowlers quickly embraced Hensell's creation, abandoning their wooden bowls in droves. Within five years, the importation of wooden bowls into Australia ceased and the country became an exporter of bowls as the popularity of Dunlop rubber bowls spread to New Zealand, South Africa, and other parts of the world.

Hensell worked under contract with Dunlop for a dozen years. By 1930, when only a small number of wooden bowls were in use on Australian greens, Hensell had turned and finished nearly 14,000 sets of Dunlop bowls. That year, Dunlop decided to take on all aspects of bowls manufacture at the company's factory in Montague, Victoria. Hensell's ties to the company were severed, presenting him with the opportunity to strike out on his own as a truly independent bowls manufacturer that same year.

HENSELL FORMS HENSELITE: 1930

In his new endeavor, Hensell had a partner, his son, Ray W. Hensell. Ray Hensell had been helping his father since shortly after the debut of rubber bowls, spending a decade learning the intricacies of bowls manufacture. The father-and-son team resolved to make a new type of bowl, a bowl made of a composite superior to rubber, and they began researching plastic materials. They settled on phenol formaldehyde, which a firm in Sydney had just begun to manufacture. The properties of the material were enticing, promising a durable product less affected by heat and climatic changes than the vulcanized rubber they had been using. One daunting challenge prevented the pair from moving forward with production, however, a technological dilemma that stood in the way of their goal to make a solid bowl without a core. The Hensells needed to make an object five inches thick, but no one had been able to mold phenol formaldehyde at a thickness greater than one-half inch.

Early experiments at molding a five-inch bowl failed, but the Hensells pressed forward. They enlisted the technical expertise of a Dr. Lang, a leading authority on phenol formaldehyde, and continued their pioneering work. Different formulas were developed and different manufacturing techniques were used before the trio succeeded in producing a solid, 3.5-pound, five-inch bowl, an impressive achievement that attracted interest throughout the global plastics industry.

Once the Hensells had produced their first one-piece plastic bowl with the assistance of Dr. Lang, they began outfitting their headquarters for the production of phenol formaldehyde bowls. Molds were made and a molding plant was installed, as the Hensells geared up to begin commercial production. In April 1931 the first sets of Henselite bowls were produced, a product line that included bowls available in black, mahogany, and chocolate colors. Inserted discs, which indicated the bias side of a bowl, also were available in several colors.

FROM RUBBER TO PLASTIC: 1931–39

The reaction to Henselite plastic bowls aped the reaction to Hensell's rubber bowls. The leading players in the country switched to the phenol formaldehyde sets, finding them to be more durable, more consistent bowls. Sales at Henselite grew, forcing Hensell to move to larger quarters to fulfill the increasing demand for his bowls. In 1937 he moved his headquarters, the third relocation of Henselite since 1930, to 16-22 Wreckyn Street, North Melbourne, where the company would remain into the 21st century.

The popularity of Henselite bowls soon spread outside Australia. At first, trial bowls were sent to South Africa, where they were embraced enthusiastically, encouraging the Hensells to be more aggressive in their distribution efforts. Henselite bowls soon were shipped to the United Kingdom, New Zealand, Canada, the United States, and a handful of other countries. The domestic and international growth fueled the rise of the company's sales. By the end of the 1930s the Hensells were selling more than 4,000 sets of bowls annually, becoming one of the largest manufacturers of bowls in the world.

POST-WORLD WAR II EXPANSION: 1946–80

The momentum achieved during Henselite's first decade of business was interrupted by the outbreak of World War II, but the company reemerged stronger than ever during the postwar economic boom period. Production of bowls at the company's factory ceased between 1942 and 1945. Its manufacturing operations were instead used to make plastic moldings for the turn-and-bank indicators on aircraft for the Royal Australian Air Force. William Hensell retired during the period, no longer taking an active roll in running the company after 1944. The responsibility for leading the company fell to his son, who designed and installed a new molding plant that incorporated a new process of electronic preheating as well as a series of automatic, high-precision turning and biasing machines. Production commenced in 1946 with new manufacturing operations capable of producing 10,000 sets of bowls per year. Demand outpaced supply and the company was forced to expand its operations again, enabling it to sell 20,000 sets in 1948, four times the total produced less than a decade earlier.

The following decade, Ray Hensell was joined by his two sons in running the business, which operated under the name R.W. Hensell & Sons Pty. Ltd. Growth continued during the 1950s, lifting annual production to more than 33,000 sets by the end of the decade. Remodeling efforts added another floor to the Henselite complex at the beginning of the 1960s, giving the company additional production space as well as room for a suite of offices.

Ray Hensell, after more than a half-century of involvement in the business of making bowls, retired in 1976. His sons, representing the third generation of Hensells, took the reins of command and quickly steered the company in a new direction. Henselite began distributing an array of sporting goods in Australia in 1977, adding showrooms and warehouses to accommodate the diversification two years later. The production of lawn bowls remained its mainstay business, however, a business that reached an impressive milestone in 1980. In March, the company produced its four millionth bowl, completing its one millionth set of Henselites. The brand had developed into an international force, having penetrated markets in North America, Europe, South America, Africa, and Asia.

A BIAS FOR EVERY MARKET: 1988–2000

The era of modern lawn bowling demanded innovation from bowls manufacturers such as Henselite. The era began in 1988 with the introduction of the World Biased Bowls (W.B.B.) Rules, which paved the way for the emergence of narrow biased bowls, bowls that took a narrower line to the jack than their predecessors. The increasing pace of bowling greens, or green speeds, drove the movement for narrow biased bowls. The faster the green, the greater the severity of the arc a bowl traveled, and the bigger its draw. As greenskeeping techniques improved, greens became faster, leading bowlers to call for a bowl that took a more direct path to the jack. Since 1930 Henselite had produced various models, but each model had the same bias, a bias designated by the company as the Henselite Standard Bias. After the adoption of the W.B.B. Rules, Henselite rebranded its Standard Bias as the Henselite Classic and released the Henselite Classic II, a bowl with a narrower bias than the Henselite Classic.

The introduction of the Classic II was a comprehensive success, quickly becoming the bowl of choice on faster greens. The enthusiastic response to a bowl with a different bias led Henselite to begin developing a range of bowls with differing bias profiles, profiles designed for different geographic markets. Green speeds varied from country to country because of climatic conditions, with the hot, arid conditions common in Australia demanding a narrow biased bowl and the damp, cool conditions common in England demanding a wider biased bowl. New models tailored for specific markets began to appear, greatly expanding the Henselite product lineup. The Maestro bowl debuted in 1992, followed by the ABT-2000 in 1994, two models that were narrower than the Classic II.

HENSELITE IN THE 21ST CENTURY: 2000–11

Henselite moved to a new headquarters location at the beginning of the 21st century, unable to effectively manage its business at its North Melbourne factory because of its volume of business. In 2002 the company moved eight kilometers north of downtown Melbourne to the suburb of Fairfield, where larger quarters enabled more efficient manufacturing and distribution operations. New product introductions followed in 2003, including the debut of the Dreamline, a narrow biased bowl that became one of the world's most popular model of bowls, and the release of the Tiger, a model intended for the U.K. market. The company also began making colored bowls during the year, releasing blue, green, and burgundy models.

Henselite held sway as the largest manufacturer and distributor of bowls in the world at the end of the decade, controlling 70 percent of the global market. In 2008 the company became the first manufacturer to produce seven million bowls, continuing to set benchmarks for other bowls manufacturers to chase. New models made their entry into the market as the decade wound to a close. The Alpha, designed for fast synthetic greens, was released in 2009 and a new version of the Dreamline, the Dreamline XG, was introduced in 2011. In the years ahead, further innovations and new models were expected to appear as the largest bowls manufacturer in the world looked to maintain its leadership position.

Jeffrey L. Covell

PRINCIPAL COMPETITORS

Drakes Pride Ltd.; Greenmaster Bowls Ltd.; Thomas Taylor (Bowls) Ltd.

FURTHER READING

Henselite (Australia) Pty. Ltd. "Henselite's History." Accessed October 10, 2011. http://www.henselite.com.au/history.

Munro, J. P. "The Romance of Bowl Manufacture." Accessed October 10, 2011. http://www.oxnardlbc.com/the_romance_of_bowl_manufacture.html.

Hess Corporation

---■---

1185 Avenue of the Americas, 40th Floor
New York, New York 10036
U.S.A.
Telephone: (212) 997-8500
Fax: (212) 536-8390
Web site: http://www.hess.com

Public Company
Founded: 1919 as Amerada Corporation
Incorporated: 1920
Employees: 13,800
Sales: $33.86 billion (2010)
Stock Exchanges: New York
Ticker Symbol: HES
NAICS: 211111 Crude Petroleum and Natural Gas Extraction; 221110 Electric Power Generation; 221122 Electric Power Distribution; 221210 Natural Gas Distribution; 324110 Petroleum Refineries; 424710 Petroleum Bulk Stations and Terminals; 424720 Petroleum and Petroleum Products Merchant Wholesalers (Except Bulk Stations and Terminals); 447110 Gasoline Stations with Convenience Stores; 447190 Other Gasoline Stations

■ ■ ■

Hess Corporation is a leading independent integrated energy concern involved in the exploration for and production of crude oil and natural gas, in refining, and in marketing refined petroleum products, natural gas, and electricity. Hess's proven reserves total around 1.54 billion barrels of oil equivalent (BOE), with about 72 percent of this consisting of crude oil and 28 percent of natural gas. The company produces about 418,000 BOE per day. Hess and partner Petróleos de Venezuela S.A. jointly operate the Hovensa refinery on St. Croix in the U.S. Virgin Islands, one of the dozen or so largest refineries in the world with an operating capacity of 350,000 barrels a day.

Hess also owns and operates a smaller refinery in Port Reading, New Jersey, with a capacity of 70,000 barrels per day and is involved in retail marketing through a chain of more than 1,350 Hess gas stations in the eastern United States (mainly in New York, New Jersey, Pennsylvania, Florida, Massachusetts, North Carolina, and South Carolina). The vast majority of these stations have convenience stores on the sites. Around 98 percent of Hess's capital spending is related to the search, development, and production of crude oil and natural gas.

EARLY HISTORY OF AMERADA

Prior to May 2006, Hess Corporation was known as Amerada Hess Corporation, a name resulting from the 1969 merger of Amerada Petroleum Corporation and Hess Oil and Chemical Corporation. The story of the Amerada side of Hess Corporation's history begins with the English oil entrepreneur Lord Cowdray, who early in 1919 set up Amerada Corporation to explore for petroleum in the United States, Canada, and Central America. At this time, Everette DeGolyer, a geophysicist and engineer with a record of important technical innovations, was made Amerada's first vice president and general manager. DeGolyer repeatedly stressed the importance of both geological competence and the then-newly evolving technologies of gravimetric and seismic reflection exploration, arguing that Amerada's ultimate success lay in making accurate and timely scientific estimates and appraisals of oil well production, as well as in the equally difficult economic estimates of oil market futures.

The company's first operations centered on wildcat and development fields in Kansas, Oklahoma, Texas, Louisiana, and Alabama. As well as having ties to the Mexican Eagle Oil Company, Amerada Corporation by 1920 controlled two subsidiaries, Goodrich Oil Company and Cameron Oil Company. Early successes were in major fields in Kansas, such as the Urschel, and in Oklahoma (the Osage, Seminole, Cromwell, and others). In 1923 DeGolyer was one of the first and most vocal advocates for systematic, as opposed to guesswork, exploration for certain kinds of oil traps around salt domes, frequently found in the Gulf of Mexico states. After state, congressional, and private rumblings about the large land and financial holdings of foreign-controlled oil companies in the United States, Lord Cowdray between 1924 and 1926 sold Amerada stock on the U.S. market at $26 a share, principally through Rycade Corporation, to fund the acquisition of oil field holdings in Texas.

As many explorationists and historians acknowledge, much of the drama and success of Amerada Corporation before and during the Great Depression was tied closely to its pioneering use of geophysical exploration methods. In 1922 DeGolyer conducted what was apparently the first survey of an oil deposit at the famous Spindletop Salt Dome in Texas using advanced geophysical techniques. To further develop and perfect these methods, in 1925, after oil's recovery from approximately 50 cents to $3 a barrel, DeGolyer together with J. Clarence Karcher organized a subsidiary company, Geophysical Research Corporation (GRC) of New Jersey, which established numerous patents and which eventually spawned Geophysical Service,

Incorporated, later known as Texas Instruments Inc. Pioneering many early joint ventures, Amerada's first major success in new field prospecting by geophysical methods came with the discovery of the Nash dome, along with 10 others elsewhere, on a lease held by Louisiana Land and Exploration Company (LL&E), systematically exploring over three million acres of southern Louisiana swamps in a fraction of the time of prior surveys. GRC undertook another major survey for Amerada Corporation in 1927 and 1928, finding oil deposits in the Wilcox sands, which had been missed by many other major and independent oil companies. De-Golyer's innovations and discoveries led to his becoming president in 1929, and chairman of the board in 1930. Notwithstanding continued exploration successes because of geophysical innovations developed during the Great Depression, DeGolyer in 1932 resigned from the company to continue work as an independent consultant and head his own exploration companies.

A SERIES OF MAJOR FINDS

After extensive joint seismic exploration surveying in 1933, Amerada and Stanolind Oil & Gas made the first discoveries in the famous Katy, Texas, oil and gas fields. Further extension surveys led to other discoveries near Houston, Texas. In 1945 Amerada was responsible for finding another major reservoir in the Permian Basin of West Texas. The history of the famous North Dakota Williston Basin oil fields emerged into geological and public attention when Amerada, between 1951 and 1953, completed major reconnaissance seismic surveys leading to an important wildcat discovery in the Nesson anticline.

In 1941 Amerada Corporation merged with its principal operating subsidiary and became Amerada Petroleum Corporation. Throughout the World War II period, Amerada operated exclusively within the United States and Canada. In December 1948 Amerada Petroleum Corporation, Continental Oil Company (later Conoco), and Ohio Oil Company (later Marathon) formed the Conorada Petroleum Corporation. Conorada was charged with petroleum exploration outside the United States and Canada and negotiated major concessions in Egypt around the Qatiara Depression near the Libyan border. In January 1963 Amerada acquired the stock interests of Conorada held by Continental and Marathon, becoming full owner of Conorada. In 1964 Amerada joined with Marathon, Continental, and Shell to form the major Oasis petroleum consortium in Libya, reportedly holding half of Libyan production (estimated at one million barrels a day) and paying only 30 cents a barrel in taxes compared to Exxon's 90 cents.

KEY DATES

1919: Lord Cowdray establishes Amerada Corporation to explore for petroleum.

1933: Amerada and Stanolind Oil & Gas make the first discoveries in the Katy, Texas, oil and gas fields.

1941: Amerada merges with its principal subsidiary to form Amerada Petroleum Corporation.

1962: Leon Hess takes his company public as Hess Oil and Chemical Corporation.

1966: Leon Hess purchases nearly 10 percent of Amerada's common stock.

1969: Hess and Amerada merge to form Amerada Hess Corporation.

1985: Monsanto Oil Company is acquired.

1998: Amerada Hess sells a 50 percent interest in its U.S. Virgin Islands refinery.

2001: Company acquires Triton Energy Limited.

2006: Company name is shortened to Hess Corporation.

2010: Hess increases its holdings in the Bakken shale oil play to more than 900,000 net acres.

In 1950 Amerada became active in petroleum pipe-lining and refining. By 1954, Amerada Petroleum Corporation was one of a group of small producers that sold its output at the wellhead. By the mid-1960s, the company held full or partial interest in over six million acres in both the United States and Canada, and some 68 million acres overseas. During this period, Amerada Petroleum had been producing natural gas in the North Sea in partnership with Standard Oil Company of Indiana. In the spring of 1966, Leon Hess bought nearly 10 percent of Amerada's outstanding common stock from the Bank of England, which had acquired it during World War II.

EARLY DEVELOPMENT OF HESS OIL AND CHEMICAL

Shortly before World War II, Leon Hess had initiated expansion of his father's original fuel oil business. His father, Mores Hess, founded the small business in 1925. In the late 1930s, Leon Hess refocused the business on post-refinery residual oil, usually treated as waste and used as fuel only for large boilers and utility operations. Hess apparently recognized that as power companies and industrial consumers progressively switched from coal to oil, residual oil had the potential to become a profitable commodity. Hess subsequently created a tank-truck fleet specifically designed to transport residual oil to power plants. The trucks were equipped with heaters that kept the oil hot and thus still useful. Adding more distribution depots and a provision terminal, Hess was able to underbid his competition for a variety of federal fuel contracts, a traditional source of significant revenue throughout the company's history. It is probable that Hess's own World War II experience in the army as a petroleum supply officer was a notable source of his later ideas about organization and discipline in business.

The late 1940s marked the start of Hess's first large profits from residual oil sales, serving customers such as Public Service Electric & Gas. Hess competed on a tight price basis, establishing large stations at prime locations close to refineries and depots and pioneering gasoline sales without services. After a period of further expansion through debt, the high debt-to-equity ratio forced Hess to take his company public by means of a merger with Cletrac Corporation. Under terms of the May 1962 merger, the new company became Hess Oil and Chemical Corporation, with Leon Hess becoming CEO and chief stockholder.

FORMATION OF AMERADA HESS IN 1969

At this point, all of Hess's operations were exclusively in refining, transportation, distribution, and retailing. Because of the opportunities, and possible vulnerability, Hess considered a merger with a larger integrated independent oil company. The Amerada-Hess merger that ultimately ensued was generally acknowledged as an extremely well-planned and well-timed success, resulting in a sizable gain in crude supply coupled with a dramatic reduction in federal income tax liabilities at a time when oil prices were low and expected to remain so. At the time of the merger, Amerada Petroleum had no debt and had proven oil reserves exceeding 500 million barrels in the United States and 750,000 barrels in Libya through the Oasis consortium. Hess made an initial purchase of Amerada stock in 1966. Amerada's chairman tried to stop the takeover, first by an arranged merger with Ashland Oil, then later by an agreement with Phillips Petroleum. By offering a notable over-market price, Hess invested more than $250 million in the transaction. In the spring of 1969, Phillips withdrew from the contest for ownership, and despite a May 1969 suit filed in federal district court to nullify the merger, Amerada's stockholders approved it by an overwhelming margin.

Because of what several analysts consider some surprising similarities in strategy and outlook, the two companies integrated so smoothly that the new Amerada

Hess Corporation rapidly pursued an aggressive and successful exploration program. In May 1970 Amerada Hess drilled the first successful wildcat well in Prudhoe Bay on Alaska's North Slope. In mid-1971 Amerada Hess was one of seven oil companies invited by the Canadian government to explore the building of pipelines from oil fields in Alaska's North Slope through Canada to the United States. In September 1974 the U.S. Department of the Interior reported that the company was the first to apply for permits to unload supertankers from the Trans-Alaska Pipeline.

Between 1966 and 1967, Hess Oil and Chemical Corporation had built a refinery on St. Croix in the U.S. Virgin Islands. In late 1967, following negotiations involving Hess, the local government, and the U.S. Department of the Interior, approval was reached on a 10-year plan to promote economic development in the Virgin Islands by U.S. industry, reciprocally permitting Hess the right to ship 15,000 barrels per day of finished oil products made from foreign crude to the U.S. mainland. The reported rationale was the need for cost-efficient heating oil in the northeastern United States, where Hess was a major refiner and fuel dealer to the government and industry. Some adverse attention and controversy arose following the announcement from Stewart L. Udall, the U.S. secretary of the interior, that a similar proposal by Coastal States Gas Producing Company had been finally rejected in favor of Hess.

In November 1970 Amerada Hess was charged by the U.S. Interior Department with import-rules violation from claims that it had made no significant expenditures for upgrading its Virgin Islands facilities and employee quota and apparently had not paid the agreed-upon royalty of 50 cents per barrel to the local development and conservation fund. By 1979, the company's St. Croix refinery output was reported as 700,000 barrels per day, the world's largest. A longtime supplier of jet and fuel oil to the Defense Supply Agency, the Defense Logistics Agency, and the Defense Fuel Supply center, Amerada Hess had also long been a chief supplier of residual and fuel oil to numerous community power and light companies. In April 1975 Amerada Hess was one of several oil companies charged by the Federal Energy Administration with pricing violations. In August 1978 Amerada Hess was one of five firms convicted on federal charges of fixing retail gasoline prices.

OIL EMBARGOS AND OTHER CRISES

In 1973 Amerada Hess received permission from U.S. President Richard Nixon's Office of Emergency Preparedness to import an extra six million barrels per day of heating oil to ease the nation's shortages but received some unfavorable notice by selling primarily to the East instead of the more energy-needy Midwest regions. With the price of crude oil increasing threefold in less than six months, Amerada Hess gained notable profits. Reported net earnings of $133 million in 1971 increased to $246 million in 1973 and to $577 million by 1980.

Including its role as major partner (with Hunt, Getty, and Louisiana Land and Exploration Company) on Alaska's North Slope, Amerada Hess invested more than $1.2 billion in exploration and production between 1973 and 1979. In the early 1970s, Amerada Hess was one of many companies negotiating with Portugal for oil and gas exploration concessions in and off the shore of Angola, and later Gabon. In 1975 Amerada Hess and Mississippi Chemical Corporation initiated a five-year joint venture of exploration and evaluation in southern Mississippi and Alabama. In 1981 Petro-Canada initiated the operation of drill ships off Labrador on behalf of a consortium that included Amerada Minerals Corporation of Canada Ltd., with considerable exploration success continuing through 1984, when it also made major natural discoveries offshore of Grand Isle, Louisiana, and further Alaskan strikes off Seal Island in 1986. In 1985 Amerada Hess acquired Monsanto Oil Company in the United Kingdom, and it became a wholly owned subsidiary.

In response to U.S. President Ronald Reagan's June 1986 deadline, Amerada Hess officially ended its Libyan operations. In 1987 Amerada Hess and Chevron were reported as the top U.S. crude and product importers of the year. In August 1989, in a $911 million deal, Amerada Hess acquired a 37 percent interest in major offshore oil and gas properties in the northern Gulf of Mexico from TXP Operating Company, a Texas limited partnership affiliated with Transco Energy Company, increasing Amerada Hess's total natural gas reserves by 25 percent. Included were major efforts at development and production in the North Sea Scott and Rob Roy fields. Natural gas was reported to make up approximately half the company's total hydrocarbon reserves in 1990. In September of that year, Amerada Minerals Corporation of Canada acquired assets from Placer Cego Petroleum Ltd. in Alberta and British Columbia. Amerada Hess Norge A/S maintained 25 percent interests in several major offshore fields.

In December 1989 the company settled its part in a 13-year suit brought by the state of Alaska concerning the North Slope oil pipeline. More notably, Amerada Hess survived apparent takeover plans in the mid-1980s. In late 1988, despite much published speculation about the flaws in corporate management, the company's overall picture remained strong. Its future was considered uncertain, however, because its five-year record was reported to be among the lowest for the entire petroleum industry. The clear trend of reserve acquisitions in the United States, Canada, and overseas reportedly pushed company debt to approximately 45 percent of total capital.

A major goal for Amerada Hess in the 1990s was to substantially reduce overall debt levels. At the same time, low oil prices and the costs of compliance with federal pollution control regulations hampered Amerada Hess's profitability throughout the decade. Net income dropped from $483 million in 1990 to only $7.5 million in 1992, and in 1993 and 1995 Amerada Hess suffered staggering net losses of $268 million and $394 million, respectively. Its decision to pump $1.1 billion into an upgrade of its St. Croix refinery, which had been damaged by Hurricane Hugo in 1989, was partly to blame, but Amerada Hess's vast network of East Coast storage facilities also imposed burdensome inventory costs when oil supplies were abundant, as they were throughout the decade.

Between 1989 and 1993 alone, Amerada Hess's $7.3 billion in capital expenditures was three times higher than the total for the period from 1984 to 1988, and by the end of 1993 the tab for developing its North Sea oilfields and for the St. Croix refinery upgrade totaled more than $42 billion. In 1993 the company finished construction on its Central Area Transmission System pipeline between the North Sea and the United Kingdom. By the end of 1995, however, Amerada Hess's stock had been unable to regain its high of four years earlier, and a decade and a half separated it from its earnings peak of 1980. In the words of *Forbes* magazine (December 4, 1995), Amerada Hess was "visibly bleeding."

"REPOSITIONING" PROGRAM
UNDER JOHN HESS

In May 1994 Leon Hess retired after six decades at the company's helm (he died in 1999), and a year later his son John was named chairman and CEO. As production began at Amerada Hess's new South Scott oil field in the North Sea, John Hess announced his intention to sell off marginal properties, consolidate the company's U.S. exploration and production operations in Houston, downsize its workforce, and reduce the company's debt. In 1995 he initiated a top-down review of the company's operations to reassess its strategy and prospects. With the goal of producing 500,000 barrels of crude oil a day by the end of the century, John Hess began building the company's hydrocarbon reserves and production through acquisitions, continued its debt-

reduction efforts, laid off some 20 percent of the workforce, and disposed of noncore properties, including the company's Canadian subsidiary, which alone had accounted for 10 percent of its assets.

Now reduced to its core operations, primarily in the North Sea and the Gulf of Mexico, Amerada Hess moved into the Brazilian market in 1996 in a joint venture with Petrobas, and in 1997 pursued the Venezuelan market through negotiations with Petróleos de Venezuela S.A. It also gained stakes in oil fields in Thailand and the Falkland Islands and explored oil development prospects in Namibia. On the marketing side, it expanded its 548-store East Coast HESS gas station chain by acquiring 66 Pick Kwik retail stores in Florida and four Sears outlets in New York, and in 1997 the company initiated a gas retail marketing venture in the United Kingdom.

By 1997, the "first phase" of Amerada Hess's "repositioning" program was announced as complete. Net income for 1996 had rebounded more than $1 billion from 1995's loss, to $660 million, and Amerada Hess's debt-to-capitalization ratio had been cut by almost $800 million to 36.4 percent. With $1 billion worth of exploration and production properties jettisoned, five new high-return oil and gas fields fully developed, and a commitment to streamline its administrative operations by adopting SAP's enterprise planning software, Amerada Hess viewed its goal of moving into the top one-third of U.S. oil companies by 2000 with some optimism.

As Amerada Hess pressed on to achieve that goal, it faced some distinct challenges. Profits at its St. Croix refinery began to dwindle during the mid-1990s, prompting the firm to seek out a partner. Amerada Hess subsequently sold a 50 percent interest in the Virgin Islands refinery to Petróleos de Venezuela in 1998, creating the Hovensa L.L.C. joint venture. That same year, oil prices began dropping off. In an attempt to bolster profits, Amerada Hess launched yet another aggressive cost-cutting campaign, slashing capital spending by 38 percent and cutting 20 percent of its U.S. and U.K. exploration workforce.

During 1998, revenues fell and the firm reported a net loss of $459 million, due in part to the sale of several assets. During 1999, however, both profits and revenues rebounded. The company sold off pipeline and terminal holdings in the Southeast and also various Gulf Coast terminals. By this time, over $2 billion of noncore assets had been sold and operating costs had been reduced by $100 million. Overall, Amerada Hess reported a rise in net income to $438 million while revenue climbed to $7.4 billion.

Under the leadership of John Hess, Amerada Hess entered the new century intent on securing its position as a leading independent, integrated energy company. The company's main focus centered on exploration and production, while marketing and refining remained secondary concerns. During 2000, Amerada Hess attempted to strengthen its international holdings when it made a play for Lasmo plc, a British exploration and production firm. The company offered Lasmo $3.5 billion in cash and stock. Its plans were thwarted, however, when Italy-based ENI S.p.A. came in with a higher offer.

This failed merger did little to dampen Amerada Hess's appetite for expansion, and in 2001 the company set its sights on Triton Energy Limited, an international exploration and production company focused on the West African, Latin American, and Southeast Asian regions. The $3.2 billion merger was completed in August 2001 and was expected to increase company production from 425,000 barrels of oil equivalent (BOE) per day to 535,000 BOE per day. The deal also gave Amerada Hess access to Triton's lucrative assets in Equatorial Guinea and Gabon. The firm added additional international holdings to its arsenal during 2002, including three deepwater tracts in the offshore regions of Senegal, Gambia, and Guinea-Bissau.

During 2002, energy prices fell and global economies weakened. Amerada Hess's financial situation faltered as a result, with revenues falling by 11 percent over the previous year. The firm also reported a net loss of $218 million just one year after securing net income of $914 million, which was the second highest in its history. While economic conditions did indeed play a role in Amerada Hess's fluctuating financial results, the majority of the company's loss stemmed from a $530 million charge related to the write-down of its Ceiba oil field, which proved to be less fertile than expected. This field was part of the Triton purchase, and the write-down left analysts speculating as to whether the merger would be as lucrative as Amerada Hess had originally hoped.

INCREASING RESERVES AND IMPROVED FINANCIAL STANDING

Amerada Hess bounced back in 2003, posting net income of $643 million on revenues of $14.31 billion. Aiming to increase its reserves and production outside the mature and high-costs regions of the United States and the North Sea, the company significantly reshaped its upstream asset portfolio during the year. Among other actions, Amerada Hess sold 26 shallow-water oil fields in the Gulf of Mexico to Anadarko Petroleum Corporation for $225 million. In addition, Amerada Hess restructured its exploration and production operations, reducing the unit's headcount by about 30 percent, or 700 positions, as it aimed to secure annual after-tax cost savings of $30 million. Proceeds from asset sales as well as the issuance of $675 million in preferred stock enabled the company to reduce its debt by more than $1 billion and cut its debt-to-capitalization ratio from 52 percent to 42.5 percent.

Over the next few years, as the company's profits and revenues skyrocketed during a boom period of high crude oil prices, Amerada Hess continued to overhaul its upstream asset portfolio, shedding additional mature properties in favor of exploration and production assets with higher growth potential. In a simultaneous asset swap completed in January 2006, for instance, Amerada Hess sold its interests in eight fields in the Permian Basin of West Texas and New Mexico to Apache Corporation for $269 million and purchased Apache's 55 percent interest in the deepwater section of Egypt's West Mediterranean Concession for $413 million. Later in 2006 Amerada Hess sold off substantially all of its remaining onshore oil- and gas-producing assets along the Gulf Coast of Texas, Louisiana, and Mississippi.

The company was also able to return to Libya with the lifting of U.S. sanctions against that nation, and it rejoined the Oasis consortium along with ConocoPhillips and Marathon, holding an 8 percent interest in the Waha concessions. In May 2006 the company shortened its name to Hess Corporation, adopting the brand that was already firmly established with its refining and marketing customers and was becoming increasingly identified with the company's global exploration and production operations.

By 2008 Hess had increased its proven reserves to 1.43 billion BOE. More importantly, the company's reserve life (proven reserves divided by current production) improved to 10 years, increasing for the sixth consecutive year. Despite heavy capital spending, nearly all of which went toward exploration and development and which totaled $4.83 billion in 2008, Hess continued to bolster its financial standing. By the end of 2008 it managed to reduce its debt-to-capitalization ratio to 24.3 percent. Soaring crude oil prices coupled with growth in Hess's global crude oil and natural gas production resulted in record profits of $2.36 billion in 2008 on record revenues of $41.17 billion.

During the second half of 2008, however, crude oil and natural gas prices dropped dramatically as a result of the financial crisis and a slowing global economy. Hess responded by cutting its capital spending budget for 2009 to $3.2 billion. In the poor economic climate of 2009, Hess's net income plunged to $740 million, while revenues fell 28 percent to $29.61 billion. That year, in addition to increasing its interests in the Valhall and Hod fields of the Norwegian sector of the North Sea, Hess committed to invest $1 billion per year over the following five years in the Bakken shale oil field of western North Dakota and northeastern Montana. The company aimed to increase its Bakken production from 11,000 BOE per day to 80,000 BOE per day.

DELVING INTO UNCONVENTIONAL PLAYS

Bakken was part of a larger company push into unconventional oil and gas plays. The oil trapped in Bakken and other shale formations had to be released through a technique known as hydraulic fracturing, or "fracking." This controversial technique involved the injection of huge amounts of water, sand, and chemicals deep underground at high pressure to crack the rock and enable the oil (or gas) flow. Critics pointed to water wells that had been contaminated with either oil, gas, or chemicals through fracking, and there were fears of wider contamination of underground water supplies. Proponents, however, noted the huge potential of shale oil and gas, both in the United States and elsewhere. The Bakken shale formation, for instance, was believed to contain billions of barrels of oil and had the potential to eventually produce a million barrels of oil a day.

In 2010 Hess substantially increased its Bakken holdings by purchasing 167,000 net acres in the field from TRZ Energy, LLC, for $1.075 billion and acquiring American Oil & Gas Inc., which owned 85,000 net acres in the Bakken, in a $450 million stock swap. Following these deals, Hess held more than 900,000 net acres in the Bakken. The company committed to invest $1.8 billion, or one-third of its 2011 capital budget, on drilling and associated infrastructure to boost its Bakken production to 40,000 BOE per day. In September 2011 Hess entered into two transactions that gave it a total of 185,000 net acres in another emerging unconventional play, the Utica Shale field in Ohio. The company paid about $593 million to enter into a joint venture with coal giant CONSOL Energy Inc. and also acquired Marquette Exploration LLC for $750 million. In addition to Bakken and Utica Shale, Hess was also a significant player in the Eagle Ford shale formation in southern Texas and was involved overseas in partnerships exploring shale oil plays in France and China.

In the wake of the Utica Shale deals, Hess increased its 2011 capital budget to $7.2 billion, with nearly half of this earmarked for unconventional plays, including $2.1 billion for the Bakken and $800 million for the Utica Shale. Also in 2011, the company announced that the capacity of the Hovensa refinery on St. Croix would

be reduced from 500,000 barrels per day to 350,000 barrels per day. A difficult environment for refinery operations prompted this action, which by mothballing older, less efficient units was expected to improve the overall efficiency and profitability of the facility. At the same time, Hess's energy marketing unit, which was the largest provider of electricity, natural gas, and fuel oil to commercial and industrial customers in its 18-state East Coast market area, was in the process of building two natural gas-fueled electric power plants in New Jersey. Jointly owned by Hess and ArcLight Capital Partners, the Bayonne Energy Center was a 512-megawatt facility slated to provide electricity to New York City on completion in 2012. Through these and other refining and marketing initiatives, as well as the push into unconventional oil and gas plays, Hess seemed likely to maintain its position as a leading U.S.-based independent integrated energy company.

Gerardo G. Tango
Updated, Paul S. Bodine;
Christina M. Stansell; David E. Salamie

PRINCIPAL SUBSIDIARIES

Hess Capital Services Corporation; Hess Energy Exploration Limited; Hess International Holdings Corporation; Hess (Luxembourg) Exploration and Production Holding S.à.r.l.; Hess (Netherlands) Oil & Gas Holdings C.V.; Hess (Netherlands) U.S. GOM Ventures B.V.; Hess Egypt West Mediterranean Limited (Cayman Islands); Hess Equatorial Guinea Inc. (Cayman Islands); Hess International Holdings Limited (Cayman Islands); Hess Libya (Waha) Limited (Cayman Islands); Hess Limited (UK); Hess Norge AS (Norway); Hess Oil and Gas Holdings Inc. (Cayman Islands); Hess Oil Company of Thailand (JDA) Limited (Cayman Islands); Hess Oil Virgin Islands Corp.; Hess UK Investments Limited (Cayman Islands); Hess West Africa Holdings Limited (Cayman Islands).

PRINCIPAL OPERATING UNITS

Worldwide Exploration & Production; Marketing and Refining.

PRINCIPAL COMPETITORS

BP p.l.c.; Chevron Corporation; ConocoPhillips; Exxon Mobil Corporation; Marathon Oil Corporation; Murphy Oil Corporation; Royal Dutch Shell plc.

FURTHER READING

"Amerada Hess Pursues Specific Opportunities Upstream, Downstream." *Petroleum Finance Week*, February 21, 2000.

Buurma, Christine. "Hess Bets on Gas Prices." *Wall Street Journal*, November 18, 2009.

Easton, Thomas. "Boot the Coach?" *Forbes*, December 4, 1995, 64.

"Hess Aims for Transformation." *World Petroleum Argus*, May 15, 2006, 14.

Norman, James. "Hess Makeover Pays Off Despite Wall Street Doubts." *Platt's Oilgram News*, July 27, 1999.

"Refiner Seeks Oil for Troubled Waters." *Crain's New York Business*, January 21, 2002, 4.

Seeley, Rachael. "Hess Strikes Again in Ohio's Utica Shale." *Oil Daily*, September 9, 2011.

Sethuraman, Dinakar. "Conoco, Hess Sign Asian Deals Worth $3 Billion." *Oil Daily*, July 22, 2003.

Tinkle, Lon. *Mr. De: A Biography of Everette Lee DeGolyer*. Boston: Little, Brown, 1972.

Wetuski, Jodi. "Triton Will Do." *Oil and Gas Investor*, August 2001, 65.

Williams, Christopher C. "A Bold Explorer with Big, Undervalued Assets." *Barron's*, May 11, 2009, 28–29.

Hostess Brands, Inc.

6031 Connection Drive, Suite 600
Irving, Texas 75039-2609
U.S.A.
Telephone: (972) 502-4500
Fax: (972) 892-7694
Web site: http://www.hostessbrands.com

Private Company
Founded: 1930 as Interstate Baking Company
Incorporated: 1987 as IBC Holdings Corp.
Employees: 20,000
Sales: $2.5 billion (2010 est.)
NAICS: 311812 Commercial Bakeries; 445291 Baked
Goods Stores

■ ■ ■

Hostess Brands, Inc., is one the largest wholesale bakers in the United States, producing breads and sweet goods in about three dozen bakeries across the country. The company, which changed its name from Interstate Bakeries Corporation in 2009 after emerging from a nearly four-and-a-half-year stint in Chapter 11 bankruptcy, distributes its products through a system of about 6,000 routes and 600 distribution centers delivering to 50,000 customers, including supermarkets, convenience stores, and mass merchandisers, as well as Hostess's more than 600 retail outlet stores. The company's flagship Hostess brand includes such top-selling and famous products as Twinkies, CupCakes, Ding Dongs, Ho Ho's, Sno Balls, and Donettes. Other sweet snack brands include Drake's cakes, which is a

leading brand in the northeastern United States, and Dolly Madison cakes. Hostess Brands' bread offerings are led by the iconic Wonder brand and also include another national brand, Nature's Pride. Among the company's regional bread brands are Merita, Home Pride, Beefsteak, Butternut, Millbrook, Eddy's, J.J. Nissen, Sweetheart, and Sunbeam. Hostess Brands emerged from bankruptcy in 2009 controlled by New York City-based private-equity firm Ripplewood Holdings L.L.C., but in early 2012 the company was once again forced to file for Chapter 11 bankruptcy protection as it struggled with a high debt load and increasing labor costs.

ORIGINS AND EXPANSION

Interstate Baking Company was founded in Kansas City, Missouri, in 1930 by baker Ralph Leroy Nafziger. Nafziger came from a family of bakers, and he produced wholesale bread loaves packaged in a distinctive country-gingham wrapper, which were resold in grocery stores. Seven years after its founding, Interstate merged with another, much better established Kansas City baker, Schulze Baking Company, Inc., which had been founded in 1893. This move was the first of a series of acquisitions and mergers that Interstate undertook over the course of the next several decades, as the bread baking industry changed from a highly fragmented field, made up of a large number of small, independent, local operations, to a more consolidated industry, with a few big producers of national brands.

Interstate's next acquisition came at the end of 1943, when the company bought Supreme Baking Company of Los Angeles, whose plant it had previously

COMPANY PERSPECTIVES

Hostess Brands is a diverse and talented team, united in our commitment to baking America's finest bread and snack cake products. We are proud of our iconic American products, our popular brands and each other. We work hard to meet the high expectations of our customers. We enjoy making our beloved products and we like nothing better than putting smiles on the faces of our many fans.

rented. Seven years later, the company also bought O'Rourke Baking Company of Buffalo, New York. With these purchases, Interstate sought to extend its geographic coverage into new areas.

THE POSTWAR CAKE BOOM

Interstate's growth through acquisitions remained steady throughout the 1950s. In 1951 the company bought Mrs. Karl's Bakeries, located in Milwaukee. Three years later, the company moved aggressively into the cake baking industry, purchasing Ambrosia Cake Company, Remar Baking Company, and Butter Cream Baking Company. Four years later, Interstate also acquired Campbell-Sell Baking Company, based in Denver, Colorado. At the end of the decade, Interstate added to its cake franchise when it purchased Kingston Cake Bakery, based in Kingston, Pennsylvania.

In 1960 the company strengthened its standing in the Midwest when it acquired Cobb's Sunlit Bakery, of Green Bay, Wisconsin. Over the next two years, Interstate purchased Schall Tasty Baking Company of Traverse City, Michigan, and Sweetheart Bread Company. Other important acquisitions during the 1960s included Hart's Bakeries, Inc. After its long period of steady expansion, Interstate also undertook a consolidation of its operations, closing some plants. The company's Buffalo bakery, once owned by O'Rourke's Baking Company, was sold. In addition, Interstate closed its Butter Cream Baking Company plant and its Schall Tasty Baking Company factory. By 1962 the company's net sales had reached $191 million, up from $124 million in 1959, through a period of steady growth.

Interstate began to expand again in the late 1960s. In March 1968 the company bought the Millbrook bread division of the National Biscuit Company. This division included seven bakeries, located in upstate New York, which produced bread, rolls, cakes, and doughnuts for distribution throughout the region. In addition, Interstate took possession of a fleet of about 700 delivery vehicles in the acquisition. This brought Interstate's overall total of motor delivery trucks to about 4,000.

In August 1968 Interstate moved outside the baking industry for the first time, acquiring a food processor, the Baker Canning Company, and its subsidiaries, Shawano Farms, Inc. and the Shawano Canning Company, companies that canned peas, beans, and corn at three canneries in Wisconsin. Its products were sold mainly to institutions and were distributed through six warehouse facilities.

By the end of the 1960s, Interstate was baking bread in 30 different cities throughout the United States, in a total of 36 different plants. The company's regional strengths were in the Midwest, the West, and upstate New York. On July 25, 1969, Interstate changed its name to Interstate Brands Corporation, to reflect the broader scope of its activities, which now included canning as well as baking. The company had become the third-largest wholesale baker in the United States. Its best-known products were Dolly Madison cakes and the Butternut and Blue Seal bread brands, which were distributed across the country. Interstate sold its canning operation in 1974 and resumed acquisition of properties that fit in with its core line of business, baking. In December of that year, Interstate bought Nolde Brothers, Inc. for $500,000.

HARD TIMES IN THE SEVENTIES

Then, in 1975, Interstate became the object of an acquisition itself. The company's unwanted suitor had been founded in 1961 as Data Processing Financial and General Corporation, with its headquarters in Hartsdale, New York, a suburb of White Plains, where International Business Machines Corporation (IBM) was located. Data Processing, which changed its name to DPF, Inc. in 1971, leased IBM computers to other businesses throughout the 1960s. In 1970 IBM introduced a new computer model, and DPF's equipment instantly became obsolete. The company lost $43 million over the next five years, until it finally got back on its feet in 1974 and began to look for a company to acquire that would allow it to diversify its activities, because the computer leasing field no longer seemed tenable, as IBM continued to step up its pace of new product introductions.

DPF decided that Interstate Brands would be a good business to buy as it was seeking a low-technology company with a solid history. In June 1975 DPF offered

KEY DATES

1930: Interstate Baking Company is formed in Kansas City, Missouri.

1937: Interstate merges with Schulze Baking Company, Inc.

1969: Company changes its name to Interstate Brands Corporation.

1975: DPF, Inc. acquires Interstate Brands.

1981: Interstate Brands becomes Interstate Bakeries Corporation.

1987: Interstate Bakeries is purchased and taken private by the newly formed IBC Holdings Corp.

1991: IBC Holdings is renamed Interstate Bakeries Corporation and goes public.

1995: Company acquires Continental Baking Company, gaining the Wonder and Hostess brands.

2004: Interstate files for Chapter 11 bankruptcy protection.

2009: Company emerges from bankruptcy, moves its headquarters to Irving, Texas, and renames itself Hostess Brands, Inc.

2012: Hostess Brands files for Chapter 11 bankruptcy protection once again.

to buy 43 percent of the outstanding shares of Interstate. Immediately, the baker sued to block the acquisition, but its request was denied. Interstate Brands then, in turn, announced that it would purchase Farmbest Foods, a dairy products processor, from Philadelphia-based I.U. International Corporation. Interstate planned to issue a block of 375,000 shares of common stock to purchase Farmbest, which would have reduced the amount of stock DPF could control to only 37 percent of the total outstanding shares. DPF sued to block this move, and finally, after additional wrangling, DPF acquired Interstate for $37 million.

In the wake of this purchase, Interstate's headquarters were transferred to Hartsdale, New York. The company's new owners set out to wring greater profits out of its operations by upgrading facilities, some of which had not seen any capital improvements for a number of years. To modernize Interstate's plants, DPF embarked on a program that saw 17 factories closed and 19 new properties purchased during the last five years of the 1970s.

As part of this program, Interstate announced in 1976 that it would undertake the construction of a new $5 million bakery in Montana. The following year, the company shed the Nolde Brothers subsidiary and purchased Spokane, Washington-based Silver Loaf Baking Company. Other acquisitions during this time included Lewiston, Idaho-based Holsum Baking Company; General Host Corporation's Eddy Bakeries division, which included several production and distribution facilities in Montana, Idaho, Utah, and North Dakota; and Mrs. Cubbison's Foods, Inc., a bread stuffing maker.

On February 27, 1979, DPF fully completed its merger with Interstate. Two years later, the acquiring firm sold what was left of its computer operations to a group of former managers and changed the entire company's name to Interstate Bakeries Corporation. Although Interstate earned a $50 million tax break from the collapse of the computer outfit, ultimately, the bakery operations were left with a heavy financial burden to bear.

By the start of the 1980s, Interstate was operating 36 different plants, selling bread and cakes in 30 different markets. Seventy percent of the company's revenues came from bread, with 30 percent derived from cakes. Although sales of white bread had grown stagnant, as people became more health conscious, sales of variety breads, such as Interstate's Pritikin diet bread and Sun-Maid raisin bread, which carried a higher price tag and had a longer shelf life, had benefited from this trend.

In addition, Interstate looked to benefit from the general recession gripping the country, because a poor economy, paradoxically, meant good news for bakers as people typically ate more bread than they might in better times. Interstate's cake business, which was supported through heavy advertising, offered higher profits than its bread sales and also was relatively immune from the effects of a poor economy, because, some analysts noted, people tended to keep treating themselves to sweets when they could not afford more expensive luxuries.

BACK ON SOLID GROUND BY THE LATE EIGHTIES

With the separation of Interstate's computer business from the core baking operations, Dale Putnam, head of Interstate's bakery division, was named CEO of Interstate in January 1982. Putnam moved Interstate headquarters back to Kansas City, its historical base of operations. The company then looked to focus all of its attention on baking, as well as on improvements in two areas: plant efficiency and market penetration. Although the company had already spent $100 million upgrading its manufacturing facilities in the late 1970s, it planned to continue its efforts in this area, in hopes of increasing its profitability to a level consistent with that of its two largest competitors.

Despite these efforts, Interstate struggled in the early 1980s. The company was saddled with the financial consequences of DPF's failed computer business, the declining demand for white bread, its staple product, and stiff competition from other national bakers. A proposed merger with another independent baker, American Bakeries Company, never materialized, and Interstate was forced to close additional baking plants that were no longer profitable. In fiscal 1983 Interstate closed out a four-year period of declining financial returns with a loss.

The bad news continued in 1984, as Interstate racked up $4.2 million in red ink. At that time, the company appointed a new president, Robert Hatch, a veteran of General Mills, Inc., who came onboard just days before Interstate's bankers demanded payment on $36 million worth of loans. In an effort to get the company out of the shadow of its computer-leasing losses, Interstate took another $21 million write-off and cashed in its $37 million pension fund to pay off the banks. The pension plan was replaced by another retirement package as this financial maneuvering was designed to provide Interstate more time to evaluate and make changes to its product lines.

Interstate next decided to emphasize strong brand marketing, rather than relying on price to differentiate its products from those of its competitors. The company, therefore, increased its spending on advertising by two-thirds. Interstate also attempted to sell its western operations to Good Stuff Food Company of Los Angeles for $55.1 million, but this deal ultimately was abandoned.

As Interstate moved into the late 1980s, its efforts to recover appeared to be bearing fruit. Sales of white bread had stabilized, and the company also began to introduce new products, such as coffee cakes, pecan rolls, pudding pies, and a wider variety of breads. To keep manufacturing efficiency high, Interstate shut down five plants and spent $109 million to modernize 27 others.

In addition, in 1986, the company also made a series of acquisitions, in the hope of filling in marketing gaps. In May, it purchased Purity Baking Company, of Decatur, Illinois, which made Sunbeam breads, and Stewart Sandwiches, Inc. of Utah was brought into the Interstate fold that December. Stewart Sandwiches sold frozen and refrigerated products, such as roast beef and turkey sandwiches.

Interstate reported $13.4 million in earnings for the fiscal year ending in May 1987. Later that year, the company continued its string of acquisitions, purchasing Landshire Food Products, Inc. and Stewart of Northern California, Inc., the partner of its earlier acquisition. In addition, Interstate bought the Langedorf cake and cookie operations of Good Stuff Food Company.

LEVERAGED BUYOUT

Interstate's most significant financial move during 1987, however, was its withdrawal from the financial markets through a leveraged buyout. IBC Holdings Corp. was formed to buy all of Interstate's outstanding stock, and Interstate was taken private by its management, with the help of a group of investment banking houses, in September 1987.

Following this move, IBC Holdings made a major acquisition in 1988, purchasing the 10 bakeries of the Merita/Cotton's Bakeries division of American Bakeries Company for $132 million. Shortly after this purchase, the president of Merita, Charles A. Sullivan, moved over to take command of IBC Holdings, becoming president and CEO. With the contribution of the new Merita unit, as well as its own revitalized operations, IBC's sales grew strongly in the last years of the 1980s. The company reported sales of $855 million for fiscal 1988, which rose to $1.1 billion by May 1989.

In May 1991 IBC Holdings Corp. changed its name to Interstate Bakeries Corporation, before the company held its initial public offering (IPO) in July 1991. Through this IPO, Interstate was able to raise $250 million to pay down debt, which had been holding down the company's profits, despite the company's increased efficiency and sales. With improved cash flow and a reduced debt level, Interstate was able to decrease its expenditures on interest.

In the early 1990s, Interstate saw the popularity of its main product, bread, increase, as the federal government put forth new dietary guidelines. The company sought to take advantage of this new demand by decentralizing its operations, so that local facilities could run as efficiently as possible. This decentralized structure was seen as more efficient than trying to continue managing more than 30 bakeries, spread across the United States, from the central headquarters.

ACQUISITION OF CONTINENTAL BAKING IN 1995

By the mid-1990s, this strategy had succeeded so well that Interstate was in a position to make a major acquisition. In July 1995 the company purchased one of its primary competitors, Continental Baking Company, for about $463 million in cash and stock. Continental, acquired from Ralston Purina Company, produced the widely popular lines of Wonder and Wonder Lite breads, as well as the snack cakes, donuts, pies, muffins, and cookies marketed under the Hostess name. As Continental's plants were located in parts of the country not yet tapped by Interstate, the company immediately gained a greater national presence. The Continental acquisition also made Interstate the largest producer of wholesale bread and cake in the United States.

Interstate Bakeries wasted little time taking advantage of the name value of its recently acquired brands, launching an aggressive marketing campaign in January 1996. A key part of the strategy involved airing a series of national television advertisements, including the first Wonder Bread ads in almost 10 years, which employed the slogan "Remember the Wonder." The company also reversed Continental's ill-advised policy of shrinking the size of Hostess snack cakes, restoring them to their original sizes, and in some instances even making them larger, without raising prices. This concentrated brand building resulted in fiscal 1997 sales of $3.21 billion, an increase of 11.6 percent over the previous year. During this time the company also introduced a number of new products, including fat-free Wonder and Butternut breads and Hostess Lights.

The Continental purchase evoked a certain amount of apprehension, however, within the U.S. Justice Department. Wary of potential antitrust issues, the agency ordered Interstate to divest one of its other holdings. The company quickly complied, agreeing to sell the Butternut Bakery in Chicago in January 1997. This sale was followed in 1998 by the removal of Weber's brand products from certain markets in Southern California.

The divestiture order did not stop the company's expansion entirely, however. During this same period the company broadened its holdings to include a wider range of products in certain key markets. In March 1997 the company acquired the San Francisco French Bread Company, famous for its line of hearth breads. In January 1998 it purchased the John J. Nissen Baking companies of Biddeford, Maine, thereby strengthening its position as a leading baked goods supplier in the Northeast. The Nissen purchase soon was followed by other acquisitions in the region, including Wayne, New Jersey-based cake maker Drake's and New Bedford, Massachusetts-based My Bread Baking Co. This growth allowed the company to diversify its product line, while at the same time simplifying its distribution process. With sales in fiscal 1998 up slightly to $3.27 billion, Interstate spent almost $100 million on new operations, including a 280,000-square-foot facility in Biddeford,

Maine, one of the largest showcase bakeries in the world, and a Toledo, Ohio, bakery with a capacity of 250,000 loaves of bread a day.

TROUBLES BEGINNING IN 1998

Interstate's fortunes took a sharp nosedive in October 1998, however, when the company announced that its second-quarter earnings would fall below expectations. The investment markets were not kind. On October 30, Interstate stock plunged 25 percent in just two hours, after attaining a yearlong high of more than $34 only three weeks earlier. A year later the company's stock was still stranded at $22.75, far below analysts' expectations of $30. Although there were no actual buyout inquiries, the company, fearing a possible takeover, created a shareholder rights plan designed to discourage possible predators.

Interstate announced another financial setback in fiscal 2000, as net income amounted to just $89.4 million, a 29 percent drop from the previous year's total. Organized labor troubles and rising fuel prices, along with the unexpected flooding of the Rocky Mount, North Carolina, Merita baking facilities, were blamed for the decline. Interstate also suffered a setback of a different sort in August 2000, when a San Francisco court awarded $132 million to 18 Wonder/Hostess bakery employees who had filed a racial discrimination suit against the company. The trial judge later reduced the damages to $27.3 million.

Beginning in March 2001 and continuing through the end of the 2002 fiscal year, Interstate rolled out its extended shelf life program, which altered the ingredients in its products to double the shelf life of its cakes to up to 28 days and its breads to 10 days. The program was designed to shave costs as the company subsequently cut its number of delivery routes from 10,500 to 9,500 and also reduced how often deliveries were made to certain outlets. Initial results from the program appeared positive, with Interstate crediting it with boosting performance in the fourth quarter of fiscal 2002. In October 2002 James R. Elsesser, a former CFO at Ralston Purina who had joined the Interstate board of directors following its acquisition of Continental Baking in 1995, was named CEO, with Sullivan remaining chairman.

HOST OF PROBLEMS, LEADING TO 2004 BANKRUPTCY FILING

By 2003 the extended shelf life program had at least partially backfired as issues arose in some locations about the quality of the reformulated products. In addition, some store owners began complaining about inconsistent stocking of store shelves with Interstate products. The company was forced to reinstate some of its canceled routes and increase delivery frequencies, reversing some of the promised efficiencies.

The difficulties with the extended shelf life program was just one of a host of problems that began besetting Interstate Bakeries around this time. During fiscal 2003 sales were down in volume terms for both the company's cakes and breads. The cake lines suffered from heightened competition from the increasing variety of candy bars, energy bars, and miniature cookies available on store shelves, while analysts criticized Interstate's bread business for missing out on a key trend at this time: increasing consumer interest in premium and superpremium breads. It took until the spring of 2004 for Interstate to debut a premium multigrain bread brand (Baker's Inn), which at the time was one of the bread industry's hot products. During 2003 and into 2004 sales were further hurt by the rising popularity of low-carbohydrate diets. Earnings were under pressure from rising costs associated with employee pay, health care expenses, energy use, and raw ingredients.

In response to these challenges, Interstate in September 2003 launched a restructuring that entailed the closure of five of its 58 bakeries and 96 of its 1,250 company-owned retail outlet stores. In a reversal of its earlier decentralizing efforts, the company also announced plans to centralize some of its operations, while also focusing more keenly on its core national brands, including Hostess and Wonder, and de-emphasizing its regional brands and local private-label lines.

During 2004, however, further difficulties arose. The Securities and Exchange Commission (SEC) launched an investigation of the company's reserves for workers' compensation, and glitches in a newly installed financial reporting system prevented Interstate from being able to file its annual report for the fiscal year ending in May 2004. Saddled with a heavy debt load of $748 million and unable to staunch the flow of red ink, Interstate filed for Chapter 11 bankruptcy protection on September 22, 2004.

PROLONGED BANKRUPTCY RESTRUCTURING

Prior to the filing, with the aid of turnaround firm Alvarez & Marsal LLC, Interstate had already secured $200 million in financing that enabled it to continue operating as it began a major overhaul. The company also changed CEOs, replacing Elsesser with Antonio C. (Tony) Alvarez II, the managing director of Alvarez & Marsal. Starting in the spring of 2005, Interstate began

a dramatic program of consolidation to eliminate underperforming operations, increase overall efficiency, and ultimately create a profitable, if smaller, company. Within two years, the company had reduced its number of bakeries to 45, cut its delivery routes to 6,400 and its distribution centers to 650, and slashed its outlet stores to about 800. Its workforce was cut from 32,000 to 25,000. Interstate continued to operate deeply in the red, however, and its sales for fiscal 2007 had fallen to $2.92 billion.

As the restructuring progressed, efforts were made to revitalize the firm's core product lines. In a belated reaction to consumer demand, Interstate launched its first 100 percent whole-grain Wonder bread in mid-2005. In addition, the first major overhaul of Hostess packaging in 25 years was rolled out, featuring a modernized Twinkie the Kid character and other changes. The company also launched in certain southwestern U.S. markets a new line called Las Delicias de Hostess that catered to Hispanic customers.

To oversee a second stage of restructuring and create a plan for the company's emergence from bankruptcy, Interstate hired a new CEO in February 2007, Craig D. Jung. The new leader was a former CEO of Panamerican Beverages, Inc., a bottler of Coca-Cola soft-drink products. In one of the key developments that Jung spearheaded, Interstate was eventually able to gain concessions from the International Brotherhood of Teamsters that were a prerequisite to the company securing $600 million in post-bankruptcy financing. The concessions, in addition to including reductions in pay and benefits, enabled Interstate to begin implementing a more cost-effective distribution system that included different delivery options for customers based on customer size, while in particular allowing for direct delivery to warehouses for certain major customers. In return for agreeing to these and other concessions, Teamsters and workers represented by other unions were promised an equity stake in the company if a return to growth occurred in the future.

EMERGING FROM BANKRUPTCY IN 2009 AS HOSTESS BRANDS

On February 3, 2009, Interstate Bakeries finally emerged from bankruptcy, nearly four and a half years after the filing. It emerged as a private company controlled by New York City-based private-equity firm Ripplewood Holdings L.L.C. Later in the year, the company moved its headquarters to Irving, Texas, although its operational base remained in Kansas City. In November 2009 Interstate changed its name to Hostess Brands, Inc., taking the name of its best-selling brand. At the time, the Hostess line was generating more than $1 billion of the company's overall sales of around $2.5 billion.

Although out of bankruptcy, Hostess Brands still faced some major challenges, including rising costs for sugar, flour, and other raw ingredients and higher fuel prices for its delivery trucks. Cost-cutting thus remained a main priority, leading to further closures of bakeries, distribution centers, and outlet stores and additional cutbacks in delivery routes. The company enjoyed some success in revitalizing its product offerings, in particular through the 2009 launch of Nature's Pride, which Hostess touted as the "first brand of 100% all natural breads available across the country." In a 2010 report, the market research firm SymphonyIRI Group, Inc. named Nature's Pride one of the year's top 10 new food brands. Hostess also responded to consumer demand for more healthful bread options by launching Wonder Smartwhite, a white bread featuring added fiber and less salt, in 2010, followed a year later by a whole-wheat version of Wonder called Wonder Smartwheat. In the meantime, Jung retired in June 2010 and was replaced by Brian J. Driscoll, who had been president of sales, customer service, and logistics at Kraft Foods Inc.

By September 2011 Hostess Brands' financial problems, which included continued high labor costs and debt in excess of $700 million, led the firm to hire restructuring advisers once again. The company entered into extensive negotiations with the unions representing much of its workforce, seeking further concessions to preclude another bankruptcy filing, or even a complete financial collapse. Ripplewood was reportedly also seeking permission to explore selling off individual brands, including Hostess and Wonder, to raise capital and repair the balance sheet. On January 12, 2012, Hostess Brands was forced to file once again for Chapter 11 bankruptcy protection as it sought to find a more lasting solution to its financial difficulties through another court-supervised restructuring.

Elizabeth Rourke
Updated, Stephen Meyer; David E. Salamie

PRINCIPAL SUBSIDIARIES

IBC Sales Corporation; IBC Services, LLC; IBC Trucking, LLC; Interstate Brands Corporation.

PRINCIPAL COMPETITORS

Flowers Foods, Inc.; George Weston Limited; Grupo Bimbo, S.A.B. de C.V.; Kellogg Company; Kraft Foods Inc.; Krispy Kreme Doughnuts, Inc.; McKee Foods Corporation; Pepperidge Farm, Incorporated; Rich Products Corporation; Sara Lee Corporation.

FURTHER READING

Adamy, Janet. "Half a Loaf: At Giant Baker, Freshness Project Takes Sour Turn." *Wall Street Journal*, September 23, 2004, A1+.

Grow, Brian. "Can Wonder Bread Rise Again?" *Business Week*, October 18, 2004, 108+.

"IBC Now Goes by Hostess Brands." *Snack Food and Wholesale Bakery*, December 2009, 30.

"IBC Searches for New Solutions to Its Woes." *Snack Food and Wholesale Bakery*, July 2003, 8, 10.

"Losses Pile Up as IBC Begins Restructuring." *Snack Food and Wholesale Bakery*, May 2005, 8, 10.

Mann, Jennifer. "Feeling the Heat: KC-Based Interstate Bakeries Looks to Turn Its Fortunes around after a Rough Couple of Years." *Kansas City (MO) Star*, August 29, 2000.

———. "Problems Pile Up, Overwhelm Interstate: KC Baker Hopes to Reverse Its Fortunes While in Bankruptcy." *Kansas City (MO) Star*, September 26, 2004, A1.

Palank, Jacqueline, Mike Spector, and Julie Jargon. "Hostess Files for Chapter 11." *Wall Street Journal*, January 12, 2012, B3.

Palmer, Eric. "Interstate Bakeries Emerges from Bankruptcy, Has Financing Plan Finalized." *Kansas City (MO) Star*, February 4, 2009, C1.

———. "Interstate Bakeries Moving Its HQ to Dallas." *Kansas City (MO) Star*, February 18, 2009, C1.

Spector, Mike. "Hostess Again Hires Advisers." *Wall Street Journal*, September 2, 2011, B6.

Twiddy, David. "Bankruptcy Is No Wonder for Twinkies Maker Interstate." *St. Louis Post-Dispatch*, October 4, 2005, C4.

Houlihan's Restaurant Group, Inc.

———◼———

8700 State Line Road, Suite 100
Leawood, Kansas 66206
U.S.A.
Telephone: (913) 901-2500
Web site: http://www.houlihans.com

Private Company
Incorporated: 1962 as Gilbert/Robinson Restaurants
Employees: 8,300
Sales: $262 million (2008 est.)
NAICS: 722110 Full-Service Restaurants

◼ ◼ ◼

Houlihan's Restaurant Group, Inc., is a chain of about 100 casual dining restaurants. The company was one of the pioneers of a dining concept that translated an elegant atmosphere and a made-from-scratch menu into a more relaxed and lower-priced kind of restaurant. The company operates restaurants in 17 states across the United States, with most company owned and some run under franchise. In addition, the company operates four seafood restaurants, and a small chain of J. Gilbert's Wood-Fired Steak and Seafood restaurants, with locations in five cities. After initiating a dining trend that became ubiquitous in the 1980s, the company suffered rapid reshuffling of ownership, leading to financial instability. Houlihan's revamped its image beginning in 2005, opting for a younger, hipper, more irreverent take on the dining experience. With a new menu and updated architecture and design, the company has since undergone a wave of expansion.

KANSAS CITY ROOTS

Houlihan's began as just one division of a storied Kansas City, Missouri, company called Gilbert/Robinson Restaurants. Founder Joseph Gilbert began working in restaurants in Kansas City as a young man in the 1920s. His father-in-law owned a chain of lunch counters, and Joseph worked his way up from dishwasher to manager. He showed his skill as an entrepreneur by taking one of his father-in-law's ailing restaurants and turning it around. He opened a variety of restaurants beginning in the 1940s, from a concession stand at the Kansas City airport to swanky downtown eateries. His son joined the business in the 1950s. In 1962 the company incorporated as Gilbert/Robinson Restaurants, taking on a new partner, Paul Martin Robinson.

The company expanded into running a variety of restaurants all across the United States. These operated under many names, but retained some signature Gilbert/Robinson touches, including certain menu items. In 1972 the company opened Houlihan's Old Place. This Kansas City restaurant deviated somewhat from the Gilbert/Robinson blueprint in that it was a bit more casual than others the company operated. It became in fact the pattern for many popular restaurant chains that flourished in the 1980s.

Houlihan's hit on a theme that resonated with restaurant patrons. In a March 2009 profile of Houlihan's Restaurant Group CEO Robert Hartnett, the *Corporate Leader* asserted, "It's hard to imagine a time in American dining when eating potato skins, onion rings and stuffed mushrooms under a Tiffany-style lamp was considered novel and fun." The journal thus implied that from a perspective of almost 40 years later, the style that Houlihan's championed in the 1970s seemed dated, and somewhat overdone. When Houlihan's first opened, however, its menu items were adventurous and relatively unknown. Its dark, lamplit atmosphere spoke of upscale luxury, but the restaurant appealed to a mixed demographic of young diners. Houlihan's was a timely innovation, and the fact that it was widely copied spoke to the power of its concept.

Gilbert/Robinson expanded the Houlihan's chain, so that it had some 50 Houlihan's within 10 years of the opening of the Kansas City unit. Houlihan's came to make up the bulk of the Gilbert/Robinson stable, which included some 70 restaurants of many names and locales by the early 1980s. Not only was Houlihan's a hit, but it inspired many imitators, such as Bennigan's, T.G.I. Friday's, and Ruby Tuesday's. Restaurants of the Houlihan's casual dining pattern became quite popular in the 1980s, and Houlihan's was able to keep opening new units until changes in ownership led to retrenching.

SERIES OF NEW OWNERS

With founder Joseph Gilbert well past retirement age, the restaurant company let itself be bought out by a conglomerate in 1982. The buyer, W.R. Grace and Co., traced its roots back to the 19th century, and operated in a variety of industries, principally chemicals and shipping. It had also at one time owned the brewing company Miller, and it was not so odd in that era for companies to be involved in many disparate kinds of businesses. Under W.R. Grace, the Houlihan's chain continued to expand.

Although Gilbert/Robinson did well under W.R. Grace, its leadership eventually changed. Partner and cofounder Paul Robinson was described by *Nation's Restaurant News*, in October 1988, as "the master designer and concept genius" of the chain. He became less involved in the company in the years after the buyout. Another key player, Gilbert/Robinson President Kenneth Hill, also left the company, and went on to

develop the T.J. Cinnamons restaurant chain. Gilbert/Robinson then broke into two parts, with Houlihan's and the casual dining chain Darryl's falling into the casual dining division, and the company's other restaurants falling under its specialty dining division. Both divisions were part of a deal in the mid-1980s that made them part of a California company called Restaurant Enterprises Group.

Restaurant Enterprises Group had paid $537 million for 690 restaurants owned by W.R. Grace. The deal brought considerable debt to the new owner, paid by selling off chunks of the business it had acquired. In 1989, Gilbert/Robinson changed hands again. Parts of the specialty restaurant division were acquired by Paul Robinson and a partner. An assortment of roughly 100 other restaurants, including 56 Houlihan's and 11 Darryl's, went for roughly $200 million to a New York company, The Riese Organization.

Two brothers, Murray and Irving Riese, had run The Riese Organization for decades. They already owned all the Houlihan's franchises in New York, and also ran a slew of other New York restaurant franchises, including Pizza Hut and Dunkin' Donuts. The casual dining theme that Houlihan's had pioneered had become incredibly popular by the late 1980s, and another Riese relative operated a key Houlihan's competitor, T.G.I. Friday's, in New York. The Riese Organization saw enormous potential in Houlihan's, and immediately after the sale announced plans for major expansion of the chain. It planned to open hundreds of new Houlihan's, getting the restaurant into major markets across the country.

FIRST BANKRUPTCY

The expansion was not easy, as the deal The Riese Organization had made again left Gilbert/Robinson burdened with excessive debt. After two years of struggle, the company filed for bankruptcy. A new investor rescued the company in 1992. Malcolm Glazer, a Palm Beach, Florida, businessman who owned the Tampa Bay Buccaneers football team, arranged a deal where he acquired just over 70 percent of Gilbert/Robinson. The company he acquired was principally known for Houlihan's and Darryl's, and included several other chains and restaurants. Emerging from bankruptcy with the Glazer deal, the company then aligned into some smaller operating divisions, so that decisions could be made adequately for the different restaurant units. Because Houlihan's remained the single best known restaurant in the company's product line, Gilbert/Robinson changed its name in 1995 to Houlihan's Restaurant Group.

KEY DATES

■

1962: Gilbert/Robinson Restaurants is founded in Kansas City, Missouri.
1982: Gilbert/Robinson is sold to W.R. Grace.
1989: Riese Organization buys restaurant group.
1991: Company files for bankruptcy.
1992: Company emerges from bankruptcy with sale to Malcolm Glazer.
1995: Name is changed to Houlihan's Restaurant Group.
1998: Company is sold to Dallas-based Malibu Entertainment.
2003: Company emerges from its second bankruptcy.
2005: New restaurant design debuts.

The company had considered launching a public offering in 1994, but then withdrew. The company was thinly traded over the counter, mainly by its bondholders, and Malcolm Glazer continued as the single biggest owner. Houlihan's made an arrangement in 1996 to be acquired by Zapata Corporation, an energy company based in Houston. Zapata was another Glazer venture. He owned one-third of the company, which had been founded in 1954 by former president George H. W. Bush. Houlihan's seemed to be doing better after the bankruptcy, with plans to expand its 99 units by about 15 more a year. Its plans for growth, however, seemed to be interrupted by its ongoing changes in ownership.

The deal with Zapata had to be dropped after Zapata's stockholders protested that the only beneficiary of the arrangement would be the chairman of both companies, Malcolm Glazer himself. Nonetheless, Houlihan's was known to be for sale, and as many as six investment groups looked into buying it over the next two years. The company had revenue of about $375 million in 1997. Houlihan's itself owned and operated 61 Houlihan's restaurants. Combined with franchised units, the chain comprised close to 100 locations. In addition, Houlihan's ran 28 Darryl's Restaurants, five seafood restaurants, two J. Gilbert's, and five more restaurants under various names. The company had seemed ripe for expansion at least since the Riese acquisition in 1989, and several firms took a look at buying it in the late 1990s. In 1998, after a plan to be acquired by an unnamed New York investment group fell through, Houlihan's went instead to the Dallas-based Malibu Entertainment Worldwide for $130

million. A new holding company was then formed to run Houlihan's.

Under its new owners, Houlihan's made changes. Its new chief executive came from T.G.I. Friday's, Dan Scoggin. Scoggin moved to turn around the sagging Darryl's chain, which had been losing about 5 percent of its customer base annually in recent years. More Houlihan's opened through franchise, and Scoggin began to plan menu and concept redesigns for the chain. Scoggin was ousted in 2000 apparently under pressure from lenders, and another chief executive was brought in, lasting only until the fall of 2001. At this time, Houlihan's gained a new leader, Robert Hartnett. Houlihan's had reported a profit in 2000, and then moved to shut about 20 percent of its restaurants. Months after Hartnett took over, Houlihan's declared bankruptcy again. Hartnett was faced with two problems: one, the ongoing debt from the several buyouts, and two, that the Houlihan's concept was by this time tired and outdated.

EXPANSION BEGINS

Hartnett stuck with the company through the next decade, and oversaw its gradual return to health. Houlihan's closed underperforming units, seeing sales drop from $232 million in 2001 to $204 million in 2003. It emerged from bankruptcy in 2003 and set its sights on revitalizing the Houlihan's concept for the new century. The restaurant group worked on updating the menu to provide more contemporary and ethnic fare. It began plans for new buildings that moved away from the old fern bar and memorabilia look that had been elegant in the 1970s and now looked outmoded. The company hoped to grow by opening more franchised units, envisioning six or seven new locations a year by the end of the decade.

The first Houlihan's with the new design opened in Pittsburgh in 2005. The new model showed off its made-from-scratch cooking with an open kitchen, and also let guests eat and drink in an enclosed central bar and patio. The new Houlihan's menu was slightly lower in price than that of its competitors, setting it apart in its market niche. The company was ahead of schedule in new unit openings, with six company-owned stores coming online in 2005, as well as 23 more units owned by franchisees. Same-store sales grew substantially in 2005, at least among company-owned restaurants.

The new design managed to look modern without losing some of the touches that had marked the Houlihan's brand in the past. While the new models were far less cluttered than the traditional Houlihan's, they retained warm lighting and used colors such as orange and sage green that harked back to a mid-20th-century color palette. By late 2006, Houlihan's planned to do one or two total remodels a year, but hoped to open more than 20 new restaurants annually, speeding growth beyond what it had first predicted in 2003. This was at last the rapid expansion that had seemed the company's due way back in the early 1990s.

CAPITAL INFUSION

Robert Hartnett seemed to provide a stability in leadership that Houlihan's had long needed. The chain looked different by the last years of the decade, and was for the most part justifying expectations as it moved into new markets. Sales ran to approximately $318 million in 2007, as the chain grew to over 90 units. That year, Houlihan's attracted an investment of $68 million from two private investment groups. These funds were earmarked specifically for building the new-format restaurants. It had at least 30 new locations for company-owned restaurants in various stages of development in 2007, with plans to open 10 or 20 a year.

Hartnett increased the company's advertising budget by 25 percent, and incorporated new music into the restaurants. The menu contained humor and whimsy, much written by restaurant staff, to give the ambience a lighter, less serious note. This way, Houlihan's stretched its appeal across several demographic groups, targeting 25- to 54-year-olds. Clearly Houlihan's was in better shape than it had been a decade ago. Although it was smaller, it was showing solid growth and innovative leadership. In addition, it had moved beyond the "potato skins, onion rings and stuffed mushrooms under a Tiffany-style lamp" that had marked its beginnings, without losing the essentials of its brand and market niche.

Unfortunately, just when Houlihan's was realizing its long-delayed growth potential, the U.S. economy slammed into a downturn that hit casual dining restaurants hard. The industry journal *Nation's Restaurant News* noted in March 2010 that the poor economy had affected the entire casual dining segment, forcing chains to come up with creative ways to set themselves apart from their competitors. Houlihan's brought in a small-plate, tapas-style menu, and also put more emphasis on its bar business. It worked through social media both to build customer loyalty and to get valuable feedback on its menu. New menu items focused more on the younger end of its demographic spectrum, angling for groups of drinkers in their 20s and 30s rather than older diners. Although market conditions were probably not what the company would have liked, Houlihan's showed that it could adapt to

changing conditions, with the advantage of stable management thinking about long-term growth.

A. Woodward

PRINCIPAL COMPETITORS

The Cheesecake Factory, Inc.; Ruby Tuesday, Inc.; T.G.I. Friday's Inc.

FURTHER READING

Bernstein, Charles. "The Rieses: Too Much of a Good Thing." *Nation's Restaurant News*, October 10, 1988, F3.

Bertagnoli, Lisa. "Coming of Age." *Chain Leader*, July 2005, 31–42.

———. "Less Is More." *Chain Leader*, July 2006, 20–24.

Carlino, Bill. "Gilbert/Robinson Resumes Houlihan's Expansion." *Nation's Restaurant News*, October 17, 1994, 4.

"Downturn Forces Casual-Dining Operators to Retool." *Nation's Restaurant News*, March 7, 2010.

Farkas, David. "Up for the Challenge." *Chain Leader*, December 2007, 65–67.

"Gilbert/Robinson Renamed Houlihan's Restaurant Group." *Nation's Restaurant News*, April 3, 1995, 2.

Hayes, Jack. "Houlihan's Files for Ch. 11 Shield after Mass Closures." *Nation's Restaurant News*, February 4, 2002, 1, 11.

"Houlihan's Gets $68M to Fund New Prototype Expansion." *Nation's Restaurant News*, June 4, 2007, 10.

Jordan, Herbert. "Joe Gilbert." *Rotarian*, June 1983, 22–24.

"Joseph Gilbert, Restaurateur from Kansas City, Dies at 84." *New York Times*, October 2, 1983, 44.

"Paul Robinson, Houlihan's Co-founder, Dies." *Nation's Restaurant News*, December 6, 2010, 6.

Prewitt, Milford. "Investment Firm Eyes Houlihan's Acquisition." *Nation's Restaurant News*, March 30, 1988, 1.

———. "Zapata Corp. Agrees to Acquire Houlihan's." *Nation's Restaurant News*, May 13, 1996, 1.

Romeo, Peter J. "Franchisees Seize the Reins." *Nation's Restaurant News*, October 17, 1988, 86.

"Shareholders Try to Stop Houlihan's Zapata Merger." *Nation's Restaurant News*, May 20, 1996, 4.

Vinzant, Carol. "Rebranding for the Twenty-First Century." *Corporate Leader*, March 2, 2009.

Walkup, Carolyn. "Having Words with Bob Hartnett." *Nation's Restaurant News*, August 14, 2006, 94.

———. "Houlihan's Readies Menu Revamp, Post-Ch. 11 Expansion Bid." *Nation's Restaurant News*, June 14, 2004, 8, 124.

———. "Houlihan's Unveils Prototype, Menu Items in New Bid for Elusive Growth." *Nation's Restaurant News*, April 18, 2005, 4, 6.

Hunter Douglas N.V.

Piekstraat 2
Rotterdam, 3071
Netherlands
Telephone: (31 10) 486-9911
Fax: (31 10) 485-0355
Web site: http://www.hunterdouglasgroup.com

Public Company
Incorporated: 1971
Employees: 17,127
Sales: $2.45 billion (2010)
Stock Exchanges: Amsterdam Frankfurt Over the Counter (OTC)
Ticker Symbols: HDG; HUD
NAICS: 337212 Custom Architectural Woodwork, Millwork, and Fixtures; 337920 Blind and Shade Manufacturing; 551112 Offices of Other Holding Companies

■ ■ ■

Hunter Douglas N.V. is the world leader in the development and marketing of window coverings and is also a major manufacturer of architectural products. It offers fabric shades and a fully integrated line of fashion and color-coordinated window coverings. In addition, Hunter Douglas is a manufacturer of suspended ceilings, aluminum-facade panel systems, and sun-control solutions. The company also engages in metal trading. It maintains its head office in the Netherlands and has 68 manufacturing and 99 assembly operations and marketing organizations in more than 100 countries. Its

products do not reach the retailer directly but rather through a network of fabricators. The Hunter Douglas brand is used in North America and Asia, and for the company's architectural products worldwide. Luxaflex is the brand for residential window coverings in the rest of the world.

MACHINE TOOLS AND ALUMINUM BLINDS: 1919–56

Henry Sonnenberg founded a machine-tool distribution company in Düsseldorf, Germany, in 1919. It subsequently became a manufacturing company as well. In 1933, soon after the accession of Adolf Hitler to power, Sonnenberg relocated to the Netherlands and established a machine-tool operation in Rotterdam, where he had moved his entire stock of machines in 150 railroad cars to an abandoned shipyard.

With the fall of the Netherlands to German occupation in 1940, Sonnenberg moved to the United States, where he founded Douglas Machinery Company. In 1946 he established a joint venture with Joe Hunter, developing new technology and equipment for the continuous casting and fabrication of lightweight aluminum. This led to the production of lightweight aluminum-alloy slats for venetian blinds, at first in New Hyde Park, Long Island. A new plant opened in Flemington, New Jersey, in 1956.

Hunter Douglas aluminum blinds quickly won leadership in the United States and Canada and were also in Australia by 1956. The company developed a network of more than 1,000 independent fabricators

COMPANY PERSPECTIVES

The Company's objectives are to: expand its Window Coverings and Architectural Products businesses at a growth rate exceeding that of the market while continuing to be the best Company in the industry; develop and introduce innovative new products; seek acquisitions that add to the Company's organic growth by expanding product lines or distribution and that meet its return targets; continue with an efficient decentralized entrepreneurial organization, based on the principle of "maximum accountability with minimum interference."

who sold the blinds by day and custom-assembled them in their workrooms at night.

OTHER PRODUCTS, OTHER SITES: 1956–89

Policy differences led to the sale of the U.S. business in 1956. Sonnenberg moved company headquarters to Montreal. During the next two decades Hunter Douglas expanded its operations in Europe and Latin America. In 1962 it developed the 84R system for ceilings, facades, and sun louvers, and in 1966 it devised a linear aluminum-ceiling system. In 1969 the company became publicly traded, listing on Canadian and Dutch stock exchanges as Hunter Douglas Ltd.

The company moved its headquarters to Rotterdam in 1971, when, as Hunter Douglas N.V., it became the parent or holding company of the group. It reacquired its former business in the United States in 1976 and continued its global growth in 1980, when it entered Asia. The company began issuing American Depositary Receipts, the equivalent of shares of common stock, over the counter in 1994.

Montreal-based Alcan Aluminium Ltd. purchased 24.9 percent of Hunter Douglas's common stock in 1975 for shares of its own stock valued at about $13 million. This purchase reduced the Sonnenberg family's own holding from about 85 to 60 percent of the stock. By then Henry Sonnenberg had yielded active management of the company to his son Ralph, who was president and chief executive.

Hunter Douglas entered the U.S. aluminum-siding market in 1977 with the acquisition of the Crown Aluminum Industries division of Whittaker Corporation, which had a manufacturing plant in Roxboro,

North Carolina. Within a few years, Hunter Douglas had introduced Laxaclad, a new system of aluminum and vinyl siding and accessories for the do-it-yourself market.

In addition to its window coverings and architectural metal products, Hunter Douglas was trading in nonferrous metals and was also continuing to develop, manufacture, and sell machinery, machine tools, and equipment. By 1984 the company had installed, in Europe, its Wotan-Werke GmbH flexible manufacturing systems for handling large heavy components. The largest of these machines were brought across the Atlantic, where they were assembled with considerable U.S. content.

Alcan Aluminium sold its share of Hunter Douglas N.V. on the public markets in 1986, recording what it reported as a $29 million after-tax profit. Three years later, however, Alcan bought Hunter Douglas Canada Ltd. for an undisclosed price. Also in 1989, Wotan Machine Tools Inc., Hunter Douglas's machine-tool distribution company in the United States, was sold to Pratt & Whitney Inc.

EMPHASIS ON WINDOW COVERINGS: 1985–2000

As a result of the petroleum shortages and high oil prices of the 1970s, interest grew in developing energy-saving products. Around this time Hunter Douglas acquired the rights to a honeycomb, two-layer fabric structure that would provide more window insulation by trapping air within the blind. The result was the introduction, in 1985, of Duette honeycomb shades, a kind of venetian blind made of soft fabric. It was still the company's most popular product 25 years later. A new Duette collection with triple honeycomb pleated shades was introduced in 1991.

Hunter Douglas grew measurably during the next two decades. A window-fashions subsidiary in Japan was established in 1989. In 1993 Hunter Douglas established two companies in China to assemble and distribute window coverings and architectural products. In 2003 it acquired five blindmakers in four European companies, a British window-covering assembler, a Dallas-based fabricator of window-covering and interior-shutter products, and a Toronto-based distributor of shutter components.

Hunter Douglas also continued to roll out new products. Silhouette window shades, a cross between a blind and a soft window treatment, were introduced in 1991. Vignette Modern Roman shades were put on the market in 1994, the PowerRise battery-powered remote-control system in 1996, a ventilated-facade system called

KEY DATES

1919: The company that later becomes Hunter Douglas is founded in Germany.
1946: Hunter Douglas is established to fabricate items of lightweight aluminum.
1971: Company moves its headquarters to the Netherlands.
1985: Hunter Douglas introduces its most successful product, Duette honeycomb shades.
2010: Window coverings account for 83 percent of the company's sales.

QuadroClad in 1998, and the UltraGlide retractable-cord system in 1999. In 1997 Hunter Douglas introduced Luminette Privacy Sheets. They could be rotated like vertical blinds to let in varying degrees of light. When closed, they assumed the appearance of draperies.

Most of Hunter Douglas's custom products were being marketed in North America through 32 distributors that assembled the components as well as sold them to retailers and home-design consultants. Only eight of these were owned by the company. In 1994 Hunter Douglas decided to establish a "Windows to the World" incentive program to stimulate sales by this mostly independent sales network. The company's goods were high-end, and it needed a marketing strategy that would distinguish its products from less costly alternatives.

Hunter Douglas formed Tapestria, an international online market for decorative fabrics, in 2000. The program was targeted to interior designers, enabling them to shop for fabrics quickly and determine in-stock availability without the need for sample books.

ACQUISITIONS, PRODUCTS, AND SALES: 2001–11

During the first decade of the 21st century, Hunter Douglas continued to grow by means of new acquisitions and new products. In 2007 the company acquired 3form, Inc., the leading manufacturer of translucent resin panels, an architectural product that encapsulated a wide variety of materials, giving architects and interior designers the flexibility to create a range of designs and applications. Also that year, it acquired NBK Keramik GmbH & Co. KG, a pioneering German manufacturer of terra-cotta facades. Innovations in window coverings included the Platinum solar-energy sensor, which raised or lowered its window coverings to better insulate the

space, and GreenScreen, the first line of PVC-free solar-shading fabrics.

Interviewed in early 2008, as housing had entered a downturn, president and CEO of North American operations Marvin B. Hopkins told *New York Times* reporter Patricia R. Olsen that his unit's average sale to consumers was between $1,500 to $3,000. He added that in custom window coverings, it had a larger market share than the next two companies combined, between 25 and 30 percent. Questioned about his unit's relation to the parent company, he explained, "As a private part of a public company, we don't have to worry about quarterly performance and can focus on the long term."

Hunter Douglas Inc. announced in 2010 that it would no longer sell merchandise through the Internet in the United States and Canada. It said that an expected short-term loss in sales would be more than compensated by the long-term benefits of diverting sales to the company's network of 7,000 retailers, who were in a better position to offer quality service and advice to customers. A company executive said the action would affect a relatively small sector of its business: the sale of more-standardized wood and metal blinds and pleated shades. Higher-end brands such as Duette and Silhouette were not available online.

Hunter Douglas offered retailers who carried its products incentives such as merchandising and advertising support. These incentives were based on dollar volume, but in 2011 the company also began rewarding dealer loyalty based on the percentage of a retailer's overall business that the firm commanded. By late summer the company reported that 10 percent of its best dealers were making at least 75 percent of their sales with Hunter Douglas products.

PRODUCTS AND FINANCES IN 2010

Hunter Douglas's proprietary fabric shades in 2010 were Duette honeycomb shades, Silhouette and Pirouette window shadings, Luminette privacy sheets, Vignette Modern Roman shades, and Facette shades. In addition to these proprietary design innovations, Hunter Douglas offered a fully integrated and premium line of standard window-covering styles, including venetian and vertical blinds; roman, roller, pleated, and woven wood shades; wood and alternative-wood blinds and custom shutters; and exterior venetian blinds, screen products, shutters, and awnings.

Hunter Douglas's sun-control solutions, suspended ceilings, ventilated-facade systems, and translucent materials belonged to its architectural products line. These products included not only the QuadroClad system and terra-cotta facades but also Luxalon metal-ceiling systems and Techstyle acoustical panels.

After achieving record net profits of $327 million in 2006 and record net sales of $3.03 billion in 2007, Hunter Douglas struggled to overcome the legacy of the world financial crisis of 2008 and the housing meltdown in the United States and such European countries as Spain and Ireland. That year its sales were down only slightly, but it suffered a $160 million net loss in its investment portfolio, which led to a $35 million company loss for the year.

Sales fell 24 percent in 2009 because of the company's heavy reliance on new-home construction and home renovation. Hunter Douglas was profitable again in 2009, but only because of cost-cutting and staff reductions. The company closed 10 plants in the United States, concentrating much of its production in three remaining ones, in Sacramento, Salt Lake City, and Maryland. It also cut employment in the United States by 20 percent.

The results for 2010 showed a slight gain in sales and a sizable increase in profit. Window coverings accounted for 83 percent of sales, and architectural products for the bulk of the rest. Hunter Douglas was no longer in the machine-tool business, and its profits from metals trading and its investment portfolio were minuscule. In terms of geographical area, Europe and North America accounted for 40 percent of sales each. Latin America comprised 9 percent; Asia, 7 percent; and Australia, 4 percent. In all, there were 161 Hunter Douglas facilities in 100 countries.

Ralph Sonnenberg was chairman and chief executive officer of the company. His sons David and Marko were copresidents and chief operating officers. Rotterdam was headquarters for European operations as well as world headquarters. North American operations were conducted from Upper Saddle River, New Jersey. São Paulo, Brazil, was operational headquarters for Latin America, and Kuala Lumpur, Malaysia, for Asia. Hunter Douglas also maintained a management office in Lucerne, Switzerland.

Robert Halasz

PRINCIPAL SUBSIDIARIES

Hunter Douglas do Brasil (Brazil); Hunter Douglas Europe (Netherlands); Hunter Douglas International (Netherlands Antilles); Hunter Douglas Malaysia; Hunter Douglas Management (Switzerland); Hunter Douglas North America (USA); Hunter Douglas, Sydney (Australia).

PRINCIPAL OPERATING UNITS

Architectural Products; Window Covering Products.

PRINCIPAL COMPETITORS

Newell Rubbermaid, Inc.; Springs Window Fashions LLC; Tachikava Corp.

FURTHER READING

"Alcan to Buy 24.9% of Hunter Douglas for $13 Million Stock." *Wall Street Journal*, November 4, 1975, 18.

Alonzo, Vincent. "Hunter Douglas Window Fashions." *Incentive*, April 1998, 23+.

"Dutch Hunter Acquires Crown." *American Metals Market*, February 24, 1977, 2.

Kingman, Nancy. "Hunter Douglas Targets FMS Niche in US Mart." *American Metals Market*, March 26, 1984, 12.

Morley, Hugh R. "Company Ends Online Blinds Sales." *Record* (Bergen County, NJ), March 30, 2010, L07.

———. "Hunter Douglas' Future Hangs on Innovation." *Record* (Hackensack, NJ), November 9, 2009.

Olsen, Patricia R. "Timing and a Lucky Star." *New York Times*, February 13, 2005, Sec. 3, 10.

———. "With Housing in a Downturn, a Company Renovates." *New York Times*, February 23, 2008, C2.

Shoulberg, Warren. "The 75 Percent Solution." *Gifts & Decorative Accessories*, August 2011, 16.

Sloan, Carole. "Hunter Douglas Leads Online Initiative." *Home Textiles Today*, December 18, 2000, 1+.

Inchcape PLC

22A St James's Square
London, SW1Y 5LP
United Kingdom
Telephone: (+44 20) 7546 0022
Fax: (+44 20) 7546 0010
Web site: http://www.inchcape.com

Public Company
Incorporated: 1958 as Inchcape & Co. Ltd.
Employees: 13,900
Sales: £5.89 billion (2010)
Stock Exchanges: London
Ticker Symbol: INCH
NAICS: 441110 New Car Dealers; 551112 Offices of
Other Holding Companies

■ ■ ■

Inchcape PLC, with 19th-century roots in a shipping and trading firm, evolved into a diversified global conglomerate before reinventing itself at the end of the 20th century. The company is the world's largest independent automotive distribution group, operating in more than two dozen international markets, including the United Kingdom, Australia, Belgium, China, Greece, Hong Kong, Russia, and Singapore. In the United Kingdom, Inchcape operates about 125 retail outlets and a fleet-leasing business. Worldwide, the company serves as both a new and used car retailer and distributor, offering about a dozen brands, with its key partners including Toyota/Lexus, Audi, BMW, Ferrari, Jaguar, Mazda, Mercedes-Benz, Peugeot, Subaru, and

Volkswagen. In addition, the company provides parts for the brands it markets and offers insurance and financial products as well as after-sales servicing.

19TH-CENTURY ORIGINS

Inchcape PLC was launched as an overseas trading company in 1958, yet the origins of its constituent companies date back to the late 18th and early 19th centuries. Thus, the creation of Inchcape dates to Scottish merchants' early expansion of commerce in India. In 1847 a meeting took place in Calcutta between William Mackinnon and Robert Mackenzie, two merchants from Campbeltown, which led to the formation of their general merchanting partnership, Mackinnon Mackenzie & Company. Realizing the benefits of combining trading with ocean transport, especially with the gold rush to Australia in 1851, the business expanded and diversified.

In 1856 Mackinnon, at age 34, founded the Calcutta & Burmah Steam Navigation Company (C&B), secured from the East India Company the contract for carrying the mails between Calcutta and Rangoon, and incorporated the company in London with a capital of £35,000, of which Mackinnon Mackenzie & Company invested £7,000, becoming agents for the new shipping line. As a result of their success in carrying troops from Ceylon (now Sri Lanka) to India during the Indian Mutiny of 1857 to 1859, and through Mackinnon's contacts with the influential civil servant Sir Henry Bartle Frere, the partners obtained further contracts to support a fleet of coastal steamers carrying mails around the Indian coast with extensions to the Persian Gulf and

COMPANY PERSPECTIVES

Inchcape is a leading, independent international automotive distributor and retailer operating in 26 markets. Inchcape has diversified multi-channel revenue streams including sale of new and used vehicles, parts, service, finance and insurance. Inchcape's vision is to be the world's most customer-centric automotive retail group and represents some of the world's leading automotive brands, including Audi, BMW, Jaguar, Land Rover, Lexus, Mercedes-Benz, Porsche, Rolls-Royce, Subaru, Toyota and Volkswagen.

Singapore. In 1862, C&B raised sufficient additional capital to float the company under the new name of the British India Steam Navigation Company (BI). Mackinnon Mackenzie & Company continued to act as agents for the BI for nearly 100 years.

Sir William Mackinnon also promoted steamer traffic to the Dutch East Indies, establishing a Dutch-registered shipping line around Java and forming the Netherlands India Steam Navigation Company in 1868. With the opening of the Suez Canal in 1869, BI ships entered the Mediterranean Sea, establishing a trunk line between London and India via the Suez Canal in 1876. In the process, Mackinnon Mackenzie & Company became one of the greatest Eastern agency houses, and the BI posed a mighty challenge to all other shipping lines operating between the United Kingdom and the East, including the giant Peninsular & Oriental Steam Navigation Company (P&O).

LORD INCHCAPE'S ORIGINS

These events were the backdrop to the formative years of James Lyle Mackay, named Lord Inchcape in 1911. Born in 1852, the son of an Arbroath shipmaster, Mackay left Scotland at the age of 20 and worked in the customs department of Gellatly, Hankey and Sewell. Mackay, who joined Mackinnon Mackenzie & Company's Calcutta office in 1874, was to become the heir to the Mackinnon businesses after the death of Mackinnon in 1893. Mackay first became a partner after saving the BFS Bombay office from bankruptcy and became president of the prestigious Bengal Chamber of Commerce a record three times between 1890 and 1893. A member of the Viceregal Council and a close friend and confidant of Lord Lansdowne,

Viceroy of India, Mackay gained knighthood for his contribution to the solution of India's currency problems and the ultimate adoption of the gold standard in India.

Mackay returned to the United Kingdom in 1894 as a director of the BI, replacing William Mackinnon's nephew, Duncan Mackinnon, as chairman in 1913. Continuing his work on the Council of India, Mackay's growing reputation as an outstanding public servant led to his being offered the viceroyalty of India in 1909. Prime Minister Herbert Asquith opposed Mackay's nomination, however, on the grounds of his commercial interests in the subcontinent, and Mackay was offered a peerage in 1911 by way of compensation. He chose the name of Baron Inchcape of Strathnaver, commemorating the Inchcape Rock, located 12 miles from Arbroath, and expressing his loyalty to the clan Mackay, whose home is in Strathnaver. Between 1913 and 1932, Lord Inchcape personified Britain's shipping industry serving as chairman of the BI and the P&O after effecting a merger between the two lines in 1914.

Less well known than Lord Inchcape's shipping activities is his consolidation of an extensive group of commercial interests in India and beyond. These began with his accumulation of shares in Mackinnon Mackenzie & Company. Sir William Mackinnon had no son, his nephew Duncan died in 1914, and his great-nephews were killed in World War I. As a result, Inchcape became the sole-surviving senior partner of the Mackinnon enterprise, and by 1950 the Inchcape family held a controlling interest. Inchcape's chairmanship of the BI and P&O resulted in a very close connection between Mackinnon Mackenzie & Company and the shipping line, to the extent that many observers came to believe that they were one company.

EARLY DIVERSIFICATION

Mackinnon Mackenzie & Company spawned a variety of other enterprises to serve the BI routes. BI originally employed small private firms in local ports of call as agents but eventually replaced them with firms within the Mackinnon complex. These all came under the control of the senior partners and ultimately under Lord Inchcape himself. To separate the trading businesses from the shipping line, the Macneill & Barry partnership was developed to take over the extensive tea and merchanting operations that Lord Inchcape had acquired in 1915.

Amalgamated in 1949, Macneill & Barry Ltd. comprised three merchant partnerships formed in the second half of the 19th century: Barry & Company, Macneill & Company, and Kilburn & Company, which

KEY DATES

1847: William Mackinnon and Robert Mackenzie form Mackinnon Mackenzie & Company.

1958: Mackinnon group interests are consolidated to form Inchcape & Company, Ltd.; company goes public.

1981: Company is reincorporated as Inchcape PLC.

1998: Inchcape announces its restructuring plan to focus solely on its international motors operations.

2007: Company acquires European Motor Holdings PLC (EMH) with 52 U.K. retail outlets.

2010: After a two-year downturn in business due to a global recession, company sales and earnings rebound.

were involved in tea, coal, jute, river steamers, and various trading enterprises. Their principals included the Assam Company, the oldest tea company in India; the River Steam Navigation Company; and the India General Steam Navigation and Railway Company. Between 1951 and 1956, Macneill & Barry took over Kilburn & Company, and the three groups set up Pakistan-based companies. In 1965 the two river steamer businesses were sold to the government of India.

In 1906, Mackay made a successful strategic acquisition, of Binny's, a South India-based textile business. Founded in 1799, Binny's originally carried out banking and general merchanting, diversifying in the 1840s into agriculture and textiles. Indian production of textiles boomed in the 1860s, when the U.S. Civil War interrupted cotton supplies. By the late 19th century, Binny's mills managed 70,000 spindles with over 1,500 looms. In 1906, however, with the crash of the great Arbuthnot & Company banking house with which it was closely involved, Binny's faced bankruptcy. Its greatly undervalued assets were acquired by Mackay and a consortium of Mackinnon partners for £53,000. Binny & Company Ltd., as it had become known in 1906, made record profits in World War I with the production of khaki cloth. By 1917 it was supplying over a million yards per month. Binny & Company was subsequently restructured, setting up an engineering department, and rose to greater prominence during World War II, producing one billion yards of cloth a year by 1942.

Owing to the need to supply shipping-agency services to the BI, Mackinnon group enterprises were established in East Africa, the Persian Gulf, Australia, and London. In East Africa, as Sir William Mackinnon began to open up the region to British influence, the BI operated a steam shipping service. In 1872, Archibald Smith, a member of the staff of William Mackinnon & Company in Glasgow, Scotland, together with a Mackenzie man from Calcutta, established an agency to operate as BI agents and general traders.

In 1887, Sir William Mackinnon won from the sultan of Zanzibar in East Africa the right to administer a coastal strip of land in return for customs revenue, which led to the founding of the Imperial British East Africa Company (IBEA), partly in response to the buildup of German interests in this area. Smith Mackenzie & Company took a stake in IBEA and acted as its agents until the charter was surrendered in 1897. Smith Mackenzie & Company and the agency for Shell in East Africa became joint coaling agents to the admiralty during World War I and in the 1930s gained the agencies for British American Tobacco, Imperial Chemical Industries, and British Overseas Airways Corporation.

BENEFITING FROM DEVELOPMENT OF THE OIL INDUSTRY

In 1862, when a contract was won to carry mail eight times a year up and down the Persian Gulf, the merchant partnership that became Gray Mackenzie & Company was formed, helping to develop navigation on the Euphrates and Tigris Rivers and establishing a diversified trading business in an area that also faced German expansionism. In World War II, Gray Mackenzie & Company acted as agents for the British government in unloading military cargoes. The growth of its business was helped by the spectacular development of the oil industry and the rapidly growing need to service the expanding ports of the Middle East.

The Mackinnon complex also branched into Australia, with BI services at first managed by the British India and Queensland Agency Company Ltd. The Mackinnon partners invested in the formation of a major Australian shipping conglomerate in 1887, the Australasian United Steam Navigation Company (AUSN), formed with a capital of £600,000. In 1894, Mackay was appointed to the board of the AUSN. In 1900 he spent several months in Australia successfully restructuring the business. In 1915 he created a new merchant partnership, Macdonald Hamilton & Company, formed by two trusted Mackinnon appointees, B. W. Macdonald and David Hamilton. The AUSN, which had once owned 42 steamers, declined in the face of increasing competition from railways in the 1920s, and Macdonald Hamilton & Company diversified its activities into mining, pastoral management, and operating the P&O agencies in Australia.

The P&O acquired Macdonald Hamilton's P&O-related activities in 1959 and 1960. The London partnership of Gray Dawes & Company was set up to serve the BI as a shipping and brokering agency and eventually became a bank and a travel agency. It represented the interests of Smith Mackenzie & Company and Binny & Company in London, and established a secretarial department to administer the estate of James Mackay, the first Lord of Inchcape, after his death in 1932.

CONSOLIDATION AND EXPANSION: LATE FIFTIES THROUGH SEVENTIES

These diverse Mackinnon group interests were consolidated and reorganized during the 1950s, coming together as Inchcape & Company Ltd. in 1958 at the initiative of the third Lord of Inchcape. Tax considerations necessitated the conversion of these companies into private limited companies (whose former partners became the principal shareholders) controlled through London-based subsidiaries. Inchcape & Company in 1958 also became a public company through a public offering of 25 percent of its equity and in 1958 embarked on a program of growth and diversification, principally through acquisitions.

During the 1960s and 1970s, under the leadership of the third Lord of Inchcape, the company expanded to over 150 times its previous capitalization, due principally to a series of acquisitions. These acquisitions included The Borneo Company in 1967; Gilman & Company in 1969; Dodwell & Company in 1972; Mann Egerton & Company in 1973; Anglo-Thai Corporation in 1975; A.W. Bain Holdings in 1976; and Pride & Clarke, which held the Toyota agency for the United Kingdom, in 1978. During this period, through several capitalization issues, 64 original shares costing £80 in total in 1958 were worth nearly £2,000 by 1975. The merger with The Borneo Company almost doubled the size of Inchcape overnight, bringing in new interests in Canada, the Caribbean, Hong Kong, Malaysia, Singapore, Brunei, and Thailand. The Borneo Company operated jointly with Inchcape in the United Kingdom and Australia, but it introduced two new activities into the group's portfolio: motor vehicle distribution and timber and construction businesses. This merger, in which Inchcape entered new geographical regions in familiar businesses and entered new businesses in regions that it knew well, established a pattern for subsequent acquisitions and allowed considerable local autonomy.

Through Peter Heath, originally a director of The Borneo Company, Inchcape acquired Gilman & Company, one of the great trading groups of Hong Kong. Gilman & Company was seeking an acquirer but did not wish to be taken over by an existing Hong Kong business. The acquisition of Dodwell & Company gave the group further interests in this region, which it maintained as quasi-independent companies rather than forming one large entity. Dodwell & Company was founded in Shanghai in 1858, and by the 1970s had established extensive businesses in shipping, motors, and business-machine trading in Hong Kong, Japan, and many other Far Eastern locations.

Mann Egerton & Company, acquired in 1973, laid the foundations for Inchcape's motor-distribution business. Founded at the end of the 19th century in Norwich by an electrical engineer and an early motoring pioneer, Mann Egerton sold cars manufactured by de Dion, Renault, and Daimler, initially from branches in the eastern counties of England. By the 1970s Mann Egerton distributed British Leyland cars, as well as an extensive range of luxury cars, but faced a possible takeover bid from an unwanted source and felt increasingly vulnerable as a result of a wave of oil shocks.

The acquisition of Anglo-Thai Corporation involved the issue of nearly nine million Inchcape £1 ordinary shares, three times the number issued before, increasing Inchcape's market value by about 90 percent and adding to the group's assets in the Far East and Southeast Asia. In one of the group's few predatory bids, valuable businesses such as Caldbeck Macgregor & Company, a well-known importer and distributor of wines and spirits, were included. In 1976, with A.W. Bain Holdings, Inchcape developed an important insurance business through a share issue second only to that involved in the acquisition of the Anglo-Thai Corporation. With Pride & Clarke, the group gained the valuable concession of exclusive Toyota distribution in the United Kingdom after an issue of £1 million in £1 ordinary shares and £6.9 million in cash in what some observers called the biggest bargain of the century. By 1989 the motors segment was contributing two-thirds of group revenues and 53.6 percent of profits, the greater part contributed by Toyota.

ACQUISITIONS AND FINANCIAL TROUBLES: EIGHTIES AND NINETIES

Inchcape was reincorporated as Inchcape PLC in 1981. During the 1980s the company, under the chairmanship of George Turnbull, reinforced its concentration on its core businesses. Inchcape's key operations at that time were organized into three main areas: services, marketing and distribution, and resources. The service businesses consisted of buying, insurance, inspection and testing, and shipping. The marketing and distribution businesses covered business machines, consumer and industrial services, and motors. The resource-based businesses covered tea and timber.

In April 1990 Toyota paid Inchcape £110 million in cash for a 50 percent stake in Inchcape's U.K.-based distributing business known as Toyota. With this acquisition Toyota also acquired nearly 5 percent in Inchcape itself. Inchcape had a difficult time in the early 1990s during CEO Charles Mackay's tenure, in part because it had in prior decades overdiversified into areas not related to its core distribution business. The company continued to expand in the early 1990s particularly in the shipping services and insurance areas. Through a variety of acquisitions from 1990 through 1993, Inchcape expanded its shipping businesses in China, Korea, Vietnam, Indonesia, Canada, Turkey, Ecuador, and the United States. The U.S. acquisitions were seen as particularly strategic as Inchcape was able to secure operations for the Pacific, Atlantic, and Gulf Coasts of the United States, with the goal of operating a broad shipping agency covering all three coasts.

Inchcape's Bain Clarkson Ltd. insurance broker was bolstered through the 1994 acquisition of Hogg Group PLC for £176.6 million ($264.9 million). The newly named Bain Hogg Group instantly joined the ranks of the world's 10 largest brokers, and Inchcape gained a presence in the U.S. insurance market for the first time through Hogg Robinson Inc. Meanwhile, Inchcape's marketing operation was enhanced in a smaller way with the 1992 acquisition of the Spinneys group of companies, which ran a chain of supermarkets in the Middle East.

A combination of factors plunged Inchcape into its two most difficult years ever, 1994 and 1995. Difficult economic conditions in some of the company's key markets dampened consumer spending, while the strength of the yen made Inchcape's Japanese products, notably the Toyota automobiles, less attractive than those of competitors based outside Japan. In certain areas such as marketing, Inchcape had also become a more bureaucratic organization than in the past and lost touch with some of the local markets it served. As a result, pretax profits fell 15.8 percent from 1993 to 1994 and 92.4 percent from 1994 to 1995. The resulting plunge in Inchcape stock caused the company to be dropped from the prestigious FTSE 100 index in late 1995. David Plastow retired as chairman of Inchcape at the end of 1995 and was replaced by Colin Marshall, who at the same time was chairman of British Airways PLC and deputy chairman of British Telecommunica-

tions PLC. Then in March 1996, Mackay stepped aside as CEO, and Philip Cushing, who was managing director, took his place.

The new management team determined that Inchcape had to focus on its core international distribution businesses in order to turn things around. As a result, Inchcape began making significant business divestments, including selling the Bain Hogg insurance brokerage subsidiary to Aon Corporation in the United States for £160 million in 1996. The company began jettisoning unprofitable businesses and significantly reducing its workforce.

RESTRUCTURING: FOCUS ON CAR SALES, DISTRIBUTION

In March 1998 Inchcape, spurred by the fact that the Asian economic crisis had more than split in half the company's shares, was completely restructured to focus exclusively on worldwide car distribution, the most successful part of the group. One of the first major businesses divested was the company's Russian soft-drink bottling business, which was accumulating millions of pounds in losses. The sales of bottling businesses in South America, marketing services in Asia and the Middle East, and the Asia-Pacific office automation business were some of the wide-ranging divestments that quickly followed. The company also sold for £47.5 million its global shipping business, representing the world's largest independent shipping business. In July 1999, through another management reshuffling, Peter Johnson succeeded Cushing as CEO. That same month the new motors-only Inchcape was officially born. The June 2000 appointment of Sir John Egan, replacing Marshall as chairman, rounded out the leadership for the newly refocused Inchcape.

In 1999 Inchcape expanded into the rapidly developing market of e-commerce with the launch of Autobytel UK, the result of a partnership with Autobytel.com, an Internet-based new and used car purchasing service. In 2000 Inchcape invested $10 million to acquire a 7.3 percent equity stake in Autobytel Europe. By that time Inchcape already owned 100 percent of Autobytel in the United Kingdom and hoped its European version (which planned to cover the Netherlands, Germany, France, Italy, and Spain) would generate additional business. That same year Inchcape sold its 49 percent share in Toyota to Toyota Motor Corporation for £42.1 million, providing the company with funds for investments. The partnership between Inchcape and Toyota remained strong, and Inchcape remained Toyota's largest independent distributor, representing the company in Belgium, Greece, Hong

Kong, Singapore, and other locations as Inchcape expanded its automobile distribution and sales activities.

Inchcape began its transition to a vehicles-only focus with already established distribution businesses in Australia, Belgium, Greece, Hong Kong, and Singapore. The transition to a motors-only focus was not entirely smooth, though. The automobile industry in the United Kingdom was thrown into chaos in 2000 when the Competition Commission issued report findings showing that U.K. new car prices were between 10 and 12 percent higher than in other countries. Consumer confidence plummeted, and the industry suffered. Inchcape's operating profit in the United Kingdom fell from £25 million in 1999 to £0.7 million in 2000. The auto industry scrambled to respond to the report, offering lower interest rates and price reductions. The consumers came back, and in 2001 the U.K. new car market grew by more than 10 percent, and Inchcape's U.K. operating profit improved.

EXPANSION THROUGH ACQUISITIONS: 2000–03

Between 2000 and 2001 Inchcape acquired, for £25.2 million, 100 percent of Eurofleet Limited, a U.K. automotive services provider focused on sales fulfillment and logistics. The additional services allowed Inchcape to offer fully integrated services to its automobile manufacturers, rental agencies, and fleet customers. Inchcape's Asian investments by the early 2000s rebounded from that region's economic crisis. In particular, the company realized a spike in profits from Hong Kong, due largely to the strength of taxi sales, driven by government incentives that encouraged taxi drivers to switch from diesel to liquefied petroleum gas (LPG) cars. Taxi sales surged 130 percent in 2001 as a result. With Toyota dominating 90 percent of the taxi market, Inchcape saw its Hong Kong operating profit leap from £40.7 million to £48.9 million between 2000 and 2001.

During the first decade of the 2000s, Inchcape grew its U.K. auto-sales business. In August 2001 Inchcape purchased for £22.3 million the U.K.-based Bates Motor Group Ltd. with 10 Audi and BMW dealerships in the country. The acquisition bolstered Inchcape's relationship with its two primary specialty automobile manufacturers. That same year Inchcape sold its Mazda business in France, which had been losing money since the beginning of the decade. In 2002 the company acquired two U.K. Ford dealerships and a Mercedes-Benz dealership in Oxford. By 2002 Inchcape boasted that it was the world's leading independent auto-services business and the largest U.K. automobile retailer. The company had developed a niche selling such luxury models as Audi, BMW, Ferrari-Mazerati, and Mercedes-Benz as well as Ford and Volkswagen. Inchcape's sales during 2002 rose 6 percent to £3.5 billion, driven in particular by its distribution businesses in Australia, Brunei, and Singapore.

In August 2003 Inchcape spent £12 million to acquire six BMW dealerships in southeastern England, making it the second-leading BMW distributor in Britain. The following year the company purchased, for £28 million, five Mercedes-Benz and Smart dealerships, giving it eight U.K. outlets for those brands. Inchcape also acquired three Mazda dealerships, two in Estonia and one in Latvia.

U.K., EUROPEAN, AND ASIAN EXPANSION

In December 2004 Inchcape established an auto-delivery and customer-handoff service that removed the dealer from the delivery process. The firm, which already was performing vehicle inspections before delivery, purchased 40 two-vehicle transporters that Inchcape staff could drive. The company's number of transporters grew exponentially as it acquired more dealerships. That same month Inchcape established BMW and Mini dealerships in Poland and announced plans to enter Eastern Europe. Inchcape also planned to expand its Singapore-Brunei and Hong Kong operations, the former generating nearly 18 percent of company revenues due to exclusive import and sales contracts with auto manufacturers and the ability to charge higher fees.

Investors urged the company to spend its available cash on acquisition of dealerships in order to build economies of scale. Inchcape responded. In March 2005 the company acquired seven dealerships from its U.K. rival Robert Smith Group for £18 million, including six Mercedes-Benz outlets and one Smart dealership. In September 2005 Inchcape invested £7.5 million in a new Mercedes-Benz showroom in Nottingham, expected to be one of the largest U.K. retail outlets.

In January 2006 Egan retired as chairman and was replaced by Johnson, who stood down from his CEO post to replace Egan. André Lacroix was named the new CEO. The 45-year-old Lacroix came to Inchcape from Euro Disney S.C.A., where he was chairman and CEO. In 2006 Inchcape management devised a strategy to further develop its existing business and expand into identified emerging markets. Inchcape under Lacroix decided to focus primarily on six automobile brands (BMW, Mazda, Mercedes, Subaru, Toyota, and Volkswagen) in eight countries: Australia, Belgium, China, Great Britain, Greece, Hong Kong, Russia, and

Singapore. These eight countries already generated nearly 85 percent of the company's revenues. Lacroix also thought Audi and Honda could be profitable and fit the company's portfolio, while Lexus overseas and Mini and Smart brands in the United Kingdom also remained part of the company's important operations as it continued to sell more than two dozen brands worldwide. With record profits coming from Australia, Belgium, and Greece, and the company maintaining its market share in the United Kingdom, Hong Kong, and Singapore, Inchcape in 2006 entered Russia through two deals. Inchcape formed a joint venture with Independence Group of Companies in Russia involving two Toyota retail and service outlets in Moscow. The venture, 51 percent owned by Inchcape, involved construction of two new dealerships. That same year Inchcape purchased a 75.1 percent share in a Toyota and Lexus outlet in St. Petersburg. In 2006 the company also entered China with the construction of a Toyota showroom in Shaoxing and, after securing a Lexus franchise, during the next two years constructed Lexus showrooms in Shaoxing and Shanghai.

In 2006 the company also acquired Keystar Motors in Australia, a Mitsubishi, Hyundai, Kia, and Subaru dealership. Inchcape also expanded its U.K. business with the acquisition of Lind Automotive with 21 U.K. retail outlets that included those for Audi, BMW, Honda, Land Rover, Mini, Mitsubishi, and Volkswagen brands. Inchcape in 2006 also sold its stake in Inchroy Credit Corporation, a Hong Kong-based joint venture financing company, for £92 million. For 2006 the company's revenue and operating profit both rose, to £4.8 billion and £214 million, respectively.

EXPANSION IN EASTERN EUROPE AND CHINA: 2007–08

In 2007 Inchcape continued its U.K. expansion with the £262.9 million mega-acquisition of European Motor Holdings PLC (EMH) with 52 retail outlets, including those for Audi, Bentley, BMW, Jaguar, Land Rover, Mini, Volkswagen, and Volvo. The dealerships provided new and used car and light-commercial vehicle sales along with parts and repairs. In 2007 Inchcape also strengthened its Baltic operations, purchasing, for £60 million, two Latvian companies in the region's quickest-growing market, including Baltic Motor Corporation, which represented BMW, Ford, and Land Rover. The company also purchased UAB Vitvela, a retailer of Mazda, Ford, Hyundai, and Mitsubishi in Lithuania. The acquisitions made Inchcape the leading Lithuanian auto retailer. That same year the company began a two-year program of selling noncore assets, including Inchcape Automotive Limited, an auto logistics and remar-

keting services provider, a pair of former non-retail EMH companies, five of its six U.K. Vauxhall dealerships, and retail outlets selling Bentley, Ferrari, and Maserati models. The divestitures were in line with the company's strategy to streamline U.K. operations, focus on premium brands, and generate capital to expand in growing and emerging markets.

By 2007 Inchcape was Europe's third-leading independent automobile retailer. Sales and earnings were climbing in the emerging markets it had targeted. In 2007 the firm sold its U.K. Ferrari and Maserati dealerships and planned to sell another 20 Land Rover and Jaguar dealerships, many acquired through the acquisitions of Lind Group and EMH. Having completed certain noncore-asset divestitures, the company by September 2007 had EUR 1.2 billion available for acquisitions and investments. The company planned to triple its presence in targeted emerging markets that had annual double-digit sales growth. For 2007 Inchcape logged sales of nearly £6.1 billion, up 25 percent from the year prior, and a record £176.4 million in earnings. While a majority of the company's retail business came from Britain, 75 percent of earnings were generated abroad, mostly through distribution businesses.

In 2008 Inchcape also bolstered Russian operations with the purchase of Olimp Group and its two St. Petersburg retailers, an Audi and a Peugeot dealership. Inchcape in March 2008 also acquired for £100.3 million a 75.1 percent interest in Musa Motors Group, a leading Russian car dealer specializing in top-tier brands, including BMW, Jaguar, and Rolls-Royce as well as Chrysler, Dodge, Jeep, Land Rover, Mini, Renault, and Volvo. (Three years later Inchcape gained complete control of Musa.) The Moscow-based Musa controlled 16 dealerships around the city as well as a Rolls-Royce showroom in St. Petersburg. Musa planned to add an additional four retail outlets around Moscow as well as new brands by 2011.

RESPONSE TO GLOBAL RECESSION: 2008–11

In 2008 Inchcape continued to hone its brand focus and sold five of its six Volvo dealerships in the United Kingdom. By the end of 2008, a global recession was beginning to substantially reduce revenues for the company. While annual revenues rose slightly, earnings plunged to £51.4 million.

Inchcape responded in early 2009 by offering nine new ordinary shares of its stock for every one existing share. The move was expected to help the company reduce debt and interest payments and extend repayment of certain credit facilities to 2012. The company also essentially halted its acquisition program between 2009 and 2011. In 2009 revenues fell to £5.6 billion, from £6.3 billion a year earlier. By 2010 both sales and earnings were on the upswing, and the company logged £127.9 million in earnings on sales of £5.89 billion.

As of late 2011, Inchcape had operations in more than two dozen developed and emerging automobile markets. While Britain dominated its sales activities, its distribution wing generated the most profits, particularly operations in Singapore, Belgium, Australia, and Greece, which collectively represented about three-quarters of the company's distribution business. Inchcape not only had clear lines of business (retail and distribution of automobiles) but also had developed a niche for particular brands and was tapping emerging markets at what appeared to be opportune times.

Stephanie Jones
Updated, David E. Salamie; Linda M. Gwilym; Roger Rouland

PRINCIPAL SUBSIDIARIES

Autobytel Ltd.; Borneo Motors (Singapore) Pte Ltd; The Cooper Group Limited; Crown Motors Limited (Hong Kong); Gerard Mann Limited; Inchcape Finance plc (UK); Inchcape Fleet Solutions Limited; Inchcape Independence LLC (Russia; 51%); Inchcape International Holdings Limited; Inchcape Moscow Motors BV (Netherlands; 75.1%); Inchcape Motors Finland OY; Inchcape Olimp OOO (Russia); Inchcape Retail Limited; The Motor & Engineering Company of Ethiopia Ltd S.C. (94.1%); Subaru (Australia) Pty Limited (90%); Tefin SA (Greece; 50%); Toyota Belgium NV/SA; Toyota Hellas SA (Greece); Unitfin SA (Greece; 60%).

PRINCIPAL COMPETITORS

Hyundai Motor; Jardine Cycle & Carriage Limited; Mitsui O.S.K. Lines, Ltd.; Pendragon PLC.

FURTHER READING

"Cash-Rich UK Dealer Giant Looks East; Inchcape CEO Lacroix Has [Euro] 1.2 Billion to Spend." *Automotive News Europe*, September 3, 2007, 4.

de Saint-Seine, Sylviane. "Inchcape Makes Gains Thanks to Lind Acquisition." *Automotive News Europe*, July 24, 2006, 22.

————. "Talk of Management Buyout Gives HR Owen a Big Boost." *Automotive News Europe*, October 16, 2006, 20.

"Inchcape Steps Up Acquisition Programme." *Finance Week*, April 13, 2005, 8.

"Inchcape to Deal Direct with Car Buyer." *Motor Transport*, December 9, 2004, 24.

"UK: Inchcape Buys Five Mercedes/Smart Dealerships." *just-auto.com*, June 28, 2004.

"UK: Inchcape Profit up 9.9% in 2007." *just-auto.com*, February 27, 2008.

"UK: Inchcape Pushes into Emerging Markets." *just-auto.com*, October 24, 2007.

"UK: Some Inchcape Markets Doing Better Than Expected." *just-auto.com*, June 28, 2004.

International Coffee & Tea, LLC

1945 South La Cienega Boulevard
Los Angeles, California 90034
U.S.A.
Telephone: (310) 237-2326
Toll Free: (800) 832-5323
Web site: http://www.coffeebean.com

Private Company
Incorporated: 1963
Employees: 5,000
Sales: $195 million (2009 est.)
NAICS: 722213 Snack and Nonalcoholic Beverage Bars

■ ■ ■

International Coffee & Tea, LLC, is a Los Angeles-based chain of coffee and tea shops operating under the Coffee Bean & Tea Leaf banner. The stores offer coffee and tea sourced from around the world and roasted in-house and pastries baked at an in-house facility. The privately held company operates some 350 company-owned stores, including full-service kiosks inside Ralph's supermarkets, and about 400 franchised units in the western and southwestern United States, Hawaii, and more than 20 foreign countries, mostly in Southeast Asia and the Middle East. Coffee Bean bagged coffee and tea and bottled beverages are also sold at supermarket chains, including Albertsons and Vons. In addition, the company sells products online, including vanilla and chocolate powders, coffee extracts, caramel sauce, gift boxes, tumblers and mugs, coffee- and tea-making accessories, and the CBTL single-serve beverage system.

HUSBAND AND WIFE FORM COMPANY: 1963

The Coffee Bean chain was founded by Herman Hyman and his wife Mona. According to *Los Angeles Business* (November 15, 2004), the couple were inspired to enter the business "during a trip to Europe, where they saw that coffee was treated in a far different way than in the United States." A graduate of the University of California, Los Angeles (UCLA) and cigarette vendor, Hyman persuaded some of his college friends to invest and in September 1963, he and his wife opened a coffee store in the Brentwood section of Los Angeles under the Coffee Bean name. Initially, Hyman sold only coffee beans and tea leaves. To spur interest in the products, he created a beverage-sampling bar. In time, the bar was expanded to offer a full range of hot beverages.

Because of Brentwood's proximity to Beverly Hills, home to numerous movie and television stars, Hyman made an effort to attract the business of celebrities. Many of them became customers, but Hyman refrained from putting their pictures on the wall or exploiting his relationship to the celebrities that kept his home telephone number in order to address any emergency shortages of their favorite coffees. Johnny Carson was known to have his own blend. Even after he became governor of California, Ronald Reagan continued to drop by the shop. Hyman shipped packages of coffee to famed explorer and television celebrity Jacques Cousteau. Actor Lee Marvin even enjoyed working behind the counter with Hyman on occasion.

INTRODUCTION OF ICE BLENDED

Hyman expanded beyond Brentwood, and by the mid-1970s was operating a dozen coffee shops in Southern California. A major turning point for the chain took place when, according to *Jewish Journal* (October 30, 2003), an "employee threw some coffee and ice into a blender in the mid-1980s." Called "Ice Blended," known generally as the frappé, the drink helped to improve popularity and drove further expansion. Soon, the emerging Starbucks coffeehouse chain recognized the potential of the frappé and began emulating Coffee Bean.

While Hyman was less concerned with the number of units in the Coffee Bean chain, the same could not be said of Starbucks, which in the late 1980s began to expand beyond its Seattle base. In 1991 Starbucks approached Hyman with an offer to purchase the Coffee Bean chain as part of an effort to move into the Los Angeles market. It also issued a warning that if Hyman refused, Starbucks would blanket his stores with competing Starbucks stores.

Hyman turned down the offer and soon one of his stores found itself competing with a new Starbucks coffee shop. Rather than be driven out of business, however, Hyman found that the addition of Starbucks to the market only increased his business. The marketing clout of Starbucks raised the profile of specialty coffees, greatly increasing the number of potential customers. People who never visited a specialty coffee shop became curious about Coffee Bean, and many of the new customers found that they preferred the types of coffee Hyman had to offer. While Starbucks thrived in Southern California, Hyman enjoyed excellent growth as well in the 1990s, building his chain to about 60 units.

Coffee Bean was still very much a Southern California institution in 1995 when an opportunity arose to gain an international presence for the chain. Singapore businessman Victor Sassoon, while visiting his brother Sunny in Los Angeles, stumbled upon a Coffee Bean store and became enamored with the concept. Born in Singapore of Iraqi-Jewish descent, Sassoon inherited his father's design watch import business in the early 1980s. As teenagers, the Sassoon brothers moved to Los Angeles but remained connected to Singapore. While involved in the watch business, Victor Sassoon became an entertainment promoter in Singapore. In 1990 he brought the illusionist David Copperfield to Singapore, and then began promoting concerts for Michael Jackson, Phil Collins, Tina Turner, Metallica, Paula Abdul, and others. While in Los Angeles, Sassoon had coffee with Abdul, who was a Coffee Bean enthusiast, and she urged him to not just franchise Coffee Bean in Southeast Asia but to buy the entire company.

SALE OF ASIA FRANCHISE RIGHTS: 1996

Sassoon had difficulty enough persuading Hyman to license the Coffee Bean concept to him, however. After several months of talks, Hyman finally agreed in 1996 to sell the Asia franchise rights for Coffee Bean. Sassoon's brother-in-law, attorney Mel Elias, drew up the contract and became interested in the business. Elias left his position at a law firm to take charge of business development for Coffee Bean's Asian franchise operations. In November 1996, Elias opened the first Coffee Bean shop in Singapore at the Scotts Shopping Centre, relying on beans roasted in California and shipped in vacuum-sealed packages. The store was immediately popular, especially with younger customers who favored the frappés over the hot drinks. More stores followed in Singapore, and in late 1997 the first Coffee Bean store opened in Malaysia.

Convinced that the Coffee Bean chain possessed a great deal of untapped potential in both the United States and overseas, Victor Sassoon decided to buy International Coffee & Tea. The Hymans, by this time, were in their 70s and ready to retire. An undisclosed purchase price was agreed upon, and in 1998 Sassoon and his brother, along with Severin Wunderman, the former chair of Swiss luxury watchmaker Corum, bought the company. Elias was installed as chief executive officer.

While little changed on the surface, the new owners quickly established a new company headquarters and upgraded the backroom systems. Reverse osmosis water filtration systems were also installed to ensure a consistent product, and the chain gained kosher status for its products. A training program was implemented to ensure that employees knew the basics of coffee and tea making. More visible changes soon followed. The

International Coffee & Tea, LLC

KEY DATES

1963: First Coffee Bean store opens in Brentwood, California.
1996: First store in Singapore opens.
1998: Founders sell company.
2007: Coffee Bean opens 500th unit.
2010: Line of bottled coffee and tea drinks is introduced.

décor and signage became consistent. In addition, the chain began to devote more attention to its tea business. Coffee Bean had long relied on tea wholesalers and paid little attention to the origin of the product or its quality. The company now began sourcing tea on its own from India and other locales.

NEW CENTURY, GLOBAL EXPANSION

Coffee Bean's new owners opened stores in the United States, Singapore, and Malaysia as well as Taiwan and Israel. Worldwide sales increased to $60 million in 1999 and grew to about $100 million a year later. By the start of 2001, there were nearly 40 stores spread across the globe. Over the next few years, Coffee Bean expanded into a number of other new markets. A deal was made in 2003 to open stores in the Philippines. The first shop opened in Kuwait in 2005. In that same year, an agreement was reached to introduce Coffee Bean to Hawaii. The chain also continued to make strides in its home market. Coffee Bean reached a deal with UCLA's Dining Services in 2004 to be the exclusive provider of coffee products to the school's eight dining halls. A kiosk at the on-campus Bruin Café would also serve Coffee Bean products. With about 380 units, Coffee Bean looked to add to that number in Southern California through a deal struck in early 2006 with the Ralph's supermarket chain. Under the terms of the agreement, Ralph's committed to the opening of 24 full-range in-store Coffee Bean units over the next three years.

Coffee Bean established kiosks at a variety of other locations as well. Operations were found at sports arenas in Phoenix and Los Angeles, plus McCarran International Airport in Las Vegas and other airports. As a result of growth on a variety of fronts, annual sales increased to about $160 million by 2006. To support further expansion, the chain considered an initial public offering (IPO) of stock, but the idea was never finalized. Although Coffee Bean harbored no illusions about pos-

ing a direct challenge to Starbucks, content to grow at a more measured pace on its own terms, it did emulate its much larger rival in some respects. In 2007, for example, it began selling CDs in stores two years after Starbucks pioneered the concept. Not only did musical sales provide a new revenue stream, it helped to reinforce the Coffee Bean brand with customers.

CHAIN OPENS 500TH UNIT: 2007

Coffee Bean reached a significant milestone in April 2007 when it opened its 500th unit, housed in a Century City office tower in the Los Angeles area. Around the same time, the chain completed a notable achievement by becoming the largest multiunit chain to reach 100 percent certified green status from The Green Restaurant Association. The company's green program had begun in its San Diego stores in 2003 when high-efficiency lighting and energy- and water-efficient spray valves were installed. To cut down on the use of paper cups, porcelain cups were made available to customers and mandatory for employees. Moreover, the stores turned to recycled non-bleached paper cups and instituted recycling programs. Aside from good citizenship, the move toward green practices saved the company money. The first 200 stores involved in the effort would account for about $1 million in savings over a four-year period.

As the first decade of the new century came to a close, Coffee Bean continued to improve on multiple fronts despite difficult economic conditions. A new public relations firm was hired in 2008 to improve the chain's marketing efforts. Better marketing was especially important because of the poor business conditions.

Although Coffee Bean opened 100 new stores around the world in 2008, it closed 20 stores. Same-store sales were also depressed. The company responded by renegotiating leases when possible and adding to the menu. To provide better service, a spice bar was added. Greater emphasis was also placed on breakfast to drive sales. Other revenue streams were developed in 2010 with the introduction of a new line of bottled coffee and tea drinks and a single-serve beverage dispenser. Despite the challenges, the Coffee Bean concept was far from exploited and would likely enjoy steady growth in the years to come. Whether its owners would decide to take the company public still remained to be seen.

Ed Dinger

PRINCIPAL SUBSIDIARIES

CBTL Ventures, LLC.

PRINCIPAL COMPETITORS

Caribou Coffee Company, Inc.; Peet's Coffee & Tea, Inc.; Starbucks Corporation.

FURTHER READING

Berry, Kate. "Home Grown Brew." *Los Angeles Business Journal*, November 15, 2004, 15.

Clark, Taylor. *Starbucked: A Double Tall Tale of Caffeine, Commerce, and Culture*. New York: Little, Brown, 2007.

Elan, Elissa. "Coffee Bean Brews Higher Profile in Deal with Ralph's Markets." *Nation's Restaurant News*, January 23, 2006, 4.

Hopkins, Brant. "Something's Brewing." *Los Angeles Daily News*, July 30, 2003, B1.

Meineirt, Maya. "Something Brewing." *Los Angeles Business Journal*, February 16, 2009, 12.

Sieroty, Chris. "Coffee Bean Making Push in Café Wars." *Los Angeles Business Journal*, January 15, 2001, 10.

Wenig, Gaby. "Where the End Justifies the Beans." *Jewish Journal*, October 30, 2003.

iridium®
Everywhere

Iridium Communications Inc.

1750 Tysons Boulevard, Suite 400
McLean, Virginia 22102
U.S.A.
Telephone: (703) 287-7400
Fax: (703) 287-7450
Web site: http://www.iridium.com

Public Company
Incorporated: 1991 as Iridium Inc.
Employees: 174
Sales: $348.2 million (2010)
Stock Exchanges: NASDAQ
Ticker Symbol: IRDM
NAICS: 517410 Satellite Telecommunications

■ ■ ■

A NASDAQ-listed company, McLean, Virginia-based Iridium Communications Inc. is a provider of satellite communications. Through a "constellation" of 66 low-earth-orbit satellites networked with ground stations and supported by several orbiting backup satellites, the company offers mobile voice, data, and Internet services to regions of the world not served by typical cellular and wired communication systems. The U.S. military is Iridium's largest customer. Other sectors served include adventure travel, aviation, emergency response, heavy industry, maritime, and transportation. Products include satellite phones, transceivers, modems, two-way radios, tracking and monitoring devices, and postpaid calling plans. Iridium's Satellite Network Operations Center is located in Leesburg, Virginia, and the company's

Gateway Earth Station operates in Tempe, Arizona. Satellite Earth Stations are located in Fairbanks, Alaska, and Svalbard, Norway. A pair of Canadian Telemetry, Tracking, and Control Stations also play important roles in the Iridium network.

ORIGINS

The origins of Iridium can be traced to 1985 when Karen Bertiger, the wife of a Motorola Inc. engineer, was vacationing in the Bahamas and was unable to place a call to the United States using her cell phone. She persuaded her husband, Barry Bertiger, that there was a need for a mobile telephone that could be used anywhere in the world. He took the idea to his colleagues at Motorola, engineers Raymond J. Leopold and Ken Petersen, and in their spare time they considered various schemes. In 1987, Motorola allowed them to conduct formal research on the idea.

The engineers developed a plan for a global telephone and paging service that used a network of 77 orbiting satellites to communicate with each other and directly to telephones on the ground. Unlike geostationary communication satellites that hovered in one spot 22,300 nautical miles above Earth, the Iridium satellites would maintain an orbit just 420 nautical miles above Earth. Because they were not stationary, the satellites needed to relay information between one another, thus increasing the complexity of the system. On the other hand, their low orbits allowed the satellites to transmit tightly focused beams, permitting a higher quality of communication signals. In 1988, Leopold made the key suggestion that the satellites be connected to "gateways," stations placed around the world to connect the satellite signals to terrestrial telephone networks.

The number of satellites required by the system was based on a recent study published in the *Journal of the Astronautical Sciences*. The number 77 also provided a name for the proposed system. Because the satellite constellation reminded Motorola engineer Jim Williams of orbiting electrons of an atom, he turned to the periodic table of the elements and found that Iridium featured 77 electrons. Although the number of satellites in the network would be trimmed to 66 when one of the orbital planes was deemed unnecessary, the name stuck, especially when it was compared to the name of the element with 66 electrons: Dysprosium.

Originally involved in car radios, Motorola had become involved in a wide range of products over the years but had now narrowed its focus to wireless communications, making a global wireless telephone network a natural fit for the company. Nevertheless, Motorola's top executives were hesitant to pursue an expensive and technically challenging project that had no certain market for its service. Motorola's chairman, Robert Galvin, learned of the idea and met twice with Bertiger. He then told the company's president that if Motorola did not fund the idea, he would pay for it out of his own pocket.

MOTOROLA UNVEILS IRIDIUM PLAN: 1990

Motorola unveiled the Iridium plan in a major news conference in the summer of 1990. Because of the high cost of constructing the Iridium network, originally estimated at $2 billion, Motorola looked to mitigate the risk. It recruited other companies and consortia to serve as owners and operators of the gateway. Not only would these partners fund the construction of the ground stations, they were urged to invest in the project, which in 1991 was packaged into a company called Iridium Incorporated. In August 1993, a first round of funding raised $800 million from 11 companies or company pools, including Lockheed, Raytheon, and Sprint. For its part, Motorola retained a 25 percent stake in the venture and guaranteed about $1 billion in debt. A second round of fundraising in September 1994 brought another $800 million. At $1.6 billion, Iridium enjoyed the largest private placement of equity in history. In June 1997, the company was taken public and $240 million was raised in an initial public offering (IPO) of stock, which then began trading on the NASDAQ. Priced at $20, the shares quickly tripled in value. A further $800 million in high-yield debt financing was secured in July 1998.

The Iridium plans called for the first satellites to be launched in 1996 and the system to be operational two years later. The company ran into some problems, however. Two failed satellites had to be replaced. The deployment of a final slate of "birds" was delayed by a hurricane, a lightning strike, and a rocket explosion. Complicating matters further were computer problems on the ground and delays in the development of the phone developed for the system, forcing the postponement of commercial service. Voice service was finally launched on November 1, 1998, with Vice President Al Gore and the National Geographic Society making the first call, but the paging service was delayed because of technical problems.

BANKRUPTCY: 1999

Iridium had anticipated serving as a competitor to cellular services, primarily catering to traveling professionals and corporate users as well as governments, in particular the military. Since the time the system had been conceived, however, cellular service had become widespread, resulting in lower prices and a competitive edge against a more expensive, albeit more expansive, satellite service. Moreover, cellular providers subsidized the price of handsets, while Iridium handsets were bulky and cost as much as $3,400. Iridium set an early target of 27,000 subscribers, but five months after its introduction, the service attracted less than 11,000 subscribers. The repercussions of the shortfall were swift. The price of Iridium stock tumbled, and CEO Edward Staiano and his chief financial officer resigned in April 1999. Two months later, the company began laying off people and prices were cut to attract new business as the company repositioned itself as a niche provider. When these steps failed to provide much relief, Iridium filed for Chapter 11 bankruptcy protection in August 1999 after defaulting on $1.5 billion in loans, and trading of the company's stock was halted.

KEY DATES

1991: Iridium Inc. is formed.
1993: First round of funding nets $800 million.
1997: Company is taken public on the NASDAQ.
1999: Iridium declares bankruptcy after $1.5 billion loan default.
2009: Iridium Communications Inc. is formed.

The future for Iridium appeared bleak. Although its system was a marvel of engineering, the company appeared to lack a large enough market to ever become a profitable concern. Any further investment, it was feared, would be simply wasted. By March 2000, it became apparent that if no buyer for Iridium appeared, the satellites would be programmed to drop out of orbit and burn up over the Indian Ocean. Although a few interested parties appeared, nothing seemed viable. Iridium's obituary was all but written and the company's place among history's greatest technological failures assured when in December 2000 Iridium was sold for $25 million to an investment group headed by Daniel A. Colussy. The former president of Pan American World Airways, he formed Iridium Satellite LLC to acquire the assets of Iridium LLC, which included the satellites and network operations center.

TRAGEDY BRINGS ACCEPTANCE: 2001

The new Iridium completed the shift in focus from commercial service to business-to-business and business-to-government. The U.S. Department of Defense quickly stepped in to sign a two-year $72 million contract for unlimited airtime for as many as 20,000 employees. To attract further customers, the Iridium system was upgraded, allowing for the introduction of data and Internet services in June 2001. Compared to terrestrial services, the speeds were extremely slow, yet reliable. The importance of reliability would soon become apparent to many of Iridium's potential customers. On September 11, 2011, the terrorist attacks that struck the World Trade Center towers in New York City and the Pentagon in Washington, D.C., brought home this point when cellular and landline systems failed. Iridium's vice president of marketing, Wayne D'Ambrosio, was paying a sales call to a Defense Department client in Virginia near the Pentagon. Quickly, his satellite became the only means for people at the site to call home.

In the wake of the terrorist attacks, more than 1,000 Iridium phones were dispatched to New York for use by disaster workers, and 50 assigned to trade shows were driven from Iridium's Virginia headquarters to the Pentagon. Sales for Iridium phones surged, as did usage. Pending deals with the Army and Navy were quickly consummated and new service contracts were sold to companies involved in such industries as oil, forestry, construction, mining, and maritime. New services were also launched. In 2003, Iridium introduced short burst data services, ideal for asset tracking and monitoring, and short messaging services. By the summer of 2004, Iridium topped the 100,000 mark in subscribers.

Iridium made technical improvements in the early 2000s. Additional spectrum was granted by the U.S. Federal Communications Commission in 2004, allowing the company to meet growing demand for its service. In that same year, Iridium introduced a smaller, lighter handset that was better suited for travel and work in rugged terrains. In 2006, a new compact, less-expensive satellite data transceiver became available. Of even greater importance was the 2007 announcement that a second-generation satellite constellation, dubbed Iridium NEXT, was in development, a necessity given that the original satellites would begin to fail in the next few years. Scheduled to begin deployment in 2015, the new system would offer greater bandwidth and higher speeds. In addition, the satellites would offer Iridium a secondary source of income by hosting secondary payloads.

TAKEN PUBLIC: 2010

Iridium hoped to establish the second-generation satellite system at half the cost of the original, or about $2.7 billion. Although business was improving and the company would earn $54 million on revenues of $320 million in 2008, it was unable to generate enough cash to pay for such an investment. After efforts to secure private-equity financing failed to bear fruit, the company turned to New York City investment bank Greenhill & Co. and an investment entity it ran called GHL Acquisition Corp., a special-purpose acquisition company. In September 2008, an agreement was signed to merge Iridium with GHL. In September of the following year, the transaction was completed, resulting in a public company called Iridium Communications Inc. An IPO raised $200 million. In October 2010, $1.8 billion in financing was arranged to provide further funding for Iridium NEXT.

While Iridium continued to formulate plans for its new satellite systems, it expanded on a number of fronts. A machine-to-machine business grew, allowing customers to monitor equipment on remote locations or track shipments en route. Smaller and more powerful handsets and transceivers were also introduced. In September 2011, the company unveiled the Iridium Extreme satellite phone, which included a Wi-Fi accessory that would allow smartphones and other devices to be connected anywhere in the world. Should it successfully deploy its next generation satellite network, Iridium appeared to be well positioned to enjoy even further growth in the years to come.

Ed Dinger

PRINCIPAL SUBSIDIARIES

Iridium Satellite LLC; Iridium Constellation LLC; Iridium Government Services LLC; Iridium Carrier Services LLC.

PRINCIPAL COMPETITORS

Globalstar, Inc.; ICO Global Communications (Holdings) Limited; LightSquared Inc.

FURTHER READING

Barboza, David. "Planet Earth Calling Iridium." *New York Times*, September 7, 1999, 1.

Bhide, Amar V. *The Origin and Evolution of New Business*. New York: Oxford University Press, Inc., 2000.

Elstrom, Peter. "Iridium Is Looking a Little Star-Crossed." *BusinessWeek*, April 14, 1997, 40.

Hawn, Carleen. "High Wireless Act." *Forbes*, June 14, 1999, 60.

Hesseidahl, Arik. "The Second Coming of Iridium." *BusinessWeek*, October 19, 2009, 29.

Nelson, Robert A. "Iridium: From Concept to Reality." *Via Satellite*, September 1998.

Woolley, Scott. "Extraterrestrial Dreams." *Forbes*, April 13, 2009, 36.

Jefferies Group, Inc.

520 Madison Avenue, 10th Floor
New York, New York 10022-4213
U.S.A.
Telephone: (212) 284-2300
Fax: (212) 284-2111
Web site: http://www.jefco.com

Public Company
Incorporated: 1962 as Jefferies & Company
Employees: 3,084
Sales: $2.8 billion (2010)
Stock Exchanges: New York
Ticker Symbol: JEF
NAICS: 523120 Securities Brokers; 551112 Offices of Other Holding Companies

■ ■ ■

Jefferies Group, Inc., is a New York City-based global securities and investment banking firm listed on the New York Stock Exchange. Through Jefferies & Company and other subsidiaries, the company offers investment banking services, including equity financing, leveraged financing, restructuring and recapitalization, and mergers and acquisition advice; the sale and trading of securities to institutional investors; asset management services for American and European investors; wealth management for high net worth individuals, senior executives, and private equity firms; global research and analysis services for hedge funds and institutional investors; and execution and securities services to institutional investors and broker dealers. Jefferies

maintains offices in about 20 U.S. locations and a dozen cities in Europe and Asia.

PHONE BOOTH START LEADING TO THIRD MARKET SPECIALTY

The company was started in 1962 in a telephone booth at the Pacific Coast Stock Exchange by Boyd Jefferies. Jefferies, who had been a partner at Noble, Tulk, Marsh & Jefferies, borrowed $30,000 to launch his own operation. Jefferies had one employee, whom he directed as floor broker. The year 1962 was not an easy one in which to start a company: The stock market collapsed in June and fell again in August after the Cuban missile crisis, with an annual loss of over 79 points (the worst since 1931). Despite this difficult environment, Jefferies' first year was successful, and the company expanded its staff and opened a real office, using a closed-circuit television and speaker box to link Boyd Jefferies with his office staff.

In the early years, Jefferies was extremely successful in its manipulation of the emerging "third market," which involved trading listed stocks in an over-the-counter (OTC) style, providing an attractive anonymity to buyers who preferred to keep their interests from becoming public. For these clients, the stock exchange was too public and fixed commission rates were too high. Jefferies' third market offerings, on the other hand, provided privacy and negotiated commissions to banks, mutual funds, and other financial institutions.

In addition to the third market niche, Jefferies pioneered use of the split commission, or "give up," in 1964. The split commission meant that Jefferies could act on behalf of a client, charge full commission, and then share that commission with other brokerage firms that had worked with the client. This commission sharing helped Jefferies build and expand its market. Jefferies joined the Detroit, Midwest, Boston, and Philadelphia stock exchanges by 1965. In 1967, the company joined the New York Stock Exchange (NYSE), opening a five-person office in New York. From 1967 to 1968, the third market surged 40 percent in volume. The growing third market helped Jefferies become the seventh-largest firm in size and trading on the NYSE.

Members of the NYSE were dismayed by the burgeoning third market, and campaigned to eliminate it. Exchange members felt that negotiated commission rates were destructive to free competition, that the third market was irresponsible, and that the market was fragmented. In 1969, a study of the structure of securities markets was conducted by former Federal Reserve Board Chairman William McChesney Martin, who recommended the elimination of the third market and the barring of institutions trading in the market from Big Board membership. The study was followed by Securities and Exchange Commission (SEC) hearings on the issue.

THE IDS ACQUISITION: 1969

Meanwhile, Jefferies & Company was acquired in 1969 by Minneapolis-based Investors Diversified Services, Inc. (IDS), the second-largest financial services company in the country at the time. Jefferies saw the acquisition as a means to bypass the restrictions of the NYSE and increase the size of its institutional business through sizable capital outlay. The details of the acquisition called for an earn-out, which meant that Jefferies & Company would receive shares of IDS preferred stock upon the condition that earnings met expectations for four years. If earnings achieved as planned, the deal would be valued at $45 million. Because IDS did not derive at least 50 percent of its gross income from broker-dealer operations, Jefferies had to quit the New York exchange under Exchange Rule 318. Unhampered by the concerns of NYSE members, Jefferies concentrated on third market business.

The economy entered a downturn in the 1970s. While other Wall Street companies made cutbacks, Jefferies actually increased its staff commission rates to 30 percent (the industry standard was 10 to 20 percent). The result was the attraction and retention of highly qualified staff in a difficult period. Jefferies returned to the regional exchanges, with the exception of New York. Texas became a new site of expansion in 1971, with an office opened in Dallas.

In 1971 the company reapplied for membership in the Big Board of the NYSE. Upon rejection (based on Rule 318), IDS and Jefferies filed an antitrust lawsuit against the exchange, seeking $6 million in damages. Jefferies and its parent company claimed that the NYSE Big Board was an illegal monopoly, and that exclusion had placed the company at a competitive disadvantage. In 1973 the presiding judge informed the NYSE that he planned to rule in Jefferies' favor. Membership was opened to brokerage firms owned by other kinds of companies, so long as 80 percent of brokerage was conducted with the public. Jefferies rejoined the exchange in March 1973.

Jefferies had met financial expectations according to its ownership agreement with IDS for the first three years. An internal conflict of interest, however, caused an earnings dip in 1973. Almost a third of Jefferies' previous clients were lost due to competition with IDS, which always competed with investment brokerages for the best price. For its part, IDS did not yield the expected capital to Jefferies, nor did it conduct any trades with the firm. In August 1973 Boyd Jefferies bought back his company over dinner for $2.5 million. The story of the Jefferies acquisition was the subject of a later case study at Harvard Business School.

Later that year, Jefferies & Company resigned from the Big Board, only to rejoin the following spring. The NYSE raised its commission rates, and Jefferies reentered the third market in full force. Management salaries and other expenses were cut back, and Jefferies began anew without IDS's parentage.

REBUILDING IN THE SEVENTIES AND EIGHTIES

The mid-1970s marketplace continued to slump, and Congress moved to ease industry restrictions with the Exchange Act of 1975, finally signaling the end of fixed commission rates. As the third market became more attractive to many institutions, Jefferies was poised with familiarity and experience. By the late 1970s, many of Jefferies' clients who had left during the IDS period returned to the firm. In 1977, Jefferies had expanded with offices in Los Angeles, New York, Chicago, Dallas, Boston, and Atlanta. The company was a top broker for

```
┌─────────────────────────────────────────────┐
│                                               │
│              KEY DATES                        │
│                   ■                           │
│ ─────────────────────────────────────────    │
│                                               │
│  1962:  Company is founded in Los Angeles.    │
│  1969:  Jefferies is acquired by Investors    │
│         Diversified Services, Inc.            │
│  1983:  Jefferies is taken public.            │
│  1999:  Investment Technology Group, Inc. is  │
│         spun off.                             │
│  2001:  Headquarters moves to New York.       │
│  2009:  Company is named a primary dealer by  │
│         Federal Reserve Bank of New York.     │
│                                               │
└─────────────────────────────────────────────┘
```

regional banks including St. Louis Union Trust, Hartford National Bank & Trust, and First National Bank of Minneapolis, and for big volume companies including Citibank, Morgan Guaranty, and Bank of America.

Seeking to expand into the high-net-worth market, Jefferies Group, Inc. (the holding company for Jefferies & Company) took over and reorganized Wagenseller & Durst, a Los Angeles-based retail brokerage. The new company, W&D Securities, first offered secondary stocks and new issues, then became a clearing business for research, and ultimately served as a soft dollar firm, exchanging research activities for commissions.

In 1981 Jefferies achieved its largest transaction ever. Jefferies assisted drug, food, and liquor conglomerate Foremost-McKesson in a $65 million buyback from industrialist Victor Posner. The company purchased its first computer in 1982, and became accessible 24 hours a day. In December 1982, the company began to take advantage of trading halts. When Warner Communications' Atari division announced losses, Warner trades were closed on the exchange, and Jefferies was the only company moving the stock. In two days, Jefferies traded about six million shares, generating business and new international clients. Later, Jefferies took advantage of similar halts in PepsiCo, Inc. and Alleghany Corporation.

The company, on October 13, 1983, held an initial public offering (IPO) of 1.75 million shares at $13 per share. By 1984, Jefferies was among the 10 most profitable publicly held brokerages. International expansion during trade halts led the company to develop a new overseas office in London, headed by Frank Baxter. In 1986 Baxter became president and chief operating officer, returning to New York to manage the company. Later that year, Jefferies managed the first public trade

transfer of ownership, trading 25.8 million shares of Alied Stores for Robert Campeau.

MANAGING A CRISIS: 1987

After 25 years in business, the company reached a potentially disastrous turning point in 1987. Boyd Jefferies, founder and CEO, was charged by the government and the SEC with two securities violations: "parking" stock for customer Ivan Boesky and a customer margin violation. Jefferies pleaded guilty, receiving a fine and a probation barring him from the securities industry for five years. The company itself was not charged, but its brokerage unit was censured by the SEC. Jefferies resigned from the company. To make matters worse, the stock market crashed on October 19, 1987. Plummeting prices led to a $6.5 million loss on the company's principal holdings. As the new CEO, Baxter had quite a job on his hands.

Baxter's unique leadership style was peppered with personal idiosyncrasy. A disciple of New Age guru Deepak Chopra and an avid practitioner of transcendental meditation, Baxter installed a meditation room in Jefferies' headquarters (which was later closed for lack of use). On his desk sat framed photos of Mahatma Gandhi and Martin Luther King Jr. Nicknamed "the smiling assassin," Baxter had a New Age demeanor covering a hard-edged business sense.

Baxter's first action was geared toward building staff morale in a time of crisis: He retained the company's name and implemented 20 percent bonuses for the company's 180 traders. The generosity worked: Not one trader left the company. To compensate for a dip in business, Baxter cut costs by 15 percent through back office automation, and he limited capital use to $50 million (from $300 million in 1985). What could have been an institutional nightmare was salvaged by Baxter's shrewd managerial techniques. The company earned net income of $6.1 million in 1987, increasing that figure to $16 million (on sales of $145 million) in 1988. Shares rose from $7.50 in 1987 to $14.50 in mid-1989. By 1990, the company traded its highest-ever volume: 3.5 percent of the consolidated NYSE tape.

REBIRTH AND DIVERSIFICATION: LATE EIGHTIES AND NINETIES

In its second life, under Baxter's leadership, the company focused on diversification, delving beyond its third market niche. Baxter's expansion plans included global expansion in electronic trading, corporate finance, international convertible sales, and derivative sales (all of which were quick moneymakers). Jefferies moved quickly into the fourth market: off-exchange, computer-based (electronic) trading. In the fourth market, the broker's position was eliminated by the Portfolio System for Institutional Trading (POSIT), which traded portfolios and matched buyers and sellers automatically. POSIT was supplemented with the Quantitative Executive System (QUANTEX), which allowed traders to access buy and sell recommendations throughout the day. The company added a wholly owned subsidiary (Investment Technology Group) in 1987 to run POSIT. Jefferies' fourth market activities resulted in a new role for the firm's account executives, who were now referred to as JeffCAT, or Jefferies Computer Assisted Traders.

The high-yield bond trading business was another new area for Jefferies' expansion, made possible by the collapse of Drexel Burnham Lambert. Jefferies hired 18 former Drexel employees and became one of the top three junk bond trading companies. Taxable fixed income and corporate finance departments made Jefferies capable of handling bank debt capabilities and products. By 1992, junk bonds became the company's second most profitable sector. That year, the company made plans to open a Hong Kong office. In 1993, the company landed its first public equity-related deal, and 14 employees of Howard Weil Labouisse Friedrichs (including the firm's entire corporate finance department) were recruited. With 125 sales traders (the largest institutional equity sales force in the country), Jefferies was well equipped to secure equity deals. In 1992, equity trading constituted almost two-thirds of revenues ($108.2 million). The company that year earned a stunning net of $18.7 million or $3.08 a share.

At this time, the company was the biggest U.S. third market trader, as well as the largest in computer-based trading. Rapid expansion under Baxter's helm, an efficient new accounting method, and the larger boom in securities spelled success for Jefferies in the 1990s. The company's stock price jumped from $11 at the beginning of 1992 to $35 in September 1993, more than a 200 percent gain in less than two years. Since 1989, Jefferies had bought back almost three million shares of its own stock, including Boyd Jefferies' remaining 800,000 shares.

INTEGRATION: A GLOBAL INVESTMENT BANK

In the 1990s, the company positioned itself to entrepreneurial companies as a "custom shop" full investment bank, offering better pricing and financing options than Wall Street. Beginning in 1993, Baxter sought to maximize earnings per share by integrating the different departments of the firm's diversification effort (business lines, fixed income, and electronic trading). Baxter also continued to explore new industries. In

1993, Jefferies formed a new subsidiary group to compete in the public energy equity market. By 1993, the company had 38 equity analysts, and revenue from investment banking for midsized companies had jumped 127 percent over the previous year. In 1994, the company built a new analytical trading division to trade equities and futures. In 1998, Jefferies launched a series of intranet-based data marts to support its transition to investment banking and entry into the corporate, finance, and research markets.

By 1997, it was clear that Baxter had truly saved the company from its potential demise at the time of Boyd Jefferies' indictment. The company had not had a losing year since Baxter took over. Revenues for 1997 approached $800 million (a 47 percent increase over 1996), with earnings of $63.6 million. Rumors of a takeover more than doubled 1997 stock prices, which reached an all-time high of $89.63 a share in December. With high employee ownership of stock and an even higher level of personal investment in the newly focused company, Baxter gave no indications of selling, and indeed, the company remained independent.

A major cause for speculation that Jefferies was on the verge of being acquired by a major bank were reports in late 1997 that the firm had hired J.P. Morgan & Co. for an unknown reason. A few weeks later, the purpose became evident when Jefferies announced that it would split into two companies. In April 1999, the New York equity trading and research firm Investment Technology Group, Inc., was spun off in a tax-free transaction for Jefferies shareholders. Jefferies continued to maintain a presence in New York City, however. It owned several seats on the NYSE and a large portion of its revenues came from stock trading.

HEADQUARTERS MOVES TO NEW YORK: 2001

The new century brought a change of leadership at Jefferies. In 2000, Baxter relinquished his positions as president and CEO, while staying on as chairman. At the start of the following year, he was succeeded as chief executive by 39-year-old Richard B. Handler, the head of the firm's junk bond business who worked out of the Stamford, Connecticut, office. Under Handler, Jefferies expanded its New York brokerage business. Lawrence Helfant L.L.C. was acquired in 2001, adding 12 NYSE seats. It was also during this time that Boyd Jefferies died at the age of 70. A further break from the company's roots took place in February 2002 when Baxter stepped down as chairman, turning over that post as well to Handler. At that point, the firm's headquarters had essentially moved from Los Angeles to New York. In September 2001 the change became formal.

In the early 2000s, Jefferies expanded through the acquisition of sector-specific boutique advisory firms. The 2002 addition of Quarterdeck Investment Partners supplemented Jefferies' aerospace and defense business. A year later, Jefferies acquired Broadview International, a technology advisory firm. In 2005, Randall & Dewey, a mergers and acquisitions adviser for the oil and gas industry, was acquired, creating Jefferies' Energy Investment Group. Further external growth followed mid-decade. Private equity fund placement firm Helix Associates was acquired in 2005, and two years later Jefferies added London media advisory firm LongAcre Partners and financial services advisory firm Putnam Lovell, an arm of National Bank of Canada.

Jefferies also beefed up its executive ranks, adding specialists in health care, energy, and equity derivatives. For the most part, Jefferies, which had avoided the credit exposure of larger concerns, was not impacted by the banking crisis of 2008. The firm cut staff and temporarily shuttered some international offices, but it also took advantage of conditions to make strategic hires and acquisitions. In September 2008, for example, the firm's British office hired 25 former Bear Stearns executives in London. In 2009, Jefferies entered the municipal bonds sector by acquiring Depfa First Albany Securities LLC from Depfa Bank PLC.

Jefferies' ability to diversify its operations during poor economic conditions, as well as the demise of other Wall Street firms, set the stage for the firm being named a primary dealer by the Federal Reserve Bank of New York in 2009. As such, it became one of just 17 firms allowed to participate in the New York Fed's open-market buying and selling of securities and Treasury auctions and provide market information to the New York Fed. At the close of the first decade of the new century, Jefferies continued to expand. In 2011, it paid $430 million for Prudential Bache Commodities Ltd., a provider of brokerage and clearing services across all of the world's major futures and options exchanges. Also in 2011, Jefferies opened an equity sales, trading, and research office in India. Late in the year, Jefferies faced market uncertainty in the wake of the collapse of MF Global Holdings. As a smaller player in the global securities and investment banking field, Jefferies remained more susceptible to sudden and steep market shifts. Nonetheless, CEO Richard Handler remained confident that the company could safely navigate the MF Global debacle and such related and wide-reaching events as the European debt crisis.

Heidi Feldman
Updated, Ed Dinger

PRINCIPAL SUBSIDIARIES

Jefferies & Company, Inc.; Jefferies Asset Management, LLC; Jefferies Financial Products, LLC; Jefferies International Limited.

PRINCIPAL COMPETITORS

Deutsche Bank Alex. Brown; RBC Wealth Management; UBS Financial Services Inc.

FURTHER READING

Cole, Benjamin Mark. "Baxter Role Change." *Los Angeles Business Journal*, December 4, 2000, 32.

———. "Power Base Shifting to East." *Los Angeles Business Journal*, February 11, 2002, 27.

De La Merced, Michael J. "Jefferies Is Named a Primary Dealer." *New York Times*, June 17, 2009.

Glater, Jonathan D. "Boyd L. Jefferies Dies at 70." *New York Times*, August 25, 2001.

Herman, Jack, and Dan Seymour. "Jefferies Ventures into Munis with Depfa Buy." *Bond Buyer*, February 17, 2009, 1.

Hoffman, Thomas. "Intranet Helps Market Shift; Web Data Mart Expands Bank Investment Service." *Computerworld Magazine*, May 25, 1998.

Marcinek, Laura. "Jefferies Chief Sees Turmoil Easing as Memories of MF Global Failure Fade." *Bloomberg News*, November 17, 2011.

Pratt, Tom. "Jefferies' Equity Effort Expands into New Issues." *Investment Dealers Digest*, April 19, 1993, 14.

Schwimmer, Anne. "Something to Cheer About." *Investment Dealers Digest*, September 27, 1993, 16.

Sommar, Jessica. "Jefferies Recruits Kipnis to Build Equity Derivatives." *Investment Dealers Digest*, February 4, 1994, 6.

Toal, Brian A. "New Jefferies Energy Group Gets Off to Fast 1993 Deal Pace." *Oil & Gas Investor*, October 1993, 16.

Vrana, Deborah. "Jefferies' New Age: When Frank Baxter Took Over in the '80s." *Los Angeles Times*, March 22, 1998, D1.

KEEN, Inc.

———■———

926 NW 13th Avenue, Suite #210
Portland, Oregon 97209
U.S.A.
Telephone: (503) 542-1520
Toll Free: (866) 676-5336
Web site: http://www.keenfootwear.com

Private Company
Incorporated: 2003
Employees: 100
Sales: $250 million (2011 est.)
NAICS: 316213 Men's Footwear (Except Athletic) Manufacturing; 316214 Women's Footwear (Except Athletic) Manufacturing; 316219 Other Footwear Manufacturing; 448210 Shoe Stores

■ ■ ■

KEEN, Inc., began by making sandals with "patented toe protection technology," but has expanded its line of footwear to include casual shoes, boots, tote bags, and socks. The company provides products for youths, toddlers, and infants as well as different collections for men and women. Since the beginning, KEEN has been dedicated to innovation and conservation, from designing recyclable shoe boxes to creating 100 percent vegan shoes to incorporating sustainable practices into the way it conducts business. Its shoes are available through the company's Web site and at the KEEN Garage in Portland, Oregon. There are also distributors that sell KEEN products at more than 1,000 retail locations in the United States and throughout Europe, North America, Central America, Australia, and New Zealand.

ORIGINS

In 2003, Martin Keen, a shoe designer and world-class sailor, and Rory Fuerst, the owner of an athletic shoe company, founded KEEN, Inc. in Alameda, California. Their mission was to create a shoe for competitive sailors and for use during other outdoor activities. KEEN's sandal-like shoe was lightweight, like a sneaker, and designed to protect the toes from harm by a patented rubber toe guard. It delivered the breathability, comfort, and quick-drying qualities of open-toed shoes.

Martin Keen was responsible for the creation of the first KEEN shoe. He had "shoes coursing through his veins," a trait he attributed to his upbringing, he told *Providence Journal* in February 2006. Keen's father, Peter Keen, had been a pattern maker for C&J International, a footwear company in England, when Keen was a boy. After the family moved to the United States in 1971, Peter Keen worked for Rockport and Keds and other shoe companies, and the younger Keen sometimes helped his father make shoes.

After studying industrial design at Ohio State University, Martin Keen went on to work as a designer for several California-based shoe companies. During this period of his life, he sailed competitively. As a member of the 1995 J-24 team, he won the world championship. It was while sailing that Keen came up with the idea that eventually became his Jamestown sandal, prototype of the first KEEN shoe.

```
┌─────────────────────────────────────────┐
│                                          │
│      COMPANY PERSPECTIVES                │
│                   ●                      │
│  ──────────────────────────────────     │
│  KEEN's mission is to bring the opposing │
│  elements of design and life together to │
│  create Hybrid products that encourage   │
│  everyone to pursue a HybridLife. What-  │
│  ever we do: We simplify, include and    │
│  engage. Whenever we do it: We Create,   │
│  Play and Care. It's a way of life, we   │
│  call it HybridLife.                     │
│                                          │
└─────────────────────────────────────────┘
```

In preparation for making the Jamestown, Keen cast friends' feet in plaster to create a "library of feet" on which to base an anatomical last. Then using an auto-body repair material called Bondo Body Filler, he built the model for a shoe in 2001 that he had manufactured in China. Keen wore his Jamestown sandals for two years before meeting up with Rory Fuerst at an outdoor products retail show.

In short order, the two men attracted top industry talent to KEEN, Inc.'s management team. Angel Martinez, with 25 years of experience in the footwear industry, mostly at Reebok and Rockport, and *Footwear News*'s 1997 Man of the Year, became chief executive and chairman of the board. Jim Van Dine, who had held executive posts at both Reebok and Deckers Outdoor Corporation, became president. The new company farmed out aspects of its operation, such as billing, sales, and manufacturing, and set out to refine and market Keen's creation as its Newport hybrid sandal.

The Newport retained the patented large toe guard that enclosed the front of the foot, but also had a compression-molded EVA midsole and a razor-siped rubber sole. Elastic cord-lock strings allowed the wearer to tighten the front of the shoe. A sandal-like strap held the heel in place. It was available for both men and women in leather and in tough fabric lined with the material used in wetsuits.

The Newport sold for just under $100 and rang up $1 million in sales during the first nine weeks after it was introduced at the Outdoor Retailer and the World Shoe and Accessories trade shows in February 2003. Paragon, REI, and The Walking Company began carrying it and other KEEN models in the spring. Blogs and social networking sites generated powerful marketing buzz for the new start-up's products. *Footwear News*, the shoe industry's leading trade publication, labeled KEEN, Inc. the "Launch of the Year" in 2003.

FROM INDUSTRY NOBODY TO BRAND SOMEBODY

In April 2004, the Newport won the Design Innovation Award, recognizing "the best in the world of design and business," at the seventh annual Success by Design conference held jointly by the Rhode Island School of Design and Bryant College. REI named KEEN Vendor Partner of the Year when the company became its largest footwear vendor for 2004. By June, KEEN's shoes were being sold by 900 retailers nationwide. Just one year after its launch, KEEN had sold $30 million worth of shoes. *Business 2.0* magazine, in June 2005, heralded KEEN as one of the new "instant companies" that go from "industry nobody to brand somebody" at warp speed.

In 2004 Keen and Fuerst ended their partnership. Keen left the company, although he continued to own its second-largest share. In 2005, he teamed up with Timberland to develop and sell his latest shoe-sandal hybrid, the Mion ("my-own") line. Also in 2005, Martinez resigned as KEEN's chief executive officer and chairman of the board to become chief of Deckers Outdoor Corporation, which marketed the Teva, Simple, and Ugg brands.

Despite the turnover in management, however, KEEN had sales of $60 million in 2005. That year it branched out into other lines of footwear, including light hiking boots, trail running shoes, and winter boots. It had also branched out into children's shoes.

BEGINNING THE HYBRIDLIFE IN PORTLAND, OREGON: 2006–08

In 2006, KEEN moved its headquarters to Portland, Oregon, home to more than 20 footwear companies and another 20 outdoor gear and apparel companies. Van Dine explained the motivation behind the move in *Sporting Goods Business* in October 2005: "It's [got] the richest pool of talent on the planet. Add the close proximity to outstanding outdoor recreation with world class running, hiking, climbing, skiing, and cycling, the availability of affordable housing and you have what we think is needed to take KEEN to the next level." The company, which maintained production in China, offered relocation assistance to its 40-odd employees, about half of whom elected to make the move to the Pacific Northwest.

Van Dine did not follow suit, however. Instead, he left the company in 2006 along with four top KEEN executives to found Ahnu Inc., an outdoor shoe manufacturer in Alameda, California. KEEN tapped Kirk Richardson of Nike to become its new president. Richardson's career at Nike had included several leader-

KEY DATES

2003: Martin Keen and Rory Fuerst found KEEN in Alameda, California.

2004: KEEN is named Vendor Partner of the Year by REI.

2006: KEEN moves its headquarters to Portland, Oregon.

2007: Company purchases 360,000 kilowatt hours of wind power to cover 100 percent of its headquarters' electrical power usage.

2010: KEEN opens the KEEN Garage where it sells products directly to consumers.

ship positions within the company's footwear and apparel product marketing areas, including general manager of Nike Outdoor and international marketing and merchandising positions in Europe and Japan. Richardson, asked about the young company's frequent changes in management in a June 2006 *Oregonian* article, denied concern, saying: "There has been turnover at KEEN, but I'm not worried about losing momentum. We've gone from really good people … and people who were strong professionally to people with even stronger, better professional skills."

To support KEEN's marketing potential, the company worked with Forty Forty of Berkeley, a branding agency, which opened a branch in Portland to provide ongoing support to KEEN's HybridLife national marketing campaign. This campaign emphasized the importance of living a balanced life, replete with personal satisfaction, giving back to one's community, and practicing a sustainable, green lifestyle.

FASHIONING A CORPORATE CULTURE

With regard to its corporate culture, KEEN attempted to walk the walk it espoused. It prided itself on being more than an outdoor company. "We believe that supporting good causes is an obligation of financial success and that respecting the environment is simply a matter of conscience," read its company literature. In 2004, the company scrapped its plans for its first marketing campaign and devoted its $1 million advertising budget to Southeast Asia disaster relief. It also started a charitable giving program in partnership with the Conservation Alliance.

Focusing on philanthropy was unusual for a company as young as three-year-old KEEN, but

management wagered that charitable giving was an effective brand-building strategy among both consumers and employees. Between 2004 and 2006, KEEN distributed several million dollars to organizations promoting clean water, exposing urban youth to wildernesses, maintaining an urban forest park, giving bikes to children, and delivering medical and educational supplies to remote populations around the world.

In 2006, KEEN founded The KEEN Foundation, a nonprofit arm committed to environmental preservation. In subsequent years, it formed partnerships with nonprofits worldwide as part of its Hybrid Care Program, which helped raise awareness of other programs that were dedicated to making a positive impact on the environment worldwide.

KEEN also introduced a line of Hybrid Transport sport bags made from repurposed leather and aluminum scraps found on its production floors. Focusing on its materials, packing, and manufacturing, it partnered with outdoor retailer REI to introduce a 100 percent biodegradable box.

THE GREENING OF THE OUTDOOR INDUSTRY

With Richardson at the helm, KEEN became increasingly identified with sustainable growth. In 2007 it purchased 360,000 kilowatt-hours of wind power-based energy to cover 100 percent of its headquarters' electrical power usage. It hired a sustainability coordinator to make its China production facilities greener, and it began to look into buying carbon offset credits.

Richardson explained the company's perspective in the Fall 2007 *Lewis & Clark Chronicle*: "You look for alternatives, and that's what KEEN is doing. Over half of the cost of shoe materials is derived from a barrel of petroleum. That's a reality. … That's one of the reasons it's so important to mitigate waste in the waste stream."

By late 2007, slightly more than a year after KEEN had moved to Portland, its staff numbered 65, up from about 45 a year earlier. In early 2008, Richardson became KEEN's newly created chief of sustainability, and James Curleigh assumed the roles of president and chief executive. Curleigh, an environmental advocate and outdoor footwear, apparel, and accessories veteran, came to KEEN from Salomon North America, where he had been president and chief executive since 2001. Under Curleigh, the company leased 4,800 square feet of warehouse space close to its headquarters in 2008.

KEEN products began to appear in popular health and fitness magazines, cousin to the hard-core outdoor enthusiast markets that had earlier embraced them, in

2009. In the spring, the Madrid Mary Jane shoe was featured in *Women's Health*, the Coronado Sandal and the Parisi were featured in *Shape*, and the Genoa Peak WP was featured in *Fitness*. Curleigh attributed the back-to-basics attitude that made the rugged look more appealing to the financial downturn with its concomitant emphasis on comfort, durability, and multifunctionality.

EXPANSION IN PORTLAND: 2009–11

As hard economic times gripped the United States, KEEN continued to prosper with revenue increases in 2009 and 2010 of 10 and 20 percent, respectively. By the close of 2010, KEEN had more than 150 footwear styles, produced five million pairs of shoes each year in Asia, and had reached annual sales of about $200 million. Seventy percent of KEEN's business was domestic (compared to Nike's 40 percent share in North America). During these years KEEN began to sell its product online directly to consumers as well as through its existing network of retailers. In August 2010 it opened the KEEN Garage, an on-site store for its products. For each pair of shoes sold at the Garage during its first week, KEEN donated a backpack full of school supplies to local students in need of support.

In 2010, the company also opened a 15,000-square-foot factory in Portland where it began to assemble and box KEEN's new steel-toed Portland work boot. KEEN had earlier begun to produce socks in Mount Airy, North Carolina, and its scrap-based cargo bags in Chico, California.

KEEN also hired a new vice president of merchandising to increase its presence in retail outlets and elevate its profile worldwide in 2010, and added three more styles of boots to its assembly lines in Portland in 2011. Boot uppers continued to be assembled in Asia at one of KEEN's five or six factories there because of the expense of acquiring equipment and sourcing domestically.

The following year it launched its new ad campaign called HybridLife. The concept of the "Create-Play-Care dynamic" was one KEEN had embraced earlier and even attempted to implement in its workplace. The ad campaign featured stories showcasing "amazing everyday people around the planet, Creating, Playing, and Caring for the world around them."

The HybridLife campaign kicked off with the message "Recess is Back" in the spring of 2011. KEEN's goal, starting with its own workforce, was to inspire people to reclaim the playtime of their youth. The eight-year-old company wanted everyone to experience "the freedom they feel as an eight-year-old at recess." At headquarters it installed a Recess Center with a recess tracker, a map of nearby recess spots, and a collection of Frisbees, yoga mats, and bicycles. The Recess Team was empowered to rally other employees to make use of KEEN's "open door" policy and to get outside for 15-minute breaks and to play. In addition, 60 of KEEN's 2,000 retailers displayed a recreated jungle gym in their front display window.

It had been less than a decade since the Newport sandal, and KEEN had grown to encompass an ever-growing number of products sold in 5,000 retail outlets in 60 countries, online through keenfootwear.com, and at the KEEN Garage. With anticipated revenues of $250 million for 2011, about 100 employees in Portland, and ongoing growth of 20 percent, KEEN attributed its meteoric rise to what Richardson called "purposeful innovation, thoughtful innovation," likening KEEN's success to Nike's in the *Lewis & Clark Chronicle*. Curleigh had this to say in an online interview posted on the KEEN blog in 2009: "The important thing—at least for us—is to stay on the front end of that sustainability dynamic, but to remain balanced in the way we run our business and the way we evolve our brand and speak to people." As KEEN prepared to roll out its Recess Revolution in 2011, it was anyone's educated guess how far, how fast, or how high KEEN could go.

Carrie Rothburd

PRINCIPAL COMPETITORS

Ahnu, Inc.; C&J Clark International, Ltd.; Columbia Sportswear Company; Decker's Outdoor Corporation; Mephisto SA; Nike, Inc.; The Rockport Company LLC; The Timberland Company.

FURTHER READING

Blevins, Jason. "Color These Retailers Green: Avoiding Impact on the Environment Becomes a Popular Way of Doing Business for Clothiers." *Denver Post*, August 22, 2006, D1.

Brettman, Allan. "Keen on Portland." *Oregonian*, December 12, 2010.

Copeland, Michael V. "The New Instant Companies." *Business 2.0*, June 1, 2005.

Carofano, Jennifer. "Shades of Green: Footwear Companies Are Stepping Up Environmental Efforts to Save Energy, Cut Costs and Help the Planet—and It's Not Just about Image." *FN*, July 31, 2006, 48.

Helickson, Jennifer. "'Recess Is Back' and Aims to Improve the Well-Being of the Bay Area." *San Jose Examiner*, April 18, 2011.

Hill, Gail Kinsey. "Warming to 'Carbon Neutrality.'" *Oregonian*, May 9, 2007.

Jung, Helen. "Keen Sprints into Giving." *Oregonian*, June 27, 2006.

"Keen Footwear to Move Corporate Headquarters to Portland." *Sporting Goods Business*, October 28, 2005.

Kushner Resnick, Susan. "He's Sure-Footed: Jamestown Man Launches Second Shoe Line." *Providence Journal*, February 23, 2006, G1.

Larabee, Mark. "Companies Putting Green Foot Forward." *Oregonian*, July 26, 2007.

Meyer, Shelly. "Kirk Richardson B.S. '75 Leads Keen Footwear in Its Sprint to Success." *Lewis & Clark Chronicle*, Fall 2007.

Rogers, Kelli. "Daily Journal of Commerce Newsmaker 2011: KEEN Footwear." *Daily Journal of Commerce* (Portland, OR), February 22, 2011.

Waggoner, Bethany. "The Green Line Series: James Curleigh + KEEN Blaze a Trail in Sustainable Footwear." KEEN Blog: KEEN People & Places. Accessed January 19, 2012. http://www.keenfootwear.com/us/en/blog/index.php/2009/08/the-green-line-series-james-curleigh-keen-blaze-a-trail-in-sustainable-footwear/.

Kerr Drug, Inc.

3220 Spring Forest Road
Raleigh, North Carolina 27616
U.S.A.
Telephone: (919) 544-3896
Fax: (919) 544-3796
Web site: http://www.kerrdrug.com

Private Company
Founded: 1951 as Village Pharmacy
Employees: 2,400
Sales: $665 million (2008 est.)
NAICS: 446110 Pharmacies and Drug Stores

∎ ∎ ∎

Kerr Drug, Inc., is a privately held North Carolina drugstore chain with about 90 units. Unlike national competitors, Kerr focuses on its pharmacy business, which contributes about two-thirds of sales. The chain further differentiates itself by incorporating resource centers into the stores to offer clinical medical services. Kerr does not offer the gifts, groceries, snacks, and general merchandise carried by large drugstore chains. Rather, it maintains such departments as Naturally Kerr, offering more than 3,000 natural, organic, and homeopathic products; Kerr Hearing, providing hearing screening and hearing aid products; and Kerr Optical, offering eyewear. Many of the stores also offer photo service and house Kerr Cafés, which serve coffee, tea, muffins, bagels, and pastries.

NORTH CAROLINA ROOTS

Kerr Drug draws its name from Banks Dayton Kerr, who was born on a farm near Charlotte, North Carolina, in 1922. While growing up, he was drawn to the drugstore business. During his high school years, he worked the soda fountain at a local drugstore and then studied pharmacy at the University of North Carolina at Chapel Hill, graduating in 1943. He managed a drugstore owned by a doctor in Norfolk, North Carolina, but in 1944 joined the Army Medical Corps to serve his country during World War II. Following the war, he went to work for the Liggett Drug Store chain, managing a store in Charlotte before taking charge of another Liggett store in Greensboro, North Carolina.

Kerr was eager to own his own drugstore, and in 1950 he was presented with an opportunity when real estate developer Willie J. York constructed North Carolina's first shopping mall in Raleigh, called Cameron Village Shopping Center. York had learned about the young pharmacist from a Whitman's candy salesman and invited the 27-year-old Kerr and his wife to pay a visit to Raleigh. Rather than the typical drugstore of the day in which clerks waited on customers, York wanted to lease a space for a self-service store. Kerr liked the idea. Two days later he signed a lease, and in 1951 opened his first drugstore under the Village Pharmacy name.

In 1954, Kerr added a second store in Goldsboro, North Carolina, in another York development. York introduced Kerr to other developers, which led to the opening of a third drugstore in Durham, North Carolina, in 1956. Kerr added more stores in eastern

North Carolina and opened a warehouse in Raleigh, where he also maintained his home offices. In November 1963, Kerr opened his 10th store in Tarrytown Center in Rocky Mount, North Carolina. All this time, Kerr continued to serve as a pharmacist, filling orders and interacting directly with customers. Soon, however, managing his chain of drugstores commanded all of his time and attention.

By the early 1970s, there were 30 North Carolina stores, all of them east of Chapel Hill. To stimulate growth of the chain, key employees were awarded shares in the company, although the Kerr family maintained majority control. In order to expand more rapidly than the two stores per year that could be supported by cash flow, the company secured financing in the late 1970s. An additional loan was taken out in 1986.

SECOND GENERATION IN CHARGE

By this time, Kerr was nearing retirement age. His son John became president-elect while two sons-in-law held top positions in the 76-unit drugstore company. Under the leadership of the younger Kerr, following the retirement of his father, Kerr Drug continued to open new units and remodel existing ones. By 1990 the chain numbered 94, 40 of which were less than three years old. Annual sales were in the $150 million range. Faced with new competition, in particular Wal-Mart, the stores underwent a change in format at this time. Giftware and soft drinks, which had diminished in performance, received less prominence. Instead, the chain focused on pharmacy, home health care, incontinence products, and skin care. Kerr Drug also upgraded its distribution center, adding 54,000 square feet and installing a new conveyor/picking system.

To remain competitive, Kerr Drug continued to modify its format in the early 1990s. A new division, DirectCare, was launched in 1992 to provide a 24-hour monitoring service for senior citizens and other people that dispatched help as required. A year later, the chain added a 25,000-square-foot deep-discount store format. Over the years, larger chains had made offers to buy Kerr Drug, but Banks Kerr rejected them. Changes in the health care industry, however, made it apparent to him that the days of family pharmacies were numbered.

THRIFT DRUG ACQUIRES CHAIN

In early 1995, Banks Kerr sold the 97-unit Kerr Drug chain for about $72 million in J.C. Penney Company stock to Penney subsidiary Thrift Drug Company, a chain of 525 stores, mostly located in Pennsylvania, that included five stores in the Raleigh/Durham area. By adding the number one drugstore chain in North Carolina in Kerr Drug, Thrift established a major beachhead in the mid-Atlantic region. A year later, Thrift added to its holdings in the area by acquiring 190 Rite Aid stores in North and South Carolina.

A much larger deal was also in the offing. In November 1996, Penney reached an agreement to merge its 1,000 Thrift Drug stores spread across 15 eastern and midwestern states with Eckerd Corporation's more than 1,700 stores, mostly located in the South and Southeast. As a result of the combination, the Eckerd chain would hold a dominant position in the Carolinas. In the Raleigh/Durham area, for example, Eckerd would have a market share of about 50 percent. In order to approve the merger, the Federal Trade Commission (FTC) ordered Penney to sell 164 stores in North Carolina and South Carolina.

A group of Thrift executives who were being put out of jobs because of the merger elected to bid on the available drugstores, 34 of which operated under the Kerr Drug name and the remainder under the Rite Aid name. The group, led by executives Anthony Civello and Richard Johnson and provided with funding by Pennsylvania businessman Laurence Ross, received permission from the FTC to purchase the stores in May 1997. Included in the deal was a Raleigh distribution center and the Kerr Drug name. Because of goodwill built up over the years and brand recognition in the area, the stores would be operated under the Kerr Drug banner. While the new Kerr Drug was taking shape, the original Kerr stores retained by Eckerd were converted to the Eckerd brand. By late September 1997, the new Kerr Drug had completed the transition process.

NEW CHAIN TAKES SHAPE

Civello and Johnson brought 30 other Thrift executives with them from Pittsburgh, where they had run Thrift Drug. Although transplants to North Carolina, they were seasoned in the drugstore field and wasted no time in nurturing their new assets. For fiscal 1997, Kerr posted sales of $427 million. As the 1990s came to a close, Kerr made progress on several fronts. An agree-

KEY DATES

1951: Banks Kerr opens first drugstore in Raleigh, North Carolina.
1995: Kerr sells chain to Thrift Drug.
1997: Merger forces Kerr Drug divestment.
2005: First Community Healthcare Center opens.
2009: South Carolina stores are sold.

ment was reached with Cardinal Distribution to serve as the chain's primary pharmaceutical supplier. A new Kerr Drug private-label line of products was also successfully introduced. While the previous Kerr Drug chain had its own private-label program in place, these stock-keeping units (SKUs) were entirely new and employed new packaging. About 600 store brand products would soon be introduced. The company also separated its corporate headquarters from its distribution center in Research Triangle Park in Raleigh, and moved it to the North Raleigh residential and commercial development of Wakefield, where many of the company's executives lived.

The most significant development of this period, however, was the 1998 opening of the Kerr Drug Enhanced Pharmaceutical Care Center, a patient care facility that offered such services as health screenings, immunizations, wellness programs, and disease management counseling. The center was developed in collaboration with the University of North Carolina's School of Pharmacy.

The new century brought the death of the company's founder, Banks Kerr, in August 2000. Although only a handful of the stores he opened retained the Kerr brand, his name continued to grace a chain of pharmacy-oriented drugstores that reflected his core values. Sales increased to $641 million in fiscal 2000, this despite a reduction in the number of stores to 153. Several underperforming stores were closed while a number of others were replaced by a new format that favored locations in smaller communities. By concentrating on what consumers bought most often, these stores were able to reduce inventory while increasing revenues.

As the new century unfolded, Kerr continued to reduce inventory and focus more attention on its pharmacies and the growth of clinical services to maintain an edge in the increasingly competitive drugstore industry. By the summer of 2001, the chain increased the number of its Enhanced Pharmaceutical Care Centers to five. New robotic technology that improved the efficiency of drug dispensing was also installed at several stores. Unprofitable stores continued to be shed as well, and several stores that had low pharmacy sales were converted into Smart Dollar closeout stores.

FIRST COMMUNITY HEALTHCARE CENTER OPENS: 2005

The evolution of Kerr took a major step in October 2005 with the opening of the chain's first Community Healthcare Center in Lenoir, North Carolina, near Charlotte. At 9,000 square feet in size, it was large enough to offer a score of specialty departments. It would soon be certified by the American Diabetes Association for its patient education program. What was lacking were cosmetics, snacks, and greeting cards. Other new stores that followed would also include the new Healthcare Centers, as well as the Kerr Café, the chain's coffee bar concept.

In fiscal 2008, annual sales totaled $665 million, two-thirds of which stemmed from pharmacy operations. The number of units had been reduced to 102, and would grow smaller in 2009 when the chain elected to exit the South Carolina market, selling the 11 stores in the state to CVS Caremark Corporation. Kerr was content to focus on its core North Carolina market and pursue its innovative and successful approach to the drugstore business. In 2009, the chain began rolling out a new store-within-a-store concept, Naturally Kerr, to offer customers a wide range of natural, organic, and homeopathic products and services. At the same time, general merchandise, including automotive and hardware products, was eliminated.

In addition to improving community health services, Kerr explored business-to-business opportunities, making its clinical services available to health plans and other companies. In addition, the chain looked to partner with the public sector. Kerr, for example, worked through the ChecKmeds program in North Carolina to provide medication therapy management to state seniors on Medicare. In late 2010, Kerr reached an agreement with ActiveCare, Inc. to provide around-the-clock living assistance emergency response solutions through the ActiveOne PAL (Personal Assistance Link) device and service. ActiveCare would also work with Kerr to provide pharmacy-related services to its members, such as prescription refill reminders. Kerr was clearly committed to its unique drugstore approach and appeared well positioned to remain a strong regional competitor for years to come.

Ed Dinger

PRINCIPAL DIVISIONS

Kerr Health.

PRINCIPAL COMPETITORS

CVS Caremark Corporation; Rite Aid Corporation; Walgreen Co.

FURTHER READING

Fleming, Harris, Jr. "Kerr II a Hit." *Drug Topics*, April 17, 2000, 81.

Frederick, Jim. "Kerr Drug Marks 10-Year Anniversary Milestone." *Drug Store News*, June 25, 2007, 5.

Fried, Lisa I. "Former Thrift Execs Aim to Revive Kerr." *Drug Store News*, April 7, 1997, 3.

Johnston, Steve. "Coming Home." *Charlotte Observer*, September 28, 1987, 3C.

"Kerr Dazzles with Health Center Concept." *Drug Store News*, November 7, 2005, 1.

"Kerr Drugs Planning to Open New Store Here in November." *Rocky Mount Evening Telegram*, August 1, 1963, 13.

McDonald, Thomasi. "Drugstore Titan, Kerr, Dies at 78." *Raleigh (NC) News & Observer*, August 26, 2000, B1.

Persaud, Babita. "Kerr's New Prescription—Relaxing." *Raleigh (NC) News & Observer*, January 22, 1995, C1.

Pinto, David. "Kerr Fortifies Position with Store Sale to CVS." *Chain Drug Review*, June 29, 2009, 24.

"Rebirth of Kerr Shakes up Raleigh/Durham Market." *Chain Drug Review*, June 23, 1997, 391.

Kimco Realty Corporation

3333 New Hyde Park Road
New Hyde Park, New York 11042
U.S.A.
Telephone: (516) 869-9000
Fax: (516) 869-7250
Web site: http://www.kimcorealty.com

Public Company
Incorporated: 1966 as Kimco Realty Development
Employees: 687
Sales: $849.5 million (2010)
Stock Exchanges: New York
Ticker Symbol: KIM
NAICS: 531110 Lessors of Residential Buildings and
   Dwellings

■ ■ ■

A real estate investment trust (REIT) listed on the New York Stock Exchange, Kimco Realty Corporation is one of the world's largest owners and operators of neighborhood and community shopping centers. The New Hyde Park, New York-based company owns or has interests in some 950 shopping center properties in 44 states, Puerto Rico, Canada, Mexico, and South America. Kimco's portfolio comprises about 138 million square feet of leasable space. Typically, the centers are anchored by a supermarket or such big box retailers as Home Depot and Wal-Mart. Through taxable subsidiaries, Kimco develops and sells shopping centers, offers retail real estate management and disposition services, and acts as an agent or principal in connection with tax-deferred exchange transactions. The company also provides management, leasing, and operational support for shopping centers in which it owns only a small equity interest.

COMPANY ORIGINS

The Kimco name was derived from the last names of its cofounders, Martin S. Kimmel and Milton Cooper. Cooper was an associate at a law firm in which Cooper's brother was a partner. The two were brought together when a client of the firm asked for a review of a real estate project in Sackets Harbor, New York. Cooper, who focused on the financials, was impressed by Kimmel's knowledge and work on the assignment. In 1958, Cooper was engaged by Zayre Department Stores to open a discount store in Miami, Florida. The project was fraught with a myriad of leasing and construction problems, prompting Cooper to track down Kimmel in California and suggest they work together. Kimmel wasted little time in flying back to New York, and he was soon living in an apartment in Florida supervising the construction of a shopping center. It was a partnership based on a handshake but one that would endure for a lifetime.

The Kimco Development Corporation was established when Kimmel and Cooper joined with other shopping center owners and investors to combine their resources to build and manage new shopping centers. Cooper served as president, while Kimmel assumed the chairmanship. Immediately after its inception, Kimco began building new shopping centers across the United States. In 1967, it erected facilities in Florida, Indiana,

Kimco's culture radiates entrepreneurial spirit. Empowerment, accountability, team collaboration, recognition, and genuine caring for the well-being and development of our associates are the key ingredients of Kimco's positive and dynamic work environment. Over 50 years ago, Kimco was founded on the integrity of a handshake which today stands as a symbol of the trusted partnership between the company and our associates whose personal contributions make us a leader in the shopping center industry.

Ohio, and Utah. Throughout the late 1960s and early 1970s, Kimco focused on the construction of several shopping centers in Florida, while also adding several new centers in Pennsylvania, Illinois, New York, Ohio, Texas, and Virginia.

By the mid-1970s, Kimco owned and operated about 50 shopping centers, most of which were located in Florida and the Midwest. Kimco funded most of its developments by borrowing, or through joint ventures with other investors or real estate developers. Most of the shopping centers that Kimco built were relatively small in comparison to the regional malls that would become popular in the 1970s and 1980s. Kimco's projects were classified as neighborhood and community shopping centers and were designed to attract local customers seeking day-to-day necessities, rather than high-priced luxury items. Such centers were typically anchored by supermarkets, large drugstores, or discount department stores, including Winn-Dixie, Poston's World, Payday's Orlando, Save-A-Lot, and Hills Department Stores.

During this time, Kimco's development strategy was regarded as unique in the industry. Many development companies employed the services of real estate companies to serve specific functions in the development process, such as overseeing construction and financing or finding tenants to lease the property. Often, a development company would simply employ a property management and leasing company to handle the day-to-day operations of the property. Kimco, however, sought to profit by managing the entire process in-house, including construction, financing, legal and accounting functions, leasing, and maintenance. Cooper believed that total control of its holdings would allow

the company to reduce costs, achieve higher-quality projects, and build long-term wealth.

EXPANSION TO NEW MARKETS

Throughout the 1970s, Kimco continued to add new projects to its list of holdings. While Florida remained a target market, Kimco also expanded into different northeastern, mid-Atlantic, and midwestern states and engaged in a few projects in the West. Toward the end of the decade, however, the U.S. commercial real estate industry experienced a cyclical downturn, causing Kimco's development activity to continue at a much slower pace. Nevertheless, Kimco did generate a few new projects and, by 1981, the company owned and operated 77 shopping centers. Its total portfolio of properties would provide an important base of assets and cash flow that would contribute to Kimco's rapid growth during the next decade.

Real estate industry woes that lingered into the early 1980s prompted Cooper to shift Kimco's development strategy for the 1980s. For the past 15 years, Kimco had built most of its projects from the ground up. In 1981, only nine of its centers had been purchased after construction. However, Cooper found that ground-up construction had become too risky for developers seeking long-term profitability. "The theory was that if you developed anything new, you had to buy land, pay for construction, and have market rents," Cooper explained in the May 1992 issue of *Chain Store Age Executive*, adding that "The safety depended on the credit of the tenant." In addition, Kimco's executives thought that existing, undervalued properties were available for acquisition.

Bucking commercial real estate industry trends, Kimco embarked on a program of growth founded almost entirely on acquisitions. As the U.S. real estate development industry recovered and boomed in the mid- and late 1980s, office buildings and shopping centers were erected at a feverish pace. Billions of investment dollars became available for new construction. Favorable tax laws, foreign investment, and deregulation of U.S. financial markets all contributed to the hot market for new projects. Nevertheless, Kimco stuck to its acquisition strategy, building less than 5 percent of the properties it would add to its portfolio throughout the decade.

PENNSYLVANIA GROWTH: 1986

Kimco's expansion activity remained low-key in the early 1980s. The company added a few shopping centers in New Orleans and Pennsylvania to its portfolio in

KEY DATES

1958: Martin Kimmel and Milton Cooper develop Florida shopping center.
1991: Kimco Realty Corporation is taken public as a real estate investment trust.
1998: The Price REIT is acquired.
2001: Taxable subsidiary is established.
2006: Kimco is added to Standard & Poor's 500 Index.

1983 and purchased a few undervalued centers in New York, New Jersey, Ohio, and West Virginia during 1984 and 1985. The following year, however, Kimco launched an aggressive growth initiative, prompted by strong capital markets and the boom in the real estate industry. Shifting its focus away from Florida, Kimco purchased a string of properties in Pennsylvania during 1986 and then began to focus on Ohio, where it would eventually amass about 30 properties. At the same time, Kimco continued to acquire new shopping centers throughout the eastern half of the country. By the late 1980s, Kimco had accumulated more than 150 properties and was generating annual sales of nearly $60 million. While about 90 percent of its revenues came from its core of community and neighborhood shopping centers, Kimco was also operating two regional malls.

By 1989, however, the real estate business was spiraling into a deep recession. Besides general U.S. economic malaise, most sources of lending for acquisitions and new construction had dried up, and the profitability of many existing projects was rapidly declining. Importantly, the Tax Reform Act of 1986 had dealt a deathly blow to the industry. That act essentially wiped out many of the important tax advantages granted to investors in commercial real estate, including companies such as Kimco. As a result, Kimco and its industry peers had difficulty funding growth. Furthermore, the value, liquidity, and profitability of their existing properties was diminished.

Although Kimco's revenues climbed 11 percent in 1991, to $66 million, the company experienced a disappointing net loss of $15 million, which reached $16 million the following year. Despite setbacks, Kimco's problems were minor compared to those of most other developers, many of whom had relied on tax breaks and extreme financial leverage to achieve profits. Kimco's properties were relatively well managed, and the company had positioned itself for long-term growth and stable cash flow. As many other developers grappled for

cash to meet their debt obligations, Kimco survived the downturn. It did suffer from an excessive debt load, however, which had swelled past a staggering $400 million by early 1991.

TAKEN PUBLIC AS REIT: 1991

In an effort to diminish its burdensome liabilities and to generate cash for continued expansion, Cooper again bucked convention and pioneered a new growth strategy. Noting the plethora of vastly undervalued shopping centers on the market in the early 1990s, and the dearth of capitalized investors, he took Kimco Realty Corporation public in 1991. A real estate investment trust (REIT) was created, containing most of Kimco's properties, and the sale of shares in that trust raised about $150 million. Kimco used most of this money to reduce its debt, which declined to about $290 million after the public offering. "Traditional real estate financing was over," Cooper recalled in the *Chain Store Age Executive* article, noting that "We saw that in order to have the kind of growth we wanted … we would have to become public, and have a permanent base of equity."

Kimco's move to a REIT was unique and influential. As a financing technique, the REIT was generally regarded as risky and had never been used on such a large scale to securitize shopping centers. Nevertheless, the REIT provided an important advantage in that its shares could easily be liquidated by sale on the stock market. In addition, REIT owners enjoyed tax advantages not available in other forms of real estate investing. Encouraged by Kimco's success, about 35 other developers created REITs during the next two years. "Before that, people thought it would be impossible to sell real estate stock," Cooper recollected in the September 27, 1993, issue of *Newsday*.

A corollary of Kimco's move to a REIT was the formation of KC Holdings, Inc. Kimco formed KC Holdings before the public offering and moved 45 of its 178 properties into that corporation's subsidiaries. The holdings consisted primarily of poorly performing shopping centers, projects that were joint ventures, and miscellaneous properties, such as a bowling alley. By removing those assets from under the Kimco umbrella, the company was able to offer a higher-quality, lower-risk REIT. The stock of the newly formed KC Holdings remained in the hands of Cooper and other Kimco stockholders prior to the public offering.

Pleased with their first stock sale, Kimco's management sold more shares in 1992 and 1993. The two offerings brought an additional $161 million to Kimco, most of which was used for new acquisitions. In fact,

Kimco picked up 30 more properties during 1992 and 1993, raising its total asset base from about $400 million in 1991 to $450 million in 1992, and then to $650 million by the end of 1993. These gains were regarded as impressive, particularly since the company's total debt load remained below $300 million.

THE IMPORTANCE OF GOOD MANAGEMENT

Kimco's savvy financing strategies during the early 1990s were lauded by industry analysts. Investors, too, were pleased, as Kimco's REIT shares rocketed more than 100 percent between 1991 and 1993. However, it was Kimco's continuing commitment to quality management and long-term growth that allowed it to survive the commercial real estate shakeout of the early 1990s and then to prosper going into the mid-1990s. Indeed, as Kimco financiers jockeyed in financial markets, the operations team was busy streamlining the organization for improved efficiency and profitability in a changing real estate and retail environment. "The key to successful real estate investing is no longer 'location, location, location,' but 'management, management, management,'" Cooper observed in Kimco's 1993 annual report.

Kimco's strengths were also reflected in its longtime commitment to sophisticated information systems, which were used to track and manage its properties and investment activities. Such integrated systems allowed small leasing staffs to easily access and track the entire portfolio of Kimco holdings. In addition, Kimco sustained its legacy of vertical integration, handling its leasing, acquisition, property management, accounting, architecture, and other functions in-house. Kimco accomplished those varied tasks with a small, highly efficient workforce. About 80 people in its headquarters and 52 workers stationed at several of its larger properties managed the entire multimillion-dollar operation.

As Kimco bolstered its profit margins and increased its holdings, the U.S. economy began to recover. Kimco's revenues grew to $79 million in 1992, and it posted its first positive income figure, $19 million, since the late 1980s. In 1993, moreover, Kimco gleaned $35 million in profits from nearly $100 million in receipts and invested a record $164 million in new properties. Kimco continued to post solid gains early in 1994, raising an additional $150 million through two stock offerings, most of which was used to further pare its slimming debt load. The company also bought several more shopping centers, boosting its holdings to over 150 properties with about 20 million square feet of retail space in 24 states, figures that did not include the properties held by KC Holdings, Inc.

ACQUISITION OF PRICE REIT: 1998

In the second half of the 1990s, Kimco significantly added to its holdings. One of the largest transactions was the 1998 acquisition of La Jolla, California-based The Price REIT for $840 million in securities and the assumption of debt. Spun off from discount retailer Price Co. in 1991, Price REIT had interests in 37 properties in 15 states. The combination resulted in the creation of the first true national non-mall retail shopping center REIT. When Kimco closed the 1990s, its portfolio consisted of 473 property interests, including 405 neighborhood and community shopping centers. Revenues grew to $433.9 million in 1999. Despite the company's strong performance, investors paid little respect, entranced instead at the time by the prospects of new Internet and high-technology ventures. When the dot-com bubble soon burst, however, Kimco was viewed with renewed interest.

The new century brought changes in REIT law. The REIT Modernization Act that went into effect on the first day of 2001 allowed Kimco to be involved in profit-making activities and services that had not been previously allowed. Kimco immediately launched a taxable subsidiary for which the groundwork had already been laid. A key step was the hiring a year earlier of David B. Henry as Kimco's chief investment officer, a post he had previously held at GE Capital Real Estate. Henry now became CEO of the taxable subsidiary, which was broken into several diversified companies.

These included Kimco Developers Inc. for shopping center development; Retail Property Solutions, providing capital and consulting to retailers; Kimco Select Investment, a vehicle for secondary market investment in real estate and retail-related securities; Kimco Preferred Equity, providing financing for shopping center acquisitions; and Kimco Exchange Place to facilitate 1031 exchanges of real estate, which allowed investors to defer capital gains taxes on the exchange of like-kind properties. Kimco Developers took the company back to its development roots. It was run by Jerry Friedman, who had come to Kimco with the acquisition of Price REIT, which also brought a backlog of development projects.

Henry helped to grow Kimco in other ways as well. While at GE Capital, he had been active in Canadian and Mexican real estate. As soon as he joined Kimco, he urged the company to become involved in the Canadian market. In the fall of 2001, he engineered a joint venture with RioCan Real Estate Investment Trust, Canada's largest trust and the only REIT in the country that focused exclusively on retail real estate. Taking advantage of favorable exchange rates between U.S. and Canadian currency, the joint venture began to quickly assemble an extensive slate of shopping centers. For several years Kimco had the field to itself before other REITs recognized the opportunity presented by Canada. Henry played a key role in Kimco looking to its southern borders as well. In 2002, the company made its first investments in Mexico.

ADDED TO STANDARD & POOR'S 500

Ever since it had gone public in 1991, Kimco posted a string of record-breaking results. In 2006, it was added to the coveted Standard & Poor's 500. By now, one-tenth of the company's revenues came from abroad, prompting Kimco to look for other markets to pursue, including Puerto Rico, Argentina, Brazil, and Chile. The banking crisis of 2008, which limited the amount of available capital, put a damper on Kimco's expansion plans, but the firm was well diversified and remained in a strong cash position.

While Kimco sold some assets during this difficult stretch, it also made some opportunistic acquisitions. Kimco also had no difficulty in late 2009 in raising $346 million in an equity offering that had little advance buildup. In June 2010, Kimco acquired a controlling interest in 15 U.S. shopping centers from Big Shopping Centers Ltd. for $422 million. The following year, Kimco sold 11 shopping centers while adding three major shopping centers. Kimco possessed a long and successful track record in a far from glamorous yet highly reliable sector of the real estate market and was likely to enjoy continued success.

Dave Mote
Updated, Ed Dinger

PRINCIPAL SUBSIDIARIES

Kimco Development Corporation; The Kimco Corporation.

PRINCIPAL COMPETITORS

DDR Corp.; The Macerich Company; Regency Centers Corporation.

FURTHER READING

Colwell, Carolyn. "REIT Rush: Real Estate Investment Trusts—Hot Property in a Revived Market." *Newsday*, September 27, 1993, 25.

Hardesty, Dawn Wotapka. "Kimco Realty Finds Success on Long Island." *Long Island Business News*, August 5, 2005.

Jochum, Glenn. "Slicing Up Li's High Income Pie." *LI Business News*, May 9, 1994, 23.

"Kimco Realty Corporation." *Research*, January 2005, 72.

"Kimco Realty Enters Canadian Market." *National Mortgage News*, November 5, 2001, 28.

McQuaid, Kevin L. "Gambling Real Estate Futures on REITs." *Warfield's Business Record*, June 12, 1992, 1.

"Public Was the Way to Go at Kimco." *Chain Store Age Executive*, May 1992, 102.

Rudnick, Michael. "Kimco Looking to Expand beyond U.S. Borders." *HFN—The Weekly Newspaper for the Home Furnishing Network*, August 6, 2007, 55.

Talley, Karen. "Kimco Planning Big Stock Sale." *LI Business News*, October 21, 1991, 3.

"Thinking Small Leads to Big Things for Kimco Realty." *Long Island Business News*, May 5, 2006.

The Lampo Group Inc.

1749 Mallory Lane, Suite 100
Brentwood, Tennessee 37027-2931
U.S.A.
Telephone: (615) 371-8881
Fax: (615) 371-5007
Web site: http://www.daveramsey.com

Private Company
Incorporated: 1991
Employees: 280
NAICS: 541611 Administrative Management and
General Management Counseling; 514199 All
Other Information Services

∎ ∎ ∎

The Lampo Group Inc. is a Brentwood, Tennessee-based company that operates the various business interests of David L. Ramsey, a prominent financial advice author, radio host, television personality, and motivational speaker who espouses the virtues of people living within their means and avoiding debt. His syndicated radio program, *The Dave Ramsey Show,* is aired on more than 500 radio stations in the United States with a weekly listening audience of about 4.5 million. He is also the author of several books, including three *New York Times* best sellers: *Financial Peace, More Than Enough, The Total Money Makeover,* and *EntreLeadership.* Ramsey also presents his approach to financial responsibility at live events, and speaks to budding entrepreneurs at limited seating events. In addition, Lampo Group runs Financial Peace University, which offers a 13-week program to help participants climb out of debt and gain control of their finances.

RAMSEY, CHILD ENTREPRENEUR

David Ramsey was born in 1960 and raised in Antioch, Tennessee, where his father was a builder and an advocate of self-reliance. When at the age of 12 Ramsey asked his father for some money, he was told he did not need money, he needed a job. In short order, Ramsey was taken to a print shop to have business cards made up for "Dave's Lawn Service," and he was in business for himself. Ramsey continued cutting grass during high school while managing to post excellent grades. Although he was planning to enroll in college, Ramsey took a real estate exam and began buying and selling real estate all through his four years at the University of Tennessee–Knoxville, where he earned a degree in finance. After graduation in 1982, he began buying residential properties in Nashville, renovating them, and then selling them at a profit. His portfolio of properties reached $4 million, and he maintained a lavish lifestyle with his wife and two young children. His real estate holdings were financed by a group of short-term loans, however. He had encountered no difficulty in securing local financing, but his small business empire came crashing down in 1986 due to changes that resulted from the Banking Act of 1986.

With the rules for bank ownership changed, the industry underwent a wave of consolidation in the 1980s, resulting in larger concerns acquiring local banks. The bank where Ramsey did business was one of many small institutions that were quickly swallowed up. The

COMPANY PERSPECTIVES

The Lampo Group, Inc. is providing biblically based, common-sense education and empowerment which gives HOPE to everyone from the financially secure to the financially distressed.

new owners of the bank had no relationship with Ramsey and were not willing to back him further. When his short-term loans came due at the same time, they refused to renew them and he was forced to pay off the loans. Ramsey was given 90 days to sell off $1.2 million of properties. Unable to comply, he defaulted on the loans and had to contend with foreclosures and lawsuits. He ultimately declared bankruptcy in 1990.

BEGINNING TO PROVIDE FINANCIAL COUNSELING: 1991

Ramsey's experience with debt led him to study the question of how to responsibly manage money. He looked to popular authors, interviewed wealthy people, and turned to the Bible. He began using what he learned to offer financial counseling at his church. In 1991, he formed The Lampo Group Inc. to provide financial counseling. He then codified his financial principles in a book, *Financial Peace*, which he self-published in 1992. He sold the book out of his car and by mail. Having established a platform for his message, Ramsey was invited to be a guest on a Nashville radio station. He was subsequently asked to host his own show on the station to provide callers with financial advice. Because the station was in bankruptcy, it could not afford to pay him for his work, but he agreed to do the show for free. With friend and business partner Roy Matlock, he launched *The Money Game*, which would later be renamed *The Dave Ramsey Show*. (Ramsey parted ways with Matlock in 1998.)

Ramsey was well suited for the radio. Not only did he prefer it over one-on-one counseling, which he found tedious, the utter certainty of his opinions played well on commercial radio. The radio program led to other opportunities. In 1994, he launched Financial Peace University (FPU) and began working with families in weekly sessions that lasted six months. A year later, he was meeting with families five days a week, while also conducting more than 20 seminars.

Ramsey decided to syndicate his radio show in 1996. The first to pick it up was a station in Oak Ridge, Tennessee. A year later, *The Money Game* would be

broadcast in a dozen cities. At the same time, Ramsey expanded his personal brand on a number of fronts. A Web site, FinancialPeace.com, was launched. *Financial Peace* was picked up by a major publisher, Viking, which led to a 21-city book tour that helped to make the book a *New York Times* best seller. An audio version was also released by Penguin. His growing popularity led to numerous television appearances, including *The Today Show* and *CBS This Morning*. *People* magazine also profiled Ramsey in a major article. As a result of his increased exposure, Ramsey was able to launch a LIVE event tour that attracted nearly 5,000 participants over the course of 1997.

THE DAVE RAMSEY SHOW ON THE RISE

Lampo Group expanded on multiple fronts as the 1990s came to a close. *The Money Game* was renamed *The Dave Ramsey Show* in 1999, and by the end of the year it was available in 33 cities, including eight top 100 markets. The *Financial Peace Planner* was released in 1998 and became a best seller by some measures. A year later, *More Than Enough* was published by Penguin Books and became Ramsey's second *New York Times* best seller. Lampo Group released other products as well. In 1998 the company released the *1997 Taxpayer Relief Act* video, and a pair of software products: *The Envelope System* and *Dumping Debt* followed in 1999 and won the Ziff-Davis Financial Software of the Year Award. Ramsey's greater name recognition spurred interest in Lampo Group's other activities. Ramsey's LIVE events attracted more than 20,000 attendees in both 1998 and 1999. More than 10,000 families enrolled in the FPU program from 1997 to 1999.

Lampo Group continued to grow as the new century unfolded. The radio network expanded to 56 stations, which now included two top 20 markets as well as 14 top 100 markets. In 2000, the company built its own in-house radio studio. Lampo Group also looked to expand its reach to a younger generation. *Financial Peace Junior* was released, and the Financial Peace for the Next Generation program was introduced and made available at a dozen schools. Also in 2000, the company formed a church department and FPU began working with churches.

While Ramsey never hid his religious convictions, he had an uneasy relationship with secular radio stations that felt uncomfortable with the constant references to God during his conversations with listeners. Following the September 11, 2001, terrorist attacks on the United States, a tragic event that led many to embrace their religion, Ramsey decided to overtly integrate his beliefs with his financial principles. Rather than limit his audi-

KEY DATES

1991: Dave Ramsey founds The Lampo Group.
1992: Ramsey self-publishes *Financial Peace*.
1996: Ramsey begins syndicating radio show.
2003: Ramsey writes third best seller.
2011: Radio network reaches 500 stations.

ence, Ramsey grew only more popular as he surpassed other religious-oriented financial advisers to reach an ever widening audience.

FIRST LIVE SIMULCAST EVENT: 2002

The syndicated network for *The Dave Ramsey Show* grew to 96 stations in 2001 and reached 137 stations a year later, including eight of the top 20 markets and 35 of the top 100. In the meantime, Lampo Group launched a subscription Web site, "Dave's Club" (subsequently renamed MyTotalMoneyMakeover.com). The same year, FPU established the Workplace and Financial Literacy programs and began working with the military. Ramsey also expanded his motivational speaking business. In 2002, he held his first LIVE simulcast event. All told, more than 32,000 people attended LIVE events that year.

As the decade continued, Lamp Group expanded in several directions. Ramsey wrote his third *New York Times* best seller in 2003. Support for *The Total Money Makeover* included a 32-city tour that included 11 LIVE events. Attendance for these and other LIVE events that year approached 45,000 people. Also in 2003, Viking released *Financial Peace Revisited*, while Lampo Group released a children's book series and a Spanish translation of *Financial Peace*. In addition, Ramsey's writings led to a newspaper column, "Dave Says," that began to run on a syndicated basis in 2003. A year later, the column was dropped by several newspapers after it was revealed that some of the identities of the letter writers were duplicated or falsified. Although he laid the blame on a low-level employee, Ramsey apologized and offered to issue refunds to the newspapers.

Ramsey had become a major brand by the middle years of the decade. He was interviewed on *60 Minutes* and made a guest appearance on *The Oprah Winfrey Show*, where he dispensed financial advice. The number of radio stations that carried his radio program grew to 250 in 2005. The program was now available in more than half of the top 100 markets. Lampo Group also

introduced a new radio product, Daily Money Makeover, 90 vignettes that were made available to radio stations for broadcast. The company established Wealth-Coach, a unit that provided financial advice to people in the arts and professional sports. In 2006, Ramsey signed a development deal with CBS Entertainment to produce a reality show. Although he recorded a pilot and six episodes, it never aired. Ramsey was able to secure a show on Fox Business Network in 2007. Also called *The Dave Ramsey Show*, it aired on the network until it was canceled in June 2010.

GROWTH ON ALL FRONTS

In the final years of the first decade of the new century, The Lampo Group pursued growth in all of its core businesses. The radio program reached the 350 mark in affiliates in 2008 and was now available in about three-quarters of the top-100 markets and half of the top-20 markets. The number of stations grew to 450 in 2009. The newspaper column enjoyed strong growth as well. It reached more than five million people in 2008, a number that increased to 14 million readers in 2009 and more than 16 million readers a year later. Ramsey continued to enjoy success as a motivational speaker as well. The LIVE events were now attended by more than 80,000 people a year. FPU also added to its program offerings for schoolchildren and military families.

Because of a poor economy and a growing number of people saddled with credit card debt and mortgage payments they could not afford, Ramsey's message resonated more than ever. For Lampo Group that meant more opportunity to market Ramsey's financial advice in all forms. A co-publishing agreement was reached with Simon and Schuster's Howard Books, which in the fall of 2011 released *EntreLeadership*. At the heart of Ramsey's business empire, however, was his radio program. In October 2011, *The Dave Ramsey Show* syndicated network added its 500th station. Only time would tell how much further Ramsey could grow his brand and business.

Ed Dinger

PRINCIPAL OPERATING UNITS

The Dave Ramsey Show; Dave Ramsey's Financial Peace University.

PRINCIPAL COMPETITORS

Suze Orman Media, Inc.

FURTHER READING

Bellafante, Ginia. "The Anti-debt Crusader." *New York Times Magazine*, October 30, 2005, 26.

Drury, Susan. "The Gospel According to Dave." *Nashville Scene*, May 31, 2007.

McArdle, Megan. "Lead Us Not into Debt." *Atlantic*, October 26, 2009.

Moll, Rob. "Beyond Credit Card Shredding." *Christianity Today*, August 2011, 30.

Ross, Bobby, Jr. "Cover Story." *Houston Chronicle*, June 26, 2009, 6.

Stengel, Marc. "Get Used to It; Off the Floor." *Nashville Scene*, July 23, 1998.

Landmark Media Enterprises, LLC

■

150 Granby Street
Norfolk, Virginia 23510-1604
U.S.A.
Telephone: (757) 222-5416
Toll Free: (800) 446-2004
Fax: (757) 446-2489

Private Company
Incorporated: 1905 as Norfolk Newspapers Inc.
Employees: 5,000
Sales: $1.13 billion (2011 est.)
NAICS: 511110 Newspaper Publishers; 511120 Periodical Publishers; 515112 Radio Stations; 515120 Television Broadcasting; 515210 Cable and Other Subscription Programming; 541850 Display Advertising

■ ■ ■

Landmark Media Enterprises, LLC, is the privately owned holding company for a variety of media entities. It owns four daily newspapers in the southeastern United States: the *Virginian-Pilot*, of Norfolk, Virginia; the *Roanoke Times*, of Roanoke, Virginia; Greensboro, North Carolina's *News & Record*; and the *Annapolis Capital*, of Annapolis, Maryland. The company also owns over 120 community and special interest newspapers. Its Dominion Enterprises subsidiary operates some 100 different Internet-related businesses such as classified ad and real estate marketing firms. In addition, Landmark owns the television stations KLAS-TV in Las Vegas, Nevada, and WTVF-TV in Nashville,

Tennessee. The company was the longtime owner of The Weather Channel, which it founded in the 1980s and sold in 2008. Landmark is controlled by the Batten family.

SAMUEL SLOVER AND THE FOUNDING OF NORFOLK NEWSPAPERS

Landmark was founded by Samuel Leroy Slover, an enterprising gentleman immersed in the Virginia newspaper business for 55 years. A native of Tennessee, Slover migrated to Virginia in 1900, hoping to change his fortune. He had been the 20-year-old business manager of the financially troubled *Knoxville Journal*. Despite his efforts, the paper went bankrupt and Slover, then 22, assumed its liabilities ($36,400) as a debt of honor. After arriving in Virginia, Slover sold ads for a New York trade journal before approaching the well-connected Joseph Bryan, owner of the *Richmond Times*, for a loan to purchase a newspaper in neighboring Norfolk. Bryan, aghast, refused the young man. Slover, undaunted, asked to sell advertising for the *Times*. When he received a second rejection, Slover tried another tack: What if he sold ads, on a commission basis, to area merchants who were not current clients? With this proposition, Bryan had nothing to lose and everything to gain, so he accepted the offer and was soon rewarded with a multitude of new advertisers.

It was then Bryan's turn to make an offer to Slover: rescue a Newport newspaper from going under within one year and gain half interest in its ownership. Samuel took the challenge, triumphed, and was named

KEY DATES

1900–1920s: Samuel Slover becomes publisher and half-owner of the *Newport News Times-Herald*.

1964: Norfolk Newspapers purchases two cable TV franchises, forming the core of the TeleCable Corporation.

1965: The *Greensboro Daily News* and the *Greensboro Record* are acquired; they are later combined as the *Greensboro News & Record*.

1967: Company changes its name to Landmark Communications, Inc.

1969: Landmark buys its fourth metro daily paper, the *Roanoke Times & World-News*.

1982: Landmark launches The Weather Channel, a 24-hour, national cable weather service.

1984: TeleCable is spun off to Landmark stockholders as an independent company.

1995: Tele-Communications Inc. pays more than $1 billion to acquire TeleCable.

2008: The Weather Channel is sold for estimated $3.5 billion.

publisher of the *Newport News Times-Herald*. In 1909, relinquishing his title as publisher, Slover moved on to papers in Richmond, Petersburg, and other cities in southeast Virginia.

During the next several decades, he dominated the state's newspaper trade, owning outright or controlling six of Virginia's biggest papers. His modus operandi was to swoop in and rescue an ailing paper, nurse it from red to black ink, then move on. Through Slover's machinations, small, struggling papers were often merged to create large, healthier ones, usually resulting in hyphenated names such as two of Landmark's backbone publications, the *Virginian-Pilot* and the *Ledger-Star*.

By centering his company, Norfolk Newspapers Inc., near a major military installation, Slover capitalized on the region's immense growth, not only with newspapers, but other media as well. In 1930, as the Great Depression deepened, Slover took a gamble and purchased Norfolk's WTAR-AM, Virginia's first radio station, for $10,000. Although many had little faith in the sensibility of an aural medium and even less in another experimental medium, television, Slover believed in both and was later responsible for bringing Virginia its second television station.

FRANK BATTEN, TAKING OVER IN THE FIFTIES

Throughout Slover's career, his exploits would prove both interesting and educational to his young nephew, Frank Batten, who joined the Slover household after the death of his father, Frank Batten, Sr., when the youngster was only two years old. After serving in the merchant marines during World War II, Batten graduated from the University of Virginia in 1950 and received an M.B.A. from Harvard University in 1952. His initiation into the business world was fast and furious: He began as a reporter for the *Norfolk Ledger-Dispatch* (forerunner of the *Ledger-Star*), moved to the circulation and advertising departments of the *Ledger-Dispatch* and *Virginian-Pilot*, progressed to vice president in 1953, and was appointed publisher by Slover at the age of 27 in 1954.

Having absorbed much under the tutelage of his uncle and mentor, Batten learned the ropes in record time, accelerating his pivotal role in Norfolk Newspapers Inc., the forerunner of Landmark Communications. While Batten settled into his role as publisher of two of the area's most prosperous newspapers, Slover, 81, slowed down and contemplated retirement. He also sought to share the fruits of his illustrious career by liberally offering stock to his employees. With Batten at the helm a mere five years, Samuel L. Slover died in 1959, at age 86, leaving Batten a vast legacy.

Like his uncle before him, Batten's prescience would firmly move Landmark into the future. Just as Slover had envisioned the many possibilities of radio and television, Batten had been studying an extension of traditional television called "cable" programming. Batten considered cable a medium with vast potential and decided to invest in its promise. Within a year of his initial interest, in 1964, Batten acquired two cable franchises: one in Roanoke Rapids, North Carolina, and a second in Beckley, West Virginia. These two stations were the cornerstone for the development of the Tele-Cable Corporation, of Greensboro, North Carolina, which would eventually operate 21 cable systems in 15 states, reaching 740,000 subscribers nationwide. Tele-Cable's success led to a bountiful opportunity for Landmark stockholders in 1984, when it was spun off into an independent corporation. In late 1994, an offer of more than $1 billion in stock was made by rival TCI (Tele-Communications Inc.), the largest cable TV operator in the United States, to acquire TeleCable's assets. The deal was closed in January 1995.

In 1965, Batten further expanded the company by purchasing the *Greensboro Daily News*, the *Greensboro Record*, and a television station, WFMY-TV, all owned by the prominent Jeffress family. Landmark later combined the Greensboro papers into the *Greensboro News & Record*, which celebrated its centennial in 1990, and sold WFMY-TV. Two years after the Greensboro acquisitions, in 1967, Batten was named chairman of the board of Norfolk Newspapers, which at the same time changed its name to Landmark Communications, Inc. Within another two years, he was on the move again acquiring the *Roanoke Times & World-News* in Virginia's third-largest market (combined daily and Sunday circulation of over 240,000), bringing the Norfolk-based company's metro newspaper holdings to four.

In the 1970s, Landmark became home to community papers as well, including four dailies (*Carroll County Times, Citrus County Chronicle, News-Enterprise,* and *Los Alamos Monitor*); four triweeklies (the *Gazette, Lancaster News, Kentucky Standard,* and *Roane County News*); six semiweeklies; 21 weeklies; and 38 free "shoppers" available throughout the region and beyond.

In 1978 Landmark departed from its tradition of local and regional expansion by taking a leap to the West Coast, acquiring two television stations: KNTV in San Jose, for $24.5 million and KLAS-TV in Las Vegas, for $8 million. Although KNTV was later sold, KLAS, a CBS affiliate, became Las Vegas's top-ranked news station with 351,000 households, while another television acquisition, CBS-affiliate WTVF in Nashville, known as "NewsChannel 5" (purchased in 1992), delivered award-winning specials and highly rated newscasts to 738,000 households. WTVF was also known for another distinction: the hiring of a college student in 1974 who went on to conquer the media industry, Oprah Winfrey.

LAUNCHING THE WEATHER CHANNEL

Three years later, still seeking opportunities to expand the company in both scope and value, Batten considered a leap into the national broadcasting arena. In 1981 the Landmark think tank developed what is probably regarded as the company's greatest achievement, a 24-hour cable weather service called The Weather Channel. In less than 10 months, plans progressed from paper to programming reality. "The Weather Channel was the most challenging task we had undertaken," Batten admitted. "It was Landmark's first national venture, with all the complexities of marketing and distribution a national enterprise must consider." Despite jitters and numerous naysayers from within and outside the industry, Landmark was determined to live up to its name while also providing the quality of the major networks. On May 2, 1982, The Weather Channel (TWC) officially debuted, with the expressed purpose of

becoming "the nation's primary source of weather information."

Part of TWC's success was its universalization of the weather. Because everyone was affected by Mother Nature, an uncontrollable force, viewers could at least tune in, be informed, and prepare, which constituted a form of control in itself. Subscribers also appreciated TWC's format and flow: "Viewers can find a constantly varied presentation of scientific information, friendly advice, and spontaneous philosophy," said Andrew Ross, in his 1991 book, *Strange Weather: Culture, Science, and Technology in the Age of Limits.* Moreover, with programming Ross called "accessible, concrete displays of otherwise abstract weather events," viewers kept coming back for more, especially during catastrophic weather. Ratings skyrocketed during August 1991, as Hurricane Bob terrorized the coast; in March 1993 with the Northeast's unexpected blizzard; and again in December of the same year when heavy snow once again threatened the East Coast.

TWC became a staple of contemporary programming, with what Batten termed "one of the most loyal consumer audiences in television." Numbers proved him correct: At any given moment in the mid-1990s, 130,000 homes tuned in, while TWC programming was available to 56.7 million households that regularly watched its early morning and evening local forecasts, as well as a multitude of regular features (Boat & Beach Reports, Business Traveler's Reports, International Forecast, Michelin Drivers' Report, and Schoolday Forecast) and specials about weather-related health matters or seasonal hazards such as hurricanes and tornados. By 1995, TWC was available in 90 percent of all homes with cable television.

NEW VENTURES IN THE NINETIES

In 1990, Michael Eckert took over as president of what became Landmark's Video Networks and Enterprises Division. From 1991 through 1993, Paul FitzPatrick, formerly of C-Span, was The Weather Channel's president and chief operating officer. During that time, TWC's viewership increased from 48 million to 56.7 million. By 1994, TWC's staff of 325 employees (65 as on-camera meteorologists) used over $20 million worth of specialized equipment to ply their trade, including the state-of-the-art Weather STAR system, implemented in late 1993. The STAR system allowed TWC to insert local forecasts for the United States' 750 weather zones, along with tags from local advertisers, into the channel's continuous transmission.

Once TWC was firmly into black ink, its skeptics and detractors were silenced, but just until Landmark's next national undertaking, The Travel Channel (TTC). Founded in 1987 by Trans World Airlines to help sell tickets, TTC was regarded as the bane of the cable industry for its blatant self-promotion. Landmark acquired a 97 percent share of TTC in 1992 for $50 million. Although TTC had never shown a profit and continued to lose $7 million annually, Landmark increased its stagnant viewership by 2.5 million during a concerted media campaign in 1993. Up to 20 million in 1994, Landmark hoped selling TWC and TTC as a team would bolster subscribers even more. Both the Travel and Weather channels won the attention of their peers and received cable ACE awards. In 1991, The Weather Channel was given the industry's highest programming accolade, the Golden ACE.

In April 1991, Landmark joined with Atlanta-based Cox Enterprises, Inc. to form Trader Publishing Company, a 50-50 joint venture that combined the classified advertising publications operations of Landmark Target Media and Cox's Trader Publications. Headquarters for Trader Publishing were established in Norfolk.

As the 1990s advanced, Landmark initiated the first of several new ventures, each in different directions. Mid-May 1992 marked the acquisition of the nine-year-old Summary Scan! (renamed Promotion Information Management [PIM] in 1993), a tracking service of print media promotions (in-store circulars, coupons, direct mail, etc.) for packaged-goods manufacturers. Purchased from the Chicago-based Advertising Checking Bureau, PIM maintained offices in both Chicago and Overland Park, Kansas, selling its findings to customers on a weekly or monthly basis. Also in 1992, Landmark acquired Antique Trader Publications, which became a key part of Landmark Specialty Publications.

This year was also pivotal for personnel, as John O. Wynne was named corporate CEO in addition to his duties as Landmark's president. At the same time, E. Roger Williams joined The Travel Channel as president (and later CEO) after leaving ESPN. In 1994 Douglas Fox, formerly vice president of marketing for the Times-Mirror Newspaper Group, was named COO for Landmark.

INTERNATIONAL EXPANSION

In the fall of 1993, further demonstrating its progressive nature and support of the underdog, Landmark's Tele-Cable Corp. was one of six cable operators agreeing to carry the new Fox network's programming. In June 1994, the company went online by forming a joint venture (70 percent ownership) with another Norfolk-based company, Wyvern Technologies Inc., to create In-

fiNet, a service bringing Virginia subscribers access to the Internet as well as establishing and maintaining Web sites for newspapers and other media outlets. In the fall of 1994, The Weather Channel was in the news, too: CEO Michael Eckert announced plans for international expansion. A Spanish-language weather channel began serving the Latin American market in 1996, followed by a Portuguese channel for Brazil. These channels proved moderately successful, but a venture to develop several weather channels for the European market failed.

In February 1994, Travel, a London-based travel channel, was launched. In 1995, it served nearly one million cable households throughout the United Kingdom and all of Scandinavia. In May 1995, Landmark announced plans to expand further internationally by launching a new Travel Channel for Latin America, which would appeal, according to a press release, "not only to those who travel, but to those who are interested in learning about the world." The new channel, based in Miami, began broadcasting later in the year. A further travel-related venture launched in 1995 was The Vacation Store. This was a mass-market travel agency that sold vacations nationwide, primarily at first through promotional programs that aired on The Travel Channel. The agency later ran such programs on other cable networks, such as Lifetime and Discovery.

Also in 1995, Landmark purchased full control of InfiNet and then sold a 50 percent stake in that venture to Knight-Ridder, Inc. InfiNet could now draw on the holdings and attempt to attract the subscribers of two major newspaper publishers. In February 1996 another leading newspaper publisher, Gannett Co., Inc., became an InfiNet partner. The three firms held equal one-third stakes in the venture, which was based in Norfolk.

LEDGER-STAR FOLDS

Meantime, in August 1995, the number of Landmark metropolitan daily newspapers fell to three when the *Ledger-Star* ceased publication. Thus ended a decades-long run in which the *Ledger-Star* was Norfolk's afternoon newspaper and the *Virginian-Pilot* was the morning daily. The two papers, despite their common ownership, had been run independently and had maintained a fierce rivalry until 1982, when the staffs were combined in a cost-saving move precipitated by the declining fortunes of the newspaper industry. The differences between the two papers began to fade away, and circulation at the *Ledger-Star* went into a steep fall. By the end, circulation had plummeted to less than 10,000, compared to the more than 100,000 in the mid-1970s.

Late in 1996, Landmark expanded its international weather channel interests by purchasing a 50 percent stake in Pelmorex, Inc. This Canadian firm operated The Weather Network, a weather channel that reached 95 percent of the Canadian cable market, and a French-language weather channel called Meteo Media. Another 1996 development was Landmark's decision to begin divesting its travel-related holdings. In December of that year the company sold The Vacation Store to an investor group led by the agency's top executives. In the middle of the following year, after a prolonged search for a buyer, Landmark sold the troubled Travel Channel to Paxson Communications Corporation for $20 million in cash and $55 million in Paxson stock. Then in 1998, Travel Channel Latin America was sold to Discovery Communications Inc. Landmark retained ownership of Travel, its London-based travel channel.

In a somewhat incongruous development during this same period, Landmark purchased two publishers of travel guides at the same time that it was divesting The Vacation Store and the travel channels. In April 1997 the company bought The Insiders' Guides Inc., producer of a 45-title guidebook series from its headquarters in Manteo, North Carolina, and in October of that same year Landmark purchased Helena, Montana-based guidebook publisher Falcon Publishing Co. The two companies were merged, as Landmark hoped to grow the combined business by creating a new revenue stream in the form of paid advertising. This strategy did not work, and the business was soon deemed to be a noncore asset and was sold to Morris Communications Corporation in 2000.

Another new venture for Landmark was the formation in 1997 of American Outdoor Advertising Inc. This billboard advertisement subsidiary developed a network of 960 billboards in 11 southeastern states by the early 2000s. Landmark also began acquiring college sports fan magazines in 1997, placing them within the Landmark Community Newspapers unit. In January of the next year, Frank Batten turned over control of Landmark Communications to his son, Frank Batten, Jr., who became chairman. The senior Batten remained involved at the company as chairman of the board's executive committee. Batten, Jr., had served as executive vice president with responsibility for new ventures and new media since 1995. Prior to that, he had a four-year stint as president and publisher of the *Virginian-Pilot*, following precisely in his father's footsteps. Wynne continued in his capacity of president and CEO.

In early 1999, Landmark moved into the education field, specializing in career education. Company officials saw this as an extension of its core business of delivering information, because they viewed career education as a type of information business. Landmark Education Services, Inc. was created, and it bought Salt Lake City-based Certified Careers Institute, which focused on computer training. Schools focusing on allied health were later added. In another 1999 development, Landmark Specialty Publications, which included antiques and collectible titles such as *Antique Trader*, was sold to Krause Publications, Inc.

ENTERING THE NEW MILLENNIUM

Landmark began the 2000s with two major acquisitions. Early in 2000, the company paid about $120 million to Litton Industries Inc. for its Weather Services International (WSI) unit. Using National Weather Service data, WSI packaged weather presentation systems for television stations (including The Weather Channel), the aviation industry, and the government. Later in 2000, Trader Publishing spent $520 million to acquire UAP, Inc., the U.S. classified advertising publication unit of London-based United News & Media plc. The deal combined the two largest U.S. publishers of classified advertising publications. UAP published 300 free advertising titles in 38 states. Landmark extended its hold on the Norfolk area media market through a third 2000 acquisition. The *Virginian-Pilot* bought Norfolk-based Military Newspapers of Virginia, Inc., publisher of several base-related newspapers that were distributed free of charge.

In 2001, Landmark ventured further into the Internet services sector by establishing Continental Broadband LLC. This Norfolk-headquartered company was a provider of fixed wireless (wireless broadband) Internet services for medium-sized businesses. A sharp drop in advertising in the wake of three circumstances—the bursting of the Internet bubble, the start of a prolonged recession in the United States, and the September 11, 2001, terrorist attacks on the United States—resulted in a decline in revenue for Landmark Communications from an estimated $805 million in 2000 to $732 million the following year.

At the beginning of 2002, Wynne retired as president and CEO. Decker Anstrom was named president and COO of Landmark. Anstrom had been president and CEO of The Weather Channel. Before that, he had served as president of the National Cable Television Association, and he was thus the first Landmark president to have not spent the majority of his career with the company.

Alterations to the company's portfolio of businesses continued under the new president. In June 2002 Landmark sold its American Outdoor Advertising billboard subsidiary, which had been deemed a noncore asset, to Lamar Advertising Company. One month later, the company purchased a majority interest in Shorecliff Communications LLC. Headquartered in San Juan Capistrano, California, Shorecliff was a trade show enterprise specializing in industries related to telecommunications infrastructure. The firm produced two major trade shows, one serving the cellular tower industry and the other serving the fixed wireless industry. The investment in Shorecliff meshed well with the previous establishment of Continental Broadband, and Landmark's entrance into trade shows was not unexpected given that many media companies were heavily involved in the business.

In December 2002, meantime, Landmark elected to shut down its two weather channels in Latin America after six years of operating in the red. Deepening economic problems in the region contributed to the decision. In March 2003, however, The Weather Channel announced that it was developing a Spanish-language weather channel that would be aimed at the rapidly growing Hispanic population in the United States. The latter move exemplified Landmark's willingness to continue to pursue new, innovative ventures. While not all of the company's ventures proved successful, Landmark had managed over the 1980s and 1990s to add two major businesses (The Weather Channel and Trader Publishing) to its core operations in newspapers and television stations.

ATTEMPT TO DIVEST

The competitive landscape for media meanwhile changed rapidly in the first decade of the 2000s. With the rise of the Internet came severe losses in print media. According to industry analysts, U.S. newspapers lost half their value between 2002 and 2008. This was due to deep drops in advertising revenue and in circulation. While Landmark, as a private company, did not need to publish revenue figures for its newspapers, presumably the factors that influenced the industry as a whole also took their toll on the company's print outlets. The company first brokered a huge deal to sell one of its premiere properties, The Weather Channel. Then it announced its intention to put all the Landmark properties on the block.

Landmark, in 2008 operating under the new name Landmark Media Enterprises, began negotiations to sell The Weather Channel early that year. The company at first indicated that it sought as much as $5 billion for TWC. This would have nearly equaled the record set for a cable property in 2001, when The Walt Disney Company bought the Fox Family Channel for $5.3 billion. Other significant media deals, however, had come in with much smaller price tags. After sorting out bids from players such as Viacom, Time Warner, Inc.,

and Liberty Media, talk progressed with NBC Universal and two private equity groups. NBC was already a major player in weather news, with its WeatherPlus division. Ultimately, NBC Universal, along with Bain Capital and the Blackstone Group, paid an estimated $3.5 billion for The Weather Channel. The deal closed in late 2008.

While negotiations for The Weather Channel were taking place, Landmark Media offered up for bids all its other properties. In a sweeping move, it put for-sale notices on its two television stations, its four major newspapers, its Dominion Enterprises subsidiary, and all its other assets. The financial services firm Lehman Brothers was to handle the sales. The goal was to divest the company of all its assets by the end of 2008.

Landmark penciled an agreement in July 2008 to sell its Nashville television station WTVF-TV to Bonten Media Group. Bonten was a television broadcasting group formed by the private equity firm Diamond Castle Holdings. At this time, other media companies were also looking to sell off television assets. The News Corporation had just jettisoned a batch of its smaller-market stations, also to a venture capital group. However, the summer and fall of 2008 proved a wretched time for the financial markets. While Bonten announced in July its joy in taking over WTVF, by mid-October the deal was scotched. Bonten was not able to raise the credit it needed in what turned out to be the most tumultuous period financial markets had seen in over 50 years.

UNCERTAIN ECONOMY AND SALE PLANS ON HOLD

Lehman Brothers, at that time the fourth-largest investment bank in the United States, was caught in ballooning debt. Problems began to surface in the summer, and the situation moved rapidly to a shocking denouement. After an emergency meeting on September 14, Lehman Brothers declared bankruptcy on September 15, 2008, setting off a 500-point stock market drop. The company disappeared, and the U.S. economy locked into a deep recession. Given the situation, Landmark revised its plan, and declared that its assets were no longer for sale. It decided to hold onto them until the credit market stabilized and prospects improved. It seemed that the deal for The Weather Channel had come through in the nick of time, and Landmark would have to wait and see whether it could divest the rest of its media holdings.

Frank Batten, Sr., died in September 2009. He was 82 years old, and had lived with the after-effects of throat cancer that had left him without a larynx since 1979. At the time of his death, his net worth was estimated at $1.7 billion. This put him at number 430 on the *Forbes* magazine list of the world's wealthiest people. His son, Frank Batten, Jr., continued at the helm of Landmark Media Enterprises. As economic uncertainty continued in the United States into 2011, the company held onto its newspapers and other media assets. It made no mention of reviving its plan to divest all its holdings.

Taryn Benbow-Pfalzgraf
Updated, David E. Salamie; A. Woodward

PRINCIPAL SUBSIDIARIES

Continental Broadband, Inc.; Dominion Enterprises, Inc.; Landmark Community Newspapers LLC; Landmark Education Services, Inc.; Shorecliff Communications LLC; Trader Publishing Co.

PRINCIPAL COMPETITORS

Community Newspaper Holdings, Inc.; Gannett Co., Inc.; The McClatchy Co.; Media General, Inc.; Tribune Company; The Washington Post Company.

FURTHER READING

"Armed with Assets, Landmark Still Selling." *Mergers and Acquisitions*, July 21, 2008, 1–2.

Batten, Frank, and Jeffrey L. Cruikshank. *The Weather Channel: The Improbable Rise of a Media Phenomenon.* Boston: Harvard Business School Press, 2002.

Blackwell, John Reid, and Ellen Robertson. "F. Batten Sr., Retired Chairman of Landmark Communications, Dies at 82." *Richmond (VA) Times-Dispatch*, September 11, 2009.

Dinsmore, Christopher. "Landmark President and CEO to Pass Leadership Torch." *Norfolk Virginian-Pilot*, May 23, 2001, D1.

————. "Landmark Sells Billboard Subsidiary." *Norfolk Virginian-Pilot*, June 5, 2002, D1.

————. "Landmark to Close Second Business in Three Months." *Norfolk Virginian-Pilot*, December 4, 2001, D1.

————. "Norfolk Publisher to Expand: Deal Would Make Trader Publisher One of the Largest Firms Based Here." *Norfolk Virginian-Pilot*, May 10, 2000, D1.

————. "The Weather Channel Turns 20." *Norfolk Virginian-Pilot*, May 2, 2002, D1.

Farrell, Mike. "Weather Deal Could Break Soon." *Multichannel News*, July 7, 2008, 23.

Hevesi, Dennis. "Frank Batten Sr., Media Executive and Founder of Weather Channel, Dies at 82." *New York Times*, September 11, 2009, A17.

"Landmark Aims to Empty Portfolio in 08." *Mergers and Acquisitions*, June 23, 2008, 1, 3.

Lowe, Cody. "Touch Economic Climate Prompts Landmark to Halt Sales." *Roanoke Times*, October 30, 2008.

Mayfield, Dave. "Gannett Buys Stake in InfiNet." *Norfolk Virginian-Pilot*, February 15, 1996, D1.

————. "Knight-Ridder Buys into InfiNet." *Norfolk Virginian-Pilot*, June 8, 1995, D1.

Ross, Andrew. *Strange Weather: Culture, Science, and Technology in the Age of Limits.* London: Verso Press, 1991, 237–46.

"Samuel L. Slover, Virginia Publisher" (obituary). *New York Times*, November 30, 1959, 31.

Swift, Earl. "The Final Edition: The *Ledger-Star* Stops the Presses after 119 Years." *Norfolk Virginian-Pilot*, August 25, 1995, A1.

Wagner, Lon. "Newspaper Leader Hands Company Over to Son." *Roanoke (VA) Times & World-News*, December 17, 1997, A13.

Walzer, Philip. "Landmark Suspends Sale of Assets, but not The Pilot." *Norfolk Virginian-Pilot*, October 30, 2008.

"Weather Channel Sold by Landmark." *Mergers and Acquisitions*, July 14, 2008, 2.

Legrand SA

128 av du Marechal de Lattre de Tassigny
Limoges, F-87045
France
Telephone: (+33 5) 55 06 87 87
Fax: (+33 5) 55 06 13 41
Web site: http://www.legrand.fr

Public Company
Founded: 1860
Incorporated: 1926
Employees: 31,000
Sales: EUR 3.89 billion ($5.45 billion) (2010)
Stock Exchanges: Euronext Paris
Ticker Symbol: LR:FP
NAICS: 335999 All Other Miscellaneous Electrical Equipment and Component Manufacturing; 334419 Other Electronic Component Manufacturing; 335311 Power, Distribution, and Specialty Transformer Manufacturing

■ ■ ■

Legrand SA is the world's leading manufacturer of wiring devices and cable management products, focused primarily on the commercial, residential, and industrial building sectors. Legrand has gained control of an 18 percent share of the global market, in large part through the acquisition of a list of local companies in such markets as China, Russia, Brazil, and Australia. Legrand tailors its products to the requirements and specifications of each market. In this way, Legrand has expanded its sales reach from its home in France to cover 180 countries worldwide. In two-thirds of these markets, Legrand products hold the number one or number two positions. Legrand is listed on the Euronext Paris stock exchange, where it entered the CAC 40 index in December 2011. The company is led by CEO and Chairman Gilles Schnepp.

A PORCELAIN MAKER FROM THE SECOND FRENCH EMPIRE

Legrand's origins can be traced back to 1860, when Barjaud de Lafont founded a small studio for making porcelain tableware on the Route de Lyon in Limoges. In 1865, the company's activities were taken over by the brothers Vultry, who maintained the business into the next century. In 1904, Frédéric Legrand assumed ownership of the business, giving the company his name. Over the next 40 years, Legrand grew to become one of the best-known names in the porcelain tableware industry in the Limoges area. Just after World War I, however, in 1919, the company added a second business, a small factory producing electrical fittings, using the company's porcelain as insulating material. Incorporating as a "société anonyme" (SA, or "anonymous society") in 1926, the company continued to build on its reputation for fine porcelain, winning the Gold Medal at the Universal Exposition in 1937. By then, the company employed some 1,000 people. Legrand died in 1936.

The outbreak of World War II put a halt to the company's growth. Sales collapsed and the company saw its employee base cut by more than half. As the war drew to a close, Legrand was bought by Pierre Verspieren, who had founded Lloyd Continental, an insur-

COMPANY PERSPECTIVES

Ambition: To strengthen its leading position in the markets for electrical and digital infrastructures for building. To become the reference for smart electrical systems and services with innovative, highly energy-efficient solutions.

ance company, in the north of France in 1920. In 1945, Verspieren turned over direction of the company to his son, Jean Verspieren, and son-in-law, Edouard Decoster. The brothers-in-law would continue to lead the company until well into the 1980s.

The Legrand factory was destroyed by fire in 1949. Verspieren and Decoster rebuilt the factory on its original site on the Route de Lyon, which by then had been renamed the Avenue de-Lattre-de-Tassigny. The company's focus, however, turned to its still-small electrical fittings business. In 1950, Legrand abandoned the porcelain business altogether.

The company's timing could not have been better. France was entering a new period of growth as Europe underwent postwar reconstruction. Although luxury goods, such as porcelain, remained out of reach for most until the economic boom years of the late 1950s and 1960s, housing construction and renovations and the rebuilding and modernization of French industry brought a huge demand for Legrand's electrical fittings and accessories. The company expanded its headquarters factory. Then, in 1953, it extended beyond its original Avenue de-Lattre-de-Tassigny location, opening two new plants in Limoges.

The company's first acquisition came in 1956, when it acquired Electro Sécurit, renamed Legrand Antibes, in that French colony. By 1964, Legrand had begun to expand throughout the French Limousin region, opening a factory in Châlus. Company facilities spread beyond Limousin, including plants in Pau, in the Pyrénées region, and in the Normandy region.

INTERNATIONAL EXPANSION FROM THE MID-SIXTIES

Legrand's taste for international expansion came with the opening of the company's first subsidiary beyond France's borders, in Belgium, in 1966. While continuing to extend its reach throughout much of France itself, the company began its long program of expansion through acquisition, concentrating at first on the European

market. In 1970, in part to fuel this expansion, Legrand went public, trading on the Paris exchange. In that year, the company's net earnings passed the FRF 10 million mark. In 1972, with sales rising across Europe, the company opened a central distribution facility for its finished products in La Valoine. By the middle of the decade, international sales accounted for 19 percent of the Legrand group's consolidated net revenues.

Two years later, Legrand made its first move outside of Europe, entering the South American market by acquiring Pial in Brazil. The company's growth continued through the second half of the decade, including the company's move into the British market with the acquisition of a small company in Milton Keynes. On the home front, Legrand acquired Arnauld Fae, then a subsidiary of Compagnie Générale d'Electricité, in 1979. By 1982, sales had grown sufficiently to warrant the opening of a second distribution center for the company's finished products, in Marly-la-Ville.

The following year, Verspieren, who had been acting as chair of the company, died. He was replaced in that position by Decoster, who continued to serve as company president as well. In that year, however, François Grappotte, who had spent six years conducting international trade negotiations within the French government's trade department before working for Rothschild's Bank and then the engineering concern CEM, joined Legrand as the company's general manager. In 1988, Decoster retired to the position of honorary chair, naming Grappotte as chair and chief executive of the business, still largely controlled by the Verspieren-Decoster families. Under Grappotte, who would step up the company's expansion, the family remained influential in the company's management. As Grappotte told the *Daily Telegraph* in July 1990, "I am given all the latitude I want to do well—and none to do badly."

In 1984, Legrand took its first step into North America, acquiring rival companies Pass & Seymour and Slater Electric and forming the company's Pass & Seymour Legrand subsidiary, selling products under the Trade-Master brand name. Meanwhile, the company was also expanding its presence in the New World, entering Chile, Venezuela, Canada, and Mexico by the end of the decade. By the mid-1980s, the company's revenues had grown past FRF 4.5 billion, for operating earnings of more than FRF 567 million. Sales came from 22 countries, making Legrand continental Europe's leading supplier of low-voltage electrical fittings and accessories. In that year, sales outside of France accounted for 35 percent of the company's consolidated net revenues, compared to 19 percent just 10 years before.

ITALIAN ACQUISITION IN 1989

By then, however, the company began looking for a larger-sized acquisition. In 1987, it made an attempt to trump the takeover bid of RTZ Corp. for MK Electric PLC of England. The acquisition of MK Electric, which generated nearly £141 million in 1986, would have represented a substantial increase in Legrand's U.K. sales, which remained at about £20 million at the time. When RTZ raised Legrand's bid by £8 million, Legrand backed off from the takeover, considering the price to be too high. As Grappotte told the *Daily Telegraph*, "We do not consider it a defeat. It was a cold, purely rational decision."

The failure to acquire MK Electric sent Legrand looking elsewhere for its next major acquisition. In 1989, the company found this in B Ticino of Italy. The company paid FRF 1.1 billion to acquire 45 percent of the Italian company in June of that year and completed the acquisition of total control of B Ticino in December 1989. Adding B Ticino's FRF 2 billion in revenues, 4,500 employees, and dominant share of the Italian market to the Legrand Group of companies had an additional benefit over the failed MK Electric bid: The Italian market's electrical fittings were based on the common European standards, presenting Legrand with greater synergy. The acquisition also helped drive the Legrand group's total sales to nearly FRF 10 billion by the end of the decade and further solidified the company's position as the leader in the European market. International sales had by then come to represent 57 percent of the company's consolidated net sales.

Despite the increasingly important position of the international market for Legrand's revenues, the company remained true to its Limoges roots. In 1992, the company inaugurated a state-of-the-art production facility in its hometown, built for a cost of FRF 600 million. At 6,900 square meters, the Site Électronique Limousin (SITEL) brought the company into new territory, combining its growing activities in electronics production onto one site. At the same time, Legrand began construction on a new, 10,000-square-foot headquarters facility, maintaining the company's presence on the Avenue de-Lattre-de-Tassigny.

BUILDING SCALE IN THE NINETIES

Moving into the 1990s, Legrand ran headlong into the worldwide recession. Its core French market experienced a slump, as did much of Europe; its Brazilian subsidiary slipped into the red; and the company's U.S. subsidiaries, saddled with aging production facilities, were losing money. Supported by the Verspieren-Decoster families, Grappotte and Legrand's response to the difficult market conditions was to continue to invest in the company's long-term growth, maintaining a capital investment budget of as high as 10 percent or more of the company's annual sales, while spending as much as a third of revenues on the development of new products. At the same time, the company resisted the urge to diversify, maintaining its focus on electrical fittings markets.

While internal growth faltered with the continuing recession, Legrand continued its steady trail of acquisitions, adding Molveno of Italy, Bufer in Turkey, and Pieron and Baco, both in France, in 1992. In January of the following year, the company moved into Hungary with the purchase of 98 percent of that country's Kontavil and increased its U.K. holdings with the purchase of Tenby Industries Limited, a specialist in electrical installation accessories. Although the company saw its net earnings drop during the initial years of the decade (from a profit of FRF 700 million in 1990 to a profit of FRF 578 million in 1993), the company remained on solid financial ground and largely debt free. Meanwhile, Legrand continued its policy of investing about 10 percent of annual revenues in new acquisitions each year.

With the company's 1994 revenues topping FRF 10 billion and net income on the rise again, reaching FRF 785 million for the year, the company launched another series of acquisitions, bringing Britain's Power Centre and Italy's RTGama into the group. By the end of 1995, the company's net revenues had risen past FRF 11 billion, and the company's net earnings climbed to FRF 923 million.

DEVELOPING MARKETS INTO 2000

The following year, the company added four more subsidiaries, introducing Legrand to Poland with the $31.4 million purchase of 75 percent of Fael, in Zabkowice; bringing the company into India with the purchase of MDS, the largest producer of miniature circuit breakers in that country; adding Colombia to the group with the purchase of Luminex, Colombia's leading manufacturer of electrical fittings, which also held operations in Brazil and Mexico; and finally consolidating its position in the United States with the purchase of The Watt Stopper, the leading U.S. maker of occupancy and motion sensor products. These acquisitions helped raise the company's percentage of revenues from international sales to 60 percent and further enhanced Legrand's position as the worldwide leader in the FRF 140 billion low-voltage electrical fittings industry.

The continuing economic crisis in France, as well as in many of Legrand's principal European markets, modified the company's growth in 1996. Net revenues rose to FRF 11.5 million for the year, while net earnings remained flat, at FRF 927 million. Nonetheless, Legrand's steady policy of investment gave the company the promise of renewed growth, particularly as Legrand began taking the first steps to enter the burgeoning Asian markets. As Grappotte told *Le Monde* in December 1996, "To wait until the economy is healthy to invest is the best way of being left behind by the market. Developing our products is the surest way of winning added value and finding additional growth that the market is no longer offering spontaneously."

Legrand's growth remained strong through the end of the decade. The company completed a string of new acquisitions, including in France, Spain, Australia, and Italy. In the United States, Legrand picked up Ortronics, specialized in prewiring for voice-data-video systems, and Florida-based Reiker Enterprises, which specialized in ceiling support products, such as for ceiling fans and light fixtures. In 2000, the company acquired another U.S. company, Horton Controls. The purchase of Wiremold Company in July of that year nearly doubled the company's U.S. operations. By the end of the decade, Legrand's North American business accounted for 17 percent of its total revenues.

Legrand made good on its strategy of targeting positions in developing markets. The company entered South Korea, buying up the Anam group in 1999. Legrand targeted Brazil in 2000, purchasing the electrical equipment division of that country's Lorenzetti. These purchases were later followed by an entry into the mainland China market.

FAILED MERGER IN 2002

If Legrand had risen to become a giant in its core market (in the United States, for example, Legrand's share of low-voltage products had reached 23 percent), the company remained a tiny player among such electrical products giants as Siemens, General Electric, and ABB. In 2001, however, the Decoster and Verspieren families, which controlled 40 percent of the group's total stock but 56 percent of voting rights, agreed to a merger with larger compatriot Schneider. The merger would have given the new Schneider-Electric a market value of more than $16 billion, and a combined revenue of nearly $12 billion. Schneider paid nearly EUR 8 billion ($7 billion), acquiring 98 percent of Legrand.

Legrand's minority shareholders protested the sale, however, and won support from the European Commission, which blocked the merger in October 2001. While an oversight in the merger agreement had nonetheless forced Schneider to complete the original purchase, the company was barred from exerting control over Legrand. Rather than submit a new bid more favorable to minority shareholders, Schneider agreed to sell Legrand to private equity groups Wendel Investissement and Kohlberg Kravis Roberts (KKR) in 2002 for just EUR 3.6 billion.

The failure of the merger permitted Grappotte, joined by future CEO Gilles Schnepp, to resume the group's strategy of international expansion. The company restructured its organization, creating four global product divisions to replace its former region-based strategy. Legrand revamped its industrial operations, developing a new policy of specialized factories. The company also turned more and more to outside suppliers, which rose from just 10 percent of its product development to 35 percent by the middle of the decade.

PUBLIC OFFERING IN 2006

The company strategy targeted the electrical installations market, which remained marked by a myriad of local standards and specifications. Legrand launched a new acquisition drive focused on the purchases of leading companies in local or regional markets. Backed by Wendel and KKR, Legrand's acquisitions added more than EUR 300 million in revenues in 2005 alone. The company's purchases that year included key components of TCL, the leading Chinese producer of wall switches. By the end of that year, the group's revenues had climbed to EUR 3.2 billion.

Legrand made its return to the stock market in April 2006 with a listing on the Euronext Paris exchange. Wendel and KKR remained strategic investors in the company. Legrand quickly put its new capital base to work, announcing the purchase of Brazil's Cemar, a leading producer of electrical systems components in that market. The company added Utah-based Vantage Controls in October 2006, then strengthened its presence in Australia, buying HPM, the number two player in that market, in January 2007.

Other acquisitions followed shortly. The company acquired Kontaktor, in Russia, in July 2007, boosting its position in that market to number one in electrical equipment and cabling systems, and number two in modular switches. By the end of the year, the company had also added TCL Wuxi in China, UStec in the United States, Macse in Mexico, and Alpes Technologies in France. Legrand's acquisitions also included PW Industries in the United States, Turkey's Estap, Electrak in the United Kingdom, and HDL in Brazil, all in 2008.

DEVELOPING MARKET FOCUS FOR 2015

Legrand's acquisition drive was cut short by the global economic crisis at the end of the decade. The company felt the pain particularly in its North American operations. The crisis nonetheless represented an opportunity for the company, which moved to restructure its product offering. By then, the company's catalog boasted some 180,000 products across nearly 100 product families, which were grouped around 29 basic platforms, as the company called them. Instead, Legrand set out to reduce its number of product lines and platforms. By 2011, the company had already repositioned its production around nine core platforms, and forecasted a reduction in its product lines to just 60. In this way, the company expected to economize as much as 70 percent on its component costs.

Through the worst of the crisis, Legrand's total sales had slipped below EUR 3.6 billion in 2009, from EUR 4.2 billion the year before. The company returned to growth by 2010, however, posting total sales of nearly EUR 3.9 billion ($5.5 billion). Legrand also resumed its acquisition strategy.

This effort targeted especially an expansion of the group's presence in developing markets. These already accounted for 33 percent of group sales in 2011. By 2015, Legrand expected these markets to account for 50 percent of sales. Toward this end, Legrand acquired Inform, in Turkey, in 2010, followed by the switchgear operations of Indo-Asian Fusegear, in India. Through 2011, the company added SMS, the leading producer of power backup systems in Brazil. This was followed by an agreement to acquire three businesses from Malaysia's U-Li Corp.

Legrand also continued to fill in its European and North American operations, buying Italy's Meta System Energy, a producer of advanced electronic security systems, in December 2010, and acquiring Middle Atlantic Products, in the United States, in May 2011.

By then, CEO Gilles Schnepp had begun to look forward to a new growth period for the company, announcing plans to spend as much as EUR 500 million on new acquisitions. Legrand's shareholder base also underwent a transformation during the year, as Wendel and KKR, which held 52 percent of voting rights at the beginning of 2011, began a progressive exit. By the end of the year, the private equity groups held just 5.8 percent each in Legrand. The increased liquidity of the company's title enabled it to join the Paris exchange's prestigious CAC 40 index in December 2011. From a small porcelain workshop in the 19th century, Legrand had transformed itself into a global electrical equipment giant in the 21st century.

Updated, M. L. Cohen

PRINCIPAL SUBSIDIARIES

Arnould-FAE; Baco; Inovac; Legrand snc; Martin & Lunel; Planet-Wattohm; BTicino (Italy); BTicino de Mexico; Legrand Gmbh (Germany); Legrand Austria Gmbh; Legrand Electric Ltd (UK); Legrand Electricia (Portugal); Legrand Electrique (Belgium); Legrand Espanola (Spain); Pass & Seymour Legrand (USA); Pial (Brazil); Legrand (Italy); Tenby Industries (UK).

PRINCIPAL DIVISIONS

Energy Distribution and Industrial Applications; Wiring Services and Home Systems.

PRINCIPAL COMPETITORS

ABB Ltd.; Aichi Electric Company Ltd.; Alstom S.A.; China Chang Jiang Energy Corp.; General Electric Company; Koninklijke Philips Electronics N.V.; Matsushita-Kotobuki Electronics Industry; Mitsubishi Electric Corporation; Robert Bosch GmbH; Siemens AG.

FURTHER READING

"Legrand Announced the Acquisition of Vantage Controls, Located in Orem, UT." *Engineered Systems*, October 2006, 65.

"Legrand Eyes Electric Parts' Market in North." *Financial Express*, March 14, 2009.

"Legrand Launches IPO on French Exchange." *Electrical Wholesaling*, May 1, 2006.

"Legrand Refuses to Sacrifice Long-Term Development for Short-Term Gain." *Le Monde*, December 4, 1996.

"Legrand to Buy Cablofil." *Electrical Wholesaling*, January 10, 2006.

"Legrand to Buy Indo Asian's Switchgear Biz." *Industry 2.0*, July 26, 2010.

Tunbridge, Tim. "Legrand Plans to Grow but to Stick to Core Businesses of Fittings and Wiring Accessories." *Electrical Review*, June 11, 1992.

"Verspieren/Decoster Family." *Forbes*, July 15, 1996, 195.

Waller, David. "Chance for Big UK Push." *Financial Times*, December 9, 1987, 26.

Wheatcroft, Patience. "Grappotte Switches on to Legrand Plan." *Daily Telegraph*, July 9, 1990, 27.

Leona's Pizzeria, Inc.

3931 South Leavitt Street
Chicago, Illinois 60609
U.S.A.
Telephone: (773) 523-7676
Fax: (773) 247-8468
Web site: http://www.leonas.com

Private Company
Incorporated: 1952
Employees: 1,100
Sales: $35 million (2011 est.)
NAICS: 722110 Full-Service Restaurants

■ ■ ■

Leona's Pizzeria, Inc., named for its founder and matriarch, is one of Chicago's best-known Italian eateries. The chain consists of more than a dozen locations throughout the Chicagoland area in northeastern Illinois. Still family-run, the business has captured the hearts and appetites of thousands of midwesterners with great food and a bit of attitude.

GREAT PIES: THE FIFTIES

By all accounts, Leona Pianetto Molinaro Scemla was a great cook and a headstrong woman. Her family had ventured to the United States from Calabria, Italy, and she grew up around the aromas and unforgettable taste of traditional Italian cooking. As the years passed, Leona took great pride in her culinary skills and loved nothing more than gathering around the table with family and friends.

After years of praise for her Italian dishes, especially her homemade thin-crust pizza, Leona partnered with her brother Pat to open a restaurant called Pat's Pizza on Belmont Avenue in Chicago in a building owned by their father. Unfortunately, the siblings had disagreements and Leona left the business months later to go out on her own. She did not go far, though. A block away from the original pizza restaurant, she opened Leona's Pizzeria, on the corner of Belmont and Sheffield in the Lakeview neighborhood of Chicago's North Side.

Luckily for the family, the area was big enough to support both Leona and Pat, and each eatery not only survived but thrived selling her little-known Sicilian dish called pizza. It was 1950 and a heady time in the Windy City: Population had reached just over 3.6 million for the city itself and nearly six million if the outlying suburbs were included. Progress came in the form of buses replacing streetcars, and the city's first one-way streets were in development.

In the early days of the restaurant, Leona would bake her famous pizza pies (with thin crust, not the deep dish many identify with Chicago) and take them to nearby bars and taverns. The excellent taste soon brought many of these patrons to her small restaurant, and word of mouth took care of the rest. Some credit Leona with the concept of pizza delivery, as it was not a normal part of restaurant business at the time. Not only did it become a mainstay of the growing business, but later required an entire fleet of vehicles dedicated solely to delivery orders.

COMPANY PERSPECTIVES

Leona's ... a never trendy, almost sexy, vegetarian friendly, carnivorous compatible, hearty American, festive Italian, tourist tolerant, family owned, neighborhood restaurant with nocturnal kitchens and divine delivered dining that's been nourishing Chicagoland with good food and real hospitality since 1950. Whew!

EARLY GROWTH: SIXTIES TO EIGHTIES

In the early 1960s Chicago was a city full of promise with the dedication of O'Hare airport, the opening of several expressways from the city to the suburbs, and top-notch sports teams including the Blackhawks, which won hockey's Stanley Cup and the Bears, which won the National Football League championship. It was also when Leona's father and son-in-law Leonardo, sometimes called Ben, became immersed in the family business.

As the second Leona's was slated for nearby Sheridan Road, another location became available on West Augusta Boulevard and earned the distinction of being the family's second eatery in the northeast side of Chicago. By this time, part of the restaurant's charm was not just excellent Italian cooking in good-sized portions but the homey feel of its locations and a staunch loyalty to their neighborhood. This included staff comprised primarily of workers who lived within a mile or two of each eatery, something the family took great pride in. Leona's Pizzeria was an extension of its surroundings, promoted neighborhood happenings and causes, and was a place where locals went for good food, conversation, and most of all, friendly faces.

As the 1970s turned into the 1980s Leona's had opened more Chicago locations in and around the North Side and was venturing outside city limits into the suburbs. Although the same Italian fare was on the menu, the name varied, including Leona's Daughters and Leona's Neighborhood Place. Founder Leona had retired and another generation had also joined the ranks with Leonardo's sons, Leon and Salvatore (Sam) Toia, grandsons of Leona.

Leon Toia steered the eateries in new directions, diversifying the menu to offer a broader selection of entrees, appetizers, and sandwiches for carryout and delivery. Among the new items were both Italian and non-Italian dishes with chicken and salads, to differenti-

ate Leona's from the many pizzerias that dotted Chicago and its suburbs. The restaurant's immensely popular lasagna was also given an overhaul with new exotic flavors as well as the traditional. The pizzas now featured a number of ingredient combinations.

Another way Leona's made its mark in the crowded causal restaurant and pizza delivery sector was with ultimate customer service. Managers were required to check on every table and if a patron was dissatisfied, entrees were replaced. Carryout customers were invited into the restaurant for an evening of food and drink on the house. This devotion later became the impetus for a cheeky summer bash or "Stinkin' Picnic" for any and all dissatisfied customers to enjoy a huge array of food and plenty of alcohol at Leona's expense.

Among the other issues the restaurant chain dealt with in the 1980s was a parking snafu in the Lakeview neighborhood, due to night games for the Cubs baseball team at Wrigley Field. Because of increased traffic, parking became highly restricted and significantly affected area merchants, including Leona's, for a time, until the city officials and the Lakeview Central Business Association (headed by Sam Toia) resolved the situation.

RECOGNITION AND FURTHER EXPANSION

In the next decade, Leona's continued to gain acclaim. In 1990, the original, 40-year-old restaurant on Sheffield made *Restaurant Institution*'s Top 100 for the Chicagoland area, ranking at number 98 along with several well-known eateries including sports-themed Harry Caray's (from baseball sportscaster Harry Caray) and Bears coach Mike Ditka's restaurant. It also marked the ascension of the Chicago Bulls basketball team to greatness, with superstar Michael Jordan leading the team to six championships over the next several years beginning in 1991 and ending in 1998.

It was during 1998 that Leona's got a boost from a convention at the McCormick Center. When publishing professionals descended on the city for the American Booksellers Association's annual convention, Book Expo, the industry's top periodical *Publishers Weekly* hailed Leona's pizza as the best in the city. Its signature dish was so popular by this time that Leona's had a full-time staff of 250 dedicated solely to delivery of its pies.

In 2000, Leona's celebrated its 50th anniversary. Five decades of family leadership and food had resulted in a dozen city locations and several more in the outlying suburbs by 2002. Land was purchased for the company's 17th location that year. Brothers Sam and Leon continued to run the business along with a retinue of family members including their parents Leonardo and Sue; aunt Marie (Leona's middle daughter); sister Jacquie; and cousin Len. The Toia brothers also owned and operated a real estate firm, the aptly named Toia Building Properties, which sought out new locations for eateries throughout the Chicagoland region.

In the early 2000s Leona's tried to stay ahead of the casual restaurant pack by continually trying new dishes. Among the newer menu ideas were "you-choose" mix and match pasta dishes, where patrons chose two of five different raviolis, including multiple stuffings and the ravioli itself (tomato, spinach, whole wheat, or egg) for their entree; several new lasagnas including cream-based and traditional red sauce varieties; new vegetarian and vegan dishes; rich and decadent desserts; and variations on its ever-popular thin and thick-crust pizzas.

LEONA'S GETS A SIBLING: 2006 AND BEYOND

By mid-decade the restaurants were bringing in combined revenue of more than $25 million annually and had a workforce totaling more than 600. Locations were sprinkled throughout the city and its surrounding suburbs, including Oak Park to the west, Des Plaines in the northwest, Oak Lawn in the southwest, Homewood in the far southern suburbs, and Calumet City near the Indiana state line. The menu, although still based on Leona's traditional Italian cooking, included literally something for everyone from vegetarian fare with tofu and soy cheeses, a number of fish and seafood options, big burgers, and of course, pizza and pasta.

In 2007 the Toia family launched a new, sports-themed restaurant venture. Called Hop Haus, the first location was opened in the city on Franklin, closely followed by a second. The restaurant-pubs touted gourmet burgers (20 different kinds including exotic meats such as ostrich, buffalo, boar, and lamb), and dozens of beer varieties, along with wide-screen TVs for patrons to watch the sport of their choice. A departure from the family-style of Leona's sites, the new concept appealed to a younger, hipper crowd with a kitchen that stayed open until 4 a.m. on Fridays and Saturdays.

As the decade came to a close, the Leona's name no longer represented casual dining restaurants but a bona fide Chicago "brand." Leon and Sam Toia, along with the rest of the Italian clan, continued to run a successful operation with big plans for the future. In addition, Sam's duties outside of the restaurant continued to grow, including his role as chairman for the Illinois Restaurant Association and a bid for Cook County's Zoning Board of Appeals. In July 2011, Toia's loyalty and financial backing of Chicago's new mayor, Rahm Emanuel, paid off with his appointment to the board.

As Sam's political ambitions pulled him away from the business, his family took up the slack. Not only were there more Leona's restaurants (both sit-down and express carryout outlets) on the way, but Hop Haus pubs were in development for both Chicago and the suburbs as well. How far the two concepts would go was anyone's guess. Founder Leona Pianetto Molinaro Scemla probably never envisioned that her little pizzeria on Sheffield would lead to such success.

Nelson Rhodes

PRINCIPAL COMPETITORS

Bravo Restaurants, Inc.; Buona Companies, LLC; Giordano's Enterprises, Inc.; Portillo's Restaurant Group, Inc.

FURTHER READING

Almada, Jeanette. "City Sells Land for Leona's." *Chicago Tribune*, June 16, 2002, 3A.

Dardick, Hal. "Ald. Schulter Drops Reelection Bid; North Side Veteran Eyes Tax Board Post." *Chicago Tribune*, January 18, 2011, 6.

Davidson, Staci. "An Evolving Brand." *Food and Drink*, Summer 2009, 48.

Laureman, Connie. "All in the Family." *Chicago Tribune*, January 17, 1988.

Lobdell, Emily H. "Lasagna King of Chicago?" *NBC5 Chicago*, May 27, 2009.

Petersen, Chris. "Local Hangout." *Food and Drink*, May/June 2008.

Pridmore, Jay. "Leona's Expansion Grows Unexpectedly." *Chicago Tribune*, October 2, 1987.

Seigel, Jessica. "Wrigleyville Parking Ban Drives Away Merchants' Customers." *Chicago Tribune*, August 23, 1988, B3.

Sweet, Lynn. "Rahm Emanuel Rewards Backers with Board Appointments." *Chicago Tribune*, July 1, 2011.

Ver Berkmoes, Rayn. "Choice Chitown Chow." *Publishers Weekly*, May 4, 1998, 65.

Life Technologies Corporation

5791 Van Allen Way
Carlsbad, California 92008
U.S.A.
Telephone: (760) 603-7200
Toll Free: (800) 955-6288
Fax: (760) 602-6500
Web site: http://www.lifetechnologies.com

Public Company
Incorporated: 1989 as Invitrogen Corporation
Employees: 11,000
Sales: $3.58 billion (2010)
Stock Exchanges: NASDAQ
Ticker Symbol: LIFE
NAICS: 325414 Biological Product (Except Diagnostic) Manufacturing; 334516 Analytical Laboratory Instrument Manufacturing

■ ■ ■

Life Technologies Corporation develops, manufactures, and markets more than 50,000 products for customers involved in life sciences research and the commercial manufacture of genetically engineered products. Life Technologies' products and systems are found in more than 90 percent of research laboratories. The company's research kits are used to simplify and to improve gene cloning, gene expression, and gene analysis. Invitrogen also is involved in cell structure activities, which provides customers with the material to grow cells in the laboratory and to produce pharmaceutical and other materials made by cultured cells. Life Technologies has a presence in more than 160 countries.

ORIGINS

Although Invitrogen occupied a dominant position in the biotechnology industry, its rise to the industry's elite started fitfully. The company began as a partnership formed in California in 1987 before incorporating in 1989. The company's founders included researchers from the San Diego area, members of the scientific community who worked for local companies such as Syntro, Mycogen, and Scripps Clinic. One member of the founding group rose to the fore, a graduate of the University of California at San Diego's chemistry department named Lyle C. Turner. Turner was attempting to shape Invitrogen into a developer of biomedical research kits used for genetic research. His efforts were hampered early on, however, during the initial, critical phase of the company's development.

In late 1989 founding partner Bill McConnell left the organization to form his own company called McConnell Research. McConnell's departure forced Turner to use most of Invitrogen's capital to purchase the departing founder's interest in the company. The leveraged buyout left the fledgling company in a precarious position. Without the collateral required to secure a bank loan, Turner searched for another source of financing and found aid from the California Export Finance Office (CEFO). CEFO was a division of the World Trade Commission, an organization chartered to help small and midsized California businesses that needed capital to expand into foreign markets.

The aid provided by CEFO resolved Invitrogen's financial crisis, enabling the young company to gain its footing and expand internationally. By 1990 the company's distributors were located in eight countries in North America, Europe, and Asia. Sales, which totaled $2 million in 1989, were expected to reach $4 million in 1990. The company's payroll, which began with three employees in 1987, swelled to 42 employees by 1990.

BUSINESS STRATEGY YIELDS FIRST SUCCESS: 1991–99

The encouraging growth recorded by Invitrogen as it entered the 1990s provided a stable foundation for the company's progress throughout the decade. As Invitrogen developed, it targeted two main markets, the life sciences research market and the commercial production market. Invitrogen's customers in the life sciences research market included laboratories, medical research centers, government institutions such as the National Institutes of Health, and companies involved in biotechnology, pharmaceutical, energy, chemical, and agricultural activities.

Within the life sciences market, Invitrogen positioned itself to address the needs of two disciplines, cellular biochemistry and molecular biology. Cellular biochemistry included the study of genetic functioning and the biochemical composition of cells, yielding information that was used in developmental biology. Molecular biology involved the study of deoxyribonucleic acid (DNA) and ribonucleic acid (RNA), the genetic information systems of living organisms. Invitrogen's involvement in the commercial production market centered on serving industries engaged in the commercial production of rare or difficult to obtain substances through genetic engineering. A broad collection of industries was involved in such activity, ranging from the biotechnical industry to the food processing and agricultural industries.

Invitrogen's essence was its development, manufacture, and marketing of research tools in kit form that simplified and improved gene cloning, gene expression, and gene analysis techniques. These techniques were used to promote gene-based drug discovery, the success of which was expected to be greatly aided by the Human Genome Project. A multiyear, global effort, the Human Genome Project sought to identify the three billion building blocks of the human genetic code. The project, which was nearing completion at the dawn of the 21st century, was endeavoring to provide the blueprint of humanity. With such a blueprint, scientists were expected to develop new medicines that would be safer and more effective than any pharmaceutical products on the market.

Although Invitrogen marketed scores of products, one stood out among the rest. The company's patented TOPO Cloning technology dramatically accelerated the cloning process, reducing the time it took for one step in the process from 12 hours to five minutes. With the success of its patented cloning technology and the litany of other Invitrogen products, the company was able to record respectable growth throughout the 1990s, moving well beyond the $4 million recorded at the beginning of the decade. By the company's 10th anniversary, it had eclipsed the $50 million-in-sales mark, generating $55.3 million in revenues. Much of Invitrogen's financial growth arrived later in its development, coming via acquisition. Invitrogen's acquisition spree exponentially increased its revenue volume and its product portfolio, engendering a company that within a few short years was fast in pursuit of the $1 billion-in-sales mark.

ACQUISITIONS FUEL FINANCIAL GROWTH: 1999–2000

The launch of Invitrogen's acquisition campaign coincided with its conversion to public ownership. In 1999 the company completed its initial public offering (IPO) of stock, debuting on the NASDAQ. In August 1999 the company completed its first pivotal transaction, merging with San Diego-based NOVEX, a developer of products used for gene and protein analysis, in a $52 million deal. NOVEX developed and manufactured precast electrophoresis gels, which was a technique used to visualize the results of many different types of molecular biology experiments. Next, in December 1999, the company signed a letter of intent to acquire Huntsville, Alabama-based Research Genetics, Inc., a leading supplier of products and services for gene-based drug discovery research. (At roughly the same time, the Human Genome Project celebrated a major breakthrough, when scientists succeeded in mapping the entire genetic pattern of a human chromosome.)

In anticipation of Research Genetics' inclusion within the Invitrogen fold, Turner explained the impact

KEY DATES

1987: Invitrogen is formed as a partnership.
1989: Invitrogen is incorporated.
1999: Invitrogen completes its initial public offering of stock.
2000: Invitrogen acquires Life Technologies, Inc.
2003: Gregory T. Lucier replaces founder Lyle C. Turner as CEO and embarks on an acquisition campaign that sextuples annual revenues.
2008: Invitrogen acquires Applied Biosystems, Inc., and becomes Life Technologies Corporation.
2010: Life Technologies acquires Ion Torrent for $700 million.

of the acquisition in a December 13, 1999, interview with the *San Diego Business Journal.* "We will now be able to serve customers from the earliest phases of gene identification and target validation," he said, "and continuing through the various stages of cloning, protein expression, and analysis." The acquisition was completed on February 2, 2000, making Research Genetics, a $23 million-in-sales company prior to the acquisition, an Invitrogen subsidiary.

Financial growth, which had occurred at a measured pace throughout much of the 1990s, exploded as Invitrogen exited the decade and entered the 21st century. Acquisitions fueled the increase in the company's revenue volume, lending worldwide recognition to the Carlsbad, California-based company. While the final details of the Research Genetics deal were being hashed out, the company centered its sights on its next target, an Israeli company named Ethrog Biotechnologies Ltd. Ethrog had developed and patented a system for the electrophoretic separation of macromolecules. Invitrogen spent $15.1 million to acquire Ethrog, completing the deal in June 2000. The purchase of Ethrog was followed by an acquisition of astounding scale for a company of Invitrogen's size, its inclusion vaulting Turner's company toward market dominance.

On the heels of the $15 million Ethrog acquisition, Invitrogen announced a cash and stock merger valued at $1.9 billion. In July 2000 Invitrogen neared the end of negotiations to acquire Dexter Corporation. Under the terms of the agreement, Dexter was to be dissolved, marking the end of the oldest company listed on the New York Stock Exchange. Dexter traced its roots back to a decade before the American Revolution, to Seth Dexter II, who began operating a sawmill along the

Connecticut River in 1767. Dexter's business had evolved far beyond sawmill operations in the intervening years, growing to include the molecular biology operations of Life Technologies, Inc., the object of Invitrogen's desire. Founded in 1983, Life Technologies developed, manufactured, and supplied products used in life sciences research and the commercial manufacture of genetically engineered products. Invitrogen's merger with Life Technologies promised to add to the Carlsbad company's already powerful presence in the gene cloning, expression, and analysis market.

The life sciences community applauded the merger, which was expected to create the largest competitor in the molecular biology reagent business. One analyst, in a July 17, 2000, interview with *Chemical Market Reporter,* assessed the impact of the business combination, saying, "This will enable Invitrogen to become the leader in supplying researchers in all aspects of molecular biology from basic bench labwork to cutting-edge genomic and proteinics." Another analyst, in the same article, added, "We view the proposed transaction as confirmation of Invitrogen's continued emerging role as the industry's leading consolidator of enabling research tools and technologies."

The effect of the merger on Invitrogen's stature was immense, adding Life Technologies' $409 million in 1999 sales to create a company with more than $500 million in sales and operating income ranging between $80 million and $100 million annually. Upon completion of the merger, the company's product portfolio swelled to more than 5,500 products, its employee ranks increased by 2,300 workers, and it controlled about 40 percent of the market for kits and products used in gene cloning, gene expression, and gene analysis.

GROWTH REQUIRES REORGANIZATION: 2000

The merger was completed in September 2000. The following month, Invitrogen reorganized its business into two divisions as part of the formidable task of integrating Life Technologies within the company's operations. The molecular biology division was formed to spearhead the company's involvement in gene cloning, gene expression, and gene analysis. Invitrogen's COO, Lewis Shuster, was tapped to head the new division. At the same time, Invitrogen's cell culture division was formed to focus on the markets for cell culture media and serum production.

Stark Thompson, Life Technologies' president and CEO, was selected to lead the cell culture division, which was expected to generate one-third of Invitrogen's annual revenues. The bulk of the company's revenue-generating capabilities fell to the molecular biology division, which was expected to contribute three-quarters of Invitrogen's total sales. In the years ahead, the molecular biology division was expected to record 21 percent annual growth, while the cell culture division was expected to record more modest annual growth of 4 percent.

Invitrogen's sales increased to roughly $630 million in 2001, the first full year of Life Technologies' inclusion within Invitrogen. The total represented a more than sixfold increase over that recorded before the company's IPO sparked its acquisition campaign. In 2002, the process of dealing with the merger was still underway, as the company endeavored to consolidate its operations. In May, Invitrogen announced that it planned to close the Huntsville, Alabama, facility it gained from the Research Genetics acquisition. Production was to be shifted to several of the company's other facilities, a move that was expected to save as much as $10 million annually. The company also was in the process of shuttering both Invitrogen and Life Technologies facilities in the Netherlands as part of a general restructuring of European operations. Additional integration efforts included the elimination of product lines that Invitrogen's management determined were not compatible with the company's strategic goals. The company expected to discontinue product lines representing as much as $55 million in annual sales, most of which were obtained from the merger with Life Technologies.

GREGORY T. LUCIER TAKES THE HELM: 2003

As Invitrogen celebrated its 15th anniversary and planned for the future, it was expected to continue playing the role of industry consolidator. It did so in spectacular fashion, but under the direction of a new leader. Turner announced his retirement in late 2002, which led to the appointment of Gregory T. Lucier as Invitrogen's new CEO in mid-2003. Lucier, 39 years old, earned an undergraduate degree in engineering from Pennsylvania State University and a master's of business administration degree from Harvard Business School. Before joining Invitrogen, Lucier served as president and CEO of General Electric's Medical Systems Information Technologies. During his three years at the General Electric unit, Lucier increased sales from $700 million to $1.8 billion, demonstrating talents on the acquisition front that attracted Invitrogen's board of directors.

Lucier's skills would be on full display during his time at Invitrogen. In less than a decade, the company's payroll swelled from 2,600 employees to 11,000 employees and its annual revenue total nearly sextupled,

leaping from $630 million to nearly $3.6 billion. Lucier accomplished the feat largely by acquiring other companies, a strategy he began employing two months after his arrival, when Invitrogen spent $325 million to acquire Molecular Probes, an Oregon-based firm that made fluorescent markers used in biomedical research. Molecular Probes was the first of eight acquisitions Lucier would complete during his first two years at the helm.

The purchases expanded the company's collection of protein and antibody products that were used to conduct basic medical research in genes and proteins. Invitrogen completed a series of relatively small acquisitions, buying Zymed Laboratories for $60 million, which gave it more than 2,000 antibodies, and purchasing Caltag Laboratories for $20 million, a deal that added 3,000 antibodies to the company's portfolio of biological content. The bigger acquisitions understandably attracted more attention, purchases such as the $386 million transaction for Norwegian biotechnology company Dynal Biotech ASA in 2005, which gave Invitrogen magnetic bead technologies used in microbiology.

INVITROGEN BECOMES LIFE TECHNOLOGIES: 2008

By far the largest acquisition of the decade occurred in 2008, a deal that stole the headlines in the biotechnology community. Before the mammoth acquisition, Invitrogen's annual revenues neared $1.3 billion, roughly twice the total posted four years earlier. The company controlled 25 percent of its market and it ranked as the world's largest producer of the specialty products used in academic and industrial laboratories dedicated to investigating and developing cell-based medicine. Lucier envisioned an even larger company and he set his sights on the competitor he cited as his most respected foe when he arrived at Invitrogen: Foster City, California-based Applied Biosystems, Inc. In June 2008 Invitrogen agreed to purchase Applied Biosystems for $6.4 billion in cash and stock, striking a deal that virtually doubled its size. After the acquisition, Invitrogen became Life Technologies Corporation, a company with $3.5 billion in revenues, 10,000 employees in more than 100 countries, and 50,000 products built on 3,600 licenses and patents.

Life Technologies ended the decade as one of the largest biotechnology companies in the world, possessing one of the largest intellectual property portfolios in the life sciences. The company had evolved from a homespun business into a sprawling corporation approaching $4 billion in revenues in less than 25 years and it showed no signs of slackening its pace of growth. Lucier remained active on the acquisition front as he concluded his first decade at the helm, spending $700 million in 2010 to acquire Ion Torrent, a manufacturer of gene-sequencing hardware. In the years ahead, further deals were expected as Life Technologies continued to assert itself as the dominant competitor in its field.

Jeffrey L. Covell

PRINCIPAL SUBSIDIARIES

Acoustic Cytometry Systems, Inc.; AcroMetrix Corporation; Ambion, Inc.; Applied Biosystems China, Inc.; Applied Biosystems International, Inc.; Applied Biosystems Taiwan Corporation; Applied Biosystems, LLC; Biotrove Corporation; Boston Probes, Inc.; CellzDirect, Inc.; Geneart, Inc.; Genomic Nanosystems Corporation; Invitrogen Finance Corporation; Invitrogen Holdings Inc.; Invitrogen IP Holdings, Inc.; Invitrogen Real Estate Services, Inc.; Ion Torrent Systems Incorporated; Kettlebrook Insurance Co. Ltd.; Molecular Probes, Inc.; Protometrix, Inc.; Sentigen Holding Corp.; Visigen Biotechnologies, Inc.; Acrometrix Europe B.V. (Netherlands); Ambion Europe Ltd. (UK); Applied Biosystems Austria GmbH (Austria); Applied Biosystems BV (Netherlands); Applied Biosystems Europe BV (Netherlands); Applied Biosystems Finland OY; Applied Biosystems Ltd. (UK); Geneart AG (Germany); Genomed GmbH (Germany); Invitrogen AB (Sweden); Invitrogen AG (Switzerland); Invitrogen AS (Denmark); Invitrogen Dynal AS (Norway); Invitrogen Dynal Holding AS (Norway); Invitrogen Europe Limited (Scotland); Invitrogen GmbH (Germany); Invitrogen Holdings Limited (UK); Invitrogen OY (Finland); Invitrogen S.r.l. (Italy); Life Technologies B.V. (Netherlands); Life Technologies Ceska Republika s.r.o. (Czech Republic); Bodensee Wohnstatten GmbH (Germany); Life Technologies Europe B.V. (Netherlands); Life Technologies GmbH (Germany); Life Technologies Israel Ltd.; Life Technologies Limited (Scotland); Life Technologies Magyarorszag Kft. (Hungary); Life Technologies Polska Sp.z.o.o. (Poland); Life Technologies s.r.o. (Slovakia); Life Technologies SA (Spain); Life Technologies SAS (France); Mr. Gene GmbH (Germany); N.V. Invitrogen S.A. (Belgium); PE AG (Switzerland); PE GB Ltd. (UK); PE Manufacturing GmbH (Germany); PE Stockholm AB (Sweden); PE Sweden AB; PNA Diagnostics ApS (Denmark); Stokes Bio Limited (Ireland); ZAO PE Biosystems (Russia);

Applied Biosystems (Shanghai) Trading Company Ltd. (China); Applied Biosystems Asia Pte Ltd. (Singapore); Applied Biosystems Hong Kong Ltd.; Applied Biosystems Malaysia Sdn. Bhd.; Applied Biosystems Pty Ltd. (Australia); Applied Biosystems Thailand Limited; Dynal Biotech Beijing Ltd. (China); Invitrogen Australia Pty Limited; Invitrogen Bioservices India Private Limited; Invitrogen Hong Kong Limited; Invitrogen New Zealand Limited; Invitrogen Singapore Pte Limited; Invitrogen Taiwan Limited; Invitrogen Trading (Shanghai) Co. Limited (China); Life Technologies Japan Limited; Shanghai Invitrogen Biotechnology Co. Limited (China); Applied Biosystems Canada; Applied Biosystems de Mexico S. de R.L. de C.V.; Geneart, Inc. (Canada); Invitrogen Argentina SA; Invitrogen Canada Inc.; Life Technologies Brasil Comercio e Industria Ltda (Brazil); Applied Biosystems South Africa (Proprietary) Limited.

PRINCIPAL COMPETITORS

Affymetrix, Inc.; Agilent Technologies, Inc.; BD Biosciences.

FURTHER READING

Chang, Joseph. "Invitrogen to Acquire Dexter and Life Tech. in $1.8 Bn Deal." *Chemical Market Reporter*, July 17, 2000.

Edgecliffe-Johnson, Andrew. "International: Invitrogen Makes Bid for Life Technologies." *Financial Times*, July 19, 2000.

"Invitrogen Most Recognised Life Science Company." *GenomiKa*, July 3, 2002.

Sinovic, Steve. "Firm Makes Gene Sequencing Faster, More Affordable: $1.5 Billion Market for Hardware Might Hit $100 Billion in 20 Years." *San Diego Business Journal*, January 10, 2011.

Van Arnum, Patricia. "Invitrogen's Purchase of Life Tech Creates Leader in Molecular Biology." *Chemical Market Reporter*, July 17, 2000.

Webb, Marion. "Invitrogen Adheres to Aggressive Growth Strategy: Carlsbad Firm Acquires 4th Company in Last Five Months." *San Diego Business Journal*, February 14, 2005.

———. "Invitrogen Names Lucier as CEO to Replace Lyle Turner." *San Diego Business Journal*, June 9, 2003.

———. "Invitrogen Plans More Expansion with Buyout." *San Diego Business Journal*, December 13, 1999.

White, Suzanne. "Human Genome Sciences." *Washington Business Journal*, March 16, 2001.

Luxottica Group S.p.A.

Via C. Cantu 2
Milan, 20123
Italy
Telephone: (+39 02) 863341
Fax: (+39 02) 86334636
Web site: http://www.luxottica.com/en

Public Company
Founded: 1961
Employees: 62,000
Sales: EUR 5.8 billion ($8.6 billion) (2010)
Stock Exchanges: New York
Ticker Symbol: LUX
NAICS: 339115 Ophthalmic Goods Manufacturing

■ ■ ■

Luxottica Group S.p.A. is the world's leading designer, manufacturer, and distributor of eyeglasses and sunglasses. Luxottica's brand family includes such leading names as Ray-Ban, Oakley, Vogue, REVO, Arnette, and Oliver Peoples. The company also produces eyewear under such licenses as Armani, Burberry, Chanel, Dolce & Gabbani, Donna Karan, Polo Ralph Lauren, Tiffany, Versace, and Coach.

Luxottica has long pursued a vertical integration strategy, and has established the world's largest eyewear distribution business. The company's wholesale distribution operations span 130 countries, backed by a network of 18 distribution centers and 40 sales and marketing

subsidiaries. Luxottica is also a world-leading eyewear and vision care retailer, owning the LensCrafters, Pearle Vision, Eye Med, OPSM, Laubman & Pank, Opticas GMO, Econopticas, Sun Planet, and Budget Eyewear chains. Altogether, the company operates approximately 7,000 retail locations. In 2010, Luxottica's distribution arm moved nearly 20.5 million prescription eyeglass frames and nearly 38.5 million sunglasses. The company is led by founder and Chairman Leonardo Del Vecchio and CEO Andrea Guerra. In 2010, the company's total revenues reached EUR 5.8 billion ($8.6 billion).

EYEWEAR CRAFTSMANSHIP IN THE SIXTIES

Born in 1935 in Milan, Luxottica founder Leonardo Del Vecchio has been called "Italy's version of Horatio Alger." His father, a street merchant who hawked vegetables, died five months before Leonardo was born, leaving the family so destitute that the youngster spent seven years of his childhood in an orphanage. As a youth, Del Vecchio apprenticed as a designer in a tool and die factory specializing in small metal components. After studying drawing and engraving at the Brera Academy of Art, the young designer struck out on his own in 1958, manufacturing molded plastic eyeglass components in Milan. With financial backing from two key customers, he moved his 14-man shop in 1961 to Agordo, a picturesque mountain town in a region of northern Italy known for its handcrafted jewelry.

Although he had no formal training in economics, the young entrepreneur soon realized that he could retain more profits through vertical integration. Del Vecchio renamed the business Luxottica and set out to expand its capacity to include the full range of eyeglass components. Over the course of the decade, he added metalworking capabilities, plastic milling, and other processes to his company. This process culminated in the 1969 launch of Luxottica's first complete set of optical frames.

Luxottica had a brush with oblivion in 1971, when the company's two outside investors called in their ITL 190 million in loans to Del Vecchio. Del Vecchio's fortunes quickly reversed when the entrepreneur brought in a new partner, Scarrone. He then bought out this former competitor within the year.

DRIVE FOR INTEGRATED PRODUCTION IN THE SEVENTIES

Del Vecchio continued to systematically integrate his eyeglass business, focusing on technological advances throughout the 1970s. Noting that it was not materials, but retooling to accommodate fashion changes, that drove cost increases, Del Vecchio began to tackle that side of his business. Having taken courses in advanced machine design in 1969, he began to devise automated molding and milling equipment. He also adopted techniques from allied industries, borrowing specialized electroplating procedures from local jewelers, for example. Ample funding for research and development in plastics compounding, metallurgy, and basic chemistry ensured the quality of future products.

Perhaps most important, Del Vecchio guided Luxottica's implementation of computerization. By the end of the decade, the company had integrated all facets of its process, from design to manufacturing and inventory control. This early application of computer technology not only gave Luxottica a significant cost advantage over its competitors, but also helped make small production runs more efficient. This factor would become increasingly important as the influence of ever-changing fashion trends impacted the eyewear industry.

GEOGRAPHIC CONSOLIDATION THROUGH ACQUISITION IN THE EIGHTIES

Luxottica concentrated on consolidating its international distribution network in the 1980s. International sales had been vital to Luxottica's success. In fact, the very first sets of the company's frames were not sold in Italy, as one might expect, but in the United States. In 1970, the company assigned exclusive rights to distribute its eyewear in the United States to Avant Garde. The Luxottica line was not offered in Italy until 1975. After taking control of Avant Garde in 1982, Luxottica increased its U.S. market share from less than 2 percent to more than 7 percent, enough to lead this highly fragmented industry.

Under the direction of Leonardo Del Vecchio's son and expected successor, Claudio, revenues from the U.S. division, which constituted more than half of the Italian firm's total sales, increased from $28 million in 1982 to $143 million by 1990. Over the course of the decade, Luxottica acquired nine of its 12 international distributors and took significant equity positions in the remainder with an eye toward full ownership. The company applied its own finely honed standards to its new affiliates, winning opticians' and retailers' loyalty by offering computerized ordering, inventory services, and just-in-time delivery. In the early 1990s, Luxottica found itself in the unusual position of increasing brand awareness and penetration in Europe, where it had only about 5 percent of the market.

Fueled by acquisitions and continual economizing, Luxottica's revenues increased from ITL 16 billion in 1979 to ITL 194 billion in 1985. In spite of this spectacular financial and geographic expansion, Leonardo Del Vecchio remained "Signor Nessuno" (Mr. Nobody) among Italy's leading businessmen.

DESIGNER LINES SPARK LATE EIGHTIES GROWTH SPURT

Three principal trends converged in the late 1980s to jump-start Luxottica's sales and earnings growth. Prescription eyeglasses evolved from a fashion liability into an important accessory, to the point that even those who did not need to correct their vision might wear frames with noncorrective lenses just to complete a particular "look." Luxottica capitalized on this trend by amassing a collection of designer labels in the late 1980s and early 1990s. To its own Luxottica and Sferoflex ophthalmic frames and Sfersol sunglasses, the company added Giorgio Armani, Genny, Byblos, Giugiaro, Valentino, and Yves Saint Laurent. Del Vecchio correctly reasoned that people who might not be able to afford a

KEY DATES

1958: Leonardo Del Vecchio starts up a business making tools and parts for eyeglasses in Milan.

1961: Del Vecchio and two financial partners establish Luxottica in Agordo.

1969: Company begins production of its own Luxottica branded eyeglass frames.

1982: Company acquires a U.S. distributor to begin sales operations in the United States.

1990: Luxottica goes public on the New York Stock Exchange.

1995: Luxottica acquires LensCrafters and becomes a retail optical leader.

1999: Luxottica acquires the sunglasses division of Bausch & Lomb, including Ray-Ban and other brands; company launches the managed vision care subsidiary EyeMed Vision Care.

2001: Luxottica acquires Sunglass Hut International and becomes the world's leading eyewear retailer.

2007: Luxottica acquires Oakley in the United States.

Giorgio Armani suit might opt instead for the designer's eyewear.

As the share of company sales generated by designer glasses increased from nil to more than 38 percent, Luxottica's revenues and earnings mounted. Sales increased from ITL 194 billion in 1985 to more than ITL 460 billion in 1991, by which time net income exceeded ITL 60 billion. By the early 1990s, designer eyewear drove the company's gross margins to an astonishing 70 percent.

Luxottica went public on the New York Stock Exchange with a January 1990 floatation of 23 percent of the company's equity in the form of American Depositary Receipts (ADRs). Luxottica was the first Italian company ever to bypass the Milan Stock Exchange to list on the New York Stock Exchange. Company executives treated financial analysts to their stylish sunglasses to help promote the initial public offering (IPO). In an April 1991 interview, Del Vecchio told *Forbes*'s Katherine Weisman: "If we listed [on the Milan Exchange], we would have been a piccolissima cosa [teeny thing]. On the NYSE, c'e rispetto [there's respect] for everybody, piccolo e grande." The founder retained the $80 million proceeds of the IPO for

himself. Debt-free Luxottica did not need the money, and he had certainly earned the reward. By 1994, the shares had quadrupled in value.

HOSTILE TAKEOVER IN 1995

In 1995, Luxottica took its largest single step toward vertical integration with the hostile $1.4 billion takeover of United States Shoe Corporation. This initially surprising development was precipitated by heightened competition in the frame industry and reduced reimbursements from third-party payers such as insurers and health maintenance organizations. Luxottica had traditionally sold to individual opticians, and had more than 28,000 clients in the United States by the early 1990s. At that time, the company increasingly found itself squeezed between shrinking insurance allowances for frames and its competitors' price cuts to match those limits. Del Vecchio knew he could not rely on the designer market alone for continued profitable growth, but he also did not want to start chasing the industry's lowest common denominator. He found an oblique solution to the dilemma in United States Shoe Corporation.

Luxottica was not interested in the target's shoe manufacturing business or its retail apparel subsidiaries. Instead, Del Vecchio was eager to capitalize on its chain of nearly 700 LensCrafters optical stores and that operation's $767 million in annual sales. Established in 1983, LensCrafters was one of the first businesses to combine vision professionals, eyeglass frames, and prescription lens processing in one easily accessed mall location. The company's "about an hour" turnaround time completed the convenient package. Anticipating the immense potential of this new concept, United States Shoe acquired the budding three-store chain barely a year after it was founded. The financial backing of this billion-dollar conglomerate helped LensCrafters become the largest retail eyewear chain in the United States by 1988. It achieved global sales leadership in 1992.

As part of the 1995 transaction with Luxottica, United States Shoe sold its footwear group to Nine West Group Inc. for $600 million prior to its own acquisition. Luxottica was unable to find a buyer for United States Shoe's 1,300 money-losing apparel retailers, which included the Casual Corner, Petite Sophisticate, August Max, Casual & Co., and Capezio chains. As a result, the parent transferred this division to La Leonarda Finanziaria SRL, a separate Del Vecchio interest. The addition of LensCrafters more than doubled Luxottica's annual revenues from ITL 812.7 billion in 1994 to ITL 1.8 trillion in 1995.

Luxottica faced the end of the 20th century with an array of growth strategies in its arsenal. The company hoped to further increase sales of designer eyewear, which had already topped 50 percent of annual revenues, by placing stronger emphasis on these more expensive lines in LensCrafters stores. At the same time the company sought to boost its sales of its own brands in the U.S. market. Previously, Luxottica's brands had represented only a tiny portion of LensCrafters' business. Taking control of that company enabled Luxottica to step up its presence in the retail chain, eventually increasing its share of LensCrafters' stock to some 70 percent.

PUBLIC OFFERING IN 2000

Luxottica continued its diversification into sunglasses and sports eyewear with the 1995 acquisition of Italian sunglass manufacturer Persol SpA. By that time, sunglasses constituted more than one-third of annual sales. In addition, in a radical shift from its traditional trade-only promotions, Luxottica planned to boost its consumer advertising with an image-oriented campaign.

Through the late 1990s, Luxottica continued to build up its strong brand portfolio, adding licenses from such designers as Bulgari in 1996, Ferragamo and Ungaro in 1998, and Chanel in 1999. Meanwhile, Luxottica's revenues were growing strongly, jumping from EUR 419 million in 1994 to EUR 1.9 billion in 1999.

The year 1999 marked a new milestone for Luxottica. In that year the company reached an agreement to acquire the sunglasses division of optical maker Bausch & Lomb for $640 million. That purchase brought the company one of the world's strongest stables of sunglasses brands, notably, the famed Ray-Ban brand, and others, including Killer Loop, Revo, and Arnette. By then, Luxottica had taken its quest for vertical integration into another direction, setting up EyeMed Vision Care to group managed vision care provider operations in the United States, with a network of some 19 million members and 8,000 practitioners.

Luxottica finally listed on the Milan Stock Exchange in 2000. The company then sought new expansion opportunities, including planning a move into Poland, as a first point of entry into the Eastern European market. Luxottica struck again in 2001 when it announced that it had succeeded in acquiring Sunglass Hut International, the world's leading sunglasses retailer with nearly 2,000 shops worldwide. The purchase price, hammered out after a year of negotiations, reached $690 million, including nearly $200 million in debt.

ASIAN EXPANSION FROM 2006

Following the Sunglass Hut acquisition, Luxottica merged its two North American retail businesses headquarters, helping to cut costs. The company also persuaded its largest suppliers to cut their prices, in part by replacing a strong percentage of Sunglass Hut's stock with the company's own sunglasses brands. Luxottica also put the squeeze on Sunglass Hut's largest supplier, the Oakley brand, which made up some 20 percent of the chain's sales. When Oakley balked at Luxottica's demands for lower pricing, Luxottica simply dropped the brand altogether.

The company's sales topped EUR 3 billion at the end of 2001. Acquisitions remained the fuel for the group's growth through the decade. The company expanded its presence in 2003, buying OPSM, the leader of the Australian and New Zealand markets with a 35 percent share. In the United States, the company acquired Cole National for $401 million in 2004, gaining control of Cole Vision, operator of optical departments for Wal-Mart, Target, Sears, and other retailers. Cole also held a 21 percent stake in Pearle Europe, which operated nearly 1,500 stores in 14 European markets, including under the Synoptic banner. Next, Luxottica acquired Detroit-based DOC Optics, acquiring that company's 100 stores, in 2006. This was followed by the $2 billion purchase of Oakley in 2007. As a result, Luxottica gained control of one of the world's leading sports sunglasses brands.

In the second half of the decade, Luxottica targeted further expansion into developing markets, especially the Asian region, with a focus on the Indian and Chinese markets. In 2005, the company acquired the high-end optical chain Xueliang Optical, based in Beijing, which operated 77 stores in China and 68 stores in Hong Kong. The company also bought Ming Long Optical, based in Guangdong Province, and its 133 stores.

ENTERING LATIN AMERICA IN 2009

Luxottica's growth slowed amid the global economic crisis. Nonetheless, the company remained on the lookout for new acquisitions. This brought Luxottica into the Latin American market for the first time, through the acquisition of 40 percent of Multiopticas Internacional, subsidiary of Spain's Multiopticas, in 2009. By the end of the decade, Luxottica raised its share in Multiopticas Internacional to 57 percent, gaining control of the group's 470 stores in Chile, Peru, Ecuador, and Colombia. In December 2011, Luxottica raised its South American profile again, buying Brazilian leader Grupo Tecnol, in a EUR 110 million deal expected to be completed early in 2012.

These acquisitions helped fuel Luxottica's growth into the next decade as the company's sales reached EUR 5.8 billion at the end of 2010. By then, the company had extended its reach into 130 countries, producing and distributing more than 55 million eyeglasses and sunglasses each year. The company had become the world's largest eyewear retailer, marketing nearly 30 internationally recognized brands. These included the Armani brand family, which had left Luxottica for rival Safilo in 2001. In November 2011, however, Luxottica and Armani agreed to bring the brand back to Luxottica starting in 2013. Leonardo Del Vecchio remained as the head of the company, founded as a small workshop just 50 years earlier, while also preparing for his succession, naming Andrea Guerra as CEO. Moving forward, Luxottica could be expected to focus on continued growth within the field it had come to dominate.

April Dougal Gasbarre
Updated, M. L. Cohen

PRINCIPAL SUBSIDIARIES

Luxottica (Switzerland) Ag; Luxottica Argentina S.R.L.; Luxottica Australia Pty Ltd.; Luxottica Belgium N.V.; Luxottica Canada Inc.; Luxottica Do Brasil Ltda. (Brazil); Luxottica Fashion Brillen (Germany); Luxottica France S.A.R.L.; Luxottica Gozluk Tic. A.S. (Turkey); Luxottica Gulf L.L.C. (UAE); Luxottica Hellas Ae (Greece); Luxottica Iberica Sa (Spain); Luxottica Malaysia Sdn Bhd; Luxottica México S.A. De C.V.; Luxottica Nederland B.V. (Netherlands); Luxottica Norge As (Norway); Luxottica Retail North America, Inc. (USA); Luxottica Optics Ltd. (Israel); Luxottica Poland Sp.Zo.O.; Luxottica Portugal Sa; Luxottica S.R.L.; Luxottica South Africa (Pty) Ltd.; Luxottica Sun Corporation (USA); Luxottica Sweden A.B.; Luxottica U.K. Ltd.; Luxottica Vertriebs G.M.B.H. (Austria); Mirari Japan Co., Ltd.; Mirarian Marketing Pte. Ltd. (Singapore); Oakley Inc. (USA); OPSM Group Limited (USA); Oy Luxottica Finland Ab; Rayban Sun Optics India Ltd.; Sunglass Hut Trading, LLC.

PRINCIPAL DIVISIONS

House Brands; License Brands; Wholesale Distribution; Retail Distribution; Sun and Luxury Retail.

PRINCIPAL OPERATING UNITS

Ray-Ban; Oakley; Persol; Arnette; K&L; Luxottica; Mosley Tribes; Oliver Peoples; Sferoflex; Vogue.

PRINCIPAL COMPETITORS

Allergan Inc.; B Braun Melsungen AG; Carl-Zeiss-Gruppe; Essilor International S.A.; Gucci Group N.V.; Hoya Corporation; Nikon Corporation; Nippon Sheet Glass Company Ltd.; Novartis International AG.

FURTHER READING

Burke, Erica. "Seeing Is Believing." *US Business Review*, August 2005, 84.

Costin, Glynnis. "Luxottica's Designing Eyes." *WWD*, September 14, 1990, 6–7.

Goldoni, Luca. *A Far-Sighted Man*. Verona, Italy: Luxottica SpA, 1991.

Hessen, Wendy. "Customers Eye Luxottica's Big Move." *WWD*, May 1, 1995, 20–21.

Kroll, Luisa. "Lens Master." *Forbes*, February 4, 2002, 60.

"Leonardo Del Vecchio; Chairman and Chief Executive, Luxottica." *Business Week*, June 17, 2002, 76.

"Luxottica Wins Back Armani." *Optician*, November 25, 2011.

Lyons, David. "Persistence Paid Off for Suitor of Sunglass Hut." *Daily Business Review*, March 7, 2001, A1.

Morais, Richard C. "Luxottica's Golden Spectacles." *Forbes*, May 20, 1996, 98.

Saporito, Bill. "Luxottica Group Cutting Out the Middleman." *Fortune*, April 6, 1992, 96.

Sullivan, Ruth. "One Man's Vision Which Put Luxottica in the Frame." *European*, October 14, 1994, 32.

Weisman, Katherine. "Piccolissima cosa No More." *Forbes*, April 29, 1991, 70.

Willan, Philip. "Leonardo Looks Good in Glasses." *European*, September 7, 1995, 32.

Mail.Ru Group Limited

Presnenskaya Nab. 10
Block C, 57th Floor
Moscow, 123317
Russia
Telephone: (+7 49 5) 725-6357
Web site: http://corp.mail.ru

Public Company
Founded: 2005 as Digital Sky Technologies
Employees: 2,089
Sales: $324.74 million (2010)
Stock Exchanges: London
Ticker Symbol: MAIL
NAICS: 519130 Internet Publishing and Broadcasting
and Web Search Portals

■ ■ ■

Mail.Ru Group Limited is the largest Internet company in the Russian-speaking world. Mail.Ru Group operates Russia's largest e-mail service, the country's two largest instant-messaging networks, and two of Russia's three largest social networks. Through its Internet businesses, the company addresses an audience of approximately 300 million people in more than a dozen countries. Mail.Ru Group's brands include its instant messaging networks Mail.Ru Agent and ICQ, its social networks Moi Mir (My World) and Odnoklassniki (OK), and a number of Web sites such as travel.mail.ru, news.mail. ru, and hi-tech.mail.ru. The company also owns minority stakes in Facebook Inc., Zynga Game Network Inc., and Groupon Inc.

FOUNDER'S BACKGROUND

Behind the market dominance of Mail.Ru Group stood Yuri Milner, the billionaire whose shrewd deal making and foresight created a media empire largely without rival in the Russian-speaking world. Milner's stunning success in the business world came after an aborted attempt to follow in his father's footsteps in the academic world. Milner's father, the chief deputy director at the Institute of Economics of the Russian Academy of Sciences, was a professor specializing in U.S. management practices. Milner joined his father at the Russian Academy of Sciences after completing his studies in theoretical physics at Moscow State University in 1985. The 24-year-old Milner began working at the Russian Academy of Sciences' Institute of Physics while pursuing his doctorate degree in particle physics, but he dropped out before earning his degree.

The business world did not beckon yet, but it soon captured Milner's attention. After abandoning the study of particle physics, he accepted a scholarship at the University of Pennsylvania's Wharton School of Business, becoming the first Soviet citizen to study at the institution. He earned a master's of business administration (M.B.A.) degree and moved to Washington, D.C., where he worked for the World Bank as a banking specialist focused on the development of private sector banking. Later in life, Milner characterized his years in Washington, D.C., as being wasted. From nearly 5,000 miles away, Milner surveyed the upheaval in his native land, watching the privatization of government holdings once owned by the defunct Soviet state and standing in the wings as fortunes and business empires were being made. Soon, he made the move that led to his return to

---

COMPANY PERSPECTIVES

Our focus is not only on the population of Russia, but also on the Russian-speaking audience worldwide, which comprises between 250 and 300 million people. Our significant customer base creates the foundation from which we are able to launch new services and to generate revenue from display and contextual advertising, a range of internet value-added services (IVAS), including online games and virtual gifts, and to achieve our goal of becoming the leading integrated communications and entertainment platform in the Russian-speaking Internet market.

Moscow, where he would become a member of Russia's new class of immensely successful business titans.

The turning point in Milner's career occurred in 1995. In the spring he was appointed CEO of Alliance-Menatep, an investment brokerage company owned by fellow Muscovite Mikhail Khodorkovsky, who was on his way towards amassing assets worth more than $15 billion. Khodorkovsky had formed Alliance-Menatep through Menatep Bank, one of Russia's first privately owned banks, an institution that Khodorkovsky used to become an oil tycoon and an institution that provided Milner with entry into investing in the business opportunities engendered by the collapse of the Soviet Union.

Milner worked in several capacities within the Menatep Bank organization, serving as head of investment management for the bank after his stint at Alliance-Menatep and going on to serve as the deputy chairman of the bank. The experience, a period encompassing the latter half of the 1990s, brought the changing Russian business landscape before his eyes. It also introduced him to the individuals who would help him become one of the influential business leaders shaping and defining Russian commerce.

MILNER LAUNCHES NET BRIDGE: 1999

During the second half of the 1990s, Milner began considering forming a company that conducted its business on the Internet. A review he read by a Morgan Stanley analyst, Mary Meeker, about the glowing prospects for online businesses convinced him to move forward with his plan. This led him to reach out to a former Menatep colleague, Gregory Finger, who led the

Russian branch of a U.S. investment fund named New Century Holding. The meeting between Milner and Finger proved germinative, convincing New Century Holding to commit $2.25 million to an Internet start-up firm provided Milner and Finger each contributed $750,000 to the cause. Milner's proceeds from his investment deals supplied his portion of the investment capital, enabling the formation in 1999 of Netbridzh Services Ltd. (NetBridge), an Internet incubator and investment fund that looked to Milner as its president.

Through NetBridge, Milner began to build his business empire. The company bought stakes in Russian Internet companies that had modeled themselves on successful U.S. companies. NetBridge invested in the portal List.ru, an online auction site based on eBay, Molotok.ru, a free Web-hosting site based on GeoCities, Boom.ru, and an online shopping site called 24x7 that borrowed heavily from Amazon.com. The companies Milner invested in struggled to shine during the collapse of the dot-com sector at the start of the 21st century, but Milner, nevertheless, brokered an important deal from his weakened stance. He managed to spearhead the merger of the online portal, Port.ru, which owned Mail.ru, the largest e-mail service provider in Russia, with NetBridge, the owner of less popular Internet brands. Milner became CEO of the combined entities, which operated under the name Mail.Ru after the fall of 2001.

Although Milner served as CEO of Mail.Ru, he took little responsibility for managing the business. He handed much of the responsibility for running and building the business to Chief Technology Officer Dmitry Grishin, a 22-year-old graduate of Moscow State Technical University. Highlights of the first several years of Grishin's de facto leadership included the launch of an instant messaging service called Mail.Ru Agent and a search partnership with Google in 2003. In 2004 the company began mobile e-mail service and added voice calls to Mail.Ru Agent. The following year a blogging service was introduced, video calls were added to Mail.Ru Agent, and Lady.Mail.Ru, which catered to women, debuted. By 2005 Mail.ru was the most popular Russian Web site on the Internet, counting more than 30 million users.

MILNER BEGINS INVESTING THROUGH DIGITAL SKY TECHNOLOGIES: 2005

Milner, meanwhile, began to move in another direction. He resigned from the post of CEO at Mail.Ru in 2003 and two years later founded Digital Sky Technologies (DST) as an investment holding company. DST's primary asset was Mail.Ru, accounting for roughly two-

KEY DATES

1999: Yuri Milner founds NetBridge, an Internet incubator and investment fund.

2001: NetBridge and the Web portal Port.ru merge, creating Mail.Ru.

2005: Digital Sky Technologies is formed as an investment fund.

2009: Digital Sky Technologies acquires a 1.96 percent stake in Facebook Inc.

2010: Digital Sky Technologies takes Mail.Ru public, creating Mail.Ru Group.

thirds of the investment company's portfolio, and it served as the instrument used to expand Mail.Ru's interests.

By 2005 Mail.Ru was one of three companies vying for control of the Russian Internet, known as *Runet*. Yandex, a search engine, and Rambler, a portal similar to Yahoo!, stood as Mail.Ru's main rivals, each trying to gain control of the Russian-language Internet traffic. During mid-decade, Rambler lost market share because of a series of management changes and Mail.Ru benefited from the faltering steps of its foe. The company, which initially had gained its leadership position by copying the business models of successful U.S. brands, began to innovate, becoming a leader rather than a follower. Mail.Ru delved into virtual credits and online gaming before Facebook ventured into the realm. It also integrated instant messaging with e-mail in 2007, a year before Facebook released its instant messaging service, Chat.

Mail.Ru focused its efforts on developing its social networks during the latter half of the decade. The company also adopted an aggressive posture on the acquisition front, investing, through DST, $1 billion in 30 businesses during a six-year period beginning in 2005. The investments included a 32.5 percent stake in vKontakte.ru, the largest Russian social network, 21.4 percent of Qiwi.ru, the leading Russian online payment service, a $180 million stake in Zynga, the world's largest social gaming company, and the $187.5 million purchase of ICQ, the leading instant messaging service in Russia and several other Eastern European countries. By the end of the decade, DST's investments had turned Mail.Ru into an Internet powerhouse, drawing more than 70 percent of all page views in Runet and reaching approximately 300 million social networking site users in more than 13 countries.

MILNER TARGETS FACEBOOK AND COMPLETES STOCK OFFERING: 2009–10

Milner's stranglehold on Runet put him in the spotlight, but the greatest attention cast his way came from an investment made in Facebook. In 2009 he invested $200 million in Facebook, securing a 1.96 percent stake in the world's largest social network. The investment was the beginning of Milner's financial involvement with Facebook. Within the next two years he increased his stake in the company to 2.33 percent, spending $800 million to secure an asset that was valued at a staggering $5 billion by 2011. Milner, already held in high regard as a savvy investor before the series of Facebook transactions, became the stuff of legend after the enormous profit projection following his Facebook investments.

Milner's high-profile investments in Internet businesses continued after he made his initial financial commitment to Facebook. Notably, he made a $135 million investment in Groupon, a discount social commerce Web site, and furthered his commitment as part of Groupon's $950 million round of financing in 2011. He also invested $800 million in Twitter, the social networking and microblogging service, in 2011, but by the time these investments were made the relationship between DST and Mail.Ru had changed dramatically, separating the two companies into distinct entities.

In the fall of 2010, investors large and small were given the opportunity to profit from the Russian Internet empire built by Milner. In November DST was used to take Mail.Ru public on the London Stock Exchange, a maneuver that recast Mail.Ru as Mail.Ru Group, a publicly traded company that raised $900 million on the public market and boasted a market valuation of $8 billion. DST became DST Global and severed its ties to Mail.Ru Group as part of the transaction, looking to Milner as its CEO. Milner became chairman of Mail.Ru Group and Dmitry Grishin became the company's CEO.

Mail.Ru Group emerged at the end of 2010 as the new name for the entity that ranked as the largest Internet company in the Russian-speaking world. The company operated Russia's largest e-mail service, the country's two largest instant messaging networks, and held a substantial stake in the country's largest social network.

As a publicly traded concern, the company was required to disclose the financial details of its operations and holdings for the first time. Mail.Ru Group generated $324.7 million in revenue in 2010, a 64 percent increase from the previous year's total, and it posted $77.3 million in net income, a 66 percent increase from the previous year's total. In market share, the company held sway, and in Milner it enjoyed an overseer of proven capabilities. Mail.Ru Group promised to be a company of considerable influence in the years ahead, its geographic stance poised to widen as both the aspirations of Milner and the evolution of the Internet expanded.

Jeffrey L. Covell

PRINCIPAL SUBSIDIARIES

Mail.Ru Internet N.V. (Netherlands); Mail.Ru Cooperatief UA (Netherlands); Port.ru Inc. (USA); NetBridge Limited (Cyprus); Mail.Ru, LLC; Mail.Ru, LLC (Ukraine); New Trinity Investment, LLC; Port.ru Msk, LLC; Astrum Online Entertainment Limited (British Virgin Islands); Benstar Limited (British Virgin Islands); Nessly Holdings Limited (Cyprus); Mail.Ru GmbH (Germany); Astrum Nival, LLC; Dark Joker, LLC; Express Gold, LLC (75%); IT Territory Nord, LLC; Mail.Ru Games LLC; Online Games Holding Limited (British Virgin Islands); Time Zero, LLC; HeadHunter Group Limited (British Virgin Islands; 91.3%); Metajob LLC (91.3%); CV Keskus AS (Estonia; 91.3%); Odnoklassniki LLC; Odnoklassniki Ltd. (UK); Radikal LLC (80%); Forticom Group Limited (British Virgin Islands); SIA Forticom (Latvia); ICQ LLC (USA); ICQ Ltd. (Israel); Data Center M100 LLC.

PRINCIPAL COMPETITORS

Google Inc.; Yahoo! Inc.; Yandex N.V.

FURTHER READING

"Digital Sky Technologies to Acquire AOL's Instant Messaging Service." *Bezinga.com*, April 28, 2010.

"Facebook Receives Investment from Digital Sky Technologies." *CNW Group*, May 26, 2009.

Harvey, Mike. "Big Shot: Yuri Milner Makes Logical Expansion of His Network." *Times* (London), May 30, 1999.

Olson, Parmy. "The Billionaire Who Friended the Web." *Forbes*, March 9, 2011.

"Zynga Receives Investment from Digital Sky Technologies." *Investment Weekly News*, January 9, 2010.

Mark Anthony Group Inc.

———————————— ■ ————————————

887 Great Northern Way
Vancouver, British Columbia V5T 4T5
Canada
Telephone: (604) 263-9994
Toll Free: (888) 394-1122
Fax: (604) 263-9913
Web site: http://www.markanthony.com

Private Company
Founded: 1972 as Mark Anthony Wine Merchants
Employees: 500
NAICS: 312130 Wineries; 424820 Wine and Distilled
   Alcoholic Beverage Wholesalers; 424810 Beer and
   Ale Merchant Wholesalers

■ ■ ■

Mark Anthony Group Inc. is the parent company for several businesses run by Canadian entrepreneur Anthony von Mandl. Assets include Mark Anthony Brands, a distributor of wine, beer, spirits, and specialty beverages; Mission Hill Family Estate Winery, a winery with roughly 1,000 acres of vineyards in West Kelowna, British Columbia; and Seattle, Washington-based Mike's Hard Lemonade Co., a maker of flavored malt beverages. Mark Anthony Brands distributes nearly 90 brands of wine produced in more than a dozen countries and seven brands of beer originating from Canada, the Czech Republic, Italy, the Netherlands, New Zealand, and South Africa. Award-winning Mission Hill, situated in the Okanagan Valley wine appellation, produces approximately 2.5 million bottles of wine annually. Mike's Hard Lemonade ranks as the second best-selling brand of malt beverages, trailing only Smirnoff Ice.

VON MANDL BEGINS AS A DISTRIBUTOR: 1972

Mark Anthony Group's founder, Anthony von Mandl, was best known for turning Mission Hill Family Estate into an internationally recognized winery, but before he worked his magic he created the business foundation that enabled him to buy the winery. Born in Vancouver, British Columbia, to European parents in 1950, von Mandl returned to Europe with his parents at the age of nine. He attended schools in Switzerland, Austria, and Germany before returning to his native province to earn an undergraduate degree in economics from the University of British Columbia. Once he had his degree, he headed back to Europe to become an apprentice in the wine trade. Once his apprenticeship was concluded, von Mandl made his way back to Vancouver, his crisscrossing pattern of overseas travel concluded. Von Mandl was ready to start his entrepreneurial career.

The 22-year-old von Mandl established himself in 1972 as an importer and merchant of fine wines. His trappings were austere, nothing more than a 100-square-foot office in the back of a Vancouver movie theater. His rent was CAD 29.95, a sum he struggled to pay each month. Von Mandl lived a frugal existence during his first years running Mark Anthony Wine Merchants. When he ventured to Los Angeles two years after starting his business, he occupied a former oriental carpet store, using the space as his office, warehouse, and sleep-

COMPANY PERSPECTIVES

We are the leading privately-owned importer and distributor of fine wine, premium beer, and specialty beverages in Canada. Our company is built upon a foundation of true entrepreneurial spirit, innovation, and a deep respect for brand building. We proudly represent many of the world's leading brands, providing seamless service from producer to consumer, from coast to coast.

ing quarters, tucking an Army surplus, metal-framed cot in the corner. He made sales door-to-door, calling on the city's finest hotels and restaurants, offering his selection of wines imported from Europe.

He returned to Vancouver, practicing the same method of cultivating business as he had in Los Angeles. His efforts over the course of a decade pay dividends. By the end of the 1970s, Mark Anthony Wine Merchants conducted business across Canada, and von Mandl was credited with turning St. Jovian, a Bordeaux he imported, into Canada's best-selling white wine.

Once von Mandl firmly established himself as a successful wine merchant, the opportunity for Mission Hill arose. Von Mandl was approached to assist in a feasibility study for growing grapes in Okanagan Valley, north of Vancouver. The study was completed for Josef Milz, a Germany-based winery, which declined to make any investment in the region, but von Mandl was struck by his introduction to the area. The climatic conditions were ideal for making high-quality wines, he believed, convincing him to take a bold step forward and begin his career as a vintner.

THE DEVELOPMENT OF MISSION HILL: 1981–94

Using the money he had made as an importer, von Mandl set his acquisitive sights on Mission Hill Winery, which had been established by a group of Okanagan business leaders in 1966 for approximately CAD 500,000. When von Mandl viewed the property, it was in total disrepair. The winery had foundered, having slipped into receivership on two occasions. Only a decrepit collection of aluminum-sided sheds remained as the vestiges of a failed business. The fruit flies in the sheds, according to von Mandl's recollection, numbered in the billions.

To most eyes, Mission Hill was a broken-down winery and the Okanagan Valley was a lackluster appellation. Grapes had first been planted in the region in 1860, but the area had done little to distinguish itself in the wine world during the ensuing century. The appellation was known for producing jug wines and unimpressive varietals, far from the quality of wine von Mandl hoped to produce at Mission Hill. Von Mandl brushed aside consensus, believing in both the promise of Mission Hill and Okanagan Valley.

Von Mandl was ready to jump headlong into transforming Mission Hill's stature, but his financial position was weak. "I'd pulled together all the money I had, all the financing available, and I was still about $100,000 short," von Mandl remembered in a February 2004 interview with *Food & Wine*. With nowhere else to turn, and knowing the seller he was dealing with had a fondness for gambling, von Mandl offered a proposition. "I suggested we toss coins for $20,000 off the asking price per toss," he told *Food & Wine*. "I won enough tosses to make up the difference."

In 1981 von Mandl took over Mission Hill, which became Mission Hill Family Estate under his ownership, and set out to make exemplary wine. He purchased grapes from other vineyards in Okanagan Valley and began making wine while continuing to run his import and distribution business. At Mission Hill, the first steps were arduous. Interest rates leaped to 25 percent a year after he acquired the winery, nearly leading him to suffer the same fate as Mission Hill's founders. He managed to survive, however, saved by his own astute decisions. At Mission Hill, he relaunched a hard apple cider originally produced by his predecessors, rapidly increasing annual production from 18,000 cases to 300,000 cases. At Mark Anthony Wine Merchants, he secured the Canadian rights to distribute California Cooler, a highly popular wine and fruit juice alcoholic beverage, and top-selling Corona beer, which had yet to be introduced to the Canadian market.

A turning point in von Mandl's pursuit of becoming a prestigious vintner occurred in the early 1990s. After searching for a winemaker, von Mandl found the ideal candidate, John Simes, who was the chief winemaker at New Zealand-based Montana Wines. Simes, who had won an award for his Sauvignon Blanc in 1990 at London's influential International Wine & Spirit Competition, agreed to join Mission Hill in 1992 and began working on Mission Hill's Grand Reserve Barrel Select Chardonnay. In 1994 Mission Hill shocked the wine community when Simes's creation won the Avery's Trophy for Best Chardonnay at the International Wine & Spirit Competition. (The judges were stunned as well, insisting upon a re-tasting once they learned of the wine's origin, but a second tasting yielded the same result.) The coveted prize put Okanagan Valley on the

KEY DATES

1972: Anthony von Mandl begins importing wines through Mark Anthony Wine Merchants, the predecessor of Mark Anthony Brands.

1981: Von Mandl acquires Mission Hill Winery and begins producing his own wine.

1994: Mission Hill wins the Avery's Trophy for Best Chardonnay at the International Wine & Spirit Competition.

1999: Von Mandl founds Mike's Hard Lemonade Co.

2008: After losing his distribution contract for Corona beer, von Mandl starts his own brewery, Vancouver-based Turning Point Brewery.

map, conferring legitimacy to the appellation, and it represented a leap forward toward von Mandl's dream of making Mission Hill an elite winery.

MARK ANTHONY GROUP EXPANDS, MIKE'S HARD LEMONADE DEBUTS: 1996–99

After garnering their first international award, the partnership of von Mandl and Simes broadened the scope of Mission Hill's operations. The winery had relied on third-party growers for its grapes since von Mandl took over the property, but, flush with success in London, von Mandl decided to begin acquiring his own vineyards, making his first purchase in 1996. Von Mandl focused his efforts in the southern Okanagan terroir, acquiring approximately 1,000 acres of vineyards during the ensuing 15 years, which represented roughly 12 percent of all the vineyard acreage in British Columbia.

As Mission Hill rose in prominence, von Mandl did not neglect his distribution business, which operated under the name Mark Anthony Brands. The distribution of Okanagan Cider, California Cooler, and Corona beer represented only a fraction of von Mandl's wholesale business. He built Mark Anthony Brands into one of Canada's largest distributors of wine, beer, and spirits, amassing a product portfolio that included brands from nearly 20 countries. Von Mandl also created his own brands, none more successful than a product he launched in 1999.

During a trip to Australia, von Mandl was inspired by the popularity of the country's spiked lemonades. He

was not fond of the taste of the alcoholic beverages, however, and returned to Canada determined to make a better-tasting product. The result was Mike's Hard Lemonade, which was introduced into the Canadian and U.S. markets in 1999. The brand was an immediate success. Von Mandl established Mike's Hard Lemonade Co., which was owned by Mark Anthony Group, in Lakewood, Colorado, where the company remained until 2005, when it moved to Seattle, Washington. At the time of the relocation of its corporate offices, Mike's Hard Lemonade maintained six manufacturing plants and dominated the flavored malt-beverage category along with Smirnoff Ice. Together, the two brands controlled 74 percent of the $1.7 billion market.

MISSION HILL EXPANDS AND A BREWERY BEGINS: 1996–2010

Back at Mission Hill, von Mandl's dreams of bringing prestige to Okanagan Valley were being realized. Selected by *Wine Access* as Canadian "Winery of the Year" in 2001 (an award also garnered in 2007), the winery and its expanding vineyards acreage had become a popular tourist destination. In 1996, the same year he started buy vineyards, von Mandl began a six-year-long capital improvement project, investing an estimated CAD 35 million in elevating the grandeur of the property. "It was clear to me that a landmark showcase winery was absolutely essential to the future of the Okanagan," he said in an interview published in the December 2007/January 2008 issue of *Wine Access*. The Estate Room, featuring a double vaulted ceiling and housing numerous pieces from von Mandl's art collection, abutted the outdoor terrace, which overlooked rows of Pinot Noir and Chardonnay vines. The facility boasted an amphitheater, an 800-barrel wine cellar, and a 12-story bell tower with four bronze bells cast in France by the Paccard Foundry. In 2002 a 60-seat restaurant was built overlooking Okanagan Lake, a facility *Travel + Leisure* magazine selected as one of the world's five best winery restaurants.

As von Mandl's entrepreneurial career approached its 40th anniversary, the companies operating under the umbrella of Mark Anthony Group were exuding strength in their respective markets. A new member to the family arrived late in the decade, its creation motivated by von Mandl's loss of his distribution contract for Corona beer in 2008. Instead of finding another beer to distribute, von Mandl decided to build his own brewery, resulting in the establishment of Turning Point Brewery in Vancouver, which produced Stanley Park 1897 Amber. The brewery likely was not the last venture in Mandl's entrepreneurial career, promising the further expansion of Mark Anthony Group in the years ahead.

Jeffrey L. Covell

PRINCIPAL OPERATING UNITS

Mark Anthony Brands; Mike's Hard Lemonade Co.; Mission Hill Family Estate Winery; Turning Point Brewery.

PRINCIPAL COMPETITORS

Beringer Blass Wine Estates; Diageo Canada Inc.; Hainle Vineyards Estate Winery.

FURTHER READING

Cook, John. "Mike's Malt Execs Like Flavor of Seattle." *Seattle Post-Intelligencer*, February 16, 2005.

"Mike's Hard Invades Premium Category: Company Plans 'Mike-arita' as Incremental Step for Beer Drinkers." *AD-WEEK*, May 22, 2006.

Schreiner, John. "Mission Hill Family Estate." *Wine Access*, December 2007/January 2008.

Taylor, Timothy. "Man with a Mission." *Food & Wine*, February 2004.

———. "The New Brewery." *Vancouver Magazine*, July 1, 2010.

Mueller Industries, Inc.

—■—

8285 Tournament Drive, Suite 150
Memphis, Tennessee 38125-1743
U.S.A.
Telephone: (901) 753-3200
Fax: (901) 753-3250
Web site: http://www.muellerindustries.com

Public Company
Founded: 1917 as Mueller Metals Company
Incorporated: 1990
Employees: 3,846
Sales: $2.06 billion (2010)
Stock Exchanges: New York
Ticker Symbol: MLI
NAICS: 326122 Plastics Pipe and Pipe Fitting
Manufacturing; 326191 Plastics Plumbing Fixture
Manufacturing; 331316 Aluminum Extruded
Product Manufacturing; 331421 Copper Rolling,
Drawing, and Extruding; 332112 Nonferrous Forg-
ing; 332911 Industrial Valve Manufacturing;
332912 Fluid Power Valve and Hose Fitting
Manufacturing; 332913 Plumbing Fixture Fitting
and Trim Manufacturing; 332919 Other Metal
Valve and Pipe Fitting Manufacturing; 332996
Fabricated Pipe and Pipe Fitting Manufacturing

■ ■ ■

Mueller Industries, Inc., is a leading U.S.-based
manufacturer of copper, brass, plastic, and aluminum
products. The company's Standard Products Division
produces copper tube, holding a leading position in air-
conditioning and refrigeration tubes; both copper and
plastic fittings for plumbing and heating applications;
and valves. The products of this division are mainly sold
to wholesalers in the heating, ventilation, air-
conditioning, plumbing, and refrigeration markets.
Other customers include distributors to the
manufactured housing and recreational vehicle industries
as well as building material retailers. The Industrial
Products Division, which primarily serves original
equipment manufacturers (OEMs) in the plumbing,
refrigeration, fluid power, and automotive industries,
produces brass and copper alloy rod, bar, and shapes;
aluminum and brass forgings; and aluminum and copper impact extrusions. Also serving as a supplier to
OEMs is the Engineered Products Division, which
produces valves and custom OEM products for
refrigeration and air-conditioning, gas appliance, and
barbecue grill applications, as well as shaped and formed
tube for baseboard heating units, appliances, and medical instruments. Mueller Industries operates about two
dozen factories, most of which are located in the United
States, with the exception of two plants in China and
single plants in Canada, Mexico, and the United
Kingdom. About 24 percent of Mueller's sales originate
outside the United States.

EARLY HISTORY OF INNOVATION

The story of Mueller Industries begins in 1852 when
20-year-old Hieronymous Mueller immigrated to the
United States. Mueller was an inventor with an interest
in plumbing, particularly plumbing using copper. In
1872 he patented an improved water tapping machine.

In 1877 he became the first to pour castings using brass, an alloy of copper and zinc. Mueller parlayed these inventions into manufacturing facilities, and in 1893, with $68,000 in capital, he incorporated his business in Decatur, Illinois, as H. Mueller Manufacturing Company.

The firm prospered throughout the next two decades, surviving Mueller's death in 1900, after which the company was owned and operated as a partnership between the founder's six sons. In 1917, with the United States' entrance into World War I, Oscar Mueller, the youngest of the six sons, persuaded his brothers to build the first commercial brass forging facility in the nation at a site in Port Huron, Michigan, in order to produce munitions. The plant, which was established as Mueller Metals Company, opened on December 17, 1917.

After the war, shifting to civilian work, Mueller Metals made technological advances, key to the growth of significant industries. For the nascent mechanical refrigeration industry, the company provided brass forging that did not leak refrigeration gas like the porous castings previously in use. In addition, the Port Huron plant pioneered high-strength brass forging for gears, bearings, and pumps used by manufacturers of mechanical devices.

Mueller Metals directed its primary efforts at the plumbing supply business. In 1923 the company introduced soft copper tube for underground water supplies and, in 1924, hard copper tube for indoor water supplies. By 1927, Mueller Brass Company (the new name having been adopted in 1925) was firmly established in the plumbing business and was producing a full line of fittings and valves. That same year, Oscar Mueller secured full control of the firm, after which Mueller Brass was entirely separate from the company his father had founded. (Mueller Co., the name under which H. Mueller Manufacturing began operating in 1924, remained in business into the 21st century, eventually becoming one of the main operating units of Atlanta-based Mueller Water Products, Inc.)

A REVOLUTIONARY NEW FITTING

Perhaps the company's most important innovation came in 1930 when Mueller Brass introduced the revolutionary Streamline solder-type fitting. Previously, fittings (the parts that join pieces of tube) had been the weakest sections of pipes. The new solder-joined fittings, however, were actually stronger than the tubes they connected. It was because of this development that all-copper plumbing and heating systems were established as industry standards.

After the stock market crashed in 1929, Mueller fell victim to the same types of pressures other industrial companies were experiencing. Moreover, as a company that provided supplies to industrial firms, especially in the area of housing construction, Mueller experienced sales that generally reflected the low level of economic activity in the country. This being the case, Mueller canceled dividends and tightened its belt during the first half of the 1930s.

Surprisingly, Mueller returned to profitability by the mid-1930s, reinstating dividends in 1935. Toward the end of the decade, the war in Europe and a reviving economy at home spurred production. Mueller became highly profitable, a fact borne out by generally increasing dividends, including the record $2.25 dividend the company paid in 1941.

POSTWAR EXPANSION

After World War II, Mueller remained profitable, especially during the 1950s when earnings fluctuated between $2.50 and $5.50 per share, and sales averaged around $59 million. Given positive economic conditions, Fred L. Riggin, the company president and CEO, decided to embark on an expansion program. In

KEY DATES

1917: Mueller Metals Company begins operation as a commercial brass forging facility in Port Huron, Michigan.

1925: Company changes its name to Mueller Brass Company.

1965: U.S. Smelting Refining and Mining (USSRAM, later changed to UV Industries, Inc.) acquires full control of Mueller.

1979: Sharon Steel Corporation acquires UV Industries.

1987: Sharon Steel files for bankruptcy; Mueller remains a viable enterprise and does not file for Chapter 11.

1990: Mueller emerges from the Sharon Steel bankruptcy proceedings as an independent company called Mueller Industries, Inc.

1991: Mueller moves its headquarters from Port Huron, Michigan, to Wichita, Kansas.

1996: Headquarters are moved to Memphis, Tennessee.

1997: European beachhead is established through the purchases of U.K. firm Wednesbury Tube Company and French company Desnoyers S.A.

2002: Company completes the divestment of its noncore natural resources assets by selling Utah Railway.

2006: Mueller reports record net income of $148.87 million as the U.S. housing bubble reaches its peak.

December 1951 he paid $1.25 million for Valley Metal Products Co. of Plainwell, Michigan. He bought, and later sold, Sheet Aluminum Corporation, of Jackson, Mississippi, and in March 1958 he acquired American Sinteel Corporation, a Yonkers, New York, manufacturer of powder metal parts.

Along with acquisitions, Riggin upgraded existing facilities and built new ones. In 1954 he launched an eight-year program to expand and diversify the production of fabricated goods. In this effort, he placed particular emphasis on specially engineered, copper-based alloys. In addition, Riggin opened an impact extrusion facility in Marysville, Michigan, in 1958. The plant, which shaped aluminum and copper by forcing it through a die, adapted the inherent strength and minimal weight of extrusions to the specialized needs of customers who ranged from aerospace manufacturers to home appliance suppliers.

During the early 1960s, Mueller continued to do well, adding a larger proportion of defense subcontracting to its mix of customers. At this time the company was producing rods, forgings, tubes, and castings made from aluminum, copper, brass, bronze, and other alloys. Among the many semifinished and fabricated items the company produced were powdered metal, screw machine parts, machined castings, forgings and impact extrusions, refrigeration valves and fittings, chromium- and nickel-plated fabricated items, electrotinned and hot-dipped fabricated items, and copper pipes, tubes, and fittings used in plumbing, heating, and air-conditioning. Mueller continued to grow, reporting profits of $2.35 million on sales of $80.8 million in 1963. The company also acquired the assets of Bay Engineering Company of Bridgeport, Michigan, the following year. Management, however, did not cling to the idea of a large, independent Mueller with an indefinite future.

1965–79: THE USSRAM ERA

For some time, U.S. Smelting Refining and Mining (USSRAM) had been acquiring Mueller stock and by 1965 had amassed a 72 percent share of the company. That year USSRAM made an offer to acquire the remainder of Mueller through a stock swap, a proposal that was approved overwhelmingly by both companies. Technically, Mueller Brass and USSRAM merged to become a new Mueller subsidiary called Mueller Brass Corp. Upon completion of the consolidation, however, the subsidiary's name was changed to U.S. Smelting, Refining, & Mining Company and USSRAM's management took over the new company, in effect absorbing Mueller.

USSRAM was a mining company whose primary products were gold, silver, lead, and zinc. Founded in 1906, the company was relatively stable until the early 1960s when a proxy fight led to the ascension of Martin Horwitz to the offices of president and CEO in 1964. Under Horwitz, USSRAM had followed an aggressive path of acquisitions and had begun to develop the Continental Copper Mine in New Mexico. In acquiring Mueller, Horwitz was looking to join copper mining and smelting with the production of copper products.

The merger proved to be profitable from the start. In 1969, after Horwitz invested $17 million in Mueller's interests and $16 million in the copper mine, USSRAM's sales reached an all-time high of $170 million, while income hit a record $12 million.

In fact, the merger provided Mueller with the capital to introduce new products, modernize old facilities, and build new plants. In 1967 the company began to offer plastic pipe and fittings. The Port Huron rod mill was modernized in 1971, which doubled its copper alloys capacity. That same year construction of a Fulton, Mississippi, tube mill, including a 6,300-ton automated extrusion press, was completed. In a speech reprinted by the *Wall Street Transcript* in December 1976, Horwitz called the Fulton plant "possibly the most efficient tube mill in the United States." He concluded that given the plant's low-cost operation, it had "enabled Mueller to report profits when other mills were reporting losses and still others were closing down."

In the early 1970s, USSRAM changed its name to UV Industries, Inc. to better represent an increasingly diverse product mix that, by then, also included electrical equipment. Mueller, in the meantime, continued to expand, although not quite at the pace it did in the late 1960s. In 1973 the company purchased plants in Hartsville, Tennessee, to produce refrigerator and airconditioning components. By 1976, however, slow housing starts had led to a performance that, while acceptable, was nowhere near what it might be in a boom economy.

1980–90: THE SHARON STEEL ERA

In 1977 Victor Posner, chairman of Sharon Steel Corporation, offered to buy UV Industries. Posner was a Miami Beach businessman who had dropped out of high school and made a fortune in real estate by the time he was 30. He got involved in mergers and acquisitions and eventually used his NVF Company to gain control of Sharon, then the 12th-largest steel company in the United States. One of Posner's tactics was to use subordinate debentures (bonds subordinate to other claims and backed by the general credit of the issuer) rather than a specific lien on particular assets in order to fund his activities.

This was the means of payment he proposed in the acquisition of UV Industries. UV, however, was wary of Posner, and the two sides went back and forth with extensive negotiations. Finally, on November 26, 1979, it was agreed that Sharon would acquire UV for an interim note worth $517 million and the assumption of UV's liabilities. However, Sharon could not sell any UV assets until the interim note was exchanged for cash. This particular clause was important because it was widely assumed that Posner would pay for the deal by selling UV's large portfolio of investments and marketable securities. According to a July 1980 *Wall Street Journal* article, some analysts thought that cash would be hard to come by and that Posner had "erred badly in trying to swallow UV."

Under the Posner regime, Mueller remained profitable, and in 1983 the company's Canadian subsidiary in Strathroy, Ontario, began manufacturing metric fittings. Sharon, however, had difficulties. The company's debts were too high, and in 1985 Sharon defaulted on $33 million in interest payments. Bondholders could have forced the business into bankruptcy immediately. Instead, they negotiated with Posner, who wanted them to swap their subordinated debentures for a package of common shares and low-interest and zero-coupon notes.

The largest bondholder was Quantum Overseas N.V., an investment fund based in Curaçao that was headed by high-stakes investor George Soros. Quantum and the other holders allowed payments on the debentures to be extended more than 20 times while they tried to negotiate a settlement. In 1986 it was rumored that Sharon would sell Mueller to Quantum for $55 million, but that exchange never took place.

Finally, in 1987, Quantum called in the $96.9 million in Sharon securities it held and in April of that year, Sharon filed for Chapter 11 bankruptcy. Over the next two years, Quantum officials and Sharon's other creditors worked to hammer out a plan to divide Sharon's assets and help the company emerge from bankruptcy.

During this time, Mueller was not static. The company had never filed for Chapter 11 and remained a viable enterprise. In 1990 Mueller acquired U-Brand Corporation, an Ashland, Ohio, company whose plants in Ashland and Upper Sandusky, Ohio, manufactured plastic valves, pipe couplings, steel pipe nipples, malleable iron pipe fittings, iron castings, and plastic pipe fittings for wholesalers and hardware stores. In addition, Mueller continued to innovate, bringing out (coincident with strict new Environmental Protection Agency regulations) the SRD-1, which allowed customers in the refrigeration and climate control industries to capture and recover fluorocarbons during repair operations.

REGAINING INDEPENDENCE AS MUELLER INDUSTRIES

The issues surrounding Sharon were finally resolved on December 28, 1990, when negotiators, headed by Raymond Wechsler, an adviser to the Quantum Fund, hammered out a plan to divide up the company. After 25 years as a subsidiary, Mueller reemerged as an independent company called Mueller Industries, Inc. The new Mueller was an industrial concern that held its traditional plumbing and flow control equipment operation as well as natural resource holdings centered around a division called Arava Natural Resources Company, Inc. This new sector of the business included the Utah Railway Company (a short line that carried coal to Provo, Utah, for transshipment by major rail carriers), Alaskan gold mining operations, and a variety of mining interests in Canada and the West. (Sharon's steel assets were spun off into a new firm called Sharon Specialty Steel, Inc.) During 1991 Mueller moved its headquarters from Port Huron, Michigan, to Wichita, Kansas.

In its first year as an independent company, Mueller announced a loss of $43.7 million on sales of $441 million. Almost all of the 1991 loss was due to a revaluation of assets, coupled with costs related to the bankruptcy proceeding and restructuring of the business following the reorganization. Harvey L. Karp, who became chairman and CEO on October 8, 1991, moved quickly to shape up the company. He enhanced the balance sheet by selling $25 million worth of investment grade notes and negotiated for expanded borrowing capabilities that provided $40 million. In an effort to focus on the company's core manufacturing business, the sale of the malleable iron business, which had not been profitable for Mueller, was arranged in 1992.

To help upgrade operations neglected for many years, Karp made a commitment to allocate more capital and undertake improvement projects. He also negotiated settlements of litigation that asserted a $16.5 million guarantee obligation for the Sharon Steel business. This settlement turned out to be very favorable when Sharon filed Chapter 9 in the fourth quarter of 1992. Finally, among other key executives, Karp recruited William D. O'Hagan, who had 32 years of experience in the industry, to be Mueller's president and COO. Karp's efforts paid off handsomely. For the 1992 fiscal year, earnings were up significantly, reaching $16.6 million on sales of $517.3 million.

After Mueller emerged from Sharon Steel's shadow, the Quantum Fund held about 46 percent of the common stock, with the remainder owned by Sharon Steel's creditors. The stock initially traded on the NASDAQ, but the company was listed on the New York Stock Exchange in February 1991. During 1993 the Quantum Fund sold the bulk of its stake to the public through a secondary offering. Then in 1994 Mueller bought Quantum's remaining 9.6 percent stake for $25.9 million. Also in 1994, O'Hagan was promoted to president and CEO, with Karp remaining chairman.

The steadily expanding economy in the mid-1990s fueled growth in housing starts, which was the key economic indicator for Mueller given the large portion of sales that were generated from the construction industry. Both revenues and earnings advanced steadily during this period, culminating in the 1996 figures of

$61.2 million in net income on net sales of $729.9 million. During 1995 the company declared a two-for-one stock split and also announced that its headquarters would be moved from Wichita to Memphis, Tennessee. The move, completed in May 1996, was taken in order to place the head office closer to Mueller's core manufacturing operations in Tennessee and Mississippi. The mid-1990s were also marked by major capital outlays in which Mueller invested about $100 million in plant improvements that increased production capacity and improved efficiency in the company's manufacturing operations.

TURNING ACQUISITIVE LATE IN THE CENTURY

During the late 1990s, as Mueller continued to enjoy annual increases in revenues and profits, the company stepped up its growth efforts by completing a string of significant acquisitions. The first came in late December 1996 when Precision Tube Company, Inc. of North Wales, Pennsylvania, was purchased for $6.6 million. Founded in 1948, Precision Tube produced copper, copper alloy, and aluminum tubing and fabricated tubular products, with its main product line being copper tubing for the baseboard heating industry. These products were produced at the company's mill in North Wales, while a second plant in Salisbury, Maryland, manufactured semirigid and flexible coaxial cables and assemblies used in the defense industry and in microwave technology. The company achieved sales of about $20 million in 1996.

In the first half of 1997, Mueller established its first significant European beachhead through the acquisition of two copper tube manufacturers. In February the company spent $21.3 million for Wednesbury Tube Company, based in Bilston, West Midlands, England. Then, three months later, a French firm, Desnoyers S.A., was acquired for $13.5 million. Desnoyers operated two plants near Paris, in Laigneville and Longueville, and during 1996 produced 60 million pounds of tube, resulting in net sales of $100 million. The Laigneville mill was later shut down and its operations consolidated into those of the other two European plants.

With the company's streak of record results continuing, another two-for-one stock split was declared in early 1998. Three acquisitions were completed later in the year. In August Mueller acquired B&K Industries, Inc., an Elk Grove Village, Illinois-based importer and distributor of residential and commercial plumbing products with sales in 1997 of about $50 million. A key in this deal was that B&K distributed its products to all major distribution channels, including the retail market (hardware stores and home centers), which Mueller had not previously penetrated to any great extent.

Next, Mueller bought Lincoln Brass Works, Inc., a metal fabrication firm with plants in Jacksboro and Waynesboro, Tennessee, and annual sales of $35 million. Lincoln's product line complemented Mueller's brass forging operations and included custom control valve assemblies, custom metal assemblies, gas delivery systems, and tubular products, mainly for the gas appliance market. Finally, in November 1998 Mueller completed the acquisition of Halstead Industries, Inc. for about $92 million in stock. The privately held Halstead, which was founded in Pittsburgh in 1936 and which had sales in 1997 of approximately $250 million, produced copper tubing for plumbing, air-conditioning, and refrigeration applications at plants in Wynne, Arkansas, and Clinton, Tennessee. Following the acquisition, Halstead was renamed Mueller Copper Tube Products, Inc.

In addition to its series of acquisitions and its continued investment of tens of millions of dollars to modernize and update existing plants, Mueller during the late 1990s also divested a number of its natural resources operations as these businesses were increasingly viewed as noncore. At the end of 1997 the company sold off a coal mining business whose operations had been shut down earlier in the decade. Alaska Gold Company, a subsidiary that operated an open pit gold mine in Alaska, was sold to Novagold Resources, Inc. for $5.5 million in April 1999. This left Mueller with one main natural resources operation, Utah Railway, the short-line coal-carrying railroad. Mueller recorded its sixth straight year of revenue growth and its eighth consecutive year of earnings growth in 1999. Net sales surpassed the $1 billion mark for the first time, totaling $1.2 billion, while net income increased 31.7 percent, reaching $99.3 million.

RIDING HOUSING BOOM AND BUST IN EARLY 21ST CENTURY

The economic downturn that coincided with the beginning of the 21st century halted Mueller's string of record results, although the company was able to stay in the black. For 2001, sales fell 15 percent while net income declined 28 percent. To minimize the effects of the downturn, Mueller instituted a number of cost saving measures, including a wage freeze, and streamlined its sales and manufacturing operations. The company's plant in Clinton, Tennessee, was closed down, and Mueller also exited from the metric copper fittings sector, closing its Canadian plant in the process. In August 2002 the company completed the divestment of its non-core assets with the sale of Utah Railway to Genesee &

Wyoming, Inc. for $55.4 million. A difficult business environment in France also led Mueller to divest its manufacturing operations in that country during 2003.

With its fortunes tied so closely to fluctuations in the housing market, Mueller Industries enjoyed another boom period between 2004 and 2006, the peak years of the U.S. housing bubble. Revenue skyrocketed from just under $1 billion in 2003 to $2.51 billion in 2006, while net income reached a record $148.87 million in the latter year. During this period, Mueller expanded its operations through a handful of acquisitions. In 2004 the company acquired Vemco Brasscapri Limited, a U.K.-based import distributor of plumbing products to plumbers' merchants and builders' merchants, as well as the assets of the Mexican steel pipe nipples manufacturer Nipples Del Norte. The latter assets were reorganized within a newly formed subsidiary called Mueller Comercial S.A.

Pursuing growth in an important emerging market, Mueller in 2005 entered into a joint venture in China with Jiangsu Xingrong Hi-Tech Co., Ltd., and Jiangsu Baiyang Industries Ltd. Mueller owned 50.5 percent of the venture, which was named Jiangsu Mueller-Xingrong Copper Industries, Ltd. Based in Jintan City, located in Jiangsu Province, the venture specialized in engineered, inner-grooved copper tube products, manufactured primarily for China-based air-conditioning manufacturers. Early in 2007 Mueller spent $32.8 million to acquire Extruded Metals, Inc., a producer of brass rod products headquartered in Belding, Michigan. Extruded Metals reported $355.5 million in revenues for its fiscal year ending in November 2006.

Mueller's fortunes turned south beginning in 2007 when housing starts fell 24.8 percent and it became clear that the U.S. housing bubble had burst. The small revenue increase that year, up to a record $2.7 billion, was entirely attributable to the acquisition of Extruded Metals. Net income tumbled 22.4 percent to $115.48 million. During the year, the high price of copper prompted Mueller to end casting operations at its copper tube plant in Wynne, Arkansas. The plant instead began producing plastic tube, which was gaining ground in the marketplace as a less expensive alternative to copper tube. Late in the year, the company announced that O'Hagan had been diagnosed with lung cancer. He remained on the job, assisted by Gregory L. Christopher, the newly installed COO, until his death in October 2008. Christopher, who prior to serving as COO had headed the Standard Products Division, was then promoted to the CEO position.

By 2009 housing starts in the United States had dropped to an extremely low level, while the economy overall began only a very tentative recovery from the nation's deepest and longest post-World War II downturn. That year, Mueller managed to barely eke out a profit amounting to $4.68 million thanks to aggressive streamlining efforts that included a workforce reduction of 15 percent. Revenues plunged 40 percent to $1.55 billion not only because of sharply reduced demand but also because of the lower cost of copper (which was Mueller's chief raw material, the price of which generally determined the price at which the company sold its products). Also in 2009, one worker was killed and several others were injured in an explosion at the company's copper tube plant in Fulton, Mississippi. The Occupational Safety and Health Administration (OSHA) later cited Mueller for more than 100 health and safety violations at the Fulton and other company plants. Mueller appealed OSHA's proposed fine of $683,000 for the violations, and the penalties were eventually reduced to around $400,000.

ON GOOD FINANCIAL FOOTING

With a healthy amount of cash on hand and a relatively low level of debt, Mueller began pursuing acquisitions again. Late in 2010 the company acquired Tube Forming, L.P., from Wolverine Tube, Inc. for $6.9 million. From its facilities in Carrollton, Texas, and Guadalupe, Mexico, Tube Forming produced precision copper return bends and crossovers, and custom-made tube components and brazed assemblies, including manifolds and headers, for heating, air-conditioning, and refrigeration systems. Although Mueller's revenue total rebounded to $2.06 billion in 2010, the increase was largely attributable to the sharply higher cost of copper that year compared to 2009. Profits were a much healthier $86.17 million.

As it prepared to ramp up production once the residential and commercial construction markets pulled out of their lengthy downturn, Mueller faced a new challenge in the form of a possible takeover attempt from New York-based holding company Leucadia National Corporation, which had been slowly building up a stake in Mueller. In September 2011 the two companies reached a so-called standstill agreement stipulating that Leucadia would not increase its stake beyond 27.5 percent over the following two years. This deal secured Mueller's continued independence for the time being, but in return Mueller agreed to add two Leucadia executives to its board of directors. Later in the year, Karp announced his intention to resign from the company board at year's end, ending his two-decade stint as chairman. Alexander P. Federbush, a board member since early 2005, was named the new nonexecutive chairman.

Jordan Wankoff
Updated, David E. Salamie

PRINCIPAL SUBSIDIARIES

Metals, Inc.; Micro Gauge Inc.; Mueller Brass Forging Company, Inc.; Mueller Copper Fittings Company, LLC; Mueller Copper Tube Company, Inc.; Mueller Copper Tube Products, Inc.; Mueller Fittings Company, Inc.; Mueller Impacts Company, Inc.; Mueller Packaging, LLC; Mueller Plastics Corporation, Inc.; Mueller Refrigeration, LLC; Mueller Streamline Company; Precision Tube Company, Inc.; Propipe Technologies, Inc.; Streamline Copper & Brass Ltd. (Canada); Mueller Comercial de Mexico, S. de R.L. de C.V.; Mueller de Mexico, S.A. de C.V.; Mueller Europe Limited (UK); Mueller PrimaFlow Limited (UK); Jiangsu Mueller-Xingrong Copper Industries, Ltd. (China; 50.5%); Changzhou Mueller Refrigerant Valve Manufacturing Co., Ltd. (China).

PRINCIPAL DIVISIONS

Standard Products Division; Industrial Products Division; Engineered Products Division.

PRINCIPAL COMPETITORS

Cambridge-Lee Industries LLC; Cerro Flow Products, LLC; Charlotte Pipe & Foundry Company; Chase Brass & Copper Company, Inc.; CMC Howell Metal Company; Copper Products LLC; Elkhart Products Corporation; NIBCO Inc.; Wolverine Tube, Inc.

FURTHER READING

Banton, O. T., and Frank H. Mueller. *Mueller Story*. Decatur, IL: Mueller Co., 1980.

Barton, Christopher. "Mueller Industries Gears to Take Advantage of Economic Rebound." *Memphis (TN) Commercial Appeal*, May 10, 2002, C2.

Daniel, Fran. "Mueller Industries Agrees to Buy Halstead." *Winston-Salem (NC) Journal*, August 11, 1998, D1.

Harrigan, Susan. "Victor Posner Faces Hair-Raising Month as Exchange for UV Note Is Postponed." *Wall Street Journal*, July 21, 1980, 2.

Manas, Robert. "Mueller Acquires Brass Rod Producer Extruded for $32M." *American Metal Market*, February 28, 2007.

Mazzilli, Meredith. "Construction Mart Nearing Cyclical Low: Mueller Exec." *American Metal Market*, July 27, 2011, 9.

———. "Mueller Sees Better Prospects as Construction Bottoms Out." *American Metal Market*, February 2, 2011, 3.

"Mueller Industries Acquires Wolverine Tube Subsidiary." *American Metal Market*, January 6, 2011, 11.

Sacco, John E. "Mueller Acquires Precision Tube." *American Metal Market*, January 9, 1997, 2.

Scott, Jonathan. "Mueller Quietly Approaches $1 Billion in Sales Mark." *Memphis (TN) Business Journal*, October 1, 1999, 32.

Shearer, Brent. "Mueller Completes One Deal, Planning Another." *American Metal Market*, September 10, 1998, 1.

Shumsky, Tatyana. "Mueller Logs Fourth-Quarter Loss, Looks for Acquisition Targets." *American Metal Market*, February 2, 2010.

"UV Industries, Inc." *Wall Street Transcript*, December 13, 1976.

VanValkenburgh, Jaan. "Mueller Acquires Precision Tube." *Memphis (TN) Commercial Appeal*, January 8, 1997, B8.

Muscular Dystrophy Association

Muscular Dystrophy Association

3300 East Sunrise Drive
Tucson, Arizona 85718
U.S.A.
Telephone: (520) 529-2000
Toll Free: (800) 572-1717
Fax: (520) 529-5300
Web site: http://www.mda.org

Nonprofit Organization
Founded: 1950 as Muscular Dystrophy Associations of
America
Employees: 1,400
Operating Revenues: $177.82 million (2010)
NAICS: 813212 Voluntary Health Organizations

■ ■ ■

Muscular Dystrophy Association (MDA) is a nonprofit organization devoted to curing muscular dystrophy by funding worldwide research. The MDA also provides support, advocacy, and educational services, as well as health care through 225 hospital-affiliated clinics. The MDA targets more than 40 neuromuscular disorders classified as muscular dystrophies, supporting more than 330 research projects throughout the world. A major source of the organization's funding comes from the annual *MDA Labor Day Telethon*, a program broadcast by approximately 160 television stations on the Sunday before Labor Day. Historically, the program aired for 21.5 hours, but in 2011 the length of the show was reduced to six hours. The MDA is the largest,

nongovernmental sponsor of muscle and nerve disease research in the United States.

ORIGINS

In the summer of 1950 a group of people affected by muscular dystrophy took it upon themselves to accelerate the search for a cure for the disease. Members of the group included several adults suffering from muscular dystrophy, several parents of children afflicted with the disease, and a physician who was studying the disorder. Leading the meeting was a prominent New York businessman named Paul Cohen who had organized the gathering at his office in Rye, New York.

Cohen led the way, stressing the urgency to finance research on the disease. With greater resources, the medical community, it was hoped, could find treatments for the disease and perhaps a cure. The meeting led to the formation, before the end of 1950, of Muscular Dystrophy Associations of America, the name the MDA would use until the 1970s.

Cohen and his supporters faced the daunting challenge of raising vast sums of cash to solve the riddle of muscular dystrophy. Generally a hereditary disease, muscular dystrophy referred to a group of genetic diseases that caused skeletal, or voluntary, muscles to degenerate. Little was known about the various forms of muscular dystrophy and little was known about the disease outside the muscular dystrophy community. The MDA needed to raise money to fund further research and it needed to raise the awareness of the disease throughout the country. To help accomplish both objectives, Cohen made an astute decision during the first months of the nonprofit organization's development.

FIRST ASSOCIATION WITH JERRY LEWIS: 1951

Cohen believed both public awareness of muscular dystrophy and money could be raised by linking the organization with well-known personalities. He began recruiting celebrities, soliciting their support in the cause, and succeeded in convincing the comedy team of Dean Martin and Jerry Lewis to champion the MDA's efforts. At the end of 1951 Martin and Lewis ended their popular NBC network television show with an appeal to the audience to support muscular dystrophy research. Several weeks later, the duo repeated their request on their nationally broadcast radio program. Before the end of 1952, Martin and Lewis formalized their relationship with the fledgling organization, becoming national co-chairs of the MDA.

Collaboration with the luminaries of the entertainment world proved to be a powerful partnership for the MDA. Cohen was early to recognize the effectiveness of television to promote the organization, a realization that led him to stage telethons broadcast by local television stations. Between 1952 and 1953, he organized five telethons that featured a variety of Hollywood stars, including Robert Alda, Dick Van Dyke, and Virginia Graham, on programs aired in Cleveland, Atlanta, Washington, D.C., Grand Rapids, Michigan, and Madison, Wisconsin.

He also secured the MDA's first national sponsor during the period, signing on the National Association of Letter Carriers in 1953. The agreement led to a nationwide, door-to-door campaign conducted by the members of the National Association of Letter Carriers, which was promoted by a special two-hour, coast-to-coast television program with the ungainly title of *Television Party for Muscular Dystrophy Honoring the Letter Carriers of America for Their Volunteer March for Mercy*. The program was hosted by Martin and Lewis.

FIRST ASSOCIATION WITH FIREFIGHTERS: 1954

Important strides were achieved on other fronts during the MDA's first five years of existence. In 1954 a group of Boston families affected by muscular dystrophy turned to a local fire station, Local 718, to ask for help in raising money for the MDA. The firefighters began canvassing neighborhoods, using their boots to collect donations, marking the first "Fill the Boot" campaign, which became a registered trademark of the MDA. Later that same year, in August, the International Association of Fire Fighters' membership passed a resolution to support the MDA. It was a significant moment in the history of the MDA, giving it what became its most important fundraising organization for the next six decades.

No other sponsor gave more money to the MDA than the International Association of Fire Fighters, but the organization's contributions to the MDA's coffers paled in comparison to the fundraising might of nationally broadcast television specials. Martin and Lewis returned to the airwaves two years after hosting the program that promoted the efforts of the Letter Carriers of America. In 1955, one year before Martin and Dean parted ways, the pair hosted *The Martin and Lewis Roundup*, a telethon broadcast in parts by a single station, New York's WABD-TV. The event was held at Carnegie Hall in New York City, where Martin and Lewis presided over a 16.5-hour show at the end of June that raised $600,000 for the MDA. Lewis, serving as the sole national chairman of the MDA after his estrangement from Martin, hosted telethons during the Thanksgiving holiday in 1957 and 1959, but because of his film commitments Lewis's appearances were sporadic. Soon, however, Lewis's commitment became perennial, introducing generations of television viewers to the fight against muscular dystrophy.

THE FIRST LABOR DAY TELETHON: 1966

Annual telethons became the driving force behind the MDA's fundraising efforts from 1966 forward. The year marked the first *MDA Labor Day Telethon* (Telethon), known variously at different times as the *Jerry Lewis MDA Telethon* and the *Jerry Lewis MDA Labor Day Telethon*. The site of the event was the Americana Hotel in New York City. A local television station, WNEW-TV, agreed to televise provided the event was held during the Labor Day weekend, the only available slot on the station's calendar.

The 1966 Telethon featured rows of telephone operators ready to accept donations from WNEW-TV's

KEY DATES

1950: Paul Cohen and a small group of individuals affected by muscular dystrophy establish the Muscular Dystrophy Associations of America.

1954: International Association of Fire Fighters commits to supporting the MDA, marking the beginning of the "Fill the Boot" fundraising campaign.

1966: Jerry Lewis hosts the first *MDA Telethon* broadcast on Labor Day.

1976: Number of television stations airing the *MDA Telethon* reaches its peak.

2011: *MDA Telethon* is reduced in length to a six-hour program, without Lewis as its host for the first time in the history of the fundraising event.

broadcast area and it exceeded beyond expectations. The tote board manned by Lewis was capable of displaying only a six-figure amount, which proved inadequate when donations and pledges eclipsed $1 million, forcing Lewis to climb a ladder and paint the numeral one in front of the tote board's digits. The 1966 Telethon raised $1,002,114, becoming the first fundraising event of its kind to raise more than $1 million.

From the impressive 1966 showing, the Telethon grew in stature, increasing its ability to raise money for the MDA. In 1968, after seeing the ratings enjoyed by WNEW-TV, other television stations began to air the Telethon and the parade of stars and variety acts drawn to Lewis's annual event. Two stations in New York, WHEC-TV in Rochester, WGR-TV in Buffalo, and two stations in Massachusetts, WTEV-TV in New Bedford and WKBG-TV in Boston, broadcast the 1968 Telethon, marking the beginning of what the MDA referred to as the "Love Network." The year's Telethon also saw the debut of Ed McMahon as the program's anchor, a post he would occupy until his death in 2009.

One of the Love Network's original members, WHEC-TV, pioneered an effective fundraising technique on its own initiative, a technique that became a tradition and one used by the producers of other telethons. The producers of the 1969 Telethon noticed the station in Rochester raised significantly more than any other station, prompting them to call WHEC-TV's station manager, Glover Delaney, for help in determining the anomaly. Delaney confessed he had cut away from the Telethon for several minutes each hour to show

volunteers in Rochester accepting donations via telephone. In succeeding years, Delaney's technique was used by all stations composing the Love Network, eventually giving rise to local segments featuring local celebrities and local sponsors.

THE LOVE NETWORK STRETCHES FROM COAST TO COAST: 1970

The Love Network expanded quickly, growing to include more than 200 stations in less than a decade. In 1970, when there were 64 stations broadcasting the telethon, coverage became coast-to-coast with the inclusion of stations in Los Angeles and San Francisco. The tote board total increased nearly 150 percent during the 21.5-hour program, eclipsing $5 million.

The Telethon switched locations as the Love Network expanded. After six years of staging the program in New York City, the show's producers began broadcasting from Las Vegas in 1973. The 150 stations carrying the program, which originated from the Sahara Hotel, helped bring donations and pledges above the $10 million mark for the first time, to $12.3 million in contributions. Several years later, in 1976, the Love Network reached its peak, comprising 213 stations. The tote board surpassed $20 million at the end of the year's Telethon, reaching $21.7 million, the 10th consecutive year the donation total had increased.

With the proceeds from the Telethon and other major sources such as the International Association of Fire Fighters, the MDA became the largest, nongovernmental sponsor of muscle and nerve disease research in the United States. The organization's scope covered more than 40 diseases grouped within the nine forms of muscular dystrophy (myotonic, Duchenne, Becker, limb-girdle, facioscapulohumeral, congenital, oculopharyngeal, distal, and Emery-Dreifuss). The MDA funded research, established advocacy programs, and set up offices and clinics across the country. The clinics, affiliated with hospitals, enabled MDA to offer medical care from doctors, nurses, and therapists experienced in dealing with neuromuscular diseases. The clinics also functioned as the proving ground for experimental drugs and therapies in the form of clinical trials.

During the 1980s and 1990s, the MDA continued to rely heavily on the Telethon for funding its array of programs and research projects. The Telethon moved to Caesars Palace in 1982, the first year donations and pledges suffered a decline, dropping nearly 10 percent to $28.4 million. The program remained at Caesars Palace until 1989, when production of the show was moved to the Cashman Center in Las Vegas. From there, the program moved back and forth between Las Vegas and Southern California. In 1990 the Telethon originated from the Aquarius Theater in Los Angeles and then returned to the Sahara Hotel in Las Vegas until 1995 before moving to CBS Television City in Los Angeles. By the end of the 1990s the Telethon was raising more than $50 million annually.

A NEW ERA BEGINS: 2006–11

The first decade of the 21st century was a period of loss and change for the MDA. In 2006 the organization's longest-serving executive, Robert Ross, died, succumbing to pneumonia while being hospitalized for a broken hip. Ross joined the organization in 1955 as its public information director, a post he held until being promoted to executive director in 1962. Appointed vice president in 1973, Ross became senior vice president in 1991, ultimately becoming the MDA's president and CEO five years before his death. He was succeeded by Gerald C. Weinberg, who joined the MDA in 1957 and served as campaign director and director of field operations before being appointed senior vice president and COO. In 2009 the organization lost another well-known figure when Ed McMahon died, leaving the Telethon without the co-host it had relied on for 40 years.

The fundraising strength of the Telethon began to show signs of weakness during the decade. Between 1966 and 2010, the amount raised declined on only six occasions, but four of the percentage declines occurred during the first decade of the 21st century, in 2004, 2005, 2009, and 2010. Origination of the show moved to Beverly Hills in 2005 and returned to Las Vegas the following year, occupying the South Point Hotel, Casino & Spa. After the move, the program's producers began to consider making profound changes to the broadcast, changes that would appear as the Telethon approached its 50th anniversary.

In 2011 producers of the Telethon announced a dramatic reduction in the length of the broadcast, cutting the program from 21.5 hours to six hours. The change was announced in an effort to boost audience numbers, which hovered in the 40 million range, ap-

pease sponsors, and increase the fundraising appeal of the program. Under the new format, the Telethon was slated to begin at 6 p.m. and to end at midnight in all time zones, airing live only on the East Coast. The MDA also announced the 2011 Telethon would be the last hosted by Lewis, who was expected to limit his duties to those of national chairman after the Telethon.

In the months leading up to the 2011 edition, however, further changes occurred. In August 2011 the MDA announced that Lewis was no longer its national chairman. It also revealed that *American Idol* Executive Producer Nigel Lythgoe would host the program, ending Lewis's 45-year reign as the host of the annual fundraiser. Neither Lewis nor the MDA publicly explained the reasons for the sudden dissolution of their partnership.

The MDA began a new era in 2011, a new chapter in its history without Lewis as the public face of the organization. The abbreviated 2011 Telethon proved to be a success, surpassing the totals raised in 2009 and 2010. The six-hour program raised $61.5 million. In the years ahead, with the Telethon as its financial anchor, the MDA's search for a cure would continue, pressing forward with the mission articulated by Paul Cohen and his supporters 60 years earlier.

Jeffrey L. Covell

PRINCIPAL DIVISIONS

Television Production; Online Services; Publications; ALS; Advocacy.

FURTHER READING

Clolery, Paul. "'Hey Lay-Dee ...' MDA's Telethon Makeover Must Remake Jerry, Too." *Non-Profit Times*, November 1, 2010.

"Jerry Lewis Urges $100 Million Increase in Government Funding to Fight Muscular Dystrophy." *Fund Raising Management*, April 2001.

"MDA Telethon Alters Script." *Houston Chronicle*, August 19, 2011.

National Bank of Greece S.A.

86 Eolou St.
Athens, GR-102 32
Greece
Telephone: (+30 210) 334-1000
Fax: (+30 210) 334-6510
Web site: http://www.nbg.gr

Public Company
Founded: 1841
Employees: 24,091
Total Assets: EUR 120.75 billion ($170.81 billion) (2010)
Stock Exchanges: Athens New York
Ticker Symbols: ETE; NBG
NAICS: 522110 Commercial Banking

■ ■ ■

Founded in 1841, National Bank of Greece S.A. operates the largest bank and automated teller machine (ATM) network in its home country. There are about 575 domestic banking units and nearly 1,500 ATMs. There are also over 1,100 branches overseas. National Bank of Greece has a presence in 12 countries. The bank and its network can provide customers with a full range of financial products and services including investment banking, brokerage, insurance, asset management, leasing, and factoring. These services can be provided to both corporate customers and private customers. Internet banking is available through the Web site.

19TH-CENTURY ORIGINS

When National Bank of Greece (NBG) was founded in March 1841, Greece had been a free state for only about a dozen years. For nearly four centuries, Greece had been part of the Ottoman Empire, but in 1821 the Greeks began a fight for independence that lasted until 1829. After Greece won its independence, it set about creating government and administrative institutions. Although NBG was not created as the nation's central bank, it grew steadily after its founding and played a prominent role in Greek finance throughout the 19th century.

Within a short time after its founding in 1841, NBG began to expand its services beyond basic commercial banking. Eventually, NBG became involved in agriculture, transportation, and real estate. It developed an agrarian credit program and was given the right to invest capital in Greek industries. Occasionally, the bank would issue public loans and even participate in various public works. Most important to NBG's influence, however, was that it was the only bank in Greece authorized to issue bank notes.

Greece during the 19th century was not a particularly calm and stable place. Greece borders the Aegean Sea, the outlet for the Black Sea that is Russia's only link to the Mediterranean. Although the country became a constitutional monarchy in 1845, the king, Otto I (son of Bavaria's Ludwig I), was hardly popular. His rule was despotic, and he involved Greece in the Crimean War during the 1850s. Eventually he was deposed and the crown was offered to the Danish Prince William, who would become George I. There were

COMPANY PERSPECTIVES

One of the Bank's main strengths is the confidence shown in it by its customers, who hold over 9 million deposit accounts and more than 1.5 million lending accounts with NBG. Having reaffirmed its leading position in the Greek market, the Bank is further modernizing its operations, backed by investment in new technology, so as to better serve its customers and enhance its profitability.

other clashes with the Ottoman Turks during these years, and the British Empire and France in particular still held considerable sway over the country's politics. Institutions such as the National Bank of Greece were important to the country not only for the obvious services they performed but because they also had a stabilizing effect.

Through the 19th and early 20th centuries NBG continued to grow. In 1880, the Athens Stock Exchange was established, and NBG was one of the first companies listed. NBG also began to acquire other banks, such as the Privileged Bank of Epirothessaly in 1899 and the Bank of Crete in 1919.

THE WORLD WARS SHAPE
GREECE

Since gaining independence, Greece had gradually been gaining territory through a series of uprisings culminating with the Balkan Wars that occurred just before the outbreak of World War I. Greece, one of the Allied nations, benefited considerably when the war ended. When the boundaries of Europe were redrawn, Greece had nearly twice as much land as it did before the war. Some of those gains were reversed when Turkish nationalist forces under Mustafa Kemal recaptured parts of Asia Minor, including the port city of Izmir (Smyrna). The boundaries of modern Greece were established definitively by the Treaty of Lausanne, signed in 1923. By now, NBG was a powerful force in Greek life, both political and financial.

The League of Nations, which had been formed after World War I, believed that NBG's position as both a commercial and state bank was untenable. In fact, the league said, this arrangement left open too many possibilities for conflicts of interest. In accordance with the league's policies as outlined under the Geneva Protocol,

Greece agreed to establish a new state bank. The Bank of Greece was thus established on May 15, 1928. Assets in the form of gold and government debt were transferred to the new bank, as were liabilities, primarily in the form of government deposits.

Events of the 1930s had a profound effect in every corner of the world, beginning with the Great Depression and continuing with the unrest that led to World War II. By 1939, war seemed inevitable, and even established institutions such as NBG were subject to the fears of Greek citizens. A run on commercial banks began in the summer of that year. Between July and September notes in circulation increased from GRD 8 million to GRD 10 million. The Bank of Greece acted by making more cash available to the commercial banks to meet their obligations. This calmed the public and the bank run subsided.

In October 1940, Italy attacked Greece after the Greeks refused to cede parts of the country over to Benito Mussolini's Fascist dictatorship. Thanks in part to the British government, which honored an earlier commitment and made significant loans to Greece, the economy managed to remain relatively stable. Moreover, the Greeks were doing quite well in keeping Italian forces at bay. Overall, 1940 proved to be a year of relative financial calm for Greece.

All that changed in April 1941, when Germany decided to attack Greece. Within a month, the Germans had taken Athens. At that point NBG had just turned 100 years old. The Greek government, including the royal family and the governor of the Bank of Greece, went into exile. The bank's gold and foreign exchange reserves were taken to Egypt and transferred to the South African Reserve Bank in Pretoria for the duration of the war.

The war ravaged Greece as it did all of Europe, and by its end in 1945 the economic infrastructure had to be rebuilt. The government-in-exile returned to Greece in 1946, along with the country's gold and foreign reserve supplies. International agencies such as the United Nations Relief and Rehabilitation Administration and private charities helped get Greece and other countries on its feet. Moreover, the British government dropped all claims to the loans it had made to Greece in 1940. However, industrial output was roughly at one-third what it had been before the war, and bank deposits in real terms were at one-thirtieth what they had been in 1939. The Greek government created the Currency Committee, whose members included the Minister of National Economy, other government ministers, and the governor of the Bank of Greece. All monetary, credit,

KEY DATES

1841: National Bank of Greece (NBG) is founded as a commercial bank.

1928: A new bank, The Bank of Greece, is established as the nation's central bank in accordance with Geneva Protocol.

1953: NBG merges with Bank of Athens, becoming National Bank of Greece and Athens.

1958: National Bank of Greece and Athens officially adopts name National Bank of Greece.

1998: Company merges with National Mortgage Bank of Greece; new bank retains NBG name.

1999: NBG becomes first Greek bank to list on New York Stock Exchange.

2011: NBG announces plans to establish a holding company for its Balkan States operations.

and foreign exchange policy was set by the Currency Committee.

POSTWAR GAINS AND DRAWBACKS

Despite the Bank of Greece's prominent role, NBG was still the largest commercial bank in the country, and its role remained significant. In 1953, NBG merged with the Bank of Athens and briefly changed its name to the National Bank of Greece and Athens (the NBG name was restored in 1958). By the mid-1960s, NBG accounted for roughly two-thirds of all commercial bank deposits, as well as industry and trade financing.

In the years following World War II, however, the Greek government had been unstable. Communist forces had tried to overthrow the monarchy in the late 1940s but were defeated. All through the 1950s and 1960s, the government was divided into factions supporting communism, royalism, and the growing right wing. This right wing, in the form of a military junta, overthrew the monarchy in April 1967 and established a dictatorship led by Colonel George Papadopoulos. Although some would later suggest that the dictatorship was actually beneficial to the economy, in fact it served to divide the various factions even more sharply. Although the junta established Greece as a republic in 1973, it continued to rule until July 1974 when it was forced out and democratic civilian government (without the monarchy) was returned.

REACHING FROM PAST TO FUTURE

In 1977, NBG formed a committee to work on a project not commonly embarked upon by banks: the creation of a comprehensive Historical Archives Unit. From its founding, NBG had kept historical archives. Realizing the historical and research value of these archives, NBG had begun to compile historic documents for a central archives department years before, in 1938. The outbreak of war in 1941 suspended activity on the archives project, and it was revived in 1962, only to be suspended once again when Papadopoulos seized power in 1967.

This time, NBG created a committee including senior bank officials and historians to maintain its archives, as well as to establish a Historical Research Program on Economic History. The goal of this committee was to acquire, compile, and preserve all historical documents from NBG's founding, the records of banks and other companies that were merged with or acquired by NBG, and the personal archives of NBG's top officials. The original documents continued to be both preserved and microfilmed.

BUILDING THE MODERN BANK

In the 1970s and 1980s Greece went through a transition to mainstream democratic government. The conservative New Democracy Party held control until 1981, when the Panhellenic Socialist Movement (Pasok) gained control and elected Andreas Papandreou prime minister. Papandreou, an economist, favored a strong socialist agenda including universal health care and a pension system. The government borrowed heavily to finance its goals and inflation rose dramatically. By the end of the decade, the Pasok government had fallen out of favor and the New Democrats were voted back in.

One of the most important decisions Greece had to make during this period was whether it wanted to be part of the European Monetary Union. To do this would mean that the Greek government would have to put its economic house in order.

During this time NBG continued to pursue a strategy of growth and diversification. It purchased several companies, established others, and consolidated its holdings. The company also embarked on a restructuring and modernization program. This included merging the bank's two mortgage companies, absorbing the National Mortgage Bank of Greece in 1998, merging the bank's four insurance companies into one unit, and divesting assets it deemed noncore. NBG also worked to reduce the number of nonperforming loans. The number of new nonperforming loans was down to 0.19 percent by the end of 2000.

In addition, NBG enhanced its technological infrastructure, thereby streamlining operations and making it easier for the bank to be a truly global presence. NBG was one of the first Greek banks to offer its customers Internet banking. In October 1999, NBG became the first Greek bank (and only the second Greek company) to list on the prestigious New York Stock Exchange.

BALKAN STATES EXPANSION IN 2000

NBG, viewing the Balkans as an important strategic market, began acquiring stakes in regional banks. In the words of the bank, it wanted to take "a decisive step toward transforming itself from the Bank of 11 million Greeks to the Bank of 60 million inhabitants of the Balkans." In 2000 it acquired a 65 percent stake in Stopanska Bank A.D., the largest commercial bank of the former Yugoslav republic of Macedonia, and an 89.89 percent stake in United Bulgarian Bank, one of that country's largest. These acquisitions expanded NBG's operations to 18 countries on four continents, including offices in major internal banking centers such as New York, London, and Frankfurt. Domestically, the bank had more than 600 branches by the end of 2000, as well as more than 840 ATMs, while its international operations already included 328 branches. The company's total assets by then topped $44.5 billion.

NBG raised its investment in Stopanska Bank in 2001, through a capital injection of EUR 22 million. This boosted NBG's share to 70 percent. Back at home, NBG began talks to acquire its chief rival, Alpha Bank, for EUR 4.1 billion ($3.6 million). The merger fell through at the beginning of 2002, when the two banks were unable to agree on terms, while also citing, according to a January 2002 *New York Times* article, "radical differences in their management styles."

Following the collapse of the merger, NBG restructured in order to boost its earnings. Both the company's domestic and international operations were placed under review, as the group instituted an early retirement program. In this way, NBG reduced its headcount by 7 percent. The company also sold off its Canadian subsidiary, and its 10 branches, to Scotiabank in 2005. Leading the bank's restructuring was new Chairman and CEO Efstratios George Arapoglou, who had previously worked with Citigroup. Under Arapoglou's leadership, NBG transformed itself into a true commercial bank, raising total assets past EUR 60 billion ($77 billion) by 2005. In that year, net profits topped EUR 727 million. By then, the Greek government had sold the last of its stake in NBG, maintaining an interest in the bank only through a 15 percent share

held through government pension funds.

ENTERING TURKEY IN 2006

In the meantime, NBG continued to build up its Balkans presence. The company acquired Banca Romaneasca, in Romania, in 2003. This gave the group a network of 40 branches serving a population of 23 million. NBG next targeted expansion into the region's largest market: Turkey. In 2006, the company outbid Citigroup in order to acquire a controlling 46 percent stake in Finansbank. The purchase cost National Bank of Greece EUR 5.5 billion ($6.7 billion), and aroused some controversy given the ongoing animosity between the two companies.

NBG's other Balkans operations grew strongly as well, as the company added more than 100 branches in 2006. The company also acquired full control of United Bulgarian Bank. Under NBG's leadership, this bank had grown from a mere 3 percent share of Bulgaria's banking market to become the number three player with a 13 percent share. In Romania, Banca Romaneasca expanded its branch network to 80 locations, with a target of 150 by 2008.

NBG also expanded its operations in the Serbian market in 2006, paying EUR 360 million to the Serbian government in order to acquire Vojvodanska Bank. This purchase added 200 branches to NBG's own 25-branch operation in that country. The company also expanded into Albania as well, forming a six-branch network under NBG Albania. By 2007, the bank's operations also included a first step into Egypt.

NBG's international expansion had helped shield it somewhat from the turmoil surrounding Greece's sovereign debt crisis at the end of the decade. The company even managed the successful float of a EUR 1.5 billion bond issue, in 2010. By midyear, however, the bank was forced to deny it was looking to sell some of its assets, including a 30 percent stake in Finansbank. Instead, the bank reinforced its position in Stopanska, buying 20 percent from the European Bank for Reconstruction and Development and the International Finance Corporation to boost its stake to 95 percent.

BALKANS HOLDING COMPANY IN 2011

Back at home, the debt crisis opened a new opportunity for NBG to merge with its largest rival, Alpha Bank. In February 2011, NBG announced its plans to take over Alpha, with an offer of eight of its own shares for every 11 shares of Alpha. Shareholders at Alpha, however, quickly rejected the proposal. NBG was once again forced to put on hold its plans for the merger between the two banks, which would create a true national champion in Greece's banking sector.

NBG's international component appeared, therefore, to be the main vehicle for NBG's future growth. By 2011, the group's international branch operations had already outpaced its domestic network, with more than 1,100 foreign branches, including 461 in Turkey alone, compared to just 575 branches in Greece. In order to provide a structure for the group's Balkans region business, the company announced plans to establish a holding company for these operations, exclusive of Finansbank in Turkey, in late 2011. By then, NBG reported total assets of EUR 120.75 billion ($170.81 billion). In just 10 years, National Bank of Greece transformed itself from Greece's leading bank to become one of the region's banking powerhouses in the 21st century.

George A. Milite
Updated, M. L. Cohen

PRINCIPAL SUBSIDIARIES

Banca Romaneasca SA (Romania); Finans Factoring AS (Turkey); Finans Invest (Turkey); Finans Leasing AS (Turkey); Finans Portfolio Management AS (Turkey); Finansbank SA (Turkey); Garanta SA (Romania); IB Tech (Turkey); National Bank of Greece (Cyprus) LTD; NBG (Malta) Ltd; NBG International Ltd (UK); NBG Leasing DOO (Serbia); NBGI Private Equity Ltd (UK); NBGI Private Equity SEE (UK); Stopanska Banka AD Skopje (FYR Macedonia); The South African Bank of Athens Ltd; United Bulgarian Bank AD; Vojvodjanska Banka AD (Serbia).

PRINCIPAL DIVISIONS

Retail Banking; Business Banking; Asset Management; International Operations.

PRINCIPAL OPERATING UNITS

Finansbank; United Bulgarian Bank; Stopanska Banka; Banca Romaneasca; Vojvodjanska Banka; National Bank of Greece (Cyprus); South African Bank of Athens.

PRINCIPAL COMPETITORS

Alpha Bank S.A.; Bank of Cyprus Public Company Ltd.; Bank of Greece S.A.; EFG Eurobank Ergasias S.A.; Emporiki Bank of Greece S.A.; Piraeus Bank S.A.; TT Hellenic Postbank S.A.

FURTHER READING

Canadis, Wray O. *The Economy of Greece, 1944–66.* New York: Praeger, 1966.

Country Profile 2000: Greece. London: The Economist Intelligence Unit, 2000.

"From the Bank's Standpoint: 125 Years in the Service of the Nation." *Greece Today*, January 1966, 4.

Kouzos, Nick. "The Greek Banking Industry." Speech given at the Greek-Turkish Information Society Forum, May 27, 2000.

"National Bank of Greece Rides the Growth Wave." *Euromoney*, September 2007.

"NBG Shifts Its Focus to Retail Banking." *Institutional Investor*, March 2003, SS5.

Pantelakis, Nikos, "Business Archives in Greece: The Example of the Historical Archives of the National Bank of Greece." Paper presented at the CLIR/Library of Congress Conference, April 1999.

"2 Banks in Greece End Planned Merger." *New York Times*, January 21, 2002, C4.

The New York Times Company

620 Eighth Avenue
New York, New York 10018
U.S.A.
Telephone: (212) 556-1234
Fax: (212) 556-7389
Web site: http://www.nytco.com

Public Company
Incorporated: 1851 as Raymond, Jones & Company
Employees: 7,414
Sales: $2.4 billion (2010)
Stock Exchanges: American
Ticker Symbol: NYT
NAICS: 511110 Newspaper Publishers; 519110 News
   Syndicates

■ ■ ■

The New York Times Company (NYTC) is a diversified media company. The company publishes three major daily newspapers, the *New York Times* (the *Times*), the *International Herald Tribune*, and the *Boston Globe*, and 16 regional newspapers. It operates eight network-affiliated television stations and two New York City radio stations. The Times Syndicate, the largest syndicate in the world specializing in text, photos, graphics, and other noncartoon features, sells columns, magazine and book excerpts, and feature packages to more than 2,000 newspapers, and other media to clients in more than 50 countries.

19TH-CENTURY FOUNDING AND DEVELOPMENTS

The principal founders of the *New York Times* were Henry Jarvis Raymond, a sometime politician, reporter, and editor who learned his trade working for Horace Greeley on the *New York Tribune*, and George Jones, an Albany, New York, banker who had also once worked for Greeley as a business manager for the *Tribune*. Raymond proposed a newspaper that would present the news in a conservative and objective fashion, in contrast to the yellow journalism of the day, which emphasized crime, scandal, and radical politics. They raised $70,000 to establish Raymond, Jones & Company, in large part by selling stock to wealthy upstate New York investors, and set up their editorial offices in a dilapidated six-story brownstone on Nassau Street in downtown New York City. The first issue of the *New York Daily Times* (the word "Daily" was dropped from the title in 1857) was dated September 18, 1851, and it announced an editorial policy that would emphasize accurate reporting and moderation of opinion and expression.

Jones handled the company's business affairs, and Raymond, as editor, provided journalistic leadership. Under their management, helped by booming population growth in New York City, the *Times* grew rapidly, reaching 10,000 circulation within 10 days and 24,000 by the end of its first year. In 1858 the paper moved into a new five-story building containing the most modern printing equipment. As the *Times* prospered, Raymond established and continually encouraged high standards of journalism. The *Times* also became a newspaper of record. For example, it carried the entire text of Abraham Lincoln's Gettysburg Address on the front page on November 20, 1863. Among other journalistic successes, the *Times* provided outstanding coverage of the U.S. Civil War, with Raymond himself reporting on the Battle of Bull Run.

Raymond was active in Republican politics throughout the war. He was present at the creation of the party in Pittsburgh in 1856 and wrote its first statement of principles. He wrote most of the party platform in 1864. Between political activity and journalism, Raymond was chronically overworked for years, and his health suffered. On June 19, 1869, at the age of 49, he died. Jones assumed the editorial leadership of the *Times*.

By the time of Raymond's death, each of the 100 shares of stock in the company had increased in value from the original $1,000 to about $11,000, with 34 shares held by Raymond and 30 by Jones. In 1871, after a series of *Times* articles on the misdeeds of corrupt New York City politicians headed by William Marcy (Boss) Tweed, an attempt was made by Tweed interests to buy Raymond's 34 shares from his widow. Jones quickly arranged to have the shares purchased by one of his associates, thus establishing his control of the newspaper. In 1884 Jones chose to oppose the nomination by the Republican Party of James G. Blaine for president, thus losing the much needed support of Republican readers and advertisers. The paper's profits fell steadily until Jones's death in 1891. His heirs had little aptitude for the newspaper business, and the panic and depression of 1893 brought the *Times* close to failure.

In 1893 the *Times*'s editor-in-chief, Charles Ransom Miller, bought control of the paper from Jones's heirs with $1 million raised from Wall Street interests. Miller, a fine editor, had no business aptitude and was unable to maintain the newspaper's capital requirements. Staff reductions and declining journalistic quality brought the *Times* to its historic low point, and by 1896 it was on the verge of bankruptcy and dissolution. During this critical year salvation came in a dramatic fashion.

A group of Wall Street investors in what was then called the New York Times Publishing Company arranged to save the firm by placing it in receivership and recapitalizing it as a new company, The New York Times Company. The new capitalization was 10,000 shares with 2,000 being paid out in exchange for the original *Times* stock. A large stock position with contractual assurance of eventual majority stock ownership was purchased with borrowed money by a then little known but respected newspaper editor and publisher from Chattanooga, Tennessee, Adolph Simon Ochs.

Ochs, the son of German immigrants, had received little formal schooling but had learned the newspaper business from the ground up as newsboy, printer's devil, journeyman printer, business manager, and reporter. He was hardworking and ambitious. In 1878, at the age of 20, he borrowed $250 to buy the controlling interest in a failing Tennessee newspaper, the *Chattanooga Times*, thus beginning his career as a newspaper publisher before he was old enough to vote. He promoted high standards of journalism in the Chattanooga paper and soon brought it back to financial health. In 1896, looking for new challenges, he heard about the *New York Times*'s troubles. Ochs offered to take over as publisher in return for a contract that would give him a majority of the paper's stock if he succeeded in making it profitable for three consecutive years. One of his early acts after becoming publisher of the *Times* on August 18, 1896, was to add the slogan, "All the News That's Fit to Print," thus serving notice that the *Times* would continue to avoid sensationalism and follow high editorial standards.

ARRIVAL OF ADOLPH OCHS AT THE END OF THE 19TH CENTURY

Ochs's first two years with the *Times* were a continual struggle to carry on operations and improve the paper with inadequate capital. The expenses of covering the Spanish-American War in 1898 came close to ruining the paper, which sold then for three cents a copy. Some *Times* executives advised raising the price, but Ochs made the brilliant and daring decision to reduce the price to one cent. Within a year paid circulation tripled from 26,000 to 76,000. Advertising linage increased by nearly 40 percent, and the paper was profitable. Despite subsequent price increases, this was the beginning of a long upward trend in circulation and profitability.

The *Times*'s success under Ochs was due to much more than price-cutting. He improved financial and Wall Street coverage, added a Sunday magazine supplement, and a Saturday book review section, which was later moved to Sunday. With a brilliant managing editor,

Carr Van Anda, the *Times* carried out numerous journalistic coups. It scooped the world on the Japanese-Russian naval battle in 1904 by sending the first wireless dispatches from a war area. It again scooped the world on the *Titanic* shipwreck in 1912 and outdid all competition in reporting the events of World War I. The paper warned of the excesses of the 1920s, but was well equipped financially to survive the Great Depression thanks to Ochs's conservative policy of plowing back into the paper a major portion of its profits.

On August 14, 1900, Ochs received the NYTC stock certificates that established his control over the paper and the company, a controlling interest that remained in the Ochs family. Under Ochs, the NYTC followed a general policy of avoiding diversification, although Ochs himself continued as the personal owner and publisher of the *Chattanooga Times* and had a private investment in a Philadelphia paper between 1901 and 1913. In 1926, however, the NYTC did take part ownership, along with Kimberly & Clark Company, in a Canadian paper mill, the Spruce Falls Power and Paper Company, to assure its supplies of newsprint.

The *Times* did relatively well during the Great Depression, with daily circulation holding in the 450,000 to 500,000 range. Ochs's health declined during the early 1930s, and he died on April 8, 1935. On May 7, 1935, the company's directors elected as president and publisher Ochs's son-in-law, Arthur Hays Sulzberger, who had married Ochs's daughter Iphigene in 1917 and subsequently worked his way up through the executive ranks of the newspaper.

NEW LEADERSHIP IN THE POSTWAR PERIOD

Under Sulzberger the *Times* improved steadily in news coverage, financial strength, and technical progress. In a diversification move in 1944 the NYTC purchased New York City radio stations WQXR and WQXR-FM. Sulzberger opposed without success the unionization of *Times* employees. The company's first published financial statement in 1958 showed 60 consecutive years of increasing profits. In 1957 a recapitalization split the common stock into A and B common stock, with the B shares, mostly held by the Ochs trust, having voting control over the company. Sulzberger's health began to fail in the late 1950s. He retired in 1961. His successor as president and publisher was his son-in-law, Orvil E. Dryfoos. Dryfoos died in 1963. On June 20, 1963, he was succeeded in turn as president and publisher by Arthur Hays Sulzberger's son, Arthur Ochs Sulzberger, who continued in 1991 to lead the NYTC as chairman and chief executive officer.

Although Sulzberger made some administrative changes and broadened the scope of the *Times* news coverage, the company continued to earn a relatively low profit margin on revenues, partly because of his policy of spending freely for thorough reporting, even to the extent of throwing out advertisements to make room for news. A second bitter strike against the paper in 1965 unsettled the management, and a decision was made to undertake a significant program of diversification. In 1967 the company's book and educational division was enlarged, and in 1968 the *Times* purchased a 51 percent interest in Arno Press.

In 1969 the A common stock was given the vote for three members of the nine-member board. This action together with a public offering qualified the A stock for listing on the American Stock Exchange. The B stock, which controlled the company, continued to be held mostly by the Ochs family trust. In 1971 the NYTC paid Cowles Communications Company 2.6 million shares of class A stock to purchase substantial Cowles newspaper, magazine, television, and book properties, including *Family Circle* and other magazines; a Florida newspaper chain; a Memphis, Tennessee, TV station; and a textbook publisher.

ACQUISITIONS, SALES, AND RECAPITALIZATIONS: SEVENTIES AND EIGHTIES

During the 1970s the newspaper's profit margins continued to be under pressure because of competition, especially in New York City suburban areas. The former Cowles properties helped buoy earnings despite the 1976 sale of some medical magazines acquired from Cowles. In 1980 the NYTC paid about $100 million for a southern New Jersey cable television operation, its largest acquisition since the Cowles deal. In 1984 the book publishing operation was sold to Random House. In 1985 the NYTC, flush with record profits, spent about $400 million on the purchase of five regional newspapers and two TV stations. In 1986 yet another recapitalization converted every 10 shares of B stock into nine shares of A and one share of B, with the B stock still controlling the company. Since more than 80 percent of the B stock was held by the Ochs trust, this move gave the trustees more liquidity without sacrificing control of the company.

The years 1989 and 1990 continued to be profitable. In 1989 the NYTC, admitting it was not making progress with cable, sold all of its cable TV properties to a consortium of Pennsylvania cable companies for $420 million. Also in 1989 the company acquired *McCall's* magazine, which, together with the acquisitions in 1988 of *Golf World* and *Sailing World*, substantially strengthened the NYTC's magazine group. The company's large new automated printing and distribution facility in Edison, New Jersey, which had been under construction for several years, was scheduled to become operational in late 1990.

DIVERSIFICATION IN THE NINETIES

Throughout the 1990s, the company bought and sold properties in the areas of print, cable broadcasting, and electronic media as the decline in newspaper readership in the United States continued. In 1993, NYTC bought Affiliated Publications, which owned the *Boston Globe* and specialty magazines published by its division, BPI Communications. In 1994, the company sold its one-third interest in BPI, along with a group of women's magazines, including *Family Circle* and *McCall's*, to Germany's Bertelsmann AG. Also in 1994, NYTC began construction on a state-of-the-art printing plant that would allow adding more color to newspapers and accommodate later deadlines.

In 1995, NYTC purchased a majority interest in Video News International, a video newsgathering company. It returned to cable by buying a minority stake in the cable arts network, Ovation, and launched two cable news channels in Arkansas. Also in 1995, the company entered cyberspace when it joined with eight other newspaper companies in an online news service, New Century Network. It also created the New York Times Electronic Media Company as a wholly owned subsidiary to develop new products and distribution channels for the *Times*, such as on the Web, America Online (AOL), and the New York Times Index.

Two years later, in 1997, a new, expanded version of the AOL site debuted with a new design and content areas, improved navigation and functionality, and expanded advertising opportunities, such as allowing advertisers to target ads to readers of particular sections. The new content, available only to AOL members, included People in the News area, enhancements to Science Times, live crosswords and news chats, a weekly news quiz, a Topic of the Day message board for discussions based on Page One articles, monthly *Times* retrospectives, free access to *Times* bridge and chess columns, a themed monthly crossword puzzle, and access to the *New York Times Magazine* and a weekly column by the Duchess of York, Sarah Ferguson.

AMBITIOUS EXPANSION EFFORTS FOR THE 21ST CENTURY

In 1997, the NYTC, under the directorship of new President and CEO Russell T. Lewis, embarked on an ambitious program of expansion focused on transforming its flagship product, the *New York Times* newspaper, from a regional to a national publication. Integral to the goal of building widespread brand recognition was a new, $20 million advertising campaign featuring the slogan, "Expect the World." That year, the newspaper also implemented the most extensive changes to its operations and format since the 1970s. With more advanced production equipment, the paper was able to include later-breaking news and sports scores, as well as new sections and features. On October 16, the paper introduced color printing to its front page.

Further, as 1997 marked the culmination of a 10-year, $1 billion program of capital investments to shore up the paper's strengths, its print facilities, and its customer base, the company enjoyed a dramatic increase in cash flow, which it began to allocate toward two long-term goals, both aimed at increasing shareholder value. First, the company launched an aggressive share repurchasing initiative in order to improve its overall leverage and increase stock dividends. Starting with three million shares valued at $145.6 million that year, the initiative grew every year with the company allocating $623.7 million for the repurchase of 15 million shares in 2001. Second, the company sought strategic

3acquisitions to expand its portfolio of products and services, enter new markets, and facilitate distribution by opening new print sites around the country.

Among other efforts to increase the appeal of its nationally distributed newspaper, the *New York Times* added new features such as Circuits, a weekly technology section introduced in 1998, which was soon generating about $1 million per month in advertising revenue. In 1999, with the economic boom of the 1990s still holding, the company enjoyed earnings per share growth of 20.5 percent, its fifth consecutive year of double-digit growth. Revenues for 1999 reached an unprecedented $3.1 billion.

Even while the company focused on expansion, it continued to keep a firm grasp on its expenses, and to hone its focus on core businesses. In 1997 the Magazine Group sold six of its smaller, low-margin publications in order to channel more resources into its high-margin golf publications, especially the award-winning *Golf World*.

To keep pace with the growing Internet economy, in 1999 the company established New York Times Digital, an independent business unit, to oversee the operations of NYTimes.com (then boasting more than 10 million registered users) and to establish synergies between its traditional print media and its electronic offerings. To this end, in 1999 the NYTC invested $15 million in TheStreet.com, one of the top Internet providers of financial information and investment news and commentary, a digital publication with which the *Times* shared a key customer base. It sold TheStreet in 2000 at a significant loss and purchased the *Worcester Telegram & Gazette*, Massachusetts' third-largest daily.

The year 2001 proved turbulent for the NYTC, as the dot-com bubble burst, the economic slowdown bloomed into a full recession, and the nation, particularly New York City, weathered the terrorist attacks of September 11 (9/11). Nonetheless, the company managed to perform well in the midst of the chaos, with earnings per share growth of 8 percent in a year when the S&P 500 dropped by 13 percent, and an impressive six Pulitzer prizes to show for the *New York Times*'s coverage of 9/11.

The company also continued to invest in its regional media properties in 2001 (it reached 235 markets in 2002, up from 62 markets in 1997) and to lay the groundwork for penetrating international markets by introducing branded pages into respected foreign newspapers such as France's *Le Monde*. It also sold its Magazine Group, which included its four popular golf magazines, to Advance Publications, Inc., and joined a group of investors called New England Sports Ventures in purchasing the Boston Red Sox, Fen-

way Park, and the cable network New England Sports Network.

In 2002 the company formed a joint venture with Discovery Communications to run the Discovery Times Channel and unveiled plans for the construction of its new headquarters, a building to be constructed along Eighth Avenue between 40th and 41st Streets, designed by architect Renzo Piano. Piano's building, with its exposed steel and appearance of disappearing into the sky, was intended to express the qualities of lightness, strength, and stability. At the close of the year, The NYTC strong-armed the Washington Post Company into selling the Post's 50 percent stake in the International Herald Tribune (IHT) by threatening to pull out and start a competing paper. The takeover ended a 35-year partnership between the two domestic competitors and made the IHT into "The Global Edition of the New York Times."

REPORTER SCANDAL

Crisis followed upon intrigue when in the spring of 2003 news emerged that a *Times* reporter had written numerous fraudulent and even plagiarized stories that had gone undetected by his supervisors. The scandal resulted in the resignation of two of the paper's top editors, Howell Raines (replaced by Bill Keller as executive editor) and Gerald M. Boyd, and a serious blemish on the record of the otherwise revered paper.

President and CEO Lewis announced his retirement the following year. Leaving the company at the end of 2004, he was succeeded by Janet Robinson, who had been with the company for 21 years and was then its chief operating officer. During his tenure, Lewis had overseen the transformation of the *New York Times* from a local paper to one that attracted 50 percent of its readers from outside the New York region, owned eight network-affiliated television channels, two New York City radio stations, and more than 40 Web sites.

NYTC got into the free newspaper market in 2005, with the launch of *MarketPlace Weekly*, a free paper aimed at commuters in their 20s and 30s, with a classified ad focus. It also purchased a stake in a free daily paper, *Metro Boston*, from Metro International, and later it acquired an information portal called About.com and a minority share in Indeed.com in its search for a larger share of the online advertising market. At the same time, it instituted layoffs in the face of declining ad revenue: close to 200 employees at the *New York Times* and the New England Media Group (which included the *Boston Globe*) in May, followed by 500 more in September. The second round of layoffs included 80 newsroom staff at the NYTC's newspapers. In another cost-cutting measure, the company went to lighter-weight newsprint.

THESE TIMES DEMAND THE *TIMES*

In 2006 NYTC added Baseline StudioSystems, an online database and research service for information on the film and television industries, to its New York Times Media Group. Robinson announced, as reported in the *Hollywood Reporter* in August, that the acquisition would help the company become "the authoritative online alternative destination for the entertainment consumer and the industry." That year the company launched a branding campaign with the tagline "These Times Demand the *Times*." The following year the company purchased nine television stations from Oak Hill Capital Partners, including ABC, NBC, and CBS networks in eight states. The company's Internet-related businesses also grew by 30 percent in 2007.

The growth in online ad revenues, however, was insufficient to make up for losses the company suffered overall during the first quarter of 2008. Robinson predicted in an April 2008 *Globe and Mail* article that 2008 would be a "year that will pose continued challenges for everyone in the media industry." Nevertheless, hardship for the *Times* spelled opportunity for some investors. In 2006 billionaire Maurice Greenberg purchased a share in the company, and in February 2008, hedge funds Harbinger Capital and Firebrand Partners together bought 20 percent of the company's Class A stock and secured four seats on its board. In September, as online advertising revenues declined, Carlos Slim, the world's second-richest man, lent the NYTC $250 million to refinance $400 million in debt and acquired a 6.5 percent share of the company.

Following the dire events of 2008, the NYTC threatened to close the *Boston Globe*, in addition to other cost-saving moves it implemented during 2009. Later in that year, it cut 100 newsroom staff, after *Times* employees took a 5 percent pay cut that proved insufficient to stem the flow of losses. In 2010 the company announced plans to launch a metered pay model for online readers at its NYTimes.com Web site. In 2011 it sold another 8 percent of its stake in the Sports Network. In mid-December, Robinson announced that she would step down as CEO by the end of the year. The venerable and highly respected NYTC was showing signs of the crises affecting all media, but was intent on weathering these changes and remaining one of the world's outstanding news sources.

Bernard A. Block
Updated, Dorothy Kroll; Erin Brown; Carrie Rothburd

PRINCIPAL SUBSIDIARIES

NYT Capital, Inc.; NYT Holdings Inc.; The New York Times Syndication Sales Corporation; The New York Times Distribution Corporation; The New York Times Electronic Media Company; The New York Times Sales Company.

PRINCIPAL COMPETITORS

Advance Publications, Inc.; Agence France-Presse; AOL Inc.; BBC Worldwide Limited; CNN America, Inc.; Daily News, L.P.; Dow Jones & Company, Inc.; Financial Times Group Ltd.; Gannett Co., Inc.; The Hearst Corporation; Herald Media, Inc.; MSN; The News Corporation Limited; Newsday LLC; Tribune Company; The Washington Post Company; Wikimedia Foundation, Inc.

FURTHER READING

Berger, Meyer. *The Story of the New York Times, 1851–1951.* New York: Simon and Schuster, 1951.

Carr, David. "President to Retire from Times Co.; Successor Named." *New York Times*, February 20, 2004, 1.

Choi, Amy. "Designing the New York Times." *New York Construction*, September 2003, 59.

Goulden, Joseph C. *Fit to Print.* Secaucus, NJ: Lyle Stuart Inc., 1988.

"Keeping the Gray Lady Spry: CEO Russell Lewis Explains How Constant Investment, Even in Bad Times, Ensures New York Times Co.'s Long-Term Health." *Business Week Online*, November 8, 2002.

Kolodny, Laura. "N.Y. Times Swings for Baseline." *Hollywood Reporter*, August 29, 2006.

Learmonth, Michael. "What Does Carlos Slim Want with the New York Times?" *Advertising Age*, January 26, 2009, 4.

"New York Times Puts Boston Globe up for Sale." *Brand Republic News Releases*, June 15, 2009, 1.

"New York Times Slashing 500 Jobs." *Mediaweek.com*, September 20, 2005.

Paterno, Susan. "International Intrigue." *American Journalism Review*, February/March 2006, 50.

"Piano's N.Y. Times Tower Moves Forward." *Architectural Record*, January 2002, 24.

Schechner, Sam, and Shira Ovide. "U.S. Slump Hammers Newspaper Giants; New York Times Posts Unexpected Loss; Tribune Signals Asset Sales Are Likely." *Globe and Mail*,

April 18, 2008, B11.

Schwartz, Matthew. "Changing 'Times' Heralds New Direction." *BtoB*, October 9, 2006, 3.

Steinberg, Jacques. "Changes at the Times: The Overview." *New York Times*, June 6, 2003, 1.

Talese, Gay. *The Kingdom and the Power*. New York: World Publishing Company, 1969.

———. "Times Company Buys a Stake in Boston Metro, a Free Paper." *New York Times*, January 4, 2005, 9.

White, Christina. "A French Beau for the *New York Times*: The Paper's New English-Language Supplement in *Le Monde* Could Be a Long-Sought Short-Cut into Europe's Mainstream Readership." *Business Week Online*, April 12, 2002.

Nexans S.A.

8 rue du General Foy
Paris, 75008
France
Telephone: (+33 01) 56 69 84 00
Fax: (+33 01) 56 69 84 84
Web site: http://www.nexans.com

Public Company
Founded: 1994
Incorporated: 2000
Employees: 23,700
Sales: EUR 6.17 billion ($8.69 billion) (2010)
Stock Exchanges: Paris
Ticker Symbol: NEX
NAICS: 331421 Copper (Except Wire) Rolling, Drawing, and Extruding; 331411 Primary Smelting and Refining of Copper; 331525 Copper Foundries; 335931 Current-Carrying Wiring Device Manufacturing; 335932 Noncurrent-Carrying Wiring Device Manufacturing

■ ■ ■

Nexans S.A. is the world's leading specialist in cabling technologies. The Paris-based company produces and services a wide range of cables and cabling systems targeted toward four key markets: Infrastructure, Industry, Buildings, and Local Area Networks. Infrastructure accounts for more than half of the group's revenues. Europe is the group's largest geographical region, accounting for 57 percent of revenues. The North American and Asia-Pacific region each add 12

percent to sales, while South America accounts for 11 percent and the Middle East, Russia, and Africa add 8 percent. Nexans is listed on the Euronext Paris stock exchange and is led by CEO and Chairman Frédéric Vincent.

CABLING PIONEER

Waterproof electric cable was invented in 1879 by François Borel, of Switzerland, who later formed Berthoud, Borel & Company to develop the system, which consisted of wrapping wire with bituminous paper, which was then sealed with lead. The invention caused a revolution in a number of nascent industries, notably in the telecommunications and electrical power industries.

In 1897, the Société Française de Câbles was formed to manufacture cables using the Berthoud, Borel system in Lyon, France. By 1912, that firm, which became known as Société des Câbles Electriques, found an important shareholder in Compagnie Générale d'Electricité (CGE). CGE had been founded only in 1898, but by then had already become one of the most prominent companies in France's growing electrical power sector, with operations spanning both power generation and distribution and manufacturing.

CGE's growing business helped to drive the expansion of Société des Câbles Electriques as well. The close relationship between the two companies was highlighted by renaming the cable manufacturing business Compagnie Générale des Câbles de Lyon in 1917. By 1925, CGE had completed the acquisition of Câbles de Lyon, which became a separate division of CGE. The division grew again in 1938 after CGE's acquisition of Société

Industrielles de Téléphones, which operated cable manufacturing facilities in Bezons and Calais. These were placed under the Câbles de Lyon division.

Following World War II (in which CGE, taken over by the German occupying forces, had seen a large number of its facilities bombed), the French government nationalized the country's utilities operations. CGE then concentrated on its manufacturing operations, focusing especially on electrical and telecommunications components and systems, including cables and wires. During the 1950s, CGE diversified rapidly, entering various fields including consumer appliances, forcing a restructuring of its operations in the 1960s, with Câbles de Lyon taking over all of the company's cable and wire operations.

In 1969, CGE acquired Alcatel, founded in 1879 as the Société Alsacienne de Construction Mécanique, and ranking as one of the leading manufacturers of telecommunications technologies. The Alcatel acquisition boosted CGE's own telecommunications operation, CIT (the two companies were merged to form CIT-Alcatel) and also stepped up Câbles de Lyon's business as well.

JOINING THE WORLD'S LEADERS IN THE EIGHTIES

Câbles de Lyon began building scale during the 1970s, acquiring French rival Câbles Geoffrey et Delore in 1970. At the end of that decade, the company added to its French holdings with the purchase of Câbleries de Lens in 1979. The following year, Câbles de Lyon added a subsidiary in Greece, with the acquisition of Chandris

Cables. In 1981, the company moved into the United States, with the purchase of a stake in that country's Chester Cables.

By the beginning of the 1980s, Câbles de Lyon already held a leading position in the European cable market, with annual sales of some FRF 3 billion. In 1982, however, the company neared the industry's top spot with the acquisition of Kabel- und Metallwerke, Germany's fourth-largest manufacturer of cables and wires. That acquisition added another FRF 2 billion to Câbles de Lyon's sales, boosting it into Europe's second-place position.

CGE was nationalized by the French government in 1982. The following year, the government transferred another nationalized company, Thomson, into CGE. As a result of that merger, Câbles de Lyon absorbed two Thomson subsidiaries, Kabeltel and Thomson Jeumont Câbles. That year, also, Câbles de Lyon took over another cable manufacturer, Gorse. The cable division continued acquiring scale in the mid-1980s, adding Tréfilerie et Laminoir de la Méditerranée and Belgium's Câbleries de Charleroi, both in 1986.

That year, however, marked an even more significant change for Câbles de Lyon, after CGE and ITT announced their agreement to merge their telecommunications operations into a new joint venture, Alcatel NV, to be held at 65 percent by CGE. Under an extension to the original joint venture agreement, CGE agreed to add a 65 percent stake in Câbles de Lyon, which was then combined with ITT's Valtec fiber-optics and other cable operations to create a newly enlarged Câbles de Lyon.

CGE was re-privatized in 1987, in one of France's largest ever public offerings. Câbles de Lyon continued its acquisition drive, buying, in that year, Thomson Cuivre, in a move toward vertical integration. The following year, Câbles de Lyon, shortly to become known as Alcatel Cable, purchased France's Société Nouvelle de Câblerie Barelec; Greece's Manouili Hellas Cables; and Italy's Manuli Cavi, the second-largest cable maker in that country, behind Pirelli. The latter purchase, which added more than FRF 1.3 billion to Alcatel Cable's revenues, helped boost the company's total revenues to nearly FRF 15 billion in 1988. The following year, the company raised its European position still higher with the acquisition of Belgium's Câbleries de Dour.

ACQUISITIONS IN THE NINETIES

Not all of Alcatel Cable's growth came through acquisitions. In 1990, the company began construction of a new fiber-optic cable plant in the United States. By the end of that year, Alcatel Cable's sales had swollen to

ment to acquire STC Submarine Systems, part of Northern Telecom, for £600 million ($800 million). That acquisition received approval in February 1994. Later that year, Alcatel Cable acquired Switzerland's Cortaillod-Cossonay, which had inherited the original Berthoud, Borel & Cie.

Alcatel hit a bump during the mid-1990s, however. Caught off-guard by the rise of fiber optics-based cables, and by the increasing internationalization of the telecommunications market in the wake of a wave of privatization efforts, Alcatel Cable found itself facing losses. The company underwent a vast restructuring effort, which deepened its losses to nearly FRF 4 billion ($800 million) by 1996. In that year, Alcatel NV took over the remainder of Alcatel Cable, and the company became a wholly owned subsidiary of the larger group.

PURE PLAY APPROACH

By 1997, Alcatel was once again turning out profits. That year saw the company enter Asia with two Indonesian joint ventures to produce fiber-optic and submarine cables for the Asian market. The company's Swiss interests were enhanced with the creation of Alcatel Cable Switzerland, bundling its Cortaillod-Cossonay operations with those of Cabloptic and BK Breitenbach Kabel. The following year, the company acquired the North American and Portuguese subsidiary of Japan's Optec Dai-Ichi Denko Co., part of the Mitsubishi Group.

Alcatel NV began preparing to streamline its own operations in the late 1990s in order to focus on its core communications business. In May 2000, the company announced its intention to spin off Alcatel Cable as a separate company, called Nexans. Plans called for an initial public offering (IPO) of Nexans by the end of that year. Poor market conditions, however, forced Alcatel to wait until June 2001. The IPO, which reduced Alcatel's stake to just 30 percent, was oversubscribed by some 6.5 times.

The newly independent Nexans, led by Gérard Hauser, was now able to plot its own growth strategy. Acquisitions nonetheless remained a key part of the company's future, as it raced to regain its top spot, having lost out to Italy's Pirelli and Japan's Sumitomo during the 1990s. By the end of 2001, the company had already found its first takeover target, South Korea's Daesung. In mid-2002, the company struck again, picking up Germany's Petri, a maker of power cable accessories.

Hit by the difficult economic climate, Nexans engaged in a new round of restructuring, including shutting a number of its plants, which led to a loss of

KEY DATES

1879: François Borel invents waterproof electrical cables.
1897: Société Française de Câbles is formed in Lyon.
1925: Compagnie Générale d'Electricité (CGE) acquires Câbles de Lyon.
1938: CGE acquires Société Industrielles de Téléphones, and transfers its cable manufacturing facilities to Câbles de Lyon.
1982: Câbles de Lyon acquires Kabel- und Metallwerke of Germany.
1983: Company acquires Thomson Jeumont Cables and Kabeltel.
1986: Company merges with ITT's cable operations after CGE and ITT merger.
1991: Now named Alcatel Cable, company acquires AEG, Vacha Kabel, Lacroix & Kress, Ehlerskabelwerk, and Canada Wire & Cable.
1996: Alcatel NV takes full control of Alcatel Cable.
2000: Alcatel spins off cable manufacturing operations as Nexans.
2001: Nexans lists on Euronext Paris stock exchange.
2006: Nexans completes largest-ever acquisition of Olex in Australia.

FRF 24.8 billion. Acquisitions nonetheless remained a primary growth vehicle in the early 1990s for the company. In 1991, Alcatel Cable bought Canada Wire and Cable, a subsidiary of Canada's Noranda and the largest cable and wire manufacturer in the country, with 11 plants in Canada and three in the United States. The Canada Wire and Cable purchase also gave Alcatel Cable an entry into the South American market.

Germany, however, received Alcatel Cable's primary expansion efforts, when the company bought four companies there, Vacha Kabel, located in the former East Germany; Lacroix & Kress, which had been part of Raytheon since the early 1970s; another cable manufacturer, Ehlerskabelwerk; and lastly, AEG Kabel, a division of Daimler-Benz. The company also picked up operations in Turkey, acquiring that company's Erkablo.

Two more significant acquisitions came in 1993. In November of that year, the company acquired U.S. firm Berk-Tek Inc., based in Pennsylvania, adding that company's electronic and fiber-optic cable operations. By then, the company had also entered into an agree-

EUR 40 million, on EUR 4.3 billion in 2002 revenue. Nonetheless, the company expected to return to profitability by the end of 2003.

NEW MARKETS FROM 2002

Nexans quickly returned to the acquisition trail. In 2002, the company bought Petri, a producer of power cable accessories based in Germany. This was followed by a deal for a controlling stake of South Korea's Kukdong Electric Wire Company, in December 2002. The purchase made Nexans the world's leading producer of shipboard and marine cables, while adding more than $100 million to the company's annual sales. The addition of Kukdong also allowed Nexans to expand its operations in the Japanese and Chinese markets.

Soon after, Nexans boosted its presence in South America, with an agreement in January 2003 to acquire Furukawa Cabos de Energia SA, in Brazil, a company that specialized in the production of aluminum cables for the transport and energy distribution sectors. This purchase was followed in 2004 by the acquisition of Cabloswiss, focused on the production of specialized cables for robotics applications. In January 2006, the company added Switzerland's Confecta Holding AG, which specialized in cabling and cabling systems for industrial applications and the railway sector.

At the end of that year, Nexans completed its largest-ever acquisition, paying $397 million for Olex, based in Australia. The purchase doubled Nexans' Asia-Pacific operations, while adding EUR 330 million to group revenues. The company also gained a 40 percent share of the Australia and New Zealand cables markets. In 2007, Nexans turned toward the United States, where it acquired Connecticut-based The Valley Group (TVG). Although a small company with just $2 million in annual revenues, TVG brought Nexans its industry-leading thermal rating technology, used for providing power line monitoring.

ADDING SHAREHOLDERS IN 2011

Nexans continued to add new operations through the end of the decade. In 2008, the company acquired Italian special cables producer Intercond, paying EUR 90 million. This purchase came as part of the company's expansion of its Industrial cables division. Nexans also completed the purchase of the cable production division of Chile's Madeco, controlled by the Luksic family, who also controlled the Antofagasta mining group. The acquisition came in the form of a share swap, giving Madeco a 9 percent stake in Nexans. In March 2011, Nexans announced an agreement to raise Madeco's

shareholding to 20 percent over the next three years, for a total cost of around EUR 210 million.

In the meantime, Nexans completed two joint ventures. The first of these was in India, where the company joined with that country's cable leader Polycab, to create a new company producing cables for shipbuilding, material handling, railways, wind power, and other markets, as well as marketing agreement to introduce Nexans' own cables into the Indian market. The company followed this partnership with a second, now in Belgium, joining with Japan's Sumitomo Electric Industries to acquire Opticable. Both joint ventures were operational by 2009.

Nexans sought further expansion of its European operations, which by then still accounted for 57 percent of group sales. The company launched a takeover offer for Draka, based in the Netherlands, in 2010. This effort failed, however, as Draka teamed up with Prysmian. As a result, Nexans temporarily lost its position as leader of the global cables market.

Nexans in the meantime set its sights on the Chinese market, paying EUR 140 million for 75 percent of Shandong Yanggu, a producer of cables for the energy sector. The purchase gave Nexans control of three factories, and more than doubled the company's Chinese business to EUR 270 million. Nexans announced plans to expand Shandong Yanggu in order to double its size by 2015. The company announced its intention to seek out other acquisitions in China, as well as in the Middle East, into the new decade, as the company sought to defend its position as the world's leading cables and cable systems producer.

M. L. Cohen

PRINCIPAL SUBSIDIARIES

Nexans France; Nexans Wires; Société de Coulée Continue du Cuivre; Société Lensoise du Cuivre SA; Nexans Deutschland Industries AG & Co. (Germany); Lacroix & Kress GmbH (Germany); Nexans Benelux (Belgium); Nexans Holding Norway A/S; Nexans IKO Sweden A/B; Nexans Suisse SA (Switzerland); Nexans Italia Spa (Italy); Nexans Iberia SL (Spain); Nexans USA Inc.; Nexans Canada Inc.

PRINCIPAL DIVISIONS

Buildings; Infrastructure; Industry; Local Area Networks.

PRINCIPAL COMPETITORS

Alcan France S.A.S.; Boliden AB; Commercial Metals Company; Hitachi Cable Ltd.; Industrias Nacobre S.A.

de C.V.; Jiangxi Copper Company Ltd.; LS-Nikko Copper Inc.; MAN SE; Phelps Dodge International Corporation.

FURTHER READING

François, Ingrid. "Nexans Signe une Acquisition pour Doubler de Taille en Chine." *Les Echos*, June 22, 2011, 21.

Minder, Raphael. "Nexans Lowers Forecast as US Slowdown Bites." *Financial Times*, October 11, 2001, 32.

Moullakis, Joyce, and Nicolas Johnsons. "Nexans Buys Cable-Maker Olex, Expands in Asia-Pacific." *Bloomberg*, November 9, 2006.

"Nexans Cherche des Acquisitions en Chine et au Moyen Orient." *Les Echos*, February 15, 2011, 22.

"Nexans' Eu473m IPO Draws Strong Investor Support in Aftermarket amid More Bad News." *Euroweek*, June 15, 2001, 22.

"Nexans Fait Monter le Chilien Madeco à Son Capital." *Les Echos*, March 29, 2011, 24.

"Nexans Rachète l'Italien Intercond pour se Renforcer sur les Cables Speciaux." *L'Usine Nouvelle*, May 29, 2008.

"Nexans Snaps Up Furukawa." *Brazil Business News*, January 15, 2003.

"Nexans to Acquire Kukdong Electrical Wires." *Safety at Sea International*, January 2003, 22.

"Nexans Veut Lancer une OPA Sur Son Concurrent Néerlandais Draka." *L'Expansion*, October 18, 2010.

Owen, David. "Alcatel Delays Nexans IPO for New Ideas." *Financial Times*, November 1, 2000, 32.

North American
Breweries, Inc.

━━━━━■━━━━━

445 St. Paul Street
Rochester, New York 14605
U.S.A.
Telephone: (585) 546-1030
Web site: http://www.nabreweries.com

Private Company
Incorporated: 2009
Employees: 1,043
Sales: $280 million (2009 est.)
NAICS: 312120 Breweries

■ ■ ■

Based in Rochester, New York, North American Breweries, Inc. (NAB), owns and manages four brewery operations in the United States. They include Genesee Brewery in Rochester, which in addition to the Genesee line of beers, produces Dundee Ales & Lager, the Original Honey Brown Lager, and the Seagram's Escapes line of fruit-flavored malt beverages; the California and Washington breweries that make the handcrafted Pyramid Beers line; Vermont-based Magic Hat Brewing Company, a producer of craft beer; and Portland, Oregon-based MacTarnahan's Brewing Company, maker of MacTarnahan's Amber Ale and other craft beers. NAB is the U.S. distributor of Imperial beer from Costa Rica and also controls the exclusive rights to import and market Canada's Labatt Blue and other Labatt malt products and nonalcoholic beverages.

NAB makes further use of its brewing capabilities to offer a full range of contract brewing and packaging

services for both alcoholic and nonalcoholic beverages, with the capability to produce barrel batches or beverages in glass bottles or cans. The private company is majority owned by New York private-equity firm KPS Capital Partners, LP.

INDUSTRY CONSOLIDATION
OPENS DOOR FOR NAB

The formation of North American Breweries, Inc. was very much tied to changes in the beer industry that took place in the early 2000s. For years, sales of beer had fallen in the United States as drinkers increasingly turned to spirits and other alcoholic beverages. Around the world, brewers were also consolidating, resulting in fewer but more powerful competitors. In the United States, Anheuser-Busch was the dominant player by a wide margin, but in early 2008 its nearest rivals, Miller and Coors, agreed to merge. As a result, this new combination would command a 28 percent market share compared to Anheuser-Busch's 49 percent. While Miller and Coors consolidated their operations, Anheuser-Busch found itself the subject of an unsolicited takeover bid in July 2008 from giant InBev SA, a company that had been formed four years earlier when Brazil's AmBev merged with Belgium's Interbrew.

Anheuser-Busch and InBev were well familiar with one another. Only two years earlier, Anheuser-Busch acquired the Rolling Rock brand from InBev, and Anheuser-Busch distributed Stella Artois, Beck's, Bass, and other InBev products in the United States. The two companies also operated jointly in Canada and South Korea. InBev offered $65 a share for Anheuser-Busch, a

35 percent premium, for a total purchase price of $46.4 billion. The deal was quickly rejected and the two companies engaged in some public posturing for the next few months before the hostile takeover was recast as friendly and the two sides agreed on $70 a share, or a $52 billion purchase price.

The deal still had to pass regulatory muster before it could be completed, however. In November 2008, InBev was notified by the U.S. Department of Justice that it would have to sell its Labatt USA unit. InBev had acquired Canada's venerable Labatt Brewing Company in 1995. Thus, a third party would have to be employed to market, sell, and distribute Labatt brands in the United States.

FORMATION OF NAB: 2009

In February 2009, New York private-equity firm KPS Capital Partners reached an agreement to buy Labatt USA from Anheuser-Busch InBev. KPS was a relatively young firm, established in 1997 by longtime investment banker Eugene Keilin, Michael Psaros, and David Shapiro. KPS generally focused on industrial companies that were in bankruptcy or default. In conjunction with the Labatt USA acquisition, KPS formed a company called North American Breweries to house its investments in beer and malt beverages. At the same time, KPS reached an agreement to acquire Rochester, New York-based High Falls Brewing Co.

High Falls Brewing possessed a long history, dating back to 1878 when Mathius Knodolf established Genesee Brewing Company in Rochester, New York. Its name was drawn from the Indian word for the valley where the city was located. With the advent of Prohibition in 1919, the brewery was shuttered. After Prohibition was repealed in 1933, the Genesee brewery was reopened and thrived as a regional concern. The introduction of Genesee Cream Ale in 1960 spurred further popularity of the brand.

In the 1980s, however, beer consumption fell off and the industry saw a wave of consolidation. Finding it difficult to remain profitable, Genesee cut costs and looked for new revenue streams, such as the acquisition

of Ontario Foods, maker of drink mixes and other dry food products. Genesee also introduced new products, such as JW Dundee's Honey Brown Lager to appeal to younger drinkers. In the late 1990s, Genesee added to its food division but the growth in this segment was not enough to offset the losses incurred by the brewing division. In 2000, the company was split in two. The brewery business was sold to management, which renamed the company High Falls Brewing Co., part of an effort to emphasize its specialty beers.

High Falls upgraded its production facility and expanded contract production. The Brewery produced Sam Adams beers, Mike's Hard Lemonade, and Smirnoff Ice, a malt-based vodka drink. Unfortunately, when the Smirnoff contract came to an end in December 2002, High Falls found itself unable to meet a $1 million payment to the former owner of Genesee. Matters grew only worse, as the company was unable to recapitalize the business. At the end of 2003 it was also unable to meet a $3 million payment. High Falls was in decline for a full decade before its acquisition by KPS and being folded into NAB, which now made Rochester its corporate home. Labatt USA's headquarters in Buffalo became the home for NAB's sales and marketing operation.

NEW LABATT PRODUCT: BLUE LIGHT LIME

In addition to the High Falls brewery operation and its proprietary brands as well as the Labatt brands, NAB acquired the perpetual license for the Seagram's Cooler Escapes and Seagram's Smooth brands from Pernod Ricard USA, LLC. The company soon added to its portfolio by introducing a new Labatt product, Blue Light Lime. Although NAB was devoted to preserving the Canadian heritage of Labatt and remained committed to the Canadian brewing of Labatt products to maintain brand integrity, it made an exception with Blue Light Lime because it was a proprietary product that it wanted to bring to market as quickly as possible.

NAB posted $280 million in net sales in 2009. For most of the year, however, the company focused on establishing its infrastructure, especially in making the transition away from the Labatt Canada systems. On other fronts, NAB upgraded its brewery equipment and beefed up its sales force. On the marketing side, the company began to reposition its brands, developing a discernible target consumer for each one to set the stage for a major marketing effort in 2010.

Genesee products, for example, were recast to better appeal to 21- to 29-year-old male drinkers, customers who were more attracted to value beers. The Dundee

KEY DATES

1878: Genesee Brewing Company is established.
2000: Genesee Brewing is renamed High Falls Brewing Co.
2008: Merger creates Independent Brewers United.
2009: North American Breweries, Inc. (NAB) is formed to acquire High Falls Brewing and Labatt USA.
2010: NAB acquires Independent Brewers United.

craft beers, on the other hand, targeted older males possessing greater disposable income. The Seagram's business focused on 32- to 40-year-old women, especially working mothers pressed for time. The Seagram's Escapes products would also receive new packaging that used a transparent label to allow consumers to see more of the product. NAB conducted an advertising agency review in the summer of 2009 and awarded the business for the three brands to Via, a Portland, Maine-based independent agency. The Labatt brands were left out of review and remained with Publicis.

COMPANY PURCHASES INDEPENDENT BREWERS UNITED: 2010

In addition to organic growth, KPS had indicated at the time it created NAB that it would continue to pursue external growth. In August 2010, NAB reached an agreement to acquire Burlington, Vermont-based Independent Brewers United, parent company of Magic Hat Brewing Company. Magic Hat was founded in Vermont in 1994 by Alan Newman and Bob Johnson. Newman had previously operated an eco-friendly mail-order business called Seventh Generation. After leaving the mail-order business, he decided to become involved in manufacturing. It was Johnson, an avid home brewer, who persuaded him that they should begin making craft beer together. With the specialty sector growing rapidly in popularity, the new partners were able to enter the market just before it became saturated. Magic Hat made its mark with brews produced from imported barley malts and such unusual names as Blind Faith, Fat Angel, and Humble Patience. In 2008 Magic Hat acquired Seattle, Washington-based Pyramid Breweries, Inc. and Independent Brewers United was formed as the parent company of both Magic Hat and Pyramid.

Pyramid was already a thriving company in the Pacific Northwest when Magic Hat took shape on the other side of the country. It comprised two craft brewing operations: Hart Brewing, Inc., established in 1984 (its first beer was called Pyramid Pale Ale), and The Thomas Kemper Brewery, launched a year later. In 1992 the two breweries merged under the Hart Brewing name. By the mid-1990s, it was the country's fourth-largest craft brewer, mostly selling its products in 13 western states. The company went public in 1995 and the following year changed its name to Pyramid Breweries, Inc. Some of the $34.2 million raised in the stock offering was used to opened a major new brewery in Berkeley, California.

In 2004 Pyramid expanded further with the acquisition of Portland, Oregon-based MacTarnahan's Brewing Company, a craft brewer with origins that dated to 1986 when it was the Portland Brewing Company. As the craft beer industry grew more crowded, however, Pyramid found that being a public company proved to be more of a problem than a benefit. In order to comply with new filing regulations in the early 2000s, Pyramid had to spent about $1 million to remain in compliance. Given that the company recorded a loss of nearly $500,000 in 2007, the cost of remaining public was more than Pyramid could afford. Magic Hat's chief executive, R. Martin Kelly, was well familiar with Pyramid's situation, having served as the company's CEO until leaving for Magic Hat in 2004. He arranged for Magic Hat to acquire Pyramid for $2.65 a share and the assumption of $10 million in debt as part of a deal valued at $35 million.

Pyramid was a larger company than Magic Hat, but even their combined heft did not significantly improve their competitive position in a sector that had to contend with the rising price of ingredients and a poor economy that made it difficult to raise prices on what was already an expensive product. Moreover, the company that financed the Pyramid acquisition, Basso Capital Management, was experiencing its own problems and decided to exit the beer business. Thus, selling Independent Brewers United to KPS Capital was a logical decision for both parties. NAB, which wanted to bolster its slate of craft beers, was also delighted to bring Independent Brewers United into the fold. In addition to a slate of new brands, NAB added breweries in Burlington, Portland, and Berkeley.

NAB REFINANCES

In November 2010, KPS Capital refinanced NAB, providing a $120 million loan and a $25 million revolving credit facility. The company held a diverse portfolio of popularly priced beers, craft beers, and malt beverages, and appeared well positioned for ongoing growth. Especially promising was the opportunity to leverage

NAB's sales force to grow sales of Magic Hat brews in western states and the Pyramid lines in eastern states. With the financial backing of its corporate parent, the company was likely to pursue further acquisitions in the years to come.

Ed Dinger

PRINCIPAL SUBSIDIARIES

Genesee Brewing Company; Magic Hat Brewing Company; Pyramid Breweries, Inc.; MacTarnahan's Brewing Co.

PRINCIPAL COMPETITORS

Anheuser-Busch InBev SA/NV; The Boston Beer Company, Inc.; SABMiller plc.

FURTHER READING

Allison, Melissa. "Public-Company Costs Drive Pyramid Brewing to Combine with Magic Hat." *Seattle Times*, April 30, 2008.

Farrell, Colleen M. "Deal Official for Acquisition of Rochester-Based High Falls Brewing Co." *Daily Record of Rochester*, February 24, 2009.

Grandoni, Dino. "Brewery Expands Holdings." *Buffalo News*, August 12, 2010.

Holman, Kelly. "InBev Brews Tasty Deal with A-B." *Investment Dealers' Digest*, January 19, 2009, 20.

Johnson, Sally West. "Newman's Magic." *Rutland (VT) Herald*, December 23, 2001.

"Labatt USA's Parent Aims to Really Pour It On." *Buffalo News*, April 4, 2010, C1.

Mullman, Jeremy, and Rupal Parekh. "Old-Time Brands Genesee, Seagram Coolers Rise Again." *Advertising Age*, October 12, 2009, 6.

Northeast Utilities

56 Prospect Street
Hartford, Connecticut 06103
U.S.A.
Telephone: (860) 947-2000
Web site: http://www.nu.com

Public Company
Incorporated: 1966
Employees: 6,182
Sales: $4.9 billion (2010)
Stock Exchanges: New York
Ticker Symbol: NU
NAICS: 221122 Electric Power Distribution; 221210
Natural Gas Distribution; 551112 Offices of Other
Holding Companies

■ ■ ■

Northeast Utilities (NU) is a holding company whose
subsidiaries constitute the largest utility in New
England, providing electricity to nearly two million
consumers in Connecticut, New Hampshire, and Massachusetts and gas to 200,000 customers in
Connecticut. NU operates four regulated energy
distribution subsidiaries: Connecticut Light & Power
Company (CL&P), Public Service Company of New
Hampshire (PSNH), Western Massachusetts Electric
Company (WMECO), and Yankee Gas. The company's
power grid includes 35,000 miles of pole-based distribution lines and 3,100 miles of overhead transmission
lines. In 2011 NU was ranked number 459 in the
Fortune 500 and was listed on the S&P 500.

COMPANY ORIGINS

Northeast Utilities (NU) was formed in 1966 through
the merger of Western Massachusetts Electric Company
(WMECO) with Connecticut Light & Power Company
(CL&P) and Hartford Electric Light Company.
WMECO, a voluntary association, had been organized
in 1927 to acquire 11 utility companies in western
Massachusetts. These were subsequently consolidated
into the Springfield, Massachusetts-based WMECO,
which in 1959 added Huntington Electric Light
Company to its holdings.

To the newly formed NU, WMECO brought four
New England nuclear power plants known as the Yankee
Rowe, Vermont Yankee, Maine Yankee, and Connecticut
Yankee plants. In 1968 a proponent of nuclear power,
Lelan F. Sillin, Jr., became president of NU. The
region's electricity prices were higher than the national
average, and Sillin viewed nuclear power as the least
expensive, most efficient, and cleanest energy option. In
1969 NU began the construction of a million-kilowatt,
$72 million pumped-storage hydroelectric power project
on the Connecticut River in Franklin County,
Massachusetts. During the late 1960s, NU also formed
the Millstone Point Company to construct and operate
what became known as the Millstone Point nuclear
power station, whose first unit went into commercial
operation in 1970.

In 1972, the company launched a new program for
nuclear fuel financing in which the fuel itself served as
security on long-term debt. In 1973 NU generated 24
percent of its energy from nuclear units. By 1974, it was
33 percent. The second Millstone Point unit was

RECOVERY IN THE EIGHTIES

By the early 1980s, NU had revamped its demand outlook considerably. The company during the previous decade had overestimated its growth in demand for power. NU changed its direction during the 1980s, largely due to its new chief executive officer, William B. Ellis, who replaced Sillin in that post in 1983. Ellis had joined the company in the 1970s at Sillin's behest and became president in 1978. Ellis took over a company that had revenues of $1.8 billion but earnings of only $151 million. By 1986, however, margins had improved, with sales of $2 billion and income of $300.9 million.

Ellis was able to create a more friendly relationship with regulators. One of his most successful negotiations was a Connecticut rate case that was settled in 1986, the year Millstone's third unit came into full production. NU initially requested a $155.5 million increase, $133 million of which would go toward the Millstone unit's expenses. The request was denied, and the state ordered NU to put $46.5 million in a fund to offset rate increases in 1987. NU sued to protest the state's demand for this fund. Eventually, in an out-of-court settlement, the state agreed to restore the $46.5 million previously demanded as well as to allow a rate increase phased in over five years, beginning in 1988, to cover Millstone. NU's Connecticut Light and Power subsidiary agreed not to ask for any more rate increases until 1988.

NU's financial-recovery strategy also included a massive conservation effort. The utility planned to reduce all energy consumption, especially oil-generated energy. Oil-based production, which had been reduced from 74 percent in 1973 to 47 percent in 1980, was to be 10 percent by 1987. The Massachusetts legislature and the regulatory commissions of both Connecticut and Massachusetts allowed the company to use two-thirds of the fuel-cost savings to fund the conversion from oil- to coal-burning facilities. The other third was passed on to customers immediately.

The Mount Tom plant was converted to coal in 1981 at a cost of about $35 million, recovered through oil-cost savings in about three years, followed by the conversion of more plants. Other conservation efforts included ongoing research on "fuel cells," modular plants that cleanly and efficiently converted various fuels directly into electricity without burning them. NU also offered conservation tips to customers and gave school districts rebates for switching to energy-efficient equipment, such as fluorescent rather than incandescent lighting.

Despite these efforts, Connecticut regulators in a 1988 rate-increase hearing ordered NU to substantially expand its conservation efforts. The company

completed in 1975 when plans were established for a third unit and two more installations at Montague, Massachusetts.

During the 1970s, the Middle East oil embargo, escalating inflation, and rising construction cost and time requirements began eroding NU's financial viability. The Montague units, originally set for 1981 and 1983, were rescheduled to start up in 1988 and 1992. The third Millstone unit's in-service date was first pushed back three times, finally to 1986, to reduce the company's financial burden. The delay in the Millstone unit, along with inflation and regulatory requirements, increased its cost from $400 million to $2.49 billion.

The 1970s were punctuated by annual tussles with the regulatory boards in Connecticut and Massachusetts. In all, the company filed eight rate increase requests in Connecticut and six in Massachusetts. Never successful in obtaining its full request, NU averaged about 51 percent of the total amount for which it applied. In 1976, for instance, the Connecticut regulatory commission answered the company's request for a $56 million increase with a rate reduction of $22 million. The company had borrowed all that it could under federal laws by 1976 but still did not have enough money to remain financially stable. NU stock fell from 120 percent of book value in 1970 to 65 percent in 1981. Bond ratings deteriorated from AA to BAA standing in the same period.

KEY DATES

1966: Western Massachusetts Electric Company (WMECO) and Connecticut Light & Power Company (CL&P) join to form Northeast Utilities (NU).

2000: CL&P and WMECO, to comply with new state regulations, become strictly energy-delivery providers.

2001: Company ends merger talks with Consolidated Edison.

2005: Company launches its strategy to exit the competitive-generation business.

2009: NU and the Massachusetts-based utility NSTAR seek approval to develop a transmission interconnection to deliver Canadian hydroelectric power to New England.

2010: NU and NSTAR announce merger plans.

2011: CL&P's perceived slow response to an October 2011 snowstorm sparks consumer and government complaints, leading to resignation of CL&P's president and new delays for the proposed NU-NSTAR merger.

subsequently invested $250,000 to fund a collaborative project with the Conservation Law Foundation of New England and attorneys general, consumer counsels, and other agencies in Massachusetts and Connecticut. The first project began in Connecticut in February 1988, and a multi-utility process followed in Massachusetts, with WMECO as a participant. This effort identified new areas for conservation by bringing the company into closer contact with the communities it served. For example, a conservation program for public housing projects was one result of the process.

CHANGES AND CRISES IN THE NINETIES

In April 1990 NU took over management of Public Service Company of New Hampshire (PSNH), which two years earlier had filed for bankruptcy largely because of its investment in the Seabrook nuclear power plant. The NU-PSNH merger was approved in spite of anti-competitive concerns from other utilities in the region, and NU bought PSNH outright in a deal valued at $2.36 billion. In a major regulatory change, the Energy Policy Act, approved in 1992, allowed utilities to compete for wholesale customers. The PSNH acquisition was timely and gave NU enough generating capac-

ity to annually sell over $100 million worth of excess electricity to other utilities. In addition, the Seabrook nuclear plant eliminated NU's need for significant construction during the next decade.

In May 1992, one of NU's nuclear plants went offline for seven months, costing the company $190 million. This problem recurred in late 1995 and 1996, when the Nuclear Regulatory Commission shut down NU's Millstone and Connecticut Yankee plants. Connecticut Yankee was closed permanently by March 1996, while two of the three remaining Connecticut nuclear plants (one partially owned) were offline, costing NU $30 million a month for replacement power.

In September 1996 NU hired former South Carolina Electric & Gas Co. executive Bruce D. Kenyon to head its nuclear operations. At the time, only one of NU's five nuclear plants, PSNH-run Seabrook, was operating. Deregulation and the huge costs associated with fixing its nuclear plants dropped net income to $1.8 million in 1996 from $282.4 million the previous year. Bernard Fox, chairman since 1987 and CEO since 1993, retired in the summer of 1997. He was succeeded by Michael G. Morris, former president and chief executive officer of Consumers Energy, the principal subsidiary of CMS Energy.

In response to the new competitive environment, NU broadened its offerings. The company's unregulated, or "competitive," businesses included Select Energy, Inc., New England's largest energy marketer; Select Energy Services, Inc. (formerly HEC Inc.), an energy engineering firm; Northeast Generation Company; Northeast Generation Services Company; and high-speed telecom specialist Mode 1 Communications. Northeast Generation in 1999 acquired several Connecticut power plants. While expanding through acquisitions, NU also began shedding certain assets. In 1999 WMECO and CL&P sold off most of its fossil-hydroelectric power plants in Connecticut and Massachusetts. NU also sold its Millstone nuclear power plants for $1.3 billion.

MERGER AND ADAPTATION TO DEREGULATION: 1999–2005

In 1999 NU announced it would enter the gas business through a merger with Yankee Energy System Inc., whose subsidiary Yankee Gas Services Company was the largest gas concern in Connecticut, serving more than 180,000 Connecticut customers. That same year NU announced that it would be acquired by and merge with Consolidated Edison Inc. (Con Ed), a power company with three million customers. The Yankee Gas acquisition was formalized in 2000, but the Con Ed deal, also expected to be consummated in 2000, ultimately disintegrated in 2001.

In 2000 Select Energy joined Enermetrix, an online exchange that matched natural gas and electrical needs with energy providers in real time. In 2000 CL&P and WMECO, to comply with new state regulations, became strictly energy-delivery providers, conveying to their customers electricity generated by other companies. As a result, CL&P and WMECO sold several generating stations to the nonregulated NU subsidiary Northeast Generation Services Company. NU in 2001 established its transmission operations as a distinct business unit. In May 2001, with electrical deregulation in New Hampshire set to take effect, PSNH completed a two-phase 15 percent electric-rate reduction, hoping to keep its 430,000 customers who were given the right to select their own energy provider.

Between 2001 and 2002, Yankee Gas began a $23 million multiyear, 70-mile extension of service program from Southbury to Woodbury. The company also announced plans for a $4.5 billion installation of new gas mains to service Ellington, Oxford, South Windsor, and East Lyme, Connecticut, the latter which never had gas service before. During the same period, NU and its subsidiaries sold the Holyoke Water Power hydroelectric dam, Mount Tom Station, to the city of Holyoke; NU's minority stake in Vermont Yankee Nuclear power plant; and the company's remaining 40 percent stake in the Seabrook Station. Meanwhile, between 2001 and 2002, NU's competitive generation subsidiaries acquired the Maine-based high-voltage electricity contractor E.S. Boulos Company; New York-based Niagara Mohawk Energy Marketing, renamed Select Energy New York; and Woods Electrical Company and Woods Network Services.

The New Hampshire legislature in 2003 approved legislation giving PSNH permission to keep its power plants through at least April 2006. PSNH in 2003 gained an additional 11,000 customers through the acquisition of Connecticut Valley Electric Company. At the end of 2003, Morris retired as chairman, CEO, and president. He was succeeded in 2004 by Charles Schivery.

Between 2002 and 2004, Select Energy won several contracts to provide wholesale-generation service to utilities in New Jersey and Massachusetts. In 2004 PSNH began construction on its Northern Wood Power Project designed to cut emissions by transitioning from a coal-fired boiler at Portsmouth's Schiller Station to a clean-wood-burning unit. In 2005 Yankee Gas began building a 1.2 billion-cubic-foot storage facility for LNG in Waterbury, Connecticut, the company's largest construction project in its history.

FOCUS ON REGULATED UTILITY OPERATIONS

In 2005 NU launched its strategy for bowing out of the competitive-energy wholesale-generation business and selling all but its regulated utility operations by 2006, using the proceeds to reduce debt and develop its networks. Among the divestitures were all of NU's Connecticut and Massachusetts competitive-generation operations, the Select Energy retail marketing business, and Select Energy Services. The company expected the divestitures would simplify its business structure and make NU a more-focused firm in line with New England's energy-infrastructure requirements. At the same time, company officials believed that focusing on the regulated utility business would make NU's income more predictable, decrease its financial risk, and improve stockholder value and dividends.

Having been pushed out of power generation by deregulation, NU could make money for its shareholders by only its transmission business. NU invested $2 billion in a multiyear program to upgrade its power-grid infrastructure and address New England's need to import electricity. Indeed, the power system in southeastern Connecticut, for example, remained one of the country's most energy-starved areas, using more electricity than it generated.

At mid-decade, NU initiated four major infrastructure upgrades. Projects included a $350 million, 21-mile, 345-kilovolt Bethel-to-Norwalk transmission line, providing electrical power for southwest Connecticut; the Middletown-to-Norwalk project, a 45-mile overhead transmission line joint-endeavor upgrade with United Illuminating Co. (UI) to improve service reliability; the Glenbrook Cables project, connecting Norwalk and Stamford, Connecticut, with a 345-kilovolt transmission system; and the Long Island Replacement Cable project, lengthening the 345-kilovolt transmission system with 11 miles of underwater cables between New York and southwestern Connecticut. All the projects aimed at improving the reliability and security of New England's power-grid infrastructure and saving consumers the cost of government mandated charges.

In 2009 NU and the Massachusetts-based utility NSTAR received initial regulatory approval for a transmission interconnection with Hydro-Quebec to facilitate the acquisition of hydroelectric power for New England. The proposal of the two utilities included construction of the U.S. side of a high-voltage line running from Quebec to northern New England designed to reduce greenhouse gases by cutting gas-fired power generation. That same year NU separated the management of Yankee Gas and WMECO. In August 2009 NU relocated its corporate headquarters to Hartford,

Connecticut. Its former Berlin, Connecticut, headquarters building then was taken over by CL&P, Yankee Gas, and NU's transmission unit. In July 2010 CL&P and UI sought approval for UI to become a partial investor in new CL&P projects.

NEW MERGER PROPOSAL AND STORM RESPONSE PROBLEMS

In November 2010 NU announced it would acquire NSTAR for $9.5 billion, forming one of the biggest U.S. utilities. Boston-based NSTAR was the largest investor-owned gas and electric utility in Massachusetts, serving more than 1.1 million customers. The deal, planned to be consummated through a stock exchange, was expected to leave NU owning six regulated utilities serving about 3.5 million customers in three New England states. The proposed merger, which initially was expected to close in 2011, met with opposition from Massachusetts Governor Deval Patrick, whose office sought to delay the deal pending a review of rates.

An unexpected early winter snowstorm struck the Northeast on October 29, 2011, dumping 19 to 31 inches on the region's cities and cutting off the power of 830,000 CL&P customers. With a record number of Connecticut residents without electricity, NU crews worked more than 10 days before all power was restored. In the process, the company failed to meet its own announced deadline of having 99 percent of power restored by November 6. In the fallout of massive customer and government complaints, Jeffrey D. Butler, CL&P president, resigned and was replaced by NU's president of transmission, James A. Muntz.

NU Chairman Charles Schivery announced measures to improve future storm responses, offered to waive late-payment fees to customers whose service and lives were disrupted, announced an independent review of the company's storm response, and offered to establish a $10 million fund for Connecticut residents who suffered losses due to the storm, with the state government to distribute the monies. Connecticut Governor Dannel P. Malloy refused to accept the money from NU, noting it was not enough and that the utility, not the state government, should distribute funds to consumers.

CL&P's response to the snowstorm created a potentially new roadblock to the proposed NU-NSTAR merger. In November 2011, Connecticut state regulators began seeking public feedback to the utility's storm response. Along with pending legal action, the inquiry could prompt a review of the proposed merger by Connecticut Public Utilities Regulatory Authority, which earlier had stated that it had no authority to conduct such a review. No decision on the matter was expected until January 2012 at the earliest. As it neared 2012, NU was seeking to reverse negative publicity it had suffered after the October 2011 storm and complete its merger with NSTAR. As New England's largest utility, the company continued to be at the forefront of improving and making more secure and reliable the region's transmission network. How well the company could improve its own image of reliability was another challenge NU faced going forward.

Elaine Belsito
Updated, Frederick C. Ingram; Roger Rouland

PRINCIPAL SUBSIDIARIES

The Connecticut Light and Power Company; Public Service Company of New Hampshire; Yankee Gas Services Company; Western Massachusetts Electric Company.

PRINCIPAL COMPETITORS

American Electric Power Company, Inc.; Bangor Hydro-Electric Company; Central Vermont Public Service Corporation.

FURTHER READING

Celebrating Our 35th Anniversary: Diversity Fuels Our Success. Berlin, CT: Northeast Utilities, June 2001.

"CL&P Completes Construction of Overhead Portion of Middletown-Norwalk Transmission Project." *Transmission & Distribution World*, September 11, 2008.

Clark, James M. "CL&P Upgrades the Grid." *Transmission & Distribution World*, September 1, 2007.

"Malloy Rejects Northeast Utilities' $10 Million Offer." *New London (CT) Day*, November 19, 2011.

McGeehan, Patrick. "Connecticut Utility Chief Quits after Delays in Restoring Power." *New York Times*, November 18, 2011, A24.

"Northeast Utilities and NSTAR Merge." *Manufacturing Close-Up*, October 21, 2010.

"Northeast Utilities, NSTAR Pursue Interconnection with Quebec." *Transmission & Distribution World*, December 15, 2008.

"Northeast Utilities to Focus on Its Regulated Businesses, Divest All Competitive Businesses by End of 2006." *Transmission & Distribution World*, November 7, 2005.

Podsada, Janice. "State Regulators, Prodded by a Generating Firm, Might Formally Review NU-NSTAR Merger." *Hartford Courant*, December 16, 2011.

Strempel, Dan. "Con Ed and NU Fight over Failed Merger." *Fairfield County Business Journal*, March 2001, 2.

Office DEPOT.

Office Depot, Inc.

6600 North Military Trail
Boca Raton, Florida 33496
U.S.A.
Telephone: (561) 438-4800
Toll Free: (800) 937-3600
Fax: (561) 438-4001
Web site: http://www.officedepot.com

Public Company
Incorporated: 1986
Employees: 40,000
Sales: $11.63 billion (2010)
Stock Exchanges: New York
Ticker Symbol: ODP
NAICS: 453210 Office Supplies and Stationery Stores;
454110 Electronic Shopping and Mail-Order
Houses

■ ■ ■

Office Depot, Inc., ranks as the second-largest operator of office supplies superstores in North America, trailing only category leader Staples, Inc. The company operates about 1,100 retail stores in the United States and Canada that offer a full range of office supplies, office furniture, business machines, computers, and computer software. Most of the stores also include a copy and print center offering multiple services such as printing, reproduction, mailing, and shipping. These stores principally serve consumers and small to medium-sized businesses. Beyond its brick-and-mortar stores, Office Depot's distribution channels include direct mail, contract delivery, and both retail and business-to-business e-commerce. Office Depot also owns Viking Office Products, Inc., the leading direct-mail marketer of office products in the world. The firm's international operations serve customers in more than 50 countries in Europe, Asia, and Latin America via more than 400 retail stores (some operated as joint ventures or by franchisees), and a mix of direct-mail, e-commerce, and contract sales.

BEGINNINGS

Along with rival companies Staples and Office Club, Inc., Office Depot was a pioneer in the field of discount office supplies. The three companies were founded within months of each other in 1986 in three different corners of the United States: Office Depot in Florida, Staples in Massachusetts, and Office Club in California. All of them saw opportunities in selling office supplies to small businesses at bulk discount rates that had previously been the privilege of larger companies.

Since small businesses had never purchased supplies in quantities large enough to receive bulk discounts, they had been at the mercy of conventional retailers who, in the absence of price competition, could sell at manufacturers' suggested retail prices and take markups of as much as 100 percent. Buying directly from manufacturers instead of wholesalers and keeping overhead low, a discount retailer could offer goods from 20 to 75 percent off of full retail. Another trend that proved advantageous for these three companies was the advent of warehouse-style discount retailers in the 1980s. What Price Club had done for general

Office Depot, Inc.

merchandise and what Circuit City had done for consumer electronics, Office Depot, Office Club, and Staples sought to do for ballpoint pens and legal pads.

Office Depot was founded in Boca Raton, Florida, by entrepreneur F. Patrick Sher and two partners, Jack Kopkin and Stephen Dougherty. The company opened its first retail store in Fort Lauderdale in October 1986, and it proved successful enough that two more Office Depot stores appeared in Florida by the end of the year. The company continued to grow rapidly. In 1987 it opened seven more stores in Florida and Georgia and sales topped $33 million. Sher did not have long to savor his success, however, for he died of leukemia scarcely a year after his first store had opened. He was succeeded as CEO by David Fuente, an experienced retail executive whom Office Depot lured away from Sherwin-Williams, where he had been president of the paint stores division.

Fuente's strategy was for Office Depot to grow at a breakneck pace, to trap market share before copycats got into the act. He planned to enter 10 new markets a year and add 50 stores a year. Although Office Depot opened only 16 stores in 1988, expanding into Kentucky, North Carolina, Tennessee, and Texas, Fuente met his goal in 1989 and 1990. Sales topped $132 million in 1988, and Office Depot went public in June with an initial offering of more than six million shares at $3.33 per share. Office supply discount retail as a whole was proving wildly successful. Although they accounted for only a small fraction of office supply retail sales by the end of the decade, at least one analyst predicted in 1989 that

discounters would form the fastest-growing specialty-retail segment for several years to come.

Office Depot gained the distinction of being the first of the three original discount chains to turn a profit for a period of four consecutive quarters, which it did during the last two quarters of 1988 and the first two of 1989. The company achieved its success with stores that resembled nothing so much as warehouses. Their decor was functional and unassuming, in a style described by a reporter for *Fortune* in July 1989 as "plain pipe rack," with merchandise stacked floor-to-ceiling on steel shelves. As Fuente explained it, "Customers pick only from the first six feet of 'shelf' space anyway. So we use the area above 'for storage.'" By 1989 Office Depot stores were averaging $150,000 in sales per week. Of course, lack of concern for the aesthetics of interior design characterized the company's competitors, as well. Office Depot held an edge in that commercial rents were lower in the South than elsewhere in the United States, allowing the company to build exceptionally large stores and still keep overhead costs relatively low.

Office Depot continued to grow dramatically in 1989 and 1990, expanding beyond its regional base in the South into the Midwest. By the end of 1990 the company boasted 122 stores scattered across 19 states and sales of $625 million. Much of that expansion was financed by the sale of 3.6 million shares of stock for $41 million to Carrefour, a French chain-store concern with subsidiaries throughout Europe.

PURCHASE OF OFFICE CLUB IN 1991

The office supply discount field became more crowded and competitive in the early 1990s as other companies, including OfficeMax and BizMart, joined the lucrative industry. With the struggle for market share becoming more vigorous, Office Depot and Office Club decided to merge in 1991. The move solidified Office Depot's position on the Pacific Coast in one swoop by eliminating a major competitor and giving it 59 new stores in a regional market where the company previously had only a slim presence. For its part, Office Club had not fared quite as well as its fellow discounting pioneers. During the four quarters that constituted Office Depot's first profitable one-year period, Office Club lost $2.7 million, compared to Office Depot's gain of $5.1 million and Staples' narrower loss of $1.9 million. The merger, therefore, proved advantageous to Office Club as well.

Office Club had been founded in Northern California in 1986 by Mark Begelman (previously an executive with British American Tobacco) in partnership with a friend who had been selling office products to

Price Club. They reasoned that the same marketing principles that allowed Price Club to retail office supplies at deep discounts would work for stores specializing in that kind of merchandise. The first Office Club store opened in January 1987 in Concord, California. Office Club grew quickly, although not as frantically as Office Depot. By the end of 1987 Office Club had opened five stores. At the time of the merger, it operated 59 stores, most of them in California, and had posted annual sales of $300 million.

The merger was approved by Office Depot shareholders in April 1991. As a result of the agreement, which entailed a stock swap worth $137 million, Begelman became president and chief operating officer of Office Depot, with Fuente remaining chairman and CEO. Over the next 13 months, all Office Club stores were either closed or converted into Office Depot outlets, and the membership fee that Office Club had been charging its regular customers was dropped.

Even after the merger, Office Depot continued to expand. In June 1991 it sold another 1.8 million shares of stock to Carrefour for $40 million to finance expected growth, making Carrefour an 18 percent owner. In addition to the outlets acquired from Office Club, the company opened 57 new stores in 1991. At the end of the year, Office Depot had 229 stores and posted sales of $1.3 billion.

At about the same time, Office Depot saw its sales of office machines, including personal computers (PCs), begin to grow by leaps and bounds, and the company began to emphasize this side of its business more

strongly. In December 1992, Begelman claimed in an interview that 10 percent of all fax machines sold in the United States were sold by Office Depot. Store layouts were redesigned so that more machines could be put on display. The company began selling not only PC clones by Packard-Bell and Compaq, but also the real thing. In August 1991 IBM agreed to let Office Depot sell its PS/1 computers and around that time Apple gave permission for them to sell the Macintosh Performa line as well.

EXPANSION INTO CANADA IN 1992

In 1992 Office Depot made its first move beyond the U.S. market, acquiring HQ Office International, Inc., the parent company of the Great Canadian Office Supplies Warehouse chain, which operated seven stores in western Canada. HQ Office International had been founded in 1990 by Robert McNulty as a Canadian extension of his unsuccessful California-based HQ Office Supplies Warehouse chain, which was carved up and bought out by Staples and BizMart in 1990. Office Depot immediately replaced the HQ Office International name with its own and began expanding its presence in Canada, opening two stores in Manitoba. Office Depot's entry into the Canadian market set the company up for an eventual confrontation with Business Depot, a small chain based in eastern Canada, in which Staples held a minority stake.

In addition to expanding into new geographic areas, Office Depot began expanding its customer base. Originally catering to businesses with 20 or fewer employees, Office Depot decided to attract larger firms by acquiring contract stationers and integrating them into its retail business. In May 1993 Office Depot bought the office supply operations of contract stationer Wilson Stationery & Printing, a subsidiary of Steelcase Inc. The deal was valued at $16.5 million. In the next year the company also bought three more contract stationers.

Having successfully moved into the established retail office supply market, Office Depot was confident it could challenge the existing system that served larger businesses. Staples and OfficeMax clearly felt Office Depot was on the right track: they both followed suit by acquiring their own contract stationers. Two years later, however, Office Depot had yet to see big returns on its investment. Integrating the contract stationers into its core retail business had cost more than expected, but the firm remained confident that the more diverse customer base would make the investment worthwhile in the long run.

The company saw $2.6 billion in sales in 1993, with $63 million in profit. By 1994 Office Depot had grown to 362 stores, which still followed the company's original concept: warehouse-like buildings that stocked office supplies at 30 to 60 percent off manufacturers' list prices. The company's closest competitor, the Kmart Corporation subsidiary OfficeMax, was only half its size. Not satisfied, Office Depot planned to double the number of its stores in the next five years.

BLOCKED MERGER WITH STAPLES: 1997

In September 1996 Office Depot agreed to be acquired by Staples, its largest competitor, in a deal estimated at $4 billion. As these companies were number one and two, respectively, among discount chains, questions about antitrust violations were quickly raised. The Federal Trade Commission (FTC) found that the combined company would control prices in many metropolitan areas and that in cities where Office Depot and Staples competed head to head, prices might be expected to rise 5 to 10 percent. The FTC sought a court order to stop Staples from buying Office Depot.

In response, the two companies agreed to sell 63 stores to OfficeMax to open competition in certain areas, a proposal that had to be approved by the FTC. They also argued that, with only 5 percent of the office supply market, their merger was not threatening. Unappeased, the FTC argued that office superstores were a market to themselves and that Office Depot and Staples controlled 75 percent of that market. The FTC sued to stop the deal, and in late June 1997 a federal judge granted a preliminary injunction to block the transaction. At this point, Staples and Office Depot abandoned their merger plans, conceding defeat.

Aside from the failed merger, the mid-to-late 1990s were noteworthy for Office Depot's steady expansion of its overseas operations. From 1995 to 1998 the company opened stores in Poland, Hungary, and Thailand under licensing agreements, and in Mexico, France, and Japan through joint ventures. In 1998 Office Depot bought out its joint venture partner in France and did likewise in Japan the following year. Also important to this international push was the August 1998 acquisition of Viking Office Products, Inc. for about $2.7 billion in stock. Based in Torrance, California, Viking was the largest direct-mail marketer of office products in the world. Of Viking's $1.29 billion in 1997 revenues, 60 percent was generated outside the United States. It operated 11 delivery centers in Europe and Australia.

In 1998 Office Depot added to its growing channels of distribution with the launch of its first Web site, www.officedepot.com. The company's first European e-commerce site, www.viking-direct.co.uk, was launched in the United Kingdom a year later. In 1999 Office Depot also entered into a partnership with United Parcel Service, Inc. (UPS) to begin offering UPS packaging and shipping services at its U.S. stores. That year, revenues surpassed the $10 billion mark for the first time, hitting $10.2 billion, while profits were a record $257.6 million. Office Depot ended the decade with 825 stores in the United States and Canada, and 32 overseas.

Despite the record results for 1999, all was not well at Office Depot. As the ill-fated Staples deal unfolded, Office Depot had placed its expansion plans on hold. Then when the deal died, the company scrambled to make up for lost time, entering new markets where competitors were already entrenched and making some poor choices in regard to specific store locations. Office Depot was also hurt by heightened competition from warehouse discounters, particularly Costco Wholesale Corporation and Wal-Mart Stores, Inc.'s Sam's Club, which made aggressive moves into some of the most profitable office supplies categories, including computer paper, toner, and ink, forcing price cuts. Sales and profits were negatively affected, and Office Depot began missing some analysts' projections. After second-quarter 2000 earnings dropped 22 percent, the company's board reacted by easing Fuente out of the CEO slot and into the position of nonexecutive chairman. Bruce Nelson was promoted to CEO from his previous position as international president. Nelson had joined Office Depot as the president of Viking Office Products, and earlier in his career had garnered more than two decades of senior management experience at Boise Cascade Office Products.

NEW CEO MOVES TO CUT COSTS IN 2001

Nelson spent the next several months making changes to top management and launching a thorough review of the firm's operations to identify underperforming outlets and weak markets. In January 2001 he announced that Office Depot would close 70 of its 888 North American stores, leaving Cleveland and Columbus, Ohio; Phoenix; and Boston altogether. Expansion for 2001 was pared back to 50 new stores, with the new outlets being about 20,000 square feet each, about 5,000 square feet smaller than the average existing store.

Nelson also aimed to refocus the stores on small and medium-sized businesses by eliminating a great deal of consumer-oriented merchandise, such as DVD players and children's computer software. In all, about 1,800 products were to be cut. These represented about 20 percent of the total number of products but generated only about 2 percent of sales. In connection with this restructuring, Office Depot recorded an after-tax charge of $260.6 million for the fourth quarter of 2000, leaving profits for that year at a much reduced $49.3 million.

Continuing its ongoing overseas expansion, Office Depot in early 2001 acquired Sands & McDougall, an office products firm that was the largest contract stationer in Western Australia. The company also expanded its business services operations into Ireland, the Netherlands, and France that year. In December 2001 Nelson was named to the additional position of chairman, succeeding Fuente, who nevertheless remained on the company board. The Viking direct-mail business expanded into Switzerland, Spain, and Portugal during 2002, and Office Depot's business services division expanded into Italy. Through its Mexican joint-venture partner, Grupo Gigante, S.A. de C.V., the company expanded into Central America that same year, opening stores in Guatemala and Costa Rica.

In early 2003, however, Office Depot elected to exit from the Australian market in order to concentrate its international attention mainly on Europe. It sold its Australian operations to Officeworks, a subsidiary of Coles Myer Ltd. that was the leading office supplies retailer in Australia. It took little time for Office Depot to make a major move that nearly doubled its European operations. In June 2003 the company acquired the France-based Guilbert S.A. from Pinault-Printemps-Redoute S.A. for $945.2 million. Guilbert was one of the largest contract stationers in Europe, with operations in nine European countries and 2002 revenues of $1.6 billion. The acquisition of Guilbert, based in Senlis (outside Paris), not only accelerated Office Depot's penetration of the market for large business customers in Europe, it also gave the company the number one position among the continent's office supply firms.

In April 2004 Office Depot gained its first wholly owned operations in Eastern Europe by acquiring its licensee in Hungary, which had been operating three Office Depot stores in that nation. The company planned to use its Hungarian subsidiary as a base for expansion into the 10 countries in the region that had recently joined the European Union.

RETURN TO STABILITY IN 2004

After nearly four years of declines in quarterly same-store sales (sales at stores open for more than one year), Office Depot appeared to have turned the corner during the first half of 2004 when it posted two consecutive quarters of 3 percent increases in same-store sales. The company was also busy with a number of new initiatives. In February it rolled out its first-ever customer loyalty program, Office Depot Advantage, which rewarded customers who spent as little as $200 in a three-month period with a gift certificate good for future purchases.

To help ramp up expansion efforts, the company agreed to buy 124 former Kids "R" Us stores from Toys "R" Us, Inc. for $197 million in cash. The deal was later reduced to 109 stores, and Office Depot planned to resell or sublet about half of the total, but 45 to 50 of the stores were to be converted to the Office Depot format. Many of the acquired stores were in the Northeast, and the company announced an aggressive expansion into that region, a stronghold for its two main rivals, Staples (now the number one U.S. operator of office supplies superstores) and OfficeMax.

Overall, in an attempt to close the gap with Staples, which had 1,400 stores, the 900-unit-strong Office Depot aimed to open 80 new stores in 2004 and then 100 new stores in each of the following three years. The outlets were to feature a new format called Millennium2. The format offered enhanced convenience by emphasizing grouping product categories together in the way customers use them and also featured increased cross-merchandising. Also significant was that the stores began showcasing a new line of fashion-forward furniture created by Emmy Award-winning designer Christopher Lowell.

Office Depot was also moving to enhance its "green" credentials, and during 2004 partnered with Conservation International, NatureServe, and The Nature Conservancy to establish the Forest & Biodiversity Conservation Alliance, a five-year program to conserve forests. It also added in-store recycling programs for electronic devices and established goals for future environmental performance.

STEVE ODLAND BECOMES CEO IN 2005

In October 2004 Nelson left the firm after clashing with the board about the company's future direction. His place was taken on an interim basis by Director Neil Austrian, and in March 2005 former AutoZone CEO Steve Odland was named chairman and CEO. The firm was now having problems integrating the former Kids "R" Us stores and during the year closed 27 locations in the United States and abroad, as well as dropping use of the Viking brand name in the United States. The firm instituted other cost-cutting measures that included outsourcing some work, consolidating call centers, restructuring European management, and installing energy-efficient lightbulbs and conserving cash-register receipt tape. More than 600 employees in North America lost their jobs.

The following year Office Depot boosted its Asian and European operations by purchasing Best Office Co., Ltd., of Korea, AsiaEC of China, and Papirius s.r.o. of the Czech Republic, as well as adding New Jersey-based Allied Office Products. Sales topped $15 billion for the first time, with net profit hitting $558 million. More than a quarter of sales came from online operations, with 30 percent from contract sales and direct marketing in North America. Office Depot now employed 50,000 and had more than 1,100 North American stores, which it eventually expected to double by opening 100-plus new locations per year.

After strong sales growth in 2005 and 2006, same-store sales began to contract, in part due to the prolonged housing crisis. In 2007 the firm's third-quarter financial results were delayed when accounting errors were discovered via a whistle-blower complaint. Four executives subsequently lost their jobs, and the company was forced to restate the previous four quarters' results. Office Depot's stock price dropped by 50 percent during the year, while the projected number of store openings was reduced by more than half.

MORE CUTBACKS IN 2008

Financial problems continued to mount, and in mid-2008 the firm recorded a first-ever quarterly loss for North American operations of $4 million. It subsequently slowed new-store openings, as well as closed some locations and abandoned plans to remodel others. Jobs were also being cut, with 130 headquarters employees taking early buyouts during the quarter. As Moody's Investor Service reduced the company's bond rating to junk status, its stock price continued to slide. Disgruntled shareholders began seeking changes to the board, although they were unsuccessful. For the year, the company had sales of $14.5 billion and a loss of $1.48 billion. Its employee ranks now stood at 42,000 worldwide, including 6,000 in Florida.

In November 2008 Office Depot moved into a new $100 million headquarters in Boca Raton, three miles from Delray Beach. The custom-built facility, which would house a staff of 2,000, had been financed in part with $15 million in state and local incentives. During 2008 the firm also launched a new private-label green product line and opened its first "green" store, in Austin, Texas. New facilities were added in Germany and the Netherlands, and business partnerships were formed with AGE in Sweden, bigboXX.com in Hong Kong,

Netbizz Office Supplies in Singapore, and Google, which would offer Office Depot Customers online marketing assistance.

In the summer of 2009 the still-struggling company sold a 20 percent stake to private-equity firm BC Partners for $350 million. BC would receive a newly authorized category of preferred stock, and take three seats on the board. Sales for the year fell by 16 percent, to $12.1 billion, although losses narrowed to $627 million. Office Depot had closed 150 stores in Asia and the United States, many of them in hard-hit Florida and California.

ODLAND RESIGNS AS CEO IN OCTOBER 2010

In October 2010 the U.S. Securities and Exchange Commission (SEC) announced a settlement of charges that CEO Steve Odland and former CFO Patricia McKay had improperly shared confidential information with analysts in 2007. The firm would pay $1 million and the two executives $50,000 each, while admitting no guilt. On October 25 Odland announced his resignation, and longtime board member and former National Football League CEO Neil Austrian took his place on an interim basis, before later being named permanently to the post. Austrian, 71, had originally come to the firm as a member of the Viking Products board.

Meanwhile, Office Depot had come under investigation by seven states, numerous cities, and several federal government agencies for deceptive contract-order practices that involved shifting customers to a different price structure without their permission, sparked by the revelations of an executive who departed in 2008. The firm reached multimillion-dollar settlements with Florida, Missouri, Colorado, and the city of San Francisco, while continuing to be investigated by California, Ohio, Texas, New York, and the U.S. Department of Justice. The impact was heightened by the loss of some $515 million in business from state and federal agencies that canceled contracts in the wake of the investigations.

By the end of 2010 Office Depot had about 1,150 North American stores, with as many closings as openings now taking place, and had recently sold its Japanese and Israeli operations. The company was trying new initiatives to boost retail sales, including offering in-store document shredding, adding U.S. Postal Service products, and rewarding schools for their recycling efforts. Business remained challenging into 2011, however, and Austrian announced new plans to downsize stores and cut fixed costs.

As it celebrated its 25th anniversary, Office Depot, Inc. was attempting to move beyond a difficult period of falling sales and legal problems. The firm remained the number two office products retailer in the world, behind Staples, and continued to operate more than 1,100 stores in the United States and Canada, as well as more than 400 others worldwide, with other business sectors including contract sales and e-commerce. Although new CEO Neil Austrian was taking steps to right the ship, the company still faced a variety of challenges and its future success appeared far from certain.

Douglas Sun
Updated, Susan Windisch Brown;
David E. Salamie; Frank Uhle

PRINCIPAL SUBSIDIARIES

The Office Club, Inc.; Office Depot International (UK) Ltd.; Office Depot International B.V. (Netherlands); Office Depot Deutschland GmbH (Germany); Office Depot Overseas Ltd. (Bermuda).

PRINCIPAL COMPETITORS

OfficeMax, Inc.; Staples, Inc.; Target Corporation; Wal-Mart Stores, Inc.

FURTHER READING

Brooks, Rick. "Office Depot to Buy Viking in Stock Deal." *Wall Street Journal*, May 19, 1998, A3.

Caminiti, Susan. "Seeking Big Money in Paper and Pens." *Fortune*, July 31, 1989.

Frogameni, Bill. "Office Depot Won't Renew Los Angeles Contract Worth $515M a Year." *South Florida Business Journal*, July 22, 2010. Accessed November 15, 2011. http://www.bizjournals.com/southflorida/stories/2010/07/26/story7.html.

Giovia, Jaclyn. "Four Office Depot Employees Fired after Review Finds Accounting Errors." *South Florida Sun-Sentinel*, November 10, 2007. Accessed November 15, 2011. LexisNexis Academic 20071110.

Hirsh, Michael. "But Nary a Trust to Bust." *Newsweek*, June 2, 1997, 44–45.

Libbin, Jennifer. "Office Depot CEO Outlines Future." *DSN Retailing Today*, May 21, 2001, 4, 59.

Liebeck, Laura. "Office Depot Ventures into Canada, Magazine Business." *Discount Store News*, February 3, 1992.

Ostrowski, Jeff. "Office Depot Closing 70 Stores." *Palm Beach (FL) Post*, January 4, 2001, 1D.

Owers, Paul. "Acquisition to Put Office Depot on Top." *Palm Beach (FL) Post*, April 9, 2003, 8B.

Pounds, Marcia Heroux. "Investment Group Buys 20% of Office Depot." *South Florida Sun-Sentinel*, June 23, 2009. Accessed November 15, 2011. LexisNexis Academic 20090623.

———. "Office Depot Chief Steve Odland Resigns in Wake of SEC Settlement Disclosure." *South Florida Sun-Sentinel*, October 25, 2010. Accessed November 15, 2011. LexisNexis Academic 20101025.

Troy, Mike. "Change Is in the Air at Office Depot." *DSN Retailing Today*, August 7, 2000, 3, 88.

———. "Office Depot Shifts Store Expansion to M2 Format." *DSN Retailing Today*, July 19, 2004, 4, 21.

Onex Corporation

161 Bay Street, 49th Floor
Toronto, Ontario M5J 2S1
Canada
Telephone: (416) 362-7711
Fax: (416) 362-5765
Web site: http://www.onexcorp.com

Public Company
Founded: 1984 as Onex Capital Corporation
Employees: 238,000
Sales: CAD 24.36 billion ($23.84 billion) (2003)
Stock Exchanges: Toronto
Ticker Symbol: OCX
NAICS: 541618 Other Management Consulting Services; 551112 Offices of Other Holding Companies

■ ■ ■

Onex Corporation is the largest investment firm in Canada, having completed nearly 300 acquisitions with a total value of CAD 49 billion during the first three decades of its existence. Onex acquires a wide range of businesses, including companies involved in the health care, financial services, building products, manufacturing, and transportation markets. Onex maintains offices in Toronto and New York City, managing approximately CAD 10 billion of third-party capital through various funds.

FOUNDER'S BACKGROUND: 1970–83

Behind the development of Onex is its founder, Gerald Schwartz. A young man with ambition and bold ideas, Schwartz graduated from the University of Manitoba with degrees in commerce and law. Upon graduation, he headed for Harvard University and earned a degree in business administration in 1970. Schwartz then took a job in Europe, working for Bernard Cornfield, a rather eccentric and flamboyant international financier based in Switzerland. When Cornfield's company, Investors Overseas Services, was investigated for fraud and then collapsed in 1973, Schwartz moved on to the United States, seeking work in the financial caverns of Wall Street in New York City. Hired by Bear Stearns & Company, Schwartz learned the intricacies of hostile takeovers and corporate mergers. Two of his most renowned and notorious colleagues included Henry Kravis and Jerome Kohlberg.

After a stint of four years in the United States, Schwartz decided to return to his hometown of Winnipeg. There, he formed a partnership with a lawyer, Israel Asper, an astute and driven entrepreneur, and together they founded CanWest Capital Corporation, the forerunner of CanWest Global Communications Corporation, which would own numerous broadcasting businesses throughout western Canada. The partnership acquired several small to midsized Canadian firms during the late 1970s and early 1980s. The collaboration seemed to be heading in a promising direction, but Schwartz and Asper began to quarrel about strategic issues surrounding acquisitions, venture capital, and timing, and before long decided to end their partnership.

ONEX SETS OUT: 1983–87

In 1983 Schwartz relocated to Toronto and, with the financial backing of former investors at CanWest, formed Onex Capital Corporation, which he intended to use as a holding company for widely diversified acquisitions. The first such acquisition was Onex Packaging, the Canadian subsidiary of the American Can Company based in Connecticut. With a purchase price of approximately $220 million, the acquisition was the largest leveraged buyout in the history of Canada.

Schwartz was not afraid of debt. His strategy was to use debt or other innovative financing to purchase undervalued companies, and then initiate a comprehensive restructuring of the company purchased. He would then sell either parts of the company or the whole at a profit. Onex Packaging, a manufacturer of rigid packing materials, offered an initial public offering (IPO) of its stock in 1987 to cover the costs of the restructuring and to raise additional funds for the expenses incurred in modernizing the company. Unfortunately, by 1987, Onex Packaging was losing money and Schwartz decided to take the company private once again. Not long afterward, he sold Onex Packaging for less than he had originally anticipated.

Having learned a hard business lesson with Onex Packaging, Schwartz was not about to make the same mistake twice. During 1987, as Onex Packaging began to flounder, Schwartz acquired both Norex Leasing, a leading leasing company owned and operated by Citibank, and Purolator Courier Ltd., the leading overnight delivery service in Canada. At the same time, Schwartz decided to make more acquisitions in the United States and began to decrease his holdings in Canada, although his company would always remain based in his native country. This strategy led him to one of the most

important acquisitions during the late 1980s, the purchase of the airline catering company called Sky Chefs.

GROWTH THROUGH ACQUISITIONS: 1990–95

One of the first huge successes of Schwartz's acquisition strategy was Beatrice Foods Canada, Ltd. The company was purchased in 1987 when its parent firm was in the course of being dismantled in Chicago. Schwartz paid a bargain-basement cash price of $21.9 million for the company, although it was valued at a purchase price of slightly more than $300 million. In 1991, the entrepreneur resold the company for $475 million, after a complicated but productive restructuring plan that involved merging Beatrice Foods Canada with two other Canadian dairy firms. Additional acquisitions followed at a quick pace, including ProSource Distribution, a foodservice distributor in both the United States and Canada, and Dura Automotive Systems and Tower Automotive, two high-quality automotive parts manufacturers.

Schwartz's goal with Sky Chefs was to transform it into a leader in the in-flight catering industry. The first step in this direction was an alliance formed between Sky Chefs and LSG Lufthansa Service in 1993. The alliance was formed to give Sky Chefs access to international airline customers that it did not previously have. Revenues for Sky Chefs remained relatively the same from 1991 through 1994, hovering around $470 million annually. During this time, however, Sky Chefs was transformed into the leading low-cost producer of in-flight meals for the airline industry. A policy of cycle-time reduction was implemented in 1992 and resulted in a 30 percent labor production increase over a three-year period.

Although many innovative alliances and policies had been implemented at Sky Chefs during the early 1990s, it was not until 1995 that the company developed a worldwide reputation. Much of this was due to the takeover of Caterair International Corporation, one of the preeminent in-flight catering companies. Funded entirely by third-party lenders, the acquisition of Caterair International propelled Sky Chefs to the top of the industry with slightly less than 50 percent of the U.S. domestic airline catering market and 30 percent of the international airline catering market. The acquisition of Caterair International and the earlier alliance with LSG Lufthansa gave Sky Chefs access to airline customers around the world, including new contracts in Central and South America, as well as in Australia.

```
┌─────────────────────────────────────────┐
│                                           │
│              KEY DATES                    │
│                  ■                        │
│  ─────────────────────────────────────   │
│                                           │
│  1983:  Gerald Schwartz forms Onex        │
│         Capital Corporation with the      │
│         intention of using it as a        │
│         holding company.                  │
│  1987:  Company acquires Beatrice         │
│         Foods Canada, Ltd.                │
│  1995:  In-flight catering company Sky    │
│         Chefs attains global status.      │
│  1996:  Company buys a controlling        │
│         interest in IBM Canada            │
│         subsidiary Celestica.             │
│  1999:  Onex name gains notoriety with    │
│         a failed takeover bid for Air     │
│         Canada and Canadian Airlines.     │
│  2001:  Company's holdings in the         │
│         entertainment industry are        │
│         expanded.                         │
│  2003:  Onex creates its first major      │
│         private-equity fund, Onex         │
│         Partners I.                       │
│  2007:  Onex completes the CAD 2.6        │
│         billion acquisition of Eastman    │
│         Kodak Company's Health            │
│         Group.                            │
│  2010:  Onex joins forces with Canada     │
│         Pension Plan Investment Board     │
│         to complete the acquisition of    │
│         Tomkins plc, a transaction        │
│         valued at $5 billion.             │
│                                           │
└─────────────────────────────────────────┘
```

As the consolidation of in-flight catering services continued through 1995, additional contracts were signed with British Airways, Delta Airlines, USAir, and Midway. By the end of 1995, Sky Chefs counted more than 250 airline customers located in every part of the world, while revenues shot up to $739 million, an increase of 58 percent over the previous year.

As a holding company, one of Onex's top priorities was to enhance the value of shareholder equity. During 1995 this goal was pursued by a number of strategic investments, made primarily under the direction of Schwartz. Onex invested $20 million in Phoenix Pictures, a new film production company owned by Onex, Sony Pictures Entertainment, and Britain's Pearson PLC. The company also purchased Vencap Equities Alberta, Ltd., a promising venture capital fund located in western Canada. Finally, management at Onex formed Rippledwood Holdings, an acquisition fund developed to hold the 52 percent of the company's interest in Dayton Superior Corporation. Other continuing strategic investments included a 19 percent share of Purolator Courier (down from majority ownership a few years earlier), 16 percent of Scotsman

Industries, a manufacturer of ice machines, freezers, food preparation workstations, and refrigerators, and an 8.1 percent share in Alliance Communications, the leading producer and distributor of television entertainment in Canada.

LABATT TAKEOVER ATTEMPT: 1995–96

In the spring of 1995 Schwartz decided to launch a $2.3 billion hostile takeover of John Labatt Ltd., one of the most prominent brewers in Canada. Located in Toronto, Labatt had a long and distinguished history starting as a brewer of fine beers in London, England, in 1847. Controlling approximately 45 percent of the Canadian beer market in North America, second only to Molson, Labatt also had diversified into businesses unrelated to the brewing industry. At the time of Schwartz's attempted takeover, Labatt owned The Sports Network, Le Reseau des Sports, an 80 percent interest in The Discovery Network, a 42 percent interest in Toronto's SkyDome, and a 90 percent stake in the Toronto Blue Jays baseball team.

Unwilling to join the Onex Corporation holdings, management at Labatt began looking for a "white knight" to foil the hostile takeover attempt. After meetings with a number of possible suitors, Labatt finally arranged a deal with Interbrew S.A., a Belgian-based brewery that had been attempting to break into the North American beer market for years. Interbrew cooked up a deal that amounted to $2.7 billion, successfully outbidding Onex Corporation for control of Labatt. After the acquisition was finalized, Interbrew began to sell off Labatt's nonbrewing operations, which had been the sole purpose of Schwartz's attempted takeover of the company.

Although Schwartz was frustrated in his attempt to acquire Labatt, he continued to seek out undervalued companies for acquisition. While committed to running his company from Canadian headquarters, he was reportedly increasingly interested in looking south toward the United States to expand his operations.

NOTABLE DEALS: 1996–99

To appease the markets, many conglomerates shed companies to concentrate on core businesses, but Onex stayed the course. In September 1996, the company announced it was buying a controlling interest in a subsidiary of IBM Canada Ltd. Celestica Inc., a maker of electronic components for computer and telecommunications systems, had sales of about CAD 3 billion in 1995. Onex joined forces with Celestica management in the $700 million transaction, putting up $199 million for a 43 percent equity interest and voting control. Celestica's new circumstances put the company in position to sell to competitors of IBM and thus broaden its customer base.

Celestica completed its IPO in 1998. With a total value of $610 million, it was the largest offering by an electronics manufacturing services (EMS) company and the largest IPO by a technology company in Canadian history. In another 1998 deal, Onex purchased Sofbank Services Group Inc., a U.S. outsourced customer care and fulfillment company. Joining with Canadian contact center North Direct Response, Onex would form ClientLogic.

During 1999, Celestica expanded its capabilities in Europe and South America. With 18 acquisitions over three years and a spate of new global customers, Celestica was the fastest-growing EMS provider in its industry. Onex purchased J.L. French Automotive Castings, a leading supplier of aluminum die-cast components to the automotive industry. In addition, Onex established MAGNATRAX as a growth platform, following the purchase of American Building Company, the third-largest U.S. producer of metal building systems. At year-end, Onex and several of Canada's largest pension funds and financial institutions joined together to form ONCAP, to support small- to midcap investments.

Overall, 1999 was a stellar year for growth. Revenues climbed 69 percent to $14.9 billion. Earnings were up 66 percent to $293.9 million. It was a failed deal, however, that planted the name Onex in the mind of the public. Schwartz bid $1.2 billion to take over and merge Canada's two national airlines, Air Canada and Canadian Airlines. The move was contentious, pulling the Canadian government into the row. Ultimately, the courts assisted Air Canada in blocking the Onex purchase.

TRANSACTIONS AT THE MILLENNIUM

In order to sustain returns Schwartz had to up the ante dealwise. "Net of fees, Onex's annual returns on its 17 deals have averaged 35% over the past 15 years. That's double the average rate of all private-equity outfits and better than KKRs," wrote Bernard Condon for *Forbes* in March 2000.

Onex differed from other buyout companies in some significant ways, such as reliance on public capital to fund deals and retention of purchased companies as a base for consolidation. Onex still held 47 percent of Sky Chefs 13 years after buying into the company. Over the

nine years it held Dura Automotive, 13 car parts businesses had been added to the fold.

In April 2000 Onex withdrew a planned IPO of ClientLogic, citing market instability. Onex and the Ontario Municipal Employees Retirement System (OMERS) took part in a $105 million equity financing of the company in September. ClientLogic had 36 facilities in nine North American and European countries. Revenues for the customer management services provider had been growing from new business and through acquisitions, but the company's net income in 2000 was hurt by infrastructure investment, particularly in Europe. Other businesses needed some tweaking. In the building sector, MAGNATRAX was not getting expected results from its early 2000 acquisition of Jannock Limited. J.L. French's integration of Nelson Metal Products, an aluminum casting company purchased in late 1999, also failed to go as hoped.

In February 2001 Onex bought LeBlanc Ltd. and BMS Communications Services Ltd. Combined, the pair was the largest full-service provider of wireless infrastructure in Canada. Onex formed Radian Communication in the wake of the acquisitions. Other deals in 2001 included the sale of Sky Chefs to Lufthansa. Onex achieved a compound annual return of 30 percent over its 16 years of ownership. Troubled economies hurt some of Onex's business segments in 2001. North American car and light truck as well as building construction industries declined. The high-tech sector also was in trouble. Celestica's growth slid dramatically due to a steep decline in customer demand. In response, the company eliminated jobs and manufacturing plants and turned to low-cost regions for its new acquisitions.

During 2001, Onex prepared for an expansion in the entertainment industry. The company invested in the debt of and developed a restructuring plan for one of the largest owners of movie theaters in North America. Onex and partner Oaktree Capital completed the acquisition of Loews Cineplex following its emergence from bankruptcy in 2002. Onex and Oaktree also purchased a leading theater exhibition company in Mexico, engaged in a Spanish joint venture, and made theatrical purchases in South Korea and Michigan.

DIVERSIFICATION AND NEW INVESTMENT STRATEGY: 2003

Onex moved into a new line of business in 2003. Maryland-based Magellan Health Services, market leader in behavioral managed health care, needed a bailout. Onex Partners LP, a new Onex fund, invested $101 million for approximately 24 percent ownership and controlling interest in the company. Magellan's 2002 revenue was approximately $2.8 billion. Customers included health plans, corporations, unions, and government agencies. Magellan offered administrative services, risk-based services, and employee assistance program services.

The year also marked the beginning of a new way of investing for Onex. Typically, the company invested directly in its transactions, raising funds on a transaction-by-transaction basis. In 2003 Onex began investing through private-equity funds, funds comprising financial commitments from Onex and from institutional investors. The first such fund, Onex Partners I LP, closed in 2003, a CAD 1.65 billion fund that was the first of three private-equity funds launched during the decade.

With a massive war chest at its disposal, Onex began making a series of large, high-profile acquisitions, securing its stature as Canada's largest buyout firm. In 2005 Onex furthered its involvement in the health care sector substantially. The company purchased American Medical Response, Inc., the largest U.S. provider of ambulance transport services, and EmCare Holdings, Inc., the leading U.S. provider of hospital physician staffing and management services, for roughly CAD 1 billion. The company spent another CAD 745 million to acquire Skilled Healthcare Group, Inc., an operator of 70 skilled nursing and assisted living facilities in California, Texas, Kansas, and Nevada.

The year's most notable deal was the purchase of Boeing Co.'s commercial airplane manufacturing facilities in Wichita, Kansas, and Tulsa and McAlester, Oklahoma. Onex paid CAD 1.5 billion for the operations, which made fuselage sections and wing elements, and renamed the business Spirit AeroSystems, Inc.

MAJOR ACQUISITIONS: 2006–11

Major acquisitions followed during the second half of the decade, financed in part by Onex Partners II LP, which closed in 2006. Onex contributed $1.4 billion to the $3.45 billion fund and began making investments, encouraged by the CAD 1 billion the company posted in net earnings during the year. The company acquired The Warranty Group, one of the world's largest providers of extended warranty contracts, for CAD 800 million, in late 2006. At roughly the same time, it collaborated with Goldman Sachs & Co. to acquire Raytheon Aircraft Company, a leading manufacturer of business aircraft, for CAD 3.8 billion. In 2007 three major transactions turned heads in the investment community. Onex completed the CAD 2.6 billion acquisition of Eastman Kodak Company's Health

Group and renamed it Carestream Health, Inc. Next, in partnership with another private-equity firm, The Carlyle Group, Onex acquired Allison Transmission, which designed and produced automatic transmissions for trucks, buses, off-highway equipment, and military vehicles, for $5.5 billion. Before the end of the year, Onex spent CAD 960 million to purchase Husky Injection Molding Systems Ltd., one of Canada's largest manufacturers of injection molding equipment used in the plastics industry.

The size of Onex's third fund, which closed in 2009, reflected the esteem of Schwartz's firm among large, institutional investors. Onex Partners III exceeded its fundraising goal by 60 percent, becoming a $4.3 billion fund, $800 million of which was contributed by Onex. There were several large acquisitions completed during the first two years of the fund's existence, a period that also saw Onex cash in on several of its investments. Onex sold 31 percent of its interest in Spirit AeroSystems, realizing a profit of seven times its original investment. The company sold 35 percent of its interest in EmCare, realizing another sevenfold gain on its investment. It also sold Husky to Berkshire Partners and OMERS Private Equity for $2.1 billion, more than doubling its original investment of CAD 960 million.

The divestitures, which occurred between 2009 and 2011, were made at the same time a series of major acquisitions were completed, purchases financed by Onex Partners III. In 2010 the company purchased the 75 percent it did not already own of ResCare, Inc., the leading U.S. provider of in-home care, job training, and educational support for individuals with developmental and intellectual disabilities, for $340 million. The year also included the purchase of Tomkins plc, a $4.1-billion-in-sales company with substantial holdings in the automotive and building product markets. Onex joined forces with Canada Pension Plan Investment Board to complete the acquisition, a transaction that was valued at $5 billion.

In 2011 Onex invested $871 million in JELD-WEN Holding, Inc., one of the world's leading manufacturers of interior and exterior doors, windows, and related products. Further deals were expected as Onex tapped into the funds within Onex Partners III and prepared for the likely creation of Onex Partners IV, which would give Schwartz and his team the opportunity to display their investing talents on a large scale. During the first three decades of the company's existence, management recorded a 29 percent compound return on its investments, setting a high standard that Onex executives hoped to match in the years ahead.

Thomas Derdak
Updated, Kathleen Peippo; Jeffrey L. Covell

PRINCIPAL OPERATING UNITS

Onex Partners I LP; Onex Partners II LP; Onex Partners III LP; Oncap II; Oncap III; Onex Real Estate Partners; Onex Credit Partners; Direct Investments.

PRINCIPAL COMPETITORS

Berkshire Hathaway Inc.; The Blackstone Group L.P.; Clayton, Dubilier & Rice, Inc.

FURTHER READING

Bagnell, Paul. "Conglomerate No Longer a Dirty Word." *Financial Post*, January 4, 1997.

Condon, Bernard. "Kravis of the North." *Forbes*, March 6, 2000.

Dalglish, Brenda. "A Private Play: Onex Bids $2.3 Billion to Take Over Labatt." *MacLean's*, May 29, 1995.

Henry, John. "Canadian Firm Buys Windsor Door Parent." *Arkansas Business*, April 19, 1999.

"Onex Increases Commitment to Its Flagship Private Equity Fund." *Marketwire Canada*, January 4, 2010.

"Onex to Invest $675 Million in JELD-WEN, World's Largest Residential Door & Window Maker." *Marketwire Canada*, May 4, 2011.

Pearce, Ed. "Gerry Schwartz of Onex." *Ivey Business Journal*, July 2000.

Piotrowski, Julie. "Sailing with Magellan." *Modern Healthcare*, June 2, 2003.

Watson, Thomas. "The Countdown Continues: 49 Onex." *Canadian Business*, May 26, 2003.

Pan American Energy LLC

Avenida Leandro N. Alem 1180
Buenos Aires, C.F. C1001AAT
Argentina
Telephone: (54 11) 4310-4100
Fax: (54 11) 4310-4319
Web site: http://www.pan-energy.com

Private Company
Founded: 1948 as Bridas S.A.
Employees: 1,515
Sales: $2.78 billion (2009)
NAICS: 213111 Drilling Oil and Gas Wells; 213112
Support Activities for Oil and Gas Field Explora-
tion; 325110 Petrochemical Manufacturing;
447190 Other Gasoline Stations

■ ■ ■

Pan American Energy LLC (PAE) is the second-largest
producer of petroleum and natural gas in Argentina and
is also the nation's leading gas exporter. It also has
operations in Bolivia and Chile. The limited liability
company is owned by energy-producing giant BP p.l.c.
(formerly The British Petroleum Company PLC) and
Bridas Corporation, which is owned by Argentina-based
Bridas Energy Holdings Limited and China National
Offshore Oil Corporation International Limited.

OIL-FIELD CONTRACTOR:
1948–80

The origin of Pan American Energy can be traced to
Alejandro Ángel Bulgheroni. The son of a prosperous

businessman in Santa Fe, Argentina, he arrived in Buenos Aires in 1940 and soon learned that Yacimientos
Petróleos Fiscales (YPF), the nation's state-owned oil
company, required a ring, known as a *brida*, in order to
drill for oil. He called a friend who had a small
metalworking shop for support and subsequently won
the bid to supply YPF with *bridas* by offering a low
price.

Bridas S.A. was founded in 1948 and became an
importer of metal parts and machinery needed in the oil
fields not only by YPF but also Shell Oil Company's
Argentine subsidiary. In 1958 the industry was opened
up to other private companies. When contracts extended
by the previous military government were voided in
1963, Pan American International Oil Corporation, an
affiliate of Standard Oil Company (Indiana), lost its
contract with YPF to develop and operate reserves in
three areas of southern Argentina. Bridas took advantage
of the occasion to buy Pan American's drilling rigs in
Argentina for 15 or 20 percent of face value. Bridas's
close ties to the military governments that ruled
Argentina from 1966 to 1983 helped it to win exploration and drilling contracts.

Bridas consisted of seven companies, not all
engaged in hydrocarbons, in 1974, when Bulgheroni
was taken hostage and held for ransom by his own
nephew, a right-wing Peronist guerrilla. He reportedly
never got over the shock, and the direction of what had
become the Bridas group passed to his sons Carlos and
Alejandro. Carlos was the public face of the enterprise,
responsible for its finances and the all-important relations with the government and political go-betweens.

COMPANY PERSPECTIVES

Our mission is to create economic value by exploring and developing new hydrocarbon reserves, and by producing oil and natural gas.

Alejandro was known for technical expertise, strategic planning, and rigorous control of operations.

OIL AND GAS POWERHOUSE: 1980–97

Bridas's revenues totaled MXN 363.63 billion ($189.38 million) in 1980. It advanced to 17th place in Argentina in 1985 with sales of 263 million australes ($210 million). However, the financial crisis that gripped Latin America in this period almost brought down the company, whose debts came to $619 million, fourth-largest among Argentine private groups. Later in the decade, Bridas was accused of taking government funds to finance nonexistent exports and of irregularities in applying government subsidies to make paper from sugarcane bagasse.

In 1990 the group consisted of 17 companies with combined annual revenue of $400 million to $500 million. Petroleum and gas operations represented perhaps 60 percent of this total, but the holding company also had four other divisions. Río Colorado S.A. was the most important Bridas company in the division of petrochemicals and petroleum services. The group also owned a big paper company and various agroindustrial and industrial-services enterprises. Shortly after, however, Bridas divested almost all activities not related to hydrocarbons.

Bridas S.A.P.I.C. was the largest privately owned producer of natural gas in Argentina and had contracts with Gas del Estado, the state-owned transport and distribution company in this sector, to cap, treat, compress, transport, and distribute the gas. It was also taking part in an international consortium developing Argentina's first offshore oil field, in the far south of the country.

The related petrochemical and petroleum services division, led by Río Colorado, included 28 drilling teams, many of them working on contract to YPF or private companies. Servoil S.A. provided engineers, technicians, and personnel for 18 teams in the field. Two other companies produced, marketed, and sold petrochemicals. The most important was Polibutenos

Argentinos, opened in 1982 in Ensenada, Buenos Aires. Supplied by a nearby YPF refinery, it made polybutanes for use in lubricants, additives, and adhesives.

A law came into effect in 1992 enabling the privatization of state activities in the hydrocarbons industry, including pipelines, refineries, shipping terminals, and miscellaneous services. YPF and Gas del Estado were opened to private investment soon after. By 1997 Bridas was the third-largest hydrocarbons producer in Argentina and second in terms of area explored. It was producing about 30,000 barrels of oil a day and 225 million cubic feet of natural gas from 20 fields in Argentina. The company was also operating gas compression and treatment units; participating in the control and operation of oil pipelines and petroleum storage and loading facilities; and producing polybutanes. Through Servoil, it was providing petroleum services in different parts of the world. Since 1978, Bridas had also been producing petroleum in Talara, Peru.

THE CENTRAL ASIAN IMBROGLIO: 1992–96

In 1992 Bridas won two concessions in Turkmenistan, the second-largest natural-gas producer in the former Soviet Union and, reportedly, holder of the world's fourth-largest proven reserves of natural gas. By the end of 1996, when Turkmenistan accounted for 11 percent of Bridas's annual revenue of $367 million, the company was rumored to be ready to sell its Argentine assets and stake everything on its future in Central Asia. Bridas had organized a consortium to propose construction of a pipeline that would transport the gas through neighboring Afghanistan to Pakistan. A 30-year agreement between this consortium and Afghanistan for the construction and operation of the pipeline was signed in 1996.

By this time, however, Turkmenistan had signed a rival deal with California-based Unocal Corporation. Moreover, the internationally recognized government of Afghanistan controlled only a small part of the country, with most of the rest ruled by the Taliban, who were being courted by both Unocal and Bridas. The proposed 790-mile-long conduit became known as "the pipeline from hell," although the venture was again entertained soon after the U.S.-led military intervention in Afghanistan in late 2001. Eight years later, the China National Petroleum Company was completing the world's longest natural gas pipeline, carrying gas from Turkmenistan through Uzbekistan and Kazakhstan to eastern China.

KEY DATES

1948: Bridas is founded as a supplier to oil companies in Argentina.
1990: Bridas has become the nation's largest privately owned producer of natural gas.
1997: Bridas merges with Amoco Argentina Oil to form Pan American Energy (PAE).
2008: PAE's oil output has risen 48 percent and its gas output 95 percent in seven years.
2010: Chinese company CNOOC buys half of Bridas, and hence 20 percent of PAE.

PAN AMERICAN ENERGY: 1997–2000

Regardless of the progress of its Central Asian venture, Bridas remained committed to finding a partner to buttress its finances. The company was reported to have annual revenues of $310 million but debt of at least $400 million and perhaps $600 million, not counting various back taxes allegedly owed the Argentine government. In 1997 it agreed to merge its oil and gas businesses in southern South America with Amoco Argentina Oil Co., a subsidiary of Amoco Corporation. Bridas's interests in Turkmenistan were not included.

The resulting company, Pan American Energy LLC, was 60 percent owned by Amoco and 40 percent by Bridas. It became Argentina's largest hydrocarbons producer next to YPF (which had become an affiliate of Repsol YPF S.A.). Alejandro Bulgheroni was named chairman of the company, while Amoco Argentina's general manager became chief executive officer. However, Amoco merged in 1998 with one of the world's largest energy-producing companies, BP p.l.c. The merged company, BP Amoco p.l.c., was renamed BP p.l.c. in 2000.

YEARS OF GROWTH AND PROSPERITY: 2001–08

Among the Amoco holdings that Pan American Energy inherited was Cerro Dragón, a concession area in the river valley delta bordering Patagonia's San Jorge Gulf. BP's deep pockets and technical knowhow enabled PAE to triple output from this field, which had been deemed past its prime. By 2005 Cerro Dragón was the major oil-producing deposit in Argentina, yielding more than 15,000 cubic meters (92,000 barrels) of oil a day and almost nine million cubic meters of gas a day. All but a small portion of the Rhode Island-sized area lay in the

province of Chubut, and taxes on its yield provided 40 percent of the provincial budget. PAE later extended its concession from the province until 2027, agreeing to invest $2 billion by the end of 2017 and an additional $1 billion through 2027.

In 2001 Pan American's 142,000 barrels a day accounted for 9 percent of Argentina's oil production. By the end of 2002 it had advanced, in terms of annual sales, to 25th in Argentina, with revenues of MXN 2.17 billion ($589.67 million) and a comfortable profit in a year when the country was in deep recession following its recent repudiation of government debt and subsequent devaluation of its currency.

The following years also saw big gains for Pan American Energy. While Argentina's production of oil fell 20 percent between 2001 and 2008, Pan American's own oil production rose by 48 percent. Although Argentina's production of natural gas rose only 6 percent during this period, PAE's gas production rose by 95 percent. The company's proven reserves rose by 43 percent, outstripping even YPF's reserves.

In 2007 Pan American received a $550 million loan from the International Finance Corporation (IFC), part of the World Bank, to aid the company in its exploitation of Cerro Dragón. This loan was the largest ever given to a company by the IFC. The sum was earmarked for investment in drilling wells to obtain oil, natural gas, and water, besides the expansion of treatment systems and electricity-generating plants, among other projects.

CHINESE PARTNER: 2010–11

In 2010 state-owned China National Offshore Oil Company International Limited (CNOOC), the nation's largest international producer of oil, purchased a half-share in Bridas Corporation for $3.1 billion, an acquisition that gave it, in effect, 20 percent of Pan American Energy. It was the Chinese company's largest foreign acquisition ever and was seen as providing China with an energy beachhead in Latin America.

A greater opportunity for the Chinese fell into place later in 2010, after BP found itself in serious need of cash owing to the cost of the pending cleanup of its offshore oil spill in the Gulf of Mexico. Bridas announced, in November, the purchase of BP's 60 percent share of Pan American Energy for $7.06 billion, giving it full control of the company. Nevertheless, a year later the deal had yet to be consummated, owing, BP claimed, to difficulties in obtaining the necessary government permits in both Argentina and China. There was speculation that BP, Bridas, or both parties were dissatisfied with the price that had been agreed upon. Bridas canceled the deal in November 2011.

Pan American Energy was engaged only in the exploration and production of petroleum and natural gas. It had no oil refineries or service stations. However, Bridas entered into these downstream activities in March 2011, when it purchased Exxon Mobil Corporation's 720 Esso service stations in Argentina, Uruguay, and Paraguay. The acquisition also included an oil refinery and two distribution terminals in Argentina, and firms engaged in the wholesale distribution of industrial, marine, and aviation fuels. The purchase price was estimated as at least $700 million.

PRODUCTION, PROFITS, AND PROSPECTS: 2009–11

Pan American Energy was an extremely profitable company in 2009, achieving a net income of $630 million on revenue of $2.78 billion. Its share of oil and gas production in Argentina came to 18 percent of the total in 2010, twice its 9 percent share in 2001. It produced 240,000 barrels a day of petroleum during the year, compared to 142,000 in 2001. It was producing oil and gas in Argentina on its own from three fields and in partnership with other firms from seven additional fields. It also had a quarter-share in a consortium that was operating two Bolivian gas fields. Under exploration and development were 10 concession areas, of which Pan American held three on its own, with the others in partnership. In addition, the company held half of the Coirón concession in Chile. PAE also held minority stakes in an Argentine oil pipeline and gas pipeline, a joint Argentine-Uruguayan gas pipeline, a Uruguayan gas-distribution company, an Argentine marine-storage terminal, and, an Argentine electricity-generation company.

Despite Pan American Energy's favorable results, the business climate for hydrocarbons producers in Argentina was far from ideal. They were required to sell their output in Argentina at half the world price. Producing companies blamed the decline in oil produc-

tion and stagnation in gas production on such disincentives, but the depletion of the nation's biggest deposits was also a major factor.

Pan American Energy's future production was expected to depend on the willingness of BP and CNOOC to spend money in searching for new oil deposits. Without a significant infusion of funds, one expert predicted, reserves in Argentina would continue to fall. PAE said that it planned to invest $1 billion in 2012.

Robert Halasz

PRINCIPAL COMPETITORS

Chevron Argentina S.R.L.; Petrobras Argentina S.A.; Total Austral S.A.; YPF S.A.

FURTHER READING

"Argentina: A Beachhead for China." *Business Latin America*, March 29, 2010, 1–2.

"The Battle to Buy Bridas." *Petroleum Economist*, January 14, 1998, 7.

"Bridas compra activos de Exxon Mobil." *Mercado*, April 2011, 50.

Cohen, Ariel. "'Soy optimista.'" *Perfil*, March 21, 2010, 18–20.

De la Merced, Michael J. "BP's Sale of Argentine Oil Stake Collapses." *New York Times*, November 7, 2011, B5.

Evans, Judith. "The Great Game." *LatinFinance*, September 1997, 73–74.

Gallego-Díaz, Soledad. "China pone un pie en Suramérica." *El País* (Madrid), March 21, 2010, 2.

Majul, Luis. *Los dueños de la Argentina*. Buenos Aires: Editorial Sudamericana, 1992, 61–117.

Manaut, Sergio. "Los Bulgheroni." *Apertura*, March/April 1990, 48–50, 52–54.

Moyano, Julio, ed. *The Argentine Economy*. Buenos Aires: Moyano Comunicaciones, 1997, 338 and 354–55.

Pope, Hugh, and Peter Fritsch. "Pipeline Dreams." *Wall Street Journal*, January 19, 1998, A1, A9.

Petróleo Brasileiro S.A.

Av Republica do Chile 65 - 22 andar, Centro
Rio de Janeiro, RJ 20031-912
Brazil
Telephone: (+55 21) 3224 9901
Fax: (+55 21) 2262 3678
Web site: http://www.petrobras.com

Public Company
Incorporated: 1953
Employees: 80,492
Sales: BRL 213.27 billion ($120.05 billion) (2010)
Stock Exchanges: São Paulo New York
Ticker Symbols: PETR3; PBR
NAICS: 213111 Drilling Oil and Gas Wells; 213112
Support Activities for Oil and Gas Field Exploration; 324110 Petroleum Refineries

■ ■ ■

Petróleo Brasileiro S.A., or Petrobras, is the largest company in Brazil, and is ranked the second-largest oil company in the world by market value. Petrobras is a fully integrated oil and gas company, with operations spanning exploration and production, refining, transport, petrochemicals production, and wholesale and retail distribution. The proven reserves under the company's control include 13.4 billion barrels of oil and 2.6 billion barrels of oil equivalent (BOE) of natural gas. In 2010, Petrobras unveiled a $224 billion investment program designed to boost its proven reserves past 30 billion BOE, and raise production past 6.4 million BOE per day by 2020.

In addition to its assets in Brazil, Petrobras has been developing diversified international operations, including in Argentina, Bolivia, Chile, Colombia, Cuba, Curaçao, Ecuador, Mexico, Paraguay, Peru, the United States, Uruguay, and Venezuela. The company also produces oil in Nigeria, and operates refineries in Japan and the United States. Petrobras's distribution operations span more than 7,300 service stations in Brazil, as well as direct deliveries to more than 11,000 corporate customers. The company is the fourth-largest worldwide in terms of market capitalization. The Brazilian government maintains a majority stake in the company, holding 54 percent directly and another 10 percent indirectly. Petrobras is led by Chairman José Sergio Gabrielli de Azevedo. The company's total revenues topped BRL 213 billion ($120 billion) in 2010, generating net profits of more than BRL 30 billion ($13 billion).

BRAZILIAN OIL INDUSTRY IN THE PRE-WORLD WAR II ERA

Brazil's economic situation prior to the formation of Petrobras reflected long-standing inflation problems and the need to earn foreign exchange. At the end of the 1940s, foreign exchange reserves were dwindling, inflation was creeping upward, and the country was heading for a balance of payments crisis. Ambitious development plans necessitated large-scale imports of energy products. During the first half of the 1950s, Brazil's energy demands, especially for oil and its derivatives, doubled. However, the lack of foreign exchange reserves constrained energy imports and thus industrial expansion. The campaign to develop a domestic oil

COMPANY PERSPECTIVES

Mission: To operate in a safe and profitable manner in Brazil and abroad, with social and environmental responsibility, providing products and services that meet clients' needs and that contribute to the development of Brazil and the countries in which it operates. 2020 Vision: We will be one of the world's five largest energy companies and the preferred choice of our stakeholders.

industry was partly founded on the desire to relieve Brazil of this development constraint.

Politics played a major part in the birth of Petrobras and continued to exercise an unusually strong influence on the affairs of the company throughout most of its existence. The process leading to the creation of Petrobras took several years and ignited a lively political debate. The central issue was whether foreign companies should be allowed to invest in Brazil's domestic oil industry.

Economic nationalists wanted the country's natural resources to be exploited by and for Brazilians. They were a powerful force and fought an effective *o petróleo é nosso* (the oil is ours) campaign. Consequently, Law 2004 of October 3, 1953, which set up Petrobras, created a monopoly over most areas of oil activity within Brazil with no scope for foreign participation.

Implicit in the efforts to set up Petrobras was the unproved assumption that Brazil had large-scale oil reserves. The first attempts to find oil in Brazil took place in the late 19th century on a very small scale. The first explorers tended to be maverick individuals, and foreign companies were not involved. In 1917, the Geographical and Mineralogical Service of Brazil, a state-owned organization, set up a department for oil exploration, but activity by domestic interests was limited in the 1920s. Foreign companies carried out sporadic drilling, mostly in the south.

In the 1930s, the influence of state control and corporatism grew. There were desultory attempts by private Brazilian companies to find oil, but these were unsuccessful. Rumors abounded about the duplicitous designs of international oil companies on Brazil's natural resources.

In 1938, the National Petroleum Council (CNP) was formed by the state. It was placed in overall control of the oil industry and charged with carrying out systematic exploration for oil. CNP remained the official oil policy-making body after the formation of Petrobras. It was CNP that in 1939 made the first proven oil discovery on Brazilian territory, at Lobato. By the end of 1941, CNP had discovered three more fields, all in Recôncavo in the Bahia state in the north of Brazil.

LAUNCHING PETROBRAS IN 1954

Difficulties in obtaining equipment from abroad during World War II held up further development of Brazil's oil industry. By the end of 1943, domestic oil production was only 300 barrels per day, or about 1 percent of total oil consumption. Immediately after the war, there was some relaxation of the strict corporatism of the Estado Novo, the nonsocialist system under which all elements of economic life were directed by the state, and some recognition that domestic capital might be insufficient to develop the industry. However, international investment was not forthcoming. U.S. business was preoccupied with the reconstruction of Europe, and Brazil was a relatively small market with unattractive geology and a history of hostility to foreigners.

The hesitation of the U.S. companies was justified. Brazilian economic nationalism quickly reasserted itself and had strong attractions for many sections of the population. The *o petróleo é nosso* campaign started among students but quickly spread to intellectuals. The army favored tight control over natural resources for reasons of national security, and the xenophobia of the campaign exerted an emotive appeal for a large part of the general populace. By 1950, when domestic production had reached 950 barrels per day, the prospect of a private approach to the development of the oil industry was nil.

The Brazilian government passed legislation establishing a national oil company, Petróleo Brasileiro (Petrobras). The legislation also gave Petrobras a monopoly over most aspects of the country's oil business. Petrobras officially commenced business in 1954, starting up its first refinery the following year.

During the company's first decade of operation, further activities were brought within the scope of its monopoly. In January 1963, Petrobras was granted the monopoly over the distribution of petroleum derivatives to the public sector. This move intensified the company's financial problems, as the government was notoriously slow to pay its debts. In December 1963, Petrobras gained the monopoly over the imports of crude oil into Brazil. Private refiners, Petrobras, and the distributors had previously arranged their own imports. In March 1964, a decree was passed for the nationalization of the private refineries.

Petróleo Brasileiro S.A.

KEY DATES

1954: Petróleo Brasileiro, or Petrobras, begins operations as a government-owned company in Brazil.
1972: Petrobras launches its first international operations.
1990: Petrobras loses its fertilizer and petrochemicals operations as a first phase of its privatization.
1997: Petrobras officially loses its monopoly over the Brazilian market.
2000: Petrobras lists its ADRs on the New York Stock Exchange.
2002: Petrobras purchases majority ownership of Pecom in Argentina for $1 billion.
2011: Petrobras announces plans to invest $225 billion through 2015.

INTERNATIONAL EXPLORATION FROM 1972

Although Petrobras had many successes during its early years, politics came to play an increasingly important role in the management of the company. This politicization arose from Petrobras's failure to find enough oil to free itself from a continuing reliance on government revenue and from the continuing belief that Brazil had massive oil wealth. This belief gave rise to massive misplaced investment. There were frequent politically inspired changes in the top management (Petrobras had no fewer than five presidents in its first decade) and policy continuity was virtually nonexistent.

Stories of ineptitude and even corruption, both in the government and Petrobras, emerged in the early 1960s and Brazil experienced a military coup in early 1964. The removal of Petrobras from the political arena for some time was a direct result of the coup, and the company was able to concentrate on its commercial activities, in which it had some success. By 1966, only 13 years after its formation, Petrobras was listed by *Fortune* as the 88th-largest company in the world outside the United States.

From the beginning, the primary task of Petrobras was to locate and develop Brazil's oil wealth. In 1956, when Juscelino Kubitschek became president of Brazil, domestic oil production was 6,500 barrels per day. Kubitschek set a goal of 40,000 barrels per day for 1960, a target that was already exceeded by 1957. At this time, production was still confined to the Bahia Recôncavo region. Exploration activity was intensified. In the mid-

1960s, activity was concentrated on Bahia, Sergipe, and Maranhão and by the end of 1966 production had reached 150,000 barrels per day. It peaked at 172,000 barrels per day in 1969 before falling to 166,000 barrels per day in 1970 as production from Recôncavo began to decline. In 1970, reserves were estimated at 857 million barrels and new discoveries were only just replacing production.

In 1972, Petrobras began to explore in other countries through its subsidiary Braspetro, as part of a strategy to hold Brazil's oil resources in reserve. The company formed a long list of joint venture partnerships, soon adding operations in 16 countries. The company also took operational responsibility of a number of its joint ventures in such markets as Iraq, Egypt, Algeria, Libya, South Yemen, Colombia, and Ecuador. At the beginning of the 1990s, Braspetro was active to some degree in Angola, Argentina, Colombia, the Congo, Ecuador, the Gulf of Mexico, Libya, Ghana, and the Norwegian and British sectors of the North Sea.

CAMPOS BASIN DISCOVERY IN 1974

Exploration activity continued in Brazil throughout the 1970s. A major breakthrough took place in 1974 with the first discovery of oil in the Campos Basin off the coast of the state of Rio de Janeiro. Subsequent discoveries were made in the next few years. The first commercial production took place in 1977. Ten years later, oil production from the basin was 370,000 barrels per day or about 60 percent of domestic production. The performance of the continental shelf quickly compensated for the depletion of the onshore fields. Offshore deposits accounted for about 75 percent of known reserves, and their location in deep waters encouraged Petrobras to develop its expertise in deep-sea technology.

The discovery of the Albacora and the Marlim fields in the Campos Basin, in November 1984 and February 1985, respectively, marked further milestones in the company's history. The company planned a massive investment effort for these two fields, Brazil's first giant fields, with a view to output of 725,000 barrels per day by the end of the century.

Although exploration and production had been Petrobras's primary activities over the years, the company was active in all phases of the oil business. Refining had always been important to Petrobras. Initially, Brazilian refineries were ill-equipped to deal with the high paraffin content of the crude found in Bahia Recôncavo. At the end of the 1950s, only the Mataripe refinery was up to the task, and domestic crude

340   INTERNATIONAL DIRECTORY OF COMPANY HISTORIES, VOLUME 133

was exported. The majority of the crude processed in Brazilian refineries during this period consisted of imports.

By 1960, Petrobras refineries were processing 250,000 barrels per day of crude oil, equivalent to about 80 percent of Brazilian refined product demand, and domestic refineries were being upgraded to deal with domestic crudes. By 1970, only 2 percent of petroleum product requirements were imported, and Petrobras operated five refineries with a combined throughput capacity of 419,000 barrels per day. A 120,000 barrels per day refinery in São Paulo was built, and expansions were underway at two of the existing refineries.

EXPANDING IN THE EIGHTIES

Petrobras initiated an ongoing "bottom of the barrel campaign," an attempt to yield higher-value products, to bring its products yielded by the refining of crude oil in line with final demand. The aim was to yield lower quantities of heavy fuel oil and greater quantities of diesel oil. Petrobras also experimented with heavy ends cracking (secondary refining of heavy fuel oil to produce lighter products), which enabled the company to refine surplus fuel oil further into diesel oil and liquefied petroleum gas (LPG). By 1989, Petrobras was operating 10 refineries and one asphalt plant, which had a combined maximum processing capacity of 1.4 million barrels per day of oil. That year an average of 1.2 million barrels per day of crude oil was processed to yield LPG (8 percent), gasoline (16.1 percent), diesel oil (34.9 percent), fuel oils (17.9 percent), and other oil products (23.1 percent).

Petrobras's refining profile was influenced by the Proalcool campaign (National Alcohol Program), which began in 1975 as a reaction to the 1973 oil price hike. The plan was to substitute the use of gasoline in private cars with alcohol produced from sugarcane. Initially, this policy had some success. However, production problems and the massive subsidies needed to make alcohol competitive with gasoline during the mid-1980s plunged the program into chaos. This caused Petrobras to revise its gasoline production capacity upward.

Despite Brazil's increasing oil production, a large proportion of the oil refined in Brazil came from abroad. In order to save valuable foreign exchange, Petrobras maintained a major stake in the National Tanker Fleet (Fronape), which ended the 1980s with 68 ships and 21 vessels under construction. In 1989, Fronape transported 89 million tons of crude oil, refined products, alcohol, and related products. Petrobras-owned vessels were responsible for 57 percent of this total.

DISTRIBUTION LEADER IN 1989

Petrobras also bolstered operations in distribution through its subsidiary Petrobras Distribuidora. Distribution was not included in the company's monopoly, and international oil companies were allowed to continue to participate in this sector. Petrobras opened its first service station in 1961. By 1966 the company had become the third-largest distribution firm in Brazil, with 174 service stations. By 1989, its distribution arm was firmly established as the nation's leading oil and hydrated alcohol product retailer with a 37.3 percent share of the domestic market and sales amounting to the equivalent of $4.3 billion.

Diversification into petrochemicals was another obvious option for Petrobras, which, even when it was not directly involved in the production of chemicals, was the major supplier of raw materials, mainly naphtha and natural gas, to the private sector in Brazil. During the 1950s Petrobras constructed a unit for ammonia and nitrogenous fertilizers in São Paulo and a styrene butadiene rubber unit at Duque de Caxias in the state of Rio de Janeiro.

During the 1960s, the Brazilian petrochemical industry expanded rapidly, and Petrobras established its first subsidiary, Petrobras Química (Petroquisa), in which it held a 51 percent interest, to oversee its role in this development. The Petroquisa system grew to include Petroquisa itself and 35 other companies in which it had a direct share. The product range included the major plastics, aromatics, synthetic rubbers, methanol, caprolactam, caustic soda, detergents, ethylene oxide, and monoethylene glycol.

ECONOMIC LIBERALIZATION PROGRAM IN 1990

The arrival of the free-market-oriented Collor government introduced a new era in Petrobras's history. As part of its economic liberalization campaign, the Collor government began plans to break up the Petroquisa system through a series of privatizations and shutdowns, a fate that also awaited other Petrobras subsidiaries. As part of this process, Petrobras Fertilizantes (Petrofértil), comprising five subsidiaries and two affiliated companies, responsible for supplying 84 percent of the nitrogenous and 45 percent of the phosphate fertilizers consumed in Brazil, was sold at the beginning of the 1990s.

Interbras and Petrobras Mineração (Petromisa), two subsidiaries, were to be closed. Interbras, the company's international trading arm, was founded in 1976, and handled exports of coffee, cocoa, soybeans, sugar, processed foods, petroleum products and alcohol, vehicles, heavy machinery and equipment, chemicals and petrochemicals, steel and metal products, minerals, and fertilizers. Petromisa was originally set up to produce potassium fertilizers. It subsequently diversified into other mineral products.

In this way, Petrobras refocused around a core of oil exploration and production, while remaining the largest player in Brazil's distribution sector as well. The company maintained its monopoly on oil exploration and production through the first half of the 1990s, while facing increasing competition in its liberalized distribution market. Nonetheless, with a network of more than 7,000 service stations into the next decade, Petrobras remained a dominant player in this market.

INCREASING PRODUCTION IN THE NINETIES

Petrobras set out to achieve the Brazilian government's ambitious oil production goals as the company sought to reduce its dependence on the international oil market during the 1990s. This effort included a major investment program designed to increase Petrobras's capacity from 726,000 barrels per day to more than one million per day by the middle of the decade. As part of its investments, Petrobras launched its first deepwater and ultra-deepwater drilling and oil production projects in the Campos Basin oil fields. Petrobras soon established itself as the world's leader in deepwater technologies.

Petrobras's exploration efforts bore fruit during the decade, raising its reserves to 10.3 billion BOE, of which 5.1 billion BOE had already been proven. By 1995, the company's oil production had already reached 800,000 BOE, and was on track to reach the one million mark by 1997. Petrobras's refinery operations had also grown strongly, with a total of 11 refineries processing more than 1.5 million barrels per day. The company planned to expand both its oil production and processing volumes, announcing a $20 billion investment plan through the end of the decade.

The Brazilian government began reducing its shareholding in Petrobras during the 1990s, listing the company on the Bolsa de Valores de São Paolo. This dropped the government's stake to just 81.4 percent in 1992. In 1995, the government pushed ahead with the liberalization of the country's oil sector, amending the constitution to end Petrobras's monopoly. This legislation took effect in 1997. Petrobras nonetheless remained the overwhelming leader in the Brazilian market, and continued to enjoy a de facto monopoly for some years to come, particularly in the refining and transportation segments.

The government soon signaled its willingness to open up its oil exploration market. In 1999, for example, when the ANP (Brazil's National Petroleum Agency) awarded a round of 12 concessions, 10 foreign companies were among the winners. Seven of the concessions were awarded without Petrobras as a partner, the first time in the company's history.

The loss of its monopoly status led Petrobras to step up its efforts to increase its international position. In 1998, the company won an oil exploration contract off of the north coast of Cuba. Petrobras also took its first steps to reenter the petrochemicals market, forming the Petroquisa petrochemicals division, which gathered a 15 percent stake in Brazil's three petrochemical plants. Petrobras's oil output had also risen strongly, passing 1.13 million BOE per day by the end of 1999.

WORLD RECORD IN 2000

Petrobras marked the new millennium with a major new oil discovery in Santos Basin, holding reserves as high as 700 million BOE. The company also broke its own record for deepwater drilling in 1999, reaching a depth of 6,079 feet (1,870 meters) in the Roncador Field in the Campos Basin. Roncador, with estimated reserves of 2.7 billion BOE, was initially slated to produce 180,000 barrels per day, with future plans to drill another 21 wells expected to increase its output dramatically. In addition, Petrobras announced a new investment plan for nearly $33 billion through 2005.

Nearly 70 percent of this figure was earmarked for further exploration projects as part of an effort to transform Petrobras into a major player on the global oil market. The company targeted an increase in crude oil production, to 1.8 million BOE per day, and a rise in revenues from $22 billion in 1999 to as much as $35 billion in 2005. The company's plans included a further push into the international market, targeting concessions in West Africa and the Gulf of Mexico, as well as in other markets in South America.

Petrobras entered the new decade in crisis mode, however, when a ruptured pipeline at its refinery in Rio de Janeiro poured more than 1.3 million liters (117,000 barrels) of fuel oil into Guanabara Bay in 2000. The spill became the worst in Brazil's history. In 2001, the company suffered a new setback when an explosion sank its P-36 platform, which had been the largest floating oil platform in the world.

On a more positive note, however, the company had celebrated a listing on the New York Stock Exchange, in the form of American Depositary Receipts (ADRs), in September 2000. The successful listing boosted the group's market capitalization, raising the company into the ranks of the world's top 10 publicly traded oil companies. The company soon made good on its promise to enter the U.S. market, acquiring 13 blocks in the Garden Banks oil field in the Gulf of Mexico in 2000, followed by the purchase of an oil refinery there for $600 million, in 2001. In that year, the company made a major discovery in the Garden Banks oil field, with estimated reserves of 40 million BOE.

ARGENTINA ENTRY IN 2002

The company soon pursued its Latin American expansion as well. In 2002, the company paid over $1 billion to acquire 59 percent of Perez Companc, or Pecom, the second-largest oil producer in Argentina, and then spent another $88.5 million buying its smaller oil and natural counterpart Petrolera Santa Fe. Petrobras had also begun negotiations for acquisitions in Venezuela and Uruguay. In 2004 the company also spent $20 million to construct a refinery in Cuba for producing lubricants. This investment was followed by an agreement with the Bolivian government to acquire oil concessions there for $5 billion.

At mid-decade, Petrobras also quietly began investing in the petrochemicals sector, acquiring a low-density polyethylene plant in Argentina, and raising its stake in Petroquimica Triunfo to 80 percent. The Pecom acquisition had also given the company control over a number of thermoplastic production subsidiaries, as well as a majority stake in Brazilian styrene and polystyrene producer Innova. The company quickly came out of the shadows, constructing a $240 million polypropylene plant in São Paulo in partnership with Braskem.

In the meantime, Petrobras had made progress in increasing its oil and natural gas production, topping two million BOE per day by 2003. In 2006, the company announced a new investment program, of $87.1 billion to be spent between 2007 and 2011, in order to increase its capacity to 3.49 million BOE per day. That year, the company marked a new milestone, when it began production at its P-50 platform in Campos Basin. The addition of this new production capacity meant that Brazil, through Petrobras, had now joined the ranks of oil exporter nations.

WORLD'S LARGEST FOR 2020

Petrobras's exploration operations continued their successful run. In 2007, the company discovered a massive gas field in the Santos Basin. This was soon followed by the discovery of what was described as the largest oil find of the century, in deep-sea fields with reserves estimated to be the third largest in the world. These discoveries led Petrobras to revise its investment program upward. In 2009, the company announced plans to spend $174 billion through 2014. Just one year later, Petrobras proposed spending $225 billion through 2015, with more than half to be spent on exploration and production.

Part of this funding came from a new share offering, in 2010, which raised $70 billion. This became the largest share offering in history. With a market value of $226 billion, Petrobras had joined the ranks of the world's top five largest companies, and ranked behind only Exxon Mobil among the world's largest oil companies. The company's investment program was designed to position the company still higher, boosting its total production from 2.77 million BOE per day to four million in 2015 in order to match Exxon Mobil's own output. By 2020, however, Petrobras expected its total output to reach 6.4 million BOE. Petrobras planned to become not only the world's largest oil company, but also the largest publicly traded corporation as well. Since its beginnings as a small oil producer in the 1950s, Petrobras had succeeded in becoming the largest corporation in Latin America and one of the global oil industry's leaders in the new century.

Debra Johnson
Updated, M. L. Cohen

PRINCIPAL SUBSIDIARIES

Transpetro, Petrobras Transporte S.A.; Petrobras Distribuidora SA; Petrobras Química S.A.; Gaspetro SA.

PRINCIPAL DIVISIONS

Gas and Power; Exploration and Production; Refining, Transportation and Marketing; International; Services.

PRINCIPAL OPERATING UNITS

Petroquisa; Petrobras Distribuidora/Liquigas; TBG; Transpetro.

PRINCIPAL COMPETITORS

China National Petroleum Corporation; Elf Aquitaine S.A.; Royal Dutch Shell PLC; Saudi Arabian Oil Co.; SINOPEC Jianghan Oilfield Co.; Uzbekneftegaz State Holding Co.

FURTHER READING

Fontevecchia, Agustino. "Petrobras CFO on Becoming Bigger Than Exxon and Apple: I Buy Oil Every Day, iPads Every 2

Years." *Forbes*, July 29, 2011.

Giromel, Richard. "Will Petrobras Become the World's Largest Company?" *Forbes*, August 18, 2011.

Kepp, Michael. "Petrobras Explores Abroad." *Latin Trade*, April 2003, 34.

———. "Plastic Fantastic." *Latin Trade*, July 2004, 54.

"New Horizons." *Banker*, March 1, 2009.

"Over a Barrel." *Economist*, September 4, 2010, 72.

"Petrobras: Massive Discoveries and the Case for Downstream."

Forbes, November 14, 2011.

"Petrobras Pursuing Ultradeep Oil and Sugarcane Ethanol." *Technology Review*, September–October 2010, 96.

"Plunging In." *Economist*, February 14, 2009, 57.

Sissell, Kara. "Petrobras Slowly Makes a Return to Petrochemicals." *Chemical Week*, May 12, 2004, 17.

"Welcome to the NYSE, Petrobras." *Oil & Gas Interests*, September 1, 2000.

Pioneer Natural Resources Company

5205 North O'Connor Boulevard, Suite 200
Irving, Texas 75039
U.S.A.
Telephone: (972) 444-9001
Fax: (972) 969-3576
Web site: http://www.pxd.com

Public Company
Incorporated: 1997
Employees: 2,248
Sales: $2.47 billion (2010)
Stock Exchanges: New York
Ticker Symbol: PXD
NAICS: 211111 Crude Petroleum and Natural Gas
Extraction

■ ■ ■

Pioneer Natural Resources Company is a gas and oil exploration, development, and production company, with onshore and offshore properties in the United States and South Africa. Domestic properties are divided into a number of operating areas, including south Texas, the Rockies, Mid-Continent, Alaska, Barnett Combo, Eagle Ford Shale, and Permian. Through its Oooguruk project in Alaska, Pioneer became the first independent industry player to operate a producing field on the North Slope. The company has proven reserves of one billion barrels of oil equivalent (BOE) and averages daily production of 115,000 BOE.

ORIGINS

Pioneer Natural Resources Company was formed in April 1997 through the merger of Parker & Parsley Petroleum Company and Mesa, Inc. The two companies' histories in the oil and gas industry dated back to the 1950s and 1970s, respectively. Mesa CEO Jon Brumley initiated the merger after Richard Rainwater, a wealthy investor who saved Mesa from bankruptcy in 1996, hired Brumley for the purpose of helping Mesa grow beyond its debt-ridden state.

Brumley found an interest and a good strategic fit in Parker & Parsley. Upon shareholder approval in August, Pioneer opened on the New York Stock Exchange at slightly more than $37 per share. Parker & Parsley Chairman Scott Sheffield took the positions of president and CEO and Brumley became chairman.

The merger formed the third-largest independent oil and gas exploration and production company at that time. The new company owned reserves primarily located in the West Panhandle and Spraberry Trend fields in Texas and the Hugoton field in Kansas. These long-lived resources provided a dependable base of low-risk revenues that could be invested to expand the company.

EARLY GROWTH

Pioneer planned to increase development and production in these areas, including 600 development wells in Spraberry Trend. Pioneer also planned exploration and development in 200 locations at the Greenhill Petroleum properties in the Gulf of Mexico just

COMPANY PERSPECTIVES

Pioneer Natural Resources is a large independent exploration and production company focused on delivering competitive and sustainable results.

purchased by Mesa. Pioneer's goal was to double its growth over five years, primarily through acquisition, seeking opportunities in the east Texas basin, the Rocky Mountain region, and Canada. The company prepared to increase exploration as well, by expanding its team of geoscientists, particularly with expertise in deepwater exploration.

Seeking to improve the company's cash flow, Pioneer expanded immediately through two acquisitions. In September Pioneer announced an agreement to acquire Chauvco Resources Ltd., of Calgary, Alberta, involving properties in western Canada and Argentina with 153 million proven BOE of gas and oil properties and a backlog of 1,700 drilling locations. The $1.2 billion stock transaction involved a stock exchange valued at $975 million and $220 million in assumed debt.

In October Pioneer announced that it would acquire assets in the west Texas Permian Basin from subsidiaries of Belgium's Electrafina, for $157 million in cash and stock. Pioneer obtained producing wells, land, seismic data and royalties, and a gathering system, pipeline, and gas processing plant. Pioneer became one of the largest holders of acreage in the east Texas basin, with assets producing 25 million cubic feet per day (MMcfd) of gas.

To fund acquisitions and maintain cash flow Pioneer sold several properties that no longer fit with the company's goals. Pioneer sold properties in the Permian Basin for $55 million in cash and properties in Oklahoma, the Texas Panhandle, and along the Gulf of Mexico in Texas and Louisiana for $50 million. The company placed for sale another 425 properties originally owned by Parker & Parsley, accounting for 95 percent of domestic fields but only 15 percent of cash flow.

OVERSUPPLY CONSTRICTS REVENUES

Pioneer's pursuit of growth encountered major difficulties when gas and oil prices declined significantly in late 1997. This decreased the value of certain reserves and forced the company to sell many properties. In the fourth quarter Pioneer took a noncash write-down of $863 million on certain reserves, resulting in a loss of $890.7 million on revenues of $546 million in 1997.

As prices continued to decline in 1998, to as low as $10 per barrel of oil, Pioneer reduced its 1998 capital budget from $600 million to $480 million, allocating $265 million to develop producing wells, $115 million for exploration, and $60 million in property acquisitions. Other cost reduction activities included consolidation of administration activities to the Irving, Texas headquarters and closure of the Corpus Christi, Texas, office, eliminating 200 staff positions. In 1999 the company closed offices in Houston and Oklahoma City, eliminating an additional 150 jobs.

NEW DISCOVERIES

Pioneer's new emphasis on exploration resulted in significant oil and gas discoveries in 1998 and 1999. Using the latest 3-D seismic imaging technology, Pioneer made a significant discovery at the Greenhill properties along the Gulf Coast off Louisiana, which tested at 3,000 barrels per day (Bbl/d) of oil and 7 MMcfd of gas. Through a joint venture with state-owned Soeker Exploration & Production Pty, Ltd., in which Pioneer owned a 49 percent interest, the company made the Sable oil discovery in shallow water offshore South Africa in June 1998. In the deepwater Gulf, a joint venture made the March 1999 Aconcagua discovery in a lease property known as Mississippi Canyon Block 35, in which Pioneer owned a 25 percent interest. Exploration continued in South Africa, Gabon, Argentina, and gas fields in Canada.

For 1999 the $300 million capital budget was cut further as low gas and oil prices hindered cash flow. In April 1999 Pioneer halted plans for exploratory drilling at offshore sites in South Africa and the U.S. Gulf Coast Transition Zone. Exploration continued in both the deepwater Gulf and onshore wells in Louisiana and Texas. Pioneer also allocated $100 million to develop gas wells in Canada, Argentina, and the U.S. mainland.

To service a high level of debt Pioneer divested properties in 1999, including many along the Gulf Coast, for a total of $410 million. In May the company sold a package of 400 domestic oil fields to Prize Energy, formed by executives and directors of Pioneer who resigned their positions to lead the new company. Pioneer received $215 million in cash and $30 million in stock from Prize.

Pioneer sold additional properties through 10 separate deals for a total of $105 million. The largest sale, at $62.3 million, involved natural gas properties in south Texas. The company sold noncore Canadian

KEY DATES

1997: Pioneer is formed through a merger of Mesa, Inc. and Parker & Parsley Petroleum Company.

1999: Pioneer divests properties and halts certain exploration projects.

2000: Higher commodity prices support expansion and profitability.

2001: Exploration yields discoveries in the Gulf of Mexico and offshore of Gabon.

2003: Production begins at the Falcon discovery; exploration yields three satellite discoveries.

2006: Company begins emphasizing lower-risk onshore drilling projects in North America.

2010: A $1.15 billion joint venture is established with Reliance Industries Ltd.

properties and the west Texas field, but kept its northeast British Columbia property, the Chinchaga gas field, where a gas pipeline was under construction.

The sale of property resulted in a profit for the third quarter of 1999, but Pioneer ended the year with a loss of $22.5 million on revenues of $644.6 million. While revenues represented a 9 percent decline from 1998, these were derived from fewer working assets, as Pioneer had become a more streamlined company.

A NEW MILLENNIUM

Pioneer's capital investment focused on opportunities that would provide long-term reserves. In November 1999 Pioneer acquired two properties in Argentina's Neuquén Basin for $40 million, involving eight blocks over 230,000 acres. The properties held net proven reserves of 7.7 million BOE with existing wells producing 2,000 Bbl/d and 9 MMcfd. Pioneer planned to invest $1.2 billion during the course of 17-year concession contracts. Exploration at the new property procured a discovery with the first well in the Al Sur de la Dorsal Block in February 2000.

Pioneer continued to improve its operating cash flow in 2000, selling shares of Prize Energy for $18.6 million in March 2000. The company also divested $102.7 million in properties located in Oklahoma, Louisiana, and New Mexico. The company sought funding through the issuance of $400 million in 10-year bonds, but stopped the plan when interest lagged. Oil and gas prices continued to rise during 2000, however.

This allowed Pioneer to improve its balance sheet without the bonds and to expand its holdings through incremental increases in existing interests.

In late 2000 Pioneer invested a total of $38 million in development properties, notably in the deepwater Gulf of Mexico discoveries and Chinchaga gas fields. For $23 million the company acquired 12 nonproducing blocks in the Gulf of Mexico, including a 33.3 percent interest in the Camden Hills gas discovery in Mississippi Canyon, for a total 18 percent interest in the Canyon Express development project where the Aconcagua discovery was located. Pioneer increased to 20 percent its interest in the Devil's Tower oil discovery in Mississippi Canyon. Pioneer became sole owner of the Chinchaga gas field in British Columbia, acquiring the remaining 13 percent interest in that property. The company planned 70 extension and infill wells at Chinchaga over the next three drilling seasons.

PROFITABILITY

During 2000, Pioneer became a profitable company. Although the company's producing assets had declined significantly, higher gas and oil prices offset the changes. Revenues of $852.7 million and net profit of $152.2 million originated from 4,717 gross productive wells.

Pioneer prepared for long-term growth through exploration and development. Of 1,168 gross development and exploratory wells drilled from 1998 to 2000, 92 percent were successfully completed as productive. As immediate demand and commodity prices rose, Pioneer increased production and development.

In 2000 Pioneer put 86 oil wells into production at Spraberry Trend and 51 gas wells at the West Panhandle field, and two development wells were completed at the Hugoton field in 2000. In Canada 17 of 21 development wells and 12 of 14 development wells were successfully completed. In Argentina, 28 of 30 development wells and 38 of 54 exploratory wells were successfully completed.

CONSOLIDATING ASSETS AND DEVELOPING NEW DISCOVERIES

As Pioneer returned to profitability, the company increased its 2001 capital budget to $430 million. Pioneer expected its hedging contracts to produce more cash flow than the capital budget required. This allowed the company to apply excess funds to debt reduction, stock repurchase, core area acquisitions, and further development. With the help of higher oil and natural gas prices, the company reduced its debt from $1.6 billion to $700 million during the second quarter of 2001.

Overseas, Pioneer was successful in finding significant oil and gas in the Boomslang prospect south of Mossel Bay, South Africa. Pioneer owned a 49 percent working interest in the joint venture with the state-owned Soeker. In May Pioneer made a discovery in Gabon at Olowi block in offshore West Africa, a wholly owned working interest.

Deepwater Gulf of Mexico exploration resulted in the Falcon discovery in April and the Ozona Deep discovery in October, with Pioneer owning a 45 percent interest and a 32 percent interest in the properties, respectively. The Ozona Deep discovery represented the company's 13th successful discovery of 17 exploration wells drilled in the Gulf of Mexico since 1998. Exploration of deepwater locations resulted in a discovery at the Turnberry prospect as well, where Pioneer owned a 40 percent working interest.

MERGER OF 42 PARKER & PARSLEY

Pioneer completed the merger of 42 Parker & Parsley Limited Partnerships, involving privately and publicly owned stock. Shareholders approved the merger in December 2001. Four partnerships, however, did not approve the merger and remained partially owned subsidiaries of the company.

Pioneer issued $99.2 million in a stock exchange. Aggregate reserves of the partnerships involved 29 million BOE of gas and oil reserves, including the dependable Spraberry Trend. In other business, Pioneer increased its interests in the Aconcagua field and Canyon Express pipeline project, to 37.5 percent and 23.5 percent, respectively, for $25.5 million.

In the spring of 2002 Pioneer offered 11 million new shares of stock at $21.40 per share, netting $235 million to fund $193 million in acquisitions. In addition, the company sold $150 million in senior notes to refinance debt. Acquisitions involved increasing the company's working interest in several development projects.

Pioneer acquired a 25 percent interest in the Falcon field, increasing its interest to 75 percent. The project became the first deepwater Gulf project for Pioneer to operate. Pioneer acquired an additional 25 percent working interest in 11 blocks in the vicinity of the Falcon field, as well as a 100 percent interest for 10 development blocks in the area. In addition, Pioneer became the sole owner of field and gathering systems at the West Panhandle gas field.

DEVELOPMENT FOCUS

With a capital budget of $425 million in 2002, Pioneer prepared to exploit its discoveries with several projects in development for initial production in 2002 and 2003. Development of discoveries in the deepwater Gulf involved the Falcon and Devil's Tower discoveries, with production expected to begin in 2003 and 2004, respectively. The Sable oil well development project began in late 2001, with initial production slated to begin within 12 to 18 months. Gas production began at the Camden Hills discoveries at Canyon Express in September 2002, extracting 110 to 120 MMcfd of gas with prices rising to new highs. During 2002 Pioneer placed 89 new wells on production at the Spraberry Trend and 40 wells at West Panhandle and began evaluation of new development sites at Hugoton.

In September 2002 Pioneer found oil in Tunisia's Ghadames Basin, where the company owned a 40 percent working interest. The primary zone at Adam 1 well tested at 3,500 Bbl/d. Through use of nearby production facilities development of the well progressed quickly and production began in May 2003, with first sales expected by the end of the year. Pioneer continued development and exploration in the Adam concession as well as exploration in the Anaquid permit, the latter operated by Anadarko.

Progress in other international locations involved renegotiation of Pioneer's exploration interests in Gabon and initial production at the Sable field, after some delays due to problems with leased equipment, in late 2003. In Argentina's Neuquén Province a $23 million liquefied petroleum gas plant began production. Pioneer concentrated activities on extension and development wells in the oil reserves in the Neuquén Basin.

CONTINUED GROWTH

The company acquired a 70 percent working interest in oil exploration on Alaska's North Slope. Pioneer operated 10 leases covering 14,000 acres in the Kuparuk River field for its partner Armstrong Resources. In early 2003 the company drilled three exploration wells in NW Kuparuk, testing for possible extension wells in shallow waters offshore. Potential production at the Kuparuk prospects was estimated at one half billion BOE, with production expected to begin in 2005, increasing to 50,000 to 75,000 barrels of oil per day by 2008.

Pioneer acquired full interest in 32 blocks at the Falcon discovery area in June 2003 for $113 million cash. The acquisitions included the Harrier field, a satellite discovery made in early 2003. Production began at Falcon in April and tie-back production from the Harrier field was expected to be completed in early 2004.

Pioneer estimated that together the Falcon and Harrier wells would produce 275 MMcfd in gas. Exploration procured two additional discoveries, the Tomahawk prospect and the Raptor field, in August and September, respectively. Pioneer planned to tie-back the Tomahawk and Raptor wells to Falcon platform for production in 2004. The tie-back system provided a cost-efficient method of expanding production and the Falcon facility accommodated up to 400 MMcfd. In early 2004 Pioneer established a joint exploration venture in West Africa with Kosmos Energy. The enterprise would concentrate on a coastal area stretching from Angola to Morocco. A major deal unfolded midway through the year when Pioneer announced plans to acquire Denver, Colorado-based Evergreen Resources for $2.1 billion. Evergreen was engaged in the production of gas in the Rocky Mountains. The two companies finalized the deal later in the year.

A SHARPER FOCUS

Pioneer began 2005 by selling its oil and gas fields in Canada to Ketch Resources in a $207 million deal. During the middle part of the year the company also sold its stake in the African Olowi Block in a $49 million deal. In addition, by early 2006 Pioneer was finalizing the sale of its deepwater assets in the Gulf of Mexico, as well as the company's oil and gas properties in Argentina.

Moving forward, CEO Scott Sheffield said that Pioneer would be a smaller, more focused organization. Although analysts were skeptical about the company's growth plans, Sheffield said that Pioneer would attempt to achieve growth of at least 10 percent over the following five years. At this time the company also planned to begin emphasizing lower-risk onshore drilling projects in North America. This was reflected in the company's land holdings in south Texas, which grew to exceed 170,000 acres.

By mid-2007 Pioneer had established publicly traded master limited partnerships in southern Colorado's Raton basin field and Spraberry field. Around the same time, the company announced that it was shutting down its exploration efforts in Nigeria. In addition, it announced plans to make an initial public offering (IPO) of Pioneer Southwest Energy Partners LP, which had been formed to focus on the ownership of oil and gas properties in Permian Basin.

Pioneer ended 2007 by finalizing several large transactions. In addition to investing $150 million in the Barnett Shale play, the company expanded its presence in the Raton and Spraberry field via an investment of $295 million. In all, these efforts netted Pioneer an additional 1,000 drilling sites.

INCREASED CAPITAL SPENDING

The Pioneer Southwest Energy Partners IPO took place in April 2008. The company offered 8.3 million shares of Pioneer Southwest Energy common stock, which began trading under the symbol PSE on the New York Stock Exchange. After weathering challenging times in 2009, when the company's capital spending budget totaled $300 million, Pioneer announced it would ramp up spending to nearly $900 million in 2010.

By early 2010 Pioneer was seeking a joint venture partner, so that it could accelerate development efforts in south Texas' Eagle Ford Shale gas play. In June the company announced that it had found a partner in Reliance Industries Ltd., with which it established a $1.15 billion joint venture. It also was in 2010 that Pioneer made plans to double gross production in the Permian Basin. Specifically, the company set its sights on increasing the number of operational rigs in the basin from 12 to 24 by the end of the year. By 2012 Pioneer said it would have 40 rigs in operation.

Pioneer began 2011 by announcing the divestiture of its subsidiaries in Tunisia. In a deal worth $866 million, the company sold its Tunisian operations to a subsidiary of the Austrian industrial company OMV AG. In August Pioneer announced that it was increasing its 2011 capital budget by 17 percent, to $2.1 billion. The increased spending would enable the company to deepen wells in west Texas. Heading into 2012, Pioneer appeared to have a sharp focus and excellent prospects for continued growth.

Mary Tradii
Updated, Paul R. Greenland

PRINCIPAL SUBSIDIARIES

Pioneer Natural Resources USA, Inc.; Pioneer International Resources Company; Pioneer Shelf Properties Incorporated.

PRINCIPAL COMPETITORS

Anadarko Petroleum Corporation; Exxon Mobil Corporation; Hess Corporation.

FURTHER READING

Kelly, Andrew. "Pioneer Sets Double-Digit Growth Target for Next Five Years." *Oil Daily*, March 10, 2006.

"Pioneer Announces Commencement of Pioneer Southwest Energy Partners Initial Public Offering." *Business Wire*, April 22, 2008.

"Pioneer Natural Resources and Evergreen Resources Have Completed Their $2.1bn Merger." *Petroleum Economist,* November 2004, 44.

"Pioneer Natural Resources Announces Closing of $1.15 Billion Eagle Ford Shale Joint Venture with Reliance Industries." *Business Wire,* June 29, 2010.

"Pioneer Natural Resources Divests Tunisia Subsidiaries for USD866m." *M2 EquityBites,* January 6, 2011.

"Pioneer to Exit Nigeria." *Oil Daily,* July 18, 2007.

Spencer, Starr. "Pioneer Ups Capex by 17% to $2.1 Billion." *Platt's Oilgram News,* August 5, 2011.

The Procter & Gamble Company

---■---

One Procter & Gamble Plaza
Cincinnati, Ohio 45202-3315
U.S.A.
Telephone: (513) 983-1100
Fax: (513) 983-9369
Web site: http://www.pg.com

Public Company
Founded: 1837 as Procter & Gamble
Incorporated: 1890
Employees: 129,000
Sales: $82.56 billion (2011)
Stock Exchanges: New York Euronext Paris
Ticker Symbols: PG (New York); PGP (Paris)
NAICS: 311111 Dog and Cat Food Manufacturing; 322291 Sanitary Paper Product Manufacturing; 325412 Pharmaceutical Preparation Manufacturing; 325611 Soap and Other Detergent Manufacturing; 325612 Polish and Other Sanitation Good Manufacturing; 325620 Toilet Preparation Manufacturing; 332211 Cutlery and Flatware (Except Precious) Manufacturing; 335129 Other Lighting Equipment Manufacturing; 335211 Electric Housewares and Household Fan Manufacturing; 335911 Storage Battery Manufacturing; 335912 Primary Battery Manufacturing; 339994 Broom, Brush, and Mop Manufacturing

■ ■ ■

The Procter & Gamble Company (P&G) is a giant in the area of consumer goods. The leading maker of household products in both the United States and the world, P&G has operations in about 80 countries around the world and markets its strong portfolio of brands in more than 180 countries; about 63 percent of the company's revenues are derived outside the United States. Among its products are 50 of what the company calls "leadership" brands, which account for 90 percent of P&G's sales and profits. Out of these 50 are 24 that generate more than $1 billion in annual revenues: Ace, Ariel, Downy, Gain, and Tide (laundry care); Always (feminine protection); Bounty (paper towels); Braun, Fusion, Gillette, and Mach3 (razors and other grooming products); Charmin (bathroom tissue); Crest and Oral-B (toothpaste, toothbrushes, and other dental care products); Dawn (dish detergent); Duracell (batteries); Febreze (odor eliminators); Head & Shoulders, Pantene, and Wella (hair care); Iams (pet food); Olay (skin care); Pampers (diapers); and Pringles (snacks).

Committed to remaining the leader in its markets, P&G is one of the most aggressive marketers and is the largest advertiser in the world. Many innovations that are now common practices in corporate America, including extensive market research, the brand-management system, and employee profit-sharing programs, were first developed at Procter & Gamble.

1837 LAUNCH: MAKER OF CANDLES AND SOAP

In 1837 William Procter and James Gamble formed Procter & Gamble, a partnership in Cincinnati, Ohio, to manufacture and sell candles and soap. Both men had

COMPANY PERSPECTIVES

We will provide branded products and services of superior quality and value that improve the lives of the world's consumers, now and for generations to come. As a result, consumers will reward us with leadership sales, profit, and value creation, allowing our people, our shareholders, and the communities in which we live and work to prosper.

emigrated from the United Kingdom. Procter had emigrated from England in 1832 after his woolens shop in London was destroyed by fire and burglary. Gamble came from Ireland as a boy in 1819 when famine struck his native land. Both men settled in Cincinnati, then nicknamed "Porkopolis" for its booming hog-butchering trade. The suggestion for the partnership apparently came from their mutual father-in-law, Alexander Norris, who pointed out that Gamble's trade, soap making, and Procter's trade, candle making, both required use of lye, which was made from animal fat and wood ashes.

Procter & Gamble first operated out of a storeroom at Main and Sixth Streets. Procter ran the store while Gamble ran the manufacturing operation, which at that time consisted of a wooden kettle with a cast-iron bottom set up behind the shop. Early each morning Gamble visited houses, hotels, and steamboats collecting ash and meat scraps, bartering soap cakes for the raw materials. Candles were Procter & Gamble's most important product at that time.

Procter & Gamble was in competition with at least 14 other manufacturers in its early years, but the enterprising partners soon expanded their operations throughout neighboring Hamilton and Butler Counties. Cincinnati's location on the Ohio River proved advantageous as the company began sending its goods downriver. In 1848 Cincinnati was also linked to the major cities of the East via rail, and Procter & Gamble grew.

Around 1851, when P&G shipments were moving up and down the river and across the country by rail, the company's famous moon-and-stars symbol was created. Because many people were illiterate at this time, trademarks were used to distinguish one company's products from another's. Company lore asserts that the symbol was first drawn as a simple cross on boxes of Procter & Gamble's Star brand candles by dockhands so that they would be easily identifiable when they arrived at their destinations. Another shipper later replaced the

cross with an encircled star, and eventually William Procter added the familiar 13 stars, representing the original 13 U.S. colonies, and the man in the moon.

The moon-and-stars trademark became a symbol of quality to Procter & Gamble's base of loyal customers. In the days before advertising, trademarks were a product's principal means of identification, and in 1875 when a Chicago soap maker began using an almost-identical symbol, P&G sued and won. The emblem, which was registered with the U.S. Patent Office in 1882, changed slightly over the years until 1930, when Cincinnati sculptor Ernest Bruce Haswell developed its modern-day form.

During the 1850s Procter & Gamble's business grew rapidly. In the early part of the decade the company moved its operations to a bigger factory. The new location gave the company better access to shipping routes and stockyards where hogs were slaughtered. In 1854 the company leased an office building in downtown Cincinnati. Procter managed sales and bookkeeping, while Gamble continued to run the manufacturing. By the end of the decade, the company's annual sales were more than $1 million, and Procter & Gamble employed about 80 people.

PROSPERING DURING THE CIVIL WAR

Procter & Gamble's operations were heavily dependent on rosin (derived from pine sap), which was supplied from the South. In 1860, on the brink of the Civil War, two young cousins, James Norris Gamble and William Alexander Procter (sons of the founders), traveled to New Orleans to buy as much rosin as they could, procuring a large supply at the bargain price of $1 a barrel. When wartime shortages forced competitors to cut production, Procter & Gamble prospered. The company supplied the Union army with soap and candles, and the moon and stars became a familiar symbol with Union soldiers.

Although Procter & Gamble had foreseen the wartime scarcities, as time wore on, its stockpile of raw materials shrank. In order to keep up full production the company had to find new ways of manufacturing. Until 1863 lard stearin was used to produce the stearic acid for candle making. With lard expensive and in short supply, a new method was discovered to produce the stearic acid using tallow. What lard and lard stearin was available was instead developed into a cooking compound. The same process was later adapted to create Crisco, the first all-vegetable shortening. When P&G's supply of rosin ran out toward the end of the war, the company experimented with silicate of soda as a

KEY DATES

1837: William Procter and James Gamble form Procter & Gamble (P&G).

1890: P&G is incorporated.

1931: Brand management system is formally introduced.

1957: Charmin Paper Company and Clorox Chemical Company are acquired; P&G is forced to divest the latter in 1967.

1961: Test marketing of Pampers disposable diapers begins.

1985: P&G purchases Richardson-Vicks Company, owner of the Vicks and Oil of Olay brands.

1999: Premium pet food maker Iams is purchased.

2001: P&G acquires the Clairol hair-care business from Bristol-Myers Squibb Company.

2003: Company purchases a controlling interest in German hair-care firm Wella AG.

2005: P&G acquires The Gillette Company.

substitute, which later became a key ingredient in modern soaps and detergents.

LAUNCHING IVORY SOAP IN 1878

After the war Procter & Gamble expanded and updated its facilities. In 1869 the transcontinental railroad linked the two coasts and opened still more markets to Procter & Gamble. In 1875 the company hired its first full-time chemist to work with James Gamble on new products, including a soap that was equal in quality to expensive castile soaps but could be produced less expensively. In 1878 Procter & Gamble's White Soap hit the market and catapulted P&G to the forefront of its industry.

The most distinctive characteristic of the product, soon renamed Ivory soap, was developed by chance. A worker accidentally left a soap mixer on during his lunch break, causing more air than usual to be mixed in. Before long Procter & Gamble was receiving orders for "the floating soap." Although the office was at first perplexed, the confusion was soon cleared up, and P&G's formula for White Soap changed permanently.

Harley Procter, William Procter's son, developed the new soap's potential. Harley Procter was inspired to rename the soap by Psalm 45: "all thy garments smell of myrrh, and aloes, and cassia, out of the ivory palaces whereby they have made thee glad." Procter devoted himself to the success of the new product and persuaded

the board of directors to advertise Ivory. Advertising was risky at the time. Most advertisements were placed by disreputable manufacturers. Nevertheless, in 1882 the company approved an $11,000 annual advertising budget. The slogan "99 44/100% pure" was a welcome dose of sobriety amid the generally outlandish advertising claims of the day. Procter, committed to the excellence of the company's products, had them analyzed and improved even before they went to market. This practice was the origin of P&G's superior product development. Procter believed that "advertising alone couldn't make a product successful—it was merely evidence of a manufacturer's faith in the merit of the article."

The success of Ivory and the ability of Procter & Gamble to spread its message further through the use of national advertising caused the company to grow rapidly in the 1880s. In 1886 P&G opened its new Ivorydale plant on the edge of Cincinnati to keep up with demand. In 1890 James N. Gamble hired a chemist, Harley James Morrison, to set up a laboratory at Ivorydale and improve the quality and consistency of Procter & Gamble's products. P&G soon introduced another successful brand: Lenox soap. Marketed as a heavier-duty product, the yellow soap helped P&G reach sales of more than $3 million by 1889.

The 1880s saw labor unrest at many U.S. companies, including Procter & Gamble, which experienced a number of strikes and demonstrations. Thereafter, the company sought to avert labor problems before they became significant. Behind P&G's labor policies was William Cooper Procter, a grandson of the cofounder. William Cooper Procter had joined the company in 1883 after his father, William Alexander Procter, requested that he return from the College of New Jersey (later Princeton University) just one month before graduation to help with the company's affairs. Procter learned the business from the ground up, starting in the soap factory.

INNOVATIVE EMPLOYEE BENEFITS

In 1885 the young Procter recommended that the workers be given Saturday afternoons off, and the company's management agreed. Nevertheless, there were 14 strikes over the next two years. In 1887 the company implemented a profit-sharing plan in order to intertwine the employees' interests with those of the company. Although the semiannual dividends were received enthusiastically by employees, that enthusiasm rarely found its way back into the workplace. The next year William Cooper Procter recommended tying the bonuses to employee performance, which produced better results.

In 1890 The Procter & Gamble Company was incorporated, with William Alexander Procter as its first president. Two years later the company implemented an employee stock-purchase program, which in 1903 was tied to the profit-sharing plan. By 1915 about 61 percent of the company's employees were participating. The company introduced a revolutionary sickness-disability program for its workers in 1915 and implemented an eight-hour workday in 1918.

Meanwhile, new soaps, including P&G White Naphtha, which was introduced in 1902, kept P&G at the forefront of the cleaning-products industry. In 1904 the company opened its second plant, in Kansas City, Missouri, followed by Port Ivory on Staten Island, New York. In 1907 William Cooper Procter became president of the company after his father's death.

INTRODUCTION OF CRISCO

Procter & Gamble soon began experimenting with a hydrogenation process that combined liquid cottonseed oil with solid cottonseed oil. After several years of research, Procter & Gamble patented the procedure, and in 1911 Crisco was introduced to the public. Backed by a strong advertising budget, Crisco sales took off.

World War I brought shortages, but Procter & Gamble management had again foreseen the crisis and had stockpiled raw materials. William Cooper Procter was also active in the wartime fundraising effort.

During the 1920s the flurry of new products continued. Ivory Flakes came out in 1919. Chipso soap flakes for industrial laundry machines were introduced in 1921. In 1926 Camay was introduced, and three years later Oxydol joined the P&G line of cleaning products. The company's market research became more sophisticated when P&G chemist F. W. Blair began a six-month tour of U.S. kitchens and laundry rooms to assess the effectiveness of Procter & Gamble's products in practical use and to recommend improvements. After Blair returned, the economic-research department under D. Paul Smelser began a careful study of consumer behavior. Market research complemented Procter & Gamble's laboratories and home economics department in bringing new technology to market.

Soon after Richard R. Deupree became president of the company in 1930, synthetic soap products hit the market. In 1933 Dreft, the first synthetic detergent for home use, was introduced, followed by the first synthetic hair shampoo, Drene, in 1934. Further improvements in synthetics resulted in a host of new products years later.

DEBUT OF BRAND MANAGEMENT IN 1931

In 1931 Neil H. McElroy, a former promotions manager who had spent time in England and had an up-close view of Procter & Gamble's rival Unilever, suggested a system of "one man—one brand." In effect, each brand would operate as a separate business, competing with the products of other firms as well as those of Procter & Gamble. The system would include a brand assistant who would execute the policies of the brand manager and would be primed for the top job. Brand management became a fixture at P&G and was widely copied by other companies.

The Great Depression caused hardship for many U.S. corporations as well as for individuals, but Procter & Gamble emerged virtually unscathed. Radio took Procter & Gamble's message into more homes than ever. In 1933 P&G became a key sponsor of radio's daytime serials, soon known as "soap operas." In 1935 the company spent $2 million on national radio sponsorship, and by 1937 the amount was $4.5 million. In 1939 Procter & Gamble had 21 programs on the air and spent $9 million. That year P&G advertised on television for the first time, when Red Barber plugged Ivory soap during the first television broadcast of a major league baseball game.

In 1940 Procter & Gamble's packaging expertise was given military applications when the government asked the company to oversee the construction and operation of ordnance plants. Procter & Gamble Defense Corporation operated as a subsidiary and filled government contracts for 60-millimeter mortar shells. Glycerin also became key to the war effort for its uses in explosives and medicine, and P&G was one of the largest manufacturers of that product.

TIDE-FUELED POSTWAR GROWTH

After World War II the availability of raw materials and new consumer attitudes set the stage for unprecedented growth. Procter & Gamble's postwar miracle was Tide, a synthetic detergent that, together with home automatic washing machines, revolutionized the way people washed their clothes. The company was not ready for the consumer demand for heavy-duty detergent when it introduced the product in 1946. Within two years Tide, backed by a $21 million advertising budget, was the number one laundry detergent, outselling even the company's own Oxydol and Duz. Despite its premium price, Tide remained the number one laundry detergent into the 21st century. In 1950 Cheer was introduced as bluing detergent, and over the years other laundry products were also marketed: Dash in 1954, Downy in 1960, Bold in 1965, Ariel (an overseas brand) in 1967, Era in 1972, and Solo in 1979.

The 1950s were highly profitable for the company. In 1955, after five years of research, Procter & Gamble firmly established itself in the toiletries business with Crest toothpaste. Researchers at the company and at Indiana University developed the toothpaste using stannous fluoride, a compound of fluorine and tin, which could substantially reduce cavities. In 1960 the American Dental Association endorsed Crest. The product was on its way to becoming the country's number one toothpaste, nudging past Colgate in 1962.

Procter & Gamble began acquiring smaller companies aggressively in the mid-1950s. In 1955 P&G bought the Lexington, Kentucky-based nut company W.T. Young Foods, and it acquired Nebraska Consolidated Mills Company, owner of the Duncan Hines product line, a year later. In 1957 Charmin Paper Company and Clorox Chemical Company were also acquired.

In 1957 McElroy, who had become Procter & Gamble president in 1948, left the company to serve as secretary of defense in President Dwight D. Eisenhower's cabinet. He was replaced by Howard J. Morgens who, like his predecessor, had climbed the corporate ladder from the advertising side. In 1959 McElroy returned to P&G as chairman and remained in that position until 1971, when Morgens succeeded him. Morgens remained CEO until 1974.

PAPER PRODUCTS PUSH

Morgens oversaw Procter & Gamble's full-scale entry into the paper-goods markets. A new process developed in the late 1950s for drying wood pulp led to the introduction of White Cloud toilet paper in 1958 and Puffs tissues in 1960. P&G's Charmin brand of toilet paper was also made softer.

Procter & Gamble's paper-products offensive culminated in the 1961 test marketing of Pampers disposable diapers. The idea for Pampers came from a company researcher, Vic Mills, who was inspired while changing an infant grandchild's diapers in 1956. The product consisted of three parts: a leakproof outer plastic shell, several absorbent layers, and a porous film that let moisture pass through into the absorbent layers, but kept it from coming back. Test market results showed that parents liked the diapers but disliked the 10 cents-per-Pamper price. Procter & Gamble reduced the price to six cents and implemented a sales strategy emphasizing the product's price. Pamper's three-layer design was a phenomenal success, and within 20 years

disposable diapers had gone from less than 1 percent to more than 75 percent of all diapers changed in the United States. Procter & Gamble improved the technology over the years and added a lower-priced brand, Luvs, in 1976.

The company expanded its food business by entering the coffee market through the 1963 acquisition of the Folgers brand and by introducing stackable Pringles potato chips, which were shipped in resealable cans, in 1968. P&G, however, had to contend with charges from the Federal Trade Commission that both its Folgers and Clorox acquisitions violated antitrust statutes. In a case that found its way to the U.S. Supreme Court, Procter & Gamble was finally forced to divest Clorox in 1967. The Folgers action was dismissed after P&G agreed not to make any more grocery acquisitions for seven years, and coffee acquisitions for 10 years.

ADDRESSING EARLY
ENVIRONMENTAL CONCERNS

In the late 1960s public attention to water pollution focused on phosphates, a key group of ingredients in soap products. After initial resistance, Procter & Gamble, along with other soap makers, drastically reduced the use of phosphates in its products.

In 1974 Edward G. Harness became chairman and CEO of Procter & Gamble, and the company continued its strong growth. Many familiar products were improved during the 1970s, and new ones were added as well, including Bounce fabric softener for the dryer in 1972 and Sure antiperspirant and Coast soap in 1974.

In 1977, after three years of test marketing, Procter & Gamble introduced Rely tampons, which were rapidly accepted in the market as a result of their "super-absorbent" qualities. In 1980, however, the Centers for Disease Control published a report showing a statistical link between the use of Rely and a rare but often fatal disease known as toxic shock syndrome (TSS). In September 1980 the company suspended further sales of Rely tampons, taking a $75 million write-off on the product.

Ironically, P&G was able to capitalize on the resurgence of feminine napkins after the TSS scare. The company's Always brand pads quickly garnered market share, and by 1990 Always was the top sanitary napkin, with over one-fourth of the market.

FOOD AND OTC DRUG
ACQUISITIONS

In 1981 John G. Smale became CEO of Procter & Gamble. He had been president since 1974. Smale led the company further into the grocery business through a number of acquisitions, including Ben Hill Griffin citrus products. The company also entered the over-the-counter (OTC) drug market with the 1982 purchase of Norwich Eaton Pharmaceuticals, Inc., maker of Pepto-Bismol and Chloraseptic. The company completed its biggest purchase in 1985, with the acquisition of Richardson-Vicks Company, maker of Vicks respiratory care products, NyQuil cold remedies, and Oil of Olay skin-care products, for $1.2 billion. P&G also bought the motion-sickness treatment Dramamine and the laxative Metamucil from G.D. Searle & Company that same year. These purchases made Procter & Gamble a leader in OTC drug sales.

In 1985, unable to squelch perennial rumors linking Procter & Gamble's famous moon-and-stars logo to Satanism, the company reluctantly removed the logo from product packages. The logo began to reappear on some packages in the early 1990s, and the company continued to use the trademark on corporate stationery and on its building.

During fiscal 1985, Procter & Gamble experienced its first decline in earnings since 1953. Analysts maintained that Procter & Gamble's corporate structure had failed to respond to important changes in consumer shopping patterns and that the company's standard practice of extensive market research slowed its reaction to the rapidly changing market. The mass-marketing practices that had served P&G so well in the past lost their punch as broadcast television viewership fell from 92 percent to 67 percent in the mid-1980s. Many large companies responded to the challenge of cable TV and increasingly market-specific media with appropriately targeted "micro-marketing" techniques, and Procter & Gamble was forced to rethink its marketing strategy. In the late 1980s the company diversified its advertising, reducing its reliance on network television. Computerized market research, including point-of-sale scanning, also provided the most up-to-date information on consumer buying trends.

In 1987 the company restructured its brand-management system into a "matrix system." Category managers became responsible for several brands, making them sensitive to the profits of other P&G products in their areas. Procter & Gamble brands continued to compete against one another, but far less actively. The restructuring also eliminated certain layers of management, quickening the decision-making process. In addition, the company became more aware of profitability than in the past. Whereas previously the assumption was that as long as the company pursued market share, profits would follow, P&G in the later 1980s no longer concentrated only on market share but began seeking ways to increase profits independent of market share.

In the late 1980s health care products were one of the fastest-growing markets as the U.S. population grew both older and more health conscious. To serve this market, Procter & Gamble's OTC drug group, which had been built up earlier in the decade, entered a number of joint ventures in pharmaceuticals. P&G teamed up with Syntex Corporation to formulate an OTC version of its best-selling antiarthritic, Naprosyn. Cooperative deals were also struck with the Dutch Gist-Brocades Company for its De-Nol ulcer medicine; Up-John for its anti-baldness drug, Minoxidil; and Triton Bioscience and Cetus for a synthetic interferon.

NOXELL AND BLENDAX ACQUISITIONS IN 1988

In September 1988 Procter & Gamble made its first move into the cosmetics business with the purchase of Noxell Corporation, maker of Noxzema products and CoverGirl cosmetics, in a $1.3 billion stock swap. Procter & Gamble also planned to further develop its international operations. In 1988 the company acquired Blendax, a European health- and beauty-care goods manufacturer. The Bain de Soleil sun-care product line was also purchased that year. By 1989 foreign markets accounted for nearly 40 percent of group sales, up from 14 percent in 1985.

P&G's brand equity was threatened by the weak economy and resultant consumer interest in value in the late 1980s and early 1990s. This value orientation resulted in stronger performance by private labels, especially in health and beauty aids. Private labels' market share of that segment grew 50 percent between 1982 and 1992, to 4.5 percent. To combat the trend, P&G inaugurated "everyday low pricing" for 50 to 60 percent of its products.

In the 1990s Procter & Gamble also hopped on the so-called green bandwagon of environmental marketing. It reduced packaging by offering concentrated formulations of products in smaller packages and refill packs on 38 brands in 17 countries.

While P&G expanded its presence in cosmetics and fragrances through the July 1991 acquisition of the worldwide Max Factor and Betrix lines from Revlon, Inc. for $1.03 billion, it also divested holdings in some areas it had outgrown. In 1992 the corporation sold about one-half of its Cellulose & Specialties pulp business to Weyerhaeuser Co. for $600 million. While vertical integration had benefited P&G's paper products in the past, the forestry business had become unprofitable and distracting by the 1990s. The corporation also sold an Italian coffee business in 1992 to focus on a core of

European brands. P&G hoped to introduce products with pan-European packaging, branding, and advertising to capture more of the region's well-established markets. Meanwhile, Pantene Pro-V was introduced in 1992 and quickly became the fastest-growing shampoo in the world.

MAJOR RESTRUCTURING AND ACQUISITIONS IN MID-NINETIES

Company sales surpassed the $30 billion mark in 1993. Under the leadership of Edwin L. Artzt, the chairman and CEO, and John E. Pepper, serving as president, Procter & Gamble that year launched a major restructuring effort aimed at making the company's brand-name products more price-competitive with private-label and generic brands, bringing products to market faster, and improving overall profitability. The program involved severe cost-cutting, including the closure of 30 plants around the world and the elimination of 13,000 jobs, or 12 percent of P&G's total workforce. Culminated in 1997, the $2.4 billion program resulted in annual after-tax savings of more than $600 million. It also helped to increase Procter & Gamble's net earnings margin from 7.3 percent in 1994 to 10.2 percent in 1998.

During the restructuring period, the company continued its brisk acquisitions pace. In 1994 P&G entered the European tissue and towel market through the purchase of Vereinigte Papierwerke Schickedanz AG's European tissue unit, and added the prestige fragrance business of Giorgio Beverly Hills, Inc. That year also saw Procter & Gamble reenter the South African market following the lifting of U.S. sanctions. The company altered its geographic management structure the following year. P&G had divided its operations into United States and International but reorganized them around four regions: North America, Latin America, Asia, and Europe/Middle East/Africa. In July 1995 Artzt retired and was replaced as chairman and CEO by Pepper. Durk I. Jager was named president and COO.

In 1996 Procter & Gamble purchased the Eagle Snacks brand line from Anheuser-Busch Companies, Inc., the U.S. baby wipes brand Baby Fresh, and Latin American brands Lavan San household cleaner and Magia Blanca bleach. In celebration of the 50th anniversary of Tide's introduction, the company held a "Dirtiest Kid in America" contest. Also in 1996 P&G received U.S. Food and Drug Administration (FDA) approval to use olestra, a controversial fat substitute, in snacks and crackers. The company had developed olestra after 25 years of research and at a cost of $250 million. The FDA go-ahead came after an eight-year investigation

and included a stipulation that foods containing the substitute include a warning label about possible gastrointestinal side effects. P&G soon began test-marketing Fat Free Pringles, Fat Free Ritz, and other products made using olestra. No product containing olestra ever caught on in the market, however, and olestra was eventually considered one of the company's biggest product failures ever.

In July 1997 Procter & Gamble spent about $1.84 billion in cash to acquire Tambrands, Inc. and the Tampax line of tampons, thereby solidifying its number one position worldwide in feminine products. The company sold its Duncan Hines baking mix line to Aurora Foods of Ohio for $445 million in 1998.

FURTHER RESTRUCTURINGS AND MORE DEAL MAKING

In September 1998 P&G announced a new restructuring initiative, dubbed Organization 2005. A key element of this restructuring was a shift from an organization centered around the four geographic regions established in 1995 to one centered on seven global business units based on product lines: Baby Care, Beauty Care, Fabric & Home Care, Feminine Protection, Food & Beverage, Health Care & Corporate New Ventures, and Tissues & Towels. Jager would be the person leading the reorganization, as it was announced at the same time that he would become president and CEO on January 1, 1999, with Pepper remaining chairman only until September 1, 1999, when Jager would also assume that position.

In June 1999 Jager extended the Organization 2005 restructuring to include several new initiatives. The company said that by 2005 it would eliminate 15,000 jobs, shutter about 10 factories, and record restructuring costs of $1.9 billion. The aims were to increase innovation, get new products to the market faster, and accelerate both revenue and profit growth.

In the meantime, P&G remained on the lookout for acquisitions and completed two significant ones in the latter months of 1999. In its biggest deal to that time, Procter & Gamble laid out $2.22 billion in cash for The Iams Company, one of the leading makers of premium pet food in the United States, with annual global sales of approximately $800 million. P&G next acquired Recovery Engineering, Inc., for about $265 million. Based in Minneapolis, Recovery produced the fast-growing PUR brand of water-filter products, achieving $80 million in sales in 1998. Among new products introduced in 1999 was Swiffer, an electrostatic dusting mop that was part of a new category of household product: quick cleaning. The Swiffer line went on to

The Procter & Gamble Company

become one of P&G's fastest-growing brands of the early 21st century. Also debuting in 1999 were Febreze, a spray used to eliminate odors in fabrics, and Dryel, a home dry-cleaning kit.

Early in 2000 Procter & Gamble placed itself in the middle of a major takeover battle in the pharmaceutical industry. Late in the previous year, Warner-Lambert Company had agreed to a nearly $70 billion merger with American Home Products Corporation (AHP). Pfizer Inc. quickly stepped in with a hostile bid for Warner-Lambert that exceeded AHP's offer. Warner-Lambert attempted to fend off Pfizer, bringing P&G into the picture in January 2000 to discuss a three-way deal involving AHP. Jager was forced to abandon the white knight maneuver, which would have been a huge and risky move into the drug business, when word leaked out to the press and the company's stock price plummeted. Around this same time, Jager reportedly approached The Gillette Company, best known for its razors, about a takeover but was quickly rebuffed.

INCREASED EMPHASIS ON TOP BRANDS

In June 2000, after the company issued its third profit warning in a year, Jager resigned. Taking over as president and CEO was A. G. Lafley, who had joined the company in June 1977 as a brand assistant for Joy and had most recently been in charge of the global beauty-care unit. At the same time, Pepper returned to the company board as chairman. Lafley slowed down the rush to get products to market in order to make sure that they received the proper marketing support. At the same time, he focused more of the company's resources on shoring up its big core brands, the top dozen or so products, each of which brought in more than $1 billion in global revenues annually.

Among other developments in 2000, the Oil of Olay brand was renamed simply Olay in an effort to dispel the perception that the product was greasy. As part of an ongoing effort to focus on a smaller number of core brands, P&G sold Clearasil, the acne-treatment brand, to The Boots Company PLC for about $340 million. The company also received FDA approval for Actonel, a prescription treatment for osteoporosis. Aided by a marketing partnership with Aventis, P&G was able to achieve $1 billion in annual Actonel sales by fiscal 2004.

Extending its 1999 restructuring still further, P&G announced in March 2001 that it would shed several thousand additional jobs over the following three years and double the amount of money it would spend to fix its operational problems. By the end of fiscal 2003,

when the restructuring was declared to be complete, Procter & Gamble had cut about 21,600 jobs and incurred total pretax charges of $4.85 billion. In the meantime, the company's fiscal 2001 results clearly showed the dismal state of affairs at that time: Sales fell nearly 2 percent to $39.24 billion, while net income plunged 17.5 percent to $2.92 billion thanks to after-tax restructuring charges of $1.48 billion.

In March 2001 Procter & Gamble reached an agreement with The Coca-Cola Company to create a $4 billion joint venture designed to join Coke's Minute Maid brand and distribution network with P&G's Pringles chips and Sunny Delight drink brands. Coca-Cola pulled out of the deal just a few months later, having decided to try to build the Minute Maid brand on its own. Despite this setback, P&G succeeded in paring back its ever more marginal food business by selling the Jif peanut butter and Crisco shortening brands to The J.M. Smucker Company. The deal, completed in May 2002, was valued at about $900 million.

ADDING CLAIROL AND WELLA

In November 2001, meantime, P&G consummated its largest acquisition yet, buying the Clairol hair-care business from Bristol-Myers Squibb Company for nearly $5 billion in cash. The deal melded well with P&G's goal of securing faster-growing, more profitable product areas, such as beauty and hair care. Also acquired in 2001 was Dr. John's SpinBrush, maker of a battery-powered toothbrush featuring spinning bristles that at $5 was much less expensive than existing electric toothbrushes. Soon thereafter, the newly named Crest SpinBrush was successfully launched. Also brought out in 2001 were Crest Whitestrips, a tooth-whitening product. These two new products helped increase global sales of the Crest brand by 50 percent, propelling it past the $1 billion mark during fiscal 2002.

In July 2002 Pepper again retired, and Lafley took on the additional post of chairman. Results for the fiscal year ending in June 2003 provided strong evidence that Lafley had engineered a remarkable turnaround. In its best performance in nearly a decade, Procter & Gamble posted an 8 percent increase in net sales, to $43.38 billion, and a 19 percent jump in net earnings, to $5.19 billion. P&G built on these results with another blockbuster acquisition, one that once again ranked as the largest in company history.

In September 2003 the company acquired a controlling interest in Wella AG for $6.27 billion. Based in Germany, Wella was a leading maker of professional hair-care products with 2002 revenues of $3.6 billion. The deal provided P&G with an entrée into the salon market, where about half of Wella's sales were generated. Procter & Gamble also bolstered its dental care line by acquiring the Glide brand of dental floss from W.L. Gore & Associates, Inc. In September 2003, under a marketing and distribution agreement with AstraZeneca PLC, P&G began selling Prilosec OTC, an over-the-counter version of AstraZeneca's blockbuster heartburn medication, Prilosec.

Procter & Gamble sold its Sunny Delight and Punica drinks businesses to J.W. Childs Associates LP, a private-equity firm in Boston, in August 2004. This further paring of the foods business left P&G with just two main food brands, Pringles and Folgers. The snacks and beverages unit accounted for only 7 percent of the company's total revenues in fiscal 2004. That year, overall sales surged 19 percent, surpassing the $50 billion mark for the first time. Net earnings jumped 25 percent, hitting $6.48 billion. At the beginning of fiscal 2005 P&G realigned its business units, shifting its five previous units into three: global beauty care; global health, baby, and family care; and global household care. Pringles and Folgers were placed within the latter unit.

BLOCKBUSTER ACQUISITION OF GILLETTE IN 2005

Lafley returned the company's attention to Gillette, which his predecessor had unsuccessfully pursued five years earlier, reaching a deal in early 2005 to take over the Boston-based men's grooming product giant. The takeover, by far the largest in P&G history, was completed in October 2005 as a stock swap transaction valued at around $53.4 billion. The deal not only added several more brands that generated sales in excess of $1 billion each year, including Gillette razors and other grooming products, Braun electric razors, Oral-B dental care products, and Duracell batteries, it also provided Procter & Gamble with added negotiating power when dealing with the world's ever-larger retailers such as Wal-Mart Stores, Inc.

The purchase of Gillette also vaulted P&G over Unilever into the top position among the world's consumer product companies, as revenues surged to $76.48 billion by fiscal 2007, the first full year after the Gillette deal's completion. While the brands of P&G and Gillette were largely complementary, the companies did have some overlapping businesses, and several brands had to be divested for the deal to pass regulatory muster. P&G consequently divested its SpinBrush toothbrush business and several deodorant brands, including Sure, Right Guard, Soft & Dri, and Dry Idea.

Late in 2007, as the integration of Gillette into P&G was nearing its completion, Procter & Gamble

began exploring the sale of three of its businesses that did not mesh with its increasing concentration on fast-growing, high-margin brands: Duracell, Pringles, and Folgers. After initially announcing plans to spin off Folgers to shareholders, P&G reached a deal to sell the coffee business to The J. M. Smucker Company. The all-stock transaction, which was valued at about $2.5 billion, was completed in November 2008. For the time being, P&G retained Pringles (its last remaining food brand) and Duracell.

Also in 2008, the company sold its U.S.-based Noxzema skin-care business to Alberto-Culver Company, while keeping the Noxzema shaving, deodorant, and body-wash business that operated in parts of Western Europe. That same year, P&G boosted its hair-care business by acquiring Frédéric Fekkai & Co., owner of the Fekkai brand, a luxury hair-care brand sold in specialty chains such as Sephora and high-end department stores, including Saks Fifth Avenue and Neiman Marcus.

NEW STRATEGIES FOR CHALLENGING TIMES

For the fiscal year ending in June 2009, Procter & Gamble suffered a rare fall in sales, a 3.3 percent decline to $79.03 billion, as the global economic downturn led consumers around the world to cut back on their discretionary purchases and seek more value in their nondiscretionary buys. In response, in a marked turnabout from its historical approach, P&G announced plans to increase its offerings of lower-priced products. The company had long followed a highly successful strategy that relied on middle-class consumers' willingness to trade up to purchases of P&G's high-end, premium-priced products. In the severe recession that began in the late years of the 21st century's first decade, middle-class Americans in particular were in economic distress and this willingness to trade up largely evaporated.

Responsibility for carrying out P&G's new strategy soon fell to Lafley's successor, Robert A. McDonald, who took over as president and CEO in July 2009. Promoted from the COO spot, McDonald was a 29-year company veteran. Under his leadership, P&G pursued a high/low strategy in which it continued to sell its premium brands for higher income consumers while developing more lower-priced products for the less affluent. For example, the company in 2010 launched a new dish soap under the Gain brand, which sold for about half the price, on a per-ounce basis, of P&G's premium Dawn Hand Renewal dish soap. Gain soap quickly caught on with consumers, securing nearly 5 percent of the U.S. hand dishwashing soap market during its second year on store shelves.

Under McDonald as well, P&G continued to devote increased attention to its "leadership" brands, namely the top 50 or so brands that accounted for 90 percent of the firm's sales and profits. One of these brands, the annual sales of which was approaching the $1 billion mark, was Prestobarba, a line of disposable razors sold in Asia, Latin America, Europe, and the Middle East. The line, which included both premium and value versions, had grown to capture 35 percent of the world market for men's disposable razors by 2011. That year, sales of the Febreze line of odor eliminating products surpassed $1 billion, giving Procter & Gamble 24 billion-dollar brands. P&G in 2011 also consolidated its three global business divisions into two: Beauty & Grooming and Household Care.

While increasing the resources devoted to its key brands, P&G also pared its portfolio of a number of brands that had limited growth potential or garnered lower profit margins or both. In order to focus on the more promising CoverGirl brand, P&G in 2010 withdrew the underperforming Max Factor cosmetics line from U.S. store shelves, although Max Factor remained a key brand overseas where it was the company's fastest-growing cosmetics brand. Other divestments included the PUR line of water purification equipment and part of the Zest bar soap and body wash business.

In October 2009 P&G sold its global pharmaceuticals business to Warner Chilcott plc for $2.8 billion. During 2011, Procter & Gamble placed its OTC drug operations located outside North America into a Geneva, Switzerland-based joint venture with Israel-headquartered Teva Pharmaceutical Industries Ltd. P&G retained full control of the marketing and sales of its OTC drug business in North America, but it transferred control of its OTC drug manufacturing plants in the United States to Teva. In addition, the joint venture, which was named PGT Healthcare, was charged with developing new brands for the North American market.

In April 2011 P&G reached agreement on a deal to sell Pringles to Diamond Foods, Inc. for $1.5 billion. The move promised to mark P&G's final exit from the food industry, but the deal's consummation became clouded later in the year when questions were raised about the way Diamond had accounted for certain crop payments it had been making to walnut growers. In the meantime, in an economic environment that remained challenging, P&G's sales increased by more than 4 percent in fiscal 2011, to $82.56 billion. Procter & Gamble remained one of the most admired companies in the world, and it continued its streak of paying dividends without interruption since its 1890 incorporation, while also increasing its dividend for the 55th straight year.

Thomas M. Tucker
Updated, April S. Dougal; David E. Salamie

PRINCIPAL SUBSIDIARIES

The Gillette Company; Giorgio Beverly Hills, Inc.; The Iams Company; Noxell Corporation; Olay LLC; Oral-B Laboratories, G.P.; P&G-Clairol, Inc.; The Procter & Gamble Manufacturing Company; The Procter & Gamble Paper Products Company; PUR Water Purification Products, Inc.; Tambrands Inc.; Vidal Sassoon Co.; The Wella Corporation; Procter & Gamble Australia Proprietary Limited; Procter & Gamble do Brasil S/A (Brazil); Procter & Gamble Inc. (Canada); Procter & Gamble (Chengdu) Ltd. (China); Procter & Gamble (China) Ltd.; Procter & Gamble (Guangzhou) Ltd. (China); Procter & Gamble (Jiangsu) Ltd. (China); Procter & Gamble (Shanghai) International Trade Company Ltd. (China); Procter & Gamble Detergent (Beijing) Ltd. (China); Procter & Gamble Manufacturing (Tianjin) Co. Ltd. (China); Procter & Gamble Technology (Beijing) Co., Ltd. (China); Procter & Gamble France S.A.S.; Procter & Gamble GmbH (Germany); Procter & Gamble India Holdings, Inc.; Procter & Gamble Home Products Limited (India); Procter & Gamble Italia, S.p.A. (Italy); Procter & Gamble Nederland B.V. (Netherlands); "Procter & Gamble" O.O.O. (Russia); Procter & Gamble Switzerland SARL; Procter & Gamble Limited (UK).

PRINCIPAL OPERATING UNITS

Beauty & Grooming; Household Care.

PRINCIPAL COMPETITORS

Alberto-Culver Company; Church & Dwight Co., Inc.; The Clorox Company; Colgate-Palmolive Company; Energizer Holdings, Inc.; Henkel KGaA; Johnson & Johnson; Kimberly-Clark Corporation; L'Oréal SA; Nestlé Purina PetCare Company; Reckitt Benckiser Group plc; Revlon, Inc.; S.C. Johnson & Son, Inc.; Unilever.

FURTHER READING

Berner, Robert, Nanette Byrnes, and Wendy Zellner. "P&G Has Rivals in a Wringer." *BusinessWeek*, October 4, 2004, 74.

Blumenthal, Robin Goldwyn. "A Beauty!" *Barron's*, August 22, 2005, 21–23.

Brooker, Katrina. "The Un-CEO." *Fortune*, September 16, 2002, 88–92, 96.

Byron, Ellen. "As Middle Class Shrinks, P&G Aims High and Low." *Wall Street Journal*, September 12, 2011, A1, A16.

———. "At P&G, Beauty Makeover Needs to Prove It Has Legs." *Wall Street Journal*, January 26, 2011, B1.

———. "P&G Chief Wages Offensive against Rivals, Risks Profits." *Wall Street Journal*, August 19, 2010, A1+.

———. "P&G Chooses a New CEO as It Adapts to Era of Thrift." *Wall Street Journal*, June 9, 2009, A1+.

Crockett, Roger O. "Lafley Leaves Big Shoes to Fill at P&G." *BusinessWeek*, June 8, 2009. Accessed November 18, 2011. http://www.businessweek.com/bwdaily/dnflash/content/jun2009/db2009068_155480.htm.

Deogun, Nikhil, and Emily Nelson. "Stirring Giant: P&G Is on the Move." *Wall Street Journal*, January 24, 2000, A1+.

Deogun, Nikhil, Charles Forelle, Dennis K. Berman, and Emily Nelson. "Razor's Edge: P&G to Buy Gillette for $54 Billion." *Wall Street Journal*, January 28, 2005, A1+.

Dyer, Davis, Frederick Dalzell, and Rowena Olegario. *Rising Tide: Lessons from 165 Years of Brand Building at Procter & Gamble*. Boston: Harvard Business School Press, 2004.

Editors of *Advertising Age. Procter & Gamble: The House That Ivory Built*. Lincolnwood, IL: NTC Business Books, 1988.

Eisenberg, Daniel. "A Healthy Gamble." *Time*, September 16, 2002, 46–48.

Lief, Alfred. *It Floats: The Story of Procter & Gamble*. New York: Rinehart & Company, 1958.

P&G: A Company History, 1837–Today. Cincinnati, OH: The Procter & Gamble Company, 2006. Accessed November 18, 2011. http://www.pg.com/translations/history_pdf/english_history.pdf.

Pepper, John. *What Really Matters: Service, Leadership, People, and Values*. New Haven, CT: Yale University Press, 2007.

Schisgall, Oscar. *Eyes on Tomorrow: Evolution of Procter & Gamble*. Chicago: J.G. Ferguson Publishing, 1981.

Sellers, Patricia. "P&G: Teaching an Old Dog New Tricks." *Fortune*, May 31, 2004, 166–68+.

Swasy, Alecia. *Soap Opera: The Inside Story of Procter & Gamble*. New York: Times Books, 1993.

Wayne, Leslie. "With Sale, P&G Exits Global Drug Business." *New York Times*, August 25, 2009, B3.

Ziobro, Paul. "Costs Weigh on P&G Results." *Wall Street Journal*, October 28, 2011, B7.

Public Storage

701 Western Avenue
Glendale, California 91201
U.S.A.
Telephone: (818) 244-8080
Fax: (818) 553-2388
Web site: http://www.publicstorage.com

Public Company
Incorporated: 1980 as Storage Equities
Employees: 4,900
Sales: $1.64 billion (2010)
Stock Exchanges: New York
Ticker Symbol: PSA
NAICS: 531130 Lessors of Miniwarehouses and Self-Storage Units; 531311 Residential Property Managers

■ ■ ■

Public Storage is the largest operator of self-storage centers in the world. The company maintains direct or indirect equity interests in more than 2,048 self-storage facilities in 38 states. Through a 49 percent interest in Shurgard Self Storage Europe Ltd., Public Storage participates in the operation of 188 self-storage facilities in seven countries in Western Europe. The company's properties in the United States and Europe represent 135 million rentable square feet of real estate. Public Storage also has a 41 percent interest in PS Business Parks, Inc., which owns or manages 21 million rentable square feet of commercial and industrial space. Public Storage is a self-administered and self-managed real estate investment trust.

ORIGINS

A native of Oklahoma, Bradley Wayne Hughes built a career around real estate. After receiving his undergraduate degree from the University of Southern California, Hughes worked as a real estate developer in Southern California, but his rise to the top of the business world did not begin until he was in his 40s, and not until he took a road trip to Texas. During the early 1970s, Hughes was driving in Texas when he passed a self-storage warehouse erected by the side of the road. Self-storage facilities were rare at the time, prompting Hughes to park his car and pretend to be a customer. Hughes was told he could put his name on a waiting list because all the available space was already occupied. Hughes needed no further incentive to enter the business himself when he returned home.

Hughes was spurred to enter the self-storage business for two reasons. First, he believed there was a potentially large demand for self-storage space in Southern California, home to a particularly itinerant population. If the self-storage business foundered, Hughes reasoned, he could always raze the miniwarehouses and build apartments or office buildings in their place. The important asset was the land, while the self-storage centers, at the least, offered the chance to collect a return on the real estate investment until it could be developed into a more lucrative property.

With $50,000 and a partner, Kenneth Volk, Jr., Hughes entered the self-storage fray. It took roughly one year for the two partners to build their facility, due to time spent researching, buying land, obtaining zoning approval, and ultimately constructing the facility. When the first self-storage center was completed, built alongside a busy freeway in El Cajon, California, in 1972, Hughes hoped to experience the success he had witnessed in Texas. He hung up a sign that read, "Private Storage Spaces," and was quickly disappointed. For a frustratingly long time, no customers showed up, until finally one person arrived and asked if storage was available to the general public. Hughes realized his error and changed the sign to read: "Public Storage."

Any fears Hughes had that the self-storage business might not deliver profitable results for the land were quickly assuaged. Bulldozers would not be needed. The first miniwarehouse broke even with only a 35 percent occupancy rate, achieved within three months. In addition, construction costs for the facilities in the early 1970s were 35 percent to 40 percent lower than the construction costs for apartment buildings, yet storage rates per square foot were the same as for apartments. The financial opportunities excited Hughes and Volk, prompting the pair to open 20 miniwarehouses within the next two years. More expansion followed, occurring at an especially frenetic pace during the 1980s. The company's early and aggressive entry into the market determined its success to a large extent, but of equal importance was the manner in which the physical expansion was financed.

REAL ESTATE LIMITED
PARTNERSHIPS FUEL EXPANSION:
1977–89

Hughes loathed debt. He refused to borrow to fuel Public Storage's expansion, preferring instead to solicit investors to pay for real estate and construction. In return, the investors received a percentage of Public Storage's business. Hughes turned to the rapidly growing real estate limited partnership market for his supply of cash, forming his first partnership in 1977. It took approximately a year for the partnership to raise $3 million. Not long afterward, the money came pouring in, willingly offered by investors who had heard of the fortunes to be made in allying with Hughes.

Like Hughes, investors perceived great value in the land occupied by Public Storage's miniwarehouses. During the late 1970s and early 1980s, the Southern California land purchased by Hughes exploded in value, which greatly enriched Public Storage's investors. They saw their investments quadruple in value, creating a stir within the investment community that enabled Hughes to raise cash for expansion nearly at will. During the mid-1980s, Hughes was collecting between $200 million and $300 million a year from institutional and individual investors, providing sufficient resources for him to launch a national expansion campaign. Hughes targeted the 39 largest cities in the nation and began opening as many as 100 new self-storage centers a year. Between 1978 and 1989, more than 200,000 investors heeded Hughes's calls for cash, enabling him to raise an estimated $3 billion for expansion.

With the investments, Hughes was able to thoroughly dominate the self-storage industry by building an empire of 1,000 miniwarehouses. His preeminence was impressive. "We're bigger than our nine next-largest competitors put together," Hughes remarked in a February 5, 1990 interview with the *Los Angeles Business Journal*. "Consider them the McDonald's of the ministorage business," an analyst said in the November 28, 1989, issue of *Financial World*.

Although Hughes held a commanding lead in the industry, Public Storage was not alone in its bid to populate the landscape with self-storage units. In 1979 there were 3,500 miniwarehouses in operation in the United States. By the late 1980s, there were 18,000 self-storage outlets in the country, offering more than 900 million square feet of storage space and generating estimated annual revenues of $4 billion. In one four-year period during the 1980s, capacity in the industry doubled, threatening to glut the market. Hughes's facilities, although far outnumbering the properties operated by his rivals, felt the sting of a crowded market. Occupancy rates at many Public Storage facilities stalled at 85 percent, and rental rates stopped rising. Further, as more developers jumped into the self-storage business, the cost of land increased, taking some of the financial luster off Hughes's deals. The effect of these external factors was compounded by internal pressures and several tactical errors.

KEY DATES

1972: First Public Storage miniwarehouse opens in El Cajon, California.
1977: Bradley Wayne Hughes forms his first real estate limited partnership.
1995: Public Storage merges with Storage Equities, Inc.
1998: Storage Trust Realty is acquired.
2002: Ronald L. Havner, Jr., replaces Hughes as CEO.
2006: After several failed attempts, Public Storage acquires Shurgard Storage Centers in a $5 billion deal.
2011: Hughes resigns as chairman.

GROWING PAINS: 1985–89

Developing into a national chain was proving more difficult than expected, causing expansion to slow. The company was growing at such a frenetic pace that finding skilled managers was becoming difficult, as was contending with weather conditions and labor markets that differed from Southern California's. "What once took us seven months was now taking us 11, 12, and 13 months," recalled Harvey Lenkin, Public Storage's president, in a November 28, 1989, interview with *Financial World.*

Adding to the difficulties were several mistakes made by Hughes. He began including office parks into the deals forged in his numerous partnership agreements. Office parks, which Public Storage had difficulty in managing, suffered from severe overcapacity problems, leading to sizable losses. The financial drag of the office parks, which sometimes accounted for as much as 35 percent of the deal brokered by Hughes, dramatically affected the return earned by investors, who were dismayed to learn that they had not earned nearly as much as Public Storage's early investors had earned.

The problems were there, but as Robert Wrubel, a *Financial World* reporter, noted in the magazine's November 28, 1989, issue, "that Hughes is still around to tell the tale reflects well on him." Indeed, it was Hughes's own strengths that enabled him to overcome his foibles, particularly his criteria and method for expansion. Hughes's refusal to take on debt as a means to finance expansion enabled Public Storage to withstand economic cycles that halted the expansion of his rivals. In turn, his ability to raise vast sums of capital allowed Public Storage to grow quickly and decisively

outdistance competitors before they had an opportunity to mount a serious challenge.

Hughes further disabled competitors by adhering to his strategy of targeting the 39 largest cities and then saturating the markets within the city by opening four to six self-storage centers at a time. By employing his saturation strategy, Hughes could rely on a single development office for each city, which reduced construction and operating costs and, of particular importance, allowed Hughes to justify the expense of advertising on television, something few of his rivals could afford. "There are a lot of benefits that come from concentrating properties in the major markets where we could have 15, 20, 60, 70, 90, 100 properties in a metropolitan area as opposed to having three," Lenkin explained in a November 1998 interview with *National Real Estate Investor.*

CONSOLIDATION AND STRUCTURAL CHANGES: NINETIES

Hughes exited the 1980s pursuing a goal of reaching 2,000 self-storage centers by 1994, an objective that called for the company to double in size. Economic conditions during the early 1990s, however, proved more conducive to consolidation than expansion. The primary source of Public Storage's cash for the previous two decades, the real estate limited partnership market, had nearly disappeared as Hughes celebrated his 20th year in the self-storage industry. In response, Hughes began organizing his properties into real estate investment trusts (REITs), an enticing financial arrangement for investors. Under the terms of a REIT, investors started collecting a 10 percent yield within the first year of the REIT's operation, rather than having to wait three years as was often the case in a limited partnership. In addition, a REIT was forced to distribute at least 90 percent of its income to shareholders, thereby freeing itself from having to pay corporate taxes.

By 1995 Hughes's self-storage empire was organized into 17 REITs. In the final move of the consolidation process, Public Storage acquired Storage Equities, Inc., in 1995, creating the fourth-largest publicly traded REIT in the United States, with $1.4 billion in market capitalization. Prior to the merger, Public Storage, as a private company, had served as a property manager and tenant adviser for Storage Equities. The merger doubled Public Storage's size, putting all of Hughes's private real estate assets into a public company, the new Public Storage.

THE PURSUIT OF SHURGARD STORAGE: 2000–06

By the end of the 1990s, Public Storage consisted of 1,200 self-storage centers with 635,000 spaces. Aside from expanding through internal means, Hughes expanded through acquisition, targeting several of his largest rivals. In 1998 Public Storage acquired a stake in Storage Trust Realty, then offered to buy the company. Storage Trust rejected the offer, but later agreed to the deal, forced to concede after relenting to shareholder pressure.

In February 2000 Public Storage began investing heavily in Shurgard Storage Centers, the third-largest self-storage operator, spending roughly $50 million to become the company's largest shareholder by early April. In mid-April 2000 Public Storage representatives flew to Seattle and initiated talks with Shurgard officials about combining the two companies. Shurgard management rejected the offer, to the chagrin of some of the company's shareholders, and withstood the unsolicited advances of its larger rival. Public Storage decided against a hostile takeover, and several weeks later reduced its stake in Shurgard.

Rebuffed in his attempt to purchase Shurgard, Hughes looked to expand his empire in a more piecemeal approach. He built up his war chest and completed a series of transactions, acquiring two dozen properties at a time, spending between $100 million and $150 million to complete the deals. The number of properties under his control neared 1,500 by the middle of the decade, when he renewed his efforts to acquire Shurgard. Shurgard owned 640 self-storage properties in the United States at that time, but what interested Hughes and the rest of his management team the most was Shurgard's 130 self-storage properties in Europe. Public Storage submitted a $2.49 billion, unsolicited bid in July 2005, but the offer was rejected. Shurgard's management said the company was not for sale. Public Storage sent a letter to Shurgard's board of directors several months later, but the same negative response was received.

Public Storage's management pressed ahead with its pursuit and gained confidence after Shurgard's board of directors conducted a strategic review in late 2005. The following March Public Storage confirmed it had reached an agreement to purchase Shurgard in an all-stock deal valued at $5 billion. The acquisition, completed in August 2006, gave Public Storage, which boasted a market capitalization of $18 billion, interests in more than 2,100 self-storage facilities in 38 states and seven European countries.

PUBLIC STORAGE WEATHERS FINANCIAL CRISIS: 2008–11

An industry giant before the Shurgard acquisition, Public Storage towered over all rivals after the deal, but there was still plenty of room to grow. The company controlled only 6 percent of a highly fragmented industry, giving it a wealth of acquisition targets as it moved forward. The last years of the decade saw only a modicum of expansion, however. It was a period that stood in stark contrast to the years of aggressive expansion.

In 2008 the company surprised some industry observers by taking a step away from the European operations acquired in the Shurgard transaction. Public Storage sold 51 percent of Shurgard Self Storage Europe Ltd. for $606 million to the New York Common Retirement Fund, changing its stance on the primary rationale for the purchase of Shurgard. "When we bought Shurgard," Clemente Teng, Public Storage's vice president of investor relations, said in the April 7, 2008, issue of the *Los Angeles Business Journal*, "we were more interested in the American properties because the facilities were closely located to our existing facilities, which allowed us to gather scale advantages and cut costs."

After reducing its involvement in the European self-storage market, Public Storage officials promised a greater focus on expanding the company's domestic operations, but the global financial crisis at the end of the decade thwarted its progress. Severely harsh economic conditions forced the company to halt expansion and to offer discounted pricing. As a REIT the company was required to distribute 90 percent of its net income to shareholders, but federal regulators in 2009 agreed to special relief rules because of the deep recession. REITs were allowed to make distributions partly in cash and partly in new stock, which enabled Public Storage to retain a larger percentage of its profits and fill its coffers for future expansion. By 2010 the company had $720 million in cash and began spending it. In mid-2010 the company acquired 30 self-storage facilities from A-American Self Storage Management Co. for $189 million.

As Public Storage prepared for the return of more salubrious economic conditions, the nearly 40-year reign of Hughes ended. In 2002 Hughes passed the duties of CEO to Ronald L. Havner, Jr., a Public Storage executive since 1986, but remained the company's chairman. In 2011 the 77-year-old Hughes resigned as chairman, handing the title to Havner. Havner occupied the posts of president, CEO, and chairman, wielding considerable control over a company that dominated all competitors and promised to remain an industry behemoth for years to come.

Jeffrey L. Covell

PRINCIPAL SUBSIDIARIES

Connecticut Storage Fund; Diversified Storage Fund; PS Co-Investment Partners; PS Illinois Trust; PS Insurance Company–Hawaii, Ltd.; PS Orangeco, Inc.; PS Partners, Ltd.; PS Tennessee, L.P.; PS LPT Properties Investors; PSA Institutional Partners, L.P.; PSAC Development Partners, L.P.; PSAF Development Partners, L.P.; Public Storage Properties IV, Ltd.; Public Storage Properties V, Ltd.; Public Storage Institutional Fund; Public Storage Institutional Fund III; Secure Mini Storage; Shurgard Michigan, L.P.; Shurgard Storage Centers LLC; STOR-Re Mutual Insurance Corporation; Storage Trust Properties, L.P.; SSC Evergreen LLC; SSC Property Holdings LLC.

PRINCIPAL COMPETITORS

AMERCO; CubeSmart; Mobile Mini, Inc.

FURTHER READING

Crutsinger, Martin. "Public Storage to Buy Shurgard for $5 Billion in Stock." *America's Intelligence Wire*, March 7, 2006.

Deacon, Mitch. "Public Storage's Sell-Off in Europe Feeds U.S. Focus: Company Retains Minority Interest in Overseas Properties." *Los Angeles Business Journal*, April 7, 2008.

Heath, Tracy. "Public Storage Inc. Cashes In on Storing Your Stash." *National Real Estate Investor*, November 1998.

Newman, Morris. "Public Storage: Mini-Storage Turns Landscape Orange." *Los Angeles Business Journal*, February 5, 1990.

Proctor, Lisa Steen. "$800 Million Man Who Still Commutes." *Los Angeles Business Journal*, May 19, 1997.

Rudnitsky, Howard. "The King of Self-Storage." *Forbes*, October 23, 1995.

Russel, Joel. "In a Safer Place: Public Storage Looks to Launch an Expansion Plan and Boost Rental Fees as the Economy Stabilizes." *Los Angeles Business Journal*, July 5, 2010.

Sartor, Alexandra. "Dailey Thinking inside the Box." *ADWEEK Western Edition*, July 17, 2000.

"Shurgard Rebuffs Public Storage." *Puget Sound Business Journal*, May 5, 2000.

Wrubel, Robert. "California Cold Storage." *Financial World*, November 28, 1989.

Quebecor Inc.

612 Rue St. Jacques
Montreal, Quebec H3C 4M8
Canada
Telephone: (514) 380-1999
Fax: (514) 954-9624
Web site: http://www.quebecor.com

Public Company
Incorporated: 1965
Employees: 16,360
Sales: CAD 4.0 billion ($3.89 billion) (2010)
Stock Exchanges: Toronto
Ticker Symbol: QBR
NAICS: 511110 Newspaper Publishing; 511120 Periodical Publishers; 511130 Book Publishers; 513210 Cable Networks; 513120 Television Broadcasting

■ ■ ■

Quebecor Inc. is the parent company of Quebecor Media, a 55 percent-owned subsidiary involved in broadcasting, publishing, telecommunications, leisure, and entertainment activities. Quebecor, through Videotron, ranks as the third-largest cable operator in Canada. Through Sun Media, the company ranks as the largest newspaper publisher in Canada, responsible for publishing 190 publications, including *Journal de Montreal*, *Toronto Sun*, *Calgary Sun*, *Edmonton Sun*, and *Ottawa Sun*. Through TVA Group, the company ranks as the largest, private-sector broadcaster of French-language entertainment. Quebecor is managed by the second generation of the Péladeau family.

PAPERS AND PRESSES FORM FOUNDATION: 1950–72

Pierre Péladeau, Quebecor's founder, president, and CEO, bought his first newspaper in 1950 when he was 25 years old. His father had been successful in business, but lost his fortune by the time of his death, when Pierre Péladeau was only 10 years old. His mother managed to send Péladeau to an exclusive school and he continued his education at elite universities. A graduate of McGill University with a degree in law and of the University of Montreal with a master's degree in philosophy, Péladeau borrowed CAD 1,500 from his mother to buy the ailing weekly *Le Journal de Rosemont*, and worked hard to make the paper a success. In 1953 Péladeau bought his first printing press. More dailies and printing presses followed, until Péladeau had built the beginnings of his empire.

A 1964 strike at Quebec's leading French-language daily, *La Presse*, gave Péladeau a big opportunity. In *La Presse*'s absence, Péladeau launched his own daily, *Le Journal de Montréal*. The tabloid, which featured graphic pictures of crime scenes, heavy sports coverage, pinup girl photos, and no editorials, met with immediate success. *La Presse*'s return to the stands seven months later slowed but did not halt that success. In fact, circulation rose during the following years until *Le Journal* became Quebec and North America's leading French-language daily in the late 1970s, a status it maintained into the 1990s.

In 1967, Péladeau founded *Le Journal de Quebec*, and later added an entertainment magazine and the *Winnipeg Sun* to his newspaper holdings. Labor lawyer

Brian Mulroney, eventually to become Canada's prime minister, worked out *Le Journal*'s first labor agreement. Péladeau's generous dealings with labor cemented his positive reputation with the public. In 1972 Péladeau offered shares in Quebecor on the Toronto Stock Exchange.

INTERNATIONAL REACH: 1977–88

In 1977, Péladeau gambled in the U.S. newspaper market by launching the *Philadelphia Journal*. However, the venture turned out to be one of Péladeau's few misjudgments of the market and the competition. He thought the extensive sports coverage and tabloid format used in *Le Journal* would find a big audience in Philadelphia, but the paper's competition simply increased its sports coverage and cut advertising rates to squeeze Péladeau out of the market. Five years later, at a loss of $14 million, the paper closed its doors.

During the next several years, Péladeau undertook a more aggressive campaign to establish a presence in the U.S. market and to take the number one position in Canada. He saw that technology and economies of scale were becoming increasingly important to success in the printing and publishing industries due to changes in technology and a more competitive world economy. His strong customer orientation and grasp of client needs, both in business-to-business and consumer markets, were great assets in the strategic expansion of Quebecor. Quebecor invested in emerging technologies, allowing retailers and advertisers to regionalize product offerings and prices. Bar code technology allowed the creation of large databases from which computers could determine demographic buying patterns, making it possible to tailor publications to specific regions, neighborhoods, or even individuals. These technologies required specialized capabilities, including binding techniques that allowed customized compilation of pages destined for different markets.

Péladeau and British publishing magnate Robert Maxwell teamed up in 1987 to form Mircor Inc. The joint-venture company spent CAD 320 million to purchase a 54 percent stake in Donohue Inc., a leading forest products company in Quebec. Quebecor took a 51 percent share of the newly formed Mircor. The Donohue acquisition gave Quebecor its status as one of the most vertically integrated communications companies in the world, for it allowed the company to do everything from cutting the tree to distributing the printed product. Donohue supplied paper for Quebecor's journals and magazines and for direct-mail advertising for its retail clients.

In 1988 Quebecor bought almost all of the printing assets of BEC Inc., the owner of Bell Canada, for CAD 161 million and a 21 percent share of Quebecor capital stock. The acquisition expanded Quebecor's printing capabilities and brought in lucrative contracts for printing telephone directories, currency, and passports. This acquisition made Quebecor first in printing in Canada and gave the company significant economies of scale, positioning it well for success in the increasingly competitive and technology driven industry.

ACQUISITIONS FUEL EXPANSION: 1990–94

In 1990 Quebecor bought Maxwell Communication Corporation's 14 U.S. printing operations, forming the basis of Quebecor Printing. The $510 million deal included a noncompetition agreement and the purchase by Maxwell of a 25.8 percent interest in Quebecor Printing for $100 million. The purchase gave Quebecor access to a CAD 744 million customer list and rotogravure presses tailored to U.S. advertisers and catalog companies. Only a year later, Robert Maxwell's death revealed his holdings to be in a financial mess. Quebecor bought back its shares from Maxwell for $94.8 million, $5.2 million less than Maxwell had paid for it, giving Quebecor 100 percent ownership of Quebecor Printing.

Quebecor was not immune from the recession in the early 1990s. Plummeting newsprint prices in 1991 created heavy losses at Donohue, substantially eating into Quebecor's revenues. Advertising was down as well, putting pressure on the publishing and printing segments. In anticipation of the North American Free

KEY DATES

1950: Pierre Péladeau buys his first newspaper, *Le Journal de Rosemont*.
1964: Péladeau launches *Le Journal de Montréal*.
1972: Quebecor goes public.
1987: Company takes stake in paper firm Donohue.
1990: Printing business is launched with acquisition of Maxwell Communication Corp.'s U.S. printing operations.
1999: Quebecor acquires Sun Media and the printing division merges with World Color Press, forming Quebecor Media and Quebecor World, respectively.
2007: Acquisition of Osprey Media makes Quebecor Media the largest newspaper publisher in Canada.
2008: Quebecor World files for bankruptcy.

Trade Agreement (NAFTA), Quebecor established a foothold in Mexico by buying Mexican printer Gráficas Monte Alban S.A. The move was another step forward in Quebecor's determination to become a truly North American company and gave Quebecor a presence in all three North American countries. Gráficas printed books for Mexican and South American publishers. With about 200 employees and annual sales of $4.5 million, Gráficas was not a large acquisition. Nevertheless, it provided a starting point from which to learn the Mexican market and expand holdings in the fast-growing nation of 80 million people.

Quebecor expanded further in 1992 as it made large investments in its printing facilities and took Quebecor Printing public with an initial public offering (IPO) that left the parent company with a 67.57 percent share of its printing subsidiary. Proceeds from the offering were used to reduce bank debt. In the same year, Quebecor won two lucrative five-year contracts to print and bind Canadian telephone directories. The value of the contracts over five years was estimated at a combined total of CAD 505 million.

In 1992 and 1993 Quebecor Printing acquired Arcata Graphics and three major Arcata Corporation printing plants, bringing in clients such as *Reader's Digest*, *Parade*, and *TV Guide*. The acquisition of these plants substantially expanded Quebecor's market share and capacity in producing catalogs, magazines, and books. Advanced web offset publication, special binding, ink-jet printing, and shorter run production capabilities were

some of the technologies enhanced by the purchase. In 1994 Quebecor completed its buyout of Arcata when it exercised its option to buy the company's outstanding shares. The final acquisition added five book manufacturing plants and a distribution facility to Quebecor, making the company the second-largest book fabricator in the United States. By the end of 1993, U.S. sales represented more than 73 percent of Quebecor Printing's revenues and 64 percent of Quebecor Inc.'s revenues.

INTO FRANCE, INDIA, AND LEBANON: 1993–95

Quebecor Printing continued its international expansion with purchases and contracts in France, India, and Lebanon. Quebecor chose France because it was strategically situated to serve the European market, the world's second-largest market for printed products after the United States. In 1993, Quebecor acquired 70 percent of the shares of commercial printer Groupe Fécomme for about $12 million. The concern was renamed Imprimeries Fécomme-Quebecor S.A. The operation included three printing plants that made magazine covers, advertising inserts and circulars, and direct mail. Quebecor signed a letter of intent a few months after the Fécomme purchase to buy 49 percent of the shares of Groupe Jean Didier, the largest printer in France, for $27.6 million. The deal was completed in early 1995. The company produced magazines, catalogs, and inserts. With the two acquisitions, Quebecor established a significant foothold in Europe.

A partnership was formed in 1993 with Tej Bandhu Group in India to construct a printing plant, called Tej Quebecor Printing Ltd., for printing the majority of telephone directories in India. India, with a population of 850 million, provided great potential for future expansion for the company. In 1994 Quebecor was awarded a contract to produce bank notes for the central bank of Lebanon. The job specified at least 29 million large denomination pound notes. The new issue represented the first time Lebanon had printed its currency outside of England since its independence in 1943.

On the domestic front, 1994 saw the loss of one of Quebecor's major contracts, the printing of the U.S. edition of *Reader's Digest*, the largest paid monthly circulation magazine in the United States. Quebecor lost the $20 million-a-year, 10-year contract to its major U.S.-based competitor, R.R. Donnelley & Sons Co. Donnelley was the largest commercial printer in the world, with three times the revenues of Quebecor Printing. The contract was apparently awarded to Donnelley because of the company's technological capabilities in targeting advertising to specific subscriber groups. Another factor in the loss of the contract may have been the refusal of some unionized workers at Quebecor Printing of Buffalo Inc., where the magazine was printed, to accept a 10-year, no-strike/no-lockout amendment to the contract. Quebecor planned to make up the lost volume with growth in book printing.

CONTINUED GROWTH AFTER FOUNDER'S DEATH: 1997–99

Pierre Péladeau was 71 in 1996, and beginning to talk about leaving his company to his sons. Although Péladeau himself was evidently not in the best of health, Quebecor was still active, making acquisitions and entering new markets. Quebecor Printing's revenue was over $3 billion by the mid-1990s. Quebecor's pulp and paper subsidiary, Donohue, made a $1.1 billion acquisition in 1995, and was on the lookout for another major opportunity. Péladeau's second son, Pierre-Karl, left Quebecor's communications division in 1995 to head Quebecor Printing Europe. Within a few years, this subsidiary had made enough acquisitions to rank it as one of the largest printing companies in Europe.

In late 1996 Quebecor made a bid for Toronto Sun Publishing Company, which sold Sun papers in Toronto, Edmonton, Calgary, and Ottawa. Toronto Sun had a slim profit margin, and Péladeau was sure his company's management could convert the newspaper chain into much more of a moneymaker. However, Péladeau himself was a controversial figure, and several of the newspaper's columnists voiced outrage at the prospect of his owning the company. Eventually, Toronto Sun was sold to its own management team, and took the name Sun Media.

Pierre Péladeau died of a stroke in December 1997. He was succeeded by Pierre-Karl Péladeau. Within a year, Quebecor renewed its offer for Sun Media, which this time was accepted promptly. Quebecor paid CAD 983 million for Sun and the combined media company became the second-largest newspaper group in Canada. Quebecor filled the late 1990s with other significant acquisitions as well. The company moved into book publishing beginning in 1997, and within a few years Quebecor had bought five major Quebec publishers. The company also moved into television, buying the French-language network TQS. In 1999 the company launched a New Media division, capitalizing on the boom in Internet communications. Quebecor invested in various fledgling electronic commerce projects, and created a new company, Nurun, which was the largest so-called Web integrator in Canada, and a leader in the European market as well.

The largest acquisition of all was Quebecor's deal in 1999 to merge with its rival commercial printer World Color Press. World Color was quite similar in its operations to Quebecor Printing, producing magazines, catalogs, books, direct-mail circulars, and other printed goods at plants principally in the United States. The new combined company had roughly 175 printing facilities on five continents, and vaulted to the number one spot in the worldwide commercial printing industry. Quebecor's printing division changed its name to Quebecor World after the merger. Quebecor's partly owned paper subsidiary, Donohue, also made a major acquisition, buying Texas-based newsprint and specialty paper maker Champion International in 1998.

Then in early 2000, Quebecor announced it was selling its stake in Donohue to a third company, Abitibi-Consolidated. Quebecor then took an 11 percent share in Abitibi. Quebecor's management became embattled with Abitibi over the next year, when it insisted that Abitibi's CEO step down. Quebecor eventually dropped its demand, and then sold its stake in the company. The move allowed Quebecor to pay off debt it took on when making another major purchase, the Quebec cable television station Groupe Vidéotron.

FORTUNES REST ON TWO SUBSIDIARIES: 2001–11

Quebecor entered the decade ahead supported by two pillars, Quebecor Media and Quebecor World. The company owned 55 percent of Quebecor Media and 36 percent of Quebecor World, deriving CAD 9.78 billion of its CAD 11.63 billion in revenue in 2001 from Quebecor World. Unfortunately for the Péladeau family, the financial mainstay of the company suffered profoundly in the wake of the World Color Press acquisition, saddled with $1.3 billion in debt and hobbled by industry overcapacity and shrinking demand. The explosive growth of the Internet drained the vitality from magazine sales and other printing markets Quebecor World relied on, leading to alarming losses for the Quebecor subsidiary.

Quebecor Media, in contrast, fared well during the decade, easily factoring as the jewel of the Quebecor empire. Several acquisitions completed by the subsidiary cemented its reputation as Canada's premier media business. In 2004, through TVA Group and Sun Media Corp., Quebecor Media acquired Toronto television station Toronto 1 and rebranded the station Sun TV. The following year, when Videotron became the first major Canadian cable company to offer cable telephone service, Quebecor Media purchased Sogides Ltée, which possessed a catalog comprising approximately 3,900 titles, and became the largest publisher of French-language books in Canada. In 2007 the acquisition of

Osprey Media, the publisher of 20 daily and 34 weekly newspapers, made Quebecor Media the largest newspaper publisher in Canada. By the end of the year, the subsidiary generated CAD 3.36 billion in revenues.

As Quebecor Media grew in stature, Quebecor World floundered. Between 2003 and 2007, the company was led by six different CEOs, each of whom struggled in vain to solve the riddle of Quebecor World's problems. By the time the company came under the control of its seventh CEO in late 2007, Quebecor World was $1 billion in debt, losing $315 million per quarter, and dependent on the sale of its European division to a Dutch print company, RSDB Group, for its survival. When RSDB Group's shareholders voted against the deal in December 2007, all hope was lost. In January 2008 the company filed for bankruptcy, its more than $6 billion in annual revenue removed from Quebecor's financial results. Quebecor began the decade with 58,000 employees and CAD 11.63 billion in revenue and it ended the decade with 16,360 employees and CAD 4 billion in revenue.

Quebecor was a far smaller company after the Quebecor World debacle, but it was a far healthier company for having gone through the ordeal. Quebecor Media held sway as a Canadian powerhouse in the media industry, ranking as the third-largest cable operator through Videotron, the largest newspaper publisher through Sun Media, and as the largest, private-sector broadcaster of French-language entertainment through TVA Group. Profits were up and demand was increasing for the services offered by Quebecor Media, fueling confidence within the Péladeau family that the business created by Pierre Péladeau would remain a prominent force in Canadian business in the years to come.

Katherine Smethurst
Updated, A. Woodward; Jeffrey L. Covell

PRINCIPAL SUBSIDIARIES

Archambault Group Inc.; Canoe Inc.; CEC Publishing Inc.; Sogides Group Inc.; Le SuperClub Vidéotron Ltée; Nurun Inc.; Osprey Media Publishing Inc.; Quebecor Media Inc. (54.72%); Quebecor Media Printing Inc.; Sun Media Corporation; TVA Group Inc.; Videotron Ltd.

PRINCIPAL COMPETITORS

BCE Inc.; Canadian Broadcasting Corporation; Rogers Communications Inc.

FURTHER READING

"Abitibi's Big Holder Is Seeking Backing to Oust the CEO." *Wall Street Journal*, November 3, 2000.

"Bankruptcy Fears for Quebecor World as Roto Deal Collapses." *Print Week*, December 20, 2007.

De Santis, Solange. "Québécor Appears to Win Battle to Buy Sun Media as Torstar Won't Top Offer." *Wall Street Journal*, December 22, 1998.

Dougherty, Kevin. "The Powerful World of the Péladeaus." *Financial Post*, March 21, 1992.

Jason, Scott. "Quebecor Financial Fortunes Dwindling: Web Revolutions Hurting Traditional Business Models." *Merced Sun-Star*, December 29, 2007.

"Québécor Inc. Sells Its 11% Abitibi Stake for $393.4 Million." *Wall Street Journal*, June 8, 2001.

"Québécor Scraps Demands for Management Shake-Up." *Wall Street Journal*, December 15, 2000.

"The Rationale behind the Big Acquisition." *Graphic Arts Monthly*, August 1999.

"Separatism, No: Québécor to Acquire Sun Media." *Editor & Publisher*, December 12, 1998.

Wells, Jennifer. "Péladeau's Power Play." *Maclean's*, August 5, 1996.

Quiñenco S.A.

Enrique Foster Sur 20
Los Condes, Santiago
Chile
Telephone: (56 2) 750-7100
Fax: (56 2) 750-7101
Web site: http://www.quinenco.cl

Public Company
Incorporated: 1957 as Sociedad Forestal Quiñenco S.A.
Employees: 16,555
Sales: CLP 1.45 trillion ($2.84 billion) (2010)
Stock Exchanges: Santiago
Ticker Symbol: Quinenco
NAICS: 312111 Soft Drink Manufacturing; 312120
    Brewers; 312130 Wineries; 322996 Fabricated Pipe
    and Pipe Fitting Manufacturing; 331316
    Aluminum Extruded Product Manufacturing;
    331422 Copper Wire Drawing; 447110 Gasoline
    Stations with Convenience Stores; 515120 Televi-
    sion Broadcasting; 522110 Commercial Banking;
    531311 Residential Property Managers; 531110
    Lessors of Residential Buildings and Dwellings;
    551112 Offices of Other Holding Companies

∎ ∎ ∎

Quiñenco S.A. is the largest business conglomerate in
Chile, a diversified holding company whose assets
include stakes in one of the nation's leading banks and
in two important industrial sectors: metal products and
beverages. Although a public company, most of its
shares are held indirectly by members of the Luksic family, the wealthiest in Chile. It is the most diversified of
Chilean economic groups, with the largest international
presence and the largest presence in the banking system.

EXPLOITING NATURAL
RESOURCES: 1957–79

Andrónico Luksic Abaroa was born in Antofagasta, the
son of a Croatian immigrant who owned a general store.
His first business venture was the Ford dealership he
secured in his birthplace. There he met four French
engineers who had purchased a copper mine near the
city. He bought them out one by one, but the business
was in difficulty and short of capital when, in 1954,
Nippon Mining Co., a Japanese firm, agreed to pay him
what he first thought was CLP 500,000 but was in fact
$500,000, more than 10 times as much. Luksic said he
burned 20 packages of votive candles and prayed for the
intercession of his three favorite saints before depositing
the money in a bank to be used as collateral to finance
new enterprises.

Luksic established Sociedad Forestal Quiñenco S.A.
in 1957 in order to exploit tracts of eucalyptus trees that
would be cut down to provide supports for
underground tunnels needed for coal mining. (*Quiñenco*
is a Mapuche Indian word meaning "black lagoon.")
During the 1960s this company acquired control of
Empresas Lucchetti S.A., a pasta maker that expanded
into edible oils and soups and became one of Chile's
largest food companies, and Madeco S.A., which came
to dominate the nation in manufacturing copper cables
and pipes and aluminum pipes.

By the early 1970s Forestal Quiñenco was also engaged in electric-power distribution, shipping, and agriculture as well as fishing and foods and metals processing. The Marxist regime of President Salvador Allende nationalized many Chilean businesses. Luksic agreed to sell some of them less expensively to the government in return for being allowed to run the others without harassment. After Allende was overthrown in 1973, the government of General Augusto Pinochet registered its displeasure by barring Luksic from bidding on the state-owned companies to be privatized. Nevertheless, he was able to regain Madeco, one of the companies that had been nationalized. During the last part of the decade Hoteles Carrera S.A., a luxury chain, and Antofagasta-Bolivia Railway Co. plc were also incorporated into the group. Majority control of eight enterprises made Luksic sixth among the principal economic groups in Chile heading into the 1980s.

BANKING AND BEVERAGES: 1980–96

The financial crisis that gripped all of Latin America in the early 1980s ruined many Chilean capitalists and investors. Not having overextended itself, the Luksic group was able to go bargain shopping. It entered telecommunications by purchasing privatized CNT Telefónica del Sur S.A. for less than $7 million in 1982. This company became the foundation of a diversified telecommunications entity named VTR S.A. One-third of Compañia Cervecerias Unidas S.A. (CCU), a bankrupt brewery and soft-drink bottler at least $350 million in debt, was purchased about the same time for about $6 million. It settled with its creditors and, 15 years later, when it also owned the vintner Viña San Pedro S.A., had a market value of $1.5 billion.

The Luksic group entered the financial sector in 1981 by purchasing shares in Banco O'Higgins. Later in the decade it bought shares of Banco de Santiago as well. In 1993 it formed a joint venture with Spain's Banco Central Hispano that assumed control of banks in neighboring countries. This company, OHCH, merged Santiago and O'Higgins in 1995 to establish, under the Banco Santiago name, what was briefly Chile's largest bank.

During the early 1990s the Luksic group acted not only to diversify its holdings within Chile but also to enter other South American countries. Between 1991 and 1995 the group spent more than $300 million in Argentina in order to acquire a bank, beverage companies, manufacturers of machine tools, and factories that processed food. CCU became Argentina's second-largest beer company. Madeco invested about $550 million in subsidiaries in Argentina, Brazil, and Peru.

By this time Luksic had withdrawn from day-to-day management of his holdings. Adrónico Luksic Craig, his oldest son, was in charge of the financial properties. His second son, Guillermo Luksic Craig, the president of the conglomerate, supervised the industrial ones. Their father and his third son, Jean Paul Luksic Fontbana, directed the mining and railroad assets, which became Antofagasta Holdings plc in 1982. Quiñenco S.A. was made the holding company in 1996 for all the group properties other than Antofagasta Holdings. In 1997 Quiñenco became a public company, collecting $279 million in Santiago and New York for about 17 percent of the shares. After going public, it was ranked as the fifth-largest conglomerate in Latin America.

DIVERSIFIED PUBLIC HOLDING COMPANY: 1997–2007

Quiñenco was the third-largest economic group in Chile and the most diversified. In addition to its large stakes in banking and beverages, in the telecommunications sector it held 52 percent of VTR; in the foods sector, 77.5 percent of Lucchetti; in metal-products manufacturing, 56 percent of Madeco; in agriculture, 90 percent of Agrícola El Peñón S.A.; and in tourism and travel, 87 percent of Hoteles Carrera S.A.

The Luksic sons were supported in their stewardship of Quiñenco by a talented staff of executives, recruited from other companies, that was dubbed the "dream team." They were directed by Francisco Pérez Mackenna, who joined the group in 1991 and subsequently became managing director of Quiñenco.

Under the Luksics and Pérez Mackenna, the conglomerate had no attachment to any particular enterprise and was willing to downsize itself if it deemed divestiture to make economic sense. Quiñenco sold half its stake in VTR in 1995 to U.S.-based SBC Communications Inc. for $128.6 million and collected nearly $500 million more in 1997 and 1998 by selling its share

KEY DATES

1957: Sociedad Forestal Quiñenco is founded by Andrónico Luksic Abaroa.

1980: With eight diversified companies, the Luksic group is one of the largest in Chile.

1996: All group companies except Antofagasta Holdings are placed within Quiñenco.

2001: Quiñenco succeeds in acquiring a controlling share of Banco de Chile.

2007: Quiñenco agrees to sell half its stake in Banco de Chile to Citigroup Inc.

2011: Quiñenco buys 500 gasoline service stations in two separate transactions.

of VTR's cellular phone and long-distance operations. The holding company also sold its investment in VTR's cable television operations in 1999, for $260 million, but retained Telefónica del Sur, which was the largest company of its kind in southern Chile. Quiñenco and a partner founded Habitaria S.A., a residential real estate joint venture, in 1998, but it closed Hotel Carrera in Santiago and sold the Carrera hotels in Arica and Iquique to the Radisson chain.

OHCH suffered a mortal blow in January 1999, when Banco Central Hispano announced that it would merge with Spain's largest bank, Banco Santander, to form Banco Santander Central Hispano. Suddenly, Quiñenco's partner in Banco Santiago was a competitor as Banco Santander's Chilean subsidiary. Accordingly, Quiñenco sold its half of the joint venture and purchased a majority interest of Banco de A. Edwards for $283.3 million as well as a smaller stake in Banco de Chile.

Over the next two years, Quiñenco purchased a controlling share of Banco de Chile as well and in August 2001 announced it would merge Banco Edwards into the latter, which would become for a time Chile's largest private bank. As a result of the merger, completed in 2002, banking investments came to represent 45 percent of Quiñenco's assets.

In 2003 Heineken N.V. became the half-owner of the company that, with Quiñenco, held two-thirds of CCU. In 2004 the holding company sold Lucchetti, its principal food-processing property in Chile, but retained the Peruvian company. Luksic was credited by *Forbes* as being the richest man in Chile and the fourth-richest in Latin America in 2004. His holdings were valued at $4.3 billion. He died in 2005, leaving five children and 20 grandchildren.

Quiñenco also purchased a stake in one of Chile's leading retailers, Almacenes París S.A., that year, but was unable to keep control of the chain out of the hands of a rival and chose to sell its shares for a profit in 2005. Quiñenco withdrew its listing on the New York Stock Exchange in 2007.

BANKING PREDOMINATES: 2007–11

During the ensuing years, Quiñenco concentrated its activities on the financial sector. It held a majority of the voting shares in Banco de Chile by means of a subsidiary named LQ Inversiones Financieras S.A. (LQIF). In 2007, however, it agreed to sell one-third of LQIF to Citigroup Inc., with an option to sell another 17 percent to Citigroup. Banco de Chile and Citibank Chile merged at the beginning of 2008, but Citigroup did not exercise its option until 2010, bringing the value to Quiñenco from the total transaction to CLP 541 billion ($1.06 billion).

Meanwhile, Quiñenco was continuing its exit from the telecommunications sector. It had acquired a stake in another large company, Empresa Nacional de Telecomunicaciones S.A. (Entel) in 1999 but sold more than half of these shares in 2001 and the rest in 2007 and 2009. At the beginning of 2010 it sold its 74 percent share in Telefónica del Sur for CLP 76 billion ($156 million). This transaction brought the Quiñenco's revenues from sales of its stakes in more than 20 companies to $1.92 billion since 1997. Later in the year, however, it bought two-thirds of a Santiago-based television station with national coverage.

Quiñenco, in 2011, purchased the Chilean subsidiary of Shell Petroleum Company for $621 million, thereby acquiring its 300 service stations in the country and all associated businesses, such as its fuel distribution to industrial clients, distribution of lubricants under the Shell brand, asphalt and chemical products, storage tanks, and its stake in a pipeline company. Later in the year Quiñenco acquired the 200 service stations and 97 related convenience stores in Chile of Organización Terpel S.A. Also that year, Quiñenco paid $120 million for a 10 percent stake in Compañia Sudamericana de Vapores, Chile's leading maritime company.

Quiñenco's share of Madeco had dropped to 48 percent by the end of 2010. Through its LQ Inversiones Financieras S.A. joint venture with Citigroup, it held 31 percent of Banco de Chile, and through its Inversiones y Rentas S.A. joint venture with Heineken it held 33 percent of CCU.

The Luksic group continued to hold about 83 percent of Quiñenco S.A. in 2011. The rest remained publicly traded in Chile. The combined sales of companies in which the Luksic group held stakes came to $4.7 billion in 2010. That year, finance accounted for 53 percent of Quiñenco's revenues, foods and beverages for 38 percent, and manufacturing for 9 percent.

Quiñenco's model of doing business was to raise to its potential each enterprise in which the conglomerate was invested. In this way the enterprise would increase its value and its profitability to Quiñenco in the form of dividends and eventual sale in part or in whole.

Robert Halasz

PRINCIPAL SUBSIDIARIES

Inversiones Río Bravo S.A.; Inversiones Río Grande S.p.A.

PRINCIPAL DIVISIONS

Beverages and Food; Financial Services; Manufacturing.

PRINCIPAL COMPETITORS

Banco Santander Chile; Embotelladora Andina S.A.; Viña Concha y Toro S.A.

FURTHER READING

"Adrónico Luksic Abaroa: Corazón de Minero." *Gestión*, August 2004, 10–12, 14.

Dolan, Kerry A. "Like Father, Like Sons." *Forbes*, September 21, 1998, 136, 140.

Friedland, Jonathan. "The Family Empires: Chile's Luksics." *Wall Street Journal*, December 1, 1995, A10.

Fuentes E. and Luis Arturo. *Grandes grupos económicos en Chile.* Santiago: Dolmen Ediciones, 1997, 66–73 and annex 4.

Galloway, Jennifer. "Fair Market Value for All?" *LatinFinance*, December 2001, 21–23.

Kandall, Jonathan. "Andrónico Luksic, 78, Magnate in Chile, Dies." *New York Times*, August 29, 2005, B7.

———. "Strains in Diversity." *Institutional Investor*, March 1999, 97+.

———. "Sum of the Parts." *LatinFinance*, January–February 1998, 58–60.

Ralph Lauren Corporation

650 Madison Avenue
New York, New York 10022
U.S.A.
Telephone: (212) 318-7000
Toll Free: (800) 377-7656
Fax: (212) 888-5780
Web site: http://www.ralphlauren.com

Public Company
Incorporated: 1968 as Polo Fashions, Inc.
Employees: 11,000
Sales: $5.7 billion (2011)
Stock Exchanges: New York
Ticker Symbol: RL
NAICS: 315211 Men's and Boys; Cut and Sew Apparel Contractors; 315212 Women's, Girls', and Infants' Cut and Sew Apparel Contractors; 315222 Men's and Boys' Cut and Sew Suit, Coat, and Overcoat Manufacturing; 315223 Men's and Boys' Cut and Sew Shirt (Except Work Shirt Manufacturing; 315232 Women's and Girls' Cut and Sew Blouse and Shirt Manufacturing; 315233 Women's and Girls' Cut and Sew Dress Manufacturing; 315291 Infants; Cut and Sew Apparel Manufacturing; 316992 Women's Handbag and Purse Manufacturing; 325620 Toilet Preparation Manufacturing; 334518 Watch, Clock, and Part Manufacturing; 339115 Ophthalmic Goods Manufacturing; 446120 Cosmetics, Beauty Supplies, and Perfume Stores; 448110 Men's Clothing Stores; 448120 Women's Clothing Stores; 448140 Family Clothing Stores

∎ ∎ ∎

Ralph Lauren Corporation has become one of the best-known fashion design and licensing houses in the world. Founded by designer Ralph Lauren in the late 1960s, the company boomed in the 1980s as Lauren's designs came to be associated with a sophisticated and distinctly American attitude. By the 1980s, the Polo/Ralph Lauren name helped sell a wide array of products, including fragrances and accessories for men and women, clothing for young boys and infants, and a variety of housewares, shoes, furs, jewelry, leather goods, hats, and eyewear. Brands include Polo by Ralph Lauren, Lauren, Chaps, RRL, Rugby, Club Monaco, and American Living. The company's collections are available in 9,000 locations worldwide in both upscale and mid-tier department stores, as well as the firm's 370 Ralph Lauren, Club Monaco, and Rugby retail stores and its e-commerce sites.

ORIGINS IN THE SIXTIES

Ralph Lifshitz was born on October 14, 1939, in the Bronx to a middle-class Jewish family. Somewhere along the way he had his surname legally changed to "Lauren." His father was an artist and housepainter. His mother was reportedly disappointed Ralph did not become a rabbi. The Polo empire began in the late 1960s, when Lauren, then a clothing salesman, tired of selling other people's neckties and decided to design and sell his own. Lauren had no experience in fashion design, but he had grown up in the New York fashion world, selling men's gloves, suits, and ties. In 1967, he went to his employer, Abe Rivetz, with a proposal to design a line of ties, but Rivetz told him, "The world is not ready for Ralph Lauren." Lauren decided that it was, and he convinced clothier Beau Brummel to manufacture his Polo line of neckwear. "I didn't know how to make a tie," Lauren confessed to *Vogue* in August 1982. "I didn't know fabric, I didn't know measurements. What did I know? That I was a salesman. That I was honest. And that all I wanted was quality." Lauren's ties were wider and more colorful than other ties on the market and they soon found a niche, first in small menswear stores and later in the fashionable Bloomingdale's department store.

Within a year, Lauren decided to form his own company with help from his brother, Jerry, and $50,000 in backing from Norman Hilton, a Manhattan clothing manufacturer. The company, Polo Fashions, Inc. (which changed its name to Polo/Ralph Lauren Corporation in 1987), expanded the Polo menswear collection to include shirts, suits, and sportswear, as well as the trademark ties. The company designed, manufactured, and distributed the Polo collection, which met with the approval of both the department stores that featured the clothes and the fashion critics who praised their style. In 1970, Lauren received the coveted Coty Award for menswear. In a rare move, Lauren then began designing clothes for women as well as for men. His first designs (men's dress shirts cut for women) met with great success in 1971, and soon sales topped $10 million.

The rapid growth of Polo Fashions, Inc., proved hard to manage for the young entrepreneur, who had succeeded in crafting a brand identity but not in managing his business. By 1972, according to *Time* (September 1, 1986), "Lauren suddenly discovered that his enterprise was almost bankrupt because of poor financial management and the costs of headlong expansion." Scrambling to survive, Lauren invested $100,000 of his savings in the business and persuaded Peter Strom to leave his job with Norman Hilton and become his partner. The arrangement gave Lauren 90 percent and Strom 10 percent ownership. Strom described their duties to the *New York Times Magazine* in September 1983: "We divide the work this way: I do

everything Ralph doesn't want to do; and I don't do anything he likes to do. He designs, he does advertising, public relations; I do the rest." The Lauren brothers and Strom soon made changes in the structure of the company that set the stage for more than two decades of unparalleled success.

The first step in the reorganization was to concentrate on what they did best, design, and leave the rest to other companies. With this in mind, Polo Fashions, Inc., licensed the manufacture of Ralph Lauren brand women's wear to Stuart Kreisler, an experienced manufacturer who set out to build the reputation of the Lauren brand name. Under licensing agreements, the designer got a cut of wholesale revenues and shared in advertising costs. Such agreements would be the basis for Polo's future business. Moreover, Strom insisted that those retailers who sold the company's clothes make a commitment to selling the entire line, which meant they had to carry the $350 Polo suit. "That eliminated two-thirds of our accounts," Strom told *Vogue*. "But those who stayed with us experienced our commitment to them, and it wasn't long before we felt their loyalty in return." With business once again secure, the company was able to turn its attention to crafting a brand image as distinctive as any in the nation.

THE EIGHTIES: THE DECADE OF POLO

Beginning in the mid-1970s, Polo Fashions entered a period of phenomenal growth that carried it through the late 1980s. From being a designer and licenser of a limited number of lines of men's and women's clothing, the company expanded its products to include fragrances, eyewear, shoes, accessories, housewares, and a range of other products. Even as the number of products bearing the brand names "Polo" or "Ralph Lauren" expanded, the image of the company became more secure and more singular. Soon, people were speaking of the "Laurenification of America," crediting Ralph Lauren with creating a unique American aesthetic, and calling the 1980s the "decade of Ralph Lauren." The company's success in this period can be credited to the design skills of Ralph Lauren and to the astute image-making and marketing skills of Lauren and his principal partner, Peter Strom.

Fashion critics and journalists used such words as integrity, elegance, tradition, sophistication, WASPy, mannered, pseudo-English, and sporty to describe Lauren's many designs. No single word, though, could encompass the many themes, from the famous English Polo Club designs to the distinctly American western designs, with which Lauren experimented. Some critics complained that Lauren was a relentless borrower, pos-

KEY DATES

1968: Polo Fashions is created by tie salesman Ralph Lauren.
1986: Flagship store opens on Madison Avenue.
1997: Polo/Ralph Lauren Corporation goes public.
2003: European headquarters moves from Paris to Geneva.
2006: Company opens its first freestanding flagship store in Tokyo.
2007: Company launches its Global Brand Concepts.
2010: Company shortens its name to Ralph Lauren Corporation.

sessed of no unique vision. Lauren himself stated in *New York*, in December 1992, that he was interested in "style but not flamboyance, but sophistication, class, and an aristocratic demeanor that you can see in people like Cary Grant and Fred Astaire." As Lauren pointed out, "The things I do are not about novelty. They're things I love and can't get away from. There are some things in life that, no matter what the times are, keep getting better and better. That's really my philosophy."

Polo excelled at getting Lauren's distinctive design image across to consumers. From its very first advertisements in New York City newspapers in 1974, the company attempted to portray its products as part of a complete lifestyle. Polo pioneered the multipage lifestyle advertisement in major magazines. These ads presented a world lifted out of time, where wealthy, attractive people relaxed in Polo products during a weekend at their country estate or on safari in Africa. *Vogue* described the ads as a kind of "home movie," with a cast of "faintly sorrowful but wildly attractive people. The women are always between childhood and thirty; the men are sometimes old." Polo lavished huge amounts of money on these ads, as much as $15 million and $20 million a year, although its licensees shared some of the cost by returning 2 to 3 percent of sales into the advertising budget. An ad director for a major fashion magazine told *Time*: Polo "has some of the best advertising in the business because it sets a mood, it evokes a lifestyle."

Lauren's intuitive design sense and the company's ability to create an idealized image for its products provided the base for the company to expand the variety of products it marketed and attain greater control over retailing. From its first product lines (Polo by Ralph Lauren menswear and Ralph Lauren women's wear) the company introduced a variety of products: Polo by Ralph Lauren cologne and boys' clothing in 1978; a girlswear line in 1981; luggage and eyeglasses in 1982; home furnishings in 1983. Later brand extensions included shoes, furs, and underwear. The company introduced its collection of apparel for newborns, infants, and toddlers in 1994. These new product lines were accompanied by continual updating of the older brand names.

PRODUCT DEVELOPMENT, DISTRIBUTION, AND PROMOTION

Although Polo retained control over the design and advertising of its products, the success or failure of Polo product expansion often depended upon its licensees, as Polo's experience with fragrances and its home collection indicated. Polo's fragrances became a major income producer only when it found a licensee who was willing to help develop and promote the products. Although Polo had marketed its fragrances (Polo by Ralph Lauren for men and Lauren for women) since 1978, they were not major sellers until the mid-1980s, when the company licensed fragrance production to Cosmair, Inc. In 1990, Cosmair introduced Polo Crest for men and Safari for women, made to accompany a new line of clothing also bearing the Safari name. Cosmair hoped to sell between $25 million and $30 million wholesale by the end of the fragrance's first year. Two years later Polo and Cosmair launched Safari for Men, which they promoted in an uncharacteristic television commercial in which Ralph Lauren rode a horse bareback on a beach.

Not all licensing arrangements worked as well. In 1983, Polo began to promote the introduction of its "Home Collection," a line of products that Lauren had designed for the home. *House & Garden* in October 1984 called the collection, which numbered more than 2,500 items and included everything from sheets to furniture to flatware, "the most complete of its kind conceived by a fashion designer."

However, the collection soon ran into serious trouble as the licensee, the J.P. Stevens Company, experienced difficulties getting the products to retail outlets on time. J.P. Stevens also had trouble maintaining quality control, having themselves licensed elements of the line to other companies. In addition, Stevens demanded that stores that wanted to show the collection construct $250,000 freestanding, wood-paneled boutiques to display the items. Stores balked at the price tag. Polo/Ralph Lauren Vice Chairman Peter Strom told *Time* that the introduction was "A disaster! Disaster!" It took several years for the company to get the collection back on track.

Over the years, the company used a number of techniques to exert control over the way its merchandise was distributed and sold. Early on, the company insisted that retailers offer the entire product line instead of simply selecting items it wanted to carry, arguing that the lines had to stand as a coherent whole. Beginning in 1971, the company began to offer franchises as well. Instead of charging a franchise fee, the company made money as the wholesaler for the clothing. These franchises allowed an entire store to concentrate on the Polo/Ralph Lauren image.

FIRST OUTLET STORE OPENS

Then, in 1982, Polo/Ralph Lauren opened the first of its 50 outlet stores, in Lawrence, Kansas. The outlet stores allowed the company to control the distribution of irregulars and items that had not sold by the end of each season, thereby preventing the company's products from appearing in discount stores. These outlet stores were placed at a significant distance from the full-price retailers to ensure that they did not steal business. Such expansion occurred not only in the United States but around the world, as Polo/Ralph Lauren opened shops in London, Paris, and Tokyo.

The flagship of the Polo/Ralph Lauren retail enterprise was the refurbished Rhinelander mansion on Madison Avenue in New York City. Opened in 1986, the 20,000-square-foot mansion featured mahogany woodwork, hand-carved balustrades lining marble staircases, and sumptuous carpeting. "While men who look like lawyers search for your size shirt and ladies who belong at deb parties suggest complementary bags and shoes, you experience the ultimate in lifestyle advertising," wrote Lenore Skenazy in *Advertising Age*. Naomi Leff, who designed the interior of the company's palace, called it "a marker in retailing history. It tells manufacturers that if they're willing to put out, they'll be able to make their own statement, which is not being made in the department stores."

Establishing brand-focused retail outlets made perfect sense for Polo/Ralph Lauren, for it allowed the company to increase profits by eliminating the middleman as well as to control the environment in which the products appeared. In fact, other designers followed Polo/Ralph Lauren's lead, including Calvin Klein, Liz Claiborne, Adrienne Vittadini, and Anne Klein. However, the move caused tension between the designer and his traditional retailers, the large department stores. A *Forbes* feature on Lauren's strategy claimed that "a lot of people in business think it is in bad taste to compete with your own customers. Lauren did not agree. And such is his pull at the cash register that he may get away with this piece of business heresy."

GOING PUBLIC IN 1997

Polo/Ralph Lauren Corporation rode its expertly crafted brand image and astute retailing strategies to remarkable heights in the 1980s, as sustained economic growth and the public's fascination with Lauren's image fueled an unparalleled expansion in products bearing the Ralph Lauren name. Retail expansion slowed dramatically with the economic downturn in the early 1990s. Some stores that once thrived on the sales of Ralph Lauren's high-priced products complained that the company was unable to adjust to changes in the market and competition from lower-cost, knockoff rivals.

Polo/Ralph Lauren rolled out a plethora of other brand extensions in the 1990s, including shoes from Reebok and Rockport and a line of Polo-brand jeans, successful fragrances, the Polo Sport active-sportswear and RRL jeans, a moderately priced women's collection in collaboration with licensee Jones Apparel Group (which it canceled due to low sales volume, leaving Jones to take its case to court).

The 1994 sale of 28 percent of the company to a Goldman Sachs & Co. investment fund for $135 million prompted speculation about the future of the company. In the short term, industry observers expected the company to use the cash influx to expand its retail stores. Observers also wondered whether this sale, the first in the company's history, indicated that the company would eventually go public or that Ralph Lauren was beginning to look toward life after designing.

The company did, in fact, go public on the New York Stock Exchange, on June 13, 1997. Founder and Chairman Ralph Lauren sold nearly 18 million of his own shares for $465.4 million, retaining 90 percent of voting rights through his ownership of all outstanding class B stock. Although the shares traded at a premium, some analysts felt the stock had good growth potential due to relatively unexploited world markets and an underdeveloped women's line. The next year, moving to reduce expenses, the company restructured its divisions.

Although Polo/Ralph Lauren ended 1998 with announcements of 250 job cuts and nine store closings, it also opened a flagship store in Chicago and a fine-dining RL-branded restaurant next door a few months later. In March 1999, Polo/Ralph Lauren, with 56 stores in Canada and 13 in the United States, paid $80 million for Club Monaco Inc., a chain of trendy clothing stores based in Toronto that attracted the younger, hipper clientele that Ralph Lauren had been unable to lure away from Tommy Hilfiger and other competitors. Two years later, the company closed 11 underperforming Club Monaco locations and announced plans to shut down all of its jeans stores.

NEW FRONTIERS FOR THE NEW MILLENNIUM

In a 50-50 joint venture with NBC and its affiliates in 2000, Polo/Ralph Lauren formed Ralph Lauren Media Company to sell its products online as well as via broadcast, cable, and print media in 2000. RL's first television advertising debuted soon after. Also in early 2000 Polo/Ralph Lauren purchased its European licensee, Poloco, for $230 million, giving the company greater control of its brand overseas. Italian licensee PRL Fashions of Europe and a Belgian store were acquired in 2001. Overall Polo/Ralph Lauren was able to quadruple European sales between 1999 and 2002, but expansion was expensive. In Europe, clothing was typically sold in specialty shops, not the giant department stores that made up more than a half of Polo/Ralph Lauren's wholesale revenues in the United States.

In more developments overseas, Polo/Ralph Lauren moved its European operations from Paris to Geneva in 2003. It also acquired stores also from licensees in Germany and Argentina and paid ¥5.6 billion ($47.6 million) for a 50 percent interest in the master license of the company's men's, women's, and jeans business in Japan.

The following year, Polo/Ralph Lauren assumed responsibility for its Lauren line for women from its former licensee, Jones Apparel Group, an action later contested. It also denied an employee's claim, as reported in the *San Francisco Chronicle* in November 2002, that it had a policy of forcing store staff to buy its own pricey clothes to wear at work, and to update their wardrobes every season. Ironically, a general return to dressier work clothes, a result of a tighter job market, bode well for the company entering 2004.

PARTNERSHIP WITH USTA

Polo/Ralph Lauren entered the world of tennis in 2005 when it partnered with the United States Tennis Association (USTA) to become the official apparel sponsor of the U.S. Open through 2008. The deal, which included an official shirt for on-court officials, co-branded U.S. Open/Polo/Ralph Lauren merchandise, and joint marketing programs, paved the way for the company's agreement with The All England Club and Wimbledon to become the first official designer and the exclusive outfitter of Wimbledon from 2006 through

2010. Polo/Ralph Lauren began to create outfits for on-court officials and to sell its Wimbledon collection at its own freestanding stores, through select retailers, and Polo.com.

In another licensing agreement in 2006, the company partnered with Luxottica in a deal valued at more than $1.75 billion over a 10-year period. Luxottica's U.S. arm began to make Club Monaco-branded prescription frames and sunglasses that sold domestically and in Canada.

In 2007, Polo/Ralph Lauren kept its focus on the domestic landscape with the launch of a new group named Global Brand Concepts that developed lifestyle brands for specialty and department stores. The group designed and marketed accessories, home decor, and women's, men's, and children's apparel that sold under separate brands. The first of these was J.C. Penney's American Living Collection.

Not to overlook the development of its brand presence overseas during the last part of the decade, the company opened its flagship store in Tokyo in 2006. The next year Polo/Ralph Lauren secured a foothold in the Japanese apparel and accessories market by purchasing the 50 percent balance of Polo/Ralph Lauren Japan for some $23 million, making it a wholly owned subsidiary. The company also increased its stake in Impact 21 Co., a Japanese sub-licensee that operated the company's in-country men's, women's, and jeans apparel and accessories business.

Ralph Lauren also expanded its business through acquisitions during this time, extended the reach of its retail operations, and experienced organic growth. Its luxury brand accessories rivaled European competitors, thanks to strategic partnerships with licensees, including Richemont SA, with which it formed high-end Ralph Lauren Watch and Jewelry Co., and the Italian eyewear giant Luxottica Group, which designed, manufactured, and distributed Ralph Lauren-branded prescription frames and sunglasses. Other major licensing partners included Hanes for undergarments and sleepwear, L'Oréal for fragrances, and Warnaco for Chaps sportswear.

BRINGING LICENSEES INTO THE FOLD

To give the apparel maker more control of its operations in Asia, which represented 12 percent of sales, Polo/Ralph Lauren continued buying out its licensees. In late 2009, it bought out its licensing partner Dickson Concepts, which had been a licensee for the Polo brand in China, Hong Kong, Indonesia, Malaysia, the Philippines, Singapore, Taiwan, and Thailand. It also acquired the children's wear and golf apparel inventory of former licensee Naigai Co. Ltd. of Japan. In 2010 it bought its South Korean wholesale and retail distribution operation from licensee Doosan Corp.

As the company, which shortened its name to Ralph Lauren in mid-2010, headed into the second decade of the century, nothing seemed to impede its global reach. As an official outfitter of the U.S. Olympic team at the 2012 Summer Olympics in London, it was certain to sell millions of dollars of Olympics-branded apparel and accessories. Ralph Lauren remained at the fashion empire helm through his ownership of about 76 percent of the voting shares despite plans to sell more than a quarter of his holdings. An American icon, he would continue to spread his version of the American dream around the world.

Tom Pendergast
Updated, Frederick C. Ingram; Carrie Rothburd

PRINCIPAL SUBSIDIARIES

Acqui Polo, C.V. (Netherlands); Fashions Outlet of America, Inc.; PRL USA Holdings, Inc.; PRL International, Inc.; Ralph Lauren Media, LLC (50%).

PRINCIPAL COMPETITORS

Abercrombie & Fitch Co.; American Eagle Outfitters, Inc.; Giorgio Armani S.p.A.; Banana Republic, LLC; Benetton Group SpA; Burberry Group plc; Calvin Klein, Inc.; Christian Dior; Coach, Inc.; Donna Karan International Inc; Estée Lauder Inc.; Gianni Versace S.p.A.; Gucci NV; Guess?, Inc.; Liz Claiborne Inc.; Nautica Enterprises Inc.; Tommy Bahama Group, Inc.; Tommy Hilfiger Group.

FURTHER READING

Aronson, Steven M. L. "High Style in Jamaica." *House & Garden*, October 1984, 127–37, 230.

Curan, Catherine. "Polo Goes Solo with Lauren Line." *Crain's New York Business*, June 16, 2003, 1.

———. "Ralph Lauren Goes Nowhere." *Crain's New York Business*, May 13, 2002, 3.

Ettorre, Barbara. "'Give Ralph Lauren All the Jets He Wants.'" *Forbes*, February 28, 1983, 102–03.

Fallon, James. "Ralph to Launch First TV Campaign Next Month." *DNR*, October 16, 2000, 6.

Ferretti, Fred. "The Business of Being Ralph Lauren." *New York Times Magazine*, September 18, 1983, 112+.

Gross, Michael. "The American Dream." *New York*, December 21–28, 1992, 71–72.

Kaufman, Leslie. "NBC Helps Ralph Lauren Fulfill a Multimedia Dream." *New York Times*, February 8, 2000, C13.

Koepp, Stephen. "Selling a Dream of Elegance and the Good Life." *Time*, September 1, 1986, 54–61.

Kornbluth, Jesse. "Ralph Lauren: Success American Style." *Vogue*, August 1982, 263+.

Ling, Flora. "Ralph Lauren's Polo Game." *Forbes*, June 26, 1978, 88.

Shaw, Hollie, and Serena French. "Polo Cleaning House at Club Monaco." *National Post* (Canada), April 12, 2001, C3.

Skenazy, Lenore. "Lauren Gets Honorable Mansion." *Advertising Age*, October 20, 1986, 56.

Strasburg, Jenny. "Polo Says Dress Code Not Forced." *San Francisco Chronicle*, November 6, 2002, B1.

Talley, Andre Leon. "Everybody's All-American." *Vogue*, February 1992, 203–10, 284.

Trachtenberg, Jeffrey A. "You Are What You Wear." *Forbes*, April 21, 1986, 94–98.

Valkin, Vanessa. "Polo Plans Europe HQ in Geneva." *Financial Times* (London), November 7, 2002, 32.

Rogers Communications Inc.

———— ■ ————

333 Bloor Street East
Toronto, Ontario M4W 1G9
Canada
Telephone: (416) 935-7777
Fax: (416) 935-3597
Web site: http://www.rogers.com

Public Company
Incorporated: 1920 as Famous Players Canadian
    Corporation
Employees: 27,971
Sales: CAD 12.18 billion (2010)
Stock Exchanges: Toronto New York
Ticker Symbol: RCI
NAICS: 517212 Cellular and Other Wireless Telecom-
    munications; 515122 Radio Stations; 515120
    Television Broadcasting; 515210 Cable and Other
    Subscription Programming; 517910 Other
    Telecommunications; 511120 Periodical Publishers;
    451220 Prerecorded Tape, Compact Disc, and
    Record Stores; 551112 Offices of Other Holding
    Companies

■ ■ ■

Rogers Communications Inc. is the largest communications and media company in Canada. Rogers Communications ranks as the country's largest wireless voice
and data communications provider. It ranks as Canada's
second-largest cable service provider, offering cable
television, Internet access, and telephony products for
residential and business customers, who are served
through a chain of retail stores selling Rogers branded
wireless and home entertainment services. Through its
broadcasting arm, Rogers Communications operates 55
radio stations and television properties that include the
five-station Citytv network, five multicultural OMNI
stations, Rogers Sportsnet, and The Shopping Channel.
Through its publishing arm, Rogers Communications
produces 55 consumer magazines and trade
publications. Through subsidiary Blue Jays Holdco Inc.,
the company owns the Toronto Blue Jays Baseball Club.
The company generates 57 percent of its annual
revenues from its wireless businesses, 31 percent from its
cable businesses, and 12 percent from its media
businesses.

FOUNDER'S BACKGROUND AND
EARLY SUCCESS: 1921–62

On three notable occasions Edward S. Rogers Jr. challenged conventional wisdom while orchestrating the
development of his company, refusing to heed the
advice of those purporting to know better. Each instance
proved to be instrumental to the growth of Rogers
Communications and greatly contributed to Rogers'
personal success, helping him earn the epithet most
sought after by entrepreneurs, "self-made billionaire".
First, Rogers decided to enter the FM radio broadcasting business, which raised the eyebrows of disbelieving
critics who declared that FM radio would never be
popular. Next he made the decision to enter the cable
television business, while onlookers proclaimed that
consumers would never pay for television. Then, in the
mid-1980s, Rogers set his sights on the nascent cellular
telephone business, but the board of directors of Rogers

COMPANY PERSPECTIVES

Rogers knows that no matter where customers are, being in touch with friends, family and colleagues makes their lives more connected. And being connected to the information and entertainment that matters most makes life easier and more enjoyable. Rogers makes "place-shifting" a reality. Today Canadians can connect to their communications, information and entertainment almost anywhere they want to be, easily and seamlessly. We're enabling a shift to where watching TV on the train, conducting a virtual white boarding session from the beach, disarming a home monitoring system from a smartphone, or answering a home phone from 5,000 miles away are becoming everyday activities.

Communications rejected his proposal. Rogers reacted characteristically. He went ahead anyway, using his own money to help launch the venture. By the turn of the millennium, despite all the pessimistic predictions, Rogers Communications was one of the largest communications companies in the world.

Rogers inherited some of his pioneering and entrepreneurial spirit from his father, Edward S. Rogers Sr., who in 1921 was the first Canadian to transmit a radio signal across the Atlantic. At the time only 21 years old, Rogers went on to become much more than a historical footnote by inventing the radio amplifying tube, a device that revolutionized the radio industry by eliminating the need for cumbersome, leak-prone acid batteries, enabling consumers to operate their radios on alternating current. Rogers' invention led him to found CFRB (Canada's First Rogers Batteryless), which became the most popular radio station in the country, and Rogers Majestic Corporation, a manufacturing concern devoted to producing his invention. Rogers moved on to break ground in another direction in 1931 when he was granted the first license in Canada to broadcast experimental television. However, eight years later, when Edward S. Rogers Jr. was five years old, the elder Rogers died of overwork and a bleeding ulcer, leaving no one in charge to supervise his various business interests. The Rogers estate floundered and the popular CFRB station was lost.

The younger Rogers, who preferred to be called Ted, was affected deeply by the death of his father. He followed his father's footsteps in his first big business deal, purchasing radio station CHFI-FM in 1960 while studying for a law degree at Osgoode Hall Law School. Rogers used a life insurance policy as collateral to take out a $63,000 loan and paid $85,000 for the station, an intrepid move considering that only 5 percent of the Toronto market possessed FM receivers at the time. Undaunted by critics who dismissed the FM concept, Rogers plunged into the FM radio broadcasting business, establishing Rogers Radio Broadcasting Limited as the owner of CHFI. To help promote the station, Rogers, then 26 years old, approached Westinghouse Canada and persuaded the company to manufacture inexpensive ($39.95) FM radios, which he then sold or gave away to listeners. Two years later, a year after earning his law degree, Rogers purchased CFTR-AM, then went on to win other radio licenses, initially using money from his parents' estate and later soliciting financial assistance from the Bank of Montreal and Toronto business leaders.

ENTRY INTO CABLE BROADCASTING: 1965

By the mid-1960s Rogers was ready to steer the Canadian communications industry in a new direction. While his father had shown himself to be an ingenious engineer, the younger Rogers was carving his niche in the communications industry as a marketer, transforming existing but little-used technology into widely sought-after services. His entry into FM radio broadcasting had proved to be an insightful move, the first of his successful efforts to broaden the appeal of existing communications technology, but when he was awarded Canada's first cable franchise in 1965 his abilities produced success of a much higher magnitude. Competing against industry stalwarts such as Gulf & Western and CBS for the first rights to broadcast cable, Rogers emerged victorious, registering one of the several key licensing coups that would carry him to the top of the communications industry.

After slightly more than a decade in the cable business, Rogers had established a formidable presence, constructing a cable network that had few rivals. In 1978 he made an aggressive move to bolster his company's position further when he acquired Canada's second largest cable company, Canadian Cablesystems Limited, in an unfriendly takeover. At the same time, Rogers began collecting cable franchises in the United States. The following year he took his company public as the largest cable operator in Canada. Another leading cable company, Premier Communications Limited, was added to Rogers' stable of cable properties in two transactions during 1979 and 1980, extending the

KEY DATES

1960: Edward S. (Ted) Rogers Jr. acquires CHFI, a struggling FM radio station.

1994: Rogers Media is created following the CAD 3.1 billion hostile takeover of Maclean Hunter.

1999: Microsoft Corporation acquires 9.2 percent stake in company.

2000: Rogers Communications acquires Major League Baseball's Toronto Blue Jays franchise.

2004: The CAD 1.6 billion purchase of Microcell Telecommunications creates Canada's largest wireless carrier.

2009: After Ted Rogers dies of congestive heart failure in late 2008, Nadir Mohamed is named president and CEO.

company's coverage to British Columbia, where Premier served three urban centers.

In 1981 Rogers targeted UA-Columbia Cablevision Inc. as his next acquisition, offering his family's five radio stations, owned by a private company named Rogers Telecommunications Ltd., and his extensive cable television interests for a loan to secure UA-Columbia's 450,000 cable subscribers. Rogers bid $152 million for 51 percent of UA-Columbia, teaming up with United Artists Theater Circuit Inc. to beat out competing bids offered by Knight-Ridder Newspapers and Dow Jones. When the deal was concluded in November, Rogers Communications' cable properties served 1.75 million subscribers, making the company the largest cable operator in North America.

Rogers Communications' frenetic growth slowed during the early 1980s after the acquisition of UA-Columbia, as an economic recession inflated interest rates to 20 percent between 1982 and 1983. Saddled with $750 million in debt it had assumed to finance its growth, Rogers Communications staggered through the early and mid-1980s, divesting assets and abandoning plans to expand into Europe. "We sold off everything we could, just to keep afloat," Rogers said in a July 6, 1981, interview with *Forbes*. "It was like flying a plane, and you're just tossing stuff out of the plane just trying to keep above the trees." The company paid its price for two decades of aggressive expansion, losing more than $100 million between 1982 and 1987, but the losses were of secondary importance to Rogers. More important was securing commanding control over

emerging communications technologies, even if that goal was achieved through lackluster financial performance.

THE MOVE TO CELLULAR: 1982–88

Prompted by recent developments in cellular telephone technology, Rogers began exploring the possibility of entering the business in 1982. In February of the following year he approached the company's board of directors. Considering the financial condition of the struggling company at the time, they rejected his proposal to obtain a cellular telephone license. Rogers persevered, looking elsewhere for financial support. Assistance was obtained from the Belzerg family of Vancouver-based First City Financial Corporation and Philippe de Gaspé Beaubien of Montreal-based Telemedia Inc. Rogers then invested $2 million of his own money to launch the venture, which was incorporated in May 1984 as Rogers Cantel Mobile Communications Inc. Over the next four years, after investing an additional $5 million, Rogers bought out his partners to become the sole owner of Cantel, giving his company a third leg to stand on.

The future of the communications industry, as Rogers and others perceived it, entailed all communications services being transmitted via a single wire into businesses and individual residences, preferably by one company with broad communications capabilities. As a result, Rogers Communications sought to become a communications conglomerate capable of bundling telephone, television, and paging and wireless services in one monthly bill to consumers throughout Canada.

One important branch of the communications field was missing from this growing empire, however. Rogers Communications did not maintain a stake in providing telephone service. Rogers attempted to fill this void in 1985 by making a bid for CNCP Telecommunications Limited, a subsidiary of Canadian Pacific Limited, but his advances were thwarted. Four years later Rogers tried again, but first he made an uncharacteristic move by selling his U.S. cable properties to Houston Industries, Inc., in February 1989 for $1.58 billion. Instead of using the money to support an aggressive expansion program, he plowed the money back into Rogers Communications, with $525 million earmarked for refurbishing the company's cable operations and another $600 million dedicated to strengthening Cantel, which by this point had captured more than 50 percent of the Canadian mobile telephone market.

UNITEL AND MACLEAN HUNTER BROADEN CAPABILITIES: 1989–94

One month after Rogers Communications sold its U.S. cable properties, Rogers made another bid for CNCP Telecommunications. This time around Rogers was successful, acquiring a 40 percent stake in the company from Canadian Pacific Limited and spawning a new business arm for Rogers Communications, which was later named Unitel Communications Holdings Inc. In June 1992 Unitel received permission from the Canadian Radio-Television and Telecommunications Commission to compete against the telephone companies in the public long-distance market, making the company one of the largest of the long-distance companies in the country, trailing only Bell Canada.

Unitel, however, proved to be a drain on Rogers Communications' profits, losing a total of $600 million between 1992 and 1995. Rogers Communications had experienced its fair share of losses, sacrificing annual earnings for market share and for financing entry into new business areas, leading Rogers to note in a February 21, 1994, *Maclean's* interview, "All this company has to do to make money is stop growing." Nevertheless, more than $500 million in losses racked up between 1990 and 1994 were cause for concern, and by 1995 Rogers was beginning to pin some of the blame on Unitel.

Despite mounting losses, Rogers Communications concluded a pivotal deal in 1994 when it acquired Maclean Hunter Limited for $2.5 billion. Financed largely by bank loans, the acquisition of Maclean Hunter, a cable and publishing conglomerate, gave Rogers Communications a 62 percent stake in Toronto Sun Publishing Corporation, which owned the *Toronto Sun*; the *Financial Post*; tabloids in Edmonton, Calgary, Toronto, and Ottawa; and nearly 200 other publications, including *Maclean's*, *Chatelaine*, and *Canadian Business*. These properties were organized in late 1994 under the newly named Maclean Hunter Publishing Limited, which was set up as a subsidiary of the newly created Rogers Multi-Media Inc. (soon renamed Rogers Media Inc.), which was a direct subsidiary of Rogers Communications. Rogers Media was also responsible for Rogers Broadcasting Limited, which included Maclean and Rogers radio stations, in addition to Rogers' television stations and other broadcasting interests.

Maclean Hunter's numerous cable properties ranked the company as Canada's fourth-largest cable operator. With 700,000 cable subscribers in Canada (compared to Rogers Communications' 1.9 million), Maclean Hunter also owned U.S. cable systems in Florida, New Jersey, and the Detroit area that served more than 500,000 subscribers. The Canadian cable systems were folded into Rogers Cablesystems, while the U.S. properties

were quickly sold. Other Maclean Hunter properties that were sold in 1995 and 1996 included several radio stations, magazines in the United States and Europe, and some printing operations.

To gain regulatory approval, Rogers also had to divest Maclean Hunter's CFCN-TV, which was sold to Shaw Communications Inc. in September 1995. Maclean's paging operations were subsumed by Rogers Cantel. In 1996 Rogers sold several additional operations acquired with Maclean Hunter, including printers Davis & Henderson Ltd. and Transkrit Corporation and the 62 percent interest in Toronto Sun Publishing. All told, the divestments of Maclean Hunter properties generated nearly $3 billion, much of which was used to pay down Rogers' massive debt.

STRATEGIC PARTNERSHIPS: 1996–99

Despite the divestments, Rogers' debt continued to increase, nearing $5 billion by 1996, then hitting $5.6 billion in 1997. Throughout the mid-1990s and into the late 1990s, the company also continued to post losses every year. Like other players in the cable and cellular industries, Rogers was spending massive sums on capital expenditures ($800 million in 1996 alone) to build up a customer base of cable and cellular subscribers. A handsome payoff was expected in the long run.

Ted Rogers had viewed the acquisition of Maclean Hunter as a step toward turning his company into the Time Warner of Canada, a media conglomerate controlling both content and the networks that delivered the content. However, the mounting debt, a falling stock price, the prospect of continued losses for several more years, and increasing competition for Rogers Cantel from such newcomers as Clearnet Communications Inc. and Microcell Telecommunications Inc., forced the founder's son to at least temporarily pull back from his vision. This situation led to the divestment of Toronto Sun Publishing and its impressive content collection. Rogers Communications also gave up on the money-losing Unitel operation, taking a $99 million write-down to bring the value of its investment to zero. In late 1996 Rogers sold cable systems serving about 303,000 subscribers in Ontario to Cogeco Cable Inc. for $350 million.

In addition to asset sales, Rogers increasingly turned to alliances in an attempt to secure a significant position in the rapidly consolidating, deregulated communications world of the late 1990s. In April 1996 Rogers entered into partnership with RadioShack Canada Inc.

to open and operate about 100 shopping mall stores across Canada that would sell Cantel products and services along with RadioShack products and accessories. In November of that year Rogers Cantel and AT&T entered into an alliance whereby Cantel would co-brand its wireless services as "Cantel AT&T," and Cantel would gain access to AT&T's services, technology, and marketing. By this time, Rogers Communications had also entered the local telephone business through an entity called Rogers Network Services, which was renamed Rogers Telecom Inc. in 1997, and had become an Internet service provider through the cable-based Rogers WAVE. In April 1997 Rogers joined with At Home Corporation in a venture through which it began offering high-speed cable Internet access under the name Rogers@Home. In support of its Internet ventures, Rogers began replacing its cable systems with upgraded two-way cable, which was available to 78 percent of Rogers Cablesystems customers by year-end 1998.

In June 1998 Rogers Communications exited from the local phone market by selling Rogers Telecom to Calgary-based MetroNet Communications Corp. for $600 million in cash and 12.5 million nonvoting shares of MetroNet worth an initial $400 million. The company used the cash to pay down debt. Also in 1998 Rogers Cantel began a turnaround, thanks to streamlining, reducing costs, improving customer service, and introducing new simplified rate plans.

Rogers stepped up its alliance strategy in 1999, entering into deals with some of the biggest names in communications. In a deal announced in July and closed the following month, Microsoft Corporation paid CAD 600 million for a 9.2 percent stake in Rogers Communications. The deal provided Rogers with much needed cash for paying off debt and funding capital projects, in return for the company agreeing to use Microsoft's software in a minimum of one million set-top boxes for digital television. Rogers also deepened its relationship with AT&T in 1999.

Earlier in the year AT&T had entered into a joint venture with British Telecommunications PLC (BT) that combined the two companies' international operations. In August this joint venture spent CAD 1.4 billion for a 33 percent stake in Rogers Cantel, providing Rogers Communications with another opportunity to pay down debt. Cantel, AT&T, and BT also said that they planned to work together on the next generation of wireless technology and would develop global calling plans for a single set fee. The deal reduced Rogers Communications' stake in Rogers Cantel to 51 percent.

ACQUISITIONS DIVERSIFY AND STRENGTHEN PORTFOLIO: 2000–05

Rogers Communications continued to tighten its stranglehold on the communications and media industries in the first decade of the 21st century. The decade began with the company's purchase of Major League Baseball's Toronto Blue Jays Baseball Club in 2000. The company purchased the baseball club's home venue, the SkyDome, four years later and renamed it Rogers Centre. Other sports-related purchases included the acquisition of CTV Sportsnet in 2001. A specialty sports channel that owned the National Hockey League's Canadian cable package, CTV Sportsnet, was rebranded as Rogers Sportsnet.

Acquisitions played a vital role in the expansion of Rogers Communications' wireless business, its single most important business segment. A series of strategic moves occurred in 2004, including the acquisition of the 34 percent of Rogers Wireless owned by AT&T Wireless Services Inc. The CAD 1.8 billion transaction, which enabled Rogers Communication to take Rogers Wireless private before the end of the year, was followed days later by the CAD 1.6 billion purchase of Microcell Telecommunications Inc. Announced in November 2004, the purchase of Microcell and its popular Fido brand created Canada's largest wireless carrier with 5.5 million customers.

Rogers Communications' broadcasting business also benefited from moves on the acquisition front. In 2007 the company paid $375 million for five Citytv stations, gaining properties in Toronto (CITY-TV), Winnipeg (CHMI-TV), Edmonton (CKEM-TV), Calgary (CKAL-TV), and Vancouver (CKVU-TV).

ROGERS' DEATH FORCES LEADERSHIP CHANGE: 2009

As the decade ended, Rogers Communications suffered the loss of its visionary leader. Ted Rogers was hospitalized at the end of October 2008 for an existing cardiac condition and died in early December 2008 of congestive heart failure. Alan Horn, the company's chairman, filled in as interim CEO while the search for a new CEO was underway. In March 2009, the board of directors made their decision, hiring from within the organization. Nadir Mohamed was named president and CEO, taking the helm of a company he had joined nine years earlier after serving as an executive at B.C. Telecom. During his time at Rogers Communications, Mohamed served as president and CEO of Rogers Wireless and as president and COO of the Communications

Division, which encompassed the company's wireless and cable businesses.

The company transitioned smoothly through the change in leadership, performing well during severely harsh economic conditions. As countless businesses suffered during the global financial crisis at the end of the decade, Rogers Communications posted glowing financial results. The company's annual revenue increased 21 percent in 2009 and its earnings jumped 31 percent. The increases continued in 2010, when revenues climbed from CAD 11.73 billion to CAD 12.18 billion and net income rose from CAD 1.5 billion to CAD 1.7 billion. The company stood on stable financial ground and it continued to lead the way in Canada's wireless sector, announcing the commercial launch of the country's first Long Term Evolution (LTE) network in the summer of 2011. Delivering higher speeds and lower latency than the existing 4G network, the LTE network debuted in Ottawa, with service slated to extend to Toronto, Vancouver, and Montreal in the fall of 2011. The extension of the network to a further 21 markets was expected by the end of 2012.

Jeffrey L. Covell
Updated, David E. Salamie; Jeffrey L. Covell

PRINCIPAL SUBSIDIARIES

Fido Solutions Inc.; Rogers Communications Partnership; Rogers Media Inc.; Rogers Publishing Limited; Rogers Broadcasting Limited; Rogers Sportsnet Inc.; Blue Jay Holdco Inc.

PRINCIPAL COMPETITORS

Astral Media Inc.; Bell Media Inc.; Canadian Broadcasting Corporation.

FURTHER READING

Bank, David. "Microsoft Agrees to Pay $400 Million for 9.2% Rogers Communications Stake." *Wall Street Journal*, July 13, 1999.

"Bust It Up, Guys." *Canadian Business*, December 12, 1997.

"CRTC Approves Rogers Acquisition of Citytv." *CNW Group*, September 28, 2007.

Dummett, Ben. "Rogers' Free Spending Perturbs Critics." *Globe and Mail*, August 4, 1997.

Evans, Mark. "Rogers Sells $1.4-Billion Cantel Stake." *Globe and Mail*, August 6, 1999.

Garneau, George. "Maclean Hunter Agrees to Be Bought by Rogers." *Editor & Publisher*, March 19, 1994.

Marion, Larry. "The Legacy." *Forbes*, July 6, 1981.

Munk, Nina. "Ted Rogers' New Apartment." *Forbes*, April 24, 1995.

Newman, Peter C. "The Ties That Bind." *Maclean's*, February 21, 1994.

Noble, Kimberley. "Bill and Ted's Joint Adventure." *Maclean's*, July 26, 1999.

Osterland, Andrew W. "Cable's Other Ted." *Financial World*, October 25, 1994.

"Rogers Lights Up Canada's First LTE Network Today." *CNW Group*, July 7, 2011.

Whitfield, Paul. "Rogers' Mix: Wireless, Cable and Baseball." *Investor's Business Daily*, March 4, 2010.

Willis, Andrew. "Mr. Rogers' Stubborn Streak Pays Off Big." *Globe and Mail*, August 6, 1999.

Royal Jordanian Airlines Company PLC

Housing Bank Commercial Center
Queen Noor Street
Amman, 11118
Jordan
Telephone: (+962 6) 5202000
Toll Free: (800) 223-0470
Fax: (+962 6) 5672527
Web site: http://www.rj.com

Public Company
Incorporated: 1963 as Alia Royal Jordanian Airlines
Employees: 4,500
Sales: JOD 684.79 million ($959.8 million) (2010)
Stock Exchanges: Amman
Ticker Symbol: RJAL 131213
NAICS: 481111 Scheduled Passenger Air Transportation; 481112 Scheduled Freight Air Transportation; 481212 Nonscheduled Chartered Freight Air Transportation; 481211 Nonscheduled Chartered Passenger Air Transportation; 488190 Other Support Activities for Air Transportation

■ ■ ■

Royal Jordanian Airlines Company PLC is a small airline with a reputation for being progressive and adaptable. The flag carrier of Jordan, the airline has faced some of the most challenging conditions in the industry. A modern fleet of more than 30 aircraft connects 57 destinations worldwide. The group includes charter subsidiary Royal Wings and holdings in auxiliary businesses such as a flight school and maintenance facility that do extensive third-party work. Royal Jordanian was the first Arab airline to sign with one of the major global aviation groupings, joining the oneworld alliance led by British Airways and American Airlines in 2007.

ROYAL ORIGINS

Royal Jordanian Airlines Company PLC was founded in 1963 at the behest of King Hussein, a pilot himself. Named after his daughter, Alia Royal Jordanian Airlines replaced Jordan Airways, Ltd., which had recently folded after operating for just two years. Royal Jordanian's mission was to serve as an "ambassador of goodwill and the bridge across which we exchange culture, civilization, trade, technology, friendship and better understanding with the rest of the world." Ali M. Ghandour, a native of Lebanon, was the founding chairman and CEO.

Flight operations began with a pair of four-engine Douglas DC-7 aircraft and two twin-engine Handley Page HPR-7 Heralds. In July 1964 the airline received its first jet, a French-made Caravelle. A second followed several months later as the network extended to the world capitals of London, Paris, and Rome. One of the Heralds was destroyed in April 1965 with the loss of all 54 people aboard. Two years later the DC-7s were destroyed while parked during the 1967 Six-Day War. In spite of such setbacks, the airline grew rapidly. It carried 87,000 passengers in 1964 and posted revenues of JOD 1 million. The airline had about 350 employees around this time.

In the early 1970s Royal Jordanian extended its network in Europe and Africa while facing several bombings and hijackings. It had a small, diverse fleet. A

COMPANY PERSPECTIVES

◆

Vision: To be the airline of choice connecting Jordan and the Levant with the world.

Boeing 707 chartered to Nigerian Airways, Ltd., crashed on landing in bad weather in 1973, killing 176 passengers and crew members, in one of the worst air disasters in history. Two years later, a Boeing 707 leased to Royal Air Maroc, S.A., crashed on approach in Morocco with the loss of all 188 aboard.

In 1975 the airline had about 1,850 employees. The passenger count continued to increase, rising 25 percent in 1976 to 475,470. In the same year a charter subsidiary called Arab Wings, Ltd., was formed. Royal Jordanian received a pair of Boeing 747 jumbo jets in 1977 and the company launched a weekly service to New York. The number of workers increased by a third in 1978 to 3,100. The carrier had become consistently profitable and had revenues of $127 million for the year.

The passenger count exceeded one million in 1980. By the next year, it had 4,000 employees and was operating its third Boeing 747. Revenues exceeded $300 million in 1981 and peaked the next year at about 1.7 million. Arab Air Cargo, Ltd., was established in March 1982 and began operations the next year with a pair of Boeing 707s. At the same time, Royal Jordanian participated in the relaunch of Sierra Leone Airlines, Ltd.

The network reached to Los Angeles and Singapore in 1984. The next year the airline added a weekly service to Kuala Lumpur in partnership with Malaysian Airline System, Ltd. (This route was suspended in 2003 but resumed seven years later.) Royal Jordanian had a fleet of about 20 U.S.-made jets in the mid-1980s, including six Lockheed Tri-Stars. It was replacing its smaller Boeing aircraft with Airbus A320s.

NEW NAME IN 1986

At the end of 1986 the company was renamed Royal Jordanian Airlines. Although no longer named after a princess, the royal touch was retained in its crown logo. It then had nearly 4,600 employees. Revenues were $305.8 million in 1987 and the company turned a net profit of $3.7 million although it remained in the red on an operating basis. There were already plans to privatize the airline, which was struggling to break even in the face of Jordan's 40 percent currency depreciation.

Moving toward a more standardized and efficient fleet, Royal Jordanian began operating Airbus A310s beginning in March 1987. In July 1987 the airline launched a twice-weekly service to Montreal, later extended to Toronto. The company soon entered a code-sharing arrangement with Air Canada. Fifth freedom rights, or picking up new passengers at stopovers in foreign countries, was a very valuable component of the carrier's income stream.

Jordan had a population of no more than five million people but the country was able to attract two million travelers a year partly through its role as a gateway for the Levant, or eastern Mediterranean, a region of 120 million people. The country also had its own world-class cultural sites. The airline was deeply involved in promoting Jordan as a tourist destination. It invested in hotels and operated a tour group. It even managed the Royal Falcons aerial demonstration team. Maintaining dozens of sales offices around the world was a serious expenditure.

As war ravaged Beirut, capital of neighboring Lebanon, Jordan's Amman Airport came to be seen as the region's leading hub, observed *Air Transport World* in July 1987. The journal noted Royal Jordanian's revenue had grown an average of 25 percent a year. The company was beginning to post losses, however.

NEW DIRECTION IN 1989

The end of the decade represented the end of an era. CEO Ali Ghandour, who had led the airline for 27 years since its inception, stepped down in November 1989 and was succeeded by his second-in-command, Husam Abu Ghazaleh. The company began the 1990s with about 5,000 employees. The company had sold the last of its Boeing 747 jumbo jets and acquired new Airbus aircraft. It continued to expand its international route network, launching an Amman–Bucharest route with TAROM (Transporturile Aeriene Romane) in 1990. The maintenance unit, which was already performing service for third-party airlines from the Third World, built a new hangar.

In spite of such promising beginnings, much of the decade would be overshadowed by conflict in the region. Iraq's invasion of Kuwait and the subsequent military response resulted in less traffic and unprecedented insurance rates. Tourist traffic dried up altogether, and some European airlines canceled service to Amman, leading to less revenues from ground handling and catering. Even flight training was affected. Freight traffic increased, however, and the airline participated in airlifting immigrant workers out of the region.

Jordan was allied with Iraq during the crisis. The flag carrier's passenger traffic plunged 85 percent during

KEY DATES

1963: Alia Royal Jordanian Airlines is launched as successor to short-lived Jordan Airways.

1986: Company is renamed Royal Jordanian Airlines.

1996: Royal Wings feeder airline is launched.

2004: Royal Jordanian posts annual profit after two decades of losses.

2007: Royal Jordanian holds its initial public offering and joins the oneworld global airline alliance.

Operation Desert Storm in February 1991. Passenger bookings for the year totaled 646,890 while freight fell by 31.8 percent. The company posted a net loss of $56.7 million. The decade following the war saw a two-thirds decrease in the number of Jordanians working in the Gulf.

By 1993 the carrier had a new CEO, Mahmoud Jamal Balqez. The fleet included 16 aircraft. Millions of dollars in accumulated debt made the privatization question more urgent. In 1994 the government paid off part of the carrier's foreign debt. Millions more were owed to local banks and to the Jordanian Petrol Refinery Corp.

Royal Jordanian began 1996 with a new feeder subsidiary, Royal Wings. It was launched rather modestly in February with a lone de Havilland DHC-8. King Hussein's son-in-law Walid al-Kurdi resigned as chairman in April 1996 and was replaced by former finance minister Basil Jardanah. By this time there was also another CEO, Nader Dahabi. The airline was again carrying more than one million passengers a year, to nearly 50 destinations. Annual revenues were roughly $375 million in the late 1990s.

COOPERATIVE AGREEMENTS WITH ISRAEL AND THE UNITED STATES

Jordan and Israel had granted access to each other's airspace. The first commercial flights began in 1996, in cooperation with El Al Israel Airlines, Ltd. The next year, Royal Jordanian began jointly operating a new Amman–Amsterdam–New York route with Trans World Airlines (TWA). The United States and Jordan had signed an open skies agreement and the TWA partnership soon expanded with several more destinations.

Royal Jordanian was one of 19 government entities slated for privatization in 1997. The government hired outside advisers to help plot its course. Revenues were $345 million in 1998, producing an operating surplus of $36 million, including ancillary activities. Interest on the $850 million debt wiped this out, however. The airline cut money-losing international routes, including ones to Singapore and Canada, during the year.

END OF AN ERA IN 1999

When King Hussein died on February 7, 1999, the airline lost its greatest champion. The carrier had supplied planes to take him to the United States for cancer treatment. Royal Jordanian posted a net profit of $34 million on revenues of a little less than $360 million in 1999. The airline carried about 1.3 million passengers during the year.

Significant steps were taken on the long path to privatization. Operationally, Royal Jordanian closed some of its unprofitable international routes and sold some ancillary businesses. The duty-free stores went to Spain's Aldeasa in 2000 for $60 million. The next year, Britain's Alpha Flight Services bought an 80 percent stake in Jordan Flight Catering International Company for $20 million and FlightSafety Boeing Training School paid $18 million for Jordan Airline Training and Simulation, which had trained thousands of pilots for many Arab and Third World airlines.

Jordan Airmotive Limited Company (Jalco) and Jordan Aircraft Maintenance Limited Company (Joramco) were put up for sale at the end of 2003. The airline's once varied fleet had been streamlined to just two aircraft types. The political repercussions of supporting Iraq may have given Jordan a preference for European-made Airbus planes over U.S. aircraft.

The Jordanian government settled the company's $650 million debt in 1999, raising 30 percent of the total through asset sales and another 30 percent by issuing JOD 150 million ($211 million) worth of bonds. An outstanding JOD 160 million ($225 million) owed to Jordan Petroleum Refinery Company was written off. The group at that time had 5,500 employees. This would be reduced to 3,000 within three years as various subsidiaries were divested and several hundred were laid off.

The September 2000 Intifada in Palestine discouraged tourism and scared away potential strategic partners. Nonetheless, the sale of assets allowed the company to post a $1 million net profit for the year. In 2001, Israeli military incursions in the West Bank and the September 11 terrorist attacks on the United States reduced the number of tourists from Europe.

Samer Majali succeeded Nader Dahabi as president and CEO in 2002. Six years later the young executive was picked to serve a term as chairman of the board of governors of the International Air Transport Association. During this period, the airline was expanding in Asia, which was a source of religious traffic from Muslim countries such as Indonesia. It considered making the capital of Malaysia its Pacific hub but within a few years curtailed its scheduled destinations in Asia to just Bangkok.

Royal Jordanian posted a net loss of $11 million on revenues of about $400 million in 2003, a year that brought more serious challenges, including another war in Iraq. With potential strategic partners wary of the region's instability and weakened by such events as the SARS crisis, the company opted for an initial public offering (IPO) as a privatization route.

PROFITABLE AGAIN

In 2004 Royal Jordanian posted a net annual profit of JOD 15.5 million after decades of losses. This increased the next year to JOD 21 million. In 2007 *Air Transport World* gave the carrier its Phoenix Award.

CEO Samer Majali told *Aviation Week & Space Technology* in November 2005 that the company was developing a regional network along the lines of Spain's Air Nostrum. In October 2005 it received its first 74-seat Bombardier Q400 turboprops. It was considering acquiring regional jets. It branded its feeder network as Royal Jordanian Xpress as it shifted the Royal Wings unit exclusively to charters. In the spring of 2006 Royal Jordanian ordered seven EMB-195 regional jets. The next year it ordered two Boeing 787s, with plans to lease eight more, to replace the Airbus A340s it had been using on long-haul routes since 2002, as well as six new A320 series aircraft to restore its midsize fleet.

A year after joining five other Middle East airlines to form the Arabesk Group, in April 2007 Royal Jordanian became the first Arab airline to join a global alliance when it was inducted into oneworld, led by British Airways and American Airlines. This required a retooling of its information technology systems, among other things. The airline also announced a deal to begin operating the new Boeing 787 Dreamliner to handle its long-haul needs. The program's notorious production delays stalled these plans, however.

2007 IPO

The company finally held its IPO in December 2007, raising JOD 164.5 million ($232 million) and becoming known as Royal Jordanian Airlines Company PLC. All the new commercial developments did not offset the effect of the global economic downturn beginning in

late 2007. The airline had also been faced with record-high fuel prices.

Revenues peaked at JOD 700 million in 2008 although the company slipped into the red with a JOD 24.7 million net loss. The airline rebounded with a JOD 28.6 million gain in 2009 as sales slipped to JOD 598.3 million. Longtime company veteran Hussein Dabbas took over as CEO in August 2009 after Majali left to run Gulf Air.

In 2010 Royal Jordanian posted net earnings down 67.5 percent to JOD 9.3 million on revenues up 14.5 percent to JOD 684.8 million ($959.8 million). Passenger count exceeded three million. During the year the airline revamped the Airbus A340s it flew to North America with new in-flight entertainment systems. It had already ordered Boeing 787s to replace them beginning in 2013.

The regulatory environment was becoming more competitive. The airline's eight-year monopoly on international flights out of Amman expired in 2010, and at the end of the year Jordan signed an open skies agreement with the European Union. Royal Jordanian officials protested the lack of access to landing slots in London and Frankfurt.

A CHANGING WORLD

In December 2011, beginning with Lagos, Nigeria, and Nairobi, Kenya, Royal Jordanian began flying to destinations deep inside Africa in order to attract Muslim and Christian tourists and pilgrims. Routes to Ghana and Ethiopia were also in the works.

Regional disruptions and rising fuel costs nudged the airline into a projected net loss for 2011 on sales of roughly $1 billion. The airline was able to resume flights to Tripoli in September.

The oft-delayed Boeing 787s, on which Royal Jordanian was basing its long-haul strategy, were due to begin arriving in early 2014, more than three years behind schedule. Royal Jordanian was also investing in a new headquarters building.

STILL A BRIDGE

Royal Jordanian's role as a bridge between cultures remained relevant as the Arab Spring swept across the Levant into neighboring Syria. The threat of sanctions was an unwelcome prospect with the potential to deprive the airline of business and airspace access. The airline had weathered the challenges of regional instability before and, with a streamlined balance sheet, proved it could operate profitably.

Although something of a niche carrier, Royal Jordanian was roughly large enough to qualify as a major airline in U.S. terms. It was a different airline than the one founded at the dawn of the jet age. Publicly traded, with most shares held by private local investors, Royal Jordanian, despite profitability issues, appeared comfortable in its role as a cultural ambassador, enhanced by membership in a global aviation alliance.

Frederick C. Ingram

PRINCIPAL SUBSIDIARIES

Royal Wings; Galileo Jordan; Arab Wings.

PRINCIPAL COMPETITORS

Air Arabia Company - PJSC; Gulf Air; Jordan Aviation Company Ltd.; Middle East Airlines - Air Liban S.A.L.; Syrian Arab Airlines; Turkish Airlines.

FURTHER READING

Buyck, Cathy. "The Will of Royal Jordanian." *Air Transport World*, March 1, 2011, 24+.

Cameron, Doug. "Out of the Wilderness." *Airline Business*, June 1999, 50.

Dougherty, Pam. "Jordan: Coping in the Most Adverse of Conditions." *MEED Middle East Economic Digest*, January 18, 1991, SIV+.

———. "Privatisation Gets Serious This Time." *MEED Middle East Economic Digest*, June 5, 1998, 15+.

Lott, Steven. "Royal Growth Plan; Unlike Gulf Competitors, Royal Jordanian Plans Regional Expansion with Smaller Aircraft." *Aviation Week & Space Technology*, November 21, 2005, 56.

Mecham, Michael. "Royal Jordanian Seeks Alliance of Arab Carriers." *Aviation Week & Space Technology*, January 9, 1989, 67+.

"Phoenix Award: Royal Jordanian." *Air Transport World*, February 2007, 31.

Sabbagh, Rana. "Rebuilding Royal Jordanian." *Asia Africa Intelligence Wire*, September 1, 2002.

Sutton, Oliver. "Royal Jordanian Looks to Europe." *Interavia*, March 1989, 217–18.

Thompson, Richard. "Better Late Than Never: It Has Taken Longer Than Expected, but Jordan's Flag Carrier Is Poised for Privatisation." *MEED Middle East Economic Digest*, July 16, 2004, 34+.

Vandyk, Anthony. "Royal Jordanian Continues to Uphold Reputation as a Progressive Carrier." *Air Transport World*, July 1987, 72+.

America's
Best Salads®

Saladworks, LLC

Eight Tower Bridge
161 Washington Street, Suite 300
Conshohocken, Pennsylvania 19428
U.S.A.
Telephone: (610) 825-3080
Fax: (610) 825-3280
Web site: http://www.saladworks.com

Private Company
Founded: 1986
Employees: 34
Sales: $70 million (2010 est.)
NAICS: 722211 Limited-Service Restaurants

■ ■ ■

Saladworks, LLC, operates a chain of approximately 100 quick-casual restaurants in mall food courts, strip malls, and cafés across the United States. Most locations are franchised and extend primarily along the East Coast with additional restaurants scattered in the Midwest and California. Specializing in salads, the chain also sells hot and cold sandwiches, soups, and wrap-style sandwiches. Saladworks was founded in 1986 by a former country club chef, John Scardapane.

A NEW RESTAURANT CONCEPT: 1986

In 1986, Scardapane opened his first storefront, Foodworks, in a 460-square-foot space in a New Jersey mall food court. Scardapane had gotten the idea for his company while working his way up from busboy to chef at various country clubs in South Jersey. As the chef at the Tavistock Country Club, Scardapane had noticed that customer-ordering trends were shifting from red meat to salads, so he added meal-sized salads to the club's menu. When club members responded positively to the new salad entrées, Scardapane began exploring different concepts for a salad-only restaurant.

After visiting several mall food courts and discovering that no one was offering salads, Scardapane approached a real estate development firm, The Rouse Company, with his idea for a salad-only concept. At the time, the firm was renovating the Cherry Hill Mall in Cherry Hill, New Jersey, with a portion of the renovations reserved for the creation of a new food court. Rouse accepted Scardapane's proposal but with a caveat: He had to add sandwiches to the menu. "They said I was crazy," Scardapane recalled in a January 2002 *Nation's Restaurant News* article. "They didn't think salads would work by themselves."

At the new Foodworks, half of the menu was dedicated to salads, while the other half featured sandwiches. Customers were given two options for their salads: They could choose from one of 10 core salads, which included selections such as Niçoise, chicken Caesar, and B.L.T., or they could customize their own salads from three dozen ingredients set out in refrigerated display cases. There were three pricing categories ranging from 30 to 70 cents for items such as chicken, tuna, shrimp, cheddar, tomatoes, carrots, and cucumbers. Lettuce options were limited to iceberg and romaine. The average cost of a salad was $4.50 to $5.95.

COMPANY PERSPECTIVES

Saladworks is the nation's first and largest fresh-tossed salad franchise concept, with over 100 locations across the country. Saladworks offers a "fanatic'ly fresh" menu of America's Best Salads with signature dressings, proprietary soups, and Focaccia Fusion sandwiches. All Saladworks salads are made-to-order, chopped on-location, and assembled right in front of your eyes. With the addition of the True Nutrition menu, Saladworks' varieties of signature salads are all 500 calories or less.

By the end of its first month in business, Foodworks was the top-grossing restaurant in the food court. Notably, salads were the most popular menu item, and six months after opening Scardapane pulled sandwiches from the menu to make room for more salads. Encouraged by his early success, Scardapane opened two new stores in the Echelon Mall and the Hamilton Mall in Vorhees Township and Atlantic City, New Jersey, respectively, during his first year in operation.

RAPID GROWTH AND FRANCHISING: 1987–99

During the next three years, Scardapane quickly reinvested his profits in eight additional stores. Soon, he owned almost a dozen. To run them, Scardapane enlisted the help of about 15 to 20 family members, including his mother, brother, and sister-in-law, as well as neighborhood friends.

By 1991 Scardapane was ready to reposition his stores. Initially, he had been reluctant to associate his store with health food, which was unpopular at the time. "When I first came up with this concept, I didn't want it to be labeled a healthy food chain," said Scardapane in a September 2003 *Nation's Restaurant News* article. However, as attitudes shifted toward healthy eating in his target demographic of 25 to 55, Scardapane's approach to marketing his store also changed. In order to leverage this growing popularity and underscore the freshness of his offerings in comparison to his food court competitors, he changed his company's name to Saladworks.

At the time, the company was experiencing growing pains and Scardapane was looking for solutions. Although he was doing huge volumes, quality control had become a problem and Scardapane saw his profit

margin dipping. Franchising eventually emerged as a way to solve the company's problems. Scardapane offered the first franchise to one of his high school friends who had been working for the company since its inception. When he witnessed the store's profits steadily improve with the owner on the premises, Scardapane was convinced that franchising was the key to his future growth. He began converting all of his stores to franchises, which he sold to friends from the Pennsauken neighborhood where he had grown up. He also added new franchises along the East Coast.

In 1994 Scardapane opened Saladworks Café, his first non-mall location, with a 90-seat dining room in a 2,400-square-foot space. This new concept took off, and by 1999 the company had almost an equal number of mall and café locations. As the company transitioned, so did its menu. After many years of a salad-only menu, sandwiches were added back to the menu along with soups and wraps. Approximately 70 percent of sales were from salads, while other items helped boost the per-person check average to $6.65.

NATIONAL EXPANSION: 2000–05

By 2000 the company had grown too large to be handled effectively by seven employees working in a Pennsauken, New Jersey, warehouse. Scardapane needed to make a move. "I had reached a point where the choices were to either expand on a national basis or sell the concept," Scardapane explained in a January 2002 *Nation's Restaurant News* article. "I knew that it would die if I let it just remain where it was."

Opting for expansion, Scardapane began building a management infrastructure of experienced foodservice executives to help position the regional salad chain for national expansion through stepped up franchise activity. In 2001, he brought in foodservice veteran Thomas Romano as president and chief executive officer, moved the company's headquarters to Conshohocken, Pennsylvania, and brought in three more employees. Eventually his staff totaled more than 30.

In 2002 the original Cherry Hill mall restaurant was generating about $1.2 million per year and annual sales for the company topped $18 million. Fourteen Saladworks franchisees were operating 26 of the company's 27 restaurants, which were spread across New Jersey, Washington, D.C., Pennsylvania, and Illinois. With a new corporate team in place and six franchise deals in the pipeline, company executives projected the addition of 45 new units operating in strip malls, freestanding locations, and major shopping malls along the East Coast by year-end. Plans were in place for opening 100 more franchises during the next three years.

KEY DATES

1986: John Scardapane opens Foodworks in a New Jersey mall.
1991: Foodworks is renamed Saladworks.
1994: First Saladworks Café opens.
2001: Thomas Romano is hired as chief executive officer; company headquarters move from Pennsauken, New Jersey, to Conshohocken, Pennsylvania.
2008: Vernon W. Hill II makes a major investment; chain is redesigned with 100th store opening.

Through ambitious growth, company executives hoped to capitalize on the "fast-casual" restaurant trend, a new industry designation for restaurants that were more upscale than fast-food chains such as McDonald's but less formal than sit-down dining establishments such as T.G.I. Friday's. "We see this as an upscale option for baby-boomers to elevate from Ronald McDonald. There are also a lot of young teens who want to eat healthier," Romano said in a July 2002 *Philadelphia Business Journal* article.

Fast-casual restaurants focused on fresh, quality ingredients that were delivered consistently in a frequently updated menu. "Our goal has been to sell food [that] customers feel good about eating. This includes items they would prepare at home if they had the time," Scardapane said in a May 2003 *Restaurants & Institutions* article. This sector was growing at the fast rate of 15 percent (compared to the restaurant industry total which had a growth rate of 3 percent, according to research firm Technomic, Inc.). It included highly successful newcomers Panera Bread and Così.

The strategic plan for growth worked, and by 2003 Saladworks was operating in seven states and had sales of $30 million (up 80 percent from 2002). In 2004 sales were $38 million, and in 2005 the company had 67 locations with the ambitious plan of opening 200 more stores during the next five years.

CONTINUED NATIONAL GROWTH AND REBRANDING: 2006–08

One year later, in mid-2006, the company had 79 locations with sales expected to surpass $50 million. Company leaders were on a mission to grow Saladworks as quickly as possible in order to stay ahead of the increasing competition from grocery stores, fast-food chains, and other quick-casual restaurant chains then sprouting up. Demand for nutritious meals and salads had exploded across the country. Scardapane launched the company's first branding campaign to increase consumer awareness in 2006, featuring a "salad diva" as the chain's brand personality.

To differentiate his company, Scardapane resisted the industry trend toward using processed, precut produce to increase profitability. "It's more labor-intensive, but we just have never been able to find processed produce that's as good as what you chop yourself," he said in a January 2008 *Nation's Restaurant News* article. He also updated the store's menu options, including organic produce, gourmet ingredients, and newly available micro greens.

By 2007 Saladworks' annual revenue topped $60 million. However, company executives had scaled back their ambitious growth plans due to the difficulty of finding suitable lease agreements. During this time, the company focused on building a good support system for its franchisees, opening only 20 stores by year-end. The company hired executives with franchising expertise so that it could focus on franchisee support and adopt a strategic planning process with regular performance reviews to keep a tight grip on quality.

One year later, in 2008, Vernon W. Hill II, founder and retired chairman of Commerce Bancorp, made a major investment in Saladworks and joined the company as chairman of the executive committee. At the time, the company had 88 stores with plans to open another 500 new stores during the next five years. Locations targeted for expansion included metro areas in New York, Washington, D.C., Florida, and California.

Also in 2008 the company rolled out its Signature Series salad line. Based on a celebrity chef salad competition the company had hosted in 2007, these limited-edition salads featured seasonal gourmet ingredients, such as candied almonds, prosciutto, wild Alaskan salmon, grape tomatoes, and figs. The new menu options proved highly successful. "Comparative-store growth more than tripled in the nine weeks following the launch of [the first] salad," Patrick Pantano, company public relations supervisor, said in an August 2008 *Chain Leader* article. New salads would be launched quarterly in 2008, and the company planned to partner with a household-name chef for all salads in 2009.

Vernon Hill's influence also led company executives to upgrade the chain's image. When the company launched its 100th store in October 2008, it featured a revamped design concept that included new architecture, decor, and employee uniforms. The dining areas featured eco-friendly bamboo flooring, bright banquette seating, natural lighting, and photographs of fresh vegetables and farms. Equipment placement was reconfigured to redirect customer traffic in a circular route. Rather than written menus, the store relied on glass display cases that featured ingredients and premade tossed salads for customers to choose from. Additional new menu items were launched at the store, including toasted focaccia sandwiches and 25 additional salad ingredients, such as edamame, seared tuna, and filet mignon.

New messaging was implemented on the Web site and in the stores. Customers were referred to as "fans"; products were called "fanatic'ly fresh"; and employees were referred to as "fanatics." By this time, the average customer check had increased to $10.62. Executives projected that the new design would boost sales by as much as 25 percent.

OPTIMISTIC VIEW OF COMPANY'S FUTURE GROWTH: 2009–11

In December 2008, *Entrepreneur* magazine named Saladworks the nation's number one salad franchise. For the following three years it maintained this ranking. However, the economic crisis of 2008 to 2009 had an impact upon the company's plans for continued growth. Revenues in 2010 were at $70 million. The company had locations in 12 states, but additional store openings were at a standstill.

Although new deals for stores in Southern California and Boston moved forward, by June 2011 the company had not exceeded its 2008 total store count of 100. Unfazed by the stagnant growth, company executives projected the opening of 500 new stores by 2016. Difficult economic conditions did not seem to dampen an unbounded optimism in the unlimited potential of the Saladworks concept.

Arianna Dogil

PRINCIPAL COMPETITORS

Doctor's Associates, Inc. (dba Subway); Einstein Noah Restaurant Group, Inc.; Panera Bread Company.

FURTHER READING

Battaglia, Andy. "Profile: John Scardapane." *Nation's Restaurant News*, September 2005, 48.

Bernstein, Charles. "Reaping the Benefits." *Chain Leader*, March 2006, 86.

Boss, Donna. "Saladworks." *Foodservice Equipment & Supplies*, March 2009, 1.

Brubaker, Harold. "One Chain's Groundwork for Growth." *McClatchy–Tribune Business News*, January 8, 2007, 1.

Cebrzynski, Greg. "Saladworks Counts on Branding Campaign to Maintain Sales Growth." *Nation's Restaurant News*, July 10, 2006, 14.

Frumkin, Paul. "Regional Powerhouse Chains: Saladworks Café." *Nation's Restaurant News*, January 28, 2002, 182.

Jennings, Lisa. "Custom-Salad Chains Go West as New Concepts Sprout in California Market." *Nation's Restaurant News*, May 12, 2008, 43.

Marano, Ray. "Smart Leaders: John Scardapane, Thoughts on Running a Business." *Smart Business Philadelphia*, April 1, 2006, 9.

Rogers, Monica. "Name Dropping." *Chain Leader*, August 2008, 25.

Scarpa, James. "Easy Being Greens." *Nation's Restaurant News*, January 28, 2008, 32.

Van Allen, Peter. "Saladworks Dishing Out Ambitious Growth Plan." *Philadelphia Business Journal*, July 5, 2002, 3.

Walkup, Carolyn. "Health-Oriented Concepts Build Market Stamina." *Nation's Restaurant News*, September 1, 2003, 8.

Yee, Laura. "Fast-Casual Stars." *Restaurants & Institutions*, May 1, 2003, 44.

SCANA Corporation

220 Operation Way
Cayce, South Carolina 29033-3701
U.S.A.
Telephone: (803) 217-9000
Fax: (803) 217-8119
Web site: http://www.scana.com

Public Company
Incorporated: 1984
Employees: 5,877
Sales: $4.60 billion (2010)
Stock Exchanges: New York
Ticker Symbol: SCG
NAICS: 221121 Electric Bulk Power Transmission and Control; 221122 Electric Power Distribution; 221210 Natural Gas Distribution; 234920 Power and Communication Transmission Line Construction; 551114 Corporate, Subsidiary, and Regional Managing Offices

■ ■ ■

SCANA Corporation is a utilities holding company headquartered near Columbia, South Carolina. Its core business is focused on the production, distribution, and sale of electricity and natural gas. Through subsidiaries, SCANA provides services to more than one million natural gas customers in three southeastern states, in addition to providing electricity to roughly 660,000 customers in South Carolina. Following the deregulation of the Georgia natural gas industry in the late 1990s, SCANA quickly expanded into the promising new market, gaining nearly 500,000 new customers there and becoming its exclusive regulated natural gas provider.

EMERGENCE OF ELECTRIC AND NATURAL GAS POWER IN THE 19TH CENTURY

Although SCANA was incorporated as recently as 1984, its history dates back to the establishment of the Charleston Gas Light Company in 1846, long before the appearance of the first lightbulb or the commercial use of electricity. Lamps lighted by manufactured gas were the sleek and modern means of illumination, thanks to the inventor of manufactured gas, 17th-century Belgian chemist Jan Baptista van Helmont, and to William Murdoch, a British engineer who invented gas lighting in 1802. Free enterprise and the spirit of invention were alive in South Carolina. In the 1840s gas lamps were aglow in the graceful streets of Charleston as the result of the establishment in 1846 of the Charleston Gas Light Company by a group of progressive businessmen.

The year 1846 marked economic expansion everywhere. It was also the year that war began with Mexico, leading to the acquisition of California and most of the Southwest. The new company was also expanding: business blossomed, and street lighting in the beautiful southern port constantly improved.

The beginning of the Civil War in 1861, only 15 years after the establishment of the Charleston Gas Light Company, proved to be a severe blow to the company, mostly because of the Union blockade of

Charleston's harbor, which meant a loss of raw materials. Despite these and other hardships, Charleston's thoroughfares continued to be lighted throughout the war years, that is, when raging city fires or federal bombardments did not interrupt service. The worst fire in Charleston's history took place in the first year of the war, destroying at least 500 private homes and numerous public buildings and churches in the very heart of the city and wiping out a high percentage of the company's customers. The quality of street lighting during this time deteriorated substantially.

With no access to raw materials such as coal and oil, the company struggled to extract gas from local pine wood, which produced dim lighting for gas lamps. With the city occupied by the Union army in 1864, Charlestonians were alarmed to see Union air balloons, filled with Charleston gas, looming in the sky for observation purposes. The end of the war brought little relief to the beleaguered Charleston Gas Light Company, which for nearly two years was taken over by the federal government. Stockholders regained control of the company in 1866.

DEVELOPMENTS IN COLUMBIA AND CHARLESTON

Columbia, the state's capital and home of the University of South Carolina, was even worse off than Charleston during the war. Gas illumination had arrived somewhat later in Columbia than in Charleston since the Columbia Gas Light Company had been established in 1852, six years after its counterpart, the Charleston Gas Light Company. Despite the relatively late start, the company boomed until the onset of the Civil War, whose effects were more severe in Columbia than in Charleston because of an invasion by General Sherman's troops and a terrible fire that erupted shortly after the Union army's occupation, reducing the new company to cinder and ashes.

Nonetheless, despite the deprivations of the postwar years and occupation by federal troops, population growth and the demand for lighting and gas surged, resurrecting the Columbia Gas Light Company and instilling new vigor in its Charleston counterpart. By 1871, the Columbia Gas Light Company had rebounded to the extent that high-quality manufactured gas was efficiently carried through almost 10 miles of mains. Eight years later, the still unknown inventor Thomas Edison created the first electric lightbulb, inaugurating the revolutionary age of electricity.

Charleston was not far behind in acquiring the newfangled bulbs. By 1886 a strong competitor of the Charleston Gas Light Company emerged: the Charleston Electric Light Company. Soon the old gave way to the new, demand for electricity kept mounting, and after several mergers a newly reconstituted electric company arose in 1897 under the name Charleston Consolidated Railway, Gas and Electric Company. The company's name meant precisely what it implied: all gas and electric services in the greater Charleston area, including the city's public trolley system, would be provided by one company. The same consolidation had occurred in Columbia in 1892, when the Columbia Electric Street Railway, Light and Power Company emerged.

MERGERS, PROFITS, AND REGULATION: 1900–45

With the advent of gadgets and home appliances powered by electric current still some years in the future, utility companies in the late 19th and early 20th centuries still had to devise inducements for people to use electricity. Profits for utility companies in those days were greatest from the electric trolley car systems; therefore, customers were encouraged to ride the trolleys as often as possible. Utility companies such as Charleston Consolidated and Columbia Consolidated built dance halls, parks, even zoos, all within a stone's throw of the nearest trolley. In a state blessed with mile after mile of beautiful beaches, railcars in South Carolina did a brisk business carrying summer crowds to the coast, with trolleys shuttling them to the nearest beach.

In 1894 the first electrified textile mill in the world opened for business in Columbia. Twenty years later, a hydroelectric generating plant was built north of Columbia, at Parr Shoals. Gas manufacture was by no means dead, despite electricity being the preferred means of street and home lighting. The introduction and increasing popularity of gas stoves for cooking prompted a dramatic 160 percent increase in gas revenues for Charleston Consolidated between 1910 and

KEY DATES

1846: Charleston Gas Light Company is founded.

1852: Columbia Gas Light Company is founded.

1950: South Carolina Electric and Gas Company (SCE&G) merges with South Carolina Power Company; company retains SCE&G name.

1984: SCE&G merges with Carolina Energies, Inc. to form SCANA Corporation.

1997: SCANA sells subsidiary SCANA Petroleum Resources to Kelley Oil.

1998: SCANA begins marketing natural gas to customers in Atlanta, Georgia.

2007: SCANA headquarters move from Columbia to new campus in neighboring Lexington County.

1925. Just before the United States entered World War I, Charleston boasted at least 5,000 gas ranges.

The United States' entry into World War I in April 1917 strained utility services to the limit and drained them of able-bodied workers as well. With the timely addition of extra boilers to the Charlotte Street generating plant in Charleston, the amount of electricity produced in that city at least doubled. The strains of wartime production were exacerbated by the dire effects of a worldwide influenza epidemic that, by the time it had worn itself out in 1920, had taken the lives of more victims than the war. At least one-third of Charleston Consolidated's employees became ill and recovery for the company was slow.

Postwar population growth and the popularity of electric home appliances such as irons, vacuum cleaners, and electric toasters put increasing demands on utility companies. Meanwhile, the profitability of the trolley systems declined drastically in both Charleston and Columbia, undoubtedly because of the mass production of family cars and low oil prices. In fact, the last trolley car was replaced by bus systems in 1936.

The Roaring Twenties set some milestones for utility companies. In 1925 the ownership of Columbia Railroad, Gas and Electric Company fell to the Broad River Power Company, which was organized and owned by the New York firm of W.S. Barstow & Company. One year later, the South Carolina Power Company, in a merger of five Charleston utility companies that included the old Charleston Consolidated Railway, Gas and Electric Company, arose as a single powerful entity with a far reaching goal: rural electrification. By 1940 the South Carolina Power Company served 146 towns and villages, or 8,750 square miles. A similar expansion was undertaken in and around Columbia (the Midlands) by the Broad River Power Company, which changed its name in 1937 to South Carolina Electric & Gas Company (SCE&G).

BOOM TIMES, BAD TIMES, AND WAR

These were heady years of growth and profit. By 1930 construction in South Carolina ended on the largest earthen dam in the world, sitting astride the 50,000-acre artificial Lake Murray that would provide generating power for the Saluda River Hydroelectric Plant. Five thousand residents in the area had to be relocated to make way for the gargantuan project.

By the time the plant went into operation, the effects of the 1929 stock market crash had reverberated throughout the economy, halting the booming expansion and profits of utility companies. A particular threat was the looming power of government, as embodied in the Public Utility Holding Company Act of 1935, which led to the creation of the South Carolina Public Service Authority. This public regulatory agency, established by the South Carolina legislature, soon began to acquire ailing or weak utility companies, which would have bloated the federal agency at the expense of private ownership. On the eve of World War II, the South Carolina Supreme Court put an end to the agency's power of acquisition.

During World War II the federal government encouraged voluntary energy conservation, but the South Carolina Power Company and the SCE&G did not decrease gas and electric services. Again the utility companies temporarily lost much of their workforce, hiring women as replacements for men serving in the armed forces. With the shortage of raw materials, private automobile use declined, and the bus transportation system in both Charleston and Columbia did a profitable business.

UNPRECEDENTED EXPANSION DURING THE POSTWAR BOOM

Compared to the boom in electric use following World War I, what followed World War II was a virtual explosion. So insatiable was the demand for electricity and electric appliances (the latter unobtainable during the war) that to meet these and other future needs, the South Carolina Power Company and SCE&G undertook a merger in 1950. The new corporation retained the name of South Carolina Electric & Gas Company.

Exciting new developments in the 1950s and 1960s held much growth and profit potential. These included the discovery of immense deposits of natural gas in Louisiana, Texas, and Mississippi, resulting in full conversion to natural gas in Columbia and Charleston by 1954, and the use of nuclear power to generate electricity, the demand for which was expected to rise continually. Gas revenues rose rapidly from $2.3 million to $13 million in the decade between 1953 and 1963.

Construction began in 1973 on SCE&G's most costly project to date: its first nuclear power facility (operated by SCE&G and two-thirds owned by the company) and hydroelectric plant facility on a 7,000-acre artificial lake, close to the original atomic power facility. Named after the then-president and chief executive officer of SCE&G, Virgil C. Summer, it was not to be completed until 1984, at a cost of $1.3 billion. Obstacles repeatedly delayed its completion. Not the least of these was the skyrocketing price of energy resulting from the Arab oil embargo of the early 1970s, and the Three Mile Island nuclear power plant disaster in 1979. Leadership in this Herculean project fell to SCE&G President and CEO Arthur Williams, who retired before its completion. However, by 1990 the Summer Station was rated by the Nuclear Regulatory Commission as one of the five safest in the United States.

SCANA, RESULT OF 1984 MERGER

In 1984 SCE&G merged with Carolina Energies, Inc. (CEI), a holding company with six subsidiaries, to form SCANA Corporation. Within a few years SCANA comprised 11 subsidiaries, its latest acquisition being the Peoples Natural Gas Company of South Carolina. Three-quarters of its revenue was still derived from electricity production and service, while gas sales made up the remainder. SCE&G continued to be the largest component of SCANA.

In 1989 SCE&G faced the biggest challenge in its history: Hurricane Hugo, which left 300,000 customers without power. Well prepared for the disaster, SCE&G had enough spare parts and extra vehicles to enable its crews to work day and night to restore service. Over a two-week period, employees of SCE&G, including workers borrowed by the company from 48 different utility companies in 15 different states, installed 731,000 new fuses and replaced more than 10 million feet of wire. The following year the utility industry awarded SCE&G employees its most prestigious honor, the Edison Award, in recognition of their services.

During this period SCANA adopted an official environmental code, through which it began recycling three-quarters of the ash waste from its generators, as well as tons of office paper, and printing its annual reports on recyclable paper. Utility poles began to sport company-made nesting platforms for South Carolina's osprey population, and customers were encouraged by means of financial incentives to conserve electricity. Many of these environmental initiatives were in SCANA's best interests. For example, selling 75 percent of its ash waste to concrete and cement companies yielded a handsome savings of $2 million in dumping costs annually.

Having grown from a tiny gas light company to a huge corporation, SCANA, like all utility companies, faced formidable challenges in the closing decade of the 20th century. While an economic recession in the early 1990s left the company unscathed, and dividends on its stock actually increased, deregulation in the utility industry forced it to reexamine its strategies. SCANA's plans for the future involved continuing to expand its growing interest in natural gas production, broadening its customer base by seeking gas markets out of state, and extending its investments in real estate, fiber optics, and communications.

CHALLENGES AND OPPORTUNITIES IN THE ERA OF DEREGULATION

The early 1990s marked a period of extensive growth for SCANA Corporation. In an effort to gain a solid foothold in newly deregulated energy markets, the company began to look for ways to increase its customer base through the further diversification. In November 1990, the company took a significant step toward becoming a major producer of natural gas, with the purchase of extensive gas reserves in Texas from Houston-based Tri-C Resources Inc. The agreement, worth $29 million, gave SCANA an initial daily production capacity of 12 million cubic feet of natural gas, and marked the company's inaugural foray into the production side of the natural gas business.

The company further increased its natural gas properties the following February, with the $16 million purchase of offshore natural gas reserves from LLOG Exploration Co. in Louisiana. In June 1993 the company's oil and natural gas exploration subsidiary, SCANA Petroleum Resources, acquired NICOR Exploration and Production Company, significantly increasing SCANA's natural gas holdings in Texas and Louisiana, as well as expanding the company's production operations into Oklahoma. The purchase increased SCANA's overall natural gas reserves to 283 billion cubic feet.

During the mid-1990s, SCANA began to search for other diversification opportunities outside of its core utilities business. One area of potential growth was in the rapidly expanding telecommunications industry. SCANA already used an extensive system of fiber-optic lines in the monitoring of its electricity supply networks. By 1994 the company's telecommunications arm, MPX Systems, owned 1,600 miles of cable throughout four states, and had plans to extend its network by more than a third over the coming years. With a substantial infrastructure already in place, SCANA hoped to play a major role in the future growth of emerging telecommunications technologies. In March 1996, the company acquired $75 million worth of shares in InterCel, a telecommunications firm dedicated to creating a Personal Communications Service (PCS) network throughout the Southeast. SCANA's investment infused InterCel with the venture capital it needed to enter the lucrative Atlanta, Georgia, PCS market, giving it the potential to double its customer base in a relatively short span. SCANA made another $75 million telecom investment in June 1998, when it acquired an additional 50,000 shares in InterCel's new incarnation, Powertel. The deal increased SCANA's overall stake in the PCS company to nearly 30 percent.

However, as the new century approached SCANA found its most enticing expansion opportunities in newly opened natural gas markets outside of South Carolina. As neighboring states North Carolina and Georgia forged ahead with deregulation, SCANA began to pursue an aggressive expansion strategy. In late 1998, Georgia prepared to open its natural gas industry to increased competition, SCANA began to market its services to customers in Atlanta, investing $3 million in advertising campaigns and in establishing six regional offices throughout the state. By May 1999 the company had added nearly 300,000 new customers in Georgia, a figure it eventually hoped to increase to 700,000. Within three years, SCANA had become such a significant presence in Georgia that, in June 2002, the Georgia Public Service Commission voted unanimously to allow the company to become the official provider of regulated natural gas service to the state's low-income customers.

SHIFTING ASSETS TO FINANCE EXPANSION

During this time the company also made significant inroads into the North Carolina energy market, effectively doubling its natural gas customer base with the $900 million acquisition of Public Service Co. in February 2000. Financing this growth activity forced the company to withdraw resources from some of its other recent ventures, which included dumping a significant portion of its wireless stock. The company even unloaded its nascent natural gas exploration operations, SCANA Petroleum Resources, selling the subsidiary to Kelley Oil for $110 million in October 1997. Although the company's earnings suffered initially, by the beginning of the new century its shift in strategy was already paying off. The company's Georgia operations enjoyed profits of $4.4 million for the year 2000.

While deregulation represented growth potential in Georgia, it posed a threat to SCANA's profitability in its home state. During the late 1990s SCANA was engaged in a pitched battle against deregulation in South Carolina. In late 1997, SCANA CEO William B. Timmerman had even begun to discuss the possibility of relocating the company outside of South Carolina, in the event deregulation made the state's utilities industry too competitive. Although the company's lobbying and marketing efforts eventually helped defeat the deregulation bill in the state legislature, it was clear that the issue of freeing up South Carolina's utilities markets was not going to go away. With the possibility of in-state competition still looming on the horizon, the challenge facing SCANA in the early years of the 21st century remained twofold. While the company needed to remain aggressive in its efforts to gain market share in unregulated markets in other states, at the same time it was compelled to remain highly attentive to its core South Carolina customer base.

Total revenues had increased more than half to $3.4 billion in 2000, with profits of $261 million. Profits doubled the next year although total sales were flat. In 2002 SCANA lost $131 million on revenues of just under $3 billion. At this time the company had 5,361 employees.

EXITING BUSES IN 2002

SCANA had long desired to exit the municipal transportation system it had been obliged to operate in Columbia. Critics castigated the corporation for neglecting the system, for example, never buying any new buses in spite of available federal subsidies. SCANA seized the chance to unload the buses in 2002, when the Securities and Exchange Commission required it to unload the system before it would approve its 2002 takeover of North Carolina natural gas company PSNC. The City of Columbia took over responsibility for the buses. At the same time SCANA secured a 30-year monopoly on the city's electric service, paying a franchise fee (then 3 percent) on each account within its borders.

Rising medical insurance premiums were a big problem for the corporate giant. In 2005 SCANA added monthly surcharges for retirees and for spouses of employees who had access to other insurance through their own employment.

SCANA employed 1,000 people at the 450,000-square-foot Palmetto Center on Columbia's Main Street. In 2007 the corporation moved them to its new campus in neighboring Lexington County near Interstate 77.

BETTING BIG ON NUCLEAR

The federal government was promoting nuclear power as a cleaner alternative to coal and natural gas. The Energy Policy Act of 2005 boosted the long dormant nuclear power plant industry by offering loan guarantees for the first new U.S. reactors in nearly 30 years. In 2008 SCANA and its 45 percent partner in the venture, Santee Cooper, announced plans to build two new units to more than triple the capacity of the existing V. C. Summer plant at a total cost of $9.8 billion. The first of the plants was expected to be in service as early as 2016.

Otherwise, SCANA was rated as relatively unconcerned about controlling carbon dioxide emissions, which was becoming an issue with investors due to the impending prospect of mandated limits, or carbon caps. Nevertheless, in the summer of 2011 SCANA announced it was installing 10 acres of solar panels on the roof of Boeing Company's new 787 Dreamliner assembly plant near Charleston. It was billed as the sixth-largest solar installation in the Southeast.

SCANA reported operating revenues of $4.6 billion for 2010, up from $4.24 billion the previous year. Net income rose to a record $376 million. The company reported gains in its three business segments. Electric, the largest, saw revenues increase from $2.14 billion to $2.37 billion. Gas-Regulated business rose from $958 million to $989 million, and Gas-Nonregulated business climbed from $1.14 billion to $1.25 billion.

NEW LEADERSHIP

Chairman, President, and CEO William Timmerman was retiring at the end of November 2011, to be replaced by Kevin Marsh. Marsh had been chief financial officer of SCANA since 1996 and had previously led subsidiaries SCE&G and PSNC.

After more than a century and a half in business, SCANA held a uniquely influential place among South Carolina corporations. The only *Fortune* 500 company headquartered in the state, SCANA had the power to maintain its electricity monopoly in the Midlands while competing in natural gas markets in neighboring states. It could steer billions of dollars into nuclear reactors even as prevailing winds carried traces of fallout from Japan's Fukushima disaster into the Carolinas. Even so, it was still grappling with issues from the past as it tried to recover remediation costs from the polluted sites of utility companies it had acquired decades earlier.

Sina Dubovoj
Updated, Erin Brown; Frederick C. Ingram

PRINCIPAL SUBSIDIARIES

SCE&G; GENCO; Fuel Company; PSNC Energy; CGT; SCI; SEMI; ServiceCare, Inc.; SCANA Services, Inc.

PRINCIPAL DIVISIONS

Electric; Gas-Regulated; Gas-Nonregulated.

PRINCIPAL COMPETITORS

Dominion Resources, Inc.; Duke Energy Corporation; Progress Energy, Inc.

FURTHER READING

Leland, Isabella G. *Charleston: Crossroads of History.* Woodland Hills, CA: Windsor Publications, 1980.

Montgomery, John A. *Columbia, South Carolina: History of a City.* Woodland Hills, CA: Windsor Publications, 1979.

Pogue, Nell C. *South Carolina Electric & Gas Co., 1864–1964.* Columbia, SC: State Printing Co., 1964.

South Carolina Electric and Gas Company. *Highlights of a Long History.* Columbia, SC: SCANA Corporation, 1962.

Stock, Kyle. "Energy Demand, Climate Change Drive Big Push for Atomic Power." *Post and Courier* (Charleston, SC), October 15, 2007.

"Timmerman Announces Retirement, Kevin Marsh to Succeed Timmerman as Chairman and CEO." *Investment Weekly News,* January 29, 2011, 1219.

Warren, John A. *SCANA Corporation: A History of Service.* New York: Newcomen Society, 1987.

Wojcik, Joanne. "Consumerist Incentives Yield Savings for SCANA." *Business Insurance,* December 5, 2005, 18.

Serco Group plc

16 Bartley Wood Business Park
Bartley Way
Hook, Hampshire RG27 9UY
United Kingdom
Telephone: (+44 1256) 745 900
Fax: (+44 1256) 744 111
Web site: http://www.serco.com

Public Company
Incorporated: 1929 as RCA Ltd.
Employees: 58,799
Sales: £4.33 billion ($3.95 billion) (2010)
Stock Exchanges: London
Ticker Symbol: SRP
NAICS: 488111 Air Traffic Control; 488119 Other Airport Operations; 488190 Other Support Activities for Air Transportation; 488210 Support Activities for Rail Transportation; 488310 Port and Harbor Operations; 488330 Navigational Services to Shipping; 488390 Other Support Activities for Water Transportation; 488490 Other Support Activities for Road Transportation; 488991 Packing and Crating; 525910 Open-End Investment Funds; 541330 Engineering Services; 541611 Administrative Management and General Management Consulting; 541612 Human Resources Consulting Services; 541614 Process, Physical Distribution, and Logistics Consulting Services; 561110 Office Administrative Services; 561210 Facilities Support Services; 561320 Temporary Help Services; 561330 Employee Leasing Services; 923130 Administration of Human Resource Programs (Except Education,

Public Health, and Veterans' Affairs Programs); 611110 Elementary and Secondary Schools; 611699 All Other Miscellaneous Schools and Instruction

■ ■ ■

Serco Group plc provides facilities management and other engineering services for a variety of governmental and industrial clients in 30 countries around the world. Unlike traditional support services companies, which typically limit themselves to areas such as catering or cleaning, Serco undertakes the management of complex tasks. Its interests range from testing nuclear weapons to managing parking meters to operating tourist attractions. Less than 60 percent of the company's sales are from within the United Kingdom. Serco has grown rapidly as government agencies have privatized more and more services. It has also expanded its range of operations through numerous diversified acquisitions since the 1990s.

ORIGINS

Serco's history begins in 1929, when the Radio Corporation of America (RCA) established a U.K. subsidiary, RCA Ltd., to service the growing film industry in Britain. In the late 1950s, RCA supplied radomes (a dome structure for protecting radar antennas) for the Ballistic Missile Early Warning System (BMEWS) at RAF Flyingdale in Yorkshire. RCA Ltd. supplied most of the workers needed during its construction and won a contract to manage the facility.

The company would maintain this relationship into the new millennium.

In the 1980s, the U.K. Ministry of Defence used this program as a model for its privatization of operation and maintenance functions at defense facilities. The cost-cutting of Prime Minister Margaret Thatcher's administration in the 1980s provided many other opportunities for RCA Ltd. By the early 1980s, the company also was managing traffic light systems. The European Space Agency (ESA), formed in 1975, provided another area of expansion. RCA Ltd. contracted to maintain ESA's computer networks and satellites.

1987 MANAGEMENT BUYOUT

General Electric (GE) acquired RCA in 1986. RCA Ltd.'s managers bought their unit from GE for $24 million in 1987. The newly independent company was named Serco Limited. Serco, led by Chairman George Gray, who had been with the company since 1964, listed on the London Stock Exchange as Serco Group plc in 1988.

Revenues during Serco's first full year as a public company were about £47 million, producing profits of £3.6 million. Although Serco provided support services to private-sector clients such as British Aerospace and Marks and Spencer, the U.K. Ministry of Defence accounted for nearly half of the group's revenues.

In 1989, Serco began branching out to Asia and the Pacific Rim and launched an expansion into civil government and commercial markets. Several small acquisitions in 1990, together worth £1.4 million, brought Serco into the management of central government facilities in Australia and New Zealand and

bolstered the company's business with local governments inside the United Kingdom.

Serco was unique in not limiting itself to one or two discrete areas of support, such as catering or cleaning. The company began running hospitals for Britain's National Health Service. Total revenues approached $200 million by 1991. In May of that year, Serco entered a new market by acquiring Community Leisure Management. Several months later, the company and European Handling Management formed the Serair joint venture to provide an array of support services for airlines.

Serco entered the civil airport services market by acquiring most of International Aeradio Limited (IAL), apart from loss-making health operations, from British Telecommunications for £12.25 million ($18 million) in April 1992. IAL, which provided management services for airports, including air traffic control, had 900 employees in Germany, Sweden, Russia, and the Middle East.

TRANSATLANTIC EXPANSION

Serco continued to acquire companies, enter new markets, and form new structures in the mid-1990s. In 1993, the same year it entered the North American market, Serco bought Building Management Scotland. It soon obtained contracts to operate parts of the United Kingdom's traffic signal system. The Serco Institute was created in 1994. The launch of Serco Investments followed the next year.

Pretax profits grew 21 percent in 1995 to £15.2 million as sales rose 24 percent to £323.3 million. During the year, Serco announced new contracts worth £600 million, including a £180 million deal to manage ship movements and provide specialist support at three Ministry of Defence ports. Similar profit and sales increases were reported in 1996, spurred by increased outsourcing demand in Australia.

In the mid-1990s, Serco bid on several projects, particularly defense-related ones, as part of various consortiums. In October 1996, a group including Serco, Cobham plc, and Bristow Helicopter won a £400 million, 15-year contract to establish and operate a training school for the British military's helicopter pilots. It was the largest contract the Ministry of Defence had yet awarded under the government's private finance initiative (PFI). In the spring of 1997, a joint venture with Docklands Light Railway took over the operation and maintenance of the 10-year-old automated railway. Serco also had, as did British Telecommunications, a contract to handle railway telephone inquiries.

Serco moved into the U.S. state and local public services market via the acquisition of JL Associates in

KEY DATES

1929: RCA Ltd. is formed to service the British movie industry.
1987: RCA Ltd. is bought out by managers after General Electric acquires its parent company.
1988: Renamed Serco, the company lists on the London Stock Exchange.
1997: Serco joint venture begins running Docklands Light Railway.
1999: Nomura International and Serco set up a £1 billion infrastructure fund.
2004: Serco acquires Birmingham-based information technology (IT) firm ITNet.
2005: Company acquires U.S. defense contractor RCI Holding Corporation.
2008: U.S. IT contractor SI International and India's InfoVision Group are acquired.
2011: U.K. call center specialist The Listening Company and India's Intelenet Global Services are acquired.

1998. In Europe, it bought out the remaining shares of Serco Newsec AB, a Swedish joint venture. It also acquired Tecnodata, a technical services company active in continental Europe, in a deal worth up to £9.3 million.

The company expected the Asian financial crisis to result in increased demand for outsourced services, particularly in Japan, which was seen as ripe for economic reform. The domestic support services industry had grown considerably in the 1990s and expanded its range of offerings. Some estimates valued the U.K. market at £10 billion a year.

NEW CAPITAL IN 1999

As Serco's chief executive, Richard White, searched for new business, he pointed out to skeptical potential clients that the company's first job had been to provide the country with a four-minute warning in case of nuclear attack. Because of its strong reputation, Serco could choose the most lucrative opportunities, which were usually the most complex as well. White replaced Serco Chairman Gray upon his retirement in 1999, and was himself succeeded by former CFO Kevin Beeston.

In early 1999, Nomura International, the European division of a Japanese investment bank, established a £1 billion ($1.7 billion) fund along with Serco for the

purpose of bidding on and financing large public infrastructure projects. Two major projects coming up for bidding were those for Britain's National Air Traffic Control System and portions of the London Underground.

Serco bought the support services subsidiary of DASA, DaimlerChrysler's aerospace division, in August 1999. It paid DEM 53 million (£18 million) for Elekluft, which specialized in military and aerospace customers. Its origins were similar to Serco's: it was formed in 1961 to install and support German air defense radar systems. Elekluft billed about DEM 150 million a year and had added payroll, technical documentation, and other services to its repertoire.

After earnings and sales growth slipped slightly in 1998, Serco was again approaching its customary 20 percent returns in 1999. Expansion was coming in the United Kingdom and Australia. The company continued to renew 90 percent of its contracts. According to one analyst, Serco's main constraint was finding enough qualified managers. In December 1999, a consortium of Serco, BNFL, and Lockheed Martin won a 10-year, £2.2 billion contract to manage two of Britain's Atomic Weapons Establishment facilities.

Acquisitions continued. Serco bought the consulting firm Quality Assurance Associates in 2000 and the technical consulting division of AEA Technology in 2001. The latter deal, worth £76.8 million, was Serco's largest yet. AEA Technology focused on science and safety-based services. Serco failed to win a 46 percent share of Britain's National Air Traffic Services (NATS), although it remained busy with contract renewals and new business such as its first ever contract to operate an immigration detention center.

FACING CHALLENGES ON THE GROWTH CURVE

The group aimed to expand its business in the United States. It already had air traffic control contracts with the Federal Aviation Administration. In 2001 Serco teamed with Lockheed Martin in bidding to build an astrobiology lab for NASA in California.

Serco posted pretax profit up 20 percent to £37.7 million in 2000 on revenues of £967 million, also up a fifth. It had 9,000 employees worldwide. At it grew larger and more diverse, it was able to bid on more complex contracts. Some areas were challenging due to ingrained culture or capital costs. After Serco took over education in Bradford in 2001, it lost £8.5 million on the project in the first five years. In 2003 the company bought out WCC, its 50 percent partner in Premier Custodial Services, for £48.6 million. WCC's parent,

Wackenhut, had been acquired by correctional services company Group 4. Serco posted net income of £67 million on revenues of £1.5 billion for the year. By this time it had 2,000 employees in North America alone, where it derived $127 million of revenues.

Besides the area of education, Serco ran into difficulty with projects involving heavy construction. In 2004 it and its partner John Laing PLC withdrew from a project to build the new National Physical Laboratory (NPL) near London, sharing a combined loss of £100 million. Serco and NedRailways formed the joint venture called Northern Rail to run Arriva Trains Northern and First North Western in 2004. It was the third private firm called in to manage the rail system in 10 years.

Serco bought Birmingham-based information technology (IT) firm ITNet for £235 million in 2004. ITNet had been spun off from Cadbury Schweppes plc in 1995. In 2004 Serco also agreed to sell its New Zealand subsidiary to Transfield Services Limited for NZD 18 million including assumed debt. Serco entered its first Middle Eastern public finance initiative contract the same year, to create and staff a technical school in Oman. Other new contracts included managing driver exams in Ontario.

BUILDING A U.S. DEFENSE BUSINESS

In March 2005 Serco acquired RCI Holding Corporation for $215 million (£113 million). Based near Washington, D.C., RCI conducted three-quarters of its business with the U.S. Department of Defense. It had annual revenues approaching $300 million, more than twice that of Serco North America. In 2005 Serco had sales of £2.2 billion, 90 percent from government contracts and 25 percent from defense. Net income was £91 million.

The company employed 30,000 in the United Kingdom alone. Serco Group boasted a yearly employee turnover rate of little more than 3 percent; 40 percent of employees belonged to a union. Part of Serco's pitch was that its range of different activities allowed it to apply personnel capable of approaching problems from new angles. It could also offer employees more varied careers.

Serco Executive Chairman Beeston began a term as chair of CBI's Public Services Strategy Board, an agency overseeing privatization of U.K. public services, in July 2006. He succeeded Rod Aldridge, head of rival Capita Group plc.

CONTINUED GLOBAL EXPANSION

Another U.S. IT contractor, SI International of Reston, Virginia, was acquired at the end of 2008. The deal was worth $524 million, including assumed debt. Around the same time, Serco also acquired controlling interest in a significant operation in India, InfoVision Group. The price was Rs 200 crore ($75 million) for an initial 60 percent interest. InfoVision had 10,000 employees and was reporting growth of up to 50 percent a year. Its founder, Aditya Gupta, stayed on to lead the unit under new ownership.

In 2011 Serco added Intelenet Global Services Pvt. Ltd. to its Indian operation, Serco BPO, buying a 66 percent stake in a deal worth up to £385 million ($636.4 million). This was Serco's largest purchase to date. Intelenet employed 32,000 people, four times as many as Serco's existing operation in India. Intelenet was also much more involved with business process outsourcing for overseas companies.

The Listening Company was acquired in 2011 for £42.1 million plus up to £13.8 million in potential incentives. The call center specialist employed more than 4,300 people at eight U.K. locations and had annual revenues of about £82 million.

By the middle of 2011 the fast-growing group had 100,000 employees. Some observers believed budget crises in Europe and the United States assured outsourcing companies including Serco a central role in delivering services for less. Others doubted it could avoid widespread government spending cuts. Christopher Hyman, CEO since 2002, perceived ample expansion opportunities remained, even in Serco's home market of the United Kingdom. At the same time, the group had established significant roots in the disparate markets of the United States and India.

Frederick C. Ingram

PRINCIPAL SUBSIDIARIES

Serco Limited; NPL Management Limited; Serco GmbH (Germany); Serco Australia Pty Limited; Great Southern Rail Limited (Australia); Serco Services Inc. (USA); AWE Management Limited (33%); Merseyrail Services Holding Company Limited (50%); Northern Rail Holdings Limited (50%); Serco Sodexo Defence Services Pty Limited (Australia; 50%).

PRINCIPAL DIVISIONS

Civil Government; Defence, Science, and Nuclear; Local Government and Commercial; Americas; AMEAA.

PRINCIPAL COMPETITORS

ARAMARK Corporation; Cap Gemini S.A.; Capita Group plc; MITIE Group PLC; Rentokil Initial plc; The ServiceMaster Company.

FURTHER READING

Ahmed, Pervaiz K., Glenn Hardaker, and Martin Carpenter. "Integrated Flexibility—Key to Competition in a Turbulent Environment." *Long Range Planning* (London), August 1996, 562+.

Arkin, Anat. "Arise, Serco." *People Management*, May 4, 2006, 32–35.

Baird, Roger. "Sky's the Limit for Serco." *PFI Report*, March 2001, 9.

Beaumont, Alex. "Interview—Kevin Beeston: The Boy Done Good." *Public Private Finance*, July 18, 2006, 22.

Donaldson, Liza. "Interim Management: Troubleshooters for Hire in a Buyer's Market." *Industrial Relations Review and Report* (London), May 1993.

SHPS, Inc.

9200 Shelbyville Road
Louisville, Kentucky 40222-5144
U.S.A.
Telephone: (502) 426-4888
Fax: (502) 420-5590
Web site: http://www.shps.com

Private Company
Incorporated: 1997 as Sykes HealthPlan Services
Employees: 2,200
Sales: $211 million (2010 est.)
NAICS: 561400 Business Support Services

■ ■ ■

SHPS, Inc., is a Louisville, Kentucky-based employee benefits administration firm serving a wide variety of clients, including major corporations and midsize companies, hospitals, universities, state and federal government entities, and employee trusts and health plans. In addition to its Louisville operations, SHPS maintains branch offices in Atlanta, Georgia; Chico, California; Minneapolis, Minnesota; Philadelphia, Pennsylvania; Scottsdale, Arizona; Seattle, Washington; and Walnut Creek, California. SHPS is owned by New York investment firm Welsh, Carson, Anderson & Stowe.

COMPANY FORMATION: 1997

SHPS was created as a 50-50 joint venture in December 1997 between Sykes Enterprises, Inc. and HealthPlan

Services Corp. Sykes was an information technology company founded by John H. Sykes in Charlotte, North Carolina, in 1977 to provide design and engineering services to large companies, such as IBM, one of the firm's first clients. In the early 1990s, Sykes branched into the customer relationship management field, acquiring a call tracking software developer and a programming firm. From this foundation, Sykes began providing customer support for manufacturers on an outsourced basis. Later in the decade, Sykes, now based in Tampa, Florida, continued to expand and branched into new sectors. Recognizing a new opportunity to provide an outsourced service, Sykes teamed up with another Tampa company, HealthPlan Services, to become involved in the growing health care industry.

HealthPlan Services was a managed care company that mostly served the small business market, providing administrative, cost containment, and distribution services. Clients also included health care purchasing alliances, managed care organizations, insurance companies, and self-funded benefit plans. The alliance with Sykes was a natural one, given that Sykes had a network of call centers, including nine in the United States and 11 internationally, and HealthPlan Services possessed the necessary contacts in the health care industry. With each company contributing $25 million, they created a joint venture called Sykes HealthPlan Services, or SHPS (pronounced "ships"), to serve as a third-party benefits administrator. HealthPlan Services would transfer its existing care management services to SHPS and then become one of the first customers.

COMPANY PERSPECTIVES

In a complex and changing world, SHPS makes benefits administration easy.

EXPANSION THROUGH ACQUISITION

SHPS hoped to reach $100 million in sales within the first year, setting the stage for an initial public offering of stock a year or two later. The Tampa-based company wasted little time in expanding its business. In late 1997, it paid $10 million for Optimed Medical Systems, Incorporated, a provider of managed care software solutions and related services. In March 1998, SHPS completed two further acquisitions. The stock of publicly traded Health International (HI) was purchased for about $25.2 million. The Scottsdale, Arizona-based company provided disease management services through a managed medical care program to employers and health plan administrators. Again, by improving the health of employees, HI achieved cost savings for its clients.

Also in March 1998, SHPS paid about $50 million for Louisville, Kentucky-based Prudential Service Bureau, Inc., a unit of Prudential Insurance Company. Established in 1986, the company was a call center-based third-party administrator of employee health welfare benefit plans, including enrollment, record keeping, verifying or paying claims, and producing management reports. It served these needs for more than 600 major employers. The business was subsequently renamed Sykes HealthPlan Service Bureau, Inc.

SHPS recorded a net loss of $5.3 million on revenues of $59.7 million in 1997. Shortly after reporting the results, in April 1998, SHPS filed an initial public offering (IPO) of stock, the shares made available by Sykes and HealthPlan Services as well as the company. It was expected to raised more than $115 million. Market conditions were far from favorable, however. In July 1998, Sykes and HealthPlan Services decided to call off the stock offering. By this time, it had become apparent to SHPS's joint-venture partners that one or the other would have to take charge of the company if it were to realize its potential. Thus, in September 1998, Sykes bought out HealthPlan Services for $30.6 million in cash.

The Prudential Service Bureau acquisition had also brought with it a 230,000-square-foot service center that housed 630 employees. Because SHPS was interested in consolidating its service centers in Arizona, Florida, Georgia, Massachusetts, North Dakota, and Virginia, the Louisville site became a logical choice. Eager to bring additional employment to the state, the Kentucky Economic Development Finance Authority offered inducements to SHPS. In September 1998, a deal was struck to provide the company with $6.8 million in corporate tax credits for increasing the number of employees to 950. Discussions were also being held on a much larger project.

MOVE TO LOUISVILLE: 1999

In March 1999, SHPS reached an agreement to move its headquarters to Louisville. At an investment of $80 million, the company planned to establish a 50-acre campus at the Eastpoint Business Center, capable of housing more than 3,500 people. The local government agreed to provide the company with a $3.5 million loan and the Kentucky Economic Development Finance Authority provided additional tax credits as a further incentive. Aside from financial inducements, SHPS was attracted to Louisville for other reasons. Not only was it centrally located, but it also possessed a qualified, available workforce, and featured a reliable transportation system. Another factor was the willingness of local colleges (the University of Louisville, Spalding University, and Bellarmine College) to work with SHPS to develop training programs that the company could use for its employees around the country.

Unfortunately, Sykes encountered a number of obstacles that forced it to postpone construction of the expansion project. Poor results in the fourth quarter of 1999, due in large part to the performance of SHPS, led to a collapse in Sykes's stock price. Accounting errors also came to light that forced the restatement of previous reports, leading to further erosion in the price. In less than a year, shares of Sykes stock would fall from a high of $52.25 to about $3. Because Sykes elected to focus on its core businesses, the building and operation of call centers, which generated reliable profits, SHPS became expendable. Having bought out its partner in the venture provided a windfall of much needed funds to Sykes. In June 2000, Sykes sold SHPS for $165.5 million in cash to New York investment firm Welsh, Carson, Anderson & Stowe. Founded in 1979, Welsh, Carson focused on the information/business services and health care sectors.

CAREWISE PURCHASE: 2001

With the support of its new owner, SHPS resumed expansion. In June 2001, it acquired CareWise Inc. from Nashville's troubled PhyCor Inc. Seattle-based CareWise provided 3.5 million health plan consumers

```
┌─────────────────────────────────────────────┐
│                                               │
│              KEY DATES                        │
│                    ◼                          │
│  ─────────────────────────────────────────   │
│                                               │
│  1997:  Sykes HealthPlan Services is          │
│         established as joint venture.         │
│  1998:  Sykes Enterprises buys out            │
│         joint-venture partner.                │
│  2000:  Company is sold to New York           │
│         investment firm.                      │
│  2001:  CareWise Inc. is acquired.            │
│  2004:  Landacorp is acquired.                │
│                                               │
└─────────────────────────────────────────────┘
```

with personalized health and wellness programs. Because it also offered unlimited access to telephone decision and support counseling, as well as online resources, it was deemed a good fit with the strong call center operations of SHPS.

Another acquisition followed in April 2003. SHPS paid $98 million in cash for Minneapolis area-based eBenX, a provider of Web-based software that linked employers to health care providers, carriers, and brokers. The company was founded in 1993 as Network Management Services, and in November 1999 adopted the eBenX name as it prepared to go public a month later. Taking advantage of the popularity of dot-com issues at the time, the company raised $100 million, one of the largest amounts ever raised by a Minnesota company. On the first day of trading, the price per share surged to nearly $45. As the dot-com bubble burst, eBenX was not spared, however. When SHPS struck a deal to acquire the company, the stock had dipped below $2 a share. SHPS would pay $4.85 per share for the company.

SHPS grew further through external means in 2004. First, it paid $10 million for National Health Services Inc. It was part of Montreal, Canada-based BCE Emergis Inc. (later renamed Emergis and then bought by Telus), one of North America's largest e-business companies. Operating in Louisville, National Health Services was the company's U.S. care management subsidiary, providing case- and disease-management services for employee benefits programs as well as state Medicaid participants. Early in 2004, BCE put the business up for sale in order to focus on its claims, payments, loan processing, and other core businesses.

LANDACORP ACQUISITION: 2004

Also in 2004, SHPS acquired Landacorp, Inc., in a transaction valued at about $56 million. Based in

Atlanta, Georgia, Landacorp was founded in 1982 as Landa Management Systems Corporation in California, and was reincorporated in Delaware as Landacorp, Inc., in 1999 before going public. The following year, it acquired ProMedex, Inc., laying the foundation for Landacorp's Managing for Tomorrow chronic condition management products. They included software and Web-enabled management products.

SHPS introduced its enhanced health management delivery model in 2006. The following year it added other new products. A new health risk engine was released to help employers manage the health liabilities of their workforce. Landacorp also introduced the CareRadius product suite. It helped to improve health outcomes, leading to lower costs, by simplifying the medical management process. SHPS and its greater capabilities found a ready marketplace in 2007. Because a growing number of self-insured employers were separating their health management programs from their health plans, the desire to outsource the operation helped to increase the number of new clients in 2007, representing about two million additional new members for SHPS.

New products continued to be developed and rolled out. In 2008, SHPS unveiled its next-generation wellness solution. Marketed as the Carewise Personal Wellness Program, this integrated service suite offered personalized solutions for the improvement of employee health. The delivery of benefits was streamlined in the process and provided further support in the effort to rein in health care costs.

With a new administration in Washington bringing changes to the health care industry, SHPS faced uncertainty but also growing opportunities. The trend of outsourcing the administration of employee health benefits was likely to continue, and the need to control costs would only grow in importance. Both factors favored SHPS in the long term. With more then $200 million in annual sales, the company was poised to realize even greater returns in the years to come.

Ed Dinger

PRINCIPAL SUBSIDIARIES

Carewise Health, Inc.; Landacorp, Inc.

PRINCIPAL COMPETITORS

Accenture plc; Aon Corporation; Healthways, Inc.

FURTHER READING

Hundley, Kris. "Health Venture Sold to Partner." *St. Petersburg Times*, September 12, 1998, 1E.

———. "Sykes, HPS to Start Joint Health Venture." *St. Petersburg Times*, October 22, 1997, 1E.

Huntley, Helen. "Sykes HealthPlan Services Plans IPO." *St. Petersburg Times*, April 25, 1998, 8E.

Kamuf, Rachel. "City Could Snag Major Corporate Headquarters." *Business First-Louisville*, December 14, 1998, 1.

————. "Sykes Headquarters Coming to Eastpoint." *Business First-Louisville*, March 29, 1999, 1.

Stockfish, Jerome R. "Sykes to Sell Subsidiary, Reorganize." *Tampa Tribune*, June 14, 2000, 1.

Smashburger Master LLC

1515 Arapahoe Street, Tower 1, Suite 1000
Denver, Colorado 80202-3150
U.S.A.
Telephone: (303) 633-1500
Fax: (303) 593-3888
Web site: http://www.smashburger.com

Private Company
Founded: 2006
Employees: 780
Sales: $39.4 million (2010)
NAICS: 722110 Full-Service Restaurants; 533110 Owners and Lessors of Other Nonfinancial Assets

■ ■ ■

Smashburger Master LLC is a chain of more than 140 fast-casual restaurants specializing in freshly prepared hamburgers, off the menu or custom ordered. The core of the concept is to offer a "smashed-to-order" hamburger. A variety of sauces are among Smashburger's basic toppings, including the house "Smash" sauce. Premium add-ons include applewood smoked bacon, a fried egg, beef chili, and five choices of cheese, such as blue cheese and sharp cheddar. The company offers specialty burgers, designed for local tastes and available only in those cities.

ORIGINS OF THE "BETTER BURGER" CONCEPT

The Smashburger concept was the brainchild of Tom Ryan, a veteran of marketing, branding, and concept and product development in the fast-food industry. Educated in food science, Ryan's record of achievement includes Stuffed Crust Pizza and the Lovers line at Pizza Hut. For McDonald's, Ryan developed Fruit and Yogurt Parfaits, McGriddles, and Big 'N Tasty, as well as the Dollar Menu. As the chief marketing officer and branding officer at the Quiznos chain of submarine sandwich restaurants, Ryan developed Sammies, Prime Rib, and Steakhouse Beef Dip sandwiches.

Smashburger is Ryan's first attempt to develop a fast-casual, chain restaurant concept from inception. The opportunity stemmed from his position as managing partner and chief concept officer at Consumer Capital Partners (CCP), owners of the Quiznos franchise. CCP Chairman Rick Schaden and his father, Dick Schaden, were known for purchasing Quiznos in 1991 and turning the regional enterprise into the second-largest chain of submarine sandwich restaurants in the United States.

Ryan's association with CCP led to the company's $15 million investment in Smashburger in April 2007. CCP purchased Icon Burger in the city of Glendale, adjacent to Denver, and Ryan rebranded the concept. The prototype for the Smashburger concept opened in June 2007.

In contrast to the quick-service restaurant chains, the fast-casual system was essential to the Smashburger concept. Smashburger provided freshly prepared food quickly but inexpensively, and guests retrieved the food themselves at the counter. With burgers priced from $5 to $7, plus add-ons, side orders, and beverages, the average check per person was $8.50. While many kinds of fast-casual restaurant chains existed, Smashburger held a niche market as one of the few to offer premium hamburgers.

Once satisfied with the workings of the concept, Smashburger opened several more restaurants in the Denver area. A year later, the company operated five units and was in the process of negotiating leases for at least five more units by the end of 2008. New locations in the Denver area included Arvada, Broomfield, and Thornton. Stores opened in Colorado Springs, in central Colorado, and in Fort Collins, in northern Colorado.

2008: BUSINESS DEVELOPMENT

Smashburger's business development plan involved a mix of corporate ownership, joint-venture partnerships, and franchise contracts. One of the benefits of involving other owners and partners was the local knowledge of real estate markets and consumer tastes provided through local ownership. In particular, Smashburger wanted to find experienced, multiunit franchise operators capable of rapid franchise development. Smashburger set the investment minimum at $2 million in assets and $500,000 in liquid assets.

In marketing for its first franchise agreements, Smashburger developed the "Founders Club," to comprise the first five multiunit franchise companies to sign a contract. In October 2008, Smashburger signed its first franchise agreement with Mascott Corporation. Mascott operated its own Markers Restaurant and Markers Express chains, as well as several fast-food chains, including Popeye's Louisiana Kitchen, Carvel Ice Cream Stores, and Cinnabon World Famous Cinnamon Rolls. The contract with Mascott allowed for the development of 30 Smashburger locations in New Jersey.

The second franchise agreement involved Aerios, LLC, which operated several franchise units of Subway, Dairy Queen, and other brands. Aerios' Smashburger franchise territory included Kansas City, Missouri; South Dakota; and several Colorado mountain towns, including Steamboat Springs, Durango, and Rifle.

A joint-venture partnership developed the first two restaurants to open outside of Colorado. The joint venture with WTO included local real estate developers

and an experienced franchise operator. Smashburger WTO Acquisition, LLC, opened a Smashburger in Wichita, Kansas, in late 2008. The company planned to open as many as four additional units in Wichita and five units in Tulsa and Oklahoma City. The first Texas Smashburger opened in Houston in December 2008, a company-owned and operated unit.

Smashburger continued to sign new Founders Club franchisees in 2009. In January SB Alamo Development, LLC, owned by three veterans of the chain restaurant and fast-food industry, agreed to open 45 Smashburger units in West Texas and New Mexico over eight years' time. SunWest Burgers LLC, formed as a subsidiary to SunWest Restaurant Concepts, agreed to open 20 stores in Phoenix and surrounding areas. Three primary owners brought 40 years combined restaurant chain management experience to the endeavor.

Texas was an area of significant franchise development. SB Sizzle, Inc. signed a franchise agreement with Smashburger in May, for the development of 10 restaurants in small- and midsized east Texas cities, including Tyler, Longview, and Beaumont. In October, BIGG Capital Holdings signed an agreement to open 30 Smashburger units in the Dallas area over five years' time. Cow Town Sizzle, Inc., a subsidiary of SB Sizzle, signed an agreement to open 10 franchises in Fort Worth.

2009: FRANCHISE OPENINGS AND FURTHER CONCEPT DEVELOPMENT

With eight Smashburger restaurants in operation and several franchise agreements in place, the company's goal was to have 30 to 60 stores in operation by the end of 2009. The first franchises opened for business in the summer of 2009. These included an Aerios Smashburger unit in Grand Junction, Colorado, in early June. SB Alamo opened two units in San Antonio in late June and early July. Other new franchise openings that summer included locations in Tulsa, Oklahoma, and Meridian, Idaho. In addition, Smashburger opened at least three company-owned stores in the Houston area in 2009.

The Midwest proved to be a fruitful area for franchise development. Near Minneapolis-St. Paul, Smashburger units opened in St. Anthony and Golden Valley in June, followed by Roseville and Plymouth locations in July. A Smashburger in West Des Moines was opened by local franchisee Smashguys, LLC, in September 2009. Reload LLC opened its first unit in Omaha in October, with additional restaurants in development for the Lincoln and Omaha markets.

KEY DATES

2007: Icon Burger restaurant is purchased and re-branded as Smashburger.
2008: Smashburger signs its first franchise agreements.
2009: Smashburger develops burger specialties for local market tastes.
2011: The 100th Smashburger unit opens.

TAILORING MENUS TO SPECIFIC REGIONS

By this time Smashburger began to develop special burgers to reflect local tastes. The Minneapolis-St. Paul area stores featured the Twin Cities Smashburger, with melted sharp cheddar bar cheese, Swiss cheese, and garlic grilled onions. The Iowa Smashburger featured locally produced Maytag blue cheese, applewood smoked bacon, and haystack onions. The West Des Moines store offered the State Fair Brat, a bratwurst, as well. Beverages for Nebraska included Sioux City root beer and Third Stone Brown ale from Lincoln microbrewer Empyrean Brewing Company.

In August 2009 Smashburger opened two company-owned units in Salt Lake City. Since Utah was the Beehive State, local flavors included the Beehive Smashburger or Smashchicken sandwich, with honey barbeque sauce, applewood smoked bacon, cheddar cheese, and onion. The Grasshopper Mint shake was made with Häagen-Dazs ice cream.

The first Dallas Smashburger opened in November 2009. The specialty items for Texas followed from popularity of the Tex-Mex style. The Lone Star burger offered an open-faced chili-cheeseburger with jalapenos and wedge of lime on the side. Other items included a lime shake and the Tex-Mex influenced Cowboy Cobb salad.

Smashburger sought access to specialized locations through a franchise agreement with PhaseNext Hospitality. As an operator of several fast-casual concepts in airports, train stations, military bases, and university campuses, PhaseNext planned to open Smashburger units in seven airports in the United States. The first planned were at Dallas-Fort Worth and Houston George Bush Intercontinental in Texas and Ronald Reagan National Airport in Washington, D.C.

Mascott opened three Smashburger units in New Jersey in late 2009, the first in Hackensack in August. The menu featured the New Jersey Burger, with apple-wood smoked bacon, blue cheese, grilled onions, and haystack onions on an onion roll. Smashdogs included local brand Best's beef hot dogs and Italian hot dog with sautéed peppers and onions. New Jersey was a test market for sweet potato fries, as well. Smashburger's unique strategy garnered the company the accolade of being a 2009 Hot Concept by *Nation's Restaurant* magazine.

GROWTH APACE IN 2010 AND 2011

During the first three months of 2010, 15 restaurants opened in 11 markets. The company hoped to open 60 stores for the year, for a total of 100 stores by year end. Franchises opened in Oklahoma City; Orlando; Kansas City, Missouri; Sacramento; and Lexington, Kentucky; and at Fort Bliss Army Air Defense Base, near El Paso, Texas. In December 2010 Smashburger began opening company-owned units in the Chicago area, first in Batavia.

Smashburger began targeting the New York City area in 2010. The company signed two franchise agreements for the area. ISK Systems, LLC, contracted to open 20 restaurants on Long Island. Irwin S. Kruger brought more than 30 years experience as a McDonald's franchisee to the Smashburger concept. For Brooklyn, Smashburger found 25/20 Management to cover three outlets.

Franchise agreements included a five-unit contract with Aurora Burgers for the Pittsburgh area. Smash Venture, LLC, for Kalamazoo, in south-central Michigan, signed an agreement for six Smashburger locations. Winding River Restaurant, LLC, planned 13 units for Nashville and surrounding suburbs. Shreveport Sizzle, Inc., agreed to five franchise units in Shreveport, Bossier City, and northwest Louisiana.

Smashburger initiated plans for international franchise development in 2010. The company formed a partnership with Bridging Culture Worldwide (BCW) to find a franchisee in South Korea. BCW provided cross-cultural management, consulting, and strategic planning for companies seeking international expansion.

Other new developments in 2010 included the introduction of four new chicken sandwiches and two salad entrees. The chicken sandwiches included the BBQ Ranch Smashchicken, featuring applewood smoked bacon, haystack onions, and a mix of barbeque sauce and ranch dressing. The Buffalo Smashchicken featured Frank's Buffalo Sauce and crumbled blue cheese. The salad entrees included the Harvest Chicken Smashsalad, with marinated balsamic tomatoes, raisins, cranberries, sunflower seeds, pumpkin seeds, and blue cheese, served with balsamic vinaigrette dressing.

CHAIN REACHES 100 RESTAURANTS, CONTINUES GROWING

Chicago and Atlanta were considered important markets for expansion. Several company-owned units opened in the Chicago area with Smashburger restaurants in Bloomingdale, Daria, Bolingbrook, and Oak Lawn. In April 2011 Smashburger marked the opening of its 100th restaurant, located in Schaumburg, Illinois. Two Smashburger franchises opened in Atlanta in 2011, with additional units in the planning and development stage.

In early 2011 Smashburger announced that it had signed five new joint-venture franchise agreements. One joint-venture partnership planned 24 stores in Queens and Westchester County, New York, and Fairfield County, Connecticut. A joint-venture partnership in Cincinnati, Ohio, planned 12 Smashburger units. Other development plans included seven units in the Jacksonville, Florida, area; 10 for New Orleans and Birmingham; and 10 units for Charlotte, North Carolina.

PROMOTIONS, PLANS, AND INTERNATIONAL DEVELOPMENT

With the framework of a national chain in place, Smashburger began to push same store sales by initiating a number of promotions. For National Burger Month in May 2011, the company offered a Double FRY day every Tuesday. The company offered a Nutter Butter shake for the month as well. A Facebook promotion offered various prizes, including Smashburgers for a year. To be a contestant, customers had to post an accolade of Smashburger on Facebook.

Travel promotions involved selling specialty burgers from one city systemwide and offering a weekend getaway to that city. In early 2011 Smashburger offered Las Vegas's Sin City burger at Smashburger restaurants nationwide and a chance to win a trip for two to Las Vegas. To enter the contest, customers were required to purchase the Sin City burger then enter the validation code from the bottom of their receipt on Smashburger's Web site. The Sin City burger featured a fried egg, smoked applewood bacon, grilled and haystack onions, American cheese, and house smashsauce.

In September Smashburger offered customers a chance to win a trip to Chicago using the same method.

Nationwide Smashburger restaurants offered the Windy City burger, featuring cheddar cheese, haystack onions, and Gulden's spicy mustard on a hand-cut pretzel roll.

Smashburger continued to expand in the Midwest, with new restaurants in Grand Rapids, Michigan, during the summer of 2011. The local specialties included the Michigan Olive burger, a Michigan cherry barbecue sauce option, and a salad with cherries on it. Beverages included the Michigan cherry shake and a Vernor's float, using the popular local brand of ginger ale and vanilla ice cream (also known as a Boston Cooler).

In September 2011, Smashburger signed its first international restaurant development agreements. The Al Musbah Group planned to open Smashburger units at eight airport locations in Saudi Arabia. Georgetown Advisors, a commercial development company in Bahrain, planned to open three Smashburger franchises in Bahrain and six in Kuwait. Smashburger's next targets for international development included Canada and the United Kingdom.

Mary Tradii

PRINCIPAL COMPETITORS

The Counter; Fatburger Corporation; Five Guys Enterprises, Inc.; Good Times Restaurants, Inc.; In and Out Burgers; The Johnny Rockets Group, Inc.; Red Robin Gourmet Burgers, Inc.

FURTHER READING

Davis, Joyzelle. "Smashburger Hungry to Grow: Chain Plans 20 Locations by End of This Year, Eyes 500 Nationwide." *Rocky Mountain News*, May 9, 2008, 1B.

"Smashburger Announces First International Expansion with Development Agreement for Middle East." *Business Wire*, September 7, 2011.

"Smashburger Opens First Store outside Home State of Colorado and Brings a Better Burger to Wichita." *Business Wire*, December 7, 2008.

"Smashburger Signs Franchise Agreement for 63 New Restaurants." *Close-up Media*, May 26, 2011.

"Smashburger Spreads Its 'Better Burger' across America." *Business Wire*, April 26, 2010.

Smith & Nephew plc

15 Adam Street
London, WC2N 6LA
United Kingdom
Telephone: (+44 20) 7401 7646
Fax: (+44 20) 7960 2350
Web site: http://www.smith-nephew.com

Public Company
Incorporated: 1937 as Smith & Nephew Associated
    Companies Limited
Employees: 10,172
Sales: $3.96 billion (2010)
Stock Exchanges: London New York
Ticker Symbols: SN (London); SNN (New York)
NAICS: 334510 Electromedical and Electrotherapeutic
    Apparatus Manufacturing; 339112 Surgical and
    Medical Instrument Manufacturing; 339113 Surgi-
    cal Appliance and Supplies Manufacturing

∎ ∎ ∎

A global medical device provider operating in more than
90 countries, Smith & Nephew plc is among the
industry leaders in its three main areas: orthopedic
reconstruction and trauma, endoscopy, and advanced
wound management. In orthopedics, the company
produces hip, knee, and shoulder implants, along with
bone cement and products used in stabilizing severe
fractures and in correcting deformities. In endoscopy,
Smith & Nephew specializes in products used in
minimally invasive surgical procedures, including arthro-
scopes, digital cameras, surgical monitors, and fluid

management equipment. In wound management, Smith
& Nephew produces a wide array of products used for
treating the chronic wounds of the elderly as well as the
wounds of burn patients and surgical incisions.
Although based in the United Kingdom, Smith &
Nephew derives about 43 percent of its revenues from
the United States, the company's stock trades on the
New York Stock Exchange (in addition to its listing in
London), and the firm issues its financial statements in
U.S. dollars.

VICTORIAN ORIGINS

Thomas James Smith was born in 1827. He trained as a
pharmacist, first as an apprentice in Grantham, Lincolnshire, and then, in 1854 and 1855, at London's
University College, where Lord Lister, the antiseptic innovator, also studied. In 1856 Smith was admitted into
the newly formed Royal Pharmaceutical Society, and in
August of that year he bought his first shop at 71
Whitefriargate, Hull.

Smith soon became involved in the wholesale trade
of bandages and related materials. Smith took advantage
of his proximity to the docks and fishermen of Hull and
began supplying hospitals with cod liver oil, valued for
its therapeutic value in cases of rickets, tuberculosis, and
rheumatism (vitamins had not yet been identified). At
the time, doctors' visits were expensive and pharmacists
were often the first ones consulted. Most medicines did
not require a prescription, and factory-made pills were
only beginning to displace concoctions produced by
doctors and pharmacists.

COMPANY PERSPECTIVES

Smith & Nephew is committed to helping people regain their lives by repairing and healing the human body. We believe that this can only be achieved by establishing mutually beneficial relationships with all of our stakeholders including patients, healthcare professionals, investors and employees.

Smith's father lent him £500 in 1860 so he could convert two cottages on North Church Street into a warehouse. It was such a good year that he sought even larger accommodations in 1861, renting some buildings at 10 North Churchside, which he bought in 1880 with the help of another £500 loan from his father. Business was so good because he had traveled to Norway on a Norwegian gunboat to buy 750 gallons of cod liver oil. It was a shrewd business deal, as the Norwegian product was both less expensive and better tasting than the previous supply from Newfoundland. The solid fat (stearine) had been processed out of it.

At the same time, Smith's marketing efforts generated many new accounts among the hospitals of London. By 1880, he had even shipped once to Cairo. At the encouragement of a correspondent, Smith registered his oil under the brand name Paragon Cod Liver Oil, to punctuate its outstanding qualities. Two larger competitors established factories in Norway after medical opinion swung decidedly in favor of the Norwegian product.

T. J. Smith never married. In 1896, a few months before his death, his 22-year-old nephew Horatio Nelson Smith (named after T. J.'s father) became a partner. H. N. was known for his long hours and direct, inquisitive manner. H. N. had apprenticed for six years making draperies. The firm, now known as T.J. Smith & Nephew, shifted its production away from cod liver oil in favor of bandages. In 1907 it was registered as a limited liability company. When H. N. joined the company in 1896, staff numbered three. However, when he signed a contract with the Turkish government in 1911 after the outbreak of the war with Bulgaria, employment reached 54. Soon thereafter a small local competitor, Lambert & Lambert, was acquired.

Smith & Nephew bought sanitary towel manufacturer SASHENA Limited in 1912 (the name was an acronym for "Sanitary Absorbent Safe Hygienic Every Nurse Advocates"). The line was later known as "Lilia," which had originally referred to an industrial

cellulose towel product. The line also incorporated the 1925 acquisition of a half share of a German mill for producing cellulose sanitary towels, which had been developed to cope with the scarcity of cotton. As James Foreman-Peck records in his book *Smith & Nephew in the Health Care Industry*, the materials and methods for their manufacture were similar to surgical dressings, and women, buoyed by suffrage and a heightened role in the workforce, were becoming more affluent. In 1954 the line continued with the introduction of the Lil-Lets brand of tampons.

CONFIGURING FOR MODERN TIMES

Demand for bandages skyrocketed during World War I. Smith & Nephew staff increased to 1,200 as the company obtained contracts with several of the Allied governments as well as the American Red Cross. The firm's textile capacity also was used for producing certain military paraphernalia, such as weapons belts. In addition, legislation in the early 1920s, which stipulated that miners and factory workers have access to first-aid kits in the workplace, offered Smith & Nephew a natural opportunity. Nevertheless, after World War I, production was scaled down considerably, to 183 employees. Furthermore, the Great Depression spurred many administrative changes that helped shape the company into a modern manufacturing corporation. Marketing efforts became more specialized. The company was incorporated as Smith & Nephew Associated Companies Ltd. in 1937, and its stock was listed on the London Stock Exchange that same year.

Smith & Nephew often looked to Germany for technological innovations. H. N. Smith's knowledge of the German language appears to have served him well. In 1930 the company obtained the British rights to Elastoplast bandages, made from a specially woven cloth coated with adhesive, from Lohmann AG. The bandage, although more expensive than others, provided a quick and very effective fix for varicose ulcers in particular, noted various journals.

Smith & Nephew introduced a similar bandage called the Cellona plaster of Paris bandage in 1930. Although it seemed more expensive than the materials it would replace, the effort saved from making messy casts offset the costs and the bandage's light weight made patients more comfortable and healed them faster. Concerns over industrial accidents made the product's introduction timely. The bandages were later named Gypsona.

Much of Gypsona's complex manufacturing process originated with German companies. Several other types

KEY DATES

1856: Thomas James Smith opens his first pharmaceutical shop in England.

1896: Nephew Horatio Nelson Smith partners with his uncle, and the firm changes its name to T.J. Smith & Nephew.

1937: Firm incorporates as Smith & Nephew Associated Companies Limited; company's stock is listed on the London Stock Exchange.

1951: Company purchases Herts Pharmaceuticals Limited.

1986: Richards Medical Company of Memphis, Tennessee, is purchased.

1995: Firm makes several key acquisitions including Homecraft Holdings Ltd., Acufex, and Professional Care Products Inc.

2000: Company sells its consumer products business.

2007: Swiss firm Plus Orthopedics Holding AG is acquired.

2011: New strategy is unveiled aiming to pursue growth in emerging markets and seek acquisitions in the wound management sector.

of bandages soaked in various types of medicines were coopted from Germany and the United States. In 1946 a waterproof version was developed, and a new line known as Ultraplast (which later earned a Royal Warrant) came with the 1958 purchase of the Scottish company Wallace Cameron. In 1961 Elastoplast bandages controlled three-quarters of the market.

DIVERSIFICATION IN POSTWAR ERA

In the 1950s Smith & Nephew had to decide whether to modernize its textile operations in Britain or buy textiles from the Far East. It and the unions agreed to the former, although a media campaign to enlist the support of other employers was necessary. The firm's mills subsequently earned a great reputation for efficiency. Interestingly, its mills in England and France were poised to produce denim when the enduring blue jeans fashion trend arrived from the United States. The automation of the company's mills included the purchase of one of the earliest commercially available computers in the 1950s, called the Leo. Its 1963 replacement was so powerful for its time that the company leased processing time until the 1970s.

Before its 1951 purchase of Herts Pharmaceuticals Limited, Smith & Nephew had been dependent on technology developed outside the company. Herts, which before World War II was the U.K. subsidiary of Beiersdorf AG, was best known for PAS and other of the earliest oral treatments for tuberculosis. Like other research firms the company was to acquire later, however, Herts lacked the resources to develop and promote them properly on its own. After the merger, Herts also worked on psychotropic drugs and, closer to Smith & Nephew's core business, breathable membranes for covering wounds, the first of which was called Airstrip and was introduced in 1952. In addition to guaranteeing itself a supply of these types of films, the company was able to license these processes to other firms.

Smith & Nephew entered the hypodermic syringe market in 1954 with the purchase of S. & R.J. Everett & Co. The firm set up a recycling service to provide a more thorough sterilization than the boiling the hospitals had been doing, but disposable syringes made this obsolete.

Through Lilia Limited, the company formed a joint selling company with Arthur Berton Ltd., makers of the Dr. White's Brand, in 1955. Three years later both Arthur Berton and Southalls (Birmingham) Ltd. were acquired, making Lilia-White (Sales) Ltd. the leader of the sanitary protection market. To bolster its position, Smith & Nephew bought Johnson & Johnson's Wrexham sanitary protection factory in 1962. This line contributed the second-largest portion of Smith & Nephew's overall sales. Health care products remained first. Sanitary protection products also made up the second-largest portion of the firm's profits after health care products. The company also sold cosmetics and children's clothing.

The group bought No. 2 Temple Place in 1962 to house its headquarters. New products of the 1960s included disposable products and washable cotton blankets to prevent the spread of infection in hospitals. It introduced a standardized nurse's uniform, which was more efficient to produce than the myriad styles then existing among hospitals. A huge leap in efficiency was realized by a joint venture with Johnson & Johnson and a regional Scottish hospital board to develop individually wrapped sterilized dressings, which saved the hospitals the considerable expense of installing and running sterilizing equipment. Sales in 1964 totaled £28.3 million.

In 1968 the giant Unilever conglomerate made a bid to purchase Smith & Nephew in an emotional contest with its management, who initiated a campaign for the hearts and minds of its shareholders, touting the company's family tradition as well as its superior financial performance. The tactic worked well when Unilever's plan to slash dividends came to light, and the takeover attempt ultimately failed.

INCREASED R&D AND FURTHER ACQUISITIONS

The 1970s were characterized by pressures on margins and volume. The National Health Service, which accounted for much of the firm's U.K. business, became more demanding and cost-conscious. International competitive pressure also increased. This resulted in increased resources for research and development in the next decade. New buildings at the company's venerable Hull site were constructed in 1981 and 1986. Marketing and sales operations for the Health Care division were brought to Hull in 1982, joining the rest of the company's functions.

In the mid-1980s Smith & Nephew began licensing OpSite, a skin covering, through Johnson & Johnson. The 1985 purchase of the U.S. company Affiliated Hospital extended the firm's product line into rubber gloves and steel trolleys. 3 Sigma Inc., another U.S. company, also was purchased. In 1987 sports injury specialist Donjoy Inc. and Sigma Inc., which made peristaltic infusion pumps, were added. Pfizer Hospital Products Inc.'s United Medical Division, which made special surgical dressings in Florida, was acquired in 1988. In 1986 the company bought Richards Medical Company of Memphis, Tennessee, which specialized in trauma and orthopedics, for £192.7 million.

Smith & Nephew's 1989 purchase of Ioptex Inc. for $230 million suffered from bad timing: soon thereafter, prices for the company's cataract replacement lenses fell by nearly two-thirds, thanks to U.S. government intervention. Smith & Nephew sold the company to Allergan, Inc. for £11 million in 1994, pulverizing the company's profit that year.

An example of the company's good fortune, however, was illustrated by Nivea brand moisturizing cream. Overseas rights for the Nivea brand of moisturizing cream passed to Smith & Nephew with the acquisition of Herts Pharmaceuticals in 1951. Soon it contributed almost as much as Elastoplast bandages to the firm's consumer sales. In 1992 Beiersdorf paid £46.5 million to buy back U.K. and Commonwealth rights for what was estimated to be the largest toiletry brand in the world. Smith & Nephew continued to earn a 17 percent royalty on U.K. Nivea sales without having to spend any money on advertising. In the 1960s, the brand was extended with "Nivea Lotions" and an upscale skin care line known as "Nivea Visage" competed with L'Oréal in the 1990s.

SEARCHING FOR 21ST-CENTURY MARKETS

The transformation of Smith & Nephew into a modern multinational corporation occurred in the 1980s under Eric Kinder, the company chief executive. S&N's international trade dated back to T. J. Smith's early days. Companies had been established in Canada in 1921 and in Australia and New Zealand in the early 1950s. Kinder felt the company needed to extend its export markets beyond postimperial Commonwealth countries. By the late 1990s, Smith & Nephew had substantial holdings in Europe and Asia. Sales in the United Kingdom accounted for 54.1 percent of the group's total in 1980. Ten years later, that figure had dropped to 23.6 percent, with the United States as the company's biggest market.

The company broadened its European reach. In 1987 it bought the Spanish firm Alberto Fernandez S.A., which made latex products such as gloves and prophylactics. In France, the company bought Cogemo S.A., makers of continuous passive motion machines, and Sanortho S.A., which made orthopedic implants. A German distribution venture with B. Braun GmbH was set up in 1985 and expanded to include Switzerland in 1988. However, newly developing countries in Asia seemed to offer the best opportunities for growth. Smith & Nephew's division in Japan, established in 1990, achieved sales of more than £30 million in five years. In the 1990s the company forecast that China and India would be among the 10 largest health care markets within 30 years. By 1995, the firm had three offices in China, with plans to manufacture bandages there eventually. Sales in Africa, Asia, Australia, and the Pacific were worth £151 million in 1994, still quite less than the £239 million garnered in the United Kingdom. The United States remained the largest market, providing Smith & Nephew with 40 percent of its sales, or £470 million. Continental Europe accounted for £205 million in sales, up from £37 million in 1984.

At the same time as the geographic range was expanded, the commodity status of certain product lines had to be redressed to improve the company's profit margins. In 1991 John Robinson took over as chief executive, succeeding Kinder, who then served as chairman. Under Robinson, the company specialized in products for tissue repair and protection ("wound management"), rather than the grab bag of medical supplies it once offered. In 1993 Smith & Nephew moved its research center from an Essex mansion to a new site in York Science Park, convenient to York University, an esteemed research institution.

CONTINUING GROWTH

Sacramento-based Cedaron Medical Inc. licensed its Dexter computerized physical therapy system in 1994 to Smith & Nephew, which hoped to succeed by offering a high-tech solution at a lower than average price. The rehabilitation equipment market was growing at least 5 percent a year at the time of the acquisition, and industrial hand injuries such as carpal tunnel syndrome, which was then beginning to get its share of press attention, seemed a precipitous omen for the Dexter.

Smith & Nephew committed at least $10 million to a 1994 joint venture with California's Advanced Tissue Sciences Inc. (ATS) to culture cartilage cells for joint replacement applications. This project held the potential to open a vast new market and save patients from expensive and painful surgery. ATS benefited from Smith & Nephew's ability to fund the project through years of testing.

The firm continued its growth into the mid-1990s. In 1995 the firm made a series of key acquisitions, including Homecraft Holdings Ltd., a U.K.-based manufacturer of daily living aids; Acufex, a leading manufacturer of surgical instruments and related devices; and Professional Care Products Inc., an orthopedic accessories firm. The following year, Smith & Nephew continued on its buying spree as well as focusing on product development. That year, the firm announced another joint venture with ATS that would produce bioengineered human skin replacement called Dermagraft. The new product was targeted at the $2.5 billion chronic diabetic foot ulcer market and eventually became available in 1997 to the U.K. market.

Smith & Nephew also teamed up with the University of Massachusetts in 1996 to establish a research center that was dedicated to the development of endoscopic procedures and instrumentation. The Human Tissue Repair Research Laboratory also was opened in the biology department of the University of York and was fully funded by the firm.

LATE NINETIES RESTRUCTURING

Under Chris O'Donnell, who was named chief executive in 1997, Smith & Nephew began to restructure its operations that same year. A Health Care division was formed, integrating the operations of orthopedic and endoscopy businesses. The new division, based in Memphis, Tennessee, was ultimately formed as a means of consolidating all U.S. sales and distribution functions. The restructuring continued into the following year when Smith & Nephew adopted a new management structure as well as a new strategy that focused on core operations in orthopedics, endoscopy, and wound management.

As part of the firm's new focus, Smith & Nephew in 1999 acquired Exogen Inc, a U.S.-based manufacturer of ultrasound fracture healing devices, and 3M Company's shoulder and hip implant and instrumentation business. The company continued to look for strategic partnerships that fit into its new plan and began divesting operations that were no longer suitable, including its bracing and support business. In November 1999 Smith & Nephew's stock began trading on the New York Stock Exchange. At the time of the listing, nearly one-third of the company's employees were based in the United States and more than 40 percent of company sales originated in that country.

The firm continued with its restructuring strategy into the new millennium. In June 2000, its consumer products business, including its feminine hygiene and toiletry products, first-aid dressings, and the Nivea distribution business, was sold. In November, Orthopaedic Biosystems Ltd. Inc., a U.S.-based surgical device firm, was purchased as part of Smith & Nephew's focus on endoscopy. Operating profits for fiscal 2000 increased by 24 percent.

In 2001 Smith & Nephew sold its ear, nose, and throat business to Gyrus Group plc. In April of the same year, a joint venture with Beiersdorf AG, called BSN Medical, began operation. The venture included the wound-care, casting, bandaging, and phlebology businesses of both firms (with the exception of the Smith & Nephew's wound-management lines related to hard-to-heal wounds), and each parent owned 50 percent of BSN. In March 2002 the restructuring that O'Donnell had launched five years earlier drew to a close with the sale of the company's rehabilitation unit to AbilityOne Corporation.

From this divestment, Smith & Nephew received £71.8 million in cash plus a 21.5 percent stake in AbilityOne. Smith & Nephew sold this stake for £52 million a year later as part of Patterson Dental Inc.'s acquisition of AbilityOne. The sale of the rehabilitation business left Smith & Nephew fully focused on its three core areas: orthopedic implant and trauma products, endoscopic products used in minimally invasive surgical procedures, and advanced wound-management products for hard-to-heal wounds, particularly those associated with the elderly.

THWARTED TAKEOVER BIDS

On the acquisitions front, Smith & Nephew had traditionally pursued smaller, "bolt-on" deals, but in March 2003 O'Donnell broke with that strategy when he engineered an agreement to acquire the Swiss firm Centerpulse AG, the largest maker of artificial knees and hips in Europe, for $2.6 billion. O'Donnell's bid to vault his company into the first rank of global orthopedic companies was soon thwarted, however, when Zimmer Holdings, Inc., one of the U.S.-based giants in the field, stepped in with a superior offer of $3.2 billion. Smith & Nephew elected not to top Zimmer's offer and thus exited from the takeover battle. In the months that followed, the company returned to its bolt-on acquisition strategy by acquiring Midland Medical Technologies Ltd., the global leader in metal-on-metal hip replacement procedures, a technique that allowed for less invasive and harder-wearing hip replacements. This $142 million deal closed in March 2004.

Also in 2004, Smith & Nephew took a $154 million exceptional charge to cover compensation for patients who had received faulty replacement knee implants. The company suffered another setback the following year when the U.S. Food and Drug Administration denied approval of Dermagraft for the treatment of leg ulcers. Smith & Nephew subsequently decided to pull out of the tissue engineering market. In February 2006 Smith & Nephew and Beiersdorf sold BSN Medical to Montagu Private Equity for $1.23 billion, resulting in a net profit for Smith & Nephew of $351 million.

That year, in addition to introducing two new knee systems and gaining U.S. approval of its Birmingham hip resurfacing product, Smith & Nephew bolstered its endoscopic division by acquiring San Antonio, Texas-based OsteoBiologics, Inc. for $73 million. OsteoBiologics' operations in Europe focused on bioabsorbable bone graft substitutes used to repair defects in knee cartilage, while in the United States it offered a bone void filler called the Trufit BGS Plug.

In the fourth quarter of 2006, Smith & Nephew made another bid at a blockbuster takeover when it entered into advanced talks to acquire Biomet, Inc., another of the major U.S.-based orthopedics companies. Although Smith & Nephew reportedly made a "competitive" bid for Biomet, this second attempt at a major orthopedics deal was thwarted as well when a private-equity consortium triumphed with a bid that ultimately amounted to $11.4 billion. Smith & Nephew moved quickly, however, to snare a more modest yet still significant catch, Plus Orthopedics Holding AG, a privately owned Swiss firm specializing mainly in replacement hips and knees but also producing small joint and shoulder products from its manufacturing facilities in Switzerland and China. Announced in March 2007, the acquisition of Plus Orthopedics was completed two months later at a price of $889 million.

The deal made Smith & Nephew the fourth-largest orthopedics reconstruction company in the world.

SETTLEMENT WITH U.S. GOVERNMENT

About a month after the Plus Orthopedics purchase was finalized, O'Donnell retired after 10 years at the helm and was succeeded by David Illingworth, previously Smith & Nephew's COO. Later in 2007, Smith & Nephew was one of five orthopedic device makers to enter into a $311 million settlement with the U.S. government relating to a probe of allegations that the firms had paid kickbacks to surgeons to use their products. Smith & Nephew's portion of the settlement amounted to $28.9 million, and all the companies agreed to abide by new standards for consulting agreements with surgeons and to be monitored for 18 months to ensure that they were following the new standards.

In May 2008 Smith & Nephew revealed that it had discovered that Plus Orthopedics had been engaging in unethical sales practices in certain markets, most notably Greece. The company put a stop to these practices, with the result being a loss of $100 million in sales that year. Smith & Nephew later took legal action against the former owners of Plus Orthopedics, winning an out-of-court settlement of $136 million in early 2009. That year, revenues fell slightly to $3.77 billion. The global economic downturn dampened demand as some patients delayed operations for joint replacements, waiting for their financial fortunes to improve.

RESTRUCTURING UNDER NEW LEADER

The sluggishness in the orthopedics market continued in 2010, but growing sales in emerging markets coupled with robust growth in the company's endoscopy and advanced wound management divisions resulted in a 4 percent increase in sales to $3.96 billion. Pretax profits jumped 33 percent to $895 million. In early 2011 various news outlets reported that Smith & Nephew late in the previous year had rejected a $10.9 billion takeover offer from Johnson & Johnson. Speculation about Smith & Nephew remaining a takeover target continued to swirl for months to come without a deal emerging. In the meantime, Illingworth unexpectedly stepped down as chief executive in April 2011 for personal reasons and was replaced by Olivier Bohuon, a French executive with a background in the pharmaceutical industry.

Just a few months after taking charge, Bohuon began implementing a new strategy that targeted growth from the emerging markets of Brazil, Russia, India, and

China and sought to increase the annual sales generated in these so-called BRIC countries from $120 million to $500 million by 2016. A new division centered on the BRIC countries was created, as was another division focused on Central and Latin America, Eastern Europe, South Africa, South Korea, and Southeast Asia. These divisions were charged with handling Smith & Nephew's full array of orthopedic, endoscopy, and wound management products. In addition, the company's existing orthopedics and endoscopy divisions were merged to form the new Advanced Surgical Devices division. Both this division and the unchanged Advanced Wound Management division focused on the established markets of the United States, Canada, Europe, Japan, Australia, and New Zealand. By creating a more streamlined operation in these established markets, Smith & Nephew hoped to generate funds to invest in emerging markets and research and development. The company needed to continue to develop new products to keep pace with its rivals in its highly competitive core markets. Smith & Nephew's new strategy also called for a more aggressive approach to pursuing mergers and acquisitions to bolster the firm's wound management business.

Frederick C. Ingram
Updated, Christina M. Stansell; David E. Salamie

PRINCIPAL SUBSIDIARIES

Smith & Nephew Healthcare Limited; Smith & Nephew Medical Limited; T. J. Smith & Nephew, Limited; Smith & Nephew GmbH (Austria); Smith & Nephew SA-NV (Belgium); Smith & Nephew A/S (Denmark); Smith & Nephew OY (Finland); Smith & Nephew SAS (France); Smith & Nephew Orthopedics GmbH (Germany); Smith & Nephew Orthopedics Hellas SA (Greece); Smith & Nephew Limited (Ireland); Smith & Nephew Srl (Italy); Smith & Nephew Nederland CV (Netherlands); Smith & Nephew A/S (Norway); Smith & Nephew Sp Zoo (Poland); Smith & Nephew Lda (Portugal); Smith & Nephew SA (Spain); Smith & Nephew AB (Sweden); Smith & Nephew Orthopaedics AG (Switzerland); Smith & Nephew Inc. (USA); Smith & Nephew Pty Limited (Australia); Smith & Nephew Inc. (Canada); Smith & Nephew Medical (Shanghai) Co Limited (China); Smith & Nephew Limited (Hong Kong); Smith & Nephew Healthcare Private Limited (India); Smith & Nephew KK (Japan);

Smith & Nephew Limited (Korea); Smith & Nephew Healthcare Sdn Berhad (Malaysia); Smith & Nephew SA de CV (Mexico); Smith & Nephew Limited (New Zealand); Smith & Nephew Inc. (Puerto Rico); Smith & Nephew Pte Limited (Singapore); Smith & Nephew (Pty) Limited (South Africa); Smith & Nephew Limited (Thailand); Smith & Nephew FZE (United Arab Emirates).

PRINCIPAL OPERATING UNITS

Advanced Surgical Devices; Advanced Wound Management.

PRINCIPAL COMPETITORS

Arthrex, Inc.; ArthroCare Corporation; Biomet, Inc.; CONMED Corporation; ConvaTec Inc.; DePuy Inc.; DePuy Mitek, Inc.; Kinetic Concepts, Inc.; Mölnlycke Health Care AB; Stryker Corporation; Synthes, Inc.; Systagenix Wound Management, Ltd.; Zimmer Holdings, Inc.

FURTHER READING

Bennett, Richard, and F. A. Leavey. *A History of Smith & Nephew, 1856–1981*. London: Smith & Nephew, 1981.

Davoudi, Salamander. "S&N Names New Chief Executive and Plans Margin Improvement." *Financial Times*, May 4, 2007, 20.

———. "Smith & Nephew Abandoned at Altar Again." *Financial Times*, December 19, 2006, 22.

———. "Smith & Nephew in Swiss Move." *Financial Times*, March 13, 2007, 19.

Foreman-Peck, James. *Smith & Nephew in the Health Care Industry*. Aldershot, UK: Edward Elgar, 1995.

Jack, Andrew. "Smith & Nephew Appoints New Chief." *Financial Times*, February 11, 2011, 16.

———. "Smith & Nephew Chief Eyes Expansion." *Financial Times*, May 6, 2011, 20.

Jack, Andrew, Miles Johnson, and Lina Saigol. "Deal Talk Simulates Demand for S&N." *Financial Times*, January 18, 2011, 19.

Lorenz, Andrew. "Why Focus Favors Smith & Nephew." *Management Today*, January 1996, 32–36.

O'Doherty, John. "Smith & Nephew's Growing Pains." *Financial Times*, March 15, 2010, 18.

Urry, Maggie. "O'Donnell Focuses on Knees, Hips, and Teeth." *Financial Times*, May 9, 2003, 25.

SodaStream International Ltd.

Gilboa Street, Airport City
Ben Gurion Airport,
Israel
Telephone: (972 3) 976-2451
Fax: (972 3) 973-6673
Web site: http://www.sodastream.com

Public Company
Founded: 1903
Employees: 1,073
Sales: $212.9 million (2010)
Stock Exchanges: NASDAQ
Ticker Symbol: SODA
NAICS: 335200 Household Appliance Manufacturing

■ ■ ■

Based in Israel, NASDAQ-listed SodaStream International Ltd. is the world's largest maker and distributor of home carbonation systems and accessories. Sold under the SodaStream and Soda-Club brands, the company's core countertop system turns tap water into carbonated drinks through the use of exchangeable carbon-dioxide cylinders. The company also sells a wide variety of soda flavorings. SodaStream products are sold in over 40 countries through more than 40,000 retail stores, including supermarkets, department stores, hypermarkets, home and electrical appliance stores, and water specialists and dealers.

ORIGINS: 1903

SodaStream traces its heritage to 1903 when Englishman Guy Hugh Gilbey invented an "apparatus for aerating liquids," which used a carbon-dioxide cylinder to carbonate water. Gilbey's family owned W & A Gilbey Ltd, a major London gin distilling company. The resulting SodaStream unit operated as an associated business. Initially, the device was sold only to the upper classes. In the 1920s commercial carbonation machines were introduced, including the Vantas machine. Instead of producing just seltzer water, the SodaStream machine began producing flavored sodas through flavor concentrates such as sarsaparilla. In 1955, a home appliance that produced eight-ounce bottles of soda in 14 different flavors was introduced to broaden the appeal of the SodaStream product.

In 1962 International Distillers and Vintners purchased W & A Gilbey and the SodaStream business. In 1971 SodaStream was sold to the household products firm Reckitt & Colman. In 1973, SodaStream's management bought the company, moved its headquarters to Peterborough, England, and developed a mass market strategy. A five-year marketing and distribution agreement was reached with Kenwood Manufacturing Co. Ltd. In 1979, SodaStream took marketing and distribution in-house. The company then launched a television advertising campaign aimed at children, featuring the slogan "get bizzy with the fizzy" that catapulted the device to mainstream status. The Boots drugstore chain was especially active in selling the machines, at one point accounting for 30 percent of all sales.

NEW OWNERSHIP UNDER CADBURY SCHWEPPES: 1985

SodaStream added the Mr. Frothy Milkshake machine in 1982, but the home carbonation machine remained at the heart of the SodaStream business. In 1985, Cadbury Schweppes PLC bought the company for £22.5 million. Although SodaStream operated as an independent company, it was now able to add many Schweppes flavors. Under new ownership, SodaStream introduced a high-capacity machine, the Carnival, which was able to produce as much as a liter of carbonated drink in a plastic bottle. Another new machine eliminated the plastic bottle altogether.

Sales reached £15.1 million by the end of the 1980s, about 80 percent of which came from the United Kingdom, including £6.6 million in syrup sales. The popularity of the SodaStream machine waned in the United Kingdom in the 1990s, however. The machine was difficult to use, the flavors were not especially appealing, and the quality of the soda it produced was inconsistent, dependent as it was on the quality of the tap water it used. Moreover, the novelty factor wore off. In 1992, the company tried to revive the business through the direct marketing of a new generation machine. The effort failed, however, to restore SodaStream's popularity in the United Kingdom.

SODA-CLUB IN THE BACKGROUND: 1991–2002

In-home carbonation systems enjoyed better success overseas, due in large measure to the efforts of Peter Wiseburgh, the Israel distributor for SodaStream from 1978 to 1991. He and British engineer Peter Hulley formed their own company, Soda-Club Holdings Ltd., in 1991, introducing a new patented machine. The new company marketed the Cool machine and the larger capacity Gemini. The names were later changed to Original and Maxi. Soda-Club soon spread beyond the United Kingdom. It entered South Africa in 1992, followed by Switzerland in 1993, Austria in 1994, Germany a year later, and the Netherlands in 1996. Soda-Club did especially well in Germany, where a

tradition of sparkling water already existed. To take manufacturing in-house, the company opened a facility in 1996 in Israel, located in a former military factory outside of Jerusalem.

Cadbury Schweppes sold SodaStream to the company's management team in 1997. It was still the world's largest maker of home carbonation systems and associated flavor concentrates. A year later, Soda-Club acquired SodaStream for £15.5 million and continued to sell both the Soda-Club and SodaStream machines. SodaStream sales in South Africa and New Zealand were soon taken over as well. Annual sales were now in the £100 million range.

At the start of the new century, Soda-Club looked to spur growth through innovation. A host of new fruit-combination flavors were introduced in 2000, including Apple & Peach, Cranberry & Blackcurrant, Orange & Mango, and Pineapple & Grapefruit. SodaStream also updated the design of the carbonation machines, resulting in the 2001 launch of the Design drink maker. The company also resumed television advertising for SodaStream in the United Kingdom in 2002 after a several year hiatus. In that same year, Soda-Club entered Belgium and the United States. The following year, the Soda-Club brand was launched in Australia and South Korea and a German subsidiary was formed to take over distribution of Soda-Club and Soda Stream products from Brita Wasser Filter System GmbH. A new syrup factory was also established in Israel at this time.

NEW OWNER

The Soda-Club business stagnated in the early 2000s despite efforts to relaunch the SodaStream brand in the United Kingdom. By 2006 the company was losing money on operating expenses. It had no new products in the pipeline or any strategy in place for market development. Nevertheless, Israel-based private-equity firm Fortissimo Capital sensed the company possessed untapped potential. Fortissimo's managing director and chairman, Yuval Cohen, persuaded fellow Harvard Business School graduate Daniel Birnbaum to look into Soda-Club for him. Birnbaum, general manager of Nike Israel, agreed and was intrigued by what he found. Fortissimo elected to acquire a controlling interest in Soda-Club Holdings Ltd., and Birnbaum agreed to take over as chief executive officer in January 2007.

Under Birnbaum, SodaStream was rebranded. The logo was upgraded and the carbonation machine revamped, adopting a two-color look that complemented modern kitchens. The first dishwasher-proof bottles were added, and for the German market, the company introduced the Penguin machine model, the only drink maker in the industry that used glass carafes. SodaStream was also aggressive in pursuing new markets, installing a new distribution system that allowed the company to enter 24 new markets by the end of 2007. The SodaStream machine was relaunched in the United Kingdom, with the nostalgic "get bizzy with the fizzy" slogan revived as well. In the United States, where marketing had been limited to online efforts, SodaStream was picked up by major retailers, including Bed Bath & Beyond, Bloomingdale's, Macy's, Sears, and Williams-Sonoma. Birnbaum's previous experience at Procter & Gamble helped the company in cracking the U.S. market.

SodaStream expanded on a number of fronts in 2008. The new Genesis line of drink makers was unveiled, making use of a smaller footprint that made it more suitable for smaller kitchens. The Soda-Club business was also relaunched in France, Hungary, Italy, and the Baltic countries. As a result of these efforts, the company's revenues approached EUR 100 million in 2008. Sales grew to EUR 105 million the following year. During that year, the Dynamo model was introduced. The new drink maker was compatible with extra-large carbonators and allowed for customized carbonation levels. A number of new fruit flavors were offered as well. Targeting the family market, the concentrates were free of additives and preservatives and included Cherry Apple, Summer Fruits, Orchard Fruits, Apple, Mixed Berry, and Cola.

NAME CHANGE AND IPO: 2010

In March 2010, Soda-Club Holdings changed its name to SodaStream International Ltd. as it prepared to make an initial public offering (IPO) of stock. The sale was completed in November 2010 on the NASDAQ in the United States. Raising $125.3 million at $20 per share, it was the largest Israeli IPO in history. SodaStream

enjoyed a strong year. It increased the number of soda machines it sold to 1.9 million, almost double the amount sold in 2009. The company also sold 9.8 million carbon-dioxide refills compared to 8.2 million the previous year. As a result, revenues jumped to EUR 160.7 million in 2010, and net income improved from EUR 7.1 million to EUR 9.7 million.

A secondary stock offering was completed in the spring of 2011, raising $261.4 million, of which $52.2 million accrued to the company, with the balance attributed to profit taking. SodaStream used some of the funds to build up its operation to support further growth. New carbon-dioxide refill lines were added in Sweden in 2010 and the Netherlands a year later. Also of importance in 2011, SodaStream found a distribution partner in Japan, the world's second-largest retail market. To better appeal to environmentally conscious consumers, SodaStream introduced the Bio Bottle in the spring of 2011. It was made from a plastic that would decompose in as little as five years, a vast improvement over the roughly 450 years required to break down typical plastic bottles.

PLANNING FOR THE FUTURE

SodaStream enjoyed robust sales around the world in the early months of 2011, especially in the United States, where sales in the first quarter were 153 percent greater than the comparable quarter the previous year. The company also looked to address one area of potential concern, the location of its plant in the West Bank. Some European retailers pressured the company to print "Made in Palestine" on its packaging, a concession SodaStream refused to make. Rather, the company made the plant available to quarterly "social audits," allowing European retailers to visit the facility and speak with the employees that in addition to Palestinian Arabs included Israeli Arabs, Israeli Jews, immigrants from a variety of countries, and Darfurian refugees.

In June 2011, SodaStream opened a new factory in the Galilee town of Alon Tavor to manufacture soda makers. A month later, the company broke ground on an 850,000-square-foot plant to be built near Beersheva in anticipation of growing demand for soda makers. It was slated to open in 2013 and employ 1,000. In addition to organic growth, SodaStream looked to use some of its cash on hand to make strategic acquisitions. In October 2011, the company purchased CEM Industries S.R.L., an Italian company that designed and manufactured a variety of products for the beverage industry, including water carbonation, cooling and dispensing systems, and a micro-filtering system to remove impurities from tap water. SodaStream hoped to incorporate some of CEM's capabilities into its soda makers, allowing the company to move beyond the home carbonation market and enter such markets as restaurants, hospitality, and offices.

Ed Dinger

PRINCIPAL SUBSIDIARIES

Soda-Club USA, Inc.; SodaStream GmbH; SodaStream Israel LTD.

PRINCIPAL COMPETITORS

AGA Rangemaster Group plc; The Coca-Cola Company; Panasonic Corporation.

FURTHER READING

Delingpole, James. "Not So Useless." *Daily Mail*, May 8, 2008.

Habib-Valdhorn, Shiri. "SodaStream Files for Nasdaq IPO." *Israel Business Arena*, October 19, 2010.

Leichman, Abigail Klein. "Putting the 'Pop' Back into Soda Pop." *Jewish Journal*, March 23, 2011.

Lowrey, Annie. "SodaStream: How the At-Home Carbonation Device Has Become So Popular So Quickly." *Slate Magazine*, July 8, 2011.

Tsipori, Tali. "Rising Bubbles." *Israel Business Arena*, December 1, 2010.

Verity, Andrew. "SodaStream Sold." *Independent* (London), May 1, 1998, 26.

South African Airways (Proprietary) Limited

Private Bag X13
Kempton Park
Johannesburg, 1627
South Africa
Telephone: (+27 11) 978 5313
Toll Free: (800) 722-9675
Fax: (+27 11) 978 1106
Web site: http://www.flysaa.com

State-Owned Company
Incorporated: 1934 as South African Airways
Employees: 8,034
Sales: ZAR 22.98 billion (2011)
NAICS: 481111 Scheduled Passenger Air Transportation; 481211 Nonscheduled Chartered Passenger Air Transportation; 488190 Other Support Activities for Air Transportation; 561510 Travel Agencies; 722310 Food Service Contractors

■ ■ ■

South African Airways (Proprietary) Limited (SAA) is the largest carrier in South Africa. Although troubled in the late 1990s, its status as a major global player is evidenced by affiliations with individual world airlines and with the Star Alliance, which it joined in 2007. Auxiliaries include aircraft maintenance and flight catering operations that serve third-party airlines and a travel agency. SAA is affiliated with the small, low-cost carrier Mango. SAA is a wholly owned subsidiary of South Africa's Department of Public Enterprises.

ORIGINS

South African Airways was founded from the assets of Union Airways, a private carrier the Union of South Africa acquired on February 1, 1934. Its collection of several de Havilland and Junkers aircraft served to link Cape Town, Durban, and Johannesburg. This "Golden Triangle" would remain the company's hub center. SAA was soon flying "giant" Junkers Ju-52 aircraft as far as Kenya.

World War II interrupted civil operations, which resumed in 1943 with the Lockheed Lodestar aircraft as primary carrier. SAA began "Springbok" (gazelle) service to England in November 1945 in conjunction with British Overseas Airways Corporation (BOAC). The Johannesburg–London route had stops in Nairobi, Khartoum, and Tripoli. By 1947 SAA was flying several different types of aircraft, but in 1950 it was the Lockheed Constellation that cut flying time to England to 28 hours. In 1950 the DC-7 reduced this time further. In 1953 SAA became the first pure jetliner operator outside England, leasing a Comet from BOAC.

Technological advancements in jet aircraft expanded the airline's reach. Boeing's 707 allowed SAA to serve Europe nonstop (via Athens) in 1962. In 1969 it began flying to New York via Rio de Janeiro. The company's first Boeing 747s facilitated direct Johannesburg–London flights beginning in 1971. SAA added a weekly flight to Hong Kong in 1973.

In protest of apartheid, several African governments banned SAA from their airspace in 1963. This kept the carrier from overflying East Africa. SAA's transcontinental routes became longer and costlier as they had to follow the continent's west coast. U.S. antiapartheid sanctions began in 1986. Years of isolation would make SAA unusually self-sufficient for its size, resulting in the development of considerable training and maintenance facilities.

South Africa entered a recession in 1989. Moreover, political instability and a horrendous drought fueled the crisis, and the country's inflation rate reached 15 percent. Under this backdrop of financial pressure, privatization of the airline became an earnestly considered option. Nonetheless, SAA ordered four costly 747s, deemed necessary to handle the long-range, west coast route to Europe.

POSTAPARTHEID OPPORTUNITIES

SAA was made a division of Transnet, the South African government's holding company for transportation enterprises, on April 1, 1990, putting it in line for eventual privatization. While the Gulf War and a world recession were universally trying times for the civil aviation business, SAA experienced a fortunate turn of events in the early 1990s. At that time, world governments began lifting sanctions against South Africa after President Frederik de Klerk abolished apartheid and freed Nelson Mandela in February 1990. SAA rejoined the African tourism market in 1991 with resumed service to Nairobi and Kenya. Several other destinations in Africa and beyond opened up within a year. Soon 50,000 passengers a year were pouring in from New York City alone. SAA also flew a Miami–Cape Town route. An agreement with Aeroflot came in November 1991.

SAA collaborated with Ukrainian operator Antau in 1992 to operate three Ilyushin 11-76 freighters.

Although initially profitable (thanks in part to the relatively low salaries commanded by the Ukrainian pilots), the venture faltered due to the aircraft's unreliability and inefficiency. SAA converted an A300 (its first Airbus had been delivered in 1992) to haul freight on the same route, and discovered the Airbus used less than half the fuel. SAA also operated some of Antau's Antonov An-26 aircraft on domestic overnight express operations.

SAA entered into a code-sharing agreement with American Airlines in November 1992. Other agreements followed as SAA withdrew from operating unprofitable international routes with its own equipment. However, it did continue to try new destinations and expand services where needed. SAA preferred to fly smaller planes (such as the Boeing 767, which it first tried in 1993) more frequently on long-haul routes, rather than use ultrawide-body aircraft.

Thanks to its new routes, traffic grew 40 percent in 1992. SAA spent $1.3 billion on new 747s and Airbus A320s to match the resulting demand through 1998. However, the carrier failed to adapt quickly enough to avoid posting a loss of $23 million in 1993. Political violence frightened many international travelers away from South Africa, and this segment was a vital source of income.

The lifting of South Africa's isolation also meant new competition from outside airlines. Moreover, the company also faced two domestic challengers, Comair and start-up Flitestar. Domestic fares were a fraction of those found in Europe, much to the dislike of SAA management.

PATHWAY TO PRIVATIZATION

Rather than try to serve every domestic destination, SAA concentrated on the trunk routes that warranted the use of its jets. SA Express, founded in 1994, and SA Airlink operated other regional routes with turboprops. Their cooperation brought new routes and more flights to the marketplace. SAA took a 20 percent interest in SA Express, the founders of which included a Canadian and a black South African. SA Airlink, independent of SAA, was established in 1992, although its origins dated back to 1978. Airlink, which had placed one of the region's most experienced black pilots in charge of flight operations, served as a type of training ground for SAA pilots hired under a national affirmative action program known as "Turnaround 2000."

However, the coming to power of the left-wing African National Congress in the mid-1990s dimmed hopes of SAA privatization and other management reforms. Chief Executive Michael F. Myburgh, who

KEY DATES

1934: South African Airways (SAA) is formed from the assets of Union Airways.

1945: "Springbok" service to London is launched in conjunction with BOAC.

1963: Several African governments ban SAA flyovers in antiapartheid protest.

1990: SAA becomes division of state-owned Transnet holding company; apartheid is abolished by President Frederik de Klerk.

2004: SAA joins the Star Alliance.

2006: Low-cost subsidiary Mango is launched.

2007: SAA hires U.S. consultants to reverse losses.

replaced Gerrit D. van der Veer in the spring of 1993, was able to trim 16 percent of the workforce in 1994, however. Bureaucratic wrangling also slowed the arrival of desperately needed Boeing 777 and 747 aircraft on order.

The carrier operated a truly unique, nostalgic flight when it dispatched a restored Douglas DC-4 (the last one ever built) to an air show in Oshkosh, Wisconsin, in July 1994. The plane had first seen SAA service in 1947. It was subsequently sold to the South African Air Force. The trip took 55 hours of flying time to cover nearly 10,000 miles. The 22 passengers paid more than $6,000 each. They returned on a regular SAA jet from New York. SAA flew regional tours and chartered its Historic Flight, which operated other vintage aircraft such as the Ju-52 and DC-3.

SAA managed a profit of $72 million in 1995–96. It entered a code-share agreement with Lufthansa in 1996, to the extent of cooperating in the areas of cargo, frequent flier programs, even airport lounges. Transnet also planned to open a network of travel agencies modeled on a Lufthansa program in Germany.

A NEW LOOK IN 1997

In the late 1990s, SAA unveiled a dramatic new color scheme based on the colors of the flag, meant to evoke the richness of the country's landscape. The airline also moved its corporate headquarters from a high crime downtown area to the International Airport. By this time, SAA's worldwide network spanned 29 destinations from Japan to the Netherlands.

In spite of an increase in sales to ZAR 5.68 billion, 1996–97 showed a record loss of ZAR 323 million ($45

million), thanks to a huge increase in the price of fuel (Johannesburg International had among the world's highest fuel prices) and a 35 percent drop in the South African rand. Crime and a shortage of long-haul aircraft were other hindering factors.

SAA was by then competing with 70 international and nine domestic airlines. Virgin Atlantic and British Airways, its archrival, had together reduced SAA's market share of profitable London traffic to 40 percent. Moreover, Comair had captured nearly a fifth of the domestic market. Its licensing agreement with British Airways allowed it to operate as a virtual clone, right down to aircraft livery and flight designators.

SAA introduced a "Frequent Freighter" program in 1997, designed to foster loyalty among shipping clients. It operated one Airbus A300, two Boeing 737s, and one 747 dedicated to freight, in addition to using the cargo capacity of its passenger aircraft.

SAA appointed a new CEO in the summer of 1998 after the departure of Mike Myburgh. Coleman Andrews, who held an M.B.A. from Stanford, was credited with helping World Airways stave off bankruptcy in the early 1990s. He had also advised President Gerald Ford and had once run for lieutenant governor of Virginia. "We need to develop an airline which customers love and competitors fear," declared Andrews in SAA's in-flight magazine, *Sawubona*.

BEST AFRICAN CARRIER: 1999

The International Airline Passenger Association dubbed SAA the Best African Carrier in 1999, agreeing with *Executive Travel*, *Travel Weekly*, and the *London Evening Standard*. The service, however, was not without its complaints, and absenteeism was a significant problem. Andrews's plan to rescue SAA focused on productivity and forecast layoffs. Andrews also wanted to standardize SAA's fleet for the first time in its history to save money on spare parts, maintenance, and training. He also planned to aggressively market the carrier's expertise in technical services.

Privatization had to await untangling financial problems at Transnet, which found itself ZAR 4 billion ($730 million) in debt in 1998. Part of the government's plans for SAA involved dismantling its various components. In 1997, the Johannesburg Airport, which had itself been a part of SAA, was transferred to another state enterprise, Airport Company SA, also in the process of privatization. In 1999 Transnet planned to unbundle SAA's business units: Technical, Cargo, and Passenger. It planned to sell up to 49 percent of the company. British Airways, Virgin, Singapore Airlines, Lufthansa, and other eminent airlines were considering investing. Andrews himself preferred a European carrier over a U.S. airline for hub/feeding possibilities.

In spite of SAA's considerable difficulties, signs of a new "African Renaissance" gave cause for hope. The World Tourism Organization ranked South Africa the 25th-most-popular tourist destination in 1999. Hoping to offer "Africa's warmest welcome," SAA finally became independent of parent Transnet on March 31, 1999.

SAA was losing money in the increasingly competitive European passenger market. It had also experienced a dramatic falloff in cargo volume from the continent. At the same time, some of the smaller European airlines abandoned their operations in South Africa.

REVENUES AND PROFITS ON THE RISE

Revenues reached a record $1.3 billion in 2001, resulting in a profit of ZAR 408 million. As the carrier prepared for a public stock offering, Real Africa Holdings head Don Ncube became chairman of SAA in March 2001. A month later, CFO André Viljoen took over from Andrews as CEO. Several senior executives left the company, as during the last management shift. Staff morale was low. The group had cut 1,300 jobs the year before, leaving it about 11,000 employees.

Switzerland's SAir Group (Swissair), SAA's strategic partner, had acquired a 20 percent stake in 1999 for ZAR 1.4 billion. The South African government, through Transnet, repurchased this stake for a mere ZAR 382.5 million ($34 million) in February 2002 after the Swiss airline collapsed.

Revenue increased 26 percent to ZAR 13.6 billion in 2002. Profits were up nearly fourfold to ZAR 2.1 billion ($210 million). SAA had a fleet of about 60 aircraft. Its routes extended to more than 30 international destinations, most of them within Africa. It made a large order with Airbus in June 2002, ordering 41 aircraft to renew its fleet.

STAR ALLIANCE IN 2004

By this time foreign airlines accounted for most of the country's air traffic. President and CEO Viljoen stepped down suddenly in July 2004, being replaced by Oyama Mabandla. The company had posted a ZAR 6 billion ($900 million) loss for the previous fiscal year owing largely to unfavorable currency hedging for payments on its large Airbus order.

This pushed back the company's planned privatization. However, it was able to join the Star Alliance, the global airline grouping led by Lufthansa. SAA

was considered a prize as it was the first airline within Africa to join one of the three main alliances.

Spurred by its 2004 induction into the Star Alliance, South African Airways increased its efforts in developing a regional network within Africa. It prepared to set up a hub in Dakar, Senegal, to complement the one in Dar es Salaam, where it was an owner of Air Tanzania. Low-cost start-ups had captured a quarter of the domestic market in just a few years. In 2006 SAA launched its own low-cost subsidiary, Mango.

RESTRUCTURING AND LOOKING AHEAD

The losses continued. SAA posted a net deficit of ZAR 883 million in 2007. From February 2007 to April 2008 the company turned to Michael Cox and Scott Gibson of the U.S.-based Seabury consultancy to steer the airline through a cash crisis. They cut total staff numbers by 30 percent, including 2,000 management jobs, eliminated unprofitable international routes, and mostly grounded the fleet of Boeing 747s in favor of smaller, more fuel efficient Airbus A340s. The airline reported a ZAR 123 million net profit for 2008, apart from restructuring costs of ZAR 1.35 billion, for a net loss of ZAR 1.09 billion.

A comprehensive restructuring program was beginning to show results. In 2009 South African Airways reported net income of ZAR 398 million on revenues of ZAR 26.4 billion. Gains came from deferring delivery of 15 Airbus aircraft ordered in 2002. However, the airline lost ZAR 1 billion as its hedging program failed to keep up with explosive fuel prices. Total passenger count slipped 7 percent to 6.8 million. Revenues at the SA Express unit rose 22 percent to ZAR 1.86 billion in the fiscal year ended March 31, 2009. It produced a ZAR 235.4 million profit despite fuel prices going up by half. In December 2009 the unit launched its Congo Express offshoot.

Siza Mzimela became CEO in April 2010 after nearly 15 years with the group and several years as head of SA Express. SAA was celebrating its second consecutive year of profitability. As European economies weakened in 2011, SAA looked to the BRICs (Brazil, Russia, India, and China) to make up the slack. China and South Africa had recently become strategic partners in a number of areas. Traffic from within Africa continued to grow as well.

At the end of the 2011 fiscal year SAA was operating a fleet of more than 50 aircraft. The Mango unit had five aircraft and was carrying nearly 1.5 million passengers a year on a network of five destinations. SAA had about 10,000 employees and was hiring hundreds more. Group revenue was ZAR 22.98 billion for the year, up slightly. Profit for the year rose about one-fifth to ZAR 782 million.

SAA was resuming its refleeting in 2012 with the arrival of six leased A330s for long-haul routes, freeing its existing A340s for new routes to China and the United States. This was being followed the next year by delivery of 20 A320s it had deferred during its restructuring, which would be central to its strategy of developing its regional network in Africa.

The leading airline in a continent with vast untapped potential, South African Airways retained its strategic importance while operating in the face of some of the industry's greatest challenges. Many barriers of the past were removed and new alliances formed. A new focus on regional development marked an exciting stage in its development, and that of the communities it connected.

Frederick C. Ingram

PRINCIPAL SUBSIDIARIES

Air Chefs (Pty) Limited; SAA City Centre (Pty) Limited; SAA Technical (Pty) Limited; Mango Airlines (Pty) Limited.

PRINCIPAL OPERATING UNITS

South African Express Airways.

PRINCIPAL COMPETITORS

British Airways plc; Comair Limited; Deutsche Lufthansa AG; 1Time Airlines.

FURTHER READING

"Analyzing SAA: Low Cost Number Three." *Airfinance Journal*, May 2006, 14.

Andrews, Coleman. "The Troubleshooter." *Airfinance Journal*, July/August 1998, 22–23.

Birns, Hilka. "SAA Mulling Restructuring Options; South African Government Is Now 100% Owner Following Repurchase of 20% Stake Formerly Owned by Swissair." *Flight International*, February 19, 2002, 8.

Birns, Hilka, and James Srodes. "Deflating SAA's New Mae West." *Finance Week*, June 25, 1998, 17–19.

Collett, Naomi. "Agree to Disagree." *Airfinance Journal*, October 1997, 46–48.

"The End of Aerial Apartheid." *Economist*, September 28, 1996.

Hill, Leonard. "A New Tail but an Old Story." *Air Transport World*, June 1997, 40–43.

Kedrosky, Paul. "The Internet in Flight." *Forbes*, June 1, 1998, 32.

Keenan, Ted. "SAA's Privatisation Still on Runway." *Finance Week*, April 16, 1998, 23–24.

Kjelgaard, Chris. "SAA Takes 767 on South African Lease." *Airfinance Journal*, October 1993, 11, 13.

"Long Day's Journey …" *Air Transport World*, October 1994, 143–44.

Makings, Roger. "SAA Plans New Revenue Streams." *Airline Business*, August 2000, 32.

Marsh, Harriet. "South Africa: Missing the Tourist Bus?" *Marketing*, August 1, 1996, 22–23.

Nelms, Douglas W. "The Springbok Springs Back." *Air Transport World*, February 1993, 74–76.

Nevin, Tom. "Damned if You Do; Damned if You Don't." *African Business*, January 1998, 13–16.

O'Lone, Richard G. "SAA Outlook Uncertain Despite End of Isolation." *Aviation Week & Space Technology*, October 11, 1993, 37–39.

"SAA Adds Nine New Boeings to Fleet." *African Business*, February 1996, 38–39.

Schapiro, Stephen A. "South Africa's Shake Up." *Air Cargo World*, June 2001, 38.

"Teething Troubles." *Business Africa*, February 1, 1996, 2–3.

Vandyk, Anthony. "From Trunks to Tertiaries." *Air Transport World*, September 1995, 111–13.

Sport Clips, Inc.

110 Briarwood Drive
Georgetown, Texas 78628
U.S.A.
Telephone: (512) 869-1201
Toll Free: (800) 872-4247
Fax: (512) 869-0366
Web site: http://www.sportclips.com

Private Company
Incorporated: 1993
Employees: 59
Sales: $200 million (2010 est.)
NAICS: 812111 Barber Shops

■ ■ ■

Sport Clips, Inc., is a Georgetown, Texas-based chain of men's haircutting salons. In order to appeal to its market, the salons show sports programming on large-screen televisions in the waiting area as well as smaller screens at the haircutting stations. Rather than glamour magazines typically found at a hair salon, Sport Clips offers sports-related reading material. The décor also maintains a sports motif. The shampoo room is marked "showers," and the cutting floor is laid out like a baseball diamond. Sport Clips operates about 20 company-owned stores and some 800 franchised units spread across 40 states. In keeping with its sports focus, Sport Clips maintains affiliations with NASCAR drivers and such professional sports teams as the Houston Rockets in basketball, the Houston Astros in baseball, and the National Hockey League's Carolina Hurricanes,

Columbus Blue Jackets, Dallas Stars, and Nashville Predators. With its founder a former veteran, Sport Clips is also the official haircutter of the Veterans of Foreign Wars, and veterans are given a discount on franchise fees.

FOUNDER, MIT GRADUATE

Sport Clips' founder Gordon Baker Logan was born in South Carolina in 1946. After earning a degree in engineering from the Massachusetts Institute of Technology in 1968, he joined the U.S. Air Force to become a pilot. Upon leaving the military in 1976, he earned an M.B.A. from The Wharton School of Business at the University of Pennsylvania. He then served as an accountant at Price Waterhouse & Co. in Houston, Texas. He became involved in the full-service hair salon business in 1979 when he bought a Command Performance franchise, which he ran as president of a company called Austin Style, Inc. With partner Jerry Lewis, he opened Command Performance salons throughout Texas. In 1986 Logan became president of the chain's franchisee association.

By the early 1990s, Logan and Lewis were looking for a new concept in the hair salon business. Logan soon realized that he did not enjoy having his hair cut at his own salon, and surmised that many other men as well were not comfortable at salons that catered mostly to women. Barber shops were no longer readily available and few men were training as barbers. The ones that remained were aging and being pushed out by unisex hair salons. The male market, Logan decided, had become neglected and he looked to develop a concept that would appeal to these customers. Sports were a natural fit for a male-friendly concept. In addition, Logan was attracted to the budget portion of the hair salon market, because the most successful chains were engaged in it.

FIRST SPORT CLIPS OPENS: 1993

Logan and Lewis opened their first Sport Clips hair salon in Austin, Texas, in 1993. It featured televised sports, a nerf ball court, and sports memorabilia on display and for sale. Over the next two years, the partners perfected the concept, paying particular attention to the specific needs of men and boys, such as receding hairlines and cowlicks. In order to provide customers with a consistent haircut that was also fast, the shop developed its own training system. Logan told *Shopping Center World* in August 1999 that hair salon stylists generally employ a complicated method based on holding angles and cutting angles. "We've developed a system that is based on a clock face. It's so much easier to learn and execute," he explained.

Not only was the system less taxing on stylists, Sport Clips found that it was easier to retain stylists, all of them women and many of whom found that male customers were easier to serve than women. Moreover, stylists who focused on women customers often changed salons, taking customers with them and hurting the business of their former place of employment. Male customers were more loyal to the Sport Clips format than a particular stylist, and providing a consistent haircut lessened the possibility that a customer would follow a departing stylist. Although Sport Clips focused on basic haircuts, it eventually developed a premium "Signature" service that included a scalp massage, steamed towel, and neck-and-shoulder massage in an effort to pamper its male clientele.

FRANCHISING BEGINS: 1995

Logan and Lewis were ready to begin franchising the Sport Clips concept in 1995, using the original Austin

store as a training center. A year later, there were three company-owned stores and 10 franchised units in Austin, Houston, and San Antonio, Texas. The concept held enough promise that a national chain offered to buy Sport Clips. Lewis wanted to accept the offer, but Logan refused and finally bought out his partner. Lewis stayed on as a franchisee, however, and opened five stores in the Rochester, New York, area. To help build the necessary infrastructure to support expansion, Logan arranged for about $1 million in loans from a group of Houston investors in December 1997.

By the start of the new century, the Sport Clips chain numbered 31 units, seven of which were company owned, combining for about $8 million in annual sales. In addition to four Texas urban areas and Rochester, New York, Sport Clips had operations in Salt Lake City, Utah. Logan was careful in the rollout of the chain, preferring to concentrate on individual markets and states, creating critical mass before moving on. In this way, the chain hoped to avoid the problem of orphan operations, isolated stores that would not benefit from the marketing advantage created by a group. The next target market for Sport Clips was Denver, Colorado. To help promote the Sport Clips brand, the chain entered into a deal with former Dallas Cowboys' player Jay Novacek, who became a franchisee and spokesperson for the chain.

In 2001, Sport Clips expanded its Georgetown, Texas, headquarters and opened its 50th unit. The chain now had stores in additional Texas communities as well as Tulsa, Oklahoma, and Charlotte, North Carolina. The chain enjoyed a growth rate of more than 35 percent in 2001 and 2002, as the number of units reached the 100 mark in 2003. New states included Arkansas, Arizona, Georgia, Kansas, Missouri, Nebraska, South Carolina, and Tennessee. To support growth, Sport Clips funded a $2 million national advertising campaign in June 2003. Two months later, with the number of units now at 120, the company hired a new chief operating officer in Bernard J. Brozek, a seasoned veteran of franchising with experience at Pepsico, Pizza Hut, Taco Bell, and KFC. He was well familiar with the operational and marketing demands of a rapid rollout of a franchise concept, having been involved in the opening of 2,200 Pizza Hut Express units in a matter of just three years. A month after Brozek's arrival, Sport Clips also hired a new director of real estate to help in site selections.

NASCAR RELATIONSHIP BEGINS: 2004

Systemwide sales were about $25 million in 2003. The pace of expansion accelerated the following year. The

KEY DATES

1993: First Sport Clips store opens in Austin, Texas.
1995: Franchising begins.
2001: Company expands Georgetown, Texas, headquarters; chain has expanded to Oklahoma and North Carolina.
2003: NASCAR sponsorship deal is struck.
2008: Sport Clips opens 500th unit.

chain signed its first NASCAR sponsorship deal, teaming up with driver Mike Wallace. To drive growth in franchisees, Sport Clips forged a relationship with the Veterans Transition Franchise Initiative (VetFran) in 2004. Organized after the Gulf War in 1991, VetFran helped honorably discharged veterans acquire franchise businesses. Participating companies such as Sport Clips agreed to provide veterans with better deals than they offered otherwise qualified investors. Because Logan was a veteran of the air force, the association with VetFran was a natural one. The chain agreed to provide veterans with a $5,000 discount on a Sport Clips franchise. Sport Clips strengthened its military ties in 2005 by forging a partnership with the Veterans of Foreign Wars (VFW), becoming the official haircutter of the organization. VFW members would also receive discounts on haircuts.

Sport Clips strong growth in 2004 resulted in the chain cracking the top 100 in *Entrepreneur Magazine*'s list of the country's 500 fastest-growing franchises. By the start of 2005, Sport Clips boasted 220 stores in 25 states with more than a hundred more units slated to open over the next year. To further promote the Sport Clips brand, the chain signed additional professional sports sponsorship deals. New partners included the Round Rock Express Texas minor league team, and the NBA's San Antonio Spurs and Memphis Grizzlies. In early 2007, sponsorship deals were added with the NBA's Atlanta Hawks and the NHL's Atlanta Thrashers. By this stage, the number of stores approached 400 and the number of states increased to 32. Systemwide sales now increased to $90 million.

COMPANY OPENS 500TH STORE: 2008

In early 2008, Sport Clips opened its 500th store, located in San Diego, California, and the number of states represented increased to 34. Over the course of the next year, the chain added another 125 stores. Also

of importance, same store sales increased by 6 percent in 2009, and 9 percent in 2010. This performance was especially noteworthy given the state of the economy, proving that to some extent male haircuts were a recession-proof business. Poor business conditions also played to the benefit of Sport Clips. With the closing of some retail operations, new spaces became available in class "A" centers, allowing Sport Clips franchisees to trade up in locations.

Sport Clips continued to be highly ranked by *Entrepreneur Magazine*, and in early 2011 the chain was named a top 10 pick by Forbes.com's "Top Franchises for the Money." With 120 stores scheduled to open in 2011, the chain continued to grow at a rapid pace. In September 2011, Sport Clips opened its 800th store, in Redmond, Washington. The chain was on pace to top the 1,000 unit mark within the next two years. While represented in 40 states, the one area of the country left to target was the Northeast. In 2011, new stores opened in eastern Pennsylvania, New Jersey, and Connecticut, and the chain expanded its New York footprint beyond Rochester.

Sport Clips planned future stores in the New England region and anticipated that the market, very much interested in sports, could become a significant source of new growth. There were also ample markets in the rest of the country to backfill as well. While there was no shortage of potential customers, half the U.S. population, and a diminishing number of traditional barbershops, the chain's greatest future competition would likely come from salons that emulated its successful sports motif.

Ed Dinger

PRINCIPAL COMPETITORS

Athleticuts Incorporated; Cool Cuts 4 Kids Inc.; Regis Corporation.

FURTHER READING

Carson, Daniel. "Shop Meshes Sports, Haircuts." *Panama City (FL) News Herald*, January 22, 2009.

McLendon, Trey. "Sport Clips Franchise Hits a Homer with Men." *Sunday (Williamson County, TX) Sun*, February 27, 2005.

McLinden, Steve. "Hair Cutters Play Up Sports, Get Men out of Feminine Arena." *Fort Worth Star-Telegram*, March 6, 1999, 1.

Pesquera, Adolpho. "Georgetown, Texas-Based Barbershop Chain 'Sport Clips' Grows at a Fast Clip." *San Antonio Express*, November 14, 2003.

"Sport Clips: A Winning Franchise for Veterans." *Franchising World*, April 2011, 31.

"Sport Clips: Bringing Haircuts and Havens to Men in the Northeast." *Dealmakers—Everything Retail Real Estate*, July 5, 2011.

"Sport Clips Scores with Men." *Shopping Center World*, August 1, 1999.

Wagner, Karen. "Sports-Minded Barbers Moving into Denver." *Denver Business Journal*, February 25, 2000, 18A.

Sports Endeavors, Inc.

431 U.S. Highway 70A
Hillsborough, North Carolina 27278
U.S.A.
Telephone: (919) 644-6800
Fax: (919) 644-6808
Web site: http://www.sportsendeavors.com

Private Company
Incorporated: 1984
Employees: 700
Sales: $200 million (2009 est.)
NAICS: 454113 Mail-Order Houses

∎ ∎ ∎

Sports Endeavors, Inc. (SEI), is a privately held Hillsborough, North Carolina-based catalog and online retailer of sports equipment and merchandise, focusing on soccer, lacrosse, and rugby. The company's flagship operation is its Eurosport soccer catalog, which is published every four weeks and has an annual circulation of more than 11 million. In addition, the Team Eurosport catalog, published two to three times a year, focuses on soccer team uniforms, while the KeeperSport catalog, published on a quarterly basis, serves the equipment needs of soccer goalkeepers. In addition to its corporate headquarters and warehouse in Hillsborough, SEI maintains a distribution center in Mebane, North Carolina. SEI is owned and operated by the Moylan family.

AVID INTEREST IN SOCCER LEADS TO FOUNDING: 1984

The idea for selling soccer equipment by mail-order catalog was conceived by Michael Moylan as a high school project in the early 1980s. His parents moved him and his five siblings from Wisconsin to North Carolina, where his father, a surgeon, went to work at Duke University Medical Center. The Moylans possessed an entrepreneurial streak, as demonstrated by the extra money the Moylan boys earned by selling stray golf balls they found on the Duke golf course. The Moylans, both boys and girls, were also avid soccer players, an interest that would lead to the origin of Sports Endeavors. During high school, Michael Moylan worked part-time for a mall swimming store and mail-order business in Durham, SouthSwim Inc. Realizing that it was difficult to find quality soccer merchandise, he began brainstorming with salesman Gary Lloyd about launching a similar business to SouthSwim devoted to soccer players. In addition to fleshing out the concept for a high school project, he and Lloyd took the idea to Moylan's father, who eventually agreed in April 1984 to provide $25,000 in seed money to launch SEI and the Eurosport catalog.

After high school graduation, Michael Moylan rented a 700-square-foot space, a former Arthur Murray dance studio, to open a small retail store. At the time, the catalog industry was still taking shape and having a retail outlet was considered mandatory. In short order, the store closed and the focus of the young company was on the catalog business. Initially, the partners attempted to charge $1 for the catalog, an amount that would be refunded if an order was placed. The company printed 20,000 catalogs, but distributed only 8,000, resulting in sales of about $100,000 during the first year.

Although it was his idea, Michael left the business in the hands of Lloyd and his mother after three months in order to attend college at Georgetown University. Lloyd would also leave after 21 months to take a job with Lotto Sport Italia Spa. Although Moylan's mother could run Eurosport only in between raising her family and other obligations, she managed to grow the business 10-fold to about $900,000 in annual sales before Michael Moylan returned from college and took charge.

NEW HOME: 1991

Michael Moylan was also joined by his brother Brendan, 18 months younger, after he graduated from college. The company outgrew its original space and relocated to a 5,000-square-foot barn, but this too proved inadequate. To provide extra storage space, Eurosport used nine trailer beds and four sea containers. In early 1991, the company paid $625,000 for a recently closed White Furniture factory in Hillsborough, North Carolina, located between Durham and Chapel Hill. The property included 17.5 acres of land, eight buildings, and 40,000 square feet of space.

The Moylans quickly filled up the available space in their new facility, which was soon expanded to 80,000 square feet. The extra space allowed them to start a spin-off catalog, Acme Soccer & Widget Works, which offered the previous year's merchandise at discount prices. SEI also opened Dr. McSoccer retail stores in Raleigh and Durham. Another company venture, Socrates Soccer Tees, produced T-shirts in-house for sale in the Eurosport catalog. After accumulating losses of $950,000, SEI turned profitable in 1991 on sales of $7 million. The company increased sales to $15 million the following year.

FIRST LACROSSE CATALOG: 1994

Another business took shape in the early 1990s when one of SEI's employees, Char Watson, a lacrosse player,

urged the Moylans to start a catalog offering lacrosse equipment. Although the sport had far less participants than soccer, its enthusiasts were committed to lacrosse. Finally, in 1993, Watson was given eight months to create a plan for a lacrosse mail-order catalog business. He assembled a catalog, developed a mailing list by visiting about 50 youth lacrosse camps, and worked with Eurosport's creative group to develop a brand. They decided to pursue a nautical theme, and because lacrosse was very much an East Coast sport, they decided on the Great Atlantic Lacrosse Company name. In September 1993, Watson was given further help when he was assigned four customer service representatives and two new-hires. The first catalog, 40 pages in length, was mailed in February 1994. The catalog was not only well received, it won a design award. Great Atlantic found an enthusiastic market, and within three years reached the $1 million mark in annual sales, and the number of yearly mailings grew to seven.

SEI, facing little competition, enjoyed steady growth into the early 1990s without the benefit of an especially sophisticated operation. The company had a single personal computer, which was used to print out orders for the shipping department that were taken manually by the telephone sales representatives. With sales growing at a rapid rate, SEI reached a point at which it needed to upgrade its operations. In 1994, the company installed a new mail-order management system, but the transition proved nettlesome at the worst possible time. With the quadrennial World Cup competition being held in the United States that year spurring a great deal of interest in soccer, Eurosport found itself unable to make customer shipments for two months. Although it posted a $2 million loss in 1994, SEI was better positioned to enjoy sustained growth in the years to come. With a more sophisticated computer system in place, SEI was not only able to fill orders more efficiently, it was better able to anticipate what customers wanted while greatly reducing inventory.

DOMAIN NAME ACQUISITION: 1994

SEI wisely acquired the www.soccer.com and www.lacrosse.com domain names to launch an e-commerce side to its business in 1994. SEI expanded its business further in 2000 when it established a new catalog, Team Eurosport, to focus on soccer team uniforms. Catering to the needs of soccer teams at all levels, the catalog offered more than 600 different styles of jerseys. Two years later, another soccer specialty catalog was launched. Called KeeperSport, it focused on the unique needs of goalkeepers, offering such equipment and apparel as gloves, jerseys, pants, and practice dummies.

```
┌─────────────────────────────────────────────┐
│                                               │
│              KEY DATES                        │
│                    ─■─                        │
│                                               │
│  1984:  Company is founded.                   │
│  1991:  Company moves home offices to Hillsbor-│
│         ough, North Carolina.                 │
│  1994:  Lacrosse catalog is launched.         │
│  2001:  TSI Soccer Corp. is acquired.         │
│  2007:  Spanish-language catalogs and Web sites are│
│         added.                                │
│                                               │
└─────────────────────────────────────────────┘
```

In addition to organic growth, SEI grew through external means in 2001 when it acquired longtime rival TSI Soccer Corp. TSI was founded in North Carolina in 1989 by Duke graduate Evan Jones. Employed by Prudential-Bache Capital Funding in New York, Jones had taken notice of Eurosport and was convinced he could create a vastly improved soccer mail-order business. A friend and business partner went to work for SEI for six months to learn how his potential competitor operated, and Jones then developed a business plan, which raised $200,000 in venture capital. TSI quickly established its place in the market and in the early 1990s enjoyed a stronger growth rate than SEI. Jones also began opening retail stores. He told *Inc.*, in an October 1995 profile of the two soccer retailers, that he planned to be the top soccer retailer in the country by 1998. As for SEI, he expected it would simply "fade away or sell out."

Jones was not as devoted to the sport of soccer as the Moylans, however, and in 1997 he decided to sell TSI to dELiA*s, Inc. for about $9 million. A retailer of apparel and accessories to the youth market, dELiA*s also lacked commitment to the sport and struggled to run a chain of soccer merchandise stores. In late 2000, dELiA*s decided to close the stores and put the mail-order business up for sale. Thus, at an undisclosed price, SEI essentially doubled its inventory overnight, acquiring 28 tractor-trailers' worth of TSI inventory. More importantly, SEI was now the dominant force in soccer retailing, commanding more than 90 percent of the direct-mail soccer market, and better able to forge partnerships with both manufacturers and soccer leagues as well as develop promotional deals.

ADDING RUGBY PRODUCTS WITH 365 PURCHASE: 2005

In 2005, SEI added rugby products to the mix when it acquired Birmingham, Alabama-based 365 Inc. The company was founded in 1998 by England-born rugby player Bernard Frei to provide rugby news online and sell equipment. Like the Moylans, he had a passion and evangelical zeal for his sport. He grew his business to $6 million in 2004. Along the way, he also launched the news site www.soccer365.com and a retail arm, www.worldsoccershop.com. Frei was operating a pair of warehouses in Birmingham, but after the sale to SEI, the order processing and shipping functions were moved to North Carolina. Frei remained in Birmingham to head the marketing and creative operations. SEI quickly assembled a catalog to add a mail-order component to the 365 business.

In need of additional warehouse space, SEI looked for a suitable site to build a new distribution center. After a year of searching, it settled on Mebane, North Carolina, where a new facility opened in the spring of 2006. Sales hovered around $160 million from 2006 to 2008. In order to better serve the growing Hispanic population, an important base for soccer participation and support for the sport in general, SEI in 2007 began offering a Spanish-language version of its catalog and Web site.

The company was also able to leverage the Hispanic marketing unit it developed for other marketing opportunities. In 2009, for example, SEI worked with industrial power tools manufacturer DEWALT to introduce its new Compact Lithium-Ion product lines to three major Hispanic markets: Chicago, Houston/Austin, and Miami. Aimed at Hispanic contractors, DEWALT promotions made use of SEI print, online, and grassroots programs and included contests that awarded soccer.com gift cards and signed jerseys from Mexico's national team. Another partner, American Airlines, developed a promotion with SEI that included a contest awarding a trip to Spain and tickets to a Real Madrid game.

By the end of the first decade of the new century, SEI was generating annual sales of $200 million. While there was no shortage of competition, SEI with its stable of sports catalogs and Web sites and well-earned reputation was positioned to enjoy ongoing growth for many years.

Ed Dinger

PRINCIPAL SUBSIDIARIES

365 Inc.; The Great Atlantic Lacrosse Company.

PRINCIPAL COMPETITORS

The Finish Line, Inc.; Foot Locker, Inc.; The Sports Authority, Inc.

FURTHER READING

Cusick, Claire. "Firm Hits Big with Lacrosse." *Durham (NC) Herald-Sun*, July 1, 1997, B1.

Field, Anne. "Precision Marketing." *Inc.*, June 18, 1996, 54.

Fisher, Jean P. "Hillsborough, N.C.-Based Sports-Equipment Firm Scores Goal with Buyout." *Durham (NC) Herald-Sun*, March 2, 2001.

Hagel, Jack. "Sports Catalogs Gain Fans." *Raleigh (NC) News & Observer*, March 4, 2006, D2.

Nelson, Todd. "Hillsborough Catalog Retailer Cashes in on Soccer." *Raleigh (NC) News & Observer*, February 9, 1994, B1.

Pace, Lee. "Goal Oriented Business." *Business North Carolina*, May 1993, 54.

Roush, Chris. "Scrumtious: Retailer Gets into Another Gear." *Business North Carolina*, March 2006, 28.

Whitford, David. "The Fan versus the Businessman." *Inc.*, October 15, 1995, 34.

Wiltgen, Erin. "A Low-Key Anniversary for Eurosport." *Durham (NC) Herald-Sun*, November 21, 2009.

Yandle, C. E. "Soccer Gear Firm to Try New Arena." *Raleigh (NC) News & Observer*, September 5, 1991, C7.

Standex International
Corporation

—■—

11 Keewaydin Drive
Salem, New Hampshire 03079-2999
U.S.A.
Telephone: (603) 893-9701
Fax: (603) 893-7324
Web site: http://www.standex.com

Public Company
Incorporated: 1955 as Standard International Corporation
Employees: 4,000
Sales: $633.75 million (2011)
Stock Exchanges: New York
Ticker Symbol: SXI
NAICS: 332116 Metal Stamping; 332721 Precision Tuned Product Manufacturing; 332811 Metal Heat Treating; 332322 Sheet Metal Work Manufacturing; 332999 All Other Miscellaneous Fabricated Metal Product Manufacturing; 333319 Other Commercial and Service Industry Machinery Manufacturing; 333415 Air-Conditioning and Warm Air Heating Equipment and Commercial and Industrial Refrigeration Equipment Manufacturing; 333511 Industrial Mold Manufacturing; 334416 Electronic Coil, Transformer, and Other Inductor Manufacturing; 334417 Electronic Connector Manufacturing; 335311 Power, Distribution, and Specialty Transformer Manufacturing; 336399 All Other Motor Vehicle Parts Manufacturing

■ ■ ■

Standex International Corporation is a diverse manufacturer and provider of services, with its operations divided into five segments. The largest of these by far is the Food Service Equipment Group, which generates about 58 percent of the company's revenues. This group manufactures commercial foodservice equipment, including Master-Bilt and Kool Star refrigerated cabinets and cases and walk-in coolers and freezers; Nor-Lake walk-in coolers and freezers; commercial ranges, ovens, griddles, char broilers, and other cooking or warming equipment under a variety of brands; American Foodservice custom-made foodservice counter systems, buffet tables, and cabinets; and Federal Industries merchandising display cases.

The Air Distribution Products Group is a leading producer of metal ductwork and fittings for residential heating, ventilating, and air-conditioning applications. Among the world leaders in its industry is the Engraving Group, which specializes in texturizing molds used in the manufacture of plastic automobile parts and plastic components of consumer products. The Engineering Technologies Group custom fabricates and machines engineered components for a variety of industries. The Electronics and Hydraulics Group includes two businesses: Custom Hoists and Standex Electronics. Custom Hoists supplies telescopic and piston-rod hydraulic cylinders to manufacturers of dump trucks, dump trailers, and other material handling vehicles. Standex Electronics is a leading producer of electronic components and subassemblies, electrical connectors, sensors, relays, inductors, transformers, and magnetic components. The company generates approximately 18 percent of its revenues outside the United States.

COMPANY PERSPECTIVES

COMPANY PERSPECTIVES

Through the Company's "Focused Diversity" strategy, Standex leverages the combined strengths of its businesses to better penetrate current markets and to enter new geographic and vertical markets. Standex will also continue to acquire businesses that are synergistic with its current operating groups, and that can quickly contribute to profitability.

POSTWAR ORIGINS

The origins of Standex International may be traced to shortly after World War II, when Bolta Plastics, a vinyl sheeting company, was founded by John Bolten Sr.; his son, John Jr.; Samuel Dennis III; and Daniel Hogan, a former Navy officer and Bolten Sr.'s son-in-law. In less than a decade, Bolten and his partners grew Bolta from a $1 million-a-year start-up to a mature $28 million concern. In 1954 General Tire and Rubber bought the company for $4 million, and within a year Bolten and partners had reinvested the money in Standard Publishing, a Cincinnati-based publisher of religious materials founded in 1866, and Roehlen Engraving, a Rochester, New York-based manufacturer of steel-engraved embossing rollers for creating decorative impressions on tiles, upholstery, and other surfaces. They renamed the business Standard International Corporation.

Through early acquisitions such as Everedy cookware, Lestoil, and Bon Ami cleansing product manufacturers, as well as Coca-Cola bottling franchises in South America, Standard initiated a strategy of growth that by the mid-1990s had totaled more than 125 acquisitions. Almost without exception, all the companies Standard acquired grew at a faster, more profitable rate within the Standard umbrella than they had on their own. By focusing only on market leaders in basic U.S. industries that were largely unaffected by rapid technological change, Standard immediately positioned itself at the forefront of a new industry segment every time it acquired a company. "If you look at our stable of companies," Hogan (who early on succeeded Bolten Sr. as company president) was quoted in a November 29, 1983, *Boston Globe* article, "you'll find that in every case they have a definite niche and a small industry dominant position, in some cases almost a monopolistic position."

GOING PUBLIC IN 1964

In 1964 Hogan's management team took Standard International public and began defining the product groups in which it believed the company had the most expertise and around which its acquisition strategy should coalesce. From these early decisions the three basic product groups that would characterize the company's product identities and market niches for the next three decades were established: industrial products such as pumps, electronic assemblies and switches, and "texturizing" systems for product surfaces; institutional products such as restaurant china, casters and wheels, and commercial cooking and refrigeration equipment; and graphics/mail-order/consumer products such as religious publications, election forms, mail-order food goods, and bookbinding systems.

Early on, Standard adopted a corporate policy of balanced acquisition, ensuring a strong, even cash flow by acquiring cash-generating businesses (such as Crest Fruit, purchased in April 1972) at the same time as capital-intensive companies (such as Master-Bilt, added in November 1971). Exploiting high inflation rates to largely nullify the 4 percent and 5 percent interest charged on the loans it used to fuel its expansion, Standard acquired 11 new companies between January 1967 and June 1968 alone. Standard's growth strategy, however, was coupled with a policy of unceremoniously dumping companies whose profitability or competitiveness in their market niches showed signs of slipping. Through a system of tight financial controls in which all banking matters and cash requests passed through corporate headquarters, Standard focused on unusual requests for cash from its subsidiaries to weed out those potentially ripe for divestiture.

Beyond financial matters, however, Standard encouraged subsidiaries to run their businesses in an independent, entrepreneurial fashion. Indeed, the company's corporate headquarters long consisted of fewer than 50 people, managing everything from banking, taxes, and legal affairs to insurance, audits, and investor relations.

RAPID EXPANSION IN THE SEVENTIES

Standard continued to fill out its three basic product groups. Between 1969 and 1970, Standex acquired Jarvis and Jarvis (later Jarvis Caster Group, specializing in industrial caster and wheel manufacturing), United Service Equipment Co. (later USECO, a manufacturer of foodservice feeding systems for hospitals, prisons, and schools), and Mason Candlelight (a producer of candles and candle lamps for tabletop lighting). In 1971

```
┌─────────────────────────────────────────────┐
│                                               │
│              KEY DATES                        │
│                   ■                           │
├───────────────────────────────────────────────┤
│                                               │
│  1955:  Standard International Corporation is │
│         incorporated.                         │
│  1964:  Company goes public.                  │
│  1971:  Master-Bilt Refrigeration Manufacturing Co. │
│         is purchased.                         │
│  1973:  Company is renamed Standex International │
│         Corporation.                          │
│  1977:  Barbecue King Company is acquired.    │
│  1986:  Federal Industries, Ltd., is purchased. │
│  1988:  Firm acquires Custom Hoists, Inc.     │
│  1997:  ACME Manufacturing Company is         │
│         purchased.                            │
│  2003:  Standex acquires Nor-Lake, Incorporated. │
│  2007:  Associated American Industries, Inc. and │
│         American Foodservice Company are acquired. │
│                                               │
└─────────────────────────────────────────────┘
```

Standard added Spincraft, a Wisconsin firm specializing in the power spinning of metals, and Master-Bilt Refrigeration Co., a manufacturer of commercial refrigeration equipment ranging from ice cream dipping cabinets to refrigerated warehouses. Within a year, Standard had also added General Slicing Machine Company, a manufacturer of commercial refrigeration equipment, and Crest Fruit Company, a mail-order grapefruit distributor. Standard also continued to weed out unprofitable or uncompetitive units, usually at a profit. Of the 25 businesses the company divested in its first 40-odd years, only one was sold for a loss. In 1973 the company was renamed Standex International Corporation.

Between 1971 and 1975, Standex's net sales rose from $119 million to $176 million, a 48 percent leap. Industrial products comprised one-third of all sales, followed by consumer products at 28 percent, graphics (i. e., its publishing and printing operations) at 22 percent, and institutional products at 17 percent. In the same period, Standex acquired industrial engraving plants in West Germany, France, and Australia to capitalize on its library of 100,000 industrial embossing master rolls. Standex added further to its core of firms with the acquisition of Greenville, South Carolina-based Barbecue King Company (a manufacturer of commercial cooking equipment) in 1977, as well as three more companies a year later: Wire-O Corporation (a producer of wire bookbinding products), H. F. Coors China Company (a California-based manufacturer of china and cookware), and Williams Manufacturing (a Chicago producer of chiropractic and traction tables

that later became the core of Standex's Williams Health-care Systems operation).

Standex's strategy of maintaining a mix of varied manufacturers through a rolling series of acquisitions and divestitures amounted to a kind of self-investing diversified mutual fund. The corporation could count on the positive performance of any given segment of its product lines to offset the shaky performance of any other. Indeed, when appropriate acquisition targets were unavailable or too expensive, Standex literally did invest in itself, choosing to repurchase huge blocks of its own stock rather than invest in other companies. It thus spread the risks of dramatic cyclical downturns throughout the corporation's operations and virtually assured enhanced shareholder value and steadily rising quarterly dividend payments.

In 1977 Standex's sales broke the $200 million mark for the first time, and in the following year management launched a program of intensive capital spending that by 1981 had topped $70 million. The investments included the construction of a manufacturing facility for its Industrial Products Group in Kent, England, that was soon producing more than 20 million reed switches a year for electronic applications. As the 1970s wound down, Standex's plans for future expansion were centered on a single giant purchase in a new product area or several small acquisitions to its existing business lines. Preferring to pay cash for its new purchases, Standex arranged a four-year, $12 million loan through three banks in 1979, and the following year added James Burn Bindings Limited, a British bookbinding operation, to its Graphics/Mail Order Group.

CHALLENGES IN THE EIGHTIES

A rash of mergers and acquisitions in the 1980s coupled with rising interest rates, however, put a brake on Standex's expansion plans. As Wall Street corporate raiders drove the asking prices for available companies skyward, acquisitive conglomerates were branded guilty by association. In contrast to its 30 acquisitions during the 1970s, Standex acquired only 11 firms in the 1980s.

Partly as a result of this inactivity, by 1984 Standex's total debt-to-capital ratio had fallen from 38 percent in the mid-1970s to 20 percent, and it had accumulated $100 million of potential debt capacity for acquisitions. Sales broke the $375 million mark in 1984, and for perhaps the first time in its 30-year history Standex had no money-losing businesses. For all its emphasis on development through acquisition, by 1984 more than 60 percent of Standex's historical expansion had come through internal growth.

In May 1984 Standex's management joined with a Boston investment firm in an attempt to acquire Standex through a $250 million friendly leveraged buyout. By putting up a percentage of the purchase price and borrowing the rest, with the company itself offered as collateral, Standex's management hoped to buy up its stock and take the corporation private, thereby avoiding the requirement to disclose financial information to the Securities and Exchange Commission and its own shareholders. Within weeks, however, Standex management had withdrawn the offer, citing new uncertainty about the economy. In 1985 Standex nevertheless began aggressively repurchasing its stock on the open market. By 1996 a total of 17,860,000 shares had been bought back at a cost of over $200 million, reducing the number of outstanding common shares by 57 percent from 1985 levels.

After 37 years at the helm, Hogan stepped down as president in 1985, leaving the $480 million firm in the hands of Thomas L. King, a Standex veteran of 24 years and, like Hogan, an Ivy Leaguer and former Navy man. King continued to pursue additional acquisitions. Federal Industries, Ltd., a Belleville, Wisconsin-based manufacturer of refrigerated and nonrefrigerated display cases for the foodservice industry, was added to the Institutional Products Group in 1986. Two years later, Standex acquired Haysville, Ohio-based Custom Hoists, Inc., a manufacturer of hydraulic cylinders for dump trucks and other vehicles, and added it to the Industrial Products Group.

In 1991 Sapemo S.A.'s multiple ring binding product line was incorporated into the James Burn International bookbinding operations. A year later, Standex acquired Toastswell Company, a St. Louis-based manufacturer of commercial toasters, waffle irons, griddles, and food warmers, for its Institutional Products Group. In mid-1995, Metal Products Manufacturing of Milwaukie, Oregon, was acquired to extend Standex's Snappy Air Distribution product line into the Pacific Northwest. Reflecting the diversity of the product lines Standex sought for acquisition, in 1989 Standex acquired the assets of a massage/traction table manufacturer and two years later bought the entire product line of a Christmas tree stand manufacturer, making Standex, by 1996, the world leader in that market niche.

In the mid-1990s, Standex also added new product lines to its Master-Bilt subsidiary and increased the capacity of its cooler and pipe, duct, and fitting manufacturing operations. Standex posted record profits for the fiscal year ending in June 1995 of $38.3 million on record sales of $569.3 million. At the end of that fiscal year, King retired as Standex's CEO after 10 years at

the helm, giving way to Edward J. Trainor, a former president of the Institutional Products Group.

REFOCUSING COMPANY OPERATIONS

The late 1990s were characterized by a refocusing of company operations. Under the leadership of Trainor, Standex began investing in companies that would bolster what would become its new core segments. Philadelphia-based ACME Manufacturing Company was purchased in October 1997, enabling its Air Distribution group to enter new regional markets in the United States. It also purchased Fellowship Bookstores along with three mail-order companies, which included various assets of the Vidalia Onion Store and Salsa Express.

Starting in fiscal 1998, Standex sold several units, signaling the corporation's commitment to divest under-performing, smaller business operations. The units jettisoned included Doubleday Bros. & Co., Toastswell, SXI Technologies, and Williams Healthcare Systems, as well as the company's Christmas tree stand product line. It was during this time that the firm adopted a strategy of focusing on larger, growth-oriented business operations related to its reorganized business segments: Industrial, Consumer, and Food Service. As such, ATR Coil Company, Inc., a manufacturer catering to the industrial, automotive, and consumer markets, was purchased, complementing Standex's Industrial unit. The Industrial segment also secured a contract with the Boeing Company worth an estimated $147 million. Standex also expanded its Berean Christian Stores division, which in 1998 operated 23 stores in 10 states, as part of its growth efforts in its Consumer division. The firm's new strategy appeared to be paying off by fiscal 1999, when sales reached a record $641.4 million.

Standex entered the 21st century operating larger, more focused business units. Sales growth came to a halt in fiscal 2000, however, and while earnings remained strong in the Industrial and Consumer group segments, the Food Service group experienced a decline. Weakening economies in several of Standex's key markets and an unstable stock market were cited as culprits in the decline. In fiscal 2001 Standex began to feel the effects of the sharp, general downturn in the U.S. manufacturing sector, which led to an 11.6 percent drop in sales for the company's Industrial group. Overall sales that year fell 5.8 percent to $600.2 million. In April 2001 the Standex Electronics unit within the Industrial group was bolstered through the $15.7 million acquisition of ATC-Frost Magnetics, Inc., a manufacturer of custom magnetic components based in Oakville, Ontario, Canada. ATC-Frost maintained a greater than 50 percent share of the Canadian market for power transformers.

RESTRUCTURING AND DIVESTITURE OF CONSUMER PRODUCTS GROUP

In 2002 Standex launched a major restructuring that entailed the divestiture of a number of businesses offering little opportunity for growth. Among the operations either sold or shut down over the next three years were H. F. Coors China, Standex's engraving unit in Germany, its commercial printing operation, and James Burn International. At the same time, Standex pursued additional acquisitions to strengthen several core areas, including foodservice, electronics, hydraulics, and engraving. In June 2003 the company acquired I R International, Inc., a Richmond, Virginia-based producer of industrial, gravure, and embossing rolls and plates; and laser and gravure engraving. Standex in December of that year purchased Nor-Lake, Incorporated for about $34.8 million. Based in Hudson, Wisconsin, with annual sales of about $55 million, Nor-Lake was one of the nation's largest manufacturers of walk-in coolers and freezers for the foodservice and scientific industries.

These acquisitions provided boosts to two of the five segments that Standex realigned its operations into during fiscal 2004. The five segments were the Food Service Equipment Group, Consumer Products Group, Air Distribution Products Group, Engraving Group, and Engineered Products Group. In the meantime, in January 2003, Roger L. Fix was named president and CEO. Fix had joined Standex in 2001 as president and COO after having gained more than two decades of experience running large companies with diverse manufacturing operations. Trainor, Fix's predecessor, remained Standex's chairman.

Late in 2005, Standex announced plans to divest the three businesses that constituted the Consumer Products Group in a further effort to focus on the operations with the greatest potential for profitable growth. The group had generated $91.6 million in revenues in fiscal 2005, or about 14 percent of the overall total of $666.2 million. In March 2006 the mail-order unit Standex Direct was sold to State Street Refrig., Inc. Standard Publishing, one of the two founding Standex businesses, was sold to The Wicks Group of Companies, L.L.C., in July 2006. A month later, the divestment of the Consumer Products Group was completed with the sale of Berean Christian Stores to the private-equity firm JMH Capital. Around this same time, the company's operations were again realigned, with Custom Hoists pulled out of the Engineered Products Group into its own segment called the

Hydraulic Products Group. In addition, another Standex initiative during this period involved shifting production to lower-cost countries, including Mexico and China.

INCREASING PROMINENCE OF FOOD SERVICE EQUIPMENT GROUP

During the second half of the decade, the Food Service Equipment Group gained an increasingly prominent position within Standex. Late in 2005 the company acquired the Long Beach, California-based Kool Star division of Three-Star Refrigeration Engineering Inc., a deal that bolstered Standex's refrigerated walk-in cooler and freezer product line in particular by providing enhanced access to the southwestern U.S. market.

Then in January 2007, Standex spent about $95 million for two more foodservice equipment firms: Associated American Industries, Inc. (AAI) and American Foodservice Company (AFS). AAI, which generated sales of $72 million in 2006, was a manufacturer of "hot side" foodservice equipment, including APW Wyott countertop products used to cook, toast, and warm food in restaurants, convenience stores, and concession areas; Bakers Pride deck ovens, pizza ovens, conveyor ovens, countertop ranges, griddles, and char broilers, used in restaurants, pizzerias, supermarkets, and convenience stores; and BevLes heated proofers and holding cabinets for restaurants and bakeries. Based in Savannah, Tennessee, and generating annual sales of about $21 million, AFS specialized in stainless steel fabrication, millwork, and solid-surface stonework, producing custom-made foodservice counter systems, buffet tables, and cabinets.

By fiscal 2008, the Food Service Equipment Group's sales had increased to $381.3 million, representing about 55 percent of Standex's overall sales of $697.5 million. This amounted to a substantial boost over the 37 percent figure for fiscal 2005. In the meantime, the collapse in the U.S. housing market had a major impact on demand for ductwork, resulting in a 40 percent sales plunge for Standex's Air Distribution Products Group between fiscal 2007 and fiscal 2009. The severe economic downturn also led to an 8.1 percent decline in sales for the Food Service Equipment Group in fiscal 2009 and a company-wide revenue drop of 13 percent, to $607.1 million. During the year, Standex realigned its Engineered Products and Hydraulic Products Groups. The Spincraft metal spinning unit was shifted from Engineered Products into its own Engineering Technologies Group. The other Engineered Products unit, Standex Electronics, was moved into a new Electronics and Hydraulics Group, which also included Custom Hoists.

Standex responded to the economic downturn with aggressive cost-cutting initiatives. During fiscal 2009, eight manufacturing facilities across the corporation's groups were shut down, and Standex slashed its U.S. workforce by 25 percent, which entailed the elimination of 260 jobs. These actions were designed to cut annual operating costs by $36 million. Standex incurred $7.8 million in restructuring charges. When coupled with a $21.3 million impairment charge related to goodwill and intangible assets in the Food Service Equipment Group, this led to the company's first full-year net loss since its founding, amounting to $5.4 million in red ink.

The business environment gradually improved for Standex over the course of fiscal 2010, as the company returned to the black while still posting an overall sales decline for the year of 3.6 percent. Standex remained on the lookout for additional acquisitions to bolster its core businesses. The Engraving Group expanded overseas through the purchases of an Indian business in July 2010 and a South African concern in January 2011. In the meantime, the Food Service Equipment Group further expanded its cooking product offerings by acquiring Tri-Star Inc., a Santa Ana, California-based producer of ranges, fryers, griddles, convection ovens, broilers, and hot plates, in October 2010. The Engineering Technologies Group gained a second unit via the March 2011 acquisition of Metal Spinners Group, Ltd., headquartered in Newcastle, England, for $23.9 million. Like Spincraft, Metal Spinners manufactured metal parts on computer-controlled spinning machines. The U.K. firm served the medical, general industrial, and oil and gas markets in the United States, the United Kingdom, and China.

Boding well for the corporation's future, overall sales not only increased 8.3 percent in fiscal 2011 to $633.8 million, but all five of Standex's business segments posted higher sales in 2011 than in the previous year. In addition, three years of restructuring and cost-cutting efforts paid off with a 23.2 percent increase in profits to $35.4 million. As had been the case throughout Standex's history, shareholders shared in the company's success. In November 2011 Standex paid a dividend for the 189th consecutive quarter, a streak dating all the way back to the firm's initial public offering 47 years earlier.

Paul S. Bodine
Updated, Christina M. Stansell; David E. Salamie

PRINCIPAL SUBSIDIARIES

Associated American Industries, Inc.; ATC-Frost Magnetics, Inc. (Canada); Custom Hoists, Inc.; Nor-Lake, Incorporated; Precision Engineering International Limited (UK); S. I. de Mexico S.A. de C.V.; Snappy Air Distribution Products, Inc.; Standex Air Distribution Products, Inc.; Standex Electronics, Inc.; Standex Electronics (U.K.) Limited; Standex Engraving, L.L.C.; Standex Europe B. V. (Netherlands); Standex Financial Corp.; Standex Holdings Limited (UK); Standex International GmbH (Germany); Standex International Limited (UK); Standex (Ireland) Limited; SXI Limited (Canada).

PRINCIPAL DIVISIONS

Food Service Equipment Group; Air Distribution Products Group; Engraving Group; Engineering Technologies Group; Electronics and Hydraulics Group.

PRINCIPAL COMPETITORS

Hill Phoenix, Inc.; Hussmann International, Inc.; Lennox International Inc.; The Manitowoc Company, Inc.; The Middleby Corporation; Molex Corporation; TE Connectivity Ltd.

FURTHER READING

Cook, James. "Haphazard Conglomerate." *Forbes*, March 19, 1979, 38.

Hussey, Alan F. "Big Fish, Small Ponds: Standex's Winners Range from Electronics to Chiropractor's Tables." *Barron's*, November 12, 1984.

Paiste, Denis. "Standex Acquires Metal Spinners Group." *New Hampshire Union Leader*, March 9, 2011.

———. "Standex Buys Calif. Cooking Stove Maker." *New Hampshire Union Leader*, October 26, 2010.

Pillsbury, Fred. "Buy Homely Philosophy Has Paid Off for Standex." *Boston Globe*, November 29, 1983.

"Standex Acquires AAI and AFS." *Foodservice Equipment and Supplies*, February 2007, 15.

"Standex Continues to Divest Divisions." *Mergers and Acquisitions Report*, April 10, 2006.

Troxell, Thomas N., Jr. "Salem-Based Firm Plies Global Market." *New Hampshire Business Review*, March 23, 1990.

Wallace, Glenn. "Diversification Stands at Standex: Founder's Philosophy to Endure." *Manchester (NH) Union Leader*, January 20, 1992.

Stockland Corporation Limited

---

133 Castlereach Street, Level 25
Sydney, 2000
Australia
Telephone: (+61 02) 9035-2000
Fax: (+61 02) 8988-2000
Web site: http://www.stockland.com.au

Public Company
Founded: 1952
Employees: 132
Sales: $2.06 billion (2010)
Stock Exchanges: Australia
Ticker Symbol: SGP
NAICS: 237210 Land Subdivision; 531310 Real Estate
   Property Managers; 531210 Office of Real Estate
   Agents and Brokers

■ ■ ■

Based in Sydney, Australia, Stockland Corporation Limited is the country's largest real estate investment trust. The company's portfolio consists of more than AUD 20 billion in commercial, residential, and retirement living properties. Commercial interests include AUD 2.5 billion in office properties, AUD 1 billion in industrial properties, and AUD 4.6 billion in 42 retail centers. The company is also involved in the U.K. real estate market, maintaining a portfolio of retail, office, and mixed-use properties there. Stockland is a public company listed on the Australian Securities Exchange.

POST-WORLD WAR II ORIGINS

Stockland was founded by Ervin Graf. Born in 1924 in Hungary, Graf was the son of a prominent businessman. By 1942 he had completed his studies in architecture. He became a university lecturer in building design but with the end of World War II he became a refugee. When Graf sought to immigrate to Australia following the war, he claimed to be a bricklayer, a trade for which there was a need in the country. He arrived in Sydney in 1949 virtually penniless. He received a major break in his career in 1952 when he was hired to convert a poultry farm in Sefton into a housing development. With money borrowed from his brothers Albert Scheinberg and John Hammon, Graf constructed 19 fibrous cement houses. His low-cost houses found a ready market at a time of rapid growth in the population during the postwar years.

Graf gained a public listing for his growing business in 1957 by acquiring a controlling interest in the smallest company listed on the Australian Securities Exchange: Simon Hickey Industries Limited. It was in that same year that Graf also expanded beyond residential construction to become involved in commercial development, focusing on suburban retail properties. In 1961, he constructed one of the country's first drive-in shopping centers, located in Wollongong. The next significant milestone for Graf came when he acquired Imperial Arcade and renovated it into a mixed-use retail and office complex that opened in 1965. It was also during this period that he built his first town houses.

COMPANY PERSPECTIVES

Whether it is providing a shopping centre that meets the needs of the local community, building parks at our residential communities or contributing to programs that improve the wellbeing of our tenants we are focused on developing thriving communities.

In 1967, Graf began construction on Sydney's central business district's first major high-rise residential tower, the Park Regis, which also included commercial development. It was the second-tallest building in the country and for many years the tallest residential tower in the Southern Hemisphere. The Park Regis was a significant gamble for Graf, who ignored warnings that few Australians would choose inner-city living.

STOCKS & HOLDINGS EMERGES: 1968

In 1968 Simon Hickey Industries was delisted and replaced by Stocks & Holdings Limited. Also in the late 1960s, the company completed its first mixed-use, master-planned communities. The first stage of the 165-acre Sylvan Headland Estate opened in Kareela, New South Wales, some 25 kilometers south of Sydney's central business district. The development would include 800 homes, a school, and a shopping center. In addition, Graf became a pioneer in developing new sources of project funding in the 1960s. He tapped institutions, such as major insurance company Australian Mutual Provident Society, for venture capital funds.

Stocks & Holdings continued to expand in the 1970s. The company's first major shopping center, Merrylands, opened in 1972. Along with a shopping center in Gosford, New South Wales, it was located in the fast-growing western suburbs of Sydney. The company's first Queensland commercial project opened in 1977. In a coordinated effort with the Brisbane City Council, Stocks & Holdings constructed a 22-story office tower that also housed a tavern and retail shops.

Stocks & Holdings became an innovator in real estate investment vehicles. In June 1980, Stockland Property Trust was created to acquire the assets and activities of Stocks & Holdings, including all of its commercial and residential investment properties and development companies. The trust was then listed on the Australian Securities Exchange. When income tax

laws were modified, the trust was liquidated. A new entity, Stockland Trust Group, established in June 1982 and listed on the exchange, acquired the assets and launched operations at the end of September.

CORPORATE RESTRUCTURING: 1988

Further changes in tax laws later in the decade led to additional modifications to the Stockland organization. In particular, the new laws subjected unit holders to corporate income tax rates for Stockland's trading activities. As a result, Stockland was restructured in February 1988. The trading group was separated from the Trust and transferred to Stockland Corporation Limited, which took a listing on the exchange. The units of Stockland Trust Group and the shares of Stockland Corporation Limited would now be jointly quoted on the exchange, so that each transaction was for an equal number of units and shares that were "stapled" together. Also of note in 1988, Stockland acquired a property, 157 Liverpool Street in Sydney, that now became the company's headquarters.

Stockland made one of its most significant acquisitions in 1990, purchasing Pacific Pines on the Gold Coast of Queensland. The Park on Exhibition opened in Melbourne in the same year. By the end of the decade, Stockland's portfolio included nine shopping centers in New South Wales and Queensland; six commercial buildings in Sydney, Melbourne, and Brisbane; 30 residential properties spread across Australia; Stockland Hotels located in the country's major cities; and about 1,000 retail shops.

Graf was well past retirement age at the dawn of the new century. Even as he prepared to retire as chairman, he oversaw the major expansion of Stockland, especially in the company's portfolio of commercial and industrial properties. Three smaller trusts were acquired: Australian Commercial Property Trust, the Advance Property Fund, and Flinders Industrial Property Trust. When Graf retired at the age of 76 in October 2000, he left behind a company with assets of AUD 2.5 billion. Graf was succeeded as chairman by 30-year company veteran Peter Daly. Another handpicked man, Matthew Quinn, took charge as managing director. Graf passed away less than two years later, the victim of a heart attack.

NEW GENERATION MAINTAINS GROWTH

The new leadership at Stockland carried on the legacy of the founder by maintaining growth of the company's

KEY DATES

1952: Ervin Graf founds company.
1957: Graf takes company public with Simon Hickey Industries acquisition.
1988: Restructuring creates Stockland Corporation Limited.
2000: Graf retires as chairman.
2008: Retirement Living business is launched.

portfolio. In 2001, Perth, Australia-based Taylor Woodrow Holdings Pty Ltd. was acquired, growing Stockland's assets to the AUD 3 billion level and greatly increasing its footprint in Western Australia. Taylor Woodrow was renamed Stockland WA Holdings Pty. An even larger transaction was completed in 2003 when Stockland acquired the AMP Diversified Property Trust portfolio, a deal that increased Stockland's net worth to AUD 6 billion. Stockland also picked up 50 percent interests in three New Zealand shopping centers, which Stockland would now manage. In 2008, however, Stockland elected to sell these assets in order to concentrate on its core holdings in Australia.

To help fund the AMP purchase and other acquisitions, Stockland offered new shares for sale in 2003. A year later, Stockland acquired the Lensworth Group's master-planned community development business for AUD 846 million. As a result, Stockland emerged as Australia's largest residential property developer. Also in 2004, Stockland made an AUD 7.5 billion bid for General Property Trust. This deal did not come to fruition, however. In March 2005, Stockland elected to terminate the effort. In the meantime, Stockland pursued organic growth. In 2004, it launched the Unlisted Property Funds Division. Two years later, the division became involved in the wholesale investor market. The amount of assets under its management grew to well over AUD 500 million. Its success made Stockland one of Australia's largest diversified property groups.

U.K. ACQUISITION: 2007

Stockland grew in a number of directions as it continued to make its mark as a premier developer. In 2007, for example, it opened the Optus Centre in Macquarie Park. With six campus-style office buildings, it became Australia's largest purpose-built single-tenant complex of its kind. The project was also recognized for its innovation and excellence by the Property Council of

Australia, which awarded Stockland the BlueScope Buildings Award in 2008.

Stockland also looked beyond Australia in 2007, moving into the U.K. market by acquiring Halladale Group, which, while smaller, was a similar operation. Stockland paid £171 million for Halladale, which had about £1 billion in assets under management and development, primarily in mixed-use projects. With Stockland's backing, Halladale hoped to pursue larger development projects, especially residential projects. Initially, the development arm intended to focus on residential developments that were no larger than 200 apartments. In time, however, the goal grew to include community development projects on a scale similar to what Stockland was doing in Australia. Not only did Stockland plan for growth in the United Kingdom through the Stockland Halladale unit, it also hoped to use it as a launching pad for expansion into Europe.

In its home market, Stockland pursued a new growth sector. In 2008, it acquired the Rylands retirement business of Buston Group, picking up a pair of newly completed apartment-style retirement villages in Melbourne, consisting of 149 independent living apartments. Later in the year, Stockland completed a secondary share offering, raising AUD 300 million to pay down debt and expand its retirement business. Extra cash and a lower debt level was especially important at a time when the global economy was undergoing a banking crisis that stifled real estate development. Market conditions were especially difficult in the United Kingdom, where Stockland was forced to write down some of its assets.

Stockland also sold off noncore assets in response to the economy. In February 2009, the company divested about AUD 95 million in commercial properties. Additionally, Stockland reorganized its residential business in the summer of 2009. The Retirement Living business now became an independent unit.

The rearrangement of assets continued for Stockland in 2010. It sold its St. Kilda Road apartment development site in Melbourne for AUD 27.5 million, while at the same time it acquired The Ridge, a residential land parcel in Holmview Queensland, for AUD 23.5 million. This deal was emblematic of a strategy of the Residential unit to focus on new growth corridors in Victoria and Western Australia, and just one of several transactions that Stockland completed in 2010. Late in the year, it secured the right to develop a master-planned community in Melbourne's northern Lockerbie area with the potential to one day house 30,000 people. The company also looked to grow its

Retirement Living business. In the fall of that year, Stockland acquired Aevum Ltd., a retirement living group, essentially doubling the size of Stockland's Retirement Living portfolio.

Despite difficult economic conditions, Stockland continued to expand its portfolio in 2011. It acquired a large number of residential lots with a potential end value of AUD 6 billion. The Centro Hervey Bay shopping center in the fast-growing Fraser Coast region of Queensland was purchased. Although market conditions in Europe were volatile, bringing uncertainty to its plans in that part of the world, Stockland continued to hold a strong position in its home market and appeared well positioned for continued growth.

Ed Dinger

PRINCIPAL SUBSIDIARIES

Stockland Property Management Limited; Halladale Group plc.

PRINCIPAL COMPETITORS

Brookfield Multiplex; GPT Group; Mirvac Limited.

FURTHER READING

Cummins, Carolyn. "Architect Whose Faith in Property's Potential Paid Off." *Sydney Morning Herald*, July 29, 2002.

Denton, Tessa. "Graf Has His Last Day in the Chair." *Australian*, October 20, 2000.

Harley, Robert. "Graf Steps Down from Stockland Helm." *Australian Financial Review*, October 12, 2000.

Russell, Jonathan. "Halladale Gets Australian Owner." *Estates Gazette*, February 10, 2007.

"Stockland in UK Expansion." *Estates Gazette*, July 7, 2007.

StoneMor Partners L.P.

---

155 Rittenhouse Circle
Bristol, Pennsylvania 19007
U.S.A.
Telephone: (215) 826-2800
Fax: (215) 826-2929
Web site: http://www.stonemor.com

Public Company
Incorporated: 2004
Employees: 2,571
Sales: $197.3 million (2010)
Stock Exchanges: NASDAQ
Ticker Symbol: STON
NAICS: 812210 Funeral Homes; 812220 Cemeteries
and Crematories

■ ■ ■

Bristol, Pennsylvania-based StoneMor Partners L.P. is an operator of about 260 cemeteries in 26 states and Puerto Rico and some funeral homes, about half of which are located on the grounds of its cemeteries. While most of the cemeteries are company-owned, StoneMor operates about 20 on long-term contracts with the nonprofit organizations that own the properties. StoneMor offers its products and services on a pre-need (arranged prior to death) and at-need basis. They include interment rights for burial lots, lawn and mausoleum crypts, cremation niches, and perpetual care rights. StoneMor also sells and installs burial vaults, caskets, grave markers and bases, and memorials. The second-largest owner and operator of cemeteries in the United States, StoneMor is

a public company, its shares listed on the NASDAQ. It is the only publicly traded company in the "death care" industry that operates as a master limited partnership.

LOEWEN BANKRUPTCY LEADS TO COMPANY FOUNDING: 1999

StoneMor was created in 1999 as part of a shakeup in the death care industry. Traditionally, cemeteries and funeral homes were local, often mom-and-pop operations. The modern death care industry came into being in the 1980s as consolidation took place, due in large measure to investors recognizing that the baby boom generation was beginning to age and that soon its members would begin dying off, leading to what would likely become a "golden era" for companies involved in funerals, burials, and cremations. Two major consolidators emerged, Houston-based Service Corp. International (SCI), and Loewen Group of Canada, which began making acquisitions in the United States in 1987. The two rivals vied for supremacy in the 1990s, but Loewen took on too much debt along the way. In June 1999, it filed for Chapter 11 bankruptcy protection and soon began selling off assets. During that year, StoneMor's predecessor, Cornerstone Family Services, Inc., was created to acquire some of the Loewen assets.

Maintaining its home office in Bristol, Pennsylvania, a Philadelphia suburb, Cornerstone paid $193 million for 123 cemeteries and four funeral homes located in the northeastern United States. The new company was formed by the investment firm of Mc-Cown De Leeuw & Co., which recruited a pair of former Loewen executives, Lawrence Miller and William

R. Shane, to provide veteran leadership. In order to fund the expansion, McCown De Leeuw secured a $200 million senior credit facility and arranged for $125 million in high-yield debt.

From 1999 through 2003, Cornerstone acquired 10 cemeteries and sold one. It also acquired a funeral home and established two others. As a result, the company' portfolio included 132 cemeteries located in Pennsylvania, West Virginia, Maryland, New Jersey, Tennessee, Ohio, Rhode Island, Alabama, Connecticut, Delaware, and Georgia, and seven funeral homes located in Alabama, Maryland, Ohio, Pennsylvania, and Virginia. Revenues increased from $63.9 million in 2000 to $79.7 million in 2003, but the company was unprofitable, posting accumulated losses of more than $45 million.

FORMATION OF STONEMOR AS MASTER L.P.: 2004

StoneMor Partners L.P. was formed in April 2004 as a Delaware master limited partnership to operate the Cornerstone cemeteries and funeral homes. Units of the partnership were then sold in a public offering that was led by Lehman Brothers and completed in September 2004. The sale, including the exercise of an overallotment option, netted the company $80.8 million. The money was earmarked to pay down debt. Another $80 million was raised through the issuance of senior secured notes. The units began trading on the NASDAQ Global Market. Cornerstone retained majority control of the partnership interests and owned the general partner. Under the terms of the partnership, all available cash was to be distributed to unit holders on a quarterly basis.

StoneMor added to its holdings in November 2005, paying SCI $9 million in cash and $5.9 million in limited partnership units for 22 cemeteries and six funeral homes in North Carolina, Pennsylvania, Georgia, and Alabama. Because StoneMor was already present in these markets, the additional facilities allowed the company to operate more efficiently. They also provided modest help to StoneMor in increasing revenues from $89.3 million in 2004 to more than $100 million in 2005. More important to the bottom

line, however, was a 13.2 percent increase in pre-need sales, which played a key role in StoneMor achieving net earnings of $4.7 million.

The contribution of the SCI assets began to play a more prominent role on the balance sheet in 2006. During that year, StoneMor added further assets, due primarily to the expansion of SCI. The former Loewen Group, now the Cincinnati-based Alderwoods Group, had grown to become North America's second-largest cemetery and funeral home operator after its emergence from bankruptcy, recording sales of $700 million in 2005. It was acquired by the largest company in the industry, SCI, in 2006. In order to satisfy antitrust concerns, SCI was forced to shed some assets. On more than one occasion, StoneMor would be the beneficiary of SCI's rapid growth.

FURTHER SCI ACQUISITIONS: 2006

In September 2006, StoneMor completed another deal with SCI by paying $11.8 million in cash and units for 21 cemeteries and 14 funeral homes in Alabama, Oregon, Michigan, Kansas, Colorado, Washington, West Virginia, Kentucky, Illinois, and Missouri. These assets combined to generate $15 million in annual sales. Their partial contribution in 2006 helped StoneMor to increase revenues 14 percent to $115.1 million. The company also recorded net income of more than $3 million.

StoneMor continued to expand in 2007. A pair of cemeteries were acquired in the third quarter at an aggregate price of $2.4 million. StoneMor and SCI also teamed up late in the year for another asset sale, the largest one yet. For $68 million in cash, StoneMor added 45 cemeteries, 30 funeral homes, and one pet cemetery located in 17 states and Puerto Rico that no longer fit in with SCI's long-term strategy. Again, StoneMor strengthened its position in existing markets, with 32 cemeteries and 14 funeral homes located in states where the company already operated. In addition to Puerto Rico, new states included Arkansas, California, Florida, Hawaii, Iowa, and South Carolina. The new SCI properties were especially appealing because they included many thousands of unsold cemetery spaces, lawn crypts, mausoleum crypts, and cremation niches, as well as 600 undeveloped acres. In order to fund the acquisition, StoneMor engineered a secondary offering of partnership units in the final days of 2007, netting the company $51.8 million.

StoneMor's portfolio of properties owned or managed now totaled 223 cemeteries and 57 funeral homes. To help drive sales further, the company launched

KEY DATES

1999: Cornerstone Family Services Inc. is formed.
2004: StoneMor Partners is formed and taken public.
2005: StoneMor acquires 22 cemeteries and six funeral homes.
2007: Service Corp International sells 45 cemeteries and 30 funeral homes to StoneMor.
2010: StoneMor acquires nine Michigan cemeteries.

comprehensive Web sites for its properties. This effort and the acquired assets helped StoneMor to grow revenues 26 percent to $145.3 million in 2007, resulting in net income of $2.8 million. Although the transactions were much smaller, StoneMor continued to add to its holdings in 2008 by completing four acquisitions. They included the $2.3 million purchase of Valhalla Memory Gardens of Bloomington, Indiana, from SCI in the first quarter. StoneMor then acquired six cemeteries and two funeral homes for $1.4 million in the third quarter. In the final weeks of 2008, StoneMor completed a pair of acquisitions that added two cemeteries and one funeral home. Also of note, during 2008 StoneMor introduced a new pre-need pet memorialization service that looked to tap into the more than $40 billion that Americans spent each year on pet-related purchases.

TOP 100 HONORS: 2009

Revenues increased to $183.4 million in 2008. It was a performance that landed StoneMor on the *Fortune Small Business* (*FSB*) list of "America's Top Small Businesses." The following year, however, StoneMor took a step backward. While StoneMor did not complete any acquisitions in 2009, it was able to negotiate three long-term agreements to operate cemeteries. Nevertheless, revenues dipped to $181.2 million in 2009, due primarily to a decline in merchandise sales and poor performance in the company's western properties. In addition, a struggling economy hurt business as well. StoneMor, as a result, recorded a net loss of about $4.4 million.

StoneMor pursued further external growth in 2010. In the first quarter of the year, it acquired nine Michigan cemeteries for $14 million in cash from a dissolved company, Hillcrest Memorial Corp. The deal greatly expanded StoneMor's holdings in the state, which had been limited to three cemeteries. The company also picked up service trusts of about $45 mil-

lion, perpetual care trusts of $15 million, an inventory of cemetery merchandise, and a 75,000-square-foot warehouse in Plymouth, Michigan.

A few weeks later, StoneMor purchased several properties out of receivership. For a total consideration of $32.4 million, StoneMor acquired eight cemeteries and five funeral homes in Michigan, Indiana, and Ohio. Again, the new assets helped StoneMor to improve its market position in states where it already operated. StoneMor completed the acquisition of a cemetery in Pennsylvania for $1.5 million. The company completed 2010 by buying Fairlawn Burial Park and Heritage Funeral Home in Hutchinson, Kansas, out of receivership, paying $700,000. StoneMor also reached an agreement with the Archdiocese of Detroit to become the exclusive operator of cemeteries owned by the archdiocese.

CONTINUED EXTERNAL GROWTH: 2011

StoneMor increased revenues to $197.3 million in 2010 and narrowed its net loss on the year to $1.5 million. The following year, StoneMor completed additional acquisitions. In April, it agreed to pay $10.5 million for nine cemeteries and 10 funeral homes. StoneMor bought several properties out of receivership in October 2011. At a total cost of $5 million, it added three cemeteries and three funeral homes in Tennessee. As a result, StoneMor now owned or operated 272 cemeteries and 69 funeral homes in 26 states and Puerto Rico.

StoneMor continued to feel the impact of a poor economy in 2011. Nevertheless, sales through the first half of the year were higher than the comparable period in 2010. The company's long-term prospects appeared much brighter. It remained uniquely positioned as the only master limited partnership in the death care industry. It was a sector that also remained highly fragmented, offering StoneMor ample opportunities to grow within existing markets and enter new ones. More importantly, demographics favored StoneMor and any company associated with the death care industry.

While mortality rates had declined significantly in recent years, in time the baby boom generation, which accounted for about 30 percent of the world's population, would begin to die in large numbers. In terms of sheer volume, such a trend would increase StoneMor's business, but baby boomers were also a generation that would likely insist on more customized, higher margin products and services. In particular, such "comfort services" as estate planning assistance, grief counseling, and Web broadcasts of memorial services were likely to increase over the years. There was also a growing trend toward pre-need plans that not only allowed people to make such arrangements before their deaths but to lock in prices. Thus, StoneMor was likely to continually change to meet the demand of its customers before its customers ultimately passed on.

Ed Dinger

PRINCIPAL SUBSIDIARIES

Cemetery Management Services, LLC; Cornerstone Funeral and Cremation Services LLC; StoneMor Cemetery Products LLC; StoneMor Pennsylvania LLC.

PRINCIPAL COMPETITORS

Carriage Services, Inc.; Service Corporation International; Stewart Enterprises, Inc.

FURTHER READING

Ein, Jason. "The Future of the 'Death Care' Industry." *Forbes*, October 8, 2004.

Green, John. "Large Company Will Buy Cemetery." *Hutchinson (KS) News*, September 28, 2010.

Mandaro, Laura. "1st Union Keys on Capital Markets." *American Banker*, August 9, 1999, 4.

"Marin Investment Fund Scouts Cheap Internet Stocks." *San Francisco Business Times*, May 2, 1999.

Morin, Sarah. "Valhalla Sold to Pennsylvania Company for $2.3 Million." *Bloomington (IN) Herald Times*, March 26, 2008.

Rotstein, Gary. "Settling Debt." *Pittsburgh Post-Gazette*, April 30, 1999, D1.

TAM S.A.

Av. Jurandir, 856, Lote 4, 1° andar
São Paulo, SP 04072-000
Brazil
Telephone: (55 11) 5582 8365
Toll Free: (888) 235-9826
Fax: (55 11) 5582 8149
Web site: http://www.tam.com.br

Public Company
Incorporated: 1961 as Táxi Aéreos Marília
Employees: 26,285
Sales: BRL 11.38 billion ($6.81 billion) 2010
Stock Exchanges: New York São Paulo
Ticker Symbol: TAM
NAICS: 481111 Scheduled Passenger Air Transportation; 481112 Scheduled Freight Air Transportation; 481212 Nonscheduled Chartered Freight Air Transportation; 481211 Nonscheduled Chartered Passenger Air Transportation; 488190 Other Support Activities for Air Transportation

■ ■ ■

TAM S.A. is the holding company for TAM Linhas Aéreas S.A., Brazil's leading domestic airline, and affiliated companies such as regional carrier TAM Mercosur. TAM provides a vital commercial air link in a vast country that takes four hours to cross by plane, carrying roughly 30 million people a year. TAM and its affiliates operate a fleet of approximately 150 aircraft. Company founder Rolim Amaro is credited with building an air taxi operation into Brazil's strongest airline over the course of 30 years before he passed away in 2001. TAM joined the Star Alliance in 2010 and announced plans to merge with Chilean carrier LAN.

ORIGINS

The original air taxi operation that provided the company name was founded on January 7, 1961, as Táxi Aéreos Marília (TAM), named for a city in the state of São Paulo. It was a pilots' cooperative. TAM was eventually acquired by sugar producer Orlando Ometto. Ometto's right-hand man was Rolim Adolfo Amaro, who joined TAM in 1963. Amaro soon after left to work for Viação Aérea São Paulo (VASP), according to a November 2004 profile in *Airways* magazine. In 1968, he was flying for a farm owned by a bank, which financed the purchase of his own tiny Cessna 140.

Amaro and his brother João started another air taxi service, Araguaia Táxi Aéreo (ATA), in 1971. It ferried laborers in the states of Goiás and Paraná. By 1973, noted *Airways*, the enterprise was operating 10 planes.

Amaro became half owner of his former employer, TAM, in 1971. Two years later, local farmer Sebastiano Maia bought in. TAM's fleet was soon upgraded with Cessna 409s and even Learjets, noted *Airways*. TAM carried 2,800 passengers in 1972 and 18,000 in 1975. Headquarters was relocated to São Paulo.

FORMATION OF TAR: 1976

Around this time, the Brazilian government began promoting air service to the small communities that had

COMPANY PERSPECTIVES

We believe that we have a strong corporate culture, grounded by principles set forth by our founder, Captain Rolim Adolfo Amaro, that permeates all levels of our company and continues to guide the day-to-day activities of our management. In order to ensure that we act in accordance with best practices and provide value-added service to our passengers, we seek to embed our culture in our employee training, and believe that our entire staff is a product of this practice. Our mission is to be the people's favorite airline company, through joy, creativity, respect and responsibility, and we consistently transmit this mission statement to our employees. Our vision is to make our customers happy by working with a "spirit of serving." We seek to achieve this goal by offering comprehensive service that gives passengers superior value for their money. We are able to do this by continuing to reduce expenses and by improving the return on capital invested.

been abandoned by the major airlines in the age of the jet. Five smaller airlines were assigned exclusive rights to one of five regions, and TAM was earmarked for the wealthiest and most populous, Região Centro-Oeste.

TAM Transportes Aéreos Regionais (TAR) was established on May 12, 1976. VASP received a holding in the company in exchange for contributing a fleet of six 160-seat EMB-110 Bandeirantes, plus facilities at seven local airports. In July 12, 1976, the new venture began flying its first route, São Paulo–Ourinhos–Maringá.

In November 1976, Amaro bought out his partners. Amaro, often called "Commandante," was known for his emphasis on customer service. "The customer is king" was his motto. A red carpet was typically rolled out for passengers as they deplaned. TAM replaced its fleet of Bandeirantes with 48-seat Fokker F-27 turboprops in the early 1980s. In 1982, TAM Jatos Executivos was created to market Cessna Citation business jets.

EVOLVING IN 1986

TAM entered a new, expansive phase in its existence in 1986. Brasil-Central Linha Aérea S.A. was formed to fly in the north and central-western region of Brazil. Soon

renamed TAM Transportes Aéreos Meridionais S.A., it became the country's second-largest domestic carrier. TAM adopted the name TAM Linhas Aéreas on August 1, 1986. With a democratic government in power, the air market was liberalized and TAM was free to begin connecting major cities via downtown airports, which business travelers found to be a great convenience. TAM was allowed to begin flying the São Paulo–Rio "Air Bridge" in 1989.

TAM bought an interest in the regional airline assets of VOTEC in 1986. A new company was formed around them called Viação Brasil Central. In 1996, it was renamed Transportes Aéreos Meridionais. TAM's Central operation connected some very remote spots in Brazil with a fleet of Cessna Caravans.

The airline began flying a pair of Fokker 100 twinjets in October 1990. These allowed TAM to offer jet service from the downtown airports. The Brazilian aviation market was deregulated further in the early 1990s. This allowed for more growth, and TAM was soon operating 53 Fokker 100s. *Air Transport World* named TAM its Regional Airline of the Year for 1995. However, with a route network of 2,140 miles, TAM stretched the definition of regional airline. The airline had revenues of about $330 million in the 1994 fiscal year, when it carried 1.6 million passengers (one-quarter of them on charter flights). The company then had 1,400 employees.

In September 1996, TAM acquired 80 percent of LAPSA, Paraguay's troubled national airline. Renamed Transportes Aéreos del Mercosur (or TAM Mercosur), it became the unit responsible for flights to countries neighboring Brazil. On October 31, 1996, TAM suffered its worst disaster yet when a Fokker 100 jet crashed on takeoff, killing 90 people. This and later incidents would tarnish the jet's reputation in the eyes of the public.

In the late 1990s, TAM joined LAN Chile and TACA in the pooled purchase of 120 Airbus jets. TAM acquired 60 A320s and five of the larger A330s, one of which was used to open TAM's first international route to Miami in December 1998. Service to Paris was launched the next year.

In 1998 Itapemirim Transportes Aéreos Regionais was acquired, followed by Helisul Linhas Aéreas S.A. These two, renamed Interexpress Transportes Aéreos Regionais S.A. and TAM Express S.A., were merged into TAM Linhas Aéreas in 1999.

MERGER IN 2000

Transportes Aéreos Meridionais was merged into TAM Linhas Aéreas in late 2000. The combined company had

KEY DATES

1961: Táxi Aéreos Marília (TAM) air taxi service is formed.

1971: Rolim Amaro becomes a partner in Táxi Aéreos Marília.

1976: TAM Transportes Aéreos Regionais (TAR) is formed; Amaro acquires the rest of air taxi service.

1986: TAM is renamed TAM Linhas Aéreas.

1997: Holding company TAM S.A. is formed.

2000: TAM and TAR merge; sales exceed $1 billion.

2001: Amaro dies in midst of a major expansion program.

2010: TAM joins Star Alliance, announces merger with Chile's LAN.

about 8,000 employees. TAM was the only Brazilian airline to turn a profit that year. After losing BRL 83.7 million in 1999, the carrier posted net income of BRL 41.4 million ($17.6 million) as passenger count rose from less than eight million to 10.4 million. Sales were more than $1 billion. At the 2001 Paris Air Show, TAM announced orders for 20 Brazilian-made Embraer Regional Jets and 20 Airbus A318 airliners.

TAM launched a major international expansion in early 2001 by taking over routes to Buenos Aires and other destinations abandoned by VASP. TAM acquired Argentina's tiny Aerovip airline later in the year.

TAM's charismatic founder Rolim Amaro died in a helicopter crash on July 8, 2001. His widow, Noemy, headed the board of directors after his death. Amaro was succeeded as the company's president by his brother-in-law and longtime TAM employee, Daniel Madelli Martin.

International services extended to Zurich and Frankfurt in May 2001. TAM also had marketing arrangements with American Airlines and Air France. Most of the international routes were cut after the September 11, 2001, terrorist attacks on the United States, however. KLM Royal Dutch Airlines NV began a code-sharing arrangement with TAM on the São Paulo route in the winter of 2002–03. The flights were operated by TAM.

TAM lost BRL 607.5 million in 2002 on sales of $1.7 billion. Its passenger count was about 14 million. TAM was hurt by the devaluation of the Brazilian real. The cargo division, TAM Express, accounted for about 10 percent of sales. In the cost-cutting that followed,

TAM began unloading its fleet of Fokker 100 jets and cut 524 jobs. The airline did take delivery of two new Airbus jets worth $71 million each.

VARIG COOPERATION IN 2003

TAM began merger talks with Varig in February 2003 as both airlines struggled in a weakened Brazilian economy. They began selling seats on each other's aircraft through a code-sharing arrangement, which helped both of them gain more of the market.

TAM managed a net profit of BRL 173.8 million ($59 million) on sales of $1.26 billion in 2003. The company had focused on subsidiary TAM Mercosur's flights to neighboring countries (particularly Paraguay, Uruguay, and Bolivia) rather than long-haul routes. Company President Daniel Martin stepped down in August 2003 during merger negotiations with Varig. He was replaced by Marco Antonio Bologna, formerly vice president of finance.

In the summer of 2004, TAM added 15 new regional destinations to its offerings by partnering with local airlines Passaredo, Trip, and OceanAir. The airline was soon cleared to launch routes to Lima, Peru, and Santiago, Chile. Ten Airbus 320 jets were ordered to accommodate TAM's new growth. The company was considering an initial public offering (IPO) for 2005 to raise at least $100 million. Only 0.5 percent of shares had been available on the Bolsa de Valores de São Paulo.

By this time, merger talks with Varig were no longer a priority, although the two airlines were continuing their code-sharing arrangement. TAM was leading Brazil's domestic aviation market with more than a one-third market share. It was expanding in Latin America, and placed an order for 10 new A320s (and 20 options) with Airbus.

VARIG COOPERATION ENDS: 2005

The code-sharing agreement with Varig was canceled in February 2005 after plans for the proposed merger failed to gel. However, TAM had entered arrangements for feeder traffic from five smaller carriers (Passaredo, Ocean Air Total Trip, and Panatal). TAM's total passenger count rose 45 percent in 2005 to 19.6 million. The company added nearly 1,300 employees during the year, giving it a total of 9,669.

Meanwhile, a formidable rival had emerged. Gol Linhas Aéreas Inteligentes S.A., a budget airline launched in 2001, had captured more than 20 percent of the domestic market by early 2005. TAM still controlled 35 percent. In the March 2005 issue of *Latin Trade*, TAM President Marco Antonio Bologna confessed to gleaning lessons from Gol's rise. However, TAM continued to focus on the higher end of the market, retaining its signature red carpet treatment.

TAM made an initial equity offering of preferred shares primarily to U.S. institutional investors in June 2005. In March 2006 the company listed its American Depositary Shares on the New York Stock Exchange. Net income increased nearly 30 percent in 2007, to BRL 10.5 billion.

TRAGEDY IN 2007

In July 2007 the airline lost an Airbus A320 jet trying to land at one of the notoriously short runways at São Paulo's Congonhas Airport. It was Brazil's worst airliner crash to date. All 186 people aboard were killed, eclipsing the disastrous loss of a Boeing 737 from rival Gol the previous year.

TAM introduced an extended-range version of the Boeing 777 to its long-haul fleet in 2008. At the end of the year, it had 129 aircraft in all and was still buying more. It retired its Fokker F-100 turboprops, replacing them on regional routes with the larger Airbus A320 jet.

In October 2009 a new company called Multiplus was launched to manage airline loyalty programs, which TAM had pioneered in Brazil. TAM reduced its ownership in Multiplus to about 73 percent in a February 2010 IPO.

The group was carrying 30 million passengers a year by the end of the decade. TAM agreed to acquire one of its regional partners, Pantanal Linhas Aéreas S.A., in December 2009. In March 2010, Marco Antonio Bologna became president of TAM S.A., the holding company that had been formed in 1997.

ALLIED IN 2010

After two years of marketing and operational preparations, in May 2010 TAM was formally admitted to the Star Alliance. This was the largest of the global marketing groupings among world airlines. The carrier had also added code-share agreements with several world airlines.

In August 2010, TAM and Chilean carrier LAN announced a plan to join together in the new LATAM Airlines Group. The two airlines were to continue to operate independently. TAM was bigger by one-third both in terms of revenues ($4.9 billion to $3.7 billion) and in the number of employees (26,285 to LAN's 17,700). In October the companies appealed some of the mitigation measures required by Chile's antitrust authority, aiming to have the merger completed in early 2012.

LAN had a fleet of about 140 aircraft, including 14 freighters. TAM operated 151 at the end of 2010, a record. It had scaled back its fleet expansion plan due to the poor global economy, but planned to have 179 aircraft by 2015. The airline was beginning to experiment with biofuels. It was also the first in the Western Hemisphere to offer in-flight cell-phone service.

TAM retook its position as Brazil's leading domestic carrier after a brief run by Gol at the top. TAM also easily dominated Brazil's international aviation market with a nearly 90 percent share. There was a new local player in the market, Azul Linhas Aéreas Brasileiras S.A., launched by JetBlue founder David Neeleman., while industry consolidation had produced another rising regional powerhouse in Colombia-based AviancaTaca Holding S.A. In December 2011 Brazil's antitrust regulator approved the merger between TAM and LAN, while requiring that one of the global alliances be dropped. LAN was a member of oneworld.

TAM and LAN were both, like many of the major airlines in Latin America, still controlled by individual families. According to a November 2011 *Aviation Week & Space Technology* article, the idea for the LAN-TAM merger originally came from TAM founder Rolim Amaro before he died in 2001. After 50 years, the shape of the company was still influenced by the vision of its founder.

Frederick C. Ingram

PRINCIPAL SUBSIDIARIES

TAM Linhas Aéreas S.A.; Pantanal Linhas Aéreas S.A.; Fidelidade Viagens e Turismo Limited; Transportes Aéreos Del Mercosur S.A. (Paraguay; 94.98%); TP Franchising Ltda. (99.99%); TAM Milor–Táxi Aéreo, Representaçoes, Marcas e Patentes S.A.; TAM Capital Inc. (Cayman Islands); Multiplus S.A. (73.17%).

PRINCIPAL DIVISIONS

MRO; TAM Cargo; Multiplus Fidelidade; TAM Aviaçao Executiva; TAM Museum; TAM Viagens; TAM Service Academy.

PRINCIPAL COMPETITORS

AviancaTaca Holding S.A.; Azul Linhas Aéreas Brasileiras S.A.; Gol Linhas Aéreas Inteligentes S.A.; Viação Aérea Rio Grandense S.A. (Varig).

FURTHER READING

Adese, Carlos. "Fasten Your Seatbelts: Cutting Costs, TAM Airlines follows Low-Cost Gol's Model to Cater to Brazil's

Growing Airline Business." *Latin Trade*, March 2005, 29+.

"Airlines Caught Up in Price War—But Varig Tries to Remain Aloof from Cutting Contest." *Latin American Newsletters*, April 24, 2001.

Beting, Gianfranco. "TAM Has Reason to Smile." *Airways*, November 2004, 8–17.

"Brazil's 2 Largest Airlines Deny Canceling Merger Plans." *Dow Jones International News*, March 17, 2004.

Flottau, Jens. "Cleared for Takeoff." *Aviation Week & Space Technology*, July 26, 2010, 50.

———. "Latin Liason; LAN-TAM Merger Will Reset Global Airline Alliances." *Aviation Week & Space Technology*, November 21, 2011, 48+.

———. "TAM Brazil Regroups after Death of Founder." *Aviation Week & Space Technology*, July 30, 2001, 45.

Manera, Roberto. "TAM Bets on Rolim's Style to Stay on Top." *Gazeta Mercantil*, April 29, 2004.

Moorhouse, Neil. "KLM Says Has Codeshare Deal with TAM." *Dow Jones International News*, October 4, 2002.

"Regional Airline of the Year: TAM." *Air Transport World*, February 1, 1996, 32.

"Rolim Amaro, Founder of TAM, Killed in Helicopter Crash in Brazil." *Weekly of Business Aviation*, July 16, 2001, 32.

"Serious Competition as Varig and TAM Merge." *Latin American Economic and Business Report*, March 27, 2003.

"TAM Focus on Cargo Division." *Gazeta Mercantil*, December 26, 2002.

"TAM to Implement Cutbacks, as Varig Consolidates Fleet and Network." *Airclaims Airline News*, September 20, 2002.

TECHNE Corporation

—■—

614 McKinley Place NE
Minneapolis, Minnesota 55413-2610
U.S.A.
Telephone: (612) 379-8854
Fax: (612) 379-6580
Web site: http://www.techne-corp.com

Public Company
Incorporated: 1981
Employees: 834
Sales: $289.96 million (2011)
Stock Exchanges: NASDAQ
Ticker Symbol: TECH
NAICS: 551112 Holding Companies, Not Elsewhere
    Classified; 325413 In-Vitro Diagnostic Substance
    Manufacturing; 325414 Biological Product (Except
    Diagnostic) Manufacturing; 324516 Analytical
    Laboratory Instrument Manufacturing

■ ■ ■

TECHNE Corporation is a holding company whose main operating subsidiary is Research and Diagnostic Systems, Inc. (R&D Systems), based, like its parent, in Minneapolis, Minnesota. Since 1976, R&D Systems has been making hematology controls, which are used to verify the accuracy of blood analysis instruments. Starting in the late 1980s, however, the company's developing Biotechnology Division began to eclipse the Hematology Division as the centerpiece of TECHNE's operations. The Biotechnology Division, which accounts for around 93 percent of TECHNE's revenues,

manufactures specialized proteins, including cytokines, enzymes, and related reagents, that are used by scientists in research laboratories. TECHNE's products are used to investigate possible therapies for cancer, wound healing, AIDS, diabetes, and a variety of other diseases and conditions. TECHNE is the world's leading manufacturer of cytokines, which are purified proteins that act as communicators between cells, stimulating or halting growth, or changing a cell's function. The company also sells immunoassay kits, which are prepackaged kits used to test for the presence of a particular protein in biological fluids such as serum, plasma, or urine. TECHNE's European biotechnology operations are conducted through its U.K. subsidiaries, R&D Systems Europe Ltd. and Tocris Holdings Limited; a sales subsidiary in Germany called R&D Systems GmbH; and a sales office in France. Its products are distributed in China through the subsidiary R&D Systems China Co., Ltd. TECHNE's chairman, president, CEO, and treasurer is Thomas E. Oland, who first came to the company as a consultant in 1980. Oland's work ethic and stable, frugal management style are often cited as the basis for TECHNE's record of steadily increasing revenues for more than a decade and a half.

A ROUGH START: 1977–85

David Mundschenk founded Research and Diagnostics Systems, Inc. in Minneapolis in 1976. The company specialized in hematology controls, precisely measured blood samples that could be used to calibrate laboratory instruments and act as controls in blood tests. R&D

Systems' first product, a platelet-rich-plasma control, was introduced in 1977.

The company performed poorly in its early years. By 1980 R&D Systems was faltering, directionless, and deep in debt. Late that year Roger Lucas, a company executive and former professor of biochemistry at the State University of New York, met an accountant named Thomas E. Oland. Lucas hired Oland to liquidate the company. Oland, however, saw potential in R&D Systems' hematology products and negotiated with creditors to give the company time to introduce its newest blood product. In 1981 R&D Systems became only the second manufacturer in the world to introduce a whole blood control with platelets. The product was well-received and bought time for the company to get back on its feet. Oland continued working with R&D Systems as a consultant.

In 1983, however, a misstep by the company founder plunged the company back into an unfavorable situation. Mundschenk bought control of Hycel, a French maker of hematology products, for only $50,000, unaware that the company had an oversized debt load. Oland examined the company's finances and found that Hycel owed a corporate client $800,000. When R&D Systems' board of directors learned of the ill-advised acquisition, they threatened to shut the company down unless Oland took control. As a result, Oland became CEO, and biochemist Roger Lucas headed a division as chief scientific officer.

The competent leadership now in charge at R&D Systems attracted the attention of two venture capitalists. Investors George Kline and Peter Peterson owned a shell company known as TECHNE Corporation. They had founded the company in 1981 to pursue profitable acquisitions and took it public in 1983. In 1985, acting on faith in Oland's management

ability, TECHNE bought R&D Systems for about $1.9 million. R&D Systems was subsumed into the corporate shell.

DEVELOPMENT OF GROWTH FACTORS: 1986–90

That year R&D Systems also began development of a new product line. The new products were specialized proteins known as human cytokines. Cytokines are produced naturally by the body and control the growth, development, and functioning of cells. Researchers saw great therapeutic potential in the molecules, including making wounds heal faster, stimulating bone growth, and stopping the growth of certain cancer cells. A full understanding of cytokines would allow researchers to determine exactly how a protein would act on a cell and give them the ability to target specific health problems with few side effects. As a result, cytokines were in demand at government and university laboratories.

TECHNE's investment in the development of cytokine growth factors contributed to a $487,000 loss in 1985. The next year, TECHNE spent $675,000 on research in the new field. Research focused on a protein known as TGF-beta, short for "transforming growth factor." At the time, TGF-beta was the second of only three proteins that were able to stimulate or suppress the growth of cell tissue. R&D Systems was the only commercial supplier of the product, selling it mainly to researchers for laboratory applications.

The development of growth factors followed naturally from TECHNE's hematology operations. The company's hematology controls were produced largely from pig blood. TGF-beta was found in the blood's platelets, so TECHNE was able to use its ready blood supply to isolate the protein using a proprietary method. Oland saw great potential for TECHNE's protein growth factors. He told the *Minneapolis Star and Tribune* on October 23, 1986, "We think that our long-range future will be in growth factors. We think it's the hottest new field in science, and we just hope we can keep pace with it." His optimistic view seemed to be corroborated when, in October of that year, the scientists who had discovered growth factors 30 years earlier received a Nobel Prize for medicine.

TECHNE's research operations took another step forward in 1988, when the company hired several molecular biologists who had been laid off by another Twin Cities company, Molecular Genetics. The biologists helped TECHNE reduce its production costs by developing a way to grow materials in bacteria rather than buying blood and tissue for processing from vendors. That year the company officially formed its Biotechnology Division.

<table>
<tr><th colspan="2">KEY DATES</th></tr>
<tr><td>1976:</td><td>David Mundschenk founds Research and Diagnostics Systems, Inc.</td></tr>
<tr><td>1980:</td><td>Thomas E. Oland comes to R&D Systems as a consultant.</td></tr>
<tr><td>1981:</td><td>George Kline and Peter Peterson found TECHNE Corporation.</td></tr>
<tr><td>1983:</td><td>Oland becomes head of R&D Systems.</td></tr>
<tr><td>1985:</td><td>Shell company TECHNE buys R&D Systems.</td></tr>
<tr><td>1988:</td><td>TECHNE forms a Biotechnology Division to produce specialized proteins.</td></tr>
<tr><td>1991:</td><td>Amgen Inc.'s research reagent and diagnostic assay kit business is acquired.</td></tr>
<tr><td>1993:</td><td>TECHNE buys a British biotechnology company and founds a European division.</td></tr>
<tr><td>2005:</td><td>Fortron Bio Science, Inc. and BiosPacific, Inc. are acquired.</td></tr>
<tr><td>2011:</td><td>Company acquires Boston Biochem, Inc. and Tocris Holdings Limited.</td></tr>
</table>

STEADY GROWTH IN THE NINETIES

The production of growth factors became a central aspect of TECHNE's operations. By the early 1990s the company was positioned to make acquisitions that would confirm its reputation as a leading producer of cytokines. In August 1991 TECHNE bought the research reagent and diagnostic assay kit business of Amgen Inc., a California-based biotechnology firm. The acquisition went smoothly because it involved a transfer mainly of inventory and property, rather than personnel. The sale gave TECHNE the right to sell Quantikine diagnostic kits.

Later that fall, TECHNE sold its French subsidiary Hycel, the company that had aroused such dismay when Mundschenk first bought it in 1983. Although the sale of Hycel resulted in some lost revenue at TECHNE, growth in the company's main subsidiary, R&D Systems, made up for the loss. Revenues for 1991 were $22.3 million, and net income reached $1.96 million, a 17 percent increase over the previous year. Under Oland's leadership, similar growth rates continued through the end of the decade.

Several factors accounted for TECHNE's steady increase in revenues. Because the company's products were developed for use in biotechnology research rather than for the therapeutic market, TECHNE did not have

to contend with stringent product approval guidelines at the U.S. Food and Drug Administration. The company was able to cultivate long-term relationships with university and government research centers, which ensured reliable demand for its products.

Industry insiders also gave Oland much of the credit for TECHNE's success. When he took over the leadership position in 1983, he applied his personal habits of careful money management to the company. *Corporate Report-Minnesota* said he ran the company with a "miser's touch" in a July 1999 article in which Oland was profiled as one of the top underpaid CEOs in Minnesota. In the article, analysts praised Oland's work ethic, noting that he left the office at 9 p.m. most nights. Coworkers agreed that he worked incredibly hard and said he had few interests outside the company. Kline, one of the founders of TECHNE, was quoted as saying, "He is one of the rare people who puts shareholders and employees first and his own financial well-being second." *Minneapolis/St. Paul CityBusiness* also took note of Oland's low-key, effective management style. A July 7, 2000, article said he was hardworking and media-shy, preferring to let the company's performance speak for itself. "Tom is absolutely dedicated to the company. It's his baby, so to speak, and he likes to be very much involved in all aspects," research analyst Chad Simmer told *CityBusiness*.

EXPANSION OVERSEAS

TECHNE's steady growth continued through the 1990s. The company bought British Biotechnology Products Limited (BBP) in 1993 for $2.3 million. The firm had maintained a distribution agreement with R&D Systems for several years before the sale. BBP eventually became the headquarters for TECHNE's European research and development unit. The company was renamed R&D Systems Europe, Ltd., and continued to distribute products from R&D Systems in Minneapolis. The acquisition of BBP pushed TECHNE's revenue to $40.3 million for 1994, up from $28.7 million the year before.

Overseas expansion continued in 1995, when TECHNE established a sales subsidiary in Germany with an office near Frankfurt. Germany was TECHNE's largest European market. Expansion at home also continued apace. TECHNE added 80,000 square feet to its offices in 1993 and planned another 90,000-square-foot expansion in 1996.

In 1997 TECHNE carried out a restructuring of its European operations. The company decided to focus on its core cytokine-related products and pulled some underperforming molecular biology products from the market. In the summer of 1998 TECHNE managed to remove its chief competitor from the market, acquiring Genzyme Corporation's research products business for about $65.5 million. The Genzyme unit had reported sales of about $15 million in 1997. The acquisition added approximately 4,000 customers and 350 products, including antibodies, proteins, and research kits, to TECHNE's existing base of 8,000 customers and 1,900 products. It also made TECHNE the world's leading source for cytokines and related products.

The Genzyme unit's sales were lower than expected after the acquisition, but only because former Genzyme customers rapidly converted to R&D Systems products. Overall sales for 1998 once again showed steady growth. Net income for 1998 reached $15.2 million on sales of $67.3 million, compared to net income of $6.7 million on sales of $47.7 million three years earlier.

PURSUING ACQUISITIONS AND INVESTMENTS

The biotechnology market as a whole experienced substantial growth in the late 1990s, and TECHNE blazed ahead with a series of acquisitions and investments. TECHNE bought the reagent business and immunoassay patents of Cistron Biotechnology, Inc. in 1999. Cistron had worked with TECHNE as a partner for many years but decided that it wanted to withdraw from the production of research reagents and concentrate on the research and development of therapeutic applications instead. TECHNE paid $750,000 for Cistron's unit. The following year TECHNE increased its ownership in the drug developer ChemoCentryx, Inc. and acquired research and diagnostic market rights to all products developed by the firm.

Over the previous decade, TECHNE had been a well-kept secret on the stock market. Oland avoided media attention and expected the company's performance to speak for itself. In late 1999, however, investors discovered TECHNE and pushed the company's share price from $30 to $160 a share in the 10-month period ending July 2000.

In the fall of 2000 TECHNE filed a lawsuit against Amgen, from whom it had bought two units in 1991. Since the sale, Amgen had been supplying TECHNE with a product known as Erythropoietin in a cooperative agreement. Amgen said that it had mistakenly failed to invoice for the product and demanded $27 million in back payments. Oland countered that it was unreasonable to demand payment after failing to notify TECHNE for nine years that payment was due, especially because TECHNE had made only $2.7 mil-

lion in sales related to Amgen's product. The companies went to court, and in January 2002 the court judged in Amgen's favor. TECHNE settled the litigation in May 2002 with a $17.5 million cash payment to Amgen.

The lawsuit had little effect on TECHNE's ever-increasing revenues. Net income was up 60 percent in fiscal 2000 to $26.6 million on revenues of $103.8 million. In the fall of 2001 TECHNE invested in Discovery Genomics, a company located in Minneapolis that worked on determining the function of individual genes. In an arrangement similar to the ChemoCentryx deal, TECHNE acquired about 40 percent of Discovery Genomics and won the right to develop antibodies and immunoassays for proteins discovered by the company, and sell them on the research market free of royalties.

The September 11, 2001, terrorist attacks against the United States, coupled with the litigation settlement with Amgen and a general cutback in the biotechnology industry, hurt TECHNE's stock price in 2002. Nevertheless, the company continued to perform well in the area of operations. Sales in fiscal 2002 were $130.9 million, compared to the prior year's figure of $115.4 million. Because of the Amgen settlement, net income fell slightly from $34 million to $27.1 million.

TECHNE continued introducing hundreds of new products each year, thus bolstering revenue as the sales of older products leveled off. In the meantime, TECHNE's investments in companies involved in early-stage research, including ChemoCentryx and Discovery Genomics, were slow to pay off. In 2004 TECHNE wrote off its investment in Discovery Genomics because of the start-up's lack of revenues, although it retained its stake in the firm. That same year, TECHNE acquired a 10 percent interest in Hemerus Medical, LLC, for $3 million, later increasing this stake to nearly 18 percent. Founded in 2001, Hemerus had acquired and further developed technology for separating leukocytes from red blood cells and extending the shelf life of the isolated blood products. In September 2006 TECHNE invested $7.2 million in Nephromics, LLC, gaining a 16.8 percent stake. Nephromics specialized in developing diagnostic assays for the detection of preeclampsia, a potentially life-threatening condition that occurs during pregnancy.

FURTHER ACQUISITIONS AND INTERNATIONAL INITIATIVES

While new product development continued to drive TECHNE's growth during this period, given that products introduced within the previous five years typically accounted for about three-quarters of the Biotechnology Division's revenue growth each year, acquisitions were pursued as well. In keeping with its reputation for prudent, conservative management, TECHNE pursued only those acquisition opportunities that were synergistic, likely to yield a sufficient return on investment, and within the company's range of management and scientific expertise. In the summer of 2005, TECHNE acquired Fortron Bio Science, Inc. and its distribution partner, BiosPacific, Inc., for $20 million. Fortron was a developer and manufacturer of monoclonal and polyclonal antibodies, antigens, and other biological reagents, while BiosPacific was a global supplier of biologics to manufacturers of in vitro diagnostic systems and immunodiagnostic kits. Combined, the two companies had generated revenues of $8.7 million in 2004.

This acquisition helped push TECHNE's sales up to a record $202.6 million by fiscal 2006, which represented a 13 percent increase over the previous year. The profits of $73.4 million were also an all-time high. That year, TECHNE introduced 1,390 new products, increasing the total number of products it offered to more than 10,000.

With biotechnology research growing rapidly in China as a result of major governmental investment as well as Western companies establishing research operations there to take advantage of lower labor costs, TECHNE made a concerted push into the rapidly growing Asian economic giant. During fiscal 2007, the company set up a Shanghai-based subsidiary called R&D Systems China Co., Ltd., to provide warehousing, marketing, sales, and technical services for the Chinese market. By fiscal 2011 this subsidiary was contributing nearly 3 percent of TECHNE's overall sales, and its revenues increased 26 percent that year. TECHNE late in fiscal 2011 established a sales office in Hong Kong.

Despite the worldwide economic downturn, TECHNE continued to post record results through fiscal 2011, although its rate of growth significantly moderated. Sales increased only 2.5 percent and 1.9 percent in 2009 and 2010, respectively, before surging 7.8 percent in 2011. Even the latter gain, however, was well below the increases of more than 10 percent that were typical in the first years of the 21st century. While revenues were reaching a record of just under $290 million in fiscal 2011, TECHNE also enjoyed its ninth-straight year of record profits, with that year's net totaling $112.3 million.

TECHNE positioned itself for a sure boost in future revenues by completing two acquisitions in April 2011. The smaller of these was the $7.9 million purchase of Cambridge, Massachusetts-based Boston Biochem, Inc. Founded in 1997, Boston Biochem was the developer of more than 800 products related to

ubiquitin, a protein associated with the regulation of numerous disease states, including Alzheimer's, cystic fibrosis, diabetes, and various forms of cancer.

TECHNE also paid about $124 million for Tocris Holdings Limited. Based in Bristol, England, Tocris was a leading supplier of biologically active chemicals used in life-science research and the initial drug discovery process to understand biological processes and diseases. At the time of the acquisition, Tocris was offering more than 2,900 chemical, peptide, and antibody products. The firm had generated $18.2 million in revenues in 2010. The entirely complementary nature of the respective product lines of TECHNE and Tocris promised to make TECHNE even more of a one-stop shop for life science researchers.

Sarah Ruth Lorenz
Updated, David E. Salamie

PRINCIPAL SUBSIDIARIES

Research and Diagnostic Systems, Inc. (R&D Systems); BiosPacific, Inc.; Boston Biochem, Inc.; Tocris Cookson, Inc.; Tocris Holdings Limited (UK); Tocris Investments Limited (UK); Tocris Cookson Limited (UK); R&D Systems Europe Ltd. (UK); R&D Systems GmbH (Germany); R&D Systems China Co., Ltd.; R&D Systems Hong Kong Ltd.

PRINCIPAL OPERATING UNITS

Biotechnology; Hematology.

PRINCIPAL COMPETITORS

Abbott Laboratories; Abcam plc; Beckman Coulter, Inc.; Becton, Dickinson and Company; Bio-Rad Laboratories, Inc.; Cayman Chemical Company, Incorporated; Enzo Biochem, Inc.; General Electric Company; Life Technologies Corporation; Merck KGaA; PeproTech Inc.; Santa Cruz Biotechnology, Inc.; Siemens Healthcare Diagnostics Inc.; Sigma-Aldrich Corporation; Streck, Inc.; Sysmex Corporation; Thermo Fisher Scientific Inc.

FURTHER READING

Fiedler, Terry. "Building Blocks of the Biotech Boom." *Minneapolis Star-Tribune*, September 4, 2000, 1D.

Griffith, Jessica. "Oland Is Quiet, Hands-On." *Minneapolis/St. Paul CityBusiness*, September 7, 2001, 12.

Gross, Steve. "Local Firm Has a Sizable Interest in Growth Factors." *Minneapolis Star and Tribune*, October 23, 1986, 1M.

Haeg, Andrew. "Oland Drives Techne with a Miser's Touch." *Corporate Report-Minnesota*, July 1999, 24.

Lau, Gloria. "Big Gains, Small Risks in Test Kits." *Investor's Business Daily*, September 19, 2005, A11.

Lee, Wendy. "Techne Buys U.K. Chemical Supplier." *Minneapolis Star-Tribune*, May 4, 2011, 1D.

———. "Techne Tackles China." *Minneapolis Star-Tribune*, August 23, 2010, 1D.

Levy, Melissa. "Techne to Acquire Research Products Unit from Genzyme." *Minneapolis Star-Tribune*, June 24, 1998, 1D.

Niemela, Jennifer. "Techne's Low-Key CEO Gets High-Impact Results." *Minneapolis/St. Paul CityBusiness*, July 7, 2000, S25.

"Optimistic Techne Buys Room for Growth." *Minneapolis/St. Paul Business Journal*, February 13, 2005. Accessed November 8, 2011. http://www.bizjournals.com/twincities/stories/2005/02/14/story3.html.

Thomas Cook Group plc

The Thomas Cook Business Park
Coningsby Road
Peterborough, PE3 8SB
United Kingdom
Telephone: (+44 20) 7557-6400
Fax: (+44 20) 7557-6401
Web site: http://www.thomascookgroup.com

Public Company
Incorporated: 2007
Employees: 31,097
Sales: £9.8 billion (2011)
Stock Exchanges: London
Ticker Symbol: TCG
NAICS: 551112 Offices of Other Holding Companies; 481211 Nonscheduled Chartered Passenger Air Transportation; 522320 Financial Transactions Processing, Reserve, and Clearing House Activities; 524210 Insurance Agencies and Brokerages; 561510 Travel Agencies; 561520 Tour Operators

■ ■ ■

Thomas Cook Group plc is a leading provider of leisure travel services, with more than 23 million customers and approximately 3,400 owned or franchised travel outlets. The company's operations focus on six business segments: Central Europe; West & East Europe; Northern Europe; United Kingdom, Ireland, India, and the Middle East; Airlines Germany; and North America. Among the travel giant's brands are Thomas Cook, Nelson, Direct Holidays, Club 18-30, and Airtours. In

2011 the company was active in 22 countries and posted sales of £9.8 billion.

THOMAS COOK IS FOUNDED

Thomas Cook Group Ltd. was the eponymous creation of an industrious English entrepreneur. From a humble beginning chartering a train to a temperance rally in 1841, Cook expanded his business into one of the world's first full-service travel firms. After the resounding success of his first venture, Cook quickly expanded his operations, providing rail trips and making hotel reservations for customers for journeys all over the British Isles.

Cook's excursions proved so popular that he began offering trips to Europe, North America, and, beginning in 1871, around the world. Buoyed by these successes, Cook's company was able to open 120 travel offices in the United Kingdom and abroad by 1885, and Cook himself branched out to write guidebooks. The company also remained on the cutting edge of developments in the travel industry. Thomas Cook Ltd. began offering cruise trips as early as the mid-1870s, pioneered an early form of traveler's check, and was booking air travel by 1911, a mere eight years after the Wright brothers made history at Kitty Hawk, North Carolina.

The company also had a long history in the United States. Just months after the Civil War ended in 1865, Cook's Tours (as the company was then known) ran its first U.S. tour, which included stops at various battlefields. Six years later, Cook formed a partnership with an American businessman that they dubbed Cook, Son & Jenkins. This relationship subsequently dissolved acrimoniously, but by then it had helped Cook's entrench itself in the U.S. market.

To bolster its business further, the company took a pavilion at the Centennial Celebration in Philadelphia in 1876. It later expanded its offerings to include not just traditional sightseeing trips but even travel packages for immigrants coming to the United States and Canada. By 1896 Cook's U.S. business made travel arrangements to the Klondike for gold prospectors.

COOK FAMILY EXITS

Control of the company remained with the Cook family until the late 1920s. Thomas Cook himself had died in 1892, and his son and business partner did the same eight years later. His three grandsons then ran the company until the last of them retired in 1928, at which point it was sold to a Belgian travel concern, Compagnie des Wagons-Lits et des Grands Express Européens. When Germany occupied Belgium in World War II, the company was taken over by the German Custodian of Enemy Properties. However, the British government arranged for it to be reacquired by several railway companies at the close of the war. When the railroads were nationalized in 1948, ownership of Thomas Cook Ltd. passed to the crown as well.

Although Thomas Cook had become an institution both in the United Kingdom and the United States, the company risked losing touch with younger consumers in the 1960s. As a state-run business, Thomas Cook was unable to invest the same level of funding into its operations that its private rivals could. While other travel agencies crafted new strategies to attract more customers and increase revenue, such as purchasing airlines, Thomas Cook saw its sales flatten. As a result, the British government tentatively explored selling the travel agency.

LEGAL RESTRAINTS

Midland Bank acquired Thomas Cook in 1974. Since U.S. banking laws prohibited any national bank, such as

Midland, from owning domestic travel agencies, Midland sold Thomas Cook's U.S. operations to Dun & Bradstreet in 1975. Midland did not relinquish control of the Thomas Cook name, but Dun & Bradstreet was allowed to continue to operate the U.S. travel agencies under the Cook name through a licensing agreement.

Although Thomas Cook Group Ltd. had no equity in the U.S. operations, it did link the agencies into its travel network. More importantly, the British branch could supply the independent U.S. offices with traveler's checks, which represented an increasing portion of Thomas Cook Group Ltd.'s revenues. Only American Express outperformed Cook in this segment of the travel industry.

RISE OF CRIMSON TRAVEL

At about the same time that Dun & Bradstreet made this pivotal purchase, Crimson Travel Service (the Cambridge, Massachusetts-based travel agency that would later carry the Thomas Cook franchise in the United States) began to expand. Founded in 1965 by the husband-and-wife duo David and Linda Paresky, Crimson quickly grew through creative marketing efforts. Graced with the same gift for travel innovation as Thomas Cook, David Paresky launched a number of bold initiatives. As a competitor explained in the September 18, 1994, *Boston Globe*, "Paresky saw before most of us that the masses wanted to go, and he knew where they wanted to go."

Crimson chartered several immensely popular "Cruises to Nowhere," that brought the luxury of a cruise vacation to middle-class consumers. In 1968 the company forged a strategic alliance with a Western-themed television show called *Boomtown*, whereby Crimson chartered mass trips for kids (guided by Trailer, the show's host) and received ample exposure in the process. The "Boomtown" trips were a huge success and continued through the 1990s. By 1969 Crimson had opened its third Boston-area branch office, and its leisure travel business soared. By 1987 the company reported billings of $150 million.

As Crimson saw its fortune rise, the travel industry as a whole experienced tectonic changes in the 1980s. The frenetic globalization of American business meant that corporate employees traveled more frequently and purchased a growing percentage of airline tickets. Because Crimson's revenues came mostly from vacationers, not businesspeople, the company would risk its future profitability if it did not develop the corporate side of its operations. In 1988 Crimson purchased Heritage Travel, a rival Cambridge agency. Not only was

KEY DATES

1841: English entrepreneur Thomas Cook organizes his first charter.

1928: Company is sold to Compagnie des Wagons-Lits et des Grands Express Europeens.

1948: Thomas Cook falls under the control of the British government.

1994: Thomas Cook Travel Inc. is sold to American Express.

2000: Thomas Cook is acquired by Germany-based C&N Touristic AG for $794 million and is renamed Thomas Cook AG.

2007: Company merges with MyTravel Group plc in a deal worth £2.8 billion and changes its name to Thomas Cook Group plc.

2011: Regulatory approval for the acquisition of Co-operative Group is received, allowing the formation of the largest multichannel travel retailer in the United Kingdom.

Heritage equipped with cutting-edge computer technology, but it also ran a formidable corporate business.

MORE OWNERSHIP CHANGES

In 1988 Dun & Bradstreet put Thomas Cook up for sale in order to concentrate on its core marketing, credit risk, finance, and directory information divisions. Publishing magnate Robert Maxwell purchased Thomas Cook in 1989, and immediately renewed the licensing agreement with Midland to use the storied Cook name. At the time of Maxwell's acquisition, Thomas Cook was a sizable operation, generating sales of $365 million and operating 60 full-service locations and nine regional reservation centers. Many industry analysts speculated that Maxwell would quickly sell the company, since publishing was his primary concern. However, Maxwell pledged to expand Thomas Cook through a series of acquisitions that would make the franchise the leading U.S. travel service firm.

Despite his protestations to the contrary, Maxwell sold a 50 percent stake in Thomas Cook to the Pareskys' Crimson/Heritage business in 1988. With Maxwell, the Pareskys presided over the third-largest agency in the country, with revenues topping $1.3 billion. David Paresky served as president, chairman, and chief executive of his new empire, and he moved Thomas Cook's corporate headquarters from New York City to Cambridge. The co-owners quickly turned to bolstering Thomas Cook's roster of corporate clients.

While the ownership of Thomas Cook changed hands in the United States, the keeper of the coveted license, Thomas Cook Group Ltd., went through its own shifts. In 1992 Midland sold its subsidiary to LTU Group, one of Germany's largest tour operators, and Westdeutsche Landesbanke, a German bank. Westdeutsche Landesbanke purchased 90 percent of Thomas Cook Group Ltd.'s shares, while LTU Group controlled the remaining 10.

PARESKYS GAIN CONTROL

Although Thomas Cook Travel Inc. had no problems with the license, the company did endure some turbulent times in 1991 when Maxwell died suddenly. One of his privately held companies, Headington Holdings Limited, went into bankruptcy. Headington owned Maxwell Travel Inc., which in turn owned Maxwell's 50 percent share of Thomas Cook. A number of potential buyers hungrily eyed the stake in Thomas Cook, including Midland Bank, which had by then divested the bank that had prevented it from owning the chain in 1979. David Paresky had right of first refusal, and in 1993 he and his wife purchased the Maxwell stake.

Even with complete control of Thomas Cook Travel, Paresky planned no major changes. "We're continuing with the same strategy we've had before, differentiating our service through innovation and quality," he told the *Boston Globe* on January 12, 1993. "I don't think our operating philosophy will change." Sales for 1993 soared to over $1.7 billion, and the company ran approximately 500 offices throughout the United States.

Paresky's efforts to bolster Thomas Cook's corporate accounts had succeeded. At the close of 1993, 84 percent of the company's sales were from businesses. Thomas Cook's list of clients was impressive. Ford Motor Co., Fidelity Investment, Hewlett-Packard, and John Hancock Mutual Life Insurance Co. all made their travel arrangements through Thomas Cook. In 1994 the company won three more substantial accounts: the British Embassy, Walsh America, and Pharmaceutical Marketing Services Inc.

SALE TO AMERICAN EXPRESS

Despite their success, the Pareskys approached archrival American Express about selling Thomas Cook. "American Express will bring more size and more strength and more ability to invest in our people," David Paresky explained to *Travel Weekly* on September 15, 1994. To the *Boston Globe*, Paresky admitted that the cost of upgrading technology to better serve global business travelers was a factor in the decision to sell.

American Express had much to gain from the purchase. Already gigantic, with over 1,700 travel offices in more than 120 nations, American Express would boost its annual sales an additional 33 percent with this new division. The acquisition also had significant prestige value. Although American Express had recently snapped up five other large agencies, the Cook deal was to be the largest takeover in the history of the travel industry.

The transaction was finalized in September 1994 with American Express paying $375 million for the company. Although they had relinquished their ownership interests, the Pareskys remained involved in the business. Both were appointed vice presidents, and in 1995, David Paresky was reported to be "in line" to become president of American Express Travel.

American Express also moved to acquire the corporate accounts of Thomas Cook Group Ltd. (which represented about 10 percent of the British company's total revenues). While this segment of the business was lucrative, the group was willing to part with it in order to concentrate on servicing leisure travelers and on its burgeoning financial services division. However, American Express was not able to obtain from the group the rights to the venerable Thomas Cook name. As a result, all former Thomas Cook offices were to be rechristened American Express.

LEISURE TRAVEL FOCUS

After selling its business travel operation to American Express in September 1994, a number of significant changes occurred within Thomas Cook Group as the business restructured its operations. Westdeutsche Landesbanke continued to hold a 90 percent stake in the company. In early 1995 CEO Christopher Rodrigues resigned and was replaced by Hans-Ulrich Zierke, who headed Westdeutsche Landesbanke's London branch. A number of other staff changes also were made within the ranks of middle and senior management, and approximately 200 positions were eliminated organization-wide, resulting in annual savings of approximately £5 million.

Moving forward, Thomas Cook concentrated on leisure travel, traveler's checks, and foreign exchange. Westdeutsche Landesbanke also expressed a desire to better integrate the operations of Thomas Cook with its own. Following its restructuring efforts, sales increased 14 percent, reaching £750 million. In addition, operating profits skyrocketed to £46.8 million, more than double the 1994 figure of £21.5 million.

Growth continued in July 1996 when Thomas Cook parted with £38 million to acquire Sunworld, which at the time was the fifth-largest tour operator in the United Kingdom. Another acquisition followed later in the year when the city breaks tour operator Time Off was acquired. In 1997 the company made its foray into e-commerce when Thomas Cook On-Line was introduced and the company began engaging in the on-line sale of traveler's checks, guidebooks, foreign currency, and vacations.

Another important deal took place in late 1998 when Thomas Cook merged its package vacation business with Carlson Companies' U.K.-based leisure division, Carlson Worldchoice. In December Westdeutsche Landesbanke sold a 24.9 percent interest in Thomas Cook to Germany-based Preussag, which at the time was the largest travel conglomerate in Europe.

By August 1999 Preussag had a 50.1 percent ownership interest in Thomas Cook, making it the company's largest shareholder. At that time Carlson Companies revealed that, by 2002, it had an option to increase its ownership of Thomas Cook from 22 percent to 49 percent. More changes were in store when the company began taking steps to sell its financial services business in late 1999.

OWNERSHIP CHANGES CONTINUE

By mid-2000 Preussag had acquired the largest tour operator in the United Kingdom, Thomson Travel Group. In order to satisfy anticompetition concerns surrounding the deal, Preussag was required to sell its interest in Thomas Cook. At the same time, Westdeutsche Landesbanke also indicated that it would sell its stake in Thomas Cook, leaving nearly 80 percent of the company's shares available.

Rumors immediately began circulating that Carlson Companies would acquire Preussag's shares. However, in late 2000 Thomas Cook was instead acquired by Germany-based C&N Touristic AG for $794 million. Following the deal, the company was renamed Thomas Cook AG. CEO Alan Stewart stepped down and was succeeded by Managing Director Manny Fontenla-Novoa. In early 2003 headquarters were relocated from London to Peterborough. That year, the company also commenced operations of Thomas Cook Airlines in the United Kingdom.

Rapid changes continued at Thomas Cook as the company headed into the latter years of the decade. In 2007 the company merged with MyTravel Group plc in a deal worth £2.8 billion. Following the deal, the company's name became Thomas Cook Group plc, shares of which began publicly trading on the London Stock Exchange in June. C&N Touristic shareholder Arcandor AG continued to control nearly 53 percent of Thomas Cook's stock. Fontenla-Novoa continued to lead the company as CEO. Approximately 150 stores and six office locations were slated to close following the merger, impacting up to 2,800 jobs.

Thomas Cook began 2008 by agreeing to acquire Hotels4U.com. In addition, the company secured nearly 75 percent of Thomas Cook India Limited, as well as all of the Egyptian businesses operating under the Thomas Cook brand. In the Middle East, Thomas Cook also obtained licenses in 15 countries. Other acquisitions in 2008 included Jet Tours, TriWest Travel Holdings, Elegant Resorts, and Gold Medal.

It also was in 2008 that plans were made to shutter the company's sales center in Glasgow, which employed more than 150 people. The company revealed that it would relocate operations to nearby Falkirk. In mid-2009 Fontenla-Novoa revealed that, over the coming five years, Thomas Cook would likely reduce the number of physical locations in its network to 100.

CONTINUING GROWTH

In 2010 Thomas Cook Group acquired Think W3, which owned the travel-related products provider Essential Travel. Specifically, Essential Travel sold services such as airport parking and hotels, as well as travel insurance. After acquiring Germany-based Öger Tours, Thomas Cook agreed to acquire Co-operative Group and Midlands Co-operative Society in 2010. The proposed merger created a stir among independent travel agents, who claimed the deal would hinder competition. By the end of the year the United Kingdom's Office of Fair Trading was investigating the matter.

In August 2011 Fontenla-Novoa stepped down as CEO of Thomas Cook. Group Deputy Sam Weihagen assumed the role on an interim basis, while a search for a new leader was underway. That month the company also received regulatory approval to move forward with the Co-operative Group merger, which would create the largest multichannel travel retailer in the United Kingdom. Another leadership change took place in

September when Frank Meysman was designated to become the company's new chairman following the retirement of Michael Beckett in December 2011.

Thomas Cook had evolved considerably since the 1840s, when its founder organized his first tours. In the years that followed, the company had undergone tremendous changes and ownership situations. As the company looked to the future, it appeared to be well-positioned for continued success.

Wendy J. Stein
Updated, Rebecca Stanfel; Paul R. Greenland

PRINCIPAL DIVISIONS

Central Europe; West & East Europe; Northern Europe; United Kingdom, Ireland, India, and the Middle East; Airlines Germany; North America.

PRINCIPAL COMPETITORS

American Express Company; JTB Corp.; Kuoni Travel Holding Ltd.

FURTHER READING

Ackerman, Jerry. "Crimson to Cook to Gold." *Boston Globe*, September 18, 1994.

Carroll, Cathy. "American Express Buys Thomas Cook." *Travel Weekly*, September 15, 1994.

"Cook Acquires Hotels4U." *Travel Trade Gazette UK & Ireland*, February 15, 2008, 3.

"Cook Clears Last Merger Hurdle." *Travel Trade Gazette UK & Ireland*, June 1, 2007, 6.

Gill, Rob. "Cook/Co-op Deal Is 'Tesco of Travel.'" *Travel Trade Gazette UK & Ireland*, May 13, 2011, 4.

"IN BRIEF: Thomas Cook Acquires Essential Travel." *Travel Trade Gazette UK & Ireland*, March 12, 2010, 5.

Sit, Mary. "Executives Buy Thomas Cook Travel." *Boston Globe*, January 12, 1993.

Swinglehurst, Edmund. *Cook's Tours: The Story of Popular Travel*. Dorset, England: Blandford Press, 1982.

———. *The Romantic Journey: The Story of Thomas Cook and Victorian Travel*. New York: Harper & Row, 1974.

Tran, Mark. "AmEx Set to Snap Up US Travel Rival." *Guardian*, September 10, 1994.

Vallourec S.A.

27, avenue du General Leclerc
Boulogne-Billancourt, 92100
France
Telephone: (+33 1) 49 09 35 00
Fax: (+33 1) 49 09 36 94
Web site: http://www.vallourec.com

Public Company
Founded: 1895 as Société Française de Fabrication de
    Corps Creux
Incorporated: 1957
Employees: 20,000
Sales: EUR 4.49 billion ($6.45 billion) (2010)
Stock Exchanges: Euronext Paris
Ticker Symbol: VK
NAICS: 331210 Iron and Steel Pipes and Tubes
    Manufacturing from Purchased Steel

■ ■ ■

Vallourec S.A. is a world-leading producer of specialty steel tubular products and systems used in the oil and gas, power generation, petrochemicals, and other industries, including automotive and mechanical engineering applications. The energy sector represented 78 percent of Vallourec's total revenues of EUR 4.49 billion ($6.45 billion) in 2010. The Paris-based company is also a global player, claiming the number one position in the premium tubes segment, and generating 74 percent of its sales from outside of the European Union. Vallourec operates from 51 factories located in 20 countries. North America and South America are its two largest regions, each accounting for 25 percent of sales. Asia and the Middle East add 17 percent to sales, while Germany is its largest European market, at 14 percent of sales. France accounted for just 4 percent of revenues in 2010. Vallourec is listed on the Euronext Paris stock exchange and is led by Chairman Philippe Crouzet.

MERGING INDUSTRIAL GROUPS IN THE THIRTIES

The Vallourec name first appeared in 1930 upon the merger of several companies that produced steel tubing in France's North region, yet those companies had all been active since the end of the 19th century. The name Vallourec stemmed from an amalgam of the sites of the combined companies' tubing mills: Valenciennes, Denain, Louvroil, and Recquignies. That company then came under control of the Société Denain Anzin, which later evolved into French industrial giant Usinor.

Nonetheless, Vallourec's origins also lay in the Burgundy region, in the town of Montbard, where the Société Française de Fabrication de Corps Creux had been founded in 1895. In 1899, the company's name was changed to Société Métallurgique de Montbard and was listed on the Paris exchange the same year.

The Montbard company began acquiring other steel mills in the region. In 1907, Montbard acquired a company in Aulnoye, changing its name to Montbard-Aulnoye. In 1937, Montbard-Aulnoye merged with Société Louvroil et Recquignies, forming Louvroil Montbard Aulnoye. The Louvroil site had been in operation since 1890 as the Société Française pour la Fabrication des Tubes à Louvroil. That company had then merged with the Société des Forges de Recquignies, which had started operations in 1907.

Louvroil Montbard Aulnoye acquired Vallourec in 1957 as part of France's great industrial realignment begun under General Charles de Gaulle, which also saw Denain combine with fellow French steel leader Nord-Est to form Usinor (later Arcelor). Following the acquisition, Louvroil Montbard Aulnoye adopted the Vallourec name as its own, and renamed its new subsidiary Sogestra. At the same time, Usinor became the company's major shareholder.

Usinor proved more than a passive shareholder, as the consolidation of the French steel industry continued through the 1960s. In 1966, Usinor acquired another of France's largest steel products producers, Lorraine-Escaut. That company was itself the product of a merger, in 1953, among three steelworks: Société des Aciéries de Longwy, Société Escaut et Meuse, and Société Métallurgique de Senelle-Meubeuge. Following the acquisition, Usinor turned over Lorraine-Escaut's steel tubes operations to Vallourec in 1967.

NEW STEELWORKS IN THE SEVENTIES

Vallourec was by then on its way to becoming the leading tube maker in France, particularly after launching its VAM connection system in 1967. The company continued making acquisitions into the 1970s, enabling it to establish itself not only as the country's leading producer of welded and drawn tubes, but also as the only manufacturer in France producing seamless and large-scale welded tubes.

In 1975, Vallourec consolidated its position in the tubes market with the acquisition of Compagnie des Tubes de Normandie. That company dated its history back to 1729, when it began producing lead linings. In 1899, then known as Compagnie Française des Métaux, it switched production to steel tubes. That activity led it to change its name again to Compagnie des Tubes de Normandie in 1957. In 1961, it became part of the Union Sidérurgique Lorraine (Sidelor), which, after merging in 1968 with another major steel group, De Wendel, ultimately became Sacilor. In the mid-1970s,

the French government took control of both Usinor and Sacilor, moving them toward a merger in the mid-1980s.

In the late 1970s, Vallourec moved in two directions. It built its own steelworks, in Saint-Saulve, in a step toward vertical integration. Those works enabled Vallourec to supply its own raw steel for its seamless tube production. Vallourec had begun also to move toward more specialized production. In 1979, the company spun off its small welded tubes operations to Usinor subsidiary Tubes de 1a Providence, which then became known as Valexy. Vallourec remained the majority shareholder of that company, with 64 percent of its shares.

DIVERSIFYING IN THE EIGHTIES

In the early 1980s, Vallourec made a move to diversify its activities, notably with the acquisition of a major stake in construction and public works company GTM. Formed in 1891 as Grands Travaux de Marseille, GTM's origins as a pipe layer for the Marseille sewer system placed it close to Vallourec's product line. GTM had long since diversified, adding electrical works, harbor, tunnel, and other underground construction, by the time of World War I, and extending into oil platforms and structures, nuclear power plants, and parking lots and other concessions from the 1950s.

Following its acquisition by Vallourec, GTM merged with longtime partner Entrepose, founded in 1935 and owned at 90 percent by Vallourec. GTM-Entrepose, as the new company became known in 1982, then became controlled at 41 percent by Vallourec.

The collapse of the steel industry at the beginning of the 1980s had sunk Vallourec into losses by mid-decade. By 1987, the company's losses had mounted to FRF 452 million.

Vallourec was forced to undergo a major reorganization. This took place through several steps. In 1985, the company spun off its large welded tubes operations to Usinor subsidiary GTS Industries. By the end of that year, the company had relinquished its shares in both GTS and Valexy to Usinor. Vallourec then became a specialist producer of seamless tubes.

RESTRUCTURING IN 1985

Next, Vallourec began divesting its noncore operations, such as its Société Industrielle de Banque, divested in 1985. The following year, the company restructured as a holding company, creating three primary divisions: Val-

KEY DATES

1895: Société Française de Fabrication de Corps Creux is founded in Montbard, France.

1930: Vallourec is formed.

1957: Louvroil Montbard Aulnoye acquires Vallourec, adopting that name as its own.

1985: Vallourec spins off its large welded tubes operations to Usinor subsidiary GTS Industries, then relinquishes its shares in both GTS and Valexy to Usinor, becoming a specialist producer of seamless tubes.

1988: Vallourec begins to sell its stake in GTM Entrepose to Dumez.

1997: Carbon and alloy steel seamless tube operations are merged with those of Mannesmann, creating V&M Tubes.

2000: V&M Tubes acquires Mannesmann SA, of Brazil.

2002: V&M Tubes acquires North Star Tubes of the United States.

2010: Vallourec announces plans to build a $650 million factory in Youngstown, Ohio.

lourec Industries, for its tubes production; Sopretac, for its steel production and other metals-related operations; and Valinco, which took over its shareholding in GTM-Entrepose and other civil engineering and construction holdings. In 1987, Vallourec Industries was renamed Valtubes.

In that year, also, Vallourec turned to its major shareholders, Usinor and Nord-Est, to help it put together a rescue package worth some FRF 300 million. Nord-Est balked, however, and instead announced its desire to sell its stake in Vallourec. The company's management, then led by Arnault Leenhardt, took the risk and put together a buyout of Nord-Est's nearly 20 percent stake in the company. By the following year, Vallourec had returned to profitability, posting earnings of FRF 770 million on sales of FRF 7 billion.

In 1988, Vallourec's streamlining continued, with the sale of 49.5 percent of Valinco and its holding in GTM-Entrepose to French construction giant Dumez. By 1991, Vallourec had turned over all of Valinco to Dumez, thus exiting completely the civil engineering and construction sectors. GTM-Entrepose and Dumez later became GTM Group, which became one of the core members of the later Vinci group.

INTERNATIONALIZATION IN THE NINETIES

Vallourec began targeting new markets in the 1990s, particularly the international market. This effort transformed the company's operations in barely more than a decade, from a reliance on the domestic market (France represented more than half of Vallourec's sales at the beginning of the decade) to a company that generated some 85 percent of sales internationally, and more than half outside of the European Union. At the same time, Vallourec began targeting new markets, with a special emphasis on the oil and gas power generation industries, for its seamless tubes.

Meanwhile, despite the difficult economic period, Vallourec remained in good shape, thanks in part to the sell-off of its noncore holdings during the 1980s. With a war chest of some FRF 1 billion, the company began targeting acquisitions. In 1992, the company acquired the automotive division of Usinor-Sacilor's Tubeurop subsidiary. The purchase added five factories and three subsidiaries, Ficam, Lita Tubi, and Valexy Automobile Haumont, as well as additional revenues of FRF 800 million. It also positioned Vallourec at the forefront of the market as the automotive industry increasingly adopted seamless tubing as a number of systems, such as power steering, became standard features.

A step toward the internationalization of the company's operating base came in 1994 with the purchase of British Steel's Tubular Industries, based in Scotland, which had previously held a license to manufacture products using the VAM connection system. Similarly, Vallourec acquired Mexico's Prinver, which held the VAM license in that country.

FORMING VALLOUREC & MANNESMANN IN 1997

In 1994, also, Vallourec joined with Germany's Mannesmann and Italy's Dalmine to form DMV Stainless, combining the three groups' seamless stainless steel tube operations. Initially held up by the European Commission, the DMV Stainless venture became the second largest in the market, behind Sweden's Sandvik.

Vallourec's international drive continued into the second half of the 1990s, notably with the entry into the South American market and the construction of two factories in Brazil dedicated to the production of seamless tubes for the automotive industry. The company also entered China, forming the Changzhou Valinox Great Wall Welded Tube Co. Ltd. joint venture in 1996.

In 1997, Vallourec and Mannesmann joined together to form a new joint venture, Vallourec & Mannesman Tubes (V&M Tubes), which took over both companies' carbon and alloy steel seamless tube production. Owned at 55 percent by Vallourec, V&M Tubes boosted Vallourec's position with the worldwide oil and gas industry. As part of the joint venture, Mannesmann took over Usinor's 30 percent shareholding in Vallourec.

Following the merger, Vallourec reorganized its holdings into three primary businesses: V&M Tubes, Valtubes, and Sopretac. The company then sought a strategic alliance with Belgium's Timet, which operated a welded tubing division in Boulogne, France. In 1997, Vallourec agreed to merge its Valinox Welded Tubing division with the Timet division, forming Valtimet as a maker of specialty welded tubing products.

NORTH AMERICAN GROWTH IN 2002

In 2000, V&M Tubes extended its international reach by acquiring Mannesmann's 76 percent share in its Mannesmann SA subsidiary in Brazil. V&M Tubes later increased its share in the Brazil operation to nearly 100 percent.

Vallourec next targeted expansion in the United States. In 2002, the company took a major step forward in that market when it announced the acquisition, through V&M Tubes and in conjunction with long-term partner Sumitomo, of Japan, of the North Star Tubes subsidiary of Cargill. The acquisition, which gave V&M Tubes an 80 percent stake in North Star Tubes, was completed for a price of $380 million, and established V&M Tubes as one of the world's leading manufacturers of seamless tubes for the oil and gas industry. It also completed the shift in Vallourec's revenues, boosting U.S. sales to half of overall revenues.

At the beginning of 2003, Vallourec continued to boost its U.S. presence. In January of that year, the company announced its acquisition of International Tubular Products, a specialist manufacturer of stainless steel and titanium pipes and condensers for electricity generation. By then, Vallourec had boosted its revenues to more than EUR 2.5 billion, with a worldwide workforce of more than 17,000.

Mannesmann was acquired by Vodafone in 2000, which sold its 45 percent stake in V&M Tubes to Germany's number two steelmaker, Salzgitter, soon after. In 2005, Vallourec acquired Salzgitter's stake, gaining full control of V&M Tubes, in a transaction that gave Salzgitter a major share of Vallourec. Salzgitter, which had acquired parts of Mannesmann's precision tubes operations, sold off its shares in Vallourec S.A. in 2006. Following that sale, Vallourec joined the Paris exchange's CAC 40 index.

FOCUSING ON CHINA IN 2007

In the meantime, Vallourec had expanded its North American business, acquiring Omsco in 2005 and SMFI in 2006. These purchases positioned the company as the world's second-largest producer of drill pipes for the oil and gas industry. The companies were combined into a new entity, VAM Drilling. By the end of the decade, North America represented 25 percent of the group's operations, while the United States had become the company's single-largest market.

Vallourec now targeted growth in China, which was rushing to expand its infrastructure in order to support its rapid growth. In 2006 alone this country had outlined plans to add nearly 2,750 miles of new power lines and forecasted an electric power shortfall of some two million kilowatts. The demand for premium and specialty steel tubes required to achieve the country's infrastructure objectives led Vallourec to expand its Chinese operations. The company completed construction of two factories, V&M Changzhou and VAM Changzhou, in 2007. The former produced large-sized steel tubes for electric power stations and the latter focused on threaded tubes for the oil and gas industry.

The strong growth of the South American oil and gas industry during the decade also led Vallourec to target this region. The company teamed up with Sumitomo Metal Industries to found the joint venture Vallourec & Sumitomo do Brasil, with Vallourec as the majority partner at 56 percent. This company then began construction of a tube mill located in Jeceaba, which launched production in 2011.

Vallourec appeared set to become part of the global steel industry's consolidation wave, when rumors surfaced that the company would be acquired by Arcelor Mittal in 2007. The steel giant, however, bought just two of Vallourec's subsidiaries. Instead, Vallourec continued to strengthen its relationship with Sumitomo, creating VAM USA LLC in 2009. This partnership involved the merger of their previous U.S. joint venture into another Vallourec subsidiary, V&M Atlas Bradford. Vallourec had acquired Atlas Bradford in 2008, along with two other oil country tubular goods (OCTG) specialists, Tube Alloy and TCA. Vallourec and Sumitomo also agreed to purchase each other's shares, with Sumitomo acquiring 2 percent of Vallourec, and Vallourec acquiring 1 percent of Sumitomo. VAM USA became the U.S. market's largest producer of seamless steel pipe.

CHINA AND SAUDI PURCHASES IN 2011

Vallourec also expanded its operations in Indonesia and the Middle East. In France, the company invested EUR

80 million in order to triple its production of nuclear plant steam generator tubes in 2009. In 2010, the company launched construction of a $650 million tube mill in Youngstown, Ohio, a move meant to position the company for the soon-to-boom market for shale gas production. The site was scheduled to begin production by the end of 2011.

Vallourec completed a new acquisition, of Serimax for $150 million, in May 2010. This purchase boosted Vallourec's expertise in welding services and solutions for marine pipelines. In 2011, Vallourec's attention turned once again to China, where it acquired a 19.5 percent stake in Tianda Oil Pipe Co., a Hong Kong–listed company and producer of thread pipe for the Chinese OCTG sector. Vallourec also announced plans to spend $220 million expanding its Changzhou factory and another $76 million in order to build a new factory for the production of nuclear power steam generator tubes in 2012.

In the middle of 2011, Vallourec boosted its presence in the Middle East markets, paying $135 million to acquire Saudi Seamless Pipe Factory, based in Dammam. Also that year, Vallourec and Sumitomo officially inaugurated the VSB plant in Brazil, which expected to reach full capacity by 2013. Vallourec had transformed itself from a French-focused steel company to become the world's leading producer of premium steel tubes in the 21st century.

M. L. Cohen

PRINCIPAL SUBSIDIARIES

Changzhou Valinox Great Wall Welded Tubes (China); CST Valinox Ltd (India); Interfit SAS; P.T. Citra Tubindo (Indonesia; 78.2%); Seamless Tubes Asia Pacific (Singapore); Serimax Ltd; Serimax North America Llc (USA); Serimax Russia SAS; Serimax SAS; Valinox Nucléaire SAS; Valinox Nucléaire Tubes Guangzhou Co. Ltd (China); Vallourec Industries Inc. (USA); Vallourec & Mannesmann Holdings Inc. (USA); Vallourec & Mannesmann Tubes SAS; VAM Canada; VAM Drilling USA Inc.; V & M Star (USA).

PRINCIPAL COMPETITORS

Lone Star Technologies Inc; Sumitomo Corporation; Tenaris SA; United States Steel Corporation.

FURTHER READING

Leboucq, Valérie. "Les Etats-Unis pèsent de plus en plus lourd dans Vallourec." *Les Echos*, March 6, 2003, 15.

———. "Vallourec négocie le rachat de certaines activités de Mannes mann." *Les Echos*, March 10, 2000, 18.

———. "Vallourec veut travailler d'avantage avec les grands constructeurs automobiles." *Les Echos*, March 16, 1998, 13.

Omnes, Catherine. *De l'atelier au groupe industriel, Vallourec 1882–1978*. Paris: éditions de la MSH, 1980.

"Tubes: Vallourec achete l'americain ITP." *Les Echos*, January 8, 2003, 10.

Viacom Inc.

1515 Broadway
New York, New York 10036
U.S.A.
Telephone: (212) 258-6000
Fax: (212) 258-6464
Web site: http://www.viacom.com

Public Subsidiary of National Amusements Inc.
Incorporated: 1971
Employees: 10,900
Sales: $14.91 billion (2011)
Stock Exchanges: New York
Ticker Symbol: VIA
NAICS: 515210 Cable and Other Subscription Programming; 512110 Motion Picture and Video Production; 532230 Video Tape and Disc Rental; 551112 Offices of Other Holding Companies

■ ■ ■

One of the largest media companies in the world, Viacom Inc. operates well-established cable television and motion picture production companies. Viacom cable products include music channels MTV, MTV2, VH-1, and CMT. Children's and family programming from Nickelodeon includes Nick at Night, Nick Jr., Teen-Nick, and NickToons. BET Networks offers African American and multicultural entertainment on the Black Entertainment Television (BET) channel, CENTRIC, BET Gospel, and BET Hip Hop. Other entertainment channels include Spike TV, Comedy Central, and TV Land.

The Filmed Entertainment division produces and distributes original motion pictures, led by legendary Paramount Pictures. Other original film companies under Viacom's purview include Paramount Vantage, MTV Films, and Nickelodeon Movies. Paramount Classics distributes classic films. Viacom distributes movies on DVD and Blu-ray, and licenses content to cable movie stations, including its own joint venture, EPIX, and through online, digital outlets.

FORMATION AND EXPANSION: 1970

Viacom was formed by Columbia Broadcasting System (CBS) in the summer of 1970. CBS did so to comply with regulations by the Federal Communications Commission (FCC) barring television networks from owning cable TV systems or from syndicating their own programs in the United States. Viacom formally became a separate company in 1971 when CBS distributed Viacom's stock to its stockholders at the rate of one share for every seven shares of CBS stock.

Viacom began with 70,000 stockholders and yearly revenues of $19.8 million. It had about 90,000 cable subscribers, making it one of the largest cable operators in the United States. It also had an enviable stable of popular, previously run CBS television series, including *I Love Lucy*, available for syndication, which accounted for a sizable percentage of Viacom's income.

By 1973 there were about 2,800 cable systems in the United States, with about 7.5 million subscribers. This market fragmentation, along with the lack of an infrastructure in many communities and tough federal regulations, slowed the development of cable television. In 1973, Viacom had 47,000 subscribers on Long Island, New York, but a drive to find 2,000 more added only 250.

In 1976, to compete with Home Box Office (HBO), the leading outlet for films in cable, Viacom established the Showtime movie network. Like HBO, Showtime sought to provide its audience with feature films recently released in theaters. Viacom retained half interest in the network while Warner Amex owned the other half. Despite a federal ruling that removed many restrictions on the choice of movies and sports available on pay-TV and allowed a wider variety of programming, Showtime lost $825,000 in 1977. Nevertheless, Viacom earned $5.5 million that year on sales of $58.5 million. Most of the company's earnings represented sales of television series. It also reflected the growth of its own cable systems, which at this time had about 350,000 subscribers.

Showtime continued to compete aggressively with HBO. In 1977 it began transmitting its programming to local cable stations via satellite, at a cost of $1.2 million a year. The following year it worked out a deal with Teleprompter Corp., then the largest cable systems operator in the United States. Teleprompter started to offer its customers Showtime rather than HBO. Showtime also began offering a service channel called Front Row. Dedicated to family programming, including classic movies and children's shows, Front Row cost consumers less than $5 a month and was aimed at smaller cable systems where subscribers could not afford a full-time pay-TV service.

Viacom's forays into the production of original programming in the late 1970s and early 1980s had mixed results. Competition was stiff, the odds of producing a successful television series or film were long, and Viacom experienced several failures. The *Lazarus Syndrome* and *Dear Detective* series were failures, and CBS canceled *Nurse* after 14 episodes.

GROWTH THROUGH ACQUISITION

Cable systems were a capital-intensive business, and Viacom constantly invested money in building its cable infrastructure. In the early 1980s Viacom started on a program of rapid growth across a range of media categories. Company President Terrence A. Elkes told *Business Week* that Viacom hoped to become a billion-dollar company in three to five years. Because management viewed cable operations as not a strong enough engine for that growth, Viacom looked to communications and entertainment. In 1981 it bought Chicago radio station WLAK-FM for $8 million and disclosed its minority stake in Cable Health Network, a new advertiser-supported cable service. It also bought Video Corp. of America for $16 million. That firm's video production equipment stood to save Viacom a great deal of money on production costs.

While its increased size would give Viacom clout with advertisers and advertising agencies, some industry analysts believed that the acquisitions were partly intended to discourage takeover attempts. Buying radio and TV stations increased the firm's debt, and added broadcast licenses to Viacom's portfolio. The transfer of such licenses was a laborious process overseen by the FCC, thereby slowing down attempts to act quickly in taking over a company.

By 1982 Showtime had 3.4 million subscribers, earning $10 million on sales of $140 million, and was seeking to distinguish itself from other pay-TV sources by offering its own series of programs. While Viacom had sales of $210 million, syndication still accounted for a large percentage of Viacom's profits, 45 percent in 1982. The growth rate of syndication had declined, however, while that for cable had increased. By 1982 Viacom had added 450,000 subscribers to the 90,000 it inherited from CBS, making it the ninth-largest cable operator in the United States.

However, a decline in pay-TV's popularity began in 1984, and growth in the industry was virtually halted. In early 1984, Showtime became a sister station to Warner Amex's The Movie Channel in a move calculated to increase sales for both of them. HBO and its sister channel Cinemax were being offered on 5,000 of the 5,800 cable systems in the United States, while Showtime or The Movie Channel were available on 2,700. Besides having a far larger share of the market,

KEY DATES

1970: Viacom is formed by Columbia Broadcasting System (CBS).
1971: Formally made a separate company, Viacom becomes one of the largest cable firms in the United States.
1986: Debt-weakened Viacom is purchased by Sumner M. Redstone.
1994: Company purchases Paramount and Blockbuster.
1996: Viacom spins off cable systems.
2000: Viacom buys CBS Corporation.
2004: Redstone announces intention to step down as CEO; he retains post as chairman.
2005: Company unveils plan to divide Viacom and CBS into two separate companies.
2011: CEO Philippe Dauman restructures Viacom to gain direct control of MTV Networks.

HBO already featured many of the films shown by Showtime and The Movie Channel, removing some of the incentive for subscribing to both groups of services. That year Viacom earned $30.9 million on revenue of $320 million.

MTV NETWORKS PURCHASE: 1985

In September 1985, Viacom purchased MTV Networks and the other half interest in Showtime from Warner Communications, a company that needed cash because its cable interests were suffering in the unfavorable market. As part of the deal Viacom paid Warner $500 million in cash and $18 million in stock warrants. Viacom also offered $33.50 a share for the one-third of MTV stock that was publicly held. The year before Viacom bought it, MTV had made $11.9 million on sales of $109.5 million. Again, these purchases increased Viacom's debt load, making it less attractive for a takeover.

MTV Networks included MTV, a popular music video channel; Nickelodeon, a channel geared toward children; and VH-1, a music video channel geared toward an older audience than that of MTV. The most valuable property in MTV Networks was MTV itself. Its quick pace and flashy graphics were becoming highly influential in the media, and its young audience was a chief target of advertisers.

Established by Warner Amex in 1979 in response to a need for children's cable programming, Nickelodeon

had not achieved any notable success until acquired by Viacom. Viacom quickly revamped Nickelodeon, giving it the slick, flashy look of MTV and unique programming that both appealed to children and distinguished the network from such competitors as The Disney Channel. Viacom also introduced "Nick at Night," a block of classic sitcoms aired late in the evening, popular among an adult audience. In the next few years Nickelodeon went from being the least popular channel on basic cable to the most popular.

Showtime, however, lost about 300,000 customers between March 1985 and March 1986, and cash flow dropped dramatically. In 1986 Showtime embarked on an expensive and risky attempt to gain market share. While Showtime and archrival HBO had each featured exclusive presentations of some films, many films were shown on both networks. In order to eliminate this duplication, Showtime gained exclusive rights to several popular films and guaranteed its customers a new film, unavailable on other movie channels, every week. However, Showtime's move increased the price of acquiring even limited rights to a film at a time when many industry observers felt that the price of buying films for pay-TV should be decreasing since the popularity of videocassette recorders had lowered their worth. Consequently, the cost of programming was raised, and Showtime was forced to increase marketing expenditures to make certain potential viewers were aware of the new policy.

Weakened by the $2 billion debt load it incurred, in part, to scare off unfriendly buyers, Viacom lost $9.9 million on sales of $919.2 million in 1986 and, ironically, became a takeover target. First Carl Icahn made an attempt to buy the company, and then a management buyout led by Terrence Elkes failed. Finally, after a six-month battle, Sumner M. Redstone, president of the National Amusements Inc. movie theater chain, bought Viacom for $3.4 billion in March 1986. Some industry analysts felt that he had vastly overpaid, but Redstone believed Viacom had strong growth potential. Aside from its cable properties and syndication rights that now included the popular series *The Cosby Show*, Viacom owned five television and eight radio stations in major markets.

Redstone had already built National Amusements, the family business, from 50 drive-in movie theaters to a modern chain with 350 screens. Now faced with the task of turning Showtime around, he brought in Frank Biondi, former chief executive of HBO, who began organizing the company's many units into a cooperative workforce. Biondi in turn brought in HBO executive Winston Cox to run the network. Cox immediately doubled Showtime's marketing budget. Showtime also obtained exclusive contracts with Paramount Pictures and Walt Disney films, which included the rights to air seven of the top 10 films of 1986.

TURNING VIACOM AROUND: LATE EIGHTIES

Redstone's banks were demanding $450 million in interest in the first two years following the takeover, but several fortuitous events aided him in paying off this debt. Shortly after the buyout Viacom began to earn millions from television stations wanting to show reruns of *The Cosby Show*. Furthermore, when Congress deregulated cable in 1987, prices for cable franchises soared. When Redstone sold some of Viacom's assets to help pay off its debt, he was thus able to get large sums for them. In February 1989 Viacom's Long Island and suburban Cleveland cable systems were sold to Cablevision Systems Corporation for $545 million, or about 20 times their annual cash flow. Cablevision also bought a 5 percent stake in Showtime for $25 million, giving it a tangible interest in the channel's success.

After Redstone restructured MTV and installed a more aggressive advertising-sales staff, MTV experienced continued growth, against the expectations of many industry analysts. In 1989, for example, MTV Networks won 15 percent of all dollars spent on cable advertising. MTV was expanding throughout the world, broadcasting to Western Europe, Japan, Australia, and large portions of Latin America, with plans to further expand into Eastern Europe, Poland, Brazil, Israel, and New Zealand.

These successes enabled Redstone and Biondi to significantly cut Viacom's debt by September 1989 and negotiate more favorable terms on its loans. Even so, it was rough going at first. Viacom lost $154.4 million in 1987, although its sales increased to about $1 billion.

Under its new leadership Viacom branched out. Along with The Hearst Corporation and Capital Cities/ABC Inc. it introduced Lifetime, a channel geared toward women. It also started its own production operations in 1989, Viacom Pictures, which produced 10 feature films in 1989 at an average cost of $4 million a film. These films appeared first on Showtime. Viacom's television productions also achieved success after years of mixed results. Viacom produced the hit series *Matlock* for NBC and *Jake and the Fatman* for CBS. It also added the rights for *A Different World* and *Roseanne* to its rerun stable. In addition, Viacom continued to spend heavily on new and acquired productions for Nickelodeon and MTV.

In October 1989, Viacom sold 50 percent of Showtime to TCI, a cable systems operator, for $225 million.

TCI had six million subscribers, and Viacom hoped the purchase would give TCI increased incentive to market Showtime, thus giving the network a wider distribution. By 1989 Viacom owned five television stations, 14 cable franchises, and nine radio stations. In November of that year the company bought five more radio stations for $121 million. Sales for the year were about $1.4 billion, with profits of $369 million. In 1990, Viacom introduced a plan that halved the cost of Showtime but forced cable operators to dramatically increase the number of subscriptions to it. This strategy was designed to increase Showtime's market share at a time when many consumers were starting to feel that pay-TV channels were no longer worth their price.

Several months after HBO introduced its Comedy Channel in 1989, Viacom began transmitting HA!, a channel similar in format. Both channels provided comedy programs, but HA! primarily showed episodes of old sitcoms, while the Comedy Channel showed excerpts from sitcoms, movies, and standup comedy routines. Both channels started with subscriber bases in the low millions, and most industry analysts believed that only one of them would survive. Viacom management expected to lose as much as $100 million over a three-year period before HA! broke even. The two companies considered merging their comedy offerings, but HBO parent Time Warner would move forward with the idea only if Viacom agreed to settle its $2.4 billion antitrust suit against HBO.

Showtime had filed the lawsuit in 1989, alleging that HBO was trying to put Showtime out of business by intimidating cable systems that carried Showtime and by trying to corner the market on Hollywood films to prevent competitors from airing them. The suit attracted wide attention and generated much negative publicity for the cable industry.

In August 1992 the suit was finally settled out of court, after having cost both sides tens of millions of dollars in legal fees. Time Warner agreed to pay Viacom $75 million and buy a Viacom cable system in Milwaukee for $95 million, about $10 million more than its estimated worth at the time. Time Warner also agreed to more widely distribute Showtime and The Movie Channel on Time Warner's cable systems, the second largest in the United States. Furthermore, the two sides also agreed to a joint marketing campaign to revive the image of cable, which had suffered since deregulation. In a move that surprised many industry analysts, HBO and Viacom agreed to merge their struggling comedy networks. HA! and the Comedy Channel became Comedy Central, which ultimately experienced great success.

Overall, Viacom appeared to be thriving. In 1993 the company's net income reached $66 million, earned on revenues of $1.9 billion. Nickelodeon, meanwhile, was going to 57.4 million homes, and was watched by more children between ages two and 11 than the children's programming on all four major networks combined. Nickelodeon's earnings were estimated as $76 million in 1992 on sales of $190 million.

By the mid-1990s, Redstone was ready for a new challenge. The 70-year-old media mogul found it by expanding Viacom into the motion picture and video rental markets. In July 1994 Viacom purchased Paramount Communications Inc., one of the world's largest and oldest producers of motion pictures and television shows. The deal, which cost approximately $8 billion, elevated Viacom to the fifth-largest media company in the world. The acquisition vastly expanded the company's presence in the entertainment business, giving it a motion picture library that included the classics *The Ten Commandments* and *The Godfather* and an entree into the premier movie market. Moreover, in the Paramount deal Viacom gained ownership of Simon & Schuster, Inc., one of the world's largest book publishers.

Later that same year, the company again expanded into a new segment of the entertainment industry by acquiring Blockbuster, the owner, operator, and franchiser of thousands of video and music stores. The Blockbuster group of subsidiaries was one of Viacom's most quickly growing enterprises. By 1997, Blockbuster boasted 60 million cardholders worldwide and over 6,000 music and video stores.

Viacom's acquisition of Paramount and Blockbuster gave the company thriving new enterprises, but left the company in significant debt. To both relieve that debt and focus the company's energies, Viacom divested several segments of its business. In 1995 the company sold the operations of Madison Square Garden to a partnership of ITT Corporation and Cablevision Systems for $1.07 billion. In 1996, the company spun off its cable systems in a deal with TCI. Although the split-off represented a break with Viacom's origins as a cable provider, the deal relieved the company of $1.7 billion in debt. The following year, Viacom left the radio broadcasting business by selling its 10 radio stations to Evergreen Media Corporation. The approximately $1.1 billion deal reduced Viacom's debt even further.

Although Viacom was no longer a cable service provider, its cable networks remained a significant portion of its business. MTV Networks, which included MTV, Nickelodeon, and VH1, accounted for almost $625 million in operating profits in 1997, ap-

proximately 32 percent of Viacom's estimated earnings for the year.

By June 1998, Viacom more than recovered from the hit it had taken from the Blockbuster purchase. A joint production of the movie *Titanic* saw spectacular box-office receipts, and the sell-off of most of Simon & Schuster book publishing operations brought in $4.6 billion. A new strategy for Blockbuster drove up its sagging market share. Furthermore, Viacom was on a global expansion drive, selling broadcast rights to Paramount's film library, for example. Under Tom Freston, MTV became an international brand as well. Following from these successes, the company's stock equaled its 1995 high.

CREATING SYNERGY: 1999–2004

In 1999, Redstone held about $9 billion worth of Viacom shares. The company's stock outshined rivals Time Warner, Disney, and News Corporation. That year, Viacom announced plans to buy out CBS Corporation for $37 billion in stock. The heydays of network television were in the past. CBS's cash flow for the year would come from cable, radio, stations, and billboards. Cable ranked first among profitable segments of the entertainment business during the decade, with radio close behind.

CBS had made an early stab into cable in 1981, but the effort tanked. The "Tiffany Network" steered away from the medium after that, but its direct competitors, ABC, NBC, and Fox, made inroads. The tide turned thanks to CEO Mel Karmazin and his predecessor Michael Jordan. "Not until 1997 did Jordan and Karmazin lead CBS back into cable by buying two music channels, the Nashville Network and County Music Television, for $1.5 billion," Marc Gunther wrote for *Fortune.*

Redstone had his eye on those channels and proposed an exchange of Viacom television stations for the country channels. Karmazin, however, convinced Redstone of the synergistic benefits of merging the two media giants and the deal was completed in May 2000. Redstone relinquished "effective operating control" of the merged company to Karmazin, according to the *Wall Street Journal* in 2003. Wall Street applauded the move, respectful of Karmazin's record in financial management and operational details as head of CBS.

A few years down the road, it became less and less likely that Karmazin would succeed Redstone. Not only did the pair have an uneasy relationship, but Karmazin failed to meet earnings targets from 2001 to 2003. Moreover, Redstone wanted back some of the power he had relinquished.

Despite the three-year deal they arrived at in 2003, in June 2004 Karmazin resigned. Redstone named MTV's Tom Freston and CBS's Leslie Moonves copresidents, setting up a competition between them for his heir apparent. Television, radio, and outdoor segments reported to Moonves, and cable networks, entertainment, and video, to Freston. Television had produced 29 percent of Viacom's 2003 consolidated revenues; followed by video at 22 percent; cable networks, 21 percent; entertainment, 15 percent; radio, 8 percent; and outdoor, 5 percent.

Significantly, Redstone was prepared to finally step down as CEO, something he said he would do within the next three years. Gunther wrote for *Fortune*, "Until now the 81-year-old Redstone had stubbornly refused to set a date for his retirement. No one can force him out, because he controls 71% of the shareholder votes at $27 billion-a-year Viacom."

SPIN-OFF OF CBS AND OTHER SURPRISES: 2006–11

In June 2005 Redstone announced a plan to split CBS and Viacom into two independent public companies. The value of the shares would be evenly split, with Viacom stockholders receiving one share of CBS and one share of Viacom stock in exchange for two shares of existing Viacom stock.

Redstone stepped down as CEO, and operations were split along the lines of responsibilities previously assigned to Moonves and Freston. Hence, Moonves became chief executive officer of CBS, and Freston chief executive of Viacom, which retained MTV Networks and Paramount Pictures. Blockbuster had become a separate company in 2004. Redstone remained active as chairman of Viacom.

Redstone intended the split to allow the value of each company to emerge. However, that did not happen. With investors concerned whether Viacom could meet new competition from Internet companies, Viacom's stock value dropped. Redstone blamed Freston, especially after he lost a negotiation to acquire social networking site myspace.com to News Corp. Over Labor Day weekend in 2006, Redstone shocked the industry when he fired Freston.

Redstone moved longtime board member Philippe Dauman to the chief executive position. Dauman brought in board member James Tooley as chief administrative officer, later chief operating officer. Dauman was expected to bring an entrepreneurial attitude to the company, particularly in finding opportunities on the Internet to attract young audiences.

Other shakeups at Viacom involved Paramount Pictures. Redstone canceled Paramount's contract with Tom Cruise's production company, due to Cruise's recent odd behavior. However, it was expected that DreamWorks SKG, purchased in 2005, would more than compensate for the loss of revenue. During its short time as a subsidiary of Paramount, DreamWorks produced successful films, including *Norbit*, *Disturbia*, *Transformers*, and *Iron Man*. Creative conflicts, however, led to the separation of the two companies in 2007.

An unexpected development at Paramount in 2008 involved a decision not to sell movie rights to Showtime. Instead, Dauman planned to establish a new cable channel with Lions Gate and MGM, also suppliers to Showtime. To industry observers, it seemed odd that two cable channels owned by Redstone would be competing against each other. Nevertheless, Viacom launched EPIX in 2009. Although Viacom offered the cable channel at low rates, with consumers spending less on entertainment, EPIX did not generate much enthusiasm.

The Internet continued to be a major concern as the chief new competitor, particularly for young audiences. During this time Viacom became embroiled in a number of lawsuits in regard to copyright infringement. Streaming digital content provided new opportunities for movie licensing and distribution, and Viacom wanted to control those profitable opportunities. The online site Hulu presented new opportunities for distribution of television content. MTV Networks' Comedy Central licensed *The Daily Show with Jon Stewart* and *The Colbert Report*, available online the day after airing on television. *Jersey Shore* was offered on Hulu Plus, the paid subscription service.

Industry observers thought that Brad Grey, at the helm of Paramount since 2004, might be the next executive to be fired. Grey was having a highly successful run of films, including *There Will Be Blood* (2007), *No Country for Old Men* (2008), *Star Trek* (2009), *Paranormal Activity* (2009), and *True Grit* (2010).

At Nickelodeon ratings improved significantly with original programming, such as *Big Time Rush*, a series about a rock band comprising young boys. The live-action show *iCarly*, popular with children 11 and under, featured a girl creating her own online show. New channels targeted specific audiences, such as Nicktoons for boys ages six to 11, Nick Jr. for preschoolers, and Teen-Nick for young people ages 12 to 17. Nickelodeon struggled to create animation series that would compete with The Disney Channel, however.

Nickelodeon Movies sought to compete with Disney on family movies. Following the eponymous film inspired by the Nickelodeon TV series *SpongeBob SquarePants* (2004), and after some delay due to management shakeups, Nickelodeon produced some promising movies. Among these was the animated production *Rango* (2011), featuring the voice talents of popular actor Johnny Depp, among others. *The Last Airbender* (2010), although a critical failure, was a box-office success. Films in development included one designed for Miranda Cosgrove, star of *iCarly*.

Dauman sought to exert direct control over more of the programming at Viacom. In January 2011 he created Viacom International Media Networks and moved MTV Networks International under its umbrella. Despite the success MTV Networks was having at Nickelodeon and with MTV hit shows *Jersey Shore* and *Teen Mom*, Dauman fired Judy McGrath, head of MTV Networks, the following May. He eliminated her position and all of the executives heading Nickelodeon, Comedy Central, VH-1, and MTV began reporting directly to Dauman.

Scott M. Lewis
Updated, Susan Windisch Brown;
Kathleen Peippo; Mary Tradii

PRINCIPAL SUBSIDIARIES

Paramount Classics; Paramount Pictures; Paramount Vantage; MTV Films; MTV Networks; Nickelodeon Movies; BET Networks; VH-1, Inc.

PRINCIPAL DIVISIONS

Filmed Entertainment; Media Networks.

PRINCIPAL OPERATING UNITS

BET Networks; The Entertainment Group; Kids and Family Group; MTV Networks International; Music and Logo Group; Theatrical Group; Home Entertainment Group.

PRINCIPAL COMPETITORS

Dreamworks SKG; Liberty Media Corporation; NBCUniversal Media, LLC.; News Corporation; Time Warner, Inc.; The Walt Disney Company.

FURTHER READING

Atlas, Riva. "Paramount, Anyone?" *Forbes*, May 23, 1994, 264.

Barnes, Brooks. "Making Sure Nickelodeon Hangs with the Cool Kids." *New York Times*, October 31, 2010, 1.

Berkowitz, Harry. "Company President Leaves, Karmazin Steps Down at Viacom, Surprise Resignation follows Often-Rocky Relationship with CEO Redstone." *Newsday*, June 2, 2004, A2.

Carter, Bill, and Geraldine Fabrikant. "Another Split at Viacom." *New York Times*, September 6, 2006, C1.

"Dauman Digs in; Viacom Chief Fills McGrath Role after Ouster." *New York Post*, May 6, 2011, 47.

Flint, Joe. "Final Cut: Karmazin Leaves Post, Ending a Stormy Marriage." *Wall Street Journal*, June 2, 2004.

Gubernick, Lisa. "Sumner Redstone Scores Again." *Forbes*, October 31, 1988.

Gunther, Marc. "Behind the Shakeup at Viacom." *Fortune*, June 28, 2004, 34.

———. "Sumner ♡? Mel: CBS, Viacom, and the Triumph of Cable." *Fortune*, October 11, 1999, 54+.

———. "This Gang Controls Your Kids' Brains." *Fortune*, October 27, 1997, 172–78.

———. "Viacom: Redstone's Remarkable Ride to the Top." *Fortune*, April 26, 1999, 130+.

"How Much for Ads on Children's TV? A Million and a Half Dollars, if They Violate F.C.C. Rules." *New York Times*, October 22, 2004.

Impoco, Jim. "America's Hippest Grandpa." *U.S. News & World Report*, September 27, 1993, 67.

Lazaroff, Leon. "Viacom Prepares to Battle FCC over $550,000 Indecency Fine." *Knight-Ridder/Tribune Business News*, November 10, 2004.

Lenzner, Robert, and Peter Newcomb. "The Vindication of Sumner Redstone." *Forbes*, June 15, 1998, 50+.

Lieberman, David. "Is Viacom Ready to Channel the World?" *Business Week*, December 18, 1989.

Peers, Martin. "Leading the News: Viacom Is near Deal to Retain Top Management." *Wall Street Journal*, March 20, 2003, A3.

"Viacom Completes Split into 2 Companies." *New York Times*, January 2, 2006, C2.

"Viacom's Risky Quest for Growth." *Business Week*, June 21, 1982.

Vulcan, Inc.

505 Fifth Avenue South, Suite 900
Seattle, Washington 98104
U.S.A.
Telephone: (206) 342-2000
Fax: (206) 342-3000
Web site: http://www.vulcan.com

Private Company
Incorporated: 1986 as Vulcan Northwest Inc.
Employees: 500
Sales: $982.3 million (2010 est.)
NAICS: 511210 Software Publishers; 523910 Miscellaneous Intermediation; 711211 Sports Teams and Clubs; 813211 Grantmaking Foundations

■ ■ ■

Vulcan, Inc., manages the business and philanthropic interests of Paul Allen, the billionaire cofounder of Microsoft. Vulcan's holdings include the Portland Trail Blazers and Seattle Seahawks pro sports teams, the Experience Music Project rock-and-roll museum, the Paul Allen Institute for Brain Science, numerous investments in new-technology businesses, and 60 acres of real estate in Seattle. Allen also continues to hold a minority stake in Microsoft, and controls about a third of cable giant Charter Communications, which filed for bankruptcy protection in 2009. His charitable giving, made in part through the Paul G. Allen Family Foundation, has provided nearly $1 billion to support community development, forest conservation, science,

education, and the arts, and he has pledged to eventually give away more than half his fortune.

BEGINNINGS

Vulcan Inc. dates its founding to 1986, when Paul Allen created Vulcan Northwest to manage his business and charitable interests. Allen, born in Seattle in 1953 to a pair of University of Washington librarians, had developed a passionate interest in computers as a teen, and dropped out of college to write software with childhood friend Bill Gates. In 1975 the pair founded Micro-Soft in Albuquerque, New Mexico, and after moving back to Seattle four years later, Microsoft (the hyphen having been dropped) was chosen to create the operating system for IBM's first personal computer. After its successful 1981 debut, the small company's sales mushroomed, and Gates and Allen became millionaires, and within a decade billionaires.

In 1983 Allen was diagnosed with Hodgkin's disease, a cancer, and quit Microsoft to focus on his family and grueling treatments that included a bone marrow transplant and radiation. Although no longer involved with Microsoft's day-to-day operations, he retained a sizable minority ownership stake and a position on the company's board.

Two years later Allen was declared cancer-free, but rather than rejoining Microsoft he decided to focus on other interests. He first founded a software company, Asymetrix, which began work on a spreadsheet/database program, and in 1986 created Vulcan Northwest (named after the Roman god of fire) to act as a holding company. During the year Microsoft made its initial

COMPANY PERSPECTIVES

Paul G. Allen founded Vulcan Inc. in 1986 with Jo Lynn Allen to manage his business and charitable endeavors.

Those endeavors include the creation of innovative technologies, award-winning films and vibrant new neighborhoods. They're about the revolution of rock 'n roll, the humanity of science fiction, and the poetry of a fingertip catch. They're about reaching from the tiniest genome to the very stratosphere, and most importantly, about improving the way people live, learn, do business, and experience the world.

Ours is compelling and diverse work, driven by strong business strategies and a unique vision. Take a look at our portfolio and you'll find an impressive range of projects, a track record of growth, and an abiding commitment to the part of the world in which we live.

Vulcan is focused on where the future lies, and we're excited to be on the journey there.

public offering (IPO), which whittled Allen's ownership stake down to 28 percent and netted him $175 million on the sale of 200,000 shares.

PORTLAND TRAIL BLAZERS PURCHASE: 1988

In 1988 sports fan Allen bought the National Basketball Association's Portland Trail Blazers for $70 million, and later put up a sizable portion of the funding for a new arena, the $262 million Rose Garden. During the year Allen launched the first of what would become six charitable giving organizations, whose grants included the single largest conservation gift in Washington history to preserve thousands of acres of pristine forest. Like many of his other ventures, Allen's charitable arm was managed by his sister Jo Lynn (Jody) Allen Patton, 41, who had taken on the duties of overseeing and implementing her brother's visions.

In 1990 Allen also launched investment arm Vulcan Ventures, which bought a stake in such new-technology businesses as software retail chain Egghead and satellite broadcaster SkyPix, although these, as well as a number of others, did not bear fruit. Seeking to generate innovative start-ups himself, in 1992 Allen formed a think tank with David Liddle called Interval Research in

Silicon Valley, pledging $100 million to fund it for 10 years. He also founded a company called Starwave to package data on discs and online, and bought stakes in nascent Internet-based services Telescan, SureFind, and dial-up provider America Online.

The following year more investments were made in communication services Metricom and Lone Wolf, software maker Harbinger-EDI Services, computer hardware manufacturer Cardinal Technologies, and display developer Virtual Vision. Allen also paid $300 million to buy 80 percent of Ticketmaster in 1992, which was the leading provider of tickets to concerts and sporting events in the United States.

In 1994 the Paul Allen Group was founded to manage his investment portfolio, which had grown in value to $800 million. A key area of focus was Allen's vision of the future in which the Web, cable television, and entertainment would converge, which he called the Wired World.

SALE OF AMERICA ONLINE STAKE: 1994

Allen had been steadily acquiring shares of America Online, gaining control of about a quarter of the firm and reportedly selling some 700,000 shares of Microsoft stock to help finance the investment. As his stake grew he began to butt heads with CEO Steve Case, who resisted Allen's suggestions to connect subscribers to the World Wide Web rather than just its own internal network. After Allen was refused a seat on the company's board and a "poison pill" rule was adopted to limit his ownership, he sold his entire stake. He made a profit of $75 million, although just five years later the shares would have been worth $40 billion and topped the value of his Microsoft holdings, before later crashing following the AOL/Time Warner merger debacle.

In late 1994 Allen also invested $500 million in DreamWorks SKG, making him the single largest investor in the new film studio founded by Hollywood titans Steven Spielberg, Jeffrey Katzenberg, and David Geffen, although his official stake would be 18.5 percent. Allen would also later bankroll other film and entertainment ventures including children's film company Storyopolis, independent moviemaker Clear Blue Sky, and Vulcan Productions. The latter would go on to produce films and television programs that included award-winning titles *Far from Heaven* (2002), PBS miniseries *The Blues* (2003), and *This Emotional Life* (2010).

Having become frustrated with Ticketmaster's slow adoption of online sales, in 1997 Allen traded his stake in the company for an 11 percent share of USA Networks, Inc., also giving up investments in Lone

Wolf, Cardinal, and Virtual Vision. His sports holdings expanded dramatically during the year with the purchase of the Seattle Seahawks NFL football team, however, with his investment of $194 million later followed by $130 million to help build a new $425 million stadium.

MOVE INTO CABLE IN 1999

In 1999 Allen took his Wired World concept to a new level by purchasing cable TV providers Marcus Cable and Charter Communications for $2.8 billion and $4.5 billion, respectively. They were soon merged and in November Charter Communications, as Allen's cable holdings would be known, became a publicly held firm with Allen retaining a majority stake. It continued to roll up other cable providers including Falcon Communications, the third-largest cable company in Los Angeles, in a $20 billion spending spree that added a dozen firms in all. In 1999 Allen also sold one of his most successful ventures to date, ESPN Web site operator Starwave, to Disney for $350 million.

As he pursued the vision of a Wired World, Allen's portfolio grew to include stakes in more than 100 companies including CNET, N2K, U.S. Satellite Broadcasting, Oxygen Media, ZDTV, and Priceline.com. Allen's wealth was now put at $40 billion by *Forbes* in its annual ranking of the well-to-do, making him the second-richest American after Bill Gates. His Microsoft holdings now stood at a reported 5.1 percent.

Paul Allen's interests included rock and roll music, especially that of the late Seattle-born guitar legend Jimi Hendrix, whose musical catalog he had helped his family take control of. He had also assembled a huge collection of memorabilia from Hendrix and other stars, and in June 2000 he opened the Experience Music Project (EMP) museum in Seattle to display his holdings. Allen

had personally funded the $240 million, Frank Gehry-designed building (which cost nearly five times its original estimate) that also housed a foundation to support music and the arts in the region.

In 2000 the bursting of the stock market's technology bubble seriously impacted Allen, who had to write off a number of investments in start-ups that failed. He subsequently restructured Vulcan and let a number of employees go, while boosting the power of his sister Jody, the firm's CEO. During the year he also left Microsoft's board and shuttered Interval Research, which at its peak had employed 120. Although much effort had been put into creating products ranging from video games to wearable computers, and it had received some 300 patents, the think tank had not spawned any successful companies.

Allen lived on a private island in Lake Washington where his sister and mother also had homes, and in addition to several other residences (including Rock Hudson's former Beverly Hills mansion), he had numerous real estate investments in Seattle and elsewhere. In 2001 he spent a reported $100 million for a 303-foot yacht, to which he later added a custom-built, 414-foot model, *Octopus*, whose amenities included two helicopters, a recording studio, and a $12 million, eight-person submarine. The $200 million yacht was ranked the world's largest at the time of its 2003 launch.

FORMATION OF BRAIN SCIENCE INSTITUTE: 2003

In 2003 Allen announced the creation of the Paul Allen Institute for Brain Science. The $100-plus million, multiyear project was charged with mapping the human brain in full detail. Meanwhile, cable operator Charter Communications, which had been struggling to turn a profit in a fiercely competitive industry, had amassed debt of $20 billion and had lost 90 percent of its stock value. The firm was being investigated by the Securities and Exchange Commission (SEC) over accounting irregularities, and several top executives later pleaded guilty to fraud.

In 2004 Allen's six giving units were consolidated into The Paul G. Allen Family Foundation, which would dispense close to $30 million per year to nonprofit organizations in the areas of science and technology, community development and social change, education, and arts and culture. By decade's end it would reach a tally of more than $400 million in grants, with Allen's total charitable giving topping $1 billion. The firm had also adopted the shortened name of Vulcan, Inc. by this time.

Allen also funded numerous projects of a personal nature that included rebuilding his Washington State

University fraternity house for $3 million and buying the tattered Cinerama Theater, which he had attended as a child. He financed a thorough restoration of the landmark 875-seat venue, which had been built to show movies from three synchronized 35-millimeter film projectors onto a huge curved screen. He also underwrote the restoration of Seattle's Union Station, which was next to an office building he had built, donated $18 million to the University of Washington library to build a new wing named after his late father, and funded the $5 million Faye G. Allen Center for Visual Arts, in honor of his mother.

Other endeavors included the creation of the Hospital Club in London to offer a haven for artists, artificial intelligence research unit Project Halo, the online Living Computer Museum, and the STARTUP Gallery in Albuquerque's New Mexico Museum of Natural History and Science, which focused on early microcomputer developments including the beginnings of Microsoft.

SPACESHIPONE WINS X PRIZE IN 2004

In the late 1990s Allen had begun working with aviation pioneer Burt Rutan on an aircraft capable of suborbital flight some 200,000 feet above the earth. *SpaceShipOne* completed two successful flights in the fall of 2004 and was awarded the $10 million X Prize for the first privately funded suborbital space flight. Although it was intended to ultimately carry ticket-buying "space tourists," it was instead donated to the Smithsonian Institution where it was hung in the National Air and Space Museum beside Charles Lindbergh's famed *Spirit of St. Louis*.

In 2004 Allen also opened a limited-access museum called the Flying Heritage Collection at Arlington, Washington, to house a collection of more than a dozen vintage warplanes, primarily from World War II, which he had been buying and restoring. Four years later it would move to a larger site at Paine Field in Everett, Washington. While Allen's pocketbook was sometimes seen as unlimited, he had recently been cutting back staff at Vulcan, the Trail Blazers, and the EMP, where a third of the workforce was let go, bringing the total to less than half its original 500. Attendance at the museum had fallen by 30 percent in the last two years, and since its opening income had dropped by half. During the year the $20 million Science Fiction Museum and Hall of Fame was added to the building, to help boost attendance as well as to display a portion of Allen's collection. Efforts were also being made to broaden the EMP's donor base, with only 1 percent previously having come from sources other than Allen.

In 2007 Allen began reducing his stake in the now publicly traded DreamWorks and also launched the Allen Telescope Array in Northern California to search for signs of intelligent life in the universe. Allen had earlier helped fund the SETI (Search for Extra-Terrestrial Intelligence) Institute, after its federal underwriting was canceled. He also took a minority stake in the new Seattle Sounders FC professional soccer team, and took back ownership of the Trail Blazers' Rose Garden arena, which had fallen into bankruptcy in 2004 over unpaid construction debt.

During 2007 Vulcan Capital and Bankers Group Atlanta formed a joint venture called Vulcan Bankers Group LLC, and the Vulcan FlipStart debuted. The $1,999 lightweight Windows computer was discontinued the following year, however, due to poor sales. In 2008 Allen also sold his remaining shares of DreamWorks SKG for approximately $123 million.

In 2009 Charter Communications and set-top TV recorder maker Digeo, which Allen had invested $110 million in, filed for bankruptcy protection. Digeo was shut down and its assets were liquidated, but in November Charter emerged from bankruptcy. Allen subsequently resigned as board chairman and reduced his voting stake from 98 to 35 percent. At the same time Vulcan also cut its staff of 600 by about 8 percent. During the year Allen was diagnosed with another cancer called non-Hodgkin's lymphoma, but after treatment that included chemotherapy he was again declared cancer-free.

ALLEN PLEDGES TO GIVE HALF HIS WEALTH TO CHARITY IN 2010

In 2010 Bill Gates and Warren Buffett issued a "Giving Pledge" to billionaires to donate half of their wealth to charity, and Allen signed on. Business ventures of this period included a $20 million investment in mobile phone software maker Kiha, $15 million in voice recognition firm Audience, and the creation of Xiant, which would develop software to organize items in Microsoft's Outlook e-mail/scheduling program. Charitable gifts of 2010 included $26 million to Washington State University's School for Global Animal Health, which would help build a new facility and support the school's programs in Africa.

In August 2010 Allen filed suit against a group of major companies including Apple, Google, Facebook, Yahoo!, eBay, Netflix, Staples, and Office Max, alleging infringement on four Interval Licensing patents. The suit was later dismissed because it had not mentioned the specific products involved, and Allen immediately refiled an amended complaint.

Vulcan Real Estate now owned 60 acres in the South Lake Union neighborhood of Seattle, where it managed more than 1.7 million square feet of office space that would soon house the headquarters of Amazon.com and the Bill and Melinda Gates Foundation, among others. The development also included residential units. Vulcan's other real estate holdings included an eight-story office tower in Tempe, Arizona, that had been purchased for $35 million.

In January 2011 Allen further reduced his involvement with Charter Communications by converting his 2.2 million Class B voting shares of stock to Class A common shares, giving up his voting interest as well as his right to appoint board members. He had invested more than $7 billion in the company, but his stock was now worth less than $100 million. During the year Allen also sold 24 wireless-spectrum licenses that he had acquired in Washington and Oregon to AT&T Mobility, and cut the staff of mobile phone software start-up Kiha. The Brain Science institute released its completed map of the human brain, as well.

In April, Allen's memoir *Idea Man* was published, generating mild controversy over its portrayal of early clashes with Bill Gates. He had begun writing the book while undergoing chemotherapy in 2009. By now Allen had fallen in the *Forbes* rankings of the wealthy to number 57, with an estimated $13 billion. Bill Gates, with $56 billion, was second.

Twenty-five years after its founding, Vulcan, Inc. had grown in direct relationship to the ideas and passions of Paul Allen. Although he had not always picked winners in the world of business, Allen's gifts had made immense contributions to the cultural, environmental, and scientific spheres in the Pacific Northwest and elsewhere. In addition to a sizable real estate portfolio and stakes in numerous technology companies including Microsoft, Vulcan operated professional sports teams, museums, entertainment venues, and a research facility, and funded many nonprofit organizations. As long as

Allen continued to follow his heart, it appeared that Vulcan's future would remain vibrant.

Frank Uhle

PRINCIPAL DIVISIONS

The Experience Music Project; Interval Licensing; The Paul G. Allen Family Foundation; Vulcan Capital; Vulcan Productions; Vulcan Real Estate; Vulcan Sports and Entertainment; Vulcan Warbirds.

PRINCIPAL COMPETITORS

Accel Partners; Benchmark Capital Holdings Co., L.L.C.; Bill & Melinda Gates Foundation; Hummer Winblad Venture Partners; Institutional Venture Partners; Kleiner Perkins Caufield & Byers; Seattle Mariners.

FURTHER READING

Allen, Paul. *Idea Man: A Memoir by the Cofounder of Microsoft.* New York: Penguin Group, 2011.

Farrell, Mike. "Charter: Up from the Ashes." *Multichannel News*, December 7, 2009. Accessed November 8, 2011. http://www.multichannel.com/article/438666-Charter_Up_From_The_Ashes.php.

Letzing, John. "Paul Allen's Patent Lawsuit Dismissed." *Marketwatch*, December 13, 2010. Accessed November 8, 2011. http://www.marketwatch.com/story/paul-allens-patent-lawsuit-dismissed-2010-12-13.

Lynch, Jim. "Serious Money: Playful on Outside, Paul Allen Tightens Grip on His Fortune." *Wall Street Journal*, February 29, 2004.

"Paul Allen." In *Leaders of the Information Age*, edited by David Weil. New York: H.W. Wilson, 2003.

Rich, Laura. *The Accidental Zillionaire: Demystifying Paul Allen.* Hoboken, NJ: John Wiley and Sons, 2003.

Richman, Dan. "Building S. Lake Union." *Seattle Post-Intelligencer*, March 10, 2008, E1.

Timmerman, Luke. "Paul Allen Creates New Brain Project with $100 Million." *Seattle Times*, September 16, 2003, 1.

Yardley, William. "Long after Microsoft, Allen and Gates Cast Shadows over City." *New York Times*, April 27, 2011, 16A.

GRACE

W. R. Grace & Co.

7500 Grace Drive
Columbia, Maryland 21044
U.S.A.
Telephone: (410) 531-4000
Fax: (410) 531-4367
Web site: http://www.grace.com

Public Company
Incorporated: 1899
Employees: 6,000
Sales: $2.67 billion (2010)
Stock Exchanges: New York
Ticker Symbol: GRA
NAICS: 325110 Petrochemical Manufacturing; 325131 Inorganic Dye and Pigment Manufacturing; 325188 All Other Inorganic Chemical Manufacturing; 325220 Adhesive Manufacturing; 325998 All Other Miscellaneous Chemical Product and Preparation Manufacturing; 326113 Unsupported Plastics Film and Sheet (Except Packaging) Manufacturing; 326122 Plastics Pipe and Pipe Fitting Manufacturing; 326150 Urethane and Other Foam Product (Except Polystyrene) Manufacturing

■ ■ ■

W. R. Grace & Co. is a specialty chemicals and specialty materials company. Through Grace Davison, which accounts for 67 percent of the company's annual sales, Grace manufactures silica-based products, chemical catalysts, packaging sealants, and refining catalysts. Through the company's Construction Products business segment, Grace manufactures concrete and cement additives, specialty building materials, and fireproofing chemicals. The company operates in more than 40 countries, deriving approximately 70 percent of its annual sales from outside the United States.

PERUVIAN ORIGINS: 1854–65

In 1854 William Russell Grace and his father, James Grace, traveled to Callao, Peru. James, a prosperous Irish landowner, wanted to establish an Irish agricultural community. He hoped to rebuild the family fortune which had been depleted during the Irish famine of 1847–48 when he provided employment to a large number of people from the countryside around his estate. Not finding the prospects he had hoped for in Peru, James soon returned to Ireland.

William, however, remained in Peru and became a clerk in the trading firm of Bryce & Company. His value to the company was recognized after a few years when he was made a partner in the firm, which was then renamed Bryce, Grace & Company. Under William's direction, the commercial house soon became the largest in the country.

Poor health forced William to retire from the Peruvian business in 1865. He returned to New York City where he had spent a year during his youth. His brother, Michael P. Grace, who had joined him earlier in South America, remained behind to manage the growing family business in Peru which was soon named Grace Brothers & Company. With his health fully recovered, William established W. R. Grace & Co. in New York. William had long been a confidant of the Peruvian president, and through this connection the company became the Peruvian government's agent for the sale of nitrate of soda.

The Chile-Peruvian war of 1887–81 severely weakened Peru's economy, and the government had difficulty repaying its foreign debt. In 1887 a group of foreign bondholders in the Peruvian government, mostly British, called on Grace Brothers & Co. to attempt a settlement of the debt.

Michael Grace accepted the offer and in the settlement he negotiated, known as the Grace-Donoughmore Contract, two Peruvian bond issues amounting to $250 million were canceled in exchange for equally valuable concessions to the bondholders. Bondholders received shares in a newly established company, The Peruvian Corporation, which received the rights to two state-owned railroads for 66 years, all Peruvian guano output up to three million tons (except for that on Chincha Island), a government promise to pay shareholders £80,000 annually for 30 years, and ownership of the lucrative Cerro de Pasco silver mines. In return, the shareholders agreed to finish uncompleted railroads and repair existing ones within certain time limits. (Most of the contracts for supplying the railroad-building program went to the Grace company.)

LEADERSHIP CHANGES: 1904–46

When William Grace died in 1904, control of the company passed to his brother Michael, who became chairman. In 1907, he negotiated a new agreement with the Peruvian government annulling the terms of the previous agreements and extending the Peruvian corporation's lease for 17 years. The government agreed to continue paying £80,000 annually to shareholders for 30 years, but made claims to one-half of the company's net proceeds.

William's son, Joseph, who started working for the company's corporate offices in New York in 1894 when he graduated from Columbia University, became president in 1909. The company underwent a period of rapid growth during Joseph's presidency, and, in the process, greatly expanded South American production and trade.

In 1929, the year Joseph became chairman of the board, W. R. Grace and Pan American Airways together established the first international air service down the west coast of South America, Pan American Grace Airways, otherwise known as Panagra.

After suffering from a stroke in 1946, Joseph retired. A feud subsequently broke out among family members over who should run the company. Eventually, Joseph prevailed, and his son, J. Peter, after some misgivings of his own, became president.

GEOGRAPHIC EXPANSION: 1946–69

At the age of 32, Peter inherited a company with $93 million in assets and whose primary interests were in Grace Steamship Lines, Grace National Bank, Panagra, sugar plantations, and cotton mills in Peru and Chile. The company also produced paper and biscuits, mined tin, and grew coffee.

From the very beginning, Peter was concerned about the political and economic instability of South American nations, which he believed threatened Grace's operations. In particular, many companies had shown resistance to U.S. domination of their economies. With what proved to be remarkable foresight, Peter embarked on a plan of diversifying into U.S. and European investments, seeking to reduce South American investments from 100 percent to 5 percent. To raise the capital necessary for his expansion the company went public on the New York Stock Exchange in 1953. The board of directors resisted his plan of broadening investment and, although the Grace family owned more than one-half of the company's stock, he nearly lost his position as CEO.

Attracted by profits achieved by Du Pont, Peter began searching for investments in the chemical industry. He purchased two major chemical companies which made Grace the nation's fifth-largest chemical producer. In 1954 Grace completed a merger with Davison Chemical Corporation, a manufacturer of agricultural and industrial chemicals. Later that year, Grace purchased Dewey & Almy Chemical Company. A producer of sealing compounds and batteries, Dewey & Almy grew rapidly and earnings quickly surpassed the $35 million purchase price.

This became the foundation for one of the world's largest specialty chemical operations. Over the next 11 years, Grace acquired 23 more chemical companies for four million shares of stock. Seeking to enter markets that could compensate for the cyclic nature of the fertil-

KEY DATES

1854: William Russell Grace becomes a partner in Bryce, Grace & Company, in Peru.

1865: The company, now called W. R. Grace & Co., moves to New York.

1953: W. R. Grace & Co. lists on New York Stock Exchange.

1954: Davison Chemical Company and Dewey & Almy Chemical Company are acquired.

1992: First asbestos-related lawsuit is filed against W. R. Grace.

1999: Headquarters are relocated from Boca Raton, Florida, to Columbia, Maryland.

2001: W. R. Grace files for bankruptcy protection.

2008: Company agrees to pay $1.8 billion to settle asbestos-related lawsuits.

2011: Federal judge confirms Grace's bankruptcy reorganization plan.

izer industry, Grace set out to build the "General Foods of Europe." Over the decade, Peter Grace purchased a chocolate producer in the Netherlands, a Danish ice cream maker, and an Italian pasta company.

Peter continued selling the company's old businesses and using the money to acquire new ones. In 1965 he sold Grace National Bank to Marine Midland Trust (later named Marine Midland Bank). The next year he acquired a 53 percent interest in Miller Brewing Company, but relations soon soured with an heir to the brewing company's founder, leading to the sale of the equity stake for $130 million in 1969. In 1967 Peter sold the company's 50 percent interest in Pan American Grace Airways to Braniff Airways for $15 million.

In the early 1960s, the company management had reversed its previous policy in regard to South American investment and began pouring funds into paper, food, and chemical companies. Later that year, however, Grace's fears about these investments came true when the Peruvian government seized the company's sugar mills and a 25,000-acre sugar plantation. Earnings on South American operations tumbled from $12 million the previous year to zero on sales of $256 million.

DIVERSIFICATION: 1971–79

In the early 1970s, W. R. Grace made a move into consumer goods. In 1970 the company purchased Baker & Taylor, a supplier of books to libraries, as well as FAO

Schwarz, the New York toy store. Hoping to cash in on the country's love affair with leisure-time activities, the company acquired Herman's World of Sporting, a landmark in New York's financial district. Grace saw a chance for substantial returns in the sporting goods business. Involvement in the market was especially attractive since there were no national sporting goods chain stores. Department stores, preferring the profits and turnover of apparel and other soft product lines, had shunned sporting goods. The company sought to expand Herman's from three stores with $10 million in sales into the first national chain. As part of the plan, Grace bought Mooney's of Boston, Atlas of Washington, and Klein's of Chicago and converted them to Herman's sporting goods stores.

In 1974 Peter began to reduce the company's holdings by selling a grocery products venture, and began to concentrate company investments in three areas: consumer goods, chemicals, and natural resources. Fertilizer profits had rebounded because of low supply and high worldwide demand, but the consumer groups showed lackluster profits even with large sales in sporting goods. In addition, Grace's final investment in Peru was severed later in the year. The Peruvian government nationalized its paper and chemical operations, leading to a loss of $11.5 million for the company, despite $23.6 million in compensation from the government.

By 1976 the company was ready to continue its move into consumer goods and services. Later in the year, when the company was about to make a public stock offering to raise capital for further expansion, it received an offer from Peter's old friend Friedrich Karl Flick, who during the 1950s had worked for Grace National Bank for three years. Flick, head of Friedrich Flick Industrial Corporation, Germany's largest family-owned company, was looking for somewhere to invest the $900 million it had recently made from the sale of its 29 percent interest in Daimler-Benz to Deutsche Bank. Wanting to take advantage of German laws that granted tax-free capital gains and dividends earned on investments of more than 25 percent ownership in foreign companies, Flick eventually bought a 30 percent stake in Grace.

The consumer division's growth accompanied increasing internal strife at the company. In 1979, after years of watching the company's stock trading at low earnings multiples, management proposed splitting up the company into seven or eight separate companies which would command higher stock prices. Worried about the company's increasing reliance on consumer products, they also suggested selling the energy division whose market value could have been as much as $1 billion over book value. Peter, unwilling to give up his control of the company which might also have resulted from these proposals, rejected both ideas.

THE BEGINNING OF SPECIALIZATION: 1981–89

At the beginning of the 1980s, Grace's move into natural resources appeared as if it was going to be as profitable as its venture into chemicals. The company's energy reserves had grown to 73 million barrels of oil, 300 billion cubic feet of natural gas, and 239 million tons of coal. Specialty chemicals sales and earnings, meanwhile, rose an average of 15 percent annually over the last decade. The company had 85 product lines, ranging from plastic packaging materials to petroleum cracking catalysts, many of which were market leaders.

However, the company suffered with falling energy prices in 1981. Moreover, in 1982, the combination of a poor natural resources profit and a further decline in the fertilizer business led to a 50 percent decrease in the company's profitability. As a result, Grace petroleum was put up for sale in 1984. The retail and consumer goods divisions, which were returning just 14 percent of profits on 36 percent of sales, looked as if they might be next.

At the same time, however, Grace began to pursue business interests that would eventually become the main focus of the company, specialty chemicals and materials. Particularly significant was the 1985 acquisition of Chomerics, Inc., a packaging and coating manufacturer. The company, which had been losing money, was acquired through a $99 million stock swap. The company's problems were compounded in 1984, when Flick became the target of a government bribery scandal and was forced to confront a $260 million tax bill. Rumors abounded in West Germany that Flick was looking for someone to buy the family business, putting Grace at risk of a hostile takeover.

THE END OF THE PETER GRACE ERA: 1993

The rumors about Flick proved true when Deutsche Bank acquired the company and put its holdings in Grace on the market. The company immediately seized the attention of takeover specialists. GAF Corporation Chairman J. Heynian approached Grace about a friendly takeover, causing Grace's stock to rise 30 percent. Although already strapped for cash, Peter, fearing a takeover, was forced to buy Flick's holdings for $598 million. The acquisition put Grace's debt at $2.6 billion and caused a downgrade of Grace's credit rating.

Critics, both inside and outside the company, regarded this as an unthinking decision. Complaints

about Peter's domination of the company and an incoherent business strategy put mounting pressure on him to sell the consumer division. Because Grace was desperate for cash, this forced Peter to comply. Energy and fertilizer investments were reduced. Herman's was sold to Dee Corporation for $227 million, realizing a profit of $144 million. The remaining consumer goods businesses were sold for $500 million, but because of high expansion costs at the 317-store home center operations, Grace barely broke even on the sale. In addition, in 1986, Peter agreed to sell 51 percent of the restaurant division to its management in a leveraged buyout, although Grace did not bail out of the newly created Restaurant Enterprises Group until 1993.

In January 1993 Peter Grace stepped down as CEO, ending the longest term of any CEO until that time. His successor, J. P. Balduc, had been groomed for the position since joining Grace in 1983, eventually becoming COO and president in 1990. Balduc took the reins of an ambitious restructuring plan. First announced in 1991, this plan was to cut back Grace's operations to two lines of business, specialty chemicals and health care, and called for a divestment of 25 percent of the company's assets. Although Peter Grace retained his position as chairman, it was clear that Balduc was in charge as the company began to lose all resemblance to a family-run operation, becoming more like a standard corporation.

NEW LEADERSHIP AND DIVESTITURES: 1993–99

This transformation, it seemed, was long overdue. Although Grace topped $6 billion a year in sales in 1993, its profit on those sales was only $26 million, and the sprawling company was so heavily diversified that it owned over 100 subsidiaries. When Balduc trimmed it to six core businesses, the sold-off assets, which included divisions ranging from organic chemicals to restaurants to book distribution, were worth nearly $1.5 billion. Some argued, reflecting the emphasis on specialization in business that had become a 1990s trend, that even six was too much, particularly when the six ranged from specialty chemicals to health care to food packaging. Under Balduc's leadership, health care emerged as the most prominent part of Grace's business, in the form of the National Medical Care division, and the company's goal of $10 billion by 2000 seemed possible.

In March 1995 Balduc abruptly resigned from Grace, citing philosophical differences with the board of directors, paving the way for the appointment of Albert J. Costello as CEO. If anything, Costello was more aggressive about streamlining the company than his predecessor. This included spinning off Grace's medical care division, National Medical Care, in a sale to German-based medical company Fresenius AG. A series of divestitures followed. Grace sold its Dearborn water treatment business, then the third largest in the United States, to Betz Laboratories. It sold its transgenic plant business to Monsanto, its TEC systems division to Sequa Corporation, its specialty polymers business to National Starch and Chemical Co., and its cocoa business to Archer Daniels Midland. Other actions included a buyback of 10 million shares of common stock, amounting to approximately 10 percent of the total, as well as a new two-year corporate reorganization, begun late in 1995.

Costello was not focused only on selling, however. While Grace's divestments had increased its value and decreased its liability, its CEO sought acquisitions and joint ventures in keeping with the company's newer, narrower focus. In April 1998 Grace's remaining divisions essentially split. The specialty chemicals divisions, consisting of Grace Davison, Grace Construction Products, and Darex Container Products, kept the W. R. Grace name, while the Cryovac packaging business merged with Sealed Air Corporation. Now in essence a chemicals company, W. R. Grace & Co. bore no remaining resemblance to its namesake's initial venture.

In November 1998 leadership changed hands again. This time the new name was former Allied-Signal executive Paul Norris, who was named president and CEO, and was slated to take the chairman position as well. Norris immediately announced a plan of divestiture, streamlining, and job cutting. The following year, Grace moved its corporate headquarters from Boca Raton, Florida, where it had been quartered since 1991, to Columbia, Maryland, the location of its specialty chemicals division. The move cut costs both by reducing staff and by moving the headquarters closer to its business divisions. Also in 1999, Grace cut 370 jobs, or approximately 8 percent of its workforce, as part of a restructuring designed to streamline the company still further.

By 2000 it appeared that Norris had succeeded in his aim. W. R. Grace had slimmed down from a $5.7 billion conglomerate to a $1.5 billion company specializing in chemicals. Instead of 30 business divisions, it had only two, Grace Davison and its performance chemicals division. In 1999 the company had $1.47 billion in sales, with a goal of 15 percent earnings growth for 2000. By 2001 Norris intended to reach the $2 billion sales mark, partly through acquisitions, partly through the introduction of new products, and to boost the company's sagging stock price.

ASBESTOS LITIGATION PORTENDS DISASTER: 2001

With the new millennium, Grace faced formidable problems on the legal front, not the first time the company had faced a courtroom battle. A high-profile pollution case in 1986 pitted Grace against eight families in Woburn, Massachusetts, over the question of drinking-water contamination, which Grace settled for a reported $8 million. In 1995 Grace's patent on the extraction of the natural pesticide azadirachtin from Indian neem trees was challenged, as the substance had been used for that purpose in India for hundreds of years.

In 1998 the company agreed in a settlement to pay $32 million for remediation of a radioactive waste site, and the Securities and Exchange Commission sued Grace that same year over reserves pertaining to former subsidiary National Medical Care (the suit was settled out of court). In 1999 the Environmental Protection Agency (EPA) issued an emergency order to clean up ammonia near Lansing, Michigan, which threatened the local water supply. The ammonia was a by-product of Grace fertilizer production from the 1960s. In 2000 Grace agreed to pay the major portion of a $15.5 million settlement against book distributor and former subsidiary Baker & Taylor.

As the new century began, Grace faced litigation related to asbestos. The trouble had been brewing for a while. In 1994 Grace settled charges, first issued in 1992, of violating asbestos standards at its Libby, Montana, tremolite mine, for over half a million dollars. In 2000 the EPA ordered Grace to spend an additional $5 million to clean up the site. Then, in 1999, Grace was party to a $200 million settlement to residents of Cook County, Illinois, who were exposed to asbestos in the 1960s and 1970s.

By mid-2000, Grace was named in over 53,000 asbestos lawsuits and had paid out a total of $1.15 billion in judgments and settlements. By April of the following year, that amount had risen to $1.9 billion, and the number of personal injury claims against the company topped 325,000. By early 2001, Grace's stock price had fallen to under $2 a share, and President and CEO Norris admitted in the company's fourth-quarter conference call that Grace was reviewing the choice of actions available, which included resolving the company's asbestos liability through a reorganization under Chapter 11. The decision was not long in coming. Grace filed for Chapter 11 on April 2, 2001. The filing included 61 of Grace's 70 domestic subsidiaries, but none of its foreign subsidiaries.

PROTRACTED LEGAL BATTLE: 2001–11

Grace entered into bankruptcy in no hurry to exit from the protective cloak of Chapter 11. The company braced itself for a lengthy battle, one it would be able to fight without having to answer to shareholder demands. "This bankruptcy is about litigation, and through litigation we will emerge," Norris said in the May 24, 2004, issue of *Chemical Market Reporter*. Litigation centered on whether the company's Zonolite attic insulation was harmful and to what degree the company was culpable in the deaths and illnesses related to its mining activities in Libby, Montana, which produced the asbestos-contaminated vermiculite used in the insulation.

While the company attempted to resolve its profound legal difficulties under the cover of Chapter 11, it remained an active, growing company. Within the first three years of bankruptcy, Grace completed seven acquisitions, increasing its sales to $2.25 billion by 2004, the year of its 150th anniversary. Norris stepped down as CEO at the end of the year, paving the way for the promotion of the company's COO, Fred E. Festa, who was appointed CEO in mid-2005. By the time Festa took the reins of command, seven of Grace's current or former executives had been indicted on charges that they knowingly put their workers and the public in danger through exposure to vermiculite ore contaminated with asbestos from the company's mine in Libby and conspired to hide the danger from the public and the U.S. government.

For Grace, the situation was bleak as Festa's leadership tenure began, but judicial rulings began to favor the company. At the end of 2006, a federal judge, Judith Fitzgerald, ruled that the Zonolite insulation manufactured by Grace did not pose an unreasonable risk of harm, writing in her opinion, as quoted in the December 22, 2006, edition of the *Baltimore Sun*, that the risk of exposure to the insulation was "less than that of dying in a bicycle accident." In 2008 Grace agreed to pay $1.8 billion to settle thousands of asbestos personal injury claims, well below the estimated $6 billion that claimants had sought. The following year, Grace and its executives were acquitted on all criminal charges, giving Grace what was widely considered to be an unexpected victory.

With the legal decisions behind it, Grace began plotting its exit strategy from bankruptcy. Closing arguments on its plan to emerge from Chapter 11 ended in 2010, when the company held its first quarterly investor call since it filed for bankruptcy nine years earlier. In 2011, a federal judge approved the company's reorganization plan, setting the stage for Grace's exit from bankruptcy and the beginning of a new chapter in the company's lengthy history.

Genevieve Williams
Updated, Jeffrey L. Covell

PRINCIPAL SUBSIDIARIES

Alltech Associates, Inc.; AP Chem Incorporated; Construction Products Dubai, Inc.; GR 2008 LLC; Grace Asia Pacific, Inc.; Grace Chemicals, Inc.; Grace Collections, Inc.; Grace Germany Holdings, Inc.; Grace Latin America, Inc.; Grace Management Services, Inc.; Grace Receivables Purchasing, Inc.; Ichiban Chemical Co., Inc.; Synthetech, Inc.; W. R. Grace Argentina S.A.; Alltech Associates (Australia) Pty. Ltd.; Grace Australia Pty. Ltd.; Grace Construction Products N.V.; Grace S.A. (Belgium); Grace Silica N.V. (Belgium); Inverco Benelux N.V. (Belgium); Grace Brasil Ltda. (Brazil); Grace Davison Ltda. (Brazil); GEC Divestment Corporation Ltd. (Canada); Grace Canada, Inc.; W. R. Grace Finance (NRO) Ltd. (Canada); Grace Quimica Compania Limitada (Chile); Grace China Ltd.; Grace Trading (Shanghai) Co., Ltd. (China); Grace Columbia S.A.; Envases Industriales y Comerciales, S.A. (Cuba); Papelera Camagueyana, S.A. (Cuba); Alltech France S.A.R.L.; Grace Produits de Construction SAS (France); W. R. Grace S.A. (France); Graced Europe Holding GmbH (Germany); Grace GP GmbH (Germany); Grace Management GP GmbH (Germany); Grace Silica GmbH (Germany); Grace Hellas E.P.E. (Greece); Alltech Applied Science Labs (HK) Limited (Hong Kong); Alltech Scientific (China) Limited (Hong Kong); W. R. Grace (Hong Kong) Limited; Grace Ertekesito Kft. (Hungary); Grace Davison Chemicals India Pvt. Ltd.; W. R. Grace & Co. (India) Private Limited; Amicon Ireland Limited; Grace Construction Products (Ireland) Limited; Trans-Meridian Insurance (Dublin) Ltd.; Alltech Italia S.R.L. (Italy); W. R. Grace Italiana S.p.A. (Italy); Grace Chemicals K.K. (Japan); Grace Japan Kabushiki Kaisha; Grace Kores Inc.; W. R. Grace (Malaysia) Sendiran Berhad; W. R. Grace Specialty Chemicals (Malaysia) Sdn Bhd.; Grace Container, S.A. de C.V. (Mexico); W. R. Grace Holdings, S.A. de C.V. (Mexico); Alltech Applied Science B.V. (Netherlands); Amicon B.V. (Netherlands); Denac Nederland B. V. (Netherlands); W. R. Grace B.V. (Netherlands); W. R. Grace N.V. (Netherlands Antilles); Grace (New Zealand) Limited; W. R. Grace (Panama) S.A.; W. R. Grace (Philippines), Inc.; Grace Sp. z.o.o. (Poland); Darex CIS LLC (Russia); W. R. Grace (Singapore) Private Limited; Grace Davison (Proprietary) Limited (South Africa); W. R. Grace Africa (Proprietary) Limited (South Africa); Grace, S. A. (Spain); Pieri Especialidades, S.L. (Spain);

Grace AB (Sweden); Grace Construction Products S.A. (Switzerland); W. R. Grace Taiwan, Inc.; W. R. Grace (Thailand) Limited; W. R. Grace Limited (UK); Grace Venezuela, S.A.; W. R. Grace Vietnam Company Limited.

PRINCIPAL OPERATING UNITS

Grace Davison; Grace Construction Products.

PRINCIPAL COMPETITORS

Ameron International Corporation; Cabot Corporation; E.I. du Pont de Nemours and Company.

FURTHER READING

Boraks, David. "In Brief: Grace's Chapter 11 Filing Names Big Banks." *American Banker*, April 3, 2001.

Brennan, Terry. "W.R. Grace Probe Gets Messy." *Daily Deal*, July 19, 2001.

Clayton, Lawrence. *Grace: W.R. Grace & Co., the Formative Years, 1850–1930*. New York: Jamison Books, 1985.

Schneider, Andrew. "Judge's Ruling Gives W. R. Grace a Break: Attic Insulation Found Not a Risk to Homeowners." *Baltimore Sun*, December 22, 2006.

Schwartz, Jody. "Saving Grace." *Adhesives Age*, May 2001.

Steele, Karen Dorn. "W.R. Grace Accused of Shifting Assets to Avoid Asbestos Liability." *Spokesman-Review*, January 28, 2001.

Wilton, Bill. "W. R. Grace & Co." *Zacks*, May 5, 2011.

Wipperfurth, Heike. "Problem Loans Dog N.Y. Banks." *Crain's New York Business*, February 12, 2001.

"W. R. Grace Manages through Bankruptcy." *Chemical Market Reporter*, May 24, 2004.

W.W. Grainger, Inc.

100 Grainger Parkway
Lake Forest, Illinois 60045-5201
U.S.A.
Telephone: (847) 535-1000
Fax: (847) 535-0878
Web site: http://www.grainger.com

Public Company
Incorporated: 1928
Employees: 18,596
Sales: $7.18 billion (2010)
Stock Exchanges: New York Chicago
Ticker Symbol: GWW
NAICS: 423610 Electrical Apparatus and Equipment, Wiring Supplies, and Related Equipment Merchant Wholesalers; 423730 Warm Air Heating and Air Conditioning Equipment and Supplies Merchant Wholesales; 423830 Industrial Machinery and Equipment Merchant Wholesalers; 423840 Industrial Supplies Merchant Wholesalers; 423990 Other Miscellaneous Durable Goods Merchant Wholesalers

∎∎∎

W.W. Grainger, Inc., is the largest distributor of maintenance, repair, and operating (MRO) supplies to the commercial, industrial, contractor, and institutional markets in North America. The company serves a number of specialty markets as well, such as towing, agriculture, woodworking, fleet maintenance, and forestry. W.W. Grainger, Inc. specializes in assisting businesses with "unplanned purchases" that are needed quickly to effect continuous business operations. Grainger ensures rapid delivery through 24 distribution centers, including 17 in the United States, six in Canada, and one each in Mexico, Colombia, and Japan. Grainger China, in Shanghai, operates one sales branch, one distribution facility, and one regional warehouse. Operations in India originate from 19 regional warehouses.

EARLY HISTORY

In the late 1920s, William W. Grainger, a motor designer, salesman, and electrical engineer, sought to tap a segment of the market for wholesale electrical equipment sales. He set up an office in Chicago in 1927 and incorporated his business one year later. The company sold goods primarily through MotorBook, an eight-page catalog, which would become the backbone of the company's name recognition. It contained electrical motors that Grainger himself, his sister Margaret, and two employees would ship. The catalog also included extensive technical and application data.

The market for electric motors was so expansive in the late 1920s and into the 1930s that many companies developed with it. In 1926 two of the 10 largest U.S. corporations were electrical companies. City utilities made the switch from direct current (DC) to alternating current (AC) for nearly every apparatus driven by electricity. Manufacturers moved away from uniform, DC-driven assembly lines and toward separate workstations, each with individually driven AC motors. This development created a vast market, and distributors such as Grainger could reach segments untapped by volume-minded manufacturers.

Grainger established its first branch in Philadelphia in 1933. Atlanta, Dallas, and San Francisco branches opened in 1934. Sales in 1932 fell below the previous year's, to $163,000, the first of only four years where sales would not increase. In 1937 Grainger had 16 branches and sales of more than $1 million.

The complexity of the industry allowed Grainger to decentralize marketing efforts and strengthen its regional presence by adding an outside sales force in 1939, but the company limited it to one sales representative for every branch for the first 10 years. Branches opened around the country at a brisk pace, with 24 operating by 1942.

Grainger did not expand solely through the number of outlets. In 1937 it began merchandising selected products under the Dayton trademark, Grainger's first private label. In order to stimulate summer business, a line of air circulators and ventilating fans was designed, assembled, and offered for sale by the company in 1938. Grainger acted as a distributor of electric motors for government use during World War II. With its normal market disrupted, Grainger offered furniture, toys, and watches through MotorBook for a brief period. Grainger continued expansion during the war as sales grew from 1941's $2.6 million to $7.8 million in 1948, and earnings increased almost tenfold to $240,000 in 1948.

POSTWAR GROWTH: 1948–74

The rapid growth continued immediately after the war. Sales more than doubled from 1948 to 1952, calling for organizational adjustments. A single sales representative could no longer serve an entire branch, and in 1948 Grainger expanded the sales force for the first time. The postwar transition also required renewed efficiency. In 1949 Grainger had a branch office built to its own specifications for the first time. Most new branches since have also been built specifically for Grainger. Branches built after 1949 were automated to keep administrative and personnel costs low.

Beginning in 1953 the company created a regional warehousing system that replenished branch stock and

filled larger orders. Called regional distribution centers, they were eventually located in Chicago; Atlanta; Oakland, California; Fort Worth, Texas; Memphis, Tennessee; and Cranford, New Jersey.

As alternating current became standard in the United States, Grainger's market changed. No longer processing large orders, the company intensified its focus on the secondary market that existed throughout the country: small manufacturers, servicers, and dealers who purchased with high frequency but low volume. Grainger could anticipate the needs of this market and purchase from manufacturers in high volume. Grainger's distribution system, warehousing, and accounting allowed manufacturers to produce at low cost for Grainger's customers. These customers were otherwise difficult for manufacturers to reach.

Most of the increases in sales volume after World War II were due to large-scale geographic expansion. This expansion continued through the 1950s and 1960s at a consistent pace. By 1967 Grainger operated 92 branches. In 1962 sales were $43.5 million. By 1966 sales nearly doubled to $80.2 million. Automation helped build the company's reputation as a reliable supplier and brought in accounts with bigger clients. Average branch sales grew from $596,000 in 1962 to more than $2.1 million in 1974.

In 1966 Grainger acquired those shares of Dayton Electric Manufacturing Company that it did not already own. Also in the 1960s, Grainger acquired a producer of home accessories, which was divested in the 1970s. In 1967 the company went public.

In 1969 the company purchased Doerr Electric Corporation, a manufacturer of electric motors, and three Doerr affiliates. Two thirds of Doerr's sales volume was already to Grainger. In 1972 Grainger acquired McMillan Manufacturing, another maker of electric motors. That year the branch network expanded to 123 units in 40 states, and the company employed 218 territory sales representatives. By 1974 sales more than tripled, garnering the company a listing on the New York Stock Exchange.

SALES AND SERVICE EXPANSION: 1975–89

Brands exclusive to Grainger (Dayton, Teel, Demco, Dem-Kote, and Speedaire) accounted for about 65 percent of the company's 1975 sales. As Grainger's branches became larger, the need for a centralized stock diminished. The company eliminated the regional distribution centers by the mid-1970s. Grainger discontinued its McMillan Manufacturing operations in 1975.

KEY DATES

1927: Company is founded as an electrical equipment wholesaler; business incorporates a year later.
1967: Grainger goes public.
1990: Company enters the safety-products distribution business through the acquisition of Allied Safety, Inc.
1999: Company adds three Internet businesses to facilitate ordering and help customers locate hard-to-find products.
2005: Grainger lays out eight-year expansion plan.
2008: Deep recession causes sales slump.
2010: Revenues rebound with growth in manufacturing sector.

Investment in computer automation allowed Grainger to resurrect its centrally managed regional distribution centers. In 1983 the company opened a heavily automated distribution center in Kansas City, Missouri, and in 1989 opened a third such operation in Greenville County, South Carolina.

Grainger returned to its origins, trying to reach larger institutional customers. Although essentially the same business since its inception, Grainger expanded the scope of its services. Starting in 1986, through acquisition and internal development, the company began building specialty distribution businesses that were intended to complement the market position held by Grainger. These businesses included replacement parts, general industrial products, safety products, and sanitary supplies. Parts distribution continued to expand under the Parts Company of America (PCA) name. PCA provided parts service for more than 550 equipment manufacturers and offered 80,000 parts.

Grainger's prominence allowed it to count on sales increases due to population growth. In addition, the replacement market for small motors exceeded that of the repair market. Slimmed-down operations and reduced long-term debt, however, poised the company for more aggressive growth through the 1980s.

Unlike in the 1960s, the company saw no need to diversify during the 1980s, recognizing that the electrical industry itself could provide enough opportunity for growth. The transition from electromechanical equipment to electronics provided long-term growth during boom and bust periods. The period was comparable to the motor market upgrades of the 1920s and 1930s, when growth in domestic business activity led to broad-scale upgrades and system replacements. This resulted in increased orders for Grainger and more disposable cash for its own expansion. By the end of 1984, annual revenues exceeded $1 billion for the first time.

At this time Grainger began to recognize that its profitability lay in product sales, and the company divested its manufacturing business. In 1986 the company sold Doerr to Emerson Electric Company for $24.3 million. The change allowed the company to focus on sales and customer service. A study showed that while Grainger sold products in every county in the United States, it held less than a 2 percent share of a $70 billion to $90 billion industry. The study also indicated that most Grainger customers had fewer than 100 employees and valued immediacy over breadth of product line or price. In response, Grainger accelerated its decades-old expansion rate of six branches a year. It opened more than 100 new branches between 1987 and

ACQUISITIONS AND REORGANIZATION: 1989–97

General industrial distribution expanded in the late 1980s and early 1990s through a series of acquisitions. In 1989 Grainger purchased Vonnegut Industrial Products. The following year, the company acquired Bossert Industrial Supply, Inc. Bossert, positioned in the midwestern market, provided manufacturing and repair operations products, cutting tools and abrasives, and other supplies used in manufacturing processes. Also in 1990, the company entered into the safety-products distribution business through the acquisition of Allied Safety, Inc. The new safety products line included such items as respiratory systems, protective clothing, and other equipment used by individuals in the workplace and in environmental cleanup operations. Grainger added to the line in 1992 by purchasing Lab Safety Supply.

JANI-SERV Supply was created in 1990 to service the sanitary supply market. It offered more than 1,200 items, representing a full range of sanitary products. The subsidiary was expanded in 1991 with the purchase of Ball Industries, Inc., a distributor of sanitary and janitorial supplies based in California. Product expansions prompted Grainger to publish two editions of its general catalog, the successor to MotorBook, offering more than 35,000 items.

In 1993 Grainger began a three-year reorganization of the company and its subsidiaries with the goal of streamlining its sales force and eliminating redundant inventories. Grainger began by dismantling JANI-SERV

Supply in 1993 and incorporating its product line into its core business. The following year Grainger began the same process with Allied Safety, the company's safety products subsidiary, and Bossert, finishing the integration in 1995. In addition to this streamlining, Grainger opened zone distribution centers in Dallas and Atlanta in 1994.

Costs related to the reorganization and upgrades to information systems contributed to lower gross margins in the mid-1990s. A more important factor in these lower margins was Grainger's decision to lower prices on some products to attract new customers and expand existing accounts. As part of the company's effort to return to national accounts and larger industrial customers, the strategic pricing helped expand Grainger's customer base. Although the stock price fell in response to the lower margins, this effect was temporary.

LEADERSHIP CHANGE

Leadership of the company left the hands of the Grainger family for the first time when David Grainger, son of the founder, retired as chief executive officer in 1995. He remained as chair of the board and was succeeded as CEO by Richard Keyser. In another change from the status quo, the company moved its headquarters to Lincolnshire, Illinois, the same year. By 1999, however, the company had shifted addresses once again, relocating to Lake Forest, Illinois, outside of Chicago.

During the late 1990s, Grainger established operations outside the United States for the first time. In 1996 the company opened a branch in Monterrey, Mexico. The same year, Grainger purchased a division of Acklands, Ltd., a Canadian manufacturer of industrial safety and automotive aftermarket products.

The company made great strides in adding large national accounts in the mid- and late 1990s. In 1996 it signed supply agreements with several large companies, including Lockheed Martin, Procter & Gamble, and American Airlines. In 1998 Grainger announced a materials management outsourcing agreement with Compaq Computer Corporation. With the addition of new accounts and new products, sales at Grainger almost quadrupled in a decade, growing from $1.3 billion in 1987 to $4.1 billion in 1997. That year, the company was recognized by *Industrial Distribution* magazine as the number one industrial distributor in North America in terms of sales.

STRIDES INTO THE NEW
MILLENNIUM: 1990–2005

In the 21st century W.W. Grainger became one of the first old-economy companies to use the power of the In-

ternet for direct business-to-business ordering. By 1999 Grainger had developed three separate Internet businesses (Grainger.com, OrderZone.com, and FindMRO. com). All three were specifically designed to facilitate ordering and to help customers locate hard-to-find products. In that year the corporation also announced a deal with Netscape that would allow customers to access and order from Grainger's online catalog using Netscape's Netcenter, one of the leading Internet portal sites. Online resources gave Grainger about $160 million in sales in 1999.

However, the new Internet economy also created problems for Grainger. Although its Internet businesses exploded onto the market, they did not initially increase the value of the parent company's stock. While stock prices hit a high of $58 a share in 1999 shortly after the launch of OrderZone.com, by the following year stock had sunk to around $34. Existing customers loved the convenience that ordering through Grainger.com gave them, but OrderZone.com did not attract as many new paying customers as management had hoped it would. As a result, in 2000 Grainger announced a deal with Works.com, an e-commerce business based in Texas that would bolster the corporation's Internet visibility by merging OrderZone into Works.com. In 2001 Grainger also announced that customers of FacilityPro would have access to the entire line of Grainger products through FacilityPro's own online market.

The economic slowdown of the early 21st century led Grainger to try to intensify its relationships with its existing customers. In February 2001 the corporation opened an onsite facility at Florida State University, and the following year it created a similar facility for the U.S. Armed Forces at Langley Air Force in Virginia. At the same time Grainger became one of several companies that supplied the U.S. Navy's Norfolk, Virginia, base with maintenance equipment and supplies.

Grainger sought to grow by expanding its line of safety equipment. In 2003 Lab Safety Supply acquired Gempler's, a direct market supplier of agricultural and maintenance products. The 2005 Safety Lab acquisition of A.W. Direct expanded Lab Safety's product line to general towing and work truck equipment and related products. Direct market sales customers included automobile service centers, utilities, construction companies, and government entities, adding $28 million to Grainger's annual revenues.

The acquisitions were part of a long-term growth and efficiency plan. Grainger's plan involved capturing a greater percentage of market share in North America. The program focused particularly on markets in Denver, Atlanta, Seattle, Chicago, St. Louis, Tampa, Cincinnati,

Southern California, Connecticut, and northern New Jersey. The company increased the size of existing branches and expanded their staff in order to make needed products and customer service more available.

Grainger improved its ability to supply customers with supplies by opening new distribution centers or redesigning old ones. In addition, the company sought to provide customers with options in purchasing outsourced products. Grainger streamlined the supply and distribution system by consolidating its integrated supply segment into the branch-based operations. The installation of a state-of-the-art logistics network and an SAP Enterprise Resource Planning System facilitated the change. Along with expansion of its sales force, Grainger intended the upgrades in efficiency and customer service to add $1 billion in revenues by 2013.

IMPACT OF THE DEEP RECESSION: 2008–11

Grainger's long-term plans were stymied by a steady decline in sales in the United States that began by the spring of 2008 and intensified with the oncoming economic crisis. Grainger sought to compensate for the decline by establishing operations in countries where the economy was growing. The company opened its first branch in Panama and added branches in Mexico and eastern Canada. The acquisition of Excel Industriel, of Quebec, expanded access to potential customers in eastern Canada.

Grainger acquired a 50 percent interest in Asia Pacific Brands of India for $5.4 million. With 27 outlets and more than 6,000 dealers throughout India, the company distributed wholesale industrial and electrical supplies. Asia Pacific Brands went aground when its largest supplier filed for bankruptcy, however. Grainger took a write-down for its investment, revamped operations, and acquired complete ownership for $1.2 million by June 2009. Grainger bought a trimmed down company, with 20 locations and 4,000 dealers. After acquisition of the remaining interest, the subsidiary was renamed Grainger Industrial Supply India Private Limited.

Another strategy to offset slow growth involved extending the product base with specialty goods. In August 2008 Lab Safety Supply acquired Highsmith, which added library and school equipment, furniture, and supplies. The acquisition of McFeeley's Square Drive Screws added specialty woodworking tools, fasteners, and hardware. In October 2009 Grainger purchased Imperial Supplies Holding, Inc. a supplier of aftermarket components for fleet and facility maintenance.

Dissatisfied with stagnant sales of Lab Safety, in November 2008 Grainger decided to combine the supply lines of Lab Safety and Grainger Industrial Supply in Janesville. Grainger sought to create a more efficient supply and distribution infrastructure, including marketing through one sales force, Internet site, and catalog. A decline in the manufacturing sector of the economy led Grainger to initiate layoffs and retirement buyouts at Lab Safety in February 2009, as well as to take other cost-cutting measures. Grainger rearranged its distribution network by shifting some work activity from the Janesville facility to sites in California and South Carolina. The new structure was intended to meet a need for rapid order fulfillment in those regions.

With manufacturing on the rebound in 2010, Grainger looked to reinvigorate Janesville operations. The company obtained a loan from the city, forgivable on the condition that Grainger created 130 jobs over three years. Grainger continued to add new brands for processing through the facility, such as Ben Meadow forestry equipment, renamed GHC Specialty Brands. Acklands-Grainger expanded with three acquisitions in eastern Canada, a new distribution center in British Columbia, and expansion of distribution centers in Alberta, Manitoba, and Ontario.

After revenues dropped from $6.85 billion in 2008 to $6.22 billion in 2009, Grainger experienced 15 percent sales growth in 2010, to $7.18 billion. Grainger attributed this rebound to a number of factors. Some growth stemmed from the need for safety products in the aftermath of BP's oil spill in the Gulf of Mexico. Manufacturers, which accounted for 25 percent of sales, began refilling depleted inventories. The rise in manufacturing activity meant customers required more MRO supplies.

OPTIMISTIC PLANS FOR THE FUTURE

Grainger successfully convinced customers that they could improve efficiency by purchasing all their MRO supplies from one company. To become the sole supplier to more of its customers, Grainger increased the number of products in the catalog from 183,000 in 2008 to 307,000 in 2010. Reviews of 16 product lines improved the quality and appropriateness of its product offerings. To support customer service, staffing of outside sales representatives increased from 2,433 in 2008 to 3,079 in 2010.

Grainger continued to expand into overseas markets. New sales opportunities in Japan and a joint venture with an affiliate of Torhefe, Grainger Colombia, S.A., operating five branch offices, contributed to revenue growth in 2010. The company opened a new warehouse in South China in 2010 as well. Grainger established operations in Europe for the first time, through the August 2011 acquisition of industrial distributor Forbay of the Netherlands for $344 million.

Grainger planned to continue its strategy to become the one-stop supplier for its MRO customers. Toward that end, Grainger aimed to carry 354,000 products by the end of 2011, with an ideal goal of carrying 450,000 to 500,000 products over the next few years. To accommodate new products and new business, Grainger planned to establish two new distribution centers in San Francisco by the end of 2011 and on the outskirts of Chicago in late 2012. Grainger planned several technology improvements to improve its customers' online purchasing experience. Grainger expected further consolidation of a fragmented industry to provide opportunities for future acquisitions.

Ray Walsh
Updated, Susan Windisch Brown;
Kenneth R. Shepherd; Mary Tradii

PRINCIPAL SUBSIDIARIES

Acklands-Grainger Inc. (Canada); Grainger Colombia S.A.S. (80%); Grainger Industrial Supply India Private Limited; Grainger China, LLC; Grainger S.A. de C.V. (Mexico); Lab Safety Supply, Inc.

PRINCIPAL COMPETITORS

Airgas Safety, Inc.; Applied Industrial Technologies, Inc.; Fastenal Company; HD Supply, Inc.; Home Depot, Inc.; K+K America Corporation; McMaster-Carr Supply Company; MSC Industrial Direct Company, Inc.

FURTHER READING

Cohen, Andy. "Practice Makes Profits: Sales Training Spurs Double-Digit Increases Every Year for W.W. Grainger." *Sales and Marketing Management*, July 1995, 24–25.

Daniels, Steve. "Old-Line Company Tangles with Net; Grainger's Dilemma: Float Stock in Online Venture?" *Crain's Chicago Business*, November 29, 1999.

Gondo, Nancy. "W.W. Grainger Expanding in U.S., Overseas." *Investor's Business Daily*, August 4, 2008, B9.

"Grainger: The Positive View." *Forbes*, November 21, 1994, 248–49.

"How the Big Get Bigger." *Industrial Distribution*, February 1988.

Johnson, John R. "1997 Top 100 Distributor." *Industrial Distribution*, June 1997, 50.

Knapp, Kevin. "Grainger Defends Move; Says OrderZone Equity Swap a Wise Decision." *B to B*, July 3, 2000, 6.

Maddox, Kate. "Growing Wiser." *B to B*, September 9, 2002, 1.

Saito-Chung, David. "Manufacturing Rebound Aids W.W. Grainger." *Investor's Business Daily*, September 1, 2011, B3.

60 Years of Growth. Skokie, IL: W.W. Grainger, Inc., 1987.

Walgreens

Walgreen Co.

---

200 Wilmot Road
Deerfield, Illinois 60015-4620
U.S.A.
Telephone: (847) 940-2500
Toll Free: (800) 289-2273
Fax: (847) 914-2804
Web site: http://www.walgreens.com

Public Company
Incorporated: 1916
Employees: 247,000
Sales: $72.2 billion (2011)
Stock Exchanges: New York Chicago
Ticker Symbol: WAG
NAICS: 446110 Pharmacies and Drug Stores

■ ■ ■

Walgreen Co. is the largest drugstore chain in the United States, with more than 8,200 locations in all 50 states, Washington, D.C., and Puerto Rico. Walgreen operates more than 7,785 drugstores, more than three-quarters have drive-through pharmacies, and nearly all of them offer one-hour photofinishing; about one-fourth of these locations are open 24 hours. About 80 percent of Walgreens stores are freestanding locations. The typical store has 11,000 square feet of sales space carrying more than 18,000 items. Average store sales are $9 million. Walgreens also operates health care and wellness centers at more than 350 work sites and more than 350 health and wellness centers at its stores. The company serves more than six million customers daily and fills more than 819 million prescriptions annually.

EARLY YEARS OF RAPID GROWTH

The company had its origin in 1901, when Charles R. Walgreen bought the drugstore on the south side of Chicago at which he had been working as a pharmacist. He bought a second store in 1909. By 1915, there were five Walgreen drugstores. He made numerous improvements and innovations in the stores, including the addition of soda fountains that also featured luncheon service. Walgreen also began to make his own line of drug products. By doing so, he was able to control the quality of these items and offer them at lower prices than competitors.

By 1916, there were nine Walgreen stores, all on Chicago's South Side, doing a business volume of $270,000 annually. That year, the stores were consolidated as Walgreen Co. with the aim of ensuring economies of scale.

By 1919 Walgreen operated 20 stores, 19 of which were on Chicago's South Side while the other was on the near north side. Also in 1919, the company opened its first photofinishing studio. It promised faster service than most commercial studios.

The 1920s were a booming decade for Walgreen stores. In 1921 the company opened a store in Chicago's downtown, its first outside a residential area. Walgreen stores introduced the malted milkshake at their fountain counters in 1922. To meet the demand for ice cream and to ensure its quality, Walgreen

COMPANY PERSPECTIVES

Our Vision: To be "My Walgreens" for everyone in America—the first choice in health and daily living … owning the strategic territory of "well." Our Mission: To be the most trusted, convenient multichannel provider and advisor of innovative pharmacy, health and wellness solutions, and consumer goods and services in communities across America. A destination where health and happiness come together to help people get well, stay well and live well.

established its own ice cream manufacturing plants during the 1920s. The company continued to add to its number of stores. By mid-1925, there were 65 stores with total annual sales of $1.2 million. Fifty-nine of the stores were in Chicago and its suburbs, with others in Milwaukee, Wisconsin, and St. Louis, Missouri. Before the year was out, the company had expanded into Minneapolis and St. Paul, Minnesota.

The company opened its first East Coast store, in New York's theater district, in 1927. That year, the company went public. By the end of 1929, there were 397 Walgreen stores in 87 cities. Annual sales were $47 million with net earnings of $4 million.

GREAT DEPRESSION YEARS

At first, the company suffered little from the 1929 stock market crash and the subsequent Great Depression. Sales actually rose in 1930, to $52 million. The same year, the company opened a 224,000-square-foot warehouse and laboratory on Chicago's southwest side. Early in the 1930s, the company expanded on a project begun in 1929 setting up an agency system by which independent drugstores could sell Walgreen products. By 1934, 600 Walgreen agency stores were functioning in 33 states, mostly in midwestern communities with populations of less than 20,000.

By 1932, however, the company was feeling the Depression's pinch. Sales dipped to $47.6 million, and wage cuts were instituted. The company set up a benefit fund to assist retirees and needy families inside and outside the company. The company continued promoting itself, however. In 1931 it had become the first drugstore chain in the United States to advertise on radio.

There were several major events for Walgreen in 1933. The company paid a dividend on its stock for the

first time, its concessions at Chicago's Century of Progress exposition helped boost sales, and Charles R. Walgreen, Jr., became a vice president of the company. With the repeal of Prohibition late that year, Walgreen Co. acquired liquor licenses and soon was selling whiskey and wine in 60 percent of its stores.

In 1934 the company opened its first Walgreen Super Store, in Tampa, Florida. At 4,000 square feet, the store was nearly double the size of the typical store. It had a much larger fountain and more open displays of merchandise than an average store. Other Super Stores followed in Salt Lake City, Utah; Milwaukee, Wisconsin; Miami, Florida; and Rochester, New York. Also in 1934 the company's stock began trading on the New York Stock Exchange.

Walgreen's business recovered by the late 1930s. However, by 1939 the founder's health was failing. Charles Walgreen, Sr., resigned the presidency of the company in August. His son was named to succeed him, and Justin Dart, who had been with the company in various capacities since 1929, was named general manager. Dart had been married to and divorced from Ruth Walgreen, the founder's daughter. Charles Walgreen, Sr., died in December 1939 at the age of 66.

CONTINUED EXPANSION IN THE FORTIES

The company began the 1940s with the opening of a Super Store in downtown Chicago. The store featured a two-way, high-speed escalator to provide access between the two floors of the store, the first of its kind in any drugstore in the world. It also contained a full-service restaurant-tea room. In April 1940 the Marvin Drug Co., which operated eight stores and a warehouse in Dallas, merged with Walgreen Co. At year-end, Walgreen Co. announced the establishment of a pension plan, with an initial contribution of more than $500,000 from the proceeds of Charles Walgreen, Sr.'s life insurance policy.

In 1941 there was a split between Charles Walgreen, Jr., and Justin Dart. In November of that year Dart resigned and joined United Drugs Inc., where he built a substantial career and diversified beyond the drug business.

Walgreen Co. put continued growth and expansion on hold with the United States' entry into World War II after the Pearl Harbor attack in December 1941. The company felt the war's impact in a variety of ways. Certain foods became scarce, as did film and tobacco products. More than 2,500 Walgreen employees served in the armed forces; 48 did not survive. Walgreen stores sold war bonds and stamps. In 1943 the company opened a store in the Pentagon, in Washington, D.C.

KEY DATES

1901: Charles R. Walgreen buys the drugstore on the south side of Chicago where he had been working as a pharmacist.

1916: Now operating nine drugstores, the founder incorporates his business as Walgreen Co.

1927: Company goes public.

1952: Walgreen begins transition to self-service with the opening of its first self-service drugstore.

1975: Sales surpass the $1 billion mark.

1984: The 1,000th Walgreens store is opened.

1986: Company acquires 66-unit Medi Mart chain.

1992: First freestanding Walgreens store opens; drive-through pharmacies make their debut.

2008: Walgreens changes its business model to bring health care to the customer.

2010: Acquisition of Duane Reade stores in New York City influences marketing strategies.

After the war, expansion was once again possible. In 1946 the company acquired a 27 percent interest, later increased to 44 percent, in a major Mexican retail and restaurant company, Sanborns. More Walgreen Super Stores were opened in the late 1940s, including one on Chicago's Michigan Avenue, a street of elegant shops and restaurants. In 1948 the company expanded its corporate headquarters in Chicago. That year, Walgreen began advertising on television.

TRANSITION TO SELF-SERVICE BEGINNING IN THE FIFTIES

The 1950s ushered in the era of self-service in drug retailing, a concept Walgreen had tried on an experimental basis at three stores in the 1940s. In 1949 the company canceled plans for a merger with Thrifty Drug Co., a California chain, largely because Thrifty's clerk-service style would hamper a conversion of the entire company to self-service. In the course of the merger negotiations, however, Charles Walgreen, Jr., had researched Thrifty's competitors and had been impressed by the self-service Sav-on chain, which fueled his interest in taking his stores in that direction.

The first self-service Walgreens opened on Chicago's South Side in June 1952. The second followed in a few months at Evergreen Plaza, Chicago's first major shopping center. The self-service stores offered lower prices than traditional stores but often actually required more employees, because the stores were larger and carried more products. By the end of 1953, there were 22 self-service Walgreens. Self-service continued to grow throughout the 1950s. With the opening of a self-service store in Louisville, Kentucky, at the end of 1960, self-service units outnumbered traditional ones. Another major event of 1960 was the opening of the first Walgreens in Puerto Rico.

DIVERSIFYING BEYOND DRUGSTORES IN THE SIXTIES AND SEVENTIES

In 1962 Walgreen Co. entered the discount department store field by paying about $3 million for the assets of United Mercantile Inc., which owned three large Globe Shopping Center stores and seven smaller Danburg department stores, all in the Houston, Texas, area. The company expanded the Globe chain throughout the South and Southwest. By 1966, there were 13 Globe stores generating annual sales of more than $120 million.

Operating Globe gave Walgreen Co. experience in running larger stores, and the company began to open ever larger stores under the Walgreens name. The first Walgreens Super Center opened in 1964 in the Chicago suburb of Norridge. By 1969 there were 17 Super Centers around the country.

Walgreen Co. changed and diversified its restaurant operations in the 1960s. A detailed analysis early in the decade showed that the return on investment of Walgreen's fountains and grills was generally less than that of the rest of a store. Therefore, the company decided not to include fountains and grills in new stores and began closing them in others. Instead of getting out of foodservice altogether, however, the company went into full-scale restaurants. The first of these was the Villager Room, located within a Walgreens in Oak Park, a Chicago suburb. Also added during the 1960s were the fast-food chain Corky's and the medieval-decor Robin Hood restaurants.

A third generation of Walgreens ascended to the company presidency in 1969. Charles R. (Cork) Walgreen III was named president, succeeding Alvin Borg, who had become president when Charles Walgreen, Jr., became chairman of the board during a 1963 corporate reorganization. This made Walgreen Co. one of the few companies headed by second- and third-generation descendants of the founder, although the Walgreen family no longer owned a controlling share of company stock. Also in 1963, the company elected its first outside directors to the board.

Several changes occurred in the mid-1970s. In 1974 the company opened its first Wag's restaurant. Wag's were freestanding family restaurants, many open 24 hours a day. That year it also acquired the Liggett chain of 29 Florida drugstores. In 1975 Walgreen Co. moved into a new corporate headquarters in Deerfield, a suburb of Chicago. Also in 1975, the company completed the first phase of a new drug and cosmetics laboratory in Kalamazoo, Michigan; expanded its distribution center in Berkeley, Illinois; and, in Chicago, replaced its plastic container plant and photo processing studio with new ones. The company surpassed the $1 billion mark in sales in 1975.

In 1976 Charles Walgreen III succeeded his father as chairman of the board, and Robert L. Schmitt, who had been with the company since 1948, became president. Schmitt oversaw the liquidation of the Globe chain, which had been showing significant losses. He also was charged with forming a partnership with Schnuck's, a St. Louis grocery store operator, to establish combined supermarkets and drugstores, and with opening optical centers in Walgreen stores. Schmitt's tenure ended, however, when he died suddenly in October 1978. Fred F. Canning, a 32-year company veteran, succeeded him. In 1979 Walgreen Co. acquired 16 Stein drugstores in the Milwaukee area.

REFOCUSED ON DRUGSTORES IN THE EIGHTIES

The company began the 1980s by refocusing on drugstores and eliminating certain businesses. In 1980 it ended the agency program, begun in 1929, which accounted for only 2 percent of sales. This step did not sit well with some former agency stores. A group of store operators in Wisconsin sued Walgreen Co., eventually winning a $431,000 judgment. The following year, Walgreen closed its 27 optical centers and ended the partnership with Schnuck's. The company also eliminated many in-store restaurants, concentrating on Wag's instead.

Expanding the drugstore business, Walgreen Co. bought the Rennebohm chain, based in Madison, Wisconsin, in 1980. Rennebohm had 17 drugstores, two clinic pharmacies, two health- and beauty-aid stores, a card shop, and six cafeterias. In 1981 Walgreen bought 21 Kroger SuperX drugstores in Houston. In 1982 the company added additional services to its drugstores: It made next-day photofinishing available chainwide and put grocery departments in some stores located in urban areas.

In 1983 Walgreen completed chainwide installation of its Intercom computerized pharmacy system. By the end of the decade Intercom connected each store in the chain via satellite to a mainframe computer in Des Plaines, Illinois. This system enabled customers to have their prescriptions filled at any Walgreens in the country.

Walgreen opened its 1,000th store, on the near north side of Chicago, in 1984. The company continued expanding in the drugstore area, while divesting other businesses. In 1984 it sold its interest in Sanborns, by then 46.9 percent, to Sanborns' other principals for about $30 million, a move spurred by Mexico's high inflation rate.

In 1986 Walgreen bought the 66 Medi Mart store chain, located primarily in New England, in the company's largest single acquisition. That year, the company also bought 25 stores from the Indiana chain Ribordy, and opened 102 new stores, making 1986 Walgreen's biggest year for expansion yet.

In 1988, continuing to trim non-drugstore businesses, Walgreen sold its 87 freestanding Wag's restaurants to Marriott Corporation. In 1988 the Haft family sought regulatory clearance to acquire a block of Walgreen stock, a move that company officials feared would lead to an unfriendly takeover bid, as the Hafts had tried to acquire other retailers. Walgreen responded with a move that was seen as an antitakeover device, the establishment of "golden parachutes," payments to be made to executives if they left the firm after a takeover. No bid came through, however.

In 1989 the company opened four mini-drugstores called Walgreens RxPress, which offered a full-service pharmacy and popular nonprescription items in areas where full-sized store locations were difficult to find. By the mid-1990s, these 2,000-square-foot units, some of which offered one-hour photofinishing services, also featured convenient drive-through pharmacies. There were 25 RxPress locations by 1996.

ACCELERATED EXPANSION IN THE NINETIES

For Walgreen, the 1990s were dominated by an unprecedented rate of expansion. Walgreen ended the 1980s with 1,484 units. By mid-1997 the company had more than 2,200 units and was aiming for the 3,000 mark by the new century. Although most of this growth was accomplished organically, the 1990s began with an acquisition, the 1990 purchase of Lee Drug, a nine-unit drugstore chain in New Hampshire and Massachusetts. That same year Fred Canning retired as president. L. Daniel Jorndt, who had been senior vice president and treasurer, succeeded him.

For the pharmacy industry as a whole, the 1990s were a decade of profound change. Demographically, there were more and more people over the age of 50. As a result, more prescriptions were being filled each year, making pharmacies a hot commodity. Competition became fiercer as aggressive chains such as Wal-Mart Stores, Inc. challenged Walgreen's leading position in prescription drugs. Additionally, managed care health plans grew increasingly important as the decade progressed, putting pressure on drugstores to lower prices on prescriptions, thereby squeezing margins. Walgreen responded to these challenges by investing heavily in technology and by launching new initiatives aimed directly at taking advantage of the trend toward managed care.

On the technology side, the company improved its inventory management capabilities when it rolled out point-of-sale scanning equipment chainwide in late 1991. The chain-wide completion in 1994 of SIMS (Strategic Inventory Management System) united all elements of the purchasing-distribution-sales cycle. By 1997 Walgreen was rolling out a second-generation Intercom Plus system, which performed more than 200 functions and enabled customers to order prescription refills using the keys on a push-button phone. The system also cut in half the time customers had to wait to receive their prescriptions.

In response to the managed care boom, one byproduct of which was the growth in cost-effective mail-order pharmacies, Walgreen formed a subsidiary, Healthcare Plus, in 1991 to offer managed care providers a pharmacy mail service of its own. In the fall of 1995 Walgreen expanded Healthcare Plus into WHP Health Initiatives, Inc., a pharmacy benefits manager, in order to offer additional products and services to managed care providers, including long-term care pharmacies, durable medical equipment, and home infusion services. WHP was aimed at small and medium-sized employers and HMOs in Walgreens' top 28 retail markets.

Meanwhile, the expansion of the Walgreens chain continued apace, supported by the opening of two more distribution centers (in Lehigh Valley, Pennsylvania, in June 1991, and in Woodland, California, in July 1995) bringing to eight the number of such centers. The Woodland center was particularly important as it supported an aggressive expansion in California, as well as the opening of the first Walgreens in Portland, Oregon. Walgreens also expanded into several other new markets in the mid-1990s, including Dallas/Fort Worth, Detroit, Kansas City, Las Vegas, and Philadelphia.

In May 1997 Walgreen entered foreign territory for the first time since the failed Sanborns venture. That month the company formed a joint venture, RX Network Inc. (RXN), with Itochu Corp. and five other Japanese companies to set up a drugstore chain in Japan. RXN aimed to create a 500-unit chain by 2002.

In January 1998 Charles Walgreen III retired as CEO, with Jorndt succeeding him. Walgreen III remained chairman until 1999, when Jorndt took over that position as well.

A STEADY PERFORMER

In the late 1990s and into the early years of the 21st century, Walgreen achieved a remarkable record of steady growth and profitability. As revenues more than doubled from $15.31 billion in 1998 to $32.51 billion in 2003, profits increased at a similar pace, jumping from $511 million to $1.18 billion. Throughout this entire period, the net profit margin stayed within a narrow band, between 3.3 percent and 3.7 percent. Moreover, the results for 2003 marked the company's 29th consecutive year of record sales and earnings. Walgreen added about 350 stores per year in this period, opening its 3,000th store in Chicago in March 2000 and its 4,000th store in Van Nuys, California, in March 2003.

This growth was achieved almost entirely organically. Walgreen eschewed the acquisition route to growth of its competitors, who were participating in a huge consolidation wave that was sweeping the drugstore industry. Walgreen preferred to carefully select its own sites for new stores rather than take on the hodgepodge of stores with some undesirable locations and/or store formats that the typical large acquisition involves. This strategy also supported a more rapid transition of the store base to Walgreen's preferred format, freestanding stores with drive-through pharmacies, usually located on high-traffic corners.

There were a number of other important developments during this period. In 1999 Walgreen launched a comprehensive online pharmacy that enabled customers to order prescriptions for in-store pickup or mail delivery. The Web site also offered access to the health and wellness content of Mayo Clinic Health Information. The following year the Web site was expanded to include front-of-the-store merchandise, such as nail polish and shampoo.

After the company celebrated its 100th anniversary in 2001, another change in leadership occurred. In January 2002 David Bernauer, a former pharmacist and lifelong Walgreen employee who most recently served as president and chief operating officer, was named CEO, succeeding Jorndt. Bernauer inherited Jorndt's position of chairman as well one year later.

In support of its rapid expansion, Walgreen opened major new distribution centers in Jupiter, Florida, and Dallas (both in 2002); in Perrysburg, Ohio (2003); and in Moreno Valley, California (2004), bringing the total number of such facilities to 11. Late in 2003 Walgreen ended 17 years on the acquisition sideline when it purchased 11 stores and the pharmacy files of five others from Hi-School Pharmacy. The stores were located in the Portland, Oregon, and Vancouver, Washington, metropolitan areas.

Although Walgreen's competition seemed to grow increasingly fierce both at the retail level and in the form of the nascent mail-order pharmacy industry, no clear evidence had arisen suggesting that the company's steady growth was likely to come to an end. The aging U.S. population, coupled with the introduction of innovative new drugs, was fueling prescription growth. The portion of revenues that Walgreen derived from prescriptions continued to increase, surging from less than 50 percent in 1996 to 62 percent by 2003. The company was seeking to add a net 365 stores during 2004, supported by capital expenditures of $1 billion, toward a longer term goal of 7,000 stores by 2010. Among the markets targeted for major expansion was New York City, where Walgreen had only a small presence.

NEW COMPETITIVE STRATEGY: 2006–10

Competition between CVS and Walgreens intensified when CVS acquired Caremark in 2006, forcing Walgreens executives to look for ways to expand market position. The company sought acquisition opportunities among independent pharmacies struggling with lower Medicare payments. Walgreens acquired several new stores, including the Happy Harry's chain of 76 drugstores, located primarily in Delaware. The 2007 acquisition of Option Care added a network of 100 pharmacies in 34 states. The company reached the 50th state in 2007, opening its first store in Hawaii, in Honolulu. That year, Walgreens also opened its 6,000th store, located in New Orleans.

An attempt to acquire Longs Drug Stores was halted in 2008, on the basis of a poor economy and the inability of Longs and Walgreens to come to an agreement. After this Walgreens decided to completely change its business strategy. The company began to focus on providing health care services, both in-store and at corporate workplaces. Walgreens tested Health Corner Clinics opened at stores in St. Louis, Kansas City, Chicago, and Atlanta. In 2007 the acquisition of Take Care Health Systems contributed to establishment of 400 clinics by the end of 2008. Walgreens brought health care services to its retail customers as well, with the launch of Take Care in-store health clinics. Such clinics provided convenience for customers while it alleviated the pressure on primary care physicians to

provide such basic services as flu shots. Preventive care and wellness became a new focus of merchandise development.

Under new CEO Greg Wasson, Walgreens pursued growth by taking health care products and services closer to customers. Walgreens' Complete Care and Well-Being initiative, which capitalized on employer paid benefits, provided pharmacy, health, and wellness programs at corporate workplaces. For instance, Disney World in Orlando housed a health care center and exercise facility operated by Walgreens. A long-term contract with Caterpillar provided employees with generic medications without a co-pay.

Walgreens experimented with wireless technologies to improve service. QuickShop allowed customers to preorder over-the-counter drugs via e-mail or on the new Walgreens Web site. For orders of $20 or more, curbside pickup was available. For smartphone users, Walgreens experimented with a technology that employed the phone's camera and picture messaging capabilities to scan prescription bar codes in order to place pharmacy orders.

EXPANSION AND MERCHANDISING STRATEGIES

Walgreens continued to expand through new store development and acquisitions. The company opened its 7,000th store in October 2009, in Brooklyn, New York. Acquisitions included 7 Rite Aid stores in San Francisco; 17 Ike's and Super-D stores in Memphis; 18 ApothecaryRx pharmacies in Colorado, Minnesota, Missouri, Oklahoma, and Illinois; and 10 Carle RxExpress pharmacies in east and central Illinois.

The 2010 acquisition of the Duane Reade chain of 258 drugstores met the long-held goal to establish a strong presence in the New York market. A local retailing icon, Duane Reade retained its New York identity and influenced Walgreens to adopt customer loyalty and beauty products merchandising strategies. At appropriate locations Walgreens planned to install skin care centers offering skin analysis and upscale products.

Walgreens strengthened its online retail opportunities through the acquisition of Drugstore.com Inc. Walgreens gained a customer base of three million people, plus ready access to established vendors. The acquisition included the Web sites beauty.com and skinstore.com, from which Walgreens gained knowledge of online beauty marketing. In conjunction with its Duane Reade adaptations, Walgreens established its own site, discoverbeautywithin.com. Walgreens promoted beauty products by engaging bloggers to try free samples and write about the products.

Structural changes involved the sale of Walgreens Health Initiatives to Catalyst Health Solutions for $525 million. The sale followed from conflicts with CVS over pharmacy benefits reimbursement. In 2010 CVS Caremark severed its relationship with Walgreens due to concerns that Walgreens' demands would increase the cost of obtaining prescriptions. Catalyst Health Solutions agreed to provide pharmacy benefit management services to Walgreens. The sale allowed Walgreens to pursue its new merchandising and marketing initiatives.

Walgreens revamped its line of private-label merchandise. In October 2011 the company introduced the Nice! brand, marketed with a simpler, bolder look. The new line offered more than 400 grocery and household products, priced as much as 30 percent lower than name-brand goods. As it started stocking the new products, Walgreens eliminated its existing private-label brands. However, the company retained the new Good & Delish premium brand of snacks and beverages. In addition, the company added "food oases" to provide customers with fresh produce. Walgreens expected the transition to be complete in early 2012 and to add more Nice! brand products over the next few years.

Trudy Ring
Updated, David E. Salamie; Mary Tradii

PRINCIPAL SUBSIDIARIES

Duane Reade; Take Care Health Systems; Walgreen Arizona Drug Co.; Bond Drug Company of Illinois; Walgreens Home Care, Inc.; Walgreens Healthcare Plus, Inc.; Walgreens.com, Inc.; Walgreen Louisiana Co., Inc.; Walgreen Hastings Co.; Walgreen Eastern Co., Inc.; Walgreen of Puerto Rico, Inc.; Walgreen of San Patricio, Inc.

PRINCIPAL OPERATING UNITS

Take Care Consumer Solutions; Take Care Health Employer Solutions.

PRINCIPAL COMPETITORS

CVS Caremark Corporation; The Jean Coutu Group (PJC) Inc.; Rite Aid Corporation; Wal-Mart Stores, Inc.

FURTHER READING

Bacon, John U. *America's Corner Store: Walgreens' Prescription for Success.* Hoboken, NJ: Wiley, 2004, 255 p.

Baeb, Eddie. "Headaches Awaiting Walgreen's New CEO: Grow Store Base, Guard Margins." *Crain's Chicago Business,* July 23, 2001, 3.

Byrne, Harlan S. "Prescription for Profits." *Barron's,* January 12, 2004, 23.

———. "Rx for Growth." *Barron's,* January 7, 2002, 14.

"A Century of Growth Comes Full Circle." *Chain Store Age,* December 2000, 250, 252.

"CVS Caremark Announces Plan to Remove Walgreens from PBM Pharmacy Network and Transition Pharmacy Care to Participating Providers." *Benzinga.com,* June 9, 2010, 1.

Frederick, Jim. "Walgreens' 2010 Results Affirm Strategy Change." *Drug Store News,* October 11, 2010, 10.

Garbato, Debby. "A Model of Efficiency," *Retail Merchandiser,* June 2004, 16, 18, 20.

Heller, Laura. "Steering Chain along a Profitable Course." *Drug Store News,* March 25, 2002, 20, 22.

Hundley, Kris. "Drugstores' Dilemma Is Walgreens Opportunity." *St. Petersburg Times,* June 2, 2006, 1D.

Jones, Sandra. "Walgreen Doctoring Stores." *Crain's Chicago Business,* September 8, 2003, 3.

Kogan, Herman, and Rick Kogan. *Pharmacist to the Nation: A History of Walgreen Co., America's Leading Drug Store Chain.* Deerfield, IL: Walgreen Co., 1989.

Kramer, Louise. "Walgreen to Take on New York City." *Crain's New York Business,* July 5, 2004, 3.

Kruger, Renée Marisa. "Walgreens: America's Corner Drugstore." *Retail Merchandiser,* December 2000, 25–27.

Lambert, Emily. "In the Pill Box." *Forbes,* April 26, 2004, 54–56.

Prior, Molly, and Faye Brookman. "Walgreens' Battle Plan: Win Big in Beauty Biz." *WWD,* April 29, 2011, 4.

"Walgreens Launches Nice! Store Brand Chainwide, Continues Building Value and Loyalty with Its Private Brands." *Benzinga.com,* October 29, 2011.

Wolters Kluwer N.V.

Zuidpoolsingel 2
Alphen aan den Rijn, 2408 ZE
Netherlands
Telephone: (+31 172) 641 400
Fax: (+31 172) 474 889
Web site: http://www.wolterskluwer.com

Public Company
Founded: 1836
Employees: 18,237
Sales: EUR 3.57 billion ($5.11 billion) (2010)
Stock Exchanges: Euronext Amsterdam
Ticker Symbol: WKL
NAICS: 511140 Database and Directory Publishers;
511120 Periodical Publishers; 511130 Book
Publishers; 518111 Internet Service Providers;
514199 All Other Information Services

■ ■ ■

Wolters Kluwer N.V. is one of the world's top five
publishing companies, generating total revenues of EUR
3.57 billion ($5.11 billion) in 2010. As the company
has shifted its operations to Internet, mobile, and
software-based products, however, the company has
positioned itself as an "information services company."
At the beginning of 2011, the group's print operations
represented just 31 percent of its overall sales. Founded
as a textbook publisher, Wolters Kluwer has refocused
on four core business areas: Legal & Regulatory, which
generates nearly 43 percent of group revenues; Tax &
Accounting (26 percent); Health & Pharma Solutions

(23 percent); and Financial & Compliance Services (8.6
percent). Wolters Kluwer is headquartered in Amsterdam and is listed on the Euronext Amsterdam Stock
Exchange. Nancy McKinstry is the company's chairman
and CEO.

19TH-CENTURY ROOTS

The modern incarnation of Wolters Kluwer traced its
origins to four Dutch publishing families of the 19th
century: Wolters, Noordhoff, Kluwer, and Samson. During that century, the Industrial Revolution, combined
with constitutional and legal reforms that more closely
united the formerly loose association of Dutch
provinces, prompted a growing demand for educational
and informational literature. Many publishers, print
shops, and typographers responded to this demand,
numbering some 600 by the end of the 1880s. Until the
20th century, however, publishing in the Netherlands
remained the province of small-scale, often family-run
businesses with fewer than 10 employees. The first large
publishing house, the Elsevier Bookselling and Publishing Company, appeared in Amsterdam in 1881, but
remained an exception for some time to come.

J. B. Wolters founded the Schoolbook publishing
house (later to be called the J.B. Wolters Publishing
Company) in the provincial capital city of Groningen in
1836, providing educational and instructional materials
for a country just beginning the transformation to a
modern industrial economy. Wolters was childless, and
upon his death in 1860, his brother-in-law, E. B. ter
Horst, took over the company. Under ter Horst the
company began a period of expansion, adding a printing

shop and bindery to its editorial functions. Ter Horst brought his son, E. B. ter Horst, Jr., into the company in 1885, and ter Horst, Jr., was made a partner in the company eight years later.

Disagreements between father and son led the senior ter Horst to leave the company soon afterward. Ter Horst, Jr., led the company until his death in 1905. By then, the company's fortunes had fallen, to the point where the heirs to the company, ter Horst, Jr.'s half-brothers F. R. and A. ter Horst, considered closing the company. Instead, the brothers reorganized the company from a partnership into a corporation, and for the first time brought in directors from outside the family. F. R. ter Horst, formerly a banking professional, became the company's managing director, overseeing the editorial portions of its textbook and academic publishing activities from his home in The Hague. The company's production facilities remained in Groningen.

In 1915 a separate office was opened in The Hague. Two years later Dr. Anthony M. H. Schepman, who was married to a niece of F. R. ter Horst, joined the J.B. Wolters Company and was soon named a director of the company, a position he held for more than 40 years. Under the joint leadership of ter Horst and Schepman, the company continued to expand its operations. In 1920 the company opened an office in what is now known as Jakarta, Indonesia, to provide books for the Dutch-speaking population there. Setbacks for the company came with the Great Depression of the 1930s,

and the introduction of modern Dutch spelling, which removed many Germanisms from the Dutch grammar and spelling and rendered many of Wolters' titles obsolete.

These setbacks resulted in a shutdown of its Hague offices. World War II, during which Schepman was interned as a member of the Dutch elite in a German concentration camp, added to the company's difficulties. After the war, and especially after Indonesia achieved its independence in 1949, the company enjoyed a period of enhanced prosperity. Wolters also moved into the Flemish-speaking areas of Belgium, especially with the promotion of Algemeen Beschaafd Nederlands (or ABN, a standardization of the language similar to Standard Received English) over the many Dutch and Flemish dialects still spoken throughout both countries. However, in 1954, the Republic of Indonesia moved to prohibit the importation of Indonesian-language books printed outside the country. The J.B. Wolters-Djakarta division attempted to set up printing facilities in Indonesia, but in 1959, Indonesia nationalized many of the foreign companies operating there, including J.B. Wolters-Djakarta.

CONVERGENCE: LATE SIXTIES AND EARLY SEVENTIES

By then, a postwar wave of mergers across Dutch industry had begun to affect the publishing industry as well. The era of the small family publishing house was fading. The Noordhoff publishing house, founded in 1858 by P. Noordhoff to serve the educational and vocational market, was located directly next door to Wolters' offices in Groningen, and was still managed by the Noordhoff family.

Driven by the increasingly competitive nature of the Dutch publishing industry, Noordhoff approached Wolters about merging the two companies. Wolters, nearly three times the size of Noordhoff but facing the same competition from much larger publishing companies, agreed. The merger of the two houses was accomplished in 1968, literally by the breaking down of the wall that had long separated their offices. The next phase in Wolters' history followed four years later, when it merged with the Information and Communication Group, which had been formed from an earlier merger with the Samson publishing family.

Nicolaas Samson's publishing career began as an offshoot of his civil service career in the Dutch village of Hazerswoude. As the recent modernization of Dutch law was slowly reaching from the larger cities to the outlying provinces, the need arose for new administrative materials and forms, which Samson provided. Sam-

KEY DATES

1836: J. B. Wolters founds Schoolbook publishing house.
1891: Ebele E. Kluwer publishes his first textbook.
1968: Schoolbook (now known as J.B. Wolters Publishing Company) and Noordhoff merge.
1970: Samson publishing merges with A.W. Sijthoff to form the Information and Communications Union (ICU).
1972: Wolters-Noordhoff merges with ICU and takes its name.
1983: ICU changes its name to Wolters-Samson.
1987: Kluwer merges with Wolters-Samson to fend off hostile takeover bid by Elsevier; new entity is called Wolters Kluwer.
1990: Company purchases J.B. Lippincott and Company from HarperCollins.
1996: Wolters Kluwer spends $1.9 billion for tax and business materials publisher CCH, Inc.
2003: Nancy McKinstry becomes the company's first non-Dutch and first female CEO.
2007: Company sells its education division.

son operated first in an office of the town hall. By 1883 he had moved his publishing activities, including printing shop, bindery, and warehouse, to offices next to his home in Alphen aan den Rijn.

In 1886 Samson left the civil service to operate his publishing business full time. At first Samson's business concentrated on administrative forms, but he soon added periodicals and books for the administrative market. In 1888 Samson's oldest son, Jacobus Balthus, joined the company. He was joined by his younger brothers Nicolaas and Willem in 1914 and 1915. After a brief period of financial difficulty, Samson's sons took over the company and expanded its operations.

The elder Nicolaas Samson died in 1917. By then, the company had achieved a national reputation. It also maintained strong ties with the government. The company added educational materials and related forms and services to its list in 1920. Samson continued to prosper, yet always remained close to its core business. In 1970 Samson merged with the publisher A.W. Sijthoff, forming the Information and Communication Union (ICU), which merged with Wolters-Noordhoff two years later. The new company adopted the ICU name but in 1983 changed its name again, to Wolters-Samson.

The final branch of Wolters-Kluwer was founded in the 1880s in Deventer, in the eastern Netherlands, by Ebele E. Kluwer. Kluwer began as a bookseller. By 1891 he had published his first book, on arithmetic, called *The Thinker*, which was directed at the secondary school market. For many years, Kluwer concentrated on the educational and academic market, including children's books. In 1892 Kluwer published one of the first trade papers aimed at the educational market, called *De Sollicitant*. Several years later he initiated a successful series of picture books. Another of Kluwer's publications was *De Nederlandsche Jager*, a trade periodical for hunters.

Within a decade, Kluwer expanded to include business information and technical works, and soon after into tax and professional publications as well. In 1909 Kluwer published *De Vakstudie* tax series, which provided purchasers with periodic supplements of updated information. By 1920 Kluwer was publishing similar works for other professional areas, by then in a more easily updated looseleaf binder form. These series were extremely profitable for the company, fueling its expansion and remaining one of its most important markets. Kluwer's sons, Evert, Nico, and Eben, joined the firm between 1914 and 1921. His daughters and their husbands also became involved in the company. Kluwer died in 1929, leaving the company to his sons. Kluwer Publishers remained a family concern, growing to become the Netherlands' third-largest publisher, with subsidiaries in the United States and elsewhere, with revenues of NLG 966 million, by 1986.

CONSOLIDATION IN THE EIGHTIES

The Netherlands were largely untouched by the wave of hostile takeovers that marked the 1980s. That changed in 1987, when Elsevier, the country's largest publishing house, announced its intention to buy up Kluwer's stock. A year earlier, Elsevier had initiated talks with Kluwer to suggest a merger between the two companies. Kluwer rejected the plan, pointing to differences in corporate cultures. In June 1987, Elsevier announced a bid of NLG 390 per Kluwer share, which had been worth only NLG 266 per share two weeks before. Kluwer responded by issuing another 2.5 million common shares and beginning talks with Wolters Samson about a possible friendly merger between the two companies.

Kluwer's preference for a merger with the smaller house of Wolters Samson was explained by the greater similarity between the two companies' corporate cultures, and in the similarity in their publishing focus. Shortly thereafter, Kluwer issued an additional two million shares of preferential stock to Wolters Samson, vowing to do whatever necessary to stop Elsevier's takeover bid. By August 3, however, Elsevier had won control of 48.2 percent of Kluwer's stock, spending NLG 25 million in the final days to acquire it. By August 14, however, Wolters Samson was able to announce that it had acquired 50.9 percent of Kluwer's outstanding common stock, effecting the merger of their two companies.

The new company, called Wolters Kluwer N.V., moved its headquarters to Amsterdam. In the final count, Elsevier retained approximately 33 percent of the new company's shares. In 1990 it announced its intention to sell these shares, surrendering, for the time being, the idea of a merger between the two companies. Analysts, however, continued to predict that the firms would eventually join forces.

ADDING LIPPINCOTT IN 1990

With the merger, Wolters Kluwer became the Netherlands' second-largest publisher. With international holdings including the U.S. subsidiaries Kluwer Law Book Publishing Company, Raven Press, and Aspen Systems, Wolters Kluwer entered a period of foreign acquisitions. Over the next two years the company extended into France, West Germany, and Spain. By 1989, roughly 44 percent of its revenues were earned in foreign markets.

The pending formation of the European market opened a lucrative arena for the company's well-developed tax and legal publishing arms. The company increased its focus on these areas, dropping several of its Dutch trade and consumer publishers, including Bert Bakker and Martinus Nijhoff International. Its acquisitions continued, with purchases of the IPSOA Editore of Italy, Kieser Verlag of Germany, Tecnipublicaciones of Spain, and Tele Consulte of France. In 1990 the company moved to strengthen its share of the U.S. medical market, completing the $250 million purchase of the 200-year-old J.B. Lippincott and Company from HarperCollins. By that year, Wolters Kluwer included nearly 100 companies, posting annual revenues of more than NLG 2 billion.

Lippincott had been founded in 1836, when Joshua B. Lippincott opened J.B. Lippincott & Co. in Philadelphia. Lippincott's 1849 purchase of Grigg, Elliot & Co., then the world's largest book distributor, allowed him to extend his company's anniversary to the other company's 1792 founding date. The company grew quickly, with medical publications featuring prominently among its titles. After overseeing the incorporation of his company in 1885, Lippincott died the following year, leaving the firm to his three sons.

By the end of the century, Lippincott was one of the three largest U.S. publishers. In addition to its medical list, it published for the educational market. Nevertheless, it was best known for its trade books, which accounted for approximately 50 percent of its business. In the 1950s, however, the company reasserted its interest in other markets, particularly in medical and nursing books and journals. It also expanded its educational and college offerings, placing less and less emphasis on trade books. A major event occurred in 1972, when, finding itself undercapitalized, the company was forced to go public, with the Lippincott family retaining majority ownership.

The new corporation launched a period of aggressive expansion, entering new markets and extending its established divisions. By 1977, however, rising costs and other factors had increased the company's debt-to-equity ratio to two to one. The following year, Lippincott was purchased by Harper & Row. Lippincott's activities were pared down to a core focused around medical and nursing books and journals. This formula proved successful. By the time Lippincott was purchased by Wolters Kluwer, its revenues had risen by 500 percent.

The opening of European borders in 1992 meant increasing numbers of new laws and regulations that would need to be translated into many languages. Wolters Kluwer stepped up the internationalization of its activities, concentrating on the most highly developed countries of the European Union. By 1993 its international sales represented 62 percent of its yearly revenues. Its European sales outside of the Netherlands accounted for 45 percent of its total revenues, the United States for 11 percent, and the Netherlands for 37 percent.

Wolters Kluwer continued acquiring companies, including Liber in Sweden in 1993. The company established its first Eastern European subsidiary, IURA Edition, in Bratislava, Slovakia, and announced intentions for further Eastern European expansion. Electronic media, including computer diskettes, CD-ROMs, and CD-I technology, had become another growing area for Wolters Kluwer, accounting for 6 percent of its sales in 1994.

CCH ACQUISITION IN 1996

The year 1995 proved to be another busy one for the company, as it acquired a slew of businesses, including Jugend & Volk (Austria); Dalian (France); Fateco Firlag and Juristfirlaget (Sweden); Deutscher Kommunal-Verlag Dr. Naujoks & Behrendt (Germany); and Colex Data (Spain). The same year, Lippincott and Raven Press, a medical publisher, were merged to form Lippincott-Raven Publishers. By then, Wolters Kluwer operated in 16 countries and had over 8,000 employees.

In 1996, Wolters Kluwer completed a significant purchase when it spent $1.9 billion to take over a prominent U.S. publisher of tax and business materials, CCH, Inc. This acquisition greatly strengthened Wolters Kluwer's position in that segment of the U.S. publishing market. To build on this achievement, the company bought several other businesses over the next few years (including Bankers Systems, Inc. and two divisions of the West Group's Information America unit) and rolled them into CCH's operations. This division also came to play a prominent role in Wolters Kluwer's operations in Asia, as CCH arms did business in Australia, New Zealand, Japan, Singapore, and Hong Kong.

The company enjoyed continued success in 1997. Total sales and net income both rose 21 percent over 1996 levels, thanks mainly to strategic acquisitions. Wolters Kluwer's operations in Germany, France, the United Kingdom, and the United States were particularly profitable. Despite these gains, speculation remained rife that Wolters Kluwer would be taken over by Elsevier (now Reed Elsevier, after the latter's merger with another publishing powerhouse, Reed International PLC). These predictions were nearly borne out when the firms announced a proposed merger in October 1997. The deal fell through in March 1998, however, when Wolters Kluwer decided that the divestments that would be required to secure regulatory approval for the transaction were too high a price to pay.

NEW STRATEGY FOR 2002

In the wake of this incident, Wolters Kluwer convened a working group of managers from its operations around the world to devise a plan for the next phase of the company's growth and development. The resulting "Strategic Agenda 2002" led the company to decide to refocus its business on several core competencies. Specifically, Wolters Kluwer opted to concentrate on its operations in the legal and tax publishing, business publishing, medical/scientific publishing, and educational publishing/professional training realms.

To achieve this goal, the company continued to acquire firms that could bolster its efforts in these areas, and to divest holdings that fell outside them. For example, in August 1999, Wolters Kluwer sold its Wayland Publishers unit, because that division published children's books, a field in which the company no longer wished to compete. On the other hand, the company made three acquisitions in 1998 that dramatically heightened its profile in the medical/scientific publishing industry, bringing Waverly, Inc., Ovid Technologies, Inc., and Plenum Publishing Corporation into its fold.

"Strategic Agenda 2002" also identified the growing importance that electronic and online media would have in the publishing world. Wolters Kluwer was acutely aware of the risk that its traditional paper offering could be rendered obsolete if it failed to stay abreast of the technological developments cascading through the industry. As a result, the company rededicated itself to integrating new media into its traditional methods of presentation (electronic publishing had provided nearly 19 percent of the firm's revenues as far back as 1996, a figure the company expected to grow significantly in subsequent years).

To this end, the company's Kluwers Academic Publishers division joined a 12-firm consortium in November 1999 that was striving to revamp the way scientists use the Internet to conduct research. The aim of this partnership was to bridge gaps between otherwise independent and disconnected databases (the databases' proprietary owners remained free to set the terms of access, however). Moreover, Wolters Kluwer stepped up its efforts to provide high-level customer service and to develop innovative hardware and software in order to expand the range of options its customers had at their disposal to access the breadth of the company's information sources.

RESTRUCTURING IN 2003

In the new decade, Wolters Kluwer's shift toward electronic media took on steam. The company completed a flurry of acquisitions, including Loislaw.com Inc. in 2000, and Tsoft, CBF Systems Inc., ePace! Software, SilverPlatter Information, Medi-Span, and Execusite in 2001. These acquisitions nearly doubled the group's Internet-based sales. In 2002, the company launched its own online digital bookstore, ebooks.kluweronline.com, starting with 150 titles. The company also announced its intention to continue its acquisition drive, targeting companies with annual revenues as high as EUR 400 million.

Wolters Kluwer's shift from print publisher toward digitally oriented information provider necessitated the shedding of a number of noncore operations. These included Kluwer Academic Publishers, sold in 2002, and its trade publisher unit, Ten Hagen & Stam, sold in 2004. In their place, the company acquired U.K.-based ABG Professional Information, which joined the group's Legal Tax & Business division. In 2003, the company bought Transwide, a provider of e-logistics for the European market. In that year, however, the company posted a loss of nearly $87 billion.

The appointment of Nancy McKinstry as the company's CEO and chairman in 2003 marked the start of a new era for the company. The American-born McKinstry, formerly CEO of the company's U.S. operations, became the first non-Dutch national, as well as the first woman, to lead the company. McKinstry quickly led Wolters Kluwer through a major restructuring effort. The three-year plan involved the loss of 1,600 jobs and a cost reduction of EUR 240 million. The new strategy also included plans to spend EUR 800 million on new acquisitions in order to reinforce the company's "information provider" identity.

McKinstry's leadership helped the company rebound, with a profit of $184 million on $4.4 billion in revenues in 2004. In that year, the company acquired PCi Corp., followed by the purchase of Michigan-based Entyre, a provider of mortgage document services in 2005. Wolters Kluwer also boosted its Health division, spending $382 million for Arizona-based NDC Health Information Management, focused on the pharmaceutical, bioresearch, and medical research markets. The company also acquired the assets of Pennsylvania's Boucher Communications, specialized in publishing ophthalmic journals such as *Retinal Physician*, *Content Lens Spectrum*, *Ophthalmology Management*, and *Optometric Management*.

ADDING INDIA IN 2006

Wolters Kluwer continued both its restructuring and its acquisition drive in the second half of the decade. The company acquired ProVation Medical, providing document managing applications for the health care industry, and GulfPak, developer of account origination and lending software, both in 2006. The latter purchase became part of Wolters Kluwer's Financial & Compliance Services division.

Much, if not most, of the company's expansion had focused on the group's North American operations, which grew to account for more than half of the company's total revenues through the end of the decade. Europe remained a core market for the company, adding more than 40 percent to group sales. Wolters Kluwer nonetheless began to prepare for the future, with plans to extend its reach into a number of fast-developing Asian markets. In 2006, the company entered India, setting up a dedicated subsidiary there and launching a number of localized editions of its journals and other products. By 2010, the company's Financial Services division had also expanded into the Indian market.

The following year, Wolters Kluwer joined a trend among its major competitors, including Reed Elsevier and Thomson, as it moved to shed its education division. The company reached an agreement to sell Wolters Kluwer Education to a private-equity group,

Bridgepoint, for EUR 774 million in March 2007. Following that sale, Wolters Kluwer reorganized around four core divisions, Legal & Regulatory; Tax & Accounting; Health & Pharma Solutions; and Financial & Compliance Services.

CHINESE EXPANSION FROM 2011

The sale of its education division formed part of the company's continued shift to digital and online platforms. The company embraced mobile trends, developing a series of apps for the burgeoning smartphone market, such as the Emanuel Bar Review series, made available for the Apple iPhone in 2010. The company also produced mobile applications for its CCH IntelliConnect, while Lippincott Williams & Wilkins launched a Web site capable of responding to clinical questions within 30 seconds. The company also introduced an iPad-compatible version of its annual report that year. The company expected online software and services revenues to account for 75 percent of sales by 2012.

Through Corsearch, the company acquired Edital, adding its brand management products, while the Tax & Accounting division bought up the tax compliance product line of Ernst & Young Australia. By the end of the year, the company had also acquired FRSGlobal, a financial services provider, and Pharmacy OneSource, a producer of pharmacy software for hospitals.

In 2011, Wolters Kluwer judged that the time was right to enter the Chinese market. The company announced its intention to seek out partnerships in that country, in order to tailor its products for the requirements of the Chinese market. The company expected strong growth there for its legal publishing division, as the number of lawyers in China grew from zero in the 1980s to 170,000 by 2011, with expectations of more than two million by 2020.

The company's other divisions made progress in that market as well. Among the group's first moves was the creation of a joint venture with Medicom, a drug information provider, formed in 2011. The entry into China formed part of Wolters Kluwer's transformation from a Dutch textbook publisher to a global information services provider in the 21st century.

M. L. Cohen
Updated, Rebecca Stanfel; M. L. Cohen

PRINCIPAL SUBSIDIARIES

CCH, Inc.; Aspen Publishers; Ovid Technologies, Inc.; Lippincott-Raven Publishers; Stanley Thornes.

PRINCIPAL DIVISIONS

Legal & Regulatory; Tax & Accounting; Health & Pharma Solutions; Financial & Compliance Services.

PRINCIPAL COMPETITORS

Bertelsmann AG; Education Media and Publishing Group Ltd.; Hachette Livre SA; McGraw-Hill Cos.; Pearson Plc; Reed Elsevier; Thomson Corporation.

FURTHER READING

de Vries, Johan. *Four Windows of Opportunity: A Study in Publishing.* Amsterdam: Wolters Kluwer, 1995.

duBois, Martin. "Reed Elsevier and Wolters Kluwer End Merger Plans after Concerns at EU." *Wall Street Journal,* March 10, 1998.

Feldman, Gayle. "Going Dutch." *Publishers Weekly,* June 21, 1991.

"Going Dutch." *Chief Executive (U.S.),* September 2006, 12F.

Hagerty, Bob. "Esoteric Publisher Avoids the Obvious." *Wall Street Journal (Europe),* April 25, 1990.

"John Wiley and Sons: Reference Linking Service Announces Name." *M2 Presswire,* December 10, 1999.

"Kluwer's New Strategy Excites Investors." *Bookseller,* February 13, 2004, 8.

Milliot, Jim. "Wolters Kluwer to Buy Waverly." *Publishers Weekly,* February 16, 1998.

"On the Information Super Highway." *Business Daily Update,* October 13, 2011.

Scott, Robert W. "With $1.9 Billion Sale, CCH Gains Dutch Uncle." *Accounting Today,* December 11, 1995.

"Wolters Kluwer Bolsters Healthcare Unit with $200 Million Ovid Buy." *Electronic Information Report,* October 16, 1998.

"Wolters Kluwer Goes on a Healthy Acquisition Spree." *Information World Review,* October 24, 2005, 4.

"Wolters Kluwer Health Acquires Lexi-Comp." *Manufacturing Close-up,* June 2, 2011.

"Wolters Kluwer Seeks Partnerships in China." *Business Daily Update,* February 25, 2011.

"Wolters Kluwer Treads Water as Recession Bites." *Information World Review,* March 2010, 4.

WWF-World Wide Fund For Nature

Avenue du Mont Blanc
Gland, 1196
Switzerland
Telephone: (+41 22) 364 91 11
Fax: (+41 22) 364 48 921250
Web site: http://www.panda.org

Nonprofit Organization
Incorporated: 1961 as World Wildlife Fund
Employees: 429
Operating Revenues: $224.2 million (2010)
NAICS: 813312 Environment, Conservation, and
Wildlife Organizations

■ ■ ■

WWF-World Wide Fund For Nature (WWF) calls itself the "world's leading independent conservation organization." It is a global network, working in more than 100 countries, that strives to protect the diversity of life on the planet by addressing issues ranging from the survival of species and habitats to climate change, sustainable business, and environmental education. In carrying out its work, WWF cooperates with local and international partners, including United Nations' organizations, the International Union for Conservation of Nature, development agencies such as USAID and the World Bank, and businesses. WWF operates about 1,300 projects at any one time in Africa, Asia, Latin America, North America, and Eurasia, and has national affiliates (formerly called appeals) in about 100 countries. WWF is governed by a board of trustees under an international president.

SAVING SPECIES FROM EXTINCTION IN THE SIXTIES

On April 29, 1961, a small but influential group of European scientists, naturalists, and business and political leaders signed the "Morges Manifesto," which became the blueprint for the first global green organization, the World Wildlife Fund. The manifesto called for urgent worldwide action to stop the hunting of large numbers of wild animals and halt the destruction of habitats. Its signatories (among them noted British biologist Julian Huxley) undertook as their mission to raise funds and educate the public to save species from extinction worldwide.

The Morges Manifesto expressly supported the development of a new nongovernmental organization. The World Wildlife Fund (WWF) was registered as a charity on September 11, 1961, and its first offices opened in Morges, Switzerland, at the headquarters of the International Union for Conservation of Nature and Natural Resources (IUCN). Prince Bernhard of the Netherlands became its first president and naturalist and painter Peter Scott its first chairman. The organization's soon-famous logo was designed by Scott and inspired by Chi-Chi, the giant panda then recently arrived at the London Zoo.

At the first major meeting of its founders, WWF was established as an international fundraising organization that worked through national appeals. Prince Philip, Duke of Edinburgh, became president of the

WWF's mission is to stop the degradation of the planet's natural environment and to build a future in which humans live in harmony with nature, by: conserving the world's biological diversity; ensuring that the use of renewable natural resources is sustainable; and promoting the reduction of pollution and wasteful consumption.

British National Appeal, WWF's first national organization, known as World Wildlife Fund-UK. The second national appeal was incorporated in the United States in the District of Columbia on December 1, 1961, with President Dwight D. Eisenhower as President of Honor.

During its first decade WWF focused on protecting individual endangered species. Beginning in 1961, it focused on drawing public attention to the destruction of Africa's rhino and elephant populations, taking action to stop poaching and to protect habitats. Two years later, it was influential in setting up the Mweka Wildlife Management College in Tanzania, which trained park rangers and wildlife managers to serve in protected areas throughout sub-Saharan Africa. In 1969, WWF helped establish Coto Doñana National Park, one of Europe's most important wetland reserves, a major site for migrating birds, and one of the last refuges for Iberian lynx.

The leadership of the WWF recognized its need for an enduring, independent financial base. Under Fritz Vollmar, who became secretary general beginning in 1962, it established an international secretariat and began building a network of national fundraising organizations among its founding members. In 1970 WWF undertook an initiative to establish an organizational endowment. Called "The 1001: A Nature Trust," the effort sought to find 1,001 individuals to each contribute $10,000 toward a $10 million fund, the interest from which helped to cover WWF's basic administrative costs. With these costs assured, WWF could guarantee the donating public that contributions would go directly to benefit wildlife and habitat conservation.

CONSERVING HABITATS AS WELL AS SPECIES IN THE SEVENTIES

At the time of its 10th anniversary in 1971, World Wildlife Fund had set up 16 national organizations and

financed 550 projects in 59 countries. Vollmar was appointed to the new post of director general, where he served until he retired in 1978. During the 1970s, the organization's focus expanded to India, with the 1972 launch of Operation Tiger, operating in concert with the Indian government's Project Tiger, and resulting in nine national tiger reserves in India. Another three reserves opened soon after in Nepal, another one in Bangladesh, and six more in India.

Mid-decade saw the arrival of Charles de Haes as director general. (He served jointly with Vollmar for two and a half years.) The year 1975 also saw the broadening of WWF's focus to encompass ecosystems, with a tropical rain-forest campaign to set aside and manage several dozen forests in Africa, Southeast Asia, and Latin America as national parks or reserves. This was followed by an attempt to end international trade in animals and plants for commodities such as ivory and rhino horn. Working with IUCN and the Convention on International Trade in Endangered Species of Wild Fauna and Flora (CITES), which it had earlier helped found, WWF helped to set up a nonprofit wildlife monitoring body called Trade Records Analysis of Fauna and Flora in Commerce (TRAFFIC) in 1976. TRAFFIC represented a global network "committed to delivering innovative and practical solutions to wildlife trade issues."

WWF also launched its first marine program in 1976. It began by protecting marine turtle nesting sites and establishing sanctuaries for whales, dolphins, and seals. Three years later, following upon China's estimate that only about 2,400 wild pandas still existed, WWF set out to establish the Wolong Nature Reserve for the preservation of pandas in China. Working in cooperation with the People's Republic of China, WWF signed an agreement to establish a six-member WWF-China committee to act as a liaison between conservation organizations and authorities in China and WWF's worldwide conservation network. The decade drew to a close with a campaign that raised more than $1 million to combat rhino poaching.

PROMOTING THE CONCEPT OF SUSTAINABLE DEVELOPMENT IN THE EIGHTIES

During the late 1970s and early 1980s, WWF's work broadened again to encompass not only the conservation of wildlife and habitats, but also the impact of human activities on the environment. WWF began to promote the concept of sustainable development. From its new home in a modern office block in Gland, where it had moved in 1979, it published its *World Conservation Strategy* with IUCN, and the United Nations

KEY DATES

1961: World Wildlife Fund (WWF) is founded and is registered as a charity in Switzerland.

1970: WWF establishes a $10 million trust to cover administrative costs.

1971: Fritz Vollmar assumes the new post of director general.

1975: Charles de Haes becomes director general.

1981: WWF has one million regular supporters worldwide.

1986: Organization changes its name to WWF-World Wide Fund For Nature.

2005: James P. Leape becomes director general of WWF.

Environmental Program (UNEP) in 1980. The strategy was endorsed by the United Nations Secretary General, and soon 50 countries had initiated their own national conservation strategies based on its recommendations. A simplified version, *How to Save the World*, was published in several languages. Meanwhile, WWF continued to build its base of popular support. In 1981, the organization had one million regular supporters worldwide. Fundraising efforts received a boost in 1983, with the launch of the "Conservation Stamp Collection" whereby WWF worked with postal authorities in more than 200 countries to develop stamps featuring threatened species. In 1985, the organization helped bring about an international moratorium on whaling.

When it turned 25 in 1986, WWF and its network of appeals decided to publicize its expanded mandate by changing its name from World Wildlife Fund to WWF-World Wide Fund For Nature. With the exception of the United States and Canada, all national appeals took on the new name. As part of its anniversary celebrations, WWF invited leaders from the world's five main religions to attend a two-day retreat in Assisi, Italy. The gathering led to the formation of an international network through which WWF and religious groups worked together toward the common cause of conservation.

WORKING WITH INDIVIDUALS AND BUSINESSES IN THE NINETIES

The 1990s began with an international moratorium on the ivory trade and the release of the organization's expanded mission, reiterating WWF's commitment to

nature conservation, and classifying the organization's work into three interdependent categories: preservation of biological diversity, promotion of the concept of sustainable use of resources, and reduction of wasteful consumption and pollution. The accompanying 1990 strategy decentralized WWF's decision making and increased cooperation with individuals at the local level.

The following year, WWF, IUCN, and UNEP joined forces again to publish *Caring for the Earth—A Strategy for Sustainable Living*. Launched in more than 60 countries, the report listed 132 actions that people at all social and political levels could take to safeguard or improve their environment, such as cutting back on their consumption of fossil fuels.

WWF also founded the WWF 1995 Group, composed of 20 British companies dedicated to responsible management of the world's forests, in 1991. (The group later changed its name to WWF1995+ Group and later still to Global Forest Trade Network, or GFTN.) At the end of 1993, with Claude Martin as its new director general, WWF completed a two-year network-wide evaluation of its conservation work and resolved to focus its activities on three key geographic areas: forests, freshwater ecosystems, and oceans and coasts. Martin had served as director of several protected areas in the Western Region of Ghana, before becoming director of WWF-Switzerland in 1980.

WWF continued to lobby governments and policy makers, conduct research, and work with business and industry to address global threats by seeking long-term solutions. In 1998, it joined forces with the World Bank to set up a worldwide network of protected areas, including 200 million hectares of well-managed forests by 2005. In 1999 it lobbied successfully to include sustainable development in the new National Curriculum for schoolchildren in England.

MAKING THE ENVIRONMENT A MATTER OF WORLD CONCERN

In the early 2000s, WWF worked to ensure sustainable development throughout the Danube-Carpathian region, to protect freshwater habitats in the United Kingdom, Brazil, China, and along the U.S.-Mexico border, and to make it an arrestable offense to trade in endangered animals and their body parts in the United Kingdom.

WWF's direction and momentum continued under James P. Leape, a Harvard College and Law School graduate, who had coauthored the leading American text on environmental law. He became director general in 2005. In 2006, WWF launched its "Heart of Borneo" program to preserve one of the most important centers of biological diversity in the world.

In 2007 WWF's focus fell on the United Kingdom. Its "One Million Sustainable Homes" campaign resulted in a British national code used to rate the green quotient of all new homes in the United Kingdom from 2008 on. Its 2007 efforts to ensure passage of The U.K. Climate Change Act, the first legislation in the world aimed at setting binding targets to reduce greenhouse gas emissions, yielded success in 2008. In 2009 the passage of the Marine and Coastal Access Act crowned WWF's 10-year campaign to assign the United Kingdom a legal duty to conserve and protect species and habitats in and around its seas.

FIRST GLOBAL EARTH HOUR

Also in 2009, WWF launched its first annual global Earth Hour. Begun in Sydney in 2007, Earth Hour (organized globally on the last Saturday of March), asked households and businesses to turn off their nonessential lights and electrical appliances for one hour to raise awareness and put pressure on leaders to take action on climate change.

As WWF management sought to move forward, it worked to maximize operational efficiencies. Austerity measures put in place in fiscal 2009 required that 83 percent of expenses be directed toward conservation efforts (with the remainder toward administration). Operating revenue totaled $224.2 million in 2010, a 1.3 percent increase over 2009 as the organization's membership kept growing.

By January 2010, with its release of the paper "The Copenhagen Accord: A Stepping Stone?" analyzing how the world might prevent dangerous climate change, WWF had become instrumental in making the environment a matter of world concern. In addition to funding and managing countless conservation projects throughout the world, it had assumed the role of a global leader in the field, influencing both public opinion and policy. Its *Living Planet Report* posts on Facebook were viewed more than half a million times in 2010, and hundreds of thousands of people signed its petition to double the number of tigers in the wild in Asia by 2022. Earth Hour 2010 involved more than a billion people around the world, calling for action on climate change. WWF vowed to continue its advocacy and action in the years to come.

Carrie Rothburd

FURTHER READING

Huxley, Sir Julian. "Cropping the Wild Protein." *Observer*, November 20, 1960, 23.

———. "The Treasure House of Wild Life." *Observer*, November 13, 1960, 23.

———. "Wild Life as a World Asset." *Observer*, November 27, 1960, 23.

Kellaway, Kate. "How the *Observer* Brought the WWF into Being." *Observer*, November 6, 2012. Accessed January 20, 2012. http://www.guardian.co.uk/environment/2010/nov/07/wwf-world-wildlife-fund-huxley.

"Pretoria Inquiry Confirms Secret Battle for the Rhino." *Independent*, January 16, 1996.

Scott, Peter. *The Launching of a New Ark; First Report of the President and Trustees of the World Wildlife Fund, 1961–1964*. London: Collins, 1965.

Xanterra Parks & Resorts, Inc.

———— ■ ————

6312 South Fiddlers Green Circle, Suite 600N
Greenwood Village, Colorado 80111
U.S.A.
Telephone: (303) 600-3400
Fax: (303) 600-3600
Web site: http://www.xanterra.com

Private Company
Incorporated: 2002
Employees: 7,400
Sales: $305.35 million (2010)
NAICS: 721110 Hotels (Except Casino Hotels) and
Motels; 721199 All Other Traveler Accommoda-
tion; 722110 Full-Service Restaurants; 722211
Limited-Service Restaurants

■ ■ ■

Xanterra Parks & Resorts, Inc., is the largest parks
management company in the United States, operating as
a concessionaire at eight national parks and 10 state
parks. Xanterra, under management contracts, operates
31 hotels and lodges with more than 5,200 rooms. The
company manages 68 restaurants, 55 retail stores, 3
marinas, 10 golf courses, and approximately 1,700
campsites. Xanterra owns the Kingsmill Resort near
Williamsburg, Virginia, a property that includes a 425-
room hotel and five restaurants, and Seattle-based
Windstar Cruises, which operates a three-ship fleet of
luxury yachts that sail in the Caribbean, Europe, and
the Americas. Xanterra is owned by The Anschutz

Corporation, a privately owned company controlled by
billionaire Philip Anschutz.

THE BIRTH OF HARVEY HOUSES: 1875–78

In name, Xanterra originated in 2002, but the history of
its assets stretched back more than a century earlier,
back to the pioneering efforts of England-born Fred
Harvey in 1875. Harvey, credited with creating the first
restaurant chain in the United States, began establishing
cafes at railroad stops in 1875 while he was working as a
freight agent for the Chicago, Burlington, and Quincy
Railroad (Burlington). Harvey found the foodservice options at railroad stops (typically where locomotives took
on water) to be deplorable, usually consisting of rancid
meat and cold beans served by surly proprietors. His
first two railroad eating houses, located near Wallace,
Kansas, and Hugo, Colorado, stopped operating within
a year because Harvey was less than impressed by his
business partner, but Harvey was committed to the
cause and convinced he could make a handsome profit
in the business.

Harvey, who established his first dining facilities
along the Kansas Pacific Railway, turned to his
employer, Burlington Railroad, for support in his second
endeavor. Burlington Railroad, presented with a plan to
establish a systemwide foodservice operation at all
railroad meal stops, turned down Harvey's proposal, but
another railroad, the Atchison, Topeka and Santa Fe
Railway (Santa Fe), expressed interest in trying Harvey's
idea on an experimental basis. Harvey purchased the
lunchroom at the railroad's depot in Topeka, Kansas, in

COMPANY PERSPECTIVES

Our legacy of hospitality leadership spans more than a century. Over the years we have become entrusted with the care and preservation of some of the country's most prized examples of historic national park architecture. Throughout our existence we have been dedicated to providing superior visitor services. We have conducted our business not only in accordance with all applicable environmental laws, but also in a fashion that extends beyond environmental regulations to include sustainability practices that conserve natural resources on public lands.

1876 and impressed both the railroad and customers with his superior service and food.

Santa Fe agreed to expand Harvey's operations, which led to the establishment of the first Harvey House in Florence, Kansas, in 1878. Established in the Clifton Hotel, the first Harvey House served meals on fine China and Irish linens, offering travelers large portions (pies, for example, were cut into fourths rather than sixths, as was the practice in the restaurant industry) served by courteous wait staff in a cleanly kept dining room. Harvey developed a system with the railroad that alerted the kitchen staff via telegraph of the number and the time of arriving of passengers, enabling Harvey's concession to serve all the passengers on an incoming train within 30 minutes.

FRED HARVEY WORKS IN CONCERT WITH SANTA FE RAILWAY: 1878–1930

Harvey, through his company, the Fred Harvey Company, flourished. The Santa Fe Railway encouraged him to open Harvey Houses, some of which provided lodging, all along the railroad's line, agreeing to transport fresh meat and produce at no cost to any Harvey House with its own refrigerator cars. After Harvey established a strict dress policy and code of conduct for the wait staff at his establishments in 1883, the company's service personnel, all females between the ages of 18 and 30, became known as the Harvey Girls. They provided the highest standards of service and decorum along the westward routes of the Santa Fe Railway. By the late 1880s there was a Harvey House located every 100 miles along the Santa Fe Railway line, enabling the railroad to advertise "Fred Harvey Meals

All the Way" in promotional materials during the late 19th century.

As Harvey's hospitality chain grew, so too did his aspirations for the grandeur of his business. He commissioned Charles Whittlesey, the chief architect for the Santa Fe Railway, and Mary Colter, who became Fred Harvey Company's principal architect, to design prestigious hotels incorporating landscape-integrated design principals. Landmark Harvey House hotels were the result of the collaboration, engendering impressive lodging facilities situated in pristine settings. Only a handful of Harvey House facilities existed in the 21st century, notable among them, the El Tovar Hotel, which was built 20 feet from the south rim of the Grand Canyon in 1905 before the region fell under the jurisdiction of the National Park Service. Properties such as the El Tovar Hotel became signature properties managed by Xanterra in the 21st century.

The relationship between the Fred Harvey Company and the Santa Fe Railroad was mutually beneficial and it would exist for nearly a century, but the expansion of Harvey's company was not limited to the routes served by the railroad. The company began developing a presence in geographic locations beyond the reach of the railroad in the 1930s. Restaurants were established at the Chicago Union Station, the San Francisco Business Terminal, the Los Angeles Union Passenger Terminal, and at rest stops along toll ways in Illinois. The company became multifaceted, growing in several directions, but only certain aspects of its operations became relevant to Xanterra because the Fred Harvey business was dismantled more than a century after its creation.

FROM FRED HARVEY TO AMFAC PARKS & RESORTS: 1968–95

Management of the company remained within the Harvey family until the death of Fred Harvey's grandson in 1965. Shortly thereafter, in 1968, the company was purchased by Amfac, Inc., the largest private landowner in Hawaii. The properties once owned by the Fred Harvey Company became part of Amfac's diverse holdings, organized as such until 1988, when Chicago-based JMB Realty Corporation, the largest real estate syndicator in the United States, acquired Amfac for $920 million. JMB, in the midst of a $4.5 billion spending spree, broke up the Amfac assets and separated them into independent corporations. Amfac Resorts was one of the companies created in the restructuring, a company that operated as the concessionaire at Grand Canyon National Park and Death Valley National Park.

Leadership of Amfac Resorts was handed to Andrew N. Todd, who served as the company's president and

KEY DATES

1878: First Harvey House is established in Florence, Kansas.

1968: Fred Harvey Company is acquired by Amfac, Inc.

1988: JMB Realty acquires Amfac and creates Amfac Resorts.

1995: Amfac Resorts acquires TW Recreational Services and becomes Amfac Parks & Resorts, the country's largest parks management company.

2002: Amfac Parks & Resorts changes its name to Xanterra Parks & Resorts.

2011: A year after acquiring Kingsmill Resort in Virginia, Xanterra acquires Windstar Cruises.

CEO. Todd, a certified public accountant, started his career at the accounting and consulting firm KPMG after earning an undergraduate degree in accounting from Indiana University. At JMB, Todd rose to the post of senior vice president of portfolio management before being handed the duties of leading Amfac Resorts in 1994. Under Todd's leadership, the company completed a pivotal deal the following year, one that would make it the leader of its industry.

TW RECREATIONAL SERVICES ACQUISITION: 1995

In 1995 Amfac Resorts negotiated a deal to purchase TW Recreational Services, which served as the concessionaire at Yellowstone National Park, Mount Rushmore National Memorial, Bryce Canyon, and several other popular national and state parks. Amfac Parks Inc. was formed to complete the $110 million acquisition, which created Amfac Parks & Resorts, the largest national and state park concessionaire in the United States.

After completing the acquisition, the company relocated its headquarters from Flagstaff, Arizona, to Colorado, where it established its main offices in Aurora, an eastern suburb of Denver. There, Todd presided over the country's largest operator of lodges, restaurants, and other concessions at national and state parks and resorts. Amfac Parks & Resorts operated under contract with federal and state agencies, typically securing 10-, 15-, or 20-year leases to manage every aspect of a park's guest-oriented operations. Amfac Parks & Resorts was responsible for hiring employees, housing employees, selling the souvenirs, booking the rooms at

the lodges, and feeding all the guests at a bevy of national and state parks. The company also made capital improvements to the properties it managed when it deemed the investment necessary and when federal and state authorities agreed to the improvements.

As CEO and president of Amfac Parks & Resorts, Todd contended with operating constraints not faced by conventional hoteliers, restaurateurs, and shop owners. He managed the company's business under the watchful eye of the National Park Service (and state regulators for the company's operations in state parks). All pricing at Amfac Parks & Resorts-managed properties was subject to National Park Service approval. "Even though you may have a room with Old Faithful out the window," Todd said in the November 2002 issue of *ColoradoBiz*, "if they [the National Park Service] say $80, it's $80." In an interview published in the April 22, 2002, edition of the *Denver Post*, Todd explained further, saying, "You can't get greedy. You have to know you can only expect a reasonable return. It's a trade-off. You don't make a fortune, but it's a stable business." To keep Amfac Parks & Resorts stable, Todd worked to maintain a steady flow of business. The company needed to retain its existing contracts, ensuring, for example, that a 15-year contract was renewed for another 15 years upon expiration, and it needed to bid on other concessionaire contracts as they expired.

AMFAC PARKS & RESORTS AT THE MILLENNIUM

By the end of the 1990s, Amfac Parks & Resorts watched over the activities at numerous prestigious tourist destinations. The company managed operations at Yellowstone, Grand Canyon, Mount Rushmore, Bryce Canyon, Zion, Death Valley, Everglades, and Petrified Forest national parks, as well as at seven state parks in Ohio. At these locations, the company occasionally added new properties in addition to the refurbishing efforts that went along with maintaining attractive commercial enterprises. In the years following the acquisition of TW Recreational Services, for instance, the company built a 10,000-square-foot cafeteria and gift shop at Mount Rushmore and the $18 million Old Faithful Snow Lodge in Yellowstone.

A new property became part of Amfac Park & Resort's portfolio in early 2002. The company secured a 15-year contract to operate the concessions at Oregon's Crater Lake National Park, which included a 71-room lodge, a dining room, campgrounds, gift shops, and a boating and gasoline station. The following month, in April 2002, the company changed its name to Xanterra Parks & Resorts. At roughly the same time, the company renewed its Grand Canyon contract for a 10-

year term, securing a vital component of its business for the near future. By 2005 Xanterra operated 33 lodges with 5,431 guestrooms at national and state parks.

ACQUISITIONS AND NEW OWNERSHIP: 2006–11

During the second half of the decade, Xanterra expanded its business. Several significant events also occurred that changed the company's corporate profile. In 2006 the company was awarded a 10-year contract to manage the Trail Ridge Restaurant and Gift Shop at Rocky Mountain National Park in Colorado, Xanterra's first property in its home state. The following year, the company acquired Grand Canyon Railway, which included the train route from Williams, Arizona, to the South Rim of the Grand Canyon; the Grand Canyon Railway Hotel; a restaurant; and a recreational vehicle park. The railroad, originally owned by the Santa Fe Railway, linked Williams with the former Harvey House, the El Tovar Hotel, as well as the seven other lodging facilities operated by Xanterra at the South Rim.

Not long after the Grand Canyon Railway acquisition, Xanterra's relationship with JMB ended. In 2008 Xanterra was acquired by The Anschutz Corporation, a company owned by Denver billionaire Philip Anschutz. Under new ownership, Xanterra's involvement in businesses operating outside the purview of federal and state parks regulators increased. In 2010 the company purchased the Kingsmill Resort near Williamsburg, Virginia, a property developed by Anheuser-Busch during the 1970s as part of the brewing giant's diversification efforts. The acquisition included a 425-room hotel, five restaurants, a marina, and three golf courses. In 2011 Xanterra purchased Windstar Cruises from its bankrupt parent company, Ambassadors International, Inc. Based in Seattle, Windstar Cruises operated three luxury yachts that offered cruises to nearly 50 countries, calling on 100 ports in Europe, the Caribbean, and the Americas.

As Xanterra prepared for the future, the company held a commanding lead in the parks management sector. The company's increasing involvement in business ventures not operating on federal or state owned land opened a new path for the growth in the years ahead, adding a new dimension to the Fred Harvey legacy that underpinned Xanterra's financial strength.

Jeffrey L. Covell

PRINCIPAL SUBSIDIARIES

Xanterra South Rim, L.L.C.; Grand Canyon Railway Hotel, L.L.C.; Xanterra Kingsmill, LLC; Windstar Cruises, LLC.

PRINCIPAL COMPETITORS

Delaware North Corporation; Forever Resorts; Levy Restaurant Holdings, LLC.

FURTHER READING

Blevins, Jason. "Concessionaire for National, State Parks Changes Name to Xanterra." *Denver Post*, April 22, 2002.
"National Parks Are Xanterra's Turf." *ColoradoBiz*, November 2002.
"Xanterra Bid for Railway on Track." *AZ Daily Sun*, January 25, 2007.
"Xanterra Parks & Resorts Completes Purchase of Windstar Cruises." *Investment Weekly News*, June 18, 2011.

Zayo Group, LLC

400 Centennial Parkway, Suite 200
Louisville, Colorado 80027-1286
U.S.A.
Telephone: (303) 381-4683
Fax: (303) 604-6869
Web site: http://www.zayo.com

Private Company
Founded: 2006 as Zayo Bandwidth, Inc.
Employees: 530
Sales: $287.24 million (2011)
NAICS: 517110 Wired Telecommunications Carriers

■ ■ ■

Zayo Group, LLC, is a national provider of fiber-optic network and bandwidth services, including colocation interconnection services. The company's network covers 44,000 route miles. The infrastructure connects 4,500 buildings, 450 points of presence, and 2,100 cell towers on the network. Zayo's products are available in 70 metropolitan markets in 39 states and the District of Columbia. Zayo operates three carrier hotels, two in New York City and one in Newark, New Jersey, plus 12 colocation facilities in major cities in California, Nevada, Minnesota, Tennessee, Ohio, Pennsylvania, New York, and New Jersey. The company's 60 Hudson Street "Meet-Me-Room" in New York City provides interconnection services for more than 200 global networks.

PRIOR EXPERIENCE AND 2006 FOUNDING

Before the establishment of Zayo in 2006, company cofounder Dan Caruso had a long career in telecommunications. After being employed at Bell/Ameritech and MFS Communications, in 1997 he participated in the founding of Level 3 Communications, a provider of Internet-based telecommunications. Initially, Caruso managed the company's engineering, construction, and operations segments. Between 2001 and 2003 he oversaw several business lines, as well as the marketing functions of those businesses.

Caruso's career went in a new direction when he became president and chief executive officer of ICG Communications, another telecommunications company, in 2004. ICG had already undergone extensive reorganization under bankruptcy protection between 2000 and 2002. ICG was a casualty of telecommunications investment speculation and the ensuing market crash due to network oversupply. When Caruso took the helm, ICG still had $100 million in debt, and it was spending $8 million a month to run the company, with $30 million in cash remaining.

Caruso proceeded to lead a private buyout of the company, supported by an $8.7 million investment from Columbia Capital and M/C Venture Partners. He turned ICG around and then sold the company to Level 3. The success of this endeavor brought Caruso funding for a new venture in telecommunications, Zayo Bandwidth.

Caruso and John Scarano, another Level 3 executive, founded Zayo Bandwidth, Inc., in November

2006. As an operator of fiber-optic networks, Zayo planned to provide broadband services to third-party communications carriers and Internet service providers and to corporations requiring private data transmission and communications access. Although demand for fiber-optic infrastructure had not yet met supply, Caruso anticipated that the development of faster, more sophisticated communications devices would require fiber-optic infrastructure.

ESTABLISHING OPERATIONS THROUGH ACQUISITIONS AND INVESTMENT: 2007

Zayo Group, LLC, was formed as the operating company in May 2007. Zayo acquired a number of small fiber-optics telecommunications companies, targeting opportunities with at least 15 percent annual growth. Significant acquisitions at this time included two fiber-optic networks, Pennsylvania-based PPL Telcom and Memphis Networx in Tennessee.

Zayo obtained venture capital investments to fund acquisitions in August 2007. The company secured $225 million from five venture capital firms, Columbia Capital, M/C Venture Partners, Oak Investment Partners, Centennial Ventures, and Battery Ventures. The capital enabled Zayo to complete the acquisitions of Minneapolis-based Onvoy and Indiana Fiber Works.

Upon completion of these acquisitions at the end of 2007, Zayo provided services over 8,400 fiber route miles connected to 830 buildings. That year the company generated revenues of $125 million. Despite being based in Louisville, Colorado, the company's core networks were located in the eastern United States, particularly New York, New Jersey, Pennsylvania,

Virginia, Washington, D.C., Tennessee, and Indiana. The Minnesota network was the only core asset west of the Mississippi River.

Venture capital and $30 million in debt financing supported the acquisition of Citynet Fiber Network. Completed in February 2008 for $102.2 million, the acquisition expanded Zayo's existing network in western Pennsylvania, adding 8,500 route miles. The network provided broadband links to New York, Washington, D.C., Chicago, and several smaller cities, with operations in 12 states. Citynet customers included hospitals, universities, government agencies, and wireless and landline telephone service providers.

In March 2009, Zayo obtained another $95 million in private-equity funding from new investors Charlesbank Capital Partners and Morgan Stanley Alternative Investment Partners. The funding allowed Zayo to pay cash for acquisitions. The following May a merger with FiberNet Telecom Group brought colocation facilities (facilities housing and interconnecting the communications infrastructure of several companies) to Zayo's asset base. The $104.1 million acquisition included high bandwidth, fiber-optic networks in the states of New York and New Jersey, plus the cities of Chicago, Miami, and Los Angeles.

NEW INFRASTRUCTURE, SERVICES, AND ACQUISITIONS

Zayo continued to expand in 2010, supported by funds from investors and the U.S. Recovery Act Broadband Technology Opportunities Program. In 2010 Zayo received Recovery Act funding to build two fiber-optic networks. In February, Zayo received $25.10 million to expand its Indiana network by 626 miles. The new fiber-optic lines connected 80 rural communities through 21 community colleges in Indiana. The project was completed in early 2011.

Recovery Act funds contributed $13.4 million to build new broadband infrastructure in Minnesota. Anoka County, a partner in the project, and Zayo invested an additional $5.7 million. Upon completion, the Connect Anoka County Community Broadband Network would consist of 286 miles of fiber-optic lines, connecting city and county government buildings, schools, colleges, libraries, and businesses. The network would provide overall improvement of bandwidth accessibility for local Internet service providers, as well.

In March 2010 Zayo issued $250 million in senior secured notes, at 10.25 percent interest. The company paid the $30 million debt financing used to purchase Citynet assets. The company followed with another $100 million offering in September. Both notes would

KEY DATES

2006: Company is founded as Zayo Bandwidth, Inc.

2007: Venture capital of $225 million funds acquisitions.

2010: Zayo restructures operations into three business units, spins off noncore assets.

2011: Acquisition of 360Networks doubles fiber-optic network, adds new markets.

come due in March 2017. A revolving credit facility with SunTrust Bank provided another $100 million for acquisitions.

Acquisitions at this time added new telecommunications services. The $73.7 million acquisition of AGL Networks, LLC, paid with cash on hand in July 2010, included 786 route miles consisting of more than 190,000 fiber miles. AGL operated in Georgia, North Carolina, and Arizona markets, primarily. Zayo used AGL's dark fiber operations to form the Zayo Fiber Solutions (ZFS) business unit, then consolidated dark fiber operations from Zayo Bandwidth and Zayo Enterprise Networks into ZFS.

ZFS offered dark fiber for lease to customers who would use their own optronics or telecommunications transmission equipment to light the fiber-optic network. By leasing inactive fiber infrastructure, ZFS provided customers with the flexibility to customize their use of the available bandwidth. The dark fiber network supported new technology reliant on extensive bandwidth and wireless capacity for data transfer, video communications, and cloud computing. Customers included third-party carriers and communications, Internet, and wireless service providers, as well as major media and content companies.

AMERICAN FIBER SYSTEMS PURCHASE

In October Zayo acquired American Fiber Systems Holdings Corporation for $110 million in cash plus a $4.5 million unsecured promissory note due in 2012. Assets included 1,200 route miles, with 160,000 fiber miles connecting more than 600 buildings in nine metropolitan markets: Atlanta, Nashville, Cleveland, Las Vegas, Reno, Boise, Salt Lake City, Minneapolis, and Kansas City, Missouri.

Zayo reorganized operations according to type of service, with the intention of reducing operations to

three business units. In September 2010 Zayo made a minor acquisition of Dolphini Corporation for $200,000, for colocation assets in Nashville.

Zayo sought to generate revenue by expanding its customer base for its existing and growing fiber-optic network. For instance, the company leveraged 100 new miles of fiber-optic lines in Denver in 2010 to support a January 2011 service agreement with Forethought.net. A provider of Ethernet voice and data services in Colorado, Forethought required dark fiber access to provide interconnectivity among carrier central offices and customer buildings in metropolitan Denver.

2011: BUILDING A NATIONAL INFRASTRUCTURE

In 2011 Zayo focused its expansion goals on the South and Southwest, where the company had limited operational capacity. In March Zayo expanded its infrastructure in metropolitan Dallas, including eight new local switching offices. Five carrier hotel and data center facilities were also added to the network. The expansion allowed Zayo to offer both dark and lit fiber connectivity to certain businesses and carriers in Dallas.

In August Zayo announced construction of a fiber network in Los Angeles Central Business district, to support data center operations at CoreSite Realty Corporation. The network provided high-count fiber cable for bandwidth and dark fiber services. The company expected the network to be operational in early 2012.

In western Ohio Zayo began construction of a 366-mile fiber-optic network traversing 28 counties from Toledo to Columbus as well as several smaller towns. Supported by the Recovery Act Broadband Technology Opportunities Program, Com Net, Inc. was awarded $30 million for the project to enhance connectivity. Zayo, as a member of the GigE Plus Availability Coalition, added to its network in Ohio.

Activities in the South included joining the Telx's Ethernet Exchange, a competitor in interconnection and colocation services. Joining Telx enhanced Zayo's ability to use its 500-plus-mile fiber-optic network in Atlanta. In November Zayo announced plans to build a 12-mile fiber-optic network in Birmingham, Alabama. The infrastructure, located in the central business district and surrounding communities, provided a foundation for further development.

Zayo added 38 route miles in the Nashville area, where certain communities gained dark fiber, Gigabit

Ethernet, and wavelength services. Construction was completed in December 2011.

In November 2011 Zayo began construction on new fiber-optic networks in the San Diego area. The network covered the downtown area, then traveled north to Oceanside and east to Escondido. The new infrastructure added dark fiber access and improved existing services as it increased local infrastructure to more than 400 route miles.

360NETWORKS ACQUISITION

Zayo completed the $345 million acquisition of 360Networks of Seattle on December 1. Assets included 18,500 miles of fiber-optic networks across 22 states and British Columbia, including networks within several metropolitan areas. The intercity network covered more than 70 markets in the central and western United States, with overlap in 24 of Zayo's existing markets. City markets overlapping included San Diego, Sacramento, Salt Lake City, Denver, Colorado Springs, and Omaha. New markets included Tucson, San Francisco, Albuquerque, Bismarck, and Des Moines. Zayo planned to transfer 360Network's wholesale voice-over-Internet-protocol services to Onvoy, but did not know whether it would keep the Butte, Montana, and Broomfield, Colorado, offices.

Zayo closed 2011 as a private company, despite expectations of going public to satisfy investors seeking midterm returns. Zayo expected the demand for fiber networks to grow with increased use of Smartphones and as Internet providers focused on home uses, such as viewing movies and other content. Other applications expected to stimulate demand included online learning programs at colleges and universities and health care digital files accessed from a central storage facility.

Mary Tradii

PRINCIPAL OPERATING UNITS

Zayo Bandwidth; Zayo Fiber Solutions; zColo; Zayo Networks.

PRINCIPAL COMPETITORS

AboveNet, Inc.; AT&T, Inc.; CenturyLink, Inc.; Equinix, Inc.; Fibertech Networks, LLC; Level 3 Communications, Inc.; Sidera Networks; The Telx Group, Inc.; Verizon Communications, Inc.

FURTHER READING

Jackson, Margaret. "Zayo Gains Project Funds: The Louisville-Based Company Will Build Out Fiber to Give Broadband to Parts of Minnesota." *Denver Post*, July 7, 2010, B6.

Smith, Jeff. "Startup Telco Lands $225 Million." *Rocky Mountain News*, August 30, 2007, 4B.

Suzukamo, Leslie Brooks. "Onvoy Rings up a Buyer." *St. Paul Pioneer Press*, August 23, 2007, C1.

Voug, Andy. "Fiber Networks Regain Black-Gold Footing; Zayo Group Is Riding a Post-glut Optic Wave Fueled by Net Video and Mobile Broadband Needs." *Denver Post*, March 6, 2011, K11.

"Zayo and Partners in Ohio Telecommunications Coalition Continue Construction on New Broadband Fiber Network in Western Ohio." *Internet Wire*, October 5, 2011, 1.

"Zayo to Build Los Angeles Fiber Network in Support of Coresite's Southern California Data Center Ecosystem." *Investment Weekly News*, August 13, 2011, 1.

Cumulative Index to Companies

Advanced Micro Devices, Inc., 6
215–17; 30 10–12 (upd.); 99 12–17
(upd.)
Advanced Neuromodulation Systems,
Inc., 73 14–17
Advanced Technology Laboratories, Inc.,
9 6–8
Advanced Web Technologies *see* Miner
Group Int.
Advanstar Communications, Inc., 57
13–17
Advanta Corporation, 8 9–11; 38 10–14
(upd.)
Advantica Restaurant Group, Inc., 27
16–19 (upd.) *see also* Denny's
Corporation
Adventist Health, 53 6–8
The Advertising Council, Inc., 76 3–6
The Advisory Board Company, 80 1–4
see also The Corporate Executive Board
Co.
Advo, Inc., 6 12–14; 53 9–13 (upd.)
Advocat Inc., 46 3–5
AECOM Technology Corporation, 79
10–13
Aecon Group Inc., 121 17–21
Aeffe S.p.A., 119 21–25
AEG A.G., I 409–11
Aegean Marine Petroleum Network Inc.,
89 18–21
Aegek S.A., 64 6–8
Aegis Group plc, 6 15–16
AEGON N.V., III 177–79; 50 8–12
(upd.) *see also* Transamerica–An
AEGON Company
AEI Music Network Inc., 35 19–21
AEON Co., Ltd., V 96–99; 68 6–10
(upd.)
AEP *see* American Electric Power Co.
AEP Industries, Inc., 36 17–19
Aer Lingus Group plc, 34 7–10; 89
22–27 (upd.)
Aero Mayflower Transit Company *see*
Mayflower Group Inc.
Aeroflex Holding Corporation, 128
13–17
Aeroflot - Russian Airlines JSC, 6
57–59; 29 7–10 (upd.); 89 28–34
(upd.)
AeroGrow International, Inc., 95 20–23
Aerojet-General Corp., 63 6–9
Aerolíneas Argentinas S.A., 33 17–19;
69 9–12 (upd.)
Aeronca Inc., 46 6–8
Aéroports de Paris, 33 20–22
Aéropostale, Inc., 89 35–38
Aeroquip Corporation, 16 7–9 *see also*
Eaton Corp.
Aerosonic Corporation, 69 13–15
The Aerospace Corporation, 130 9–12
The Aérospatiale Group, 7 9–12; 21
8–11 (upd.) *see also* European
Aeronautic Defence and Space
Company EADS N.V.
AeroVironment, Inc., 97 13–16
The AES Corporation, 10 25–27; 13
12–15 (upd.); 53 14–18 (upd.); 133
20–25 (upd.)

Aetna Inc., III 180–82; 21 12–16
(upd.); 63 10–16 (upd.); 133 26–33
(upd.)
Aetna Insulated Wire *see* The Marmon
Group, Inc.
AFC Ajax NV, 132 5–8
AFC Enterprises, Inc., 32 12–16 (upd.);
83 9–15 (upd.)
Affiliated Computer Services, Inc., 61
12–16
Affiliated Foods Inc., 53 19–21
Affiliated Managers Group, Inc., 79
14–17
Affiliated Publications, Inc., 7 13–16
Affinia Group Inc., 128 18–22
Affinion Group, Inc., 121 22–24
Affinity Group Holding Inc., 56 3–6
Affymetrix Inc., 106 18–24
Aflac Incorporated, 10 28–30 (upd.); 38
15–19 (upd.); 109 6–11 (upd.)
African Rainbow Minerals Ltd., 97
17–20
Africare, 59 7–10
After Hours Formalwear Inc., 60 3–5
Aftermarket Technology Corp., 83
16–19
AG Barr plc, 64 9–12
Ag-Chem Equipment Company, Inc., 17
9–11 *see also* AGCO Corp.
Ag Services of America, Inc., 59 11–13
Aga Foodservice Group PLC, 73 18–20
AGCO Corp., 13 16–18; 67 6–10
(upd.)
Agence France-Presse, 34 11–14; 125
16–20 (upd.)
Agere Systems Inc., 61 17–19
Agfa Gevaert Group N.V., 59 14–16
Aggregate Industries plc, 36 20–22
Aggreko Plc, 45 10–13; 133 34–38
(upd.)
Agilent Technologies Inc., 38 20–23; 93
28–32 (upd.)
Agilysys Inc., 76 7–11 (upd.)
AGL Resources Inc., 116 12–15
Agland, Inc., 110 6–9
Agnico-Eagle Mines Limited, 71 11–14
Agora S.A. Group, 77 5–8
AGRANA *see* Südzucker AG.
Agri Beef Company, 81 5–9
Agria Corporation, 101 9–13
Agricultural Bank of China, 116 16–19
Agrigenetics, Inc. *see* Mycogen Corp.
Agrium Inc., 73 21–23
Agrofert Holding A.S., 117 5–9
AgustaWestland N.V., 75 18–20
Agway, Inc., 7 17–18; 21 17–19 (upd.)
see also Cargill Inc.
AHL Services, Inc., 27 20–23
Ahlers, 123 1–5
Ahlstrom Corporation, 53 22–25; 125
21–25 (upd.)
Ahmanson *see* H.F. Ahmanson & Co.
AHMSA *see* Altos Hornos de México,
S.A. de C.V.
Ahold *see* Koninklijke Ahold NV.
AHP *see* American Home Products Corp.
AIA Engineering Ltd., 119 26–30

AICPA *see* The American Institute of
Certified Public Accountants.
AIG *see* American International Group,
Inc.
AIMCO *see* Apartment Investment and
Management Co.
Ainsworth Lumber Co. Ltd., 99 18–22
Air & Water Technologies Corporation,
6 441–42 *see also* Aqua Alliance Inc.
Air Berlin GmbH & Co. Luftverkehrs
KG, 71 15–17
Air Canada, 6 60–62; 23 9–12 (upd.);
59 17–22 (upd.); 125 26–32 (upd.)
Air China Limited, 46 9–11; 108 15–19
(upd.)
Air Express International Corporation,
13 19–20
Air France–KLM, 108 20–29 (upd.)
Air India Limited, 6 63–64; 27 24–26
(upd.); 130 13–18 (upd.)
Air Jamaica Limited, 54 3–6; 129 5–8
(upd.)
Air Liquide *see* L'Air Liquide SA.
Air Mauritius Ltd., 63 17–19
Air Methods Corporation, 53 26–29
Air Midwest, Inc. *see* Mesa Air Group,
Inc.
Air New Zealand Limited, 14 10–12; 38
24–27 (upd.); 119 31–36 (upd.)
Air Pacific Ltd., 70 7–9
Air Partner PLC, 93 33–36
Air Products and Chemicals, Inc., I
297–99; 10 31–33 (upd.); 74 6–9
(upd.)
Air Sahara Limited, 65 14–16
Air T, Inc., 86 6–9
Air Wisconsin Airlines Corporation, 55
10–12
Air Zimbabwe (Private) Limited, 91 5–8
AirAsia Berhad, 93 37–40
Airborne Freight Corporation, 6
345–47; 34 15–18 (upd.) *see also*
DHL Worldwide Network S.A./N.V.
Airborne Systems Group, 89 39–42
AirBoss of America Corporation, 108
30–34
Airbus Industrie *see* G.I.E. Airbus
Industrie.
Airgas, Inc., 54 7–10
Airguard Industries, Inc. *see* CLARCOR
Inc.
Airlink Pty Ltd *see* Qantas Airways Ltd.
Airsprung Group PLC, 121 25–27
Airstream *see* Thor Industries, Inc.
AirTouch Communications, 11 10–12
see also Vodafone Group PLC.
Airtours Plc, 27 27–29, 90, 92
AirTran Holdings, Inc., 22 21–23
Aisin Seiki Co., Ltd., III 415–16; 48
3–5 (upd.); 120 10–14 (upd.)
Aitchison & Colegrave *see* Bradford &
Bingley PLC.
Aiwa Co., Ltd., 30 18–20
AIXTRON AG, 118 11–14
Ajegroup S.A, 92 1–4
Ajinomoto Co., Inc., II 463–64; 28
9–11 (upd.); 108 35–39 (upd.)

Bed Bath & Beyond Inc., 13 81–83; 41 49–52 (upd.); 109 63–70 (upd.)

Bedoukian Research, Inc., 127 29–32

Beech Aircraft Corporation, 8 49–52 *see also* Raytheon Aircraft Holdings Inc.

Beech-Nut Nutrition Corporation, 21 53–56; 51 47–51 (upd.)

Beef O'Brady's *see* Family Sports Concepts, Inc.

Beer Nuts, Inc., 86 30–33

Beggars Group Ltd., 99 61–65

Behr GmbH & Co. KG, 72 22–25

Behr Process Corporation, 115 47–49

Behring Diagnostics *see* Dade Behring Holdings Inc.

BEI Technologies, Inc., 65 74–76

Beiersdorf AG, 29 49–53

Bekaert S.A./N.V., 90 53–57

Bekins Company, 15 48–50

Bel *see* Fromageries Bel.

Bel-Art Products Inc., 117 35–38

Bel Fuse, Inc., 53 59–62

Bel/Kaukauna USA, 76 46–48

Belco Oil & Gas Corp., 40 63–65

Belden CDT Inc., 19 43–45; 76 49–52 (upd.)

Belfor Holdings Inc., 128 66–70

Belgacom, 6 302–04

Belk, Inc., V 12–13; 19 46–48 (upd.); 72 26–29 (upd.)

Belkin International, Inc., 121 67–71

Bell and Howell Company, 9 61–64; 29 54–58 (upd.) *see also* ProQuest LLC.

Bell Atlantic Corporation, V 272–74; 25 58–62 (upd.) *see also* Verizon Communications.

Bell Canada International, Inc., 6 305–08 *see also* BCE, Inc.

Bell Helicopter Textron Inc., 46 64–67

Bell Industries, Inc., 47 40–43

Bell Media, Inc., 126 86–89

Bell Resources *see* TPG NV.

Bell Sports Corporation, 16 51–53; 44 51–54 (upd.) *see also* Easton-Bell Sports, Inc.

Bell's Brewery, Inc., 117 39–42

Bellcore *see* Telcordia Technologies, Inc.

Belle International Holdings Limited, 133 59–62

Belleek Pottery Ltd., 71 50–53

Belleville Shoe Manufacturing Company, 92 17–20

Bellisio Foods, Inc., 95 51–54

BellSouth Corporation, V 276–78; 29 59–62 (upd.) *see also* AT&T Corp.

Bellway Plc, 45 37–39

Belo Corporation, 98 19–25 (upd.)

Beloit Corporation, 14 55–57 *see also* Metso Corp.

Belron International Ltd., 76 53–56

Belships ASA, 113 41–44

Belvedere S.A., 93 77–81

Bemis Company, Inc., 8 53–55; 91 53–60 (upd.)

Ben & Jerry's Homemade, Inc., 10 146–48; 35 58–62 (upd.); 80 22–28 (upd.)

Ben Bridge Jeweler, Inc., 60 52–54

Ben E. Keith Company, 76 57–59

Ben Hill Griffin, Inc., 110 43–47

Benchmark Capital, 49 50–52

Benchmark Electronics, Inc., 40 66–69

Benckiser N.V. *see* Reckitt Benckiser plc.

Bendix Corporation, I 141–43

Beneficial Corporation, 8 56–58

Benesse Corporation, 76 60–62

Bénéteau SA, 55 54–56

Benetton Group S.p.A., 10 149–52; 67 47–51 (upd.)

Benfield Greig Group plc, 53 63–65

Benguet Corporation, 58 21–24

Benihana, Inc., 18 56–59; 76 63–66 (upd.)

Benjamin Moore & Co., 13 84–87; 38 95–99 (upd.); 115 50–55 (upd.)

Benninger AG, 107 40–44

BenQ Corporation, 67 52–54

Benton Oil and Gas Company, 47 44–46

Berean Christian Stores, 96 40–43

Berendsen plc, 128 71–76 (upd.)

Berentzen-Gruppe AG, 113 45–49

Beretta *see* Fabbrica D' Armi Pietro Beretta S.p.A.

Bergdorf Goodman Inc., 52 45–48

Bergen Brunswig Corporation, V 14–16; 13 88–90 (upd.) *see also* AmerisourceBergen Corp.

Berger Bros Company, 62 31–33

Beringer Blass Wine Estates Ltd., 22 78–81; 66 34–37 (upd.)

Berjaya Group Bhd., 67 55–57

Berkeley Farms, Inc., 46 68–70

Berkshire Hathaway Inc., III 213–15; 18 60–63 (upd.); 42 31–36 (upd.); 89 92–99 (upd.)

Berkshire Realty Holdings, L.P., 49 53–55

Berlex Laboratories, Inc., 66 38–40

Berliner Stadtreinigungsbetriebe, 58 25–28

Berliner Verkehrsbetriebe (BVG), 58 29–31

Berlinwasser Holding AG, 90 58–62

Berlitz International, Inc., 13 91–93; 39 47–50 (upd.)

Bernard C. Harris Publishing Company, Inc., 39 51–53

Bernard Chaus, Inc., 27 59–61

Bernard Hodes Group Inc., 86 34–37

Bernard L. Madoff Investment Securities LLC, 106 58–62

Bernard Matthews Ltd., 89 100–04

The Bernick Companies, 75 62–65

Bernina Holding AG, 47 47–50

Bernstein-Rein, 92 21–24

Berry Bros & Rudd *see* BB&R Limited.

The Berry Company *see* L. M. Berry and Company

Berry Petroleum Company, 47 51–53; 130 85–89 (upd.)

Berry Plastics Group Inc., 21 57–59; 98 26–30 (upd.)

Bertelsmann A.G., IV 592–94; 43 63–67 (upd.); 91 61–68 (upd.)

Bertrandt AG, 126 90–93

Bertucci's Corporation, 16 54–56; 64 51–54 (upd.)

Berwick Offray, LLC, 70 17–19

Berwind Corporation, 100 61–64

Besix Group S.A./NV, 94 66–69

Besnier SA, 19 49–51 *see also* Groupe Lactalis

Best Buy Co., Inc., 9 65–66; 23 51–53 (upd.); 63 61–66 (upd.)

Best Kosher Foods Corporation, 82 41–44

Best Maid Products, Inc., 107 45–48

Best Western International, Inc., 124 35–38

Bestfoods, 22 82–86 (upd.)

Bestseller A/S, 90 63–66

Bestway Transportation *see* TNT Freightways Corp.

BET Holdings, Inc., 18 64–66

Beter Bed Holding N.V., 123 39–43

Beth Abraham Family of Health Services, 94 70–74

Beth Israel Medical Center *see* Continuum Health Partners, Inc.

Bethlehem Steel Corporation, IV 35–37; 7 48–51 (upd.); 27 62–66 (upd.)

Betsey Johnson Inc., 100 65–69

Betsy Ann Candies, Inc., 105 28–31

Better Made Snack Foods, Inc., 90 67–69

The Betty Ford Center at Eisenhower, 126 94–97

Bettys & Taylors of Harrogate Ltd., 72 30–32

Betz Laboratories, Inc., I 312–13; 10 153–55 (upd.)

Beverly Enterprises, Inc., III 76–77; 16 57–59 (upd.) *see also* Golden Living.

Bewag AG, 39 54–57

BFC Construction Corporation, 25 63–65

The BFGoodrich Company, V 231–33; 19 52–55 (upd.) *see also* Goodrich Corp.

BFI *see* The British Film Institute; Browning-Ferris Industries, Inc.

BFP Holdings Corp. *see* Big Flower Press Holdings, Inc.

BG&E *see* Baltimore Gas and Electric Co.

BG Products Inc., 96 44–47

Bharat Electronics Limited, 113 50–53

Bharat Heavy Electricals Limited, 119 88–92

Bharat Petroleum Corporation Limited, 109 71–75

Bharti Airtel Limited, 128 77–82

Bharti Tele-Ventures Limited, 75 66–68

BHC Communications, Inc., 26 32–34

BHP Billiton, 67 58–64 (upd.)

Bhs plc, 17 42–44

Bianchi International (d/b/a Gregory Mountain Products), 76 67–69

Bibby Line Group Ltd., 128 83–88

Bibliographisches Institut & F.A. Brockhaus AG, 74 30–34

BIC Corporation, 8 59–61; 23 54–57 (upd.)

Columbia Manufacturing, Inc., 114 138–41

Columbia Sportswear Company, 19 94–96; 41 100–03 (upd.)

Columbia TriStar Motion Pictures Companies, II 135–37; 12 73–76 (upd.)

Columbia/HCA Healthcare Corporation, 15 112–14

Columbian Home Products, LLC, 121 106–09

Columbus McKinnon Corporation, 37 95–98

Com Ed *see* Commonwealth Edison.

Comair Holdings Inc., 13 171–73; 34 116–20 (upd.)

Combe Inc., 72 79–82

Comcast Corporation, 7 90–92; 24 120–24 (upd.); 112 96–101 (upd.)

Comdial Corporation, 21 132–35

Comdisco, Inc., 9 130–32

Comerci *see* Controladora Comercial Mexicana, S.A. de C.V.

Comerica Incorporated, 40 115–17; 101 120–25 (upd.)

Comex Group *see* Grupo Comex.

COMFORCE Corporation, 40 118–20

Comfort Systems USA, Inc., 101 126–29

Cominco Ltd., 37 99–102

Comisión Federal de Electricidad, 108 178–81

Command Security Corporation, 57 71–73

Commerce Bancshares, Inc., 116 140–43

Commerce Clearing House, Inc., 7 93–94 *see also* CCH Inc.

Commercial Credit Company, 8 117–19 *see also* Citigroup Inc.

Commercial Federal Corporation, 12 77–79; 62 76–80 (upd.)

Commercial Financial Services, Inc., 26 85–89

Commercial Metals Company, 15 115–17; 42 81–84(upd.); 125 86–91 (upd.)

Commercial Union plc, III 233–35 *see also* Aviva PLC.

Commercial Vehicle Group, Inc., 81 91–94

Commerzbank AG, II 256–58; 47 81–84 (upd.); 122 91–96 (upd.)

Commodore International, Ltd., 7 95–97

Commonwealth Bank of Australia Ltd., 109 138–42

Commonwealth Edison, V 583–85

Commonwealth Energy System, 14 124–26 *see also* NSTAR.

Commonwealth Telephone Enterprises, Inc., 25 106–08

CommScope, Inc., 77 112–15

Community Coffee Co. L.L.C., 53 108–10

Community Health Systems, Inc., 71 111–13

Community Newspaper Holdings, Inc., 91 128–31

Community Psychiatric Centers, 15 118–20

Compagnia Italiana dei Jolly Hotels S.p.A., 71 114–16

Compagnie de Saint-Gobain, III 675–78; 16 119–23 (upd.); 64 80–84 (upd.)

Compagnie des Alpes, 48 106–08

Compagnie des Cristalleries de Baccarat *see* Baccarat.

Compagnie des Machines Bull S.A., III 122–23 *see also* Bull S.A.; Groupe Bull.

Compagnie Financière de Paribas, II 259–60 *see also* BNP Paribas Group.

Compagnie Financière Richemont AG, 50 144–47

Compagnie Financière Sucres et Denrées S.A., 60 94–96

Compagnie Générale d'Électricité, II 12–13

Compagnie Générale des Établissements Michelin, V 236–39; 42 85–89 (upd.); 117 52–57 (upd.)

Compagnie Générale Maritime et Financière, 6 379–81

Compagnie Maritime Belge S.A., 95 110–13

Compagnie Nationale à Portefeuille, 84 55–58

Compagnie Plastic Omnium S.A., 127 71–75

Compal Electronics Inc., 117 58–61

Companhia Brasileira de Distribuiçao, 76 111–13

Companhia de Bebidas das Américas, 57 74–77

Companhia de Tecidos Norte de Minas - Coteminas, 77 116–19

Companhia Energética de Minas Gerais S.A., 65 118–20

Companhia Siderúrgica Nacional, 76 114–17

Companhia Suzano de Papel e Celulose S.A., 94 130–33

Companhia Vale do Rio Doce, IV 54–57; 43 111–14 (upd.) *see also* Vale S.A.

Compañía Anónima Nacional Teléfonos de Venezuela, 123 85–88

Compania Cervecerias Unidas S.A., 70 61–63

Compañia de Minas BuenaventuraS.A.A., 92160–63

Compañia Española de Petróleos S.A. (CEPSA), IV 396–98; 56 63–66 (upd.); 123 89–93 (upd.)

Compañia Industrial de Parras, S.A. de C.V. (CIPSA), 84 59–62

Compañia Sud Americana de Vapores S.A., 100 121–24

Compaq Computer Corporation, III 124–25; 6 221–23 (upd.); 26 90–93 (upd.) *see also* Hewlett-Packard Co.

Compass Bancshares, Inc., 73 92–94

Compass Diversified Holdings, 108 182–85

Compass Group plc, 34 121–24; 110 97–102 (upd.)

Compass Minerals International, Inc., 79 109–12

CompDent Corporation, 22 149–51

Compellent Technologies, Inc., 119 114–18

CompHealth Inc., 25 109–12

Complete Business Solutions, Inc., 31 130–33

Complete Production Services, Inc., 118 103–06

Comprehensive Care Corporation, 15 121–23

Comptoirs Modernes S.A., 19 97–99 *see also* Carrefour SA.

Compton Petroleum Corporation, 103 120–23

CompuAdd Computer Corporation, 11 61–63

CompuCom Systems, Inc., 10 232–34

CompuDyne Corporation, 51 78–81

CompUSA, Inc., 10 235–36; 35 116–18 (upd.)

CompuServe Interactive Services, Inc., 10 237–39; 27 106–08 (upd.) *see also* AOL Time Warner Inc.

Computer Associates International, Inc., 6 224–26; 49 94–97 (upd.)

Computer Data Systems, Inc., 14 127–29

Computer Learning Centers, Inc., 26 94–96

Computer Sciences Corporation, 6 227–29; 116 144–49 (upd.)

Computer Services, Inc., 122 97–100

ComputerLand Corp., 13 174–76

Computervision Corporation, 10 240–42

Compuware Corporation, 10 243–45; 30 140–43 (upd.); 66 60–64 (upd.)

CompX International Inc., 130 148–51

Comsat Corporation, 23 133–36 *see also* Lockheed Martin Corp.

comScore, Inc., 119 119–23

Comshare Inc., 23 137–39

Comstock Resources, Inc., 47 85–87; 126 119–23 (upd.)

Comtech Telecommunications Corp., 75 103–05

Comverse Technology, Inc., 15 124–26; 43 115–18 (upd.)

Con Ed *see* Consolidated Edison, Inc.

Con-way Inc., 101 130–34

ConAgra Foods, Inc., II 493–95; 12 80–82 (upd.); 42 90–94 (upd.); 85 61–68 (upd.)

Conair Corporation, 17 108–10; 69 104–08 (upd.)

Conaprole *see* Cooperativa Nacional de Productores de Leche S.A. (Conaprole).

Concentra Inc., 71 117–19

Concepts Direct, Inc., 39 93–96

Concha y Toro *see* Viña Concha y Toro S.A.

Concord Camera Corporation, 41 104–07

Concord EFS, Inc., 52 86–88

Finlay Enterprises, Inc., 16 206–08; 76 148–51 (upd.)

Finmeccanica S.p.A., 84 119–123

Finnair Oyj, 6 87–89; 25 157–60 (upd.); 61 91–95 (upd.); 122 158–64 (upd.)

Finning International Inc., 69 167–69

Firearms Training Systems, Inc., 27 156–58

Fired Up, Inc., 82 111–14

Firehouse Restaurant Group, Inc., 110 151–54

Fireman's Fund Insurance Company, III 250–52

Firmenich International S.A., 60 125–27

First Advantage Corporation, 119 175–78

First Albany Companies Inc., 37 146–48

First Alert, Inc., 28 133–35

First American Financial Corporation, 52 125–27; 123 155–59 (upd.)

First Artist Corporation PLC, 105 168–71

First Aviation Services Inc., 49 140–42

First Bank System Inc., 12 164–66 *see also* U.S. Bancorp

First Brands Corporation, 8 180–82

First Busey Corporation, 105 172–75

First Cash Financial Services, Inc., 57 138–40

First Chicago Corporation, II 284–87 *see also* Bank One Corp.

First Choice Holidays PLC, 40 185–87

First Citizens Bancshares Incorporated, 116 225–28

First Colony Coffee & Tea Company, 84 124–126

First Commerce Bancshares, Inc., 15 161–63 *see also* Wells Fargo & Co.

First Commerce Corporation, 11 105–07 *see also* JPMorgan Chase & Co.

First Data Corporation, 30 195–98 (upd.); 116 229–35 (upd.)

First Empire State Corporation, 11 108–10

First Executive Corporation, III 253–55

First Fidelity Bank, N.A., New Jersey, 9 221–23

First Financial Management Corporation, 11 111–13

First Hawaiian, Inc., 11 114–16

First Industrial Realty Trust, Inc., 65 146–48

First International Computer, Inc., 56 129–31

First Interstate Bancorp, II 288–90 *see also* Wells Fargo & Co.

First Look Studios, Inc., 111 132–35

The First Marblehead Corporation, 87 168–171

First Mississippi Corporation, 8 183–86 *see also* ChemFirst, Inc.

First Nationwide Bank, 14 191–93 *see also* Citigroup Inc.

First Niagara Financial Group Inc., 107 131–35

First of America Bank Corporation, 8 187–89

First Pacific Company Limited, 18 180–82

First Security Corporation, 11 117–19 *see also* Wells Fargo & Co.

First Solar, Inc., 95 146–50

First Team Sports, Inc., 22 202–04

First Tennessee National Corporation, 11 120–21; 48 176–79 (upd.)

First Union Corporation, 10 298–300 *see also* Wachovia Corp.

First USA, Inc., 11 122–24

First Virginia Banks, Inc., 11 125–26 *see also* BB&T Corp.

First Wind Holdings, Inc., 133 137–40

The First Years Inc., 46 191–94

Firstar Corporation, 11 127–29; 33 152–55 (upd.)

FirstEnergy Corp., 112 170–75 (upd.)

FirstGroup plc, 89 216–19

FirstMerit Corporation, 105 176–79

FirstService Corporation, 121 178–82

Fischerwerke GmbH & Co. KG, 123 160–64

Fiserv, Inc., 11 130–32; 33 156–60 (upd.); 106 186–90 (upd.)

Fish & Neave, 54 109–12

Fisher Auto Parts, Inc., 104 152–55

Fisher Communications, Inc., 99 164–168

Fisher Companies, Inc., 15 164–66

Fisher Controls International, LLC, 13 224–26; 61 96–99 (upd.)

Fisher-Price Inc., 12 167–69; 32 190–94 (upd.)

Fisher Scientific International Inc., 24 162–66 *see also* Thermo Fisher Scientific Inc.

Fishman & Tobin Inc., 102 124–27

Fisk Corporation, 72 132–34

Fiskars Corporation, 33 161–64; 105 180–86 (upd.)

Fisons plc, 9 224–27; 23 194–97 (upd.)

Five Guys Enterprises, LLC, 99 169–172

Five Star Quality Care, Inc., 125 145–47

Fives S.A., 107 136–40

FJ Management, 121 183–87 (upd.)

FKI Plc, 57 141–44

Flagstar Companies, Inc., 10 301–03 *see also* Advantica Restaurant Group, Inc.

Flammarion Group, 131 108–12

Flanders Corporation, 65 149–51

Flanigan's Enterprises, Inc., 60 128–30

Flatiron Construction Corporation, 92 119–22

Fleer Corporation, 15 167–69

FleetBoston Financial Corporation, 9 228–30; 36 206–14 (upd.)

FleetCor Technologies, Inc., 132 121–24

FleetPride, Inc., 128 213–16

Fleetwood Enterprises, Inc., III 484–85; 22 205–08 (upd.); 81 159–64 (upd.)

Fleming Companies, Inc., II 624–25; 17 178–81 (upd.)

Fletcher Building Limited, 125 148–51

Fletcher Challenge Ltd., IV 278–80; 19 153–57 (upd.)

Fleury Michon S.A., 39 159–61

Flexsteel Industries Inc., 15 170–72; 41 159–62 (upd.)

Flextronics International Ltd., 38 186–89; 116 236–240 (upd.)

Flight Options, LLC, 75 144–46

FlightSafety International, Inc., 9 231–33; 29 189–92 (upd.)

Flint Ink Corporation, 13 227–29; 41 163–66 (upd.)

Flintco, LLC, 130 220–23

FLIR Systems, Inc., 69 170–73

Flo *see* Groupe Flo S.A.

Floc'h & Marchand, 80 119–21

Florida Crystals Inc., 35 176–78

Florida East Coast Industries, Inc., 59 184–86

Florida Gaming Corporation, 47 130–33

Florida Power & Light Company *see* FPL Group, Inc.

Florida Progress Corp., V 621–22; 23 198–200 (upd.) *see also* Progress Energy, Inc.

Florida Public Utilities Company, 69 174–76

Florida Rock Industries, Inc., 46 195–97 *see also* Patriot Transportation Holding, Inc.

Florida's Natural Growers, 45 160–62

Florists' Transworld Delivery, Inc., 28 136–38 *see also* FTD Group, Inc.

Florsheim Shoe Group Inc., 9 234–36; 31 209–12 (upd.)

Flotek Industries Inc., 93 217–20

Flour City International, Inc., 44 181–83

Flow International Corporation, 56 132–34

Flowers Foods Inc., 12 170–71; 35 179–82 (upd.); 119 179–84 (upd.)

Flowserve Corporation, 33 165–68; 77 146–51 (upd.)

FLSmidth & Co. A/S, 72 138–40

Fluke Corporation, 15 173–75

Fluor Corporation, I 569–71; 8 190–93 (upd.); 34 164–69 (upd.); 112 176–82 (upd.)

Fluxys SA, 101 188–91

FlyBE *see* Jersey European Airways (UK) Ltd.

Flying Boat, Inc. (Chalk's Ocean Airways), 56 135–37

Flying Food Group, LLC, 130 224–27

Flying J Inc., 19 158–60 *see* FJ Management.

Flying Pigeon Bicycle Co. *see* Tianjin Flying Pigeon Bicycle Co., Ltd.

FMC Corp., I 442–44; 11 133–35 (upd.); 89 220–27 (upd.)

FMR Corp., 8 194–96; 32 195–200 (upd.)

FN Manufacturing LLC, 110 155–59

Guardian Life Insurance Company of America, 116 262–66

Guardian Media Group plc, 53 152–55

Guardsmark, L.L.C., 77 171–74

Gucci Group NV, 15 198–200; 50 212–16 (upd.); 115 227–32 (upd.)

Gudang Garam *see* PT Gudang Garam Tbk

Guenther *see* C.H. Guenther & Son, Inc.

Guerbet Group, 46 214–16

Guerlain, 23 240–42

Guess, Inc., 15 201–03; 68 187–91 (upd.)

Guest Supply, Inc., 18 215–17

Guggenheim Foundation *see* John Simon Guggenheim Memorial Foundation

Guida-Seibert Dairy Company, 84 171–174

Guidant Corporation, 58 149–51

Guilbert S.A., 42 169–71

Guilford Mills Inc., 8 234–36; 40 224–27 (upd.)

Guillemot Corporation, 41 188–91, 407, 409

Guillin *see* Groupe Guillin SA

Guinness Peat Group PLC, 119 213–16

Guinness/UDV, I 250–52; 43 212–16 (upd.) *see also* Diageo plc.

Guinot Paris S.A., 82 158–61

Guitar Center, Inc., 29 221–23; 68 192–95 (upd.)

Guittard Chocolate Company, 55 183–85

Gulf + Western Inc., I 451–53 *see also* Paramount Communications; Viacom Inc.

Gulf Agency Company Ltd., 78 133–36

Gulf Air Company, 56 146–48

Gulf Island Fabrication, Inc., 44 201–03

Gulf States Toyota, Inc., 115 233–36

Gulf States Utilities Company, 6 495–97 *see also* Entergy Corp.

GulfMark Offshore, Inc., 49 180–82; 126 182–86 (upd.)

Gulfport Energy Corporation, 119 217–20

Gulfstream Aerospace Corporation, 7 205–06; 28 169–72 (upd.)

Gund, Inc., 96 159–62

Gunite Corporation, 51 152–55

The Gunlocke Company, 23 243–45

Gunnebo AB, 53 156–58

GUS plc, 47 165–70 (upd.)

Guthy-Renker Corporation, 32 237–40; 119 221–26 (upd.)

Guttenplan's Frozen Dough Inc., 88 151–54

Guy Degrenne SA, 44 204–07

Guyenne et Gascogne S.A., 23 246–48; 107 173–76 (upd.)

GVT S.A., 127 165–68

Gwathmey Siegel & Associates Architects LLC, 26 186–88

GWR Group plc, 39 198–200

Gymboree Corporation, 15 204–06; 69 198–201 (upd.)

H

H&E Equipment Services, 128 254–58

H&M Hennes & Mauritz AB, 98 181–84 (upd.)

H&R Block, Inc., 9 268–70; 29 224–28 (upd.); 82 162–69 (upd.)

H-P *see* Hewlett-Packard Co.

H.B. Fuller Company, 8 237–40; 32 254–58 (upd.); 75 179–84 (upd.)

H. Betti Industries Inc., 88 155–58

H.D. Vest, Inc., 46 217–19

H. E. Butt Grocery Company, 13 251–53; 32 259–62 (upd.); 85 164–70 (upd.)

H.F. Ahmanson & Company, II 181–82; 10 342–44 (upd.) *see also* Washington Mutual, Inc.

H. J. Heinz Company, II 507–09; 11 171–73 (upd.); 36 253–57 (upd.); 99 198–205 (upd.)

H.J. Russell & Company, 66 162–65

H. Lundbeck A/S, 44 208–11

H.M. Payson & Co., 69 202–04

H.O. Penn Machinery Company, Inc., 96 163–66

H.P. Hood L.L.C., 117 130–33

The H.W. Wilson Company, 66 166–68

Ha-Lo Industries, Inc., 27 193–95

The Haartz Corporation, 94 223–26

Habasit AG, 121 230–33

Habersham Bancorp, 25 185–87

The Habitat Company LLC, 106 213–17

Habitat for Humanity International, Inc., 36 258–61; 106 218–22 (upd.)

Hach Co., 18 218–21

Hachette Filipacchi Medias S.A., 21 265–67

Hachette S.A., IV 617–19 *see also* Matra-Hachette S.A.

Haci Omer Sabanci Holdings A.S., 55 186–89 *see also* Akbank TAS

Hackman Oyj Adp, 44 212–15

Hadco Corporation, 24 201–03

Häfele GmbH & Co Kommanditgesellschaft, 127 169–73

Haeger Industries Inc., 88 159–62

Haemonetics Corporation, 20 277–79; 122 192–96 (upd.)

Haftpflichtverband der Deutschen Industrie Versicherung auf Gegenseitigkeit V.a.G. *see* HDI (Haftpflichtverband der Deutschen Industrie Versicherung auf Gegenseitigkeit V.a.G.).

Hagemeyer N.V., 39 201–04

Haggar Corporation, 19 194–96; 78 137–41 (upd.)

Haggen Inc., 38 221–23

Hagoromo Foods Corporation, 84 175–178

Hahn Automotive Warehouse, Inc., 24 204–06

Haier Group Corporation, 65 167–70

Haights Cross Communications, Inc., 84 179–182

The Hain Celestial Group, Inc., 27 196–98; 43 217–20 (upd.); 120 152–56 (upd.)

Hair Club For Men Ltd., 90 222–25

Hajoca Corporation, 131 137–40

Hakuhodo, Inc., 6 29–31; 42 172–75 (upd.)

HAL Inc., 9 271–73 *see also* Hawaiian Airlines, Inc.

Hal Leonard Corporation, 96 167–71

Hale-Halsell Company, 60 157–60

Half Price Books, Records, Magazines Inc., 37 179–82

Halfords Group plc, 110 200–04

Hall, Kinion & Associates, Inc., 52 150–52

Halliburton Company, III 497–500; 25 188–92 (upd.); 55 190–95 (upd.); 127 174–81 (upd.)

Hallmark Cards, Inc., IV 620–21; 16 255–57 (upd.); 40 228–32 (upd.); 87 205–212 (upd.)

Halma plc, 104 179–83

Hamilton Beach/Proctor-Silex Inc., 17 213–15

Hammacher Schlemmer & Company Inc., 21 268–70; 72 160–62 (upd.)

Hammerson plc, IV 696–98; 40 233–35 (upd.); 133 165–69 (upd.)

Hammond Manufacturing Company Limited, 83 179–182

Hamon & Cie (International) S.A., 97 190–94

Hamot Health Foundation, 91 227–32

Hampshire Group Ltd., 82 170–73

Hampson Industries PLC, 122 197–200

Hampton Affiliates, Inc., 77 175–79

Hampton Industries, Inc., 20 280–82

Hancock Fabrics, Inc., 18 222–24; 129 150–53 (upd.)

Hancock Holding Company, 15 207–09

Handleman Company, 15 210–12; 86 185–89 (upd.)

Handspring Inc., 49 183–86

Handy & Harman, 23 249–52

Hanesbrands Inc., 98 185–88

Hang Lung Group Ltd., 104 184–87

Hang Seng Bank Ltd., 60 161–63

Hanger Orthopedic Group, Inc., 41 192–95; 129 154–58 (upd.)

Hangzhou Wahaha Group Co., Ltd., 119 227–30

Haniel *see* Franz Haniel & Cie. GmbH.

Hanjin Shipping Co., Ltd., 50 217–21

Hankook Tire Company Ltd., 105 200–03

Hankyu Corporation, V 454–56; 23 253–56 (upd.)

Hankyu Department Stores, Inc., V 70–71; 62 168–71 (upd.)

Hanmi Financial Corporation, 66 169–71

Hanna Andersson Corp., 49 187–90

Hanna-Barbera Cartoons Inc., 23 257–59, 387

Hannaford Bros. Co., 12 220–22; 103 211–17 (upd.)

HealthTronics, Inc., 117 134–38

The Hearst Corporation, IV 625–27; 19 201–04 (upd.); 46 228–32 (upd.); 130 247–53 (upd.)

Hearst Television, Inc., 125 202–06

Hearth & Home Technologies, 107 177–80

Heartland Express, Inc., 18 225–27; 120 163–67 (upd.)

Heartland Payment Sytems, Inc., 116 279–82

The Heat Group, 53 164–66

Heaven Hill Distilleries, Inc., 132 170–74

Hebei Iron & Steel Group, 111 189–93

Hechinger Company, 12 233–36

Heckler & Koch GmbH, 125 207–10

Hecla Mining Company, 20 293–96

Heekin Can Inc., 13 254–56 see also Ball Corp.

Heelys, Inc., 87 213–216

Heery International, Inc., 58 156–59

HEICO Corporation, 30 236–38; 133 177–81 (upd.)

Heidelberg Cement AG, 109 293–99 (upd.)

Heidelberger Druckmaschinen AG, 40 239–41

Heidelberger Zement AG, 31 250–53

Heidrick & Struggles International, Inc., 28 180–82

Heifer Project International, 112 207–10

Heijmans N.V., 66 176–78

Heileman Brewing Co see G. Heileman Brewing Co.

Heilig-Meyers Company, 14 235–37; 40 242–46 (upd.)

Heineken N.V., I 256–58; 13 257–59 (upd.); 34 200–04 (upd.); 90 230–36 (upd.)

Heinrich Bauer Verlag, 122 214–17 (upd.)

Heinrich Deichmann-Schuhe GmbH & Co. KG, 88 173–77

Heinz Co see H.J. Heinz Co.

Heiskell see J.D. Heiskell & Company

Helen of Troy Corporation, 18 228–30

Helene Curtis Industries, Inc., 8 253–54; 28 183–85 (upd.) see also Unilever PLC.

Helix Energy Solutions Group, Inc., 81 173–77

Hella KGaA Hueck & Co., 66 179–83

Hellenic Petroleum SA, 64 175–77

Heller, Ehrman, White & McAuliffe, 41 200–02

Helly Hansen ASA, 25 205–07

Helmerich & Payne, Inc., 18 231–33; 115 237–42 (upd.)

Helmsley Enterprises, Inc., 9 278–80; 39 209–12 (upd.)

Helzberg Diamonds, 40 247–49

HEMA B.V., 111 194–97

Hemisphere GPS Inc., 99 210–213

Hemlo Gold Mines Inc., 9 281–82 see also Newmont Mining Corp.

Henan Zhongpin Food Company, Ltd. see Zhongpin Inc.

Henderson Land Development Company Ltd., 70 113–15

Hendrick Motorsports, Inc., 89 250–53

Hengdeli Holdings Ltd., 127 182–85

Henkel KGaA, III 31–34; 34 205–10 (upd.); 95 174–83 (upd.)

Henkel Manco Inc., 22 257–59

The Henley Group, Inc., III 511–12

Hennes & Mauritz AB, 29 232–34 see also H&M Hennes & Mauritz AB

Henry Boot plc, 76 175–77

Henry Crown and Company, 91 233–36

Henry Dreyfuss Associates LLC, 88 178–82

Henry Ford Health System, 84 183–187

Henry Lambertz see Aachener Printen- und Schokoladenfabrik Henry Lambertz GmbH & Co. KG.

Henry Modell & Company Inc., 32 263–65

Henry Schein, Inc., 31 254–56; 70 116–19 (upd.)

Hensel Phelps Construction Company, 72 174–77

Henselite (Australia) Pty. Ltd., 133 182–86

Hensley & Company, 64 178–80

HEPCO see Hokkaido Electric Power Company Inc.

Her Majesty's Stationery Office, 7 215–18

Heraeus Holding GmbH, IV 98–100; 54 159–63 (upd.); 130 254–60 (upd.)

Herald Media, Inc., 91 237–41

Herbalife Ltd., 17 226–29; 41 203–06 (upd.); 92 162–67 (upd.)

Herbst Gaming, Inc., 124 119–22

Hercules Inc., I 343–45; 22 260–63 (upd.); 66 184–88 (upd.)

Hercules Technology Growth Capital, Inc., 87 217–220

The Heritage Foundation, 114 218–22

Herley Industries, Inc., 33 187–89

Herlitz AG, 107 181–86

Herman Goelitz, Inc., 28 186–88 see also Jelly Belly Candy Co.

Herman Goldner Company, Inc., 100 215–18

Herman Miller, Inc., 8 255–57; 77 180–86 (upd.)

Hermès International S.A., 14 238–40; 34 211–14 (upd.)

Hero Group, 100 219–24

Héroux-Devtek Inc., 69 205–07

Herr Foods Inc., 84 188–191

Herradura see Grupo Industrial Herradura, S.A. de C.V.

Herschend Family Entertainment Corporation, 73 173–76

Hersha Hospitality Trust, 107 187–90

Hershey Company, II 510–12; 15 219–22 (upd.); 51 156–60 (upd.); 110 205–12 (upd.)

Herstal see Groupe Herstal S.A.

Hertie Waren- und Kaufhaus GmbH, V 72–74

The Hertz Corporation, 9 283–85; 33 190–93 (upd.); 101 240–45 (upd.)

Heska Corporation, 39 213–16

Hess Corporation, 133 187–94 (upd.)

Hettich Holding GmbH & Company oHG, 123 179–82

Heublein Inc., I 259–61

Heuer see TAG Heuer International SA.

Heuliez see Groupe Henri Heuliez S.A.

Hewitt Associates, Inc., 77 187–90

Hewlett-Packard Company, III 142–43; 6 237–39 (upd.); 28 189–92 (upd.); 50 222–30 (upd.); 111 198–204 (upd.)

Hexagon AB, 78 154–57

Hexal AG, 69 208–10

Hexcel Corporation, 28 193–95; 132 175–80 (upd.)

Hexion Specialty Chemicals, Inc., 116 283–86

HFF, Inc., 103 218–21

hhgregg Inc., 98 189–92

HI see Houston Industries Inc.

Hibbett Sporting Goods, Inc., 26 189–91; 70 120–23 (upd.)

Hibernia Corporation, 37 187–90

Hickory Farms, Inc., 17 230–32

HickoryTech Corporation, 92 168–71

High Falls Brewing Company LLC, 74 144–47

High Liner Foods Inc., 123 183–87 (upd.)

High Tech Computer Corporation, 81 178–81

Highland Gold Mining Limited, 95 184–87

Highlights for Children, Inc., 95 188–91

Highmark Inc., 27 208–11

Highsmith Inc., 60 167–70

Highveld Steel and Vanadium Corporation Limited, 59 224–27

Hikma Pharmaceuticals Ltd., 102 166–70

Hilb, Rogal & Hobbs Company, 77 191–94

Hildebrandt International, 29 235–38

Hilding Anders AB, 102 171–74

Hill International, Inc., 124 123–26

Hillenbrand Industries, Inc., 10 349–51; 75 188–92 (upd.)

Hillerich & Bradsby Company, Inc., 51 161–64

The Hillhaven Corporation, 14 241–43 see also Vencor, Inc.

Hills Industries Ltd., 104 200–04

Hill's Pet Nutrition, Inc., 27 212–14

Hills Stores Company, 13 260–61

Hillsdown Holdings, PLC, II 513–14; 24 218–21 (upd.)

Hillyard, Inc., 114 223–26

Hilmar Cheese Company, Inc., 98 193–96

Hilo Hattie see Pomare Ltd.

Hilti AG, 53 167–69

Hilton Group plc, III 91–93; 19 205–08 (upd.); 62 176–79 (upd.); 49 191–95 (upd.)
Hindustan Lever Limited, 79 198–201
Hindustan Petroleum Corporation Ltd., 116 287–90
Hines Horticulture, Inc., 49 196–98
Hino Motors, Ltd., 7 219–21; 21 271–74 (upd.)
Hipercor S.A., 123 188–91
HiPP GmbH & Co. Vertrieb KG, 88 183–88
Hiram Walker Resources Ltd., I 262–64
Hiroshima Bank Ltd., 131 145–49
Hispanic Broadcasting Corporation, 35 219–22
HIT Entertainment PLC, 40 250–52
Hitachi, Ltd., I 454–55; 12 237–39 (upd.); 40 253–57 (upd.); 108 254–61 (upd.)
Hitachi Construction Machinery Co., Ltd., 119 231–36
Hitachi Data Systems Corporation, 128 259–63
Hitachi Metals, Ltd., IV 101–02
Hitachi Zosen Corporation, III 513–14; 53 170–73 (upd.)
Hitchiner Manufacturing Co., Inc., 23 267–70
Hite Brewery Company Ltd., 97 204–07
Hittite Microwave Corporation, 106 229–32
HKS, Inc., 124 127–30
HMI Industries, Inc., 17 233–35
HMS Holdings Corp., 122 218–21
HMV Group plc, 59 228–30
HNI Corporation, 74 148–52 (upd.)
Ho-Chunk Inc., 61 125–28
HOB Entertainment, Inc., 37 191–94
Hobby Lobby Stores Inc., 80 139–42
Hobie Cat Company, 94 236–39
Hochtief AG, 33 194–97; 88 189–94 (upd.)
The Hockey Company, 34 215–18; 70 124–26 (upd.)
Hodes see Bernard Hodes Group Inc.
Hodgson Mill, Inc., 88 195–98
Hoechst AG, I 346–48; 18 234–37 (upd.)
Hoechst Celanese Corporation, 13 262–65
Hoenig Group Inc., 41 207–09
Hoesch AG, IV 103–06
Hoffman Corporation, 78 158–12
Hoffmann-La Roche & Co see F. Hoffmann-La Roche & Co.
Hogan & Hartson L.L.P., 44 220–23
Hogg Robinson Group PLC, 105 216–20
Hohner see Matth. Hohner AG.
HOK Group, Inc., 59 231–33
Hokkaido Electric Power Company Inc. (HEPCO), V 635–37; 58 160–63 (upd.)
Hokuriku Electric Power Company, V 638–40
Holberg Industries, Inc., 36 266–69

Holden Ltd., 62 180–83
Holderbank Financière Glaris Ltd., III 701–02 see also Holnam Inc
N.V. Holdingmaatschappij De Telegraaf, 23 271–73 see also Telegraaf Media Groep N.V.
Holiday Companies, 120 168–71
Holiday Inns, Inc., III 94–95 see also Promus Companies, Inc.
Holiday Retirement Corp., 87 221–223
Holiday RV Superstores, Incorporated, 26 192–95
Holidaybreak plc, 96 182–86
Holland & Barrett Retail Limited, 118 188–91
Holland & Knight LLP, 60 171–74
Holland America Line Inc., 108 262–65
Holland Burgerville USA, 44 224–26
Holland Casino, 107 191–94
The Holland Group, Inc., 82 174–77
Hollander Home Fashions Corp., 67 207–09
Holley Performance Products Inc., 52 157–60
Hollinger International Inc., 24 222–25; 62 184–88 (upd.)
Holloway Sportswear Inc., 127 186–89
Holly Corporation, 12 240–42; 111 205–10 (upd.)
Hollywood Casino Corporation, 21 275–77
Hollywood Entertainment Corporation, 25 208–10
Hollywood Media Corporation, 58 164–68
Hollywood Park, Inc., 20 297–300
Holme Roberts & Owen LLP, 28 196–99
Holmen AB, 52 161–65 (upd.); 111 211–17 (upd.)
Holnam Inc., 8 258–60; 39 217–20 (upd.)
Hologic, Inc., 106 233–36
Holophane Corporation, 19 209–12
Holson Burnes Group, Inc., 14 244–45
Holt and Bugbee Company, 66 189–91
Holt's Cigar Holdings, Inc., 42 176–78
Holtzbrinck see Verlagsgruppe Georg von Holtzbrinck.
Homasote Company, 72 178–81
Home Box Office Inc., 7 222–24; 23 274–77 (upd.); 76 178–82 (upd.)
Home City Ice Company, Inc., 111 218–22
The Home Depot, Inc., V 75–76; 18 238–40 (upd.); 97 208–13 (upd.)
Home Hardware Stores Ltd., 62 189–91
Home Inns & Hotels Management Inc., 95 195–95
Home Insurance Company, III 262–64
Home Interiors & Gifts, Inc., 55 202–04
Home Market Foods, Inc., 110 213–16
Home Product Center plc, 104 205–08
Home Products International, Inc., 55 205–07
Home Properties of New York, Inc., 42 179–81

Home Retail Group plc, 91 242–46
Home Shopping Network, Inc., V 77–78; 25 211–15 (upd.) see also HSN.
HomeAway, Inc., 116 291–94
HomeBase, Inc., 33 198–201 (upd.)
Homestake Mining Company, 12 243–45; 38 229–32 (upd.)
Hometown Auto Retailers, Inc., 44 227–29
HomeVestors of America, Inc., 77 195–98
Homex see Desarrolladora Homex, S.A. de C.V.
Hon Hai Precision Industry Company, Ltd., 59 234–36; 117 139–43 (upd.)
HON Industries Inc., 13 266–69 see HNI Corp.
Honam Petrochemical Corp., 131 150–53
Honda Motor Company Ltd., I 174–76; 10 352–54 (upd.); 29 239–42 (upd.); 96 187–93 (upd.)
Honest Tea, Inc., 132 181–84
Honeywell International Inc., II 40–43; 12 246–49 (upd.); 50 231–35 (upd.)109 300–07 (upd.)
Hong Kong and China Gas Company Ltd., 73 177–79
Hong Kong Dragon Airlines Ltd., 66 192–94
Hong Kong Telecommunications Ltd., 6 319–21 see also Cable & Wireless HKT.
Hongkong and Shanghai Banking Corporation Limited, II 296–99 see also HSBC Holdings plc.
Hongkong Electric Holdings Ltd., 6 498–500; 23 278–81 (upd.); 107 195–200 (upd.)
Hongkong Land Holdings Ltd., IV 699–701; 47 175–78 (upd.)
Honshu Paper Co., Ltd., IV 284–85 see also Oji Paper Co., Ltd.
Hood see H.P. Hood L.L.C.
Hoogovens see Koninklijke Nederlandsche Hoogovens en Staalfabricken NV.
Hooker Furniture Corporation, 80 143–46
Hooper Holmes, Inc., 22 264–67
Hooters of America, Inc., 18 241–43; 69 211–14 (upd.)
The Hoover Company, 12 250–52; 40 258–62 (upd.)
Hoover's, Inc., 108 266–69
HOP, LLC, 80 147–50
Hops Restaurant Bar and Brewery, 46 233–36
Hopson Development Holdings Ltd., 87 224–227
Horace Mann Educators Corporation, 22 268–70; 90 237–40 (upd.)
Horizon Food Group, Inc., 100 225–28
Horizon Lines, Inc., 98 197–200
Horizon Organic Holding Corporation, 37 195–99

Lewis-Goetz and Company, Inc., 102 224–27

LEXIS-NEXIS Group, 33 263–67

Lexmark International, Inc., 18 305–07; 79 237–42 (upd.)

LG&E Energy Corporation, 6 516–18; 51 214–17 (upd.)

LG Corporation, 94 277–83 (upd.)

LHC Group, Inc., 122 263–66

Li & Fung Ltd., 59 258–61; 127 231–36 (upd.)

Libbey Inc., 49 251–54

The Liberty Corporation, 22 312–14

Liberty Livewire Corporation, 42 224–27

Liberty Media Corporation, 50 317–19; 111 278–82 (upd.)

Liberty Mutual Holding Company, 59 262–64

Liberty Orchards Co., Inc., 89 302–05

Liberty Property Trust, 57 221–23

Liberty Travel, Inc., 56 203–06

The Library Corporation, 113 214–17

Library Systems & Services, LLC, 122 267–70

Libya Insurance Company, 124 194–97

Libyan National Oil Corporation, IV 453–55 see also National Oil Corp.

Liebherr-International AG, 64 238–42

Liechtensteinische Landesbank AG, 121 286–89

Life Care Centers of America Inc., 76 246–48

Life Fitness, Inc., 132 245–48

Life is good, Inc., 80 213–16

Life Technologies Corporation, 17 287–89133 265–69 (upd.)

Life Time Fitness, Inc., 66 208–10

LifeCell Corporation, 77 236–39

Lifeline Systems, Inc., 32 374; 53 207–09

LifeLock, Inc., 91 314–17

LifePoint Hospitals, Inc., 69 234–36

Lifetime Brands, Inc., 27 286–89; 73 207–11 (upd.)

Lifetime Entertainment Services, 51 218–22

Lifetouch Inc., 86 243–47

Lifeway Foods, Inc., 65 215–17

LifeWise Health Plan of Oregon, Inc., 90 276–79

Ligand Pharmaceuticals Incorporated, 10 48; 47 221–23

Lighting Science Group Corporation, 129 206–09

LILCO see Long Island Lighting Co.

Lillian Vernon Corporation, 12 314–15; 35 274–77 (upd.); 92 207–12 (upd.)

Lilly & Co see Eli Lilly & Co.

Lilly Endowment Inc., 70 157–59

Limagrain see Groupe Limagrain.

Limelight Networks, Inc., 129 210–13

Limited Brands Inc., V 115–16; 20 340–43 (upd.); 109 362–67 (upd.)

Limoneira Company, 110 288–91

LIN Broadcasting Corp., 9 320–22

Linamar Corporation, 18 308–10; 114 274–79 (upd.)

Lincare Holdings Inc., 43 265–67

Lincoln Center for the Performing Arts, Inc., 69 237–41

Lincoln Educational Services Corporation, 111 283–86

Lincoln Electric Co., 13 314–16

Lincoln National Corporation, III 274–77; 25 286–90 (upd.); 113 218–24 (upd.)

Lincoln Property Company, 8 326–28; 54 222–26 (upd.)

Lincoln Snacks Company, 24 286–88

Lincoln Telephone & Telegraph Company, 14 311–13

Lindal Cedar Homes, Inc., 29 287–89

Linde AG, I 581–83; 67 236–39 (upd.)

Lindley see Corporación José R. Lindley S.A.

Lindsay Corporation, 20 344–46; 130 303–07 (upd.)

Lindt & Sprüngli see Chocoladefabriken Lindt & Sprüngli AG.

Line 6, Inc., 117 243–46

Linear Technology Corporation, 16 332–34; 99 254–258 (upd.)

Linens 'n Things, Inc., 24 289–92; 75 239–43 (upd.)

Linfox Logistics Proprietary Limited, 129 214–17

Link Snacks, Inc., 131 230–33

LinkedIn Corporation, 103 246–49

Linklaters LLP, 130 308–11

Lintas: Worldwide, 14 314–16

The Lion Brewery, Inc., 86 248–52

Lion Corporation, III 44–45; 51 223–26 (upd.)

Lion Nathan Limited, 54 227–30

Lionbridge Technologies Inc., 127 237–40

Lionel L.L.C., 16 335–38; 99 259–265 (upd.)

Lions Gate Entertainment Corporation, 35 278–81; 118 259–64 (upd.)

Lipman Electronic Engineering Ltd., 81 236–39

Lipton see Thomas J. Lipton Co.

Liqui-Box Corporation, 16 339–41

Liquidity Services, Inc., 101 309–13

Liquidnet, Inc., 79 243–46

LIRR see The Long Island Rail Road Co.

Litehouse Inc., 60 198–201

Lithia Motors, Inc., 41 238–40

Littelfuse, Inc., 26 266–69

Little Caesar Enterprises, Inc., 7 278–79; 24 293–96 (upd.); 121 290–94 (upd.)

Little Switzerland, Inc., 60 202–04

Little Tikes Company, 13 317–19; 62 231–34 (upd.)

Littleton Coin Company Inc., 82 201–04

Littlewoods plc, V 117–19; 42 228–32 (upd.)

Litton Industries Inc., I 484–86; 11 263–65 (upd.) see also Avondale Industries; Northrop Grumman Corp.

LIVE Entertainment Inc., 20 347–49

Live Nation, Inc., 80 217–22 (upd.)

LivePerson, Inc., 91 318–21

The Liverpool Football Club and Athletic Grounds PLC, 105 280–83

Liz Claiborne, Inc., 8 329–31; 25 291–94 (upd.); 102 228–33 (upd.)

LKQ Corporation, 71 201–03

Lloyd Aéreo Boliviano S.A., 95 239–42

Lloyd's, III 278–81; 22 315–19 (upd.); 74 172–76 (upd.)

Lloyds TSB Group plc, II 306–09; 47 224–29 (upd.)

LM Ericsson see Telefonaktiebolaget LM Ericsson.

Loblaw Companies Limited, 43 268–72; 108 322–26 (upd.)

Localiza Rent a Car S.A., 111 287–90

L'Occitane International S.A., 132 249–52

Lockheed Martin Corporation, I 64–66; 11 266–69 (upd.); 15 283–86 (upd.); 89 306–11 (upd.)

Loctite Corporation, 8 332–34; 30 289–91 (upd.)

Lodge Manufacturing Company, 103 250–53

LodgeNet Interactive Corporation, 28 240–42; 106 285–89 (upd.)

Loehmann's Holdings Inc., 24 297–99; 107 243–47 (upd.)

Loewe AG, 90 280–85

Loewe S.A., 104 272–75

The Loewen Group, Inc., 16 342–44; 40 292–95 (upd.) see also Alderwoods Group Inc.

Loews Corporation, I 487–88; 12 316–18 (upd.); 36 324–28 (upd.); 93 297–304 (upd.)

Loganair Ltd., 68 235–37

Logan's Roadhouse, Inc., 29 290–92

Logica plc, 14 317–19; 37 230–33 (upd.)

Logicon Inc., 20 350–52 see also Northrop Grumman Corp.

Logitech International S.A., 28 243–45; 69 242–45 (upd.)

LogMeIn, Inc., 124 198–202

LoJack Corporation, 48 269–73; 120 214–19 (upd.)

Lojas Americanas S.A., 77 240–43

Lojas Arapuã S.A., 22 320–22; 61 175–78 (upd.)

Lojas Renner S.A., 107 248–51

Lojas Riachuelo S.A. see Guararapes Confecções S.A.

Loma Negra C.I.A.S.A., 95 243–46

London Drugs Ltd., 46 270–73

London Fog Industries, Inc., 29 293–96

London Regional Transport, 6 406–08

London Scottish Bank plc, 70 160–62

London Stock Exchange Limited, 34 253–56

Lone Star Steakhouse & Saloon, Inc., 51 227–29

Lonely Planet Publications, 55 253–55; 124 203–07 (upd.)

The Long & Foster Companies, Inc, 85 221–24

Long Island Bancorp, Inc., 16 345–47

NetCracker Technology Corporation, 98 253–56
NetEase.com, Inc., 131 279–82
Netezza Corporation, 69 276–78
Netflix, Inc., 58 248–51; 115 350–55 (upd.)
NETGEAR, Inc., 81 261–64
NetIQ Corporation, 79 278–81
NetJets Inc., 96 303–07 (upd.)
Netscape Communications Corporation, 15 320–22; 35 304–07 (upd.)
NetScout Systems, Inc., 122 294–97
Netto International, 103 281–84
Network Appliance, Inc., 58 252–54
Network Associates, Inc., 25 347–49
Network Equipment Technologies Inc., 92 265–68
Neuberger Berman Inc., 57 268–71
NeuStar, Inc., 81 265–68
Neutrogena Corporation, 17 340–44
Nevada Bell Telephone Company, 14 345–47 see also AT&T Corp.
Nevada Power Company, 11 342–44
Nevamar Company, 82 255–58
New Balance Athletic Shoe, Inc., 25 350–52; 68 267–70 (upd.)
New Belgium Brewing Company, Inc., 68 271–74
New Britain Palm Oil Limited, 131 283–87
New Brunswick Scientific Co., Inc., 45 285–87
New Chapter Inc., 96 308–11
New Clicks Holdings Ltd., 86 295–98
New Dana Perfumes Company, 37 269–71
New England Business Service, Inc., 18 361–64; 78 237–42 (upd.)
New England Confectionery Co., 15 323–25
New England Electric System, V 662–64 see also National Grid USA.
New England Mutual Life Insurance Co., III 312–14 see also Metropolitan Life Insurance Co.
New Enterprise Associates, 116 366–70
New Era Cap Company, Inc., 122 298–301
New Flyer Industries Inc., 78 243–46
New Holland N.V., 22 379–81 see also CNH Global N.V.
New Horizons Worldwide, Inc., 120 263–66
New Jersey Devils, 84 281–285
New Jersey Manufacturers Insurance Company, 96 312–16
New Jersey Resources Corporation, 54 259–61
New Jersey Sports and Exposition Authority, 130 361–64
New Line Cinema, Inc., 47 271–74
New Look Group plc, 35 308–10
New NGC Inc., 127 294–99 (upd.)
New Orleans Saints LP, 58 255–57
The New Piper Aircraft, Inc., 44 307–10
New Plan Realty Trust, 11 345–47
The New School, 103 285–89

New Seasons Market, 75 272–74
New Street Capital Inc., 8 388–90 (upd.) see also Drexel Burnham Lambert Inc.
New Times, Inc., 45 288–90
New Valley Corporation, 17 345–47
New Wave Group AB, 128 354–57
New World Development Company Limited, IV 717–19; 38 318–22 (upd.)
New World Pasta Company, 53 241–44
New World Restaurant Group, Inc., 44 311–14
New York & Company Inc., 113 269–72
New York City Health and Hospitals Corporation, 60 214–17
New York City Off-Track Betting Corporation, 51 267–70; 115 356–60 (upd.)
New York Community Bancorp, Inc., 78 247–50
New York Daily News, 32 357–60
New York Eye and Ear Infirmary see Continuum Health Partners, Inc.
New York Health Care, Inc., 72 237–39
New York Jets Football Club Inc., 125 274–77
New York Knickerbockers, 129 254–57
New York Life Insurance Company, III 315–17; 45 291–95 (upd.); 118 303–11 (upd.)
New York Philharmonic see Philharmonic-Symphony Society of New York, Inc.
New York Presbyterian Hospital see NewYork-Presbyterian Hospital.
New York Restaurant Group, Inc., 32 361–63
New York Shakespeare Festival Management, 92 328–32
New York State Electric and Gas Corporation, 6 534–36
New York Stock Exchange, Inc., 9 369–72; 39 296–300 (upd.)
The New York Times Company, IV 647–49; 19 283–85 (upd.); 61 239–43 (upd.); 133 300–06 (upd.)
New York Yacht Club, Inc., 103 290–93
New Young Broadcasting Holding Co., Inc., 125 278–82 (upd.)
New Zealand Post Group, 129 258–62
New Zealand Railways Corporation, 125 283–86
The Newark Group, Inc., 102 302–05
Neways, Inc., 78 251–54
Newbury Comics, Inc., 123 283–86
Newcom Group, 104 345–48
Newcor, Inc., 40 332–35
Newcrest Mining Limited, 129 263–66
Newedge Group S.A., 122 302–05
Newegg Inc., 107 291–94
Newell Rubbermaid Inc., 9 373–76; 52 261–71 (upd.); 120 267–76 (upd.)
Newfield Exploration Company, 65 260–62
Newhall Land and Farming Company, 14 348–50

Newly Weds Foods, Inc., 74 201–03
Newman's Own, Inc., 37 272–75; 125 287–91 (upd.)
NewMarket Corporation, 116 371–74
Newmont Mining Corporation, 7 385–88; 94 331–37 (upd.)
NewPage Corporation, 119 333–38
Newpark Resources, Inc., 63 305–07
Newport Corporation, 71 247–49
Newport News Shipbuilding Inc., 13 372–75; 38 323–27 (upd.)
News America Publishing Inc., 12 358–60
News Communications, Inc., 103 294–98
News Corporation, IV 650–53; 7 389–93 (upd.); 46 308–13 (upd.); 109 408–15 (upd.)
Newsday Media Group, 103 299–303
Newsquest plc, 32 354–56
NewYork-Presbyterian Hospital, 59 309–12
Nexans S.A., 54 262–64; 133 307–11 (upd.)
NEXCOM see Navy Exchange Service Command.
Nexen Inc., 79 282–85
Nexity S.A., 66 243–45
Nexsan Corporation, 129 267–71
Nexstar Broadcasting Group, Inc., 73 238–41
Next Media Ltd., 61 244–47
Next plc, 29 355–57
Nextel Communications, Inc., 10 431–33; 27 341–45 (upd.) see also Sprint Nextel Corp.
NextWave Wireless Inc., 112 291–94
Neyveli Lignite Corporation Ltd., 65 263–65
NFC plc, 6 412–14 see also Exel plc.
NFL see National Football League Inc.
NFL Films, 75 275–78
NFO Worldwide, Inc., 24 352–55
NG2 S.A., 120 277–80
NGC Corporation, 18 365–67 see also Dynegy Inc.
NGK Insulators Ltd., 67 264–66
NH Hoteles S.A., 79 286–89
NHK, III 580–82; 115 361–65 (upd.)
Niagara Corporation, 28 314–16
Niagara Mohawk Holdings Inc., V 665–67; 45 296–99 (upd.)
NICE Systems Ltd., 83 280–283
Nichii Co., Ltd., V 154–55
Nichimen Corporation, IV 150–52; 24 356–59 (upd.) see also Sojitz Corp.
Nichimo Company Ltd., 123 287–90
Nichirei Corporation, 70 203–05
Nichiro Corporation, 86 299–302
Nichols plc, 44 315–18
Nichols Research Corporation, 18 368–70
Nicklaus Companies, 45 300–03
Nicole Miller, 98 257–60
Nicor Inc., 6 529–31; 86 303–07 (upd.)
Nidec Corporation, 59 313–16
Nielsen Business Media, Inc., 98 261–65

Nigerian National Petroleum Corporation, IV 472–74; 72 240–43 (upd.)

Nihon Keizai Shimbun, Inc., IV 654–56

NII *see* National Intergroup, Inc.

NIKE, Inc., V 372–74; 8 391–94 (upd.); 36 343–48 (upd.); 75 279–85 (upd.)

Nikken Global Inc., 32 364–67

The Nikko Securities Company Limited, II 433–35; 9 377–79 (upd.)

Nikon Corporation, III 583–85; 48 292–95 (upd.); 132 319–25 (upd.)

Nilson Group AB, 113 273–76

Niman Ranch, Inc., 67 267–69

Nimbus CD International, Inc., 20 386–90

Nine West Group Inc., 11 348–49; 39 301–03 (upd.)

Nintendo Co., Ltd., III 586–88; 7 394–96 (upd.); 28 317–21 (upd.); 67 270–76 (upd.)

NIOC *see* National Iranian Oil Co.

Nippon Credit Bank, II 338–39

Nippon Electric Glass Co. Ltd., 95 301–05

Nippon Express Company, Ltd., V 477–80; 64 286–90 (upd.)

Nippon Life Insurance Company, III 318–20; 60 218–21 (upd.); 127 300–04 (upd.)

Nippon Light Metal Company, Ltd., IV 153–55

Nippon Meat Packers, Inc., II 550–51; 78 255–57 (upd.)

Nippon Mining Holdings Inc., IV 475–77; 102 306–10 (upd.)

Nippon Oil Corporation, IV 478–79; 63 308–13 (upd.); 120 281–87 (upd.)

Nippon Paint Company Ltd., 115 366–68

Nippon Paper Group Inc., 132 326–31 (upd.)

Nippon Professional Baseball Association, 132 332–35

Nippon Seiko K.K., III 589–90

Nippon Sheet Glass Company, Limited, III 714–16

Nippon Shinpan Co., Ltd., II 436–37; 61 248–50 (upd.)

Nippon Soda Co., Ltd., 85 303–06

Nippon Steel Corporation, IV 156–58; 17 348–51 (upd.); 96 317–23 (upd.)

Nippon Suisan Kaisha, Limited, II 552–53; 92 269–72 (upd.)

Nippon Telegraph and Telephone Corporation, V 305–07; 51 271–75 (upd.); 117 279–85 (upd.)

Nippon Television Network Corporation, 126 256–59

Nippon Yusen Kabushiki Kaisha (NYK), V 481–83; 72 244–48 (upd.)

Nippondenso Co., Ltd., III 591–94 *see also* DENSO Corp.

NIPSCO Industries, Inc., 6 532–33

NiSource Inc., 109 416–20 (upd.)

Nissan Motor Company Ltd., I 183–84; 11 350–52 (upd.); 34 303–07 (upd.); 92 273–79 (upd.)

Nisshin Seifun Group Inc., II 554; 66 246–48 (upd.)

Nisshin Steel Co., Ltd., IV 159–60

Nissho Iwai K.K., I 509–11

Nissin Food Products Company Ltd., 75 286–88

Nitches, Inc., 53 245–47

Nixdorf Computer AG, III 154–55 *see also* Wincor Nixdorf Holding GmbH.

NKK Corporation, IV 161–63; 28 322–26 (upd.)

NL Industries, Inc., 10 434–36

NN, Inc., 129 272–75

Noah Education Holdings Ltd., 97 303–06

Noah's New York Bagels *see* Einstein/Noah Bagel Corp.

Nobel Biocare Holding AG, 119 339–42

Nobel Industries AB, 9 380–82 *see also* Akzo Nobel N.V.

Nobel Learning Communities, Inc., 37 276–79; 76 281–85 (upd.)

Nobia AB, 103 304–07

Noble Affiliates, Inc., 11 353–55

Noble Group Ltd., 111 338–42

Noble Roman's Inc., 14 351–53; 99 297–302 (upd.)

Nobleza Piccardo SAICF, 64 291–93

Noboa *see also* Exportadora Bananera Noboa, S.A.

Nocibé SA, 54 265–68

NOF Corporation, 72 249–51

Nokia Corporation, II 69–71; 17 352–54 (upd.); 38 328–31 (upd.); 77 308–13 (upd.)

Nokian Tyres Plc, 126 260–63

NOL Group *see* Neptune Orient Lines Ltd.

Noland Company, 35 311–14; 107 295–99 (upd.)

Nolo.com, Inc., 49 288–91

Nomura Securities Company, Limited, II 438–41; 9 383–86 (upd.)

Noodle Kidoodle, 16 388–91

Noodles & Company, Inc., 55 277–79

Nooter Corporation, 61 251–53

Noranda Inc., IV 164–66; 7 397–99 (upd.); 64 294–98 (upd.)

Norcal Waste Systems, Inc., 60 222–24

The NORDAM Group, Inc., 121 317–20

Norddeutsche Affinerie AG, 62 249–53

Norddeutsche Landesbank Girozentrale, 124 267–70

Nordea Bank AB, 40 336–39; 117 286–90 (upd.)

Nordex AG, 101 362–65

NordicTrack, 22 382–84 *see also* Icon Health & Fitness, Inc.

Nordisk Film A/S, 80 269–73

Nordson Corporation, 11 356–58; 48 296–99 (upd.)

Nordstrom, Inc., V 156–58; 18 371–74 (upd.); 67 277–81 (upd.)

Nordzucker AG, 121 321–24

Norelco Consumer Products Co., 26 334–36

Norfolk Southern Corporation, V 484–86; 29 358–61 (upd.); 75 289–93 (upd.)

The Norinchukin Bank, II 340–41; 125 292–95 (upd.)

Norit International N.V., 130 365–69

Norm Thompson Outfitters, Inc., 47 275–77

Norrell Corporation, 25 356–59

Norseland Inc., 120 288–91

Norsk Hydro ASA, 10 437–40; 35 315–19 (upd.); 109 421–27 (upd.)

Norske Skogindustrier ASA, 63 314–16

Norstan, Inc., 16 392–94

Nortek, Inc., 34 308–12 *see also* NTK Holdings Inc.

Nortel Networks Corporation, 36 349–54 (upd.)

North American Breweries, Inc., 133 312–15

North American Fur Auctions, 130 370–73

North American Galvanizing & Coatings, Inc., 99 303–306

North Atlantic Trading Company Inc., 65 266–68

North Carolina National Bank Corporation *see* NCNB Corp.

The North Face, Inc., 18 375–77; 78 258–61 (upd.)

North Fork Bancorporation, Inc., 46 314–17

North Pacific Group, Inc., 61 254–57

North Star Steel Company, 18 378–81

The North West Company, Inc., 12 361–63

North West Water Group plc, 11 359–62 *see also* United Utilities PLC.

Northeast Utilities, V 668–69; 48 303–06 (upd.); 133 316–20 (upd.)

Northern and Shell Network plc, 87 341–344

Northern Foods plc, 10 441–43; 61 258–62 (upd.); 126 264–69 (upd.)

Northern Reflections Ltd., 130 374–77

Northern Rock plc, 33 318–21

Northern States Power Company, V 670–72; 20 391–95 (upd.) *see also* Xcel Energy Inc.

Northern Telecom Limited, V 308–10 *see also* Nortel Networks Corp.

Northern Trust Corporation, 9 387–89; 101 366–72 (upd.)

Northland Cranberries, Inc., 38 332–34

Northrop Grumman Corporation, I 76–77; 11 363–65 (upd.); 45 304–12 (upd.); 111 343–53 (upd.)

Northwest Airlines Corporation, I 112–14; 6 103–05 (upd.); 26 337–40 (upd.); 74 204–08 (upd.)

Northwest Natural Gas Company, 45 313–15; 125 296–300 (upd.)

NorthWestern Corporation, 37 280–83

Northwestern Mutual Life Insurance Company, III 321–24; 45 316–21 (upd.); 118 312–18 (upd.)

Norton Company, 8 395–97

Printronix, Inc., 18 434–36

PRISA *see* Promotora de Informaciones S.A.

Prison Rehabilitative Industries and Diversified Enterprises, Inc., 53 277–79; 129 297–301 (upd.)

Pro-Build Holdings Inc., 95 344–48 (upd.)

Pro-Football, Inc., 121 343–46

The Procter & Gamble Company, III 50–53; 8 431–35 (upd.); 26 380–85 (upd.); 67 304–11 (upd.)133 351–61 (upd.)

Prodigy Communications Corporation, 34 360–62

Prodware S.A., 102 339–42

Proeza S.A. de C.V., 82 288–91

Professional Basketball Club, LLC, 124 301–06

Professional Bull Riders Inc., 55 310–12

The Professional Golfers' Association of America, 41 318–21

Proffitt's, Inc., 19 323–25 *see also* Belk, Inc.

Programmer's Paradise, Inc., 81 324–27

Progress Energy, Inc., 74 249–52

Progress Software Corporation, 15 371–74; 120 330–35 (upd.)

The Progressive Corporation, 11 405–07; 29 395–98 (upd.); 109 451–56 (upd.)

Progressive Enterprises Ltd., 96 339–42

The Progressive Inc., 110 381–84

ProLogis, 57 300–02

Prometheus Global Media, LLC, 122 349–52

Promotora de Informaciones S.A., 121 347–50

Promus Companies, Inc., 9 425–27 *see also* Hilton Hotels Corp.

ProQuest LLC, 131 305–11 (upd.)

ProSiebenSat.1 Media AG, 54 295–98

Proskauer Rose LLP, 47 308–10

Prosper De Mulder Limited, 111 411–14

Protection One, Inc., 32 372–75

Provell Inc., 58 276–79 (upd.)

Providence Health System, 90 343–47

The Providence Journal Company, 28 367–69; 30 15

The Providence Service Corporation, 64 309–12

Provident Bankshares Corporation, 85 340–43

Provident Life and Accident Insurance Company of America, III 331–33 *see also* UnumProvident Corp.

Providian Financial Corporation, 52 284–90 (upd.)

Provigo Inc., II 651–53; 51 301–04 (upd.)

Provimi S.A., 80 292–95

PRS *see* Paul Reed Smith Guitar Co.

Prudential Financial Inc., III 337–41; 30 360–64 (upd.); 82 292–98 (upd.)

Prudential plc, III 334–36; 48 325–29 (upd.)

PSA Peugeot Citroën S.A., 28 370–74 (upd.); 124 307–12 (upd.)

PSF *see* Premium Standard Farms, Inc.

PSI Resources, 6 555–57

Psion PLC, 45 346–49

PSS World Medical, Inc., 115 397–402 (upd.)

Psychemedics Corporation, 89 358–61

Psychiatric Solutions, Inc., 68 297–300

PT Astra International Tbk, 56 283–86

PT Bank UOB Buana Tbk, 60 240–42; 124 313–16 (upd.)

PT Gudang Garam Tbk, 103 339–42

PT Indosat Tbk, 93 354–57

PT Semen Gresik Tbk, 103 343–46

PTT Public Company Ltd., 56 287–90; 127 327–31 (upd.)

Pubco Corporation, 17 383–85

Public Radio International, Inc., 132 365–68

Public Service Company of Colorado, 6 558–60

Public Service Company of New Hampshire, 21 408–12; 55 313–18 (upd.)

Public Service Company of New Mexico, 6 561–64 *see also* PNM Resources Inc.

Public Service Enterprise Group Inc., V 701–03; 44 360–63 (upd.); 130 394–99 (upd.)

Public Storage, 21 52 291–93; 133 362–66 (upd.)

Publicis Groupe, 19 329–32; 77 346–50 (upd.)

Publishers Clearing House, 23 393–95; 64 313–16 (upd.)

Publishers Group, Inc., 35 357–59

Publishing and Broadcasting Limited, 54 299–302

Publix Super Markets, Inc., 7 440–42; 31 371–74 (upd.); 105 345–51 (upd.)

Puck Lazaroff Inc. *see* The Wolfgang Puck Food Company, Inc.

Pueblo Xtra International, Inc., 47 311–13

Puerto Rico Electric Power Authority, 47 314–16

Puget Sound Energy Inc., 6 565–67; 50 365–68 (upd.)

Puig Beauty and Fashion Group S.L., 60 243–46

Pulaski Furniture Corporation, 33 349–52; 80 296–99 (upd.)

Pulitzer Inc., 15 375–77; 58 280–83 (upd.)

Pulsar Internacional S.A., 21 413–15

Pulte Homes, Inc., 8 436–38; 42 291–94 (upd.); 113 310–15 (upd.)

PUMA AG Rudolf Dassler Sport, 35 360–63; 120 336–41 (upd.)

Pumpkin Masters, Inc., 48 330–32

Pumpkin Patch Limited, 129 302–05

Punch International N.V., 66 258–60

Punch Taverns plc, 70 240–42

Puratos S.A./NV, 92 315–18

Pure World, Inc., 72 285–87

Purina Mills, Inc., 32 376–79

Puritan-Bennett Corporation, 13 419–21

Purolator Products Company, 21 416–18; 74 253–56 (upd.)

Putt-Putt Golf Courses of America, Inc., 23 396–98

PVC Container Corporation, 67 312–14

PW Eagle, Inc., 48 333–36

PWA Group, IV 323–25 *see also* Svenska Cellulosa.

Pyramid Breweries Inc., 33 353–55; 102 343–47 (upd.)

Pyramid Companies, 54 303–05

PZ Cussons plc, 72 288–90

Q

Q.E.P. Co., Inc., 65 292–94

Qantas Airways Ltd., 6 109–13; 24 396–401 (upd.); 68 301–07 (upd.)

Qatar Airways Company Q.C.S.C., 87 404–407

Qatar National Bank SAQ, 87 408–411

Qatar Petroleum, IV 524–26; 98 324–28 (upd.)

Qatar Telecom QSA, 87 412–415

Qdoba Restaurant Corporation, 93 358–62

QIAGEN N.V., 39 333–35; 121 351–55 (upd.)

QinetiQ Group PLC, 128 384–88

QLT Inc., 71 291–94

QRS Music Technologies, Inc., 95 349–53

QSC Audio Products, Inc., 56 291–93

QSS Group, Inc., 100 358–61

Quad/Graphics, Inc., 19 333–36

Quaker Chemical Corp., 91 388–91

Quaker Fabric Corp., 19 337–39

Quaker Foods North America, II 558–60; 12 409–12 (upd.); 34 363–67 (upd.); 73 268–73 (upd.)

Quaker State Corporation, 7 443–45; 21 419–22 (upd.) *see also* Pennzoil-Quaker State Co.

QUALCOMM Incorporated, 20 438–41; 47 317–21 (upd.); 114 337–43 (upd.)

Quality Chekd Dairies, Inc., 48 337–39

Quality Dining, Inc., 18 437–40

Quality Food Centers, Inc., 17 386–88 *see also* Kroger Co.

Quality King Distributors, Inc., 114 344–47

Quality Systems, Inc., 81 328–31

Quanex Corporation, 13 422–24; 62 286–89 (upd.)

Quanta Computer Inc., 47 322–24; 110 385–89 (upd.)

Quanta Services, Inc., 79 338–41

Quantum Chemical Corporation, 8 439–41

Quantum Corporation, 10 458–59; 62 290–93 (upd.)

Quark, Inc., 36 375–79

Quarto Group Inc., 131 312–16

Québéc Hydro-Electric Commission *see* Hydro-Québec.

Quebecor Inc., 12 412–14; 47 325–28 (upd.); 133 367–71 (upd.)

Shearson Lehman Brothers Holdings
  Inc., II 450–52; 9 468–70 (upd.) *see
  also* Lehman Brothers Holdings Inc.
Shed Media plc, 104 414–17
Shedd Aquarium Society, 73 297–99
Sheetz, Inc., 85 387–90
Sheffield Forgemasters International
  Ltd., 115 425–28
Shelby Williams Industries, Inc., 14
  435–37
Sheldahl Inc., 23 432–35
Shell Oil Company, IV 540–41; 14
  438–40 (upd.); 41 356–60 (upd.) *see
  also* Royal Dutch/Shell Group.
Shell Transport and Trading Company
  p.l.c., IV 530–32 *see also* Royal Dutch
  Petroleum Company; Royal
  Dutch/Shell.
Shell Vacations LLC, 102 380–83
Sheller-Globe Corporation, I 201–02 *see
  also* Lear Corp.
Shells Seafood Restaurants, Inc., 43
  370–72
Shenandoah Telecommunications
  Company, 89 390–93
Shenhua Group *see* China Shenhua
  Energy Company Limited
Shepherd Neame Limited, 30 414–16
Sheplers, Inc., 96 387–90
The Sheridan Group, Inc., 86 357–60
Shermag, Inc., 93 392–97
The Sherwin-Williams Company, III
  744–46; 13 469–71 (upd.); 89
  394–400 (upd.)
Sherwood Brands, Inc., 53 302–04
Shikoku Electric Power Company, Inc.,
  V 718–20; 60 269–72 (upd.)
Shimano Inc., 64 347–49
Shimizu Corporation, 109 492–97
Shine Ltd., 118 402–06
Shionogi & Co., Ltd., III 60–61; 17
  435–37 (upd.); 98 350–54 (upd.)
Shire PLC, 109 498–502
Shiseido Company, Limited, III 62–64;
  22 485–88 (upd.); 81 364–70 (upd.)
Shive-Hattery, Inc., 123 366–69
Shochiku Company Ltd., 74 302–04
Shoe Carnival Inc., 14 441–43; 72
  326–29 (upd.)
Shoe Pavilion, Inc., 84 346–349
Shoney's North America Corp., 7
  474–76; 23 436–39 (upd.); 105
  397–403 (upd.)
Shopko Stores Operating Company,
  L.L.C., 21 457–59; 58 329–32
  (upd.); 123 370–74 (upd.)
Shoppers Drug Mart Corporation, 49
  367–70; 130 434–39 (upd.)
Shoppers Food Warehouse Corporation,
  66 290–92
Shorewood Packaging Corporation, 28
  419–21
Showa Shell Sekiyu K.K., IV 542–43;
  59 372–75 (upd.); 120 396–401
  (upd.)
ShowBiz Pizza Time, Inc., 13 472–74
  see also CEC Entertainment, Inc.

Showboat, Inc., 19 400–02 *see also*
  Harrah's Entertainment, Inc.
Showtime Networks, Inc., 78 343–47
SHPS, Inc., 133 408–11
Shred-It Canada Corporation, 56
  319–21
Shriners Hospitals for Children, 69
  318–20
Shubert Organization Inc., 24 437–39;
  112 372–75 (upd.)
Shuffle Master Inc., 51 337–40
Shure Inc., 60 273–76
Shurgard Storage Centers, Inc., 52
  309–11
Shutterfly, Inc., 98 355–58
SHV Holdings N.V., 55 344–47
The Siam Cement Public Company
  Limited, 56 322–25
Sideco Americana S.A., 67 346–48
Sidel *see* Groupe Sidel S.A.
Siderar S.A.I.C., 66 293–95
Siderúrgica del Orinoco Alfredo
  Maneiro, 120 402–05
Sidley Austin LLP, 40 400–03; 122
  397–401 (upd.)
Sidney Frank Importing Co., Inc., 69
  321–23
Siebe plc *see* BTR Siebe plc.
Siebel Systems, Inc., 38 430–34
Siebert Financial Corp., 32 423–25
Siegel & Gale, 64 350–52
Siemens AG, II 97–100; 14 444–47
  (upd.); 57 318–23 (upd.)
The Sierra Club, 28 422–24
Sierra Health Services, Inc., 15 451–53
Sierra Nevada Brewing Company, 70
  291–93
Sierra Nevada Corporation, 108 448–51
Sierra On-Line, Inc., 15 454–56; 41
  361–64 (upd.)
Sierra Pacific Industries, 22 489–91; 90
  369–73 (upd.)
SIFCA S.A., 131 353–57
SIFCO Industries, Inc., 41
SIG plc, 71 334–36
SIG Sauer, Inc., 125 368–71
SIGG Switzerland AG, 130 440–43
Sigma-Aldrich Corporation, I 690–91;
  36 429–32 (upd.); 93 398–404 (upd.)
Sigma Pharmaceuticals Ltd., 121
  393–97
Sigma Plastics Group, 119 415–18
Signet Banking Corporation, 11 446–48
  see also Wachovia Corp.
Signet Group PLC, 61 326–28
Sika AG, 130 444–47
Sikorsky Aircraft Corporation, 24
  440–43; 104 418–23 (upd.)
Silgan Holdings Inc., 128 409–14
Silhouette Brands, Inc., 55 348–50
Silicon Graphics Inc., 9 471–73 *see also*
  SGI.
Siliconware Precision Industries Ltd., 73
  300–02
Siltronic AG, 90 374–77
Silver Lake Cookie Company Inc., 95
  378–81
Silver Wheaton Corp., 95 382–85

SilverPlatter Information Inc., 23
  440–43
Silverstar Holdings, Ltd., 99 415–418
Silverstein Properties, Inc., 47 358–60
Silvio Santos Participações Ltda., 123
  375–79
Simba Dickie Group KG, 105 404–07
Simco S.A., 37 357–59
Sime Darby Berhad, 14 448–50; 36
  433–36 (upd.)
Simmons Company, 47 361–64
Simon & Schuster Inc., IV 671–72; 19
  403–05 (upd.); 100 393–97 (upd.)
Simon Property Group Inc., 27
  399–402; 84 350–355 (upd.)
Simon Transportation Services Inc., 27
  403–06
Simplex Technologies Inc., 21 460–63
Simplicity Manufacturing, Inc., 64
  353–56
Simpson Investment Company, 17
  438–41
Simpson Thacher & Bartlett, 39 365–68
Sims Metal Management, Ltd., 109
  503–07
Simula, Inc., 41 368–70
SINA Corporation, 69 324–27
Sinclair Broadcast Group, Inc., 25
  417–19; 109 508–13 (upd.)
Sinclair Oil Corporation, 111 432–36
Sine Qua Non, 99 419–422
Singapore Airlines Limited, 6 117–18;
  27 407–09 (upd.); 83 355–359 (upd.)
Singapore Press Holdings Limited, 85
  391–95
Singapore Telecommunications Limited,
  111 437–41
Singer & Friedlander Group plc, 41
  371–73
The Singer Company N.V., 30 417–20
  (upd.)
The Singing Machine Company, Inc.,
  60 277–80
SingTel *see* Singapore Telecommunications
  Limited
Sinochem Group, 129 345–48
Sir Speedy, Inc., 16 448–50
Sirius Satellite Radio, Inc., 69 328–31
Sirona Dental Systems, Inc., 117
  392–96
Sirti S.p.A., 76 326–28
Siskin Steel & Supply Company, 70
  294–96
Sistema JSFC, 73 303–05
Sisters of Charity of Leavenworth
  Health System, 105 408–12
Sitel Worldwide Corporation, 128
  415–18
Six Flags, Inc., 17 442–44; 54 333–40
  (upd.)
Sixt AG, 39 369–72
SJM Holdings Ltd., 105 413–17
SJW Corporation, 70 297–99
SK Group, 88 363–67
SK Telecom Co., Ltd., 128 419–23
Skadden, Arps, Slate, Meagher & Flom
  LLP, 18 486–88; 120 406–10 (upd.)
Skalli Group, 67 349–51

Vanguard Health Systems Inc., 70 338–40

Vann's Inc., 105 467–70

Van's Aircraft, Inc., 65 349–51

Vans, Inc., 16 509–11; 47 423–26 (upd.)

Vapores *see* Compañia Sud Americana de Vapores S.A.

Varco International, Inc., 42 418–20

Vari-Lite International, Inc., 35 434–36

Varian, Inc., 48 407–11 (upd.)

Varian Medical Systems, Inc., 12 504–06; 122 465–70 (upd.)

Variety Wholesalers, Inc., 73 362–64

Variflex, Inc., 51 391–93

VARIG S.A. (Viação Aérea Rio-Grandense), 6 133–35; 29 494–97 (upd.)

Varity Corporation, III 650–52 *see also* AGCO Corp.

Varlen Corporation, 16 512–14

Varsity Brands, Inc., 15 516–18; 94 436–40 (upd.)

Varta AG, 23 495–99

VASCO Data Security International, Inc., 79 460–63

Vastar Resources, Inc., 24 524–26

Vattenfall AB, 57 395–98; 126 418–23 (upd.)

Vaughan Foods, Inc., 105 471–74

Vaupell Inc., 121 426–29

Vauxhall Motors Limited, 73 365–69

VBA - Bloemenveiling Aalsmeer, 88 431–34

VCA Antech, Inc., 58 353–55; 129 429–32 (upd.)

VDL Groep B.V., 113 447–50

Veba A.G., I 542–43; 15 519–21 (upd.) *see also* E.On AG.

Vebego International BV, 49 435–37

Vecellio Group, Inc., 113 451–54

VECO International, Inc., 7 558–59 *see also* CH2M Hill Ltd.

Vector Aerospace Corporation, 97 441–44

Vector Group Ltd., 35 437–40 (upd.)

Vectren Corporation, 98 429–36 (upd.)

Vedanta Resources plc, 112 457–61

Vedior NV, 35 441–43

Veeco Instruments Inc., 32 487–90

Veeder-Root Company, 123 417–20

Veidekke ASA, 98 437–40

Veit Companies, 43 440–42; 92 398–402 (upd.)

Velan Inc., 123 421–24

Velcro Industries N.V., 19 476–78; 72 361–64 (upd.)

Velocity Express Corporation, 49 438–41; 94 441–46 (upd.)

Veltins *see* Brauerei C. & A. Veltins GmbH & Co. KG.

Velux A/S, 86 412–15

Venator Group Inc., 35 444–49 (upd.) *see also* Foot Locker Inc.

Vencor, Inc., 16 515–17

Vendex International N.V., 13 544–46 *see also* Koninklijke Vendex KBB N.V. (Royal Vendex KBB N.V.).

Vendôme Luxury Group plc, 27 487–89

Venetian Casino Resort, LLC, 47 427–29

Venoco, Inc., 119 494–98

Ventana Medical Systems, Inc., 75 392–94

Ventura Foods LLC, 90 420–23

Venture Stores Inc., 12 507–09

Veolia Environnement, SA, 109 566–71

Vera Bradley Inc., 130 474–77

Vera Wang Bridal House Ltd., 126 424–27

VeraSun Energy Corporation, 87 447–450

Verband der Vereine Creditreform e. V., 117 448–52

Verbatim Corporation, 14 533–35; 74 371–74 (upd.)

Verbrugge Terminals B.V., 131 408–12

Vereinigte Elektrizitätswerke Westfalen AG, IV V 744–47

Veridian Corporation, 54 395–97

VeriFone, Inc., 18 541–44; 76 368–71 (upd.)

Verint Systems Inc., 73 370–72

VeriSign, Inc., 47 430–34; 119 499–505 (upd.)

Veritas Software Corporation, 45 427–31

Verity Inc., 68 388–91

Verizon Communications Inc., 43 443–49 (upd.); 78 432–40 (upd.)

Verlagsgruppe Georg von Holtzbrinck GmbH, 35 450–53

Verlagsgruppe Weltbild GmbH, 98 441–46

Vermeer Manufacturing Company, 17 507–10

The Vermont Country Store, 93 478–82

Vermont Pure Holdings, Ltd., 51 394–96

The Vermont Teddy Bear Co., Inc., 36 500–02

Versace *see* Gianni Versace SpA.

Vertex Pharmaceuticals Incorporated, 83 440–443

Vertis Communications, 84 418–421

Vertrue Inc., 77 469–72

Vesta Corporation, 128 508–12

Vestas Wind Systems A/S, 73 373–75

Vestey Group Ltd., 95 433–37

Vêt'Affaires S.A., 120 472–75

Veuve Clicquot Ponsardin SCS, 98 447–51

VEW AG, 39 412–15

VF Corporation, V 390–92; 17 511–14 (upd.); 54 398–404 (upd.); 119 506–14 (upd.)

VHA Inc., 53 345–47

Viacom Inc., 7 560–62; 23 500–03 (upd.); 67 367–71 (upd.); 133 475–81 (upd.)

Viad Corp., 73 376–78

Viag AG, IV 229–32 *see also* E.On AG.

ViaSat, Inc., 54 405–08; 132 441–45 (upd.)

Viasoft Inc., 27 490–93; 59 27

VIASYS Healthcare, Inc., 52 389–91

Viasystems Group, Inc., 67 372–74

Viatech Continental Can Company, Inc., 25 512–15 (upd.)

Vibram S.p.A., 126 428–31

Vicarious Visions, Inc., 108 529–32

Vicat S.A., 70 341–43

Vickers plc, 27 494–97

Vicon Industries, Inc., 44 440–42

VICORP Restaurants, Inc., 12 510–12; 48 412–15 (upd.)

VicSuper Pty Ltd, 124 438–41

Victor Company of Japan, Limited, II 118–19; 26 511–13 (upd.); 83 444–449 (upd.)

Victor Hasselblad AB, 123 425–28

Victoria Coach Station Ltd. *see* London Regional Transport.

Victoria Group, III 399–401; 44 443–46 (upd.)

Victorinox AG, 21 515–17; 74 375–78 (upd.)

Victory Refrigeration, Inc., 82 403–06

Vicunha Têxtil S.A., 78 441–44

Videojet Technologies, Inc., 90 424–27

Vidrala S.A., 67 375–77

Viel & Cie, 76 372–74

Vienna Sausage Manufacturing Co., 14 536–37

Viessmann Werke GmbH & Co., 37 411–14

Viewpoint International, Inc., 66 354–56

ViewSonic Corporation, 72 365–67

Viking Office Products, Inc., 10 544–46 *see also* Office Depot, Inc.

Viking Range Corporation, 66 357–59

Viking Yacht Company, 96 446–49

Village Roadshow Limited, 58 356–59; 125 446–50 (upd.)

Village Super Market, Inc., 7 563–64

Village Voice Media, Inc., 38 476–79

Villeroy & Boch AG, 37 415–18

Vilmorin Clause et Cie, 70 344–46

Vilter Manufacturing, LLC, 105 475–79

Vin & Spirit AB, 31 458–61 *see also* V&S Vin & Sprit AB.

Viña Concha y Toro S.A., 45 432–34

Viña San Pedro Tarapacá S.A., 119 515–19

Vinci S.A., 27 54; 43 450–52; 113 455–59 (upd.)

Vincor International Inc., 50 518–21

Vineyard Vines, LLC, 132 446–49

Vinmonopolet A/S, 100 434–37

Vinson & Elkins L.L.P., 30 481–83; 129 333–36 (upd.)

Vintage Petroleum, Inc., 42 421–23

Vinton Studios, 63 420–22

Vion Food Group NV, 85 438–41

Viracon, Inc., 131 413–16

Virbac Corporation, 74 379–81

Virco Manufacturing Corporation, 17 515–17

Virgin Media Inc., 12 513–15; 32 491–96 (upd.); 89 479–86 (upd.); 132 450–54 (upd.)

Virginia Dare Extract Company, Inc., 94 447–50

Warner Communications Inc., II
175–77 *see also* AOL Time Warner Inc.

Warner-Lambert Co., I 710–12; 10
549–52 (upd.) *see also* Pfizer Inc.

Warner Music Group Corporation, 90
432–37 (upd.)

Warners' Stellian Inc., 67 384–87

Warrantech Corporation, 53 357–59

Warrell Corporation, 68 396–98

Warren Equipment Company, 127
434–37

Warrnambool Cheese and Butter
Factory Company Holdings Limited,
118 469–72

Warsteiner Group, 113 460–64

Wärtsilä Corporation, 100 442–46

Warwick Valley Telephone Company, 55
382–84

Wascana Energy Inc., 13 556–58

The Washington Companies, 33
442–45; 127 438–43 (upd.)

Washington Federal, Inc., 17 525–27

Washington Football, Inc., 35 462–65

Washington Gas Light Company, 19
485–88

Washington H. Soul Pattinson and
Company Limited, 112 486–91

Washington Mutual, Inc., 17 528–31;
93 483–89 (upd.)

Washington National Corporation, 12
524–26

Washington Nationals Baseball Club,
LLC, 124 442–48

Washington Natural Gas Company, 9
539–41 *see also* Puget Sound Energy
Inc.

The Washington Post Company, IV
688–90; 20 515–18 (upd.); 109
577–83 (upd.)

Washington Scientific Industries, Inc.,
17 532–34

Washington Water Power Company, 6
595–98 *see also* Avista Corp.

Wasion Group Holdings Ltd., 127
444–47

Wassall Plc, 18 548–50

Waste Connections, Inc., 46 455–57

Waste Holdings, Inc., 41 413–15

Waste Management Inc., V 752–54; 109
584–90 (upd.)

Water Pik Technologies, Inc., 34
498–501; 83 450–453 (upd.)

Waterford Wedgwood plc, 12 527–29;
34 493–97 (upd.) *see also* WWRD
Holdings Ltd.

WaterFurnace Renewable Energy, Inc.,
124 449–52

Waterhouse Investor Services, Inc., 18
551–53

Waters Corporation, 43 453–57

Waterstone's Booksellers Ltd., 131
417–20

Watkins-Johnson Company, 15 528–30

Watsco Inc., 52 397–400

Watson Pharmaceuticals, Inc., 16
527–29; 56 373–76 (upd.); 122
471–76 (upd.)

Watson Wyatt Worldwide, 42 427–30

Wattie's Ltd., 7 576–78

Watts of Lydney Group Ltd., 71 391–93

Watts Water Technologies, Inc., 19
489–91; 115 479–83 (upd.)

Wausau-Mosinee Paper Corporation, 60
328–31 (upd.)

Wave2Wave Communications Inc., 132
455–58

Waverly, Inc., 16 530–32

Wawa Inc., 17 535–37; 78 449–52
(upd.)

The Wawanesa Mutual Insurance
Company, 68 399–401

WAXIE Sanitary Supply, 100 447–51

Waxman Industries, Inc., 9 542–44

WAZ Media Group, 82 419–24

WB *see* Warner Communications Inc.

WD-40 Company, 18 554–57; 87
455–460 (upd.)

We-No-Nah Canoe, Inc., 98 460–63

WE: Women's Entertainment LLC, 114
506–10

Weather Central Inc., 100 452–55

The Weather Channel Companies, 52
401–04 *see also* Landmark
Communications, Inc.

Weather Shield Manufacturing, Inc.,
102 444–47

Weatherford International Ltd., 39
416–18; 130 488–92 (upd.)

Weaver Popcorn Company, Inc., 89
491–93

Web.com Group, Inc., 130 493–96

Webasto Roof Systems Inc., 97 449–52

Webber Oil Company, 61 384–86

Weber et Broutin France, 66 363–65

Weber-Stephen Products Co., 40
458–60

WebEx Communications, Inc., 81
419–23

WebMD Corporation, 65 357–60

Webster Financial Corporation, 106
486–89

Weekley Homes, L.P., 125 455–58

Weeres Industries Corporation, 52
405–07

Weetabix Limited, 61 387–89

Weg S.A., 78 453–56

Wegener NV, 53 360–62

Wegmans Food Markets, Inc., 9
545–46; 41 416–18 (upd.); 105
488–92 (upd.)

WEHCO Media, Inc., 125 459–62

Weider Nutrition International, Inc., 29
498–501

Weight Watchers International Inc., 12
530–32; 33 446–49 (upd.); 73
379–83 (upd.)

Weil, Gotshal & Manges LLP, 55
385–87; 127 448–52 (upd.)

Weinbrenner Shoe Company, Inc., 120
476–79

Weiner's Stores, Inc., 33 450–53

Weingarten Realty Investors, 95 442–45

The Weinstein Company LLC, 118
473–76

The Weir Group PLC, 85 450–53

Weirton Steel Corporation, IV 236–38;
26 527–30 (upd.)

Weis Markets, Inc., 15 531–33; 84
422–426 (upd.)

The Weitz Company, Inc., 42 431–34

Welbilt Corp., 19 492–94; *see also*
Enodis plc.

Welch Foods Inc., 104 470–73

Welcome Wagon International Inc., 82
425–28

Weleda AG, 78 457–61

The Welk Group, Inc., 78 462–66

Wella AG, III 68–70; 48 420–23 (upd.)

WellCare Health Plans, Inc., 101
487–90

WellChoice, Inc., 67 388–91 (upd.)

Wellco Enterprises, Inc., 84 427–430

Wellcome Foundation Ltd., I 713–15 *see
also* GlaxoSmithKline plc.

Wellman, Inc., 8 561–62; 52 408–11
(upd.)

WellPoint, Inc., 25 525–29; 103 505–14
(upd.)

Wells Enterprises, Inc., 36 511–13; 127
453–57 (upd.)

Wells Fargo & Company, II 380–84; 12
533–37 (upd.); 38 483–92 (upd.); 97
453–67

Wells-Gardner Electronics Corporation,
43 458–61

Wells Rich Greene BDDP, 6 50–52

Welsh Rugby Union Limited, 115
484–87

Wendell *see* Mark T. Wendell Tea Co.

Wendy's/Arby's Group, Inc., 8 563–65;
23 504–07 (upd.); 47 439–44 (upd.);
118 477–83 (upd.)

Wenner Bread Products Inc., 80 411–15

Wenner Media, Inc., 32 506–09

Werhahn *see* Wilh. Werhahn KG.

Werner Enterprises, Inc., 26 531–33

Weru Aktiengesellschaft, 18 558–61

WESCO International, Inc., 116
459–62

Wesfarmers Limited, 109 591–95

Wessanen *see* Koninklijke Wessanen nv.

West Bend Co., 14 546–48

West Coast Entertainment Corporation,
29 502–04

West Corporation, 42 435–37

West Fraser Timber Co. Ltd., 17
538–40; 91 512–18 (upd.)

West Group, 34 502–06 (upd.)

West Linn Paper Company, 91 519–22

West Marine, Inc., 17 541–43; 90
438–42 (upd.)

West One Bancorp, 11 552–55 *see also*
U.S. Bancorp.

West Pharmaceutical Services, Inc., 42
438–41

West Point-Pepperell, Inc., 8 566–69 *see
also* WestPoint Stevens Inc.; JPS Textile
Group, Inc.

West Publishing Co., 7 579–81

Westaff Inc., 33 454–57

Westamerica Bancorporation, 17
544–47

Westar Energy, Inc., 57 404–07 (upd.)

Zumiez, Inc., 77 493–96
Zumtobel AG, 50 544–48
Zurich Financial Services, III 410–12;

42 448–53 (upd.); 93 502–10 (upd.)
Zweigle's Inc., 111 534–37
Zygo Corporation, 42 454–57

Zynga Inc., 124 462–65
Zytec Corporation, 19 513–15 *see also*
Artesyn Technologies Inc.

Index to Industries

Accounting

American Institute of Certified Public
    Accountants (AICPA), 44
Andersen, 29 (upd.); 68 (upd.)
Automatic Data Processing, Inc., III; 9
    (upd.); 47 (upd.); 126 (upd.)
BDO Seidman LLP, 96
BKD LLP, 96
CPP International, LLC, 103
CROSSMARK, 79
Deloitte Touche Tohmatsu International,
    9; 29 (upd.)
Ernst & Young Global Limited, 9; 29
    (upd.); 108 (upd.)
FTI Consulting, Inc., 77
Grant Thornton International, 57
Huron Consulting Group Inc., 87
JKH Holding Co. LLC, 105
KPMG International, 33 (upd.); 108
    (upd.)
L.S. Starrett Co., 13
LarsonAllen, LLP, 118
McLane Company, Inc., 13
NCO Group, Inc., 42
Paychex Inc., 15; 46 (upd.); 120 (upd.)
PKF International, 78
Plante & Moran, LLP, 71
PRG-Schultz International, Inc., 73
PricewaterhouseCoopers International
    Limited, 9; 29 (upd.); 111 (upd.)
Resources Connection, Inc., 81
Robert Wood Johnson Foundation, 35
Rothstein, Kass & Company, P.C., 131
RSM McGladrey Business Services Inc.,
    98
Saffery Champness, 80
Sanders\Wingo, 99
Schenck Business Solutions, 88

StarTek, Inc., 79
Travelzoo Inc., 79
Univision Communications Inc., 24; 83
    (upd.)

Advertising & Business Services

1-800-FLOWERS.COM, Inc., 26; 102
    (upd.)
4imprint Group PLC, 105
24/7 Real Media, Inc., 49
ABM Industries Incorporated, 25 (upd.);
    128 (upd.)
Abt Associates Inc., 95
Accenture Ltd., 108 (upd.)
AchieveGlobal Inc., 90
Ackerley Communications, Inc., 9
ACNielsen Corporation, 13; 38 (upd.)
Acosta Sales and Marketing Company,
    Inc., 77
Acsys, Inc., 44
Adecco S.A., 36 (upd.); 116 (upd.)
Adelman Travel Group, 105
Adia S.A., 6
Administaff, Inc., 52
The Advertising Council, Inc., 76
The Advisory Board Company, 80
Advo, Inc., 6; 53 (upd.)
Aegis Group plc, 6
Affiliated Computer Services, Inc., 61
Affinion Group, Inc., 121
AHL Services, Inc., 27
Alibaba.com, Ltd., 119
Alion Science and Technology
    Corporation, 128
Allegis Group, Inc., 95
AlliedBarton Security Services LLC, 128
    (upd.)

Alloy, Inc., 55
Amdocs Ltd., 47
American Building Maintenance
    Industries, Inc., 6
Amey Plc, 47
Analysts International Corporation, 36
APAC Customer Services Inc., 127
aQuantive, Inc., 81
The Arbitron Company, 38
Ariba, Inc., 57
Armor Holdings, Inc., 27
Asatsu-DK Inc., 82
Ashtead Group plc, 34
Astral Media Inc., 126
Avalon Correctional Services, Inc., 75
Bain & Company, 55
Barrett Business Services, Inc., 16
Barton Protective Services Inc., 53
Bates Worldwide, Inc., 14; 33 (upd.)
Bearings, Inc., 13
Belfor Holdings Inc., 128
Berlitz International, Inc., 13; 39 (upd.)
Bernard Hodes Group Inc., 86
Bernstein-Rein, 92
Big Flower Press Holdings, Inc., 21
Billing Concepts, Inc., 26; 72 (upd.)
Billing Services Group Ltd., 102
The BISYS Group, Inc., 73
bofrost Dienstleistungs GmbH and
    Company KG, 123
Booz Allen Hamilton Inc., 10; 101 (upd.)
Boron, LePore & Associates, Inc., 45
The Boston Consulting Group, 58
Bozell Worldwide Inc., 25
Brambles Limited, 42; 129 (upd.)
BrandPartners Group, Inc., 58
Bright Horizons Family Solutions, Inc., 31
Broadcast Music Inc., 23; 90 (upd.)

Xerox Corporation, III; 6 (upd.); 26 (upd.); 69 (upd.)
Yelp Inc., 132
Young & Rubicam, Inc., I; 22 (upd.); 66 (upd.)
Ziment Group Inc., 102
Zogby International, Inc., 99

Aerospace

A.S. Yakovlev Design Bureau, 15
AAR Corp., 28; 127 (upd.)
Aerojet-General Corp., 63
Aeronca Inc., 46
Aerosonic Corporation, 69
The Aerospace Corporation, 130
The Aerospatiale Group, 7; 21 (upd.)
AeroVironment, Inc., 97
AgustaWestland N.V., 75
Airborne Systems Group, 89
Alliant Techsystems Inc., 30 (upd.)
Allison Gas Turbine Division, 9
Antonov Design Bureau, 53
Arianespace S.A., 89
Astronics Corporation, 35; 130 (upd.)
Astrotech Corporation, 129
Aviacionny Nauchno-Tehnicheskii Komplex im. A.N. Tupoleva, 24
Aviall, Inc., 73
Avions Marcel Dassault-Breguet Aviation, I
B/E Aerospace, Inc., 30
BAE Systems plc, 108 (upd.)
Ballistic Recovery Systems, Inc., 87
Banner Aerospace, Inc., 14
BBA Aviation plc, 90
Beech Aircraft Corporation, 8
Bell Helicopter Textron Inc., 46
The Boeing Company, I; 10 (upd.); 32 (upd.); 111 (upd.)
Bombardier Inc., 42 (upd.); 87 (upd.)
British Aerospace plc, I; 24 (upd.)
CAE USA Inc., 48
Canadair, Inc., 16
Cessna Aircraft Company, 8; 27 (upd.)
Cirrus Design Corporation, 44
Cobham plc, 30
CPI Aerostructures, Inc., 75
Curtiss-Wright Corporation, 122 (upd.)
Daimler-Benz Aerospace AG, 16
Dassault Aviation S.A., 114 (upd.)
DeCrane Aircraft Holdings Inc., 36
Derco Holding Ltd., 98
Diehl Stiftung & Co. KG, 79
DigitalGlobe, Inc., 116
Ducommun Incorporated, 30
Duncan Aviation, Inc., 94
EADS SOCATA, 54
Eclipse Aviation Corporation, 87
EGL, Inc., 59
Elano Corporation, 14
Embraer S.A., 36; 133 (upd.)
Esterline Technologies Corporation, 15; 132 (upd.)
European Aeronautic Defence and Space Company EADS N.V., 52 (upd.); 109 (upd.)
Fairchild Aircraft, Inc., 9
Fairchild Dornier GmbH, 48 (upd.)

Finmeccanica S.p.A., 84
First Aviation Services Inc., 49
G.I.E. Airbus Industrie, I; 12 (upd.)
GE Aircraft Engines, 9
GenCorp Inc., 8; 9 (upd.)
General Dynamics Corporation, I; 10 (upd.); 40 (upd.); 88 (upd.
GKN plc, III; 38 (upd.); 89 (upd.)
Goodrich Corporation, 46 (upd.); 109 (upd.)
Groupe Dassault Aviation SA, 26 (upd.)
Grumman Corporation, I; 11 (upd.)
Grupo Aeropuerto del Sureste, S.A. de C.V., 48
Gulfstream Aerospace Corporation, 7; 28 (upd.)
Hampson Industries PLC, 122
HEICO Corporation, 30; 133 (upd.)
Héroux-Devtek Inc., 69
International Lease Finance Corporation, 48
Irkut Corporation, 68
Israel Aircraft Industries Ltd., 69
JBT AeroTech, 131
Kaman Corporation, 118 (upd.)
Kolbenschmidt Pierburg AG, 97
Kreisler Manufacturing Corporation, 97
Lancair International, Inc., 67
Latécoère S.A., 100
Learjet Inc., 8; 27 (upd.)
Lockheed Martin Corporation, I; 11 (upd.); 15 (upd.); 89 (upd.)
Loral Space & Communications Ltd., 54 (upd.)
Magellan Aerospace Corporation, 48
Martin Marietta Corporation, I
Martin-Baker Aircraft Company Limited, 61
McDonnell Douglas Corporation, I; 11 (upd.)
Meggitt PLC, 34
Messerschmitt-Bölkow-Blohm GmbH., I
Moog Inc., 13
Mooney Aerospace Group Ltd., 52
N.V. Koninklijke Nederlandse Vliegtuigenfabriek Fokker, I; 28 (upd.)
The New Piper Aircraft, Inc., 44
Northrop Grumman Corporation, I; 11 (upd.); 45 (upd.); 111 (upd.)
Orbital Sciences Corporation, 22; 107 (upd.)
Pemco Aviation Group Inc., 54
Pratt & Whitney, 9; 125 (upd.)
Raytheon Aircraft Holdings Inc., 46
Raytheon Company, II; 11 (upd.); 38 (upd.); 105 (upd.)
Robinson Helicopter Company, 51
Rockwell Collins, 106
Rockwell International Corporation, I; 11 (upd.)
Rohr Incorporated, 9
Rolls-Royce Allison, 29 (upd.)
Rolls-Royce plc, I; 7 (upd.); 21 (upd.)
Rostvertol plc, 62
Russian Aircraft Corporation (MiG), 86
Safe Flight Instrument Corporation, 71
Sequa Corporation, 13; 54 (upd.); 130 (upd.)

Shannon Aerospace Ltd., 36
Sikorsky Aircraft Corporation, 24; 104 (upd.)
Smiths Industries PLC, 25
Snecma Group, 46
Société Air France, 27 (upd.)
Spacehab, Inc., 37
Spar Aerospace Limited, 32
Spirit AeroSystems Holdings, Inc., 122
Sukhoi Design Bureau Aviation Scientific-Industrial Complex, 24
Sundstrand Corporation, 7; 21 (upd.)
Surrey Satellite Technology Limited, 83
Swales & Associates, Inc., 69
Teledyne Technologies Inc., 62 (upd.)
Textron Lycoming Turbine Engine, 9
Thales S.A., 42
Thiokol Corporation, 9; 22 (upd.)
TransDigm Group Incorporated, 119
Triumph Aerostructures—Vought Aircraft Division, 123 (upd.)
Triumph Group, Inc., 31; 126 (upd.)
Umeco plc, 114
United Technologies Corporation, I; 10 (upd.); 34 (upd.); 105 (upd.)
Van's Aircraft, Inc., 65
Vector Aerospace Corporation, 97
Vought Aircraft Industries, Inc., 49
Whittaker Corporation, 48 (upd.)
Williams International Co., L.L.C., 118
Woodward Governor Company, 13; 49 (upd.); 105 (upd.)
Zodiac S.A., 36

Agribusiness & Farming

AeroGrow International, Inc., 95
Ag-Chem Equipment Company, Inc., 17
AGCO Corporation, 13; 67 (upd.)
Agland, Inc., 110
Agrium Inc., 73
Alamo Group Inc., 32
The Andersons, Inc., 31
BayWa AG, 112
Bou-Matic, 62
Corn Products International, Inc., 116
CTB International Corporation, 43 (upd.)
DeBruce Grain, Inc., 112
Fonterra Co-operative Group Limited, 58; 124 (upd.)
Garst Seed Company, Inc., 86
George W. Park Seed Company, Inc., 98
Incitec Pivot Limited, 129
Kubota Corporation, III; 26 (upd.)
Mumias Sugar Company Limited, 124
Pennington Seed Inc., 98
Perdue Incorporated, 7; 23 (upd.); 119 (upd.)
Riceland Foods, Inc., 128
Ridley Corporation Ltd., 129 (upd.)
Sinochem Group, 129
SLC Participaçoes S.A., 111
Staple Cotton Cooperative Association (Staplcotn), 86
Sun Gro Horticulture Inc., 129
W. Atlee Burpee & Co., 27
Wilbur-Ellis Company, 114
Wyllie Group Pty Ltd, 124

Airlines

Automotive

Beverages

Bio-Technology

Chemicals

Education & Training

Electrical & Electronics

Pacific Aerospace & Electronics, Inc., 120
Palm, Inc., 36; 75 (upd.)
Palo Alto Research Center Incorporated, 129
Palomar Medical Technologies, Inc., 22
Parlex Corporation, 61
Peak Technologies Group, Inc., The, 14
Peavey Electronics Corporation, 16
Philips Electronics N.V., II; 13 (upd.)
Philips Electronics North America Corp., 13
Pioneer Electronic Corporation, III; 28 (upd.)
Pioneer-Standard Electronics Inc., 19
Pitney Bowes Inc., III; 19 (upd.); 47 (upd.)
Pittway Corporation, 9; 33 (upd.)
Pixelworks, Inc., 69
Planar Systems, Inc., 61
Plantronics, Inc., 106
Plessey Company, PLC, The, II
Plexus Corporation, 35; 80 (upd.)
Polaroid Corporation, III; 7 (upd.); 28 (upd.); 93 (upd.)
Polk Audio, Inc., 34
Potter & Brumfield Inc., 11
Powell Industries, Inc., 130
Premier Industrial Corporation, 9
Protection One, Inc., 32
QUALCOMM Incorporated, 114 (upd.)
Quanta Computer Inc., 47; 79 (upd.); 110 (upd.)
Racal Electronics PLC, II
RadioShack Corporation, 36 (upd.); 101 (upd.)
Radius Inc., 16
RAE Systems Inc., 83
Ramtron International Corporation, 89
Raychem Corporation, 8
Raymarine plc, 104
Rayovac Corporation, 13; 39 (upd.)
Raytheon Company, II; 11 (upd.); 38 (upd.); 105 (upd.)
RCA Corporation, II
Read-Rite Corp., 10
Real Goods Solar, Inc., 122
Redback Networks, Inc., 92
Reliance Electric Company, 9
Research in Motion Ltd., 54
Rexel, Inc., 15
Richardson Electronics, Ltd., 17
Ricoh Company, Ltd., III; 36 (upd.); 108 (upd.)
Rimage Corp., 89
Rittal Corporation, 127
Rival Company, The, 19
Rockford Corporation, 43
Rogers Corporation, 61; 80 (upd.)
Roku, Inc., 121
Roper Industries, Inc., 122 (upd.)
S&C Electric Company, 15
SAGEM S.A., 37
St. Louis Music, Inc., 48
Sam Ash Music Corporation, 30
Samsung Electronics Co., Ltd., 14; 41 (upd.); 108 (upd.)
SanDisk Corporation, 121
Sanmina-SCI Corporation, 109 (upd.)

SANYO Electric Co., Ltd., II; 36 (upd.); 95 (upd.)
Sarnoff Corporation, 57
Satcon Technology Corporation, 124
ScanSource, Inc., 29; 74 (upd.)
Schneider Electric SA, II; 18 (upd.); 108 (upd.)
SCI Systems, Inc., 9
Scientific-Atlanta, Inc., 45 (upd.)
Scitex Corporation Ltd., 24
Seagate Technology, 8; 34 (upd.); 105 (upd.)
SEGA Corporation, 73
Semitool, Inc., 79 (upd.)
Semtech Corporation, 32
Sennheiser Electronic GmbH & Co. KG, 66
Sensormatic Electronics Corp., 11
Sensory Science Corporation, 37
SGI, 29 (upd.)
Sharp Corporation, II; 12 (upd.); 40 (upd.); 114 (upd.)
Sheldahl Inc., 23
Shure Inc., 60
Siemens AG, II; 14 (upd.); 57 (upd.)
Sierra Nevada Corporation, 108
Silicon Graphics Incorporated, 9
Siltronic AG, 90
Skullcandy, Inc., 123
SL Industries, Inc., 77
Sling Media, Inc., 112
SMA Solar Technology AG, 118
SMART Modular Technologies, Inc., 86
Smiths Industries PLC, 25
Solectron Corporation, 12; 48 (upd.)
Sonus Networks Inc., 126
Sony Corporation, II; 12 (upd.); 40 (upd.); 108 (upd.)
Spansion Inc., 80
Spectrum Control, Inc., 67
Spire Corporation, 129
SPX Corporation, 10; 47 (upd.); 103 (upd.)
Square D, 90
Standex International Corporation, 17; 44 (upd.); 133 (upd.)
Sterling Electronics Corp., 18
STMicroelectronics NV, 52
Strix Ltd., 51
Stuart C. Irby Company, 58
Sumitomo Electric Industries, Ltd., II
Sun Microsystems, Inc., 7; 30 (upd.); 91 (upd.)
Sunbeam-Oster Co., Inc., 9
SunPower Corporation, 91
Suntech Power Holdings Company Ltd., 89
Suntron Corporation, 107
SunWize Technologies, Inc., 114
Synaptics Incorporated, 95
Syneron Medical Ltd., 91
SYNNEX Corporation, 73
Synopsys, Inc., 11; 69 (upd.)
Syntax-Brillian Corporation, 102
Sypris Solutions, Inc., 85
SyQuest Technology, Inc., 18
Taiwan Semiconductor Manufacturing Company Ltd., 47

Tandy Corporation, II; 12 (upd.)
Tatung Co., 23
TDK Corporation, II; 17 (upd.); 49 (upd.); 114 (upd.)
TEAC Corporation, 78
Technitrol, Inc., 29
Tech-Sym Corporation, 18
Tektronix, Inc., 8
Teledyne Technologies Inc., 62 (upd.)
Telxon Corporation, 10
Teradyne, Inc., 11; 98 (upd.)
Tesla Motors, Inc., 124
Texas Instruments Incorporated, II; 11 (upd.); 46 (upd.); 118 (upd.)
Thales S.A., 42
Thomas & Betts Corporation, 11; 54 (upd.); 114 (upd.)
THOMSON multimedia S.A., II; 42 (upd.)
THQ, Inc., 92 (upd.)
Titan Corporation, The, 36
TiVo Inc., 75
TomTom N.V., 81
Tops Appliance City, Inc., 17
Toromont Industries, Ltd., 21
Trans-Lux Corporation, 51
Trimble Navigation Limited, 40
Trio-Tech International, 129
TriQuint Semiconductor, Inc., 63
TT electronics plc, 111
Tweeter Home Entertainment Group, Inc., 30
Ultimate Electronics, Inc., 69 (upd.)
Ultrak Inc., 24
Uniden Corporation, 98
Unisys Corporation, 112 (upd.)
United Microelectronics Corporation, 98
Universal Electronics Inc., 39; 120 (upd.)
Universal Security Instruments, Inc., 96
Varian, Inc., 12; 48 (upd.)
Veeco Instruments Inc., 32
VIASYS Healthcare, Inc., 52
Viasystems Group, Inc., 67
Vicon Industries, Inc., 44
Victor Company of Japan, Limited, II; 26 (upd.); 83 (upd.)
Vishay Intertechnology, Inc., 21; 80 (upd.)
Vitesse Semiconductor Corporation, 32
Vitro Corp., 10
Vizio, Inc., 100
VLSI Technology, Inc., 16
Volterra Semiconductor Corporation, 128
Vorwerk & Co. KG, 112 (upd.)
VTech Holdings Ltd., 77
Wells-Gardner Electronics Corporation, 43
WESCO International, Inc., 116
Westinghouse Electric Corporation, II; 12 (upd.)
Winbond Electronics Corporation, 74
Wincor Nixdorf Holding GmbH, 69 (upd.)
Wistron Corporation, 126
WuXi AppTec Company Ltd., 103
Wyle Electronics, 14
Xantrex Technology Inc., 97

Engineering & Management Services

Vinci, 43
Volkert and Associates, Inc., 98
VSE Corporation, 108
Weir Group PLC, The, 85
Willbros Group, Inc., 56
Wisconsin Lift Truck Corp., 130
WS Atkins Plc, 45
WSP Group plc, 126

Entertainment & Leisure

4Kids Entertainment Inc., 59
7digital Limited, 125
19 Entertainment Limited, 112
24 Hour Fitness Worldwide, Inc., 71
40 Acres and a Mule Filmworks, Inc., 121
155 East Tropicana, LLC, 124
365 Media Group plc, 89
888 Holdings plc, 124
A&E Television Networks, 32
Aardman Animations Ltd., 61
ABC Family Worldwide, Inc., 52
Academy of Motion Picture Arts and
    Sciences, 121
Academy of Television Arts & Sciences,
    Inc., 55
Acclaim Entertainment Inc., 24
Activision, Inc., 32; 89 (upd.)
Acushnet Company, 64
Adams Golf, Inc., 37
Adelman Travel Group, 105
AEI Music Network Inc., 35
AFC Ajax NV, 132
Affinity Group Holding Inc., 56
Airtours Plc, 27
Alaska Railroad Corporation, 60
Aldila Inc., 46
All American Communications Inc., 20
All England Lawn Tennis & Croquet
    Club, The, 54
Allen Organ Company, 33
Allgemeiner Deutscher Automobil-Club
    e.V., 100
Alliance Entertainment Corp., 17
Alternative Tentacles Records, 66
Alvin Ailey Dance Foundation, Inc., 52
Amblin Entertainment, 21
AMC Entertainment Inc., 12; 35 (upd.);
    114 (upd.)
Amer Group plc, 41
American Golf Corporation, 45
American Gramaphone LLC, 52
American Kennel Club, Inc., 74
American Museum of Natural History,
    121
American Skiing Company, 28
Ameristar Casinos, Inc., 33; 69 (upd.)
AMF Bowling, Inc., 40
Amscan Holdings, Inc., 61; 124 (upd.)
Anaheim Angels Baseball Club, Inc., 53
Anchor Gaming, 24
AOL Time Warner Inc., 57 (upd.)
Apollo Theater Foundation, Inc., 109
Applause Inc., 24
Apple Corps Ltd., 87
Aprilia SpA, 17
Arena Leisure Plc, 99
Argosy Gaming Company, 21
Aristocrat Leisure Limited, 129 (upd.)

Aristocrat Leisure Limited, 54
Arizona Cardinals Football Club LLC,
    129
Arsenal Holdings PLC, 79
Art Institute of Chicago, The, 29
Arthur C. Clarke Foundation, The, 92
Arthur Murray International, Inc., 32
Artisan Entertainment Inc., 32 (upd.)
Asahi National Broadcasting Company,
    Ltd., 9
Aspen Skiing Company, 15; 129 (upd.)
Aston Villa plc, 41
Atari S.A., 9; 23 (upd.); 66 (upd.); 132
    (upd.)
Athletics Investment Group, The, 62
Atlanta National League Baseball Club,
    Inc., 43
Atlantic Group, The, 23
Augusta National Inc., 115
Autotote Corporation, 20
Avedis Zildjian Co., 38
Aztar Corporation, 13
Bad Boy Worldwide Entertainment
    Group, 58
Baker & Taylor Corporation, 16; 43
    (upd.)
Baldwin Piano & Organ Company, 18
Ballet Theatre Foundation, Inc., 118
Bally Total Fitness Holding Corp., 25
Baltimore Orioles L.P., 66
Barden Companies, Inc., 76
Baseball Club of Seattle, LP, The, 50
Basketball Club of Seattle, LLC, The, 50
Beggars Group Ltd., 99
Bell Media, Inc., 126
Bell Sports Corporation, 16; 44 (upd.)
BenQ Corporation, 67
Bertelsmann A.G., IV; 15 (upd.); 43
    (upd.); 91 (upd.)
Bertucci's Inc., 16
Big Fish Games, Inc., 108
Big Idea Productions, Inc., 49
BigBen Interactive S.A., 72
The Biltmore Company, 118
BioWare Corporation, 81
Black Diamond Equipment, Ltd., 62; 121
    (upd.)
Blockbuster Inc., 9; 31 (upd.); 76 (upd.)
Blue Note Label Group, 115
Boca Resorts, Inc., 37
Bonneville International Corporation, 29
Booth Creek Ski Holdings, Inc., 31
Boston Basketball Partners L.L.C., 14;
    115 (upd.)
Boston Professional Hockey Association
    Inc., 39
Boston Sox Baseball Club Limited
    Partnership, 124
Boston Symphony Orchestra Inc., The, 93
Boy Scouts of America, The, 34
Boyd Gaming Corporation, 43; 132
    (upd.)
Boylesports Holdings Ltd., 129
Boyne USA Resorts, 71
Brass Eagle Inc., 34
Bravo Company, 114
Brillstein-Grey Entertainment, 80

British Broadcasting Corporation Ltd., 7;
    21 (upd.); 89 (upd.)
British Film Institute, The, 80
British Museum, The, 71
British Sky Broadcasting Group plc, 20;
    60 (upd.)
Broadway Video Entertainment, 112
Brooklyn Academy of Music, 132
Brunswick Corporation, III; 22 (upd.); 77
    (upd.)
Burgett, Inc., 97
Burton Snowboards Inc., 22
Busch Entertainment Corporation, 73
bwin.party digital entertainment plc, 129
C. Bechstein Pianofortefabrik AG, 96
C.F. Martin & Co., Inc., 42
Cablevision Systems Corporation, 7; 30
    (upd.); 109 (upd.)
California Sports, Inc., 56
Callaway Golf Company, 15; 45 (upd.);
    112 (upd.)
Camelot Group plc, 110
Canadian Broadcasting Corporation, 109
    (upd.)
Canlan Ice Sports Corp., 105
Canterbury Park Holding Corporation, 42
Capcom Company Ltd., 83
Capital Cities/ABC Inc., II
Capitol Records, Inc., 90
Carlson Companies, Inc., 6; 22 (upd.); 87
    (upd.)
Carlson Wagonlit Travel, 55
Carmike Cinemas, Inc., 14; 37 (upd.); 74
    (upd.)
Carnegie Hall Corporation, The, 101
Carnival Corporation, 6; 27 (upd.); 78
    (upd.)
Carrere Group S.A., 104
Carsey-Werner Company, L.L.C., The, 37
Carvin Corp., 89
Cavaliers Operating Company, LLC, 124
CBS Inc., II; 6 (upd.)
Cedar Fair Entertainment Company, 22;
    98 (upd.)
Celtic PLC, 122
Central European Media Enterprises Ltd.,
    61
Central Independent Television, 7; 23
    (upd.)
Century Casinos, Inc., 53
Century Theatres, Inc., 31
Championship Auto Racing Teams, Inc.,
    37
Channel Four Television Corporation, 93
Charles M. Schulz Creative Associates,
    114
Chello Zone Ltd., 93
Chelsea Ltd., 102
Chelsea Piers Management Inc., 86
Chicago Bears Football Club, Inc., 33
Chicago Blackhawk Hockey Team, Inc.,
    132
Chicago National League Ball Club, Inc.,
    66
Chicago Symphony Orchestra, 106
Chicago White Sox, Ltd., 125
Chris-Craft Corporation, 9, 31 (upd.); 80
    (upd.)

Financial Services: Banks

Financial Services: Excluding Banks

Food Products

Food Services, Retailers, & Restaurants

Health, Personal & Medical Care Products

Health Care Services

Information Technology

Yahoo! Inc., 27; 70 (upd.)
YouTube, Inc., 90
Zanett, Inc., 92
Zapata Corporation, 25
Ziff Davis Media Inc., 36 (upd.)
Zillow, Inc., 129
Zilog, Inc., 15; 72 (upd.)

Insurance

Accident Exchange Group Plc, 125
ACE Limited, 116
Admiral Group, PLC, 109
AEGON N.V., III; 50 (upd.)
Aetna Inc., III; 21 (upd.); 63 (upd.); 133 (upd.)
Aflac Incorporated, 10 (upd.); 38 (upd.); 109 (upd.)
Alexander & Alexander Services Inc., 10
Alfa Corporation, 60
Alleanza Assicurazioni S.p.A., 65
Alleghany Corporation, 10
Allianz SE, III; 15 (upd.); 57 (upd.); 119 (upd.)
Allmerica Financial Corporation, 63
The Allstate Corporation, 10; 27 (upd.); 116 (upd.)
AMB Generali Holding AG, 51
American Family Corporation, III
American Family Insurance Group, 116
American Financial Group Inc., III; 48 (upd.)
American General Corporation, III; 10 (upd.); 46 (upd.)
American International Group Inc., III; 15 (upd.); 47 (upd.); 109 (upd.)
American National Insurance Company, 8; 27 (upd.)
American Physicians Service Group, Inc., 114
American Premier Underwriters, Inc., 10
American Re Corporation, 10; 35 (upd.)
AOK-Bundesverband (Federation of the AOK), 78
Aon Corporation, III; 45 (upd.); 113 (upd.)
Arch Capital Group Ltd., 116
Arthur J. Gallagher & Co., 73
Assicurazioni Generali S.p.A., III; 15 (upd.); 103 (upd.)
Assurances Générales de France, 63
Assured Guaranty Ltd., 93
Atlantic American Corporation, 44
Aviva plc, 50 (upd.); 119 (upd.)
AXA Colonia Konzern AG, 27; 49 (upd.)
AXA Equitable Life Insurance Company, III; 105 (upd.)
AXA Group, 114 (upd.)
Baldwin & Lyons, Inc., 51
Bâloise-Holding, 40
Benfield Greig Group plc, 53
Berkshire Hathaway Inc., III; 18 (upd.); 42 (upd.); 89 (upd.)
Blue Cross and Blue Shield Association, 10
Botswana Life Insurance Limited, 116
British United Provident Association Limited (BUPAL), 79
Brown & Brown, Inc., 41

Business Men's Assurance Company of America, 14
Capital Holding Corporation, III
Cathay Life Insurance Company Ltd., 108
Catholic Order of Foresters, 24; 97 (upd.)
Catlin Group Limited, 133
China Life Insurance Company Limited, 65
ChoicePoint Inc., 65
Chubb Corporation, The, III; 14 (upd.); 37 (upd.); 113 (upd.)
CIGNA Corporation, III; 22 (upd.); 45 (upd.); 109 (upd.)
Cincinnati Financial Corporation, 16; 44 (upd.)
CNA Financial Corporation, III; 38 (upd.)
CNP Assurances, 116
Commercial Union PLC, III
Connecticut Mutual Life Insurance Company, III
Conseco, Inc., 10; 33 (upd.); 112 (upd.)
Continental Corporation, The, III
Crawford & Company, 87
Crum & Forster Holdings Corporation, 104
Dai-Ichi Life Insurance Company, Limited, 116
Debeka Krankenversicherungsverein auf Gegenseitigkeit, 72
Delta Dental of California, 112
Doctors' Company, The, 55
Donegal Group Inc., 123
Ebix, Inc., 119
EmblemHealth Inc., 113
Empire Blue Cross and Blue Shield, III
Enbridge Inc., 43
Endurance Specialty Holdings Ltd., 85
Engle Homes, Inc., 46
Equitable Life Assurance Society of the United States Fireman's Fund Insurance Company, The, III
ERGO Versicherungsgruppe AG, 44
Erie Indemnity Company, 35
Fairfax Financial Holdings Limited, 57
Farm Family Holdings, Inc., 39; 117 (upd.)
Farmers Insurance Group of Companies, 25
Federal Deposit Insurance Corporation, 93
Fidelity National Financial Inc., 54
First American Corporation, The, 52
First Executive Corporation, III
Foundation Health Corporation, 12
Gainsco, Inc., 22
GEICO Corporation, 10; 40 (upd.); 132 (upd.)
General Accident PLC, III
General Re Corporation, III; 24 (upd.)
Genworth Financial Inc., 116
Gerling-Konzern Versicherungs-Beteiligungs-Aktiengesellschaft, 51
GMAC, LLC, 109
GraceKennedy Ltd., 92
Grange Mutual Casualty Company, 119
Great-West Lifeco Inc., III
Groupama S.A., 76

Gryphon Holdings, Inc., 21
Guardian Financial Services, 64 (upd.)
Guardian Holdings Limited, 111
Guardian Life Insurance Company of America, 116
Guardian Royal Exchange Plc, 11
Harleysville Group Inc., 37
Hartford Financial Services Group, Inc., 116
HCC Insurance Holdings Inc., 116
HDI (Haftpflichtverband der Deutschen Industrie Versicherung auf Gegenseitigkeit V.a.G.), 53
HealthExtras, Inc., 75
HealthMarkets, Inc., 88 (upd.)
Hilb, Rogal & Hobbs Company, 77
Home Insurance Company, The, III
Horace Mann Educators Corporation, 22; 90 (upd.)
Household International, Inc., 21 (upd.)
Hub International Limited, 89
HUK-Coburg, 58
Humana Inc., III; 24 (upd.); 101 (upd.)
Humphrey Products Company, 110
Inventec Corp., 113
Irish Life & Permanent Plc, 59
Jackson National Life Insurance Company, 8
Japan Post Holdings Company Ltd., 108
Jefferson-Pilot Corporation, 11; 29 (upd.)
John Hancock Financial Services, Inc., III; 42 (upd.)
Johnson & Higgins, 14
Kemper Corporation, III; 15 (upd.)
LandAmerica Financial Group, Inc., 85
Legal & General Group Plc, III; 24 (upd.); 101 (upd.)
Liberty Corporation, The, 22
Liberty Mutual Holding Company, 59
Libya Insurance Company, 124
LifeWise Health Plan of Oregon, Inc., 90
Lincoln National Corporation, III; 25 (upd.); 113 (upd.)
Lloyd's, 74 (upd.)
Lloyd's of London, III; 22 (upd.)
Loewen Group Inc., The, 40 (upd.)
Lutheran Brotherhood, 31
Manulife Financial Corporation, 85
Mapfre S.A., 109
Markel Corporation, 116
Marsh & McLennan Companies, Inc., III; 45 (upd.); 123 (upd.)
Massachusetts Mutual Life Insurance Company, III; 53 (upd.); 127 (upd.)
MBIA Inc., 73
Medical Mutual of Ohio, 128
Meiji Mutual Life Insurance Company, The, III
Mercury General Corporation, 25
Metropolitan Life Insurance Company, III; 52 (upd.)
MGIC Investment Corp., 52
Midland Company, The, 65
Millea Holdings Inc., 64 (upd.)
Mitsui Marine and Fire Insurance Company, Limited, III
Mitsui Mutual Life Insurance Company, III; 39 (upd.)

Legal Services

Manufacturing

Materials

Advanced Drainage Systems, Inc., 121
AK Steel Holding Corporation, 19; 41 (upd.)
American Biltrite Inc., 16; 43 (upd.)
American Colloid Co., 13
American Standard Inc., III; 30 (upd.)
Ameriwood Industries International Corp., 17
Andersen Corporation, 10
Anhui Conch Cement Company Limited, 99
Apasco S.A. de C.V., 51
Apogee Enterprises, Inc., 8
Asahi Glass Company, Ltd., III; 48 (upd.)
Asbury Carbons, Inc., 68
Bairnco Corporation, 28
Bayou Steel Corporation, 31
Berry Plastics Group Inc., 21; 98 (upd.)
Blessings Corp., 19
Blue Circle Industries PLC, III
Bodycote International PLC, 63
Boral Limited, III; 43 (upd.); 103 (upd.)
British Vita plc, 9; 33 (upd.)
Brush Engineered Materials Inc., 67
Bryce Corporation, 100
Burger Iron Company, 131
California Steel Industries, Inc., 67
Callanan Industries, Inc., 60
Cameron & Barkley Company, 28
CARBO Ceramics, Inc., 108
Carborundum Company, 15
Carl Zeiss AG, III; 34 (upd.); 91 (upd.)
Carlisle Companies Inc., 8; 82 (upd.)
Carpenter Co., 109
Carter Holt Harvey Ltd., 70
Cementos Argos S.A., 91
CEMEX, S.A.B. de C.V., 20; 59 (upd.); 122 (upd.)
Century Aluminum Company, 52
Ceradyne, Inc., 65
CertainTeed Corporation, 35
Chargeurs International, 6; 21 (upd.)
Chemfab Corporation, 35
Cimentos de Portugal SGPS S.A. (Cimpor), 76
Ciments Français, 40
Cold Spring Granite Company Inc., 16; 67 (upd.)
Columbia Forest Products Inc., 78
Compagnie de Saint-Gobain, III; 16 (upd.); 64 (upd.)
Cookson Group plc, III; 44 (upd.)
Corning Inc., III; 44 (upd.); 90 (upd.)
CRH plc, 64
CSR Limited, III; 28 (upd.); 85 (upd.)
Dal-Tile International Inc., 22
David J. Joseph Company, The, 14; 76 (upd.)
Dexter Corporation, The, 12 (upd.)
Dickten Masch Plastics LLC, 90
Dyckerhoff AG, 35
Dynamic Materials Corporation, 81
Dyson Group PLC, 71
ECC Group plc, III
Edw. C. Levy Co., 42
ElkCorp, 52
Empire Resources, Inc., 81

English China Clays Ltd., 15 (upd.); 40 (upd.)
Entegris, Inc., 112
Envirodyne Industries, Inc., 17
EP Henry Corporation, 104
Feldmuhle Nobel A.G., III
Fibreboard Corporation, 16
Filtrona plc, 88
Florida Rock Industries, Inc., 46
FLSmidth & Co. A/S, 72
Foamex International Inc., 17
Formica Corporation, 13
GAF Corporation, 22 (upd.)
Geon Company, The, 11
Gerresheimer Glas AG, 43
Giant Cement Holding, Inc., 23
Gibraltar Steel Corporation, 37
Glaverbel Group, 80
Granite Rock Company, 26
GreenMan Technologies Inc., 99
Groupe Sidel S.A., 21
Grupo Bimbo S.A. de C.V., 128 (upd.)
Harbison-Walker Refractories Company, 24
Harrisons & Crosfield plc, III
HeidelbergCement AG, 109 (upd.)
Heidelberger Zement AG, 31
Hexcel Corporation, 28; 132 (upd.)
Holderbank Financière Glaris Ltd., III
Holnam Inc., 8; 39 (upd.)
Holt and Bugbee Company, 66
Homasote Company, 72
Howmet Corp., 12
Huttig Building Products, Inc., 73
Ibstock Brick Ltd., 14; 37 (upd.)
Imerys S.A., 40 (upd.)
Imperial Industries, Inc., 81
Internacional de Ceramica, S.A. de C.V., 53
International Shipbreaking Ltd. L.L.C., 67
Jaiprakash Associates Limited, 101
Joseph T. Ryerson & Son, Inc., 15
K-Tron International Inc., 115
Knauf Gips KG, 100
La Seda de Barcelona S.A., 100
Lafarge Cement UK, 28; 54 (upd.)
Lafarge Coppée S.A., III
Lafarge Corporation, 28
Lamson & Sessions Co., 13; 61 (upd.); 132 (upd.)
Lehigh Portland Cement Company, 23
Loma Negra C.I.A.S.A., 95
Lyman-Richey Corporation, 96
Manville Corporation, III; 7 (upd.)
Material Sciences Corporation, 63
Matsushita Electric Works, Ltd., III; 7 (upd.)
McJunkin Corporation, 63
Medusa Corporation, 24
Mitsubishi Materials Corporation, III; 131 (upd.)
Monarch Cement Company, The, 72
Muralo Company Inc., 117
National Gypsum Company, 10
Nevamar Company, 82
New NGC Inc., 127 (upd.)
Nippon Sheet Glass Company, Limited, III

North Pacific Group, Inc., 61
Nuplex Industries Ltd., 92
OmniSource Corporation, 14; 125 (upd.)
Onoda Cement Co., Ltd., III
Otor S.A., 77
Owens-Corning Fiberglass Corporation, III
Pacific Clay Products Inc., 88
Pilkington Group Limited, III; 34 (upd.); 87 (upd.)
Pioneer International Limited, III
PMC Global, Inc., 110
PolyOne Corporation, 87 (upd.)
PPG Industries, Inc., III; 22 (upd.); 81 (upd.)
PT Semen Gresik Tbk, 103
R.T. Vanderbilt Company, Inc., 117
Recticel S.A./NV, 123
Redland plc, III
Rinker Group Ltd., 65
RMC Group p.l.c., III; 34 (upd.)
Rock of Ages Corporation, 37
Rogers Corporation, 80 (upd.)
Royal Group Technologies Limited, 73
Rugby Group plc, The, 31
Scholle Corporation, 96
Schuff Steel Company, 26
Sekisui Chemical Co., Ltd., III; 72 (upd.)
Severstal Joint Stock Company, 65
Sherwin-Williams Company, The, III; 13 (upd.); 89 (upd.)
Siam Cement Public Company Limited, The, 56
SIG plc, 71
Simplex Technologies Inc., 21
Siskin Steel & Supply Company, 70
Smith-Midland Corporation, 56
Solutia Inc., 52
Sommer-Allibert S.A., 19
Southdown, Inc., 14
Spartech Corporation, 19; 76 (upd.)
Ssangyong Cement Industrial Co., Ltd., III; 61 (upd.)
Steel Technologies Inc., 63
Strongwell Corporation, 110
Sun Distributors L.P., 12
Symyx Technologies, Inc., 77
Taiheiyo Cement Corporation, 60 (upd.); 124 (upd)
Tarmac Limited, III; 28 (upd.); 95 (upd.)
Tergal Industries S.A.S., 102
Thermotech, 113
Tilcon-Connecticut Inc., 80
Titan Cement Company S.A., 64
Tong Yang Cement Corporation, 62
TOTO LTD., III; 28 (upd.)
Toyo Sash Co., Ltd., III
Tulikivi Corporation, 114
Tuscarora Inc., 29
U.S. Aggregates, Inc., 42
Ube Industries, Ltd., III; 38 (upd.); 111 (upd.)
United States Steel Corporation, 50 (upd.)
Universal Forest Products, Inc., 122 (upd.)
USEC Inc., 124
USG Corporation, III; 26 (upd.); 81 (upd.)

Mining & Metals

Hampton Affiliates, Inc., 77
Herlitz AG, 107
Holmen AB, 52 (upd.); 111 (upd.)
Honshu Paper Co., Ltd., IV
International Paper Company, IV; 15 (upd.); 47 (upd.); 97 (upd.)
James River Corporation of Virginia, IV
Japan Pulp and Paper Company Limited, IV
Jefferson Smurfit Group plc, IV; 49 (upd.)
Jujo Paper Co., Ltd., IV
Kadant Inc., 96 (upd.)
KapStone Paper and Packaging Corporation, 122
Kimberly-Clark Corporation, III; 16 (upd.); 43 (upd.); 105 (upd.)
Kimberly-Clark de México, S.A. de C.V., 54
Klabin S.A., 73
Koninklijke Houthandel G Wijma & Zonen BV, 96
Kruger Inc., 17; 103 (upd.)
Kymmene Corporation, IV
Longview Fibre Paper and Packaging, Inc., 8; 37 (upd.); 130 (upd.)
Louisiana-Pacific Corporation, IV; 31 (upd.); 126 (upd.)
Mackay Envelope Corporation, 45
MacMillan Bloedel Limited, IV
Mail-Well, Inc., 28
Marvin Lumber & Cedar Company, 22
Matussière et Forest SA, 58
Mead Corporation, The, IV; 19 (upd.)
MeadWestvaco Corporation, 76 (upd.)
Menasha Corporation, 8; 59 (upd.); 118 (upd.)
Mercer International Inc., 64
Metsa-Serla Oy, IV
Metso Corporation, 30 (upd.); 85 (upd.)
Miquel y Costas Miquel S.A., 68
Mo och Domsjö AB, IV
Mohawk Fine Papers, Inc., 108
Monadnock Paper Mills, Inc., 21
Mondi Ltd., 131
Mosinee Paper Corporation, 15
M-real Oyj, 56 (upd.)
Myllykoski Oyj, 117
Nashua Corporation, 8
National Envelope Corporation, 32
NCH Corporation, 8
Newark Group, Inc., The, 102
NewPage Corporation, 119
Nippon Paper Group Inc., 132 (upd.)
Norske Skogindustrier ASA, 63
Nuqul Group of Companies, 102
Oji Paper Co., Ltd., IV; 128 (upd.)
P.H. Glatfelter Company, 8; 30 (upd.); 83 (upd.)
Packaging Corporation of America, 12
PaperlinX Limited, 129
Papeteries de Lancey, 23
Plum Creek Timber Company, Inc., 43; 106 (upd.)
Pope & Talbot, Inc., 12; 61 (upd.)
Pope Resources LP, 74
Potlatch Corporation, 8; 34 (upd.); 87 (upd.)
PWA Group, IV

Rayonier Inc., 24; 130 (upd.)
Rengo Co., Ltd., IV
Reno de Medici S.p.A., 41; 129 (upd.)
Rexam PLC, 32 (upd.); 85 (upd.)
RIS Paper Company, Inc., 120
Riverwood International Corporation, 11; 48 (upd.)
Rock-Tenn Company, 13; 59 (upd.); 118 (upd.)
Rogers Corporation, 61
St. Joe Company, The, 8; 98 (upd.)
Sanyo-Kokusaku Pulp Co., Ltd., IV
Sappi Ltd., 49; 107 (upd.)
Schneidersöhne Deutschland GmbH & Co. KG, 100
Schweitzer-Mauduit International, Inc., 52
Scott Paper Company, IV; 31 (upd.)
Sealed Air Corporation, 14; 57 (upd.); 121 (upd.)
Sierra Pacific Industries, 22; 90 (upd.)
Simpson Investment Company, 17
Smead Manufacturing Co., 17
Smurfit Kappa Group plc, 112 (upd.)
Sonoco Products Company, 8; 89 (upd.)
Specialty Coatings Inc., 8
Stimson Lumber Company, 78
Stone Container Corporation, IV
Stora Enso Oyj, IV; 36 (upd.); 85 (upd.)
Sveaskog AB, 93
Svenska Cellulosa Aktiebolaget SCA, IV; 28 (upd.); 85 (upd.)
TAB Products Co., 17
Tapemark Company Inc., 64
Tembec Inc., 66
Temple-Inland Inc., IV; 31 (upd.); 102 (upd.)
Thomsen Greenhouses and Garden Center, Incorporated, 65
TimberWest Forest Corp., 114
TJ International, Inc., 19
Tolko Industries Ltd., 114
U.S. Timberlands Company, L.P., 42
Union Camp Corporation, IV
Unipapel S.A., 131
Unisource Worldwide, Inc., 131
United Paper Mills Ltd. (Yhtyneet Paperitehtaat Oy), IV
Universal Forest Products, Inc., 10; 59 (upd.)
UPM-Kymmene Corporation, 19; 50 (upd.); 126 (upd.)
Wausau-Mosinee Paper Corporation, 60 (upd.)
West Fraser Timber Co. Ltd., 17; 91 (upd.)
West Linn Paper Company, 91
Westvaco Corporation, IV; 19 (upd.)
Weyerhaeuser Company, IV; 9 (upd.); 28 (upd.); 83 (upd.)
Wickes Inc., 25 (upd.)
Willamette Industries, Inc., IV; 31 (upd.)
Worthen Industries, Inc., 131
WTD Industries, Inc., 20

Personal Services

24 Hour Fitness Worldwide, Inc., 71
Adelman Travel Group, 105
ADT Security Services, Inc., 12; 44 (upd.)

Akal Security Incorporated, 119
Alderwoods Group, Inc., 68 (upd.)
Ambassadors International, Inc., 68 (upd.)
American Retirement Corporation, 42
Ameriwood Industries International Corp., 17
Aquent, 96
Arbor Memorial Services Inc., 122
Aurora Casket Company, Inc., 56
Bidvest Group Ltd., 106
Blackwater USA, 76
Bonhams 1793 Ltd., 72
Brickman Group, Ltd., The, 87
CareerBuilder, Inc., 93
Carriage Services, Inc., 37; 129 (upd.)
CDI Corporation, 6; 54 (upd.)
Central Parking System, 18; 104 (upd.)
CeWe Color Holding AG, 76
Chemed Corporation, 13; 118 (upd.)
Chubb, PLC, 50
Correctional Services Corporation, 30
CUC International Inc., 16
Curves International, Inc., 54
eHarmony.com Inc., 71
Elis G.I.E., 123
Franklin Quest Co., 11
Gateway Group One, 118
Gold's Gym International, Inc., 71
Granite Industries of Vermont, Inc., 73
Greg Manning Auctions, Inc., 60
Gunnebo AB, 53
Hair Club For Men Ltd., 90
Herbalife Ltd., 17; 41 (upd.); 92 (upd.)
I Grandi Viaggi S.p.A., 105
Imperial Parking Corporation, 58
Initial Security, 64
Jazzercise, Inc., 45
Jostens, Inc., 7; 25 (upd.); 73 (upd.)
Kayak.com, 108
Kiva, 95
Lifetouch Inc., 86
Loewen Group Inc., The, 16; 40 (upd.)
Mace Security International, Inc., 57; 124 (upd.)
Manpower, Inc., 9
Martin Franchises, Inc., 80
Match.com, LP, 87
Meetic S.A., 129
Michael Anthony Jewelers, Inc., 24
Michael Page International plc, 45
New Zealand Post Group, 129
OGF S.A., 113
Orkin, Inc., 104
PHS Group Holdings Ltd., 123
PODS Enterprises Inc., 103
Prison Rehabilitative Industries and Diversified Enterprises, Inc., 53; 129 (upd.)
Randstad Holding nv, 113 (upd.)
Regis Corporation, 18; 70 (upd.)
Rollins, Inc., 11; 104 (upd.)
Rose Hills Company, 117
Rosenbluth International Inc., 14
Screen Actors Guild, 72
Secom Company Ltd., 131
Segway LLC, 48; 125 (upd.)
Service Corporation International, 6; 51 (upd.)

Shutterfly, Inc., 98
Smarte Carte, Inc., 127
Snapfish, 83
SOS Staffing Services, 25
Spark Networks, Inc., 91
Sport Clips, Inc., 133
Stewart Enterprises, Inc., 20
StoneMor Partners L.P., 133
Supercuts Inc., 26
Teleflora LLC, 123
Town & Country Corporation, 19
Travelport Limited, 125
UAW (International Union, United
    Automobile, Aerospace and Agricultural
    Implement Workers of America), 72
Weight Watchers International Inc., 12;
    33 (upd.); 73 (upd.)
Yak Pak, 108
York Group, Inc., The, 50
YTB International, Inc., 108

Petroleum

Abraxas Petroleum Corporation, 89
Abu Dhabi National Oil Company, IV;
    45 (upd.); 114 (upd.)
Adani Enterprises Ltd., 97
Aegean Marine Petroleum Network Inc.,
    89
Agland, Inc., 110
Agway, Inc., 21 (upd.)
Aker ASA, 128
Alberta Energy Company Ltd., 16; 43
    (upd.)
Alon Israel Oil Company Ltd., 104
Amerada Hess Corporation, IV; 21 (upd.);
    55 (upd.)
Amoco Corporation, IV; 14 (upd.)
Anadarko Petroleum Corporation, 10; 52
    (upd.); 106 (upd.)
ANR Pipeline Co., 17
Anschutz Corp., 12
Apache Corporation, 10; 32 (upd.); 89
    (upd.)
Aral AG, 62
Arctic Slope Regional Corporation, 38;
    131 (upd.)
Arena Resources, Inc., 97
Ashland Inc., 19; 50 (upd.); 115 (upd.)
Ashland Oil, Inc., IV
Atlantic Richfield Company, IV; 31 (upd.)
Atwood Oceanics, Inc., 100
Aventine Renewable Energy Holdings,
    Inc., 89
Badger State Ethanol, LLC, 83
Baker Hughes Incorporated, 22 (upd.); 57
    (upd.); 118 (upd.)
Basic Earth Science Systems, Inc., 101
Belco Oil & Gas Corp., 40
Benton Oil and Gas Company, 47
Berry Petroleum Company, 47; 130 (upd.)
BG Products Inc., 96
Bharat Petroleum Corporation Limited,
    109
BHP Billiton, 67 (upd.)
Bill Barrett Corporation, 71
BJ Services Company, 25
Blue Rhino Corporation, 56
Blue Sun Energy, Inc., 108

Boardwalk Pipeline Partners, LP, 87
Bolt Technology Corporation, 99
Boots & Coots International Well
    Control, Inc., 79
BP p.l.c., 45 (upd.); 103 (upd.)
Brigham Exploration Company, 75
British Petroleum Company plc, The, IV;
    7 (upd.); 21 (upd.)
British-Borneo Oil & Gas PLC, 34
Broken Hill Proprietary Company Ltd.,
    22 (upd.)
Bronco Drilling Company, Inc., 89
Burlington Resources Inc., 10
Burmah Castrol PLC, IV; 30 (upd.)
Callon Petroleum Company, 47
Caltex Petroleum Corporation, 19
Calumet Specialty Products Partners, L.P.,
    106
CAMAC International Corporation, 106
Canadian Oil Sands Limited, 133
Cano Petroleum Inc., 97
Carrizo Oil & Gas, Inc., 97
Chesapeake Energy Corporation, 132
Chevron Corporation, IV; 19 (upd.); 47
    (upd.); 103 (upd.)
Chiles Offshore Corporation, 9
The China National Offshore Oil Corp.,
    118
China National Petroleum Corporation,
    46; 108 (upd.)
China Petroleum & Chemical
    Corporation (Sinopec Corp.), 109
Chinese Petroleum Corporation, IV; 31
    (upd.)
Cimarex Energy Co., 81
CITGO Petroleum Corporation, IV; 31
    (upd.)
Clayton Williams Energy, Inc., 87
Coastal Corporation, The, IV; 31 (upd.)
Compañia Española de Petróleos S.A.
    (CEPSA), IV; 56 (upd.); 123 (upd.)
Complete Production Services, Inc., 118
Compton Petroleum Corporation, 103
Comstock Resources, Inc., 47; 126 (upd.)
Conoco Inc., IV; 16 (upd.)
ConocoPhillips, 63 (upd.)
CONSOL Energy Inc., 59
Continental Resources, Inc., 89
Cooper Cameron Corporation, 20 (upd.);
    58 (upd.)
Cosmo Oil Company, Limited, IV; 53
    (upd.); 126 (upd.)
CPC Corporation, Taiwan, 116
Crimson Exploration Inc., 116
Crown Central Petroleum Corporation, 7
Daniel Measurement and Control, Inc.,
    16; 74 (upd.)
Dead River Company, 117
Deep Down, Inc., 129
DeepTech International Inc., 21
Delek Group Ltd., 123
Den Norse Stats Oljeselskap AS, IV
Denbury Resources, Inc., 67
Deutsche BP Aktiengesellschaft, 7
Devon Energy Corporation, 61
Diamond Shamrock, Inc., IV
Distrigaz S.A., 82
DOF ASA, 110

Dominion Resources, Inc., V; 54 (upd.);
    130 (upd.)
Double Eagle Petroleum Co., 114
Dril-Quip, Inc., 81
Duvernay Oil Corp., 83
Dyneff S.A., 98
Dynegy Inc., 49 (upd.)
E.On AG, 50 (upd.)
Edge Petroleum Corporation, 67
Egyptian General Petroleum Corporation,
    IV; 51 (upd.)
El Paso Corporation, 66 (upd.)
Elf Aquitaine SA, 21 (upd.)
Empresa Colombiana de Petróleos, IV
Enbridge Inc., 43; 127 (upd.)
EnCana Corporation, 109
Encore Acquisition Company, 73
Energen Corporation, 21; 97 (upd.)
ENI S.p.A., 69 (upd.)
Enron Corporation, 19
ENSCO International Incorporated, 57
Ente Nazionale Idrocarburi, IV
Enterprise GP Holdings L.P., 109
Enterprise Oil PLC, 11; 50 (upd.)
Entreprise Nationale Sonatrach, IV
EOG Resources, 106
Equitable Resources, Inc., 54 (upd.)
Ergon, Inc., 95
Etablissements Maurel & Prom S.A., 115
Exxon Mobil Corporation, IV; 7 (upd.);
    32 (upd.); 67 (upd.)
F.L. Roberts & Company, Inc., 113
Ferrellgas Partners, L.P., 35; 107 (upd.)
FINA, Inc., 7
FJ Management, 121 (upd.)
Flotek Industries Inc., 93
Fluxys SA, 101
Flying J Inc., 19
Forest Oil Corporation, 19; 91 (upd.)
Frontier Oil Corporation, 116
Galp Energia SGPS S.A., 98
GDF SUEZ, 109 (upd.)
General Sekiyu K.K., IV
GeoResources, Inc., 101
Giant Industries, Inc., 19; 61 (upd.)
Global Industries, Ltd., 37
Global Marine Inc., 9
Global Partners L.P., 116
GlobalSantaFe Corporation, 48 (upd.)
Grant Prideco, Inc., 57
Grey Wolf, Inc., 43
Gulf Island Fabrication, Inc., 44
Gulfport Energy Corporation, 119
Halliburton Company, III; 25 (upd.); 55
    (upd.); 127 (upd.)
Hanover Compressor Company, 59
Hawkeye Holdings LLC, 89
Helix Energy Solutions Group, Inc., 81
Hellenic Petroleum SA, 64
Helmerich & Payne, Inc., 18; 115 (upd.)
Hess Corporation, 133 (upd.)
Hindustan Petroleum Corporation Ltd.,
    116
Holly Corporation, 12; 111 (upd.)
Hunt Consolidated Inc., 7; 27 (upd.); 132
    (upd.)
Hunting plc, 78
Hurricane Hydrocarbons Ltd., 54

Husky Energy Inc., 47; 118 (upd.)
Idemitsu Kosan Company Ltd., IV; 49 (upd.); 123 (upd.)
Imperial Oil Limited, IV; 25 (upd.)
Indian Oil Corporation Ltd., IV; 48 (upd.); 95 (upd.); 113 (upd.)
INPEX Holdings Inc., 97
Input/Output, Inc., 73
Iogen Corporation, 81
Ipiranga S.A., 67
Irving Oil Limited, 118
Kanematsu Corporation, IV; 24 (upd.); 102 (upd.)
KBR Inc., 106 (upd.)
Kerr-McGee Corporation, IV; 22 (upd.); 68 (upd.)
Kinder Morgan, Inc., 45; 111 (upd.)
King Ranch, Inc., 14
Knot, Inc., The, 74
Koch Industries, Inc., IV; 20 (upd.), 77 (upd.)
Koppers Industries, Inc., 26 (upd.)
Korea Gas Corporation, 114
Kuwait Petroleum Corporation, IV; 55 (upd.); 124 (upd.)
Libyan National Oil Corporation, IV
Louisiana Land and Exploration Company, The, 7
Lufkin Industries Inc., 78
Lyondell Petrochemical Company, IV
Mansfield Oil Company, 117
MAPCO Inc., IV
Marathon Oil Corporation, 109
Mariner Energy, Inc., 101
Marquard & Bahls AG, 124
Maxus Energy Corporation, 7
McDermott International, Inc., III; 37 (upd.)
MDU Resources Group, Inc., 114 (upd.)
Merit Energy Company, 114
Meteor Industries Inc., 33
Mexichem, S.A.B. de C.V., 99
Mitchell Energy and Development Corporation, 7
Mitsubishi Oil Co., Ltd., IV
Mobil Corporation, IV; 7 (upd.); 21 (upd.)
MOL Rt, 70
Motiva Enterprises LLC, 111
Murphy Oil Corporation, 7; 32 (upd.); 95 (upd.)
N.V. Nederlandse Gasunie, V; 111 (upd.)
Nabors Industries Ltd., 9; 91 (upd.)
National Fuel Gas Company, 6; 95 (upd.)
National Iranian Oil Company, IV; 61 (upd.)
National Oil Corporation, 66 (upd.)
National Oilwell, Inc., 54
Neste Oil Corporation, IV; 85 (upd.)
Newfield Exploration Company, 65
Nexen Inc., 79
NGC Corporation, 18
Nigerian National Petroleum Corporation, IV; 72 (upd.)
Nippon Oil Corporation, IV; 63 (upd.); 120 (upd.)
Noble Affiliates, Inc., 11
NuStar Energy L.P., 111

OAO Gazprom, 42; 107 (upd.)
OAO LUKOIL, 40
OAO LUKOIL, 109 (upd.)
OAO NK YUKOS, 47
OAO Siberian Oil Company (Sibneft), 49
OAO Surgutneftegaz, 48; 128 (upd.)
OAO Tatneft, 45
Occidental Petroleum Corporation, IV; 25 (upd.); 71 (upd.)
Odebrecht S.A., 73
Oil and Natural Gas Corporation Ltd., IV; 90 (upd.)
Oil States International, Inc., 77
Oil Transporting Joint Stock Company Transneft, 93
OMV AG, IV; 98 (upd.)
Orlen Lietuva, 111
Oryx Energy Company, 7
Pacific Ethanol, Inc., 81
Pakistan State Oil Company Ltd., 81
Pan American Energy LLC, 133
Parallel Petroleum Corporation, 101
Paramount Resources Ltd., 87
Parker Drilling Company, 28
Patina Oil & Gas Corporation, 24
Patterson-UTI Energy, Inc., 55
Pengrowth Energy Trust, 95
Penn Virginia Corporation, 85
Pennzoil-Quaker State Company, IV; 20 (upd.); 50 (upd.)
Pertamina, IV; 56 (upd.)
Petrobras Energia Participaciones S.A., 72
Petro-Canada, IV; 99 (upd.)
Petrofac Ltd., 95
PetroFina S.A., IV; 26 (upd.)
Petrohawk Energy Corporation, 79
Petróleo Brasileiro S.A., IV; 133 (upd.)
Petróleos de Portugal S.A., IV
Petróleos de Venezuela S.A., IV; 74 (upd.)
Petróleos del Ecuador, IV
Petróleos Mexicanos (PEMEX), IV; 19 (upd.); 104 (upd.)
Petroleum Development Oman LLC, IV; 98 (upd.)
Petroliam Nasional Bhd (PETRONAS), IV; 56 (upd.); 117 (upd.)
Petron Corporation, 58
Petroplus Holdings AG, 108
Phillips Petroleum Company, IV; 40 (upd.)
Pilot Flying J Inc., 49; 121 (upd.)
Pioneer Natural Resources Company, 59; 133 (upd.)
Plains Exploration & Production Company, 118
Pogo Producing Company, 39
Polski Koncern Naftowy ORLEN S.A., 77
Premcor Inc., 37
Premier Oil plc, 130
Pride International Inc., 78
PrimeEnergy Corp., 131
PTT Public Company Ltd., 56; 127 (upd.)
Qatar Petroleum, IV; 98 (upd.)
Quaker State Corporation, 7; 21 (upd.)
RaceTrac Petroleum, Inc., 111
Range Resources Corporation, 45
Reliance Industries Ltd., 81

Repsol YPF S.A., IV; 16 (upd.); 40 (upd.); 119 (upd.)
Resource America, Inc., 42
Rosneft, 106
Rowan Companies, Inc., 43
Royal Dutch Shell plc, IV; 49 (upd.); 108 (upd.)
RPC, Inc., 91
RWE AG, 50 (upd.); 119 (upd.)
St. Mary Land & Exploration Company, 63
SandRidge Energy, Inc., 112
Santa Fe International Corporation, 38
Santos Ltd., 81
Sapp Bros Travel Centers, Inc., 105
Sasol Limited, IV; 47 (upd.)
Saudi Arabian Oil Company, IV; 17 (upd.); 50 (upd.)
Schlumberger Limited, III; 17 (upd.); 59 (upd.); 130 (upd.)
Seadrill Ltd., 131
Seagull Energy Corporation, 11
Seitel, Inc., 47
Shanghai Petrochemical Co., Ltd., 18
Shell Oil Company, IV; 14 (upd.); 41 (upd.)
Showa Shell Sekiyu K.K., IV; 59 (upd.); 120 (upd.)
Sinclair Oil Corporation, 111
Sinochem Group, 129
Smith International, Inc., 15; 59 (upd.); 118 (upd.)
Société Nationale Elf Aquitaine, IV; 7 (upd.)
Sonangol E.P., 124
Sonatrach, 65 (upd.)
Spinnaker Exploration Company, 72
Statoil ASA, 61 (upd.)
Suburban Propane Partners, L.P., 30
SUEZ-TRACTEBEL S.A., 97 (upd.)
Sun Company, Inc., IV
Suncor Energy Inc., 54; 119 (upd.)
Sunoco, Inc., 28 (upd.); 83 (upd.)
Superior Energy Services, Inc., 65
Superior Plus Corporation, 125
Swift Energy Company, 63
Syncrude Canada Ltd., 125
Talisman Energy Inc., 9; 47 (upd.); 103 (upd.)
TAQA North Ltd., 95
Teck Resources Limited, 112 (upd.)
Tengasco, Inc., 99
TEPPCO Partners, L.P., 73
Tesoro Corporation, 7; 45 (upd.); 97 (upd.)
Teton Energy Corporation, 97
Texaco Inc., IV; 14 (upd.); 41 (upd.)
Tidewater Inc., 37 (upd.)
TNK-BP, 129
TODCO, 87
Tom Brown, Inc., 37
Tonen Corporation, IV; 16 (upd.)
TonenGeneral Sekiyu K.K., 54 (upd.)
Tosco Corporation, 7
Total S.A., IV; 24 (upd.); 50 (upd.); 118 (upd.)
Transammonia Group, 95
TransCanada Corporation, 93 (upd.)

Publishing & Printing

Real Estate

Retail & Wholesale

Ace Hardware Corporation, 12; 35 (upd.)
Action Performance Companies, Inc., 27
Adams Childrenswear Ltd., 95
AEON Co., Ltd., 68 (upd.)
After Hours Formalwear Inc., 60
Alimentation Couche-Tard Inc., 77
Alldays plc, 49
Allders plc, 37
Alliance Boots plc, 83 (upd.)
Allou Health & Beauty Care, Inc., 28
Alon Holdings Blue Square—Israel Ltd., 125 (upd.)
Altmeyer Home Stores Inc., 107
AMAG Group, 102
Amazon.com, Inc., 25; 56 (upd.)
AMCON Distributing Company, 99
American Coin Merchandising, Inc., 28; 74 (upd.)
American Eagle Outfitters, Inc., 24; 55 (upd.)
American Furniture Company, Inc., 21
American Girl, Inc., 69 (upd.)
American Tire Distributors Holdings, Inc., 117
America's Collectibles Network, Inc., 123
Ames Department Stores, Inc., 9; 30 (upd.)
Amscan Holdings, Inc., 61; 124 (upd.)
Anderson-DuBose Company, The, 60
AnnTaylor Stores Corporation, 13; 37 (upd.); 67 (upd.)
Anton Schlecker, 102
Applied Industrial Technologies, Inc., 130 (upd.)
Arbor Drugs Inc., 12
Arcadia Group plc, 28 (upd.)
Army and Air Force Exchange Service, 39
Art Van Furniture, Inc., 28
Ashley Furniture Industries, Inc., 122 (upd.)
Ashworth, Inc., 26
ASI Computer Technologies, Inc., 122
Au Printemps S.A., V
Audio King Corporation, 24
Auto Value Associates, Inc., 25
Autobytel Inc., 47
AutoNation, Inc., 50; 114 (upd.)
AutoTrader.com, L.L.C., 91
AutoZone, Inc., 9; 31 (upd.); 110 (upd.)
AVA AG (Allgemeine Handelsgesellschaft der Verbraucher AG), 33
Aveve S.A./NV, 123
Aviall, Inc., 73
Aviation Sales Company, 41
AWB Ltd., 56
B & H Foto and Electronics Corporation, 126
B. Dalton Bookseller Inc., 25
B2W Companhia Global do Varejo, 117
Babbage's, Inc., 10
Baby Superstore, Inc., 15
Baccarat, 24
Bachman's Inc., 22
Bailey Nurseries, Inc., 57
Baker & Taylor, Inc., 122 (upd.)
Ball Horticultural Company, 78
Banana Republic Inc., 25

Barnes & Noble, Inc., 10; 30 (upd.); 75 (upd.)
Barnes & Noble College Booksellers, Inc., 115
Barnett Inc., 28
Barneys New York Inc., 28; 104 (upd.)
Barrett-Jackson Auction Company L.L.C., 88
Barrow Industries, Inc., 123
Basketville, Inc., 117
Bass Pro Shops, Inc., 42; 118 (upd.)
Baumax AG, 75
BB&R Limited, 122
Beacon Roofing Supply, Inc., 75
Beate Uhse AG, 96
bebe stores, inc., 31; 103 (upd.)
Bed Bath & Beyond Inc., 13; 41 (upd.); 109 (upd.)
Belk, Inc., V; 19 (upd.); 72 (upd.)
Ben Bridge Jeweler, Inc., 60
Benetton Group S.p.A., 10; 67 (upd.)
Berean Christian Stores, 96
Bergdorf Goodman Inc., 52
Bergen Brunswig Corporation, V; 13 (upd.)
Bernard Chaus, Inc., 27
Best Buy Co., Inc., 9; 23 (upd.); 63 (upd.)
Bestseller A/S, 90
Beter Bed Holding N.V., 123
Bhs plc, 17
Big 5 Sporting Goods Corporation, 55
Big A Drug Stores Inc., 79
Big Dog Holdings, Inc., 45
Big Lots, Inc., 50; 110 (upd.)
Big O Tires, Inc., 20
Birks & Mayors Inc., 112
Birthdays Ltd., 70
Blacks Leisure Group plc, 39
Blair Corporation, 25; 31 (upd.)
Blish-Mize Co., 95
Blokker Holding B.V., 84
Bloomingdale's Inc., 12
Blue Nile, Inc., 61; 121 (upd.)
Blue Square Israel Ltd., 41
Bluefly, Inc., 60
BlueLinx Holdings Inc., 97
Bob's Discount Furniture LLC, 104
Bombay Company, Inc., The, 10; 71 (upd.)
Bon Marché, Inc., The, 23
Bon-Ton Stores, Inc., The, 16; 50 (upd.)
Booker Cash & Carry Ltd., 68 (upd.)
Books-A-Million, Inc., 14; 41 (upd.); 96 (upd.)
Bookspan, 86
Boots Company PLC, The, V; 24 (upd.)
Borders Group, Inc., 15; 43 (upd.)
Boscov's Department Store, Inc., 31
Boston Proper, Inc., 131
Boulanger S.A., 102
Bowlin Travel Centers, Inc., 99
Bradlees Discount Department Store Company, 12
Bricorama S.A., 68
Briscoe Group Ltd., 110
Brodart Company, 84
Broder Bros. Co., 38

Brooks Brothers Inc., 22; 115 (upd.)
Brookstone, Inc., 18
The Buckle, Inc., 18; 115 (upd.)
Buhrmann NV, 41
Build-A-Bear Workshop, Inc., 62; 129 (upd.)
Burdines, Inc., 60
Burkhart Dental, Inc., 121
Burlington Coat Factory Warehouse Corporation, 10; 60 (upd.); 130 (upd.)
Buttrey Food & Drug Stores Co., 18
buy.com, Inc., 46
C&A, V; 40 (upd.)
C&J Clark International Ltd., 52
C.C. Filson Company, 130
Cabela's Inc., 26; 68 (upd.)
Cablevision Electronic Instruments, Inc., 32
Caché, Inc., 124 (upd.)
Cache Incorporated, 30
Cactus S.A., 90
Caldor Inc., 12
Calloway's Nursery, Inc., 51
Camaïeu S.A., 72
Camelot Music, Inc., 26
Campeau Corporation, V
Campmor, Inc., 104
Campo Electronics, Appliances & Computers, Inc., 16
Car Toys, Inc., 67
Carol Wright Gifts Inc., 131
Carphone Warehouse Group PLC, The, 83
Carrefour SA, 10; 27 (upd.); 64 (upd.)
Carson Pirie Scott & Company, 15
Carter Hawley Hale Stores, Inc., V
Carter Lumber Company, 45
Cartier Monde, 29
Casas Bahia Comercial Ltda., 75
Casey's General Stores, Inc., 19; 83 (upd.)
Castorama-Dubois Investissements SCA, 104 (upd.)
Castro Model Ltd., 86
Casual Corner Group, Inc., 43
Casual Male Retail Group, Inc., 52
Catherines Stores Corporation, 15
CDS (Superstores International) Limited, 126
CDW Computer Centers, Inc., 16
Celebrate Express, Inc., 70
Celebrity, Inc., 22
CellStar Corporation, 83
Cencosud S.A., 69
Central European Distribution Corporation, 75
Central Garden & Pet Company, 23
Central Retail Corporation, 110
Cenveo Inc., 71 (upd.)
Chadwick's of Boston, Ltd., 29
Charlotte Russe Holding, Inc., 35; 90 (upd.)
Charming Shoppes, Inc., 38
Chas. Levy Company LLC, 60
Cherry Brothers LLC, 105
Chiasso Inc., 53
Children's Place Retail Stores, Inc., The, 37; 86 (upd.)
China Nepstar Chain Drugstore Ltd., 97

Rubber & Tires

Textiles & Apparel

Waste Services

Geographic Index

Albania
Albtelecom Sh. a, 111

Algeria
Sonatrach, IV; 65 (upd.)

Angola
Sonangol E.P., 124
TAAG Angola Airlines (Linhas Aéreas de Angola, E.P.), 124

Argentina
Acindar Industria Argentina de Aceros S.A., 87
Adecoagro LLC, 101
Aerolíneas Argentinas S.A., 33; 69 (upd.)
Alpargatas S.A.I.C., 87
Aluar Aluminio Argentino S.A.I.C., 74
Arcor S.A.I.C., 66
Atanor S.A., 62
Coto Centro Integral de Comercializacion S.A., 66
Cresud S.A.C.I.F. y A., 63
Grupo Clarín S.A., 67
Grupo Financiero Galicia S.A., 63
Grupo Los Grobo, 133
IRSA Inversiones y Representaciones S.A., 63
Ledesma Sociedad Anónima Agrícola Industrial, 62
Loma Negra C.I.A.S.A., 95
Mastellone Hermanos S.A., 101
MercadoLibre, Inc., 128
Minera Alumbrera Ltd., 118
Molinos Río de la Plata S.A., 61
Nobleza Piccardo SAICF, 64
Pampa Energía S.A., 118
Pan American Energy LLC, 133

Penaflor S.A., 66
Petrobras Energia Participaciones S.A., 72
Quilmes Industrial (QUINSA) S.A., 67
Renault Argentina S.A., 67
SanCor Cooperativas Unidas Ltda., 101
Sideco Americana S.A., 67
Siderar S.A.I.C., 66
Telecom Argentina S.A., 63
Telefónica de Argentina S.A., 61
YPF Sociedad Anonima, IV

Australia
ABC Learning Centres Ltd., 93
Amcor Limited, IV; 19 (upd.), 78 (upd.)
Ansell Ltd., 60 (upd.)
Aquarius Platinum Ltd., 63
Aristocrat Leisure Limited, 54; 129 (upd.)
Arnott's Ltd., 66
Asciano Limited, 129
ASX Limited, 115
Ausenco Limited, 129
Austal Limited, 75
Australia and New Zealand Banking Group Ltd., II; 52 (upd.); 120 (upd.)
AWB Ltd., 56
BHP Billiton, 67 (upd.)
Billabong International Limited, 44; 112 (upd.)
BlueScope Steel Ltd., 133
Blundstone Pty Ltd., 76
Bond Corporation Holdings Limited, 10
Boral Limited, III; 43 (upd.); 103 (upd.)
Brambles Limited, 42; 129 (upd.)
Broken Hill Proprietary Company Ltd., IV; 22 (upd.)
Burns, Philp & Company Ltd., 63
Campbell Brothers Limited, 115
Carlton and United Breweries Ltd., I

Casella Wines Pty Limited, 132
Centamin Egypt Limited, 119
Cochlear Ltd., 77
Coles Group Limited, V; 20 (upd.); 85 (upd.)
Colorado Group Ltd., 107
Commonwealth Bank of Australia Ltd., 109
CRA Limited, IV; 85 (upd.)
CSL Limited, 112
CSR Limited, III; 28 (upd.)
David Jones Ltd., 60
Downer EDI Limited, 119
Elders Ltd., I; 123 (upd.)
Fairfax Media Ltd., 94 (upd.)
Foster's Group Limited, 7; 21 (upd.); 50 (upd.); 111 (upd.)
Goodman Fielder Ltd., 52; 127 (upd.)
Harvey Norman Holdings Ltd., 56
Henselite (Australia) Pty. Ltd., 133
Hills Industries Ltd., 104
Holden Ltd., 62
The Hoyts Corporation Pty Ltd., 126
Incitec Pivot Limited, 129
James Hardie Industries N.V., 56
John Fairfax Holdings Limited, 7
Leighton Holdings Limited, 128
Lend Lease Corporation Limited, IV; 17 (upd.); 52 (upd.)
Linfox Logistics Proprietary Limited, 129
Lion Nathan Limited, 54
Lonely Planet Publications, 55; 124 (upd.)
Macquarie Bank Ltd., 69
McMillan Shakespeare Ltd., 131
McPherson's Ltd., 66
Mermaid Marine Australia Limited, 115
Metcash Limited, 58; 129 (upd.)
MYOB Ltd., 86
National Australia Bank Ltd., 111

Assured Guaranty Ltd., 93
Bacardi & Company Ltd., 18; 82 (upd.)
BW Group Ltd., 107
Catlin Group Limited, 133
Central European Media Enterprises Ltd., 61
Covidien Ltd., 91
Endurance Specialty Holdings Ltd., 85
Frontline Ltd., 45
Genpact Limited, 132
Gosling Brothers Ltd., 82
Jardine Matheson Holdings Limited, I; 20 (upd.); 93 (upd.)
Lazard LLC, 38; 121 (upd.)
Marvell Technology Group Ltd., 112
Nabors Industries Ltd., 91 (upd.)
PartnerRe Ltd., 83
Sea Containers Ltd., 29
Seadrill Ltd., 131
Tyco International Ltd., III; 28 (upd.); 63 (upd.)
VistaPrint Limited, 87
Warner Chilcott Limited, 85
White Mountains Insurance Group, Ltd., 48

Bolivia
Lloyd Aéreo Boliviano S.A., 95

Botswana
Botswana Life Insurance Limited, 116
Debswana Diamond Company Proprietary Limited, 124

Brazil
Abril S.A., 95
Aché Laboratórios Farmacéuticas S.A., 105
Algar S/A Emprendimentos e Participações, 103
Amil Participações S.A., 105
Andrade Gutierrez S.A., 102
Anhanguera Educacional Participações S.A., 122
Aracruz Celulose S.A., 57
Arthur Lundgren Tecidos S.A., 102
B2W Companhia Global do Varejo, 117
Banco Bradesco S.A., 13; 116 (upd.)
Banco do Brasil S.A., 113 (upd.)
Banco Itaú S.A., 19
Bombril S.A., 111
Brasil Telecom Participaçoes S.A., 57
Braskem S.A., 108
Brazil Fast Food Corporation, 74
Bunge Brasil S.A., 78
Camargo Corrêa S.A., 93
Casas Bahia Comercial Ltda., 75
Cia Hering, 72
Cielo S.A., 131
Companhia Brasileira de Distribuiçao, 76
Companhia de Bebidas das Américas, 57
Companhia de Tecidos Norte de Minas - Coteminas, 77
Companhia Energética de Minas Gerais S.A. CEMIG, 65
Companhia Siderúrgica Nacional, 76
Companhia Suzano de Papel e Celulose S.A., 94

Cosan Ltd., 102
Cyrela Brazil Realty S.A. Empreendimentos e Participações, 110
EBX Investimentos, 104
Embraer S.A., 36; 133 (upd.)
Embratel Participações S.A., 119
G&K Holding S.A., 95
Gerdau S.A., 59
Globex Utilidades S.A., 103
Globo Comunicação e Participações S.A., 80
Gol Linhas Aéreas Inteligentes S.A., 73
Grendene S.A., 102
Grupo Martins, 104
Grupo Positivo, 105
Guararapes Confecções S.A., 118
GVT S.A., 127
Hypermarcas S.A., 117
Ipiranga S.A., 67
JBS S.A., 100
Klabin S.A., 73
Localiza Rent a Car S.A., 111
Lojas Americanas S.A., 77
Lojas Arapua S.A., 22; 61 (upd.)
Lojas Renner S.A., 107
Magazine Luiza S.A., 101
Marcopolo S.A. 79
Meridian Industries Inc., 107
Natura Cosméticos S.A., 75
Odebrecht S.A., 73
Perdigao SA, 52
Petróleo Brasileiro S.A., IV; 133 (upd.)
Randon S.A. 79
Redecard S.A., 131
Renner Herrmann S.A. 79
Sadia S.A., 59
Sao Paulo Alpargatas S.A., 75
Schincariol Participaçóces e Representações S.A., 102
Silvio Santos Participações Ltda., 123
SLC Participaçoes S.A., 111
Souza Cruz S.A., 65
TAM S.A., 68; 133 (upd.)
Tele Norte Leste Participações S.A., 80
Tigre S.A. Tubos e Conexões, 104
TIM Participações S.A., 126
TransBrasil S/A Linhas Aéreas, 31
Tupy S.A., 111
Unibanco Holdings S.A., 73
UNIPAR – União de Indústrias Petroquímicas S.A., 108
Usinas Siderúrgicas de Minas Gerais S.A., 77
Vale S.A., IV; 43 (upd.); 117 (upd.)
VARIG S.A. (Viaçâo Aérea Rio-Grandense), 6; 29 (upd.)
Vicunha Têxtil S.A., 78
Votorantim Participaçoes S.A., 76
Vulcabras S.A., 103
Weg S.A., 78
White Martins Gases Industriais Ltda., 111

Brunei
Royal Brunei Airlines Sdn Bhd, 99

Canada
1-800-GOT-JUNK? LLC, 74

AbitibiBowater Inc., V; 25 (upd.); 99 (upd.)
Abitibi-Price Inc., IV
Aecon Group Inc., 121
Agnico-Eagle Mines Limited, 71
Agrium Inc., 73
Ainsworth Lumber Co. Ltd., 99
Air Canada, 6; 23 (upd.); 59 (upd.); 125 (upd.)
AirBoss of America Corporation, 108
Alberta Energy Company Ltd., 16; 43 (upd.)
Alcan Aluminium Limited, IV; 31 (upd.)
Alderwoods Group, Inc., 68 (upd.)
Algo Group Inc., 24
Alimentation Couche-Tard Inc., 77
Alliance Atlantis Communications Inc., 39
Andrew Peller Ltd., 101
Angiotech Pharmaceuticals, Inc., 128
Arbor Memorial Services Inc., 122
Astral Media Inc., 126
ATI Technologies Inc. 79
Axcan Pharma Inc., 85
Ballard Power Systems Inc., 73
Bank of Montreal, II; 46 (upd.)
Bank of Nova Scotia, II; 59 (upd.); 124 (upd.)
Barrick Gold Corporation, 34; 112 (upd.)
Bata Ltd., 62
BCE Inc., V; 44 (upd.); 133 (upd.)
Bell Canada, 6
Bell Media, Inc., 126
BFC Construction Corporation, 25
Biovail Corporation, 47
BioWare Corporation, 81
Birks & Mayors Inc., 112
BMO Financial Group, 130 (upd.)
Bombardier Inc., 42 (upd.); 87 (upd.)
Boston Pizza International Inc., 88
Bradley Air Services Ltd., 56
Bramalea Ltd., 9
Brascan Corporation, 67
Brick Brewing Co. Limited, 130
British Columbia Telephone Company, 6
Brookfield Properties Corporation, 89
Cameco Corporation, 77
Campeau Corporation, V
Canada Bread Company, Limited, 99
Canada Council for the Arts, 112
Canada Packers Inc., II
Canadair, Inc., 16
Canadian Broadcasting Corporation, 37; 109 (upd.)
Canadian Imperial Bank of Commerce, II; 61 (upd.)
Canadian National Railway Company, 6; 71 (upd.)
Canadian Oil Sands Limited, 133
Canadian Pacific Railway Limited, V; 45 (upd.); 95 (upd.)
Canadian Solar Inc., 105
Canadian Tire Corporation, Limited, 71 (upd.)
Canadian Utilities Limited, 13; 56 (upd.)
Canam Group Inc., 114
Canfor Corporation, 42
Canlan Ice Sports Corp., 105
Canstar Sports Inc., 16

Arianespace S.A., 89
Arkema S.A., 100
Association des Centres Distributeurs E. Leclerc, 37
Assurances Générales de France, 63
Atari S.A., 132 (upd.)
Atochem S.A., I
Atos Origin S.A., 69
Au Printemps S.A., V
Aubert & Duval S.A.S., 107
Auchan Group, 37; 116 (upd.)
Automobiles Citroen, 7
Autoroutes du Sud de la France SA, 55
Avions Marcel Dassault-Breguet Aviation, I
AXA Group, III; 114 (upd.)
Babolat VS, S.A., 97
Baccarat, 24
Banque Nationale de Paris S.A., II
Baron Philippe de Rothschild S.A., 39
Bayard SA, 49
Belvedere S.A., 93
Bénéteau SA, 55
Besnier SA, 19
BigBen Interactive S.A., 72
bioMérieux S.A., 75
BNP Paribas Group, 36 (upd.); 111 (upd.)
Boiron S.A., 73
Boizel Chanoine Champagne S.A., 94
Bonduelle SA, 51
Bongrain S.A., 25; 102 (upd.)
Boulanger S.A., 102
Bouygues S.A., I; 24 (upd.); 97 (upd.)
Bricorama S.A., 68
Brioche Pasquier S.A., 58
Brossard S.A., 102
BSN Groupe S.A., II
Buffalo Grill S.A., 94
Bugatti Automobiles S.A.S., 94
Bull S.A., 43 (upd.)
Bureau Veritas SA, 55
Burelle S.A., 23
Business Objects S.A., 25
Caisse des Dépôts et Consignations, 90
Camaïeu S.A., 72
Canal Plus, 10; 34 (upd.)
Cap Gemini Ernst & Young, 37
Carbone Lorraine S.A., 33
Carrefour SA, 10; 27 (upd.); 64 (upd.)
Carrere Group S.A., 104
Casino Guichard-Perrachon S.A., 59 (upd.)
Castorama-Dubois Investissements SCA, 104 (upd.)
Cegedim S.A., 104
Celio France S.A.S., 113
Cemoi S.A., 86
Cetelem S.A., 21
Champagne Bollinger S.A., 114
Chanel SA, 12; 49 (upd.); 128 (upd.)
Chantiers Jeanneau S.A., 96
Charal S.A., 90
Chargeurs International, 6; 21 (upd.)
Christian Dalloz SA, 40
Christian Dior S.A., 19; 49 (upd.); 110 (upd.)
Christofle SA, 40

Ciments Français, 40
Clarins S.A., 119
Club Mediterranée S.A., 6; 21 (upd.); 91 (upd.)
CNP Assurances, 116
Coflexip S.A., 25
Colas S.A., 31
Compagnie de Saint-Gobain, III; 16 (upd.); 64 (upd.)
Compagnie des Alpes, 48
Compagnie des Machines Bull S.A., III
Compagnie Financiere de Paribas, II
Compagnie Financière Sucres et Denrées S.A., 60
Compagnie Générale d'Électricité, II
Compagnie Générale des Établissements Michelin, V; 42 (upd.); 117 (upd.)
Compagnie Générale Maritime et Financière, 6
Compagnie Plastic Omnium S.A., 127
Comptoirs Modernes S.A., 19
Coopagri Bretagne, 88
Crédit Agricole Group, II; 84 (upd.)
Crédit Industriel et Commercial S.A., 116
Crédit Lyonnais, 9; 33 (upd.)
Crédit National S.A., 9
Cristal Union S.C.A., 127
Dalkia Holding, 66
Damartex S.A., 98
Darty S.A., 27
Dassault Aviation S.A., 114 (upd.)
Dassault Systèmes S.A., 25
DCN S.A., 75
De Dietrich & Cie., 31
Delachaux S.A., 76
Délifrance S.A., 113
Deveaux S.A., 41
Devoteam S.A., 94
Dexia Group, 42
Doux S.A., 80
Drouot S.A., 132
Du Pareil au Même, 43
Dynaction S.A., 67
Dyneff S.A., 98
EADS SOCATA, 54
ECS S.A, 12
Ed S.A.S., 88
Éditions Gallimard, 72
Editis S.A., 78
Eiffage S.A., 27; 117 (upd.)
Electricité de France S.A., V; 41 (upd.); 114 (upd.)
Elf Aquitaine SA, 21 (upd.)
Elior SA, 49
Elis G.I.E., 123
Emin Leydier S.A.S., 127
Entremont Alliance S.A.S., 127
Eram SA, 51
Eramet, 73
Eridania Béghin-Say S.A., 36
Essilor International, 21
Etablissements Economiques du Casino Guichard, Perrachon et Cie, S.C.A., 12
Établissements Jacquot and Cie S.A.S., 92
Etablissements Maurel & Prom S.A., 115
Etam Developpement SA, 44
Eurazeo, 80
Euro Disney S.C.A., 20; 58 (upd.)

Euro RSCG Worldwide S.A., 13
Eurocopter S.A., 80
Eurofins Scientific S.A., 70
Euronext Paris S.A., 37
Europcar Groupe S.A., 104
Eutelsat S.A., 114
Evialis S.A., 100
Exacompta Clairefontaine S.A., 102
Expand SA, 48
Facom S.A., 32
Faiveley S.A., 39
Faurecia S.A., 70
Fimalac S.A., 37
Fives S.A., 107
Flammarion Group, 131
Fleury Michon S.A., 39
Floc'h & Marchand, 80
FNAC, 21
Foncière Euris, 111
Framatome SA, 19
France Telecom S.A., V; 21 (upd.); 99 (upd.)
Fromageries Bel, 23
Fruité Entreprises S.A., 120
G.I.E. Airbus Industrie, I; 12 (upd.)
Galeries Lafayette S.A., V; 23 (upd.)
Gaumont S.A., 25; 91 (upd.)
Gaz de France, V; 40 (upd.)
GDF SUEZ, 109 (upd.)
Gecina SA, 42
Gefco SA, 54
Générale des Eaux Group, V
Geodis S.A., 67
Gévelot S.A., 96
GFI Informatique SA, 49
GiFi S.A., 74
GL Events S.A., 107
Glaces Thiriet S.A., 76
Grands Vins Jean-Claude Boisset S.A., 98
GrandVision S.A., 43
Grévin & Compagnie SA, 56
Groupama S.A., 76
Groupe Air France, 6
Groupe Alain Manoukian, 55
Groupe André, 17
Groupe Ares S.A., 102
Groupe Bigard S.A., 96
Groupe Bolloré, 67
Groupe Bourbon S.A., 60
Groupe Caisse d'Epargne, 100
Groupe Castorama-Dubois Investissements, 23
Groupe CECAB S.C.A., 88
Groupe Crit S.A., 74
Groupe Danone, 32 (upd.); 93 (upd.)
Groupe Dassault Aviation SA, 26 (upd.)
Groupe de la Cite, IV
Groupe DMC (Dollfus Mieg & Cie), 27
Groupe Dubreuil S.A., 102
Groupe Euralis, 86
Groupe Flo S.A., 98
Groupe Fournier SA, 44
Groupe Genoyer, 96
Groupe Glon, 84
Groupe Go Sport S.A., 39
Groupe Guillin SA, 40
Groupe Henri Heuliez S.A., 100
Groupe Jean-Claude Darmon, 44

Air Sahara Limited, 65
Allied Digital Services Ltd., 119
Bajaj Auto Limited, 39
Bharat Electronics Limited, 113
Bharat Heavy Electricals Limited, 119
Bharat Petroleum Corporation Limited, 109
Bharti Airtel Limited, 128
Bharti Tele-Ventures Limited, 75
Britannia Industries Ltd., 117
Coal India Limited, IV; 44 (upd.); 115 (upd.)
Dr. Reddy's Laboratories Ltd., 59
EIH Ltd., 103
Essar Group Ltd. 79
Essel Propack Limited, 115
Hindustan Lever Limited 79
Hindustan Petroleum Corporation Ltd., 116
ICICI Bank Ltd., 131
IDBI Bank Ltd., 128
Indian Airlines Ltd., 46
The Indian Hotels Company Limited, 125
Indian Oil Corporation Ltd., IV; 48 (upd.); 113 (upd.)
Infosys Technologies Limited, 38; 119 (upd.)
Jaiprakash Associates Limited, 101
Jet Airways (India) Private Limited, 65
Kotak Mahindra Bank Ltd., 131
Larsen and Toubro Ltd., 117
Mahindra & Mahindra Ltd., 120
McLeod Russel India Limited, 128
Minerals and Metals Trading Corporation of India Ltd., IV
MTR Foods Ltd., 55
Neyveli Lignite Corporation Ltd., 65
Oil and Natural Gas Corporation Ltd., IV; 90 (upd.)
Ranbaxy Laboratories Ltd., 70
Raymond Ltd., 77
Reliance Industries Ltd., 81
Rolta India Ltd., 90
Satyam Computer Services Ltd., 85
State Bank of India, 63
Steel Authority of India Ltd., IV; 66 (upd.)
Sun Pharmaceutical Industries Ltd., 57
Suzlon Energy Limited, 128
Tata Consultancy Services Limited, 119
Tata Iron & Steel Co. Ltd., IV; 44 (upd.)
Tata Motors, Ltd., 109
Tata Steel Ltd., 109 (upd.)
Tata Tea Ltd., 76
Wipro Limited, 43; 106 (upd.)

Indonesia

PT Adaro Energy Tbk, 133
PT Astra International Tbk, 56
PT Bank UOB Buana Tbk, 60; 124 (upd.)
Djarum PT, 62
Garuda Indonesia, 6; 58 (upd.)
PT Gudang Garam Tbk, 103
PT Indosat Tbk, 93
Pertamina, IV; 56 (upd.)
PT Semen Gresik Tbk, 103

Iran

IranAir, 81
National Iranian Oil Company, IV; 61 (upd.)

Ireland

Aer Lingus Group plc, 34; 89 (upd.)
Allied Irish Banks, plc, 16; 43 (upd.); 94 (upd.)
Baltimore Technologies Plc, 42
Bank of Ireland, 50
Boylesports Holdings Ltd., 129
Cahill May Roberts Group Ltd., 112
Clondalkin Group PLC, 120
Cooper Industries plc, 133 (upd.)
CRH plc, 64
CryptoLogic Limited, 106
DCC plc, 115
DEPFA BANK PLC, 69
Dunnes Stores Ltd., 58
eircom plc, 31 (upd.)
Elan Corporation PLC, 63
Fyffes PLC, 38; 106 (upd.)
Glanbia plc, 59; 125 (upd.)
Glen Dimplex, 78
Grafton Group plc, 104
Greencore Group plc, 98
Harland and Wolff Holdings plc, 19
IAWS Group plc, 49
Independent News & Media PLC, 61; 132 (upd.)
Ingersoll-Rand PLC, 115 (upd.)
IONA Technologies plc, 43
Irish Distillers Group, 96
Irish Food Processors Ltd., 111
Irish Life & Permanent Plc, 59
Jefferson Smurfit Group plc, IV; 19 (upd.); 49 (upd.)
Jurys Doyle Hotel Group plc, 64
Kerry Group plc, 27; 87 (upd.)
Musgrave Group Plc, 57
Paddy Power plc, 98
Ryanair Holdings plc, 35; 132 (upd.)
Shannon Aerospace Ltd., 36
Shire PLC, 109
SkillSoft Public Limited Company, 81
Smurfit Kappa Group plc, 112 (upd.)
Stafford Group, 110
Telecom Eireann, 7
Thomas Crosbie Holdings Limited, 81
Trinity Biotech plc, 121
United Drug PLC, 121
Waterford Wedgwood plc, 34 (upd.)
WPP Group plc, 112 (upd.)

Israel

Aladdin Knowledge Systems Ltd., 101
Alon Holdings Blue Square—Israel Ltd., 125 (upd.)
Alon Israel Oil Company Ltd., 104
Amdocs Ltd., 47
Bank Hapoalim B.M., II; 54 (upd.)
Bank Leumi le-Israel B.M., 60
Blue Square Israel Ltd., 41
BVR Systems (1998) Ltd., 93
Castro Model Ltd., 86
Check Point Software Technologies Ltd., 119

Delek Group Ltd., 123
ECI Telecom Ltd., 18
EL AL Israel Airlines Ltd., 23; 107 (upd.)
Elco Holdings Ltd., 123
Elscint Ltd., 20
Emblaze Ltd., 117
EZchip Semiconductor Ltd., 106
Galtronics Ltd., 100
Given Imaging Ltd., 83
IDB Holding Corporation Ltd., 97
Israel Aircraft Industries Ltd., 69
Israel Chemicals Ltd., 55
Israel Corporation Ltd., 108
Koor Industries Ltd., II; 25 (upd.); 68 (upd.)
Lipman Electronic Engineering Ltd., 81
Makhteshim-Agan Industries Ltd., 85
NICE Systems Ltd., 83
Orbotech Ltd., 75
Scitex Corporation Ltd., 24
SodaStream International Ltd., 133
Strauss-Elite Group, 68
Syneron Medical Ltd., 91
Taro Pharmaceutical Industries Ltd., 65
Teva Pharmaceutical Industries Ltd., 22; 54 (upd.); 112 (upd.)
Tnuva Food Industries Ltd., 111

Italy

A2A S.p.A., 133
ACEA S.p.A., 115
Aeffe S.p.A., 119
AgustaWestland N.V., 75
Alfa Romeo, 13; 36 (upd.); 132 (upd.)
Alitalia—Linee Aeree Italiana, S.p.A., 6; 29 (upd.); 97 (upd.)
Alleanza Assicurazioni S.p.A., 65
Angelini SpA, 100
Aprilia SpA, 17
Arnoldo Mondadori Editore S.p.A., IV; 19 (upd.); 54 (upd.)
Artsana SpA, 92
Assicurazioni Generali S.p.A., III; 15 (upd.); 103 (upd.)
Astaldi SpA, 131
Autogrill SpA, 49
Automobili Lamborghini Holding S.p.A., 13; 34 (upd.); 91 (upd.)
Autostrada Torino-Milano S.p.A., 101
Azelis Group, 100
Banca Commerciale Italiana SpA, II
Banca Fideuram SpA, 63
Banca Intesa SpA, 65
Banca Monte dei Paschi di Siena SpA, 65
Banca Nazionale del Lavoro SpA, 72
Barilla G. e R. Fratelli S.p.A., 17; 50 (upd.)
Benetton Group S.p.A., 10; 67 (upd.)
Brioni Roman Style S.p.A., 67
Bulgari S.p.A., 20; 106 (upd.)
Cantine Giorgio Lungarotti S.R.L., 67
Capitalia S.p.A., 65
Cavit s.c., 130
Cinecittà Luce S.p.A., 132
Cinemeccanica SpA
Compagnia Italiana dei Jolly Hotels S.p.A., 71

Consorzio del Formaggio
  Parmigiano-Reggiano, 133
Credito Italiano, II
Cremonini S.p.A., 57
Davide Campari-Milano S.p.A., 57
De Agostini Editore S.p.A., 103
De Rigo S.p.A., 104
De'Longhi S.p.A., 66
Diadora SpA, 86
Diesel SpA, 40
Dolce & Gabbana SpA, 62
Ducati Motor Holding SpA, 30; 86 (upd.)
Enel S.p.A., 108 (upd.)
ENI S.p.A., 69 (upd.)
Ente Nazionale Idrocarburi, IV
Ente Nazionale per L'Energia Elettrica, V
Ermenegildo Zegna SpA, 63
Fabbrica D' Armi Pietro Beretta S.p.A., 39
FASTWEB S.p.A., 83
Ferrari S.p.A., 13; 36 (upd.)
Ferrero SpA, 54
Ferretti Group SpA, 90
Ferrovie Dello Stato Societa Di Trasporti e
  Servizi S.p.A., 105
Fiat S.p.A., I; 11 (upd.); 50 (upd.); 120
  (upd.)
Fila Holding S.p.A., 20; 52 (upd.)
Finarte Casa d'Aste S.p.A., 93
Finmeccanica S.p.A., 84
Geox S.p.A., 118
Gianni Versace S.p.A., 22; 106 (upd.)
Giorgio Armani S.p.A., 45; 128 (upd.)
Gruppo Editoriale L'Espresso S.p.A., 131
Gruppo Coin S.p.A., 41
Gruppo Italiano Vini, 111
Gruppo Riva Fire SpA, 88
Guccio Gucci, S.p.A., 15
I Grandi Viaggi S.p.A., 105
illycaffè S.p.A., 50; 110 (upd.)
Industrie Natuzzi S.p.A., 18
Industrie Zignago Santa Margherita
  S.p.A., 67
Ing. C. Olivetti & C., S.p.a., III
Istituto per la Ricostruzione Industriale
  S.p.A., I; 11
Juventus F.C. S.p.A, 53
La Doria SpA, 101
Luxottica Group S.p.A., 17; 52 (upd.);
  133 (upd.)
Magneti Marelli Holding SpA, 90
Marchesi Antinori SRL, 42
Marcolin S.p.A., 61
Mariella Burani Fashion Group, 92
Martini & Rossi SpA, 63; 131 (upd.)
Marzotto S.p.A., 20; 67 (upd.)
Mediaset SpA, 50; 132 (upd.)
Mediolanum S.p.A., 65
Milan AC, S.p.A. 79
Miroglio SpA, 86
Montedison SpA, I; 24 (upd.)
Officine Alfieri Maserati S.p.A., 13
Olivetti S.p.A., 34 (upd.)
Pagnossin S.p.A., 73
Parmalat Finanziaria SpA, 50
Peg Perego SpA, 88
Perfetti Van Melle S.p.A., 72
Piaggio & C. S.p.A., 20; 100 (upd.)
Pirelli & C. S.p.A., 75 (upd.)

Pirelli S.p.A., V; 15 (upd.)
Poste Italiane S.p.A., 108
RCS MediaGroup S.p.A., 96
Recordati Industria Chimica e
  Farmaceutica S.p.A., 105
Reno de Medici S.p.A., 41; 129 (upd.)
Rinascente S.p.A., 71
Riunione Adriatica di Sicurtè SpA, III
Safilo SpA, 54
Salvatore Ferragamo Italia S.p.A., 62
Sanpaolo IMI S.p.A., 50
Seat Pagine Gialle S.p.A., 47
Sirti S.p.A., 76
Società Finanziaria Telefonica per Azioni,
  V
Società Sportiva Lazio SpA, 44
Stefanel SpA, 63
Targetti Sankey SpA, 86
Telecom Italia Mobile S.p.A., 63
Telecom Italia S.p.A., 43
Tiscali SpA, 48
UniCredit S.p.A., 108 (upd.)
Vibram S.p.A., 126

Ivory Coast
SIFCA S.A., 131

Jamaica
Air Jamaica Limited, 54; 129 (upd.)
Desnoes and Geddes Limited 79
GraceKennedy Ltd., 92
Wray & Nephew Group Ltd., 98

Japan
AEON Co., Ltd., 68 (upd.)
Aisin Seiki Co., Ltd., III; 48 (upd.); 120
  (upd.)
Aiwa Co., Ltd., 30
Ajinomoto Co., Inc., II; 28 (upd.); 108
  (upd.)
Alfresa Holdings Corporation, 108
All Nippon Airways Co., Ltd., 6; 38
  (upd.); 91 (upd.)
Alpine Electronics, Inc., 13
Alps Electric Co., Ltd., II; 44 (upd.)
Anritsu Corporation, 68
Aomori Bank Ltd., 123
Asahi Breweries, Ltd., I; 20 (upd.); 52
  (upd.); 108 (upd.)
Asahi Denka Kogyo KK, 64
Asahi Glass Company, Ltd., III; 48 (upd.)
Asahi National Broadcasting Company,
  Ltd., 9
The Asahi Shimbun Company, 126
Asatsu-DK Inc., 82
ASICS Corporation, 57
Astellas Pharma Inc., 97 (upd.)
Autobacs Seven Company Ltd., 76
Bandai Co., Ltd., 55
Bank of Tokyo-Mitsubishi Ltd., II; 15
  (upd.)
Benesse Corporation, 76
Bourbon Corporation, 82
Bridgestone Corporation, V; 21 (upd.); 59
  (upd.); 118 (upd.)
Brother Industries, Ltd., 14
C. Itoh & Company Ltd., I

Canon Inc., III; 18 (upd.); 79 (upd.)
Capcom Company Ltd., 83
CASIO Computer Co., Ltd., III; 16
  (upd.); 40 (upd.)
Central Japan Railway Company, 43
Chubu Electric Power Company, Inc., V;
  46 (upd.); 118 (upd.)
Chugai Pharmaceutical Co., Ltd., 50
Chugoku Electric Power Company Inc.,
  V; 53 (upd.)
Citizen Watch Co., Ltd., III; 21 (upd.);
  81 (upd.)
Clarion Company Ltd., 64
Cosmo Oil Company, Limited, IV; 53
  (upd.); 126 (upd.)
Dai-Ichi Life Insurance Company,
  Limited, 116
Dai Nippon Printing Co., Ltd., IV; 57
  (upd.)
Daido Steel Co., Ltd., IV
Daiei, Inc., The, V; 17 (upd.); 41 (upd.)
Daihatsu Motor Company, Ltd., 7; 21
  (upd.)
Dai-Ichi Kangyo Bank Ltd., The, II
Daiichikosho Company Ltd., 86
Daikin Industries, Ltd., III
Daiko Advertising Inc. 79
Daimaru, Inc., The, V; 42 (upd.)
Daio Paper Corporation, IV, 84 (upd.)
Daishowa Paper Manufacturing Co., Ltd.,
  IV; 57 (upd.)
Daiwa Bank, Ltd., The, II; 39 (upd.)
Daiwa Securities Group Inc., II; 55 (upd.)
DDI Corporation, 7
DeNA Co., Ltd., 121
DENSO Corporation, 46 (upd.); 128
  (upd.)
Dentsu Inc., I; 16 (upd.); 40 (upd.)
DIC Corporation, 115
East Japan Railway Company, V; 66
  (upd.)
Ebara Corporation, 83
Eisai Co., Ltd., 101
Elpida Memory, Inc., 83
Encho Company Ltd., 104
Ezaki Glico Company Ltd., 72
Fanuc Ltd., III; 17 (upd.); 75 (upd.)
Fast Retailing Company Ltd., 126
Fuji Bank, Ltd., The, II
Fuji Electric Co., Ltd., II; 48 (upd.)
Fuji Photo Film Co., Ltd., III; 18 (upd.);
  79 (upd.)
Fuji Television Network Inc., 91
Fujisawa Pharmaceutical Company, Ltd.,
  I; 58 (upd.)
Fujitsu Limited, III; 16 (upd.); 42 (upd.);
  103 (upd.)
Funai Electric Company Ltd., 62
Furukawa Electric Co., Ltd., The, III
General Sekiyu K.K., IV
Hagoromo Foods Corporation, 84
Hakuhodo, Inc., 6; 42 (upd.)
Hankyu Department Stores, Inc., V; 23
  (upd.); 62 (upd.)
Hanwa Company Ltd., 123
Hazama Corporation, 126
Hino Motors, Ltd., 7; 21 (upd.)
Hiroshima Bank Ltd., 131

Proeza S.A. de C.V., 82
Pulsar Internacional S.A., 21
Real Turismo, S.A. de C.V., 50
Sanborn Hermanos, S.A., 20
SANLUIS Corporación, S.A.B. de C.V., 95
Sears Roebuck de México, S.A. de C.V., 20
Telefonos de Mexico S.A. de C.V., 14; 63 (upd.); 128 (upd.)
Tenedora Nemak, S.A. de C.V., 102
Tubos de Acero de Mexico, S.A. (TAMSA), 41
TV Azteca, S.A. de C.V., 39
Urbi Desarrollos Urbanos, S.A. de C.V., 81
Valores Industriales S.A., 19
Vitro Corporativo S.A. de C.V., 34
Wal-Mart de Mexico, S.A. de C.V., 35 (upd.)

Mongolia
Newcom, LLC, 104
Maroc Telecom, 122

Nepal
Royal Nepal Airline Corporation, 41

The Netherlands
ABN AMRO Holding, N.V., 50
AEGON N.V., III; 50 (upd.)
AFC Ajax NV, 132
Akzo Nobel N.V., 13; 41 (upd.); 112 (upd.)
Algemene Bank Nederland N.V., II
Amsterdam-Rotterdam Bank N.V., II
Arcadis NV, 26
ASML Holding N.V., 50
Australian Homemade Holding B.V., 123
Avantium Technologies BV 79
Baan Company, 25
Bavaria N.V., 121
Beter Bed Holding N.V., 123
Blokker Holding B.V., 84
Bols Distilleries NV, 74
Bolton Group B.V., 86
Buhrmann NV, 41
Campina Group, The, 78
Chicago Bridge & Iron Company N.V., 82 (upd.)
CNH Global N.V., 38 (upd.); 99 (upd.)
CSM N.V., 65
DAF Trucks N.V., 123
Deli Universal NV, 66
Drie Mollen Holding B.V., 99
DSM N.V., I; 56 (upd.)
Elsevier N.V., IV
Endemol Entertainment Holding NV, 46
Equant N.V., 52
Euronext N.V., 89 (upd.)
European Aeronautic Defence and Space Company EADS N.V., 52 (upd.); 109 (upd)
Friesland Coberco Dairy Foods Holding N.V., 59
Fugro N.V., 98
Getronics NV, 39

Granaria Holdings B.V., 66
Grand Hotel Krasnapolsky N.V., 23
Greenpeace International, 74
Grontmij N.V., 110
Gucci Group NV, 50; 115 (upd.)
Hagemeyer N.V., 39
Head N.V., 55
Heijmans N.V., 66
Heineken N.V., I; 13 (upd.); 34 (upd.); 90 (upd.)
HEMA B.V., 111
Holland Casino, 107
Hunter Douglas N.V., 133
IHC Caland N.V., 71
IKEA Group, 94 (upd.)
Indigo NV, 26
ING Groep N.V., 108
Intres B.V., 82
Ispat International N.V., 30
KLM Royal Dutch Airlines, 104 (upd.)
Koninklijke Ahold N.V., II; 16 (upd.); 124 (upd.)
Koninklijke Houthandel G Wijma & Zonen BV, 96
Koninklijke Luchtvaart Maatschappij, N.V. (KLM Royal Dutch Airlines), I; 28 (upd.)
Koninklijke Nederlandsche Hoogovens en Staalfabrieken NV, IV
Koninklijke Nedlloyd N.V., 6; 26 (upd.)
Koninklijke Philips Electronics N.V., 50 (upd.); 119 (upd.)
Koninklijke PTT Nederland NV, V
Koninklijke Reesink N.V., 104
Koninklijke Vendex KBB N.V. (Royal Vendex KBB N.V.), 62 (upd.)
Koninklijke Wessanen nv, II; 54 (upd.); 114 (upd.)
KPMG International, 10; 33 (upd.); 108 (upd.)
Laurus N.V., 65
LyondellBasell Industries Holdings N.V., 109 (upd.)
Macintosh Retail Group N.V., 120
Mammoet Transport B.V., 26
MIH Limited, 31
N.V. AMEV, III
N.V. Holdingmaatschappij De Telegraaf, 23
N.V. Koninklijke Nederlandse Vliegtuigenfabriek Fokker, I; 28 (upd.)
N.V. Nederlandse Gasunie, V; 111 (upd.)
Nationale-Nederlanden N.V., III
New Holland N.V., 22
Norit International N.V., 130
Nutreco Holding N.V., 56
Océ N.V., 24; 91 (upd.)
PCM Uitgevers NV, 53
Philips Electronics N.V., II; 13 (upd.)
PolyGram N.V., 23
Prada Holding B.V., 45
QIAGEN N.V., 39; 121 (upd.)
Rabobank Group, 116 (upd.)
Rabobank Group, 33
Randstad Holding nv, 16; 43 (upd.); 113 (upd.)
Rodamco N.V., 26
Royal Boskalis Westminster NV, 127

Royal Dutch Shell plc, IV; 49 (upd.); 108 (upd.)
Royal Grolsch NV, 54
Royal KPN N.V., 30; 124 (upd.)
Royal Numico N.V., 37
Royal Packaging Industries Van Leer N.V., 30
Royal Ten Cate N.V., 68
Royal Vopak NV, 41
SHV Holdings N.V., 55
Spyker Cars N.V., 124
Telegraaf Media Groep N.V., 98 (upd.)
Tennet BV, 78
TNT Post Group N.V., V, 27 (upd.); 30 (upd.)
TomTom N.V., 81
Toolex International N.V., 26
TPG N.V., 64 (upd.)
Trader Classified Media N.V., 57
Triple P N.V., 26
Unilever N.V., II; 7 (upd.); 32 (upd.)
United Pan-Europe Communications NV, 47
Van Lanschot NV 79
VBA - Bloemenveiling Aalsmeer, 88
VDL Groep B.V., 113
Vebego International BV, 49
Vedior NV, 35
Velcro Industries N.V., 19
Vendex International N.V., 13
Verbrugge Terminals B.V., 131
Vion Food Group NV, 85
VNU N.V., 27
Wegener NV, 53
Wolters Kluwer N.V., 14; 33 (upd.); 133 (upd.)
Zentiva N.V./Zentiva, a.s., 99

Netherlands Antilles
Café Britt Coffee Corporation Holdings NV, 119
Koninklijke Wessanen nv, 114 (upd.)
Orthofix International NV, 72
Velcro Industries N.V., 72

New Zealand
Air New Zealand Limited, 14; 38 (upd.); 119 (upd.)
Briscoe Group Ltd., 110
Carter Holt Harvey Ltd., 70
Cerebos Gregg's Ltd., 100
Fletcher Building Limited, 125
Fletcher Challenge Ltd., IV; 19 (upd.)
Fonterra Co-operative Group Limited, 58; 124 (upd.)
Frucor Beverages Group Ltd., 96
Fulton Hogan Ltd, 131
KiwiRail, 131
Mainfreight Limited, 119
New Zealand Post Group, 129
New Zealand Railways Corporation, 125
Nuplex Industries Ltd., 92
Progressive Enterprises Ltd., 96
Pumpkin Patch Limited, 129
Reynolds Group Holdings Ltd., 121
Sky Network Television Limited, 125
SKYCITY Entertainment Group Limited, 132

Telecom Corporation of New Zealand Limited, 54; 128 (upd.)
Turners & Growers Ltd., 129
The Warehouse Group Limited, 125
Wattie's Ltd., 7
Weta Digital Ltd., 132

Scottish & Newcastle plc, 15; 35 (upd.)
Scottish Hydro-Electric PLC, 13
Scottish Media Group plc, 32
ScottishPower plc, 19
Stagecoach Holdings plc, 30
Standard Life Assurance Company, The, III

Singapore

Asia Pacific Breweries Limited, 59
Boustead Singapore Ltd., 127
City Developments Limited, 89
Creative Technology Ltd., 57
Flextronics International Ltd., 38; 116 (upd.)
Fraser & Neave Ltd., 54
Hotel Properties Ltd., 71
Jardine Cycle & Carriage Ltd., 73
Keppel Corporation Ltd., 73
M1 Limited, 119
Neptune Orient Lines Limited, 47; 128 (upd.)
Olam International Ltd., 122
Pacific Internet Limited, 87
RSH Ltd., 110
Singapore Airlines Limited, 6; 27 (upd.); 83 (upd.)
Singapore Press Holdings Limited, 85
Singapore Telecommunications Limited, 111
StarHub Ltd., 77
United Overseas Bank Ltd., 56
Wilmar International Ltd., 108

Slovakia

Doprastav A.S., 113

Slovenia

Lek farmacevtska druzba d.d., 130
Merkur - trgovina in storitve, d.d., 130
Mobitel, telekomunikacijske storitve, d.d., 130
Telekom Slovenije, d.d., 130

South Africa

Absa Group Ltd., 106
African Rainbow Minerals Ltd., 97
Anglo American Corporation of South Africa Limited, IV; 16 (upd.)
Aspen Pharmacare Holdings Limited, 112
Barlow Rand Ltd., I
Barloworld Ltd., 109 (upd.)
Bidvest Group Ltd., 106
City Lodge Hotels Limited, 114
De Beers Consolidated Mines Limited/De Beers Centenary AG, IV; 7 (upd.); 28 (upd.)
Dimension Data Holdings PLC, 69
Distell Group Ltd., 126
Edgars Consolidated Stores Ltd., 66
Eskom Holdings Limited, 121
Exxaro Resources Ltd., 106
Famous Brands Ltd., 86
Foschini Group, The, 110
Gencor Ltd., IV; 22 (upd.)
Gold Fields Ltd., IV; 62 (upd.)
Harmony Gold Mining Company Limited, 63

Highveld Steel and Vanadium Corporation Limited, 59
Illovo Sugar Ltd., 127
Iscor Limited, 57
JD Group Ltd., 110
Korbitec, 120
Mondi Ltd., 131
Mr Price Group Ltd., 130
MTN Group Ltd., 106
Naspers Ltd., 66
New Clicks Holdings Ltd., 86
Oceana Group Ltd., 123
Pick 'n Pay Stores Ltd., 82
Sanlam Ltd., 68
Sappi Ltd., 49; 107 (upd.)
Sasol Limited, IV; 47 (upd.)
South African Airways (Proprietary) Limited, 28; 133 (upd.)
South African Breweries Limited, The, I; 24 (upd.)
Southern Sun Hotel Interest (Pty) Ltd., 106
Telkom S.A. Ltd., 106
Tiger Brands Limited, 112
Transnet Ltd., 6
Truworths International Ltd., 107
Vodacom Group Pty. Ltd., 106

South Korea (Republic of Korea)

Anam Group, 23
Asiana Airlines, Inc., 46; 133 (upd.)
CJ Corporation, 62
Daesang Corporation, 84
Daewoo Group, III; 18 (upd.); 57 (upd.)
Daewoo Shipbuilding and Marine Engineering Co., Ltd., 128
Doosan Heavy Industries and Construction Company Ltd., 108
Electronics Co., Ltd., 14
Goldstar Co., Ltd., 12
Hanjin Shipping Co., Ltd., 50
Hankook Tire Company Ltd., 105
Hanwha Group, 62
Hite Brewery Company Ltd., 97
Honam Petrochemical Corp., 131
Hotel Shilla Company Ltd., 110
Hynix Semiconductor Company Ltd., 111
Hyundai Group, III; 7 (upd.); 56 (upd.)
Hyundai Heavy Industries Co., Ltd., 119
Hyundai Merchant Marine Co., Ltd., 128
Kia Motors Corporation, 12; 29 (upd.)
Kookmin Bank, 58
Korea Electric Power Corporation, 56; 117 (upd.)
Korea Exchange Bank, 131
Korea Gas Corporation, 114
Korean Air Lines Co., Ltd., 6; 27 (upd.); 114 (upd.)
KT&G Corporation, 62
Kumho Tire Company Ltd., 105
LG Corporation, 94 (upd.)
Lotte Confectionery Company Ltd., 76
Lotte Shopping Company Ltd., 110
Lucky-Goldstar, II
Megastudy Company Ltd., 127
Pohang Iron and Steel Company Ltd., IV
POSCO, 57 (upd.); 123 (upd.)

Samick Musical Instruments Co., Ltd., 56
Samsung Electronics Co., Ltd., I; 41 (upd.); 108 (upd.)
Samsung Heavy Industries Co., Ltd., 128
SK Group, 88
SK Telecom Co., Ltd., 128
Ssangyong Cement Industrial Co., Ltd., III; 61 (upd.)
Tong Yang Cement Corporation, 62
Young Chang Co. Ltd., 107

Spain

Abengoa S.A., 73
Abertis Infraestructuras, S.A., 65
Acciona S.A., 81
Adolfo Dominguez S.A., 72
Altadis S.A., 72 (upd.)
Áreas S.A., 104
Banco Bilbao Vizcaya Argentaria S.A., II; 48 (upd.); 130 (upd.)
Banco Central, II
Banco do Brasil S.A., II
Banco Santander, S.A., 36 (upd.); 111 (upd.)
Baron de Ley S.A., 74
Bayer Hispania S.L., 120
Campofrío Alimentación S.A, 59
Caprabo S.A., 123
Chupa Chups S.A., 38
Codere S.A., 110
Coflusa S.A., 120
Compañia Española de Petróleos S.A. (CEPSA), IV; 56 (upd.); 123 (upd.)
Corporación Alimentaria Peñasanta S.A., 120
Corporación de Radio y Televisión Española S.A., 120
Correos y Telegrafos S.A., 80
Cortefiel S.A., 64
Dogi International Fabrics S.A., 52
Duro Felguera S.A., 120
Ebro Foods S.A., 118
El Corte Inglés Group, V; 26 (upd.)
ENDESA S.A., V; 46 (upd.)
Ercros S.A., 80
Federico Paternina S.A., 69
Fomento de Construcciones y Contratas S.A., 129
Freixenet S.A., 71
Futbol Club Barcelona, 121
Gas Natural SDG S.A., 69
Grupo Dragados SA, 55
Grupo Eroski, 64
Grupo Ferrovial S.A., 40; 118 (upd.)
Grupo Ficosa International, 90
Grupo Leche Pascual S.A., 59
Grupo Lladró S.A., 52
Grupo Planeta, 94
Hipercor S.A., 123
Iberdrola, S.A., 49; 123 (upd.)
Iberia Líneas Aéreas de España S.A., 6; 36 (upd.); 91 (upd.)
Industria de Diseño Textil S.A., 64
Instituto Nacional de Industria, I
La Seda de Barcelona S.A., 100
Loewe S.A., 104
Mapfre S.A., 109
Mecalux S.A., 74

American Printing House for the Blind, 26
American Public Education, Inc., 108
American Railcar Industries, Inc., 124
American Re Corporation, 10; 35 (upd.)
American Red Cross, 40; 112 (upd.)
American Reprographics Company, 75
American Residential Mortgage Corporation, 8
American Restaurant Partners, L.P., 93
American Retirement Corporation, 42
American Rice, Inc., 33
American Safety Razor Company, 20
American Science & Engineering, Inc., 81
American Seating Company, 78
American Skiing Company, 28
American Snuff Company, LLC, 126
American Society for the Prevention of Cruelty to Animals (ASPCA), 68
The American Society of Composers, Authors and Publishers, 29; 125 (upd.)
American Software Inc., 25
American Standard Companies Inc., III; 30 (upd.)
American States Water Company, 46
American Stores Company, II; 22 (upd.)
American Superconductor Corporation, 97
American Systems Corporation, 119
American Technical Ceramics Corp., 67
American Technology Corporation, 103
American Tire Distributors Holdings, Inc., 117
American Tourister, Inc., 16
American Tower Corporation, 33
American Vanguard Corporation, 47
American Water Works Company, Inc., 6; 38 (upd.)
American Woodmark Corporation, 31
AmeriCares Foundation, Inc., 87
America's Collectibles Network, Inc., 123
America's Favorite Chicken Company, Inc., 7
America's Car-Mart, Inc., 64
Amerigon Incorporated, 97
AMERIGROUP Corporation, 69
Amerihost Properties, Inc., 30
Amerijet International, Inc., 128
Ameriprise Financial, Inc., 116
AmeriSource Health Corporation, 37 (upd.)
AmerisourceBergen Corporation, 64 (upd.)
Ameristar Casinos, Inc., 33; 69 (upd.)
Ameritech Corporation, V; 18 (upd.)
Ameritrade Holding Corporation, 34
Ameriwood Industries International Corp., 17
Amerock Corporation, 53
Ameron International Corporation, 67
Ames Department Stores, Inc., 9; 30 (upd.)
AMETEK, Inc., 9; 114 (upd.)
AMF Bowling, Inc., 40
Amfac/JMB Hawaii L.L.C., I; 24 (upd.)
Amgen, Inc., 10; 30 (upd.); 89 (upd.)
AMICAS, Inc., 69
Amkor Technology, Inc., 69

Amoco Corporation, IV; 14 (upd.)
Amoskeag Company, 8
AMP Incorporated, II; 14 (upd.)
Ampacet Corporation, 67
Ampco-Pittsburgh Corporation 79
Ampex Corporation, 17
Amphenol Corporation, 40
AMR Corporation, 28 (upd.); 52 (upd.); 126 (upd.)
AMREP Corporation, 21
Amscan Holdings, Inc., 61; 124 (upd.)
AmSouth Bancorporation, 12; 48 (upd.)
Amsted Industries Incorporated, 7
AmSurg Corporation, 48; 122 (upd.)
Amtech Systems, Inc., 127
Amtran, Inc., 34
Amway Corporation, III; 13 (upd.); 30 (upd.)
Amylin Pharmaceuticals, Inc., 67
Amy's Kitchen Inc., 76
Anacomp, Inc., 94
Anadarko Petroleum Corporation, 10; 52 (upd.); 106 (upd.)
Anaheim Angels Baseball Club, Inc., 53
Analex Corporation, 74
Analog Devices, Inc., 10
Analogic Corporation, 23
Analysts International Corporation, 36
Analytic Sciences Corporation, 10
Analytical Surveys, Inc., 33
Anaren, Inc., 33; 128 (upd.)
Ancestry.com Inc., 116
Anchor BanCorp Wisconsin, Inc., 101
Anchor Bancorp, Inc., 10
Anchor Brewing Company, 47
Anchor Gaming, 24
Anchor Hocking Glassware, 13
Andersen, 10; 29 (upd.); 68 (upd.)
Anderson Trucking Service, Inc., 75
Anderson-DuBose Company, The, 60
The Andersons, Inc., 31; 122 (upd.)
Andin International, Inc., 100
Andis Company, Inc., 85
Andretti Green Racing, 106
Andrew Corporation, 10; 32 (upd.)
Andrews Institute, The, 99
Andrews Kurth, LLP, 71
Andrews McMeel Universal, 40
Andronico's Market, 70
Andrx Corporation, 55
Angelica Corporation, 15; 43 (upd.)
Angelo, Gordon & Co., 130
AngioDynamics, Inc., 81
Anheuser-Busch InBev, I; 10 (upd.); 34 (upd.); 100 (upd.)
Anixter International Inc., 88
Annaly Capital Management, Inc., 128
Annie's Homegrown, Inc., 59
Annin & Co., 100
AnnTaylor Stores Corporation, 13; 37 (upd.); 67 (upd.)
ANR Pipeline Co., 17
Anschutz Company, The, 12; 36 (upd.); 73 (upd.)
Ansoft Corporation, 63
ANSYS, Inc., 115
Anteon Corporation, 57
Anthem Electronics, Inc., 13

Anthony & Sylvan Pools Corporation, 56
Antioch Company, The, 40
AOL Time Warner Inc., 57 (upd.)
Aon Corporation, III; 45 (upd.); 113 (upd.)
APAC Customer Services Inc., 127
Apache Corporation, 10; 32 (upd.); 89 (upd.)
Apartment Investment and Management Company, 49
Apex Digital, Inc., 63
APi Group, Inc., 64
APL Limited, 61 (upd.)
Apogee Enterprises, Inc., 8
Apollo Group, Inc., 24; 119 (upd.)
Apollo Theater Foundation, Inc., 109
Appaloosa Management L. P., 116
Applause Inc., 24
Apple Inc., III; 6 (upd.); 36 (upd.); 77 (upd.); 132 (upd.)
Apple & Eve L.L.C., 92
Apple Bank for Savings, 59
Applebee's International Inc., 14; 35 (upd.)
Appliance Recycling Centers of America, Inc., 42
Applica Incorporated, 43 (upd.)
Applied Bioscience International, Inc., 10
Applied Extrusion Technologies Inc., 126
Applied Films Corporation, 48
Applied Industrial Technologies, Inc., 130 (upd.)
Applied Materials, Inc., 10; 46 (upd.); 114 (upd.)
Applied Micro Circuits Corporation, 38
Applied Power, Inc., 9; 32 (upd.)
Applied Signal Technology, Inc., 87
Apria Healthcare Group Inc., 123
AptarGroup, Inc., 69
Aqua Alliance Inc., 32 (upd.)
aQuantive, Inc., 81
Aquarion Company, 84
Aquatic Company, 121
Aquent, 96
Aquila, Inc., 50 (upd.)
AR Accessories Group, Inc., 23
ARA Services, II
ARAMARK Corporation, 13; 41 (upd.); 122 (upd.)
Arandell Corporation, 37
Arbitron Company, The, 38
Arbor Drugs Inc., 12
Arby's Inc., 14
Arch Chemicals Inc., 78
Arch Coal Inc., 98
Arch Mineral Corporation, 7
Arch Wireless, Inc., 39
Archer Daniels Midland Company, I; 11 (upd.); 32 (upd.); 75 (upd.)
Archie Comics Publications, Inc., 63
Archipelago Learning, Inc., 116
Archon Corporation, 74 (upd.)
Archstone-Smith Trust, 49
Archway Cookies, Inc., 29
ARCO Chemical Company, 10
Arctco, Inc., 16
Arctic Cat Inc., 40 (upd.); 96 (upd.)

Benton Oil and Gas Company, 47
Berean Christian Stores, 96
Bergdorf Goodman Inc., 52
Bergen Brunswig Corporation, V; 13 (upd.)
Berger Bros Company, 62
Beringer Blass Wine Estates Ltd., 66 (upd.)
Beringer Wine Estates Holdings, Inc., 22
Berkeley Farms, Inc., 46
Berkshire Hathaway Inc., III; 18 (upd.); 42 (upd.); 89 (upd.)
Berkshire Realty Holdings, L.P., 49
Berlex Laboratories, Inc., 66
Berlitz International, Inc., 13; 39 (upd.)
Bernard C. Harris Publishing Company, Inc., 39
Bernard Chaus, Inc., 27
Bernard Hodes Group Inc., 86
Bernard L. Madoff Investment Securities LLC, 106
Bernick Companies, The, 75
Bernstein-Rein, 92
Berry Petroleum Company, 47; 130 (upd.)
Berry Plastics Group Inc., 21; 98 (upd.)
Bertucci's Corporation, 16; 64 (upd.)
Berwick Offray, LLC, 70
Berwind Corporation, 100
Best Buy Co., Inc., 9; 23 (upd.); 63 (upd.)
Best Kosher Foods Corporation, 82
Best Maid Products, Inc., 107
Best Western International, Inc., 124
Bestfoods, 22 (upd.)
BET Holdings, Inc., 18
Beth Abraham Family of Health Services, 94
Bethlehem Steel Corporation, IV; 7 (upd.); 27 (upd.)
Betsey Johnson Inc., 100
Betsy Ann Candies, Inc., 105
Better Made Snack Foods, Inc., 90
The Betty Ford Center at Eisenhower, 126
Betz Laboratories, Inc., I; 10 (upd.)
Beverly Enterprises, Inc., III; 16 (upd.)
BFGoodrich Company, The, V; 19 (upd.)
BG Products Inc., 96
BHC Communications, Inc., 26
Bianchi International (d/b/a Gregory Mountain Products), 76
BIC Corporation, 8; 23 (upd.)
Bicoastal Corporation, II
Bienstock & Michael, P.C., 131
Big A Drug Stores Inc. 79
Big B, Inc., 17
Big Bear Stores Co., 13
Big Brothers Big Sisters of America, 85
Big Dog Holdings, Inc., 45
Big Fish Games, Inc., 108
Big 5 Sporting Goods Corporation, 55
Big Flower Press Holdings, Inc., 21
Big Idea Productions, Inc., 49
Big Lots, Inc., 50; 110 (upd.)
Big O Tires, Inc., 20
Big Rivers Electric Corporation, 11
Big V Supermarkets, Inc., 25
Big Y Foods, Inc., 53; 127 (upd.)

Bill & Melinda Gates Foundation, 41; 100 (upd.)
Bill Barrett Corporation, 71
Bill Blass Group Ltd., 32; 115 (upd.)
Billing Concepts, Inc., 26; 72 (upd.)
Billing Services Group Ltd., 102
The Biltmore Company, 118
Bindley Western Industries, Inc., 9
Bing Group, The, 60
Bingham Dana LLP, 43
Binks Sames Corporation, 21
Binney & Smith Inc., 25
BioClinica, Incorporated, 129
Biogen Idec Inc., 71 (upd.)
Biogen Inc., 14; 36 (upd.)
Bio-IT World Inc., 113
Biolase Technology, Inc., 87
Biomet, Inc., 10; 93 (upd.
Bio-Rad Laboratories, Inc., 93
Bio-Reference Laboratories, Inc., 122
BioScrip Inc., 98
Biosite Incorporated, 73
Bird Corporation, 19
Birds Eye Foods, Inc., 69 (upd.)
Birkenstock USA, LP, 12; 42 (upd.); 125 (upd.)
Birmingham Steel Corporation, 13; 40 (upd.)
BISSELL Inc., 9; 30 (upd.)
BISYS Group, Inc., The, 73
BJ Services Company, 25
BJ's Wholesale Club, Inc., 94
BKD LLP, 96
Black & Decker Corporation, The, III; 20 (upd.); 67 (upd.)
Black & Veatch Corporation, 22; 130 (upd.)
Black Box Corporation, 20; 96 (upd.)
Black Diamond Equipment, Ltd., 62; 121 (upd.)
Black Hills Corporation, 20
Blackbaud, Inc., 85
Blackboard Inc., 89
Blackfoot Telecommunications Group, 60
BlackRock, Inc. 79
Blackstone Group L.P., The, 115
Blackwater USA, 76
Blair Corporation, 25; 31
Blessings Corp., 19
Blimpie, 15; 49 (upd.); 105 (upd.)
Blish-Mize Co., 95
Blizzard Entertainment, 78
Block Communications, Inc., 81
Block Drug Company, Inc., 8; 27 (upd.)
Blockbuster Inc., 9; 31 (upd.); 76 (upd.)
Blodgett Holdings, Inc., 61 (upd.)
Blonder Tongue Laboratories, Inc., 48; 132 (upd.)
Bloom Energy Corporation, 129
Bloomberg L.P., 21; 126 (upd.)
Bloomingdale's Inc., 12
Blount International, Inc., 12; 48 (upd.)
Blue Bell Creameries L.P., 30
Blue Bird Corporation, 35
Blue Coat Systems, Inc., 83
Blue Cross and Blue Shield Association, 10
Blue Diamond Growers, 28

Blue Heron Paper Company, 90
Blue Martini Software, Inc., 59
Blue Mountain Arts, Inc., 29
Blue Nile, Inc., 61; 121 (upd.)
Blue Note Label Group, 115
Blue Rhino Corporation, 56
Blue Ridge Beverage Company Inc., 82
Blue Sun Energy, Inc., 108
Bluefly, Inc., 60
Bluegreen Corporation, 80
BlueLinx Holdings Inc., 97
Blyth, Inc., 18; 74 (upd.)
BMC Industries, Inc., 17; 59 (upd.)
BMC Software, Inc., 55
Boardwalk Pipeline Partners, LP, 87
Boart Longyear Company, 26
Boatmen's Bancshares Inc., 15
Bob Evans Farms, Inc., 9; 63 (upd.)
Bobit Publishing Company, 55
Bobs Candies, Inc., 70
Bob's Discount Furniture LLC, 104
Bob's Red Mill Natural Foods, Inc., 63
Boca Resorts, Inc., 37
Boddie-Noell Enterprises, Inc., 68
Body Glove International LLC, 88
Boeing Company, The, I; 10 (upd.); 32 (upd.); 111 (upd.)
Boenning & Scattergood Inc., 102
Bogen Communications International, Inc., 62
Bohemia, Inc., 13
Boise Cascade Holdings, L.L.C., IV; 8 (upd.); 32 (upd.); 95 (upd.)
Bojangles Restaurants Inc., 97
The Boler Company, 127
Bollinger Shipyards, Inc., 61
Bolt Technology Corporation, 99
Bombay Company, Inc., The, 10; 71 (upd.)
Bon Marché, Inc., The, 23
Bon Secours Health System, Inc., 24
Bonneville International Corporation, 29
Bonneville Power Administration, 50
Bon-Ton Stores, Inc., The, 16; 50 (upd.)
Book-of-the-Month Club, Inc., 13
Books-A-Million, Inc., 14; 41 (upd.); 96 (upd.)
Bookspan, 86
Boole & Babbage, Inc., 25
Booth Creek Ski Holdings, Inc., 31
Boots & Coots International Well Control, Inc. 79
Booz Allen Hamilton Inc., 10; 101 (upd.)
Borden, Inc., II; 22 (upd.)
Borders Group, Inc., 15; 43 (upd.)
Borghese Inc., 107
Borg-Warner Corporation, III
BorgWarner Inc., 14; 32 (upd.); 85 (upd.)
Borland International, Inc., 9
Boron, LePore & Associates, Inc., 45
Borrego Solar Systems, Inc., 111
Borroughs Corporation, 110
Boscov's Department Store, Inc., 31
Bose Corporation, 13; 36 (upd.); 118 (upd.)
Boss Holdings, Inc., 97
Boston Acoustics, Inc., 22
Boston Apparel Group, 112 (upd.)

Extended Stay, Inc., 41; 123 (upd.)
EXX Inc., 65
Exxon Corporation, IV; 7 (upd.); 32 (upd.)
Exxon Mobil Corporation, 67 (upd.)
Eye Care Centers of America, Inc., 69
E-Z Serve Corporation, 17
EZCORP Inc., 43
E-Z-EM Inc., 89
F&W Publications, Inc., 71
F. Dohmen Co., The, 77
F. Korbel & Bros. Inc., 68
F.L. Roberts & Company, Inc., 113
F.W. Webb Company, 95
Fab Industries, Inc., 27
Fabri-Kal Corporation, 121
Fabri-Centers of America Inc., 16
Facebook, Inc., 90
FactSet Research Systems Inc., 73
Faegre & Benson LLP, 97
Fair Grounds Corporation, 44
Fair, Isaac and Company, 18
Fairchild Corporation, 131
Fairchild Aircraft, Inc., 9
Fairfield Communities, Inc., 36
Falcon Products, Inc., 33
FalconStor Software, Inc., 121
Fallon McElligott Inc., 22
Fallon Worldwide, 71 (upd.)
Family Christian Stores, Inc., 51
Family Dollar Stores, Inc., 13; 62 (upd.)
Family Golf Centers, Inc., 29
Family Sports Concepts, Inc., 100
Famous Dave's of America, Inc., 40
Fannie Mae, 45 (upd.); 109 (upd.)
Fannie May Confections Brands, Inc., 80
Fansteel Inc., 19
FAO Schwarz, 46
Farah Incorporated, 24
Faribault Foods, Inc., 89
Farley Northwest Industries, Inc., I
Farley's & Sathers Candy Company, Inc., 62
Farm Family Holdings, Inc., 39; 117 (upd.)
Farm Journal Corporation, 42
Farmer Bros. Co., 52
Farmer Jack Supermarkets, 78
Farmers Cooperative Society, 118
Farmers Insurance Group of Companies, 25
Farmland Foods, Inc., 7
Farmland Industries, Inc., 48
Farnam Companies, Inc., 107
FARO Technologies, Inc., 87
Farouk Systems Inc., 78
Farrar, Straus and Giroux Inc., 15
Fastenal Company, 14; 42 (upd.); 99 (upd.)
Fatburger Corporation, 64
Faultless Starch/Bon Ami Company, 55
Faygo Beverages Inc., 55
Fay's Inc., 17
Fazoli's Management, Inc., 76 (upd.)
Fazoli's Systems, Inc., 27
Featherlite Inc., 28
Fechheimer Brothers Company, Inc., 110
Fedders Corporation, 18; 43 (upd.)

Federal Agricultural Mortgage Corporation, 75
Federal Deposit Insurance Corporation, 93
Federal Express Corporation, V
Federal National Mortgage Association, II
Federal Paper Board Company, Inc., 8
Federal Prison Industries, Inc., 34
Federal Signal Corp., 10
Federal-Mogul Corporation, I; 10 (upd.); 26 (upd.); 121 (upd.)
Federated Department Stores Inc., 9; 31 (upd.)
FedEx Corporation, 18 (upd.); 42 (upd.); 109 (upd.)
FedEx Office and Print Services, Inc., 109 (upd.)
Feed The Children, Inc., 68
Feeding America, 120 (upd.)
Feesers Inc., 127
FEI Company 79
Feld Entertainment, Inc., 32 (upd.)
Fellowes Inc., 28; 107 (upd.)
Fellowship of Christian Athletes, 129
Fender Musical Instruments Company, 16; 43 (upd.); 121 (upd.)
Fenwick & West LLP, 34
Ferolito, Vultaggio & Sons, 27; 100 (upd.)
Ferrara Fire Apparatus, Inc., 84
Ferrara Pan Candy Company, 90
Ferrellgas Partners, L.P., 35; 107 (upd.)
Ferro Corporation, 8; 56 (upd.)
F5 Networks, Inc., 72
FHP International Corporation, 6
FiberMark, Inc., 37
Fibreboard Corporation, 16
Fidelity Investments Inc., II; 14 (upd.)
Fidelity National Financial Inc., 54
Fidelity Southern Corporation, 85
Fieldale Farms Corporation, 23; 107 (upd.)
Fieldcrest Cannon, Inc., 9; 31 (upd.)
Fiesta Mart, Inc., 101
Fifth Third Bancorp, 13; 31 (upd.); 103 (upd.)
Figgie International Inc., 7
Fiji Water LLC, 74
FileMaker, Inc., 125
FileNet Corporation, 62
Fili Enterprises, Inc., 70
Film Department Holdings, Inc., The, 124
Film Roman, Inc., 58
FINA, Inc., 7
Fingerhut Companies, Inc., 9; 36 (upd.)
Finisar Corporation, 92
Finish Line, Inc., The, 29; 68 (upd.)
FinishMaster, Inc., 24
Finlay Enterprises, Inc., 16; 76 (upd.)
Firearms Training Systems, Inc., 27
Fired Up, Inc., 82
Firehouse Restaurant Group, Inc., 110
Fireman's Fund Insurance Company, III
First Advantage Corporation, 119
First Albany Companies Inc., 37
First Alert, Inc., 28

First American Financial Corporation, 52; 123 (upd.)
First Aviation Services Inc., 49
First Bank System Inc., 12
First Brands Corporation, 8
First Busey Corporation, 105
First Cash Financial Services, Inc., 57
First Chicago Corporation, II
First Citizens Bancshares Incorporated, 116
First Colony Coffee & Tea Company, 84
First Commerce Bancshares, Inc., 15
First Commerce Corporation, 11
First Data Corporation, 30 (upd.); 116 (upd.)
First Empire State Corporation, 11
First Executive Corporation, III
First Fidelity Bank, N.A., New Jersey, 9
First Financial Management Corporation, 11
First Hawaiian, Inc., 11
First Industrial Realty Trust, Inc., 65
First Interstate Bancorp, II
First Look Studios, Inc., 111
First Marblehead Corporation, The, 87
First Mississippi Corporation, 8
First Nationwide Bank, 14
First Niagara Financial Group Inc., 107
First of America Bank Corporation, 8
First Security Corporation, 11
First Solar, Inc., 95
First Team Sports, Inc., 22
First Tennessee National Corporation, 11; 48 (upd.)
First Union Corporation, 10
First USA, Inc., 11
First Virginia Banks, Inc., 11
First Wind Holdings, Inc., 133
First Years Inc., The, 46
Firstar Corporation, 11; 33 (upd.)
FirstEnergy Corp., 112 (upd.)
FirstMerit Corporation, 105
Fiserv, Inc., 11; 33 (upd.); 106 (upd.)
Fish & Neave, 54
Fisher Auto Parts, Inc., 104
Fisher Communications, Inc., 99
Fisher Companies, Inc., 15
Fisher Controls International, LLC, 13; 61 (upd.)
Fisher Scientific International Inc., 24
Fisher-Price Inc., 12; 32 (upd.)
Fishman & Tobin Inc., 102
Fisk Corporation, 72
Five Guys Enterprises, LLC, 99
Five Star Quality Care, Inc., 125
FJ Management, 121 (upd.)
Flagstar Companies, Inc., 10
Flanders Corporation, 65
Flanigan's Enterprises, Inc., 60
Flatiron Construction Corporation, 92
Fleer Corporation, 15
FleetBoston Financial Corporation, 9; 36 (upd.)
FleetCor Technologies, Inc., 132
FleetPride, Inc., 128
Fleetwood Enterprises, Inc., III; 22 (upd.); 81 (upd.)
Fleming Companies, Inc., II; 17 (upd.)

International Rectifier Corporation, 31; 71 (upd.)
International Shipbreaking Ltd. L.L.C., 67
International Shipholding Corporation, Inc., 27
International Speedway Corporation, 19; 74 (upd.)
International Telephone & Telegraph Corporation, I; 11 (upd.)
International Total Services, Inc., 37
Interpool, Inc., 92
Interpublic Group of Companies, Inc., The, I; 22 (upd.); 75 (upd.)
Inter-Regional Financial Group, Inc., 15
Interscope Music Group, 31
Intersil Corporation, 93
Interstate Bakeries Corporation, 12; 38 (upd.)
Interstate Batteries, 110
Interstate Hotels & Resorts Inc., 58
InterVideo, Inc., 85
Intevac, Inc., 92
Intimate Brands, Inc., 24
Intrado Inc., 63
Intuit Inc., 14; 33 (upd.); 73 (upd.)
Intuitive Surgical, Inc. 79
Invacare Corporation, 11; 47 (upd.)
inVentiv Health, Inc., 81
Inventure Group, Inc., The, 96 (upd.)
Inverness Medical Innovations, Inc., 63
Invitrogen Corporation, 52
Invivo Corporation, 52
INX International Ink Co., 123
Iomega Corporation, 21
Ionatron, Inc., 85
Ionics, Incorporated, 52
Iowa Telecommunications Services, Inc., 85
IPALCO Enterprises, Inc., 6
Ipsen International Inc., 72
Irex Contracting Group, 90
Iridium Communications Inc., 133
IRIS International, Inc., 101
iRobot Corporation, 83
Iron Mountain, Inc., 33; 104 (upd.)
Irvin Feld & Kenneth Feld Productions, Inc., 15
Irwin Financial Corporation, 77
Island ECN, Inc., The, 48
Isle of Capri Casinos, Inc., 41
Ispat Inland Inc., 40 (upd.)
ITA Software, Inc., 132
ITC Holdings Corp., 75
Itel Corporation, 9
Items International Airwalk Inc., 17
Itron, Inc., 64
ITT Corporation, III; 116 (upd.)
ITT Educational Services, Inc., 33; 76 (upd.)
i2 Technologies, Inc., 87
Ivan Allen Workspace L.L.C., 113
Ivar's, Inc., 86
IVAX Corporation, 11; 55 (upd.)
IVC Industries, Inc., 45
iVillage Inc., 46
Iwerks Entertainment, Inc., 34
IXC Communications, Inc., 29
Ixia, 117

J & J Snack Foods Corporation, 24
J&R Electronics Inc., 26
J. & W. Seligman & Co. Inc., 61
J.A. Riggs Tractor Co., 131
J.A. Jones, Inc., 16
J. Alexander's Corporation, 65
J.B. Hunt Transport Services Inc., 12; 119 (upd.)
J. Baker, Inc., 31
J. C. Penney Company, Inc., V; 18 (upd.); 43 (upd.); 91 (upd.)
J. Crew Group. Inc., 12; 34 (upd.); 88 (upd.)
J.D. Edwards & Company, 14
J.D. Heiskell & Company, 117
J.D. Power and Associates, 32
J. D'Addario & Company, Inc., 48
J.F. Shea Co., Inc., 55; 120 (upd.)
J.H. Findorff and Son, Inc., 60
J.I. Case Company, 10
J.J. Keller & Associates, Inc., 81
J. Jill Group, Inc., The, 35; 90 (upd.)
J.L. Hammett Company, 72
J. Lohr Winery Corporation, 99
J. M. Smucker Company, The, 11; 87 (upd.)
J.P. Morgan Chase & Co., II; 30 (upd.); 38 (upd.)
J. Paul Getty Trust, The, 105
J.R. Simplot Company, 16; 60 (upd.); 130 (upd.)
J. W. Pepper and Son Inc., 86
Jabil Circuit, Inc., 36; 88 (upd.)
Jack B. Kelley, Inc., 102
Jack Henry and Associates, Inc., 17; 94 (upd.)
Jack in the Box Inc., 89 (upd.)
Jack Morton Worldwide, 88
Jack Schwartz Shoes, Inc., 18
Jackpot Enterprises Inc., 21
Jackson Family Wines, 124 (upd.)
Jackson Hewitt, Inc., 48
Jackson National Life Insurance Company, 8
Jacmar Companies, 87
Jaco Electronics, Inc., 30
Jacob Leinenkugel Brewing Company, 28
Jacobs Engineering Group Inc., 6; 26 (upd.); 106 (upd.)
Jacobson Stores Inc., 21
Jacor Communications, Inc., 23
Jacuzzi Brands Inc., 76 (upd.)
Jacuzzi Inc., 23
JAKKS Pacific, Inc., 52
Jalate Inc., 25
Jamba Juice Company, 47
James Avery Craftsman, Inc., 76
James Original Coney Island Inc., 84
James River Corporation of Virginia, IV
Jani-King International, Inc., 85
JanSport, Inc., 70
Janus Capital Group Inc., 57
Jarden Corporation, 93 (upd.)
Jason Incorporated, 23
Jay Jacobs, Inc., 15
Jayco Inc., 13
Jays Foods, Inc., 90

Jazz Basketball Investors, Inc., 55; 129 (upd.)
Jazzercise, Inc., 45
JB Oxford Holdings, Inc., 32
JBT AeroTech, 131
JBT FoodTech, 131
JDA Software Group, Inc., 101
JDS Uniphase Corporation, 34
JE Dunn Construction Group, Inc., 85
Jean-Georges Enterprises L.L.C., 75
Jefferies Group, Inc., 25; 133 (upd.)
Jefferson-Pilot Corporation, 11; 29 (upd.)
Jel Sert Company, 90
JELD-WEN, Inc., 45; 125 (upd.)
Jelly Belly Candy Company, 76
Jenkens & Gilchrist, P.C., 65
Jenner & Block LLP, 131
Jennie-O Turkey Store, Inc., 76
Jennifer Convertibles, Inc., 31
Jenny Craig, Inc., 10; 29 (upd.); 92 (upd.)
Jeppesen Sanderson, Inc., 92
Jerry's Famous Deli Inc., 24
Jersey Mike's Franchise Systems, Inc., 83
Jervis B. Webb Company, 24
JetBlue Airways Corporation, 44; 127 (upd.)
Jetro Cash & Carry Enterprises Inc., 38
Jewett-Cameron Trading Company, Ltd., 89
JG Industries, Inc., 15
Jillian's Entertainment Holdings, Inc., 40
Jim Beam Brands Worldwide, Inc., 14; 58 (upd.)
Jim Henson Company, The, 23; 106 (upd.)
Jimmy John's Enterprises, Inc., 103
Jitney-Jungle Stores of America, Inc., 27
Jive Software, Inc., 130
JKH Holding Co. LLC, 105
JLG Industries, Inc., 52
JLM Couture, Inc., 64
JM Smith Corporation, 100
JMB Realty Corporation, IV
Jo-Ann Stores, Inc., 72 (upd.)
Jockey International, Inc., 12; 34 (upd.); 77 (upd.)
Joe's Sports & Outdoor, 98 (upd.)
The Joffrey Ballet of Chicago, 52; 121 (upd.)
Johanna Foods, Inc., 104
John B. Sanfilippo & Son, Inc., 14; 101 (upd.)
John D. and Catherine T. MacArthur Foundation, The, 34
John D. Brush Company Inc., 94
John F. Kennedy Center for the Performing Arts, 106
John Frieda Professional Hair Care Inc., 70
John H. Harland Company, 17
John Hancock Financial Services, Inc., III; 42 (upd.)
John Nuveen Company, The, 21
John Paul Mitchell Systems, 24; 112 (upd.)
John Q. Hammons Hotels, Inc., 24

John Simon Guggenheim Memorial
  Foundation, 118
John Snow, Inc., 123
John W. Danforth Company, 48
John Wiley & Sons, Inc., 17; 65 (upd.)
Johnny Rockets Group, Inc., 31; 76
  (upd.)
Johns Manville Corporation, 64 (upd.)
Johnson & Higgins, 14
Johnson & Johnson, III; 8 (upd.); 36
  (upd.); 75 (upd.)
Johnson Controls, Inc., III; 26 (upd.); 59
  (upd.); 110 (upd.)
Johnson Outdoors Inc., 28; 84 (upd.)
Johnson Publishing Company, Inc., 28;
  72 (upd.)
Johnsonville Sausage L.L.C., 63
Johnston Industries, Inc., 15
Johnstown America Industries, Inc., 23
Joie de Vivre Hospitality, Inc., 122
Jones Apparel Group, Inc., 11; 39 (upd.)
Jones Day, 124
Jones Intercable, Inc., 21
Jones Knowledge Group, Inc., 97
Jones Lang LaSalle Incorporated, 49
Jones Medical Industries, Inc., 24
Jones Soda Co., 69
Jones, Day, Reavis & Pogue, 33
Jordache Enterprises, Inc., 23
Jordan Company LP, The, 70
Jordan Industries, Inc., 36
Jordan-Kitt Music Inc., 86
Jordano's, Inc., 102
Jordan's Furniture Inc., 132
Jos. A. Bank Clothiers, Inc., 31; 104
  (upd.)
Joseph T. Ryerson & Son, Inc., 15
Joseph's Lite Cookies, Inc., 132
Jostens, Inc., 7; 25 (upd.); 73 (upd.)
JOULÉ Inc., 58
Journal Communications, Inc., 86
Journal Register Company, 29
Joy Cone Company, 127
Joy Global Inc., 104 (upd.)
JPI, 49
JPMorgan Chase & Co., 91 (upd.)
JPS Textile Group, Inc., 28
JTH Tax Inc., 103
j2 Global Communications, Inc., 75
Judge Group, Inc., The, 51
Juicy Couture, Inc., 80
Jujamcyn Theaters Corporation, 112
Juniper Networks, Inc., 43; 122 (upd.)
Juno Lighting, Inc., 30
Juno Online Services, Inc., 38
Jupitermedia Corporation, 75
Just Bagels Manufacturing, Inc., 94
Just Born, Inc., 32
Just For Feet, Inc., 19
Justin Industries, Inc., 19
JWP Inc., 9
JWT Group Inc., I
K & B Inc., 12
K & G Men's Center, Inc., 21
K&L Gates LLP, 126
K-Tron International Inc., 115
K-VA-T Food Stores, Inc., 117
Kable Media Services, Inc., 115

Kadant Inc., 96 (upd.)
Kaiser Aluminum Corporation, IV; 84
  (upd.)
Kaiser Foundation Health Plan, Inc., 53;
  119 (upd.)
Kal Kan Foods, Inc., 22
Kaman Corporation, 12; 42 (upd.); 118
  (upd.)
Kaman Music Corporation, 68
Kampgrounds of America, Inc. 33
Kana Software, Inc., 51
Kansas City Power & Light Company, 6
Kansas City Southern Industries, Inc., 6;
  26 (upd.)
Kansas City Southern Railway Company,
  The, 92
Kaplan, Inc., 42; 90 (upd.)
KapStone Paper and Packaging
  Corporation, 122
KAR Auction Services, Inc., 117
Kar Nut Products Company, 86
Karl Kani Infinity, Inc., 49
Karsten Manufacturing Corporation, 51
Kash n' Karry Food Stores, Inc., 20
Kashi Company, 89
Kasper A.S.L., Ltd., 40
kate spade LLC, 68
Katy Industries, Inc., I; 51 (upd.)
Katz Communications, Inc., 6
Katz Media Group, Inc., 35
Kaufman and Broad Home Corporation,
  8
Kayak.com, 108
Kaydon Corp., 18; 117 (upd.)
Kaye Scholer LLP, 131
Kayem Foods Incorporated, 118
KB Home, 45 (upd.)
KB Toys, 15; 35 (upd.); 86 (upd.)
KBR Inc., 106 (upd.)
Keane, Inc., 56; 127 (upd.)
Keds, LLC, 118
Keebler Foods Company, 36
KEEN, Inc., 133
Keith Companies Inc., The, 54
Keithley Instruments Inc., 16
Kelley Bean Co., 123
Kelley Blue Book Company, Inc., 84
Kelley Drye & Warren LLP, 40
Kellogg Brown & Root, Inc., 62 (upd.)
Kellogg Company, II; 13 (upd.); 50
  (upd.); 110 (upd.)
Kellwood Company, 8; 85 (upd.)
Kelly Services Inc., 6; 26 (upd.); 109
  (upd.)
Kelly-Moore Paint Company, Inc., 56;
  112 (upd.)
Kelly-Springfield Tire Company, The, 8
Kelsey-Hayes Group of Companies, 7; 27
  (upd.)
KEMET Corporation, 14; 124 (upd.)
Kemper Corporation, III; 15 (upd.)
Kemps LLC, 103
Kendall International, Inc., 11
Kendall-Jackson Winery, Ltd., 28
Kendle International Inc., 87
Kenetech Corporation, 11
Kenexa Corporation, 87
Kenmore Air Harbor Inc., 65

Kennametal Inc., 68 (upd.)
Kennedy-Wilson, Inc., 60
Kenneth Cole Productions, Inc., 25
Ken's Foods, Inc., 88
Kensey Nash Corporation, 71
Kensington Publishing Corporation, 84
Kent Electronics Corporation, 17
Kentucky Electric Steel, Inc., 31
Kentucky Utilities Company, 6
Kerasotes ShowPlace Theaters LLC, 80
Kerr Drug, Inc., 133
Kerr Group Inc., 24
Kerr-McGee Corporation, IV; 22 (upd.);
  68 (upd.)
Ketchum Communications Inc., 6
Kettle Foods, Inc., 48; 132 (upd.)
Kewaunee Scientific Corporation, 25
Key Plastics, L.L.C., 121
Key Safety Systems, Inc., 63
Key Technology Inc., 106
Key Tronic Corporation, 14
KeyCorp, 8; 93 (upd.)
Keyes Fibre Company, 9
Keynote Systems Inc., 102
Keys Fitness Products, LP, 83
KeySpan Energy Co., 27
Keystone Foods LLC, 117
Keystone International, Inc., 11
KFC Corporation, 7; 21 (upd.); 89 (upd.)
Kforce Inc., 71
KI, 57
Kidde, Inc., I
Kiehl's Since 1851, Inc., 52
Kiewit Corporation, 116 (upd.)
Kikkoman Corporation, 47 (upd.)
Kimball International, Inc., 12; 48 (upd.)
Kimberly-Clark Corporation, III; 16
  (upd.); 43 (upd.); 105 (upd.)
Kimco Realty Corporation, 11; 133 (upd.)
Kimpton Hotel & Restaurant Group, Inc.,
  105
Kinder Morgan, Inc., 45; 111 (upd.)
KinderCare Learning Centers, Inc., 13
Kinetic Concepts, Inc. (KCI), 20
King & Spalding LLP, 23; 115 (upd.)
King Arthur Flour Company, The, 31
King Kullen Grocery Co., Inc., 15
King Nut Company, 74
King Pharmaceuticals, Inc., 54; 132 (upd.)
King Ranch, Inc., 14; 60 (upd.)
King World Productions, Inc., 9; 30
  (upd.)
King's Hawaiian Bakery West, Inc., 101
Kingston Technology Company, Inc., 20;
  112 (upd.)
Kinko's, Inc., 16; 43 (upd.)
Kinney Shoe Corp., 14
Kinray Inc., 85
Kintera, Inc., 75
Kirby Corporation, 18; 66 (upd.)
Kirkland & Ellis LLP, 65
Kirlin's Inc., 98
Kirshenbaum Bond + Partners, Inc., 57
Kiss My Face Corporation, 108
Kit Manufacturing Co., 18
Kitchell Corporation, 14
KitchenAid, 8
Kitty Hawk, Inc., 22

MTS Inc., 37
Mueller Industries, Inc., 7; 52 (upd.); 133 (upd.)
Mueller Sports Medicine, Inc., 102
Mueller Water Products, Inc., 113
Mullen Advertising Inc., 51
Multiband Corporation, 131
Multi-Color Corporation, 53; 126 (upd.)
Multimedia Games, Inc., 41
Multimedia, Inc., 11
Muralo Company Inc., 117
Murdock Holding Company, 127
Murdock Madaus Schwabe, 26
Murphy Family Farms Inc., 22
Murphy Oil Corporation, 7; 32 (upd.); 95 (upd.)
Musco Family Olive Co., The, 91
Musco Lighting, 83
Muscular Dystrophy Association, 133
Museum of Modern Art, 106
Musicland Stores Corporation, 9; 38 (upd.)
Mutual Benefit Life Insurance Company, The, III
Mutual Life Insurance Company of New York, The, III
Mutual of Omaha Companies, The, 98
Muzak, Inc., 18
MWH Preservation Limited Partnership, 65
MWI Veterinary Supply, Inc., 80
MXL Industries, Inc., 120
Mycogen Corporation, 21
Myers Industries, Inc., 19; 96 (upd.
Mylan Inc., I; 20 (upd.); 59 (upd.); 122 (upd.)
Myriad Genetics, Inc., 95
Myriad Restaurant Group, Inc., 87
N.F. Smith & Associates LP, 70
Nabisco Foods Group, II; 7 (upd.)
Nabors Industries, Inc., 9
NACCO Industries Inc., 7; 78 (upd.)
Naked Juice Company, 107
Nalco Holding Company, I; 12 (upd.); 89 (upd.)
Nantucket Allserve, Inc., 22
Napster, Inc., 69
NASD, 54 (upd.)
NASDAQ Stock Market, Inc., The, 92
Nash Finch Company, 8; 23 (upd.); 65 (upd.)
Nashua Corporation, 8
Nastech Pharmaceutical Company Inc. 79
Nathan's Famous, Inc., 29
National Amusements Inc., 28
National Aquarium in Baltimore, Inc., 74
National Association for Stock Car Auto Racing, Inc., 32; 125 (upd.)
National Association for the Advancement of Colored People, 109
National Association of Securities Dealers, Inc., 10
National Audubon Society, 26
National Auto Credit, Inc., 16
National Bank of South Carolina, The, 76
National Beverage Corporation, 26; 88 (upd.)

National Broadcasting Company, Inc., II; 6 (upd.); 28 (upd.)
National Can Corporation, I
National Car Rental System, Inc., 10
National Cattlemen's Beef Association, 124
National CineMedia, Inc., 103
National City Corporation, 15; 97 (upd.)
National Collegiate Athletic Association, 96
National Convenience Stores Incorporated, 7
National Council of La Raza, 106
National Discount Brokers Group, Inc., 28
National Distillers and Chemical Corporation, I
National Educational Music Co. Ltd., 47
National Envelope Corporation, 32
National Equipment Services, Inc., 57
National Financial Partners Corp., 65
National Football League, 29; 115 (upd.)
National Frozen Foods Corporation, 94
National Fuel Gas Company, 6; 95 (upd.)
National Geographic Society, 9; 30 (upd.); 79 (upd.)
National Grape Cooperative Association, Inc., 20
National Grid USA, 51 (upd.)
National Gypsum Company, 10
National Health Laboratories Incorporated, 11
National Heritage Academies, Inc., 60
National Hockey League, 35
National Home Centers, Inc., 44
National Instruments Corporation, 22
National Intergroup, Inc., V
National Jewish Health, 101
National Journal Group Inc., 67
National Media Corporation, 27
National Medical Enterprises, Inc., III
National Medical Health Card Systems, Inc. 79
National Oilwell, Inc., 54
National Organization for Women, Inc., 55
National Patent Development Corporation, 13
National Penn Bancshares, Inc., 103
National Picture & Frame Company, 24
National Presto Industries, Inc., 16; 43 (upd.); 130 (upd.)
National Public Radio, Inc., 19; 47 (upd.); 132 (upd.)
National R.V. Holdings, Inc., 32
National Railroad Passenger Corporation (Amtrak), 22; 66 (upd.)
National Record Mart, Inc., 29
National Research Corporation, 87
National Rifle Association of America, The, 37; 112 (upd.)
National Sanitary Supply Co., 16
National Semiconductor Corporation, II; VI, 26 (upd.); 69 (upd.)
National Service Industries, Inc., 11; 54 (upd.)
National Standard Co., 13

National Starch and Chemical Company, 49
National Steel Corporation, 12
National Technical Systems, Inc., 111
National TechTeam, Inc., 41
National Thoroughbred Racing Association, Inc., 58; 127 (upd.)
National Weather Service, 91
National Wildlife Federation, 103
National Wine & Spirits, Inc., 49
NationsBank Corporation, 10
Nationwide Mutual Insurance Company, 108
Native New Yorker Inc., 110
Natori Company, Inc., 108
Natrol, Inc., 49
Natural Alternatives International, Inc., 49
Natural Grocers by Vitamin Cottage, Inc., 111
Natural Ovens Bakery, Inc., 72
Natural Selection Foods, 54
Natural Wonders Inc., 14
Naturally Fresh, Inc., 88
Nature Conservancy, The, 28
Nature's Sunshine Products, Inc., 15; 102 (upd.)
Natus Medical Incorporated, 119
Naumes, Inc., 81
Nautica Enterprises, Inc., 18; 44 (upd.)
Navarre Corporation, 24
Navarro Discount Pharmacies, 119
Navigant Consulting, Inc., 93
Navigant International, Inc., 47
Navigators Group, Inc., The, 92
NaviSite, Inc., 128
Navistar International Corporation, I; 10 (upd.); 114 (upd.)
NAVTEQ Corporation, 69
Navy Exchange Service Command, 31
Navy Federal Credit Union, 33
NBBJ, 111
NBD Bancorp, Inc., 11
NBGS International, Inc., 73
NBTY, Inc., 31; 132 (upd.)
NCH Corporation, 8
NCI Building Systems, Inc., 88
NCL Corporation 79
NCNB Corporation, II
NCO Group, Inc., 42; 131 (upd.)
NCR Corporation, III; 6 (upd.); 30 (upd.); 90 (upd.)
Nebraska Book Company, Inc., 65
Nebraska Furniture Mart, Inc., 94
Nebraska Public Power District, 29
Nederlander Producing Company of America, Inc., 108
Neenah Foundry Company, 68
Neff Corp., 32
NeighborCare, Inc., 67 (upd.)
Neiman Marcus Group, Inc., The, 12; 49 (upd.); 105 (upd.)
Nektar Therapeutics, 91
Neogen Corporation, 94
NERCO, Inc., 7
NetApp, Inc., 116
NetCracker Technology Corporation, 98
Netezza Corporation, 69
Netflix, Inc., 58; 115 (upd.)

NETGEAR, Inc., 81
NetIQ Corporation 79
NetJets Inc., 96 (upd.)
Netscape Communications Corporation, 15; 35 (upd.)
NetScout Systems, Inc., 122
Network Appliance, Inc., 58
Network Associates, Inc., 25
Network Equipment Technologies Inc., 92
Neuberger Berman Inc., 57
NeuStar, Inc., 81
Neutrogena Corporation, 17
Nevada Bell Telephone Company, 14
Nevada Power Company, 11
Nevamar Company, 82
New Balance Athletic Shoe, Inc., 25; 68 (upd.)
New Belgium Brewing Company, Inc., 68
New Brunswick Scientific Co., Inc., 45
New Chapter Inc., 96
New Dana Perfumes Company, 37
New England Business Service Inc., 18; 78 (upd.)
New England Confectionery Co., 15
New England Electric System, V
New England Mutual Life Insurance Company, III
New Enterprise Associates, 116
New Era Cap Company, Inc., 122
New Horizons Worldwide, Inc., 120
New Jersey Devils, 84
New Jersey Manufacturers Insurance Company, 96
New Jersey Resources Corporation, 54
New Jersey Sports and Exposition Authority, 130
New Line Cinema, Inc., 47
New NGC Inc., 127 (upd.)
New Orleans Saints LP, 58
New Piper Aircraft, Inc., The, 44
New Plan Realty Trust, 11
New School, The, 103
New Seasons Market, 75
New Street Capital Inc., 8
New Times, Inc., 45
New Valley Corporation, 17
New World Pasta Company, 53
New World Restaurant Group, Inc., 44
New York & Company Inc., 113
New York City Health and Hospitals Corporation, 60
New York City Off-Track Betting Corporation, 51; 115 (upd.)
New York Community Bancorp Inc., 78
New York Daily News, 32
New York Health Care, Inc., 72
New York Jets Football Club Inc., 125
New York Knickerbockers, 129
New York Life Insurance Company, III; 45 (upd.); 118 (upd.)
New York Restaurant Group, Inc., 32
New York Shakespeare Festival Management, 93
New York State Electric and Gas, 6
New York Stock Exchange, Inc., 9; 39 (upd.)
The New York Times Company, IV; 19 (upd.); 61 (upd.); 133 (upd.)

New York Yacht Club, Inc., 103
New Young Broadcasting Holding Co., Inc., 125 (upd.)
Newark Group, Inc., The, 102
Neways Inc., 78
Newbury Comics, Inc., 123
Newcor, Inc., 40
Newegg Inc., 107
Newell Rubbermaid Inc., 9; 52 (upd.); 120 (upd.)
Newfield Exploration Company, 65
Newhall Land and Farming Company, 14
Newly Weds Foods, Inc., 74
Newman's Own, Inc., 37; 125 (upd.)
NewMarket Corporation, 116
Newmont Mining Corporation, 7; 94 (upd.)
NewPage Corporation, 119
Newpark Resources, Inc., 63
Newport Corporation, 71
Newport News Shipbuilding Inc., 13; 38 (upd.)
News America Publishing Inc., 12
News Communications, Inc., 103
News Corporation, 109 (upd.)
Newsday Media Group, 103
NewYork-Presbyterian Hospital, 59
Nexsan Corporation, 129
Nexstar Broadcasting Group, Inc., 73
Nextel Communications, Inc., 10; 27 (upd.)
NextWave Wireless Inc., 112
NFL Films, 75
NFO Worldwide, Inc., 24
NGC Corporation, 18
Niagara Corporation, 28
Niagara Mohawk Holdings Inc., V; 45 (upd.)
Nichols Research Corporation, 18
Nicklaus Companies, 45
Nicole Miller, 98
Nicor Inc., 6; 86 (upd.)
Nielsen Business Media, Inc., 98
NIKE, Inc., V; 8 (upd.); 36 (upd.); 75 (upd.)
Nikken Global Inc., 32
Niman Ranch, Inc., 67
Nimbus CD International, Inc., 20
Nine West Group, Inc., 11; 39 (upd.)
NIPSCO Industries, Inc., 6
NiSource Inc., 109 (upd.)
Nitches, Inc., 53
NL Industries, Inc., 10
NN, Inc., 129
Nobel Learning Communities, Inc., 37; 76 (upd.)
Noble Affiliates, Inc., 11
Noble Roman's Inc., 14; 99 (upd.)
Noland Company, 35; 107 (upd.)
Nolo.com, Inc., 49
Noodle Kidoodle, 16
Noodles & Company, Inc., 55
Nooter Corporation, 61
Norcal Waste Systems, Inc., 60
The NORDAM Group, Inc., 121
NordicTrack, 22
Nordson Corporation, 11; 48 (upd.)
Nordstrom, Inc., V; 18 (upd.); 67 (upd.)

Norelco Consumer Products Co., 26
Norfolk Southern Corporation, V; 29 (upd.); 75 (upd.)
Norm Thompson Outfitters, Inc., 47
Norrell Corporation, 25
Norseland Inc., 120
Norstan, Inc., 16
Nortek, Inc., 34
North American Breweries, Inc., 133
North American Galvanizing & Coatings, Inc., 99
North Atlantic Trading Company Inc., 65
North Face, Inc., The, 18; 78 (upd.)
North Fork Bancorporation, Inc., 46
North Pacific Group, Inc., 61
North Star Steel Company, 18
Northeast Utilities, V; 48 (upd.); 133 (upd.)
Northern States Power Company, V; 20 (upd.)
Northern Trust Corporation, 9; 101 (upd.)
Northland Cranberries, Inc., 38
Northrop Grumman Corporation, I; 11 (upd.); 45 (upd.); 111 (upd.)
Northwest Airlines Corporation, I; 6 (upd.); 26 (upd.); 74 (upd.)
Northwest Natural Gas Company, 45; 125 (upd.)
NorthWestern Corporation, 37
The Northwestern Mutual Life Insurance Company, III; 45 (upd.); 118 (upd.)
Norton Company, 8
Norton McNaughton, Inc., 27
Norwood Promotional Products, Inc., 26
Notations, Inc., 110
NovaCare, Inc., 11
NovaStar Financial, Inc., 91
Novell, Inc., 6; 23 (upd.)
Novellus Systems, Inc., 18
Noven Pharmaceuticals, Inc., 55
NPC International, Inc., 40
NPD Group, Inc., The, 68
NRG Energy, Inc. 79
NRT Incorporated, 61
NSF International, 72
NSS Enterprises Inc., 78
NSTAR, 106 (upd.)
NTD Architecture, 101
NTK Holdings Inc., 107 (upd.)
NTN Buzztime, Inc., 86
Nu Skin Enterprises, Inc., 27; 76 (upd.)
Nuance Communications, Inc., 122
NuCO2 Inc., 129
Nucor Corporation, 7; 21 (upd.); 79 (upd.)
Nugget Market, Inc., 118
Nu-kote Holding, Inc., 18
NuStar Energy L.P., 111
Nutraceutical International Corporation, 37; 124 (upd.)
NutraSweet Company, The, 8; 107 (upd.)
NutriSystem, Inc., 71
Nutrition for Life International Inc., 22
Nutrition 21 Inc., 97
NVIDIA Corporation, 54
NVR Inc., 8; 70 (upd.)
NYMAGIC, Inc., 41

San Francisco Baseball Associates, L.P., 129 (upd.)
San Francisco Opera Association, 112
Sanborn Map Company Inc., 82
Sandals Resorts International, 65
Sanders Morris Harris Group Inc., 70
Sanders\Wingo, 99
Sanderson Farms, Inc., 15
Sandia National Laboratories, 49
SanDisk Corporation , 121
SandRidge Energy, Inc., 112
Sandy Spring Bancorp, Inc., 126
Sanford L.P., 82
Sanmina-SCI Corporation, 109 (upd.)
Santa Barbara Restaurant Group, Inc., 37
Santa Cruz Operation, Inc., The, 38
Santa Fe Gaming Corporation, 19
Santa Fe International Corporation, 38
Santa Fe Pacific Corporation, V
Santarus, Inc., 105
Sapient Corporation, 122
Sapp Bros Travel Centers, Inc., 105
Sara Lee Corporation, II; 15 (upd.); 54 (upd.); 99 (upd.)
Sarnoff Corporation, 57
Sarris Candies Inc., 86
SAS Institute Inc., 10; 78 (upd.)
Satcon Technology Corporation, 124
Saturn Corporation, 7; 21 (upd.); 80 (upd.)
Saucony Inc., 35; 86 (upd.)
Sauder Woodworking Company, 12; 35 (upd.)
Sauer-Danfoss Inc., 61
Saul Ewing LLP, 74
Savannah Foods & Industries, Inc., 7
Save Mart Supermarkets, 130
Savers, Inc., 99 (upd.)
Savi Technology, Inc., 119
Sawtek Inc., 43 (upd.)
Saxton Pierce Restaurant Corporation, 100
Sbarro, Inc., 16; 64 (upd.)
SBC Communications Inc., 32 (upd.)
SBS Technologies, Inc., 25
SCANA Corporation, 6; 56 (upd.); 133 (upd.)
ScanSource, Inc., 29; 74 (upd.)
SCB Computer Technology, Inc., 29
SCEcorp, V
Schawk, Inc., 24; 129 (upd.)
Scheels All Sports Inc., 63
Scheid Vineyards Inc., 66
Schenck Business Solutions, 88
Scherer Brothers Lumber Company, 94
Schering-Plough Corporation, I; 14 (upd.); 49 (upd.); 99 (upd.)
Schieffelin & Somerset Co., 61
Schlage Lock Company, 82
Schlotzsky's, Inc., 36
Schlumberger Limited, III; 17 (upd.); 59 (upd.); 130 (upd.)
Schmitt Music Company, 40
Schneider National, Inc., 36; 77 (upd.)
Schneiderman's Furniture Inc., 28
Schnitzer Steel Industries, Inc., 19; 122 (upd.)

Scholastic Corporation, 10; 29 (upd.); 126 (upd.)
Scholle Corporation, 96
School Specialty, Inc., 68
School-Tech, Inc., 62
Schott Brothers, Inc., 67
Schott Corporation, 53
Schottenstein Stores Corporation, 14; 117 (upd.)
Schreiber Foods, Inc., 72
Schuff Steel Company, 26
Schulte Roth & Zabel LLP, 122
Schultz Sav-O Stores, Inc., 21; 31 (upd.)
Schumacher Electric Corporation, 125
Schurz Communications, Inc., 98
Schwan Food Company, The, 7; 26 (upd.); 83 (upd.)
Schwebel Baking Company, 72
Schweitzer-Mauduit International, Inc., 52
Schwinn Cycle and Fitness L.P., 19
SCI Systems, Inc., 9
Science Applications International Corporation, 15; 109 (upd.)
Scientific Games Corporation, 64 (upd.)
Scientific Learning Corporation, 95
Scientific-Atlanta, Inc., 6; 45 (upd.)
SCO Group Inc., The, 78
Scolari's Food and Drug Company, 102
The SCOOTER Store, Ltd., 122
Scope Products, Inc., 94
Score Board, Inc., The, 19
Scotsman Industries, Inc., 20
Scott Fetzer Company, 12; 80 (upd.)
Scott Paper Company, IV; 31 (upd.)
Scottrade, Inc., 85
Scotts Company, The, 22
Scotty's, Inc., 22
Scoular Company, The, 77
Scovill Fasteners Inc., 24
SCP Pool Corporation, 39
Screen Actors Guild, 72
Scripps Health, 126
Scripps Research Institute, The, 76
SDI Technologies, Inc., 125
Sea Ray Boats Inc., 96
Seaboard Corporation, 36; 85 (upd.)
SeaChange International, Inc. 79
SEACOR Holdings Inc., 83
Seagate Technology, Inc., 8; 34 (upd.)
Seagull Energy Corporation, 11
Sealaska Corporation, 60
Sealed Air Corporation, 14; 57 (upd.); 121 (upd.)
Sealed Power Corporation, I
Sealright Co., Inc., 17
Sealy Corporation, 12; 112 (upd.)
Seaman Furniture Company, Inc., 32
Sean John Clothing, Inc., 70
Sears Holding Corporation, V; 18 (upd.); 56 (upd.); 119 (upd.)
Seattle City Light, 50
Seattle FilmWorks, Inc., 20
Seattle First National Bank Inc., 8
Seattle Lighting Fixture Company, 92
Seattle Pacific Industries, Inc., 92
Seattle Seahawks, Inc., 92
Seattle Times Company, The, 15; 124 (upd.)

Seaway Food Town, Inc., 15
Sebastiani Vineyards, Inc., 28; 117 (upd.)
Second City, Inc., The, 88
Second Harvest, 29
Security Capital Corporation, 17
Security Pacific Corporation, II
SED International Holdings, Inc., 43
See's Candies, Inc., 30
Sega of America, Inc., 10
Segway Inc., 48; 125 (upd.)
SEI Investments Company, 96
Seigle's Home and Building Centers, Inc., 41
Seitel, Inc., 47
Select Comfort Corporation, 34
Select Medical Corporation, 65
Selee Corporation, 88
Selmer Company, Inc., The, 19
SEMCO Energy, Inc., 44
Seminis, Inc., 29
Semitool, Inc., 18; 79 (upd.)
Sempra Energy, 25 (upd.); 116 (upd.)
Semtech Corporation, 32
Seneca Foods Corporation, 17; 60 (upd.)
Senomyx, Inc., 83
Sensient Technologies Corporation, 52 (upd.)
Sensormatic Electronics Corp., 11
Sensory Science Corporation, 37
SENTEL Corporation, 106
Sepracor Inc., 45; 117 (upd.)
Sequa Corporation, 13; 54 (upd.); 130 (upd.)
Serologicals Corporation, 63
Serta, Inc., 28
Servco Pacific Inc., 96
Service America Corp., 7
Service Corporation International, 6; 51 (upd.)
Service Merchandise Company, Inc., V; 19 (upd.)
ServiceMaster Company, The, 6; 23 (upd.); 68 (upd.)
Servidyne Inc., 100 (upd.)
Servpro Industries, Inc., 85
Seton Company, Inc., 110
Sevenson Environmental Services, Inc., 42
Seventh Generation, Inc., 73
Seyfarth Shaw LLP, 93
SFX Entertainment, Inc., 36
SGI, 29 (upd.)
Shakespeare Company, 22
Shaklee Corporation, 12; 39 (upd.)
Shamrock Foods Company, 105
Shared Medical Systems Corporation, 14
Sharper Image Corporation, The, 10; 62 (upd.)
The Shaw Group, Inc., 50; 118 (upd.)
Shaw Industries, Inc., 9; 40 (upd.)
Shawmut National Corporation, 13
Shaw's Supermarkets, Inc., 56
Sheaffer Pen Corporation, 82
Shearer's Foods, Inc., 72
Shearman & Sterling, 32
Shearson Lehman Brothers Holdings Inc., II; 9 (upd.)
Shedd Aquarium Society, 73
Sheetz, Inc., 85

Southtrust Corporation, 11
Southwest Airlines Co., 6; 24 (upd.); 71 (upd.)
Southwest Gas Corporation, 19
Southwest Water Company, 47
Southwestern Bell Corporation, V
Southwestern Electric Power Co., 21
Southwestern/Great American, Inc., 131
Southwestern Public Service Company, 6
Southwire Company, Inc., 8; 23 (upd.); 122 (upd.)
Sovereign Bancorp, Inc., 103
Sovran Self Storage, Inc., 66
Spacehab, Inc., 37
Spacelabs Medical, Inc., 71
Spaghetti Warehouse, Inc., 25
Spangler Candy Company, 44
Spanish Broadcasting System, Inc., 41
Spansion Inc., 80
Spanx, Inc., 89
Spark Networks, Inc., 91
Spartan Motors Inc., 14
Spartan Stores Inc., 8; 66 (upd.)
Spartech Corporation, 19; 76 (upd.)
Sparton Corporation, 18
Spear & Jackson, Inc., 73
Spear, Leeds & Kellogg, 66
Special Olympics, Inc., 93
Specialized Bicycle Components Inc., 50
Specialty Coatings Inc., 8
Specialty Equipment Companies, Inc., 25
Specialty Products & Insulation Co., 59
Spec's Music, Inc., 19
Spectra Energy Corporation, 116
Spectrum Brands, Inc., 109 (upd.)
Spectrum Control, Inc., 67
Spectrum Organic Products, Inc., 68
Spee-Dee Delivery Service, Inc., 93
SpeeDee Oil Change and Tune-Up, 25
Speedway Motorsports, Inc., 32; 112 (upd.)
Speidel Inc., 96
Speizman Industries, Inc., 44
Spelling Entertainment, 14; 35 (upd.)
Spencer Stuart and Associates, Inc., 14
Spherion Corporation, 52
Spicy Pickle Franchising, Inc., 105
Spiegel, Inc., 10; 27 (upd.)
Spinnaker Exploration Company, 72
Spire Corporation, 129
Spirit AeroSystems Holdings, Inc., 122
Spirit Airlines, Inc., 31
Sport Chalet, Inc., 16; 94 (upd.)
Sport Clips, Inc., 133
Sport Supply Group, Inc., 23; 106 (upd.)
Sportif USA, Inc., 118
Sportmart, Inc., 15
Sports & Recreation, Inc., 17
The Sports Authority, Inc., 16; 43 (upd.); 120 (upd.)
Sports Club Company, The, 25
Sports Endeavors, Inc., 133
Sportsman's Guide, Inc., The, 36
Springs Global US, Inc., V; 19 (upd.); 90 (upd.)
Sprint Nextel Corporation, 9; 46 (upd.); 110 (upd.)
SPS Technologies, Inc., 30

SPSS Inc., 64
SPX Corporation, 10; 47 (upd.); 103 (upd.)
Spyglass Entertainment Group, LLC, 91
Square D, 90
Squibb Corporation, I
SRA International, Inc., 77
SRAM Corporation, 65
SRC Holdings Corporation, 67
SRG Global, Inc., 121
SRI International, Inc., 57
SSI (U.S.), Inc., 103 (upd.)
SSOE Inc., 76
STAAR Surgical Company, 57
Stabler Companies Inc., 78
Stage Stores, Inc., 24; 82 (upd.)
Stanadyne Automotive Corporation, 37
StanCorp Financial Group, Inc., 56
Standard Candy Company Inc., 86
Standard Commercial Corporation, 13; 62 (upd.)
Standard Federal Bank, 9
Standard Microsystems Corporation, 11
Standard Motor Products, Inc., 40
Standard Pacific Corporation, 52
Standard Register Company, The, 15, 93 (upd.)
Standex International Corporation, 17; 44 (upd.); 133 (upd.)
Stanhome Inc., 15
Stanley Furniture Company, Inc., 34
Stanley Works, The, III; 20 (upd.); 79 (upd.)
Staple Cotton Cooperative Association (Staplcotn), 86
Staples, Inc., 10; 55 (upd.); 119 (upd.)
Star Banc Corporation, 11
Star of the West Milling Co., 95
Starbucks Corporation, 13; 34 (upd.); 77 (upd.)
Starcraft Corporation, 30; 66 (upd.)
Starent Networks Corp., 106
Starkey Laboratories, Inc., 52
StarKist Company, 113
Starrett Corporation, 21
StarTek, Inc. 79
Starter Corp., 12
Starwood Hotels & Resorts Worldwide, Inc., 54; 119 (upd.)
Starz LLC, 91
Stash Tea Company, The, 50
State Auto Financial Corporation, 77
State Farm Mutual Automobile Insurance Company, III; 51 (upd.); 126 (upd.)
State Financial Services Corporation, 51
State Street Corporation, 8; 57 (upd.)
Staten Island Bancorp, Inc., 39
Stater Bros. Holdings Inc., 64
Station Casinos, Inc., 25; 90 (upd.)
Staubach Company, The, 62
Steak n Shake Company, The, 41; 96 (upd.)
Stearns, Inc., 43
Steel Dynamics, Inc., 52; 128 (upd.)
Steel Technologies Inc., 63
Steelcase, Inc., 7; 27 (upd.); 110 (upd.)
Stefanini TechTeam Inc., 128 (upd.)
Stein Mart Inc., 19; 72 (upd.)

Steiner Corporation (Alsco), 53
Steinway Musical Instruments, Inc., 19; 111 (upd.)
Stemilt Growers Inc., 94
Stepan Company, 30; 105 (upd.)
Stephan Company, 60
Stephens Inc., 92
Stephens Media, LLC, 91
Stericycle, Inc., 33; 74 (upd.)
Sterilite Corporation, 97
STERIS Corporation, 29; 132 (upd.)
Sterling Chemicals Inc., 16; 78 (upd.)
Sterling Drug, Inc., I
Sterling Electronics Corp., 18
Sterling Financial Corporation, 106
Sterling Mets LP, 129
Sterling Software, Inc., 11
Sterling Vineyards, Inc., 130
Steve & Barry's LLC, 88
Stevedoring Services of America Inc., 28
Steven Madden, Ltd., 37; 123 (upd.)
Stew Leonard's, 56
Stewart & Stevenson Services Inc., 11
Stewart Enterprises, Inc., 20
Stewart Information Services Corporation, 78
Stewart's Beverages, 39
Stewart's Shops Corporation, 80
Stiefel Laboratories, Inc., 90
Stiles Machinery Inc., 123
Stillwater Mining Company, 47
Stimson Lumber Company, 78
Stock Yards Packing Co., Inc., 37
Stone & Webster, Inc., 13; 64 (upd.)
Stone Container Corporation, IV
Stone Manufacturing Company, 14; 43 (upd.)
StoneMor Partners L.P., 133
Stonyfield Farm, Inc., 55; 126 (upd.)
Stop & Shop Supermarket Company, The, II; 24 (upd.); 68 (upd.)
Storage Technology Corporation, 6
Storage USA, Inc., 21
Stouffer Corp., 8
Strand Book Store Inc., 114
StrataCom, Inc., 16
Stratagene Corporation, 70
Stratasys, Inc., 67
Strategic Staffing Solutions, L.C., 128
Strattec Security Corporation, 73
Stratus Computer, Inc., 10
Strauss Discount Auto, 56
Strayer Education, Inc., 53; 124 (upd.)
StreamServe Inc., 113
Stride Rite Corporation, The, 8; 37 (upd.); 86 (upd.)
Strine Printing Company Inc., 88
Strober Organization, Inc., The, 82
Stroh Brewery Company, The, I; 18 (upd.)
Strombecker Corporation, 60
Strongwell Corporation, 110
Stroock & Stroock & Lavan LLP, 40
Strouds, Inc., 33
Structure Tone Organization, The, 99
Stryker Corporation, 11; 29 (upd.); 79 (upd.)
Stuart C. Irby Company, 58

United Defense Industries, Inc., 30; 66 (upd.)
United Dominion Industries Limited, 8; 16 (upd.)
United Dominion Realty Trust, Inc., 52
United Farm Workers of America, 88
United Foods, Inc., 21
United HealthCare Corporation, 9
United Illuminating Company, The, 21
United Industrial Corporation, 37
United Industries Corporation, 68
United Jewish Communities, 33
United Merchants & Manufacturers, Inc., 13
United National Group, Ltd., 63
United Nations International Children's Emergency Fund (UNICEF), 58
United Natural Foods, Inc., 32; 76 (upd.)
United Negro College Fund, Inc. 79
United Online, Inc., 71 (upd.)
United Parcel Service of America Inc., V; 17 (upd.)
United Parcel Service, Inc., 63; 94 (upd.)
United Press International, Inc., 25; 73 (upd.)
United Rentals, Inc., 34
United Retail Group Inc., 33
United Road Services, Inc., 69
United Service Organizations, 60
United Services Automobile Association, 109 (upd.)
Yard House USA, Inc., 126
United States Cellular Corporation, 9
United States Filter Corporation, 20
United States Masters Swimming, Inc., 131
United States Pipe and Foundry Company, 62
United States Playing Card Company, 62
United States Postal Service, 14; 34 (upd.); 108 (upd.)
United States Shoe Corporation, The, V
United States Soccer Federation, 108
United States Steel Corporation, 50 (upd.); 114 (upd.)
United States Sugar Corporation, 115
United States Surgical Corporation, 10; 34 (upd.)
United States Tennis Association, 111
United Stationers Inc., 14; 117 (upd.)
United Surgical Partners International Inc., 120
United Talent Agency, Inc., 80
United Technologies Automotive Inc., 15
United Technologies Corporation, I; 10 (upd.); 34 (upd.); 105 (upd.)
United Telecommunications, Inc., V
United Video Satellite Group, 18
United Water Resources, Inc., 40
United Way of America, 36
United Way Worldwide, 112 (upd.)
UnitedHealth Group Incorporated, 103 (upd.)
Unitil Corporation, 37
Unitog Co., 19
Unitrin Inc., 16; 78 (upd.)
Univar Corporation, 9
Universal American Corp., 111

Universal Compression, Inc., 59
Universal Corporation, V; 48 (upd.)
Universal Electronics Inc., 39; 120 (upd.)
Universal Foods Corporation, 7
Universal Forest Products, Inc., 10; 59 (upd.); 122 (upd.)
Universal Health Services, Inc., 6; 124 (upd.)
Universal International, Inc., 25
Universal Manufacturing Company, 88
Universal Music Group, 128
Universal Security Instruments, Inc., 96
Universal Stainless & Alloy Products, Inc., 75
Universal Studios, Inc., 33; 100 (upd.)
Universal Technical Institute, Inc., 81
Universal Truckload Services, Inc., 111
University of Chicago Press, The, 79
Univision Communications Inc., 24; 83 (upd.)
Uno Restaurant Corporation, 18
Uno Restaurant Holdings Corporation, 70 (upd.)
Unocal Corporation, IV; 24 (upd.); 71 (upd.)
UnumProvident Corporation, 13; 52 (upd.)
Upjohn Company, The, I; 8 (upd.)
Upper Deck Company, LLC, The, 105
Urban Engineers, Inc., 102
Urban Institute, 129
Urban Outfitters, Inc., 14; 74 (upd.)
URS Corporation, 45; 80 (upd.)
US Airways Group, Inc., I; 6 (upd.); 28 (upd.); 52 (upd.); 110 (upd.)
US Oncology, Inc., 127
US 1 Industries, Inc., 89
USA Interactive, Inc., 47 (upd.)
USA Mobility Inc., 97 (upd.)
USA Track & Field, Inc., 122
USA Truck, Inc., 42
USAA, 10; 62 (upd.)
USANA, Inc., 29
USEC Inc., 124
USF&G Corporation, III
USG Corporation, III; 26 (upd.); 81 (upd.)
UST Inc., 9; 50 (upd.)
USX Corporation, IV; 7 (upd.)
Utah Medical Products, Inc., 36
Utah Power and Light Company, 27
UTG Inc., 100
UtiliCorp United Inc., 6
UTStarcom, Inc., 77
Utz Quality Foods, Inc., 72
UUNET, 38
Uwajimaya, Inc., 60
VAALCO Energy, Inc., 128
Vail Resorts, Inc., 11; 43 (upd.); 120 (upd.)
Valassis Communications, Inc., 8; 37 (upd.); 76 (upd.)
Valero Energy Corporation, 7; 71 (upd.)
Valhi, Inc., 19; 94 (upd.)
Vallen Corporation, 45
Valley Media Inc., 35
Valley National Bancorp, 128
Valley National Gases, Inc., 85

Valley Proteins, Inc., 91
ValleyCrest Companies, 81 (upd.)
Valmont Industries, Inc., 19; 123 (upd.)
Valspar Corporation, The, 8; 32 (upd.); 77 (upd.)
Value City Department Stores, Inc., 38
Value Line, Inc., 16; 73 (upd.)
Value Merchants Inc., 13
ValueClick, Inc., 49
ValueVision International, Inc., 22
Valve Corporation, 101
Van Camp Seafood Company, Inc., 7
Vance Publishing Corporation, 64
Vanderbilt University Medical Center, 99
Vanguard Group, Inc., The, 14; 34 (upd.)
Vanguard Health Systems Inc., 70
Vann's Inc., 105
Van's Aircraft, Inc., 65
Vans, Inc., 16; 47 (upd.)
Varco International, Inc., 42
Varian Medical Systems, Inc., 12; 48 (upd.); 122 (upd.)
Variety Wholesalers, Inc., 73
Variflex, Inc., 51
Vari-Lite International, Inc., 35
Varlen Corporation, 16
Varsity Spirit Corp., 15
VASCO Data Security International, Inc. 79
Vastar Resources, Inc., 24
Vaughan Foods, Inc., 105
Vaupell Inc., 121
VCA Antech, Inc., 58; 129 (upd.)
Vecellio Group, Inc., 113
VECO International, Inc., 7
Vector Group Ltd., 35 (upd.)
Vectren Corporation, 98 (upd.)
Veeco Instruments Inc., 32
Veeder-Root Company, 123
Veit Companies, 43; 92 (upd.)
Velocity Express Corporation, 49; 94 (upd.)
Venator Group Inc., 35 (upd.)
Vencor, Inc., 16
Venetian Casino Resort, LLC, 47
Venoco, Inc., 119
Ventana Medical Systems, Inc., 75
Ventura Foods LLC, 90
Venture Stores Inc., 12
Vera Bradley Inc., 130
Vera Wang Bridal House Ltd., 126
VeraSun Energy Corporation, 87
Verbatim Corporation, 14; 74 (upd.)
Veridian Corporation, 54
VeriFone Holdings, Inc., 18; 76 (upd.)
Verint Systems Inc., 73
VeriSign, Inc., 47; 119 (upd.)
Veritas Software Corporation, 45
Verity Inc., 68
Verizon Communications, 43 (upd.); 78 (upd.)
Vermeer Manufacturing Company, 17
Vermont Country Store, The, 93
Vermont Pure Holdings, Ltd., 51
Vermont Teddy Bear Co., Inc., The, 36
Vertex Pharmaceuticals Incorporated, 83
Vertis Communications, 84
Vertrue Inc., 77

Weight Watchers International Inc., 12; 33 (upd.); 73 (upd.)

Weil, Gotshal & Manges LLP, 55; 127 (upd.)

Weinbrenner Shoe Company, Inc., 120

Weiner's Stores, Inc., 33

Weingarten Realty Investors, 95

The Weinstein Company LLC, 118

Weirton Steel Corporation, IV; 26 (upd.)

Weis Markets, Inc., 15; 84 (upd.)

Weitz Company, Inc., The, 42

Welbilt Corp., 19

Welch Foods Inc., 104

Welcome Wagon International Inc., 82

Welk Group Inc., The, 78

WellCare Health Plans, Inc., 101

WellChoice, Inc., 67 (upd.)

Wellco Enterprises, Inc., 84

Wellman, Inc., 8; 52 (upd.)

WellPoint, Inc., 25; 103 (upd.)

Wells Enterprises, Inc., 36; 127 (upd.)

Wells Fargo & Company, II; 12 (upd.); 38 (upd.); 97 (upd.)

Wells Rich Greene BDDP, 6

Wells-Gardner Electronics Corporation, 43

Wendy's/Arby's Group, Inc., 8; 23 (upd.); 47 (upd.); 118 (upd.)

Wenner Bread Products Inc., 80

Wenner Media, Inc., 32

We-No-Nah Canoe, Inc., 98

Werner Enterprises, Inc., 26

WESCO International, Inc., 116

West Bend Co., 14

West Coast Entertainment Corporation, 29

West Corporation, 42

West Group, 34 (upd.)

West Linn Paper Company, 91

West Marine, Inc., 17; 90 (upd.)

West One Bancorp, 11

West Pharmaceutical Services, Inc., 42

West Point-Pepperell, Inc., 8

West Publishing Co., 7

Westaff Inc., 33

Westamerica Bancorporation, 17

Westar Energy, Inc., 57 (upd.)

WestCoast Hospitality Corporation, 59

Westcon Group, Inc., 67

Westell Technologies, Inc., 57

Westerbeke Corporation, 60

Western Alliance Bancorporation, 119

Western & Southern Financial Group, Inc., 131

Western Atlas Inc., 12

Western Beef, Inc., 22

Western Company of North America, 15

Western Digital Corporation, 25; 92 (upd.)

Western Gas Resources, Inc., 45

Western Publishing Group, Inc., 13

Western Resources, Inc., 12

WesterN SizzliN Corporation, The, 60

Western Union Company, 54; 112 (upd.)

Western Wireless Corporation, 36

Westfield Group, 69

Westin Hotels and Resorts Worldwide, 9; 29 (upd.)

Westinghouse Air Brake Technologies Corporation, 116

Westinghouse Electric Corporation, II; 12 (upd.)

Westmoreland Coal Company, 7

WestPoint Home, Inc., 132 (upd.)

WestPoint Stevens Inc., 16

Westport Resources Corporation, 63

Westvaco Corporation, IV; 19 (upd.)

Westwood One Inc., 23; 106 (upd.)

Wet Seal, Inc., The, 18; 70 (upd.)

Wetterau Incorporated, II

Weyco Group, Incorporated, 32

Weyerhaeuser Company, IV; 9 (upd.); 28 (upd.); 83 (upd.)

WFS Financial Inc., 70

WGBH Educational Foundation, 66

Wham-O, Inc., 61

Whataburger Restaurants LP, 105

Wheatland Tube Company, 123

Wheaton Industries, 8

Wheaton Science Products, 60 (upd.)

Wheelabrator Technologies, Inc., 6; 60 (upd.)

Wheeling-Pittsburgh Corporation, 7; 58 (upd.)

Wheels Inc., 96

Wherehouse Entertainment Incorporated, 11

Whirlpool Corporation, III; 12 (upd.); 59 (upd.); 127 (upd.)

White & Case LLP, 35

White Castle Management Company, 12; 36 (upd.); 85 (upd.)

White Consolidated Industries Inc., 13

White House, Inc., The, 60

White Lily Foods Company, 88

White Rose, Inc., 24

Whitehall Jewellers, Inc., 82 (upd.)

Whiting Petroleum Corporation, 81

Whiting-Turner Contracting Company, 95

Whitman Corporation, 10 (upd.)

Whitman Education Group, Inc., 41

Whitney Holding Corporation, 21

Whittaker Corporation, I; 48 (upd.)

Whole Foods Market, Inc., 20; 50 (upd.); 110 (upd.)

WHX Corporation, 98

Wickes Inc., V; 25 (upd.)

Widmer Brothers Brewing Company, 76

Wieden + Kennedy, 75

Wikimedia Foundation, Inc., 91

Wilbert, Inc., 56

Wilbur Chocolate Company, 66

Wilbur-Ellis Company, 114

Wilco Farm Stores, 93

Wild Oats Markets, Inc., 19; 41 (upd.)

Wildlife Conservation Society, 31

Willamette Industries, Inc., IV; 31 (upd.)

Willamette Valley Vineyards, Inc., 85

William L. Bonnell Company, Inc., 66

William Lyon Homes, 59

William Morris Agency, Inc., 23; 102 (upd.)

William Zinsser & Company, Inc., 58

Williams & Connolly LLP, 47

Williams Communications Group, Inc., 34

The Williams Companies, Inc., IV; 31 (upd.); 126 (upd.)

Williams International Co., L.L.C., 118

Williams Scotsman, Inc., 65

Williams-Sonoma, Inc., 17; 44 (upd.)

Williamson-Dickie Manufacturing Company, 14; 45 (upd.); 122 (upd.)

Willkie Farr & Gallagher LLP, 95

Willow Run Foods, Inc., 100

Wilmer Cutler Pickering Hale and Dorr L.L.P., 109

Wilmington Trust Corporation, 25

Wilson Sonsini Goodrich & Rosati, 34

Wilson Sporting Goods Company, 24; 84 (upd.)

Wilsons The Leather Experts Inc., 21; 58 (upd.)

Wilton Products, Inc., 97

Winchell's Donut Houses Operating Company, L.P., 60

WinCo Foods Inc., 60

Wind River Systems, Inc., 37

Windmere Corporation, 16

Windstream Corporation, 83

Windswept Environmental Group, Inc., 62

Wine Group, Inc., The, 39; 114 (upd.)

Wine.com, Inc., 126

Winegard Company, 56

Winmark Corporation, 74

Winn-Dixie Stores, Inc., II; 21 (upd.); 59 (upd.); 113 (upd.)

Winnebago Industries, Inc., 7; 27 (upd.); 96 (upd.)

WinsLoew Furniture, Inc., 21

Winston & Strawn, 35

Wintrust Financial Corporation, 106

WinWholesale Inc., 131

Wiremold Company, The, 81

Wirtz Corporation, 72

Wisconsin Alumni Research Foundation, 65

Wisconsin Bell, Inc., 14

Wisconsin Central Transportation Corporation, 24

Wisconsin Dairies, 7

Wisconsin Energy Corporation, 6; 54 (upd.); 126 (upd.)

Wisconsin Lift Truck Corp., 130

Wisconsin Public Service Corporation, 9

Wise Foods, Inc. 79

Witco Corporation, I; 16 (upd.)

Witness Systems, Inc., 87

Wizards of the Coast LLC, 24; 112 (upd.)

WLR Foods, Inc., 21

Wm. B. Reily & Company Inc., 58

Wm. Wrigley Jr. Company, 7; 58 (upd.)

WMS Industries, Inc., 15; 53 (upd.); 119 (upd.)

WMX Technologies Inc., 17

Wolfgang Puck Worldwide, Inc., 26, 70 (upd.)

Wolohan Lumber Co., 19

Wolverine Tube Inc., 23

Wolverine World Wide, Inc., 16; 59 (upd.); 118 (upd.)

Zimbabwe

Air Zimbabwe (Private) Limited, 91